Catalogue of the Babylonian Tablets in the British Museum

Volumes IV–V

E. Leichty,
I. L. Finkel and
C. B. F. Walker

with contributions by T. G. Pinches, A. J. Sachs,
D. J. Wiseman, W. G. Lambert, M. Jursa,
M. J. Geller, J. C. Fincke and J. J. Taylor

dubsar

Altorientalistische Publikationen
Publications on the Ancient Near East

Band 10

Herausgegeben von Kristin Kleber und Kai A. Metzler

Catalogue of the Babylonian Tablets in the British Museum

Volumes IV–V

E. Leichty,
I. L. Finkel and
C. B. F. Walker

with contributions by T. G. Pinches, A. J. Sachs,
D. J. Wiseman, W. G. Lambert, M. Jursa,
M. J. Geller, J. C. Fincke and J. J. Taylor

Zaphon

Münster
2019

Cover illustration: Bookplate of Theophilus Pinches, who started the first work on this catalogue in 1894–1895. The drawing is based on an Assyrian sculpture from the South-West Palace at Nimrud drawn by A. H. Layard (Monuments of Nineveh I, pl. 32).

Catalogue of the Babylonian Tablets in the British Museum

Volumes IV–V

E. Leichty, I. L. Finkel and C. B. F. Walker

with contributions by T. G. Pinches, A. J. Sachs, D. J. Wiseman, W. G. Lambert, M. Jursa, M. J. Geller, J. C. Fincke and J. J. Taylor

dubsar 10

Printed in Germany
Printed on acid-free paper

ISBN 978-3-96327-056-7

ISSN 2627-7174

Preface

The present double volume of the Catalogue of the Babylonian Tablets presents all tablets from Babylonia excavated, purchased or donated between 1821 and 1881. Cataloguing of these collections began in 1894-5 when T. G. Pinches prepared a slip catalogue of the first part of the second Spartali collection (here Sp-II). Unfortunately the pressures on the museum's curatorial staff to register the flood of tablets which had come in from Rassam's excavations and continued to come in from dealers and later excavations meant that no further work on cataloguing was undertaken until the 1950s. At that time Abe Sachs would come to the museum every summer to work on Late Babylonian astronomical texts, and each day he and Donald Wiseman would examine more of the tablets listed here and Wiseman would record their identifications on the department's filecards. In the 1970s Irving Finkel continued the process of cataloguing the collections. He developed a vast visual knowledge of the tablets, made a considerable number of joins and continued to annotate the filecards. In the early 1990s Christopher Walker set up a computer database and input all the data from the filecards. Erle Leichty then came each summer to continue the process of cataloguing, checking each tablet in turn, revising the database, and adding identifications for any tablets which had not yet been catalogued. The result was the first draft of the present volume. Over the last 15 years Christopher Walker, with the support of Irving Finkel and Jon Taylor, has continued to edit the catalogue, add bibliography, and consult a number of cuneiform specialists. Michael Jursa re-examined the 1881,0701 collection, Wilfred Lambert helped to revise the long list of literary texts, and Mark Geller and Jeanette Fincke did the same for medical and astrological texts. Numerous other colleagues have examined smaller groups.

We also acknowledge the contribution of Cyril Bateman, Mark Wynthrop-Young and Ken Uprichard, who as conservators baked many of these tablets, making them clearer to read and ensuring their preservation for future generations to work on.

Jonathan Tubb

Keeper, Department of the Middle East, British Museum

Table of contents

Introduction

The tablets in this catalogue derive from (1) the explorations and excavations of Sir Robert Ker Porter, Claudius James Rich, Austen Henry Layard, Henry Rawlinson, William Kennett Loftus, John George Taylor, George Smith and Hormuzd Rassam, (2) purchases from the dealers Marini (Baghdad), Shemtob (London) and Spartali & Co. (London), and (3) smaller purchases from or donations by Claude Scott Steuart, Thomas Burgon, H. O. Cureton, the Duke of Somerset, George Eastwood (previously Mr Hawkins), Lieut.-Gen. Malcolm, Arthur James Lewis, James Paddle, Mme. de Valmency (née Ouseley, daughter of Sir William Ouseley), Alfred J. Lawson, S. M. Alishan (Constantinople), Herica Finnis Jr. of Lynch Bros. London, Alex Hector, Solomon Hurwitz, William St. Chad Boscawen, W. D. Cutter, Miss Erskine, J. Fremlyn Streatfield, the India Museum (London), C. D. Cobham, and Mrs. E. C. B. Chappelow. This last group (3) is only 230 in total.

Registration and numbering

We do not now know how the tablets coming from Iraq were labelled, packed, unpacked, sorted and stored in the museum in the 19th century, but it is clear that the staff had considerable difficulty in maintaining order, and quite a few tablets ended up being registered in the wrong collections. Registration was a long and slow process. For an overview of the problem in relation to many of the collections catalogued here see J. E. Reade's introduction to CBTBM VI, pp. xiii-xxxvi.

The present system of allocating a five- or six-figure number to a tablet, known to outsiders as the "BM number" (although the "BM" element does not appear in the Museum's on-line database) was first implemented by L. W. King in the 1890s. Prior to his work tablets only had their collection numbers (e.g. DT 1 or 76-11-17, 1), and copies by Strassmaier, Bertin and Pinches recorded only collection numbers.

It is clear that when King started allocating the "BM numbers" he found the early part of the collection (tablets acquired before 1871 and now mostly numbered in the range 30000-30222) in a state of considerable confusion, and he only partially succeeded in restoring order. His work was not helped by the fact that obviously some of the tablets (principally those coming from Loftus's excavations) were in a poor state of preservation and may already have lost their original numbering. His own surviving catalogue slips recording the numbering process show that a few tablets had already gone missing and that a few had to be written off in the 1890s having disintegrated beyond repair. The first attempts to conserve tablets in the 1850s seem to have been unsuccessful, and the current process of conservation was only begun by Cyril Bateman in the 1950s, when further tablets had to be written off.

Joins and probable joins

In this catalogue joins which have actually been made are indicated by "+" (e.g. 30282 + 32669) and joins which are probable but which cannot be made because there is insufficient contact between two or more fragments are indicated by "(+)" (e.g. 31425

(+) 36799). Actual joins are recorded as such in the Museum's on-line database, but probable joins are only noted as a separate comment. Unfortunately problems have arisen because students have proposed joins which the Museum's conservators were unable to make because of insufficient contact, but the students have nevertheless published the fragments as joined into a single tablet. While we hope to have presented here an accurate list of real and proposed joins, on receiving a tablet for study it will generally be useful to check that one has actually received all possible fragments of the tablet.

Chronology

Most of the tablets catalogued here are Late Babylonian, dating from the time of Eriba-Marduk and Tiglath-pileser III down to the Seleucid and Arsacid Eras (for which the abbreviations SE and AE are used).

A small number are dated as follows:

Lagaš II (Gudea, Ur-Bau, Ur-Ningirsu, Enannatum): 30044, 30046, 30047, 30049, 30064, 30067, 30071a, 30073, 30074, 30089, 30378-30391, 30393-30403, 32552, 33446, 38118, 90792a, 90845, 91007, 91008, 91056, 91058, 91060, 100691.

Pre-Sargonic: 22457, 22470, 30072, 33429, 45593, 90951.

Ur III (Ur-Nammu, Šu-Sin, Šulgi): 30045(?), 30051-30057, 30065, 30068, 30075-30088, 30090, 30097, 30220, 30222, 33262, 33443, 90826, 91075, 91148.

Old Babylonian (Abiešuḫ, Ammiditana, Ammiṣaduqa, Hammurabi, Išme-Dagan, Lipit-Ištar, Nur-Adad, Rim-Anum, Rim-Sin I & II, Samsuditana, Samsi-iluna, Sin-iddinam, Sin-kašid, Warad-Sin): K.1377, K.4248, K.4709, K.4755, K.6697, K.7855, K.8755, K.8765, K.8795, K.8860, K.8866, K.9076, K.9552, K.9569, K.9870-1, K.9920, K.9967, K.10468, K.10506, K.13720, K.13942, K.14844, K.14946, K.18634; N.1667; Sm.2224; 22455, 22456, 30009, 30010, 30012-30018, 30020-30027, 30029-30039, 30041, 30045, 30048, 30050, 30058-30060, 30062, 30063, 30066, 30069-30071, 30091-30096, 30098, 30099, 30101-30103, 30105-30116, 30181, 30183, 30184, 30215-30219, 30221, 30246, 33108, 33158-33327, 33375, 33394, 33430-33433, 33435-33438, 33440-33442, 33444, 33840, 33843, 33846, 33894, 33099-33103, 38304, 38325, 38378, 38719, 38827, 40037, 40558, 40631, 40955, 42259-42261, 42263-42266, 42270, 42279-42280, 42321, 42376, 42378, 42455, 42456, 42458, 42459, 42462, 42464, 42466-42468, 42471-42474, 42477, 41481, 41482, 42491, 42493, 42511-42521, 42526, 42529, 42531, 42534-42537, 42643, 42670, 42671, 43133, 43157, 43206, 43225, 43228, 43238, 43241, 43243, 43254, 43245, 43278, 43285, 43288, 43289, 43312, 43316, 43317, 43326-43334, 43352, 43381, 43382, 43386, 43388, 43390-43394, 43396-43405, 43411, 43425, 43428, 43450, 43482, 43503, 43532, 43559, 43638, 43653, 43703, 43731, 43789, 43795, 43802, 44731, 45599, 46513, 46918, 47165, 47244, 47312-47315, 47317-47322, 47324-47328, 47330, 47331, 47333-47339a, 90842, 90893, 90899, 90939, 91084, 91149, 91151, 91152, 91923, 92680, 92703, 93029, 139356, 139991-139993.

Old Assyrian: 30230, 90299.
Kassite / Middle Babylonian: N.2050, 1881,0701.3395, 38440, 38646, 40103, 40204, 40494.a, 40590, 47507, 89560, 90827, 90833, 90850, 90937, 90938, 91000, 91001, 91004, 104407, 104408, 104414, 104415, 137438, 137439.
Dynasty of E: 30624, 38114, 38612, 40548.
Middle Assyrian: 30211.
Neo-Assyrian: 30001-30005, 30011, 30190, 30205, 30208, 30209, 30422-30427, 30431, 32646-32650, 33019, 34089, 36448, 36543, 36711, 42439, 45607.

The dates of texts are given in the sequence king day/month/year. This is current English practice, in contrast with the original Babylonian format month/day/year king, and in contrast with Strassmaier's format king year/month/day. As a result where precise chronology is of importance for any future project it will be worth checking the original tablets. Incomplete dates are presented in a format using "-" or "[]" for missing elements. Leichty's original draft only used "-", which does not make clear whether the scribe never actually included that part of the date or whether it was later damaged or broken off. From checking publications and from recent re-examination of some tablets we have changed many cases of "-" to "[]" for lost data, but there remain many cases where the meaning of "-" is unclear. In any case we do not use "-/-/-" or "[]/[]/[]". In practice on Late Babylonian school texts the year is almost never given.

Personal and place names

All personal names are given in standard transliterations or transcriptions with the exception of royal names, which are given in the transcriptions used by J. A Brinkman in his supplement to A. L. Oppenheim's Ancient Mesopotamia (1964) pp. 335-347 (except for Amel-Marduk).

Marduk's temple can be found in current Assyriological literature transcribed variously as Esagil, Esagila, Esangil, or Esangila. In this volume it is, rightly or wrongly, transcribed as Esangila.

All city names are given in standard transliterations or transcriptions with the exception of Babylon and Borsippa. However in references to excavations and entries in the museum's registers modern names of the sites or parts of sites have often been used as follows:

Bābili	Babylon, Ibrahim al-Khalil, Jimjima, Omran, Amran
Barsip	Borsippa, Birs Nimrud, B.N.
Dilbat	Dailem, D.
Girsu	Telloh, Tel-loh
Ḫursag-kalamma	Ingharra (part of Kiš)
Kiš	Al Hymer, El Hymar, Uhaimir
Kutalla	Tell Sifr
Kūtû	Cutha, Kutha, Tell Ibrahim, T.I.
Larsa	Senkereh, Sinkara

Nibru	Nippur, Nuffar, Niffar
Ninua	Niniveh, Kouyunjik
Sippar	Abu Habba, Abu-habbah, A.H.
Sirara	Zurghul
Ur	Mugayer, Muqeyer, Muqayyar, Al Mughair
Uruk	Warka, Erech
unknown	Geraineh

At the beginning of each collection we record what the museum's register says about the provenance of tablets. In individual catalogue entries we record such provenance as is written on the tablet; this includes suggested provenances written in round brackets, e.g. (Babylon), and restored provenances written in square brackets, e.g. [Babylon], where such provenances have been suggested or restored by modern Assyriologists on archival grounds. One should also note that tablets written in one city could be archived and found in another. For instance some of the contracts found in the Egibi archive at Babylon were written at Šušan (Susa).

Series names

Copies of various series will be found in this catalogue under the following standard names:

Lexical series: Aa, An = Anum, Ana ittišu, Diri, Ea, Erimḫuš, Ḫḫ (ḪAR-ra = ḫubullu), Idu, Kunuk ḫalti, Lú = ša, Malku, Nabnitu, Reciprocal Ea, Syllabary A/B, Šammu šikinšu, Ṭup abni, Uruanna, Weidner god list.

Literary and ritual texts or series: Angim, Bīt mēseri, Counsels of Wisdom, Dialogue 5 (OB), Enmešarra's defeat, Enūma eliš, Erra, Fable of the fox (and dog), Farmer's Instructions, Gilgamesh, Giš-al hymn, Ḫulbazizi, Instructions of Šuruppak, Lamaštu, Ludlul, Maqlu, Marduk's Address, Mīs pî, Muššu'u, Prayer to Marduk no. 1 or 2, Sag-ba, Sag-gig, Šamaš Hymn, Šurpu, Theodicy, Tintir II.

Omen series: Alamdimmû, Enūma Anu Enlil, Iqqur īpuš, Sa-gig, Šumma ālu, Šumma ekallu, Šumma izbu, Šumma multabiltu, Šumma šulmu, Udug-ḫul.

Tablet shapes and direction of script

Most of the tablets catalogued here are of standard formats, nearly rectangular or circular, being turned by the scribe from bottom to top in order to inscribe the reverse and with the text written in the same direction on both obverse and reverse. There are a few exceptions to this pattern.

Tablets of unusual shape: 33016 (amulet?), 36734 (amulet), 37912 (olive shaped), 38044 (irregular shape), 38502 (bead), 39706 (irregular shape), 42291 (bead), 44765 (irregular shape), 46533 (ball-shaped), 46534 (ball-shaped), 47576 (ball-shaped), 47577 (ball-shaped), 48437 (irregular shape), 48441 (cone-shaped), 104891 (amulet), 137497 (irregular shape).

Direction of script: Tablets turning sideways from obverse to reverse: 33016, 41217, 41624, 45394, 45552, 47042, 48100. Tablets with one face inscribed in portrait format and the other in landscape format, so that the two parts of the text are at right angles to each other: 31778, 31918, 33384, 33879, 36651, 37162, 41570, 43889, 46735, 47102, 47298. On 37405 the obverse is inscribed in one column, but the reverse is inscribed in two columns of which one is upside down. On the cylinder 40134 the two columns are written in opposite directions. On 47593 two lines on the upper edge are inscribed upside down.

Copying problems

Modern Assyriologists copying tablets are usually careful to indicate where tablets and individual signs are damaged or lost, but this was not always the practice. E. A. W. Budge, The rise and progress of Assyriology (1925), p. 172, writes: "The duty of the copyist is not to make a facsimile of the tablet which he is copying and show every scratch or abrasion of the surface of the clay, but to supply the student with a copy of the text which he can read. It is useless to smother with lines a character which the copyist cannot read with certainty, and to think that the student or a fellow-scholar will be helped by such evidence of the copyist's uncertainty. It is the duty of the copyist to decide what each character is before he copies it and to make his copy as clear and neat as possible." This comment clearly reflects the practice of Strassmaier, and to a lesser extent of Bertin and Pinches. Where tablets have been copied by both Strassmaier and Bertin comparison of their copies shows that while Bertin shades many damaged areas and damaged signs Strassmaier copies damaged tablets without any indication that anything is damaged or lost. Pinches's copies are generally the best in showing just how much is damaged. In some cases tablets have been conserved and cleaned since the 19th century copy was made and the signs may have been made clearer, but in other cases tablets have deteriorated and there must be room for doubt about how accurately the 19th century copy really reflects what the original scribe wrote. This issue needs to be kept in mind when checking and editing these tablets.

Index of collections

1821,0120	Sir Robert Ker Porter
1825,0503	Mary Rich, wife of C. J. Rich
1895,0406	Miss Holmes (previously C. J. Rich)
1841,0726	Claude Scott Steuart
1842,0728	Thomas Burgon
1848,1104	A.H. Layard
N	A.H. Layard
1849,0623	Harry Osborn Cureton (previously J. R. Steuart)
1851,0101	W. K. Loftus
1851,1009	Lt. Col. H. Rawlinson
1856,0903	W. K. Loftus
1856,0908	J. G. Taylor

1856,1110	Duke of Somerset
1859,1014	J. G. Taylor
1862,0716	George Eastwood (previously Hawkins)
1868,0709	Lieut. General T. J. Malcolm
1869,1006	Arthur J. Lewis
Old collections	various
K	various
1871,0311	James Paddle
1873,0319	Mme. De Valmency
1875,0609	Alfred J. Lawson
1876,0102	S. M. Alishan
1876,0110	J. M. Shemtob
1876,0515	Herica Finnis Jr., of Lynch Bros.
1876,1016	J. M. Shemtob
DT	G. Smith
Sm	G. Smith
1876,1117	G. Smith
1877,0222	J. M. Shemtob
1877,0409	J. M. Shemtob
1877,0417	J. M. Shemtob
1877,1002	Alex Hector
1877,1114	Raphael I. Shemtob
1877,1115	Solomon Hurwitz
1877,1116	Messrs. Spartali & Co.
1877,1129	W. St. Chad Boscawen
1878,0531	William D. Cutter
1878,0730	Solomon Hurwitz
1878,0828	Miss Erskine
1878,0902	J. M. Shemtob
1878,1015	J. M. Shemtob
1878,1023	J. M. Shemtob
1878,1028	J. M. Shemtob
1878,1107	J. M. Shemtob
1878,1120	J. M. Shemtob
1878,1130	J. M. Shemtob
1878,1218	Messrs. Spartali & Co.
1879,0201	J. M. Shemtob
1879,0301	J. M. Shemtob
1879,0322	J. M. Shemtob
1879,0419	J. M. Shemtob
1879,0430	J. M. Shemtob
1879,0606	J. M. Shemtob
1879,0730	J. M. Shemtob
1879,1108	J. M. Shemtob
1879,1210	J. Fremlyn Streatfeild

B	W. K. Loftus
Rm	H. Rassam
Rm-II	H. Rassam
Rm-III	H. Rassam
Rm-IV	H. Rassam
Sp	Messrs. Spartali & Co.
Sp-II	Messrs. Spartali & Co.
Sp-III	Messrs. Spartali & Co.
1880,0126	J. M. Shemtob
1880,0130	India Museum (London)
1880,0617	H. Rassam
1880,1012	Messrs. Spartali & Co.
1880,1112	H. Rassam
1881,0201	Messrs. Spartali & Co.
1881,0324	H. Rassam
1881,0428	H. Rassam
1881,0625	Messrs. Spartali & Co.
1881,0701	H. Rassam
1881,0706	Joseph M. Shemtob
1881,0727	H. Rassam
1881,0728	H. Rassam
1881,0830	H. Rassam
1881,1008	C. D. Cobham
1881,1103	H. Rassam
Later collections	(1882-1883)
1958,0412	Mrs. E. C. B. Chappelow (previously T. G. Pinches)

1821,0120 collection

The 1821,0120 collection was presented by Sir Robert Ker Porter. For an account of his travels and researches see Ker Porter, Travels. Some of the items found or acquired by Ker Porter and by C. J. Rich (1825,0503 collection) were drawn by Carl Bellino (1791-1820); on his activity see R. D. Barnett, Charles Bellino and the beginnings of Assyriology, Iraq 36 (1974), 5-28, and W. Schramm, Carl Bellino and G. Fr. Grotefend. Briefe und Inschriften, ZA 64 (1975) 250-290; his drawings are preserved in the Niedersächsischen Staats- und Universitätsbibliothek Göttingen. A few of the items which Bellino drew came to the British Museum through the later collectors Claude Scott Steuart (1841,0726) and C. D. Cobham (1881,1008).

30042	1821,0120.3	Uninscribed brick.
90917	1821,0120.9	Brick of Nebuchadnezzar II; previously numbered 12045. CBI, no. 102.
90286	1821,0120.13	Brick of Adad-apla-iddina. (Kiš). Ker Porter, Travels II, pl. 77 (Bellino's copy); CBI, no. 72; Barnett and Walker, Iraq 36, 27, no. 8.
90908	1821,0120.11	Historical cylinder of Nebuchadnezzar II. Previously numbered 12036. Ker Porter, Travels II, pl. 78 (Bellino's copy); Berger, AOAT 4/1, Nebukadnezar Zylinder-Fragment III,1, no. 1; Barnett and Walker, Iraq 36, 27, no. 11.

1825,0503 collection

The 1825,0503 collection was purchased from Mary Rich, widow of Claudius James Rich (1787-1820) who had been resident, or agent, at Baghdad in the service of the East India Company in the years 1808-1820.

On Rich's activities in Iraq see his various publications: (1) Memoir on the ruins of Babylon (1818); (2) Narrative of a residence in Koordistan, and on the site of ancient Nineveh: with journal of a voyage down the Tigris to Bagdad and an account of a visit to Shirauz and Persepolis; edited by Rich's widow (1836); (3) Narrative of a Journey to the Site of Babylon in 1811: Memoir on the Ruins: Remarks on the Topography of Ancient Babylon by Major Rennell in Reference to the Memoir: Second Memoir on the Ruins in Reference to Major Rennell's Remarks with Narrative of a Journey to Persepolis; edited by Rich's widow (1839).

The original registration of the Rich collection ("Claudius James Rich Esq., late resident, or agent, at Basra and Baghdad, in the service of the East India Company") in the then Department of Antiquities deals with the items inscribed in cuneiform only briefly, "2. Stones, and bricks with the cuneiform character. 3. A beautiful, hollow cylinder in terra cotta, covered, on the outside, with cuneiform, or arrow-headed characters. 4. Five smaller solid cylinders, in terra cotta, with cuneiform characters. 5. Many pieces of terra cotta, in different shapes, some of them fragments: all having the cuneiform character." There is no clear indication of the numbers of items involved, and the collection included a few fakes.

The Rich collection was eventually re-registered in the Department of the Ancient Near East in the 1980s by J. E. Reade and C. B. F. Walker, Walker being responsible for the tablets, but it is not entirely clear in every case why a tablet was allocated to this collection. Thus there must be some doubt over 30123 and 30127. Many tablets are marked with "R" on a small fragment of white paper glued to the tablet, and it has generally been assumed that this means Rich; but it should be noted that in the registers for early numbers of the Kouyunjik Collection there is often a note in the right-hand margin, "R.1" or the like, which does not obviously mean Rich, but presumably reflects another numbering system. The numbers given to 30135 by Strassmaier and Bertin are also problematic.

Many of these tablets come from what is now known as the Kasr archive; see Stolper, Fs Larsen, 511-549.

	1825,0503.001ff.	Rich 1-58 are bricks. See CBI.
90837	1825,0503.099	Stele of Nabonidus. Previously numbered 12149. Purchased by Rich at Babylon in 1811. Babylon. Rich, Narrative Babylon, pl. 8, 2a-b (Bellino's copy); King, BBSt, 128-129 and pls. XCIII-XCIV, no. XXXVII; Schaudig, AOAT 256, 530-532; Barnett and Walker, Iraq 36, 27, no. 2.
90833	1825,0503.100	Boundary-stone (kudurru), recording a grant of land. Purchased at Babylon. Previously numbered 12070. Babylon. Rich, Narrative Babylon, pl. 8, 1a-c (Bellino's copy); King, BBSt, 83-84 and pls. LXXX-LXXXI and 15, no. XIV; Barnett and Walker, Iraq 36, 27, no. 1.
93029	1825,0503.101	Old Babylonian fragment of diorite monument. Royal inscription of Hammurabi. Also wrongly registered as N.1667. Ker Porter, Travels II, p. 395 and pl. 77 h (Bellino's copy), with reference to its being found by Bellino at Al Khymer (Kiš); King, LIH I, 128, no. 67 and II, 197, no. II (as N. 1667); Frayne, RIME 4.3.6.20; Barnett and Walker, Iraq 36, 27, no. 10 (under wrong number 93089).
91119	1825,0503.103	Historical cylinder of Nebuchadnezzar II. Also registered as K.1683. (Babylon). Rich, Narrative Babylon, pl. 9, 4 (Bellino's copy); 1R 52, 4; Berger, AOAT 4/1, Nebukadnezar Zylinder II, 2, no. 1; Barnett and Walker, Iraq 36, 27, no. 4.
K.5424c	1825,0503.108	Promissory note for barley and emmer; with Aramaic note; probably from the Kasr archive. Also registered as K.5424c. [Dar II] []/[]/15. [Babylon?]. Stevenson, Ass.-Bab. Contracts, no. 41; 2R 70, no. 15; Stolper, Fs Larsen, 520.

K.8485	1825,0503.109	Promissory note for dates; vitrified; probably from the Kasr archive. Also registered as K.8485. [Dar II] []/8/11. [Babylon] (Kasr archive). Bertin 3075; Stolper, Fs Larsen, 520.
K.8506	1825,0503.110	Promissory note for apples; vitrified; probably from the Kasr archive. Also registered as K.8506. Art I/II 1/2/10. Tamerat Ṭābānu (near Borsippa). Bertin 2872; Stolper, Bagh Mitt 21 (1990) 560 n. 5; Stolper, Fs Larsen, 520.
K.8133	1825,0503.112	Contract for hire of oxen; date lost. Also registered as K.8133. Stolper, JAOS 114, 625-627.
30040	1825,0503.113	Memorandum about 36 seals; not dated. (Babylon). Rich, Narrative Babylon, pl. 9, 5 (Bellino's copy); Barnett and Walker, Iraq 36, 27, no. 5.
30121	1825,0503.114	Contract; sale of real estate; sealed. For the seal cf. 30131, 30212, 68456-7, TSBA 4 256 & pl. [Art I]. [Babylon] (Kasr archive). Stolper, Fs Larsen, 520; Nisaba 28, no. 220.
30123	1825,0503.115	Promissory note for silver. Cyr 28/12/3. Uruk (Sîn-tabni archive). Bertin 1686-7.
30124	1825,0503.116	Promissory note for dates. Dar II 17/6/10. Ḫanašatu. Bertin 2186; Grotefend, ZKM 1, 212-222 and pl. after p. 254: B 2 (Bellino copy N of the date only); Barnett and Walker; Iraq 36, 27, no. 17; Stolper, Fs Larsen, 529 and 545.
30125	1825,0503.117	Contract; fragment, witnesses only. Probably part of the Kasr archive. Dar II 10/4/18. [Babylon]. Bertin 2395. Stolper, NABU 1999, 6-9, no. 6 (attribution to Darius II); Stolper, Fs Larsen, 520.
30126	1825,0503.118	Sale of a slave; finger-nail mark and caption. Dar II 1/1/7. Bīt Šurā. Bertin 2106; Stolper, ZA 79, 93-95; Stolper, Fs Larsen, 520.
30127	1825,0503.119	Promissory note for silver. Cyr 9/5/7. Uruk (Sîn-tabni archive). Bertin 1682.
30128	1825,0503.120	Receipt for rent; sealed; finger-nail marks. Art II 11/3/3. Babylon (Kasr archive). Strassmaier, 8th Orientalist Congress, no. 24; Oppert and Ménant, DJ, 278-280, no. 7; Stolper, Fs Larsen, 520; Bertin 2866; Nisaba 28, no. 228.
30129	1825,0503.121	Contract; lease of a field. Strassmaier gives registration as R, 51-1-1-? Dar II 11/6/3. Bab-surri. Dar 78; Bertin 1978; Stolper, Fs Larsen, 520.
30130	1825,0503.122	Promissory note for silver. Esarhaddon 25/1/4. Libbi-āli (Babylon). Strassmaier, 8th Orientalist Congress, no. 3; San Nicolò, BR 8/7, no. 51; Brinkman and Ken-

		nedy, JCS 35, 18, I.7; Bertin 1; Oppert and Ménant, DJ, 186-7, no. 20.
30131	1825,0503.123	Contract; sale of land; sealed; for the seal see 30121, TSBA 4, 256 and BM 68456-7. [Art I]. [Babylon]. Grotefend, ZKM 4, 43-57, and pl. after p. 258, F (Bellino's copy); Barnett and Walker, Iraq 36, 28, no. 20; Stolper, Fs Larsen, 520, 524-5 and 542; Nisaba 28, no. 221.
30133	1825,0503.124	Contract; fragment; date lost. [Babylon]. Stolper, Fs Larsen, 531 and 546 (Bellino copy P). (For 30134 see 1880,0130.13).
30135	1825,0503.125	Promissory note for silver. Dupl. 31509 (Dar 319). Dar 22/1/12. Babylon (Egibi archive). Dar 319a (as + 172); Bertin 2231 (as S†.122).
30136	1825,0503.126	Contract; sale of silver; lower left corner; sealed; vitrified. [Dar II?]. [Babylon] (Kasr archive). Stolper, Fs Larsen, 520; Nisaba 28, no. 224.
30140	1825,0503.127	Contract; fragment; witnesses; vitrified. Art I/II 11+/7?/[]. Dūru-ša-karrabbi. Bertin 2876; Stolper, Fs Larsen, 520.
30159	1825,0503.128	Contract; receipt for rent of a field; vitrified; sealed. Dar II []/12/[18]. Babylon (Kasr archive). Dar 476; Stolper, Fs Reiner, 393; Stolper, Fs Larsen, 520; Stolper, NABU 1999, 6-9, no. 6 (attribution to Darius II); Nisaba 28, no. 226.
115716	1825,0503.129	Contract for sale of a slave. [Art I/II]. [Babylon]. Stolper, ZA 79, 87 n. 13 and 99-100 (Bellino copy O); Stolper, Fs Larsen, 520, 546 (Bellino copy O).
67423	1825,0503.189	Receipt for barley; vitrified. Marked "R", but registered as 1882,0918.7420. Dar II 7/9/14. Dilbat (Kasr archive). Bertin 2312; Oppert and Ménant, DJ, 276-278, no. 6; Stolper, Iraq 54 (1992), 119-121; Stolper, Fs Larsen, 520.

Note also:

	1895,0406.2	Contract; sublease of fields; Aramaic note. Kasr archive. Presented by Miss Holmes; originally in the collection of C. J. Rich and given to Miss Holmes by Miss Hay-Erskine, Rich's great-niece; see King, ZA 10 (1895) 95-98. Art II 9/5/1. (Babylon). Copied by Carl Bellino; see Stolper, Fs Reiner (1987), 390 n. 4 and 393-394; Borger, WAO, 181, no. 1; Zadok, Israel Oriental Studies 18 (1990) 257 n. 5 (on the Aramaic note); Stolper, Fs Larsen, 520 and 533-4 and 548 (Bellino copy).

1841,0726 collection

The 1841,0726 collection was presented by Claude Scott Steuart.

	1841,0726	For bricks in this collection see CBI.
30170	1841,0726.27	Terracotta figurine.
91134	1841,0726.55	Cast of the Emaḫ cylinder of Nebuchadnezzar II. Berger, AOAT 4/1, Nebukadnezar Zylinder II,1, no. 12.
30210	1841,0726.56	List of daily offerings to gods (of Uruk) in the months Kislīmu, Ṭebētu and Šabāṭu. Zawadzki, ZA 103, 230-236.
-	1841,0726.57	Cast of the Emaḫ cylinder of Nebuchadnezzar II. Berger, AOAT 4/1, Nebukadnezar Zylinder II, 1, no. 13.
90939	1841,0726.58	Old Babylonian steatite tablet. Historical inscription of Hammurabi. Previously numbered 12068. 1R 4 xv 1; King, LIH, no. 61; Frayne, RIME 4.3.6.16.1.
68610	1841,0726.59	Legal protocol; resolution of dispute over possession of temple fields and revenues belonging to the estate of Šamaš collected by officials at Babylon; mentions Ebabbar at Larsa; sealed. The tablet is also registered as 1882,0908.8609. Alexander IV 11/[]/9. [Babylon]. Ker Porter, Travels II pl. 77g (drawn by Bellino); Oppert and Ménant, DJ, 285-290, no. IX; Barnett and Walker, Iraq 36, 27, no. 9; Oelsner, ZA 56, 267 (no. 2); Bertin 1924-1925; van der Spek, Grondbezit, 202-211, no. 5; Stolper, Achaemenid History VIII, 347; Jursa, Persika, pp. 147-148, n. 32; Searight, no. 639; van der Spek, JESHO 57, 212; Nisaba 28, no. 548.
-	1841,0726.63	Register: Square fragment, steatite, 1 + 5 lines. 2 3/4 in.
-	1841,0726.64	Register: Fragment of a brick with part of two lines of cuneiform inscription. 6 x 4 1/2 in.
30043	1841,0726.66	Brick of Nebuchadnezzar II. CBI, no. 101.
89878	1841,0726.189	Eye-stone with inscription of Nebuchadnezzar II. Berger, AOAT 4/1, p. 159
90986	1841,0726.301	Cast of the Emaḫ cylinder of Nebuchadnezzar II. Previously numbered 12119. Berger, AOAT 4/1, Nebukadnezar Zylinder II, 1, no. 16.

1842,0728 collection

The 1842,0728 collection was purchased from Thomas Burgon.

30143	1842,0728.60	Promissory note for barley. Dar II 22/12/16?. Kār-Nabû. Dar 364; Bertin 2261.

1848,1104 collection

The 1848,1104 collection comes from the excavations of Austen Henry Layard.

90937	1848,1104.284	Stone tablet; sale of land. Previously numbered as 12066. Found by Layard at Nimrud. Simbar-šipak. Saḫrītu. King, BBSt, 101-104, pls. 20-22, no. XXVII; Layard, Niniveh II, p. 40, and MN II, pl. 95a nos. 12-13, and ICC pl. 53.
30211	1848,1104.318	Middle Assyrian. List of men assigned to gates in Ashur. Līmu of Mušallim-Adad, month Muḫur-ilī, day 26. Registered by T. G. Pinches on 21/10/1891 "with the 48-11-4 collection as being, as far as date of acquisition is concerned, the most probable one", and provenance recorded as Kala'at Sherkat = Ashur. George, Iraq 50, 30-35.

N collection

The N collection comes from the excavations of Austen Henry Layard; part arrived in London in 1848 and part in 1851.

22456	N.615	Old Babylonian mace head in copper; É.GAL Ḫa-am-mu-ra-bi. Presumably one of the group found by Layard at Tell Mohammed in 1851; see Layard, Nineveh and Babylon, p. 477, and Harris, JCS 9, 31. King, LIH, no. 65; Frayne, RIME 4.3.6.18.2.
-	N.1667	See 1825,0503.101 = 93029.
-	N.2050	Middle Babylonian limestone relief; carved fragment with the ends of three lines of inscription; showing two gods in procession, one labelled Mār-bīti. (Babylon). Layard, Nineveh and Babylon, 508 (Layard misread Mār-bīti as Ninlil).

1849,0623 collection

The 1849,0623 collection was presented by H. O. Cureton; the individual items had previously been included in the sale on 22 June 1849 of the collection of J. R. Steuart.

-	1849,0623.39	Register: Babylonian brick, with impressions of seals inscribed in cuneiform characters. Length 3 5/8 in, breadth 3 in.
-	1849,0623.40	Register: Babylonian brick, with carved figure on reverse.
91135	1849,0623.42	Historical cylinder of Nebuchadnezzar II. Berger, AOAT 4/1, Nebukadnezar Zylinder II, 7, no. 2.
30212	1849,0623.43	Contract; sale of a house, sealed, finger-nail marks. Nisaba 28, no. 222.

30213	1849,0623.47	Promissory note for silver; sealed; vitrified. Art II 1/1/9. Borsippa. Nisaba 28, no. 230.

1851,0101 collection

The 1851,0101 collection comes from the excavations of William Kennett Loftus. On Loftus's travels and excavations see his book, Travels and researches in Chaldaea and Susiana; with an account of excavations at Warka, the "Erech" of Nimrod, and Shush, "Shushan the palace", of Eshtar, in 1849-52 (London 1857), and his article "Notes of a journey from Baghdad to Busrah, with descriptions of several Chaldaean remains" in Journal of the Royal Geographical Society of London 26 (1856) 131-153. The Department of the Middle East has an unpublished manuscript volume by W. K. Loftus and H. A. Churchill, Drawings in Babylonia. With the exception of 1851,0101.217 those tablets for which no five-figure museum number is given cannot now be identified or located; their descriptions are taken from the museum's register. Any attempt to identify them with tablets with missing registration numbers to which L. W. King allocated numbers in the 1890s (e.g. 30007 etc. below) or with the tablets which we re-register below as 1851,0101.360 etc. will necessarily be very speculative particularly given the number of tablets which have had to be written off having disintegrated beyond repair.

	1851,0101	For bricks in this collection see CBI.
	1851,0101.120	Register: Tablet with 25 lines of cuneiform inscription. 2 1/2 x 1 3/4 in.
30173	1851,0101.121	Promissory note for silver. Nbn 6/1/16. Uruk (Sîn-tabni archive). Bertin 669. Register: Do. 20 lines. 2 1/4 x 1 3/4 in.
	1851,0101.122	Register: Do. 36 lines (and 2 on the edge). 3 1/2 x 2 1/2 in.
	1851,0101.123	Register: Do. 24 lines. 2 1/8 x 1 5/8 in.
30174	1851,0101.124	Promissory note for silver. Nbk 17/7/12. [Uruk] (Atû archive). Nbk 95; Bertin 72. Register: Do. 21 lines (much broken). 2 1/2 x 1 7/8 in.
30175	1851,0101.125	Contract; lease of a house. Nbn []/[]/7. Uruk. Bertin 449. Marked by Bertin as 51-1-1, 25(?); it seems to correspond to no. 125. Register: Do. 21 lines. 2 1/4 x 1 5/8 in.
	1851,0101.126	Register: Do. 19 lines (broken). 2 1/4 x 1 1/2 in.
	1851,0101.127	Register: Do. 22 lines. 2 x 1 1/4 in.
	1851,0101.128	Register: Do. 24 lines. 2 1/2 x 1 3/4 in.
	1851,0101.129	Register: Do. 20 lines. 2 x 1 1/4 in.
	1851,0101.130	Register: Do. 17 lines. 1 1/5 x 1 in.
	1851,0101.131	Register: Do. 19 lines. 1 3/4 x 1 1/2 in.
	1851,0101.132	Register: Do. 16 lines. 2 x 1 1/2 in.
	1851,0101.133	Register: Do. 19 lines. 2 x 1 1/4 in.
	1851,0101.134	Register: Do. 16 lines. 2 1/4 x 1 3/4 in.

	1851,0101.135	Register: Do. 16 lines. 1 1/2 x 1 3/4 in.
30144	1851,0101.136	Promissory note for silver. Nbn 6/6/16. Uruk (Sîn-tabni archive). Nbn 977; Bertin 677. Register: Do. 16 lines. 1 1/2 x 1 1/4 in.
	1851,0101.137	Promissory note for silver. Nbn 30/1/15. Uruk(!) (Sîn-tabni archive). Bertin 646. Register: Do. 24 lines. 2 1/2 x 2 1/4 in. Presumably now written off.
	1851,0101.138	Register: Do. 21 lines (much corroded). 2 x 1 1/2 in.
	1851,0101.139	Register: Do. 25 lines. 3 x 2 1/8 in.
	1851,0101.140	Register: Do. 32(?) lines (much broken). 2 1/2 x 2 in.
	1851,0101.141	Register: Do. 15 lines. 1 1/4 x 1 1/4 in.
	1851,0101.142	Register: Do. 19 lines. 1 3/4 x 1 1/4 in.
	1851,0101.143	Register: Do. 19 lines (much damaged). 1 3/4 x 1 1/2 in.
	1851,0101.144	Register: Do. much broken and damaged. 2 3/4 x 1 3/4 in.
	1851,0101.145	Register: Do. with 22 lines (much corroded). 2 x 1 3/4 in.
	1851,0101.146	Register: Do. 14 lines (much corroded). 2 x 1 1/2 in.
	1851,0101.147	Register: Do. 18(?) lines (much corroded). 2 3/4 x 2 1/4 in.
	1851,0101.148	Register: Do. 21 lines (much corroded). 2 1/4 x 2 in.
	1851,0101.149	Register: Do. 26 lines. 3 x 2 in.
30164	1851,0101.150	Promissory note for silver; now much disintegrated. Cam 10/9/1. Uruk (Sîn-tabni archive). Cam 78; Bertin 1788. Register: Do. 20 lines (much broken). 2 1/4 x 1 1/2. 1851,0101.151 Register: Do. 22 lines. 2 5/8 x 2 in.
	1851,0101.152	Register: Do. 19 lines. 2 x 1 1/2 in.
	1851,0101.153	Register: Do. 25 lines. 2 1/2 in. x 2 in.
	1851,0101.154	Register: Do. 21 lines. 2 x 1 1/2 in.
	1851,0101.155	Register: Do. 21(?) lines (much decayed). 4 x 3 1/4 in.
	1851,0101.156	Register: Do. 15 lines. 2 x 1 1/2 in.
	1851,0101.157	Register: Do. 9 lines (on one side only). 2 x 1 1/4 in.
	1851,0101.158	Register: Do. several lines much damaged. 5 1/2 x 3 in.
	1851,0101.159	Register: Do. 14 lines. 1 1/2 x 1 1/4 in.
	1851,0101.160	Register: Do. quite decomposed. 2 x 1 1/2 in.
92707	1851,0101.161	Promissory note for silver. Nbk 15/7/21. Uruk (Atû archive). Nbk 129; Strassmaier, Warka 112. Register: Do. with 14 lines. 2 x 1 1/2 in. The tablet is also registered as K.1297, and actually marked 92707, K.1297, and in red 29+ and R.201.

30176	1851,0101.162	Contract; receipt for silver. Cam 14/3/2. Uruk (Sîn-tabni archive). Bertin 1784; Oppert and Ménant, DJ, 268-9, no. II. Register: Do. 14 lines. 1 1/2 x 1 1/8 in.
	1851,0101.163	Register: Do. 8 lines (on one side only). 1 1/2 x 1 in.
	1851,0101.164	Register: Do. 19 lines (much corroded). 1 3/4 x 1 1/4 in.
30178	1851,0101.165a	Contract; lease of a house. [Uruk?]. Bertin 3070. Bertin gives registration as "51-1-1-169, 2"; the tablet has 165. The tablet corresponds to what is registered as 165a. Register: Fragment of tablet with 12 lines (broken). 2 1/4 x 1 1/2 in.
	1851,0101.165b	Register: Fragment of tablet with 13 lines (and two seals). 1 1/2 x 1 in.
30177	1851,0101.165c	Promissory note for silver. Npl 15/12/10. [Uruk] (Atû archive). Strassmaier, ZA 4, 139, no. 7; Kennedy, JCS 38, 192, T.10.41; Bertin 5. Marked by Bertin and Strassmaier, and on the tablet, as "51-1-1, 1659". The tablet corresponds to what is registered as 165c. Register: Do. do. 9 lines. 2 x 1 in.
	1851,0101.165d	Register: Do. do. 5 lines. 2 1/2 x 1 1/8 in.
	1851,0101.165e	Register: Do. do. much broken. 2 3/4 x 2 1/4 in.
	1851,0101.165f	Register: Do. do. 16 lines. 2 x 1 1/2 in.
	1851,0101.165g	Register: Do. do. 16(?) lines. 1 5/8 x 1 1/8 in.
	1851,0101.165h	Register: Do. do. inscribed quite decayed. 2 1/4 x 1 1/4 in.
	1851,0101.165i	Register: Do. do. 19 lines (in 2 pieces). 1 3/4 x 1 1/2 in.
	1851,0101.165k	Register: Do. do. quite decayed. 1 1/2 x 1 1/2 in.
	1851,0101.165l	Register: Do. do. 7 lines. 1 1/2 x 1 in.
	1851,0101.165m	Register: Do. do. 9 lines. 1 3/4 x 1 in.
30179	1851,0101.165n	Promissory note for silver; sealed. Nbn 20/6/14. Uruk (Sîn-tabni archive). + 1851,0101.165s and bb. Bertin 626; Nisaba 28, no. 683. Register: Do. do. 11 lines. 3 x 1 in.
	1851,0101.165o	Register: Do. do. 11 lines.1 1/4 x 1 1/8 in.
	1851,0101.165p	Register: Do. do. 17 lines. 2 x 1 1/8 in.
	1851,0101.165q	Register: Do. do. 8 lines (on one side only). 2 x 1 1/2 in.
	1851,0101.165r	Register: Do. do. 19 lines. 2 1/4 x 1 1/2 in.
	1851,0101.165s	Joined to 30179. Register: Do. do. 6 lines (and 1 seal). 1 3/4 x 1 3/4 in.
	1851,0101.165t	Register: Do. do. quite decayed. 2 1/2 x 1 1/2 in.
	1851,0101.165u	Register: Do. do. quite decayed. 2 x 1 1/2 in.
	1851,0101.165v	Register: 17 lines (in 2 pieces). 2 x 1 3/4 in.
	1851,0101.165w	Register: 14 lines. 1 1/2 x 1 in.

	1851,0101.165x	Register: Do. do. quite decayed. No dimensions given.
	1851,0101.165y	Register: Do. do. quite decayed. No dimensions given.
	1851,0101.165z	Register: Do. do. quite decayed. No dimensions given.
	1851,0101.165aa	Register: Do. do. quite decayed. No dimensions given.
	1851,0101.165bb	Joined to 30179. Register: Do. do. 7 lines. 1 3/4 x 1 in.
	1851,0101.165cc	Register: Do. do. quite decayed. 1 1/2 x 1 in.
	1851,0101.165dd	Register: Do. do. 7 lines. 1 1/2 x 1 in.
	1851,0101.165ee	Register: Do. do. reduced to mud. No dimensions given.
	1851,0101.165ff	Register: Do. do. quite decayed. 1 3/4 x 1 in.
	1851,0101.165gg	Register: Do. do. 11 lines. 2 x 1 1/2 in.
	1851,0101.165hh	Register: Do. do. 6 lines. 1 1/2 x 1 1/4 in.
	1851,0101.165ii	Register: Do. do. (in two pieces). No dimensions given.
	1851,0101.165kk	Register: Do. do. (in 7 pieces). No dimensions given.
	1851,0101.165ll	Register: Do. do. (in 2 pieces). No dimensions given.
K.55	1851,0101.166	Lexical; Ḫḫ X. The tablet is also registered as K.55. (Uruk?). MSL 7, 71; CT 19, 1-2 (both as K.55).
91150	1851,0101.167	Joined to 30071.
91151	1851,0101.168	Old Babylonian cone; inscription of Sin-kašid. Frayne, RIME 4.1.8.1-2
30089	1851,0101.169	Lagaš II cone; inscription of Gudea dedicated to Nindub. Uruk. 1R 5 xxiii 1; Steible, FAOS 9/1 Gudea 39 C; Edzard, RIME 3/1 1.7.35; Layard, Nineveh and Babylon, 564; Loftus, Travels, 190.
91923	1851,0101.170	Old Babylonian stone plaque with inscription in reverse, draft for five seal inscriptions. Collon, CS III, p. 220, no. 656, pl. XLVI.
22457	1851,0101.215	Alabaster vase fragment dedicated to Geštinanna; pre-Sargonic. PreSa.
30180	1851,0101.216	Court record; first witnesses are Nabû-ušabši, governor of Uruk, and Nabû-iqiša, šatammu of Eanna. Uruk. Brinkman and Kennedy, JCS 35, 39, Kn.12 (proposing dating to the time of Šamaš-šum-ukin and Ashurbanipal).
-	1851,0101.217	Late Uruk tablet with archaic numerals. Reade, Fs Strommenger. 177-179.
30215	1851,0101.256	Old Babylonian cone; inscription of Sin-iddinam. Larsa. 1R 3 ix; CT 21, 30; Frayne, RIME 4.2.9.7.

	1851,0101.292	Register: Fragment from centre of brick, 9 lines. 3 1/2 x 3 1/4 in.
	1851,0101.296	Register: Brick, with illegible inscription. 8 1/2 x 8 1/2 in.

The following items, for which the registration number had been lost, clearly come from Loftus's excavations at Uruk and have recently been re-registered at the end of the 1851,0101 collection.

30132	1851,0101.360	Promissory note for silver; now almost illegible. 24 lines. 2 1/2 x 2 in. Nbn 6/1/16. ⌜Uruk⌝ (Sîn-tabni archive). Bertin 668.
30139	1851,0101.354	Promissory note for silver. 21 lines damaged. 2 1/8 x 1 3/4 in. Nbk 19/3/[]. ⌜Uruk⌝ (archive uncertain). Nbk 423; Bertin 854. Nbn 17/11/4.
30141	1851,0101.355	Promissory note for silver. 19 lines damaged. 2 1/8 x 1 3/4 in. Cyr 23/8/5. Uruk (Atû archive). Cyr 203; Bertin 802.
30147	1851,0101.361	Promissory note for silver. 16 lines. 2 1/8 x 1 5/8 in. Cyr 14/1/3. Uruk (Sîn-tabni archive). Bertin 772.
30149	1851,0101.362	Promissory note for silver. 7 lines. 1 5/8 x 1 in. Cyr -/-/6. [Uruk] (Sîn-tabni archive). Bertin 1770 (as R.?).
30150	1851,0101.356	Receipt for silver ilku-dues. 18 lines damaged. 1 5/8 x 1 1/4 in. Cyr 27/12/2. Uruk (Sîn-tabni archive) Cyr 89; Bertin 762.
30151	1851,0101.363	Promissory note for silver. 16+ lines damaged. 2 x 1 1/2 in. Dar 8/6/2. Uruk (Atû archive). Dar 39; Bertin 1934.
30158	1851,0101.364	Promissory note for silver. 24 lines. 2 5/8 x 1 7/8 in. Nbn 6/11/9. Ḫuṣṣēti-ša-Nabunnāya (near Uruk) (Sîn-tabni archive). Nbn 377; Bertin 482. Marked by Strassmaier, "K...? Rich Coll?".
30161	1851,0101.365	Promissory note for silver. 19 lines. 1 7/8 x 1 1/2 in. Nbn 1/6/12. Uruk (Sîn-tabni archive). Nbn 621; Bertin 571.
30162	1851,0101.357	Promissory note for barley. 17 lines. 1 5/8 x 1 1/4 in. Nbk 5/1/21. (Uruk) (archive uncertain). Nbk 124; Bertin 98.
30165	1851,0101.358	Promissory note for silver. 19 lines damaged. 2 x 1 5/8 in. Dar 8/6/3. ⌜Uruk⌝ (Atû archive). Dar 77; Bertin 1975
30169	1851,0101.366	Receipt of silver; 16 lines. 1 3/4 x 1 3/8 in. Cam 28/3/2. Uruk (Sîn-tabni archive). Cam 109; Bertin 877.

30171	1851,0101.367	Promissory note for silver; ḫarrānu. 25 lines. 2 1/2 x 2 in. Nbn -/1/15. Uruk (Sîn-tabni archive). Bertin 1560; Oppert and Ménant, DJ, 262-4, no. IV.
30172	1851,0101.368	Promissory note for silver. 20 lines. 2 1/8 x 1 1/2 in. Nbn 22/4/5. Uruk (Sîn-tabni archive). Bertin 1305; Oppert and Ménant, DJ, 260-2, no. III.
30214	1851,0101.359	Promissory note for silver. 20 lines. 2 x 1 1/2 in. Cyr 28/12/2. Uruk (Sîn-tabni archive). Bertin 1685; Oppert and Ménant, DJ, 266-8, no. I; Oppert, ROA 6, 336-7. Wrongly marked by Bertin as K.1297 (q.v.).
67419	1851,0101.369	Contract about a brewer's prebend. 34? lines damaged. 2 3/8 x 2 1/8 in. Dar 24/3/22. Uruk (Atû archive). Dar 543; Bertin 2480. Previously registered as 1882.0918.7416.
67432	1851,0101.370	Promissory note for silver. 19 lines. 1 3/4 x 1 5/8. Dar 10/4/21. Uruk (Atû archive). Dar 524; Bertin 2464. Previously registered as 1882.0918.7429.
92698	1851,0101.371	Old Babylonian; mathematical; table of measurements, squares and cubes; previously numbered 12136. Larsa. Loftus, Travels, 255-256; 4R 37 [40]; Weissbach, ZDMG 69 (1915), 305-320; Thureau-Dangin, RA 27 (1930), 115-116; Neugebauer, MKT I pp. 68-73.

The following tablets which cannot now be found, presumably having been written off, probably came from Loftus's excavations at Uruk and belonged to the 1851,0101 collection, but are copied or published without a museum number.

-	-	Contract. 15+ lines damaged. Nbk 15/-/-. Uruk (archive uncertain). Bertin 246.
-	-	Promissory note for silver. 5 + 8 lines. Nbn 26/[]/9. [Uruk?]. Bertin 489.
-	-	Contract(?); obverse effaced. 7 + 3 lines. Nbn 17/11/14. Uruk (Sîn-tabni archive). Bertin 637. Bertin copies TIN.TIR.KI; the copy rather suggests a damaged Uruk tablet.
-	-	Promissory note. 6?+ 1 + 8 lines. Nbn 10/11/9. [Uruk] (archive uncertain). Nbn 378; Bertin 724. Marked by Strassmaier, "K...? Rich Coll?". Certainly not in the K collection. Probably from the 1851-1-1 collection. Strassmaier copies a shaded TIN.TIR.KI, but Bertin does not; the copies rather suggest a damaged Uruk tablet.
-	-	Promissory note for silver. 4 + 3 lines. Cyr 27/5/2. Uruk (Sîn-tabni archive). Cyr 52; Bertin 761.

-	-	Promissory note for silver. 2 + 5 lines. Cyr 21/3/4. Uruk (archive uncertain). Cyr 165; Bertin 792.
-	-	Contract. 2 + 6 lines. Cam 10/2/1. [Uruk] (Sîn-tabni archive). Cam 37; Bertin 867.
-	-	Contract. 8 lines one side only. Cam 25/1/-. [Uruk?]. Bertin 994.
-	-	Promissory note for silver. 2 + 6 lines. Cam 2/10/-. [Uruk?]. Bertin 995.
-	-	Contract; very damaged. 10 + 11 lines. Darius []/[]/20. Uruk? Bertin 2448 (Bertin's copy of a damaged TIN.TIR.KI probably being a mistake for UNUG.KI).

1851,1009 collection

The 1851,1009 collection was presented by Lt. Col. H. Rawlinson.

	1851,1009	For bricks in this collection see CBI.
90938	1851,1009.45	Stone tablet with inscription recording grant of freedom from labour service. Dated at Babylon, but said to have been found at Za'aleh, 12 miles NW of Babylon. Previously numbered 12067. Marduk-nadin-aḫḫe -/11/1. 1R 66; King, BBSt, 98-99, pl. XCVII, no. XXV; Reade, NABU 2000, 87, no. 77.
22455	1851,1009.146	Old Babylonian mace head in copper; É.GAL Ḫa-am-mu-ra-bi. Presumably one of the group found by J. F. Jones at Tell Mohammed in 1850 (see Harris, JCS 9, 31), but said by Rawlinson to come from Kalwadka, near Baghdad. King, LIH, no. 64; Frayne, RIME 4.3.6.18.1.
22470	1851,1009.130	Pre-Sargonic. Headless stone figurine dedicated to Ninšubur by Kalkiaku. CT 10, 2.
91084	1851,1009.152	Old Babylonian stone macehead. Historical inscription of Ilum-muttabbil, viceroy of Der. Previously numbered 12227. CT 21, 1; Frayne, RIME 4.12.2.1.

1856,0903 collection

The 1856,0903 collection comes from the excavations of William Kennett Loftus. See above on the 1851,0101 collection.

30001	1856,0903.1505	Neo-Assyrian terracotta dog; inscribed. Nineveh. Barnett, Ashurbanipal, 36, pl. I.
30002	1856,0903.1506	Neo-Assyrian terracotta dog; inscribed. Nineveh. Barnett, Ashurbanipal, 36, pl. I.
30003	1856,0903.1507	Neo-Assyrian terracotta dog; inscribed. Nineveh. Barnett, Ashurbanipal, 36, pl. I.

30004	1856,0903.1508	Neo-Assyrian terracotta dog; inscribed. Nineveh. Barnett, Ashurbanipal, 36, pl. I.
30005	1856,0903.1509	Neo-Assyrian terracotta dog; inscribed. Nineveh. Barnett, Ashurbanipal, 36, pl. I.
30062	1856,0903.1476	Old Babylonian cone; inscription of En-ana-tuma, daughter of Išme-Dagan. (Išme-Dagan). Ur. 1R 2 vi 1; CT 21, 22-23; Frayne, RIME 4.2.5.2.1.
30063	1856,0903.1477	Old Babylonian cone; inscription of Lipit-Ištar. Ur. 1R 5 xvii; CT 21, 18; Frayne, RIME 4.1.5.6.1.
30064	1856,0903.1478	Lagaš II cone; inscription of Gudea dedicated to Nanše; the cone has been cut short and curiously cut down and hollowed out from either end. Zurghul. 1R 5 xxiii 2; Steible, FAOS 9/1 Gudea 29 (L); Edzard, RIME 3/1 1.7.26.
30065	1856,0903.1479	Ur III cone; inscription of Ur-Nammu. Ur. Steible, FAOS 9/2 Urnammu 22 (A); Frayne, RIME 3/2.1.1.39.1.
30066	1856,0903.1480	Old Babylonian cone; inscription of Lipit-Ištar. Ur. 1R 5 xviii; CT 21, 19; Frayne, RIME 4.1.5.5.1.
30067	1856,0903.1481	Lagaš II cone; inscription of Gudea dedicated to Nanše. Zurghul. 1R 5 xxiii 2; Steible, FAOS 9/1 Gudea 29 (L); Edzard, RIME 3/1 1.7.26.
30068	1856,0903.1482	Ur III cone; inscription of Ur-Nammu. Ur. Steible, FAOS 9/2 Urnammu 25 (A); Frayne, RIME 3/2.1.1.11.7.
30069	1856,0903.1483	Old Babylonian cone; inscription of Warad-Sin. Ur? Frayne, RIME 4.2.13.1.1.
30070	1856,0903.1484	Old Babylonian cone; inscription of Nur-Adad. Ur. 1R 2 iv; CT 21, 29; Frayne, RIME 4.2.8.2.1.
30071	1856,0903.1485	Old Babylonian cone; inscription of Sin-kašid. Uruk. + 91150. CT 21, 15-16; Frayne, RIME 4.1.8.3-4.
30072	1856,0903.1486	Cone of Elili, king of Ur on the building of the Apsu for Enki, king of Eridu: [d.e]n-ki / [] lu[gal]-eridu.ki-ra / é li li / lugal-uri.ki-ma-ke4 / zu-ab-ni / mu-na-dù. Dupl. 121343 (Smith, JRAS 1932, 305-6, obtained at Khidr). PreSa. Such-Gutiérrez, Fs Owen, 148.
30073	1856,0903.1487	Lagaš II cone; inscription of Gudea dedicated to Nin-dar-a; a paper label attached to the cone says, "Warka". Uruk. 1R 5 xxiii 1; Steible, FAOS 9/1 Gudea 38 (A); Edzard, RIME 3/1 1.7.31
30074	1856,0903.1488	Lagaš I cone; inscription of Enannatum I. Zurghul; dupl. Steible, FAOS 5/1, Enannatum I.10 lines 1-9 only.

30075	1856,0903.1489	Ur III cone; inscription of Ur-Nammu. Ur. 1R 1 i 4; CT 21, 8; Steible, FAOS 9/2 Urnammu 25 (A); Frayne, RIME 3/2.1.1.11.8.
30076	1856,0903.1490	Ur III cone; inscription of Ur-Nammu. Ur. 1R 1 i 4; CT 21, 8; Steible, FAOS 9/2 Urnammu 25 (A); Frayne, RIME 3/2.1.1.11.9.
30077	1856,0903.1491	Ur III cone; inscription of Ur-Nammu. Ur. Steible, FAOS 9/2 Urnammu 25 (A); Frayne, RIME 3/2.1.1.11.10.
30078	1856,0903.1492	Ur III cone; inscription of Ur-Nammu. Ur. Steible, FAOS 9/2 Urnammu 25 (A); Frayne, RIME 3/2.1.1.11.11.
30079	1856,0903.1493	Ur III cone; inscription of Ur-Nammu. Ur. Steible, FAOS 9/2 Urnammu 25 (A); Frayne, RIME 3/2.1.1.11.12.
30080	1856,0903.1494	Ur III cone; inscription of Ur-Nammu. Ur. Steible, FAOS 9/2 Urnammu 25 (A); Frayne, RIME 3/2.1.1.11.13.
30081	1856,0903.1495	Ur III cone; inscription of Ur-Nammu. Ur. Steible, FAOS 9/2 Urnammu 25 (A); Frayne, RIME 3/2.1.1.11.14.
30082	1856,0903.1497	Ur III cone; inscription of Ur-Nammu. Ur. Steible, FAOS 9/2 Urnammu 25 (A); Frayne, RIME 3/2.1.1.11.15.
30083	1856,0903.1498	Ur III cone; inscription of Ur-Nammu. Ur. Steible, FAOS 9/2 Urnammu 25 (A); Frayne, RIME 3/2.1.1.11.16.
30084	1856,0903.1499	Ur III cone; inscription of Ur-Nammu. Ur. Steible, FAOS 9/2 Urnammu 22 (A) and 23 (A); Frayne, RIME 3/2.1.1.39.2.
30085	1856,0903.1500	Ur III cone; inscription of Ur-Nammu. Ur. Steible, FAOS 9/2 Urnammu 25 (A); Frayne, RIME 3/2.1.1.11.17.
30086	1856,0903.1501	Ur III cone; inscription of Ur-Nammu. Ur. Steible, FAOS 9/2 Urnammu 26 (D); Frayne, RIME 3/2.1.1.17.1.
30087	1856,0903.1502	Ur III cone; inscription of Ur-Nammu. Ur. Steible, FAOS 9/2 Urnammu 25 (A); Frayne, RIME 3/2.1.1.11.18.
30088	1856,0903.1503	Ur III cone; inscription of Ur-Nammu. Ur. Steible, FAOS 9/2 Urnammu 22 (A); Frayne, RIME 3/2.1.1.39.3.
30090	1856,0903.1496	Ur III cone; inscription of Ur-Nammu. Ur. 1R 1 i 4; Steible, FAOS 9/2 Urnammu 25 (B); Frayne, RIME 3/2.1.1.11.19.

30117	1856,0903.1513	Sale of an ērib bītūtu prebend; payment in staters of Antiochus; sealed; also marked W (cf. 93002-4). SE Ant II []/[]/60. [Uruk]. Bertin 2912-2913; Loftus, Travels, 230, no. 2; Oppert and Ménant, DJ, 296-301, no. 1; Doty, CAHU, 400-2, Corò, PTES, 154-6 (as Oppert 1); Corò, STUBM, no. 35-P, p. 160, pl. XXXV.
30118	1856,0903.1514	Sale of a gerseqqūtu prebend; payment in staters of [...]; sealed; also marked W. SE Ant & Sel. []/10/[]+3 (presumably year [3]3 or [4]3). Uruk. + K.11800. Loftus, Travels, 231, no. 5; Doty, CAHU, 399 and 416-8, Oelsner, Materialien, 148; Corò, PTES, 199-201; all 30118 only; Corò, STUBM, no. 08-P, p. 116-1173, pl. VIII (including K.11800).
30119	1856,0903.1515	Sale of a prebend in a kirû ḫallatu; payment in staters of Seleucus; sealed; also marked W 68(?). Dupl. 109942. SE Sel II 7/[11]/74. Uruk. Loftus, Travels 232; Corò, PTES, 424-5; Mitchell and Searight, no. 704; Corò, STUBM, no. 47-P, p. 179, pl. XLVII.
30120	1856,0903.1516	Contract about ērib bītūtu and gerseqqūtu prebends; incomplete; sealed. SE Ant III 21/9/90. Uruk. Loftus, Travels 232; Oppert and Ménant, DJ, 313-5, no. 4; Doty, CAHU, 410-411; Corò, PTES, 375-6 (as Oppert 4); Mitchell and Searight, no. 717; Corò, STUBM, no. 67-P, p. 207, pl. LXVII.
93002	1856,0903.1517	Sale of an ērib bītūtu prebend; payment in shekels; sealed; also marked W.111 (cf. 30117 and 93003, 93004). SE Sel 18/1/68. Uruk. Bertin 2890-2891; Oppert and Ménant, DJ, 301-6, no. 2; Loftus, Travels 231, no. 4; Corò, PTES, 156-8 (as Oppert 2); Corò, STUBM, no. 44-P, p. 173, pl. XLIV.
93003	1856,0903.1518	Sale of an ērib bītūtu prebend; payment in staters of Seleucus; sealed; also marked W.112 (cf. 30117, 93002, 93004). Duplicate of 109940. SE Sel II 27/1/78. Uruk. Bertin 2892-2893; Oppert and Ménant, DJ, 306-12, no. 3; Loftus, Travels 231, no. 3; Corò, PTES, 160-2 (as Oppert 3); Corò, STUBM, no. 55-P, p. 187, pl. LV.
93004	1856,0903.1519	Sale of various prebends; sealed; also marked W.114 (cf. 30117, 93002, 93003). SE Demetrius. Uruk. Bertin 2914-2915; Oppert and Ménant, DJ, 315-22, no. 5; Loftus, Travels 230, no. 1; Corò, PTES, 378-81 (as Oppert 5); Linssen, CM 25, 38, 43-44, 49-50 for Ménant; Corò, STUBM, no. 106-P, p. 275, pl. CVI.

139437	1856,0903.1520	Five fragments of Seleucid tablets, found unnumbered, marked by T. G. Pinches as "from Warka", and presumed to belong to the 56-9-3 collection. SE. Uruk. Corò, STUBM, no. 115-P, p. 288, pl. CXV.

1856,0908 collection

The 1856,0908 collection comes from the excavations of John George Taylor at Ur. For an account of his work see his articles "Notes on the ruins of Muqeyer" and "Notes on Abu Shahrein and Tel el Lahm" in Journal of the Royal Asiatic Society of Great Britain and Ireland 15 (1855), 260-276 and 404-415.

30061	1856,0908.328	Uninscribed clay nail or jar stopper.
	1856,0908.400	Nos. 400-403 are bricks. See CBI.

1856,1110 collection

The 1856,1110 collection was presented by the Duke of Somerset.

	1856,1110.1	Cast of the Emaḫ cylinder of Nebuchadnezzar II. Berger, AOAT 4/1, Nebukadnezar Zylinder II, 1, no. 14. Berger notes a pencilled label attached, saying, "Somerset".

1859,1014 collection

The 1859,1014 collection comes from the excavations of John George Taylor at Ur. See above on the 1856,0908 collection.

	1859,1014	For bricks in this collection see CBI.
30050	1859,1014.81	Old Babylonian cone; inscription of Warad-Sin. Ur. 4R(2) 35, 6; Frayne, RIME 4.2.13.6.1-2.
91152	1859,1014.82	Old Babylonian cone; inscription of Sin-iddinam. Ur. 4R 36 [38], 2; Frayne, RIME 4.2.9.9.1-2.
91149	1859,1014.83	Old Babylonian cone; inscription of Warad-Sin. Ur. 4R(2) 35, 6; Frayne, RIME 4.2.13.16.3-4.
30051	1859,1014.85	Ur III cone; inscription of Ur-Nammu. Ur. 1R 1 i 4; CT 21, 8; Steible, FAOS 9/2 Urnammu 25 (A); Frayne, RIME 3/2.1.1.11.1.
30052	1859,1014.86	Ur III cone; inscription of Ur-Nammu. Ur. Steible, FAOS 9/2 Urnammu 25 (A); Frayne, RIME 3/2.1.1.11.2.
30053	1859,1014.87	Ur III cone; inscription of Ur-Nammu. Ur. 1R 1 i 4; CT 21, 8; Steible, FAOS 9/2 Urnammu 25 (A); Frayne, RIME 3/2.1.1.11.3.
30054	1859,1014.88	Ur III cone; inscription of Ur-Nammu. Ur. Steible, FAOS 9/2 Urnammu 25 (A); Frayne, RIME 3/2.1.1.11.4.

30055	1859,1014.89	Ur III cone; inscription of Ur-Nammu. Ur. Steible, FAOS 9/2 Urnammu 25 (A); Frayne, RIME 3/2.1.1.11.5.
30056	1859,1014.90	Ur III cone; inscription of Ur-Nammu. Ur. Steible, FAOS 9/2 Urnammu 27 (A); Frayne, RIME 3/2.1.1.19.1.
30057	1859,1014.91	Ur III cone; inscription of Ur-Nammu. Ur. Steible, FAOS 9/2 Urnammu 25 (A); Frayne, RIME 3/2.1.1.11.6.
30045	1859,1014.91a	Ur III or Old Babylonian cone; almost illegible. Ur.
30058	1859,1014.92	Old Babylonian cone; inscription of Warad-Sin. Ur. Frayne, RIME 4.2.13.20.1.
30216	1859,1014.93	Old Babylonian cylinder; inscription of Warad-Sin. Ur. Frayne, RIME 4.2.13.29.
30217	1859,1014.94	Old Babylonian brick of Sin-iddinam. Ur. CBI, no. 37; Frayne, RIME 4.2.9.13.1.
30060	1859,1014.102	Old Babylonian cone; inscription of Lipit-Ištar. Ur. Frayne, RIME 4.1.5.5.2.
30218	1859,1014.103	Old Babylonian lenticular school text. Ur.
30110	1859,1014.104	Old Babylonian lenticular school text. Ur.
30219	1859,1014.105	Old Babylonian lexical. Ur.
30181	1859,1014.106	Old Babylonian account of livestock. Warad-Sin -/12/11. Ur.
	1859,1014.107	Old Babylonian school letter. Also registered as K.8765. Ur.
30111	1859,1014.108	Old Babylonian economic. Ur.
30182	1859,1014.109	Letter; names of sender and addressee lost. Late Babylonian. Ur. Hackl et al., AOAT 414/1, no. 82.
30112	1859,1014.110	Old Babylonian letter. Ur.
30183	1859,1014.111	Old Babylonian economic; erasures; illegible. Ur.
30220	1859,1014.112.	Ur III; account; alan. Ur.
30025	1859,1014.113	Old Babylonian letter. Ur.
30113	1859,1014.114	Old Babylonian economic. Ur.
30184	1859,1014.115	Old Babylonian mathematical; table of measures of length; šu-si; fragmentary. Ur.
30186	1859,1014.116	Promissory note; mostly illegible. Late Babylonian. Ur.
30114	1859,1014.117	Old Babylonian lexical. Ur.
30114a	1859,1014.118	Old Babylonian letter. Ur.
139356	1859,1014.119	Old Babylonian tablet; fragment. Ur.
30115	1859,1014.120	Old Babylonian school text. Ur.
30221	1859,1014.121	Old Babylonian cone; inscription of Warad-Sin. Ur. Frayne, RIME 4.2.13.20.3.
30222	1859,1014.122	Ur III economic; obverse mostly eroded; dated itu á-ki-ti / mu d.Šu-d.Suen lugal. Ur.

30059	1859,1014.123	Old Babylonian cone; inscription of Warad-Sin. Ur. Frayne, RIME 4.2.13.20.2.
30116	1859,1014.124	Old Babylonian letter? Ur.
91148	1859,1014.131	Stone duck-weight, with the Sumerian inscription of an Ur III king. Ur. Frayne, RIME 3/2.1.6.1024.
90951	1859,1014.160	Pre-Sargonic. Copper cone with inscription of A'annepada, king of Ur. Ur. Reade, Iran 40 (2002) 252-253; Gadd, JRAS 1928, 626-628.

1862,0716 collection

The 1862,0716 collection was purchased from George Eastwood, having previously belonged to Mr. Hawkins.

91136	1862,0716.1	Cast of the Emaḫ cylinder of Nebuchadnezzar II. Berger, AOAT 4/1, Nebukadnezar Zylinder II, 1, no. 15.

1868,0709 collection

The 1868,0709 collection was purchased from Lieut.-General T. J. Malcolm, London.

91137	1868,0709.1	Historical cylinder of Nebuchadnezzar II. Winckler, ZA 2, 142. Berger, AOAT 4/1, Nebukadnezar Zylinder III, 3.

1869,1006 collection

The 1869,1006 collection was presented by Arthur James Lewis of Regent Street, London.

115714	1869,1006.1	Jemdet Nasr stamp seal.
30154	1869,1006.2	Receipt of silver from Marduk-nāṣir-apli. Dar 24/12/12. Babylon. Dar 338 (as A J Lewis 89); Bertin 2222; Abraham, BPPE, 406-9, no. 110.
30155	1869,1006.3	Transcript of a trial. [Nbk]. [Babylon]. Bertin 2960-2961 (as A J Lewis?); Sandowicz, dubsar 11, no. 13.
30156	1869,1006.4	Sale of a slave. Nbn 1/5/9. Šapīja. Nbn 348 (as A J Lewis 19); Strassmaier, Liverpool 97; Bertin 472.
67413	1869,1006.5	Contract about dates and silver. Also registered as 1882,0918.7410. Dar 22/10/17. Šaḫrīn. Dar 452 (as A J Lewis 39); Bertin 2376.

Old collections

The following tablets were allocated numbers by L. W. King in the 1890s without his being able to establish their original registration. One might guess that many of them, particularly those subsequently written off, came from the excavations of W. K. Loftus at Uruk, Larsa and Zurghul, although the Neo-Assyrian ones presumably come from the excavations of A. H. Layard.

30006		Number not used.

30007	-	Old Babylonian administrative account(?) in four columns.
30008	-	Joined to K.8866.
30009	-	Old Babylonian lexical; syllabary; giš.
30010	-	Old Babylonian letter.
30011	-	Neo-Assyrian. Medical omens; Sa-gig XIX. Joined to K.7009. Heeßel, AOAT 43, 226-239 and 455-456.
30012	-	Old Babylonian lexical.
30013	-	Old Babylonian lexical; giš.
30014	-	Old Babylonian lexical.
30015	-	Old Babylonian lexical; giš.
30016	-	Old Babylonian lenticular school text; illegible.
30017	-	Old Babylonian lexical.
30018	-	Old Babylonian lexical; giš.
30019	-	Joined to K.10468.
30020	-	Old Babylonian lexical.
30021	-	Old Babylonian lexical.
30022	-	Old Babylonian lexical.
30023	-	Old Babylonian lexical.
30024	-	Old Babylonian lexical; Weidner god list. + 68333.
30026	-	Old Babylonian letter? Obv. destroyed, rev. traces of 3 signs.
30027	-	Old Babylonian mathematical; calculations?
30028	-	Incantation?
30029	-	Old Babylonian letter.
30030	-	School practice text?
30031	-	Old Babylonian letter.
30032	-	Old Babylonian letter.
30033	-	Old Babylonian letter.
30034	-	Old Babylonian letter.
30035	-	Old Babylonian letter?
30036	-	Old Babylonian letter.
30037	-	Old Babylonian lenticular school text.
30038	-	Old Babylonian contract for sale of a field, sealed.
30039	-	Old Babylonian school text?
30041	-	Old Babylonian lexical cylinder; syllabary. + 90906.
30044	-	Lagaš II cone; inscription of Gudea dedicated to Ningirsu. Zurghul. Steible, FAOS 9/1 Gudea 51 (T); Edzard, RIME 3/1 1.7.41.
30046	-	Lagaš II cone; inscription of Gudea dedicated to Ningirsu. Zurghul. Steible, FAOS 9/1 Gudea 51 (T); Edzard, RIME 3/1 1.7.41.
30047	-	Lagaš II cone; inscription of Gudea dedicated to Ningirsu. Zurghul. Dupl. Steible, FAOS 9/1 Gudea 51 (T); Edzard, RIME 3/1 1.7.41.

30048	-	Old Babylonian Sumerian legal compendium. (+) 90893 (+) 33264 + 90892 + 90894. Cf. Sollberger, Fs Kraus 346-350.
30049	-	Lagaš II cone; inscription of Ur-Bau. Zurghul. Steible, FAOS 9/1 Urbaba 7 (L); Edzard, RIME 3/1.1.6.4.
30071a	-	Lagaš II cone; inscription of Gudea. Zurghul. Steible, FAOS 9/1 Gudea 51 (T); Edzard, RIME 3/1.1.7.41.
30091	-	Old Babylonian lenticular school text.
30092	-	Old Babylonian lenticular school text.
30093	-	Old Babylonian lenticular school text.
30094	-	Old Babylonian lenticular school text.
30095	-	Old Babylonian economic; commodities and names.
30096	-	Old Babylonian letter?
30097	-	Ur III; list of 14 men, summarised as lú-kin-gá gub-ba-me; undated. Ur?
30098	-	Old Babylonian Economic.
30099	-	Old Babylonian contract; sealed.
30100	-	Lexical; god list.
30101	-	Old Babylonian Economic.
30102	-	Old Babylonian lenticular school text.
30103	-	Old Babylonian Economic.
30104	-	Written off.
30105	-	Old Babylonian or Ur III label, uninscribed; sealed.
30106	-	Old Babylonian or Ur III label, uninscribed; sealed.
30107	-	Old Babylonian or Ur III label, uninscribed; sealed.
30108	-	Old Babylonian or Ur III label, uninscribed; sealed.
30109	-	Old Babylonian or Ur III label, uninscribed; sealed.
30122	-	Contract; sale of fields, houses and slaves; captions for seals but seals lost, and finger-nail marks with caption. Dupl. 32188+, 34074, 35579, 37077+. Cyr 6/3/4. [Babylon]. Cyr 160; Bertin 793; Wunsch, CM 3, no. 292; Wunsch, CM 20B, 150-158 as no. 125B. Belongs to the Egibi archive from Babylon, so presumably wrongly attributed by Strassmaier to the 1851,0101 collection.
30137	-	Written off.
30138	-	Written off.
30142	-	Written off.
30145	-	Written off; already disintegrated in 1921.
30146	-	Written off.
30148	-	Written off.
30152	-	Written off.
30153	-	Neo-Babylonian prism; royal inscription of Esarhaddon. Babylon. Borger, AfO Beih. 9, 11; Cogan, AfO 31, 75. Leichty, RINAP 4.104.5.

30157	-	Written off.
30160	-	Written off.
30163	-	Illegible; to be written off.
30166	-	Written off; already disintegrated in 1921.
30167	-	Receipt for beer; sealed. Alex III []/[]/10. Borsippa. CT 49, 2, no. 8; Nisaba 28, no. 439.
30168	-	Letter from Nabû-šum-iddina to Iddinaya; sealed. Nisaba 28, no. 207.
30185	-	Written off.
30187	-	Written off; already disintegrated in 1921.
30188	-	Written off; already disintegrated in 1921.
30189	-	Written off.
30190	-	Neo-Assyrian. Loan of silver; partly vitrified.
30191	-	Written off.
30192	-	Written off.
30193	-	Written off.
30194	-	Letter.
30195	-	Written off.
30196	-	Written off.
30197	-	No script remains.
30198	-	Written off.
30199	-	Written off.
30200	-	Written off.
30201	-	Written off.
30202	-	Written off.
30203	-	Written off.
30204	-	Astrological.
30205	-	Neo-Assyrian. Letter to the king (Sargon II) from Nergal-eṭir. van Buylaere, Fs Postgate, 651-653.
30206	-	Written off.
30207	-	Written off.
30208	-	Neo-Assyrian. Literary; namburbû ritual in second column.
30209		Neo-Assyrian. Omens; physiognomic. Böck, AfO Beih. 27, 172, no. 6, pl. 8.
90892	-	Joined to 33264.
90893	-	Old Babylonian Sumerian legal compendium. (+) 30048 (+) 33264 + 90892 + 90894. Strassmaier, Warka, no. 110 (33264 only); Sollberger, Fs Kraus 346-350 (not 30048).
90894	-	Joined to 33264.
90906	-	Joined to 30041.
92695	-	Old Babylonian. Lexical; syllabary; 12 columns.
92696	-	Old Babylonian. Lexical; syllabary; 9 columns.

92697	-	Old Babylonian. Lexical; syllabary; 9 columns. Now written off.

K collection

The following Babylonian tablets registered in the Kouyunjik Collection may have come from the excavations or collections of Rich, Rawlinson, Loftus and Taylor. The Kouyunjik Collection seems to have become a dumping ground for tablets which the Museum staff were unable to allocate to another registered collection.

	K.55	Lexical; Ḫḫ X. Originally registered as 1851,0101.166. Uruk. CT 19, 1-2; MSL 7 71 (both as K.55).
92706	K.433	Contract; sale of a house by Ina-tēšî-ēṭir. Caption for finger-nail mark but no finger-nail mark impressed. Asb 20/1/20. Uruk. S. A. Smith, MAT pp. 15-16, pl. 28; San Nicolò, BR 8/7, no. 13; Brinkman and Kennedy, JCS 35, 22, J.12; Bertin 3-4.
92707	K.1297	Promissory note for silver. The tablet is also registered as 1851,0101.161. 14 lines; 3.9 x 5.1 cm. Nbk 15/7/21. Uruk (Atû archive). Nbk 129; Strassmaier, Warka 112.
	K.1377	Old Babylonian contract; repayment of silver held on deposit by Ṣilli-Eštar. Also marked "B.5" (from Tell Sifr). [Samsuiluna]. Kutalla (Tell Sifr). Charpin, Archives, 122, 276 and pl. V, no. 103.
	K.1661	Historical cylinder of Nebuchadnezzar II. Berger, AOAT 4/1, Nebukadnezar Zylinder-Fragment IV, 1, no. 3.
91118	K.1682	Historical cylinder of Nebuchadnezzar II. Larsa. Berger, AOAT 4/1, Nebukadnezar Zylinder II, 4, no. 2.
91119	K.1683	Historical cylinder of Nebuchadnezzar II. Originally registered as Rich (1825,0503) 103. 1R 52, 4; Berger, AOAT 4/1, Nebukadnezar Zylinder II, 2, no. 1.
91120	K.1684	Historical cylinder of Nebuchadnezzar II. Larsa. 1R 51, 2; Berger, AOAT 4/1, Nebukadnezar Zylinder II, 4, no. 1.
91121	K.1685	Historical cylinder of Nebuchadnezzar II. Borsippa. 1R 51, 1; Berger, AOAT 4/1, Nebukadnezar Zylinder II, 12, no. 1.
91122	K.1686	Historical cylinder of Nebuchadnezzar II. Borsippa. Berger, AOAT 4/1, Nebukadnezar Zylinder II, 12, no. 2.
91123	K.1687	Historical cylinder of Nebuchadnezzar II. Borsippa. Berger, AOAT 4/1, Nebukadnezar Zylinder II, 12, no. 3.

91124	K.1688	Historical cylinder of Nabonidus. Ur. + 1924,0920. 243 + 244 (U.1560 and U.1560a). 1R 69 (part); Schaudig, AOAT 256, 445-466; Berger, AOAT 4/1, Nabonid Zylinder III, 4, no. 1; Langdon, AJSL 32 (1915) 102-117. Note Schaudig's comments (pp. 445-446) on the joins and the failure to join K.2746.
91126	K.1690	Historical cylinder of Nabonidus. Ur. Schaudig, AOAT 256, 350-353; Berger, AOAT 4/1, Nabonid Zylinder II, 2, no. 2.
91127	K.1691	Historical cylinder of Nabonidus. Ur. Schaudig, AOAT 256, 350-353; Berger, AOAT 4/1, Nabonid Zylinder II, 2, no. 3.
91128	K.1692	Historical cylinder of Nabonidus. Ur. Schaudig, AOAT 256, 350-353; Berger, AOAT 4/1, Nabonid Zylinder II, 2, no. 4.
91129	K.1693a	Historical cylinder of Nebuchadnezzar II. Larsa. Berger, AOAT 4/1, Nebukadnezar Zylinder II, 4, no. 3.
	K.1694	Historical cylinder of Nebuchadnezzar II. Larsa. Berger, AOAT 4/1, Nebukadnezar Zylinder-Fragment IV, 1, no. 1.
	K.2746	Historical cylinder of Nabonidus. Ur. Schaudig, AOAT 256, 445-466 and 758 Abb. 34; Berger, AOAT 4/1, Nabonid Zylinder III, 4, no. 3.
	K.2799	Historical cylinder of Nebuchadnezzar II. Berger, AOAT 4/1, Nebukadnezar Zylinder II, 4, no. 4.
	K.2841	Copy of an én é-nu-ru incantation; possibly from Babylonia? + K.9141 + K.16783. Lambert, RA 53, 123 (K 9141 only).
92680	K.3168	Old Babylonian mathematical; table of square roots. Larsa. 4R 37 [40]; Neugebauer, MKT I p. 68, no. 13, p. 70, no. 13 and p. 71 n. 2.
	K.3753	Festival calendar for the second half of the year; prayer on the upper edge; colophon. A note in Pinches's hand with the tablet says, "From the Sassanian mound, Warka". Presumably originally part of the 1856,0903 collection. SE Antiochus II 21/4/65. Uruk. Weidner, Gestirn-Darstellungen, 10-11 and pls. 11-12; Linssen, CM 25, 65-67, 69, 71, 89, 148 n. 130, 153 n. 182, 325; Hunger, AOAT 2, no. 88; Oppert and Ménant, DJ, 334-340, no. 6.
	K.3783	Aramaic note. Stevenson, Ass.-Bab. Contracts, no. 42; 2R 70, no. 17; CIS II/I, p. 40f.
	K.3787	Memorandum of a slave-girl and her owner. Marduk-apla-iddina II -/11/11. Strassmaier, 8th Orientalist Congress, no. 1.

	K.4248	Old Babylonian lexical; geographical list. + K.11985. 4R 36 [38], 1; MSL 11, 59-61.
	K.4709	Old Babylonian promulgation document for the year formula for Rim-Anum year E. Presumably originally part of the 1856,0903 collection. Rim-Anum. Uruk. 4R 35, 8.
	K.4755	Old Babylonian Sumerian literary; Nisaba hymn. + K.8551 + K.9771 + B frags. 4R 35, 7; Reisman, AOAT 25, 357-365 (part published as exemplar G). A paper label in the box in which K.4755 was stored since the 19th century says, “Outside wall of a tomb, Sinkara”.
	K.4790	Contract; captions for seals. Presumably originally part of the 1856,0903 collection. SE Demetrius. Uruk. Oelsner, Materialien, 161; Corò, STUBM, no. 107-?, p. 285, pl. CVII.
	K.5424c	Promissory note for barley and emmer; with Aramaic note. Also registered as 1825,0503.108. [Dar II] []/[]/15. [Babylon?]. Stevenson, Ass.-Bab. Contracts, no. 41; Stolper, Fs Larsen, 520.
	K.6364	Historical cylinder of Nabonidus. Larsa. Schaudig, AOAT 256, 397-409 and 756; Berger, AOAT 4/1, Nabonid Zylinder III, 1, no. 2.
	K.6697	Old Babylonian Sumerian literary; Giš-al hymn, and Farmer’s Instructions. + K.8069. Civil, Farmer’s Instructions, p. 64.
	K.7855	Old Babylonian foundation tablet of Sin-kašid of Uruk. Presumably originally part of the 1856,0903 collection; cf. 30071. Uruk. Walker, AfO 23, 88-89; Frayne, RIME 4.4.1.15.
	K.8069	Joined to K.6697.
	K.8133	Contract for hire of oxen. Stolper, JAOS 114, 625-627. Also registered as 1825,0503.112.
	K.8485	Promissory note for dates; vitrified; probably from the Kasr archive. [Dar II] []/8/11. [Babylon] (Kasr archive). Bertin 3075; Stolper, Fs Larsen, 520. Also registered as 1825,0503.109.
	K.8506	Promissory note for apples; vitrified; probably from the Kasr archive. Art I/II 1/2/10. Tamerat Ṭābānu (near Borsippa). Bertin 2872; Stolper, Bagh Mitt 21 (1990) 560 n. 5; Stolper, Fs Larsen, 520. Also registered as 1825,0503.110.
92703	K.8527	Old Babylonian mathematical; multiplication table for 45. Larsa. Neugebauer, MKT I, p. 34, no. 2 and p. 36, no. 2.

K.8712	Promissory note for dates. Wunsch, CM 20A-B, no. 233.
K.8755	Old Babylonian Sumerian literary. Reade, Iraq 67, 369.
K.8765	Old Babylonian school letter. Originally registered as 1859,1014.107. Ur. Reade, Iraq 67, 369.
K.8795	Old Babylonian Sumerian literary.
K.8847	Described in Bezold's Catalogue as, "Archaic Babylonian; not from Kouyunjik(?). Portion of a religious text, serving, perhaps, as an amulet." Now written off having disintegrated beyond repair.
K.8851	Joined to K.4755.
K.8860	Old Babylonian contract. Reade, Iraq 67, 369.
K.8866	Old Babylonian lexical; Ḫḫ forerunner. + K.9599 + 30008. MSL 10, 61 (K.8866 only).
K.9008	Literary; Marduk's chariot. Perhaps of Achaemenid date. + 1883,0118.141. Lambert, Fs Böhl, 275-280.
K.9023	Historical inscription; mentions Esangila.
K.9076	Old Babylonian Sumerian literary.
K.9141	Joined to K.2841.
K.9288	Ritual and incantations; first tablet of the series Kunuk ḫalti; includes list of stones; colophon; nu-til; scribe Mušēzib-[]. Nbk []/12/8. (+) K.9288a. Hunger, AOAT 2, no. 420; Schuster-Brandis, AOAT 46, p. 193 and pl. 39.
K.9288a	Ritual and incantations; fragment; probably (+) K.9288.
K.9463	Historical cylinder of Nebuchadnezzar II. Berger, AOAT 4/1, Nebukadnezar Zylinder II, 7, no. 2.
K.9552	Old Babylonian school text, lenticular; plus fragments; virtually illegible; cf. K.13720.
K.9569	Late Old Babylonian administrative ledger.
K.9599	Joined to K.8866.
K.9771	Joined to K.4755.
K.9870	Old Babylonian administrative; list of fields?
K.9871	Old Babylonian administrative? or list of year-names?; two columns; fragment.
K.9920	Old Babylonian lexical; geographical list. MSL 11, 138-9.
K.9967	Old Babylonian lexical; geographical list. MSL 11, 139.
K.10066	Historical cylinder, fragment. Possibly of Nabonidus; mentions Agade and Eulmaš. Cf. Sm 486 which is made from the same over-fired clay (or faience?).

	K.10468	Old Babylonian lexical; a-šà; gi. + K.14296 + 30019. Reade, Iraq 67, 369.
	K.10494	Described in Bezold's Catalogue as, "Archaic Babylonian; not from Kouyunjik(?). Part of a religious text." Now written off having disintegrated beyond repair.
	K.10506	Old Babylonian lexical; KUŠ; two columns; fragment. Reade, Iraq 67, 369.
	K.10795	Described in Bezold's Catalogue as, "Archaic Babylonian; not from Kouyunjik(?). Part of a religious(?) text." Now written off having disintegrated beyond repair.
137438	K.11596a	Brick of Kurigalzu. Ur. CBI, no. 62.
137439	K.11596b	Brick of Kurigalzu. Ur. CBI, no. 62.
137440	K.11690	Elamite brick. CBI, p. 137.
	K.11800	Contract; fragment of the upper right corner of the reverse. Joined to 30118. Presumably originally from the 1856,0903 collection. Uruk.
	K.11958	Religious.
	K.11967	Receipt.
	K.11985	Joined to K.4248.
	K.13113	Contract. Nbk 6/7/3.
	K.13720	Old Babylonian school text, lenticular; random wedges; probably a scribe learning to hold the stylus; cf. K.9552.
	K.13942	Old Babylonian Sumerian literary; Instructions of Shuruppak; marginal numbers; two columns. + B.171. Reade, Iraq 67, 369. Presumably from Taylor's excavations at Ur; see also under the B collection below.
	K.14296	Joined to K.10468.
	K.14844	Old Babylonian envelope. Joined to 33199. Kutalla. (Tell Sifr).
	K.14946	Old Babylonian triangular docket; inscribed and sealed. Larsa? Loftus, Travels, p. 255.
	K.15145	Literary; Gilgamesh I, 12-17. (+) Rm.785+. George, Gilgamesh II, pl. 47
	K.15159	Contract.
	K.15163	Contract; sale of land; sealed; finger-nail mark. [Nbn]. Nisaba 28, no. 80
	K.16783	Joined to K.2841.
	K.18634	Fragment of an Old Babylonian tablet. Reade, Iraq 67, 369.
	K.21119	Fragment of an Old Babylonian cylinder; lexical? Reade, Iraq 67, 369.

1871,0311 collection

The 1871,0311 collection was donated by James Paddle, London.

30223	1871,0311.1	Receipt of silver from Marduk-nāṣir-apli in partial payment of a debt on behalf of two other persons. Dar 9/11/11. Babylon. Dar 310; Abraham, BPPE, 400-401, no. 106; Bertin 2209.

1873,0319 collection

The 1873,0319 collection was presented by Mme. de Valmency (née Ouseley, daughter of Sir William Ouseley), London.

30224	1873,0319.12	Contract; lease of a field; finger-nail marks with caption. Art II 4/6/1. Bīt-Idija. Strassmaier, 8th Orientalist Congress, no. 23; Stolper, Fs Reiner, 394; Bertin 2877.
30225	1873,0319.13	Contract; sale of a house at the Great Gate of Uraš in Borsippa; sealed; finger-nail marks. The tablet is partly vitrified so may come from the Kasr archive. Dar II 28/[]/3. Dilbat? Dar 100; Bertin 1984; Nisaba 28, no. 225.
30226	1873,0319.14	Letter from Madān-šumu-iddin to Nabû-nādin-aḫi. CT 22, 17-18, no. 84.
30227	1873,0722.1	The number 30227 was probably reserved for the tablet 1873,0722.1, but not used as that tablet was placed in the Kouyunjik Collection.

1875,0609 collection

The 1875,0609 collection was donated by Alfred J. Lawson.

30228	1875,0609.1	Deposition. Ner 16/6/acc. Babylon. Evetts, Ner 2; Sack, AOAT 236, no. 2; Wunsch, AfO 44/45, 75, no. 4; Bertin 292.
30229	1875,0609.2	Promissory note for silver. Cam 6/10/5. Babylon. Bertin 933.

1876,0102 collection

The 1876,0102 collection was purchased from S. M. Alishan, Constantinople.

30230	1876,0102.1	Old Assyrian. About garments. CCT 5 44; Pinches, PSBA 4 (1882) 11-18, 28-32; Garelli, Assyriens, 241, no. 4.

1876,0110 collection

The 1876,0110 collection was purchased from Joseph M. Shemtob, London. The register records the provenance of the whole collection as Babylon.

30231	1876,0110.2	Promissory note for silver. Nbn 26/8/14. Nbn 807; Wunsch, AfO 42/43, 45-46; Bertin 633. Note this and 30232 are numbered in reverse order.
30232	1876,0110.1	Loan; rašūtu. AM 14/4/2. Babylon. Evetts, Ev-M 22; Sack, AOATS 4, no. 8; Bertin 285.
30233	1876,0110.3	Contract; undertaking to register a receipt of dates from Marduk-nāṣir-apli. Dar 7/12/31. Babylon. Bertin 2702; Abraham, BPPE, 206-208, no. 2.
92710	1876,0110.4	Promissory note for silver. Nbk 5/12/3. Saḫrītu. Nbk 33; Bertin 24.
92713	1876,0110.5	Purchase of inheritance share. Nbk 4/6/30. Babylon. Nbk 214; Bertin 149.
30234	1876,0110.6	Promissory note for barley. Dar 8/4/13. Babylon. Dar 347; Bertin 2252.
92711	1876,0110.7	Promissory note for silver. Nbk 2/12/4. Saḫrītu. Nbk 38; Bertin 26.
30235	1876,0110.8	Receipt of ilku-tax by Marduk-nāṣir-apli. Dar 5/1/26. Babylon. Bertin 2620; Abraham, BPPE, 208-209, no. 3.
30236	1876,0110.9	Promissory note for silver. Nbn 8/5/10. Nbn 426; Bertin 494.
30237	1876,0110.10	Promissory note for dates; dupl. 30491. Dar 14/1/20. Babylon. Dar 498b; Bertin 2456.
30238	1876,0110.11	Contract; transfer of property. Nbk 15/2/9. Bertin 57-58; Wunsch, CM 20A-B, no. 83.
30239	1876,0110.12	Promissory note for silver. Dar 8/1/11. Babylon. Dar 294; Bertin 2213.
30240	1876,0110.13	Purchase of barley. Nbk 23/10/9. Babylon. Nbk 82; Bertin 61.
30241	1876,0110.14	Promissory note for silver. Nbk 21/7/28. Babylon. Nbk 188; Bertin 126.
30242	1876,0110.15	Receipt for silver in payment for sheep. Cam 10/6b/[3]. Babylon. Cam 422; Bertin 991; Wunsch, CM 3, no. 332.
30243	1876,0110.16	Receipt of ilku-tax by Marduk-nāṣir-apli. Dar 7/8/25. Babylon. Bertin 2572; Abraham, BPPE, 210, no. 4.
30244	1876,0110.17	Contract about a promissory note for silver. Ner 17/11/1. Babylon. Evetts, Ner 30; Sack, AOAT 236, no. 30; Bertin 309.
30245	1876,0110.18	Contract; sale of a field. Nbn 13/12b/3. Nbn 133; Bertin 386.

1876,0515 collection

The 1876,0515 collection was acquired from Herica Finnis Jr., of Lynch Bros., London. The register gives the provenance of no. 1 as Baghdad and of nos. 2-5 as Babylon.

30246	1876,0515.1	Re-numbered as 90899.
90899	1876,0515.1	Old Babylonian stone tablet with dedicatory inscription of Simat-Ištar to Nin-egal. Previously numbered 12027 and 30246. Hallo, BiOr 18 10, Rim-Sin 6 i; Frayne, RIME 4.2.14.16.1.
30247	1876,0515.2	Promissory note for silver. Nbk III []/7/acc. Babylon. Nbk 5; Bertin 11; Lorenz, Nebukadnezar III/IV, p. 31.
30248	1876,0515.3	List of personal names ša SAG.DU.
30249	1876,0515.4	Silver pledge against share of an inheritance. Nbn 8/12b/1. Babylon. Nbn 51; Bertin 356.
30250	1876,0515.5	Contract; lease of a house. Dar 9/1/3. Babylon. Dar 60; Bertin 1989.

1876,1016 collection

The 1876,1016 collection was purchased from Joseph M. Shemtob, London. The register gives the provenance of nos. 1-23 as Baghdad and of nos. 25-30 as Babylon; no. 24 is given no provenance.

30251	1876,1016.1	Apprenticeship contract. Cyr 20/7/2. Babylon. Cyr 64; Pinches, BOR 1, 81-83, pl. facing p. 88; Bertin 769; Wunsch, CM 3, no. 278.
30252	1876,1016.2	Promissory note for silver with house given as pledge. Ner 15/5/1. Babylon. Evetts, Ner 24; Sack, AOAT 236, no. 24; Bertin 304; Wunsch, CM 3, no. 69.
30253	1876,1016.3	Promissory note for barley. Dar 1/11/14. Alu-ša-Zumbā. Dar 387; Bertin 2300.
30254	1876,1016.4	Hire of a slave. AM 23/9/acc. Sack, AOATS 4, no. 19; Bertin 255.
30255	1876,1016.5	Receipt for interest on a loan. Dar 6/10/22. Babylon. Dar 545; Bertin 2483.
30256	1876,1016.6	Receipt of barley from Marduk-nāṣir-apli. Dar 2/7/24. Babylon. Bertin 2537; Abraham, BPPE, 211-212, no. 5.
30257	1876,1016.7	Promissory note for silver. Nbn 8/10/12. Babylon. Nbn 655; Bertin 580.
30258	1876,1016.8	Promissory note for silver; Aramaic note on the upper edge. Nbn 15/5/11. Nbn 526; Bertin 533.
30259	1876,1016.9	Promissory note for silver. Dar 8/2/23. Šaḫrīn. Dar 561; Bertin 2504.
30260	1876,1016.10	Sale of slaves. Nbn 2/1/11. Nbn 400; cf. Wunsch, AfO 44/45, 97 (collation of date); Bertin 727.

30261	1876,1016.11	Receipt of ilku-tax by Marduk-nāṣir-apli. Dar 13/4/26?. Babylon. Bertin 2836; Abraham, BPPE, 212-214, no. 6.
30262	1876,1016.12	Promissory note for silver. Nbn 22/12/8. Babylon. Nbn 314; Wunsch, AfO 44/45, 82, no. 11; Bertin 461.
30263	1876,1016.13	Sale of slaves. Nbn 21/6/11. Babylon. Nbn 533; Bertin 538.
30264	1876,1016.14	Promissory note for dates. Dar 25/6/5. Babylon. Dar 173; Bertin 2068
30265	1876,1016.15	Promissory note for silver. Nbn 11/11/10. Babylon. Nbn 474; Bertin 511; Wunsch, CM 3, no. 181.
30266	1876,1016.16	Memorandum of the measurements of a house; not dated.
30267	1876,1016.17	Contract with Aramaic note; wife as collateral. Ner 2/6/2. Upija. 5R 67, 3 (wrongly marked S†.17); Stevenson, Ass.-Bab. Contracts, no. 29; Sack, AOAT 236, no. 82 (wrongly numbered 30297); Oppert, ZA 3, 17-22.
30268	1876,1016.18	Account of silver loan contracts. Nbn 14/2/15. Bīt-šar-Bābili. Nbn 83; Bertin 650.
30269	1876,1016.19	Slave girl given as a pledge. Nbn 21/2/13. Šaḫrīn. Nbn 700; Bertin 601; Wunsch, CM 3, no. 212.
30270	1876,1016.20	Contract; hire of a boat to Marduk-nāṣir-apli. Dar 6/12/26. Babylon. Bertin 2602; Abraham, BPPE, 214-217, no. 7.
30271	1876,1016.21	Promissory note for dates. Nbn 25/2/13. Babylon. Nbn 701; Bertin 602.
30272	1876,1016.22	Promissory note to pay a debt of silver due from Marduk-naṣir-apli. Dar 22/8/15. Nār-šarri-ša-Elam. Dar 411; Abraham, BPPE, 422-423, no. 119; Bertin 2331.
30273	1876,1016.23	Contract; ḫarrānu, with Marduk-nāṣir-apli's capital being dates from the tithes of Bēl. Dar 29 /10/13. Alu-ša-Kī-Bēl. Dar 359; Abraham, BPPE, 415-416, no. 114; Bertin 2272.
30274	1876,1016.24	Contract; release of Ardiya from army service. Dar 13/4/24. Babylon. Bertin 2540; Abraham, BPPE, 217-218, no. 8.
30275	1876,1016.25	Contract; sale of land. Dar 22/10/4. Babylon. Dar 140; Bertin 2016; dupl. 31485.
30276	1876,1016.26	Account of expenses. Nbk 10/8/42. Nbk 402; Bertin 226; Wunsch, CM 3, no. 47.
30277	1876,1016.27	Promissory note for barley. Cyr 22/12a/3. Babylon. Cyr 146; Bertin 785.
30278	1876,1016.28	Summons to bring slaves. Dar 1/1/-. Bertin 2790.

30279	1876,1016.29	Promissory note for silver. Cam 21/4/6. Babylon. Cam 315; Scheil, RA 12, 11-13; Bertin 947.
30280	1876,1016.30	Sale of a slave girl. Dar 6/[]/12. Dar 340; Bertin 2221.

DT collection

The Babylonian tablets in this collection were mostly purchased by George Smith in Baghdad during the course of his 1873 expedition sponsored by the Daily Telegraph (see J. E. Reade in CBTBM VI, p. xiv, and Budge, Rise and Progress, p. 113). There is evidence for tablets in this collection being re-numbered and re-registered, and relevant comments are made on page 30 of the department's register (volume 5).

Of the tablets listed here the register gives the provenance Babylon to nos. 15-37, 66, 84, 87, 108, 112-114, 187, 189, 233, 253, 260, 278, the provenance Babylonia to nos. 73, 110, 143, 168, 183, 195, 203, 204, 207, 208, 210, 225, and the provenance Kouyunjik to nos. 62, 72, 78, 79, 107, 109, 149, 153, 165, 181, 184, 185, 188, 193, 202, 213, 221, 239, 245, 248, 255, 268, 272, 276.

92704	DT.15	New Year festival ritual. Bought in Baghdad; see British Library, Add MSS 30413 fol. 18, no. 3. 4R(2) 40 [46-47], 1; Thureau-Dangin, RAcc, 127-146 and 149-150; Linssen, CM 25, 215-237 and 9, 11, 80.
	DT.20	Promissory note for dates. Dar 14/[]/[]. Bāb-Nār-Kūtê-labīru. Bertin 2774 (Bertin marks it as "49"); Wunsch, CM 20A-B, no. 160.
	DT.21	Contract. Dar 26/1/31. Bertin 2694 (Bertin marks it as "22").
	DT.24	Contract. Nbk 15/4/20. Babylon.
	DT.25	Sale of a slave; Egibi archive. []/[]/5?. Babylon. Bertin 3006 (Bertin marks it as "71?").
	DT.26	Contract. Nbk 5/1/19. Babylon. Bertin 1064.
	DT.27	Contract for bricks; Egibi archive. Nbk 13/2/11. Babylon. Bertin 523 (Bertin marks it as "DT 15").
	DT.29	Loan; finger-nail mark and caption on left edge.
	DT.30	Promissory note for silver. Nbn 23/9/9. Babylon. Bertin 478.
	DT.31	Promissory note. Nbk 21/2/37. Babylon. Bertin 185; Wunsch, CM 3, no. 26.
	DT.32	Receipt for onions. Nbn 18/5/6. Sippar. Nbn 232; Bertin 427.
	DT.33	Promissory note for dates. Cam 6/6/2. Babylon. Bertin 1785; Wunsch, CM 20A-B, no. 74.
92712	DT.34	Contract; sale of land; finger-nail marks. Bought in Baghdad; see British Library Add MSS 30413 fol. 19, no. 33. Esar 22/2/4. Babylon. Strassmaier, 8th Orientalist Congress, no. 5; San Nicoló, BR 8/7, no. 4; Brinkman and Kennedy, JCS 35, 18, I.8; Bertin 2.

92705	DT.35	Omens; commentary on Iqqur īpuš; colophon. SE 23/12/208 = AE 144. Frahm, NABU 2005, 43-45, no. 43.
92700	DT.36	Omen commentary on Šumma ālu 48. CT 41, 32; Labat, Commentaires, 66-69.
92683	DT.37	Omen commentary on Šumma ālu 49. CT 41, 30-31; Labat, Commentaires, 56-65; De Zorzi, NABU 2016, 131-134, no. 79; Finkel, CTMMA 2, 283.
	DT.62	Contract; lease of a house; Egibi archive. Nbn2/5/[]. Babylon. Bertin 738 (Bertin marks it as "DT 221 (74)". Nothing other than DT.62 now on the tablet. It corresponds only to DT.62 in the Register).
	DT.66	Promissory note for silver. Bought at Hillah; see Smith, Assyrian Discoveries, 316. Šamaš-šum-ukin 24/[]/11+. Bertin 718; Brinkman and Kennedy, JCS 35, 37, K.167.
92684	DT.72	Cryptographic astrological omens. Hunger, AOAT 1, 133-145; Gadd, JCS 21, 53-63; Hunger, ZA 64, 43-45, Brown, CM 18, 306.
	DT.73	Astrological omens.
92685	DT.78	Cryptographic astrological omens; colophon mentioning Ashurbanipal. Hunger, AOAT 1, 133-145; Gadd, JCS 21, 53-63; Hunger, ZA 64, 43-45; Brown, CM 18, 306; Hunger, AOAT 2, no. 496.
	DT.79	Astronomical.
	DT.84	Commentary on extispicy; colophon; prayer on upper edge. Cf. 42322. Frahm, NABU 2005, 43-45, no. 43; Finkel, CTMMA 2, 283; Hunger, AOAT 2, no. 478; Frahm, GMTR 5, 31, 172, 239, 308.
	DT.87	Commentary on Sa-gig X-XI; colophon. Frahm, NABU 2005, 43-45, no. 43; Finkel, CTMMA 2, 283; Frahm, GMTR 5, 51, 225, 308.
	DT.107	Astrological.
	DT.108	Promissory note for dates; Iddin-Marduk archive. Nbk 8/9/37. Babylon.
92708	DT.109	Joined to 32485.
	DT.110	Memorandum; undated.
	DT.112	Contract; Iddin-Marduk archive. Nbn 9/1/-. Šaḫrīn ālu ša Nabû. Bertin 739.
	DT.113	Medical commentary. Frahm, GMTR 5, 101, 240, 311.
92686	DT.114	Ritual; prayer on edge. 4R(2) 40, 2; Thureau-Dangin, RAcc, 127-146 and 152; Linssen, CM 25, 215-237.

DT.143	Astronomical; Almanac for SE 347. LBAT 1197; Sachs, AOAT 25, 384-386, pl. XV; Hunger and Sachs, ADART VII, no. 214.
DT.149	Contract; lease of a house; Egibi archive. Dar 22/[]/15. [Babylon].
DT.153	Medical.
DT.165	Contract. Nbn 20/7/-.
DT.168	Account of payments of silver.
DT.181	Contract; [RN LUGAL] E.KI. x+5/[]/1.
DT.183	Astronomical procedure text for Jupiter ACT 814; Steele, JHA 34 (2003) 269-289; Ossendrijver, BMAPT, no. 23; Ossendrijver, JNES 76, 231-247, text F.
DT.184	Literary; mentioning Tiamat, Marduk and Mummu. Lambert, JCS 10, 100; Lambert, BCM, p. 327, pl. 56.
DT.185	Promissory note for silver and onions; Iddin-Marduk archive. [Nbk] []/[]/37. Šaḫrīn.
DT.187	Contract.
DT.188	Astronomical.
DT.189	Receipt; fragment; mentions years 16 and 17 (of Antiochus III) and year 120 SE; sealed. SE Antiochus III []/[]/120. Bezold, Cat. 4, p. 1558; Rost, MVAG 2/2 (1897), 4 n. 2; cf. Oelsner, Materialien, 199; Mitchell and Searight, no. 656; Nisaba 28, no. 599.
DT.193	Contract; sale of an orchard; finger-nail marks; also numbered "7" on the tablet. RN lost 5/2/21. Borsippa. Zadok, Nisaba 21, 239.
DT.195	Literary text giving names of Zarpanitu. + DT.221 + DT.302. Lambert, BCM, p. 159, pl. 41.
DT.202	Contract; division of property; caption for a seal, but seal lost.
DT.203	Memorandum; undated. Bertin 3008. Bertin marks it as "DT 19?"; the copy corresponds to the tablet originally registered as DT.19, before the register entry was revised.
DT.204	Contract; fragment.
DT.207	Astronomical; Goal Year text for SE 256. Hunger and Sachs, ADART VI, no. 95.
DT.208	Promissory note for dates; [RN] LUGAL TIN.TIR.KI. []/12/acc. Babylon. Bertin 3072 (Bertin marks it only as "?").
DT.210	Oracle question (tamītu) to Šamaš and Adad. RN lost 4/6b/[]. Lambert, BOQ, no. 26, pl. 52.
DT.213	Contract; year 17 of Darius mentioned. Dar []/[]/17.
DT.221	Joined to DT.195.

	DT.225	Promissory note for silver. Nbn 5/12/[]. Babylon. Wunsch, CM 20A-B, no. 122.
	DT.233	Contract. Wunsch, AfO 42/43, 59, no. 9.
	DT.239	Prayer to Marduk no. 1. Lambert, AfO 19, 55 and pl. 16.
	DT.245	Literary or religious.
	DT.248	Sale of 3 slaves; finger-nail marks. [Babylon?].
	DT.253	Contract. Nbk []/1/26.
	DT.255	Bilingual religious. Bezold, Cat. 4, p. 1563.
	DT.260	Medical commentary. Frahm, GMTR 5, 261.
	DT.268	Promissory note for silver; Egibi archive; sealed; dupl. 31850. [Dar] [15]/[7]/[]. [Babylon]. Nisaba 28, no. 158.
	DT.272	Cylinder of Ashurbanipal. Frame, RIMB 2.6.32.12.3.
	DT.276	Promissory note for onions. Nbn 10/6/16. Babylon. Bertin 678; Wunsch, CM 3, no. 244.
	DT.278	Lexical; personal names.
	DT.279	Omens.
	DT.285	Memorandum about silver; undated. Bertin 3007. Bertin marks it as “18”; tablet and copy correspond to register entry for DT.366, which says “marked with red 18”; later re-registered as DT.285.
	DT.297	Bilingual incantation; Udug-ḫul fragment 15.
	DT.300	Letter order; sealed. CT 54, 440; Reynolds, SAA XVIII, 120; Nisaba 28, no. 215.
	DT.302	Joined to DT.195.
	DT.303	Astrological omens(?); badly preserved.
	DT.309	Contract. Cam 14/8/[]. Babylon. Bertin 1786. Bertin marks it as “36”.
90285	DT.381	Brick of Ashurbanipal. Purchased in Baghdad. Babylon. CBI, no. 78.
90850	DT.383	Boundary stone (kudurru) recording a grant of land by Marduk-apla-iddina I to Marduk-zakir-šumi. Bought in Baghdad, but said to have been found on the western bank of the Tigris opposite Baghdad (G. Smith, Assyrian Discoveries, pp. 236-241). 4R 38 [41]; King, BBSt, 24-29 and pls. XXXI-XLII, no. V.
	DT.519	Promissory note for silver. Nbn 24/11/5. Babylon. Nbn 211; Bertin 422. Found marked “DT” and first registered on 20/3/1980.

Sm collection

The Sm collection was the result of George Smith's second expedition to Iraq in 1873-1874. It includes two items from Babylonia. If they are correctly registered in this collection it is unclear how he obtained them. The register gives the provenance of both of them as Kouyunjik.

Sm.486	Historical cylinder; fragment. Mentions "Ištar my lady." Cf. K.10066 which is made from the same over-fired clay (or faience?).
Sm.2224	Old Babylonian fragment of a steatite tablet. Inscription of Warad-Sin. Dupl. UET I 129 and Frayne, RIME 4.2.13.9. Warad-Sin.

1876,1117 collection

The 1876,1117 collection was bought by George Smith in Baghdad from the dealer Marini. See J. E. Reade in CBTBM VI, p. xiv. The register gives the provenance Babylon to almost all items in this collection, except that it gives the provenance "Babylonia (Baghdad)" to nos. 101-125, no provenance to the Assyrian items nos. 145-150, the provenance Assyria to nos. 2413-2417, and no provenance to nos. 2611-2627 (first registered in 1982). Many of the economic texts in this collection come from the Egibi archive; for a general introduction to the archive see Wunsch, CM 20A, 1-12 (especially p. 2 n. 5 for a list of the other collections in which tablets from the archive have been found). On George Smith's own work on this collection see J. E. Reade, Iraq 55, 107-117.

30281	1876,1117.1	Contract; sale of a field. Nbk 5/12/36. Babylon. Nbk 311; Bertin 178.
30282	1876,1117.2	Contract; sale of a house. + 32669.
30283	1876,1117.3	Promissory note for barley. RN lost 4/9/-.
30284	1876,1117.4	Promissory note for silver. Nbk 4/8/28. Babylon. Nbk 189; Bertin 130.
30285	1876,1117.5	Promissory note for silver. Dar 25/12/15. Borsippa. Dar 418; Bertin 2082.
30286	1876,1117.6	Contract.
30287	1876,1117.7	Purchase of copper. Nbn 25/12a/3. Babylon. Nbn 131; Bertin 385.
30288	1876,1117.8	Contract; sale of land; sealed; finger-nail marks; dupl. 30685 (Dar 227). Dar I 3/7/7. [Babylon]. Wunsch, CM 20A-B, no. 184 B; Nisaba 28, no. 115.
30289	1876,1117.9	Promissory note for silver. Dar 15/5/10. Babylon. Dar 271; Bertin 2782.
30290	1876,1117.10	Promissory note for silver. Nbk 15/12/3. Saḫrītu. Nbk 34; Bertin 25.
30291	1876,1117.11	Promissory note for silver. Nbn 26/1/11. Babylon. Nbn 498; Bertin 518.
30292	1876,1117.12	Contract; sale of land.

30293	1876,1117.13	Promissory note for silver. Dar 21/12/15. Dar 417; Bertin 2189.
30294	1876,1117.14	Court record about a creditor's claim (rašûtu) on a slave; sealed. Nbn 15/11/13. Bāb-Nār-Šamaš. Nbn 738; Bertin 612; Nisaba 28, no. 21.
30295	1876,1117.15	Contract; sale of land. Nbn 23/2/4. Babylon. Nbn 147; Bertin 3394.
30296	1876,1117.16	Promissory note for silver. Cyr []/12/7. Babylon. Cyr 284; Bertin 820; Wunsch, CM 3, no. 306.
30297	1876,1117.17	Receipt of ilku-tax by Marduk-nāṣir-apli. Dar 6/8/24. Babylon. Bertin 2542; Abraham, BPPE, 219-220, no. 9.
30298	1876,1117.18	Receipt for payment of silver. Nbn 20/12/14. Nbn 820; Bertin 639.
30299	1876,1117.19	Contract; lease of a house; Egibi archive. Cam 16/5/2. Babylon. Cam 117; Bertin 891.
30300	1876,1117.20	Promissory note for silver. AM 13/6/1. Babylon. Evetts, Ev-M 10; Sack, AOATS 4, no. 26; Strassmaier, Liverpool, 128; Bertin 263; Wunsch, CM 3, no. 55.
30301	1876,1117.21	Sale of a slave girl. Nbk 11/6/26. Babylon. Nbk 166; Bertin 120.
30302	1876,1117.22	Promissory note for silver; rašûtu. AM 26/1/2. Babylon. Evetts, Ev-M 19; Sack, AOATS 4, no. 9; Strassmaier, Liverpool, 132; Bertin 281.
30303	1876,1117.23	Promissory note for silver. Nbn 2/10/12. Babylon. Nbn 653; Bertin 579.
30304	1876,1117.24	Purchase of vats. Nbn 7/10/1. Babylon. Nbn 44; Strassmaier, Liverpool, 49; Bertin 351.
30305	1876,1117.25	Sale of a slave. Cyr 10/1/7. Babylon.
30306	1876,1117.26	Promissory note for silver. Nbn 22/5/16. Babylon. Nbn 974; Bertin 675.
30307	1876,1117.27	Contract; sale of land. Dar 2/9/23. Babylon. Dar 571; Bertin 2505.
30308	1876,1117.28	Promissory note for silver. Nbn 25/3/2. Babylon. Nbn 67; Strassmaier, Liverpool, 57; Bertin 372.
30309	1876,1117.29	Receipt of silver paid on behalf of Marduk-nāṣir-apli in partial payment of a debt. Sealed. Dar 20/10/17. Babylon. Dar 450; Abraham, BPPE, 430-431, no. 123; Bertin 2370; Nisaba 28, no. 160.
30310	1876,1117.30	Promissory note for barley and silver. Nbn 23/2/8. Šaḫrīn. Nbn 287; Strassmaier, Liverpool, 85; Bertin 454; Wunsch, CM 3, no. 152.

30311	1876,1117.31	Promissory note for silver. Npl 13/6/16. Saḫrītu. Strassmaier, ZA 4, 143, no. 14; Kennedy, JCS 38, 201, T.16.22; Bertin 6.
30312	1876,1117.32	Contract; lease of a house; Egibi archive. Nbn 3/2/17. Bīt-šar-Bābili. Nbn 1030; Bertin 692.
30313	1876,1117.33	Promissory note for dates. Dar 16/7/2. Babylon. Dar 51; Bertin 1946.
30314	1876,1117.34	Promissory note for barley. Nbn 20/1/7. Babylon. Nbn 251; Strassmaier, Liverpool, 74; Bertin 433.
30315	1876,1117.35	Sale of a slave girl. Ner 18/11/1. Babylon. 5R 67 2; Sack, AOAT 236, no. 81; Sack, ZA 68, 146-149.
30316	1876,1117.36	Promissory note for silver. Nbk 21/5/7. Babylon. Nbk 59; Strassmaier, Liverpool, 140; Bertin 45.
30317	1876,1117.37	Contract; sale of a field.
30318	1876,1117.38	Promissory note for silver. Cyr 22/1/8. Cyr 249; Bertin 819.
30319	1876,1117.39	Promissory note for silver. Nbn 20/7/10. Babylon. Nbn 443; Bertin 504; Wunsch, CM 3, no. 178.
30320	1876,1117.40	Sale of a slave girl. Nbn 21/1/13. Babylon. Nbn 693; Bertin 599.
30321	1876,1117.41	Deed of partnership. Nbk 16/7/10. Babylon. Nbk 88; Strassmaier, Liverpool, 145; Bertin 65.
30322	1876,1117.42	Promissory note for silver. Dar 27/11/3. Babylon. Dar 95; Strassmaier, Liverpool, 173; Bertin 1976.
30323	1876,1117.43	Contract; division of an inheritance. Cyr 29/4/4. Cyr 168; Bertin 791.
30324	1876,1117.44	Promissory note for dates. Dar 6/5/9. Babylon. Dar 252; Bertin 2152.
30325	1876,1117.45	Promissory note for barley. Nbk 29/2/30. Babylon. Nbk 212; Bertin 148.
30326	1876,1117.46	Promissory note for silver. Cam 16/12/6. Babylon. Cam 348; Bertin 955.
30327	1876,1117.47	Promissory note for dates in lieu of silver. Nbn 16/4/9. Babylon. Nbn 344; Strassmaier, Liverpool, 95; Bertin 470; Wunsch, CM 3, no. 166.
30328	1876,1117.48	Contract; ḫarrānu. Nbk 8/11/18. Nbk 116; Bertin 91.
30329	1876,1117.49	Gift of a slave as dowry. Nbk 1/3/29. Babylon. Nbk 198; Bertin 138.
30330	1876,1117.50	Promissory note for silver. Nbk III 10/8/acc. Babylon. Nbk 8; Bertin 13; Lorenz, Nebukadnezar III/IV, p. 31.
30331	1876,1117.51	Promissory note for silver and barley. Ner 2/9/2. Šaḫrīn. Evetts, Ner 43; Sack, AOAT 236, no. 43; Strassmaier, Liverpool, 119; Bertin 318; Wunsch, CM 3, no. 76.

30332	1876,1117.52	Promissory note for silver. Nbn 4/6/10. Babylon. Nbn 433 (wrongly as 1876,1117.56); Bertin 497.
30333	1876,1117.53	Promissory note for silver. AM 11/9/[]. Babylon. Sack, AOATS 4, no. 10; Bertin 288.
30334	1876,1117.54	Promissory note for silver as the price of onions. Ner 2/1/4. Šaḫrīn. Evetts, Ner 69; Sack, AOAT 236, no. 69; Bertin 330; Wunsch, CM 3, no. 82.
30335	1876,1117.55	Promissory note for silver. Npl 27/4/14. Babylon. Strassmaier, ZA 4, 141, no. 11; Kennedy, JCS 38, 197-198, T.14.15.
30336	1876,1117.56	Commentary on numerically cryptographically written astrological omens. Cf. 30432, 40475, etc. Probably late (Seleucid?). Frahm, GMTR 5, 78, 173.
30337	1876,1117.57	Court record; division of an inheritance among the sons of Itti-Marduk-balāṭu; sealed. Dar 24/5/14. Babylon. Dar 379; Bertin 2303-2306; Nisaba 28, no. 32.
30338	1876,1117.58	Contract; sale of land by Nabû-šuma-uṣur to Kabti-ilāni-Marduk; captions for seals but not. Sealed; finger-nail marks; dupl. 32849. Nbn 24/7/3. Babylon. Nbn 116a; Bertin 380-381; Wunsch, CM 20A, 42-45, no. 33.
30339	1876,1117.59	Promissory note for dates. Dar 27/5/25. Bīt-Ḫaḫḫūru. Bertin 2579; Wunsch, CM 20A-B, no. 195.
30340	1876,1117.60	Promissory note for silver. Nbn 28/2/3. Šaḫrīn. Nbn 103; Bertin 377; Wunsch, CM 3, no. 112.
30341	1876,1117.61	Contract; division of property. Nbn 6/10/15. Ḫarrān-Kiš. Nbn 916; Bertin 664.
30342	1876,1117.62	Hire of a slave. Nbk 6/10/28. Babylon. Nbk 193; Strassmaier, Liverpool, 15; Bertin 133; Wunsch, AfO 44/45, 74, no. 2.
30343	1876,1117.63	Account of sheep. Nbk 2/6/34. Tagritajn. Nbk 266; Bertin 162.
30344	1876,1117.64	Promissory note for silver. Nbk 27/2/8. Babylon. Nbk 64; Bertin 49.
30345	1876,1117.65	Contract for repayment of silver loan. Nbk 5/5/37. Babylon. Nbk 320; Bertin 183.
30346	1876,1117.66	Deposition. Nbk 7/8/40. Upija. Nbk 365; Strassmaier, Liverpool, 152; Bertin 207.
30347	1876,1117.67	Promissory note for silver; sealed. Dar 11/1/20+. Šušan. Dar 497; Bertin 2428; Nisaba 28, no. 167.
	1876,1117.68	Nothing registered.
30348	1876,1117.69	Deposition. Nbk 4/1/27. Babylon. Nbk 172; Bertin 123.

30349	1876,1117.70	Promissory note for silver; rašûtu. Nbk []/2/7. Babylon. Nbk 57; Bertin 43. Duplicate registration as 1876,1117.2518.
30350	1876,1117.71	Promissory note for silver. Nbk 10/10/22. Babylon. Nbk 133; Strassmaier, Liverpool, 147; Bertin 104.
30351	1876,1117.72	Contract; transfer of silver. Nbk 8/11/32. Nbk 250; Bertin 155.
	1876,1117.73	Re-registered as 1876,1117.139.
30352	1876,1117.74	Promissory note for silver as house rent. Nbk 15/7/39. Babylon. Nbk 350; Strassmaier, Liverpool, 158; Bertin 197.
30353	1876,1117.75	Promissory note for silver. Nbk 20/6/23. Alu-ša-Nabû-immē. Nbk 138a; Strassmaier, Liverpool, 153; Bertin 111.
30354	1876,1117.76	Deed of partnership. Nbn 3/8/5. Babylon. Nbn 199; Pinches, ZA 1, 202-205; Bertin 418.
30355	1876,1117.77	Promissory note for dates. Cam 30/6/3. Babylon. Cam 174; Bertin 903.
30356	1876,1117.78	Contract; lease of a house. Cam 5/[]/2. Babylon. Cam 147; Bertin 881; Wunsch, CM 3, no. 330.
30357	1876,1117.79	Promissory note for silver. Cam 18/11/6. Babylon. Cam 341; Bertin 946.
30358	1876,1117.80	Contract; transfer of a field, slaves and household goods as dowry. Cam 22/11/3. Paširi. Cam 215; Bertin 914; Wunsch, CM 3, no. 338a.
30359	1876,1117.81	Receipt of silver for urāšu service baking bricks. Cam 14/5/1. Babylon. Wunsch, CM 3, no. 265c.
30360	1876,1117.82	Inventory and value of vats. Cam. Cam 435; Bertin 872.
30361	1876,1117.83	Receipt for silver. Cam 14/8/1. Babylon. Cam 73; Bertin 868.
30362	1876,1117.84	Sale of slave girls. Cam 4/2/6. Babylon. Cam 307; Bertin 944; Wunsch, CM 3, no. 344.
30363	1876,1117.85	Contract; sale of a field. Cam 22/6/5. Babylon. Cam 286; Bertin 937.
30364	1876,1117.86	Promissory note for dates and barley. Dar 7/12/9. Babylon. Dar 261; Bertin 2156.
30365	1876,1117.87	Contract; division of property. Dar 1/6b/3. Nāru-eššu. Dar 80; Bertin 1985-1986; dupl. 32216.
30366	1876,1117.88	Receipt of ilku-tax by Marduk-nāṣir-apli. Dar 7/8/26. Babylon. Bertin 2616; Abraham, BPPE, 220-221, no. 10.
30367	1876,1117.89	Promissory note for dates. Dar 10/6/4. Nāru-eššu. Dar 124; Bertin 2014.

30368	1876,1117.90	Contract for repayment of silver loan. Dar 17/4/17. Babylon. Dar 446; Bertin 2368.
30369	1876,1117.91	Missing.
30370	1876,1117.92	Contract; sale of a boat to Marduk-nāṣir-apli. Dar 3+/5/26. Babylon. Bertin 2615; Abraham, BPPE, 222-224, no. 11.
30371	1876,1117.93	Promissory note for dates and barley. Dar 3/[]/14. Babylon. Dar 396; Bertin 2289.
30372	1876,1117.94	Promissory note for dates; dupl. Nab 375. Nbn 18/5/12. Babylon. Nbn 619; Bertin 567; Wunsch, CM 3, no. 200.
30373	1876,1117.95	Promissory note for barley. Nbn 22/2/8. Babylon. Nbn 286; Strassmaier, Liverpool, 84; Bertin 453.
30374	1876,1117.96	Promissory note for silver. Nbn 22/4/14. Babylon. Nbn 772; Bertin 624.
30375	1876,1117.97	Sale of a slave. Nbn 26/6/10. Babylon. Nbn 434; Bertin 498.
30376	1876,1117.98	Receipt for vats. Nbn 22/10/5. Babylon. Nbn 204; Strassmaier, Liverpool, 72; Bertin 421.
30377	1876,1117.99	Payment of remainder of house rent to Nabû-aḫḫe-iddin; sealed. Nbn 22/2/6. Babylon. Nbn 224; Bertin 426; Nisaba 28, no. 145.
30378	1876,1117.100	Lagaš II cone; inscription of Gudea. Steible, FAOS 9/1 Gudea 51 (T); Edzard, RIME 3/1 1.7.41.
30379	1876,1117.101	Lagaš II cone; inscription of Gudea. Steible, FAOS 9/1 Gudea 75 (H); Edzard, RIME 3/1 1.7.73.
30380	1876,1117.102	Lagaš II cone; inscription of Gudea. Steible, FAOS 9/1 Gudea 46 (J); Edzard, RIME 3/1 1.7.48.
30381	1876,1117.103	Lagaš II cone; inscription of Gudea. Steible, FAOS 9/1 Gudea 46 (J); Edzard, RIME 3/1 1.7.48.
30382	1876,1117.104	Lagaš II cone; inscription of Gudea. Steible, FAOS 9/1 Gudea 36 (S); Edzard, RIME 3/1 1.7.31.
30383	1876,1117.105	Lagaš II cone; inscription of Gudea. Steible, FAOS 9/1 Gudea 51 (T); Edzard, RIME 3/1 1.7.41.
30384	1876,1117.106	Lagaš II cone; inscription of Gudea. Steible, FAOS 9/1 Gudea 46 (J); Edzard, RIME 3/1 1.7.48.
30385	1876,1117.107	Lagaš II cone; inscription of Gudea. Steible, FAOS 9/1 Gudea 19 (K); Edzard, RIME 3/1 1.7.16.
30386	1876,1117.108	Lagaš II cone; inscription of Gudea. Steible, FAOS 9/1 Gudea 5 (B); Edzard, RIME 3/1.1.7.6.
30387	1876,1117.109	Lagaš II cone; inscription of Gudea. Steible, FAOS 9/1 Gudea 48 (U); Edzard, RIME 3/1 1.7.37.
30388	1876,1117.110	Lagaš II cone; inscription of Gudea. Steible, FAOS 9/1 Gudea 48 (U); Edzard, RIME 3/1 1.7.37.

30389	1876,1117.111	Lagaš II cone; inscription of Gudea. Steible, FAOS 9/1 Gudea 51 (T); Edzard, RIME 3/1 1.7.41.
30390	1876,1117.112	Lagaš II cone; inscription of Gudea. Steible, FAOS 9/1 Gudea 46 (J); Edzard, RIME 3/1 1.7.48.
30391	1876,1117.113	Lagaš II cone; inscription of Gudea. Steible, FAOS 9/1 Gudea 51 (T); Edzard, RIME 3/1 1.7.41.
Istanbul	1876,1117.114	Lagaš II cone; inscription of Gudea. Presented to the Sultan in 1882; now in Istanbul.
30393	1876,1117.115	Lagaš II cone; inscription of Gudea. Steible, FAOS 9/1 Gudea 51 (T); Edzard, RIME 3/1 1.7.41.
30394	1876,1117.116	Lagaš II cone; inscription of Gudea. Steible, FAOS 9/1 Gudea 48 (U); Edzard, RIME 3/1 1.7.37.
30395	1876,1117.117	Lagaš II cone; inscription of Gudea. Steible, FAOS 9/1 Gudea 15 (K); Edzard, RIME 3/1 1.7.11.
30396	1876,1117.118	Lagaš II cone; inscription of Gudea. Steible, FAOS 9/1 Gudea 51 (T); Edzard, RIME 3/1 1.7.41.
30397	1876,1117.119	Lagaš II cone; inscription of Gudea. Steible, FAOS 9/1 Gudea 15 (K); Edzard, RIME 3/1 1.7.11.
30398	1876,1117.120	Lagaš II cone; inscription of Gudea. Steible, FAOS 9/1 Gudea 51 (T); Edzard, RIME 3/1 1.7.41.
30399	1876,1117.121	Lagaš II cone; inscription of Gudea. Steible, FAOS 9/1 Gudea 19 (K); Edzard, RIME 3/1 1.7.16.
30400	1876,1117.122	Lagaš II cone; inscription of Gudea. Steible, FAOS 9/1 Gudea 56 (B); Edzard, RIME 3/1 1.7.51.
30401	1876,1117.123	Lagaš II cone; inscription of Gudea. Steible, FAOS 9/1 Gudea 48 (U); Edzard, RIME 3/1 1.7.37.
30402	1876,1117.124	Lagaš II cone; inscription of Gudea. Steible, FAOS 9/1 Gudea 28 (F); Edzard, RIME 3/1 1.7.24.
30403	1876,1117.125	Lagaš II cone; inscription of Gudea. Steible, FAOS 9/1 Gudea 46 (J); Edzard, RIME 3/1 1.7.48.
30404	1876,1117.126	Promissory note for barley. Nbk 25/5/25. Babylon. Nbk 152; Bertin 116.
30405	1876,1117.127	Promissory note for dates. Bardija 20/6/1. Babylon. Strassmaier, ZA 4, 151, Sm 8; Bertin 1923.
30406	1876,1117.128	Promissory note for silver. Nbk 6/10/5. Saḫrītu. Nbk 46; Strassmaier, Liverpool, 13; Bertin 32.
30407	1876,1117.129	Promissory note for silver, barley and dates. Nbn 16/12b/12. Babylon. Nbn 678; Bertin 590; Wunsch, CM 3, no. 208.
30408	1876,1117.130	Securement of responsibility. Dar 14/12b/13. Babylon. Dar 366; Strassmaier, Liverpool, 179; Bertin 2260.
30409	1876,1117.131	Promissory note for silver and dates. Nbn 7/11/acc. Babylon. Nbn 11; Bertin 347; Wunsch, CM 3, no. 88.

30410	1876,1117.132	Contract; division of property. Nbn 26/12a/1. Babylon. Nbn 50; Bertin 373.
30411	1876,1117.133	Promissory note for silver. Ner 9/12b/acc. Babylon. Evetts, Ner 9; Sack, AOAT 236, no. 9; Strassmaier, Liverpool, 11; Bertin 297.
30412	1876,1117.134	Promissory note for silver. Cam 28/11/acc. Babylon. Cam 16; Bertin 859; Wunsch, CM 3, no. 319.
30413	1876,1117.135	Promissory note for sheep, wool and cows; ḫarrānu. AM 21/2/2. Babylon. Evetts, Ev-M 20; Sack, AOATS 4, no. 30 (variants); Bertin 282; Wunsch, CM 3, no. 60.
30414	1876,1117.136	Promissory note for barley. Nbk 11/1/43. Babylon. Nbk 411; Strassmaier, Liverpool, 163; Bertin 233.
30415	1876,1117.137	Promissory note for silver. Nbn 9/12/16. Babylon. Nbn 1013; Strassmaier, Liverpool, 108; Bertin 684-685.
30416	1876,1117.138	Promissory note for silver. Dar 21/5/4. Babylon. Bertin 796.
30417	1876,1117.139	Receipt in the context of a claim for silver. LM 14/2/acc. Evetts, Lab 3; Strassmaier, 8th Orientalist Congress, no. 13; Bertin 1217; Wunsch, CM 3, no. 85.
30418	1876,1117.140	Contract; sale of a field. Cyr 7/9/acc. Cyr 3; Bertin 748.
30419	1876,1117.141	Promissory note for silver. Ner 6/5/acc. Babylon. Evetts, Ner 12; Sack, AOAT 236, no. 12; Bertin 298; Wunsch, CM 3, no. 62.
30420	1876,1117.142	Receipt for sesame. Cyr 2/12/1. Babylon. Cyr 27; Bertin 752; Wunsch, CM 3, no. 270.
30421	1876,1117.143	Receipt of silver for work on the wall of the Enlil gate. Cyr []/[]/acc. Babylon. Cyr 10; Bertin 749.
91441	1876,1117.144	Duck weight; inscribed.
30422	1876,1117.145	Neo-Assyrian. Prism. Royal inscription of Ashurbanipal. Bezold, Cat. 4, p. xii.
30423	1876,1117.146	Neo-Assyrian. Joined to K.1785. Bezold, Cat. 4, p. xii.
30424	1876,1117.147	Neo-Assyrian. Physiognomic omens. + 1876,1117.2624. Bezold, Cat. 4, p. xii; Kraus, AfO Bh. 3, 48; Böck, AfO Beih. 27, 230, pl. 25
30425	1876,1117.148	Neo-Assyrian. Prism. Royal inscription of Ashurbanipal; dupl. Rm. 1 ii 49-60, etc. Bezold, Cat. 4, p. xii.
30426	1876,1117.149	Neo-Assyrian. Incantations; Maqlu III. Bezold, Cat. 4, p. xii; Meier, AfO 21, 74; Abusch, AMD 10, 79-112.

30427	1876,1117.150	Neo-Assyrian. Omens; Šumma ālu 38. Bezold, Cat. 4, p. xii; CT 38, 44; Freedman, If a city, vols. 1, 333 and 2, 274.
91058	1876,1117.151	Copper figure of a god or Gudea, kneeling with a foundation nail in front of him. Previously numbered 12201. Steible, FAOS 9/1 Gudea 51 (F); Edzard, RIME 3/1 1.7.41.
91056	1876,1117.152	Copper figure of a god or Gudea, kneeling with a foundation nail in front of him. Previously numbered 12199. Steible, FAOS 9/1 Gudea 51 (F); Edzard, RIME 3/1 1.7.41.
30428	1876,1117.153	Sale of a slave. Cam 15/9/1. Šaḫrīn. Bertin 1787; Wunsch, CM 3, no. 267.
30429	1876,1117.154	Promissory note for silver. Nbk 22/6/7. Saḫrītu. Nbk 60; Strassmaier, Liverpool, 141; Bertin 46.
92275	1876,1117.155	Terracotta figurine of a horse.
30430	1876,1117.156	Neo-Assyrian. Bilingual incantations. Bīt mēseri; Udug-ḫul 12. Joined to K.3622+. Bezold, Cat. 4, p. xii; Geller, BAM 8, 399-433.
30431	1876,1117.157	Neo-Assyrian. Omens; Šumma ālu 16, 15-33. Bezold, Cat. 4, p. xii; Freedman, If a city, vol. 1, 239.
90616	1876,1117.158	Brick of Nebuchadnezzar II. CBI, no. 99.
30432	1876,1117.159	Astrological, planetary(?) omens, with cryptographic use of numbers for signs, together with a key(?). Cf. 30336, 40475, etc. + 32593 + 32594 + 32595 + 32658 + 32712 + 32721 + 32722 + 32725 + 32735 + 8 unnum.
30433	1876,1117.160	Promissory note for dates. Dar 15/2/4. Babylon. Dar 114; Bertin 2020.
30434	1876,1117.161	Promissory note for barley and silver. Dar 14/1/4. Babylon. Dar 108; Bertin 2021.
30435	1876,1117.162	List of craftsmen and addresses.
30436	1876,1117.163	Deposition. Dar 17/5/24. Babylon. Bertin 2535.
30437	1876,1117.164	Contract for repayment of silver loan. Cam 28/4/3. Babylon. Cam 165; Bertin 905.
30438	1876,1117.165	Promissory note for silver. Nbk 21/4/23. Babylon. Nbk 137a; Bertin 110.
30439	1876,1117.166	Contract; sale of a field. Nbn 1/2/14. Babylon. Nbn 760; Bertin 1533.
30440	1876,1117.167	Promissory note for barley. Dar 10/1/26. Babylon. Bertin 2617.
30441	1876,1117.168	Promise of fields, slaves and household goods as a dowry. Dar 1/3/25. Babylon (KÁ.DINGIR.MEŠ.KI). Bertin 2580; Roth, JAOS 111, 29-30 and n. 30; Wunsch, AfO 42/43, 55-56, no. 6.

30442	1876,1117.169	Promissory note for silver as the price of a cow and calf. AM 6/9/1. Šaḫrīn. Sack, AOATS 4, no. 28; Bertin 277; Wunsch, CM 3, no. 58.
30443	1876,1117.170	Promissory note for silver. Ner 10/6/2. Babylon. Evetts, Ner 39; Bertin 315; Sack, AOAT 236, no. 39; Strassmaier, Liverpool, 118; Bertin 315.
30444	1876,1117.171	Contract; lease of a house; Egibi archive. Dar 6/6/12. Babylon. Dar 330; Bertin 2230.
30445	1876,1117.172	Promissory note for dates. Dar 21/11/17. Šuppatu. Dar 454; Bertin 2183.
30446	1876,1117.173	Receipt of persons enlisted to tow boats. Dar 4/7/24. Babylon. Bertin 2532; Abraham, BPPE, 224-226, no. 12.
30447	1876,1117.174	Promissory note for silver. Nbk 8/3/16. Babylon. Nbk 108; Bertin 80 and 82.
30448	1876,1117.175	Summons to settle debts with Marduk-nāṣir-apli; dupl. 33962. Dar 8/9/20. Babylon. Dar 509; Abraham, BPPE, 440-443, no. 129; Bertin 2443.
30449	1876,1117.176	Contract; sale of a field. Nbn 13/8/[]. Babylon. Nbn 1111; Bertin 726.
30450	1876,1117.177	Court record. Dar 25/8/9. Šaḫrīn. Dar 260; Bertin 2142-2143.
30451	1876,1117.178	Receipt of silver from Marduk-nāṣir-apli as payment of rikis qabli. Dar 24/1/5. Babylon. Dar 156; Abraham, BPPE, 377-378, no. 93; Bertin 2065.
30452	1876,1117.179	Promissory note for dates; Egibi archive. Cam 28/6/6. Babylon. Cam 319; Bertin 969.
30453	1876,1117.180	Contract; undertaking to transmit an order issued by Nergal-eṭir to Marduk-nāṣir-apli requiring him to pay silver. Dar 1/10/23. Pani-abul-Enlil. Dar 573; Abraham, BPPE, 454-455, no. 136; Bertin 2503.
30454	1876,1117.181	Sale of a slave girl. Ner 27/8/2. Babylon. Evetts, Ner 42; Sack, ZA 68 145; Sack, AOAT 236, no. 42; Bertin 317.
30455	1876,1117.182	Contract; lease of a house; Egibi archive. Nbn 1/2/11. Babylon. Nbn 499; Bertin 519.
30456	1876,1117.183	Sale of a slave girl. Nbn 21/4/12. Babylon. Nbn 609; Bertin 563.
30457	1876,1117.184	Receipt for silver. Nbn 27/6/11. Nbn 536; Bertin 539.
30458	1876,1117.185	Promissory note for dates. Dar 25/5/5. Babylon. Dar 166; Bertin 2074.
30459	1876,1117.186	Promissory note for dates. Cyr -/-/8. Cyr 331; Bertin 839.
30460	1876,1117.187	Promissory note for dates. Cam 23/9/6. Babylon. Cam 335; Bertin 940.

30461	1876,1117.188	Gift of slave girls. Nbk 16/10/40. Babylon. Nbk 368; Strassmaier, Liverpool, 160; Bertin 211.
30462	1876,1117.189	Promissory note for silver. Nbn 15/11/16. Babylon. Nbn 1005; Bertin 682.
30463	1876,1117.190	Promissory note for dates. Nbn 11/12/11. Babylon. Nbn 575; Bertin 548.
30464	1876,1117.191	Promissory note for silver. Nbn 24/3/14. Bīt-šar-Bābili. Nbn 769; Bertin 623.
30465	1876,1117.192	Promissory note for dates. Nbn 5/3/12. Babylon. Nbn 600; Bertin 557.
30466	1876,1117.193	Promissory note for dates as imittu payment. Nbn 13/7/12. Šaḫrīn. Nbn 627; Bertin 573; Wunsch, CM 3, no. 201.
30467	1876,1117.194	Purchase of vats. Cam 11/9/6. Ḫursag-kalamma. Cam 331; Bertin 943.
30468	1876,1117.195	Promissory note for silver. Nbn 9/3/8. Šaḫrīn. Nbn 294; Strassmaier, Liverpool, 88; Bertin 456.
30469	1876,1117.196	Promissory note for dates. Dar 25/7/6. Babylon. Dar 132; Bertin 2029.
30470	1876,1117.197	Witnessed correction of a promissory note. Nbn 10/4/2. Nbn 68; Strassmaier, Liverpool, 58; Bertin 365; Wunsch, CM 3, no. 104.
30471	1876,1117.198	Contract; guarantee for the presence of a man. Nbk 16/1/39. Nbk 342; Bertin 192; Wunsch, CM 3, no. 29.
30472	1876,1117.199	Promissory note for silver. Nbn 17/8/14. Babylon. Nbn 816; Bertin 632.
30473	1876,1117.200	Contract for repayment of silver. Nbk 6/[]/28. Babylon. Nbk 196; Bertin 136.
30474	1876,1117.201	Promissory note. Wunsch, CM 20A-B, no. 164.
30475	1876,1117.202	Promissory note for silver. Cam 12/3/5. Dūr-karaši-Bandada. Cam 276; Bertin 930.
30476	1876,1117.203	Promissory note for silver. Nbn 20/5/4. Babylon. Nbn 158; Bertin 401.
30477	1876,1117.204	Promissory note for silver. Nbk 21/4/23. Babylon. Nbk 137; Bertin 110.
30478	1876,1117.205	Promissory note for silver. Cyr 25/6/8. Babylon. Cyr 317; Bertin 841.
30479	1876,1117.206	Receipt for silver. Nbn 5/11/10. Babylon. Nbn 470; Bertin 509.
30480	1876,1117.207	Hire of a workman. Nbn 14/2/15. Babylon. Nbn 839; Bertin 649; Wunsch, CM 3, no. 234.
30481	1876,1117.208	Promissory note for barley. Dar 19/3/14. Alu-ša-Nabû-ēreš. Dar 374; Bertin 2293.
30482	1876,1117.209	Contract; lease of a house. Cam 4/7/3. Babylon. Cam 184; Bertin 910.

30483	1876,1117.210	Contract; lease of a house. Nbn 23/7/7. Babylon. Nbn 261; Bertin 441.
30484	1876,1117.211	Receipt for silver. Cyr []/4/7. Babylon. Cyr 261; Bertin 827.
30485	1876,1117.212	Promissory note for silver. Nbn 28/7/11. Babylon. Nbn 541; Bertin 543.
30486	1876,1117.213	Promissory note for silver. Dar 5/8/4. Babylon. Dar 134; Bertin 2017.
30487	1876,1117.214	Contract; lease of a house. Dar 2/3/20. Babylon. Dar 499; Strassmaier, Liverpool, 181; Bertin 2440.
30488	1876,1117.215	Promissory note to pay a debt of silver due from Marduk-nāṣir-apli. Dar []/[12?]/16. Šušan. Dar 437; Abraham, BPPE, 428-429, no. 122; Bertin 2345.
30489	1876,1117.216	Promissory note for silver. Nbk IV 16/7/1. Babylon. Nbk 17; Lorenz, Nebukadnezar III/IV, p. 32.
30490	1876,1117.217	Contract; hire of a boat by Marduk-nāṣir-apli. Dar 5/12/26. Babylon. Bertin 2618; Abraham, BPPE, 227-229, no. 13; Jursa, AfO Beih. 25, 181.
30491	1876,1117.218	Promissory note for dates; dupl. 30237. Dar 14/1/20. Babylon. Dar 498; Bertin 2445.
30492	1876,1117.219	Promissory note for silver; rašûtu. AM 20/10/1. Babylon. Sack, AOATS 4, no. 6; Bertin 274.
30493	1876,1117.220	Promissory note for silver. Nbn 9/4/15. Bīt-šar-Bābili. Nbn 863; Bertin 654.
30494	1876,1117.221	Contract about silver for a ḫarrānu partnership. Nbk 24/12/33. Babylon. Nbk 261; Bertin 160; Wunsch, CM 3, no. 12.
30495	1876,1117.222	Sale of a slave girl. Nbk 9/12/34. Babylon. Nbk 147; Bertin 115; Wunsch, CM 3, no. 17.
30496	1876,1117.223	Promissory note for silver and barley. Nbn 25/2/4. Šaḫrīn. Nbn 148; Bertin 395; Wunsch, CM 3, no. 125.
30497	1876,1117.224	Promissory note for dates. Dar 7/6/4. Babylon. Dar 123; Bertin 2023.
30498	1876,1117.225	Promissory note for silver. Dar 4/2/24. Babylon.
30499	1876,1117.226	Promissory note for barley?. Nbn 5/9/9. Babylon. Nbn 367; Bertin 479.
30500	1876,1117.227	Receipt for purchase of sheep.
30501	1876,1117.228	Promissory note for silver. Bertin 851.
30502	1876,1117.229	Promissory note for dates. Dar 22/6/15. Alu-ša-Bēl-ittannu. Dar 403; Bertin 2326.
30503	1876,1117.230	Promissory note for wooden beams. Nbn 11/7/10. Babylon. Nbn 441; Bertin 502; Wunsch, CM 3, no. 177.
30504	1876,1117.231	Field plan.

30505	1876,1117.232	Hire of a slave girl. Nbn 13/7/10. Babylon. Nbn 442; Bertin 503.
30506	1876,1117.233	Promissory note for silver. Nbn 3/2/5. Borsippa. Nbn 187; Bertin 412-413; Pinches, TSBA 8 (1885) 273-274, 281-282, pl. after p. 274; Wunsch, CM 3, no. 135.
30507	1876,1117.234	Receipt of dates in partial payment of a contract. Nbn 23/7/13. Šaḫrīn. Nbn 722; Bertin 613; Wunsch, CM 3, no. 215.
30508	1876,1117.235	Promissory note for silver. Nbn 24/4/12. Babylon. Nbn 613; Bertin 565; Wunsch, CM 3, no. 199.
30509	1876,1117.236	Agreement to make compensation payment if a slave sold is delivered late. Nbn 8/12/11. Babylon. Nbn 573; Bertin 547; Wunsch, CM 3, no. 193.
30510	1876,1117.237	Promissory note for silver. Nbn 22/9/11. Babylon. Nbn 552; Bertin 544.
30511	1876,1117.238	Sale of a slave. Nbn 19/5/17. Bīt-šar-Bābili. Nbn 1044; Bertin 697.
30512	1876,1117.239	Contract; division of property. Nbn 19/6/14. Babylon. Nbn 787; Bertin 628.
30513	1876,1117.240	Contract; sale of land. Nbn 10/8/12. Babylon. Nbn 633; Bertin 575.
30514	1876,1117.241	Promissory note for dates. Nbn 28/5/16. Adirtu. Nbn 973; Bertin 676.
30515	1876,1117.242	Contract; transfer of land as an additional part of an inheritance. Nbn 10/11/15. Babylon. Bertin 665; Wunsch, Bab Arch 2, 106-111, no. 33.
30516	1876,1117.243	Promissory note for silver. Nbn 4/2/17. Babylon. Nbn 1031; Bertin 693.
30517	1876,1117.244	Promissory note for silver. Nbn 19/3/1. Šubat-Gula. Nbn 30; Strassmaier, Liverpool, 46; Bertin 346; Wunsch, CM 3, no. 95.
30518	1876,1117.245	Promissory note for seed. Nbn 13/3/10. Babylon. Nbn 418; Bertin 492.
30519	1876,1117.246	Missing.
30520	1876,1117.247	Sale of a slave girl. Nbn 4/2/2. Babylon. Nbn 59; Strassmaier, Liverpool, 53; Bertin 360.
30521	1876,1117.248	Promissory note for silver. Nbn 18/1/12. Babylon. Nbn 585; Bertin 553.
30522	1876,1117.249	Sale of an ox. Nbn 28/12/5. Babylon. Nbn 216; Bertin 424.
30523	1876,1117.250	Sale of a slave girl. Nbn 1/7/12. Ḫursag-kalamma. Nbn 626; Wunsch, AfO 44/45, 82-83, no. 12; Bertin 572.

30524	1876,1117.251	Contract. Nbk 16/9/20. Ḫuṣṣēti ša-Nabû-ḫammē. Nbk 122; Bertin 97.
30525	1876,1117.252	Payment of dowry. Ner 6/6/1. Babylon. Evetts, Ner 25; Sack, AOAT 236, no. 25; Bertin 305.
30526	1876,1117.253	Promissory note for silver and onions. Ner 19/11/2. Babylon. Evetts, Ner 50; Sack, AOAT 236, no. 50; Strassmaier, Liverpool, 120; Bertin 319; Wunsch, CM 3, no. 77.
30527	1876,1117.254	Account of silver. Nbn 14/1/17. Nbn 1024; Bertin 689.
30528	1876,1117.255	Sale of a slave girl. Nbn 16/9/12. Babylon. Nbn 648; Bertin 577; Wunsch, CM 3, no. 203.
30529	1876,1117.256	Contract; sale of a field. Cyr 16/4/8. Šaḫrīn. Cyr 308; Bertin 837.
30530	1876,1117.257	Contract; sale of a field. Cyr 13/6/7. Babylon. Cyr 264; Bertin 822.
30531	1876,1117.258	Receipt for silver. Cyr 1/3/5. Babylon. Cyr 194; Bertin 803.
30532	1876,1117.259	Partial payment for a field. Cyr 11/9/8. Babylon. Cyr 346; Strassmaier, Liverpool, 166; Bertin 1713.
30533	1876,1117.260	Receipt of silver for urāšu services. Cyr 13/5/2. Babylon. Cyr 48; Bertin 756; Wunsch, CM 3, no. 275.
30534	1876,1117.261	Promissory note for dates. Bardija 1/7/1. Babylon. Strassmaier, ZA 4, 152, Sm 9; Bertin 1922.
30535	1876,1117.262	Promissory note for silver. Nbk III 17/7/acc. Babylon. Nbk 3; Bertin 8; Lorenz, Nebukadnezar III/IV, p. 31.
30536	1876,1117.263	Sale of a slave. Nbk III 20/9/acc. Babylon. Nbk 9; Bertin 14; Lorenz, Nebukadnezar III/IV, p. 32.
30537	1876,1117.264	Promissory note for dates. Dar 20/6/5. Babylon. Dar 171; Bertin 2040.
30538	1876,1117.265	Promissory note for dates. Dar 26/6/3. Babylon. Dar 79; Bertin 1981.
30539	1876,1117.266	Receipt. Dar 21/-/-.
30540	1876,1117.267	Promissory note for dates or grain. Dar -/7/-. Babylon.
30541	1876,1117.268	Promissory note to pay a debt of silver to the brother of Marduk-nāṣir-apli. Dar []/[]/25. Babylon. Bertin 2335; Abraham, BPPE, 229-230, no. 14.
30542	1876,1117.269	Deposition.
30543	1876,1117.270	Receipt of miksu-toll from Marduk-nāṣir-apli. Dar 18/4/10. Babylon. Dar 268; Abraham, NABU 1997, 46-51, no. 53; Abraham, BPPE, 392-393, no. 102; Bertin 2797.
30544	1876,1117.271	Receipt for payment of silver. Nbn 14/[]/11. Babylon. Wunsch, CM 3, no. 196.

30545	1876,1117.272	Promissory note for silver. Dar 10/6/14. Dar 380; Bertin 2297.
30546	1876,1117.273	Prayer to Šamaš and Adad.
30547	1876,1117.274	Letter from Madān-bēlu-uṣur to Iddin-Marduk. CT 22, 17, no. 81; Hackl et al., AOAT 414/1, no. 5.
30548	1876,1117.275	Promissory note for silver. [Nbn] 7/11/[]. Wunsch, CM 3, no. 356.
30549	1876,1117.276	Court record; about a woman appointed to perform a ritual sprinkling in honour of Ninlil. Nbn []/11/acc. Babylon. Nbn 16; Wunsch, AfO 44/45, 97, no. 31; Bertin 14; Waerzeggers, AH XV, p. 50.
30550	1876,1117.277	Letter.
30551	1876,1117.278	Promissory note for dates; ḫarrānu. Ner 27/4/1. Babylon. Evetts, Ner 22; Sack, AOAT 236, no. 22; Bertin 302; Wunsch, CM 3, no. 68.
30552	1876,1117.279	Promissory note for silver.
30553	1876,1117.280	Contract; sale of fields; sealed; possibly Seleucid. d.l. Nisaba 28, no. 606.
30554	1876,1117.281	Memorandum about silver payments. Dar 10/11/-.
30555	1876,1117.282	Litigation, adoption mentioned. Wunsch, CM 20A-B, no. 59.
30556	1876,1117.283	Account of silver. -/11/-.
30557	1876,1117.284	Contract. Nbk? 1/11/-.
30558	1876,1117.285	Contract; division of property.
30559	1876,1117.286	Literary; Gilgameš XII. + 32418. CT 46, 34, no. 34; Garelli, Gilgameš, 133-135 (copy of 30559 + 32418 by Wiseman); George, Gilgamesh II, pl. 147.
30560	1876,1117.287	Receipt for payment of silver.
30561	1876,1117.288	Promissory note (for silver?); fragment from centre.
30562	1876,1117.289	Letter from Kalbāya to Iddināya. CT 22, 19, no. 95; Hackl et al., AOAT 414/1, no. 26.
30563	1876,1117.290	Promissory note.
30564	1876,1117.291	Account of onions delivered as šibšu-tax. Wunsch, CM 3, no. 357.
30565	1876,1117.292	Account of silver and barley.
30566	1876,1117.293	Account of silver expenditures. Bertin 3004.
30567	1876,1117.294	Contract; deed of property in exchange for support. Nbk 23/6/42. Babylon. Nbk 403; Bertin 227.
30568	1876,1117.295	Promissory note for barley. Nbk 11/12/8. Babylon. Nbk 72; Bertin 55.
30569	1876,1117.296	Promissory note for barley. Nbk 12/8/28. Babylon. Nbk 191; Strassmaier, Liverpool, 150; Bertin 132.
30570	1876,1117.297	Promissory note for silver payment. Nbk 2/12/5. Saḫrītu. Nbk 48; Bertin 34.

30571	1876,1117.298	Marriage contract. Nbk 9/8/13. Babylon. Nbk 101; Wunsch, AfO 44/45, 73, no. 1; Bertin 75.
30572	1876,1117.299	Promissory note for silver. Nbk 4/12/6. Babylon. Nbk 54; Strassmaier, Liverpool, 1399; Bertin 41.
30573	1876,1117.300	Promissory note for onions; ḫarrānu. Ner 9/2/1. Šaḫrīn. Evetts, Ner 15; Strassmaier, Liverpool, 111; Sack, AOAT 236, no. 15; Sack, ZA 68, 144; Bertin 300; Wunsch, CM 3, no. 65.
30574	1876,1117.301	Sale of a slave. Ner 3/5/1. Babylon. Evetts, Ner 23; Sack, ZA 68 144; Sack, AOAT 236, no. 23; Strassmaier, Liverpool, 113; Bertin 303.
30575	1876,1117.302	Promissory note for silver; ḫarrānu. Ner 14/8/1. Babylon. Evetts, Ner 26; Sack, AOAT 236, no. 26; Bertin 307; Wunsch, CM 3, no. 70.
30576	1876,1117.303	Promissory note for dates. Nbn 2/12/15. Ḫumma. Nbn 931; Bertin 666.
30577	1876,1117.304	Promissory note for onions. Ner 5/11/3. Babylon. Evetts, Ner. 66; Strassmaier, Liverpool, 124; Sack, ZA 68 141; Sack, AOAT 236, no. 66; Bertin 326; Wunsch, CM 3, no. 79.
30578	1876,1117.305	Promissory note for onions. Nbn 9/3/4. Šaḫrīn. Nbn 152; Bertin 397; Wunsch, CM 3, no. 127.
30579	1876,1117.306	Sale of a slave. Nbn 4/8/14. Babylon. Nbn 801; Bertin 1534.
30580	1876,1117.307	Sale of slave girls. Nbn 13/11/7. Babylon. Nbn 273; Wunsch, CM 3, no. 147.
30581	1876,1117.308	Promissory note for barley. Nbn 21/7/10. Babylon. Bertin 542 (wrongly as S†.304).
30582	1876,1117.309	Promissory note for silver, barley and dates; ḫarrānu. Nbn 7/5/acc. Nbn 4; Bertin 331; Wunsch, CM 3, no. 86.
30583	1876,1117.310	Promissory note for dates. Nbn 27/6/10. Nbn 43; Bertin 499.
30584	1876,1117.311	Receipt of silver for urāšu service. Cyr 8/12/2. Babylon. Cyr 86; Bertin 759; Wunsch, CM 3, no. 282.
30585	1876,1117.312	Receipt for silver, slaves and household goods as dowry. Cyr 26/11/3. Babylon. Cyr 143; Bertin 775.
30586	1876,1117.313	Promissory note for dates. Cyr 16/6/8. Babylon. Cyr 316; Bertin 830.
30587	1876,1117.314	Contract; lease of a house. Cyr 9/3/6. Babylon. Cyr 228; Bertin 811.
30588	1876,1117.315	Promissory note for silver. Cyr 20/1/6. Šaḫrīn. Cyr 222; Bertin 812; Wunsch, CM 3, no. 300.

30589	1876,1117.316	Receipt of ilku-silver by Marduk-nāṣir-apli. Dar 20/3/26. Babylon. Bertin 2619; Abraham, BPPE, 230-231, no. 15; Jursa, Bēl-rēmanni, 106, 108.
30590	1876,1117.317	Contract; sale of land. Dar 19/5/10. Babylon. Dar 273; Bertin 2177.
30591	1876,1117.318	Promissory note for barley, involving Marduk-nāṣir-apli. Dar 27/7?/35. Babylon. Bertin 2739; Abraham, OLA 65, 1-9; Abraham, BPPE, 232-233, no. 16.
30592	1876,1117.319	Contract; sale of a field. Dar 12/2/14. Babylon. Dar 371; Bertin 2291.
30593	1876,1117.320	Account of barley tithes. Dar -/-/21. Dar 533; Bertin 2461-2462.
30594	1876,1117.321	Contract; lease of a house; Egibi archive. Dar 22/12/-. Babylon. Bertin 2798.
30595	1876,1117.322	Promissory note for silver. Npl 11/-/-. Saḫrītu. Strassmaier, ZA 4, 147, no. 20; Kennedy, JCS 38, 220, T.x.96; Bertin 7.
30596	1876,1117.323	Promissory note for silver. Nbk 22/9/-.
30597	1876,1117.324	Promissory note for silver. Nbk 11/11/36. Babylon. Nbk 308; Bertin 181; Wunsch, CM 3, no. 23.
30598	1876,1117.325	Sale of a slave. Nbk 13/6/29. Babylon. Nbk 203; Bertin 142.
30599	1876,1117.326	Promissory note for onions and barley. Ner 23/9/3. Babylon. 5R 67 4; Sack, AOAT 236, no. 83; Strassmaier, Liverpool, 123; Oppert, ZA 3, 17-22; Wunsch, CM 3, no. 78.
30600	1876,1117.327	Sale of a slave girl. Nbn 2/2/15. Bīt-šar-Bābili. Nbn 837; Bertin 647.
30601	1876,1117.328	Contract; lease of a house. Nbn 22/2/12. Babylon. Nbn 597; Bertin 556.
30602	1876,1117.329	Contract for silver tithe. Nbn 9/11/7. Babylon. Nbn 270; Strassmaier, Liverpool, 80; Bertin 446-447.
30603	1876,1117.330	Promissory note for barley. Nbn 14/12/11. Šaḫrīn. Nbn 577; Bertin 549; Wunsch, CM 3, no. 194.
30604	1876,1117.331	Interim account of silver receipts in payment for onions. Nbn 1/4/11. Babylon. Nbn 515; Bertin 527; cf. Wunsch, AfO 44/45, 97; Wunsch, CM 3, no. 186.
30605	1876,1117.332	Sale of a slave girl. Nbn 2/1/11. Babylon. Nbn 509; cf. Wunsch, AfO 44/45, 97, collation of date; Bertin 535.
30606	1876,1117.333	Sale of a slave. Nbn 24/2/9. Babylon. Nbn 336; Strassmaier, Liverpool, 94; Bertin 467; Wunsch, CM 3, no. 165.

30607	1876,1117.334	Witnessed declaration about an agreement. Nbn 10/4/2. Babylon. Nbn 69; Bertin 366; Wunsch, CM 3, no. 105.
30608	1876,1117.335	Inventory of furniture; dowry? Nbn 1/2/14. Babylon. Nbn 761; Bertin 620.
30609	1876,1117.336	Contract for purchase paid with dates. Nbn 12/4/7. Babylon. Nbn 254; Strassmaier, Liverpool, 76; Bertin 437.
30610	1876,1117.337	Promissory note for dates. Cyr 26/6/3. Nāru-eššu. Cyr 123; Bertin 780.
30611	1876,1117.338	Promissory note for barley. Cyr 8/1/8. Šaḫrīn. Cyr 291; Bertin 832.
30612	1876,1117.339	Promissory note for silver and onions. Cam 7/8/3. Šaḫrīn. Cam 167; Bertin 901; Wunsch, CM 3, no. 333.
30613	1876,1117.340	Disposition of slave girls. Cam 1/9/6. Šaḫrīn. Cam 329; Bertin 951.
30614	1876,1117.341	Sale of slave girls. Nbn 15/9/1. Šaḫrīn. Bertin 3071; Wunsch, CM 3, no. 99.
30615	1876,1117.342	Promissory note for silver. Dar 8/11/19. Gummānu ālu ša Nabû. Dar 490; Bertin 2416.
30616	1876,1117.343	Account of silver.
30617	1876,1117.344	Astronomical Diary.
30618	1876,1117.345	Contract; sale of a house. Dar 26/4/12. Babylon. Dar 326; Bertin 2237.
30619	1876,1117.346	Contract; sale of a field.
30620	1876,1117.347	Promissory note for sheep, wool and cows; ḫarrānu. AM 21/2/2. Babylon. Evetts, Ev-M 20; Strassmaier, Liverpool, 133; Sack, AOATS 4, no. 30; Bertin 282; Wunsch, CM 3, no. 60.
30621	1876,1117.348	Sale of a slave girl. Cyr 21/3/4. Ḫursag-kalamma.
30622	1876,1117.349	Contract; lease of a house. Nbn 27/6/6. Babylon. Nbn 239; Bertin 428.
30623	1876,1117.350	Sale of slave girls.
30624	1876,1117.351	Later copy of an administrative list of temple(?) personnel; ḫe-pí; Marduk-balassu-iqbi 2/12/1.
30625	1876,1117.352	Receipt for partial payment for a field. Cyr 11/9/8. Babylon. Cyr 323; Bertin 831.
30626	1876,1117.353	Contract; sale of a house for barley. Nbn 27/2/8. Babylon. Nbn 289; Strassmaier, Liverpool, 86; Bertin 455.
30627	1876,1117.354	Contract; inheritance division of one field with field plan. Dar 1/6b/3. Nāru-eššu. Wunsch, CM 20A-B, no. 11.
30628	1876,1117.355	Account of dates or grain.

30629	1876,1117.356	Summons to settle a payment of silver with Marduk-nāṣir-apli. Dar 12/7/6. Ḫursag-kalamma. Bertin 2093; Abraham, BPPE, 234-235, no. 17.
30630	1876,1117.357	Promissory note for barley. Dar 23/3/17. Alu-ša-Nabû-zēra-iqīša. Dar 441; Bertin 2379.
30631	1876,1117.358	Contract. 29/3/1. Babylon.
30632	1876,1117.359	Astronomical Diary. SE -/8?/97.
30633	1876,1117.360	Promissory note for flour. Cyr 5/10/6. Babylon. Cyr 239; Bertin 807.
30634	1876,1117.361	Contract about silver for a ḫarrānu partnership. Nbk 22/8/33. Babylon. Nbk 271; Bertin 164; Wunsch, CM 3, no. 11.
30635	1876,1117.362	Promissory note for onions and silver. Nbn 9/3/4. Šaḫrīn. Nbn 151; Bertin 396; Wunsch, CM 3, no. 126.
30636	1876,1117.363	Promissory note for silver. Nbk 2/12/4. Saḫrītu. Nbk 38; Bertin 26.
30637	1876,1117.364	Contract; sale of land. Dar 24/1/18. Babylon. Dar 467; Bertin 2653.
30638	1876,1117.365	Deposition. Dar 3/6/20. Bīt-Ḫaḫḫūru. Dar 505; Bertin 2436.
30639	1876,1117.366	Receipt of payment for transport costs due by Marduk-nāṣir-apli. Dar 28/7/25. Babylon. Bertin 2576; Abraham, BPPE, 235-236, no. 18.
30640	1876,1117.367	Promissory note for dates. Nbn 21/6/12. Babylon. Nbn 623; Bertin 569.
30641	1876,1117.368	Reminder about payment for a promised delivery of seeds. 30/4/no year. Abraham, BPPE, 237, no. 19, and 539, no. 1.
30642	1876,1117.369	Receipt of silver for urāšu service baking bricks. Cam 14/5/1. Babylon. Cam 88; Bertin 865; Wunsch, CM 3, no. 265a.
30643	1876,1117.370	Letter from Sūqāya to Širku. CT 22, 34-35, no. 189; Hackl et al., AOAT 414/1, no. 33.
30644	1876,1117.371	Sale of an ox. Dar 10/9/10. Alu-ša-Nūrānu ālu ša Nabû. Dar 282; Bertin 2166.
30645	1876,1117.372	Court record; captions for seals but not sealed. Nbn 26/11/12. Babylon. Nbn 668; Wunsch, AfO 44/45, 86-87, no. 16; Bertin 584-585.
30646	1876,1117.373	Contract; division of property. AM 13/8/1. Babylon. Evetts, Ev-M 13; Strassmaier, Liverpool, 129; Sack, AOATS 4, no. 15; Sack, ZA 68, 136; Bertin 289.
30647	1876,1117.374	Sale of a slave. Nbk 20/11/28. Šabilu. Nbk 195; Bertin 135.

30648	1876,1117.375	Letter from Lâbâši to Iddināya. Pinches, PSBA 33 (1911) 158 and pl. XXII; Hackl et al., AOAT 414/1, no. 30.
30649	1876,1117.376	Contract to make a payment according to a promissory note. Wunsch, CM 3, no. 358.
30650	1876,1117.377	Contract; lease of a house; on the date see Weissbach, ZDMG LV (1901) 209-210. Cam 7/[]/1. Babylon. Cam 97; Bertin 1845; Wunsch, CM 3, no. 271.
30651	1876,1117.378	Account of silver. n.d. Abraham, BPPE, 238-239, no. 20, and 540-541, no. 2.
30652	1876,1117.379	Sale of slave girls. Nbn 26/2/11. Babylon. Nbn 508; Bertin 524; Wunsch, CM 3, no. 184; cf. Wunsch, AfO 44/45, 97.
30653	1876,1117.380	Receipt for a partial payment of silver. Babylon. Wunsch, CM 3, no. 359.
30654	1876,1117.381	Sale of a slave. Nbn 22/1/14. Šaḫrīn. Nbn 756; Bertin 618; Wunsch, CM 3, no. 223.
30655	1876,1117.382	Deposition. Nbk 27/11/22. Nbk 134; Bertin 106.
30656	1876,1117.383	List of workmen.
30657	1876,1117.384	Receipt for barley. Dar []/10/10. Dar 286; Bertin 2174.
30658	1876,1117.385	Contract; hire of a boat by Marduk-naṣir-apli's son. Dar 18/8/31. Babylon. + 31690. Abraham, BPPE, 305-306, no. 56, and 556, no. 16.
30659	1876,1117.386	Promissory note for silver. Nbn 27/3/4. Babylon. Nbn 153; Bertin 398; Wunsch, CM 3, no. 128.
30660	1876,1117.387	Promissory note for dates. Wunsch, CM 20A-B, no. 232.
30661	1876,1117.388	Promissory note to pay a debt of silver due from Marduk-nāṣir-apli. Dar 12/4/22? Babylon. Dar 544; Abraham, BPPE, 49-50, no. 133; Bertin 2458.
30662	1876,1117.389	Receipt for gugallūtu tax paid in onions. <Nbn> 27/1/10. Šaḫrīn ālu ša Nabû. Wunsch, CM 3, no. 175.
30663	1876,1117.390	Promissory note for silver. Nbn 2/10/10. Babylon. Nbn 461; Bertin 507.
30664	1876,1117.391	Promissory note for [dates]; ḫarrānu. 23/6/[]. Wunsch, CM 3, no. 360.
30665	1876,1117.392	Receipt for final payment for a field. Dar 28/12/4. Babylon. Dar 151; Bertin 2025.
30666	1876,1117.393	Promissory note for silver. Dar 4/10/17. Babylon. Dar 449; Bertin 2380.
30667	1876,1117.394	Letter from Nabû-šumu-uṣur to Širku; sealed. Dar 28/8/14. Dar 385; Bertin 2301; Nisaba 28, no. 198; Hackl et al., AOAT 414/1, no. 35.

30668	1876,1117.395	Receipt of dates as imittu payment from a slave of Marduk-nāṣir-apli by a slave of Bagasaru; partly dupl. 30938. (Dar 20/3/22). Dar 534; Abraham, BPPE, 447-449, no. 132; Bertin 2477.
30669	1876,1117.396	Hemerology; list of favourable and unfavourable days.
30670	1876,1117.397	Promissory note for dates and onions. Cam 30/2/2. Šaḫrīn. Cam 104; Bertin 880.
30671	1876,1117.398	Promissory note for silver. Dar 18/4/20. Borsippa. Dar 501; Bertin 2444.
30672	1876,1117.399	Receipt for payment of silver. Nbn 29/11/12. Babylon. Nbn 669; Bertin 586; Wunsch, CM 3, no. 206.
30673	1876,1117.400	Letter from Nabû-šumu-uṣur to Širku. Nisaba 28, no. 200; Hackl et al., AOAT 414/1, no. 37.
30674	1876,1117.401	Promissory note for silver. Dar 18/1/12. Bertin 2771.
30675	1876,1117.402	Promissory note for barley and onions. Nbn 9/5/10. Babylon. Nbn 427; Bertin 495; Wunsch, CM 3, no. 176.
30676	1876,1117.403	Sale receipt. Nbk 26/2/[]. Ḫuṣṣūtu-ša-Bau-ēreš. Nbk 422; Bertin 239
30677	1876,1117.404	Promissory note for silver; unusual nail marks on upper edge. Nbk 5/6/8. Babylon. Nbk 65; Bertin 50.
30678	1876,1117.405	Sale of a slave girl. Dar 4/7/6. Babylon. Dar 207; Bertin 2092.
30679	1876,1117.406	Receipt for payment of silver. Nbn 5/12/4. Babylon. Nbn 177; Bertin 408.
30680	1876,1117.407	Promissory note for dates.
30681	1876,1117.408	Promissory note for silver. Dar 3/7/2. Babylon. Dar 44.
30682	1876,1117.409	Account of payments. 17/10/7.
30683	1876,1117.410	Receipt of wool from Marduk-nāṣir-apli by a weaver of Lugal-Marada. Dar 27/8/6. Babylon. Dar 182; Abraham, BPPE, 385-386, no. 97; Bertin 2070.
30684	1876,1117.411	Contract; sale of a field. Nbn 30/12/11. Babylon. Nbn 578; Bertin 550.
30685	1876,1117.412	Contract; sale of land; sealed; finger-nail marks. Dupl. 30288. Dar 3/7/7. Babylon. Dar 227; Strassmaier, Liverpool, 175; Bertin 2116-2117; Wunsch, CM 20A, 276, no. 184A, and CM 20B, 218-220; Nisaba 28, no. 116.
30686	1876,1117.413	Sale of barley and dates. Nbk IV []/7?/1. Babylon. Nbk 12; Bertin 17; Lorenz, Nebukadnezar III/IV, p. 32.
30687	1876,1117.414	Promissory note for dates. Dar 10/6/15. Babylon. Dar 402; Bertin 2320.

30688	1876,1117.415	Letter from Libluṭ to Dummuqu. Kleber and Hackl, ZABR 16 (2010) 56 and 68-69; Hackl et al., AOAT 414/1, no. 63.
30689	1876,1117.416	Promissory note for onions; ḫarrānu. Wunsch, CM 3, no. 361.
30690	1876,1117.417	Contract; sale of a house; finger-nail marks (on upper and lower edges, without caption). Dar 15/4/12. Babylon. Dar 325; Bertin 2226-2227.
30691	1876,1117.418	Promissory note for dates. Dar 27/[]/18. Babylon. Dar 478; Bertin 2397.
30692	1876,1117.419	Promissory note for silver as part of a dowry. [Nbn] 4/[]/6. Babylon. Wunsch, CM 3, no. 139.
30693	1876,1117.420	Promissory note for dates. Cam 15/7/4. Babylon. Cam 246; Bertin 923.
30694	1876,1117.421	Receipt for purchases. 12/-/-.
30695	1876,1117.422	Promissory note for dates. Nbn 19/7/7. Wunsch, CM 3, no. 305.
30696	1876,1117.423	Account of silver payments. Cam. Cam 436; Bertin 998.
30697	1876,1117.424	Promissory note for silver. Cyr 26/11/5. Babylon. Cyr 217; Bertin 801; Wunsch, CM 3, no. 298.
30698	1876,1117.425	Sale of slave girls. Cam 11/10/7. Ḫumadēšu. Cam 388; Bertin 974.
30699	1876,1117.426	Receipt of dates by Marduk-nāṣir-apli's slave. Dar 3/5/15. Šaḫrīn. Dar 400; Abraham, BPPE, 420-421, no. 117; Bertin 2292.
30700	1876,1117.427	Account of wool.
30701	1876,1117.428	Contract; ḫarrānu. Dar []/7/10. Babylon. Dar 280; Bertin 2165.
30702	1876,1117.429	Promissory note for silver. AM 14/[]/2.
30703	1876,1117.430	Contract. 27/-/-.
30704	1876,1117.431	Deposition; sealed. Cam 1/9/7. Ḫumadēšu. Cam 384; Bertin 981; Mitchell and Searight, no. 380; Nisaba 28, no. 149.
30705	1876,1117.432	Gift of dowry. Nbn 18/5/7. Babylon. Nbn 258; Strassmaier, Liverpool, 79; Bertin 450-451.
30706	1876,1117.433	Promissory note for dates. Dar 2/6/16. Nār-Kūtê-labīru. Dar 426; Bertin 2350.
30707	1876,1117.434	Sale of a boat; sealed. Nbn 13/5/14. Babylon. Nbn 776; Strassmaier, Liverpool, 106; Wunsch, AfO 44/45, 97-98, no. 34; Bertin 625; Nisaba 28, no. 24.
30708	1876,1117.435	Receipt of silver for urāšu service. Cyr(!) 18/6/1? Babylon. Nbn 1091; Bertin 742; Wunsch, CM 3, no. 266.
30709	1876,1117.436	Contract. 13/-/-.

30710	1876,1117.437	Sale of prebends. Nbn 21/4/9. Babylon. Nbn 346; Strassmaier, Liverpool, 96; Bertin 471.
30711	1876,1117.438	Promissory note for dates. Dar 19/5/17. Alu-ša-Ubār. Dar 443; Bertin 2375.
30712	1876,1117.439	Promissory note for silver payment. Dar 25/9/4. Babylon. Dar 137; Bertin 2024.
30713	1876,1117.440	Contract about a debt of silver. Ner. Babylon. Evetts, Ner 71; Sack, AOAT 236, no. 71; Wunsch, CM 3, no. 83.
30714	1876,1117.441	Promissory note for silver. Dar 28/7/13. Babylon. Dar 356; Bertin 2271.
30715	1876,1117.442	Promissory note for barley and cress. Dar 29/10/13. Bīt-Ṭāb-Bēl. Dar 360; Bertin 2254.
30716	1876,1117.443	Contract for vats. Dar []/6/11. Borsippa. Dar 305; Bertin 2196.
30717	1876,1117.444	Letter from Madān-bēlu-uṣur to Marduk-nāṣir-apli. CT 22, 17, no. 82; Hackl et al., AOAT 414/1, no. 38.
30718	1876,1117.445	Contract for bronze cooking vessels. Nbn 30/10/8. Babylon. Nbn 310; Bertin 460.
30719	1876,1117.446	Receipt for silver payment. Dar 19/5/24. Babylon. Bertin 2543.
30720	1876,1117.447	Receipt of silver from Marduk-nāṣir-apli, with undertaking to repay the remainder on return from Elam. Dar []/10/23. Babylon. Dar 577; Abraham, BPPE, 456-458, no. 138; Bertin 2495.
30721	1876,1117.448	Contract; allotment of a share in profits to Marduk-nāṣir-apli, his brother and a third person. Dar 21/12/11. Šaḫrīn. Dar 315; Abraham, BPPE, 401-403, no. 107; Bertin 2195.
30722	1876,1117.449	Contract; sale of a field. Cam 22/11/3. Paširi. Cam 217; Bertin 909.
30723	1876,1117.450	Promissory note for silver. Nbn 24/10/10. Babylon. Nbn 468; Bertin 508.
30724	1876,1117.451	Deposition. Cyr 22/2/8. Babylon. Cyr 302; Bertin 840.
30725	1876,1117.452	Promissory note for dates. Nbn 6/6/13. Babylon. Nbn 715; Bertin 605.
30726	1876,1117.453	Contract. Cam 28/10/-. Babylon.
30727	1876,1117.454	Contract; transfer of responsibility.
30728	1876,1117.455	Promissory note for silver payment. Cam 3/7/2. Borsippa. Cam 120; Bertin 888.
30729	1876,1117.456	Account of dates deliveries. Cam -/-/2. Cam 149; Bertin 856-857.
30730	1876,1117.457	Promissory note for dates. Dar 26/6/14. Babylon. Dar 382; Bertin 2287.

30731	1876,1117.458	Contract; record of deposit in elephant staters of Seleucus; Murānu archive; sealed. SE Ant I & Sel []/8/35. Babylon. CT 49, 19, no. 105; Bertin 2899-2900; Stolper, Annali Supp. 77, 20-23, no. 6; Jursa, Persika 9, 175, 178-179; Nisaba 28, no. 556.
30732	1876,1117.459	Deposition. Dar 2/12/20. Babylon. Dar 514; Bertin 2441.
30733	1876,1117.460	Undertaking by a man under oath to bring his fellow debtor. Dar 14/10/5. Babylon. Dar 187; Bertin 2051; Wunsch, CM 3, no. 352.
30734	1876,1117.461	Promissory note for dates. Cam []/8/7. Šaḫrīn. Cam 410; Bertin 997.
30735	1876,1117.462	Contract; lease of a house. Cam 15/7/3. Babylon. Cam 187; Bertin 915.
30736	1876,1117.463	Account of grain.
30737	1876,1117.464	Letter from Nergal-āhu-iddin to Mukīn-Marduk. Hackl et al., AOAT 414/1, no. 20.
30738	1876,1117.465	Letter from Bīt-Ir'anni-šarru-uṣur to Marduk-šumu-uṣur. CT 22, 44-45, no. 243; Hackl et al., AOAT 414/1, no. 16.
30739	1876,1117.466	Astronomical Diary for SE 117. LBAT 321; Sachs and Hunger, ADART II, no. -194 B; Bertin 2983.
30740	1876,1117.467	Sale of an ass. Dar 29/6/25. Bīt-ḫaremarē pīḫāt Dannu-Nergal. Bertin 2577; Weszeli and Baker, WZKM 87, 241-243 and 247; Weszeli, NABU 2004, 62, no. 60.
30741	1876,1117.468	Promissory note for dates. Dar []/6/5. Babylon. Dar 174; Bertin 2071; Wunsch, CM 3, no. 351.
30742	1876,1117.469	Account of grain.
30743	1876,1117.470	List of men.
30744	1876,1117.471	Sale of a slave. Dar 9/12/2. Babylon. Dar 53.
30745	1876,1117.472	Promissory note to pay a debt of silver and onions to Marduk-nāṣir-apli's brother. Dar 2/1/13. Babylon. Dar 345; Abraham, BPPE, 411-412, no. 112; Bertin 2263.
30746	1876,1117.473	Promissory note for silver and barley. Dar 6/8/20. Babylon. Dar 507; Bertin 2449.
30747	1876,1117.474	Receipt of miksu-toll from Marduk-nāṣir-apli; refers to the 10th year. n.d. Abraham, BPPE, 240-241, no. 21, and 542, no. 3.
30748	1876,1117.475	Account of dates.
30749	1876,1117.476	Letter from Bēl-iddin to Širku; sealed. Nisaba 28, no. 201; Hackl et al., AOAT 414/1, no. 42.
30750	1876,1117.477	Promissory note for silver. Dar 5/5/4. Babylon. Dar 119; Strassmaier, Liverpool, 174; Bertin 2027.

30751	1876,1117.478	Letter from Madān-bēlu-uṣur to Iddin-Marduk. CT 22, 17, no. 80; Hackl et al., AOAT 414/1, no. 7.
30752	1876,1117.479	Account of beer and barley; finger-nail marks on upper edge.
30753	1876,1117.480	Promissory note for barley. Dar 5/9/15. Babylon. Dar 413; Bertin 2329.
30754	1876,1117.481	Contract. Dar 23/9/22. Written with an unusual stylus (and marked by L W King in the register as a fake).
30755	1876,1117.482	Letter (ši-pir-tum).
30756	1876,1117.483	Account of barley income. -/2/14.
30757	1876,1117.484	Sale of a slave; finger-nail marks or scratches on right edge. Nbn 19/11/12. Babylon. Nbn 666; Bertin 583.
30758	1876,1117.485	Promissory note for silver. Nbn 3/6/3. Nbn 112; Bertin 379; Wunsch, CM 3, no. 115.
30759	1876,1117.486	Promissory note for barley. Dar 12/10/10. Babylon. Dar 284; Bertin 2176.
30760	1876,1117.487	Purchase of household utensils. Cam 27/1/3. Babylon. Cam 153; Bertin 896.
30761	1876,1117.488	Promissory note for silver. Dar 7/2/2. Babylon. Dar 31; Strassmaier, Liverpool, 172.
30762	1876,1117.489	Contract; pledge of real estate. Dar 19/4/5? Babylon. Bertin 2041; Wunsch, CM 20A, n. 364.
30763	1876,1117.490	Letter from Madān-bēlu-uṣur to Iddin-Marduk. CT 22, 16, no. 78; Hackl et al., AOAT 414/1, no. 8.
30764	1876,1117.491	Receipt of a man hired to tow boats. Dar 23/3/25. Babylon. Bertin 2566; Abraham, BPPE, 242, no. 22.
30765	1876,1117.492	Contract; ḫarrānu. Nbn 3/8/5. Babylon. Nbn 199a; Pinches, ZA 1, 202-205; Bertin 417.
30766	1876,1117.493	Account of dates or grain.
30767	1876,1117.494	Receipt for silver payment for dates. Wunsch, CM 3, no. 362.
30768	1876,1117.495	Promissory note for silver.
30769	1876,1117.496	Account of various purchases. 1/4/-.
30770	1876,1117.497	Contract for settlement of debt. Dar 18/11/3. Babylon. Dar 93; Bertin 1987.
30771	1876,1117.498	Letter from Mukīn-Marduk to Iddin-Marduk; sealed. Nisaba 28, no. 208; Hackl et al., AOAT 414/1, no. 10.
30772	1876,1117.499	Receipt of ilku-tax by Marduk-nāṣir-apli. Dar 20/12/26. Babylon. Bertin 2621; Abraham, BPPE, 243-244, no. 23.
30773	1876,1117.500	Promissory note for barley. Dar 11/10/14. Babylon. Dar 386; Bertin 2294.
30774	1876,1117.501	Missing.
30775	1876,1117.502	Promissory note for silver. Nbk 27/10/8. Babylon. Nbk 69a; Bertin 53.

30776	1876,1117.503	Promissory note for dates. Dar 25/7/5. Babylon. Dar 178; Bertin 2050.
30777	1876,1117.504	Receipt for silver payment. []/1/1. Babylon. Wunsch, CM 3, no. 363.
30778	1876,1117.505	Letter from Itti-Nabû-balāṭu to Iddināya. CT 22, 9-10, no. 43; Hackl et al., AOAT 414/1, no. 24.
30779	1876,1117.506	Receipt for oxen. Cyr 26/9/4. Šaḫrīn. Bertin 790; Wunsch, CM 3, no. 295.
30780	1876,1117.507	Account of purchases for silver. Cam 22/2/7. Cam 369; Bertin 983.
30781	1876,1117.508	Account of dates as income. -/-/16.
30782	1876,1117.509	Contract; lease of a house; Egibi archive. Dar 4?/1/32. Babylon. Bertin 2709.
30783	1876,1117.510	Promissory note for dates. Dar 25/6/8. Babylon. Dar 238; Bertin 2137.
30784	1876,1117.511	Promissory note for silver. Dar 19/6/26. Babylon. Bertin 2607.
30785	1876,1117.512	Return of a promissory note for silver. Cam 1/3/7. Babylon. Cam 370; Bertin 973; Wunsch, CM 3, no. 345.
30786	1876,1117.513	Promissory note for silver as the price of onions. Dar 15/12/12. Babylon. Dar 336; Strassmaier, Liverpool, 178; Bertin 2223.
30787	1876,1117.514	Contract to sail a boat to Babylon for Marduk-nāṣir-apli as part of the kanšu-service. Dar 7/3/5. Babylon. Dar 158; Abraham, BPPE, 379-381, no. 94; Bertin 2054.
30788	1876,1117.515	Contract for household furnishings. Dar 27/1/18. Babylon. Dar 468; Bertin 2645 (wrongly marked by Bertin as S†.315).
30789	1876,1117.516	Receipt for onions. Nbk 25/9/42. Šaḫrīn. Nbk 406; Bertin 230; Wunsch, CM 3, no. 48.
30790	1876,1117.517	Promissory note for silver. Dar 20/5/27. Babylon. Bertin 2643.
30791	1876,1117.518	Promissory note for barley; dupl. 34017. Nbn 11/8/10. Šaḫrīn. Nbn 445; Bertin 505; Wunsch, CM 3, no. 179.
30792	1876,1117.519	Promissory note for silver. Nbk 16/8/2. Babylon. Nbk 26; Bertin 19.
30793	1876,1117.520	Promissory note for silver. Dar 24/10/1. Borsippa. Dar 23; Bertin 2777.
30794	1876,1117.521	Promissory note for barley. Dar 10/4/27. Babylon. Bertin 2640.

30795	1876,1117.522	Receipt of persons and register of their enlistment. Marduk-nāṣir-apli is a witness. Dar 26/10/26. Babylon. Bertin 2606; Abraham, BPPE, 244-247, no. 24.
30796	1876,1117.523	Account.
30797	1876,1117.524	Promissory note for barley. Dar 24/11/13. Šuppatu. Dar 362; Bertin 2265.
30798	1876,1117.525	Promissory note for barley and wheat. Dar 22/1/5. Nāru-eššu. Dar 155; Bertin 2053.
30799	1876,1117.526	Contract; hire of a boat by Marduk-nāṣir-apli. Dar 26/5/4? Abraham, BPPE, 247-249, no. 25, and 543, no. 4; Wunsch, CM 20A, n. 339.
30800	1876,1117.527	Promissory note for silver.
30801	1876,1117.528	Promissory note for silver payment. Nbn 11/4/12. Babylon. Nbn 605; Bertin 561.
30802	1876,1117.529	Bilingual incantation; Udug-ḫul 16. Geller, BAM 8, 499-541, pl. 130.
30803	1876,1117.530	Promissory note for silver. Cam 28/11/3. Babylon. Cam 219; Bertin 907; Wunsch, CM 3, no. 338.
30804	1876,1117.531	Contract; lease of a house; Egibi archive. Bertin 2962.
30805	1876,1117.532	Deposition. Nbk 21/6/40. Upija. Nbk 363; Bertin 206.
30806	1876,1117.533	Deposition. Nbk 21/4/40. Upija. Nbk 361; Strassmaier, Liverpool, 159; Bertin 205.
30807	1876,1117.534	Promissory note for silver. Nbn 8/11/8. Babylon. Wunsch, CM 3, no. 159.
30808	1876,1117.535	Promissory note for silver payment. Nbn 15/9/acc. Babylon. Nbn 9; Strassmaier, Liverpool, 36; Bertin 334.
30809	1876,1117.536	Contract; sale of a field. Nbn 6/2/17. Babylon. Nbn 1032; Bertin 694.
30810	1876,1117.537	Receipt for payment of silver as the price of slaves. Nbn 15/12/9. Babylon. Nbn 392; Strassmaier, Liverpool, 101; Bertin 486; Wunsch, CM 3, no. 173.
30811	1876,1117.538	Promissory note for silver. Cam 6/3/3. Babylon. Cam 161; Bertin 902; Wunsch, CM 3, no. 331.
30812	1876,1117.539	Deposition. Cam 6/7/6. Šaḫrīn. Cam 321; Bertin 952.
30813	1876,1117.540	Contract to repair a wall. Dar 20/6/4. Babylon. Dar 129; Strassmaier, Warka, no. 113; Bertin 2026.
30814	1876,1117.541	Contract; lease of a house. Dar 14/10/22. Babylon. Dar 554; Bertin 2482.
30815	1876,1117.542	Promissory note for dates. Dar 3/12/11. Nāru-eššu. Dar 313; Bertin 2210.
30816	1876,1117.543	Promissory note for silver. Dar 24/-/-. Babylon. Bertin 2776.
30817	1876,1117.544	Contract; lease of a house. Dar 26/6/9. Babylon. Dar 256; Strassmaier, Warka, 114; Bertin 2161.

30818	1876,1117.545	Contract; lease of a field. Dar []/7/5+. Šuppatu. Bertin 2837; Wunsch, CM 20A-B, no. 145.
30819	1876,1117.546	Receipt of ilku-tax by Marduk-nāṣir-apli. Dar 5?/12/25. Šabilu. Bertin 2575; Abraham, BPPE, 249-251, no. 26.
30820	1876,1117.547	Contract; ḫarrānu.
30821	1876,1117.548	Sale of a slave. Dar 21/11/19. Babylon. Dar 492; Bertin 2409.
30822	1876,1117.549	Promissory note to pay a debt of barley, silver, and browned ghee to Marduk-nāṣir-apli. Dar 3/3/22. Bīt-Ṭāb-Bēl. Dar 541; Abraham, BPPE, 445-446, no. 131; Bertin 2476.
30823	1876,1117.550	Promissory note for dates. Dar 17/1/23. Babylon. Dar 560; Bertin 2843.
30824	1876,1117.551	Promissory note for silver with house as collateral. Dar 14/1/21. Babylon. Dar 519; Bertin 2455.
30825	1876,1117.552	Promissory note to deliver dates as imittu payment to Marduk-nāṣir-apli's slave. Dar 4/7/15. Šaḫrīn. Dar 405; Abraham, BPPE, 421-422, no. 118; Bertin 2330.
30826	1876,1117.553	Promissory note for dates. Dar 2/6/6. Šuppatu. Dar 203; Bertin 2098.
30827	1876,1117.554	Promissory note for silver. Dar 22/11/4. Šaḫrīn. Dar 142; Bertin 2015.
30828	1876,1117.555	Promissory note for silver. Dar 5/6/8. Šaḫrīn. Dar 236; Bertin 2132.
30829	1876,1117.556	Sale of a slave. [Nbk] 8/[]/30. Babylon.
30830	1876,1117.557	Astronomical Diary for SE 116. LBAT 319; Sachs and Hunger, ADART II, no. -195 E.
30831	1876,1117.558	Account of dates. 12/10/5.
30832	1876,1117.559	Receipt for barley. Dar 26/6/24. Babylon. Bertin 2521.
30833	1876,1117.560	Account of silver payments.
30834	1876,1117.561	Receipt for silver. 26/7/-.
30835	1876,1117.562	Promissory note for dates. Nbn 3/9/16. Babylon. Nbn 995; Bertin 680.
30836	1876,1117.563	Contract; transfer of promise to pay silver. Nbn 23/1/17. Borsippa. Nbn 1025; Bertin 690; Wunsch, CM 3, no. 249.
30837	1876,1117.564	Sale of a slave. Nbn 19/12/12. Babylon. Nbn 681; Bertin 593.
30838	1876,1117.565	Promissory note to pay a debt of silver and barley to Marduk-bēlšunu; repayment according to the measure of Marduk-nāṣir-apli. Dar 16/1/12. Babylon. Dar 318; Abraham, BPPE, 404-405, no. 108; Bertin 2240.

30839	1876,1117.566	Promissory note for silver. Cyr 20/1/6. Šaḫrīn. Cyr 223; Bertin 808; Wunsch, CM 3, no. 301.
30840	1876,1117.567	Receipt for purchase of bitumen. Nbn 18/8/7. Babylon. Nbn 267; Bertin 444.
30841	1876,1117.568	Sale of a slave; dupl. 31819; finger-nail marks. Nbk 26/2/12. Ḫuṣṣūtu-ša-Bau-ēreš. Nbk 94; Bertin 70 and 103.
30842	1876,1117.569	Receipt of silver in payment for work. Nbn 6/9/13. Babylon. Nbn 727; Bertin 610; Wunsch, CM 3, no. 216.
30843	1876,1117.570	Promissory note for dates. Nbn 22/4/12. Babylon. Nbn 610; Bertin 574.
30844	1876,1117.571	Contract for a garment. Nbk 23/11/14. Alu-ša-Lugal-Marada. Nbk 106; Bertin 78.
30845	1876,1117.572	Contract for a house and slave. AM 7/12/acc. Babylon. Evetts, Ev-M 7; Sack, AOATS 4, no. 55; Bertin 259.
30846	1876,1117.573	Contract for ṣapītu (plants?). Cyr 24/8/6. Babylon. Cyr 236; Bertin 816.
30847	1876,1117.574	Promissory note for barley. Dar 22/1/13. URU Tuk-lam.ki. Dar 346; Bertin 2253.
30848	1876,1117.575	Contract; lease of a house. Ner 27/2/2. Babylon. Evetts, Ner 34; Sack, AOAT 236, no. 34; Bertin 312.
30849	1876,1117.576	Promissory note for silver. Nbn 9/11/acc. Babylon. Nbn 12; Strassmaier, Liverpool, 37; Bertin 336.
30850	1876,1117.577	Purchase of a house. AM 8/9/1. Babylon. Sack, AOATS 4, no. 11; Bertin 271.
30851	1876,1117.578	Promissory note for silver. Dar 19/7/9. Babylon. Dar 258; Bertin 2162.
30852	1876,1117.579	Contract; lease of a house. Nbn 8/1/15. Babylon. Nbn 827; Bertin 642.
30853	1876,1117.580	Expenditure of silver and barley for boats, etc. n.d. Abraham, BPPE, 251-255, no. 27 (with comment on the date), and 544-545, no. 5; Wunsch, Bab Arch 2, p. 169; Wunsch, CM 20A, p. 100.
30854	1876,1117.581	List of expenditures of silver. n.d. Abraham, BPPE, 256-257, no. 28, and 546, no. 6.
30855	1876,1117.582	Letter from Nabû-šumu-uṣur to Širku; sealed. CT 22, 30, no. 162; Nisaba 28, no. 199; Hackl et al., AOAT 414/1, no. 3.
30856	1876,1117.583	Promissory note for silver; dupl. Dar 458. Dar 23/11/[17]. Babylon. Bertin 2799.
30857	1876,1117.584	Promissory note for barley. Dar 15/11/14. Alu-ša-Kināja. Dar 389; Bertin 2295.

30858	1876,1117.585	Promissory note for silver. Nbk 1/10/8. Babylon. Nbk 68; Strassmaier, Liverpool, 142; Bertin 52.
30859	1876,1117.586	Promissory note for dates. 14/-/-.
30860	1876,1117.587	Receipt for silver. Dar 19/1/9. Borsippa. Dar 249; Bertin 2157.
30861	1876,1117.588	Promissory note for dates. Dar 17/5/10. Babylon. Dar 272; Bertin 2791.
30862	1876,1117.589	Promissory note for dates. Dar 9/6/9. URU šá DUMU 1.ŠEŠ-ba-ni-i. Dar 255.
30863	1876,1117.590	Contract; fixation of interest for a silver debt by Marduk-nāṣir-apli; sealed. Dar 15/11/17. Babylon. Dar 455; Abraham, BPPE, 435-436, no. 126; Bertin 2378; Nisaba 28, no. 162.
30864	1876,1117.591	Promissory note to pay a debt of silver and onions to Marduk-bēlšunu. Dar 15/8/12. Babylon. Dar 334; Abraham, BPPE, 405-406, no. 109; Bertin 2219.
30865	1876,1117.592	Contract; lease of a field. Dar 18/[]/14. Babylon. Bertin 2309; Wunsch, CM 20A-B, no. 44.
30866	1876,1117.593	Promissory note for dates. Dar 23/5/2. Babylon. Bertin 1947; Wunsch, CM 20A-B, no. 81.
30867	1876,1117.594	Promissory note for silver. Nbk 20/6/23 Ḫuṣṣēti-ša-Nabû-ḫammē. Nbk 138; Strassmaier, Liverpool, 148; Bertin 111.
30868	1876,1117.595	Marriage of a slave girl. Nbn 25/12/12. Babylon. Nbn 682; Wunsch, AfO 44/45, 87-88, no. 18; Bertin 596.
30869	1876,1117.596	Sale of a slave. Nbn 17/8/12. Babylon. Nbn 635; Bertin 576.
30870	1876,1117.597	Receipt for telittu tax. Nbn 23/1/16. Babylon. Nbn 956; Bertin 672.
30871	1876,1117.598	Sale of a slave girl. Ner 5/6/3. Babylon. Evetts, Ner. 59; Sack, AOAT 236, no. 59; Bertin 323.
30872	1876,1117.599	Rental of slaves. Dar 22/10/13. Babylon. Dar 358; Bertin 2269.
30873	1876,1117.600	Promissory note for onions. Cyr 7/1/1. Babylon. Cyr 12; Bertin 751; Wunsch, CM 3, no. 263.
30874	1876,1117.601	Promissory note for silver for a ḫarrānu partnership. Nbk 16/8/33. Babylon. Nbk 258; S. A. Smith, MAT pp. 14-15, pl. 27; Wunsch, CM 3, no. 10.
30875	1876,1117.602	Purchase of jewellery. Nbn 2/2/11. Babylon. Nbn 501; Bertin 521.
30876	1876,1117.603	Promissory note for silver. Cam 18/5/7. Babylon. Cam 379; Bertin 980.
30877	1876,1117.604	Deposition. Dar 17/12a/-. Ḫuṣṣēti-ša-Bēl-ēṭir. Bertin 2773.

30878	1876,1117.605	Promissory note for silver. Dar 16/10/24. Dēru. Bertin 2533.
30879	1876,1117.606	Sale of a slave girl. Cam 19/9/6. Babylon. Cam 334; Bertin 967.
30880	1876,1117.607	Promissory note for silver. Nbn 12/9/[]. Babylon. Nbn 1116; Bertin 729.
30881	1876,1117.608	Contract; sale of a field. Nbn 24/2/1. Babylon. Nbn 26; Bertin 345.
30882	1876,1117.609	Contract about silver for a ḫarrānu partnership. Nbk 21/7/30. Babylon. Nbk 216; Bertin 150; Wunsch, CM 3, no. 5.
30883	1876,1117.610	Promissory note for silver. Cyr -/2/8. Babylon. Cyr 303; Bertin 829; Wunsch, CM 3, no. 308.
30884	1876,1117.611	Receipt of silver for onions and sheep. Cam 10/10/2. Cam 135; Bertin 890; Wunsch, CM 3, no. 329.
30885	1876,1117.612	Promissory note for dates. Cam 8/8/6. Babylon. Cam 325; Bertin 962.
30886	1876,1117.613	Promissory note for silver. Nbn 13/1/12. Babylon. Nbn 584; Bertin 598.
30887	1876,1117.614	Promissory note for final silver payment. Cyr 20/8/8. Cyr 320a; Bertin 847.
30888	1876,1117.615	Receipt of silver in payment for work. Nbn 24/1/14. Babylon. Nbn 757; Bertin 619; Wunsch, CM 3, no. 224.
30889	1876,1117.616	Contract for bricks. Dar 10/4/24. Babylon. Bertin 2539.
30890	1876,1117.617	Court record; about the sale of a house. Nbn 5/6/17. Bīt-šar-Bābili. Nbn 1048; Bertin 698.
30891	1876,1117.618	Promissory note for dates. Dar 19/5/12. Dūru-ša-kar (for Dūru-ša-karrabbi?). Dar 328.
30892	1876,1117.619	Receipt for small pots. Cyr 3/11/3. Babylon. Cyr 140; Bertin 771.
30893	1876,1117.620	Promissory note for dates as imittu payment. Cam 21/5/1. Šaḫrīn. Cam 54; Bertin 876; Wunsch, CM 3, no. 322.
30894	1876,1117.621	Sale of a slave. Nbn 15/5/8. Babylon. Nbn 300b; Bertin 457.
30895	1876,1117.622	Promissory note for silver. Nbk 25/5/5. Ḫuṣṣēti-ša-Iddina-Marduk. Nbk 43; Bertin 2.7
30896	1876,1117.623	Promissory note for dates. Dar 18/5/16. Babylon. Dar 423; Bertin 2420.
30897	1876,1117.624	List of people.
30898	1876,1117.625	Receipt for final payment for a field. Dar 12/1/3. Babylon. Dar 61; Bertin 1982.

30899	1876,1117.626	Sale of a slave girl. Nbn 20/12/12. Babylon. Nbn 680; Bertin 591.
30900	1876,1117.627	Promissory note for silver. Nbn 26/11/3. Babylon. Nbn 128; Bertin 382; Wunsch, CM 3, no. 119.
30901	1876,1117.628	Sale of a donkey. Nbn 21/1/4. Babylon. Nbn 140; Strassmaier, Liverpool, 65; Bertin 391.
30902	1876,1117.629	Receipt for payment of silver. Cam 23/9/1. Babylon. Cam 86; Bertin 875; Wunsch, CM 3, no. 266.
30903	1876,1117.630	Promissory note for silver. Cyr 13/2/7. Babylon. Cyr 252; Bertin 828.
30904	1876,1117.631	Promissory note for silver. Nbn 5/11/11. Babylon. Nbn 566; Bertin 354.
30905	1876,1117.632	Account of silver. 10/10/-.
30906	1876,1117.633	Promissory note for silver. Cyr 6/9/8. Babylon. Cyr 321; Bertin 833; Wunsch, CM 3, no. 309a.
30907	1876,1117.634	Promissory note for dates. Dar 13/6/4. Šuppatu. Dar 126; Bertin 2029.
30908	1876,1117.635	Deposition. Nbk 2/2/20. Babylon. Nbk 120; Bertin 96; Sandowicz, AOAT 398, 179-180, no. O.11.
30909	1876,1117.636	Contract; sale of a field. Nbn 12/7/9. Babylon. Nbn 359; Roth, Fs Oelsner, 395-396; Bertin 477.
30910	1876,1117.637	Receipt of [silver] for urāšu service. Cam []/12/7. Babylon. Wunsch, CM 3, no. 346.
30911	1876,1117.638	Sale of a slave girl. Nbn 12/1/15. Borsippa. Nbn 829; Bertin 643.
30912	1876,1117.639	Contract; lease of a field. Dar 27/4/2. Babylon. Bertin 1949; Wunsch, CM 20A-B, no. 78.
30913	1876,1117.640	Contract for sharing of a jenny and her unweaned foal for six years, between Marduk-naṣir-apli and Nabû-apla-iddin. Dar 19/8/23. Babylon. Bertin 2840; Weszeli, WZKM 86, 471-472 and 475.
30914	1876,1117.641	Promissory note for silver. Cyr 2/12/2. Babylon. Cyr 83; Bertin 767; Wunsch, CM 3, no. 281.
30915	1876,1117.642	Sale of a slave. Cyr 26/5/3. Babylon. Cyr 120; Bertin 853; dupl. 31492 (Cyr 120a).
30916	1876,1117.643	Sale of a slave girl. Cam 15/2/6. Ḫumadēšu. Cam 309; Bertin 956.
30917	1876,1117.644	Promissory note for silver. Cyr 7/10/7. Babylon. Cyr 275; Bertin 826.
30918	1876,1117.645	Medical text; colophon; partial duplicate to Köcher, BAM II, 124 and 125.
30919	1876,1117.646	Promissory note for silver. 3/11/2.
30920	1876,1117.647	Promissory note for silver. Cam 25/4/1. Babylon. Cam 46; Bertin 873; Wunsch, CM 3, no. 264.

30921	1876,1117.648	Promissory note for barley. Cam 9/8/1. Babylon. Cam 72; Bertin 870.
30922	1876,1117.649	Purchase of spades. Nbn 2/6/11. Babylon. Nbn 529; Bertin 534.
30923	1876,1117.650	Sale of a slave girl. Nbk 15/8/7. Saḫrītu. Nbk 62; Bertin 48.
30924	1876,1117.651	Receipt for repayment of a loan. Dar 2/12/28. Babylon. Bertin 2654.
30925	1876,1117.652	Sale of slaves. Nbn 21/1/15. Babylon. Nbn 832; Bertin 645.
30926	1876,1117.653	Summons to transmit crops from the land of Bagasaru and to arrange for their proper registration. Dar 18/1/11. Babylon. Dar 296; Abraham, BPPE, 393-396, no. 103; Bertin 2201.
30927	1876,1117.654	Contract; sale of a slave to Marduk-nāṣir-apli and receipt of the purchase price. Dar 26/9/6. Bīt-Ḫaḫḫūru ālu ša Kalbāya. Dar 212; Abraham, BPPE, 388-389, no. 99; Bertin 2095.
30928	1876,1117.655	Account of silver.
30929	1876,1117.656	Promissory note for dates or grain. -/6/acc. Babylon.
30930	1876,1117.657	Receipt for payment of contracted dates and barley loan. Cam 10/10/4. Bīt-Ṭāb-Bēl. Cam 257; Bertin 921.
30931	1876,1117.658	Deposition. Dar 15/7/5. Babylon. Dar 176; Bertin 2073.
30932	1876,1117.659	Summons to bring witnesses. Nbk -/-/14.
30933	1876,1117.660	Measurements of fields. Wunsch, CM 20A-B, no. 36.
30934	1876,1117.661	Receipt for interest on a loan. Cyr 3/1/9. Babylon. Cyr 334; Bertin 845.
30935	1876,1117.662	Promissory note for silver. Nbk 22/2/39. Babylon. Nbk 345; Bertin 194; Wunsch, CM 3, no. 31.
30936	1876,1117.663	Receipt for oxen. AM 19/7/1. Alu-ša-Nabû-apla-iddina. Sack, AOATS 4, no. 61; Bertin 265.
30937	1876,1117.664	Promissory note for silver and wool. Nbn 25/3/11. Babylon. Nbn 512; Bertin 526.
30938	1876,1117.665	Receipt of dates as imittu payment from a slave of Marduk-nāṣir-apli by a slave of Bagasaru; partly dupl. 30668. Dar 20/3/22. Dar 542; Abraham, BPPE, 447-449, no. 132; Bertin 2478.
30939	1876,1117.666	Receipt of silver in payment for barley. Nbn 6/5/4. Babylon. Nbn 157; Bertin 400; Wunsch, CM 3, no. 130.
30940	1876,1117.667	Contract for repayment of loan of silver with interest; sealed. Nbk 9/4/15. Babylon. Nbk 107; Strassmaier,

		Liverpool, 146; Bertin 81; Mitchell and Searight, no. 288; Nisaba 28, no. 142.
30941	1876,1117.668	Promissory note for barley. Ner 12/12/3. Šaḫrīn. Evetts, Ner 67a; Sack, AOAT 236, no. 67a; Bertin 327; Wunsch, CM 3, no. 80.
30942	1876,1117.669	Letter from Nabû-mukīn-šarri to Iddin-Marduk. CT 22, 28, no. 148; Hackl et al., AOAT 414/1, no. 11.
30943	1876,1117.670	Receipt for dates. 2/2/28.
30944	1876,1117.671	Receipt for silver to purchase a slave given as a dowry. Nbn 20/1/14. Babylon. Nbn 755; Bertin 617; Wunsch, CM 3, no. 222.
30945	1876,1117.672	Promissory note for barley; finger-nail marks (or Aramaic note?) on the reverse. Dar 15/5/13. Alu-ša-Bēl-uballiṭ. Dar 350; Bertin 2262.
30946	1876,1117.673	Promissory note for silver. Nbn 22/[]/17. Bīt-šar-Bābili. Nbn 1056; Bertin 700.
30947	1876,1117.674	Contract; lease of a house. Nbn 2/2/11. Babylon. Nbn 500; Bertin 520.
30948	1876,1117.675	Promissory note for dates. Dar 3/-/-. Ḫursag-kalamma. Bertin 2780.
30949	1876,1117.676	Contract for a delivery. Cyr 22/10/3. Babylon. Cyr 137; Bertin 770.
30950	1876,1117.677	Sale of slaves. Nbn 7/5/7. Babylon. Nbn 257; Strassmaier, Liverpool, 78; Bertin 439.
30951	1876,1117.678	Purchase of a millstone. Ner 7/9/2. Babylon. Evetts, Ner 45; Sack, AOAT 236, no. 45; Bertin 316.
30952	1876,1117.679	Apprenticeship contract. Cyr 19/1/7. Babylon. Cyr 248; Bertin 824.
30953	1876,1117.680	Promissory note for silver. Nbn 20/7/14. Bīt-ša-Nabû-mukīn. Nbn 796; Bertin 627.
30954	1876,1117.681	Sale of a slave. Nbn 15/5/8. Babylon. Nbn 300a; Bertin 457.
30955	1876,1117.682	Promissory note for dates.
30956	1876,1117.683	Promissory note for silver and sesame. Nbn 5/8/14. Bīt-šar-Bābili. Nbn 802; Bertin 631.
30957	1876,1117.684	Promissory note for silver. Dar 30/7/[]. Babylon. Bertin 2781.
30958	1876,1117.685	Marriage contract. Nbn 10/12/6. Babylon. Nbn 243; Petschow, JCS 19, 1077; Bertin 430.
30959	1876,1117.686	Receipt for jewellery components. Cam 21/12/3. Dapīni. Cam 223; Bertin 900.
30960	1876,1117.687	Promissory note for silver. Nbn 23/2/9. Babylon. Nbn 335; Bertin 466; Wunsch, CM 3, no. 164.

30961	1876,1117.688	Receipt of silver from Marduk-nāṣir-apli as purchase price of a boat; dupl. 31641. Dar 12/6/26. Babylon. Bertin 2622; Abraham, BPPE, 257-258, no. 29.
30962	1876,1117.689	Promissory note for silver. Nbn 16/1/8. Babylon. Nbn 282; Strassmaier, Liverpool, 83.
30963	1876,1117.690	Promissory note for silver. Cyr 20/3/7. Babylon. Cyr 254; Bertin 823.
30964	1876,1117.691	Gift of dowry. Cyr []/[]/3. Cyr 154; Bertin 774.
30965	1876,1117.692	Contract; undertaking to settle debts due to Madanu-bēla-uṣur with Marduk-nāṣir-apli. Dar 21/5/26. Babylon. Bertin 2603; Abraham, BPPE, 259-261, no. 30.
30966	1876,1117.693	Account of silver payments.
30967	1876,1117.694	Promissory note for onions. Nbn 13/2/2. Šaḫrīn. Bertin 2981; Wunsch, CM 3, no. 102.
30968	1876,1117.695	Promissory note for silver. Nbn 2/12/[]. Nbn 1132; Bertin 731.
30969	1876,1117.696	Promissory note for dates. 27/3/[]. URU Til-Gula. Wunsch, CM 3, no. 364.
30970	1876,1117.697	Letter.
30971	1876,1117.698	Promissory note for silver. Dar 16/7/12. Babylon. Bertin 2220.
30972	1876,1117.699	Promissory note for silver. Cam 20/8/3. Babylon. Cam 195; Bertin 904.
30973	1876,1117.700	Promissory note for silver. Dar 28/6/12. Šaḫrīn. Dar 333; Bertin 2232.
30974	1876,1117.701	Deposition. Dar 9/5/20. Babylon. Dar 502; Bertin 2450.
30975	1876,1117.702	Transfer of responsibility. Cyr 8/5/8. Babylon. Cyr 311; Bertin 838.
30976	1876,1117.703	Apprenticeship contract. Cyr 6/12/8. Babylon. Cyr 325; Lambert, RA 73, 89; Bertin 834.
30977	1876,1117.704	Promissory note for silver. Nbn 4/2/10. Babylon. Nbn 404; Bertin 491.
30978	1876,1117.705	Promissory note for barley. Nbn 14/12/11. Šaḫrīn. Nbn 576; Bertin 549; Wunsch, CM 3, no. 194.
30979	1876,1117.706	Promissory note for bricks. Nbn 22/4/7. Babylon. Nbn 256; Strassmaier, Liverpool, 77; Bertin 438; Wunsch, CM 3, no. 141.
30980	1876,1117.707	Receipt of payment for transport costs due by Marduk-nāṣir-apli. Dar 4/8/26. Babylon. Bertin 2623; Abraham, BPPE, 261-262, no. 31.
30981	1876,1117.708	Promissory note for silver to buy gold. Nbk 28/4/21. Babylon. Nbk 127; Bertin 100.
30982	1876,1117.709	Promissory note for silver. Dar 28/5/8. Babylon. Dar 235; Bertin 2133.

30983	1876,1117.710	Receipt for final payment for a field. Cyr 20/8/8. Babylon. Cyr 320; Bertin 1672.
30984	1876,1117.711	Deposition. Dar 26/10/18. Šaḫrīn. Dar 473; Bertin 2396.
30985	1876,1117.712	Promissory note for dates; ḫarrānu. Nbn 3/6/1. Šaḫrīn. Nbn 34; Strassmaier, Liverpool, 477; Bertin 347; Wunsch, CM 3, no. 96.
30986	1876,1117.713	Receipt for silver as part of the price of a house. Nbn 10/7/8. Babylon. Wunsch, CM 3, no. 157.
30987	1876,1117.714	Receipt for silver deposit. Cam 10/1/7. Babylon. Cam 356; Bertin 916.
30988	1876,1117.715	Sale of a slave girl. Nbn 7/9/15. Babylon. Nbn 903; Bertin 662.
30989	1876,1117.716	Promissory note for silver. Cam 8/10/3. Babylon. Cam 208; Bertin 939.
30990	1876,1117.717	Promissory note for dates. Nbk 21/5/36. Babylon. Nbk 301; Bertin 174; Wunsch, CM 3, no. 22.
30991	1876,1117.718	Guarantee for the sale of slave girls. Nbn 15/9/1. Šaḫrīn. Nbn 42; Bertin 350; Wunsch, CM 3, no. 100.
30992	1876,1117.719	Contract for pipes. Dar 16/11/14. Alu-ša-Nabû-ēreš. Dar 391; Bertin 2290.
30993	1876,1117.720	Promissory note for silver. Dar 15/11/15. Babylon. Dar 415; Bertin 2325.
30994	1876,1117.721	Promissory note to pay a debt of silver to Marduk-nāṣir-apli; dupl. 31722. Dar 5/7/26. Babylon. Bertin 2608; Abraham, BPPE, 262-264, no. 32.
30995	1876,1117.722	Promissory note for silver. Dar 13/7/-. Babylon. Bertin 2796.
30996	1876,1117.723	Deposition. Dar 3/2/2. Babylon. Bertin 1954.
30997	1876,1117.724	Letter from Kalbāya to Iddināya. CT 22, 19-20, no. 97; Hackl et al., AOAT 414/1, no. 28.
30998	1876,1117.725	Contract for household utensils. Nbk 21/4/[]. Babylon. Nbk 426; Bertin 236.
30999	1876,1117.726	Promissory note for silver. Nbk 16/10/28. Babylon. Nbk 194; Bertin 134; Wunsch, CM 3, no. 2.
31000	1876,1117.727	Account of dates or grain.
31001	1876,1117.728	Promissory note for silver. Cam 10/10/6. Babylon. Cam 337; Bertin 965.
31002	1876,1117.729	Promissory note for dates. Cam 28/6/6. Babylon. Cam 319; Bertin 963.
31003	1876,1117.730	Contract; lease of a house. Dar 7/8/9. Borsippa. Dar 259; Bertin 2153.
31004	1876,1117.731	Sale of slaves; dupl. 31375. Nbk 16/5/29. Borsippa. Nbk 201; Bertin 141; Wunsch, CM 3, no. 3.

31005	1876,1117.732	Promissory note for silver. Cam 1/9/6. Babylon. Cam 328; Bertin 948.
31006	1876,1117.733	Promissory note to pay a debt of barley to Marduk-nāṣir-apli. Dar 15/11/14. Alu-ša-Libbi-ālāja. Dar 390; Abraham, BPPE, 418-419, no. 116; Bertin 2286.
31007	1876,1117.734	Sale of a child. Nbk 16/11/8. Saḫrītu(?)-ša-Mušallim-Marduk. Nbk 70a; Bertin 54.
31008	1876,1117.735	Promissory note for silver. Cam 23/9/6. Babylon. Cam 33; Bertin 942.
31009	1876,1117.736	Contract for leather goods. Ner 9/4/3. Babylon. Evetts, Ner 55; Sack, AOAT 236, no. 55; Bertin 321.
31010	1876,1117.737	Promissory note for silver. Cam 19/4/7. Babylon. Cam 372; Bertin 985.
31011	1876,1117.738	Promissory note for silver. Nbk 9/6/36. Babylon. Nbk 302; Bertin 176.
31012	1876,1117.739	Contract; lease of a house. Nbn 21/1/5. Babylon. Nbn 184; Strassmaier, Liverpool, 68; Bertin 411.
31013	1876,1117.740	Promissory note for barley. Nbn 14/9/15. Babylon. Bertin 663.
31014	1876,1117.741	Promissory note for dates. Dar 6/[]/9. Wunsch, CM 20A-B, no. 28.
31015	1876,1117.742	Sale of slaves. Nbk 11/11/29. Babylon. Nbk 207; Bertin 144; Wunsch, CM 3, no. 4.
31016	1876,1117.743	Contract about silver for a ḫarrānu partnership. Nbk 25/7/34. Babylon. Nbk 269; Bertin 163; Wunsch, CM 3, no. 14.
31017	1876,1117.744	Promissory note for silver. Nbk 27/10/8. Babylon. Nbk 69; Strassmaier, Liverpool, 143; Bertin 53.
31018	1876,1117.745	Receipt of silver from Marduk-nāṣir-apli. Dar 2/5/11. Babylon. Abraham, BPPE, 264-265, no. 33, and 547, no. 7.
31019	1876,1117.746	Promissory note for barley. Dar 28/4/11. Babylon. Dar 300; Bertin 2197.
31020	1876,1117.747	Transfer of ownership of a slave. Nbn 9/2/13. Babylon. Nbn 697; Bertin 600; Wunsch, CM 3, no. 211.
31021	1876,1117.748	Account of silver payments.
31022	1876,1117.749	Division of dates. Dar 27/8/14. Alu-ša-Nabû-ēreš. Dar 384; Bertin 2302.
31023	1876,1117.750	Promissory note for barley. Dar 4/1/29. Babylon. Bertin 2675.
31024	1876,1117.751	Contract; guarantee for a slave sale. Nbk 10/2/31. Babylon. Nbk 37; Bertin 147.
31025	1876,1117.752	Promissory note for silver and onions. Nbn 26/7/4. Šaḫrīn. Nbn 169; Bertin 405; Wunsch. CM 3, no. 133.

31026	1876,1117.753	Receipt of silver from Marduk-nāṣir-apli's slave and Iddināya. Dar 3/5/15. Šaḫrīn. Bertin 2318; Abraham, BPPE, 266-267, no. 34.
31027	1876,1117.754	Promissory note to pay a debt of silver and dates to Marduk-nāṣir-apli's slave. Dar 26/7/11. Šaḫrīn. Dar 308; Abraham, BPPE, 398-399, no. 105; Bertin 2198.
31028	1876,1117.755	Promissory note for dates. Nbn. Babylon. Bertin 730.
31029	1876,1117.756	Promissory note for silver and barley. Cam 23/1/8. Šaḫrīn. Cam 409; Bertin 988.
31030	1876,1117.757	Receipt for flour. Dar 30/6/6. Babylon. Dar 205; Bertin 863 and 2101.
31031	1876,1117.758	Promissory note for barley. Nbk 12/8/19. Ḫuṣṣēti ša-Nabû-ḫammē. Nbk 118; Bertin 94.
31032	1876,1117.759	Contract; lease of a house. Cam 7/8/4. Babylon. Cam 253; Bertin 920.
31033	1876,1117.760	Promissory note for wheat. Nbk 14/6/6. Alu-ša-Mušallim-Marduk. Nbk 52; Bertin 39.
31034	1876,1117.761	Receipt of silver from Marduk-nāṣir-apli. Dar 6/11/[6]. Babylon. Bertin 2800; Abraham, BPPE, 205-206, no. 1.
31035	1876,1117.762	Contract; sale of a field. Dar 28/4/2. Babylon. Dar 35; Bertin 1944.
31036	1876,1117.763	Receipt of dates and silver from Marduk-nāṣir-apli. Dar 18/2/26. Babylon. Bertin 2613; Abraham, BPPE, 267-268, no. 35.
31037	1876,1117.764	Promissory note for onions. Nbk 25/3/42. Bīt-Ṭāb-Bēl. Nbk 397; Bertin 228; Wunsch, CM 3, no. 45.
31038	1876,1117.765	Promissory note for dates. Dar 12/7/5. Babylon. Dar 175; Bertin 2052.
31039	1876,1117.766	Promissory note for silver. Nbn 12/[]/15. Babylon. Nbn 945; Bertin 667.
31040	1876,1117.767	Promissory note for silver. Nbn 22/9/14. Babylon. Nbn 813; Bertin 634; Wunsch, CM 3, no. 228.
31041	1876,1117.768	Letter from Puršu to Širku. CT 22, 15, no. 73; Hackl et al., AOAT 414/1, no. 45.
31042	1876,1117.769	Sale of a child. Nbk 16/11/8. Saḫrītu(?)-ša-Mušallim-Marduk. Nbk 70; Bertin 191.
31043	1876,1117.770	Contract; exchange of sheep. Nbn 16/10/11. Babylon. Nbn 562; Bertin 540; Wunsch, CM 3, no. 190.
31044	1876,1117.771	Promissory note for barley; ḫarrānu. Ner 12/12/3. Šaḫrīn. Evetts, Ner 67; Sack, AOAT 236, no. 67; Bertin 328; Wunsch, CM 3, no. 80.
31045	1876,1117.772	Account of silver.
31046	1876,1117.773	Inventory of a dowry. Cam 11/9/6. Ḫursag-kalamma. Cam 330; Bertin 957.

31047	1876,1117.774	Receipt for dates or grain.
31048	1876,1117.775	Receipt for repayment of a loan. Dar 22/7/10. Babylon. Dar 279; Bertin 2173.
31049	1876,1117.776	Contract; sale of a field. Dar 5/10/19. Babylon. Dar 488; Bertin 2418; dupl. 31514.
31050	1876,1117.777	Sale of a slave girl. Cam 21/11/acc. Babylon. Cam 15; Bertin 863; Wunsch, CM 3, no. 318.
31051	1876,1117.778	Promissory note for dates. Cam 16/6/acc. Babylon. Cam 2; Bertin 860.
31052	1876,1117.779	Contract; lease of a house. Nbk 3/5/24. Babylon. Nbk 142; Bertin 114.
31053	1876,1117.780	Promissory note for silver. Nbk 23/2/22. Bāṣ (LAM.KUR.RU.ki). Bertin 105.
31054	1876,1117.781	Receipt of payment in silver; sealed. Dar 4/6/18. Babylon. Dar 470; Nisaba 28, no. 164.
31055	1876,1117.782	List of silver debtors.
31056	1876,1117.783	Promissory note for barley. Dar 21/12/10. Babylon. Dar 290; Bertin 2167.
31057	1876,1117.784	Deposition. Dar 26/12/8. Babylon. Dar 244; Bertin 784.
31058	1876,1117.785	Promissory note to pay a debt of dates to Marduk-nāṣir-apli. [Dar] 18/1/[]. Babylon. Bertin 3068; Abraham, BPPE, 269-270, no. 36.
31059	1876,1117.786	Promissory note for barley. Nbn 30/12/9. Babylon. Nbn 3; Bertin 488.
31060	1876,1117.787	Deposition. Dar 20/11/14. Alu-ša-Zumbā. Dar 392; Bertin 2310.
31061	1876,1117.788	Promissory note for silver. Dar 12/12/18. Babylon. Dar 474; Bertin 2393.
31062	1876,1117.789	Sale of a slave. Nbn 15/5/8. Babylon. Nbn 300; Strassmaier, Liverpool, 89; Bertin 457.
31063	1876,1117.790	Purchase of vats Nbk III 19/9/acc. Babylon. Nbk 10; Bertin 15; Lorenz, Nebukadnezar III/IV, p. 32.
31064	1876,1117.791	Contract for purchase of beams. Nbn 22/3/2. Babylon. Nbn 66a; Strassmaier, Liverpool, 56; Bertin 364.
31065	1876,1117.792	Receipt for final payment of loan. Nbk -/9/17. Babylon. Nbk 111; Bertin 86.
31066	1876,1117.793	Promissory note for silver. Nbk 14/1/23. Babylon. Nbk 136; Bertin 109.
31067	1876,1117.794	Account of issues of barley. Nbn 24/11/16 Nbn 1006; Bertin 683; Wunsch, CM 3, no. 245.
31068	1876,1117.795	Promissory note for barley. Nbn 1/1/8. Babylon. Nbn 280; Bertin 452; Wunsch, CM 3, no. 149.
31069	1876,1117.796	Promissory note for silver. Dar 16/10/21. Babylon. Dar 529; Bertin 2463.

31070	1876,1117.797	Receipt for purchase of a slave. Nbn 11/4/11. Babylon. Nbn 516; Bertin 528; Wunsch, AfO 44/45, 79, no. 7.
31071	1876,1117.798	Account of silver.
31072	1876,1117.799	Service contract and promissory note for silver. Nbn 21/11/5. Borsippa. Nbn 210; Bertin 528; Wunsch, CM 3, no. 136.
31073	1876,1117.800	Promissory note for barley. Nbn 4/1/[]. Šaḫrīn. Nbn 1059; Bertin 728; Wunsch, CM 3, no. 253.
31074	1876,1117.801	Field plan.
31075	1876,1117.802	Promissory note for silver. Cyr 11/12/6. Bīt-Raḫē. Cyr 240; Bertin 806.
31076	1876,1117.803	Contract for a garment. Nbk 8/9/36. Babylon. Nbk 307; Bertin 177.
31077	1876,1117.804	Sale of a donkey Nbk IV 14/6/1. Babylon. Nbk 13; Bertin 16; Lorenz, Nebukadnezar III/IV, p. 32.
31078	1876,1117.805	Receipt for silver payment. Cyr 16/9/acc. Borsippa. Bertin 746; Wunsch, CM 3, no. 259.
31079	1876,1117.806	Promissory note for silver. Nbn 25/11/4. Babylon. Nbn 176; Strassmaier, Liverpool, 66; Pinches, ZA 1, 198-202; Bertin 407.
31080	1876,1117.807	Promissory note for barley; ḫarrānu. Nbn 26/6/1. Babylon. Nbn 36; Strassmaier, Liverpool, 48; Bertin 348; Wunsch, CM 3, no. 97.
31081	1876,1117.808	Promissory note for silver. Cyr 16/6b/2. Asurukkānu. Cyr 58; Bertin 760
31082	1876,1117.809	Receipt of miksu-toll for an onion boat. Cam 19/1/5. Babylon. Cam 272; Bertin 929; Wunsch. CM 3, no. 317.
31083	1876,1117.810	Contract for remaining cost of a slave. Nbn 17/6/15. Babylon. Nbn 881; Bertin 658.
31084	1876,1117.811	Promissory note for onions and silver; ḫarrānu. Ner 25/3/2. Babylon. Evetts, Ner 35; Sack, AOAT 236, no. 35; Bertin 313; Wunsch. CM 3, no. 74.
31085	1876,1117.812	Promissory note for barley; finger-nail marks. Nbk 5/4/6. Alu-ša-Šulā. Nbk 50; Bertin 36.
31086	1876,1117.813	Promissory note for onions and barley; ḫarrānu. Nbk 2/12a/36. Babylon. Nbk 309; Strassmaier, Liverpool, 155; Bertin 179; Wunsch. CM 3, no. 24.
31087	1876,1117.814	Contract concluding a ḫarrānu partnership. Nbk 12/11/39. Babylon. Nbk 356; Bertin 200; Wunsch, CM 3, no. 33.
31088	1876,1117.815	Promissory note for silver. Nbk 7/2/37. Babylon. Nbk 317; Bertin 182.

31089	1876,1117.816	Promissory note for silver; ḫarrānu. Nbk 1/10/34. Babylon. Nbk 272; Bertin 1651; Wunsch, CM 3, no. 15.
31090	1876,1117.817	Promissory note for silver. Nbk 16/2/7. Babylon. Nbk 55; Bertin 56.
31091	1876,1117.818	Promissory note for silver. Nbk 6/12/42. Babylon. Nbk 407; Bertin 231.
31092	1876,1117.819	Promissory note for silver. Nbk 4/12b/36. Babylon. Nbk 314; Bertin 175; Wunsch, CM 3, no. 25.
31093	1876,1117.820	Deposition. Nbk 28/4/28. Babylon. Nbk 183; Bertin 128.
31094	1876,1117.821	Sale of a slave girl. Nbk 11/11/41. Babylon. Nbk 386; Strassmaier, Liverpool, 162; Bertin 222.
31095	1876,1117.822	Deposition. Nbk 21/11/34 Nbk 276; Bertin 167.
31096	1876,1117.823	Promissory note for silver. Nbk 23/11/37. Dannatu. Nbk 327; Bertin 189.
31097	1876,1117.824	Promissory note for silver as kārum payment for a boat-load of onions. Nbk 16/8/41. Bīt-Ṭāb-Bēl. Nbk 384; Bertin 219; Wunsch. CM 3, no. 41.
31098	1876,1117.825	Contract; ḫarrānu; dupl. 31488 (Nbk 429). Nbk 17/5/7. Babylon. Nbk 58; Bertin 44.
31099	1876,1117.826	Promissory note for silver. Nbk 15/5/29. Babylon. Nbk 200; Bertin 140.
31100	1876,1117.827	Promissory note for silver and sesame; ḫarrānu. AM 12/7/1. Babylon. Evetts, Ev-M 11; Sack, AOATS 4, no. 27; Bertin 267; Wunsch, CM 3, no. 56.
31101	1876,1117.828	Promissory note for silver. AM 13/10/1. Babylon. Evetts, Ev-M 15; Sack, AOATS 4, no. 16; Bertin 273.
31102	1876,1117.829	Promissory note for barley. AM 12/1/2. Babylon. Evetts, Ev-M 17; Sack, AOATS 4, no. 17; Bertin 280.
31103	1876,1117.830	Promissory note for onions in lieu of silver. AM 11/4/2. Babylon. Evetts, Ev-M 21; Sack, AOATS 4, no. 24; Bertin 284; Wunsch, CM 3, no. 61.
31104	1876,1117.831	Promissory note for silver and onions; ḫarrānu. Ner 2/6/2. Babylon. Evetts, Ner 38; Sack, AOAT 236, no. 38; Bertin 314; Wunsch, CM 3, no. 75.
31105	1876,1117.832	Sale of a slave. Ner 29/10/acc. Babylon. Evetts, Ner 7; Sack, AOAT 236, no. 7; Bertin 295.
31106	1876,1117.833	Note about silver. Nbn 5/5/15. Nbn 872; Bertin 655; Wunsch, CM 3, no. 236.
31107	1876,1117.834	Promissory note for silver. Nbn 12/9/8. Babylon. Nbn 308; Bertin 459.
31108	1876,1117.835	Contract; sale of a field. Nbn 26/9/9. Babylon. Nbn 372; Bertin 480.

31109	1876,1117.836	Sale of slave girls. Nbn 15/8/1. Bīt-Ṭāb-Bēl. Nbn 40; Bertin 349; Wunsch, CM 3, no. 98.
31110	1876,1117.837	Forfeit of land held as collateral. Cyr 22/2/9. Babylon. Cyr 337; Bertin 842.
31111	1876,1117.838	Promissory note for silver as the price of sesame. Cyr 3/5/2. Babylon. Cyr 45; Bertin 757; Wunsch, CM 3, no. 273.
31112	1876,1117.839	Promissory note for dates. Cam 20/6/acc. Babylon. Cam 3; Bertin 855.
31113	1876,1117.840	Promissory note for barley. Cam 18/3/2. Babylon. Cam 164; Bertin 913; Wunsch, CM 3, no. 324.
31114	1876,1117.841	Promissory note for silver. Cam 29/4/3. Babylon. Cam 166; Bertin 908.
31115	1876,1117.842	Promissory note for silver. Dar 3/5/13. Šaḫrīn. Dar 349; Bertin 2267.
31116	1876,1117.843	Contract; lease of a house. Dar 28/6/16. Borsippa. Dar 428; Bertin 2341.
31117	1876,1117.844	Promissory note for barley; finger-nail marks on the reverse. Dar 2/8/14. Babylon. Dar 383; Bertin 2296.
31118	1876,1117.845	Receipt for a man hired by Marduk-nāṣir-apli. Dar 4/[]/25. Babylon. Bertin 2581; Abraham, BPPE, 270-271, no. 37.
31119	1876,1117.846	Letter from Ubār to Širku. Hackl et al., AOAT 414/1, no. 50.
31120	1876,1117.847	Sale contract. Bertin 3069.
31121	1876,1117.848	Letter from Iddinaya to f.Qudāšu. CT 22, 2-3, no. 6; Hackl et al., AOAT 414/1, no. 22.
31122	1876,1117.849	List of men and women.
31123	1876,1117.850	Promissory note for dates. Cam 24/11/4. Šaḫrīn. Cam 261; Bertin 922.
31124	1876,1117.851	Letter to Širku; sealed. Nisaba 28, no. 202; Hackl et al., AOAT 414/1, no. 51.
31125	1876,1117.852	Contract. Nbk 16/1/17. Babylon.
31126	1876,1117.853	Promissory note for dates. Nbk 8/4/35. Babylon. Nbk 281; Bertin 169; Wunsch, CM 3, no. 18.
31127	1876,1117.854	Account.
31128	1876,1117.855	Promissory note for silver. Nbn []/[]/8? Babylon. Wunsch, CM 3, no. 161.
31129	1876,1117.856	Contract; sale of a house.
31130	1876,1117.857	Receipt for sale of field. Dar 16/5/6. Babylon. Dar 202; Bertin 2100.
31131	1876,1117.858	Promissory note for silver. Nbk 7/2/37. Babylon. Nbk 317a; Bertin 182.
31132	1876,1117.859	Sale of a slave. Nbn 30/6/5. Babylon. Nbn 194; Strassmaier, Liverpool, 70; Bertin 416.

31133	1876,1117.860	Promissory note for dates. Nbn 24/1/12. Babylon. Nbn 587; Bertin 554.
31134	1876,1117.861	Promissory note for dates. Nbn 28/5/15. Babylon. Nbn 875; Bertin 657.
31135	1876,1117.862	Contract for repayment of debt. Nbk 17/1/20. Babylon. Nbk 119; Bertin 95.
31136	1876,1117.863	Receipt for silver payment. Cam 17/8/2. Babylon. Cam 125; Bertin 889; Wunsch, CM 3, no. 327.
31137	1876,1117.864	Promissory note for dates or grain. Nbn []/10/8. Babylon. Nbn 311; Bertin 481.
31138	1876,1117.865	Receipt of barley from Marduk-nāṣir-apli. Dar 19/3/25. Babylon. Bertin 2568; Abraham, BPPE, 272-273, no. 38.
31139	1876,1117.866	Receipt for interest payment; sealed. SE Ant III 19/7/100. Babylon. CT 49, 29, no. 134; Bertin 2910; Stolper, Annali Supp. 77, 34-38, no. 11; Nisaba 28, no. 658.
31140	1876,1117.867	Hire of a slave. Nbk 13/1/14. Babylon. Nbk 103; Bertin 76; Sandowicz, AOAT 398, 178-179, no. O.10.
31141	1876,1117.868	Promissory note for silver. Nbk 5/12/3. Saḫrītu. Nbk 33a; Strassmaier, Liverpool, 137; Bertin 24.
31142	1876,1117.869	Contract; undertaking to transmit an order issued by Nergal-eṭir to Marduk-nāṣir-apli. Dar 1/10/22. Babylon. Dar 552; Abraham, BPPE, 450-452, no. 134; Bertin 2481.
31143	1876,1117.870	Promissory note for barley, wool, silver and animals. Ner 23/2/2. Babylon. Evetts, Ner 33; Sack, AOAT 236, no. 33; Bertin 311; Wunsch, CM 3, no. 73.
31144	1876,1117.871	Contract for exchange of dates. Dar 27/8/2. Babylon. Bertin 1948.
31145	1876,1117.872	Receipt for delivery. Nbn 2/3/-.
31146	1876,1117.873	Receipt of silver for urāšu service baking bricks. Cam 15/5/[1]. Babylon. Cam 419; Bertin 1001; Wunsch, CM 3, no. 265b.
31147	1876,1117.874	Audit of beer supplies. Nbn 3/10/14. Nbn 815a; Bertin 636.
31148	1876,1117.875	Promissory note for silver. Nbn 10/12/12. Babylon. Nbn 674; Bertin 588.
31149	1876,1117.876	Receipt for silver payment. Cyr 24/11/3. Babylon. Cyr 142; Bertin 777.
31150	1876,1117.877	Promissory note for silver. Nbn 24/3/15. Babylon. Nbn 858; Bertin 652; Wunsch, CM 3, no. 235.
31151	1876,1117.878	Contract sale of fields from a dowry. Ner 6/6/3. Babylon. Evetts, Ner 60; Sack, AOAT 236, no. 60; Bertin 324.

31152	1876,1117.879	Promissory note for silver. Nbn 21/6/11. Babylon. Nbn 534; Bertin 537; Wunsch, CM 3, no. 189.
31153	1876,1117.880	Sale of a slave. Nbk 13/4/39. Kiš. Nbk 346; Bertin 199.; Wunsch, CM 3, no.
31154	1876,1117.881	Promissory note for silver. Dar 25/7/4. Babylon. Dar 131; Bertin 2031.
31155	1876,1117.882	Letter from Bēl-aḫḫē-iddin to Iddin-Marduk. CT 22, 11, no. 48; Hackl et al., AOAT 414/1, no. 12.
31156	1876,1117.883	Guarantee for a slave sale. Nbn 7/4/17. Babylon. Nbn 1039; Bertin 695; Wunsch, CM 3, no. 252.
31157	1876,1117.884	Promissory note for silver. Nbk 6/10/17. Babylon. Nbk 112; Bertin 87.
31158	1876,1117.885	Promissory note for silver. Nbk 19/7/5. Saḫrītu. Nbk 44; Bertin 29.
31159	1876,1117.886	Contract about route of access to a house; month 12b, but the duplicate, 78145, is dated month 12a. Nbn 24/12b/1. Babylon. Nbn 53; Strassmaier, Liverpool, 51; Bertin 357.
31160	1876,1117.887	Contract; sale of a field. Nbn 14/[]/11. Babylon. Nbn 580; Bertin 552.
31161	1876,1117.888	Contract for beams. Nbn 22/3/2. Babylon. Nbn 66; Bertin 364.
31162	1876,1117.889	Deposition. Nbk 23/8/40. Upija. Nbk 366; Bertin 208.
31163	1876,1117.890	Sale of a slave girl. Nbn 9/12a/12. Babylon. Nbn 671; Bertin 587.
31164	1876,1117.891	Sale of a slave. Nbn 14/12b/6. Babylon. Nbn 244; Strassmaier, Liverpool, 82; Bertin 431.
31165	1876,1117.892	Receipt of onions. Nbn 15/12b/3. Šaḫrīn. Nbn 134; Bertin 389; Wunsch, CM 3, no. 121.
31166	1876,1117.893	Promissory note for onions. Nbn 22/12b/15. Ibri ālu ša Nabû. Nbn 943; Bertin 640; Wunsch, CM 3, no. 240.
31167	1876,1117.894	Promissory note for silver and barley. Nbn 13/6b/10. Babylon. Nbn 438; Bertin 496.
31168	1876,1117.895	Promissory note for silver. Nbn 27/12b/12. Babylon. Nbn 688; Bertin 597.
31169	1876,1117.896	Hire of a slave.
31170	1876,1117.897	Promissory note for dates. Nbn 20/6/12. Babylon. Nbn 622; Bertin 568.
31171	1876,1117.898	Promissory note for silver. Cyr 11/9/8. Babylon. Cyr 322; Bertin 1671.
31172	1876,1117.899	Sale of oxen. Cyr 8/12b/ 6. Uruk. Cyr 219; Bertin 805.
31173	1876,1117.900	Receipt for delivery of dates. Cyr 14/12b/3. Babylon. Cyr 149; Bertin 783; Wunsch, CM 3, no. 289.

31174	1876,1117.901	Promissory note for silver. Cyr 10/9/6. Babylon. Cyr 237; Bertin 817.
31175	1876,1117.902	Promissory note for dates. Cyr 20/[]/2. Babylon. Cyr 91; Bertin 755.
31176	1876,1117.903	Receipt for silver payment. Cyr 2/12/3. Babylon. Cyr 144; Bertin 778; Wunsch, CM 3, no. 289.
31177	1876,1117.904	Promissory note for silver. Cyr 4/12b/3. Babylon. Cyr 148; Bertin 784.
31178	1876,1117.905	Receipt for silver payment according to contract. Cyr 8/12b/6. Uruk. Cyr 242; Bertin 813.
31179	1876,1117.906	Promissory note for silver. Cam 25/9/1. Babylon. Cam 81; Wunsch, CM 3, no. 269.
31180	1876,1117.907	Receipt of silver for urāšu service. Cyr 21/12/acc. Babylon. Cyr 8; Bertin 747; Wunsch, CM 3, no. 261.
31181	1876,1117.908	Promissory note for silver. Cyr 26/2/2. Urāzu-mētanu. Cyr 37; Bertin 754.
31182	1876,1117.909	Contract; lease of a house. Cam 22/6b/3. Babylon. Cam 182; Bertin 887.
31183	1876,1117.910	Contract; sale of a field. Cam 22/6b/3. Babylon. Cam 226; Bertin 898.
31184	1876,1117.911	Promissory note for silver. Dar 15/11/17. Babylon. Dar 456; Bertin 2377.
31185	1876,1117.912	Promissory note for silver; dupl. 30856. Dar 23/11/17. Babylon. Dar 458; Bertin 2367.
31186	1876,1117.913	Promissory note for silver. Dar 15/12a/12+ Dar 337; Kugler, SSB II 420; Bertin 2236.
31187	1876,1117.914	Receipt of silver from Marduk-nāṣir-apli as payment for rikis qabli; ITI.KIN.2.KAM; see Abraham's comment on the date. Dar -/6b/3. Babylon. Dar 206; Abraham, BPPE, 386-387, no. 98; Bertin 2091.
31188	1876,1117.915	Receipt of a forced labourer as tower of a boat by Marduk-nāṣir-apli. Dar 25/[]/24. Babylon. Bertin 2534; Abraham, BPPE, 273-275, no. 39.
31189	1876,1117.916	Promissory note for dates. Dar 25/6/5. Lītamu. Dar 172; Bertin 2048.
31190	1876,1117.917	List of four men working? at a store house.
31191	1876,1117.918	Contract for responsibility for workmen. Nbk []/[]/9 Nbk 83; Bertin 62.
31192	1876,1117.919	List of men.
31193	1876,1117.920	List of crews of workmen for various jobs.
31194	1876,1117.921	Promissory note for sesame. Nbn 9/4/9. Babylon.
31195	1876,1117.922	Letter from Kāṣir to Bēl-rēṣu'a. CT 22, 20, no. 98; Hackl et al., AOAT 414/1, no. 46.
31196	1876,1117.923	Letter from Lābāši to Madān-bēlu-uṣur. CT 22, 20-21, no. 104; Hackl et al., AOAT 414/1, no. 32.

31197	1876,1117.924	Letter from Rēmūt to Arrabi. CT 22, 22, no. 193; Hackl et al., AOAT 414/1, no. 19.
31198	1876,1117.925	Memorandum about a previous letter.
31199	1876,1117.926	Letter from Nabû-kuṣranni to Iddin-Marduk. CT 22, 29, no. 157; Hackl et al., AOAT 414/1, no. 9.
31200	1876,1117.927	Account of dates or grain.
31201	1876,1117.928	Memorandum attesting to the presence of a lady.
31202	1876,1117.929	Promissory note for silver. 6+/[]/6.
31203	1876,1117.930	Receipt of flour, paid on behalf of Marduk-nāṣir-apli. [] 4/8/[]. Babylon. Abraham, BPPE, 275-276, no. 40, and 548, no. 8.
31204	1876,1117.931	Receipt of miksu-toll for an onion-boat. Cam -/-/4. Bertin 1908; Wunsch, CM 3, no. 339.
31205	1876,1117.932	Account of household furnishings (as dowry?). Nbk 8/12/[] Nbk 441; Bertin 250.
31206	1876,1117.933	Promissory note for onions, mustard, old vats and silver. AM 19/7/acc. Babylon. Evetts, Ev-M 2; Strassmaier, Liverpool, 125; Sack, AOATS 4, no. 25; Bertin 254; Wunsch, CM 3, no. 50.
31207	1876,1117.934	Promissory note for dates. Ner 26/6/3. Nāru-eššu. Evetts, Ner 63; Sack, AOAT 236, no. 63; Bertin 325.
31208	1876,1117.935	Promissory note for silver as part of the price of an ox; ḫarrānu. AM 18/1/2. Šaḫrīn. Evetts, Ev-M 18; Strassmaier, Liverpool, 131; Sack, AOATS 4, no. 31; Bertin 279; Wunsch, CM 3, no. 59.
31209	1876,1117.936	Contract; lease of a house. Ner 25/2/3. Babylon. Evetts, Ner 52; Strassmaier, Liverpool, 121; Sack, AOAT 236, no. 52; Bertin 320.
31210	1876,1117.937	Promissory note for silver. Nbn 24/1/9. Šaḫrīn. Nbn 325; Strassmaier, Liverpool, 92; Bertin 464; Wunsch, CM 3, no. 162.
31211	1876,1117.938	Promissory note for silver as the price of onions. Nbn 1/1/14. Bābtu. Nbn 750; Bertin 641; Wunsch, CM 3, no. 220.
31212	1876,1117.939	Promissory note for dates and silver. Nbn 26/9/14. Babylon. Nbn 808; Bertin 635; Wunsch, CM 3, no. 229.
31213	1876,1117.940	Receipt for payment of silver. Nbn 1/9/15. Babylon. Nbn 900; Bertin 661; Wunsch, CM 3, no. 238.
31214	1876,1117.941	Audit of beer supplies. Nbn 3/10/14 Nbn 815; Bertin 636.
31215	1876,1117.942	Receipt for silver for ilku duties. Nbn 13/12/13. Babylon. Nbn 741; Bertin 615; Wunsch, CM 3, no. 218.
31216	1876,1117.943	Promissory note for silver. Nbn 11/11/12. Babylon. Nbn 663; Bertin 581; Wunsch, CM 3, no. 205.

31217	1876,1117.944	Receipt of onions. Nbn 30/5/4. Šaḫrīn. Nbn 160; Bertin 402; Wunsch, CM 3, no. 132.
31218	1876,1117.945	Receipt for silver payment. Nbn 26/12/7 Nbn 276; Bertin 448; Wunsch, CM 3, no. 148.
31219	1876,1117.946	Promissory note for silver. Nbn 15/1/7. Babylon. Bertin 432.
31220	1876,1117.947	Hire of children for work. Nbn 11/2/15. Babylon. Nbn 843; Bertin 648; Wunsch, CM 3, no. 233.
31221	1876,1117.948	Receipt for partial payment of silver. Nbn 12/5/11. Babylon. Nbn 524; Bertin 532; Wunsch, CM 3, no. 188.
31222	1876,1117.949	Receipt of payment for urāšu service. Cyr 8/5/5. Babylon. Bertin 798; Wunsch, CM 3, no. 296.
31223	1876,1117.950	Promissory note for onions. Nbn 2/2/4 Nbn 141; Bertin 392; Wunsch, CM 3, no. 123.
31224	1876,1117.951	Account of barley. Cam 29/1/7. Cam 361; Bertin 982.
31225	1876,1117.952	Promissory note for silver. Dar 19/11/19. Babylon. Dar 49; Bertin 2412.
31226	1876,1117.953	Receipt of a person from Marduk-nāṣir-apli. Dar 9/7/26. Babylon. Bertin 2612; Abraham, BPPE, 276-278, no. 41.
31227	1876,1117.954	Receipt of ilku-tax by Marduk-nāṣir-apli. Dar 4/[]/25. Bāb-bitaqu. Bertin 2569; Abraham, BPPE, 279-280, no. 42.
31228	1876,1117.955	Contract; lease of a house. Dar -/2/19. Bīt-Ḫaḫḫūru. Dar 482; Bertin 2410.
31229	1876,1117.956	Promissory note for dates. Dar 10/[]/31. Šaḫrīn. Bertin 2701.
31230	1876,1117.957	Sale of a slave. Dar 4/12b/5. Babylon. Bertin 2067.
31231	1876,1117.958	Promissory note for silver. Dar 29/5/15. Babylon. Dar 401; Bertin 958.
31232	1876,1117.959	Contract; sale of a field. Dar 5/6/3 Dar 76; Bertin 1979.
31233	1876,1117.960	Promissory note for barley. Dar 8/4/21. Babylon. Dar 523; Bertin 2457.
31234	1876,1117.961	Promissory note for barley. Dar 29/8/2. Šaḫrīn. Dar 48; Bertin 1952.
31235	1876,1117.962	Deposition. Dar 3/8/13. Babylon. Dar 357; Bertin 2270.
31236	1876,1117.963	Letter from Širku to Nabû-šarrāni. CT 22, 39-40, no. 215; Hackl et al., AOAT 414/1, no. 52.
31237	1876,1117.964	Memorandum as to location of men.
31238	1876,1117.965	Receipt for silver.

31239	1876,1117.966	Contract about a dowry. Nbk 13/5/34. Babylon. Nbk 265; Strassmaier, Liverpool, 154; Bertin 161; Wunsch, CM 3, no. 13 (wrongly as 32139).
31240	1876,1117.967	Agreement to conclude a dispute about silver and barley. Nbk 25/6/41. Babylon. Nbk 379; Strassmaier, Liverpool, 161; Bertin 218; Wunsch, CM 3, no. 39.
31241	1876,1117.968	Promissory note for sheep and a garment. Nbk 23/4/38. Babylon. Nbk 333; Strassmaier, Liverpool, 156; Bertin 196; Wunsch, CM 3, no. 28.
31242	1876,1117.969	Promissory note for silver; finger-nail marks. Nbk 20/2/7. Babylon. Nbk 56; Bertin 42.
31243	1876,1117.970	Loan. Nbk 25/10/11. Bāṣ (LAM.KUR.RU.ki). Nbk 93; Bertin 69.
31244	1876,1117.971	Contract; sale of a field. AM 9/10/1. Babylon. Evetts, Ev-M 14; Strassmaier, Liverpool, 130; Sack, AOATS 4, no. 2; Bertin 272.
31245	1876,1117.972	Promissory note for silver. AM 4/5/2. Babylon. Evetts, Ev-M 24; Strassmaier, Liverpool, 135; Sack, AOATS 4, no. 60; Bertin 286.
31246	1876,1117.973	Contract; sale of a field. AM 15/12/1. Babylon. Evetts, Ev-M 16; Sack, AOATS 4, no. 4; Bertin 275.
31247	1876,1117.974	Promissory note for silver. AM 28/12/acc. Šubat-Gula. Evetts, Ev-M 8; Strassmaier, Liverpool, 127; Sack, AOATS 4, no. 59; Bertin 262; Wunsch, CM 3, no. 53.
31248	1876,1117.975	Promissory note for silver. Ner 1/3/1. Babylon. Evetts, Ner 16; Strassmaier, Liverpool, 112; Sack, AOAT 236, no. 16; Bertin 301.
31249	1876,1117.976	Slave given as dowry. Ner 29/10/acc. Babylon. Evetts, Ner 7a; Sack, AOAT 236, no. 7a; Bertin 294.
31250	1876,1117.977	Deposition. Cam 13/7/6. Babylon. Cam 322; Bertin 37.
31251	1876,1117.978	Hire of a slave. Nbn 14/5/8. Babylon. Nbn 299; Bertin 744.
31252	1876,1117.979	Promissory note for silver. Nbn 20/11/acc. Babylon. Nbn 15; Strassmaier, Liverpool, 40; Bertin 341; Wunsch, CM 3, no. 89.
31253	1876,1117.980	Contract; exchange of slave girls. Nbn 20/12a/12. Babylon. Nbn 679; Wunsch, AfO 44/45, 87, no. 17; Bertin 592.
31254	1876,1117.981	Contract; lease of a house. Nbn 25/2/15. Babylon. Nbn 845; Bertin 651.
31255	1876,1117.982	Receipt for delivery of barley. Nbn 29/11/16. Šaḫrīn. Nbn 1008; Bertin 681; Wunsch, CM 3, no. 246.

31256	1876,1117.983	Promissory note for dates. Nbn 20/11/1. Kūtû. Nbn 47; Strassmaier, Liverpool, 50; Bertin 355.
31257	1876,1117.984	Promissory note for dates. Nbn 11/5/11. Babylon. Nbn 523; Bertin 531.
31258	1876,1117.985	Promissory note for silver. Nbn 5/4/15. Bīt-šar-Bābili. Nbn 861; Bertin 653.
31259	1876,1117.986	Promissory note for barley and onions. Nbn 14/12/14. Šaḫrīn. Nbn 819; Bertin 638; Wunsch, CM 3, no. 230.
31260	1876,1117.987	Promissory note for barley; ḫarrānu. Nbn 22/1/1. Babylon. Nbn 19; Strassmaier, Liverpool, 45; Bertin 344; Wunsch, CM 3, no. 94.
31261	1876,1117.988	Receipt for payment of silver. Cyr 14/5/2. Babylon. Cyr 49; Bertin 763.
31262	1876,1117.989	Receipt of silver for urāšu service. Cyr 27/1/3. Babylon. Cyr 102; Bertin 782. Wunsch, CM 3, no. 283.
31263	1876,1117.990	Receipt of silver for urāšu service. Cyr 22/10/5. Cyr 212; Bertin 804. Wunsch, CM 3, no. 297.
31264	1876,1117.991	Receipt of silver. Cyr []/4/4. Babylon. Cyr 169; Bertin 795; Wunsch, CM 3, no. 293.
31265	1876,1117.992	Promissory note for silver. Cyr 23/12/7. Babylon. Bertin 1714; Wunsch, CM 3, no. 307.
31266	1876,1117.993	Audit of partnership under dissolution. Cyr 2/3/9. Borsippa. Cyr 338; Bertin 844.
31267	1876,1117.994	Receipt for payment of silver. Cam 22/11/6. Babylon. Cam 343; Bertin 966.
31268	1876,1117.995	Receipt for final payment for a slave girl. Cam 24/12/2. URU GU.KI. Cam 144; Bertin 885.
31269	1876,1117.996	Sale of a slave girl. Cam 30/6/5. Babylon. Cam 287; Bertin 932.
31270	1876,1117.997	Receipt for barley as imittu payment. Dar 4/7/13. Babylon. Bertin 2264.
31271	1876,1117.998	Contract; sale of a field. Dar 13/7/7 Dar 228; Bertin 2120.
31272	1876,1117.999	Contract; ḫarrānu. Dar 14/12/3. Babylon. Dar 97; Bertin 1977.
31273	1876,1117.1000	Contract; lease of a house; Egibi archive. Dar 18/10/33. Babylon. Bertin 2749.
31274	1876,1117.1001	Contract; lease of a house. Dar []/6/19. Babylon. Dar 485; Bertin 2419.
31275	1876,1117.1002	Account of vats.
31276	1876,1117.1003	Letter from Sūqāya to Nabû-aḫḫē-bulliṭ. Hackl et al., AOAT 414/1, no. 48.
31277	1876,1117.1004	Account of telittu tax payments.
31278	1876,1117.1005	Letter from Šadinnu to Širku. Hackl et al., AOAT 414/1, no. 53.

31279	1876,1117.1006	Letter from Marduk-ibni to Širku. CT 22, 22, no. 111; Hackl et al., AOAT 414/1, no. 54.
31280	1876,1117.1007	Receipt for dates or grain.
31281	1876,1117.1008	Account of silver payments.
31282	1876,1117.1009	Sale of a slave. Nbn 2/8/-. Babylon.
31283	1876,1117.1010	Account of silver payments.
31284	1876,1117.1011	Promissory note for barley.
31285	1876,1117.1012	Sale of a slave. (Ner?) 10/11/1. Wunsch, AfO 44/45, 74, no. 3.
31286	1876,1117.1013	Letter from Kalbāya to Iddināya. CT 22, 19, no. 96; Hackl et al., AOAT 414/1, no. 27.
31287	1876,1117.1014	Account of dates or grain.
31288	1876,1117.1015	Letter from Nabû-aḫu-[] to Marduk-nāṣir-apli. CT 22, 26, no. 138; Hackl et al., AOAT 414/1, no. 65.
31289	1876,1117.1016	Receipt for silver. Bertin 3005; Wunsch, CM 3, no. 365.
31290	1876,1117.1017	Letter from Nabû-zēru-šubši to f.Ṣikkû. CT 22, 28, no. 151; Hackl et al., AOAT 414/1, no. 17.
31291	1876,1117.1018	Memorandum; numbers, Aramaic note.
31292	1876,1117.1019	Letter from Kī-Bēl to Rēmūt-Bēl. CT 22, 19, no. 92; Ebeling, Neubab. Briefe, no. 92; Hackl et al., AOAT 414/1, no. 83.
31293	1876,1117.1020	Account of lumps of silver.
31294	1876,1117.1021	Letter from Rēmūt to Iddināya. CT 22, 35-36, no. 194; Hackl et al., AOAT 414/1, no. 7.
31295	1876,1117.1022	Addresses of two people.
31296	1876,1117.1023	Promissory note for silver. 1/[]/10. Babylon.
31297	1876,1117.1024	Addresses of people.
31298	1876,1117.1025	Contract; sale of a house; finger-nail marks with caption. Dar 10/12b/8 Dar 245; Bertin 2140-2141.
31299	1876,1117.1026	Sale of a slave girl; cf. 32071. Dar -/4/-. Babylon. Bertin 2795.
31300	1876,1117.1027	Sale of an ox. Dar 2/5/13. Bīt-Sikkānu. Dar 348; Bertin 2273.
31301	1876,1117.1028	Promissory note for silver. Cam 10/4/5. Babylon. Cam 279; Bertin 931; Wunsch, CM 3, no. 340.
31302	1876,1117.1029	Promissory note for dates. Dar 26/6/4. Alu-ša-Bēl-ittannu. Dar 127; Bertin 2066.
31303	1876,1117.1030	Sale of slaves. Cyr 23/5/4. Babylon. Cyr 171; Bertin 794.
31304	1876,1117.1031	Promissory note for wheat. Cam []/12/acc. Babylon. Wunsch, CM 3, no. 316.
31305	1876,1117.1032	Promissory note for silver and old vats. Nbn 29/1/9. Babylon. Nbn 326; Strassmaier, Liverpool, 93; Bertin 465; Wunsch, CM 3, no. 163.

31306	1876,1117.1033	Contract; exchange of barley and dates. Nbn []/4/12. Babylon. Nbn 616; Bertin 566.
31307	1876,1117.1034	Receipt for lime. Nbn 16/6/13. Babylon. Nbn 716; Bertin 606.
31308	1876,1117.1035	Promissory note for onions and silver. Ner 10/1/2. Babylon. Evetts, Ner 32; Sack, AOAT 236, no. 32; Bertin 310; Wunsch, CM 3, no. 71.
31309	1876,1117.1036	Promissory note for silver. AM 1/10/acc. Ḫursag-kalamma. Sack, AOATS 4, no. 77; Bertin 256.
31310	1876,1117.1037	Promissory note for silver. Cyr 6/9/8. Babylon. Cyr 321a; Bertin 833; Wunsch, CM 3, no. 309b.
31311	1876,1117.1038	Illegible.
31312	1876,1117.1039	Receipt for partial payment of debt. Nbn 27/3/12. Babylon. Nbn 603; Bertin 559.
31313	1876,1117.1040	Contract; lease of a house. Cyr 25/9/7. Babylon. Cyr 274; Bertin 825.
31314	1876,1117.1041	Promissory note for silver. Nbk 13/9/6. Borsippa. Nbk 53; Bertin 40.
31315	1876,1117.1042	Account of payments.
31316	1876,1117.1043	Contract; hire of a boat by Marduk-nāṣir-apli. Dar 9?/10/4. Babylon. Dar 138; Abraham, BPPE, 373-374, no. 90; Bertin 2030.
31317	1876,1117.1044	Promissory note for remainder of price of a slave. Dar 25/5/5. Babylon. Dar 165; Bertin 2061.
31318	1876,1117.1045	Audit of an account25/5/2. Babylon.
31319	1876,1117.1046	Receipt for payment of silver. Nbn 13/12/13. Babylon. Nbn 742; Bertin 616.
31320	1876,1117.1047	Receipt for a spade. Dar 15/5/18. Babylon. Dar 270; Bertin 2417.
31321	1876,1117.1048	Receipt for silver. Cyr 22/7/2. Babylon. Cyr 65; Bertin 764; Wunsch, CM 3, no. 279.
31322	1876,1117.1049	Receipt of ilku-tax by Marduk-nāṣir-apli. Dar 16/4/25. Babylon. Bertin 2583; Abraham, BPPE, 281-282, no. 43.
31323	1876,1117.1050	Contract for vats.7/9/4. Wunsch, CM 20A, p. 100.
31324	1876,1117.1051	Receipt for wood for building. Nbn 28/9/4. Babylon. Nbn 171; Bertin 406.
31325	1876,1117.1052	Promissory note for dates. Dar 10/6/12. Babylon. Dar 331; Bertin 2218.
31326	1876,1117.1053	Promissory note for silver as the price of a cow and onions; ḫarrānu. AM 23/7/1. Šaḫrīn. Evetts, Ev-M 12; Sack, AOATS 4, no. 32; Bertin 266, Wunsch, CM 3, no. 57.
31327	1876,1117.1054	Promissory note for dates. Nbn 22/5/15. Babylon. Nbn 874; Bertin 656.

31328	1876,1117.1055	Sale of a slave. Dar 2/5/3. Babylon. Dar 70; Bertin 1983.
31329	1876,1117.1056	Promissory note for emmer. [Cyr] 9/10/6. Babylon. Wunsch, CM 3, no. 304.
31330	1876,1117.1057	Promissory note for silver. Dar 12/12/25. URU maḫ-ra-a'. Bertin 2571 (copy confuses obv. and rev.).
31331	1876,1117.1058	Contract; lease. Nbk 16/11/-.
31332	1876,1117.1059	Promissory note for dates. Nbk 19/4/41. Babylon. Nbk 376; Bertin 214.
31333	1876,1117.1060	Promissory note for silver. Nbn 23/5/-. Babylon. Wunsch, AfO 42/43, 47, no. 1.
31334	1876,1117.1061	Promissory note for silver. Babylon. Wunsch, CM 20A, p. 17.
31335	1876,1117.1062	Promissory note for silver. Nbn []/[]/15 Wunsch, CM 3, no. 241.
31336	1876,1117.1063	Promissory note for barley. Nbn 6/1/1. Šaḫrın. Nbn 18; Strassmaier, Liverpool, 43; Bertin 343; Wunsch, CM 3, no. 92.
31337	1876,1117.1064	Receipt for payment of silver. Cam 11/10/5. Šaḫrīn. Bertin 935; Wunsch, CM 3, no. 342.
31338	1876,1117.1065	Contract; transfer of promise to pay silver. Cyr 23/6/4. Borsippa. Cyr 172; Bertin 789; Wunsch, CM 3, no. 294.
31339	1876,1117.1066	Promissory note for silver. Dar 17/7/2. Babylon. Dar 45; Bertin 1950.
31340	1876,1117.1067	Promissory note for silver. Cam 14/4/1. Babylon. Cam 43; Bertin 874; Wunsch, CM 3, no. 320.
31341	1876,1117.1068	Sale of a slave. Cam []/6/4. Babylon. Cam 245; Bertin 1000.
31342	1876,1117.1069	Deposition. Dar 5/6/20. Bīt-Ḫaḫḫūru. Dar 506; Bertin 2442.
31343	1876,1117.1070	Contract; sale of a house. -/8/-. Babylon.
31344	1876,1117.1071	Promissory note for barley. Nbn 29/8/10. Babylon. Nbn 451; Bertin 506.
31345	1876,1117.1072	Receipt for payment of silver.
31346	1876,1117.1073	Contract; sale of a field; finger-nail marks. Bertin 2984-2985; Wunsch, CM 20A-B, no. 130.
31347	1876,1117.1074	Receipt of miksu-toll from Marduk-nāṣir-apli. Dar 20/9/[]. Abraham, BPPE, 282-284, no. 44, and 550, no. 10; Abraham, NABU 1997, 46-51, no. 53.
31348	1876,1117.1075	Contract; sale of a field Wunsch, CM 20A-B, no. 173.
31349	1876,1117.1076	Promissory note for silver. Dar 10/2/-. Nār-ma-ka-si-Nār-[ ]. Bertin 2802.
31350	1876,1117.1077	Illegible.
31351	1876,1117.1078	Contract; lease of a house.

31352	1876,1117.1079	Receipt for a payment. 8/[]/6.
31353	1876,1117.1080	Account of dates owed under a contract.
31354	1876,1117.1081	Promissory note for silver. Nbn 13/8/[] Nbn 1110; Bertin 725.
31355	1876,1117.1082	Receipt for house rent agreed before judges; Egibi archive. Dar -/1/[33]. Bertin 2725; Sandowicz, dubsar 11, no. 47.
31356	1876,1117.1083	Promissory note for silver; five captions for seals but not sealed. Nbn 20/6/9. Babylon. Nbn 355; Roth, Fs Oelsner, 394-395; Bertin 474.
31357	1876,1117.1084	Contract for garments. Dar 10/11/10. Babylon. Dar 288; Bertin 2170.
31358	1876,1117.1085	Contract; lease of a house; Egibi archive. AM []/8/[]. Babylon. Sack, AOATS 4, no. 21; Bertin 290.
31359	1876,1117.1086	Summons to settle a debt of silver due to Marduk-nāṣir-apli's brother. Dar 15/1/14. Šaḫrīn. Dar 369; Abraham, BPPE, 417-418, no. 115; Bertin 2288.
31360	1876,1117.1087	Summons to settle debts with Marduk-nāṣir-apli. Dar 2/9/26. Bertin 2605; Abraham, BPPE, 284-286, no. 45.
31361	1876,1117.1088	Promissory note for silver. Nbn []/12/[]. Babylon. Bertin 721.
31362	1876,1117.1089	Promissory note for silver; ḫarrānu. Nbn 14/10/3. Babylon. Nbn 123; Bertin 383; Wunsch, CM 3, no. 117.
31363	1876,1117.1090	Contract; lease of a house; Egibi archive. Dar. Ḫursag-kalamma. Bertin 2772.
31364	1876,1117.1091	Sale of slave girls. Dar 11/12/8. Babylon. Dar 242; Bertin 2135 (as S+.1001).
31365	1876,1117.1092	Contract; lease of a house; Egibi archive.
31366	1876,1117.1093	Account of dates or grain.
31367	1876,1117.1094	Contract; division of property Wunsch, CM 20A-B, no. 47.
31368	1876,1117.1095	Promissory note for silver.
31369	1876,1117.1096	Promissory note for dates. Nbk []/[]/40. Bīt-šannabi. Nbk 373; Bertin 213.
31370	1876,1117.1097	Account Wunsch, CM 20A, n. 175.
31371	1876,1117.1098	Receipt for silver. Cam -/-/6. Bertin 949.
31372	1876,1117.1099	Receipt for delivery of dates. Dar 13/11/13. Babylon. Dar 361; Bertin 2266.
31373	1876,1117.1100	Promissory note for silver. Dar -/5/12. Babylon.
31374	1876,1117.1101	Promissory note for silver. Nbn 18/4/4. Babylon. Nbn 154; Bertin 399; Wunsch, CM 3, no. 129.
31375	1876,1117.1102	Sale of slaves; dupl. 31004 (Nbk. 201). Nbk 16/5/29. Borsippa. Wunsch, CM 3, no. 3.

31376	1876,1117.1103	Contract; lease of a house. Dar 28/12/5. Alu-ša-Kalbā. Dar 191.
31377	1876,1117.1104	List of boats rented and their owners.
31378	1876,1117.1105	Sale of a slave. Nbn []/[]/9. Babylon. Nbn 396; Bertin 490.
31379	1876,1117.1106	Receipt for payment of silver. 26/12/-. Babylon.
31380	1876,1117.1107	Memorandum about purchases with silver. Nbn 28/9/11. Nbn 557; Bertin 545.
31381	1876,1117.1108	Promissory note for silver. AM 21/8/1. Borsippa. Sack, AOATS 4, no. 1; Bertin 268.
31382	1876,1117.1109	Promissory note for dates. Cam 26/6/3. Babylon. Cam 173; Bertin 894.
31383	1876,1117.1110	Promissory note for dates; dupl. 31935. Dar 21/5/-. Babylon. Bertin 2778.
31384	1876,1117.1111	Promissory note for barley. Nbk []/3/[]. Babylon. Nbk 424; Bertin 252.
31385	1876,1117.1112	Promissory note for dates. Cam 14/4/2. Cam 110; Bertin 882.
31386	1876,1117.1113	Contract; lease. AM 11/1/2. Babylon. Sack, AOATS 4, no. 94; Bertin 278.
31387	1876,1117.1114	Promissory note for silver with interest. Nbn 22/10/[]. Nbn 1123; Bertin 445; Wunsch, CM 3, no. 257.
31388	1876,1117.1115	Promissory note for silver. Dar -/12b/8. Babylon. Dar 246; Bertin 2134.
31389	1876,1117.1116	Receipt for silver. Cam 28/9/5. Babylon.
31390	1876,1117.1117	Promissory note for silver. -/-/11. Babylon.
31391	1876,1117.1118	Receipt for delivery of [dates or barley]. 24/4/[]. Babylon. Wunsch, CM 3, no. 366.
31392	1876,1117.1119	Promissory note for silver. Nbn 10/12/9. Babylon. Nbn 389; Bertin 483.
31393	1876,1117.1120	Receipt of barley from Marduk-nāṣir-apli. Dar []/8/25. Babylon. Abraham, BPPE, 287-289, no. 46, and 549, no. 9.
31394	1876,1117.1121	Protocol of witnesses to an agreement. Nbn 17/5/acc. Bištu-ša-ṣinnatu. Nbn 5; Bertin 332; Wunsch, CM 3, no. 87.
31395	1876,1117.1122	Promissory note for dates. Nbn 8/-/-. Bertin 704.
31396	1876,1117.1123	Receipt of silver and onions. Cyr 7/4/9. Babylon. Cyr 340; Bertin 843; Wunsch, CM 3, no. 310.
31397	1876,1117.1124	Promissory note for silver. Nbk 5/[]/41. Šubat-Gula. Nbk 389; Bertin 225; Wunsch, CM 3, no. 43.
31398	1876,1117.1125	Deposition; sealed. Nbn 8/3/2. Babylon. Nbn 64; Bertin 362; Wunsch, AfO 44/45, 97, no. 32; Nisaba 28, no. 10.

31399	1876,1117.1126	Promissory note for silver. AM []/[]/1. Babylon. Evetts, Ev-M 9; Sack, AOATS 4, no. 5.
31400	1876,1117.1127	Sale for silver. 15/-/-.
31401	1876,1117.1128	Contract; lease of a field with additional clauses. Wunsch, CM 20A-B, no. 23.
31402	1876,1117.1129	Promissory note for silver. Cam []/11/6. Babylon. Cam 346; Bertin 945.
31403	1876,1117.1130	Hire of a slave.
31404	1876,1117.1131	Payment on loan of silver. -/3/10. Babylon.
31405	1876,1117.1132	Promissory note for barley?; mostly illegible.
31406	1876,1117.1133	Contract for purchase with silver. Nbn []/[]/4. Babylon. Nbn 181; Bertin 403.
31407	1876,1117.1134	Promissory note for silver. -/-/4. Babylon.
31408	1876,1117.1135	Receipt. 26/-/-. Babylon.
31409	1876,1117.1136	Receipt of payment for salaries and rations from Marduk-nāṣir-apli. Dar 20/9/23. Dar 572; Abraham, BPPE, 452-453, no. 135; Bertin 2509.
31410	1876,1117.1137	Sale of a slave. 7/6/-.
31411	1876,1117.1138	Promissory note for silver. 24/-/-. Taḫmakka.
31412	1876,1117.1139	Promissory note for silver. Cam 14/11/[]. Babylon. Cam 431; Bertin 992; Wunsch, CM 3, no. 348.
31413	1876,1117.1140	Medical; list of plants.
31414	1876,1117.1141	Promissory note for silver. Nbn 10/12/10. Babylon. Nbn 479; Bertin 515.
31415	1876,1117.1142	Contract; lease of a house. Cam 27/[]/6. Babylon. Cam 351; Bertin 941.
31416	1876,1117.1143	Letter from [] to Širku about ilku tax. (Dar I). Abraham, BPPE, 289-291, no. 47, and 551, no. 11; Hackl et al., AOAT 414/1, no. 55.
31417	1876,1117.1144	Letter from Iddin-Marduk to Madān-bēlu-uṣur. CT 22, 3, no. 8; Hackl et al., AOAT 414/1, no. 3.
31418	1876,1117.1145	Promissory note for silver; ḫarrānu. Wunsch, CM 3, no. 367.
31419	1876,1117.1146	Letter.
31420	1876,1117.1147	Text erased; doodles over original text which was an account of work of jewellers.
31421	1876,1117.1148	Promissory note for silver; ḫarrānu. Šaḫrīn. Wunsch, CM 3, no. 368
31422	1876,1117.1149	Promissory note for silver; ḫarrānu. Nbk 1/12/42. Šubat-Gula. Nbk 27; Bertin 20; Wunsch, CM 3, no. 49.
31423	1876,1117.1150	Contract; fixation of interest and pledge of property for a silver debt due to Šaddinnu from Marduk-nāṣir-apli; sealed. Dar 24/10/17. Babylon. + 31726. Dar

		453 (31726 only); Abraham, BPPE, 433-435, no. 125; Bertin 2369; Nisaba 28, no. 161.
31424	1876,1117.1151	Contract about the cultivation of dates on the property of Bēl by seven gardeners. Dar 27/[]/12. Šaḫrīn. Dar 342; Abraham, BPPE, 409-410, no. 111; Bertin 2212.
31425	1876,1117.1152	Divorce contract. [Dar] [9]/[1?]/[5]. Babylon? (+) 36799. Wunsch, Bab Arch 2, 32-39, no. 8.
31426	1876,1117.1153	Sale of slave girls. Cam 24/12/2. Upija. Cam 143; Bertin 878.
31427	1876,1117.1154	Receipt of silver from Marduk-nāṣir-apli as rent for a boat. Dar 22/10/23. Babylon. Dar 576; Abraham, BPPE, 455-456, no. 137; Bertin 2508.
31428	1876,1117.1155	Promissory note for silver and onions; ḫarrānu. Ner 7/12/acc. Babylon. Evetts, Ner 8a; Sack, AOAT 236, no. 8A; Wunsch, CM 3, no. 63.
31429	1876,1117.1156	Promissory note for onions. Cyr 7/10/2. Babylon. Cyr 76; Bertin 765; Wunsch, CM 3, no. 280.
31430	1876,1117.1157	Contract for bricks. Dupl. 31540. [10]/7/[acc]. Babylon.
31431	1876,1117.1158	Account of dates.
31432	1876,1117.1159	Deposition. Nbn 16/10/2. Babylon. Nbn 83; Bertin 370.
31433	1876,1117.1160	Contract about a ploughed field from a bow-fief, and about a plough-team of Marduk-nāṣir-apli. Dar 19/6b/11. Babylon. Dar 307; Abraham, BPPE, 396-397, no. 104; Bertin 2211.
31434	1876,1117.1161	Sale of slaves. Nbn 20/1/16. Babylon. Nbn 953; Bertin 670.
31435	1876,1117.1162	Contract about a payment of silver. []/[]/3. Wunsch, CM 3, no. 291.
31436	1876,1117.1163	Promissory note for dates with land given as pledge. Nbn [5]/[2]/[]. Šaḫrīn. Bertin 736; Wunsch, CM 3, no. 254b.
31437	1876,1117.1164	Receipt for payment of silver.
31438	1876,1117.1165	Letter from [Libluṭ] to [Dummuqu] about rikis qabli payment. (Dar I). Abraham, BPPE, 291-292, no. 48, and 552, no. 12; Kleber, ZABR 16 (2010) 67 and 69-70; Hackl et al., AOAT 414/1, no. 62.
31439	1876,1117.1166	Promissory note for silver. Nbk III 7/8/acc. Babylon. Nbk 7; Bertin 12; Lorenz, Nebukadnezar III/IV, p. 31.
31440	1876,1117.1167	Contract; sale of a field.
31441	1876,1117.1168	Receipt of purchased onions. Nbn 20/12b/3. Šaḫrīn. Nbn 130; Bertin 387; Wunsch, CM 3, no. 120.
31442	1876,1117.1169	Promissory note for silver. Nbn []/7/14. Babylon. Nbn 800; Bertin 630; Wunsch, CM 3, no. 227.

31443	1876,1117.1170	Incantation and ritual against a ghost of the dead. Ambos, Der König, 153 and 260.
31444	1876,1117.1171	Promissory note for dates. Cam 27/6/5. Babylon. Wunsch, CM 20A-B, no. 170.
31445	1876,1117.1172	Contract; ḫarrānu. -/8/3.
31446	1876,1117.1173	School text; bilingual incantation, Udug-ḫul 13-15; unidentified. Geller, Iraq 42, 27 and 48; Geller, BAM 8, 434-498, pl. 123.
31447	1876,1117.1174	List of people.
31448	1876,1117.1175	Astronomical.
31449	1876,1117.1176	Receipt of a man hired from Marduk-nāṣir-apli. Dar []/[]/23? Babylon. Abraham, BPPE, 292-293, no. 49, and 553, no. 13.
31450	1876,1117.1177	Chronicle of Artaxerxes III's 14th year. Strassmaier, 8th Orientalist Congress, no. 28; Grayson, TCS 5, Chronicle 9; S. Smith, BHT, 148-149; Bertin 2874.
31451	1876,1117.1178	Contract; ḫarrānu. -/-/12. Babylon.
31452	1876,1117.1179	Account of payments.
31453	1876,1117.1180	Promissory note for silver. 20/[]/5. Babylon.
31454	1876,1117.1181	Promissory note for silver owed to Murānu; sealed. SE RN lost []/3/[4]4. Babylon. Jursa, Persika 9, 207; Nisaba 28, no. 569.
31455	1876,1117.1182	Sale of a slave girl.
31456	1876,1117.1183	Illegible. Cyr.
31457	1876,1117.1184	Letter from Itti-Marduk-balāṭu to Iddin-Marduk. CT 22, 21-22, no. 110; Hackl et al., AOAT 414/1, no. 23.
31458	1876,1117.1185	Receipt of imittu payment. Dar []/[]/24. Wunsch, CM 20A-B, no. 196.
31459	1876,1117.1186	Promissory note for silver.
31460	1876,1117.1187	Promissory note for silver. Wunsch, CM 3, no. 369.
31461	1876,1117.1188	Promissory note for dates and barley. Cam 7/11/5. Šaḫrīn. Cam 292; Bertin 989.
31462	1876,1117.1189	Receipt for silver payment. 19/4/7.
31463	1876,1117.1190	Addresses of people.
31464	1876,1117.1191	Contract. 14/2/-.
31465	1876,1117.1192	Promissory note for silver.
31466	1876,1117.1193	Contract; sale of a house.
31467	1876,1117.1194	Promissory note for silver.
31468	1876,1117.1195	Contract; hire of a boat. 14/2/-. Babylon.
31469	1876,1117.1196	Receipt for payment of silver. Dar 25/10/[]. Wunsch, CM 3, no. 312.
31470	1876,1117.1197	Receipt of silver as the price of a house sale. AM 1/[]/[].
31471	1876,1117.1198	Promissory note for silver. -/-/6. Babylon.

31472	1876,1117.1199	Promissory note for dates. Nbn. Wunsch, CM 20A-B, no. 46.
31473	1876,1117.1200	Dialogue contract between Murānu and the administrators of Esangila; sealed. SE Ant I & Ant 13/7/46. CT 49, 23, no. 115; Jursa, Persika 9, 140-143; Nisaba 28, no. 570.
31474	1876,1117.1201	Astronomical Diary for SE 125. LBAT 334. Sachs, PTRSL A.276, 49, fig. 12; Sachs and Hunger, ADART II, no. -186 C.
31475	1876,1117.1202	Bilingual incantation.
31476	1876,1117.1203	Astronomical Diary for SE 142. LBAT 370. Sachs, PTRSL A.276, 49, fig. 11; Sachs and Hunger, ADART II, no. -169.
31477	1876,1117.1204	Promissory note for silver and onions; ḫarrānu. Wunsch, CM 3, no. 370.
31478	1876,1117.1205	Contract; division of property.
31479	1876,1117.1206	Contract; ḫarrānu. Nbk []/12b/42? Nbk 409; Bertin 21.
31480	1876,1117.1207	Contract; ḫarrānu. Nbk 9/[]/30. Šaḫrīn. Nbk 231; Bertin 151.
31481	1876,1117.1208	Account of various expenditures, ḫarrānu. [Nbn] x+4/[]/acc. Bertin 740-741; CM 20A-B, no. 54.
31482	1876,1117.1209	Names and addresses of men; census.
31483	1876,1117.1210	Field plan. Nemet-Nejat, LB Field Plans, no. 70, pls. 38-38.
31484	1876,1117.1211	Promissory note for silver. Nbn []/[]/17. Babylon. Nbn 1057; Bertin 702.
31485	1876,1117.1212	Contract; sale of a house; dupl. Dar 140. Dar 22/10/4. Babylon.
31486	1876,1117.1213	Promissory note for silver. Nbk -/5/18. Bertin 88.
31487	1876,1117.1214	Promissory note for onions. Nbk 19/5/42. Šubat-Gula. Nbk 400; Bertin 229; Wunsch, CM 3, no. 46.
31488	1876,1117.1215	Contract; ḫarrānu; dupl. 31098 (Neb 58). Nbk 17/5/[]. Babylon. Nbk 429; Bertin 242.
31489	1876,1117.1216	Deposition. Nbk 16/2/39. Babylon. Nbk 344; Bertin 193; Wunsch, CM 3, no. 20.
31490	1876,1117.1217	Promissory note for dates. Nbk 16/5/[]. Babylon. Nbk 428; Bertin 240.
31491	1876,1117.1218	Contract about division of purchased onions. AM 8/12/acc. Babylon. Sack, AOATS 4, no. 23; Bertin 260; Wunsch, CM 3, no. 51.
31492	1876,1117.1219	Sale of a slave; dupl. 30915. Cyr 26/5/3. Babylon. Cyr 120a; Bertin 853.
31493	1876,1117.1220	Contract. Nbn. Upija. Bertin 463.

31494	1876,1117.1221	Promissory note for silver as the price of wool. Nbn 20/[]/11. Babylon. Nbn 581; Bertin 551; Wunsch, CM 3, no. 195.
31495	1876,1117.1222	Account of plucked dates. Nbn -/3/13 Nbn 708; Bertin 603.
31496	1876,1117.1223	Contract for remaining dowry. Nbn 30/6/4 Nbn 165; Bertin 404.
31497	1876,1117.1224	Loan; now almost illegible. Nbn 20/[]/10. Babylon. Bertin 517.
31498	1876,1117.1225	Sale of a slave girl. Nbn 4/3/14. Babylon. Nbn 765; Bertin 622.
31499	1876,1117.1226	Promissory note for dates and onions. Nbn 18/2/3. Nbn 100; Bertin 425; Wunsch, CM 3, no. 111.
31500	1876,1117.1227	Promissory note for dates. Nbn 5/5/2. Babylon. Nbn 71; Bertin 367; Wunsch, CM 3, no. 107.
31501	1876,1117.1228	Promissory note for silver. Nbn 4/9/acc. Babylon. Nbn 8; Strassmaier, Liverpool, 35; Bertin 333.
31502	1876,1117.1229	Promissory note for dates. Nbn 10/8/13. Babylon. Nbn 724; Bertin 609.
31503	1876,1117.1230	Promissory note for silver. Cyr 30/3/3. Babylon. Cyr 114; Bertin 773.
31504	1876,1117.1231	Promissory note for barley. Cyr -/12/-. Babylon. Bertin 1769.
31505	1876,1117.1232	Sale of a slave girl. Cam []/1/7. Babylon. Cam 362; Bertin 986.
31506	1876,1117.1233	Receipt for interest on a loan. Cam 3/[]/5. Babylon. Cam 301; Bertin 934.
31507	1876,1117.1234	Receipt of silver as the price of a slave. Cam 2/9/acc. Babylon. Cam 8; Bertin 861; Wunsch, CM 3, no. 315.
31508	1876,1117.1235	Contract; sale of a house; finger-nail marks; sealed. Nbk III 20/7/acc. Babylon. Nbk 4; Strassmaier, Liverpool, 136; Bertin 9-10; Lorenz, Nebukadnezar III/IV, p. 31; Nisaba 28, no. 107.
31509	1876,1117.1236	Promissory note for silver; dupl. 30135. Dar 22/1/12. Babylon. Dar 319; Bertin 2225.
31510	1876,1117.1237	Promissory note for silver. Dar 27/2/14. Babylon. Dar 372; Bertin 2298.
31511	1876,1117.1238	Promissory note for silver. Dar 8/[]/21. Babylon. Dar 531; Bertin 2460.
31512	1876,1117.1239	Sale contract. Dar 11/11/31. Babylon.
31513	1876,1117.1240	Promissory note for dates. Dar 18/6/2. Babylon. Bertin 1940; Roth, JAOS 111, 19-37 and n. 24; Wunsch, CM 20A-B, no. 99.

31514	1876,1117.1241	Contract; sale of land; receipt of purchase price; dupl. 31049 (Dar 488). Dar 5/10/19. Babylon. Wunsch, CM 20A-B, no. 216 B; Bertin 2775.
31515	1876,1117.1242	Deposition. Dar 9/5/17. Bīt-Ṭāb-Bēl. Bertin 2384.
31516	1876,1117.1243	Promissory note for silver. Dar 25/7/24. Babylon. Bertin 2522.
31517	1876,1117.1244	Receipt of ilku-tax by Marduk-nāṣir-apli. Dar 25/[]/25. Babylon. Bertin 2557; Abraham, BPPE, 294-295, no. 50.
31518	1876,1117.1245	Receipt for partial repayment of a loan. Dar []/1/5. Babylon. Dar 157; Bertin 2062.
31519	1876,1117.1246	Purchase of vats. Dar 3/6/5. Babylon. Dar 168; Bertin 2055.
31520	1876,1117.1247	Receipt for silver. Dar 27/11/-. Bertin 2779.
31521	1876,1117.1248	Contract; exchange of fields. Dar 2/1/10. Babylon. + 42210. Dar 265; Bertin 2184-2185.
31522	1876,1117.1249	Contract; lease of a house. Dar 3/9/6. Borsippa. Dar 210; Bertin 2102.
31523	1876,1117.1250	Receipt for the return of household furnishings. Dar []/[]/2. Babylon. Dar 57; Bertin 1945; Wunsch, CM 3, no. 350.
31524	1876,1117.1251	Contract; sale of a field. Dar 13/2/10. Babylon. Dar 267; Bertin 2785.
31525	1876,1117.1252	Promissory note for dates. Dar 3/6/-. Bertin 2804.
31526	1876,1117.1253	Receipt for silver payment. Dar 7/12/9. Babylon. Dar 262; Bertin 2158.
31527	1876,1117.1254	Promissory note for dates. Dar 28/10/12. Babylon. Dar 335; Bertin 2239.
31528	1876,1117.1255	Receipt of silver by Marduk-nāṣir-apli's brother as payment for rikis qabli. Dar 26/5/26. Babylon. Bertin 2614; Abraham, BPPE, 296-297, no. 51.
31529	1876,1117.1256	Sale of a slave. Dar 9/2/22. Babylon. Dar 537; Bertin 2479.
31530	1876,1117.1257	Promissory note for silver. Dar 15/12/-. Babylon. Bertin 2805.
31531	1876,1117.1258	Deposition. Dar 8/3/5. Babylon. Dar 159; Bertin 2063.
31532	1876,1117.1259	Promissory note for barley. Dar 27/11/13. Alu-ša-Nabû-zēra-iqīša. Dar 363; Bertin 2255.
31533	1876,1117.1260	Receipt of ilku-tax by Marduk-nāṣir-apli. Dar 1/12/25. Šabilu. Bertin 2573; Abraham, BPPE, 298-299, no. 52.
31534	1876,1117.1261	List of men.

31535	1876,1117.1262	Court record; about a claim for a slave; sealed. Nbn 27/1/[11+]. Nbn 495; Bertin 708-709; Wunsch, AfO 44/45, 97-98, no. 33; Nisaba 28, no. 19.
31536	1876,1117.1263	Contract?
31537	1876,1117.1264	List of workmen.
31538	1876,1117.1265	Contract; record of deposit of silver in elephant staters; Murānu archive; sealed. SE. CT 49, 45, no. 173; Jursa, NABU 2001, 98-100, no. 102; Stolper, Annali Supp. 77, 25-28, no. 8; Jursa, Persika 9, 175, 200; Nisaba 28, no. 607.
31539	1876,1117.1266	Astronomical Diary for SE 118. Sachs and Hunger, ADART II, no. -193 C.
31540	1876,1117.1267	Contract for bricks. Dupl. 31430. 10/7/acc. Babylon.
31541	1876,1117.1268	Account of silver payments.
31542	1876,1117.1269	Account of irbu payments of barley. -/-/14.
31543	1876,1117.1270	Promissory note for barley and other commodities.
31544	1876,1117.1271	List of slaves.
31545	1876,1117.1272	Promissory note for silver. Wunsch, CM 20A-B, no. 146.
31546	1876,1117.1273	Court record; sealed. Nbn. Bertin 716; Roth, AfO 36/37, 48, no. 1; Roth, Fs Oelsner, 388-390 and 399; Nisaba 28, no. 16.
31547	1876,1117.1274	Court record. Dar 28/6/16. Dar 429; Bertin 2348.
31548	1876,1117.1275	Promissory note for silver. []/12/[]. Babylon.
31549	1876,1117.1276	Receipt for purchases. -/12/-. Babylon.
31550	1876,1117.1277	Contract; ḫarrānu.
31551	1876,1117.1278	List of names and addresses.
31552	1876,1117.1279	Receipt for payment of silver.
31553	1876,1117.1280	Promissory note for dates. 27/[]/8. Wunsch, CM 20A-B, no. 158.
31554	1876,1117.1281	Receipt of silver from Marduk-nāṣir-apli as rent for a boat; day 11 or 21. [Dar I] 11?/10/23. Babylon. Abraham, BPPE, 299-301, no. 53, and 554, no. 14.
31555	1876,1117.1282	Promissory note for silver. Dar 10+/5/-.
31556	1876,1117.1283	Contract about silver to be given as a dowry. Nbk 22/2/33. Babylon. Nbk 254; Bertin 158; Wunsch, CM 3, no. 9.
31557	1876,1117.1284	Promissory note for silver. Nbk 10/1/37. Babylon. Nbk 316; Bertin 180.
31558	1876,1117.1285	Promissory note for silver. Ner 30/8/1. Babylon. Evetts, Ner 27; Strassmaier, Liverpool, 117; Sack, ZA 68 143; Sack, AOAT 236, no. 27; Bertin 308.
31559	1876,1117.1286	Sale of a slave girl. Nbn 10/2/[]. Babylon. Nbn 1068; Bertin 732.

31560	1876,1117.1287	Promissory note for silver. Nbn 22/5/16. Babylon. Bertin 1604; Wunsch, CM 3, no. 243.
31561	1876,1117.1288	Promissory note for silver; the reverse is now disintegrated. Nbn 10/[]/[]. Babylon. Nbn 1120; Bertin 733.
31562	1876,1117.1289	Sale of a slave. Nbn 23/4/11. Babylon. Nbn 518; Bertin 529; Wunsch, AfO 44/45, 79-80, no. 8.
31563	1876,1117.1290	Contract; transfer of an obligation to deliver onions; ḫarrānu. Nbn []/[]/4. Šaḫrīn. Bertin 723; Wunsch, CM 3, no. 134.
31564	1876,1117.1291	Promissory note for silver. Nbn 11/4/9. Babylon. Bertin 1353.
31565	1876,1117.1292	Promissory note for barley. Nbn 5/5/11. Babylon. Nbn 520; Bertin 530.
31566	1876,1117.1293	Promissory note for silver and a sheep. Nbn 11/2/4. Šaḫrīn. Nbn 145; Bertin 393; Wunsch, CM 3, no. 124.
31567	1876,1117.1294	Receipt for the provision of two urāšu workmen for earth moving. Nbn 9/8/12. Babylon. Nbn 632; Bertin 1450; Wunsch, CM 3, no. 202.
31568	1876,1117.1295	Receipt of payment for urāšu service. Cyr 3/2/6. Babylon. Cyr 224; Bertin 810; Wunsch, CM 3, no. 302.
31569	1876,1117.1296	Economic. Cam 4/10/[]. Babylon. Cam 429; Bertin 999.
31570	1876,1117.1297	Promissory note for dates. Cam 27/8/6. Babylon. Cam 326; Bertin 970.
31571	1876,1117.1298	Promissory note for division of dates. Dar 1/6/16. Nāru-eššu. Dar 425; Bertin 2342.
31572	1876,1117.1299	Receipt of barley from Marduk-nāṣir-apli. Dar 7/4/25. Babylon. Bertin 2567; Abraham, BPPE, 301-303, no. 54.
31573	1876,1117.1300	Receipt for payment for a garment. Dar 29/1/19. Babylon. Dar 481; Bertin 2413.
31574	1876,1117.1301	Promissory note for dates. Dar 21/6/21. Babylon. Bertin 2453.
31575	1876,1117.1302	Promissory note for silver. Dar -/4/-. Bertin 2801.
31576	1876,1117.1303	Promissory note for silver. Dar 2/6/3. Babylon. Dar 75; Bertin 1988.
31577	1876,1117.1304	Promissory note for dates. Dar 11/6/8. Babylon. Dar 237; Bertin 2136.
31578	1876,1117.1305	Purchase of dates. Dar 28/12/20. Babylon. Dar 515; Bertin 2438.
31579	1876,1117.1306	Letter.
31580	1876,1117.1307	Receipt; Murānu archive; sealed. SE []/[]/90. CT 49, 43, no. 168; Jursa, Persika 9, 197-198; Nisaba 28, no. 655.

31581	1876,1117.1308	Astronomical Diary for SE 127. LBAT 335; Sachs and Hunger, ADART II, no. -184 A.
31582	1876,1117.1309	Account of silver for wool and telittu-tax.
31583	1876,1117.1310	Astronomical Diary for SE 119. Sachs and Hunger, ADART II, no. -192.
31584	1876,1117.1311	Account of silver payments.
31585	1876,1117.1312	Receipt for silver as the price of a slave. Cyr 21/12/[]. Babylon. Cyr 362; Bertin 852; Wunsch, CM 3, no. 313.
31586	1876,1117.1313	Contract; lower left corner.
31587	1876,1117.1314	Contract; witnesses; lower edge.
31588	1876,1117.1315	Contract; ḫarrānu.
31589	1876,1117.1316	Contract. d.l. Wunsch, AfO 44/45, 80-81, no. 9.
31590	1876,1117.1317	Promissory note for dates and date products.
31591	1876,1117.1318	Promissory note for silver.
31592	1876,1117.1319	Astronomical; Almanac for SE 245. + 31635 + 32242 + 32612 + 1876,1117.2539. LBAT 1179-1180 (32242 + 32612 only); Hunger and Sachs, ADART VII, no. 199.
31593	1876,1117.1320	Written off.
31594	1876,1117.1321	Illegible.
31595	1876,1117.1322	Account of barley deliveries. 22/3/-.
31596	1876,1117.1323	Account of deliveries.
31597	1876,1117.1324	Receipt for silver; upper edge.
31598	1876,1117.1325	Promissory note for dates and silver.
31599	1876,1117.1326	Promissory note.
31600	1876,1117.1327	Promissory note for [dates?] and onions. [Nbn] 5/[]/13. Šaḫrīn. Wunsch, CM 3, no. 219.
31601	1876,1117.1328	Contract; sale of a field.
31602	1876,1117.1329	Contract for wool. Babylon.
31603	1876,1117.1330	Contract; sale of land.
31604	1876,1117.1331	Promissory note for silver. -/-/24.
31605	1876,1117.1332	Contract; lease of a house; Egibi archive. 25/[]/3. Babylon.
31606	1876,1117.1333	Promissory note for dates or grain.
31607	1876,1117.1334	Promissory note for silver.
31608	1876,1117.1335	Promissory note for barley.
31609	1876,1117.1336	Contract; sale of a field.
31610	1876,1117.1337	Sale of slaves.
31611	1876,1117.1338	Letter from Madān-bēlu-uṣur to Širku. Dar -/-/8. + 31831. Bertin 2130 (31611 only); Hackl et al., AOAT 414/1, no. 41.
31612	1876,1117.1339	Promissory note for dates with land given as pledge. Nbn 5/2/[]. Šaḫrīn. Wunsch, CM 3, no. 254a.
31613	1876,1117.1340	Illegible.

31614	1876,1117.1341	Promissory note for beer.
31615	1876,1117.1342	Contract about a dowry.
31616	1876,1117.1343	Sale of a slave. Nbn 22/10/11. Nbn 564; Bertin 541; Wunsch, CM 3, no. 191.
31617	1876,1117.1344	Promissory note for barley. -/11/10.
31618	1876,1117.1345	Deposition. 2/3/9.
31619	1876,1117.1346	Contract for repayment of remaining silver.
31620	1876,1117.1347	Contract; lease of a house.
31621	1876,1117.1348	Contract; sale of a field.
31622	1876,1117.1349	Receipt for payment of silver. Nbn []/[]/6.
31623	1876,1117.1350	Promissory note for dates.
31624	1876,1117.1351	Contract; witnesses; lower left corner.
31625	1876,1117.1352	Inventory of household furnishings. 27/-/-.
31626	1876,1117.1353	Deposition.
31627	1876,1117.1354	Contract; sale of a field. + 32176.
31628	1876,1117.1355	Contract for repayment of remaining silver(?); upper left corner; reverse blank.
31629	1876,1117.1356	Contract; lease of a house. Dar -/10/-. Babylon.
31630	1876,1117.1357	Contract for vats. 25/[]/1.
31631	1876,1117.1358	List of names and places.
31632	1876,1117.1359	Deposition.
31633	1876,1117.1360	Astronomical.
31634	1876,1117.1361	Economic; right edge.
31635	1876,1117.1362	Joined to 31592.
31636	1876,1117.1363	Promissory note for silver; lower edge.
31637	1876,1117.1364	Note about silver; upper edge; reverse blank.
31638	1876,1117.1365	Illegible.
31639	1876,1117.1366	Contract; witnesses.
31640	1876,1117.1367	Contract; lease of a house; Egibi archive.
31641	1876,1117.1368	Receipt of silver from Marduk-nāṣir-apli as purchase price of a boat; dupl. 30961. Dar 12/6/26. Babylon. + 31667. Abraham, BPPE, 304, no. 55, and 555, no. 15.
31642	1876,1117.1369	Contract.
31643	1876,1117.1370	Contract; lower left corner.
31644	1876,1117.1371	Receipt of miksu-toll for an onion-boat. Nbn 20+/[3]/[17]. Wunsch, CM 3, no. 251.
31645	1876,1117.1372	Receipt for repayment of silver; lower right corner.
31646	1876,1117.1373	Astronomical Diary.
31647	1876,1117.1374	Promissory note for barley. Wunsch, CM 20A-B, no. 20.
31648	1876,1117.1375	Promissory note for silver; fragment from centre.
31649	1876,1117.1376	Receipt for payment.
31650	1876,1117.1377	Promissory note for silver and onions. Nbk []/2/41. Šaḫrīn. Wunsch, CM 3, no. 37.
31651	1876,1117.1378	Contract; hire of a boat.

31652	1876,1117.1379	Contract; division of fields. Dar 4/10/18. Wunsch, CM 20A, p. 167, n. 347.
31653	1876,1117.1380	Sale of slaves.
31654	1876,1117.1381	Promissory note for barley and wheat. 25/3/-. Babylon.
31655	1876,1117.1382	Contract; lease of a house; Egibi archive. Dar 15/7/7. Bertin 2110.
31656	1876,1117.1383	Promissory note for silver. Cam -/-/4.
31657	1876,1117.1384	Promissory note for dates. Nbk -/-/41. Babylon.
31658	1876,1117.1385	Promissory note for dates. Nbk 4/5/42. Babylon.
31659	1876,1117.1386	Contract; sale of a field? Dar -/1/7. Babylon.
31660	1876,1117.1387	Promissory note for silver. Dar 19/4/15. Babylon.
31661	1876,1117.1388	Sale of slaves. Nbn 8/5/13. Babylon.
31662	1876,1117.1389	Contract for wine. Nbn 15/11/16.
31663	1876,1117.1390	Contract; lower right corner.
31664	1876,1117.1391	Audit of a partnership. Babylon.
31665	1876,1117.1392	Promissory note for dates. Dar 26/2/6. Babylon.
31666	1876,1117.1393	Promissory note for wheat. Cam 11/9/-. Babylon. Bertin 1800.
31667	1876,1117.1394	Joined to 31641.
31668	1876,1117.1395	Promissory note for silver. 15/[]/32.
31669	1876,1117.1396	Promissory note for silver. Cam 1/4/-.
31670	1876,1117.1397	Deposition. Nbn 29/12/-. Babylon.
31671	1876,1117.1398	Contract; division of property. Nbk.
31672	1876,1117.1399	Court record. 29/7/9. Babylon. Wunsch, CM 20A-B, no. 84.
31673	1876,1117.1400	Contract; lease of a house. Nbn -/3/-. Babylon.
31674	1876,1117.1401	Sale of a slave. Nbn 10/6/5. Babylon.
31675	1876,1117.1402	Receipt for final payment for a house. Nbn 22/7/[]. Babylon. Nbn 1104; Bertin 734.
31676	1876,1117.1403	Court record. Nbk 21/2/3. (+) 34392 Wunsch, AfO 44/45, 90-91, no. 21.
31677	1876,1117.1404	Contract; lease of a house.
31678	1876,1117.1405	Promissory note for silver. Cyr 20/8/5. Babylon.
31679	1876,1117.1406	Promissory note for silver. Cyr 3/8/7. Babylon.
31680	1876,1117.1407	Promissory note for silver. Dar 25/-/-. + 32139.
31681	1876,1117.1408	Court record; caption for a seal, but seal lost. Nbn 7/5/5. Babylon. Wunsch, AfO 44/45, 93, no. 23.
31682	1876,1117.1409	Promissory note for silver. Dar 16/10/-. Babylon.
31683	1876,1117.1410	Receipt for barley delivery. Dar 2/[]/14.
31684	1876,1117.1411	Purchase of beer. Dar.
31685	1876,1117.1412	Sale of slaves. Nbn 6/1/-. Babylon.
31686	1876,1117.1413	Receipt for delivery of seed. Nbn 11/12/-.
31687	1876,1117.1414	Receipt. Nbn 23/6/12. Babylon.

31688	1876,1117.1415	Promissory note for silver. Nbk 21/4/41. Babylon. Nbk 377; Bertin 215.
31689	1876,1117.1416	Promissory note for dates. Dar 1/[]/8. Babylon.
31690	1876,1117.1417	Joined to 30658.
31691	1876,1117.1418	Receipt about the sale of a share in a field. Wunsch, CM 20A-B, no. 68.
31692	1876,1117.1419	Promissory note for silver.
31693	1876,1117.1420	Will of Itti-Marduk-balāṭu, disposing of land and slaves to his family; dupl. 31698. 12/10/acc. Borsippa. Wunsch, CM 3, no. 260b.
31694	1876,1117.1421	Promissory note for silver.
31695	1876,1117.1422	Contract.
31696	1876,1117.1423	Deposition. 29/9/-.
31697	1876,1117.1424	Contract; lease of a house. Cyr []/6/6. Cyr 231; Bertin 809; Wunsch, CM 3, no. 303.
31698	1876,1117.1425	Will of Itti-Marduk-balāṭu, disposing of land and slaves to his family; dupl. 31693. Cyr 12/10/acc. Borsippa. + 31743. Wunsch, CM 3, no. 260a.
31699	1876,1117.1426	Promissory note for seed.
31700	1876,1117.1427	Receipt of silver as payment for urāšu work. Nbn 16/5/13. Babylon. Nbn 713; Bertin 604; Wunsch, CM 3, no. 213.
31701	1876,1117.1428	Contract; sale of a house. Nbn 27/6/6. Babylon. Nbn 238; Bertin 429.
31702	1876,1117.1429	Purchase of dates. Babylon.
31703	1876,1117.1430	Note about onions. Cyr 24/3/2. Cyr 41; Bertin 1680; Wunsch, CM 3, no. 272.
31704	1876,1117.1431	Promissory note for dates? [Nbn] 23/[]/10. Babylon. Wunsch, CM 3, no. 183.
31705	1876,1117.1432	Contract; sale of a field. Dar 5/7/2. Nuḫšānītu. Bertin 1953; Wunsch, CM 20A, n. 274.
31706	1876,1117.1433	Contract. Cam 5/8/4. Ḫumadēšu. Cam 251; Bertin 925.
31707	1876,1117.1434	Contract; lease of a house; Egibi archive. Dar 9/11/31. Babylon. Bertin 2703.
31708	1876,1117.1435	Contract; witnesses; lower edge.
31709	1876,1117.1436	Promissory note for silver. -/-/12. Babylon.
31710	1876,1117.1437	Promissory note for silver; lower edge.
31711	1876,1117.1438	Sale of a slave girl. Nbn 15/[]/10.
31712	1876,1117.1439	Contract; lease. Dar 4/1/15. Babylon. Dar 398; Bertin 2284.
31713	1876,1117.1440	Promissory note for silver. Nbk 15/6/41. Babylon.
31714	1876,1117.1441	Promissory note for dates. Dar 2/6/25. URU Ṭa-a-bi-Bēl. Bertin 2582.
31715	1876,1117.1442	Astronomical; eclipses.

31716	1876,1117.1443	Promissory note for silver. Dar 15/7/16. Babylon.
31717	1876,1117.1444	Contract; sale of a field. + 31783. Bertin 2982 (31717 only).
31718	1876,1117.1445	Receipt of dates and barley by Marduk-nāṣir-apli. Abraham, BPPE, 306-307, no. 57, and 557, no. 17.
31719	1876,1117.1446	Promissory note for silver. Dar 28/8/15. Bīt-Ḫaḫḫūru. Dar 412; Bertin 2327.
31720	1876,1117.1447	Excerpted rituals.
31721	1876,1117.1448	Contract; transfer of property. Wunsch, Bab Arch 2, 82-83, no. 22.
31722	1876,1117.1449	Promissory note to pay a debt of silver to Marduk-nāṣir-apli; dupl. 30994. Dar 5/7/26. Babylon. + 35235. Bertin 2611 (31722 only); Abraham, BPPE, 308-309, no. 58.
31723	1876,1117.1450	Promissory note for dates. Nbn 10/6/9. Nāru-eššu. Nbn 353; Bertin 473.
31724	1876,1117.1451	Contract for dowry. Cyr 3/5/5. Babylon. Cyr 198; Bertin 799.
31725	1876,1117.1452	Astronomical Diary.
31726	1876,1117.1453	Joined to 31423.
31727	1876,1117.1454	Contract; sale of a field; finger-nail marks; dupl. 32000 (Nbn 437). [Nbn] [8]/[6b]/[10]. [Babylon]. + 32156. Wunsch, CM 20A-B, no. 64 B.
31728	1876,1117.1455	Promissory note for silver; Murānu archive; sealed. SE Ant I & Ant 2/3/51. Babylon. + 32956 + 42052. Jursa, Persika 9, 75, 189, 207, 212 (32956 + 42052 only); Nisaba 28, no. 573.
31729	1876,1117.1456	Contract.
31730	1876,1117.1457	Astronomical Diary.
31731	1876,1117.1458	Astronomical Diary for SE 45?
31732	1876,1117.1459	Promissory note.
31733	1876,1117.1460	Promissory note for dates; ḫarrānu. 29/[]/[]. Wunsch, CM 3, no. 371.
31734	1876,1117.1461	Promissory note for silver.
31735	1876,1117.1462	Contract; division of property. 4/-/-. Babylon.
31736	1876,1117.1463	Contract; sale of land.
31737	1876,1117.1464	Contract; sale of land. Dar 24/1/18. Babylon. Dar 465; Bertin 2398.
31738	1876,1117.1465	Deposition. Nbn 19/1/16. + 33145. Nbn 954 (31738 only); Bertin 671; Wunsch, CM 20A-B, no. 166.
31739	1876,1117.1466	Commentary.
31740	1876,1117.1467	Promissory note for silver with slaves as collateral.
31741	1876,1117.1468	Promissory note for silver. Nbn 1/-/-.
31742	1876,1117.1469	List of people.
31743	1876,1117.1470	Joined to 31698.

31744	1876,1117.1471	Contract; only witnesses remain; lower left corner.
31745	1876,1117.1472	Promissory note for silver.
31746	1876,1117.1473	Promissory note for silver. Dar -/7/14. Babylon.
31747	1876,1117.1474	Contract; lease of a house. Dar -/-/17. Babylon.
31748	1876,1117.1475	Omens; apodoses.
31749	1876,1117.1476	Prayer to Ishtar.
31750	1876,1117.1477	Promissory note for silver. Nabû-[] -/12/19. Saḫrītu.
31751	1876,1117.1478	List of debtors.
31752	1876,1117.1479	Promissory note for silver. Nbn 22/1/15. Babylon. Wunsch, CM 3, no. 232.
31753	1876,1117.1480	Contract; lease of a house; Egibi archive.
31754	1876,1117.1481	Promissory note for dates. Dar 27/-/-. Bīt-Ḫaḫḫūru.
31755	1876,1117.1482	Sale of a slave. Nbk 23/4/28. Babylon. Nbk 182; Bertin 127.
31756	1876,1117.1483	Receipt for repayment of a debt. Dar 13/2/22. Babylon. Dar 539; Bertin 2473.
31757	1876,1117.1484	Promissory note for dates. 8/-/-. Wunsch, CM 3, no. 372.
31758	1876,1117.1485	Receipt for onions. Cyr. Wunsch, CM 3, no. 299.
31759	1876,1117.1486	Promissory note for silver.
31760	1876,1117.1487	Contract; division of fields. Babylon.
31761	1876,1117.1488	Promissory note for silver. 19/[]/16. Babylon.
31762	1876,1117.1489	Promissory note. 25/3/-.
31763	1876,1117.1490	Contract; lease of a house. Nbn -/-/10. Babylon.
31764	1876,1117.1491	Promissory note for silver. Cam -/3/-. Babylon.
31765	1876,1117.1492	Contract; sale of a field.
31766	1876,1117.1493	Promissory note for silver. Wunsch, CM 3, no. 373.
31767	1876,1117.1494	Receipt for payment of silver. 2/12/3.
31768	1876,1117.1495	Economic; mentions LÚ.SAG LUGAL.
31769	1876,1117.1496	Promissory note for silver. Nbn 14/1/9. Babylon.
31770	1876,1117.1497	Promissory note for silver.
31771	1876,1117.1498	Literary.
31772	1876,1117.1499	Promissory note. Wunsch, CM 3, no. 374.
31773	1876,1117.1500	Contract; lease of a house. Cam -/6b/-. Babylon.
31774	1876,1117.1501	Bilingual incantation; Udug-ḫul 16. Geller, BAM 8, 499-541, pls. 28, 161.
31775	1876,1117.1502	Promissory note for silver.
31776	1876,1117.1503	Promissory note for silver; left edge.
31777	1876,1117.1504	Promissory note for silver. Dar 16/8/12.
31778	1876,1117.1505	List of people; turns at right angles.
31779	1876,1117.1506	Promissory note for silver; lower edge.
31780	1876,1117.1507	Deposition. -/5/-. Babylon.
31781	1876,1117.1508	Contract; lease of a house. Cyr 13/7/-. Babylon. Wunsch, CM 3, no. 311.
31782	1876,1117.1509	Contract; hire of a boat. Dar -/7/5.

31783	1876,1117.1510	Joined to 31717.
31784	1876,1117.1511	Inventory of household furnishings.
31785	1876,1117.1512	Promissory note for silver as the price of onions. Nbn 6/1/1. Šaḫrīn. Wunsch, CM 3, no. 93.
31786	1876,1117.1513	Receipt of barley from Marduk-nāṣir-apli. Dar []/[]/25. Babylon. Bertin 2574; Abraham, BPPE, 309-310, no. 59.
31787	1876,1117.1514	Receipt for repayment of silver.
31788	1876,1117.1515	Receipt for silver payment. Dar 11/1/27. Bertin 2638.
31789	1876,1117.1516	Promissory note for dates. 6/6b/-. Šuppatu.
31790	1876,1117.1517	Contract; sale of a field. Kandalanu 2/9/-. Babylon.
31791	1876,1117.1518	Sale of slaves. Cam 6/2/7. Babylon. Cam 365; Bertin 971.
31792	1876,1117.1519	Promissory note for dates.
31793	1876,1117.1520	Receipt of silver by Marduk-nāṣir-apli as partial repayment of a debt; year 27 or 28. Dar 11/10/27? Bertin 2159; Abraham, BPPE, 310-312, no. 60.
31794	1876,1117.1521	Promissory note for silver. Dar -/1/1. Babylon.
31795	1876,1117.1522	Contract; hire of boats. Nbn 21/2/14. Bīt-šar-Bābili. Nbn 764; Bertin 621.
31796	1876,1117.1523	Contract.
31797	1876,1117.1524	Court record. Ner 10/8/acc. Babylon. Wunsch, AfO 44/45, 75-77, no. 5.
31798	1876,1117.1525	Receipt of silver by Marduk-nāṣir-apli. Dar 8/7/[]. Bertin 2783; Abraham, BPPE, 313, no. 61.
31799	1876,1117.1526	Astronomical Diary for SE 99. Sachs and Hunger, ADART II, no. -212 A.
31800	1876,1117.1527	Promissory note for silver agreed before judges; sealed. Dar 19/[]/[]. [Babylon]. Nisaba 28, no. 45; Sandowicz, dubsar 11, no. 48.
31801	1876,1117.1528	Deposition. Dar.
31802	1876,1117.1529	Promissory note for silver. 25/7/-.
31803	1876,1117.1530	Apprenticeship contract; sealed. SE Ant II 26/6/53. Babylon. Bertin 3073-3074; Jursa, Persika 9, 204-207, 217; Nisaba 28, no. 576.
31804	1876,1117.1531	Astronomical Diary for SE 116. Sachs and Hunger, ADART II, no. -195 C.
31805	1876,1117.1532	Confirmation that a dowry in silver, slaves and household goods has not been delivered. Cam 22/11/ 3. Paširi. Cam 214; Bertin 906; Wunsch, CM 3, no. 334.
31806	1876,1117.1533	Promissory note for silver; refers to month ii of year 17. Dar []/12b/[16]. Babylon (NUN.ki). Bertin 2385 (as S†.76-11-17, 15?6).
31807	1876,1117.1534	Promissory note for silver.

31808	1876,1117.1535	Promissory note for barley. Dar 26/3/14. Babylon. Dar 375; Bertin 2299.
31809	1876,1117.1536	Promissory note for silver.
31810	1876,1117.1537	Promissory note for dates.
31811	1876,1117.1538	Promissory note for silver. 8/12/-. Babylon.
31812	1876,1117.1539	Promissory note for barley.
31813	1876,1117.1540	Contract.
31814	1876,1117.1541	Contract for rent and provision. Dar []/7/23. [URU P]a-ni-abul-Enlil. Dar 569; Bertin 2507.
31815	1876,1117.1542	Sale of a slave. Nbk 10/9/12. Babylon. Nbk 96; Bertin 74.
31816	1876,1117.1543	Hire of a slave. Cam 7/1/1. Babylon. Cam 31; Bertin 864.
31817	1876,1117.1544	Contract.
31818	1876,1117.1545	Astronomical Diary.
31819	1876,1117.1546	Sale of a slave; dupl. 30841. Nbk 26/2/12. Ḫuṣṣūtu-ša-Bau-ēreš. Nbk 94a; Bertin 71 and 103.
31820	1876,1117.1547	Promissory note for silver. Nbn 11/7/9. Babylon.
31821	1876,1117.1548	Sale of a slave girl. Nbn 30/4/[7]. Šaḫrīn. Nbn 1083; Bertin 707 and 735; Wunsch, CM 3, no. 142.
31822	1876,1117.1549	Promissory note for dates. Nbn 24/6/12. Babylon. Nbn 625; Bertin 570.
31823	1876,1117.1550	List of men. -/9/-.
31824	1876,1117.1551	Contract; lease of a house; Egibi archive. Dar 26/[]/35. Šaḫrīn. Bertin 2555.
31825	1876,1117.1552	Promissory note for barley. Dar 9/12/10. Babylon. Dar 289; Bertin 2172.
31826	1876,1117.1553	Letter from Nabû-bullissu to Širku. Hackl et al., AOAT 414/1, no. 56.
31827	1876,1117.1554	Account of barley deliveries.
31828	1876,1117.1555	Interim account of partnership expenses. Nbn 22/4/16. Bīt-šar-Bābili. Nbn 966; Strassmaier, Liverpool, 107; Bertin 674; Wunsch, CM 3, no. 242.
31829	1876,1117.1556	Promissory note for silver. Nbk 8/3/29. Babylon. Nbk 199; Bertin 139.
31830	1876,1117.1557	Letter from Širku to Zēria. Hackl et al., AOAT 414/1, no. 57.
31831	1876,1117.1558	Joined to 31611. Dar -/-/8. Bertin 2130.
31832	1876,1117.1559	Promissory note for silver. 23/4/-.
31833	1876,1117.1560	Account of deliveries of dates or grain.
31834	1876,1117.1561	Contract; sale of a field. 8/[]/[]. Wunsch, CM 20A-B, no. 126.
31835	1876,1117.1562	Receipt for barley. Dar 22/[]/9. Babylon. Dar 263; Bertin 2160.

31836	1876,1117.1563	Sale of a slave. Nbk 27/6/17. Babylon. Nbk 110; Bertin 85.
31837	1876,1117.1564	Promissory note for silver. 14/-/-.
31838	1876,1117.1565	Account of deliveries of dates or grain.
31839	1876,1117.1566	Contract.
31840	1876,1117.1567	Receipt for final payment of debt.
31841	1876,1117.1568	Promissory note for silver. Dar 26/7/28. Bertin 2655.
31842	1876,1117.1569	Contract; sale of a house. Cam 15/11/3. Babylon. Cam 213; Bertin 893.
31843	1876,1117.1570	Contract. Cam 26/12/acc. Babylon. Cam 25; Bertin 858.
31844	1876,1117.1571	Letter from Marduk-erība to Širku. Hackl et al., AOAT 414/1, no. 58.
31845	1876,1117.1572	Promissory note for dates. Nbn 10/11/10. Nāru-eššu. Nbn 473; Bertin 510.
31846	1876,1117.1573	Receipt for payment on a loan. Dar 11/6/13. Babylon. Dar 354; Bertin 2268.
31847	1876,1117.1574	Astronomical Diary for SE 140. Sachs and Hunger, ADART II, no. -171 C.
31848	1876,1117.1575	List of men.
31849	1876,1117.1576	Deposition. Dar 9/9/5. Babylon. Dar 184; Bertin 2049.
31850	1876,1117.1577	Promissory note for silver; dupl. DT.268. Dar 15/7/[]. Babylon. Bertin 2784.
31851	1876,1117.1578	Sale of a slave. Nbk []/1/[]. Nbk 420; Bertin 237.
31852	1876,1117.1579	Contract; sale of a house in Ḫursag-kalamma. Nbn -/1/16? Bīt-šar-Bābili. + 32108.
31853	1876,1117.1580	Promissory note for silver.
31854	1876,1117.1581	Gift of a slave as part of a dowry. Wunsch, CM 3, no. 355.
31855	1876,1117.1582	Receipt. 6/8/27.
31856	1876,1117.1583	Receipt.
31857	1876,1117.1584	Astronomical Diary for SE 116.
31858	1876,1117.1585	Hire of workers. Ner 19/5/3. Babylon. Evetts, Ner 58; Strassmaier, Liverpool, 122; Sack, AOAT 236, no. 58; Bertin 322.
31859	1876,1117.1586	Sale of a slave. Nbn 21/8/[]. Nbn 1114; Bertin 722.
31860	1876,1117.1587	Contract; lease of a house; Egibi archive. 12/6/5. Babylon.
31861	1876,1117.1588	Receipt for house rent. Dar []/3/6. Babylon. Dar 201; Bertin 2097.
31862	1876,1117.1589	Sale of a slave. Nbk 14/1/[]. Nbk 417; Bertin 238.
31863	1876,1117.1590	Promissory note for barley. Nbk 14/5/31. Babylon. Nbk 244; Bertin 153.
31864	1876,1117.1591	Promissory note for silver. 1/9/-. Babylon.

31865	1876,1117.1592	Sale of a slave. Nbk 16/6/19. Babylon. Nbk 117a; Bertin 93.
31866	1876,1117.1593	Receipt for repayment of silver.
31867	1876,1117.1594	Promissory note for silver. Cyr 25/2/1. Rāzu[...]. Cyr 15; Bertin 849.
31868	1876,1117.1595	Promissory note for dates. Cyr 4/1/9. Babylon. Cyr 335; Bertin 846.
31869	1876,1117.1596	Receipt of silver paid on behalf of Marduk-nāṣir-apli; dupl. 31977. Dar 3/10/18. Babylon. Dar 472; Abraham, BPPE, 320-321, no. 65; Bertin 2392.
31870	1876,1117.1597	Contract; exchange of house plots. Nbk 15/6b/21. Babylon. Bertin 101-102; Wunsch, CM 20A, n. 110.
31871	1876,1117.1598	Promissory note for silver. 2/10/-.
31872	1876,1117.1599	Contract; sale of a field. Nbn 14/12b/2. Babylon. + 34254. Nbn 132 (31872 only); Bertin 388 (31872 only).
31873	1876,1117.1600	Receipt for a payment. Dar 18/5/-. Babylon. Bertin 2770.
31874	1876,1117.1601	Letter from Sūqāya to Marduk-nāṣir-apli. Hackl et al., AOAT 414/1, no. 34.
31875	1876,1117.1602	Promissory note for dates. Cam 15/2/1. Babylon. Cam 38; Bertin 869.
31876	1876,1117.1603	Promissory note for dates. Dar -/6/25. Bēl-iqbi. Bertin 2570.
31877	1876,1117.1604	Sale of a slave. Nbk 13/6/29. Babylon. Nbk 203a; Bertin 145.
31878	1876,1117.1605	Promissory note for silver. 13/[]/[]. Wunsch, CM 3, no. 375.
31879	1876,1117.1606	Promissory note for silver. Cyr 1/4/5. Babylon. Cyr 196; Bertin 814.
31880	1876,1117.1607	Sale of a slave. Cyr 23/[]/9.
31881	1876,1117.1608	Contract; ḫarrānu.
31882	1876,1117.1609	Promissory note. -/-/14.
31883	1876,1117.1610	Contract for furnishings and textiles. Nbk 17/6/[]. Upija. Nbk 431; Bertin 243.
31884	1876,1117.1611	Sale of a slave girl. Dar 7/2/2. Babylon. Dar 30; Bertin 1951.
31885	1876,1117.1612	Promissory note. Nbk 23/11/27. Dannatu. Nbk 179; Bertin 124.
31886	1876,1117.1613	Sale of a slave. -/7/acc. Upija.
31887	1876,1117.1614	Promissory note for silver. 7/8/-.
31888	1876,1117.1615	Promissory note for silver. Nbn 1/[]/4. Nbn 182; Bertin 374.
31889	1876,1117.1616	Contract; lease of a house; Egibi archive.
31890	1876,1117.1617	Promissory note; lower edge.

31891	1876,1117.1618	Contract; hire of a boat by Marduk-nāṣir-apli. Dar 7/6/[]. Babylon. Abraham, BPPE, 314-316, no. 62, and 558, no. 18.
31892	1876,1117.1619	Promissory note for barley. Dar 7/[]/10.
31893	1876,1117.1620	Sale of a boat.
31894	1876,1117.1621	Sale of a slave. Nbk []/6/41. Nbk 380; Bertin 245; Wunsch, CM 3, no. 40.
31895	1876,1117.1622	Contract?
31896	1876,1117.1623	Deposition. [Babylon]. Dar. Sandowicz, AOAT 463 (Fs Zawadzki) 189-199.
31897	1876,1117.1624	Contract; sale of a field.
31898	1876,1117.1625	Promissory note for silver. Nbk 22/2/39. Babylon. + 31979. Nbk 345a (31898 only); Bertin 195 (31898 only); Wunsch, CM 3, no. 31.
31899	1876,1117.1626	Receipt for wine.
31900	1876,1117.1627	Sale of slaves. Cam 5/5/7. Borsippa. Cam 377; Bertin 972.
31901	1876,1117.1628	Promissory note for silver. Cam 1/11/7. Ḫursag-kalamma. Cam 393; Bertin 984.
31902	1876,1117.1629	Sale of slave girls. Nbn 15/8/1. Bīt-Ṭāb-Bēl. Nbn 39; Bertin 349; Wunsch, CM 3, no. 98.
31903	1876,1117.1630	Promissory note for dates as imittu payment. Cam 21/5/1. Šaḫrīn. Cam 53; Bertin 866; Wunsch, CM 3, no. 321.
31904	1876,1117.1631	Promissory note for dates. Dar 17/6/7. Babylon. Dar 225; Bertin 2119.
31905	1876,1117.1632	Sale of a slave. Nbk 23/6b/7. Saḫrītu. Nbk 61; Bertin 47.
31906	1876,1117.1633	Promissory note for silver. Cyr 20/8/7. Babylon. Cyr 270; Bertin 821.
31907	1876,1117.1634	Promissory note.
31908	1876,1117.1635	Promissory note for silver. Cam []/[]/5. Babylon. Cam 304; Bertin 928.
31909	1876,1117.1636	Promissory note for dates. Nbk 12/10/[39]. Nbk 367; Bertin 209.
31910	1876,1117.1637	Receipt for jewellery.
31911	1876,1117.1638	Receipt for a delivery. Nbn 28/7/10 Nbn 444; Bertin 516.
31912	1876,1117.1639	List of āšipū in the charge of Širik / Itti-Marduk-balāṭu / Egibi; Aramaic letter on the upper edge.
31913	1876,1117.1640	Contract; sale of a field. Wunsch, CM 20A-B, no. 206.
31914	1876,1117.1641	Omens.
31915	1876,1117.1642	Promissory note for barley. Dar 25/4/-. Babylon. Bertin 2792.

31916	1876,1117.1643	Contract. Dar 19/10/-. Babylon.
31917	1876,1117.1644	Purchase of cress. Dar 7/2/1. Borsippa. Dar 12; Bertin 2844.
31918	1876,1117.1645	Account of payments of silver; turns at right angles. Wunsch, CM 3, no. 376.
31919	1876,1117.1646	Account of barley deliveries. -/8/-.
31920	1876,1117.1647	Promissory note for onions. Nbn 11/12/16. Borsippa. Nbn 1014; Bertin 686; Wunsch, CM 3, no. 247.
31921	1876,1117.1648	Marriage contract. Nbk 22/3/40. Ḫursag-kalamma. Nbk 359; Bertin 203; Wunsch, AfO 44/45, 81, no. 10.
31922	1876,1117.1649	Receipt for silver as dowry. Cyr 21/8/3. Babylon. Cyr 129; Bertin 768; Wunsch, CM 3, no. 286b.
31923	1876,1117.1650	Receipt for silver; Murānu archive.
31924	1876,1117.1651	Contract?; mostly illegible; reverse blank.
31925	1876,1117.1652	Purchase of seed. Cam 23/1/7. Cam 360; Bertin 987.
31926	1876,1117.1653	Promissory note for silver. 29/-/-.
31927	1876,1117.1654	Promissory note for silver? Mostly illegible.
31928	1876,1117.1655	Promissory note for beer.
31929	1876,1117.1656	Adoption contract. Dar I -/-/28. Babylon.
31930	1876,1117.1657	Illegible.
31931	1876,1117.1658	Promissory note for dates and date products.
31932	1876,1117.1659	Contract; sale of a field; finger-nail marks.
31933	1876,1117.1660	Contract; division of property.
31934	1876,1117.1661	Promissory note for silver. 11/-/-.
31935	1876,1117.1662	Promissory note for dates; dupl. 31383. Dar 21/5/-. Babylon. Bertin 2786.
31936	1876,1117.1663	Letter from Marduk-erība and Šadinnu to Iddin-Marduk. CT 22, 21, no. 109; Hackl et al., AOAT 414/1, no. 4.
31937	1876,1117.1664	Deposition. Cam 14/[]/5. Bīt-Ṭāb-Bēl. Cam 303; Bertin 927.
31938	1876,1117.1665	Sale of a slave. 18/-/-.
31939	1876,1117.1666	Contract; sale of a field. []/8/[]. Wunsch, CM 20A-B, no. 133.
31940	1876,1117.1667	Promissory note for dates. Dar 10/6/-.
31941	1876,1117.1668	Promissory note for silver.
31942	1876,1117.1669	Promissory note for silver. Nbn []/6/8. Babylon. Nbn 305; Bertin 458.
31943	1876,1117.1670	Promissory note for silver. Nabû-[] -/12b/5. Babylon.
31944	1876,1117.1671	Account of silver payments.
31945	1876,1117.1672	Promissory note for dates.
31946	1876,1117.1673	Promissory note for silver. Dar 24/4/-. Babylon. Bertin 2787.
31947	1876,1117.1674	Promissory note.

31948	1876,1117.1675	Letter from Itti-Nabû-balāṭu to Šulāya. Hackl et al., AOAT 414/1, no. 49.
31949	1876,1117.1676	Promissory note for dates. Cam []/6/6. Babylon. Cam 320; Bertin 950.
31950	1876,1117.1677	Promissory note for date products.
31951	1876,1117.1678	Promissory note to pay a debt of silver to Marduk-nāṣir-apli. Dar []/[]/25. Šaḫrīn. Bertin 2578; Abraham, BPPE, 316-318, no. 63.
31952	1876,1117.1679	Letter.
31953	1876,1117.1680	Promissory note for silver. Dar 6/2/8. Babylon. Dar 220; Bertin 2131.
31954	1876,1117.1681	Promissory note for dates.
31955	1876,1117.1682	Contract; sale of a field. Nbn 9/7/[]. Bīt-šar-Bābili. Nbn 1102; Bertin 705.
31956	1876,1117.1683	Sale of slaves. Dar 4/-/-. Bertin 2803.
31957	1876,1117.1684	Contract; sale of a field; sealed. Nbk []/10/29. Babylon. Nbk 206; Bertin 143.
31958	1876,1117.1685	Contract; sale of a field. Artaxerxes II/III 5/9/17. Kapri-šapiri. Strassmaier, 8th Orientalist Congress, no. 29; Bertin 2875.
31959	1876,1117.1686	Contract; division of property. [Dar]. + 32047. Bertin 990 (32047 only); Wunsch, CM 20A-B, no. 10 A.
31960	1876,1117.1687	Sale of inheritance rights. Nbk 12/6b/9. Babylon. Nbk 78; Bertin 60.
31961	1876,1117.1688	Court record about land. [Nbn]. [Babylon]. Bertin 714-715; Roth, Fs Oelsner, 391-393 and 400; see Wunsch, CM 20A-B, no. 112.
31962	1876,1117.1689	Promissory note for dates.
31963	1876,1117.1690	Promissory note for silver. Nbk 15/4/[]. Babylon. Nbk 425; Bertin 249.
31964	1876,1117.1691	Promissory note for silver. Ner 15/4/1. Babylon. Evetts, Ner 20; Strassmaier, Liverpool, 116; Sack, AOAT 236, no. 20; Bertin 306; Wunsch, CM 3, no. 67.
31965	1876,1117.1692	Receipt? Wunsch, CM 3, no. 377.
31966	1876,1117.1693	Promissory note.
31967	1876,1117.1694	Promissory note for wheat. Dar 19/[]/18. Dar 477; Bertin 2139.
31968	1876,1117.1695	Sale of a slave. Nbk []/4/3. Babylon. Nbk 29; Bertin 22.
31969	1876,1117.1696	Receipt of silver as the price of a slave. Nbn []/1/13. Babylon. Wunsch, CM 3, no. 210.
31970	1876,1117.1697	Names of two people.
31971	1876,1117.1698	Receipt. Wunsch, CM 3, no. 378.
31972	1876,1117.1699	Receipt for silver.

31973	1876,1117.1700	Promissory note for silver. Nbk 2/3/33. Babylon. Nbk 256; Bertin 159.
31974	1876,1117.1701	Promissory note for silver. 7/1/-. Babylon.
31975	1876,1117.1702	Contract about a plot of land with a house built on it neighbouring Marduk-nāṣir-apli's property; sealed. Dar 10/12b/16. Šušan. Dar 435; Abraham, BPPE, 426-427, no. 121; Bertin 2347; Nisaba 28, no. 34.
31976	1876,1117.1703	Contract about two heifers belonging to the slave of Marduk-nāṣir-apli. Dar 24/3/27. Šaḫrīn. Bertin 2639; Abraham, BPPE, 318-320, no. 64.
31977	1876,1117.1704	Receipt of silver paid on behalf of Marduk-nāṣir-apli; dupl. 31869. Dar 3/10/18. Babylon. + 31978. Dar 472b (31978 only); Bertin 2399 (31978 only); Abraham, BPPE, 320-321, no. 65.
31978	1876,1117.1705	Joined to 31977.
31979	1876,1117.1706	Joined to 31898.
31980	1876,1117.1707	Receipt for payment.
31981	1876,1117.1708	Promissory note for silver. Nbk []/2/5. Babylon. Nbk 41; Bertin 33.
31982	1876,1117.1709	Promissory note for silver. Cam 8/7/3. Babylon. Cam 185; Bertin 899.
31983	1876,1117.1710	Promissory note for barley. Nbn 20/3/10. Nāru-eššu. Nbn 419; Bertin 469 and 493.
31984	1876,1117.1711	Promissory note for silver. Ner. Wunsch, CM 3, no. 84.
31985	1876,1117.1712	Promissory note for dates. Dar 1/6/9. Alu-ša-Nabû-uballiṭ. Dar 254; Bertin 2154.
31986	1876,1117.1713	Contract.
31987	1876,1117.1714	Promissory note for dates.
31988	1876,1117.1715	Contract.
31989	1876,1117.1716	Promissory note; lower edge.
31990	1876,1117.1717	Astronomical Diary.
31991	1876,1117.1718	Contract; lower edge; witnesses.
31992	1876,1117.1719	Promissory note for dates. Nbk 3/5/41. Babylon. Nbk 378; Bertin 216.
31993	1876,1117.1720	Account of dates or grain.
31994	1876,1117.1721	Promissory note for silver. Nbn 15/10/3. Babylon. Nbn 124; Bertin 384; Wunsch, CM 3, no. 118.
31995	1876,1117.1722	Contract; sale of a field?
31996	1876,1117.1723	Contract; lease of a date orchard. Dar 19/[]/12 Dar 341; Bertin 2238.
31997	1876,1117.1724	Contract; lower edge.
31998	1876,1117.1725	Purchase of dates. 14/5/-. Babylon.
31999	1876,1117.1726	Promissory note for silver; upper and lower edges lost.

32000	1876,1117.1727	Contract; sale of a field; finger-nail marks. Nbn 8/6b/10. Babylon. (+) 32037 + 32193. Nbn 437; Bertin 500; Wunsch, CM 20A-B, no. 64 A.
32001	1876,1117.1728	Receipt; Egibi archive; lower edge.
32002	1876,1117.1729	Contract; upper(?) edge.
32003	1876,1117.1730	Contract; lower edge.
32004	1876,1117.1731	Promissory note for silver. Cyr 15/7/-. Babylon.
32005	1876,1117.1732	Account of dates or grain.
32006	1876,1117.1733	Deposition.
32007	1876,1117.1734	Contract. Nbk.
32008	1876,1117.1735	Contract; lease of a house. Cyr []/[]/3. Babylon. Cyr 155; Bertin 779.
32009	1876,1117.1736	Astronomical.
32010	1876,1117.1737	Contract; lower left corner.
32011	1876,1117.1738	Copy of a contract; Nergal-[] 21/[]/2 (written [ITU].x UD 21-KAM MU 2-KAM ḫe-pí Né-iri11-gal-[...]).
32012	1876,1117.1739	Contract; lower edge.
32013	1876,1117.1740	Promissory note for barley. 21/12/-. Babylon.
32014	1876,1117.1741	Promissory note for silver. -/-/4.
32015	1876,1117.1742	Receipt; lower edge.
32016	1876,1117.1743	Contract; sale of a field. + 32064. Wunsch, CM 20A-B, no. 42.
32017	1876,1117.1744	Contract; fragment from centre and right edge.
32018	1876,1117.1745	Receipt for a delivery. Dar []/[]/9. Dar 264; Bertin 2164.
32019	1876,1117.1746	Contract; fragment from centre.
32020	1876,1117.1747	Promissory note for dates or grain.
32021	1876,1117.1748	Sale contract; fragment from centre.
32022	1876,1117.1749	Contract?; mostly illegible; lower left corner.
32023	1876,1117.1750	Court record; sealed. Nbn []/[]/[11]. [Babylon]. + 32155 + 32220. Wunsch, AfO 44/45, 77-79, no. 6; Wunsch, Fs Oelsner, 571; Nisaba 28, no. 18.
32024	1876,1117.1751	Contract; sale of a house, etc., at Babylon; sealed; finger-nail marks. Cam 4/8/[]. Babylon. + 32198. Cam 423 (32198 only); Bertin 993 (32198 only); Nisaba 28, no. 103.
32025	1876,1117.1752	Promissory note for dates.
32026	1876,1117.1753	Deposition. [Nbk] -/-/40. Sippar.
32027	1876,1117.1754	Promissory note for barley. Dar 24/5/12. Dar 329; Bertin 2243.
32028	1876,1117.1755	Promissory note for silver; right edge.
32029	1876,1117.1756	Contract; left side.
32030	1876,1117.1757	Astronomical Diary(?).
32031	1876,1117.1758	Account of deliveries.
32032	1876,1117.1759	Contract; lower left corner.

32033	1876,1117.1760	Copy of a contract for hire of a slave as baker. Nbn 20/11/10. Babylon. Nbn 475; Bertin 512; Wunsch, CM 3, no. 182.
32034	1876,1117.1761	Receipt for utensils.
32035	1876,1117.1762	Promissory note for silver; lower left corner.
32036	1876,1117.1763	Contract; lower edge.
32037	1876,1117.1764	Contract; sale of a field. [Nbn] [8]/[6b]/[10]. [Babylon]. + 32193 + 32670 (+) 32000. Wunsch, CM 20A-B, no. 64 A.
32038	1876,1117.1765	Promissory note for silver. -/10/acc. Babylon.
32039	1876,1117.1766	Incantation prayer to Ea. Abusch and Schwemer, AMD 8/2 text 9.6 d, pl. 72.
32040	1876,1117.1767	Contract. LM -/2/acc.
32041	1876,1117.1768	Sale of a slave. Dar 19/6/-. Babylon. Bertin 2757.
32042	1876,1117.1769	Purchase of barley. Dar 5/10/-. Babylon. Bertin 2793.
32043	1876,1117.1770	Contract; sale of a field.
32044	1876,1117.1771	Contract; sale of a field. Nbk 3?/3?/40. Borsippa. Nbk 374; Bertin 201 (obv.) and 717 (rev.).
32045	1876,1117.1772	Protocol of a dispute about a house. Dar 10/8/15. Babylon. Dar 410; Bertin 2319; Wunsch, CM 3, no. 353.
32046	1876,1117.1773	Promissory note for silver.
32047	1876,1117.1774	Joined to 31959.
32048	1876,1117.1775	Sale of slaves.
32049	1876,1117.1776	Letter from Nabû-nādin-aḫi to Ḫaḫḫūru; sealed. Nisaba 28, no. 209; Hackl et al., AOAT 414/1, no. 64.
32050	1876,1117.1777	Letter.
32051	1876,1117.1778	Purchase of dates or grain.
32052	1876,1117.1779	Contract; sale of land. Dar 10/[]/7. Ḫursag-kalamma. Dar 232; Bertin 2118.
32053	1876,1117.1780	Receipt for silver. Nbn 20/4/7 Nbn 255; Bertin 436.
32054	1876,1117.1781	Promissory note for silver; lower right corner.
32055	1876,1117.1782	Contract; lease of a house; Egibi archive.
32056	1876,1117.1783	Account of barley and wheat.
32057	1876,1117.1784	Contract. AM 18/10/acc.
32058	1876,1117.1785	Sale of slaves.
32059	1876,1117.1786	Contract; lower right corner.
32060	1876,1117.1787	Sumerian incantation?
32061	1876,1117.1788	Economic; obverse lost, reverse blank except for the end of one line from the obverse.
32062	1876,1117.1789	Astronomical Diary. + 32606.
32063	1876,1117.1790	Contract; lower left corner.
32064	1876,1117.1791	Joined to 32016.
32065	1876,1117.1792	Contract. Dar -/-/19 ? Babylon.
32066	1876,1117.1793	Promissory note for silver. Dar -/3/7.
32067	1876,1117.1794	Sale contract; left edge.

32068	1876,1117.1795	Letter; names of sender and addressee lost. Hackl et al., AOAT 414/1, no. 21.
32069	1876,1117.1796	Contract(?); fragment of right edge.
32070	1876,1117.1797	Sale of a slave. Wunsch, CM 3, no. 379.
32071	1876,1117.1798	Deposition. Dar 15/7/13. Babylon. Dar 355; Bertin 2821.
32072	1876,1117.1799	Contract; transfer of a field, slaves and household goods as dowry. Cam []+12/11/3. Babylon. + 41592. Cam 216 (32072 only); Wunsch, AfO 42/43, 54, no. 3 (both fragments); Bertin 892; Wunsch, CM 3, no. 336.
32073	1876,1117.1800	Envelope of a letter to Širku for an issue to Nidintu-[Bēl?]. Dar []/7/24. Bertin 2536; Hackl et al., AOAT 414/1, no. 59.
32074	1876,1117.1801	Promissory note for barley.
32075	1876,1117.1802	Contract; lower left corner.
32076	1876,1117.1803	Astronomical Diary.
32077	1876,1117.1804	Account of deliveries of various commodities. 19/5/-.
32078	1876,1117.1805	Contract. -/8/13.
32079	1876,1117.1806	Account of deliveries.
32080	1876,1117.1807	Contract; lease of a house. Dar.
32081	1876,1117.1808	Receipt for silver payment.
32082	1876,1117.1809	Contract. -/-/12.
32083	1876,1117.1810	Contract. Nbk 11/2/6. Babylon.
32084	1876,1117.1811	Receipt(?); fragment from centre.
32085	1876,1117.1812	Contract; sale of a field.
32086	1876,1117.1813	Contract; lower edge.
32087	1876,1117.1814	Contract; witnesses; lower edge.
32088	1876,1117.1815	Astronomical; Normal Star Almanac for SE 159. + 32471. Hunger and Sachs, ADART VII, no. 72.
32089	1876,1117.1816	Contract; fragment from centre.
32090	1876,1117.1817	Contract; transfer of land, involving a woman and her sons. Cam 5/5/7. Borsippa. + 32105 + 32111. Cam 399 (32105 only); Bertin 979 (32105 only); Zadok, Nisaba 21, 234.
32091	1876,1117.1818	Promissory note for silver. -/-/25.
32092	1876,1117.1819	Promissory note for date products.
32093	1876,1117.1820	Unidentified; badly abraded.
32094	1876,1117.1821	Receipt.
32095	1876,1117.1822	Receipt for house rent. AM 26+/11/[]. Babylon. Bertin 291 (as "1822").
32096	1876,1117.1823	Sale of a slave. [Cyr/Cam]. 7/11/4. Babylon.
32097	1876,1117.1824	Receipt for irbu tax. Dar 4/12/[]. + 41804. Bertin 2794 (as "1824").

32098	1876,1117.1825	Contract; sale of a field. Dar 13/5/20. Babylon. Dar 503; Bertin 2437.
32099	1876,1117.1826	Contract for tithe; sealed. Nbk 17/5/[]. Sippar. Nbk 430; Bertin 241.
32100	1876,1117.1827	Contract; lease of a house; Egibi archive.
32101	1876,1117.1828	Contract; ḫarrānu. Nbn 21/3/12. Babylon. Nbn 601; Bertin 558.
32102	1876,1117.1829	Final payment for a field. Cyr. Babylon. Cyr 366; Bertin 848.
32103	1876,1117.1830	Contract; division of property. Nbn 15/11/-. Babylon.
32104	1876,1117.1831	Contract; ḫarrānu. -/-/40.
32105	1876,1117.1832	Joined to 32090. Bertin 979.
32106	1876,1117.1833	Promissory note for dates. Wunsch, CM 3, no. 380.
32107	1876,1117.1834	Astrological omens, Enūma Anu Enlil 63, Venus Tablet of Ammiṣaduqa. Ossendrijver, NABU 2013, 7-9, no. 5.
32108	1876,1117.1835	Joined to 31852.
32109	1876,1117.1836	Contract; lower left corner.
32110	1876,1117.1837	Receipt.
32111	1876,1117.1838	Joined to 32090.
32112	1876,1117.1839	Contract.
32113	1876,1117.1840	Promissory note for silver. Wunsch, CM 3, no. 381.
32114	1876,1117.1841	Deposition.
32115	1876,1117.1842	Contract; sale of a field. Wunsch, CM 20A-B, no. 134.
32116	1876,1117.1843	Promissory note for silver. 20+/6/[]. Wunsch, CM 3, no. 382.
32117	1876,1117.1844	Medical ritual; mentions stones. Schuster-Brandis, AOAT 46, p. 86, Kette 17, p. 180. Kette 238.
32118	1876,1117.1845	Promissory note for dates. 2/[]/11.
32119	1876,1117.1846	Sale of a slave girl. 27/[]/13. Babylon.
32120	1876,1117.1847	Contract. Nbn 4/8/7. Nbn 266; Bertin 443.
32121	1876,1117.1848	Contract. Nbk.
32122	1876,1117.1849	Promissory note for dates and date products.
32123	1876,1117.1850	Receipt for silver payment. Dar []/[]/8. Dar 247; Bertin 2128.
32124	1876,1117.1851	Contract. Dar.
32125	1876,1117.1852	Names and addresses.
32126	1876,1117.1853	Contract.
32127	1876,1117.1854	Contract; lower left corner.
32128	1876,1117.1855	Promissory note for dates.
32129	1876,1117.1856	Promissory note for silver. Wunsch, CM 3, no. 383.
32130	1876,1117.1857	Promissory note for silver. [Nbn] 29/[]/11. Šaḫrīn. Wunsch, CM 3, no. 197.
32131	1876,1117.1858	Promissory note for silver; lower left corner.

32132	1876,1117.1859	Promissory note for silver; flake from obverse.
32133	1876,1117.1860	Liver omens; Šumma ekallu. (+) Rm.797.
32134	1876,1117.1861	Contract.
32135	1876,1117.1862	Sale of a slave girl. Nbn 11/7/[]. Nbn 1103; Bertin 737.
32136	1876,1117.1863	Contract. Wunsch, CM 3, no. 384.
32137	1876,1117.1864	Literary.
32138	1876,1117.1865	Contract. -/-/acc. Babylon.
32139	1876,1117.1866	Joined to 31680.
32140	1876,1117.1867	Field plan. Nemet-Nejat, LB Field Plans, no. 11.
32141	1876,1117.1868	Contract; lower edge.
32142	1876,1117.1869	Contract; lower right corner.
32143	1876,1117.1870	Astronomical Diary for SE 141. LBAT 366; Sachs and Hunger, ADART II, no. -170 D; Bertin 2907.
32144	1876,1117.1871	Contract; sale of a field.
32145	1876,1117.1872	Contract.
32146	1876,1117.1873	Contract; sale of a field. [Cyrus] 30/[]/9. Babylon. Wunsch, CM 20A-B, no. 168.
32147	1876,1117.1874	Promissory note for silver. Nbk 20/2/37 Nbk 318; Bertin 184.
32148	1876,1117.1875	Promissory note for silver. Nbn 18/3/3. Šubat-Gula. Nbn 106 (wrongly as 1876,1117.1375); Bertin 378; Wunsch, CM 3, no. 113.
32149	1876,1117.1876	Astronomical Diary. + 32886 (+) 32252 (+) 32529. LBAT 183 (32886 only); Sachs, PTRSL A.276, 49, fig. 10; Sachs and Hunger, ADART I, no. -366 A.
32150	1876,1117.1877	Promissory note for silver. 28/6/[]. Wunsch, CM 3, no. 385.
32151	1876,1117.1878	Deposition.
32152	1876,1117.1879	Contract; transfer of property; year 3 or 6 or 9; sealed. Cyr []/3/3+. Babylon. Wunsch, CM 20A-B, no. 149; Nisaba 28, no. 87.
32153	1876,1117.1880	Contract; transfer of property. []/6/[]. + 32185 + 32194 + 2 unnum. Wunsch, Bab Arch 2, 62 66, no. 16.
32154	1876,1117.1881	Astronomical; Goal Year Text for SE 81. + 1881,0625.97 + 32408. LBAT 1216-1217; Kugler, Or NS 2, 100-104, 113-114 (part); Schaumberger, AnOr 6, 1-12; Stephenson, HEER, 134, 139; Hunger and Sachs, ADART VI, no. 5.
32155	1876,1117.1882	Joined to 32023.
32156	1876,1117.1883	Joined to 31727.
32157	1876,1117.1884	Court record; sealed. [Nbn]. [Babylon]. (+) 34432. Wunsch, AfO 44/45, 92, no. 22; Nisaba 28, no. 8a.
32158	1876,1117.1885	Historical-literary epic.

32159	1876,1117.1886	Contract; sale of a field; sealed; finger-nail marks. Cam 23/[]/[]. [Babylon?]. Wunsch, CM 20A-B, no. 136; Nisaba 28, no. 104.
32160	1876,1117.1887	Contract; sale of fields; lower half only; finger-nail marks; dupl. 33057 and 41398. [Amel-Marduk] [11]/[8]/[1]. [Babylon]. Nisaba 28, no. 56.
32161	1876,1117.1888	Contract; sale of a field; sealed; finger-nail marks; dupl. 32212. Dar 29/12/4. Babylon. + 32895 Dar 152 (32895 only); Bertin 2018f (32895 only); Wunsch, CM 20A-B, no. 181 A; Nisaba 28, no. 112.
32162	1876,1117.1889	Astrological; Enūma Anu Enlil with commentary; Sin, horns. + 32364. Reiner, Fs Borger (CM 10), 292; Frahm, GMTR 5, 163.
32163	1876,1117.1890	Contract; sale of fields; sealed; finger-nail marks. Nbn. [Babylon?]. + 41697 + unnum. (+) 32201. Wunsch, CM 20A-B, no. 37; Nisaba 28, no. 77a.
32164	1876,1117.1891	Astronomical Diary for SE 133. LBAT 352; Sachs and Hunger, ADART II, no. -178 A; Bertin 2904.
32165	1876,1117.1892	Court record; about a debt with land given as pledge; sealed. Nbn 11/7/13. Babylon. + 32199 + 32763 + 141867. Nbn 720 (32199 only, wrongly as 76-11-17, 1826 following Bertin); Bertin 607-608 (32199 only); Wunsch, CM 20A-B, no. 90 A; Ménant, Notice, pl. II.9; Nisaba 28, no. 22; 141867 unpublished.
32166	1876,1117.1893	Contract; sale of a field; sealed. Nbn 6/5/[]. Babylon. Wunsch, AfO 44/45, 95-96, no. 29; Nisaba 28, no. 13.
32167	1876,1117.1894	Astronomical procedure text for the moon; System A; prayer on upper edge. + 32172 + 32451 + 32651 + 32663 + 32744 + 32752. ACT 200; Aaboe, AIHS 25/97 (1975), 208-211; Neugebauer, JCS 7, 100-102 (all 32651 only); ACT 200aa, colophon Zqb (32172 only); Ossendrijver, BMAPT, no. 53.
32168	1876,1117.1895	Contract; sale of land. Wunsch, CM 20A-B, no. 210.
32169	1876,1117.1896	Contract; sale of a field. + 42202.
32170	1876,1117.1897	Contract; lease of a house; sealed. SE Ant I [& Sel] 20/[9]/37. + 32537. CT 49, 20, no. 107 (32537 only); Zadok, NABU 1997, 138-139, no. 149; Nisaba 28, no. 559.
32171	1876,1117.1898	Chronicle of the Seleucid period. Grayson, TCS 5, Chronicle 13; BCHP 10.
32172	1876,1117.1899	Joined to 32167.
32173	1876,1117.1900	Contract; sale of fields; Šuanna mentioned in line 2; reverse all lost; finger-nail marks; sealed. d.l. [Babylon]. + 32177 + 32460. Wunsch, CM 20A, n. 284; Nisaba 28, no. 81.

32174	1876,1117.1901	Court record; year 2 is mentioned; sealed. Nbn []/[]/[2+]. [Babylon]. Wunsch, AfO 44/45, 89-90, no. 20; Nisaba 28, no. 11.
32175	1876,1117.1902	Transcript of a trial. Cyr. [Borsippa?]. Sandowicz, dubsar 11, no. 15.
32176	1876,1117.1903	Joined to 31627.
32177	1876,1117.1904	Joined to 32173.
32178	1876,1117.1905	Mathematical table of squares of regular numbers. + 1876,1117.2228 + Rm.848. Aaboe, JCS 19, 80-82; Ossendrijver, JCS 66, 149-165 and pls.; ACT 1002 (Rm 848 only).
32179	1876,1117.1906	Astrological omens (copy); probably Enūma Anu Enlil; TE-tablet. + 1876,1117.2389a. Reiner, Fs Borger (CM 10), 292.
32180	1876,1117.1907	Contract; sale of a field; finger-nail marks; sealed; dupl. RSM 1909.405.23 (= Dalley, Edinburgh, no. 75). Dar []/[]/3. Babylon. + 33125. Dar 102 (32180 only = Bertin 1971); Bertin 2986-2987 (33125 only); Nisaba 28, no. 110.
32181	1876,1117.1908	List of names and addresses.
32182	1876,1117.1909	Account of expenditures of silver.
32183	1876,1117.1910	Bilingual incantation; Gattung I. + 32318 + 32469.
32184	1876,1117.1911	Contract; sale of a date orchard. Ner 10/9/2. [Babylon]. Wunsch, CM 20A-B, no. 7.
32185	1876,1117.1912	Joined to 32153.
32186	1876,1117.1913	Account of payments of silver.
32187	1876,1117.1914	Contract; sale of a field.
32188	1876,1117.1915	Contract; sale of fields, houses and slaves; sealed; finger-nail marks. Dupl. 30122 etc. Cyr 6/3/4. Babylon. + 38111 + 41910. Cyr 161 (38111 only); Bertin 787-788 (38111 only); Wunsch, CM 20A-B, no. 125 A; Nisaba 28, no. 88.
32189	1876,1117.1916	Astrological, Enūma Anu Enlil with commentary, Sin. Reiner, Fs Borger (CM 10), 292; Frahm, GMTR 5, 163.
32190	1876,1117.1917	Astronomical Diary for SE 118. + 1876,1117.1986. LBAT 322; Sachs and Hunger, ADART II, no. -193 A.
32191	1876,1117.1918	Bilingual.
32192	1876,1117.1919	Contract; sale of a field; dupl. 41511. Nbn 2/12/3. Wunsch, CM 20A-B, no. 48 B.
32193	1876,1117.1920	Joined to 32037.
32194	1876,1117.1921	Joined to 32153.
32195	1876,1117.1922	Contract; sale of a house; sealed; finger-nail marks. Nbn 22/9/5. Babylon. + 32196 + 32540. Bertin 3052

		(32196 only); Ménant, Notice, pl. IV.20 (32196 only); Nisaba 28, no. 68.
32196	1876,1117.1923	Joined to 32195.
32197	1876,1117.1924	Contract; sale of a field; sealed; finger-nail marks. d.l. [Babylon?]. Wunsch, CM 20A-B, no. 91; Nisaba 28, no. 84.
32198	1876,1117.1925	Joined to 32024.
32199	1876,1117.1926	Joined to 32165.
32200	1876,1117.1927	Contract; sale of a field; sealed; finger-nail marks. d.l. Wunsch, CM 20A, pp. 59, 153, nn. 110, 311; Ménant, Notice, p. 221, pl. III.14; Nisaba 28, no. 105.
32201	1876,1117.1928	Contract; sale of a field; sealed; finger-nail marks. [Nbn]. (+) 32163 + 41697. Wunsch, CM 20A-B, no. 37; Nisaba 28, no. 77b.
32202	1876,1117.1929	Contract; sale of a field; sealed. [Cyrus] [30]/[12b]/[]. (+) 32500. Nisaba 28, no. 94a.
32203	1876,1117.1930	Contract; sale of a field; sealed. d.l. Nisaba 28, no. 78.
32204	1876,1117.1931	Contract; sale of a field; sealed; finger-nail marks; dupl. Archi, OrAn 14, p. 13. d.l. Babylon. + 42065 Wunsch, CM 20A-B, no. 70 B; Nisaba 28, no. 93.
32205	1876,1117.1932	Sale of slaves. Cam []/[]/acc. Babylon. + 41542 + 41561 + 41600 + 41720 + 48890. Wunsch, AfO 42/43, 48-53, no. 3.
32206	1876,1117.1933	Public ritual for Babylon in the month Kislīmu. + 32237 + 34723 (+) F.220. Cagirgan and Lambert, JCS 43/45, 89-106; Linssen, CM 25, 9, 11, 16 n. 104, 27 n. 31, 31 nn. 56 and 62, 39, 67, 69 n. 328, 70, 79, 81 n. 425, 86, 87 n. 467, 88, 90-91, 93-94, 118 and n. 718, 148 n. 129, 149 n. 136, 152 n. 172, 160 n. 260, 324.
32207	1876,1117.1934	Omens; extispicy; isru 4th tablet; colophon; SE 138 (An-ti-'-[]); compare 35556. SE (Ant IV) []/[]/138. + 1876,1117.2230 + unnum.
32208	1876,1117.1935	Literary; Ludlul I, II, IV-V. + 1876,1117.2478 + 32214 + 32371 + 32378 + 32449 + 32659 + 32694 + 4 unnum. Lambert, BWL 21-46, pl. 4 (32214 and 32694 only); Oshima, BPPS, 377-378; Lambert, MC 24, no. 149.
32209	1876,1117.1936	Astronomical; observations; lunar conjunctions with Mars and Saturn, and list of years with intercalary months, for 423-400 BC. + 41854. LBAT 1411-1412; Hunger and Sachs, ADART V, no. 58.
32210	1876,1117.1937	Contract; sale of a field; finger-nail marks. AM 6/7/1. [Babylon?]. + 41677. Sack, AOATS 4, no. 13 (32210 only); Bertin 264.

32211	1876,1117.1938	Astrological; prayer on upper edge. Steele, JCS 67, 213-214
32212	1876,1117.1939	Contract; sale of a field, dupl. 32161 (Dar 152+). Dar 29/12/[4]. [Babylon]. Wunsch, CM 20A-B, no. 181 B.
32213	1876,1117.1940	Contract for dowry.
32214	1876,1117.1941	Joined to 32208.
32215	1876,1117.1942	Astrological; commentary on Enūma Anu Enlil 35, solar eclipse omens. + 32303 + 32672 + 32761. Reiner, Fs Borger (CM 10), 292-293; Frahm, GMTR 5, 163.
32216	1876,1117.1943	Contract; inheritance division; dupl. Dar 80. Wunsch, CM 20A-B, no. 12 B.
32217	1876,1117.1944	Prayer to Zarpanitu(?); cf. Mayer, Untersuchungen, pp. 424-425.
32218	1876,1117.1945	Astronomical; tables for Jupiter. Aaboe, JCS 20, 8, 22-23, 31; see ACT, p. 310.
32219	1876,1117.1946	Account of barley.
32220	1876,1117.1947	Joined to 32023.
32221	1876,1117.1948	Promissory note for dates.
32222	1876,1117.1949	Astronomical; Goal Year Text for SE 118. + 1876,1117.2048 + 2329. LBAT 1237; Epping and Strassmaier, ZA 6, 231-233 (1876,1117.1949 only); Stephenson, HEER, 155-156, 200-201; Hunger and Sachs, ADART VI, no. 20.
32223	1876,1117.1950	Astronomical Diary; dated by Seleucus and Antiochus.
32224	1876,1117.1951	Horoscopic omens; three columns. + 32290.
32225	1876,1117.1952	Promissory note for silver; Murānu archive; sealed. SE Ant II 17/[]/56. Jursa, Persika 9, 53-155, 175, 210; Nisaba 28, no. 579.
32226	1876,1117.1953	Astrological omens.
32227	1876,1117.1954	Medical; headaches; ears. + 32277 + 32341 + 32777 + unnum.
32228	1876,1117.1955	Astronomical; Goal Year Text for SE 79. Hunger and Sachs, ADART VI, no. 3.
32229	1876,1117.1956	Ritual?
32230	1876,1117.1957	Astronomical; Normal Star Almanac for SE 208. Hunger and Sachs, ADART VII, no. 95.
32231	1876,1117.1958	Astronomical; planetary observations, Mercury for SE 14-17, Mars for SE 15. + 32273. Hunger and Sachs, ADART V, no. 71.
32232	1876,1117.1959	Astronomical Diary. + 32390.
32233	1876,1117.1960	Astronomical; Vorläufer; mentions Ḫ̮AB-rat. + 1876,1117.2049.

32234	1876,1117.1961	Astronomical; lunar eclipse table for at least 609-447 BC. LBAT 1419; Kennedy, JCS 38, 205, T.17n.3; Stephenson, HEER, 149, 152-153, 166, 173-174, 198, 208; Hunger and Sachs, ADART V, no. 4; Stolper, NABU 1999, 6-9, no. 6.
32235	1876,1117.1962	Chronicle about Seleucus I. (+) 32957. Grayson, TCS 5, Chronicle 12; BCHP 9.
32236	1876,1117.1963	Astrological procedure text; zodiacal signs, eclipses, watches. + 32336.
32237	1876,1117.1964	Joined to 32206.
32238	1876,1117.1965	Astronomical; lunar eclipse table for at least 731-317 BC. LBAT 1414; Stephenson, HEER, 149, 153-154, 162, 176-177, 195, 199, 208; Hunger and Sachs, ADART V, no. 2.
32239	1876,1117.1966	Astronomical Diary.
32240	1876,1117.1967	Joined to Rm.792.
32241	1876,1117.1968	Astronomical procedure text for the moon, System A; colophon. ACT 200aa; Ossendrijver, BMAPT, no. 62.
32242	1876,1117.1969	Joined to 31592.
32243	1876,1117.1970	Astrological? or astronomical Vorläufer?; Mars and Mercury mentioned. + 32577 + 32660 + 32780 + 32937a. Reiner, Fs Borger (CM 10), 293 (32577+).
32244	1876,1117.1971	Astronomical Diary.
32245	1876,1117.1972	Astronomical Diary for SE 50. + 32404. Sachs and Hunger, ADART I, no. -261 B.
32246	1876,1117.1973	Contract for a purchase; sealed. d.l. SE. [Babylon]. Nisaba 28, no. 608.
32247	1876,1117.1974	Astronomical; Normal Star Almanac for SE 234. + 32749. Roughton, AOAT 297, 367-378; Hunger and Sachs, ADART VII, no. 103.
32248	1876,1117.1975	Chronicle about events at Esangila. SE. + 32456 + 32477 + 32543 + unnum. BCHP 6.
32249	1876,1117.1976	Account.
32250	1876,1117.1977	Promissory note for dates owed to Murānu / Bēl-bullissu by Bēl-ušēzib / Nergal-nāṣir; sealed. SE Ant II 2/1/55. Babylon. Jursa, Persika 9, 143-145, 175, 209; Nisaba 28, no. 578.
32251	1876,1117.1978	Astronomical Diary?
32252	1876,1117.1979	Astronomical Diary. (+) 32149 (+) 32529. LBAT 184; Sachs, PTRSL A.276, 49, fig. 10; Sachs and Hunger, ADART I, no. -366 A.
32253	1876,1117.1980	Mathematical; standard table of reciprocals; fragment.
32254	1876,1117.1981	Astrological; Enūma Anu Enlil, lunar eclipses. Reiner, Fs Borger (CM 10), 292.

32255	1876,1117.1982	Astrological omens?
32256	1876,1117.1983	Astronomical Diary; prices.
32257	1876,1117.1984	Account.
32258	1876,1117.1985	Astrological; Enūma Anu Enlil, eclipses; commentary. + 32379 + 32415 + unnum. Reiner, Fs Borger (CM 10), 292.
	1876,1117.1986	Joined to 32190.
32259	1876,1117.1987	Liver omens. + 36819.
32260	1876,1117.1988	Prayer?
32261	1876,1117.1989	Astronomical Diary. + 32267.
32262	1876,1117.1990	Prayer.
32263	1876,1117.1991	Astronomical; Normal Star Almanac. Hunger and Sachs, ADART VII, no. 104.
32264	1876,1117.1992	Liver omens; copy (he-pí).
32265	1876,1117.1993	Astronomical Diary for SE 122. + 32464. Sachs and Hunger, ADART II, no. -189 B.
32266	1876,1117.1994	Chronicle referring to the Juniper Garden. SE. BCHP 8.
32267	1876,1117.1995	Joined to 32261.
32268	1876,1117.1996	Omens; extispicy orientation. + 32278 + 32307 (+) 32298. U. S. Koch, AOAT 326, 480-518 and pls. xliii-xliv.
32269	1876,1117.1997	Astronomical or astrological.
32270	1876,1117.1998	Astronomical Diary.
32271	1876,1117.1999	Astronomical.
32272	1876,1117.2000	Astronomical Diary for SE 20. + 32288 + 32422 + 32501 + 32624. LBAT 224 (32501 only); Sachs and Hunger, ADART I, no. -291 B.
32273	1876,1117.2001	Joined to 32231.
32274	1876,1117.2002	Astronomical Diary.
32275	1876,1117.2003	Contract; sealed. d.l. SE? + 32281. Nisaba 28, no. 609.
32276	1876,1117.2004	Astronomical; microzodiac rising time scheme; ziqpu stars; two columns. Steele, Rising time schemes, 96-101.
32277	1876,1117.2005	Joined to 32227.
32278	1876,1117.2006	Joined to 32268.
32279	1876,1117.2007	Lexical; list of stones. + 1876,1117.2030 + 2181 + 2384 + 2449 + unnum. Schuster-Brandis, AOAT 46, p. 276-318, Text 9, pls. 28-29.
32280	1876,1117.2008	Astronomical Diary. + 32356.
32281	1876,1117.2009	Joined to 32275.
32282	1876,1117.2010	Astrological; Enūma Anu Enlil; obverse Sin, reverse MUL. Reiner, Fs Borger (CM 10), 292.

32283	1876,1117.2011	Promissory note; Murānu archive; sealed. SE Ant I [& Sel] []/[]/42. [Babylon]. CT 49, 22, no. 112; Stolper, Annali Supp. 77, 49-50, no. 16; Jursa, Persika 9, 175, 183-184; Nisaba 28, no. 561.
32284	1876,1117.2012	Ritual mentioning eclipse of the moon.
32285	1876,1117.2013	Astronomical.
32286	1876,1117.2014	Astronomical; Goal Year Text for SE 90. LBAT 1218; Kugler, Or NS 2, 105-107, 114-115; Schaumberger, AnOr 6, 1-12. Stephenson, HEER, 155, 200; Hunger and Sachs, ADART VI, no. 6.
32287	1876,1117.2015	Astronomical; Vorläufer; two columns. + 32638. Reiner, Fs Borger (CM 10), 292.
32288	1876,1117.2016	Joined to 32272.
32289	1876,1117.2017	Contract; sale of a field.
32290	1876,1117.2018	Joined to 32224.
32291	1876,1117.2019	Bilingual historical-literary text of Nebuchadnezzar I; dupl. 47805+ (Frame, RIMB.2.4.8.4).
32292	1876,1117.2020	Astrological; TE-tablet. Reiner, Fs Borger (CM 10), 292.
32293	1876,1117.2021	Astronomical; Goal Year Text for SE 134. + 1876, 1117.2239. LBAT 1248; Hunger and Sachs, ADART VI, no. 29.
32294	1876,1117.2022	Joined to 32291.
32295	1876,1117.2023	Missing.
32296	1876,1117.2024	Astrological; Enūma Anu Enlil 15. + 32513. Rochberg-Halton, AfO Beih. 22, EAE 15 (32513 only); for 32513 see George, OLZ 1991, 380; Reiner, Fs Borger (CM 10), 292.
32297	1876,1117.2025	Incantation.
32298	1876,1117.2026	Omens; extispicy orientation. (+) 32268. U. S. Koch, AOAT 326, 480-518 and pls. xlv-xlvi.
32299	1876,1117.2027	Astronomical; Venus and lunar data from 463 to 392 BC. (+) 42083 (+) 45674. LBAT 1388; Hunger and Sachs, ADART V, no. 56.
32300	1876,1117.2028	Sumerian school letter. Civil, Fs Lambert, 109-116.
32301	1876,1117.2029	Astronomical; Vorläufer? or star catalogue?; ḫe-pí.
	1876,1117.2030	Joined to 32279.
32302	1876,1117.2031	Astronomical; System A lunar ephemeris. (+) 32531 (+) 32742. ACT 6aa; Steele, Fs Walker, 293-318, text D.
32303	1876,1117.2032	Joined to 32215.
32304	1876,1117.2033	Astronomical; three columns.
32305	1876,1117.2034	Omens; extispicy; tīrānu 4th tablet; colophon. Artaxerxes 2/[]/32. + 1876,1117.2355.

32306	1876,1117.2035	Promissory note for barley; sealed. SE [Sel I] & Ant []/2/24. [Babylon]. + 32366. CT 49, 18, no. 102; Stolper, Annali Supp. 77, 51-53, no. 17; Nisaba 28, no. 552.
32307	1876,1117.2036	Joined to 32268.
32308	1876,1117.2037	Astronomical; Mercury observations; list of dates and zodiac signs of Mercury's stationary points over 1 year. Hunger and Sachs, ADART V, no. 85.
32309	1876,1117.2038	Astronomical Diary. + 32402.
32310	1876,1117.2039	Chronicle of the Seleucid period. + 32384 + 32398. CT 49, 49, no. 188 (32398 only); Grayson, TCS 5, Chronicle 13A (32310 only); BCHP 7.
32311	1876,1117.2040	Astronomical; MUL.APIN. Scribe, Itti-Marduk-balāṭu descendant of Mušēzib; colophon; dated by Seleucus. Hunger and Pingree, AfO Beih. 24, 3; Hunger and Steele, MUL.APIN, 21.
32312	1876,1117.2041	Astronomical Diary; prayer on upper edge. Sachs, PTRSL A.276, 48, fig. 3; Sachs and Hunger, ADART I, no. -651; Casaburi, NABU 2001, 38-39, no. 32.
32313	1876,1117.2042	Ritual and prayer.
32314	1876,1117.2043	Astrological omens.
32315	1876,1117.2044	Medical.
32316	1876,1117.2045	Astronomical Diary.
32317	1876,1117.2046	Contract.
32318	1876,1117.2047	Joined to 32183.
	1876,1117.2048	Joined to 32222.
	1876,1117.2049	Joined to 32233.
32319	1876,1117.2050	Astronomical Diary for SE 38. LBAT 241; Sachs and Hunger, ADART I, no. -273 A.
32320	1876,1117.2051	Astronomical Diary for SE 22. + 32370 + 32387 + 32568. Sachs and Hunger, ADART I, no. -289.
32321	1876,1117.2052	Astronomical; Normal Star Almanac for SE 40. + 32368. Hunger and Sachs, ADART VII, no. 7.
32322	1876,1117.2053	Promissory note for silver.
32323	1876,1117.2054	Astrological; Enūma Anu Enlil, Venus, group A. On the left edge the impression of a ring seal (design lost). SE. Reiner and Pingree, BPO 3, 29, 67; Reiner, Fs Borger (CM 10), 292.
32324	1876,1117.2055	Astrological?
32325	1876,1117.2056	Contract; sale of a field. Cyr 10/5/[]. + 32399 + 41602. Wunsch, CM 20A-B, no. 128.
32326	1876,1117.2057	Astrological omens; eclipses. Reiner, Fs Borger (CM 10), 292.
32327	1876,1117.2058	Astronomical; lunar data for SE 62-93, and solstices, equinoxes and Sirius data for SE 62-69. + 1876,1117.

		2059 + 2143 + 2169 + 2250 + 32340. LBAT 1432b; Sachs, JCS 6, 110-112; Hunger and Sachs, ADART V, no. 39; Steele, Calendars and years, 144-145.
	1876,1117.2059	Joined to 32327.
32328	1876,1117.2060	Incantation.
32329	1876,1117.2061	Astronomical Diary for SE 30. + 1876,1117.2155. Sachs and Hunger, ADART I, no. -281 B; Stephenson, HEER, 133, 142 (where the reference is wrongly given to BM 41660 which is -281 A).
32330	1876,1117.2062	Astronomical Diary.
32331	1876,1117.2063	Astronomical Diary.
32332	1876,1117.2064	Joined to Rm.845.
32333	1876,1117.2065	Astronomical Diary. + 32420. Sachs and Hunger, ADART I, no. -375 C.
32334	1876,1117.2066	Astronomical Diary; mentions lunar and solar eclipse possibilities.
32335	1876,1117.2067	Contract; fragment.
32336	1876,1117.2068	Joined to 32236.
32337	1876,1117.2069	Astrological; Enūma Anu Enlil, stars. Reiner, Fs Borger (CM 10), 292.
32338	1876,1117.2070	Account of deliveries of dates.
32339	1876,1117.2071	Astrological table. + 32407 + 32645.
32340	1876,1117.2072	Joined to 32327.
32341	1876,1117.2073	Joined to 32227.
32342	1876,1117.2074	Astronomical; Goal Year Text; not datable. Hunger and Sachs, ADART VI, no. 96.
32343	1876,1117.2075	Astronomical.
32344	1876,1117.2076	Promissory note for good quality lambs. Nbk 13/11/37. Nbk 326, Bertin 187; Wunsch, CM 3, no. 27.
32345	1876,1117.2077	Receipt for repayment of a loan.
32346	1876,1117.2078	Contract. Cam -/9/-.
32347	1876,1117.2079	Contract.
32348	1876,1117.2080	Contract. AM 10+/12/[]. Babylon.
32349	1876,1117.2081	Astronomical Diary for SE 126. + 32428. Sachs and Hunger, ADART II, no. -185 A.
32350	1876,1117.2082	Contract; sale of a field Wunsch, CM 20A-B, no. 208.
32351	1876,1117.2083	Astronomical; auxiliary table for the latitude of the moon for (at least) four years. ACT 91.
32352	1876,1117.2084	Astronomical Diary for SE 50. + 41615 + 41913. LBAT 250-251 (not 32352); Sachs and Hunger, ADART I, no. -261 C (not 32352).
32353	1876,1117.2085	Contract for a dowry.
32354	1876,1117.2086	Omens about birds; dupl. CT 41, 6: K.3240, 5-22.
32355	1876,1117.2087	Religious.

32356	1876,1117.2088	Joined to 32280.
32357	1876,1117.2089	Astrological; Enūma Anu Enlil, stars and moon. Reiner, Fs Borger (CM 10), 292.
32358	1876,1117.2090	Astronomical; Goal Year Text; not datable. Hunger and Sachs, ADART VI, no. 97.
32359	1876,1117.2091	Astrological; stars (Pabilsag). Reiner, Fs Borger (CM 10), 292.
32360	1876,1117.2092	Incantations.
32361	1876,1117.2093	Economic; fragment from left edge.
32362	1876,1117.2094	Omens; Iqqur īpuš, Du'ūzu.
32363	1876,1117.2095	Astronomical; lunar eclipse table for at least 647-574 BC. LBAT 1418; Hunger and Sachs, ADART V, no. 35.
32364	1876,1117.2096	Joined to 32162.
32365	1876,1117.2097	Astronomical Diary for SE 83.
32366	1876,1117.2098	Joined to 32306.
32367	1876,1117.2099	Lexical; GI. + 32382 + 2 unnum.
32368	1876,1117.2100	Joined to 32321.
32369	1876,1117.2101	Astronomical Diary.
32370	1876,1117.2102	Joined to 32320.
32371	1876,1117.2103	Joined to 32208.
32372	1876,1117.2104	Astronomical Diary for SE 4. Sachs and Hunger, ADART I, no. -307 A.
32373	1876,1117.2105	Astrological; Enūma Anu Enlil 3. Reiner, Fs Borger (CM 10), 292; Verderame, Nisaba 2, 99-100 and Fol. V 4-5.
32374	1876,1117.2106	Incantation?
32375	1876,1117.2107	Astrological?; planets and stars.
32376	1876,1117.2108	Horoscope. SE (24-27?)/(10)/(13). Rochberg, Babylonian Horoscopes, no. 3.
32377	1876,1117.2109	Astronomical; ephemeris for at least one year. ACT 125a.
32378	1876,1117.2110	Joined to 32208.
32379	1876,1117.2111	Joined to 32258.
32380	1876,1117.2112	Illegible.
32381	1876,1117.2113	Astronomical Diary.
32382	1876,1117.2114	Joined to 32367.
32382a	1876,1117.2115	Unidentified; fragment.
32383	1876,1117.2116	Contract; sale of a house. + 42046.
32384	1876,1117.2117	Joined to 32310.
32385	1876,1117.2118	Astronomical; two columns.
32386	1876,1117.2119	Astrological omens; commentary on Enūma Anu Enlil. + 32394. Reiner, Fs Borger (CM 10), 292; Frahm, GMTR 5, 164.
32387	1876,1117.2120	Joined to 32320.

32388	1876,1117.2121	Astronomical Diary for SE 110. Sachs and Hunger, ADART II, no. -201 A.
32389	1876,1117.2122	Astronomical; mostly illegible.
32390	1876,1117.2123	Joined to 32232.
32391	1876,1117.2124	Prayer.
32392	1876,1117.2125	Sumerian incantation.
32393	1876,1117.2126	Sale of a slave girl.
32394	1876,1117.2127	Joined to 32386.
32395	1876,1117.2128	Incantations and rituals.
32396	1876,1117.2129	Astronomical. + 32411 + 32484 + 32610.
32397	1876,1117.2130	Astronomical procedure text for an outer planet. + 32421 + 32454. Ossendrijver, BMAPT, no. 48.
32398	1876,1117.2131	Joined to 32310.
32399	1876,1117.2132	Joined to 32325.
32400	1876,1117.2133	Commentary on astrological omens.
32401	1876,1117.2134	Mathematical table. + 32707. Ossendrijver, JCS 66, 149-165 and pls.
32402	1876,1117.2135	Joined to 32309.
32403	1876,1117.2136	Contract; sale of land in Babylon; sealed. SE Sel II []/7/73. Babylon. CT 49, 27, no. 130; Nisaba 28, no. 583.
32404	1876,1117.2137	Joined to 32245.
32405	1876,1117.2138	Astrological; Enūma Anu Enlil 50?; stars; ziqpu. Reiner, Fs Borger (CM 10), 292.
32406	1876,1117.2139	Astronomical procedure text for Mercury or Venus. + 32491 + 32505 + 4 unnum. Ossendrijver, BMAPT, no. 49.
32407	1876,1117.2140	Joined to 32339.
32408	1876,1117.2141	Joincd to 32154.
32409	1876,1117.2142	Astronomical Diary. + 32524.
	1876,1117.2143	Joined to 32327.
32410	1876,1117.2144	Joined to Rm.757.
32411	1876,1117.2145	Joined to 32396.
32412	1876,1117.2146	Contract.
32413	1876,1117.2147	Astronomical Diary; two columns. + 32579.
32414	1876,1117.2148	Astronomical; System A lunar ephemeris, several columns, for SE 146-149. + 32455 + 32704 + 32773 (+) 32499. ACT 4a (not 32455); Steele, AHES 60 (2006) 123-153, text E.
32415	1876,1117.2149	Joined to 32258.
32416	1876,1117.2150	Astronomical; Goal Year Text.
32417	1876,1117.2151	Astronomical Diary?
32418	1876,1117.2152	Joined to 30559.
32419	1876,1117.2153	Contract; sale of a field.
32420	1876,1117.2154	Joined to 32333.

	1876,1117.2155	Joined to 32329.
32421	1876,1117.2156	Joined to 32397.
32422	1876,1117.2157	Joined to 32272.
32423	1876,1117.2158	Contract; sale of a field. Nbn 8/7/10. Babylon. + 32609. Nbn 440 (32423 only); Bertin 501 (32423 only).
32424	1876,1117.2159	Incantations.
32425	1876,1117.2160	Contract.
32426	1876,1117.2161	Astronomical; Goal Year Text; not datable. Hunger and Sachs, ADART VI, no. 98.
32427	1876,1117.2162	Astronomical; MUL.APIN. Reiner, Fs Borger (CM 10), 292.
32428	1876,1117.2163	Joined to 32349.
32429	1876,1117.2164	Illegible.
32430	1876,1117.2165	Joined to Rm.792.
32431	1876,1117.2166	Court record; deposition; sealed. [Nbn] []/[]/[13+]. [Babylon]. Wunsch, AfO 44/45, 88, no. 19; Nisaba 28, no. 23.
32432	1876,1117.2167	Medical.
32433	1876,1117.2168	School text; lexical; erased.
	1876,1117.2169	Joined to 32327.
32434	1876,1117.2170	Astronomical; Goal Year Text; not datable. Hunger and Sachs, ADART VI, no. 99.
32435	1876,1117.2171	Astronomical Diary.
32436	1876,1117.2172	Contract. 19/-/-.
32437	1876,1117.2173	Contract; sale of fields; finger-nail marks. Nbk []/11/[30]. Babylon. (+) 32640 Wunsch, CM 20A-B, no. 5 A.
32438	1876,1117.2174	Astronomical?; fragment.
32439	1876,1117.2175	Astronomical.
32440	1876,1117.2176	Joined to Rm.757.
32441	1876,1117.2177	Astrological; Enūma Anu Enlil. Reiner, Fs Borger (CM 10), 292.
32442	1876,1117.2178	Astrological omens; DIŠ UD 28/29 etc.
32443	1876,1117.2179	Astronomical; Goal Year Text for SE 106; prayer on upper edge. + 34894 + 35386. LBAT 1231-1233; Hunger and Sachs, ADART VI, no. 15.
32444	1876,1117.2180	Incantation. + 32560.
	1876,1117.2181	Joined to 32279.
32445	1876,1117.2182	Astronomical.
32446	1876,1117.2183	Omens; extispicy.
32447	1876,1117.2184	Contract; fragment from centre.
32448	1876,1117.2185	Astronomical Diary for SE 47. + 32569 + 32697. Sachs and Hunger, ADART I, no. -264.
32449	1876,1117.2186	Joined to 32208.

32450	1876,1117.2187	Astronomical; Jupiter, oppositions and second stationary points for (at least) SE 142 to 195; System A. ACT 609.
32451	1876,1117.2188	Joined to 32167.
32452	1876,1117.2189	Joined to 32268.
32453	1876,1117.2190	Astronomical.
32454	1876,1117.2191	Joined to 32397.
32455	1876,1117.2192	Joined to 32414.
32456	1876,1117.2193	Joined to 32248.
32457	1876,1117.2194	Astronomical; Goal Year Text; not datable. Hunger and Sachs, ADART VI, no. 100.
32458	1876,1117.2195	Astronomical Diary.
32459	1876,1117.2196	Ritual.
32460	1876,1117.2197	Joined to 32173.
32461	1876,1117.2198	Astronomical; Vorläufer; "day is long, night is short". + 32478 + 32657.
32462	1876,1117.2199	Literary; mythological narrative involving Marduk and [Enme]šarra; two columns. Lambert, MC 24, no. 46.
32463	1876,1117.2200	Contract; transfer of property including prebends. 10/12/4. Wunsch, Bab Arch 2, 67-71, no. 17.
32464	1876,1117.2201	Joined to 32265.
32465	1876,1117.2202	Astronomical.
32466	1876,1117.2203	Contract; lower right corner.
32467	1876,1117.2204	Literary cylinder; hymn to Ninurta; cf. 40802. + 32911 + 40077. Mayer, Or NS 61, 17-57; Gesche, AOAT 275, 670.
32468	1876,1117.2205	Literary?; a-na ti-ik ḪAB UR.MAŠ.
32469	1876,1117.2206	Joined to 32183.
32470	1876,1117.2207	Astronomical Diary.
32471	1876,1117.2208	Joined to 32088.
32472	1876,1117.2209	Economic; right edge.
32473	1876,1117.2210	Astronomical Diary for SE 132. + 32786.
32474	1876,1117.2211	Contract; division of property; sealed. d.l. Nisaba 28, no. 138.
32475	1876,1117.2212	Astronomical Diary.
32476	1876,1117.2213	Unidentified.
32477	1876,1117.2214	Joined to 32248.
32478	1876,1117.2215	Joined to 32461.
32479	1876,1117.2216	Astronomical Diary.
32480	1876,1117.2217	Economic. -/5/-.
32481	1876,1117.2218	Unidentified.
32482	1876,1117.2219	Ritual for the month Šabāṭu with directions for the priestess who makes music in the month of Addaru;

		combined with late astrology; two columns; copy (ḫe-pí); cf. 32656. + 32621 + 32639 + 32724.
32483	1876,1117.2220	Astrological omens?; Sin? Reiner, Fs Borger (CM 10), 292.
32484	1876,1117.2221	Joined to 32396.
32485	1876,1117.2222	New Year's Festival ritual. + 92708 (DT.109). Craig, ABRT 1, 1-2 (DT.109 only); Thureau-Dangin, RAcc, 127-146 and 151-152 (DT.109 only); Linssen, CM 25, 9, 83 n. 438, 215-237 and 339 (copy of 32485).
32486	1876,1117.2223	Astrological omens. Colophon and date: [...] UD 3-KAM MU 1 me 1-šu 3-KAM šá ši-i MU 2 me 27-KAM [1.a]r-šá-ka-a ma-li-ki. SE Arsaces 3/[]/227 = AE 163.
32487	1876,1117.2224	Lexical; vocabulary.
32488	1876,1117.2225	Horoscopic omens; LÚ.TUR a-lid-ma, etc. + unnum.
32489	1876,1117.2226	Joined to Rm.792.
32490	1876,1117.2227	Astronomical Diary for SE 41. + 41848. LBAT 245-246; Sachs and Hunger, ADART I, no. -270 B.
	1876,1117.2228	Joined to 32178.
32491	1876,1117.2229	Joined to 32406.
	1876,1117.2230	Joined to 32207.
32492	1876,1117.2231	Contract; sale of an orchard. Nbn 17/6b/10. Babylon. Wunsch, CM 20A-B, no. 65.
32493	1876,1117.2232	Contract(?); fragment from centre.
32494	1876,1117.2233	Liver omens; kak.zag.ga; is-ru 4th tablet. + 1876,1117.2289 + 2 unnum.
32495	1876,1117.2234	Astronomical; Goal Year Text for SE 107. (+) 32504. LBAT 1234; Hunger and Sachs, ADART VI, no. 16.
32496	1876,1117.2235	Astrological; vertical and horizontal rulings on one side and radial rulings on the other.
32497	1876,1117.2236	Contract; sale of a field. + 32498.
32498	1876,1117.2237	Joined to 32497.
32499	1876,1117.2238	Astronomical; System A lunar ephemeris, several columns, for SE 146-149. (+) 32414+. ACT 4a; Steele, AHES 60 (2006) 123-153, text E.
	1876,1117.2239	Joined to 32293.
32500	1876,1117.2240	Contract; sale of a field; finger-nail marks; sealed. Cyr 30/12b/[]. Babylon. (+) 32202. Nisaba 28, no. 94b.
32501	1876,1117.2241	Joined to 32272.
32502	1876,1117.2242	Astronomical Diary.
32503	1876,1117.2243	Astronomical Diary.
32504	1876,1117.2244	Astronomical; Goal Year Text for SE 107. (+) 32495. Hunger and Sachs, ADART VI, no. 16.
32505	1876,1117.2245	Joined to 32406.

32506	1876,1117.2246	Astronomical Diary for SE 128. + 32521 + 32695.
32507	1876,1117.2247	Bilingual historical-literary text of Nebuchadnezzar I; dupl. 47805+ (Frame, RIMB.2.4.8.4).
32508	1876,1117.2248	Astronomical Diary.
32509	1876,1117.2249	Astronomical; Normal Star Almanac. SE -/-/130+. Hunger and Sachs, ADART VII, no. 105.
	1876,1117.2250	Joined to 32327.
32510	1876,1117.2251	Chronicle about the theft of gold from a temple. SE. BCHP 15.
32511	1876,1117.2252	Astronomical Diary; colophon. + 40865. LBAT 177 (40865); Sachs and Hunger, ADART I, no. -372 A.
32512	1876,1117.2253	Astronomical; Goal Year Text; not datable. + 1876, 1117.2258. Hunger and Sachs, ADART VI, no. 101.
32513	1876,1117.2254	Joined to 32296.
32514	1876,1117.2255	Dream omens. + 32637.
32515	1876,1117.2256	Incantations and ritual; É-gal-ku4-ra. Abusch and Schwemer, AMD 8/2 text 3.4 h.
32516	1876,1117.2257	Ritual; about a procession of gods from E-tur-kalamma in Babylon to Kiš; dupl. 41239. George, Fs Lambert, 289-299; Linssen, CM 25, 10 n. 66, 324.
	1876,1117.2258	Joined to 32512.
32517	1876,1117.2259	Astrological; tabulated; cf. LBAT 1578-1580 and K.11151+ (Weidner, Gestirndarstellungen, pl. 17); cf. 36292, 38452 (+) 39680, 39629, 42288 (+) 32716.
32518	1876,1117.2260	Astronomical Diary for SE 102. Sachs and Hunger, ADART II, no. -209 C.
32519	1876,1117.2261	Ritual.
32520	1876,1117.2262	Muššu'u tablet VII. Böck, JCS 61, 133-134; Lambert, BCM, p. 157.
32521	1876,1117.2263	Joined to 32506.
32522	1876,1117.2264	Astronomical; Normal Star Almanac for SE 101. LBAT 1009a; Hunger and Sachs, ADART VII, no. 38.
32523	1876,1117.2265	Astronomical.
32524	1876,1117.2266	Joined to 32409.
32525	1876,1117.2267	Contract; sale of a house. Dar 29/1/18. Babylon. + 41680. Dar 469; Bertin 2391.
32526	1876,1117.2268	Astrological; Enūma Anu Enlil; thunder; Adad; aku-kūtu; dupl. ACh Supp. 2 107, 108. Reiner, Fs Borger (CM 10), 293.
32527	1876,1117.2269	Ritual.
32528	1876,1117.2270	Sale of a slave. Nbk -/1/4. Babylon.
32529	1876,1117.2271	Astronomical Diary. (+) 32149 (+) 32252. LBAT 351; Sachs, PTRSL A.276, 49, fig. 10; Sachs and Hunger, ADART I, no. -366 A.
32530	1876,1117.2272	Bilingual incantation to Utu.

32531	1876,1117.2273	Astronomical; System A lunar ephemeris. (+) 32302 (+) 32742. Steele, Fs Walker, 293-318, text D.
32532	1876,1117.2274	Astronomical; ACT ephemeris.
32533	1876,1117.2275	God list; names of Marduk; colophon of Marduk-aḫḫē-erība. Lambert, BCM, p. 151-152, pls. 39-40.
32534	1876,1117.2276	Bilingual; hymn about the king's appointment.
32535	1876,1117.2277	Ritual.
32536	1876,1117.2278	Unidentified.
32537	1876,1117.2279	Joined to 32170.
32538	1876,1117.2280	Astronomical; Goal Year Text; not datable. + 32603. Hunger and Sachs, ADART VI, no. 102.
32539	1876,1117.2281	Astronomical; numbers on one side, astrological? on the other.
32540	1876,1117.2282	Joined to 32195.
32541	1876,1117.2283	Contract; sale of a field; finger-nail marks.
32542	1876,1117.2284	Ritual.
32543	1876,1117.2285	Joined to 32248.
32544	1876,1117.2286	Bilingual prayer; tablet XX of eme.gi7 (cf. Thureau-Dangin, Rituels accadiens, p. 150 vi 28).
32545	1876,1117.2287	Omens; extispicy.
32546	1876,1117.2288	Unidentified.
	1876,1117.2289	Joined to 32494.
32547	1876,1117.2290	Astronomical; Goal Year Text; not datable. Hunger and Sachs, ADART VI, no. 103.
32548	1876,1117.2291	Joined to 32507.
32549	1876,1117.2292	Bilingual literary.
32550	1876,1117.2293	Cylinder; historical inscription of Neriglissar. Langdon, VAB 4, 214-217, Ner. no. 2; Da Riva, SANER 3, 114-120.
32551	1876,1117.2294	Contract; sale of a field. d.l. Wunsch, AfO 44/45, 98-99, no. 36.
32552	1876,1117.2295	Lagaš II cone; inscription of Gudea. Steible, FAOS 9/1 Gudea 75 (H); Edzard, RIME 3/1 1.7.73.
32553	1876,1117.2296	Incantations.
32554	1876,1117.2297	Astronomical Diary. + 32558.
32555	1876,1117.2298	Astronomical Diary for SE 146. Sachs and Hunger, ADART II, no. -165 C.
32556	1876,1117.2299	Astrological omens.
32557	1876,1117.2300	Astronomical; late astronomy or Vorläufer; ḫa-la; two columns. + 32605
32558	1876,1117.2301	Joined to 32554.
32559	1876,1117.2302	Astrological omens.
32560	1876,1117.2303	Joined to 32444.
32561	1876,1117.2304	Astrological omens.
32562	1876,1117.2305	Astronomical Diary.

32563	1876,1117.2306	Astronomical Diary for SE 133. LBAT 351; Sachs and Hunger, ADART II, no. -178 D.
32564	1876,1117.2307	Medical.
32565	1876,1117.2308	Sumerian literary.
32566	1876,1117.2309	Astronomical; Goal Year Text for SE 120. Hunger and Sachs, ADART VI, no. 21.
32567	1876,1117.2310	Unidentified.
32568	1876,1117.2311	Joined to 32320.
32569	1876,1117.2312	Joined to 32448.
32570	1876,1117.2313	Contract; sale of a field.
32571	1876,1117.2314	Receipt.
32572	1876,1117.2315	Astronomical Diary for SE 136. Sachs and Hunger, ADART II, no. -175 A.
32573	1876,1117.2316	Astronomical Diary. + 32790 + 34018. LBAT 531 (34018 only).
32574	1876,1117.2317	Astrological commentary. King, STC I, 216-218; cf. Oelsner, Materialien, 214.
32575	1876,1117.2318	Contract for dowry; sealed. d.l. SE? Nisaba 28, no. 610.
32576	1876,1117.2319	Astrological; pre-Seleucid?. Reiner, Fs Borger (CM 10), 293.
32577	1876,1117.2320	Joined to 32243.
32578	1876,1117.2321	Astrological; Enūma Anu Enlil 15. + 32586. Rochberg-Halton, AfO Beih. 22, EAE 15; Reiner, Fs Borger (CM 10), 293.
32579	1876,1117.2322	Joined to 32413.
32580	1876,1117.2323	Contract. -/12/-.
32581	1876,1117.2324	Joined to Rm.757.
32582	1876,1117.2325	Lexical; Diri III. CT 12, 28; 5R 22.1; MSL 15 135.
32583	1876,1117.2326	Horoscopic omens; colophon. + 41484. LBAT 1592 (41484 only).
32584	1876,1117.2327	Mathematical; table of fourth powers.
32585	1876,1117.2328	Joined to Rm.757.
	1876,1117.2329	Joined to 32222.
32586	1876,1117.2330	Joined to 32578.
32587	1876,1117.2331	Medical.
32588	1876,1117.2332	Field plan. Nemet-Nejat, LB Field Plans, no. 7.
32589	1876,1117.2333	Omens; extispicy; cf. K.2018a and Sm 801; catch-line.
32590	1876,1117.2334	Astronomical; observation text; Mars, Greek letter phenomena for SE 27-35 and passings of Normal Stars for SE 11-12, 14-16. Hunger and Sachs, ADART V, no. 69.
32591	1876,1117.2335	Unidentified.
32592	1876,1117.2336	Omens?

32593	1876,1117.2337	Joined to 30432.
32594	1876,1117.2338	Joined to 30432.
32595	1876,1117.2339	Joined to 30432.
32596	1876,1117.2340	God-list; names of Zarpanitu. Lambert, BCM, p. 159, pl. 41.
32597	1876,1117.2341	Astronomical Diary for SE 113. Sachs and Hunger, ADART II, no. -198 B.
32598	1876,1117.2342	Adoption contract. Wunsch, AfO 50, 232-233, no. 16.
32599	1876,1117.2343	Astronomical procedure text; Venus text composed according to System A; colophon. ACT 824 and 1050; Aaboe and Hamilton, AHES 53 (1998), 215-221; Britton, AHES 55 (2001) 525-554; Ossendrijver, BMAPT, no. 10.
32600	1876,1117.2344	Unidentified.
32601	1876,1117.2345	Contract; lease of a house; Egibi archive.
32602	1876,1117.2346	Sale of a slave. Ner 9/12/1. Babylon. Sack, AOAT 236, no. 86.
32603	1876,1117.2347	Joined to 32538.
32604	1876,1117.2348	Contract; only witnesses preserved.
32605	1876,1117.2349	Joined to 32557.
32606	1876,1117.2350	Joined to 32062.
32607	1876,1117.2351	Liver omens; ekallu.
32608	1876,1117.2352	Contract; sale of a field. + 32615.
32609	1876,1117.2353	Joined to 32423.
32610	1876,1117.2354	Joined to 32396.
	1876,1117.2355	Joined to 32305.
32611	1876,1117.2356	Joined to Rm.845.
32612	1876,1117.2357	Joined to 31592.
32613	1876,1117.2358	Omens.
32614	1876,1117.2359	Astronomical Diary for SE 45. Sachs and Hunger, ADART I, no. -266 A.
32615	1876,1117.2360	Joined to 32608.
32616	1876,1117.2361	Astronomical; Goal Year Text; not datable; mentions 5th year of Antigonus. Hunger and Sachs, ADART VI, no. 104.
32617	1876,1117.2362	Contract; only witnesses preserved; upper edge.
32618	1876,1117.2363	Astronomical; Normal Star Almanac; two columns. Hunger and Sachs, ADART VII, no. 6.
32619	1876,1117.2364	Will of Iddin-Marduk son of Nabû-mukīn-apli. Cyr 10/11/8. URU Taḫ-ú-ka(?).KI. Wunsch, Bab Arch 2, 112-115, no. 34.
32620	1876,1117.2365	School text; lexical, Syllabary A, Syllabary B, Ḫḫ I-III; god-list, An = Anum; colophon. + 3 unnum. Gesche, AOAT 275, 222-224, 670.
32621	1876,1117.2366	Joined to 32482.

32622	1876,1117.2367	Astronomical Diary for SE 24. Sachs and Hunger, ADART I, no. -287.
32623	1876,1117.2368	Astronomical; numbers, etc. On rev. several lines seem to have (ina) me-me šú + dates.
32623a	1876,1117.2369	Illegible.
32624	1876,1117.2370	Joined to 32272.
32625	1876,1117.2371	Joined to 32507.
32626	1876,1117.2372	Astronomical; MUL.APIN. Hunger and Pingree, AfO Beih. 24, 3; Hunger and Steele, MUL.APIN, 21.
32627	1876,1117.2373	Astronomical. + 32760. Reiner, Fs Borger (CM 10), 293.
32628	1876,1117.2374	Astronomical; Goal Year Text for SE 127. Hunger and Sachs, ADART VI, no. 25.
32629	1876,1117.2375	Joined to 32507.
32630	1876,1117.2376	Literary.
32631	1876,1117.2377	Literary.
32632	1876,1117.2378	Incantation.
32633	1876,1117.2379	Astronomical; Goal Year Text; not datable. Hunger and Sachs, ADART VI, no. 105.
32634	1876,1117.2380	Literary; myth.
32635	1876,1117.2381	Royal inscription?
32636	1876,1117.2382	Literary.
32637	1876,1117.2383	Joined to 32514.
	1876,1117.2384	Joined to 32279.
32638	1876,1117.2385	Joined to 32287.
32639	1876,1117.2386	Joined to 32482.
32640	1876,1117.2387	Contract; sale of fields; finger-nail marks; dupl. 48351. Nbk []/[11]/[30]. (+) 32437. Wunsch, CM 20A-B, no. 5 A.
92421	1876,1117.2388	Inscribed qutāru pot. Walker, Iraq 42, 84-86. See the list from Mr. Skene, Aleppo, in M. E. Correspondence 1868-1881 SH-SPA, p. 6029, in which it is described as, "Jar with cuneiform inscription & small fragments of Arabic glass & pottery – said to have contained tablets".
	1876,1117.2389a	Joined to 32179.
32641	1876,1117.2389b	Hemerology; six columns. 5R 48-49; Labat, RA 38, 13-40; Livingstone, CUSAS 25 pp. 9.
32642	1876,1117.2390	Fragment of a boundary stone; inscribed; recording a transfer of land; various divine symbols. Marduk-apla-iddina II. (+) VA Bab 4177/8095. Paulus, AOAT 51, 709-714, pls. 59-60, MAI II 3.
32643	1876,1117.2391	Fragment of a stone statue(?) with inscription; Old Akkadian?

91007	1876,1117.2392	Stone tablet; inscription of Gudea. Previously numbered 12143. Steible, FAOS 9/1 Gudea 51 (J); Edzard, RIME 3/1 1.7.41.
91060	1876,1117.2393	Stone tablet; inscription of Gudea. Previously numbered 12203. Steible, FAOS 9/1 Gudea 51 (J); Edzard, RIME 3/1 1.7.41.
91008	1876,1117.2394	Stone tablet; inscription of Gudea. Previously numbered 12144. Steible, FAOS 9/1 Gudea 51 (J); Edzard, RIME 3/1 1.7.41.
92074	1876,1117.2395	Clay lamp.
92061	1876,1117.2396	Clay lamp.
92064	1876,1117.2397	Clay lamp.
92065	1876,1117.2398	Clay lamp.
91784	1876,1117.2399	Terracotta figurine of a woman.
92277	1876,1117.2400	Terracotta figurine of a male rider.
118760	1876,1117.2401	Terracotta female figurine.
120471	1876,1117.2402	Alabaster male figurine.
	1876,1117.2403	Terracotta female figurine; Parthian.
	1876,1117.2404	Marble female figurine.
91856	1876,1117.2405	Terracotta female figurine; Parthian.
120468	1876,1117.2406	Terracotta boy's head.
	1876,1117.2407	Uninscribed stone fragment.
	1876,1117.2408	Flint implement.
	1876,1117.2409	Uninscribed stone fragment.
32644	1876,1117.2410	Esangila ritual.
32645	1876,1117.2411	Joined to 32339.
	1876,1117.2412	Potter's mould; Islamic.
32646	1876,1117.2413	Neo-Assyrian. Prism. Royal inscription of Ashurbanipal(?). Nineveh.
32647	1876,1117.2414	Neo-Assyrian. Lexical, Ḫḫ XI 241-307 (MSL VII 138-140) or Uruanna III (Köcher, Pflanzenkunde, no. 23). Nineveh.
32648	1876,1117.2415	Neo-Assyrian. Lexical. Malku VI. Nineveh.
32649	1876,1117.2416	Neo-Assyrian. Prism. Royal inscription of Ashurbanipal. Dupl. VAB VII 52 vi 36-43. Nineveh.
32650	1876,1117.2417	Neo-Assyrian. Liver omens. Nineveh.
32651	1876,1117.2418	Joined to 32167.
32652	1876,1117.2419	Cylinder; historical inscription of Nebuchadnezzar II. Frame, Mesopotamica 28 (1993), 21-50.
32653	1876,1117.2420	Contract; sale of a house; finger-nail marks. Nbk [ ]/[ ]/37. Nbk 328; Bertin 190.
	1876,1117.2421	Clay lamp.
32654	1876,1117.2422	Literary; Enmešarra's defeat. + 38193. Pinches, PSBA 30 (1908) 53-62 and 77-85. (32654 only);

		Linssen, CM 25, 324 and 9; Lambert, BCM, pp. 290-297, pls. 44-49.
32655	1876,1117.2423	Hymn to the high priest of Esangila.
32656	1876,1117.2424	Temple ritual for E-tur-kalamma, the temple of Ištar at Babylon, for the month Simānu; cf. 32482+. George, Fs Lambert, 270-280; Linssen, CM 25, 21 n. 149-150, 69 n. 325, 70, 90, 120-121, 324.
32657	1876,1117.2425	Joined to 32461.
32658	1876,1117.2426	Joined to 30432.
32659	1876,1117.2427	Joined to 32208.
32660	1876,1117.2428	Joined to 32243.
32661	1876,1117.2429	Astronomical Diary.
32662	1876,1117.2430	Astronomical Diary.
32663	1876,1117.2431	Joined to 32167.
32664	1876,1117.2432	Contract; sale of a field.
32665	1876,1117.2433	Legal text. Nbk.
32666	1876,1117.2434	Astronomical Diary.
32667	1876,1117.2435	Unidentified.
32668	1876,1117.2436	School text.
32669	1876,1117.2437	Joined to 30282.
32670	1876,1117.2438	Joined to 32037.
32671	1876,1117.2439	Contract; sale of a field.
32672	1876,1117.2440	Joined to 32215.
32673	1876,1117.2441	Lexical; list of stones.
32674	1876,1117.2442	Contract; sale of a field; sealed; finger-nail marks. Nbn []/[]/[9]. (+) 33056. Wunsch, CM 20A-B, no. 111; Roth, Fs Oelsner, 391; Nisaba 28, no. 15a.
32675	1876,1117.2443	Astronomical; Normal Star Almanac. Hunger and Sachs, ADART VII, no. 106.
32676	1876,1117.2444	Contract, interim account about ḫarrānu. 27/1/[]. Wunsch, CM 20A-B, no. 57.
32677	1876,1117.2445	Account of dates or grain.
32678	1876,1117.2446	Contract; sale of a field in Šu-an-na.KI; sealed; finger-nail marks. Babylon. Nisaba 28, no. 59.
32679	1876,1117.2447	Promissory note; Murānu archive?; sealed. SE Ant I [& Sel] 15/[]/43. CT 49, 23, no. 114; Jursa, Persika 9, 175, 184; Nisaba 28, no. 568.
32680	1876,1117.2448	Astronomical Diary.
	1876,1117.2449	Joined to 32279.
32681	1876,1117.2450	Mathematical table. Ossendrijver, JCS 66, 149-165 and pls.
32682	1876,1117.2451	Contract; lower right corner.
32683	1876,1117.2452	Contract. (Dar) 3/[]/30. Babylon.
32684	1876,1117.2453	Astronomical Diary.
32685	1876,1117.2454	Promissory note for beer and vats. Babylon.

32686	1876,1117.2455	Astronomical Diary.
32687	1876,1117.2456	Astronomical Diary.
32688	1876,1117.2457	Astronomical Diary.
32689	1876,1117.2458	Omens?
32690a	1876,1117.2459a	Promissory note for silver. SE Ant I [& Sel] []/8/41. CT 49, 21, no. 110.
32690b	1876,1117.2459b	Only witnesses preserved; lower edge.
32691a	1876,1117.2460a	Promissory note for onions.
32691b	1876,1117.2460b	Astronomical.
32691c	1876,1117.2460c	Contract; division of property.
32692a	1876,1117.2461a	Contract; sale of a field.
32692b	1876,1117.2461b	Contract; lower right corner.
32693	1876,1117.2462	Economic; lower right corner.
32694	1876,1117.2463	Joined to 32208.
32695	1876,1117.2464	Joined to 32506.
32696	1876,1117.2465	Astronomical; procedure or Vorläufer; two columns, small fragment; ud-da-[zal ...].
32697	1876,1117.2466	Joined to 32448.
32698	1876,1117.2467	Promissory note for silver; flake from obverse.
32699	1876,1117.2468	Contract; right edge.
32700	1876,1117.2469	Contract; sale of a field.
32701	1876,1117.2470	Contract; left edge; sealed. (+) 32732.
32702	1876,1117.2471	Promissory note for silver. 3/-/-.
32703	1876,1117.2472	Promissory note; fragment from centre.
32704	1876,1117.2473	Joined to 32414.
32705	1876,1117.2474	Deposition.
32706	1876,1117.2475	Account of aromatics.
32707	1876,1117.2476	Joined to 32401.
32708	1876,1117.2477	Contract; fragment from centre.
	1876,1117.2478	Joined to 32208.
32709	1876,1117.2479	Astronomical; Normal Star Almanac. Hunger and Sachs, ADART VII, no. 107.
32710	1876,1117.2480	Contract; fragment from centre.
32711	1876,1117.2481	Incantation.
32712	1876,1117.2482	Joined to 30432.
32713	1876,1117.2483	Contract; fragment from centre.
32714	1876,1117.2484	Astronomical Diary.
32715	1876,1117.2485	Economic; left side.
32716	1876,1117.2486	Astrological; tabulated. (+) 32517.
32717	1876,1117.2487	Economic; upper edge.
32718	1876,1117.2488	Chronicle?
32719	1876,1117.2489	Lexical; ṭup abni.
32720	1876,1117.2490	Contract; upper right corner.
32721	1876,1117.2491	Joined to 30432.
32722	1876,1117.2492	Joined to 30432.

32723	1876,1117.2493	Literary.
32724	1876,1117.2494	Joined to 32482.
32725	1876,1117.2495	Joined to 30432.
32726	1876,1117.2496	Economic; flake from centre; three signs only.
32727	1876,1117.2497	Contract. Nbn -/8/-.
32728	1876,1117.2498	Contract; fragment from centre of one face.
32729	1876,1117.2499	Contract; lower edge.
32730	1876,1117.2500	Prayer.
32731	1876,1117.2501	Promissory note for silver; fragment from centre.
32732	1876,1117.2502	Contract; lower left corner; line 2′: KUŠ.GÍD.DA šá-ṭa-ri. (+) 32701.
32733	1876,1117.2503	Contract; lower left corner.
32734	1876,1117.2504	Ritual.
32735	1876,1117.2505	Joined to 30432.
32736	1876,1117.2506	Incantation.
32737	1876,1117.2507	Contract; sale of a field.
32738	1876,1117.2508	Contract; sale of fields; dupl. 33103 and 41935 (+) 42215. [Nbn] 12/12/[]. Babylon. Wunsch, CM 20A-B, no. 8 B; Mitchell and Searight, no. 325.
32739	1876,1117.2509	Contract; right edge.
32740	1876,1117.2510	Promissory note for silver. 25/9/acc.
32741	1876,1117.2511	Contract; left edge.
32742	1876,1117.2512	Astronomical; System A lunar ephemeris. (+) 32302 (+) 32531. Steele, Fs Walker, 293-318, text D.
32743	1876,1117.2513	Contract; sale of a field; sealed. Wunsch, CM 20A-B, no. 174; Nisaba 28, no. 106.
32744	1876,1117.2514	Joined to 32167.
32745	1876,1117.2515	Contract. Dar -/3/-.
32746	1876,1117.2516	Promissory note for silver; lower left corner.
32747	1876,1117.2517	Lexical; Aa II/4 = 12. MSL 14, 280.
	1876,1117.2518	Duplicate registration of 1876,1117.70.
32748	1876,1117.2519	Receipt for delivery of barley. 1/10/-.
32749	1876,1117.2520	Joined to 32247.
32750	1876,1117.2521	Literary cylinder. Gesche, AOAT 275, 670 (wrongly as 32740).
32751	1876,1117.2522	Joined to 32507.
32752	1876,1117.2523	Joined to 32167.
32753	1876,1117.2524	Promissory note for silver. Dar -/-/12.
32754	1876,1117.2525	Unidentified.
32755	1876,1117.2526	Literary; perhaps mythological. Lambert, MC 24, no. 53.
32756	1876,1117.2527	Astronomical Diary.
32757	1876,1117.2528	Hymn.
32758	1876,1117.2529	Astronomical.
32759	1876,1117.2530	Astronomical Diary.

32760	1876,1117.2531	Joined to 32627.
32761	1876,1117.2532	Joined to 32215.
32762	1876,1117.2533	Astronomical; System A lunar ephemeris; several columns, for SE 144-149. (+) 34575 + 34687 + 65831 (+) 132282. Steele, Fs Walker, 293-318, text C; Steele, AHES 60 (2006) 123-153, text D.
32763	1876,1117.2534	Joined to 32165.
32764	1876,1117.2535	Astronomical?
32765	1876,1117.2536	Astronomical Diary.
32766	1876,1117.2537	Astronomical Diary.
32767	1876,1117.2538	Astronomical.
	1876,1117.2539	Joined to 31592.
32768	1876,1117.2540	Astronomical?
32769	1876,1117.2541	Astronomical; Normal Star Almanac for SE 175. + 34263 + 34323. LBAT 1040-1042; Hunger and Sachs, ADART VII, no. 77.
32770	1876,1117.2542	Astronomical; Goal Year Text; not datable. Hunger and Sachs, ADART VI, no. 106.
32771	1876,1117.2543	Lexical; Ḫḫ XXIV. MSL 11, 77.
32772	1876,1117.2544	Joined to 32507.
32773	1876,1117.2545	Joined to 32414.
32774	1876,1117.2546	Omens; extispicy.
32775	1876,1117.2547	Astronomical Diary.
32776	1876,1117.2548	Astronomical.
32777	1876,1117.2549	Joined to 32227.
32778	1876,1117.2550	Astronomical Diary?
32779	1876,1117.2551	Medical.
32780	1876,1117.2552	Joined to 32243.
32781	1876,1117.2553	Medical.
32782	1876,1117.2554	Chronicle?
32783	1876,1117.2555	Astronomical.
32784	1876,1117.2556	Astronomical Diary?
32785	1876,1117.2557	Astronomical; System A lunar ephemeris. + 34041 + 34094 + 34734 + 34778 (+) 34253 + 34354 + 34420. ACT 5; LBAT 10-13 (34041 + 34094 + 34734 + 34778 only).
32786	1876,1117.2558	Joined to 32473.
32787	1876,1117.2559	Astronomical Diary?
32788	1876,1117.2560	Astronomical Diary?
32789	1876,1117.2561	Promissory note for dates and other items. Wunsch, CM 20A-B, no. 224.
32790	1876,1117.2562	Joined to 32573.
32791	1876,1117.2563	Medical; two columns.
32792	1876,1117.2564	Literary.
32793	1876,1117.2565	Economic; fragment from centre.

32794	1876,1117.2566	Promissory note for dates or grain.
32795	1876,1117.2567	Promissory note for silver. Cam.
32796	1876,1117.2568	Contract; lower edge.
32797	1876,1117.2569	Sale of doors. []/12b/acc.
32798	1876,1117.2570	Contract; sale of land.
32799	1876,1117.2571	Contract; upper right corner.
32800	1876,1117.2572	Contract; lower edge.
32801	1876,1117.2573	Promissory note for onions.
32802	1876,1117.2574	Promissory note for dates.
32803	1876,1117.2575	Contract; lower left corner.
32804	1876,1117.2576	Contract; lower right corner.
32805	1876,1117.2577	Astronomical?
32806	1876,1117.2578	Omens; DIŠ ina ITI [...] / DIŠ NA [...]. Cf. Reiner, Fs Borger (CM 10), 293.
32807	1876,1117.2579	Promissory note; lower edge.
32808	1876,1117.2580	Astronomical Diary.
32809	1876,1117.2581	Astronomical; procedure text?
32810	1876,1117.2582	Economic; fragment from centre.
32811	1876,1117.2583	Economic; left edge.
32812	1876,1117.2584	Contract; left edge.
32813	1876,1117.2585	Economic; fragment from centre of one face.
32814	1876,1117.2586	Economic; fragment from lower edge.
32815	1876,1117.2587	Promissory note for dates. Cam.
32816	1876,1117.2588	Contract. Cam? 9/[]/5.
32817	1876,1117.2589	Contract; lower left edge.
32818	1876,1117.2590	Contract; sale of a field. Nbk 5/3/-.
32819	1876,1117.2591	Contract; fragment from lower edge.
32820	1876,1117.2592	Receipt; fragment from lower left corner.
32821	1876,1117.2593	Contract. 11/4/-.
32822	1876,1117.2594	Receipt for barley.
32823	1876,1117.2595	Economic. 3/-/-.
32824	1876,1117.2596	Promissory note for dates.
32825	1876,1117.2597	Contract; fragment from centre of one face.
32826	1876,1117.2598	Economic; flake from centre of one face.
32827	1876,1117.2599	Contract. -/-/6.
32828	1876,1117.2600	Promissory note for silver; fragment from centre of one face.
32829	1876,1117.2601	Contract; fragment from centre of one face.
32830	1876,1117.2602	Economic; fragment from lower left corner.
32831	1876,1117.2603	Economic; flake from lower edge and reverse.
32832	1876,1117.2604	Economic. Cyr 10/5/2.
32833	1876,1117.2605	Sale of a donkey.
32834	1876,1117.2606	Promissory note for silver; lower edge.
32835	1876,1117.2607	Contract; left edge.
32836	1876,1117.2608	Astronomical?

32837	1876,1117.2609	Economic; fragment from centre of one face.
32838	1876,1117.2610	Promissory note; left edge.
	1876,1117.2611ff.	Nos. 2611-2623 are uninscribed objects.
	1876,1117.2624	Joined to 30424.
	1876,1117.2625	Uninscribed clay female head.
	1876,1117.2626	Promissory note. Cyr. Wunsch, CM 3, no. 314.
	1876,1117.2627	Contract. Wunsch, CM 3, no. 386.

1877,0222 collection

The 1877,0222 collection was purchased from Joseph M. Shemtob, London. The register gives its provenance as Babylon.

32839	1877,0222.1	Astronomical Diary for SE 170. + 41629 + 41833. LBAT 411-413; Sachs and Hunger, ADART III, no. -141 F.
32840	1877,0222.2	Joined to Rm.718.
32841	1877,0222.3	Contract for a dowry.
32842	1877,0222.4	Account of delivery of dates or grain.
32843	1877,0222.5	Astronomical Diary for SE 178. LBAT 435; Sachs and Hunger, ADART III, no. -133 A.
32844	1877,0222.6	Astronomical Diary for SE 146. LBAT 376; Sachs and Hunger, ADART II, no. -165 A. Stephenson, HEER, 140.
32845	1877,0222.7	Astronomical; lunar eclipse report for eclipse of 28 December 66 BC. SE Arsaces 246. LBAT 1450; Stephenson, HEER, 184, 205, 210; Hunger and Sachs, ADART V, no. 30.
32846	1877,0222.8	Contract; sale(?); archive of Iddin-Marduk. d.l. Wunsch, AfO 44/45, 99-100, no. 37; Nisaba 28, no. 14.
32847	1877,0222.9	Astronomical; Normal Star Almanac for SE 55. + 41842. LBAT 997-998; Hunger and Sachs, ADART VII, no. 12.
32848	1877,0222.10	Astronomical Diary for SE 226. (+) 41691 + 42100. LBAT 508; Sachs and Hunger, ADART III, no. -85 C.

1877,0409 collection

The 1877,0409 collection was purchased from Joseph M. Shemtob, London. The register gives its provenance as Babylon.

32849	1877,0409.1	Contract; sale of land by Nabû-šuma-uṣur to Kabti-ilāni-Marduk; sealed; finger-nail marks; dupl. 30338. Nbn 24/7/3. Babylon. Nbn 116; 5R 68, 1; Wunsch, CM 20A-B, no. 33; Nisaba 28, no. 65.

1877,0417 collection

The 1877,0417 collection was purchased from Joseph M. Shemtob, London. The register gives its provenance as Babylon.

32850	1877,0417.1	Receipt for silver; sealed. Cam 25/6/2. Cam 119; Bertin 883; Nisaba 28, no. 187.
32851	1877,0417.2	Contract to go to Elam for Marduk-nāṣir-apli by joining the chariot of the governor of Babylon. Dar 15/1/5. Babylon. Dar 154; Abraham, BPPE, 376-377, no. 92; Bertin 2056.
32852	1877,0417.3	Receipt for payment of remainder of dowry. Nbk 17/7/11. Babylon. Nbk 91; Bertin 68.
32853	1877,0417.4	Promissory note for silver. AM 5/4/2. Babylon. Sack, AOATS 4, no. 7; Bertin 283.
32854	1877,0417.5	Promissory note for silver. Nbk 14/12/42. Ḫursag-kalamma. Nbk 408; Bertin 232.
32855	1877,0417.6	Account of dates deliveries.
32856	1877,0417.7	Promissory note for silver. Dar 14/12/1. Babylon.
32857	1877,0417.8	Promissory note for onions; ḫarrānu. Nbk 3/1/36. Šaḫrīn. Nbk 290; Bertin 173; Wunsch, CM 3, no. 20.
32858	1877,0417.9	Receipt of silver by Marduk-nāṣir-apli; sealed. Dar 13/7/31. Babylon. Bertin 2700; Abraham, BPPE, 322-323, no. 66; Nisaba 28, no. 175.
32859	1877,0417.10	Receipt of silver by Marduk-nāṣir-apli's slave and Iddinaya. Dar 30/6/16. Šaḫrīn. Dar 430; Abraham, BPPE, 424-425, no. 120; Bertin 2346.
32860	1877,0417.11	Promissory note for barley. Nbk 8/3/31. Babylon. Nbk 235; Bertin 152.
32861	1877,0417.12	Sale of a slave girl. Nbn 13/11/12. Ḫursag-kalamma. Nbn 665; Wunsch, AfO 44/45, 85-86, no. 15; Bertin 582.
32862	1877,0417.13	Promissory note for silver. Cyr 4/1/7. Babylon. Cyr 245; Bertin 818.
32863	1877,0417.14	Promissory note for silver. Nbn 5/6/17. Bīt-šar-Bābili. Nbn 1047; Bertin 699.
32864	1877,0417.15	Promissory note for silver. Cam 23/4/7. Babylon. Cam 373; Bertin 975.
32865	1877,0417.16	Sale of an ox. Dar 6/12b/27. Šaḫrīn. Bertin 2641.
32866	1877,0417.17	Promissory note for silver. Nbk 22/9/3. Saḫrītu. Nbk 32; Bertin 23.
32867	1877,0417.18	Receipt for purchased onions. Nbn 30/12/acc. Šaḫrīn. Nbn 17; Bertin 342; Wunsch, CM 3, no. 90 (wrongly as 32864).

32868	1877,0417.19	Contract; transfer of responsibility for a person; finger-nail marks. Nbk 1/5/10. Alu-ša-Amurru. Nbk 86; Bertin 64.
32869	1877,0417.20	Promissory note for silver, barley and dates. Nbk 21/7/38. Babylon. Nbk 334; Bertin 198.

1877,1002 collection

The 1877,1002 collection was purchased from Alex Hector (London).

32870	1877,1002.1	Contract; sale of a field; finger-nail marks; sealed. Nbk 2/5/26. Babylon. Nbk 164; Nisaba 28, no. 52.
32871	1877,1002.2	Contract; sale of a house; involves Bunnānītu daughter of Ḫāriṣāya (cf. 33945 and 41459); sealed. Nbn 24/11/2. Babylon. Nbn 85; Pinches, TSBA 8 (1885) 271-273, 279-281, pl. after p. 272; Bertin 371; Wunsch, CM 3, no. 109; Wunsch, CM 20A, 290, no. 241; Nisaba 28, no. 64.

1877,1114 collection

The 1877,1114 collection was purchased from Raphael I. Shemtob, London. The register gives the provenance Babylon to nos. 4, 88, 14, 17 and 19.

32872	1877,1114.1	Contract; sale of a field; sealed; finger-nail marks. Dar 6/2/12. Babylon. Dar 321; Nisaba 28, no. 117.
32873	1877,1114.2	Contract, perhaps for an exchange of boats; Marduk-nāṣir-apli is the scribe. Dar 16/12/26. Babylon. Bertin 2610; Abraham, BPPE, 323-326, no. 67.
32874	1877,1114.3	Promissory note for silver; finger-nail marks. Dar 15/10/23. Babylon. Dar 575; Bertin 2506.
32875	1877,1114.4	Sumerian incantation; dupl. CT 17, 15. CT 51, 141; Schramm, GBAO 2, p. 90, pl. 42, text B5.
32876	1877,1114.5	Contract; sale of a field. Dar 17/12b/5. Babylon. Dar 193; Bertin 2069.
32877	1877,1114.6	Promissory note to pay a debt of barley and dates to Marduk-nāṣir-apli. Dar 25/11/4. Šaḫrīn. Dar 144; Abraham, BPPE, 375-376, no. 91; Bertin 2022.
32878	1877,1114.7	Contract; sale of a field. Nbn 20/4/16. Babylon. Nbn 964; Bertin 673.
32879	1877,1114.8	Contract; sale of a field. AM 17/7/acc. Babylon. Sack, AOATS 4, no. 14; Bertin 253.
32880	1877,1114.9	Promissory note for silver. Dar 18/4/19. Babylon. Dar 483; Bertin 2422.
32881	1877,1114.10	Deposition. Dar 8/12/5. Babylon. Dar 189; Bertin 2072.
32882	1877,1114.11	Promissory note for silver on behalf of Cambyses. Cyr 5/8/4. Cyr 177; Bertin 786.

32883	1877,1114.12	Contract; sale of a boat; Marduk-nāṣir-apli assumes warranty on behalf of the seller. Dar 10/1/10. Babylon. Bertin 2175; Abraham, BPPE, 326-327, no. 68.
32884	1877,1114.13	Astronomical Diary for SE 218. LBAT 494; Sachs and Hunger, ADART III, no. -93 A.
32885	1877,1114.14	Medical ritual.
32886	1877,1114.15	Joined to 32149.
32887	1877,1114.16	Astronomical Diary for SE 170. LBAT 408; Sachs and Hunger, ADART III, no. -141 A.
32888	1877,1114.17	Astronomical; Almanac for SE 127. LBAT 1120; Hunger and Sachs, ADART VII, no. 156.
32889	1877,1114.18	Astronomical Diary for SE 65. + 1877,1114.19 + 32967 + 41614 + 41618. LBAT 271-273; Sachs and Hunger, ADART II, no. -246. Stephenson, HEER, 117, 122; Bertin 2906.
	1877,1114.19	Joined to 32889.
32890	1877,1114.20	Astronomical Diary for SE 215. LBAT 486; Sachs and Hunger, ADART III, no. -96 A.

1877,1115 collection

The 1877,1115 collection was purchased from Solomon Hurwitz, London. The register gives the provenance Babylon to nos. 1, 5, 8-11, 15, 16, 19, 20.

32891	1877,1115.1	Receipt of barley from Marduk-nāṣir-apli. Dar 11/4/[]. Babylon. Bertin 2806; Abraham, BPPE, 328-329, no. 69.
32892	1877,1115.2	Sale of house and land by Šuzubu to Itti-Marduk-balāṭu; sealed; finger-nail marks. Cyr 13/8/6. Babylon. Cyr 345; 5R 68, 2; Nisaba 28, no. 92.
32893	1877,1115.3	Promissory note for silver. Cyr 6/1/4. Babylon. Bertin 797.
32894	1877,1115.4	Contract; transfer of a field, slaves and household goods as dowry. Cam 13/11/3. Babylon. Bertin 895; Wunsch, CM 3, no. 335b.
32895	1877,1115.5	Joined to 32161. Dar 29/12/4. Babylon. Dar 152; Bertin 2018-2019.
32896	1877,1115.6	Promissory note for dates. Dar 16/8/19. Babylon. Dar 486.
32897	1877,1115.7	Promissory note for barley. Nbn 16/11/acc. Babylon. Nbn 14.
32898	1877,1115.8	Contract; lease of a house; sealed. Dar 9/2/3. Borsippa. Dar 64; Bertin 1980; Nisaba 28, no. 153.
32899	1877,1115.9	Contract; sale of fields; finger-nail marks with caption. Dar 22/12b/5. Babylon. Dar 194; Bertin 2057-2058.

32900	1877,1115.10	Promissory note for onions. Cyr 21/12/2. Babylon. Cyr 87; Bertin 758.
32901	1877,1115.11	Deposition. Dar 11/9/11. Šaḫrīn ālu ša Nabû. Dar 309; Bertin 2208.
32902	1877,1115.12	Contract; division of property. Dar 24/1/17. Bāb-bitaqu. Dar 439; Bertin 2374.
32903	1877,1115.13	Promissory note for dates and barley. Nbk 18/8/8. Saḫrītu. Nbk 66; Bertin 51.
32904	1877,1115.14	Promissory note for silver. Nbk 26/5/6. Babylon. Nbk 51; Bertin 38.
32905	1877,1115.15	Receipt for silver as dowry. Cyr 22/8/3. Babylon. Cyr 130; Bertin 781; Wunsch, CM 3, no. 286a.
32906	1877,1115.16	Contract; division of fields as dowry. Cyr 15/8/3. Borsippa. Cyr 128; Bertin 776.
32907	1877,1115.17	Receipt for final payment for purchase of fields. Dar 14/12/6. Babylon. Dar 217; Bertin 2099.
32908	1877,1115.18	Receipt for loans of silver; mentions years 14 and 15; complete.
32909	1877,1115.19	Incantation to Marduk; én ga-aš-ru; dupl. King, BMS, no. 9: 1-25; see Mayer, Untersuchungen, 395, Marduk 2.(2).
32910	1877,1115.20	Contract; sale of fields; not sealed. Dar 24/2/12. Šaḫrīn. Dar 323; Bertin 2233-2234.

1877,1116 collection

The 1877,1116 collection was purchased from Messrs. Spartali & Co., London. The register gives its provenance as Baghdad.

90842	1877,1116.1	Fragment of a stone statue, with historical inscription of Hammurabi; bilingual. CT 21, 40-42; King, LIH, no. 60, LIH I pls. 108-117 (copy), LIH III pp. 172-176; G. Smith, Assyrian Discoveries, p. 233.

1877,1129 collection

The 1877,1129 collection was purchased from William St Chad Boscawen, who had previously been Assistant in the Department of Oriental Antiquities at the British Museum (see E. A. W. Budge, The rise and progress of Assyriology (London, 1925), 120-125, S. M. Evers, Iraq 55, 107-117, and R. Horry, Iraq 77, 107-128).

32911	1877,1129.1	Joined to 32467.

1878,0531 collection

The 1878,0531 collection was purchased from William D. Cutter, London. The register gives the provenance Babylon to nos. 1-25 and the provenance Babylonia to nos. 26a-96.

32912	1878,0531.1	Purchase of vats.
32913	1878,0531.2	Promissory note for silver. [Dar] x+5/1/15. Babylon.
32914	1878,0531.3	Audit of ginû-tax. 5/4/25. Babylon.
32915	1878,0531.4	Building plan with labels. + 32977.
32916	1878,0531.5	Promissory note for dates. Nbk 1/5/2. Saḫrītu. Nbk 24; Bertin 18.
32917	1878,0531.6	Agreement to share assets. Nbk 15/2/21. Larsa. Nbk 125; Bertin 99.
32918	1878,0531.7	Contract; transfer of an obligation to pay silver. Nbk 16/11/41. Babylon. Nbk 387; Bertin 223; Wunsch, CM 3, no. 42.
32919	1878,0531.8	Sale of a slave girl and her child. Nbk 19/9/[?]8. Babylon. Nbk 67; Bertin 247; Wunsch, CM 3, no. 1.
32920	1878,0531.9	Receipt of silver in payment for a slave girl. Nbn 12/12a/12. Nbn 675; Bertin 589; Wunsch, CM 3, no. 207.
32921	1878,0531.10	Promissory note for silver in payment for sheep and goats; ḫarrānu. Nbn 20/1/7. Šaḫrīn. Bertin 434; Wunsch, CM 3, no. 151.
32922	1878,0531.11	Sale of a slave. Nbn []/12/16. Šaḫrīn. Nbn 1020; Bertin 687; Wunsch, CM 3, no. 248.
32923	1878,0531.12	Contract; transfer of an obligation to pay silver; ḫarrānu. Nbn 27/2/2. Babylon. Nbn 63; Bertin 361; Wunsch, CM 3, no. 103.
32924	1878,0531.13	Promissory note for barley. Nbn 19/12/9. Babylon. Nbn 393; Bertin 487.
32925	1878,0531.14	Economic. Cam 1/10/[]. Babylon. Cam 428; Bertin 996.
32926	1878,0531.15	Promissory note for silver. Cam 13/6/5. Cam 285; Bertin 938; Wunsch, CM 3, no. 343.
32927	1878,0531.16	Promissory note for silver. Dar 16/7/10. Babylon. Dar 278; Bertin 2169.
32928	1878,0531.17	Promissory note for silver. Dar 13/11/20. Babylon. Dar 511; Bertin 2435.
32929	1878,0531.18	Receipt for delivery on behalf of Nabû-ušallim. Dar 4/6/6. Babylon. Dar 204; Bertin 2094.
32930	1878,0531.19	Promissory note for dates. Dar 19/6/7. Bertin 2109; Wunsch, CM 20A-B, no. 27.

32931	1878,0531.20	Receipt of silver from Marduk-nāṣir-apli as partial payment of salary. Dar 20/10/6. Babylon. Dar 215; Abraham, BPPE, 390-391, no. 101; Bertin 2096.
32932	1878,0531.21	Receipt of a man to tow boats by Marduk-nāṣir-apli. Dar 18/7/24. Babylon. Bertin 2541; Abraham, BPPE, 330-331, no. 70; Zawadzki, NABU 2001, 57-59, no. 60.
32933	1878,0531.22	Account of dates income. Dar -/-/16. Šaḫrīn. Dar 438; Bertin 2349.
32934	1878,0531.23	Deposition. Dar 18/12/18. Babylon. Dar 475.
32935	1878,0531.24	Cast of a cylinder of Nebuchadnezar II. Berger, AOAT 4/1, Nebukadnezar Zylinder II,8, no. 4; Winckler, ZA 1, 337-348 and 2, 124-125.
32936	1878,0531.25	Cast of a cylinder of Nebuchadnezar II. Berger, AOAT 4/1, Nebukadnezar Zylinder II,8, no. 5; Winckler, ZA 1, 337-348 and 2, 124-125.
32937a	1878,0531.26a	Joined to 32243.
32937b	1878,0531.26b	List of market prices for years 46-48 SE. Slotsky and Wallenfels, Tallies and Trends, text 3.
32938	1878,0531.27	Astronomical Diary.
32939	1878,0531.28	Omens; obv. astrological; rev. medical or physiognomic; colophon of [] / Iddin-Bēl / Iddin?-[]. Cf. Reiner, Fs Borger (CM 10), 293.
32940	1878,0531.29	Astrological. + 32953.
32941	1878,0531.30	Astronomical; Goal Year Text; not datable. + 32984. Hunger and Sachs, ADART VI, no. 107.
32942	1878,0531.31	Astronomical procedure text for the moon; System A. Ossendrijver, BMAPT, no. 75.
32943	1878,0531.32	Omens.
32944	1878,0531.33	Contract; lease of a house. SE [Ant &] Ant 24/[]/111. CT 49, 29, no. 135
32945	1878,0531.34	Astrological; Enūma Anu Enlil.
32946	1878,0531.35	Contract; hire of a boat; left edge.
32947	1878,0531.36	Astronomical; Goal Year Text.
32948	1878,0531.37	Astronomical; Goal Year Text; not datable. Hunger and Sachs, ADART VI, no. 108.
32949	1878,0531.38	Contract; division of property; sealed. d.l. Nisaba 28, no. 632.
32950	1878,0531.39	Astrological omens.
32951	1878,0531.40	Astronomical Diary for SE 121. Sachs and Hunger, ADART II, no. -190 E. Stephenson, HEER, 121.
32952	1878,0531.41	Lexical; syllabary.
32953	1878,0531.42	Joined to 32940.
32954	1878,0531.43	Ritual; mentions Ištar of Babylon. + 32958 + 32966.
32955	1878,0531.44	Astronomical Diary.

32956	1878,0531.45	Joined to 31728. Babylon.
32957	1878,0531.46	Chronicle about Seleucus I. (+) 32235. Grayson, TCS 5, Chronicle 12; BCHP 9.
32958	1878,0531.47	Joined to 32954.
32959	1878,0531.48	Astronomical; pre-Seleucid observations?; copy (ḫe-pí).
32960	1878,0531.49	Literary.
32961	1878,0531.50	Astronomical Diary.
32962	1878,0531.51	Astronomical Diary.
32963	1878,0531.52	Religious; mentions Gula, Ningal, Ezida and Tintir.
32964	1878,0531.53	Astronomical; Goal Year Text; not datable. Hunger and Sachs, ADART VI, no. 109.
32965	1878,0531.54	Astronomical Diary.
32966	1878,0531.55	Joined to 32954.
32967	1878,0531.56	Joined to 32889.
32968	1878,0531.57	Astronomical Diary.
32969	1878,0531.58	Receipt for silver; upper left corner.
32970	1878,0531.59	Contract; sealed. SE [Antiochus] & Seleucus. Nisaba 28, no. 544a.
32971	1878,0531.60	Lexical; syllabary.
32972	1878,0531.61	Astronomical Diary.
32973	1878,0531.62	Economic; lower right corner.
32974	1878,0531.63	Astrological; Enūma Anu Enlil, Adad. Reiner, Fs Borger (CM 10), 293.
32975	1878,0531.64	Omens.
32976	1878,0531.65	Letter from the temple assembly of Esangila to [], the quartermaster (bēl mindu) of the astrologers; sealed; prayer on the upper edge. SE. CT 49, 47, no. 183; Jursa, Persika 9, 151-153; Nisaba 28, no. 677.
32977	1878,0531.66	Joined to 32915.
32978	1878,0531.67	Astrological omens; Enūma Anu Enlil; MUL.MAR. GÍD.DA.
32979	1878,0531.68	Astronomical.
32980	1878,0531.69	Astronomical.
32981	1878,0531.70	Unidentified; upper left corner.
32982	1878,0531.71	Account of dates or grain.
32983	1878,0531.72	Astronomical Diary.
32984	1878,0531.73	Joined to 32941.
32985	1878,0531.74	Astronomical.
32986	1878,0531.75	Astronomical; Goal Year Text for SE 139. Hunger and Sachs, ADART VI, no. 33.
32987	1878,0531.76	Astronomical Diary.
32988	1878,0531.77	Astronomical Diary.
32989	1878,0531.78	Astronomical(?).
32990	1878,0531.79	Astronomical Diary?

32991	1878,0531.80	Astronomical Diary.
32992	1878,0531.81	Medical.
32993	1878,0531.82	Economic; fragment from centre of one face.
32994	1878,0531.83	Astronomical; Almanac. Hunger and Sachs, ADART VII, no. 220.
32995	1878,0531.84	Astronomical.
32996	1878,0531.85	Contract; fragment from centre.
32997	1878,0531.86	Letter to Ea-tabtanâ-bulliṭ / Murānu. SE [Ant II] []/[]/58. Jursa, Persika 9, 194, 212.
32998	1878,0531.87	Illegible.
32999	1878,0531.88	Dialogue contract about the employment of astrologers; sealed. + 33026 + 33038 + 33053a. CT 49, no. 186; van der Spek, BiOr 42, 552-553; both 33038 only; Nisaba 28, no. 611.
33000	1878,0531.89	Economic; fragment from centre of one face.
33001	1878,0531.90	Astrological. Reiner, Fs Borger (CM 10), 293.
33002	1878,0531.91	Astronomical Diary.
33003	1878,0531.92	Astronomical Diary.
33003a	1878,0531.93	Uninscribed; fragment from centre of one face.
33004	1878,0531.94	Astronomical Diary?
33005	1878,0531.95	Illegible.
33006	1878,0531.96	Astronomical.

1878,0730 collection

The 1878,0730 collection was purchased from Solomon Hurwitz, London. The register gives its provenance as Babylon.

33007	1878,0730.1	Contract for the transfer of a field, house and slaves by Nabû-apla-iddina to his father Šamaš-apla-uṣur. Cyr 19/11/7. Cyr 277; Bertin 1683-1684.
33008	1878,0730.2	Receipt for delivery of various products; sealed. Cyr 19/1/8. Dilbat. Bertin 1681; Nisaba 28, no. 186.
33009	1878,0730.3	Account of issues of silver. SE Arsaces 18/11/218. CT 49, 38, no. 156; Strassmaier, ZA 3, 145; van der Spek, Raḫimesu, 226, no. 14.
33010	1878,0730.4	Account of issues of silver. SE Arsaces 11/12/218. CT 49, 37, no. 155; van der Spek, Raḫimesu, 227, no. 15.
33011	1878,0730.5	Account of issues of silver. SE Arsaces 25/8/218. CT 49, 38, no. 157; van der Spek, Raḫimesu, 220, no. 10.
33012	1878,0730.6	Account of issues of silver. SE Arsaces 9/1/219. CT 49, 41, no. 163; van der Spek, Raḫimesu, 233-234, no. 22.
33013	1878,0730.7	Dialogue contract with the assembly of Esangila. SE Arsaces 28/1/219. Babylon. CT 49, 40, no. 160; van

		der Spek, Raḫimesu, 235-237, no. 24; van der Spek, Fs Oelsner, 440-441.
33014	1878,0730.8	Receipt for silver. SE Arsaces 30/2/219. CT 49, 40, no. 161; Strassmaier, ZA 3, 146; van der Spek, Raḫimesu, 239-240, no. 27.
33015	1878,0730.9	Account of issues of silver. SE Arsaces 18/12/218. CT 49, 37, no. 154; van der Spek, Raḫimesu, 227-228, no. 16.
33016	1878,0730.10	Incantations; Ḫulbazizi; the tablet turns sideways; the upper edge is broken, but blank space at the top of obverse and reverse suggests it may have had an amulet format. Not dated, but Seleucid / Arsacid.
33017	1878,0730.11	Issues of dates. SE Arsaces []/[]/209. CT 49, 34, no. 146; Strassmaier, ZA 3, 143; van der Spek, Raḫimesu, 212-213, no. 3.
33018	1878,0730.12	Horoscope; prayer on upper edge. SE Arsaces 22/6/187. LBAT 1468; Rochberg, Babylonian Horoscopes, no. 21; Rochberg, Centaurus 32 (1989), 153-160.

1878,0828 collection

The 1878,0828 collection was presented by Miss Erskine, London. The register gives its provenance as Assyria.

33019	1878,0828.1	Neo-Assyrian cylinder. Royal inscription of Sennacherib; fragment of cols. i-ii only; dupl. Luckenbill, Sennacherib, pp. 23-27, col. i. lines 1-9 and 68-75.

1878,0902 collection

The 1878,0902 collection was purchased from Joseph M. Shemtob, London. The register gives its provenance as Babylon.

-	1878,0902.1	Stone head of a Seljuq(?) statue; now re-registered as 1934,0316.19.
122119a	1878,0902.2	Fragment of stone stela with inscription of Nebuchadnezzar II in archaizing script,

1878,1015 collection

The 1878,1015 collection was purchased from Joseph M. Shemtob, London. The register gives its provenance as Babylon.

33020	1878,1015.1	Legal record about a tithe of arable land, involving Nergal-ina-tēšî-ēṭer, šatammu of Babylon; cf. 47926 and MMA 86.11.299 (CTMMA IV, 213-227). SE. + 33028. BCHP 16.
33021	1878,1015.2	Chronicle.

33022	1878,1015.3	Block of clay with worm tracks(?) on one side; 8 x 4 x 4.5 cms. Compare 39264 and 49083.
33023	1878,1015.4	List of market prices. + 33027. Slotsky and Wallenfels, Tallies and Trends, text 12.
33024	1878,1015.5	Astronomical Diary for SE 188. + 1878,1015.29 + 33045 + 45757. LBAT 452 (45757 only); Sachs and Hunger, ADART III, no. -123 A.
33025	1878,1015.6	Unidentified.
33026	1878,1015.7	Joined to 32999.
33027	1878,1015.8	Joined to 33023.
33028	1878,1015.9	Joined to 33020.
33029	1878,1015.10	Omens; Šumma multabiltu I, source E. + 33053. U. S. Koch, AOAT 326, 90-106; Neb 329a; Wiseman, Chronicles, 94 and pl. xxi (33053 only); Borger, AfO 18, 88; Frahm, GMTR 5, 187, 311.
33030	1878,1015.11	Religious.
33031	1878,1015.12	Astronomical Diary.
33032	1878,1015.13	Astronomical Diary?
33033	1878,1015.14	Astronomical; System A lunar ephemeris. + 33051. ACT 16a.
33034	1878,1015.15	Astronomical; Vorläufer?; two columns; small fragment; upper? edge.
33035	1878,1015.16	Astronomical Diary.
33036	1878,1015.17	Astronomical Diary; mentions an eclipse.
33037	1878,1015.18	Neo-Babylonian royal inscription; tablet fragment.
33038	1878,1015.19	Joined to 32999.
33039	1878,1015.20	Astronomical.
33040	1878,1015.21	Contract; sealed. [Darius II/III]. Nisaba 28, no. 535.
33041	1878,1015.22	Historical; report of Nebuchadnezzar II's campaign to Egypt in his 37th year. + 1878,1015.37. Nbk 329; Wiseman, Chronicles, 94-95 and pls. xx-xxi; Berger, AOAT 4/1, Nebukadnezar Tontafel-Fragment II,1.
33042	1878,1015.23	Astronomical Diary.
33043	1878,1015.24	Contract.
33043a	1878,1015.25	Uninscribed; all surfaces lost.
33044	1878,1015.26	Astronomical Diary for SE 189. + 33047. Sachs and Hunger, ADART III, no. -122 D.
33045	1878,1015.27	Joined to 33024.
33046	1878,1015.28	Brick of Nebuchadnezzar II. CBI, no. 100.
	1878,1015.29	Joined to 33024.
33047	1878,1015.30	Joined to 33044.
33048	1878,1015.31	Astronomical procedure text for Mercury and Mars. Ossendrijver, BMAPT, no. 43.
33049	1878,1015.32	Astronomical.

33050	1878,1015.33	Astronomical; System A lunar ephemeris for SE 228. Steele, SCIAMVS 11 (2010), 211-239, text D.
33051	1878,1015.34	Joined to 33033.
33051a	1878,1015.35	Uninscribed; all surfaces lost
33052	1878,1015.36	Astronomical.
	1878,1015.37	Joined to 33041.
33053	1878,1015.38	Joined to 33029.
33053a	1878,1015.39	Joined to 32999.
	1878,1015.40	Terracotta figurine, boy's head. Karvonen-Kannas, Figurines, 587.
33054	1878,1015.41	Astronomical; System A, lunar ephemeris. Steele, Fs Walker, 293-318, text E.

1878,1023 collection

The 1878,1023 collection was purchased from Joseph M. Shemtob, London. The register gives its provenance as Babylon.

33055	1878,1023.1	Description of divine symbols, with drawings.
33056	1878,1023.2	Contract; sale of a field; sealed; finger-nail marks. Nbn []/[]/[9]. [Babylon?]. (+) 32674. Wunsch, CM 20A-B, no. 111; Roth, Fs Oelsner, 391; Nisaba 28, no. 15b.
33057	1878,1023.3	Contract; sale of land; sealed; finger-nail marks; dupl. 32160 and 41398. AM 11/8/1. Babylon. + 35480 + 38112. Nisaba 28, no. 55.

1878,1028 collection

The 1878,1028 collection was purchased from Joseph M. Shemtob, London. The register gives its provenance as Babylonia

	1878,1028.1ff.	Nos. 1-7 are uninscribed objects.
137447	1878,1028.8	Brick of Nebuchadnezzar II. CBI, no. 102.
	1878,1028.9	Terracotta figurine; male head.
91444	1878,1028.10	Duck weight; uninscribed.
33058	1878,1028.11	Sale of a slave. Dar 16/11/17. Babylon. Dar 457; Bertin 2372.
33059	1878,1028.12	Promissory note for dates. Cyr 5/5/2. Babylon. Bertin 766; Wunsch, CM 3, no. 274.
33060	1878,1028.13	Promissory note for silver. Nbn 16/1/15. Nbn 830; Wunsch, AfO 42/43, 46-47; Bertin 644.
33061	1878,1028.14	Deposition. Dar 6/11/7. Babylon. Dar 229; Bertin 2115.
33062	1878,1028.15	Contract for vats. Nbk 13/11/37. Babylon. Nbk 325; Bertin 188.

1878,1107 collection

The 1878,1107 collection was purchased from Joseph M. Shemtob, London. The register gives its provenance as Babylonia.

33063	1878,1107.1	Promissory note for silver. Nbn 10/3/2. Babylon. Nbn 65; Bertin 363.
33064	1878,1107.2	Contract; sale of a date orchard; sealed; finger-nail marks. Nbn 6/10/5. Babylon. Nbn 203; Wunsch, CM 20A-B, no. 51; Bertin 419-420; Nisaba 28, no. 69.
33065	1878,1107.3	Court record; deposition. Cyr 11/5/8. Babylon. Cyr 312; Bertin 835-836.
33066	1878,1107.4	Astronomical; observation text; lunar and planetary data for Cambyses year 7 (523/2 BC). LBAT 1477; Cam 400; Pinches, BOR 2, 202-207; Epping, ZA 5, 281-288; Kugler, ZA 17, 203-238; Kugler, SSB I 61f.; Stephenson, HEER, 166-167; Hunger and Sachs, ADART V, no. 55; Britton, Fs Slotsky, 7-34; Britton and Huber, Fs Hunger, 215.

1878,1120 collection

The 1878,1120 collection was purchased from Joseph M. Shemtob, London. The register gives its provenance as Babylon.

33067	1878,1120.1	Promissory note for silver and onions; ḫarrānu. Ner 7/12/acc. Babylon. Evetts, Ner 8; Sack, AOAT 236, no. 8; Bertin 296; Wunsch, CM 3, no. 63.
33068	1878,1120.2	Contract; lease of fields, additional clauses. Dar 2/3/3. Babylon. Bertin 1972; Wunsch, CM 20A-B, no. 104.
33069	1878,1120.3	Promissory note for barley. Nbn 23/7/7. Šaḫrīn. Nbn 263; Bertin 442; Wunsch, CM 3, no. 145.
33070	1878,1120.4	Contract; transfer of property from mother to daughter with retention of a life interest. Nbk 24/7/35. Babylon. Nbk 283; Bertin 171-172; Wunsch, CM 3, no. 19.

1878,1130 collection

The 1878,1130 collection was purchased from Joseph M. Shemtob, London. The register gives its provenance as Babylon.

33071	1878,1130.1	Promissory note for silver. Nbn 24/3/7. Bīt-Ṭāb-Bēl. Nbn 253; Bertin 435; Wunsch, CM 3, no. 140.
33072	1878,1130.2	Promissory note for silver. Nbk 10/3/40. Šubat-Gula. Nbk 358; Bertin 202; Wunsch, CM 3, no. 35.
33073	1878,1130.3	Receipt for repayment of silver. Nbn 21/1/3. Babylon. Nbn 90; Bertin 375.

1878,1218 collection

The 1878,1218 collection was purchased from Messrs. Spartali & Co., London. The register gives its provenance as Babylonia.

91075	1878,1218.1	Ur III. Stone wig for a statue dedicated to Lamma by a servant of Ur-Ningirsu for the life of Šulgi. Previously numbered 12218. Frayne, RIME 3/2.1.2.2030; CT 5, 2.

1879,0201 collection

The 1879,0201 collection was purchased from Joseph M. Shemtob, London. The register gives its provenance as Babylon.

33074	1879,0201.1	Cylinder; inscription of Nebuchadnezzar II. Langdon, VAB 4, 84-85, Neb. no. 5. Berger, AOAT 4/1, Nebukadnezar Zylinder II,5.

1879,0301 collection

The 1879,0301 collection was purchased from Joseph M. Shemtob, London. The register gives its provenance as Babylon.

33075	1879,0301.1	Letter from Murānu to Širku. CT 22, 24-25, no. 129; Hackl et al., AOAT 414/1, no. 60.
33076	1879,0301.2	Letter from Mardukā to Ṣillāya. CT 22, 24, no. 127; Hackl et al., AOAT 414/1, no. 44.
33077	1879,0301.3	Letter from Gūzānu (governor of Babylon?) to Širku about soldiers; Darius I is mentioned. CT 22, 15, no. 74; Ebeling, Neubab. Briefe, no. 74; Abraham, BPPE, 368-371, no. 88; Hackl et al., AOAT 414/1, no. 61.
33078	1879,0301.4	Account of payments of silver.
33079	1879,0301.5	Sale of oxen. Nbk 10/5/9. Ḫuṣṣēti ša-Nabû-ḫammē. Nbk 76; Bertin 59.
33080	1879,0301.6	Promissory note for silver. Nbk 16/1/11. Babylon. Nbk 89; Bertin 66.
33081	1879,0301.7	Contract; transfer of responsibility for a slave. Nbk 10/8/37. Upija. Nbk 322; Bertin 186.
33082	1879,0301.8	Agreement about the service of a slave. Nbk 6/[]/41. Bīt-Bēl-rēmanni. Nbk 390; Bertin 224; Wunsch, CM 3, no. 44.
33083	1879,0301.9	Sale of a slave. Nbn 5/7/15. Babylon. Nbn 892; Bertin 660.
33084	1879,0301.10	Court record; deposition; captions for seals but not sealed; finger-nail marks. Nbn 17/8/[]. Bīt-šar-Bābili. Nbn 1113; Bertin 710-711; Strassmaier, Liverpool, no. 42.

33085	1879,0301.11	Promissory note for dates and barley. Dar 3/9/17. Alu-ša-Nabû-ēreš. Dar 448; Bertin 2373.
33086	1879,0301.12	Sale of an ox. Dar 29/6/9. Alu-ša-Nabû-uballiṭ. Dar 257; Bertin 2155.
33087	1879,0301.13	Contract; sale of a field. Dar 2/11/10. Babylon. Dar 287; Bertin 287.

1879,0322 collection

The 1879,0322 collection was purchased from Joseph M. Shemtob, London. The register gives its provenance as Babylon.

33088	1879,0322.1	Cylinder; inscription of Nebuchadnezzar II. Berger, AOAT 4/1, Nebukadnezar Zylinder II,8, no. 6.

1879,0419 collection

The 1879,0419 collection was purchased from Joseph M. Shemtob, London. The register gives its provenance as Babylon.

33089	1879,0419.1	Contract; sale of a field; caption for seals but not sealed; finger-nail marks; dupl. 41406. Nbn 6/12/4. Babylon. Nbn 178a; Bertin 409-410; Wunsch, CM 20A-B, no. 49 B.
33090	1879,0419.2	Contract; sale of a field; sealed; finger-nail marks. Nbn 24/12a/12. Babylon. Nbn 687; Bertin 594-595; Wunsch, CM 20A, 244, no. 120 (copy of seals and captions), and CM 20B, 145-147; Nisaba 28, no. 72.
33091	1879,0419.3	Promissory note for silver; Aramaic note. Cam 8/7/4. Babylon. Stevenson, Ass.-Bab. Contracts, 193, no. 32; Bertin 917.

1879,0430 collection

The 1879,0430 collection was purchased from Joseph M. Shemtob, London. The register gives its provenance as Babylon.

33092	1879,0430.1	Contract; transfer of property (husband to wife and children). Nbk 26/8/41. Bertin 220-221.
33093	1879,0430.2	Sale of a slave girl. Nbn 11/4/13. Babylon. Bertin 1519.
33094	1879,0430.3	Promissory note for silver. Cyr 16/2/6. Ailtammu. Cyr 227; Bertin 815.
33095	1879,0430.4	Contract; sale of a field; finger-nail marks with caption; dupl. 34137. Dar 8/12/1. Babylon. Dar 26; Bertin 1929-1930.
33096	1879,0430.5	Contract; lease of a house. Dar 22/5/14. Babylon. Dar 378; Bertin 2285.

1879,0606 collection

The 1879,0606 collection was purchased from Joseph M. Shemtob, London. The register gives its provenance as Babylon.

33097	1879,0606.1	Cylinder; inscription of Nebuchadnezzar II. Dupl. Langdon, VAB 4, 84-85, Neb. no. 6. Previously numbered 12042. Berger, AOAT 4/1, Nebukadnezar Zylinder II,1, no. 10.
33098	1879,0606.2	School text; lexical.
33099	1879,0606.3	Astronomical; planetary observations for the 8th-11th years; two columns; year 8 has month DIR ŠE (so Darius I or Artaxerxes I).

1879,0730 collection

The 1879,0730 collection was purchased from Joseph M. Shemtob, London. The register gives the provenance Babylonia to nos. 1-18 and the provenance Babylon to nos. 19-54.

33100	1879,0730.1	Promissory note to pay a debt of barley and dates to Marduk-nāṣir-apli. Dar 25/5/13. Babylon. Dar 351; Abraham, BPPE, 412-415, no. 113; Bertin 2251.
33101	1879,0730.2	Receipt of barley; not Dar 153, which is 33111. Dar 16/8/25. Babylon.
33102	1879,0730.3	Sale of a slave. Nbk 16/6/19. Babylon. Nbk 117; Bertin 93.
33103	1879,0730.4	Contract; sale of fields; sealed; dupl. 32738 and 41935 (+) 42215. Nbn [12]/[12]/[]+2. [Babylon]. Wunsch, CM 20A-B, no. 8A; Mitchell and Searight, no. 325; Nisaba 28, no. 75.
33104	1879,0730.5	Promissory note for dates. 26/11/-. Babylon.
33105	1879,0730.6	Promissory note for silver. Cyr 13/7/7. Babylon. Cyr 268; Bertin 800.
33106	1879,0730.7	Promissory note for silver. Nbn 2/10/12. Babylon. Nbn 652; Bertin 578.
33107	1879,0730.8	Promissory note for dates. Nbn 14/2/11. Babylon. Nbn 504; Bertin 522.
33108	1879,0730.9	Old Babylonian account. Samsu-[] []/9/[].
33109	1879,0730.10	Promissory note for dates. Cam 16/5 /5. Babylon. Cam 280; Bertin 936.
33110	1879,0730.11	Receipt for silver given for buying and selling. Dar 20+/9/-. Babylon. Bertin 2769.
33111	1879,0730.12	Promissory note for silver. Dar 12/1/5. Babylon. Dar 153 (wrongly as 79-7-30, 2); Bertin 2059.
33112	1879,0730.13	Receipt of barley from Marduk-nāṣir-apli. Dar 17/5/25. Babylon. Bertin 2587; Abraham, BPPE, 331-

		332, no. 71; Jursa, Bēl-rēmanni, 152; Zawadzki, NABU 2001, 57-59, no. 60.
33113	1879,0730.14	Contract; sale of a field. Dar 15/4/12. Babylon. Bertin 2244.
33114	1879,0730.15	Gift of silver as part of a dowry. Nbn []/11/5. Babylon. Bertin 1297; Roth, JAOS 111, 19-37, and 21 n. 4; Wunsch, CM 3, no. 137.
33115	1879,0730.16	Promissory note for silver. Cam 1/5/7. Babylon. Bertin 1798; Bertin 1798.
33116	1879,0730.17	List of people and addresses (šá áš-bu i-na...).
33117	1879,0730.18	List of dowry. Nbk 18/10/40. Upija. Nbk 369; Bertin 212.
33118	1879,0730.19	Promissory note for silver. Dar 6/-/-. Babylon. Bertin 2768.
33119	1879,0730.20	Sale of oxen. Nbk []/5/5. Babylon. Nbk 42; Bertin 28; Sandowicz, AOAT 398, 177-178, no. O.9.
33120	1879,0730.21	Promissory note for silver. Dar -/3/27. Iggur (near Ur). Bertin 2842.
33121	1879,0730.22	Contract; undertaking by a man under oath to bring his sons to Marduk-nāṣir-apli; ITI.ŠE IGI-ú. Dar 21+/12a/[]. URU Til-Gula.KI. Bertin 2825; Abraham, BPPE, 333-334, no. 71; Zadok, NABU 1997, 6-7, no. 7.
33122	1879,0730.23	Promissory note for silver to Marduk-nāṣir-apli and his brothers; sealed. Dar 9/[]/17. Abraham, BPPE, 334-337, no. 73, and 559-560, no. 19; Nisaba 28, no. 163.
33123	1879,0730.24	Promissory note for silver. Dar 24/12/-. Babylon. Bertin 2838.
33124	1879,0730.25	Promissory note for barley, onions and silver. AM 6/[]/1. Bīt-Ṭāb-Bēl. Sack, AOATS 4, no. 29; Bertin 276; Wunsch, CM 3, no. 54.
33125	1879,0730.26	Joined to 32180.
33126	1879,0730.27	Promissory note for dates. Cam 4/5/6. Bāb-Nār-Barsip. Cam 317; Bertin 968.
33127	1879,0730.28	Hire of a slave girl. Nbn 4/3/9. Babylon. Nbn 340; Bertin 468.
33128	1879,0730.29	Promissory note for dates. Nbn 27/8/7. Nbn 268; Bertin 706; Wunsch, CM 3, no. 146.
33129	1879,0730.30	Promissory note for silver. Nbn 25/12/8. Babylon. Nbn 316; Bertin 46.
33130	1879,0730.31	Account of delivery of sheep and goats. 11/1/9.
33131	1879,0730.32	Promissory note for silver. Dar 10/10/19. Babylon. Dar 489; Bertin 2411.

33132	1879,0730.33	Receipt for payment for purchase of field. Dar 4/5/11. Ḫursag-kalamma. Dar 302; Bertin 2202.
33133	1879,0730.34	Promissory note for silver; sealed. Nbn 24/10/10. Nbn 466; Bertin 352; Wunsch, CM 3, no. 180; Nisaba 28, no. 147.
33134	1879,0730.35	Contract; division of property. Cyr.
33135	1879,0730.36	Economic; mentions several women.
33136	1879,0730.37	Contract; sale of a field; sealed; finger-nail marks. Nbn 22/11/10. Babylon. Nbn 477; Bertin 513-514; Wunsch, CM 20A, 233, no. 94 and CM 220B, 119-121; Nisaba 28, no. 71.
33137	1879,0730.38	Promissory note for silver. Nbn 22/4/12. Babylon. Nbn 611; Bertin 564; Wunsch, CM 3, no. 198.
33138	1879,0730.39	Account of silver.
33139	1879,0730.40	Sale of slaves. Cam 19/7/3. Babylon. Cam 189; Bertin 897.
33140	1879,0730.41	Promissory note for dates. Cam 20/6/2. Nāru-eššu. Cam 118; Bertin 879.
33141	1879,0730.42	Promissory note for barley.
33142	1879,0730.43	Deposition. Nbk 29/1/[]. Upija. Nbk 419; Bertin 235.
33143	1879,0730.44	School practice text; wedges only.
33144	1879,0730.45	Promissory note for dates; dupl. Nab 619. Nbn (18)/(5)/(12). Nbn 375; Bertin 74; Wunsch, CM 3, no. 200.
33145	1879,0730.46	Joined to 31738.
33146	1879,0730.47	Promissory note for dates.
33147	1879,0730.48	Promissory note for silver. Nbk 1/10/8. Babylon. Nbk 68; Bertin 52.
33148	1879,0730.49	Promissory note for dates. Dar 23/6/15. Ālu-ša-Bēl-ittannu. Dar 404; Bertin 2317.
33149	1879,0730.50	Promissory note for silver. Dar 12/12/8. Šaḫrīn. Dar 243; Bertin 2138.
33150	1879,0730.51	Deposition. Dar 15/5/20. Dar 504; Bertin 2439.
33151	1879,0730.52	Contract; sale of a field. Dar 14/[]/11. Dar 316; Bertin 2200.
33152	1879,0730.53	Receipt for delivery of barley. Dar 27/8/19. Babylon. Bertin 2421.
33153	1879,0730.54	Promissory note for silver; sealed. Dar 21/1/18. Babylon. Dar 464; Bertin 2394; Nisaba 28, no. 165.

1879,1108 collection

The 1879,1108 collection was purchased from Joseph M. Shemtob, London. The register gives its provenance as Babylonia.

33154	1879,1108.1	Incantation; colophon: copied from an original from Borsippa.
33155	1879,1108.2	Religious.
33156	1879,1108.3	Receipt for payment of silver. Nbn 11/12/9. Babylon. Nbn 390; Bertin 484; Wunsch, CM 3, no. 171.
33157	1879,1108.4	Deposition. Dar 1/[]/12. Babylon. Dar 339; Bertin 2224.

1879,1210 collection

The 1879,1210 collection was purchased from J. Fremlyn Streatfeild, London. The register gives its provenance as Tel-loh.

91057	1879,1210.1	Bronze peg figure with inscription of Gudea. Previously numbered 12200. Steible, FAOS 9/1 Gudea 51 (F); Edzard, RIME 3/1 1.7.41.
	1879,1210.2-3	Nos. 2-3 are uninscribed objects.

B collection

The B collection is the product of excavations by W. K. Loftus at Tell Sifr (Kutalla) in 1854 and by J. J. Taylor at Ur. The register records no provenances. Much of the collection was published by Strassmaier as coming from Warka (Uruk) and later by Jean as coming from Tell Sifr (Kutalla). D. Charpin's recent study (Charpin, Archives) showed that in fact it is a mixture of tablets from Kutalla and Ur.

Loftus, Travels, pp. 263-271, in giving account of his excavations at Tel Sifr reports finding tablets carefully stored in an assembly of unbaked bricks and reed matting. He says, "Several were found broken but the fragments were carefully collected. There must have been, in all, about one hundred tablets of which about seventy are either quite perfect or slightly damaged".

Charpin identifies 34 tablets as coming from Ur, and suggests (Charpin, Archives, p. 26) that they are to be identified with the "about thirty small and large" fragments of tablets found by Taylor on his "Tomb Mound" (Taylor, JRAS 15, 1855, p. 274), but in fact a better comparison is with Taylor's later reference to finding "two jars, filled with clay tablets, in envelopes of the same material" (Taylor, JRAS 15, 1855, p. 414); they were found in the vaults 20 feet under ground in the extreme western mound (JRAS 15, pl. III. Fig. 1).

Since Charpin's publication numerous joins have been made to these tablets by Janet Politi from a box of unmarked inscribed fragments of B tablets (here listed as "unnum."); more fragments remain to be joined including many bearing seal impressions. The fact that there are so many fragments available to be joined must be entirely due to the remarkable circumstances in which the two collections had been stored in antiquity.

With the single exception of 33262 everything in this collection is Old Babylonian. Note that the fragment B.171 has been joined to K.13942. 33846 (Rm-IV.406) has had two unnumbered B fragments joined to it. This seems to be a clear indication that it was registered out of its proper collection and that it comes from Kutalla or Ur. Another Tell Sifr tablet marked B.5 was registered as K.1377.

33158	B.1	Contract; sale of a house. Rim-Sin -/2/4. Ur. Strassmaier, Warka, no. 76; Jean, Tell Sifr, no. 2; Charpin, Archives, 44-45 and 202, no. 2.
33158a	B.1a	Case of 33158. Rim-Sin -/2/4. Ur. Strassmaier, Warka, no. 76A (quoted as variants); Jean, Tell Sifr, no. 2a; Charpin, Archives, 44-45 and 202, no. 2a.
33159	B.2	Contract; sale of a house plot. Rim-Sin -/6/8. Ur. Strassmaier, Warka, no. 77; Jean, Tell Sifr, no. 6; Charpin, Archives, 34-35 and 204, no. 6.
33159a	B.2a	Case of 33159. Rim-Sin -/6/8. Ur. + 33312 + unnum. Strassmaier, Warka, no. 77A (quoted as variants); Jean, Tell Sifr, no. 6a; Charpin, Archives, 34-35 and 204-205, no. 6a.
33160	B.3	Letter; names of sender and addressee lost.
33161	B.4	Contract; sale of a house plot; two fragments, not joining. Samsuiluna 30/9/7. Kutalla. + 3 unnum. Strassmaier, Warka, no. 49; Jean, Tell Sifr, no. 79; Charpin, Archives, 113 and 261, no. 79.
33161a	B.4a	Case of 33181. Rim-Sin -/12/9. Ur. + 33181a + 33276 + 33303 + 5 unnum. Strassmaier, Warka, no. 92 (33181a, quoted as variants); Jean, Tell Sifr, no. 14a + 79b; Charpin, Archives, 45 and 209-210, no. 14a.
33161aa	B.4aa	Case of 33161. Samsuiluna 30/9/7. Kutalla. (+) 33161b (+) 33269 + 33320 + unnum. (+) 33316. Jean, Tell Sifr, no. 79a; Charpin, Archives, 113 and 261-262, no. 79a.
33161b	B.4b	Case of 33161. (+) 33161aa.
33161c	B.4c	Fragment of a case; line 1, [] sar é-dù-a [].
33162	B.5	Contract; sale of a house plot. Rim-Sin II -/11/b. Kutalla. Strassmaier, Warka, no. 22; Jean, Tell Sifr, no. 86; Charpin, Archives, 114-115, 195 and 267, no. 86.
33162a	B.5a	Case of 33162. Rim-Sin II -/11/b. Kutalla. Strassmaier, Warka, no. 22; Jean, Tell Sifr, no. 86a; Charpin, Archives, 114-115, 195 and 267, no. 86a.
33163	B.6	Contract; sale of a house. Rim-Sin -/12/36. Kutalla. Strassmaier, Warka, no. 24; Jean, Tell Sifr, no. 28; Charpin, Archives, 91 and 218, no. 28.

33163a	B.6a	Case of 33163. Rim-Sin -/12/36. Kutalla. Strassmaier, Warka, no. 24; Jean, Tell Sifr, no. 28a; Charpin, Archives, 91 and 219, no. 28a.
33164	B.7	Administrative; right half; month 8, year [mu ... d.e]n.ki / [...] x ki? ba-dù. Ur? + unnum.
33165	B.8	Contract; agreement about a party wall. Warad-Sin -/8/12. Ur. Strassmaier, Warka, no. 78; Jean, Tell Sifr, no. 87; Charpin, Archives, 44 and 267-268, no. 87.
33166	B.9	Contract about prebends. d.l. Ur. Strassmaier, Warka, no. 79; Jean, Tell Sifr, no. 88; Charpin, Archives, 51-52 and 268, no. 88.
33167	B.10	Record of payments for work in the temple of Gula. n.d. Ur. Strassmaier, Warka, no. 80; Jean, Tell Sifr, no. 89; Charpin, Archives, 42 and 268, no. 89.
33168	B.11	Contract involving an issue of flour. n.d. Ur. Strassmaier, Warka, no. 81; Jean, Tell Sifr, no. 90; Charpin, Archives, 53 and 268, no. 90.
33169	B.12	Record of payments for work in the temple of Nanna. Rim-Sin 28/[]/58. Ur. Strassmaier, Warka, no. 82; Jean, Tell Sifr, no. 91; Charpin, Archives, 42 and 269, no. 91.
33170	B.13	Contract; agreement about a party wall. d.l. Ur. Strassmaier, Warka, no. 83; Jean, Tell Sifr, no. 92; Charpin, Archives, 41 and 269, no. 92.
33171	B.14	Contract; sale of land. d.l. Kutalla. Strassmaier, Warka, no. 2; Jean, Tell Sifr, no. 31; Charpin, Archives, 136 and 220, no. 31.
33172	B.15	Contract; sale of a house. Rim-Sin -/[]/2. Ur. Strassmaier, Warka, no. 84; Jean, Tell Sifr, no. 93; Charpin, Archives, 28 and 269, no. 93.
33173	B.16	Contract; sale of land. Warad-Sin -/4/2. Ur. Strassmaier, Warka, no. 85; Jean, Tell Sifr, no. 94; Charpin, Archives, 39 and 269-270, no. 94.
33173a	B.16a	Case of 33173. Warad-Sin -/4/2. Ur. + 33288. Jean, Tell Sifr, no. 94a; Charpin, Archives, 39 and 270, no. 94a.
33174	B.17	Contract; gift of a prebend. Rim-Sin 24/10/24. Ur. Strassmaier, Warka, no. 86; Jean, Tell Sifr, no. 20; Charpin, Archives, 47-49 and 213, no. 20.
33174a	B.17a	Case of 33174. Rim-Sin 24/10/24. Ur. (+) 33268. Strassmaier, Warka, no. 86 (quoted as variants); Jean, Tell Sifr, no. 20a; Charpin, Archives, 47-49 and 213, no. 20a.

33175	B.18	Contract; sale of a prebend. Rim-Sin -/8/28. Ur. Strassmaier, Warka, no. 87; Jean, Tell Sifr, no. 21; Charpin, Archives, 49 and 214, no. 21.
33175a	B.18a	Case of 33175. Rim-Sin -/8/28. Ur. Strassmaier, Warka, no. 87 (quoted as variants); Jean, Tell Sifr, no. 21a; Charpin, Archives, 49 and 214, no. 21a.
33176	B.19	Contract; sale of land. Rim-Sin -/8/13. Kutalla. Strassmaier, Warka, no. 88; Jean, Tell Sifr, no. 12; Charpin, Archives, 136 and 208, no. 12.
33176a	B.19a	Case of 33176. Rim-Sin -/8/13. Kutalla. Strassmaier, Warka, no. 88 (quoted as variants); Jean, Tell Sifr, no. 12a; Charpin, Archives, 136 and 208, no. 12a.
33177	B.20	Contract; sale of land. Rim-Sin -/12b/7. Kutalla. Strassmaier, Warka, no. 89; Jean, Tell Sifr, no. 95; Charpin, Archives, 132 and 270-271, no. 95.
33177a	B.20a	Case of 33177. Rim-Sin -/12b/7. Kutalla. Strassmaier, Warka, no. 89 (note only); Charpin, Archives, 132 and 270-271, no. 95a.
33178	B.21	Contract; sale of an orchard. d.l. Ur. Jean, Tell Sifr, no. 98 (part; under wrong number B.102); Charpin, Archives, 53, 273 and pl. IV, no. 98.
33178a	B.21a	Case of 33178. d.l. Ur. Charpin, Archives, 53, 273 and pl. IV, no. 98a.
33179	B.22	Contract; sale of a house plot. Rim-Sin -/5/10. Ur. Strassmaier, Warka, no. 90; Jean, Tell Sifr, no. 8; Charpin, Archives, 46 and 205-206, no. 8.
33179a	B.22a	Case of 33179. Rim-Sin -/5/10. Ur. Strassmaier, Warka, no. 90 (quoted as variants); Jean, Tell Sifr, no. 8a; Charpin, Archives, 46 and 206, no. 8a.
33180	B.23	Contract; division of an inheritance in land and prebends. Rim-Sin -/12/7. Ur. Strassmaier, Warka, no. 91; Jean, Tell Sifr, no. 5; Charpin, Archives, 37-38 and 203-204, no. 5.
33180a	B.23a	Case of 33180. Rim-Sin -/12/7. Ur. + 2 unnum. Strassmaier, Warka, no. 91 (quoted as variants); Jean, Tell Sifr, no. 5a; Charpin, Archives, 37-38 and 204, no. 5a.
33181	B.24	Contract about an inheritance in land, prebends and furniture. The case is 33161a+. Rim-Sin -/12/9. Ur. Strassmaier, Warka, no. 92; Jean, Tell Sifr, no. 14; Charpin, Archives, 45-46 and 209, no. 14.
33181a	B.24a	Joined to 33161a.
33182	B.25	Contract; sale of a house plot. Rim-Sin -/7/8. Ur. Strassmaier, Warka, no. 93; Jean, Tell Sifr, no. 7; Charpin, Archives, 36 and 205, no. 7.

33182a	B.25a	Case of 33182. Rim-Sin -/7/8. Ur. Strassmaier, Warka, no. 93 (quoted as variants); Jean, Tell Sifr, no. 7a; Charpin, Archives, 36 and 205, no. 7a.
33183	B.26	Contract; adoption of Šat-Sîn as her daughter by Bēlessunu. Rim-Sin -/5/15. Ur. Strassmaier, Warka, no. 94; Jean, Tell Sifr, no. 13; Charpin, Archives, 46-47 and 208-209, no. 13.
33183a	B.26a	Case of 33183. Rim-Sin -/5/15. Ur. Charpin, Archives, 46-47 and 209, no. 13a.
33184	B.27	Contract; adoption of Ilî-sukkallum as her son by Ḫiššātum. Rim-Sin -/10/38. Kutalla. + 33280. Strassmaier, Warka, no. 3; Meissner, BAP, no. 93; Jean, Tell Sifr, no. 32; Charpin, Archives, 73-75 and 220-221, no. 32.
33184a	B.27a	Case of 33184. Rim-Sin -/10/38. Kutalla. Strassmaier, Warka, no. 4; Meissner, BAP, no. 93; Jean, Tell Sifr, no. 32a; Charpin, Archives, 73-75 and 221, no. 32a.
33185	B.28	Contract; sale of a house. Rim-Sin -/8/28. Ur. Strassmaier, Warka, no. 95; Jean, Tell Sifr, no. 22 (with wrong numbers B.48 and 33205); Charpin, Archives, 29-30 and 214-215, no. 22.
33185a	B.28a	Case of 33185. Rim-Sin -/8/28. Ur. Strassmaier, Warka, no. 95 (quoted as variants); Jean, Tell Sifr, no. 22a; Charpin, Archives, 29-30 and 215, no. 22a.
33186	B.29	Contract; sale of a house. Rim-Sin -/11/17. Ur. Strassmaier, Warka, no. 96; Jean, Tell Sifr, no. 16; Charpin, Archives, 28-29 and 210-211, no. 16.
33186a	B.29a	Case of 33186. Rim-Sin -/11/17. Ur. + 33293 + 33315 + 2 unnum. Strassmaier, Warka, no. 96 (quoted as variants); Jean, Tell Sifr, no. 16a; Charpin, Archives, 28-29 and 211, no. 16a.
33187	B.30	Contract; sale of a house. Rim-Sin -/7/10. Ur. Strassmaier, Warka, no. 97; Jean, Tell Sifr, no. 9; Charpin, Archives, 41 and 206, no. 9.
33187a	B.30a	Case of 33187. Rim-Sin -/7/10. Ur. Strassmaier, Warka, no. 97 (quoted as variants); Jean, Tell Sifr, no. 9a; Charpin, Archives, 41 and 206, no. 9a.
33188	B.31	Contract; sale of land. Rim-Sin -/8/4. Kutalla. Strassmaier, Warka, no. 98; Jean, Tell Sifr, no. 3 (with wrong number 33192) Charpin, Archives, 135 and 202, no. 3.
33188a	B.31a	Case of 33188. Rim-Sin -/8/4. Kutalla. Strassmaier, Warka, no. 98 (quoted as variants); Jean, Tell Sifr, no. 3a; Charpin, Archives, 35 and 202, no. 3a.

33189	B.32	Contract; sale of a house and storehouses. Rim-Sin 30/10/17. Ur. Strassmaier, Warka, no. 99; Jean, Tell Sifr, no. 15; Charpin, Archives, 47 and 210, no. 15.
33189a	B.32a	Case of 33189. Rim-Sin 30/10/17. Ur. Strassmaier, Warka, no. 99 (quoted as variants); Jean, Tell Sifr, no. 15a; Charpin, Archives, 47 and 210, no. 15a.
33190	B.33	Contract; sale of land. Warad-Sin -/12/[2]. Ur. Strassmaier, Warka, no. 100; Jean, Tell Sifr, no. 96; Charpin, Archives, 39-40 and 271, no. 96.
33190a	B.33a	Case of 33190. Warad-Sin -/12/[2]. Ur. + 33270. Strassmaier, Warka, no. 100 (quoted as variants); Jean, Tell Sifr, no. 96a; Charpin, Archives, 39-40 and 271-272, no. 96a.
33191	B.34	Lawsuit about the sale of a house. Nur-Adad -/10/b. Ur. Jean, Tell Sifr, no. 1; Charpin, Archives, 42-44 and 201, no. 1.
33191a	B.34a	Case of 33191. Nur-Adad -/10/b. Ur. Strassmaier, Warka, no. 1; Jean, Tell Sifr, no. 1a; Charpin, Archives, 42-44 and 201, no. 1a.
33192	B.35	Contract; sale of land. Rim-Sin -/5/6. Ur. Strassmaier, Warka, no. 101; Jean, Tell Sifr, no. 4 (with wrong number 33188); Charpin, Archives, 36-37 and 203, no. 4.
33193	B.36	Contract; sale of land. Rim-Sin -/11/11. Ur. Strassmaier, Warka, no. 5; Jean, Tell Sifr, no. 11; Charpin, Archives, 46 and 207, no. 11.
33193a	B.36a	Case of 33193. Rim-Sin -/11/11. Ur. Strassmaier, Warka, no. 6; Jean, Tell Sifr, no. 11a; Charpin, Archives, 46 and 208, no. 11a.
33194	B.37	Contract; sale of a house plot. Rim-Sin -/11/47. Kutalla. Strassmaier, Warka, no. 7; Jean, Tell Sifr, no. 30; Charpin, Archives, 115 and 219, no. 30.
33194a	B.37a	Case of 33194. Rim-Sin -/11/47. Kutalla. Strassmaier, Warka, no. 8; Jean, Tell Sifr, no. 30a; Charpin, Archives, 115 and 220, no. 30a.
33195	B.38	Contract; sale of a house. Rim-Sin 30/12/35. Ur. Strassmaier, Warka, no. 9; Meissner, BAP, no. 41; Jean, Tell Sifr, no. 25; Charpin, Archives, 30-34 and 216, no. 25.
33195a	B.38a	Case of 33195. Rim-Sin 30/12/35. Ur. Strassmaier, Warka, no. 10; Jean, Tell Sifr, no. 25a; Charpin, Archives, 30-34 and 217, no. 25a.
33196	B.39	Contract; sale of a house plot. Rim-Sin II 26/11/b. Kutalla. Strassmaier, Warka, no. 11; Jean, Tell Sifr, no. 85; Charpin, Archives, 110-111, 195 and 266, no. 85.

33196a	B.39a	Case of 33196. Rim-Sin II 26/11/b. Kutalla. Strassmaier, Warka, no. 12; Jean, Tell Sifr, no. 85a; Charpin, Archives, 110-111, 195 and 266, no. 85a.
33197	B.40	Contract; sale of a house. Rim-Sin 30/7/42. Kutalla. Strassmaier, Warka, no. 13; Jean, Tell Sifr, no. 29; Charpin, Archives, 141-142 and 219, no. 29.
33197a	B.40a	Case of 33197. Rim-Sin 30/7/42. Kutalla. Strassmaier, Warka, no. 14; Jean, Tell Sifr, no. 29a; Charpin, Archives, 141-142 and 219, no. 29a.
33198	B.41	Contract; sale of land. Rim-Sin -/4/11. Kutalla. Strassmaier, Warka, no. 15; Jean, Tell Sifr, no. 10; Charpin, Archives, 132-133 and 206-207, no. 10.
33198a	B.41a	Case of 33198. Rim-Sin -/4/11. Kutalla. Strassmaier, Warka, no. 16; Jean, Tell Sifr, no. 10a; Charpin, Archives, 132-133 and 207, no. 10a.
33199	B.42	Contract; adoption of Enlil-issu as their heir by Etel-pî-Sîn and his wife Sîn-nâda. Rim-Sin -/1/[]. Ur. + K.14844. Strassmaier, Warka, no. 102; Meissner, BAP, no. 98; Jean, Tell Sifr, no. 97; Charpin, Archives, 50-51 and 272, no. 97.
33199a	B.42a	Case of 33199. Rim-Sin -/1/[]. Ur. Strassmaier, Warka, no. 102 (quoted as variants); Meissner, BAP, no. 98; Jean, Tell Sifr, no. 97a; Charpin, Archives, 50-51 and 272-273, no. 97a.
33200	B.43	Contract; sale of land. Hammurabi -/7/39. Kutalla. Strassmaier, Warka, no. 103; Meissner, BAP, no. 67; Jean, Tell Sifr, no. 48; Charpin, Archives, 92 and 234-235, no. 48.
33200a	B.43a	Case of 33200. Hammurabi -/7/39. Kutalla. Strassmaier, Warka, no. 103 (quoted as variants); Meissner, BAP, no. 67; Jean, Tell Sifr, no. 48a; Charpin, Archives, 92 and 235, no. 48a.
33201	B.44	Contract; division of an inheritance in land. Rim-Sin -/11/20. Kutalla. Strassmaier, Warka, no. 17; Meissner, BAP, no. 108; Jean, Tell Sifr, no. 18; Charpin, Archives, 73 and 212, no. 18.
33201a	B.44a	Case of 33201. Rim-Sin -/11/20. Kutalla. Strassmaier, Warka, no. 18; Meissner, BAP, no. 108; Jean, Tell Sifr, no. 18a; Charpin, Archives, 73 and 212, no. 18a.
33202	B.45	Contract; sale of a house plot. Rim-Sin 10/11/57. Kutalla. Strassmaier, Warka, no. 19; Jean, Tell Sifr, no. 27; Charpin, Archives, 137-138 and 217-218, no. 27.
33202a	B.45a	Case of 33202. Rim-Sin 10/11/57. Kutalla. Jean, Tell Sifr, no. 27a; Charpin, Archives, 137-138 and 218, no. 27a.

33203	B.46	Contract; sale of a prebend. Case only. Rim-Sin 25/[]/30. Ur. Strassmaier, Warka, no. 104 (under number B 46a); Jean, Tell Sifr, no. 23; Charpin, Archives, 49 and 215, no. 23.
33204	B.47	Contract; division of an orchard. Rim-Sin -/6/34. Ur. Strassmaier, Warka, no. 105; Jean, Tell Sifr, no. 24; Charpin, Archives, 30 and 215-216, no. 24.
33204a	B.47a	Case of 33204. Rim-Sin -/6/34. Ur. Strassmaier, Warka, no. 105 (quoted as variants); Jean, Tell Sifr, no. 24a; Charpin, Archives, 30 and 216, no. 24a.
33205	B.48	Contract; renunciation of future claims against Ḫiššātum. Rim-Sin -/5/17. Kutalla. Strassmaier, Warka, no. 20; Meissner, BAP, no. 44; Jean, Tell Sifr, no. 17; Charpin, Archives, 72-73 and 211, no. 17.
33205a	B.48a	Case of 33205. Rim-Sin -/5/17. Kutalla. Strassmaier, Warka, no. 21; Meissner, BAP, no. 44; Jean, Tell Sifr, no. 17a; Charpin, Archives, 72-73 and 211-212, no. 17a.
33206	B.49	Contract; division of an inheritance in land, furniture and slaves. Case is 33286 + 33313 (+) 33295. Rim-Sin -/4/23. Kutalla. Strassmaier, Warka, no. 106; Jean, Tell Sifr, no. 19; Charpin, Archives, 62-63 and 212-213, no. 19.
33207	B.50	Contract; payment made by Ḫiššātum for regular offerings to Annunitum. Rim-Sin 30/12/36. Ur. Strassmaier, Warka, no. 107; Jean, Tell Sifr, no. 26; Charpin, Archives, 51 and 217, no. 26.
33207a	B.50a	Case of 33207. Rim-Sin 30/12/36. Ur. Strassmaier, Warka, no. 107 (quoted as variants); Jean, Tell Sifr, no. 26a; Charpin, Archives, 51 and 217, no. 26a.
33208	B.51	Contract; sale of a slave. Rim-Sin II 10/9/b. Kutalla. Meissner, BAP, no. 1; Charpin, Archives, 114, 195 and 275-276, no. 102.
33209	B.52	Contract; division of an inheritance in land, commodities and silver. Hammurabi 4/12/36. Kutalla. Strassmaier, Warka, no. 25; Jean, Tell Sifr, no. 44; Charpin, Archives, 68-69 and 231-232, no. 44.
33209a	B.52a	Case of 33209. Hammurabi 4/12/36. Kutalla. Strassmaier, Warka, no. 26; Jean, Tell Sifr, no. 44a; Charpin, Archives, 68-69 and 232, no. 44a.
33210	B.53	Contract; sale of a house. Hammurabi -/1/31. Kutalla. Strassmaier, Warka, no. 27; Jean, Tell Sifr, no. 33; Charpin, Archives, 107-108 and 221, no. 33.

33210a	B.53a	Case of 33210. Hammurabi -/1/31. Kutalla. + unnum. Strassmaier, Warka, no. 27; Jean, Tell Sifr, no. 33a; Charpin, Archives, 107-108 and 221, no. 33a.
33211	B.54	Contract; repayment of a deposit of silver. Hammurabi 10/10/41. Kutalla. Strassmaier, Warka, no. 108; Meissner, BAP, no. 28; Jean, Tell Sifr, no. 54; Charpin, Archives, 121 and 239, no. 54.
33211a	B.54a	Case of 33211. Hammurabi 10/10/41. Kutalla. Strassmaier, Warka, no. 108 (quoted as variants); Meissner, BAP, no. 28; Jean, Tell Sifr, no. 54a; Charpin, Archives, 121 and 239, no. 54a.
33212	B.55	Contract; sale of land. Hammurabi -/6/42. Kutalla. Strassmaier, Warka, no. 28; Jean, Tell Sifr, no. 55; Charpin, Archives, 95 and 239-240, no. 55.
33212a	B.55a	Case of 33212. Hammurabi -/6/42. Kutalla. (+) 33212b-e (+) 33272 + 33291 (+) 33327. Strassmaier, Warka, no. 28 (note only); Charpin, Archives, 95 and 240, no. 55a.
33212b-e	B.55a	Four fragments of case of 33212 and two more unnumbered fragments. Hammurabi -/6/42. Kutalla. (+) 33212a.
33213	B.56	Contract; sale of land; dupl. 33218. Hammurabi -/3/36. Kutalla. Strassmaier, Warka, no. 29; Meissner, BAP, no. 46; Jean, Tell Sifr, no. 40; Charpin, Archives, 99-101 and 227, no. 40
33213a	B.56a	Case of 33213. Hammurabi -/3/36. Kutalla. + 33278 + 33285 + 33314 + 33325 + 10 unnum. Strassmaier, Warka, no. 29; Jean, Tell Sifr, no. 40a; Charpin, Archives, 99-101 and 227-228, no. 40a.
33214	B.57	Lawsuit about ownership of an orchard after a mīšarum-decree of Rim-Sin. Hammurabi 4/7/41. Kutalla. Strassmaier, Warka, no. 30; Meissner, BAP, no. 43; Jean, Tell Sifr, no. 58; Charpin, Archives, 142-146 and 242-243, no. 58.
33214a	B.57a	Case of 33214. Hammurabi 4/7/41. Kutalla. + 33268a + 33283 + 33296 + 33306 + 33310 + 33321 + 33323 + 5 unnum. Strassmaier, Warka, no. 30 (note only); Charpin, Archives, 142-146 and 243-244, no. 58a.
33215	B.58	Contract; sale of a storehouse. Hammurabi 5/9/35. Kutalla. Strassmaier, Warka, no. 31; Jean, Tell Sifr, no. 39; Charpin, Archives, 92 and 226, no. 39.
33215a	B.58a	Case of 33215. Hammurabi 5/9/35. Kutalla. + 33308. Strassmaier, Warka, no. 31 (note only); Charpin, Archives, 92 and 226-227, no. 39a.

33216	B.59	Contract; sale of a house. Hammurabi -/11/[]. Kutalla. Strassmaier, Warka, no. 32; Jean, Tell Sifr, no. 59; Charpin, Archives, 90-91 and 244, no. 59.
33216a	B.59a	Fragment of case of 33216. Hammurabi -/11/[]. Kutalla. + unnum. (+) 33216b-d. Strassmaier, Warka, no. 32 (note only); Charpin, Archives, 90-91 and 244-245, no. 59a.
33216b-d	B.59a	Three fragments of case of 33216. Hammurabi -/11/[]. Kutalla. (+) 33216a. Strassmaier, Warka, no. 32 (note only); Jean, Tell Sifr, no. 59a (33216b only); Charpin, Archives, 90-91 and 244-245, no. 59a (b and d only).
33217	B.60	Contract; sale of land. Hammurabi 10/6/41. Kutalla. Strassmaier, Warka, no. 33; Jean, Tell Sifr, no. 49; Charpin, Archives, 79-80 and 235, no. 49.
33217a	B.60a	Case of 33217. Hammurabi 10/6/41. Kutalla. Strassmaier, Warka, no. 33 (quoted as variants); Jean, Tell Sifr, no. 49a; Charpin, Archives, 79-80 and 235, no. 49a.
33218	B.61	Contract; sale of land; dupl. 33213. Hammurabi -/3/36. Kutalla. Strassmaier, Warka, no. 34; Meissner, BAP, no. 46; Jean, Tell Sifr, no. 41; Charpin, Archives, 99-101 and 228, no. 41.
33218a	B.61a	Case of 33218. Hammurabi -/3/36. Kutalla. + 33319. Strassmaier, Warka, no. 34 (quoted as variants); Meissner, BAP, no. 46; Jean, Tell Sifr, no. 41a; Charpin, Archives, 99-101 and 229, no. 41a.
33219	B.62	Contract; gift of a slave and various amounts of silver by Lamassum to her children. Hammurabi -/12/34. Kutalla. Strassmaier, Warka, no. 35; Meissner, BAP, no. 109; Jean, Tell Sifr, no. 35; Charpin, Archives, 76-77 and 222-223, no. 35.
33219a	B.62a	Case of 33219. Hammurabi 2/12b/34. Kutalla. Strassmaier, Warka, no. 35 (quoted as variants); Meissner, BAP, no. 109; Jean, Tell Sifr, no. 35a; Charpin, Archives, 76-77 and 222-223, no. 35a.
33220	B.63	Contract; sale of land. Hammurabi -/10/41. Kutalla. Strassmaier, Warka, no. 36; Jean, Tell Sifr, no. 51; Charpin, Archives, 80-81 and 236-237, no. 51.
33220a	B.63a	Case of 33220. Hammurabi -/10/41. Kutalla. Strassmaier, Warka, no. 36 (quoted as variants); Jean, Tell Sifr, no. 51a; Charpin, Archives, 80-81 and 236-237, no. 51a.

33221	B.64	Contract; sale of a house plot. Hammurabi 23/11/31. Kutalla. Strassmaier, Warka, no. 37; Jean, Tell Sifr, no. 34; Charpin, Archives, 94-95 and 222, no. 34.
33221a	B.64a	Case of 33221. Hammurabi 23/11/31. Kutalla. Strassmaier, Warka, no. 37 (quoted as variants); Jean, Tell Sifr, no. 34a; Charpin, Archives, 94-95 and 222, no. 34a.
33222	B.65	Lawsuit about the sale of a house. Hammurabi -/12/34. Kutalla. Strassmaier, Warka, no. 38; Meissner, BAP, no. 39; Jean, Tell Sifr, no. 36; Charpin, Archives, 124-126 and 223, no. 36.
33222a	B.65a	Case of 33222. Hammurabi -/12/34. Kutalla. Strassmaier, Warka, no. 38 (quoted as variants); Meissner, BAP, no. 39; Jean, Tell Sifr, no. 36a; Charpin, Archives, 124-126 and 224, no. 36a.
33223	B.66	Contract; sale of a house plot. Hammurabi 13/8/41. Kutalla. Strassmaier, Warka, no. 39; Jean, Tell Sifr, no. 53; Charpin, Archives, 111-112 and 238, no. 53.
33223a	B.66a	Case of 33223. Hammurabi 13/8/41. Kutalla. Strassmaier, Warka, no. 39 (quoted as variants); Jean, Tell Sifr, no. 53a; Charpin, Archives, 111-112 and 238-239, no. 53a.
33224	B.67	Contract confirming Nirah-iddinam's ownership of inherited land. Hammurabi -/6/41. Kutalla. Strassmaier, Warka, no. 40; Jean, Tell Sifr, no. 50; Charpin, Archives, 80 and 236, no. 50.
33224a	B.67a	Case of 33224. Hammurabi -/6/41. Kutalla. Strassmaier, Warka, no. 40 (quoted as variants); Jean, Tell Sifr, no. 50a; Charpin, Archives, 80 and 236, no. 50a.
33225	B.68	Contract; sale of land. Hammurabi -/8/37. Note that the case, 33225a, is dated to year 38. Kutalla. Strassmaier, Warka, no. 41; Meissner, BAP, no. 47; Jean, Tell Sifr, no. 45; Charpin, Archives, 103-106 and 232-233, no. 45.
33225a	B.68a	Case of 33225. Hammurabi -/8/38. Note that the tablet, 33225, is dated to year 37. Kutalla. Strassmaier, Warka, no. 41 (quoted as variants); Meissner, BAP, no. 47; Jean, Tell Sifr, no. 45a; Charpin, Archives, 103-106 and 233, no. 45a.
33226	B.69	Contract; exchange of land. Hammurabi -/6/36. Kutalla. Strassmaier, Warka, no. 42; Jean, Tell Sifr, no. 43; Charpin, Archives, 101-103 and 230, no. 43.
33226a	B.69a	Case of 33226. Hammurabi -/6/36. Kutalla. Strassmaier, Warka, no. 42 (quoted as variants); Jean, Tell

		Sifr, no. 43a; Charpin, Archives, 101-103 and 230, no. 43a.
33227	B.70	Contract; receipt by Ṣilli-Šamaš of silver granted to him by the earlier contract 33219. Hammurabi 13/5/35. Kutalla. Meissner, BAP, no. 27; Jean, Tell Sifr, no. 38; Charpin, Archives, 77-78 and 225, no. 38.
33227a	B.70a	Case of 33227. Hammurabi 13/5/35. Kutalla. Meissner, BAP, no. 27; Jean, Tell Sifr, no. 38a; Charpin, Archives, 77-78 and 225-226, no. 38a.
33228	B.71	Contract; sale of a house. Hammurabi -/10/42. Kutalla. Strassmaier, Warka, no. 50; Meissner, BAP, no. 34; Jean, Tell Sifr, no. 57; Charpin, Archives, 109-110 and 242, no. 57.
33228a	B.71a	Case of 33228. Hammurabi -/10/42. Kutalla. Strassmaier, Warka, no. 50 (quoted as variants); Meissner, BAP, no. 3434; Jean, Tell Sifr, no. 57a; Charpin, Archives, 109-110 and 242, no. 57a.
33229	B.72	Contract; sale of land. Hammurabi -/11/41. Kutalla. Strassmaier, Warka, no. 43; Jean, Tell Sifr, no. 52; Charpin, Archives, 93 and 237, no. 52.
33229a	B.72a	Case of 33229. Hammurabi -/11/41. Kutalla. + 33282 + 33299 + 33318. Strassmaier, Warka, no. 43 (quoted as variants); Jean, Tell Sifr, no. 52a; Charpin, Archives, 93 and 237-238, no. 52a.
33230	B.73	Court record; agreement in settlement of a partnership (tappûtum). Hammurabi -/12/34. Kutalla. Strassmaier, Warka, no. 44; Meissner, BAP, no. 78; Jean, Tell Sifr, no. 37; Charpin, Archives, 123-124 and 224, no. 37.
33230a	B.73a	Case of 33230. Hammurabi -/12/34. Kutalla. Strassmaier, Warka, no. 44 (quoted as variants); Meissner, BAP, no. 78; Jean, Tell Sifr, no. 37a; Charpin, Archives, 123-124 and 224-225, no. 37a.
33231	B.74	Court record; about the sale of land. Hammurabi 22/3/36. Kutalla. Strassmaier, Warka, no. 45; Meissner, BAP, no. 45; Jean, Tell Sifr, no. 42; Charpin, Archives, 98-99 and 229, no. 42.
33231a	B.74a	Case of 33231. Hammurabi 22/3/36. Kutalla. Strassmaier, Warka, no. 45 (quoted as variants); Jean, Tell Sifr, no. 42a; Charpin, Archives, 98-99 and 229-230, no. 42a.
33232	B.75	Contract; sale of a house. Hammurabi -/8/38. Kutalla. Strassmaier, Warka, no. 46; Jean, Tell Sifr, no. 47; Charpin, Archives, 106-108 and 234, no. 47.

33232a	B.75a	Case of 33232. Hammurabi -/8/38. Kutalla. Strassmaier, Warka, no. 46 (quoted as variants); Jean, Tell Sifr, no. 47a; Charpin, Archives, 106-108 and 234, no. 47a.
33233	B.76	Contract; division of an inheritance in land. Hammurabi -/10/42. Kutalla. Strassmaier, Warka, no. 47; Jean, Tell Sifr, no. 56; Charpin, Archives, 64-66 and 240-241, no. 56.
33233a	B.76a	Case of 33233. Hammurabi -/10/42. Kutalla. + 33273 + 33274 + 33302 + 33309 (+) 33326. Strassmaier, Warka, no. 47 (quoted as variants); Jean, Tell Sifr, no. 56a; Charpin, Archives, 64-66 and 241-242, no. 56a.
33234	B.77	Contract; receipt of silver. Case is 33263 + 33300. Hammurabi -/7/38. Kutalla. Meissner, BAP, no. 29; Jean, Tell Sifr, no. 46; Charpin, Archives, 121-122 and 233-234, no. 46.
33235	B.78	Court record; about the ownership of land. Samsuiluna 15/6b/5. Kutalla. Strassmaier, Warka, no. 48; Jean, Tell Sifr, no. 71; Charpin, Archives, 188 and 254, no. 71.
33235a	B.78a	Case of 33235. Samsuiluna 15/6b/5. Kutalla. Strassmaier, Warka, no. 48 (quoted as variants); Jean, Tell Sifr, no. 71a; Charpin, Archives, 188 and 254-255, no. 71a.
33236	B.79	Contract; sale of a storehouse. Samsuiluna -/9/1. Kutalla. Jean, Tell Sifr, no. 61; Charpin, Archives, 94 and 246, no. 61.
33236a	B.79a	Case of 33236. Samsuiluna -/9/1. Kutalla. Strassmaier, Warka, no. 51; Jean, Tell Sifr, no. 61a; Charpin, Archives, 94 and 246, no. 61a.
33237	B.80	Contract; division of an inheritance in land. Samsuiluna 4/8/4. Kutalla. Strassmaier, Warka, no. 52; Jean, Tell Sifr, no. 68; Charpin, Archives, 66-67 and 252, no. 68.
33237a	B.80a	Case of 33237. Samsuiluna 4/8/4. Kutalla. Strassmaier, Warka, no. 52 (quoted as variants); Jean, Tell Sifr, no. 68a; Charpin, Archives, 66-67 and 252-253, no. 68a.
33238	B.81	Contract; sale of a house plot. Samsuiluna 15/6/4. Kutalla. Strassmaier, Warka, no. 53; Jean, Tell Sifr, no. 65; Charpin, Archives, 139-140 and 249, no. 65.
33238a	B.81a	Case of 33238. Samsuiluna 15/6/4. Kutalla. Strassmaier, Warka, no. 53 (quoted as variants); Jean, Tell Sifr, no. 65a; Charpin, Archives, 139-140 and 250, no. 65a.

33239	B.82	Contract; sale of a house plot. Samsuiluna 24/8/6. Kutalla. Strassmaier, Warka, no. 54; Jean, Tell Sifr, no. 75; Charpin, Archives, 86-87 and 257-258, no. 75.
33239a	B.82a	Case of 33239. Samsuiluna 24/8/6. Kutalla. Strassmaier, Warka, no. 54 (quoted as variants); Jean, Tell Sifr, no. 75a; Charpin, Archives, 86-87 and 258, no. 75a.
33240	B.83	Contract; receipt of the price of goods delivered by the palace at the kārum of Larsa. Samsuiluna 20/1/7. Kutalla. Strassmaier, Warka, no. 55; Jean, Tell Sifr, no. 78; Charpin, Archives, 127-128 and 260, no. 78.
33240a	B.83a	Case of 33240. Samsuiluna 20/1/7. Kutalla. Strassmaier, Warka, no. 55 (quoted as variants); Jean, Tell Sifr, no. 78a; Charpin, Archives, 127-128 and 260, no. 78a.
33241	B.84	Contract; sale of a house plot. Samsuiluna 15/7/6. Kutalla. Strassmaier, Warka, no. 56; Jean, Tell Sifr, no. 74; Charpin, Archives, 82 and 256-257, no. 74.
33241a	B.84a	Case of 33241. Samsuiluna 15/7/6. Kutalla. + 33271. Strassmaier, Warka, no. 56 (quoted as variants); Jean, Tell Sifr, no. 74a; Charpin, Archives, 82 and 257, no. 74a.
33242	B.85	Contract; sale of land and a storehouse. Samsuiluna 12/2/4. Kutalla. Strassmaier, Warka, no. 57; Jean, Tell Sifr, no. 64; Charpin, Archives, 112 and 248-249, no. 64.
33242a	B.85a	Part of case of 33242. Samsuiluna 12/2/4. Kutalla. (+) 33307. Jean, Tell Sifr, no. 64a; Charpin, Archives, 112 and 249, no. 64a.
33243	B.86	Contract; sale of a house plot. Samsuiluna 2/11/4. Kutalla. Strassmaier, Warka, no. 58; Jean, Tell Sifr, no. 69; Charpin, Archives, 113 and 253, no. 69.
33243a	B.86a	Case of 33243. Samsuiluna 2/11/4. Kutalla. + 33287. Jean, Tell Sifr, no. 69a; Charpin, Archives, 113 and 253, no. 69a.
33244	B.87	Contract; sale of a house plot. Samsuiluna 20/7/6. Kutalla. Strassmaier, Warka, no. 59; Jean, Tell Sifr, no. 73; Charpin, Archives, 82 and 256, no. 73.
33244a	B.87a	Case of 33244. Samsuiluna 20/7/6. Kutalla. + 33305. Strassmaier, Warka, no. 59 (quoted as variants); Jean, Tell Sifr, no. 73a; Charpin, Archives, 82 and 256, no. 73a.
33245	B.88	Contract; sale of a house plot. Samsuiluna 1/4/4. Kutalla. Strassmaier, Warka, no. 60; Jean, Tell Sifr, no. 67; Charpin, Archives, 137-139 and 251, no. 67.

33245a	B.88a	Case of 33245. Note 33245 has month 4. Samsuiluna 1/5/4. Kutalla. Strassmaier, Warka, no. 60 (quoted as variants); Jean, Tell Sifr, no. 67a; Charpin, Archives, 137-139 and 251, no. 67a.
33246	B.89	Contract; sale of a house plot. Samsuiluna 10/7/6. Kutalla. Strassmaier, Warka, no. 61; Jean, Tell Sifr, no. 72; Charpin, Archives, 82 and 255, no. 72.
33246a	B.89a	Case of 33246. Samsuiluna 10/7/6. Kutalla. Strassmaier, Warka, no. 61 (quoted as variants); Jean, Tell Sifr, no. 72a; Charpin, Archives, 82 and 255-256, no. 72a.
33247	B.90	Contract; sale of a house plot. Samsuiluna 20/8/6. Kutalla. Strassmaier, Warka, no. 62; Jean, Tell Sifr, no. 76; Charpin, Archives, 86 and 258-259, no. 76.
33247a	B.90a	Case of 33247. Samsuiluna 20/8/6. Kutalla. Strassmaier, Warka, no. 62 (quoted as variants); Jean, Tell Sifr, no. 76a; Charpin, Archives, 86 and 259, no. 76a.
33248	B.91	Contract; sale of a house plot. Samsuiluna 10/11/10. Kutalla. Strassmaier, Warka, no. 63; Jean, Tell Sifr, no. 84; Charpin, Archives, 114-115, 195 and 265, no. 84.
33248a	B.91a	Case of 33248. Samsuiluna 10/11/10. Kutalla. Strassmaier, Warka, no. 63 (quoted as variants); Jean, Tell Sifr, no. 84a; Charpin, Archives, 114-115, 195 and 265-266, no. 84a.
33249	B.92	Contract; sale of a house plot. Samsuiluna -/10/4. Kutalla. Strassmaier, Warka, no. 64; Jean, Tell Sifr, no. 63; Charpin, Archives, 141 and 248, no. 63.
33249a	B.92a	Case of 33249. Samsuiluna -/10/4. Kutalla. Strassmaier, Warka, no. 64 (quoted as variants); Jean, Tell Sifr, no. 63a; Charpin, Archives, 141 and 248, no. 63a.
33250	B.93	Contract; sale of a house plot. Samsuiluna -/-/8. Kutalla. Strassmaier, Warka, no. 65; Jean, Tell Sifr, no. 83; Charpin, Archives, 96-97 and 264-265, no. 83.
33250a	B.93a	Case of 33250. Samsuiluna -/-/8. Kutalla. + 33275 + 33297. Strassmaier, Warka, no. 65 (quoted as variants); Jean, Tell Sifr, no. 83a; Charpin, Archives, 96-97 and 264-265, no. 83a.
33251	B.94	Contract; sale of a house plot. Samsuiluna -/8/6. Kutalla. + 33324. Strassmaier, Warka, no. 66; Jean, Tell Sifr, no. 77; Charpin, Archives, 89 and 259-260, no. 77.
33251a	B.94a	Case of 33251. Samsuiluna -/8/6. Kutalla. + 33304. Strassmaier, Warka, no. 66 (quoted as variants); Jean,

		Tell Sifr, no. 77a; Charpin, Archives, 89 and 260, no. 77a.
33252	B.95	Contract; sale of a house plot. Samsuiluna 18/6/4. Kutalla. Strassmaier, Warka, no. 67; Jean, Tell Sifr, no. 66; Charpin, Archives, 140 and 250, no. 66.
33252a	B.95a	Case of 33252. Note variant day number. Samsuiluna 30/6/4. Kutalla. Strassmaier, Warka, no. 67 (quoted as variants); Jean, Tell Sifr, no. 66a; Charpin, Archives, 139-140 and 250-251, no. 66a.
33253	B.96	Contract; sale of a house plot. Samsuiluna 30/8/1. Kutalla. Strassmaier, Warka, no. 68; Meissner, BAP, no. 66; Jean, Tell Sifr, no. 60; Charpin, Archives, 93-94 and 245, no. 60.
33253a	B.96a	Case of 33253. Samsuiluna 30/8/1. Kutalla. Strassmaier, Warka, no. 68 (quoted as variants); Meissner, BAP, no. 66; Jean, Tell Sifr, no. 60a; Charpin, Archives, 93-94 and 245, no. 60a.
33254	B.97	Contract; sale of a house plot. Samsuiluna -/6b/8. Kutalla. Strassmaier, Warka, no. 69; Jean, Tell Sifr, no. 80; Charpin, Archives, 87-88 and 262, no. 80.
33254a	B.97a	Case of 33254. Note 33254 has month 6b. Samsuiluna -/7/[8]. Kutalla. Strassmaier, Warka, no. 69 (quoted as variants); Jean, Tell Sifr, no. 80a; Charpin, Archives, 87-88 and 262-263, no. 80a.
33255	B.98	Contract; sale of a house plot. Samsuiluna 8/7/8. Kutalla. Strassmaier, Warka, no. 70; Jean, Tell Sifr, no. 82; Charpin, Archives, 96 and 263-264, no. 82.
33255a	B.98a	Case of 33255. Samsuiluna 8/7/8. Kutalla. Strassmaier, Warka, no. 70 (quoted as variants); Jean, Tell Sifr, no. 82a; Charpin, Archives, 96 and 264, no. 82a.
33256	B.99	Contract; sale of a house plot. Samsuiluna 3/6/3. Kutalla. Strassmaier, Warka, no. 71; Jean, Tell Sifr, no. 62; Charpin, Archives, 84-85 and 246-247, no. 62.
33256a	B.99a	Case of 33256. Samsuiluna 3/6/3. Kutalla. + 33261. Strassmaier, Warka, nos. 62a and 75; Jean, Tell Sifr, no. 62a (33256a only); Charpin, Archives, 84-86, 247-248 and 275 nos. 62a, 101 and 101a.
33257	B.100	Contract about payment of the costs of a business partnership (ḫarrān ṣērim). Samsuiluna 20/5/5. Kutalla. Strassmaier, Warka, no. 72; Jean, Tell Sifr, no. 70; Charpin, Archives, 126 and 253-254, no. 70.
33258	B.101	Contract; sale of land(?). Samsuiluna 5/7/8. Kutalla. Strassmaier, Warka, no. 73; Jean, Tell Sifr, no. 81; Charpin, Archives, 114 and 263, no. 81.

33259	B.102	Contract; exchange of land. Samsuiluna 4?/2/4. Kutalla. Charpin, Archives, 112-113, 276 and pl. VI, no. 104.
33260	B.103	Case fragment; loan repayable at the gate of the gagûm; sealed.
33261	B.104	Joined to 33256a. Kutalla.
33262	B.105	Ur III. Receipt; Lagaš month name: amar-a-a-si. Šulgi -/10/48. Strassmaier, Warka, no. 109, as "B 70".
33263	B.106	Case of 33234. Hammurabi -/7/38. Kutalla. + 33300. Charpin, Archives, 121-122 and 234, no. 46a.
33264	B.107	Sumerian legal compendium; cylinder. + 90892 + 90894 (+) 30048 (+) 90893. Strassmaier, Warka, no. 110 (33264 only); Sollberger, Fs Kraus, 346-350 (not 30048).
33265	B.108	Contract; adoption of Šamaš-ilî as their son by Apil-irṣitim and Abikkultum. Rim-Sin 30/5/30. Ur. Charpin, Archives, 50, 277 and pl. VIII, no. 106.
33266	B.109	Contract; sale of a house plot and land. Samsuiluna -/6/6. Kutalla. (+) 33289. Strassmaier, Warka, no. 74 (33266 only); Charpin, Archives, 88-89 and 274, no. 100.
33266a	B.109a	Case of 33266 (+) 33289. Samsuiluna -/6/6. Kutalla. + 33301 + 33322. Charpin, Archives, 88-89 and 274, no. 100a.
33267	B.110	Contract about land at Kutalla and a ṣimdat šarrim. Case is 33279 + 33298. Rim-Sin -/7/25. Kutalla. Strassmaier, Warka, no. 23; Charpin, Archives, 133-134 and 273-274, no. 99.
33268	B.111	Part of case of 33174. Rim-Sin 24/10/24. Kutalla. (+) 33174a. Charpin, Archives, 47-49 and 214, no. 20a.
33268a	B.111a	Joined to 33214a. Kutalla.
33269	B.112	Part of case of 33161. Samsuiluna 30/9/7. Kutalla. + 33320 + unnum. (+) 33161a (+) 33161b (+) 33316. Charpin, Archives, 113 and 261-262, no. 79a.
33270	B.113	Joined to 33190a. Ur.
33271	B.114	Joined to 33241a. Kutalla.
33272	B.115	Case of 33212. Kutalla. + 33291 (+) 33212a (+) 33212b-e (+) 33327.
33273	B.116	Joined to 33233a. Kutalla.
33274	B.117	Joined to 33233a. Kutalla.
33275	B.118	Joined to 33250a. Kutalla.
33276	B.119	Joined to 33161b. Ur.
33277	B.120	Case fragment; sealed.
33278	B.121	Joined to 33213a. Kutalla.

33279	B.122	Case of 33267. Rim-Sin -/7/25. Kutalla. + 33298. Charpin, Archives, 133-134 and 273-274 nos. 99 and 99a.
33280	B.123	Joined to 33184. Kutalla.
33281	B.124	Case fragment.
33282	B.125	Joined to 33229a. Kutalla.
33283	B.126	Joined to 33214a. Kutalla.
33284	B.127	Case fragment.
33285	B.128	Joined to 33213a. Kutalla.
33286	B.129	Case of 33206. Rim-Sin -/4/23. Kutalla. + 33313 (+) 33295. Charpin, Archives, 62-63 and 212-213, no. 19a.
33287	B.130	Joined to 33243a. Kutalla.
33288	B.131	Joined to 33173a. Ur.
33289	B.132	Contract; sale of a house plot and land. Samsuiluna -/6/6. Kutalla. (+) 33266. Charpin, Archives, 88-89 and 274 and pl. III, no. 100.
33290	B.133	Case fragment.
33291	B.134	Joined to 33272a. Kutalla.
33292	B.135	Contract; sale of land. d.l. Ur. Charpin, Archives, 53-54, 277 and pl. VII, no. 107.
33293	B.136	Joined to 33186a. Ur.
33294	B.137	Case fragment.
33295	B.138	Case of 33206. Rim-Sin -/4/23. Kutalla. (+) 33286. Charpin, Archives, 62-63 and 212-213, no. 19a.
33296	B.139	Joined to 33214a. Kutalla.
33297	B.140	Joined to 33250a. Kutalla.
33298	B.141	Joined to 33279. Kutalla.
33299	B.142	Joined to 33229a. Kutalla.
33300	B.143	Joined to 33263. Kutalla.
33301	B.144	Joined to 33266a. Kutalla.
33302	B.145	Joined to 33233a. Kutalla.
33303	B.146	Joined to 33161b. Ur.
33304	B.147	Joined to 33251a. Kutalla.
33305	B.148	Joined to 33244a. Kutalla.
33306	B.149	Joined to 33214a. Kutalla.
33307	B.150	Part of case of 33242. Samsuiluna 12/2/4. Kutalla. (+) 33242a. Charpin, Archives, 112 and 249, no. 64a.
33308	B.151	Joined to 33215a. Kutalla.
33309	B.152	Joined to 33233a. Kutalla.
33310	B.153	Joined to 33214a. Kutalla.
33311	B.154	Contract; fragment; in-pàd.
33312	B.155	Joined to 33159a. Ur.
33313	B.156	Joined to 33286. Kutalla.
33314	B.157	Joined to 33213a. Kutalla.

33315	B.158	Joined to 33186a. Ur.
33316	B.159	Part of case of 33161; sealed. Samsuiluna 30/9/7. Kutalla. (+) 33161a (+) 33161b (+) 33269 + 33320 + unnum. Charpin, Archives, 113 and 261-262, no. 79a
33317	B.160	Contract; rent of a field. d.l. Ur. Charpin, Archives, 54, 276-277 and pl. VII, no. 105.
33318	B.161	Joined to 33229a. Kutalla.
33319	B.162	Joined to 33218a. Kutalla.
33320	B.163	Joined to 33269; now wrongly marked as B.164. Kutalla.
33321	B.164	Joined to 33214a; now wrongly marked as B.165. Kutalla.
33322	B.165	Joined to 33266a; now wrongly marked as B.163. Kutalla.
33323	B.166	Joined to 33214a. Kutalla.
33324	B.167	Joined to 33251. Kutalla.
33325	B.168	Joined to 33213a. Kutalla.
33326	B.169	Part of case of 33233. Kutalla. (+) 33233a. Charpin, Archives, 64-66 and 241-242, no. 56a.
33327	B.170	Case of 33212. Kutalla. (+) 33212a (+) 33212b-e (+) 33272 + 33291.
	B.171	Joined to K.13942. Ur?
139991	B.172	Sumerian literary; Dialogue 5. Ur? CT 58, no. 59a.
139992	B.173	Sumerian literary; Dialogue 5. Ur? CT 58, no. 59b.
139993	B.174	Sumerian literary; Nisaba hymn. Ur? CT 58, no. 52
	B.175	See Register 16/51; apparently a tablet fragment also registered as 1990,0105.1, but there is no such register entry and the tablet cannot be found.
	B.176	There is a box of unregistered B fragments stored after 33327, and a large box of B fragments and some trays of seal impressions sorted out and copied by G. Colbow.

Rm collection

The Rm collection includes Babylonian tablets purchased by Rassam in Baghdad in December 1877 which arrived at the British Museum in September 1878. See J. E. Reade in CBTBM VI pp. xxviii-xxix. The register gives the following provenances:

Babylon: nos. 673-853, 942.
Kouyunjik: nos. 914-938, 946-1027.

91131	Rm.673	Historical cylinder of Nebuchadnezzar II. Mar(a)da. Winckler, ZA 2, 142; CT 34, 19-22; Berger, AOAT 4/1, Nebukadnezar Zylinder III,1, no. 2.

	Rm.674	Historical cylinder of Nebuchadnezzar II. Mar(a)da. CT 34, 19-22; Berger, AOAT 4/1, Nebukadnezar Zylinder III,1, no. 2.
91132	Rm.675	Historical cylinder of Nebuchadnezzar II. Mar(a)da. Winckler, ZA 2, 137; Berger, AOAT 4/1, Nebukadnezar Zylinder II,10, no. 1.
91133	Rm.676	Historical cylinder of Nebuchadnezzar II. Ball, PSBA 11 (1889) 248-253; Berger, AOAT 4/1, Nebukadnezar Zylinder II,1, no. 8.
	Rm.677	Historical cylinder of Nebuchadnezzar II. Mar(a)da. Winckler, ZA 2, 137; Berger, AOAT 4/1, Nebukadnezar Zylinder II,10, no. 2.
92682	Rm.678	Joined to 34053.
	Rm.679	Promissory note for silver; sealed. Cam 2/8/1. Babylon. Cam 68; Bertin 871; Nisaba 28, no. 148.
	Rm.680	Contract; sale of a house. Dar 22/8/24. Babylon. Bertin 2538.
	Rm.681	Antichretic loan made by Nidinti-Bēl with a house given as security for five years; captions for seals but not sealed. Dar 9/11/32. [Babylon]. Bertin 2708; Roth, JAOS 111, 32-33 and n. 41; Wunsch, AfO 42/43, 61, no. 11.
	Rm.682	Promissory note for dates. Dar 1/6/30. Babylon. Bertin 2681.
	Rm.683	Promissory note for silver. Dar 16/6/5. Babylon. Dar 170; Bertin 2064.
	Rm.684	Receipt for dates. Dar 6/6b/11. Dar 306; Bertin 2199.
	Rm.685	Promissory note for silver. Dar 22/12/-. Babylon. Bertin 2822.
	Rm.686	Promissory note for barley. Dar 25/1/-. Bertin 2841.
	Rm.687	Division of dates. Dar 14/7/26. Bīt-Ḫaḫḫūru. Dar 208; Bertin 2609.
	Rm.688	Account of issues of silver. SE Arsaces 18/6/218. CT 49, 37, no. 153; van der Spek, Raḫimesu, 217-218, no. 8; Bertin 2925.
	Rm.689	Promissory note for silver and onions. Nbn 25/9/3. Babylon. Nbn 122; Bertin 703; Wunsch, CM 3, no. 116.
	Rm.690	Account of oil.
	Rm.691	Sale of a slave girl. -/-/12. Babylon.
	Rm.692	Sale of furnishings. -/-/42.
	Rm.693	Astronomical Diary for SE 129; prayer on upper edge. + Rm.734 (+) 45613. LBAT 341 (Rm.693 only); Sachs and Hunger, ADART II, no. -182 A.

Rm.694	Astronomical Diary for SE 77. + 41641 + 41930 + 41963 + 41997. LBAT 281-282, 923, 930, and 935; Sachs and Hunger, ADART II, no. -234 A.
Rm.695	Astronomical Diary for SE 224. + Sp.172. LBAT 504-505; Sachs and Hunger, ADART III, no. -87 C. (+) 41921.
Rm.696	Dowry list. Dar 2/5/11. Babylon. Dar 301.
Rm.697	Astronomical Diary.
Rm.698	Astronomical Diary for SE 174; prayer on upper edge. + Rm.730 + 41927. LBAT 425 + 426 + 428; Sachs and Hunger, ADART III, no. -137 E.
Rm.699	Contract.
Rm.700	Astronomical Diary.
Rm.701	Astronomical Diary for SE 182. + 41646 + 41478. LBAT 296 + 446; Sachs and Hunger, ADART III, no. -129 A. (+) 34040.
Rm.702	Astronomical.
Rm.703	Contract.
Rm.704	Astronomical.
Rm.705	Astronomical Diary for SE 251. + 34215 + 34458 + 41932. LBAT 547 + 569 + 924 (not Rm.705); Sachs and Hunger, ADART III, no. -60.
Rm.706	Astronomical.
Rm.707	Astronomical Diary.
Rm.708	Astronomical Diary for SE 72. Sachs and Hunger, ADART II, no. -239.
Rm.709	Chronological list; begins MU 1,41-KAM.
Rm.710	Astronomical Diary for SE 223; prayer on upper edge. + 41479 + unnum. LBAT 498 + 869; Epping and Strassmaier, ZA 6, 235 (Rm.710 only); Sachs and Hunger, ADART III, no. -88 A (Rm.710 only).
Rm.711	Commentary on Šumma izbu. Frahm, GMTR 5, 210, 311.
Rm.712	Astronomical Diary for SE 70. LBAT 276; Sachs and Hunger, ADART II, no. -241.
Rm.713	Astronomical; colophon. SE [Sel] &Ant 14/[]/100+.
Rm.714	Terracotta picture of a pig with inscription on reverse: šá 1.A-za-ru A É-sag-íl-a-a. Reade, AfO 48/49, 154 figs. 19-20.
Rm.715	Astronomical Diary.
Rm.716	Astronomical. SE Ant & Ant -/-/141. + Rm.761.
Rm.717	Catalogue of incipits and rubrics for the ašipu; dupl. BM 55148; dupl. Ebeling, KAR 44. + 34188 + 99677 + 140684. Geller, Fs Lambert, p. 257; cf. Finkel, Gs Sachs, 150

Rm.718	Astronomical Diary for SE 60. + Rm.723 + 32840 + 34130. LBAT 262-264. Aaboe, Centaurus 24 (1980) 16-20; Sachs and Hunger, ADART II, no. -251; Aaboe, Episodes, 35-36.
Rm.719	Astronomical Diary.
Rm.720	Astronomical Diary for SE 71. + Rm.732 + 41522. LBAT 277-278 + 883; Sachs and Hunger, ADART II, no. -240 Stephenson, HEER, 142-143.
Rm.721	Astronomical; System A lunar ephemeris. + Rm.810. ACT 3.
Rm.722	Astronomical Diary.
Rm.723	Joined to Rm.718.
Rm.724	Astronomical Diary.
Rm.725	Incantation.
Rm.726	Astronomical Diary. LBAT 521.
Rm.727	Astronomical; lunar six table. Huber and Steele, SCIAMVS 8 (2007) 3-36, text H.
Rm.728	Astronomical Diary for SE 81. LBAT 287; Sachs and Hunger, ADART II, no. -230 C.
Rm.729	Astronomical.
Rm.730	Joined to Rm.698.
Rm.731	Astronomical; Normal Star Almanac for SE 82. + Rm.917 + 2 unnum. LBAT 1003 (Rm.731 only); Hunger and Sachs, ADART VII, no. 23.
Rm.732	Joined to Rm.720.
Rm.733	Astronomical.
Rm.734	Joined to Rm.693.
Rm.735	Astronomical Diary; observations from months xi and xii; left edge.
Rm.736	Astronomical Diary for SE 151. LBAT 386; Sachs and Hunger, ADART III, no. -160 B.
Rm.737	Astronomical Diary?
Rm.738	Astronomical.
Rm.739	Astronomical; Goal Year Text for SE 97. LBAT 1226; Hunger and Sachs, ADART VI, no. 13.
Rm.740	Astronomical Diary for SE 33. LBAT 234; Sachs and Hunger, ADART I, no. -278 A.
Rm.741	Astronomical.
Rm.742	Astronomical.
Rm.743	Astronomical Diary.
Rm.744	Omens; extispicy.
Rm.745	Astronomical Diary.
Rm.746	Illegible.
Rm.747	Astronomical Diary.
Rm.748	Omens; colophon. RN lost 9/12a([ITU.Š]E IGI-ú)/[].

Rm.749	Astronomical.
Rm.750	Astronomical Diary.
Rm.751	Literary; Gilgameš X. + 34853 + 35546. CT 46, 34, no. 32 (35546 + Rm.751 only); Garelli, Gilgameš, 124 (copy of 35546 by Wiseman), 131; George, Gilgamesh II, pl. 116-117.
Rm.752	Astronomical Diary. + 34197.
Rm.753	Astronomical Diary.
Rm.754	Astronomical.
Rm.755	Astronomical; Normal Star Almanac for SE 101. LBAT 1009; Hunger and Sachs, ADART VII, no. 38.
Rm.756	Astronomical Diary for SE 192. + 42110 (+) 41131 + 41149 + 41206 (+) 41189. LBAT 457 + 972; Sachs and Hunger, ADART III, no. -119 B.
Rm.757	Chronicle about Antiochus the crown prince. SE. + 32410 + 32440 + 32581 + 32585 + 2 unnum. Grayson, TCS 5, Chronicle 11 (32440 + 32581 + 32585 only); BCHP 5.
Rm.758	Astronomical Diary.
Rm.759	List of furniture; dowry?
Rm.760	Astronomical Diary.
Rm.761	Joined to Rm.716.
Rm.762	Astronomical Diary.
Rm.763	Astronomical. Goal Year Text for SE 246. + Rm.946. LBAT 1301 (Rm.763 only); Hunger and Sachs, ADART VI, no. 91.
Rm.764	Astronomical.
Rm.765	Contract.
Rm.766	Note of an agreement made before the šatammu and kiništu of Esangila; wrongly listed in LBAT 305 as a Diary for 108 SE. CT 49, 34, no. 147; LBAT 305; van der Spek, Fs Oelsner, 442-444 (with comment on the date).
Rm.767	Astronomical Diary for SE 66. + Rm.818 + 41633 + 77244. LBAT 274 (41633 only); Sachs and Hunger, ADART II, no. -245 B.
Rm.768	Astronomical; Goal Year Text; not datable. Hunger and Sachs, ADART VI, no. 177.
Rm.769	Contract; sale of fields; finger-nail marks.
Rm.770	Astronomical.
Rm.771	Astronomical Diary for SE 64. (+)MNB 1876 + 1904 (for which see Durand, TBER pls. 83-84). LBAT 270; Sachs and Hunger, ADART II, no. -247 C.
Rm.772	Astrological omens.

Rm.773	Astronomical. SE -/-/92.
Rm.774	Horoscope?
Rm.775	Astronomical.
Rm.776	Letter from Guzānu to Širku.
Rm.777	Astronomical; daily positions of the moon for several months. ACT 196; Jones, AHES 29 (1983) 1-11.
Rm.778	Astronomical; Goal Year Text for SE 158; prayer on upper edge. + 41571 + 42057. LBAT 1261 and 1289-1290; Hunger and Sachs, ADART VI, no. 76.
Rm.779	Economic; about garments.
Rm.780	Astronomical Diary.
Rm.781	Astronomical; star list.
Rm.782	Astronomical.
Rm.783	Promissory note for silver. 22/[]/34.
Rm.784	Astronomical Diary for SE 224. LBAT 503; Sachs and Hunger, ADART III, no. -87 B.
Rm.785	Literary; Gilgameš I. + Rm.956 + Rm.1017 + 34248 + 34357 (+) K.15145. CT 46, 30, no. 19; George, Gilgamesh II, pl. 47; Kwasman and George, NABU 1998, 89-90, nos. 99-100 (Rm 956).
Rm.786	Astronomical; Almanac for SE 127. LBAT 1121; Hunger and Sachs, ADART VII, no. 155.
Rm.787	Astronomical Diary for SE 54. Sachs and Hunger, ADART II, no. -257 B.
Rm.788	Explanations of temple names; colophon. SE 18/4/[]. George, BTT, pl. 19.
Rm.789	Account of issues of silver. SE Arsaces []/[]/219. CT 49, 41, no. 164; van der Spek, Raḫimesu, 243, no. 31.
Rm.790	Astronomical; ruled.
Rm.791	Bilingual incantation, Udug-ḫul 8. Geller, BAM 8, 288-301, pl. 67.
Rm.792	Astronomical Diary. + 32240 + 32430 + 32489. LBAT 210 (32240) + 211 (32430); Sachs and Hunger, ADART I, no. -322 D.
Rm.793	Unidentified.
Rm.794	Astronomical Diary for SE 56. LBAT 257; Sachs and Hunger, ADART II, no. -255 B.
Rm.795	Astronomical.
Rm.796	Astronomical Diary.
Rm.797	Liver omens; Šumma ekallu. (+) 32133.
Rm.798	Astronomical.
Rm.799	Unidentified.
Rm.800	Astronomical Diary for SE 34. + Rm.837 + 34220 (+) 132279. LBAT 239 (34220 only); Sachs and Hunger, ADART I, no. -277 C.

Rm.801	Astronomical.
Rm.802	Astronomical.
Rm.803	Astronomical Diary for SE 4. LBAT 217; Sachs and Hunger, ADART I, no. -307 B; Stephenson, HEER, 154 (under wrong number BM 40122).
Rm.804	Omens; apodoses.
Rm.805	Omens.
Rm.806	Lexical; signs of Syllabary A and associated numbers. Pearce, Iraq 45, 136-137.
Rm.807	Astronomical.
Rm.808	Inventory.
Rm.809	Account of dates.
Rm.810	Joined to Rm.721.
Rm.811	Astronomical.
Rm.812	Astronomical; Normal Star Almanac. Hunger and Sachs, ADART VII, no. 149.
Rm.813	Astronomical; Normal Star Almanac. Hunger and Sachs, ADART VII, no. 150.
Rm.814	Astronomical; Normal Star Almanac or lunar six table. Hunger and Sachs, ADART VII, no. 151.
Rm.815	Promissory note; Murānu archive. SE []/[]/49. [Babylon]. CT 49, 24, no. 116; Jursa, Persika 9, 175, 185-186.
Rm.816	Astronomical Diary.
Rm.817	Astronomical.
Rm.818	Joined to Rm.767.
Rm.819	Astronomical Diary.
Rm.820	Astronomical Diary.
Rm.821	Astronomical Diary.
Rm.822	Astronomical Diary; dated by Artaxerxes; fragment.
Rm.823	Astronomical.
Rm.824	Protocol of the deliberations of the assembly of Esangila involving Bēl-lūmur, šatammu of Esangila; dated 125 AE = 189 SE. SE []/[]/189. CT 49, 34, no. 149.
Rm.825	Astronomical.
Rm.826	Lexical; Ḫḫ I. MSL 5, 7.
Rm.827	Astronomical Diary.
Rm.828	Receipt for silver.
Rm.829	Astronomical.
Rm.830	Astronomical.
Rm.831	Astronomical?; very cursive script; hard to read.
Rm.832	Horoscopic astrology; zodiologia; dupl. LBAT 1593. Reiner, Fs Lambert, 421-427.
Rm.833	Commentary?

Rm.834	Unidentified.
Rm.835	Astronomical; Goal Year Text; not datable. Hunger and Sachs, ADART VI, no. 178.
Rm.836	Astronomical.
Rm.837	Joined to Rm.800.
Rm.838	Astronomical; Normal Star Almanac. Hunger and Sachs, ADART VII, no. 152.
Rm.839	Astronomical procedure text for the moon; System A. ACT 200e; Ossendrijver, BMAPT, no. 54.
Rm.840	Economic.
Rm.841	Astronomical; Goal Year Text?
Rm.842	Astronomical Diary with historical section referring to Antiochus.
Rm.843	Incantations; Maqlu II. Abusch, AMD 10, 51-77.
Rm.844	Legal decision of the šatammu and assembly of Esangila; prayer on upper edge. SE (Arsaces) 14/4/224. (Babylon). Epping and Strassmaier, ZA 6, 230; van der Spek, Fs Oelsner, 441-442.
Rm.845	Astronomical Diary. + 32332 + 32611. LBAT 197 (32332); Epping and Strassmaier, ZA 6, 232 (Rm.845); Sachs and Hunger, ADART I, no. -328.
Rm.846	Account of wool?
Rm.847	Astronomical Diary for SE 98. + unnum. Sachs and Hunger, ADART II, no. -213; Mitsuma, NABU 2013, 90-92, no. 54.
Rm.848	Mathematical table of squares of regular numbers. + 32178. ACT 1002; Ossendrijver, JCS 66, 149-165 and pls.
Rm.849	Astronomical.
Rm.850	Hemerology.
Rm.851	Astronomical; ephemeris. ACT 127.
Rm.852	Astronomical Diary.
Rm.853	Literary; Gilgameš IV. CT 46, 30, no. 21; George, Gilgamesh II, pl. 71.
Rm.914	Unidentified.
Rm.915	Economic. 2/-/-. Babylon.
Rm.917	Joined to Rm.731.
Rm.918	Economic.
Rm.927	Promissory note for silver; sealed 12/[]/[]. Nisaba 28, no. 631.
Rm.929	Commentary.
Rm.938	Astronomical.
Rm.942	Contract; sale of a field. Wunsch, CM 20A-B, no. 97.
Rm.946	Joined to Rm.763.
Rm.956	Joined to Rm.785.

Rm.966	Mathematical astronomy.
Rm.967	Astronomical Diary.
Rm.969	Lexical; syllabary.
Rm.972	School text? God list?
Rm.974	Literary or letter. Marked T.N.; presumably an indication of provenance.
Rm.975	Contract.
Rm.979	Account of silver.
Rm.983	Astronomical Diary.
Rm.984	Astronomical.
Rm.986	Astronomical Diary.
Rm.987	Promissory note for barley. Dar -/-/12.
Rm.988	Astronomical.
Rm.990	Astronomical.
Rm.991	Astronomical.
Rm.997	Astronomical Diary.
Rm.1000	Fragment of a circular tablet or perhaps the lid of a jar of c. 10 cms. diameter; mentions year SE 221. Hackl, Fs van der Spek, 87-106, no. 11.
Rm.1006	Astronomical.
Rm.1007	Astronomical; ruled.
Rm.1008	Astronomical.
Rm.1009	Astronomical.
Rm.1011	Letter.
Rm.1014	Astronomical Diary.
Rm.1015	Astronomical; two columns.
Rm.1017	Joined to Rm.785.
Rm.1020	Astronomical.
Rm.1021	Economic; personal names.
Rm.1023	Astronomical Diary.
Rm.1024	Incantations.
Rm.1025	Astronomical.
Rm.1026	Astronomical Diary.
Rm.1027	Contract. Cam 2/4/-.

Rm-II collection

The Rm-II collection is mostly Assyrian apart from the following items which may be strays from another registered collection. See J. E. Reade in CBTBM VI, p. xxix. The register records the provenance of no. 588 as Babylon and of no. 599 as Kouyunjik.

Rm-II.588	Lexical. Bezold, Cat. 4, p. 1686; Meissner, Supp, pl. 25; Meek, AJSL 36 (1919), 154ff.
Rm-II.599	Promissory note for dates and grain. Ner -/-/3. Bezold, Cat. 4, p. 1687.

Rm-III collection

The Rm-III collection comes from Hormuzd Rassam's excavations in Babylonia, arriving at the Museum in July 1879. See J. E. Reade in CBTBM VI, p. xxix on the various problems involved in determining the origins of specific tablets and the uncertainties over their registration. No. 123 was first registered by King 11/5/98, and nos. 124-125 were registered by Reade. The register gives the provenance Babylon to nos. 1-122, but Reade corrects this to Telloh for nos. 115-122 and adds the same for nos. 123-124. No. 125 comes from Aššur. The items in this collection dated as Pre-Sargonic (no. 106), Lagaš II (nos. 123-124, Ur III (no. 120), and Old Babylonian (nos. 52, 71, 107-110, 112-119, 121) may all have come from Rassam's brief excavation at Telloh (which has traces of settlement in the Old Babylonian period); they are in very poor condition. See Verderame, Fs Sigrist, 231-244, for more fragments from this excavation.

33328	Rm-III.1	Bilingual hymn to Šamaš; dupl. 36041. Abel and Winckler, KGV, 59-60.
33329	Rm-III.2	School text; lexical; Syllabary B. 3/[]/-. MSL 3, 130; CT 12, 32.
33330	Rm-III.3	Lexical; Ḫḫ I. MSL 5, 5; 5 R 39, 3; CT 19, 8.
33331	Rm-III.4	List of 19 stones; prophylactic medical. Schuster-Brandis, AOAT 46, p. 319-321, Text 10, pl. 30.
33332	Rm-III.5	Babylonian King List A. CT 36, 24-25; Grayson, RlA 7, 90-96.
33333a	Rm-III.6a	Contract; sale of a field. Nbk 13/9/34. Babylon. + 33336 + 33404.
33333b	Rm-III.6b	Explanatory diagram and rules for playing the game of 20 squares (Royal Game of Ur); colophon of Itti-Marduk-balāṭu. SE Seleucus IV 3/8/135. Bottero, Syria 33 (1956) 30-35; Weidner, Syria 33 (1956) 175-183; Finkel, Board Games, 16-32.
33334	Rm-III.7	Cylinder; inscription of Nebuchadnezzar II; second column of a two-column cylinder. Dupl. Langdon, VAB 4, 150-175, Neb. no. 19 iv-v? + 55433.
33335	Rm-III.8	School text; lexical; syllabary.
33336	Rm-III.9	Joined to 33333a.
33337	Rm-III.10	Ritual. Maul, Bagh Forsch 18, 347-8, 548.
33338	Rm-III.11	Cylinder; inscription of Ashurbanipal on the rebuilding of the temple of Ninmaḫ at Babylon. Babylon. Frame, RIMB 2.6.32.5.2.
33339	Rm-III.12	Contract; lease of a house; sealed. Art 18/2/3. Babylon. Nisaba 28, no. 259.
33340	Rm-III.13	Neo-Babylonian copy of accounts of Ezida at Borsippa during the 10th year of Adad-apla-iddina; copy made in the reign of Nebuchadnezzar II.
33341	Rm-III.14	Lexical; god-list, An = Anum VII. CT 41, 50.

33342	Rm-III.15	Promissory note for silver; sealed. Dar II 29/11/acc; dated also year 41 (of Artaxerxes). Babylon. Bertin 2889; Stolper, AMI NF 16, 223-236; Nisaba 28, no. 240.
33343	Rm-III.16	Incantation for dedication of a bull before sacrifice. Dupl. K.6060 and VAT 8247 (Ebeling, KAR 50, and Thureau-Dangin, Rituels accadiens, 22-25).
33344	Rm-III.17	Neo-Babylonian copy of an inscription of Sin-kašid, king of Uruk. Colophon. Copy by Balaṭu, the junior scribe. Dupl. CT 21, 13-14. Nbk 21/8/2.
33345	Rm-III.18	Late Babylonian copy of a royal inscription of a king of Ur; cf. 33408 and 33413.
33346	Rm-III.19	Liver omens with historical excerpts parallel to K.2130 and BM 67404; IM.GÍD.DA 2-KAM BE BÀ a-na si-[ḫi-ir-ti-ša ...]; colophon; copied from an original from Babylon. De Zorzi, JCS 68, 144-147.
33347	Rm-III.20	School text; bilingual incantation, 10/5/-. Udug-ḫul 10. Geller, BAM 8, 323-339, pl. 81.
33348	Rm-III.21	Prayer to Šamaš.
33349	Rm-III.22	Receipt for wood deliveries. Art 10/10/5. Bertin 2888.
33350	Rm-III.23	Promissory note for silver. Ner 15/2/2. Babylon. Sack, AOAT 236, no. 85.
33351	Rm-III.24	Promissory note for silver. Cyr 2/12/2+.
33352	Rm-III.25	Contract; promise to come and take an oath about custody of silver; finger-nail mark with caption. Dar 6/2/20+. Babylon. Bertin 2751; Sandowicz, AOAT 398, 302, O.153.
33353	Rm-III.26	Contract; sale of a house. 10/12/-.
33354	Rm-III.27	Medical.
33355	Rm-III.28	Marriage contract. Nbk -/7/21. Babylon.
117870	Rm-III.29	Incantation bowl. + Rm-III.30 + 32. Segal, Incantation Bowls, no. 072A pl. 74.
	Rm-III.30	Joined to Rm-III.29.
117871	Rm-III.31	Incantation bowl. Segal, Incantation Bowls, no. 073A pl. 75.
	Rm-III.32	Joined to Rm-III.29.
33356	Rm-III.33	Sumerian litany.
33357	Rm-III.34	Medical omens; copy of 34th tablet of Sa-gig, made in the reign of Šamaš-šum-ukin; colophon.
33358	Rm-III.35	Deposition. Šamaš-šum-ukin. Kissik (ABxḪA+GIŠ). Brinkman and Kennedy, JCS 35, 38, K.170.
33359	Rm-III.36	Promissory note for silver. Cyr 26 ?/11/-. Babylon.
33360	Rm-III.37	Receipt. Cyr 17/1/8. Babylon.
33361	Rm-III.38	Promissory note for dates. Nbn 13/6/1. Aballi.
33362	Rm-III.39	Account of deliveries of silver.

33363	Rm-III.40	Account of deliveries of silver.
33364	Rm-III.41	Receipt for a repayment. Dar 1/5/10. Upija.
33365	Rm-III.42	Contract; division of land. Nbn 10/5/1. Babylon.
33366	Rm-III.43	Promissory note for dates. 14/[]/11. URU DIR? IM [KI].
33367	Rm-III.44	Promissory note for silver. Nbn -/5/-.
33368	Rm-III.45	Deposition. Ner -/7/-. Babylon.
33369	Rm-III.46	Promissory note for dates. Nbn 5/9/10.
33370	Rm-III.47	Promissory note for silver. Dar -/8/29. Babylon.
33371	Rm-III.48	Contract for baked bricks. Nbk 25 ?/5 ?/39. URU DIR IM.
33372	Rm-III.49	Note of expenditures. 7/-/-.
33373	Rm-III.50	Receipt for a delivery of reed mats. 14/10/-.
33374	Rm-III.51	Note for deliveries.
33375	Rm-III.52	Old Babylonian(?) rectangular label; hole pierced through the top; cf. 33394. Telloh?
33376	Rm-III.53	Lexical; Ḫḫ; two columns.
33377	Rm-III.54	Contract; sale of a house and bricks. Cam 26/6/-.
33378	Rm-III.55	Payment for excavation. Nbn -/5/5.
33379	Rm-III.56	Receipt for payment of rent. 24/12/2.
33380	Rm-III.57	Contract; lease of a house. Šamaš-šum-ukin 29/7/19. Babylon. Brinkman and Kennedy, JCS 35, 35, K.129.
33381	Rm-III.58	Promissory note for barley. Nbn -/11/16. Dūr-x-x-x. Bertin 1617.
33382	Rm-III.59	Horoscope. SE Sel I & Ant 24. LBAT 1459; Rochberg, Babylonian Horoscopes, no. 4; Bertin 2894.
33383	Rm-III.60	Promissory note for dates.
33384	Rm-III.61	Rectangular exercise tablet; on one side simple numbers in portrait format, on the other side a largely erased text in landscape format.
33385	Rm-III.62	Administrative note of silver, gammidatu garments and copper; sealed. Ner 30/2/1. Nisaba 28, no. 183a.
33386	Rm-III.63	Promissory note for silver. Cam 6/8/2.
33387	Rm-III.64	Promissory note for barley. Nbn 28/2/15. URU DIR IM KI.
33388	Rm-III.65	Contract; lease of a plot of land; year number 14 (collated). Nbn 4/9/14. URU Qu-ru-bu-ana-d.EN. Bertin 1582; Zadok, NABU 1995, 5, no. 6.
33389	Rm-III.66	Promissory note for dates. Nbn 2/9/-. Babylon.
33390	Rm-III.67	Contract; payment of silver in cancellation of a debt. Cam 7/6 /5. Borsippa. Zadok, Nisaba 21, 234.
33391	Rm-III.68	Promissory note for silver. Nbn 27/7/11.
33392	Rm-III.69	Medical ritual; cf. Ebeling, KAR 42.
33393	Rm-III.70	Copy (ḫe-pí) of incantation against AN.TA.ŠUB.BA; medical.

33394	Rm-III.71	Old Babylonian(?) rectangular label; hole pierced through the top; upper half only; cf. 33375. Telloh?
33395	Rm-III.72	Promissory note for silver.
33396	Rm-III.73	Contract; sale of a field.
33397	Rm-III.74	Promissory note.
33398	Rm-III.75	Omens; extispicy; isru 4th tablet.
33399	Rm-III.76	Magico-medical prescriptions against Lamaštu. Farber, Lamaštu, 52, 57, 277-278, 310-311, 337, pl. 75.
33400	Rm-III.77	Promissory note for silver.
33401	Rm-III.78	Medical.
33402	Rm-III.79	School text; bilingual incantation, Udug-ḫul 9; Tintir II; lexical, Ḫḫ IV. + 33425. George, BTT, pl. 9; Geller, BAM 8, 302-322, pl. 73.
33403	Rm-III.80	Omens; Iqqur īpuš, Nisannu.
33404	Rm-III.81	Joined to 33333a.
33405	Rm-III.82	Astrological; colophon. Reiner, Fs Borger (CM 10), 293.
33406	Rm-III.83	Omens; extispicy. + unnum.
33407	Rm-III.84	Religious.
33408	Rm-III.85	Late Babylonian copy of an earlier royal inscription; cf. 33345 and 33413.
33409	Rm-III.86	Hemerology.
33410	Rm-III.87	Astrological. Reiner, Fs Borger (CM 10), 293.
33411	Rm-III.88	Letter.
33412	Rm-III.89	Contract; sale of a field; finger-nail marks with caption. 13/[]/[].
33413	Rm-III.90	Late Babylonian copy of a royal inscription; colophon; cf. 33345 and 33408.
33414	Rm-III.91	Contract. Nabû-[] -/5/1. Babylon.
33415	Rm-III.92	Promissory note for barley.
33416	Rm-III.93	School text; lexical and literary extracts.
33417	Rm-III.94	Lexical.
33418	Rm-III.95	Religious.
33419	Rm-III.96	School text; lexical; repetition of A.
33420	Rm-III.97	Astronomical or mathematical; numbers in rows; two columns; crudely written.
33421	Rm-III.98	Contract. Cam 25/6/-.
33422	Rm-III.99	Medical.
33423	Rm-III.100	Promissory note for dates. Cam.
33424	Rm-III.101	Medical omens; Sa-gig tablet 3. Heeßel, AOAT 43, 140.
33425	Rm-III.102	Joined to 33402.
33426	Rm-III.103	Lexical; Ḫḫ XI. MSL 9, 195.
33427	Rm-III.104	Cylinder; inscription of Nebuchadnezzar II.

33428	Rm-III.105	Cylinder; inscription of Nabû-šum-imbi, governor of Borsippa, on the restoration of Ezida and events during the reign of Nabû-šuma-iškun; perhaps a later copy. Borsippa. (marked B.N.). Lambert, Gs Speiser, 123-132; Frame, RIMB 2.6.14.2001; Reade, Iraq 48, 108; Zadok, NABU 1997, 10-13, no. 11.
33429	Rm-III.106	Archaic kudurru fragment. Pre-Sargonic.
33430	Rm-III.107	Old Babylonian letter; names of sender and addressee lost.
33431	Rm-III.108	Old Babylonian letter; names of sender and addressee lost.
33432	Rm-III.109	Old Babylonian letter.
33433	Rm-III.110	Old Babylonian letter.
33434	Rm-III.111	Written off.
33435	Rm-III.112	Old Babylonian account.
33436	Rm-III.113	Old Babylonian letter.
33437	Rm-III.114	Old Babylonian contract? Its envelope was 33439, now written off.
33438	Rm-III.115	Old Babylonian list of personal names. The tablet quoted in Finkel, AuOr 9 (1991) 103 is 38438, not 33438.
33439	Rm-III.116	Old Babylonian, envelope of 33437, sealed; now written off.
33440	Rm-III.117	Old Babylonian letter.
33441	Rm-III.118	Old Babylonian practice letter (apputum).
33442	Rm-III.119	Old Babylonian letter.
33443	Rm-III.120	Ur III. Receipt for sheep which d.Sukkal-ì-dúr? received from Šu-d.Utu; witnesses; month mu-šu-du7. Šu-Sin -/9/7.
33444	Rm-III.121	Old Babylonian economic.
33445	Rm-III.122	Astronomical Diary for SE 58. (+) 45840. Sachs and Hunger, ADART II, no. -253 A.
33446	Rm-III.123	Lagaš II cone; inscription of Ur-Bau. Steible, FAOS 9/1 Urbaba 7 (L); Edzard, RIME 3/1.1.6.4.
90845	Rm-III.124	Lagaš II. Stone door-socket of Ur-Ningirsu. Steible, FAOS 9/1 Ur-Ningirsu II 1; Edzard, RIME 3/1.1.8.1; Winckler, ABK, no. 13.
90299	Rm-III.125	Old Assyrian. Brick of Erišum I from Aššur; also registered as 1979,1220.184. CBI, no. 119.

Rm-IV collection

The Rm-IV collection comes from Hormuzd Rassam's excavations in Babylonia and arrived in December 1879. See J. E. Reade in CBTBM VI pp. xix-xxx. The register gives the provenance Babylon to the whole collection except for nos. 398 (Babylon or Abu Habbah), 399 (Abu Habbah), 425 (Abu Habbah), and 426-428 (Babylonia). One may suspect that the Old Babylonian tablets in this collection (nos. 400, 403, 406, 456) are registered outside their proper collection. See the comment on no. 406.

33447	Rm-IV.1	Mathematical table. Ossendrijver, JCS 66, 149-165 and pls.
33448	Rm-IV.2	Astronomical; Normal Star Almanac for SE 183. + 33466 + 33743 + 47727 + Rm-IV unnum. LBAT 1045-1046 (33466 + 47727); LBAT 1138 (33743); Hunger and Sachs, ADART VII, no. 82.
33449	Rm-IV.3	Prayer to Ishtar?
33450	Rm-IV.4	Astronomical; Normal Star Almanac for SE 121. + 48923 + 48898 (+) 33462 + 48864. LBAT 1023 (33450 only); Hunger and Sachs, ADART VII, no. 52.
33451	Rm-IV.5	Astronomical; procedure text for the moon; System A; colophon. Ossendrijver, BMAPT, no. 61D (not 49084). + 47744 + 47924 + 49084.
33452	Rm-IV.6	Lexical; Ḫḫ III. + 33467 + 33886 + Rm-IV unnum. MSL 9, 159.
33453	Rm-IV.7	Astronomical; table for Saturn for SE 199-217. + 33473 + 33499 + 33758 + Rm-IV unnum. ACT 705a (33453 + 33473); ACT 704a (33499); ACT 704a (33758). The unnumbered fragment is unpublished.
33454	Rm-IV.8	Astronomical; largely illegible.
33455	Rm-IV.9	Contract; witnesses; caption for the seal of the mukīn šarri. SE -/-/[73+].
33456	Rm-IV.10	Astronomical.
33457	Rm-IV.11	Astronomical; Goal Year Text for SE 211. + 47916. LBAT 1293; Hunger and Sachs, ADART VI, no. 79.
33458	Rm-IV.12	Astronomical or mathematical; table of coefficients of length (šu-si, kùš), possibly in an astronomical context. + 33577 + 33585 + Rm-IV unnum.
33459	Rm-IV.13	Astronomical or mathematical; table of coefficients of length (uš, danna), possibly in an astronomical context. + Rm-IV.213.
33460	Rm-IV.14	Lexical; Ḫḫ XX. MSL 11, 3.
33461	Rm-IV.15	Astronomical Diary for SE 174; mentions Aspasine. + 33836. LBAT 427 (33836 only); Sachs and Hunger, ADART III, no. -137 D.

33462	Rm-IV.16	Astronomical; Normal Star Almanac. + 48864 (+) 33450 + 48923. Hunger and Sachs, ADART VII, no. 52.
33463	Rm-IV.17	Counsels of Wisdom. (+) 33496 + 33595 + 33819. Lambert, MC 24, no. 259.
33464	Rm-IV.18	Astronomical Diary.
33465	Rm-IV.19	Bilingual religious.
33466	Rm-IV.20	Joined to 33448.
33467	Rm-IV.21	Joined to 33452.
33468	Rm-IV.22	Astronomical; Normal Star Almanac. + 33754. Hunger and Sachs, ADART VII, no. 99.
33469	Rm-IV.23	Lexical; Ḫḫ.
33470	Rm-IV.24	Lexical; Ḫḫ.
33471	Rm-IV.25	Astronomical; Normal Star Almanac. + 33498. Hunger and Sachs, ADART VII, no. 108.
33472	Rm-IV.26	Astronomical; Goal Year Text for SE 175. + 33524 + 33721 + 2 Rm-IV unnum. Hunger and Sachs, ADART VI, no. 54.
33473	Rm-IV.27	Joined to 33453.
33474	Rm-IV.28	Astrological; Enūma Anu Enlil 35, solar eclipse omens. Reiner, Fs Borger (CM 10), 293.
33475	Rm-IV.29	Medical ritual.
33476	Rm-IV.30	Lexical; Ḫḫ I, 237.
33477	Rm-IV.31	Astronomical Diary for SE 169. + 33591 + 33613. Sachs and Hunger, ADART III, no. -142 A.
33478	Rm-IV.32	Astronomical Diary. LBAT 162; Sachs and Hunger, ADART I, no. -440; J. Koch, AfO 38/39 101-103.
33479	Rm-IV.33	List of market prices for years 184-190 SE. + 33639. Slotsky and Wallenfels, Tallies and Trends, text 8.
33480	Rm-IV.34	Astronomical procedure text for the moon; System A. Ossendrijver, BMAPT, no. 64.
33481	Rm-IV.35	Astronomical; Goal Year Text for SE 191. Hunger and Sachs, ADART VI, no. 66.
33482	Rm-IV.36	Astronomical; Normal Star Almanac for SE 178. + 33486 + 33487 + Rm-IV.85 + 3 Rm-IV unnum. LBAT 1042a-c; Hunger and Sachs, ADART VII, no. 79.
33483	Rm-IV.37	Literary; The murder of Anšar. + 33765 + 33775 + 33835. Lambert, BCM, p. 316-320, pls. 52-53.
33484	Rm-IV.38	School practice text.
33485	Rm-IV.39	Astronomical; Almanac for SE 248; prayer on upper edge. + 33822 + Rm. unnum. LBAT 1183 (33822 only); Hunger and Sachs, ADART VII, no. 202.
33486	Rm-IV.40	Joined to 33482.
33487	Rm-IV.41	Joined to 33482.
33488	Rm-IV.42	School text; religious; lexical; two columns. + 33502.

33489	Rm-IV.43	Astronomical; Almanac. Hunger and Sachs, ADART VII, no. 27.
33490	Rm-IV.44	Astronomical Diary.
	Rm-IV.45	Joined to 33482.
33491	Rm-IV.46	Tintir I. + 33826 + Rm-IV unnum. George, BTT, pl. 4.
33492	Rm-IV.47	Ritual of akitu type.
33493	Rm-IV.48	Omens; extispicy; isru. + 33503 + 33519 + 33521 + 33586 + 33831 + 48865 + 48866 + 48885.
33494	Rm-IV.49	School practice text.
33495	Rm-IV.50	Astronomical; Goal Year Text; not datable. Hunger and Sachs, ADART VI, no. 110.
33496	Rm-IV.51	Counsels of Wisdom. + 33595 + 33819 (+) 33463. Lambert, MC 24, no. 259.
33497	Rm-IV.52	Astronomical; Normal Star Almanac. + 33504 + 33510. Hunger and Sachs, ADART VII, no. 62.
33498	Rm-IV.53	Joined to 33471.
33499	Rm-IV.54	Joined to 33453.
33500	Rm-IV.55	Literary; Enmešarra's defeat. Lambert, BCM, p. 298, pl. 46.
33501	Rm-IV.56	Astronomical; Normal Star Almanac. + Rm-IV unnum. Hunger and Sachs, ADART VII, no. 49.
33502	Rm-IV.57	Joined to 33488.
33503	Rm-IV.58	Joined to 33493.
33504	Rm-IV.59	Joined to 33497.
33505	Rm-IV.60	Literary; bilingual.
33506	Rm-IV.61	Medical ritual. + 33529 + 33761.
33507	Rm-IV.62	Lexical; Ḫḫ IV. + 33659 + 33853 + 33854 + 47927 + 3 Rm-IV unnum. (+) 33858. MSL 5, 148 and 9, 168.
33508	Rm-IV.63	Ritual; akitu type. + 33729 + 33747 + 47726 + Rm-IV unnum.
33509	Rm-IV.64	Lexical; Ḫḫ III. MSL 9, 159.
33510	Rm-IV.65	Joined to 33497.
33511	Rm-IV.66	Lexical; bilingual.
33512	Rm-IV.67	Economic.
33513	Rm-IV.68	Economic.
33514	Rm-IV.69	School text; literary, Muššu'u VII, Šamaš Hymn; lexical, giš. + 33517 + 33531 + 33719 + 33738 + 33744 + 33766 + 48918 + 3 Rm-IV unnum. Lambert, BCM, p. 157; Lambert, MC 24, no. 137.
33515	Rm-IV.70	Astronomical; Almanac. Hunger and Sachs, ADART VII, no. 192.
33516	Rm-IV.71	Lexical; Ḫḫ?
33517	Rm-IV.72	Joined to 33514.
33518	Rm-IV.73	Receipt for hire of slaves.

33519	Rm-IV.74	Joined to 33493.
33520	Rm-IV.75	Lexical?
	Rm-IV.76	Nothing registered.
33521	Rm-IV.77	Joined to 33493.
33522	Rm-IV.78	Astronomical; Goal Year Text for SE 247. + 33569 + 33580 + 33814 + Rm-IV unnum. Hunger and Sachs, ADART VI, no. 92.
33523	Rm-IV.79	Lexical; Ḫḫ; giš.
33524	Rm-IV.80	Joined to 33472.
33525	Rm-IV.81	Literary. + 33526.
33526	Rm-IV.82	Joined to 33525.
33527	Rm-IV.83	Contract; sale of a field.
33528	Rm-IV.84	Astronomical Diary.
33529	Rm-IV.85	Joined to 33506.
33530	Rm-IV.86	Astrological omens.
33531	Rm-IV.87	Joined to 33514.
33532	Rm-IV.88	Astronomical.
33533	Rm-IV.89	Astronomical; Goal Year Text for SE 247. Hunger and Sachs, ADART VI, no. 93.
33534	Rm-IV.90	Bilingual incantation; colophon. CT 17, 33; Pinches, PSBA 23 (1901) 205-210 and pl. facing p. 204; Schramm, GBAO 2, p. 90, pls. 37-38, text B1.
33535	Rm-IV.91	Astrological medicine, using the microzodiac. Hunger, Fs Biggs (AS 27, 2007), 141-151.
33536	Rm-IV.92	Astrological; Enūma Anu Enlil 37?; colophon. Reiner, Fs Borger (CM 10), 293.
33537	Rm-IV.93	Contract; sale of land; finger-nail marks. Šamaš-šum-ukin 29/2/20. Babylon. Strassmaier, 8th Orientalist Congress, no. 6; Brinkman and Kennedy, JCS 35, 35, K.140; Frame, JCS 51, 105.
33538	Rm-IV.94	Account of delivery of dates. Nbn 17/11/11. Babylon. Nbn 570; Bertin 1631.
33539	Rm-IV.95	Contract; record of deposit; Murānu archive; sealed. SE Ant & Sel 20/11/37. Babylon. CT 49, 21, no. 108; Stolper, Annali Supp. 77, 24-25, no. 7; Jursa, Persika 9, 175, 180-182; Bertin 3017; Nisaba 28, no. 560.
33540	Rm-IV.96	School text; lexical, Ḫḫ IV; literary extracts. MSL 9, 168.
33541	Rm-IV.97	Literary; lament for Uruk; colophon. SE Sel & Ant 15/6/25. Babylon. Pinches, PSBA 23 (1901) 197-198 and pl. facing p. 192.
33542	Rm-IV.98	Sale of produce. Dar 5/6/4. Babylon. Dar 122; Bertin 1998.
33543	Rm-IV.99	Incantations. Abusch and Schwemer, AMD 8/2 text 3.4 g, pl. 4.

33544	Rm-IV.100	Promissory note for dates. Nbn 18/6/9. Bītāti. Nbn 354; Bertin 1360.
33545	Rm-IV.101	Letter; sealed. Bertin 3018.
33546	Rm-IV.102	Account of shepherds.
33547	Rm-IV.103	Contract; quit-claim for a repaid debt in silver; finger-nail mark. Art I/II 4/3/41. Babylon. Strassmaier, 8th Orientalist Congress, no. 30; Bertin 2884.
33548	Rm-IV.104	Sale of an ox. Nbn 27/4/-. Bertin 1644.
33549	Rm-IV.105	Promissory note for dates. Dar 14/3/27. Šaḫrīn. Bertin 2633.
33550	Rm-IV.106	Receipt for silver. SE (Arsaces) 17/[]/218. CT 49, 35, no. 151; Strassmaier, ZA 3, 143; van der Spek, Raḫimesu, 232, no. 21 (with comment on the date); Bertin 3054.
33551	Rm-IV.107	Hemerology. List of dates in months I-VIII probably of unlucky days.
33552	Rm-IV.108	Astronomical procedure text; description of a quantitative model for Venus; colophon. Britton and Walker, Centaurus 34 (1991) 97-118; Brown, CM 18, 305; Ossendrijver, BMAPT, no. 9.
33553	Rm-IV.109	Promissory note for barley. Nbn 9/9/9. Šaḫrīn. Nbn 369; Bertin 1359; Wunsch, CM 3, no. 169.
33554	Rm-IV.110	Promissory note for silver. Dar 5/7/-.
33555	Rm-IV.111	Account of purchases.
33556	Rm-IV.112	Promissory note for onions and [barley?]; ḫarrānu. Nbn 8/4/3. Babylon. Nbn 107; Bertin 1265; Wunsch, CM 3, no. 114.
33557	Rm-IV.113	Astrological?
33558	Rm-IV.114	Horoscopic predictions. SE.
33559	Rm-IV.115	Silver entrusted for payment of a debt. Nbn 25/11/9. Babylon. Nbn 383; Bertin 1367.
33560	Rm-IV.116	Contract; lease of a house. Dar 25/5/16. Babylon. Dar 424; Bertin 2351.
33561	Rm-IV.117	Receipt for sale of donkey. Dar 10/2/-. Babylon. Bertin 2818.
33562	Rm-IV.118	Promissory note for dates. Ner 27/4/1. Babylon. Evetts, Ner 21; Sack, AOAT 236, no. 21; Bertin 1205; Wunsch, CM 3, no. 66.
33562a	Rm-IV.118a	Astronomical; lunar eclipse report for eclipse of 10 April 80 BC; prayer on upper edge. SE Arsaces -/-/232. Strassmaier, ZA 3, 135 and 147-148; Epping, ZA 4, 76-82; LBAT 1445; Stephenson, HEER, 112-113, 160, 183, 189-190, 204, 209-210; Hunger and Sachs, ADART V, no. 25; Bertin 2918.

33563	Rm-IV.119	Horoscope. SE 16/10/19. Rochberg, Babylonian Horoscopes, no. 30.
33564	Rm-IV.120	Astronomical procedure text; obv. daylight; rev. shadows; colophon. Steele, SCIAMVS 14 (2013), 3-39.
33565	Rm-IV.121	Promissory note for silver. Cam 16/2/7. Babylon. Cam 3; Bertin 1909.
33566	Rm-IV.122	Omens; Šumma ālu; also has a namburbû ritual.
33567	Rm-IV.123	Mathematical; table of squares of regular numbers. Aaboe, JCS 19, 80-81.
33568	Rm-IV.124	School text; sign list; badly damaged.
33569	Rm-IV.125	Joined to 33522.
33570	Rm-IV.126	School practice text; wedges only.
33571	Rm-IV.127	Lexical; two columns.
33572	Rm-IV.128	School text; lexical; literary; Enūma eliš VI. Lambert, BCM, p. 109, pl. 26.
33573	Rm-IV.129	School text? largely illegible.
33574	Rm-IV.130	Astronomical; planetary observations; Mars and Venus. Hunger and Sachs, ADART V, no. 86.
33575	Rm-IV.131	Contract; witnesses.
33576	Rm-IV.132	Contract for a partnership. Dar -/9/4. Babylon.
33577	Rm-IV.133	Joined to 33458.
33578	Rm-IV.134	Astronomical; Normal Star Almanac. + 33615. Hunger and Sachs, ADART VII, no. 68.
33579	Rm-IV.135	Lexical; Ḫḫ IX and X. + 33860. MSL 7, 35 and 74, and 9, 181.
33580	Rm-IV.136	Joined to 33522.
33581	Rm-IV.137	Lexical; Ḫḫ?
33582	Rm-IV.138	Astronomical.
33583	Rm-IV.139	Lexical; Ḫḫ?
33584	Rm-IV.140	Incantations; Šurpu VIII. (+) 33636 + 33855.
33585	Rm-IV.141	Joined to 33458.
33586	Rm-IV.142	Joined to 33493.
33587	Rm-IV.143	Astronomical Diary.
33588	Rm-IV.144	School text; lexical.
33589	Rm-IV.145	Distribution or delivery of grain.
33590	Rm-IV.146	Illegible.
33591	Rm-IV.147	Joined to 33477.
33592	Rm-IV.148	Astronomical.
33593	Rm-IV.149	Astronomical procedure text for the moon; System A. ACT 207; Aaboe, KDVSMM 40/6 (1979) 9-10; Ossendrijver, BMAPT, no. 88.
33594	Rm-IV.150	Contract; sealed; cf. 33599 and 33602. Nisaba 28, no. 633.
33595	Rm-IV.151	Joined to 33496.
33596	Rm-IV.152	Lexical; Ḫḫ VIII. MSL 7, 6

33597	Rm-IV.153	Omens; Iqqur īpuš, Abu. Cf. Reiner, Fs Borger (CM 10), 293.
33598	Rm-IV.154	Incantation.
33599	Rm-IV.155	Contract; cf. 33594 and 33602.
33600	Rm-IV.156	Religious.
33601	Rm-IV.157	Astronomical Diary.
33602	Rm-IV.158	Contract; cf. 33594 and 33599.
33603	Rm-IV.159	Lexical; practical vocabulary. MSL 10, 102.
33604	Rm-IV.160	Astronomical; Goal Year Text; not datable. Hunger and Sachs, ADART VI, no. 111.
33605	Rm-IV.161	Lexical; giš; Ḫḫ.
33606	Rm-IV.162	Economic.
33607	Rm-IV.163	Lexical. + Rm-IV unnum.
33608	Rm-IV.164	Astronomical; Goal Tear Text; not datable. Hunger and Sachs, ADART VI, no. 112.
33609	Rm-IV.165	Promissory note for dates. Npl 12/7/[]. Babylon.
33610	Rm-IV.166	School text; metrological table; lexical; syllabary.
33611	Rm-IV.167	Astronomical; Normal Star Almanac. Hunger and Sachs, ADART VII, no. 109.
33612	Rm-IV.168	Lexical.
33613	Rm-IV.169	Joined to 33477.
33614	Rm-IV.170	Religious.
33615	Rm-IV.171	Joined to 33576.
33616	Rm-IV.172	Lexical; Ḫḫ XI. MSL 9, 195.
33617	Rm-IV.173	Chronicle.
33618	Rm-IV.174	Astronomical; Mercury, evening star, for (at least) SE 214 to 220, System A1. ACT 303.
33619	Rm-IV.175	Ritual; piristum. + 33620 + 33635.
33620	Rm-IV.176	Joined to 33619.
33621	Rm-IV.177	School text; lexical.
33622	Rm-IV.178	Medical.
33623	Rm-IV.179	Astronomical table.
33624	Rm-IV.180	School text; lexical; Ḫḫ.
33625	Rm-IV.181	Lexical; giš.
33626	Rm-IV.182	Lexical; syllabary.
33627	Rm-IV.183	Lexical; Ḫḫ. + Rm-IV unnum.
33628	Rm-IV.184	Astronomical Diary?
33629	Rm-IV.185	Astronomical; Jupiter, first visibility for (at least) SE 197 to 206. ACT 613.
33630	Rm-IV.186	School text; lexical; Syllabary A; literary extract. MSL 3, 7; CT 12, 32.
33631	Rm-IV.187	Astronomical procedure text for the moon; System A. ACT 200b; Ossendrijver, BMAPT, no. 56.
33632	Rm-IV.188	Astronomical; Normal Star Almanac. Hunger and Sachs, ADART VII, no. 99.

33633	Rm-IV.189	Astronomical; Almanac for SE 234. LBAT 1161; Hunger and Sachs, ADART VII, no. 190.
33634	Rm-IV.190	Astronomical Diary.
33635	Rm-IV.191	Joined to 33619.
33636	Rm-IV.192	Incantation, Šurpu VIII 42-54. + 33855 + Rm-IV.418 (+) 33584.
33637	Rm-IV.193	Contract. + Rm-IV unnum.
33638	Rm-IV.194	School text; lexical and literary extracts.
33639	Rm-IV.195	Joined to 33479.
33640	Rm-IV.196	Lexical.
33641	Rm-IV.197	Astronomical; Almanac for SE 209. LBAT 1152; Hunger and Sachs, ADART VII, no. 185.
33642	Rm-IV.198	Personal names. -/1/-.
33643	Rm-IV.199	Astronomical; lunar eclipse report for eclipse of 28 February 190 BC. SE 121. LBAT 1437; Stephenson, HEER, 201; Hunger and Sachs, ADART V, no. 18.
33644	Rm-IV.200	Lexical; plants.
33645	Rm-IV.201	Astronomical Diary; prices.
33646	Rm-IV.202	School text; metrological table; lexical; syllabary.
33647	Rm-IV.203	Only witnesses preserved.
33648	Rm-IV.204	Offering ledger.
33649	Rm-IV.205	Astronomical Diary. + 34648. LBAT 575 (34648 only).
33650	Rm-IV.206	Lexical.
33651	Rm-IV.207	Astronomical; Almanac or Normal Star Almanac. + 33752 + 5 Rm-IV unnum. Hunger and Sachs, ADART VII, no. 205.
33652	Rm-IV.208	School text; lexical.
33653	Rm-IV.209	Contract; Murānu archive; sealed. SE. Nisaba 28, no. 612.
33654	Rm-IV.210	Astronomical.
33655	Rm-IV.211	Astronomical Diary for SE 86. Sachs and Hunger, ADART II, no. -225; Stephenson, HEER, 84, 177, 186.
33656	Rm-IV.212	Astronomical; Jupiter, second stationary point and last visibility, for (at least) SE 188 to 222. ACT 605.
	Rm-IV.213	Joined to 33459.
33657	Rm-IV.214	Promissory note for silver; Murānu archive; sealed. SE Ant II 12/4/59. Bīt-Erū'a, Jursa, Persika 9, 175, 195-196, 213; Nisaba 28, no. 581.
33658	Rm-IV.215	Receipt for barley. Cyr -/9/7?
33659	Rm-IV.216	Joined to 33507.
33660	Rm-IV.217	Letter to Ea-tabtanâ-bulliṭ / Murānu; sealed. SE Ant II 28/12/56. CT 49, 26, no. 124; Jursa, Persika 9, 156, 192-193; Nisaba 28, no. 671.

33661	Rm-IV.218	Contract; sale of a field. Nbk 24/7/6.
33662	Rm-IV.219	Contract; sale of a field. Npl 12/9/12. Babylon.
33663	Rm-IV.220	Receipt for flour. Cam 2/12/[].
33664	Rm-IV.221	Receipt for jewellery.
33665	Rm-IV.222	Receipt for jewellery of the king; drawing. Nbn 25/6/15. URU Qu-ri-ban-a-na-d.[EN].
33666	Rm-IV.223	Contract; quit-claim mentions years 151 and 156; sealed. SE []/[]/156. CT 49, 32, no. 139; Nisaba 28, no. 604.
33667	Rm-IV.224	Horoscope. SE 8/9/54. LBAT 1461; Rochberg, Babylonian Horoscopes, no. 7; Sachs, JCS 6, 58-60, pl. IV.
33668	Rm-IV.225	Contract; lease of a house. Nbn 24/12a/1. Babylon.
33669	Rm-IV.226	Medical.
33670	Rm-IV.227	Contract; lease of a house.
33671	Rm-IV.228	Astronomical Diary for SE 112. LBAT 310; Sachs and Hunger, ADART II, no. -199 B.
33672	Rm-IV.229	Contract with oath by Marduk, Nabû and Darius. Dar I []/9/20.
33673	Rm-IV.230	Incantation. + 33696.
33674	Rm-IV.231	Incantation, Šurpu II 146-148. Linssen, Fs Stol, 47-52.
33675	Rm-IV.232	School text; lexical.
33676	Rm-IV.233	Lexical.
33677	Rm-IV.234	Lexical.
33678	Rm-IV.235	School text; lexical. + Rm-IV.245.
33679	Rm-IV.236	Lexical.
33680	Rm-IV.237	School text; lexical.
33681	Rm-IV.238	Lexical; syllabary. CT 12, 32.
33682	Rm-IV.239	Bilingual incantation.
33683	Rm-IV.240	Lexical; syllabary.
33684	Rm-IV.241	Lexical.
33685	Rm-IV.242	Medical ritual.
33686	Rm-IV.243	Literary.
33687	Rm-IV.244	Bilingual literary.
	Rm-IV.245	Joined to 33678.
33688	Rm-IV.246	School text; lexical.
33689	Rm-IV.247	School text; lexical; Diri II. MSL 15 121.
33690	Rm-IV.248	Lexical.
33691	Rm-IV.249	School text; lexical and literary extracts. 23/12/-.
33692	Rm-IV.250	School text; metrological table; lexical; syllabary.
33693	Rm-IV.251	Lexical; syllabary.
33694	Rm-IV.252	Lexical.
33695	Rm-IV.253	Astronomical.
33696	Rm-IV.254	Joined to 33673.

33697	Rm-IV.255	Literary; Enūma eliš III. Kämmerer and Metzler, AOAT 375, 93, Tafel III R, pl. XXIII; Lambert, BCM, p. 74, pl. 15.
33698	Rm-IV.256	Literary.
33699	Rm-IV.257	Lexical.
33700	Rm-IV.258	Religious.
33701	Rm-IV.259	Lexical; Ḫḫ XXIII.
33702	Rm-IV.260	Bilingual incantation.
33703	Rm-IV.261	Contract; sale of a field; sealed. Nisaba 28, no. 82.
33704	Rm-IV.262	Mathematical; metrological table; small fragment.
33705	Rm-IV.263	School text; lexical.
33706	Rm-IV.264	Lexical; Ḫḫ II. + 33881. MSL 5, 47
33707	Rm-IV.265	School text; lexical; Ḫḫ XVI-XVII. MSL 10, 3, 81
33708	Rm-IV.266	School text; lexical; Ḫḫ XXI. 21/12/-. MSL 11, 11
33709	Rm-IV.267	Contract; sale of a field.
33710	Rm-IV.268	Bilingual incantation.
33711	Rm-IV.269	Lexical; god list.
33712	Rm-IV.270	Bilingual incantation, Udug-ḫul 16. CT 16, 19-23; Geller, BAM 8, 499-541.
33713	Rm-IV.271	School text; lexical; Ḫḫ III; literary extract. MSL 5, 88 and 9, 159.
33714	Rm-IV.272	School text; lexical.
33715	Rm-IV.273	Bilingual incantation.
33716	Rm-IV.274	School text; Prayer to Marduk no. 1; lexical. Oshima, BPM, 147-148; Lambert, MC 24, no. 92.
33717	Rm-IV.275	Contract; sealed. Nisaba 28, no. 634.
33718	Rm-IV.276	Promissory note for silver; sealed; finger-nail marks. Antigonus []/9/3. CT 49, 8, no. 34; Stolper, Annali Supp. 77, 53-54, no. 18; Nisaba 28, no. 337.
33719	Rm-IV.277	Joined to 33514.
33720	Rm-IV.278	Promissory note for barley.
33721	Rm-IV.279	Joined to 33472.
33722	Rm-IV.280	Economic; market prices.
33723	Rm-IV.281	Bilingual incantation.
33724	Rm-IV.282	Astronomical; MUL.APIN. + 33779. Hunger and Pingree, AfO Beih. 24, 3 (33779 only); Reiner, Fs Borger (CM 10), 293; Fincke, JCS 69, 247-260; Hunger and Steele, MUL.APIN, 21.
33725	Rm-IV.283	School text; personal names.
33726	Rm-IV.284	Prophecy text; astrological protases. Grayson and Lambert, JCS 18, 24; Biggs, Iraq 29, 117-128.
33727	Rm-IV.285	Astronomical; Normal Star Almanac. Hunger and Sachs, ADART VII, no. 110.
33728	Rm-IV.286	Astronomical; MUL.APIN. Hunger and Pingree, AfO Beih. 24, 3; Hunger and Steele, MUL.APIN, 21.

33729	Rm-IV.287	Joined to 33508.
33730	Rm-IV.288	School text; lexical.
33731	Rm-IV.289	School text.
33732	Rm-IV.290	Lexical; Ḫḫ IV. MSL 5, 148.
33733	Rm-IV.291	Astronomical procedure text for a planet. Ossendrijver, BMAPT, no. 50.
33734	Rm-IV.292	Contract. 26/1/-. Babylon.
33735	Rm-IV.293	Astronomical.
33736	Rm-IV.294	Astronomical; Almanac for SE 237. + Rm-IV unnum. LBAT 1175; Hunger and Sachs, ADART VII, no. 193.
33737	Rm-IV.295	Tintir I. + 33818 + Rm-IV unnum. George, BTT, pl. 4.
33738	Rm-IV.296	Joined to 33514.
33739	Rm-IV.297	Astronomical procedure text; lunar latitudes. Neugebauer, JCS 21, 202 (duplicate to Atypical text E).
33740	Rm-IV.298	Astronomical.
33741	Rm-IV.299	Horoscope. SE 28/3/62. LBAT 1463; Rochberg, Babylonian Horoscopes, no. 12; Sachs, JCS 6, 61f, pl. III.
33742	Rm-IV.300	Contract. Nbn 26/11/10. Babylon.
33743	Rm-IV.301	Joined to 33448.
33744	Rm-IV.302	Joined to 33514.
33745	Rm-IV.303	School text; lexical.
33746	Rm-IV.304	Astronomical; Almanac for SE 236. + 46046. LBAT 1117 + 1172; Hunger and Sachs, ADART VII, no. 191.
33747	Rm-IV.305	Joined to 33508.
33748	Rm-IV.306	Astronomical; System A ephemeris; solar eclipses from (at least) SE 244 to 248. ACT 52.
33749	Rm-IV.307	Contract for a partnership; sealed. SE 10+/[]/100+. CT 49, 47, no. 179; Mitchell and Searight, no. 757; Nisaba 28, no. 591.
33750	Rm-IV.308	Dream omens.
33751	Rm-IV.309	Astronomical Diary.
33752	Rm-IV.310	Joined to 33651.
33753	Rm-IV.311	Astronomical.
33754	Rm-IV.312	Joined to 33468.
33755	Rm-IV.313	School text; lexical; Ea II-III. MSL 14, 245, 301; Landsberger, Gs Speiser, 133-147; Gesche, AOAT 275, 670.
33756	Rm-IV.314	Astronomical; Goal Year Text; not datable. Hunger and Sachs, ADART VI, no. 113.
33757	Rm-IV.315	School text; lexical.
33758	Rm-IV.316	Joined to 33453.
33759	Rm-IV.317	Astronomical Diary. LBAT 178; Sachs and Hunger, ADART I, no. -372 D.

33760	Rm-IV.318	School text; lexical; personal names.
33761	Rm-IV.319	Joined to 33506.
33762	Rm-IV.320	Astronomical Diary; mentions Darius in line 1; colophon.
33763	Rm-IV.321	Astronomical.
33764	Rm-IV.322	Astronomical Diary.
33765	Rm-IV.323	Joined to 33483.
33766	Rm-IV.324	Joined to 33514.
33767	Rm-IV.325	School text; lexical.
33768	Rm-IV.326	Incantation. + Rm-IV unnum.
33769	Rm-IV.327	Graeco-Babyloniaca; literary, Šamaš Hymn; lexical, Ḫḫ XXIII? Sollberger, Iraq 24, 71, and pl. XXV, C1; Geller, ZA 87, 78 and 94, no. 12 (copy); Westenholz, ZA 97, 269-273; MSL 11, 68.
33770	Rm-IV.328	Mathematical; metrological table; gú-un; fragment.
33771	Rm-IV.329	Astronomical.
33772	Rm-IV.330	Astrological omens.
33773	Rm-IV.331	School text; lexical; personal names.
33774	Rm-IV.332	Inventory of bottles, beer and other items. (+) 33829.
33775	Rm-IV.333	Joined to 33483.
33776	Rm-IV.334	School text; lexical.
33777	Rm-IV.335	Astronomical; Normal Star Almanac. Hunger and Sachs, ADART VII, no. 20.
33778	Rm-IV.336	Graeco-Babyloniaca; lexical, Ea IV. Sollberger, Iraq 24, 72, and pl. XXVI, C4; Geller, ZA 87, 75 and 90, no. 9 (copy); Westenholz, ZA 97, 268-269.
33779	Rm-IV.337	Joined to 33724.
33780	Rm-IV.338	Account of deliveries of grain.
33781	Rm-IV.339	School text; lexical and literary extracts.
33782	Rm-IV.340	Astronomical Diary; dated by Arsaces; refers to Arabia. SE Arsaces.
33783	Rm-IV.341	School text; a) traces only, b) Tintir II. George, BTT, pl. 8.
33784	Rm-IV.342	Astronomical; Almanac for SE 303. + 33790. LBAT 1191-1192; Kugler, SSB II 505-506, and 3. Erg., pls. VIII-IX; Hunger and Sachs, ADART VII, no. 210.
33785	Rm-IV.343	School text; lexical; Ḫḫ IV. MSL 9, 168.
33786	Rm-IV.344	School text; lexical; syllabary.
33787	Rm-IV.345	School text; lexical; syllabary.
33788	Rm-IV.346	School text; lexical; god list; literary extracts. + Rm-IV unnum.
33789	Rm-IV.347	School text; lexical; syllabary; literary extracts.
33790	Rm-IV.348	Joined to 33784.

33791	Rm-IV.349	Astronomical; MUL.APIN. + Rm-IV.350. Hunger and Pingree, AfO Beih. 24, 3; Hunger and Steele, MUL.APIN, 21.
	Rm-IV.350	Joined to 33791.
33792	Rm-IV.351	Astronomical Diary.
33793	Rm-IV.352	Omens; Šumma izbu 22. De Zorzi, Šumma izbu, 857.
33794	Rm-IV.353	Mathematical; problems in areas (UŠ, SAG), but obverse rather illegible. + Rm-IV.359.
33795	Rm-IV.354	Marriage contract. Wunsch, Bab Arch 2, 21-24, no. 5.
33796	Rm-IV.355	Promissory note for dates. Ner []/6/2. Babylon. Sack, AOAT 236, no. 89.
33797	Rm-IV.356	Astronomical; Almanac for SE 301; prayer on upper edge. LBAT 1190; Kugler, SSB I 104f, pl. IX; Hunger and Sachs, ADART VII, no. 209.
33798	Rm-IV.357	Astronomical; Almanac for SE 247; prayer on upper edge. LBAT 1182; Hunger and Sachs, ADART VII, no. 201.
33799	Rm-IV.358	School text; lexical and literary extracts.
	Rm-IV.359	Joined to 33794.
33800	Rm-IV.360	Lexical; Ḫḫ III. MSL 5, 89.
33801	Rm-IV.361	Astronomical procedure text for Jupiter, Saturn and Mars. ACT 811, colophon Zs; Ossendrijver, BMAPT, no. 44.
33802	Rm-IV.362	Table of calendar dates at 27 month intervals from Alexander III year 6 to SE 41.
33803	Rm-IV.363	Promissory note for silver; sealed. SE Antiochus III 28/8/[]. Nisaba 28, no. 600.
33804	Rm-IV.364	Promissory note for silver; Murānu archive; sealed. SE Ant & Sel []/[]/[35]. [Babylon]. CT 49, 20, no. 106; Stolper, Annali Supp. 77, 38-42, no. 12; Jursa, Persika 9, 175, 179-180; Nisaba 28, no. 557.
33805	Rm-IV.365	Astronomical Diary for SE 28. LBAT 230; Sachs and Hunger, ADART I, no. -283 A.
33806	Rm-IV.366	Promissory note for dates. Nbn 11/6/acc. <URU> Qur-ri-ba-an-[].EN. Nbn 7.
33807	Rm-IV.367	Lexical; Ḫḫ IV. MSL 9, 168.
33808	Rm-IV.368	Astronomical Diary for SE 110. Sachs and Hunger, ADART II, no. -201 C.
33809	Rm-IV.369	Astronomical; list of years with intercalary Ulūlu from Merodach-baladan to the Seleucid Era; colophon. Cf. Boiy, JCS 52, 115-121.
33810	Rm-IV.370	Memorandum about silver. CT 49, 46, no. 174.
33811	Rm-IV.371	School text; Prayer to Marduk no. 2; lexical; Ḫḫ VIII. MSL 7, 5 and 9, 173; Lambert, MC 24, no. 123.

33812	Rm-IV.372	Astronomical; solar eclipse report for eclipse of 14 March 190 BC. SE Antiochus III 121. LBAT 1438; Stephenson, HEER, 121, 135, 139; Hunger and Sachs, ADART V, no. 19.
33813	Rm-IV.373	School text; syllabary.
33814	Rm-IV.374	Joined to 33522.
33815	Rm-IV.375	School text; lexical; syllabary.
33816	Rm-IV.376	Contract; division of property; sealed. SE Ant & Sel 10+[]/9/[12]3. Nisaba 28, no. 602.
33817	Rm-IV.377	Contract; sealed. Nisaba 28, no. 635.
33818	Rm-IV.378	Joined to 33737.
33819	Rm-IV.379	Joined to 33496.
33820	Rm-IV.380	Astronomical Diary for SE 174. LBAT 424; Sachs and Hunger, ADART III, no. -137 C.
33821	Rm-IV.381	Literary; mentions MUL.GÍR.TAB; colophon; dated by Seleucus.
33822	Rm-IV.382	Joined to 33485.
33823	Rm-IV.383	Astronomical; Goal Year Text for SE 144. LBAT 1256; Hunger and Sachs, ADART VI, no. 39.
33824	Rm-IV.384	School text; literary, Enūma eliš IV; lexical, Ḫḫ XIX-XX; unidentified. MSL 10, 127 and 11, 3; Gesche, AOAT 275, 670; Kämmerer and Metzler, AOAT 375, 95, Tafel IV T, pl. XXII; Lambert, BCM, p. 85, pl. 18.
33825	Rm-IV.385	Astrological omens.
33826	Rm-IV.386	Joined to 33491.
33827	Rm-IV.387	Marriage contract; payment in silver of Antiochus; sealed. SE Ant III. Babylon. CT 49, 50, no. 193; Roth, AOAT 222, no. 40; Nisaba 28, no. 597.
33828	Rm-IV.388	School text; lexical; syllabary; literary extracts.
33829	Rm-IV.389	Inventory of various items. (+) 33774.
33830	Rm-IV.390	Astronomical Diary.
33831	Rm-IV.391	Joined to 33493.
33832	Rm-IV.392	Deposition; [Xerxes šar] KUR ma-da-a-a. [Xer] 25/4?/6.
33833	Rm-IV.393	Astrological; commentary on Enūma Anu Enlil; colophon. + 47931. Reiner, Fs Borger (CM 10), 293, 300; Frahm, GMTR 5, 164.
33834	Rm-IV.394	School text; lexical.
33835	Rm-IV.395	Joined to 33483.
33836	Rm-IV.396	Joined to 33461.
33837	Rm-IV.397	Astronomical Diary for SE 79. LBAT 284; Epping and Strassmaier, ZA 6, 236-241, and ZA 7, 236-254; Sachs and Hunger, ADART II, no. -232.

33838	Rm-IV.398	School text; lexical, Ḫḫ I and Lú list; personal names; copy of an administrative text dated to Philip III year 7. MSL 5, 5; Gesche, AOAT 275, 225-228, 670.
33839	Rm-IV.399	Barley ledger of the Šamaš temple. Cyr 4/2/[]. Sippar.
33840	Rm-IV.400	Old Babylonian. Sumerian literary?
33841	Rm-IV.401	Astronomical. + 48068.
33842	Rm-IV.402	Literary; dialogue. Lambert, MC 24, no. 329.
33843	Rm-IV.403	Old Babylonian. School text; exercise in Sumerian; circular tablet.
33844	Rm-IV.404	School text.
33845	Rm-IV.405	Astrological; Enūma Anu Enlil, lunar eclipses. Cf. Reiner, Fs Borger (CM 10), 293.
33846	Rm-IV.406	Old Babylonian. Larsa date list. + 2 unnum. B frags. Sigrist, RA 79, 161-168. The fact that two B fragments are joined seems to be a clear indication that 33846 was registered outside its proper collection and that it comes from Kutalla or Ur.
33847	Rm-IV.407	School text; syllabary.
33848	Rm-IV.408	School text; syllabary.
33849	Rm-IV.409	Gula hymn of Bulluṭsa-rabi. Lambert, Or NS 36, 115.
33850	Rm-IV.410	Astronomical Diary for SE 148. + 47722. LBAT 381 (33850 only); Sachs and Hunger, ADART III, no. -162.
33851	Rm-IV.411	Literary; Counsels of Wisdom; colophon. + 76672. Lambert, BWL 96-107, pls. 27, 29; King, STC II pls. LXIV-LXVI; Lambert, MC 24, no. 257.
33852	Rm-IV.412	Religious.
33853	Rm-IV.413	Joined to 33507.
33854	Rm-IV.414	Joined to 33507.
33855	Rm-IV.415	Joined to 33636.
33856	Rm-IV.416	School text; lexical and literary extracts.
33857	Rm-IV.417	List of priests and temple personnel including ērib bīt Marduk and aluzinnu.
	Rm-IV.418	Joined to 33636.
33858	Rm-IV.419	Lexical; Ḫḫ IV. (+) 33507. MSL 5, 148.
33859	Rm-IV.420	Lexical; Ḫḫ II. MSL 5, 48.
33860	Rm-IV.421	Joined to 33579.
33861	Rm-IV.422	School text; literary extracts; Ludlul II; lexical, Ḫḫ XXII-XXIV. + Rm-IV.423. MSL 11, 22, 68, 78; Oshima, BPPS, 401-402; Lambert, MC 24, no. 155.
	Rm-IV.423	Joined to 33861.
33862	Rm-IV.424	Mantic ritual and incantation to Nisaba.
33863	Rm-IV.425	Account of brick deliveries. 15/5/[]. Sippar. A note by Pinches in the register says, "Properly of the 82-9-18 or 82-7-14 col.").

33864	Rm-IV.426	Lexical; Ḫḫ IV 18-27 and 52-58. MSL 5, 147.
33865	Rm-IV.427	School practice text; mostly blank.
33866	Rm-IV.428	School text; lexical; Syllabary A. MSL 3, 95.
33867	Rm-IV.429	Astronomical; Almanac for SE 179 = AE 115 (not 125 as Pinches's copy); prayer on upper edge. LBAT 1135; Hunger and Sachs, ADART VII, no. 171.
33868	Rm-IV.430	School text; lexical; syllabary; literary extracts.
33869	Rm-IV.431	Astronomical procedure text for Jupiter. ACT 810; Ossendrijver, BMAPT, no. 32.
33870	Rm-IV.432	Chronicle about Antiochus IV and the Greek community in Babylon in the year SE 149. BCHP 14; van der Spek, RAI XLVIII, 403-404.
33871	Rm-IV.433	Lexical; syllabary.
33872	Rm-IV.434	Lexical; Ḫḫ XV. MSL 9, 4.
33873	Rm-IV.435	Astronomical; Almanac for SE 129. LBAT 1123; Kugler, SSB I 92ff, pl. VII and SSB II 481ff.; Hunger and Sachs, ADART VII, no. 158.
33874	Rm-IV.436	Lexical; syllabary.
33875	Rm-IV.437	School text; obv. lexical; syllabary; rev. mathematical table. + Rm-IV unnum.
33876	Rm-IV.438	Lexical; Ḫḫ VII A, 174-176, 178, 200, 203, 204!, 205-208.
33877	Rm-IV.439	Lexical; syllabary.
33878	Rm-IV.440	Astronomical. SE Ant 3/2/[].
33879	Rm-IV.441	Ritual for the 4th day, for the temple é-tùr-kalam-ma at Babylon; the text on the reverse is written at right angles to the main text; prayer on upper edge. Lambert, Unity and Diversity, 98-135.
33880	Rm-IV.442	Lexical; Ḫḫ III. MSL 5, 89.
33881	Rm-IV.443	Joined to 33706.
33882	Rm-IV.444	Lexical; Syllabary A; literary extract? MSL 3, 95.
33883	Rm-IV.445	Lexical; Syllabary Λ. MSL 3, 95.
33884	Rm-IV.446	Lexical; Ḫḫ VIII. MSL 9, 173.
33885	Rm-IV.447	School text; lexical, Ḫḫ I; proverb. MSL 9, 157; Lambert, MC 24, no. 300.
33886	Rm-IV.448	Joined to 33452.
33887	Rm-IV.449	Astronomical Diary.
33888	Rm-IV.450	Lexical; Ḫḫ XIV?
33889	Rm-IV.451	School text; bilingual religious, Udug-ḫul 12 and 13-15; lexical; Ḫḫ. Geller, BAM 8, 399-433, 434-498, pl. 110.
33890	Rm-IV.452	Lexical; syllabary.
33891	Rm-IV.453	School text; lexical and literary extracts; obv. Diri I-III; rev. Enūma eliš IV. MSL 15 105, 121, 135;

		Kämmerer and Metzler, AOAT 375, 96, Tafel IV Z, pl. XXVII; Lambert, BCM, p. 85, pl. 17.
33892	Rm-IV.454	Administrative; receipt?; sealed. n.d. Nisaba 28, no. 664.
33893	Rm-IV.455	Account of deliveries.
33894	Rm-IV.456	Old Babylonian. School text; lenticular; Sumerian personal names.
33895	Rm-IV.457	Receipt for onions. 7/8/-.
33896	Rm-IV.458	Receipt for silver. 5/3/[].
33897	Rm-IV.459	School text; lexical; syllabary.
33898	Rm-IV.460	School text; lexical; syllabary.
33899	Rm-IV.461	Lexical; syllabary.
33900	Rm-IV.462	Economic; list of months, days and measurements of weight. Mayer, Or NS 54, 203-215, and Or NS 57, 70-71.
33901	Rm-IV.463	Lexical; Ḫḫ I. MSL 9, 157.
33902	Rm-IV.464	Lexical; Ḫḫ.
33903	Rm-IV.465	Lexical; syllabary.
33904	Rm-IV.466	Lexical; Ḫḫ VIII and IX. MSL 7, 5 and 35, and 9, 173.
104891	Rm-IV.467	Lamaštu amulet; inscribed; made of basalt.
	Rm-IV.468ff.	Rm-IV.468-514 are uninscribed objects.

Sp collection

The Sp collection was purchased from Messrs. Spartali & Co., London, in April 1879. The register gives the provenance Babylon to nos. 1-376 (except for no. 188, Kouyunjik) and no. 536 and the provenance Babylonia to nos. 377-504 and nos. 537-652.

33905	Sp.1	Transcript of post-trial proceedings. Šamaš-šum-ukin. 28/1/12. Kūtû. Brinkman and Kennedy, JCS 35, 29, K.51; Sandowicz, dubsar 11, no. 37.
33906	Sp.2	Sale of a slave. Nbk []/7/3. Upija. Nbk 31; Bertin 234.
33907	Sp.3	Contract; sale of fields; finger-nail marks. Nbk 21/12/22. Babylon. Nbk 135; Bertin 107-108.
33908	Sp.4	Promissory note. Nbk 10/1/37. Babylon. Nbk 316a; Bertin 180.
33909	Sp.5	Promissory note for silver. AM 28/11/acc. Babylon. Evetts, Ev-M 6; Sack, AOATS 4, no. 20; Bertin 258.
33910	Sp.6	Promissory note for silver. Ner []/[]/acc. Babylon. Evetts, Ner 10; Sack, ZA 68, 140; Sack, AOAT 236, no. 10; Bertin 299.
33911	Sp.7	Deposition. Nbn 25/2/3. Babylon. Nbn 102; Bertin 376.
33912	Sp.8	Contract; sale of fields. Nbn 25/6/5. Babylon. Nbn 193; Bertin 414-415.

33913	Sp.9	Contract; transfer of a promise to deliver dates and barley. Nbn 2/7/7. Babylon. Nbn 260; Bertin 440; Wunsch, CM 3, no. 143.
33914	Sp.10	Receipt for silver in payment for work. Nbn 19/10/12. Babylon. Nbn 657; Bertin 611; Wunsch, CM 3, no. 204.
33915	Sp.11	Receipt for deposit of silver. Nbn 26/1/2. Babylon. Nbn 55; Bertin 359.
33916	Sp.12	Sale of a slave. Nbn 20/11/7+?. Babylon. Nbn 126 and 274; Bertin 712.
33917	Sp.13	Promissory note for silver. Cyr 16/12/1. Taḫmakka. Cyr 29; Bertin 750.
33918	Sp.14	Contract; lease of a house. Nbn 22/4/16. Babylon. Nbn 967; Bertin 679.
33919	Sp.15	Receipt for payment of silver. Cam 29/8/2. Babylon. Cam 127; Bertin 884; Wunsch, CM 3, no. 328.
33920	Sp.16	Promissory note for dates; Egibi archive. Cam 4/12/4. Šaḫrīn.
33921	Sp.17	Contract. Cam 26/11/4. Babylon. Cam 263; Bertin 924.
33922	Sp.18	Contract; sale of a house; Egibi archive; sealed; finger-nail marks; dupl. 41849. Cam 14/3/4. Borsippa. + 41699. Cam 233 (33922 only); Bertin 918-919 (33911 only); Nisaba 28, no. 100.
33923	Sp.19	Contract; ḫarrānu. Cam 5/5/7. Borsippa. Cam 376.
33924	Sp.20	Contract; sale of a house at Borsippa; sealed; finger-nail marks. Dar I []/8/13. Babylon. Dar 367; Bertin 2256-2257; Nisaba 28, no. 118.
33925	Sp.21	Receipt, Egibi archive. Dar 6/12/14. Bertin 2280.
33926	Sp.22	Receipt of ilku-silver by Marduk-nāṣir-apli. Dar 17/4/15. Babylon. Abraham, BPPE, 338-339, no. 74; Bertin 2321.
33927	Sp.23	Promissory note for silver. Dar 3/[]/22. Babylon.
33928	Sp.24	Receipt of silver from Marduk-nāṣir-apli's son paid on behalf of Marduk-nāṣir-apli for equipment and travel provisions; dupl. 33957. Dar 28/2/35. Babylon. Abraham, BPPE, 339-341, no. 75; Bertin 2554; Wunsch, CM 3A, p. 8 n. 33 (under wrong number 33929).
33929	Sp.25	Receipt for payment of silver. Dar 16/8/28. Babylon. Bertin 2656.
33930	Sp.26	Receipt of makkasu-dates from Marduk-nāṣir-apli for the preparation of offerings in the temple of Nergal. Dar 3/9/29. Šaḫrīn. Abraham, BPPE, 341-344, no. 76; Bertin 2626.

33931	Sp.27	Promissory note for silver; Egibi archive. Dar 13/10/13. Babylon. Bertin 2258; Abraham, NABU 1997, 46-51, no. 53.
33932	Sp.28	Contract; transfer of real estate, slaves and household goods as part of a dowry; sealed. Dar 22/8/32. Babylon. Roth, JAOS 111, 32 and n. 39; Wunsch, AfO 42/43, 60, no. 10; Bertin 2706-2707; Mitchell and Searight, no. 460; Nisaba 28, no. 38.
33933	Sp.29	Assignment of slaves and real estate in lieu of a field promised as a dowry; sealed. Dar 26/6/33. [Babylon]. Roth, JAOS 111, 19-37 and n. 43; Wunsch, AfO 42/43, 62-63, no. 12; Bertin 2716-2717; Mitchell and Searight, no. 462; Nisaba 28, no. 42.
33934	Sp.30	Contract; transfer of real estate, slaves and household goods as part of a dowry; sealed. Dar 23/9/34. Babylon. Roth, JAOS 111, 30-32 and n. 35; Wunsch, AfO 42/43, 55-57, no. 7; Wunsch, CM 3A, p. 33 n 128; Bertin 2726-2727; Mitchell and Searight, no. 466; Nisaba 28, no. 43.
33935	Sp.31	Contract; settlement of a silver debt through sale of land and slaves by Marduk-nāṣir-apli to his creditor; a previous house sale became void after the house had been seized by the Esangila temple; sealed. Dar 25/11/[]. URU Kar-AN-BÁRA. Abraham, BPPE, 344-347, no. 77; Bertin 2809-2810; Mitchell and Searight, no. 470; Nisaba 28, no. 177.
33936	Sp.32	Promissory note to pay in Babylon a debt of silver due from Marduk-nāṣir-apli to Zababa-iddin, governor of Kish, through an intermediary, Nabû-uballissu; captions for seals but not sealed; dupl. Strassmaier, Liverpool, no. 25. Dar 3/12a/[16]. Šušan. Abraham, BPPE, 347-350, no. 78; Abraham, OLP 28, 83 (copy); Zadok, NABU 1997, 6-7, no. 7; Bertin 2839.
33937	Sp.33	Promissory note for silver; Egibi archive. Dar 5/7/[]. Babylon. Bertin 2824.
33938	Sp.34	Promissory note for dates and grain. Dar 18/4/22. Bertin 2484.
33939	Sp.35	Promissory note for silver. Nbn 13/7/2. Babylon. Nbn 77; Bertin 369.
33940	Sp.36	Copy of a contract for purchase of household furnishings. Nbn -/7/2 (day lost, hé-pí). Borsippa. Nbn 75; Bertin 368.
33941	Sp.37	Contract; sale of a house; storehouse. Nbn 8/6/11. Babylon. Nbn 531; Bertin 536.

33942	Sp.38	Final payment for purchase of a slave. Nbn 8/2/12. Babylon. Nbn 593; Bertin 555.
33943	Sp.39	Promissory note for silver. Nbn 20/7/[]. Babylon. Nbn 1079; Bertin 743; Wunsch, CM 3, no. 226.
33944	Sp.40	Sale of cows and goats. Nbn 20/6/15. Babylon. Nbn 884; Bertin 659; Wunsch, CM 3, no. 237.
33945	Sp 41	Court record about the dowry and house of Bunnānītu daughter of Ḫāriṣāya (cf. 32871); dupl. 41459. Nbn 26/6/9. Babylon. Nbn 356; Bertin 475-476; Pinches, TSBA 8 (1885) 274-275, 282-286, pl. after p. 278; Wunsch, CM 3, no. 167.
33946	Sp.42	Promissory note for silver with a slave given as pledge. Nbn []/10/[]. Babylon. Nbn 1125; Bertin 719; Wunsch, CM 3, no. 258.
33947	Sp.43	Promissory note for silver. Nbn 8/4/-. Babylon. Nbn 1077; Bertin 720.
33948	Sp.44	Sale of slaves. Cam 11/10/5. Šaḫrīn. Cam 290; Bertin 926.
33949	Sp.45	Promissory note for silver and onions. Cam 13/2/6. Babylon. Cam 308; Bertin 964.
33950	Sp.46	Promissory note for barley and onions. Cam 24/10/7. Šaḫrīn. Cam 391; Bertin 978.
33951	Sp.47	Promissory note for silver. Dar 6/2/10. Babylon. Bertin 2178.
33952	Sp.48	Promissory note for silver. Dar 9/2/11. Babylon. Dar 298; Bertin 2203.
33953	Sp.49	Order for officials to appear for questioning. Dar 16/4/11. Babylon. Dar 299; Bertin 2207.
33954	Sp.50	Promissory note to deliver flour to Marduk-nāṣir-apli. Dar 25/4?/12. Babylon. Abraham, BPPE, 350-352, no. 79; Jursa, Bēl-rēmanni, 103; Zawadzki, NABU 2001, 57-59, no. 60; Bertin 2235.
33955	Sp.51	Contract for bales of hay. Dar 14/11/14. Til-būrti? Dar 388; Bertin 2281.
33956	Sp.52	Promissory note for dates. Dar 17/7/15. Babylon. Dar 406; Bertin 2322.
33957	Sp.53	Receipt of silver from Marduk-nāṣir-apli's son paid on behalf of Marduk-nāṣir-apli for equipment and travel provisions; dupl. 33928. Dar [28]/2/35. Babylon. Abraham, BPPE, 339-341, no. 75; Wunsch, CM 3A, p. 8 n. 33; Bertin 2740.
33958	Sp.54	Promissory note to pay a debt of barley to Marduk-nāṣir-apli's slave. Dar 7/12/17. Šaḫrīn. Dar 459; Abraham, BPPE, 437-438; Bertin 2364.

33959	Sp.55	Contract about promissory notes for onions from the property of Bel in Šaḫrinu; mentions Marduk-nāṣir-apli. Dar 24/10/17. Babylon. Abraham, BPPE, 353-355, no. 80; Bertin 2382.
33960	Sp.56	Contract; lease of a house from Širku / Iddinâ; Egibi archive. Dar 20/4/17. Borsippa. Zadok, Nisaba 21, 234; Bertin 2381.
33961	Sp.57	Promissory note for barley. Dar -/4/19. Bertin 2415.
33962	Sp.58	Summons to settle debts with Marduk-nāṣir-apli; dupl. 30448. Dar 8/10/20. [Babylon]. Abraham, BPPE, 355, no. 81.
33963	Sp.59	Promissory note for barley. Dar 10/1/20. Babylon. Bertin 2447.
33964	Sp.60	Contract; ḫarrānu. Dar 17/6/21. Kapar-Imba. Dar 526; Bertin 2459.
33965	Sp.61	Promissory note for silver. Dar 11/4/27. Babylon. Bertin 2637.
33966	Sp.62	Contract; lease of a house; Egibi archive. Dar 5/5/36. Babylon. Bertin 2748.
33967	Sp.63	Promissory note for dates; Egibi archive. Dar 23/7/3. Babylon. Bertin 1963.
33968	Sp.64	Contract about the delivery of a baker to Marduk-nāṣir-apli. Dar []/9/[15]. Babylon. Abraham, BPPE, 356-358, no. 82; Bertin 2823.
33969	Sp 65	Promissory note for dates; Egibi archive. Dar 3/7/5+. Babylon. Bertin 2826.
33970	Sp 66	Promissory note for dates; Egibi archive. Dar 12/2/-. Bertin 2808.
33971	Sp.67	Promissory note for silver. [Nbn]. Wunsch, CM 20A-B, no. 117; Bertin 2963.
33972	Sp.68	Promissory note to pay a debt of silver, barley and onions to Marduk-nāṣir-apli in year 6. [Dar] []/[]/[5?]. Šaḫrīn. Bertin 3065-3066; Abraham, BPPE, index.
33973	Sp.69	Contract; exchange of fields; sealed. Cam 28/12/6. Babylon. Cam 349; Bertin 953-954; Wunsch, CM 20A, 269, no. 175 (copy of seals and captions), and CM 20B, 207-208; Nisaba 28, no. 101.
33974	Sp.70	Purchase of a donkey; Egibi archive. Bertin 3016.
33975	Sp.71	Account of deliveries of various commodities.
33976	Sp.72	Letter.
33977	Sp.73	Receipt for dates. Dar 20/[]/17. Šuppatu. Dar 461; Bertin 2371.
33978	Sp.74	Adoption contract; Egibi archive. Xerxes 12+/12/acc. Babylon. Bertin 2850; Wunsch, AfO 50, 238-239, no. 20.

33979	Sp.75	Contract; lease of a house; Egibi archive. Xerxes 21/4/1. Babylon.
33980	Sp.76	Contract; lease of a house; Egibi archive. Xerxes 13/4/1. Babylon. Bertin 2851.
33981	Sp.77	Promissory note about dowry silver, pledge of a house. Xerxes 26/5/1. Babylon. Wunsch, AfO 42/43, 62-63, no. 13.
33982	Sp.78	Astronomical; lunar eclipse report for eclipse of 5 November 129 BC; prayer on upper edge. SE Arsaces -/-/183. LBAT 1441; Stephenson, HEER, 171-172, 182; Hunger and Sachs, ADART V, no. 21; Bertin 2916.
33983	Sp.79	Receipt? SE Arsaces 28/12/200. CT 49, 34, no. 145; van der Spek, Raḫimesu, 211-212, no. 2; Bertin 2917.
33984	Sp.80	Account of issues of silver; SE Arsaces 2/5/218 = AE 154. Babylon. Bertin 2924; Hackl, Fs van der Spek, 87-106, no. 1.
33985	Sp.81	Record of deposit of silver in staters of Seleucus; sealed. SE Sel & Ant 8/10/32. CT 49, 18-19, no. 103; Stolper, Annali Supp. 77, 16-20, no. 5; Bertin 2908; Mitchell and Searight, no. 654; Nisaba 28, no. 553.
33986	Sp.82	Receipt; sealed. SE Antiochus II 3/11/61. Babylon. CT 49, 27, no. 129; Nisaba 28, no. 653.
33987	Sp.83	Astronomical; Normal Star Almanac for SE 108 (Antiochus III). LBAT 1019; Bertin 2911; Hunger and Sachs, ADART VII, no. 45.
33988	Sp.84	Letter to Ea-tabtanâ-bulliṭ / Murānu. SE Antiochus II 10/7/56. CT 49, 26, no. 125; Jursa, Persika 9, 156, 193-194; Bertin 2905.
33989	Sp.85	Astronomical; Normal Star Almanac for SE 60 (Antiochus II). LBAT 1000; Bertin 2903; Hunger and Sachs, ADART VII, no. 14.
33990	Sp.86	Letter to Ea-tabtanâ-bulliṭ / Murānu; sealed. SE Antiochus II 6/10/58. CT 49, 26, no. 126; Jursa, Persika 9, 145-146; Nisaba 28, no. 674.
33991	Sp.87	Astronomical Diary for SE 143. LBAT 374; Sachs and Hunger, ADART II, no. -168 E; Bertin 2909.
33992	Sp.88	Astronomical Diary for SE 113. LBAT 311; Sachs and Hunger, ADART II, no. -198 A.
33993	Sp.89	Contract; sale of fields. 20/-/-.
33994	Sp.90	Promissory note for dates.
33995	Sp.91	Contract.
33996	Sp.92	Memorandum about payments of silver.
33997	Sp.93	Contract; sale of fields. Wunsch, AfO 42/43, 56-59, no. 8.

33998	Sp.94	Receipt for silver; sealed; RN = [...] A 1.KI.[MIN]. Alex IV 25/[]/11. Babylon. Strassmaier, ZA 3, 148; Bertin 3040-3041; Mitchell and Searight, no. 640; Nisaba 28, no. 549.
33999	Sp.95	Literary; myth of the 21 poultices. Lambert, AnSt 30, 77-83.
34000	Sp.96	Astronomical Diary for SE 144. LBAT 375; Sachs, PTRSL A.276, 49, fig. 11; Sachs and Hunger, ADART II, no. -167 A.
34001	Sp.97	Receipt for onions. 26/-/-.
34002	Sp.98	Apprenticeship contract. 1/[]/5. Bīt-Ṭāb-Bēl.
34003	Sp.99	Horoscope; prayer on upper edge. SE 9/10/223. LBAT 1470; Rochberg, Babylonian Horoscopes, no. 23.
34004	Sp.100	Mantic dream ritual.
34005	Sp.101	Account of medicaments.
34006	Sp.102	Account of silver payments.
34007	Sp.103	Receipt for barley. 22/1/-.
34008	Sp.104	Account of vats. 17/6/-.
34009	Sp.105	Promissory note for silver.
34010	Sp.106	Letter from judges to [], mentioning Iddin-Marduk. Hackl et al., AOAT 414/1, no. 18.
34011	Sp.107	Receipt for vats.
34012	Sp.108	Receipt. -/8/5.
34013	Sp.109	Account of delivery of produce.
34014	Sp.110	Contract; ḫarrānu.
34015	Sp.111	Contract; sale of fields. Wunsch, CM 20A-B, no. 95.
34016	Sp.112	Personal name only: 1.bul-lu-ṭa-a DUMU šá / 1.d.EN-DIN-iṭ / DUMU LÚ-d.É-a.
34017	Sp.113	Promissory note for barley; dupl. 30791. Nbn 11/8/[10]. Šaḫrīn. Nbn 1109; Bertin 713; Wunsch, CM 3, no. 179.
34018	Sp.114	Joined to 32573.
34019	Sp.115	Receipt for payment of silver.
34020	Sp.116	Economic; mentions 1.Šiš-ki.
34021	Sp.117	Account of vessels and containers
34022	Sp.118	Contract(?); obverse largely illegible; sealed. Alex IV? 27+/[]/[]. Nisaba 28, no. 550.
34023	Sp.119	Astronomical Diary for SE 107. LBAT 536; Sachs and Hunger, ADART II, no. -204 B.
34024	Sp.120	Hire of oxen. Nbk 26/4/-. Babylon.
34025	Sp.121	Sale of a slave girl; receipt of payment; Egibi archive. Nbn 9/5/-. Babylon.
34026	Sp.122	Sale of vats.

34027	Sp.123	Contract; sale of a house; sealed; finger-nail marks; Egibi archive. d.l. (+?) 34379. Nisaba 28, no. 57.
34028	Sp.124	List of persons; Egibi archive.
34029	Sp.125	List of household furnishings. Mayer, Or NS 57, 70-75.
34030	Sp.126	Literary; address to five deities of Babylon, participating in a ritual procession in place of older deities. Lambert, AoF 24 (1997) 158-162.
34031	Sp.127	Astrological omens; Enūma Anu Enlil 64; colophon. LBAT 1526; Reiner, Fs Borger (CM 10), 293; Casaburi, Gs Cagni, vol. I, 85-99.
34032	Sp.128	Astronomical; Normal Star Almanac for SE 201. LBAT 1059; Epping, AaB 160-167, pl. 4-6; Hunger and Sachs, ADART VII, no. 93
34033	Sp.129	Astronomical; Normal Star Almanac for SE 189. LBAT 1055; Epping, AaB 152-159, pl. 1-3; Hunger and Sachs, ADART VII, no. 87.
34034	Sp.130	Astronomical; Goal Year Text for SE 194. LBAT 1285; Stephenson, HEER, 64-65 (fig. 3.9), 129, 136-137, 188; see ACT, p. 94; Stephenson and Walker, Halley's Comet 34-35 (part); Hunger and Sachs, ADART VI, no. 69; Brack-Bernsen in Swerdlow, Astronomy, 158-166 and 173-174.
34035	Sp.131	Astrological and ritual commentary; prayer on upper edge; colophon. SE Arsaces 27/2/174. Borsippa. Epping and Strassmaier, ZA 6, 241-244; Livingstone, MMEWABS, 7, etc.; Linssen, CM 25, 3 n. 21, 10 n. 67, 324.
34036	Sp.132	Astronomical; Mars observations for SE 126-128 and 139-144. LBAT 1390; Hunger and Sachs, ADART V, no. 79.
34037	Sp.133	Astronomical; Goal Year Text for SE 167. LBAT 1264; Stephenson and Walker, Halley's Comet 36; Stephenson, HEER, 170-171; Hunger and Sachs, ADART VI, no. 47.
34038	Sp.134	Ledger.
34039	Sp.135	Astronomical Diary for SE 178. (+) 34175. LBAT 436; Sachs and Hunger, ADART III, no. -133 B.
34040	Sp.136	Astronomical Diary for SE 182. (+) Rm.701. LBAT 445; Sachs and Hunger, ADART III, no. -129 A.
34041	Sp.137	Joined to 32414.
34042	Sp.138	Astronomical; Almanac for SE 209; note that the date AE 145 = SE 208 is a scribal error for 209; colophon. LBAT 1153; Hunger and Sachs, ADART VII, no. 185.

34043	Sp.139	Astrological omens; Enūma Anu Enlil, Šamaš. LBAT 1550.
34044	Sp.140	Astronomical; Goal Year Text for SE 168. LBAT 1265; Hunger and Sachs, ADART VI, no. 48.
34045	Sp.141	Astronomical Diary for SE 168. LBAT 406; Sachs and Hunger, ADART III, no. -143 A.
34046	Sp.142	Contract; only witnesses preserved.
34047	Sp.143	Astronomical; new and full moons for SE 181. ACT 121, colophon Zmaa; LBAT 64.
34048	Sp.144	Astronomical; Goal Year Text for SE 135. LBAT 1249; Stephenson, HEER, 134-135, 139; Hunger and Sachs, ADART VI, no. 31.
34049	Sp.145	Astronomical Diary for SE 122. LBAT 530; Sachs and Hunger, ADART II, no. -189 C.
34050	Sp.146	Astronomical Diary for SE 171. + Sp.176. LBAT 420; Sachs and Hunger, ADART III, no. -140 C.
34051	Sp.147	Astronomical; Almanac for SE 178. LBAT 1134; Hunger and Sachs, ADART VII, no. 170.
34052	Sp.148	Astronomical; intermediate astronomy; moon. + 34109. LBAT 1517-1518.
34053	Sp.149	Astronomical; Goal Year Text for SE 236; prayer on upper edge. + 92682 (Rm.678). LBAT 1296-1297; Epping and Strassmaier, ZA 5, 353-366 (Rm.678 only), and ZA 6, 229-231. (Rm.678 only); Hunger and Sachs, ADART VI, no. 86.
34054	Sp.150	Astronomical; Normal Star Almanac for SE 184. LBAT 1047; Hunger and Sachs, ADART VII, no. 83.
34055	Sp.151	Account of sheep for sacrifice. CT 49, 49, no. 187.
34056	Sp.152	Astronomical; Normal Star Almanac for SE 179. + 34151. LBAT 1043-1044; Hunger and Sachs, ADART VII, no. 80.
34057	Sp.153	Liver omens; Manzazu text 10. U. S. Koch-Westenholz, Babylonian Liver Omens, 126-130, no. 16 (from a cast of 34057 at Heidelberg).
34058	Sp.154	Astrological; MUL NN SUKKAL DN ana MUL... TE. + Sp.182. LBAT 1565; Reiner, Fs Borger (CM 10), 293.
34059	Sp.155	Late astrology; intermediate astronomy; cf. 45666. LBAT 1606.
34060	Sp.156	Omens; Šumma izbu 18. + 34095. De Zorzi, Šumma izbu, 763.
34061	Sp.157	Lexical; Syllabary A. + Sp-II.425 + 641. MSL 3, 7; CT 11, 8.
34062	Sp.158	Historical-literary text; one of the "Chedorlaomer" texts. + Sp-II.962. Pinches, JTVI 29 (1897) 43-89;

		Jeremias, MVAG 21 (1916) 69-97; cf. Güterbock and Landsberger, ZA 42, 21; cf. Grayson, BHLT 42; Brinkman, PHPKB, 361, 396.
34063	Sp.159	Lexical.
34064	Sp.160	Omen commentary. + Sp-III unnum.
34065	Sp.161	Incantations; Maqlu II. Abusch, AMD 10, 51-77.
34066	Sp.162	Astronomical; new and full moons for SE 179. + Sp-II.728 + 34277 + 34400 + 34488. ACT 120; LBAT 60-63.
34067	Sp.163	Astronomical; instructions for construction of a gnomon-like instrument. + 35010. LBAT 1495 (34067 only).
34068	Sp.164	Court record; sealed; probably of Seleucid date. Nisaba 28, no. 613.
34069	Sp.165	Astronomical; full moons for four years. + 34900. ACT 126, colophon Zqa; LBAT 75-76.
34070	Sp.166	Astronomical; Goal Year Text for SE 79; prayer on upper edge. + 1881,0201.46 + 77239 + 77254. LBAT 1214-1215 (34070 + 77254 only); Hunger and Sachs, ADART VI, no. 2; Brack-Bernsen in Swerdlow, Astronomy, 174.
34071	Sp.167	Medical omens; Sa-gig VI-VII. Heeßel, AOAT 43, 142.
34072	Sp.168	School text; lexical. + Sp.368.
34073	Sp.169	List of market prices for 173-175 SE. + Sp-II.653 + 666 + 35123. Slotsky and Wallenfels, Tallies and Trends, text 6.
34074	Sp.170	Contract; sale of fields, houses and slaves. Dupl. 30122 etc. ⌊Babylon⌋. [Cyrus] [6]/[3]/[4]. + Sp.258. Wunsch, CM 20A-B, no. 125 C.
34075	Sp.171	Astronomical; lunar sixes for at least five years, -322/1 to 318/7; note beginning of Philip's reign in month iii of his year 1. LBAT 1431; Hunger and Sachs, ADART V, no. 36.
	Sp.172	Joined to Rm.695.
34076	Sp.173	Astronomical; Normal Star Almanac for SE 172; prayer on upper edge. + Sp.221. LBAT 1038; Hunger and Sachs, ADART VII, no. 75.
34077	Sp.174	Incantations; Maqlu IV. Abusch, AMD V, p. 311; Abusch, AMD 10, 113-129.
34078	Sp.175	Astronomical; Normal Star Almanac for SE 188; prayer on upper edge. + Sp-II.777 (+) 34588. LBAT 1051; Hunger and Sachs, ADART VII, no. 86.
	Sp.176	Joined to 34050.

34079	Sp.177	Astronomical procedure text for the moon; System A. + 35152 + 35324. ACT 204; LBAT 95-96; Aaboe, AIHS 25/97 (1975), 191-193; Ossendrijver, BMAPT, no. 65.
34080	Sp.178	Astronomical; Normal Star Almanac for SE 104. LBAT 1010; Hunger and Sachs, ADART VII, no. 39.
34081	Sp.179	Astronomical procedure text for Jupiter; mathematical rules for the area of a trapezoid. + 34622 + 34846 + 42816 + 45851 + 46135. ACT 813; LBAT 146-148; Steele, JHA 34 (2003) 269-289; Ossendrijver, BMAPT, no. 18; Ossendrijver, Science 351 (2016) 482-484, text C (and Supplementary Materials); Ossendrijver, JNES 76, 231-247, text G.
34082	Sp.180	Lexical; Hg VIII-X. MSL 7, 65, and 9, 185.
34083	Sp.181	Astronomical; System A ephemeris; solar and lunar eclipses from (at least) SE 298 to 353. LBAT 49; ACT 53; Aaboe, KDVSMM 40/6 (1979) 28-32.
	Sp.182	Joined to 34058.
34084	Sp.183	Šu'illa prayer to Ninurta-Sirius (Kaksisa) no. 1. Abusch and Schwemer, AMD 8/2 text 8.41 a; Mayer, Or NS 59, 466-469, 484.
34085	Sp.184	Astrological procedure text. + Sp.251 + Sp-II.323. LBAT 1599
34086	Sp.185	Astronomical Diary for SE 179. + Sp.199 (+) 34157. LBAT 441; Sachs and Hunger, ADART III, no. -132 D.
34087	Sp.186	Omens; Šumma izbu 19. + Sp.215. CT 40, 32; De Zorzi, Šumma izbu, 791.
34088	Sp.187	Astronomical; System A lunar ephemeris. + Sp-II.105 + 34493 + 35264. ACT 9; LBAT 23 + 25; 35264 is unpublished.
34089	Sp.188	Neo-Assyrian. Astrological omens; Enūma Anu Enlil, eclipses; lines 8-19 dupl. Labat, Calendrier babylonien, 158-159 section 78. Bezold, Cat. 4, p. xii; Reiner, Fs Borger (CM 10), 293.
34090	Sp.189	Hemerology. + 34416 + 34421 + 34440. Jiménez and Adali, ZA 105, 154-191.
34091	Sp.190	Lexical and literary extracts.
34092	Sp.191	Omens; Šumma ālu, tablet 17, with ritual. CT 38, 24; Caplice, Or NS 40, 148-153; Freedman, If a city, vol. 1, 253-272.
34093	Sp.192	Astronomical Diary; colophon. + Sp.544 + 35758. LBAT 212 + 213; Sachs and Hunger, ADART I, no. -321; Stephenson, HEER, 79, 131-132, 141-142.
34094	Sp.193	Joined to 32414.

34095	Sp.194	Joined to 34060.
34096	Sp.195	Astronomical Diary for SE 200. LBAT 462; Sachs and Hunger, ADART III, no. -111 A.
34097	Sp.196	Astronomical; Goal Year Text; not datable. LBAT 1306; Hunger and Sachs, ADART VI, no. 114.
34098	Sp.197	Astronomical Diary for SE 163. LBAT 535; Sachs and Hunger, ADART III, no. -148.
34099	Sp.198	Astronomical Diary for SE 34. + 41925 + 42003 (+) 41579. LBAT 237 + 917 + 944; Sachs and Hunger, ADART I, no. -277 A.
	Sp.199	Joined to 34086.
34100	Sp.200	Omens; extispicy.
34101	Sp.201	Contract. + 34502.
34102	Sp.202	Ritual; akitu type.
34103	Sp.203	Omen commentary; colophon.
34104	Sp.204	Historical-literary text about Adad-šuma-uṣur; two columns. + 34126 + 34219 + 34230 + 34256 + 34339 + 34644 + 34657 + 1881,0706.191. CT 51, 77 (34657 only); Grayson, BHLT 56-77.
34105	Sp.205	Astronomical Diary for SE 58. + 41901 + 42041 (+) 42015. LBAT 259 + 260 + 953; Sachs, PTRSL A.276, 48, fig. 5; Sachs and Hunger, ADART II, no. -253b.
34106	Sp.206	Bilingual incantation, Udug-ḫul 16; colophon. + Sp.396 (+) 34169. CT 16, 19-23; Thompson, Devils I, 88-115; Geller, BAM 8, 499-541, pls. 126-127, 147.
34107	Sp.207	Omens; extispicy.
34108	Sp.208	Astronomical Diary for SE 224. + 41482. LBAT 501-502; Sachs and Hunger, ADART III, no. -87 A.
34109	Sp.209	Joined to 34052.
34110	Sp.210	Literary; copy of an esoteric text; drawings of two snakes; colophon. Nbn 2/10/3. + 35163. Wiseman, Iraq 36, 255, pl. LVI (34110 only); Lambert, RA 68, 149-156; Reiner, Fs Slotsky, 207-210.
34111	Sp.211	Mantic dream ritual and incantation; prayer on upper edge.
34112	Sp.212	Astronomical Diary for SE 185. Sachs and Hunger, ADART III, no. -126 B.
34113	Sp.213	Historical-literary text about Amel-Marduk. Grayson, BHLT 87-92; Schaudig, AOAT 256, 589-590.
34114	Sp.214	Contract; sealed; probably of Seleucid date; cf. 41461. Nisaba 28, no. 585.
	Sp.215	Joined to 34087.
34115	Sp.216	Ritual.

34116	Sp.217	Astronomical; Normal Star Almanac for SE 146. + 34802. LBAT 1029-1030; Hunger and Sachs, ADART VII, no. 63.
34117	Sp.218	Astronomical Diary; prices.
34118	Sp.219	Astronomical Diary.
34119	Sp.220	Contract about silver; sealed; Murānu archive. SE. [Babylon]. Nisaba 28, no. 567.
	Sp.221	Joined to 34076.
34120	Sp.222	Omens; extispicy?
34121	Sp.223	Astronomical; Almanac for SE 158. LBAT 1127; Hunger and Sachs, ADART VII, no. 163.
34122	Sp.224	Omens; extispicy?
34123	Sp.225	Ration list; two columns.
34124	Sp.226	Chronicle about an Arsacid king. SE. BCHP 19.
34125	Sp.227	Astrological; stars; adir. LBAT 1545; Reiner, Fs Borger (CM 10), 293.
34126	Sp.228	Joined to 34104.
34127	Sp.229	Astronomical Diary for SE 100. + Sp.259. LBAT 532; Sachs and Hunger, ADART II, no. -211 B.
34128	Sp.230	Astronomical; Venus, evening and morning star, for SE 236 to 259; system A1. (+) 34222. ACT 410; LBAT 107.
34129	Sp.231	Lexical; Hg VII A-B. MSL 6, 108 (as 34127), and 9, 185.
34130	Sp.232	Joined to Rm.718.
34131	Sp.233	Bilingual?
34132	Sp.234	Astronomical; Goal Year Text; not datable. LBAT 1307; Hunger and Sachs, ADART VI, no. 115.
34133	Sp.235	Omens; extispicy?
34134	Sp.236	Astronomical procedure text for the moon; System A. ACT 207b; LBAT 98; Ossendrijver, BMAPT, no. 70.
34135	Sp.237	Astronomical Diary. LBAT 539.
34136	Sp.238	Lexical; stones.
34137	Sp.239	Contract; sale of fields; dupl. 33095; finger-nail marks. [Dar] [8]/[12]/[10]. + 39314. Wunsch, CM 20A-B, no. 177 B.
34138	Sp.240	Literary; Love Lyrics.
34139	Sp.241	Astronomical Diary. LBAT 538.
34140	Sp.242	Astronomical Diary for SE 150. (+) 34180 (+) 45829. LBAT 382; Sachs and Hunger, ADART III, no. -161 A.
34141	Sp.243	Unidentified; virtually illegible.
34142	Sp.244	Mantic dream ritual; colophon. SE 22/[]/127.
34143	Sp.245	Bilingual incantation. + Sp.502.
34144	Sp.246	Incantation.

34145	Sp.247	Astronomical; Goal Year Text for SE 170. LBAT 1268; Hunger and Sachs, ADART VI, no. 52.
34146	Sp.248	Contract; sale of fields.
34147	Sp.249	Literary cylinder; hymn to Nabû. + Sp.285. Lambert, Fs Matouš II, 75-111; Gesche, AOAT 275, 670
34148	Sp.250	Astronomical procedure text for the moon; System A. ACT 200d; LBAT 87; Aaboe, AIHS 25/97 (1975), 191-193; Ossendrijver, BMAPT, no. 58.
	Sp.251	Joined to 34085.
34149	Sp.252	Astronomical; Goal Year Text for SE 122. LBAT 1238; Hunger and Sachs, ADART VI, no. 22.
34150	Sp.253	Astronomical; Goal Year Text for SE 188. LBAT 1308; Hunger and Sachs, ADART VI, no. 65.
34151	Sp.254	Joined to 34056.
34152	Sp.255	Unidentified; virtually illegible.
34153	Sp.256	Incantation?; virtually illegible.
34154	Sp.257	Contract; sale of fields.
	Sp.258	Joined to 34074.
	Sp.259	Joined to 34127.
34155	Sp.260	Incantation?; two columns.
34156	Sp.261	Literary.
34157	Sp.262	Astronomical Diary for SE 179. + 34341 (+) 34086. LBAT 440 + 556; Sachs and Hunger, ADART III, no. -132 D.
34158	Sp.263	Astrological. LBAT 1603.
34159	Sp.264	Astronomical; Almanac for SE 282. LBAT 1185; Hunger and Sachs, ADART VII, no. 206.
34160	Sp.265	Literary; Gilgameš X. + 34193 + 35174 + 35348 + 35413 + 35628. CT 46, 32-33, no. 30; Garelli, Gilgameš, 128-131 (copy of 34193 + 35413 by Wiseman), 131-135 (copy of 35174 + 35628 by Wiseman); George, Gilgamesh II, pls. 114-115.
34161	Sp.266	Unidentified.
34162	Sp.267	Astronomical; eclipse magnitudes for new moons for (at least) SE 54 to 67. ACT 149; LBAT 82; Brown, CM 18, 305.
34163	Sp.268	Astronomical; Goal Year Text for SE 144. LBAT 1257; Hunger and Sachs, ADART VI, no. 40.
34164	Sp.269	Omens; excerpt of monthly omens from Šumma ālu or Iqqur īpuš.
34165	Sp.270	Astrological omens; Enūma Anu Enlil 13; colophon. LBAT 1528; Reiner, Fs Borger (CM 10), 293.
34166	Sp.271	Bilingual incantation.
34167	Sp.272	Administrative account. SE -/-/125.
34168	Sp.273	School text; god-list.

34169	Sp.274	Bilingual incantation, Udug-ḫul 16. (+) 34106. Geller, BAM 8, 499-541, pls. 126-127, 147.
34170	Sp.275	Astronomical Diary for SE 109. + Sp-III.222 + 35703. LBAT 307 + 537; Sachs and Hunger, ADART II, no. -202 B.
34171	Sp.276	Omens; extispicy. + Sp.351 + 1881,0706.211.
34172	Sp.277	Brick of Nebuchadnezzar II. + Sp.536. CBI, no. 95.
34173	Sp.278	Account of debts of silver. + 1880,0617.502.
34174	Sp.279	Astronomical Diary for SE 176. LBAT 533; Sachs and Hunger, ADART III, no. -135.
34175	Sp.280	Astronomical Diary for SE 178. (+) 34039. LBAT 437; Sachs and Hunger, ADART III, no. -133 B.
34176	Sp.281	Historical-literary text about the reign of Nabonidus. + 34375 + 34896 + 34995 + Sp. unnum. CT 46, 46, no. 48 (not 34176); Lambert, AfO 22, 1-8 (as "34167"); Schaudig, AOAT 256, 590-595 and 766 (copy of Sp. unnum.); Berger, AOAT 4/1, Nabonid Tafel-Fragment VI,2.
34177	Sp.282	Astronomical Diary for SE 179. LBAT 543; Sachs and Hunger, ADART III, no. -132 E.
34178	Sp.283	Literary cylinder; hymn to Nabû. Gesche, AOAT 275, 670.
34179	Sp.284	Literary cylinder. Cf. Lambert, Fs Matouš II, 75-111.
	Sp.285	Joined to 34147.
34180	Sp.286	Astronomical Diary for SE 150. (+) 34140 (+) 45829. LBAT 383; Sachs and Hunger, ADART III, no. -161 A.
34181	Sp.287	Omens; extispicy; Šumma tirānu. + Sp.643.
34182	Sp.288	Astronomical Diary. + 41890. LBAT 534 + 912.
34183	Sp.289	Contract; sale of a slave-girl; sealed. Art II/III 1/[]/9. Bi-ḫu.KI. + 34374 + 35192 (+) 34840 + 34869 + 35280 + 35393. Nisaba 28, no. 537.
34184	Sp.290	Bilingual incantation.
34185	Sp.291	Astronomical; System A lunar ephemeris. (+) 34619. ACT 10; LBAT 27.
34186	Sp.292	Astronomical; Goal Year Text for SE 191. LBAT 1283; Hunger and Sachs, ADART VI, no. 67.
34187	Sp.293	Omens.
34188	Sp.294	Joined to Rm.717.
34189	Sp.295	Astrological; lunar eclipses and zodiac. LBAT 1595.
34190	Sp.296	Receipt for a purchase; Egibi archive. 11/8/-. Babylon.
34191	Sp.297	Literary; Gilgameš III. + 41835. CT 46, 32, no. 28 (34191 only); George, Gilgamesh II, pl. 59.
34192	Sp.298	Astronomical Diary. LBAT 546.

34193	Sp.299	Joined to 34160.
34194	Sp.300	Astronomical.
34195	Sp.301	Astronomical Diary. LBAT 541.
34196	Sp.302	Contract; sale of fields. [Nbn] 25/9/12. [Babylon]. + 34450. Wunsch, AfO 44/45, 83, no. 13.
34197	Sp.303	Joined to Rm.752.
34198	Sp.304	Astronomical Diary. LBAT 545.
34199	Sp.305	Astronomical; Normal Star Almanac for SE 173. LBAT 1039; Hunger and Sachs, ADART VII, no. 76.
34200	Sp.306	Lexical; syllabary.
34201	Sp.307	Account of issues of silver. SE (Arsaces) -/-/218. Hackl, Fs van der Spek, 87-106, no. 8.
34202	Sp.308	Astronomical Diary. LBAT 542.
34203	Sp.309	Court record about a claim to temple income made by two women, with reference back to SE 153. CT 49, 32, no. 140; van der Spek, BiOr 42, 554-555.
34204	Sp.310	Astronomical Diary. LBAT 540.
34205	Sp.311	Lexical; syllabary.
34206	Sp.312	Hemerology.
34207	Sp.313	Astronomical; Goal Year Text; not datable. LBAT 1309; Hunger and Sachs, ADART VI, no. 116.
34208	Sp.314	Bilingual incantation; birth incantation; ruled after every line. + Sp.412 + Sp-II.365 + 599 + 695 + 701 + 4 unnum.
34209	Sp.315	Astronomical Diary for SE 153. LBAT 544; Sachs and Hunger, ADART III, no. -158 E.
34210	Sp.316	Letter from an official of the jewellers of Esangila. SE 20/[]/220.
34211	Sp.317	Lexical; Ṭup abni; perhaps part of the same tablet as 34760; two columns. + Sp.384 + 493 + 558 + Sp-II.155 + 328 + 576. CT 51, 89; Schuster-Brandis, AOAT 46, p. 333-340, Text 12; Simkó, NABU 2017, 185-188, no. 105.
34212	Sp.318	Astrological omens; Enūma Anu Enlil 19. + 82870. LBAT 1549; Rochberg-Halton, AfO Beih. 22, Enūma Anu Enlil 19; Reiner, Fs Borger (CM 10), 293 (all 34212 only); Fincke, Kaskal 13, 108-112, text III.D, 119 figure 10.
34213	Sp.319	Astronomical; ephemeris for (at least) three years. ACT 125b; LBAT 72.
34214	Sp.320	Contract; sale of a house; finger-nail marks. Cam 18/8/3. Babylon.
34215	Sp.321	Joined to Rm.705.

34216	Sp.322	Astronomical; Goal Year Text for SE 122; prayer on upper edge. + 35080. LBAT 1239-1240; Hunger and Sachs, ADART VI, no. 23.
34217	Sp.323	Receipt for purchase of onions.
34218	Sp.324	Prayer to Marduk no. 1. + 34334. Oshima, BPM, 146-151; Lambert, MC 24, no. 88.
34219	Sp.325	Joined to 34104.
34220	Sp.326	Joined to Rm.800.
34221	Sp.327	Astronomical procedure text for Jupiter and Venus. + 34299 + 35119 + 35206 + 35445 (+) 45702. ACT 812; LBAT 140-145; Ossendrijver, BMAPT, no. 46.
34222	Sp.328	Astronomical; Venus, evening and morning star, for SE 236 to 259; System A1. + Sp.545 + 548 (+) 34128. ACT 410; LBAT 110.
34223	Sp.329	Bilingual incantation; colophon. SE []/[]/129. Babylon. + Sp-III.191 + 35156 + 35397 + 45692. CT 17 15-18; Schramm, GBAO 2, p. 90, text B.
34224	Sp.330	Letter order; mentions Antiochus. SE.
34225	Sp.331	Issue of silver. SE [Arsaces] 27/1/218? CT 49, 43, no. 166; van der Spek, Raḫimesu, 214-215, no. 5.
34226	Sp.332	Astronomical Diary. LBAT 522.
34227	Sp.333	Astrological omens; Enūma Anu Enlil 63. + 42033. LBAT 1560-1561; Reiner and Pingree, BPO 1, source K and p. 65; Reiner, Fs Borger (CM 10), 293, 298.
34228	Sp.334	Astronomical; Normal Star Almanac for SE 135. LBAT 1026; Hunger and Sachs, ADART VII, no. 58.
34229	Sp.335	Astronomical; Normal Star Almanac for SE 195. LBAT 1058; Hunger and Sachs, ADART VII, no. 91.
34230	Sp.336	Joined to 34104.
34231	Sp.337	Astronomical Diary. LBAT 555.
34232	Sp.338	Astronomical; Almanac for SE 128. LBAT 1122; Hunger and Sachs, ADART VII, no. 157.
34233	Sp.339	Astronomical?
34234	Sp.340	Lexical; syllabary. + 34261.
34235	Sp.341	Medical.
34236	Sp.342	Astronomical; lunar eclipse table for at least 195-160 BC. LBAT 1436; Stephenson, HEER, 156-157, 186-187; Hunger and Sachs, ADART V, no. 16.
34237	Sp.343	Astronomical; System A lunar ephemeris. ACT 17; LBAT 41.
34238	Sp.344	Astronomical; Goal Year Text; not datable. LBAT 1310; Hunger, Hunger and Sachs, ADART VI, no. 117.
34239	Sp.345	Promissory note for dates. Wunsch, CM 20A-B, no. 198.

34240	Sp.346	Sale of a slave girl?
34241	Sp.347	Contract; sale of fields. Wunsch, AfO 42/43, 54-55, no. 4a.
34242	Sp.348	Bilingual incantation; Eršaḫunga.
34243	Sp.349	Omens; extispicy; Šumma šulmu VIII; colophon. Demetrius []/[]/[]+18.
34244	Sp.350	Astrological. LBAT 1594.
	Sp.351	Joined to 34171.
34245	Sp.352	Astronomical procedure text for the moon; System A; prayer on upper edge. + 41608. ACT 200c, colophon Zqc; LBAT 85-86 (not 41608); Ossendrijver, BMAPT, no. 57.
34246	Sp.353	Contract; sale of land in Marad; sealed; probably Late Achaemenid or Seleucid. CT 49, 44, no. 169; Mitchell and Searight, no. 590; Nisaba 28, no. 636.
34247	Sp.354	Omens; extispicy.
34248	Sp.355	Joined to Rm.785.
34249	Sp.356	Mathematical table; prayer on upper edge. Ossendrijver, JCS 66, 149-165 and pls.
34250	Sp.357	Omens; Šumma izbu 6. De Zorzi, Šumma izbu, 503.
34251	Sp.358	Field plan. Nemet-Nejat, LB Field Plans, no. 22.
34252	Sp.359	Astronomical.
34253	Sp.360	Astronomical; System A lunar ephemeris. + 34354 + 34420 (+) 32785+. ACT 5; LBAT 7-9.
34254	Sp.361	Joined to 31872.
34255	Sp.362	Astronomical Diary. LBAT 551.
34256	Sp.363	Joined to 34104.
34257	Sp.364	Astronomical; Normal Star Almanac. LBAT 1066; Hunger and Sachs, ADART VII, no. 111.
34258	Sp.365	No script remains.
34259	Sp.366	Astronomical; Normal Star Almanac. LBAT 1067; Hunger and Sachs, ADART VII, no. 112.
34260	Sp.367	Contract; sale of a house; Egibi archive.
	Sp.368	Joined to 34072.
34261	Sp.369	Joined to 34234.
34262	Sp.370	Unidentified.
34263	Sp.371	Joined to 32769.
34264	Sp.372	Bilingual incantation, Udug-ḫul 3, colophon. Geller, BAM 8, 89-132, pl. 22.
34265	Sp.373	Receipt; sealed. RN lost []/12b/[]. Nisaba 28, no. 665.
34266	Sp.374	Contract; fragment of right edge.
34267	Sp.375	Omens; extispicy.
34268	Sp.376	Literary cylinder. Cf. Lambert, Fs Matouš II, 75-111.
34269	Sp.377	Astronomical; Goal Year Text; not datable. LBAT 1311; Hunger and Sachs, ADART VII, no. 118.

34270	Sp.378	Lexical; syllabary.
34271	Sp.379	Omens; extispicy; lung omens tablet IX; BE ŠU.SI MUR.
34272	Sp.380	Omens.
34273	Sp.381	Astronomical Diary. LBAT 554.
34274	Sp.382	Astronomical Diary for SE 185. + 34739. Sachs and Hunger, ADART III, no. -126 A.
34275	Sp.383	Astrological; planets, zodiac, eclipses, locusts and earthquakes; colophon. SE Antiochus II 19/12/62. + Sp.427 + 428 + Sp-II.153 + 225 + 303 + 336 + 404 + 1029. LBAT 1604.
	Sp.384	Joined to 34211.
34276	Sp.385	Literary.
34277	Sp.386	Joined to 34066.
34278	Sp.387	Astronomical. LBAT 1202.
34279	Sp.388	School text.
34280	Sp.389	Receipt for payment of silver; Egibi archive.
34281	Sp.390	Contract; mentions Ḫaḫḫaru. + 35443 (+) 34481.
34282	Sp.391	No script remains.
34283	Sp.392	Astrological; groups of days associated with zodiac and planets. + 41584 + 42108. LBAT 1582-1584.
34284	Sp.393	No script remains.
34285	Sp.394	Astronomical Diary for SE 81. LBAT 550; Sachs and Hunger, ADART II, no. -230 B.
34286	Sp.395	Astronomical.
	Sp.396	Joined to 34106.
34287	Sp.397	Bilingual incantation.
34288	Sp.398	Lexical.
34289	Sp.399	Contract; sealed. SE Seleucus II []/[]/70. + 34308. Nisaba 28, no. 582a.
34290	Sp.400	Astronomical; Goal Year Text; not datable. LBAT 1312; Hunger and Sachs, ADART VI, no. 119.
34291	Sp.401	Literary.
34291a	Sp.402	Uninscribed fragment from the core of a tablet.
34292	Sp.403	Astronomical; Goal Year Text for SE 184. + 34388 (+) 34359. LBAT 1275-1276; Hunger and Sachs, ADART VI, no. 60.
34293	Sp.404	Physiognomic omens.
34294	Sp.405	Literary.
34295	Sp.406	Astronomical.
34296	Sp.407	Lexical.
34297	Sp.408	Contract; sale of fields.
34298	Sp.409	Astronomical; Almanac for SE 190. LBAT 1143; Hunger and Sachs, ADART VII, no. 178.
34299	Sp.410	Joined to 34221.

34300	Sp.411	Lexical.
	Sp.412	Joined to 34208.
34301	Sp.413	Astronomical; Goal Year Text; not datable. LBAT 1313; Hunger and Sachs, ADART VI, no. 120.
34302	Sp.414	Ritual.
34303	Sp.415	Astronomical Diary.
34304	Sp.416	Unidentified; mostly illegible.
34305	Sp.417	Lexical.
34306	Sp.418	Astronomical.
34307	Sp.419	Economic.
34308	Sp.420	Joined to 34289.
34309	Sp.421	Contract. Cyr 6/3/-.
34310	Sp.422	Contract; sealed. Nisaba 28, no. 613a.
34311	Sp.423	Omens; extispicy; Šumma kakku.
34312	Sp.424	Contract; sealed.
34313	Sp.425	Omens; Šumma ālu, tablet 10?
34314	Sp.426	Literary; Gilgameš. CT 46, 33, no. 31; George, Gilgamesh I, 136 and II, pl. 115.
	Sp.427	Joined to 34275.
	Sp.428	Joined to 34275.
34315	Sp.429	Sale of a slave; Egibi archive.
34316	Sp.430	Literary.
34317	Sp.431	Astronomical.
34318	Sp.432	Šu'illa prayer to Ištar no. 1; dupl. Ebeling, Handerhebung, 132: 55-59. Mayer, Or NS 59, 477, 488.
34319	Sp.433	Contract. Cyr -/4/-. Babylon.
34320	Sp.434	Literary.
34321	Sp.435	Astronomical; Goal Year Text; not datable. LBAT 1314; Hunger and Sachs, ADART VI, no. 121.
34322	Sp.436	Astronomical; intermediate astronomy? LBAT 1516.
34323	Sp.437	Joined to 32769.
34324	Sp.438	Astronomical; Almanac for SE 250. LBAT 1203; Hunger and Sachs, ADART VII, no. 203.
34325	Sp.439	Astronomical; Normal Star Almanac. LBAT 1077; Hunger and Sachs, ADART VII, no. 113.
34326	Sp.440	Contract; sale of land?
34327	Sp.441	Contract.
34328	Sp.442	Astronomical; Normal Star Almanac. LBAT 1068; Hunger and Sachs, ADART VII, no. 114.
34329	Sp.443	Literary.
34330	Sp.444	Contract.
34331	Sp.445	Contract; lease of a house.
34332	Sp.446	Contract. Cam.
34333	Sp.447	Medical.
34334	Sp.448	Joined to 34218.

34335	Sp.449	No script remains.
34336	Sp.450	Astronomical; intermediate astronomy? LBAT 1519.
	Sp.451	Joined to 34323.
34337	Sp.452	Astronomical; Goal Year Text; not datable. LBAT 1315; Hunger and Sachs, ADART VI, no. 122.
34338	Sp.453	Illegible.
34339	Sp.454	Joined to 34104.
34340	Sp.455	Medical.
34341	Sp.456	Joined to 34157.
34342	Sp.457	Literary; barely legible.
34343	Sp.458	Promissory note for silver. 23/-/-.
34344	Sp.459	Omens.
34345	Sp.460	Astronomical; Almanac for SE 160. LBAT 1129; Hunger and Sachs, ADART VII, no. 165.
34346	Sp.461	List of workmen?
34347	Sp.462	Literary.
34348	Sp.463	Astronomical Diary. + 34383. LBAT 553 + 571.
34349	Sp.464	Astronomical Diary. LBAT 549.
34350	Sp.465	Unidentified.
34351	Sp.466	Omens.
34352	Sp.467	Lexical.
34353	Sp.468	Contract. SE -/-/160+.
34354	Sp.469	Joined to 34253.
34355	Sp.470	Astronomical.
34356	Sp.471	Astronomical; Normal Star Almanac. LBAT 1069; Hunger and Sachs, ADART VII, no. 115.
34357	Sp.472	Joined to Rm.785.
34358	Sp.473	Astronomical Diary. LBAT 548.
34358a	Sp.474	Uninscribed fragment from the core of a tablet.
	Sp.475	Joined to 34095.
34359	Sp.476	Astronomical; Goal Year Text for SE 183. (+) 34292. LBAT 1316; Hunger and Sachs, ADART VI, no. 60.
34360	Sp.477	Omens; physiognomic; Šumma tirku. Fincke, Fs Geller, 203-231.
34361	Sp.478	Astrological. LBAT 1624.
34362	Sp.479	Astronomical Diary for SE 114. + 34931 + 35143 + 35422 + 35679 + 35922 + 45616 + 45769. LBAT 312 + 313 + 314 + 316 + 552 + 674 + 778 + 831; Sachs and Hunger, ADART II, no. -197 B.
34363	Sp.480	Contract; division of property. -/9/3. Babylon.
34364	Sp.481	Astronomical Diary. LBAT 560.
34365	Sp.482	Astronomical; full moons for (at least) one year. + 34394. ACT 124; LBAT 70-71.
34366	Sp.483	Prayer to Marduk no. 1. (+) 45746. Oshima, BPM, 142-157; Lambert, MC 24, no. 85.

34367	Sp.484	Astronomical Diary. LBAT 557.
34368	Sp.485	Astronomical; planetary observations; Greek letter phenomena for several planets. + 41590 (+) 42147. LBAT 1481-1482; Hunger and Sachs, ADART V, no. 87.
34369	Sp.486	Astrological omens; Enūma Anu Enlil, Sin? LBAT 1542; Reiner, Fs Borger (CM 10), 293.
34370	Sp.487	Incantation.
34371	Sp.488	Mantic dream ritual.
34372	Sp.489	No script remains.
34373	Sp.490	Astronomical Diary for SE 154. + 41879 + 41899. LBAT 392 + 573 + 902; Sachs and Hunger, ADART III, no. -157 A.
34374	Sp.491	Joined to 34183. Babylon. Nisaba 28, no. 542.
34375	Sp.492	Joined to 34176.
	Sp.493	Joined to 34211.
34376	Sp.494	Astronomical; Goal Year Text; not datable. LBAT 1317; Hunger and Sachs, ADART VI, no. 123.
34377	Sp.495	Astronomical; Normal Star Almanac. LBAT 1070; Hunger and Sachs, ADART VII, no. 116.
34378	Sp.496	Astronomical; Goal Year Text; not datable. LBAT 1318; Hunger and Sachs, ADART VI, no. 124.
34379	Sp.497	Contract; sale of fields. (+?) 34027.
34380	Sp.498	Astrological omens; Enūma Anu Enlil, Sin. LBAT 1547; Reiner, Fs Borger (CM 10), 293.
34381	Sp.499	Omens.
34382	Sp.500	Contract.
34383	Sp.501	Joined to 34348.
	Sp.502	Joined to 34143.
34384	Sp.503	Unidentified; right edge.
34385	Sp.504	Administrative note.
34386	Sp.505	Contract; sale of a field; sealed; finger-nail marks; Baker and Wunsch, RAI 45, 200, n. 14 notes a join to a Liverpool fragment (1877-11-29, 25) published as Strassmaier, 6th Orientalist Congress, no. 29. Ner 14/9/3. Babylon. + 38113. Mitchell and Searight, no. 329 (as 38113); Nisaba 28, no. 58.
34387	Sp.506	Astronomical; Astrolabe A. LBAT 1500.
34388	Sp.507	Joined to 34292.
34389	Sp.508	Astronomical procedure text; Venus. ACT 815; LBAT 150; Ossendrijver, BMAPT, no. 11.
34390	Sp.509	Astronomical Diary. LBAT 561.
34391	Sp.510	Medical.

34392	Sp.511	Court record; captions for seals but not sealed. Nbn 21/2/3. [Babylon]. + 41543 + 41700 + 41907 (+) 31676. Wunsch, AfO 44/45, 90-91, no. 21.
34393	Sp.512	Lexical; syllabary.
34394	Sp.513	Joined to 34365.
34395	Sp.514	Astronomical; Normal Star Almanac for SE 188. LBAT 1053; Hunger and Sachs, ADART VII, no. 86.
34396	Sp.515	Omens.
34397	Sp.516	Astronomical; Goal Year Text; not datable. LBAT 1319; Hunger and Sachs, ADART VI, no. 123.
34398	Sp.517	Astronomical.
34399	Sp.518	Omens; extispicy.
34400	Sp.519	Joined to 34066.
34401	Sp.520	Lexical; syllabary.
34402	Sp.521	Contract; sale of land by a woman; caption for a finger-nail mark. 10/11/[]. Ḫursag-kalamma.
34403	Sp.522	Astronomical; ziqpu stars? LBAT 1514.
34404	Sp.523	Literary.
34405	Sp.524	Astronomical; Goal Year Text for SE 201 and 202. (+) 34509 (+) 35453 (+) 41958 + 132275. LBAT 1320; Hunger and Sachs, ADART VI, no. 73.
34406	Sp.525	Receipt. 17/-/-.
34407	Sp.526	Astronomical.
34408	Sp.527	Astronomical; Goal Year Text; not datable. LBAT 1321; Hunger and Sachs, ADART VI, no. 126.
34409	Sp.528	Inventory.
34410	Sp.529	Astronomical Diary.
34411	Sp.530	Astronomical; Goal Year Text for SE 187. LBAT 1322; Hunger and Sachs, ADART VI, no. 63.
34412	Sp.531	Astronomical Diary. LBAT 562.
34413	Sp.532	Astronomical; Normal Star Almanac. LBAT 1071; Hunger and Sachs, ADART VII, no. 117.
34414	Sp.533	School text; metrological table.
34415	Sp.534	Bilingual incantation.
34416	Sp.535	Joined to 34090.
	Sp.536	Joined to 34172.
34417	Sp.537	Commentary.
34418	Sp.538	Astronomical Diary. LBAT 565.
34419	Sp.539	Astronomical Diary. LBAT 570.
34420	Sp.540	Joined to 34253.
34421	Sp.541	Joined to 34090.
34422	Sp.542	Astronomical; Goal Year Text; not datable. LBAT 1323; Hunger and Sachs, ADART VI, no. 127.
34423	Sp.543	Astronomical.
	Sp.544	Joined to 34093.

	Sp.545	Joined to 34222.
34424	Sp.546	Incantation.
34425	Sp.547	Horoscope. SE -/-/180.
	Sp.548	Joined to 34222.
34426	Sp.549	Lexical; syllabary.
34427	Sp.550	Lexical.
34428	Sp.551	Chronicle about the invasion of Babylonia by Ptolemy III. SE. + Sp-II.198 + 348 + 450 + 633 + 638 + 683 + 690 + 783. BCHP 11.
34429	Sp.552	Lexical; syllabary.
34430	Sp.553	Astronomical; Goal Year Text; not datable. LBAT 1324l. Hunger and Sachs, ADART VI, no. 128.
34431	Sp.554	Astronomical.
34432	Sp.555	Court record; datable to Nabonidus years 1-6; sealed. (+) 32157. Wunsch, AfO 44/45, 92, no. 22; Nisaba 28, no. 8b.
34433	Sp.556	Astronomical Diary with historical section, mentioning Demetrius and Arabia. SE.
34434	Sp.557	Astronomical Diary with historical section mentioning messengers of the pulitai (Greek citizens). SE.
	Sp.558	Joined to 34211.
34435	Sp.559	Astronomical?
34436	Sp.560	Astronomical Diary. LBAT 558.
34437	Sp.561	Contract.
34438	Sp.562	Astronomical; Mars observations. LBAT 1485; Hunger and Sachs, ADART V, no. 88.
34439	Sp.563	Omens; extispicy.
34440	Sp.564	Joined to 34090.
34441	Sp.565	Contract; caption for a seal.
34442	Sp.566	Astronomical Diary. LBAT 564.
34443	Sp.567	Astronomical Diary.
34444	Sp.568	Lexical; syllabary.
34445	Sp.569	Omens.
34446	Sp.570	Contract. Dar 10/3/-.
34447	Sp.571	Contract; sale of fields; sealed; finger-nail marks; datable to Nabonidus by the seal. [Nbn]. Babylon. + 41916. Wunsch, CM 20A-B, no. 238; Baker and Wunsch, RAI XLV, 211; Mitchell and Searight, no. 329; Nisaba 28, no. 60.
34448	Sp.572	Contract; caption for a seal.
34449	Sp.573	Literary; Gilgameš II. George, Gilgamesh II, pl. 53.
34450	Sp.574	Joined to 34196.
34451	Sp.575	Promissory note for silver.

34452	Sp.576	Astrological; "calendar text"; numbers, stars and cities. + 34738 + Sp 2, 824. LBAT 1586-1587; Hunger, ZA 64, 40-43.
34453	Sp.577	Contract; sale of fields?
34454	Sp.578	Letter; names of sender and addressee lost; sealed. Nisaba 28, no. 210.
34455	Sp.579	Astronomical; Goal Year Text for SE 198. + 35398. LBAT 1287 + 1325; Roughton and P. K. Koch, JCS 35, 133-134; Hunger and Sachs, ADART VI, no. 71.
34456	Sp.580	Omens; Iqqur īpuš.
34457	Sp.581	Incantation; Muššu'u tablet VIII. Böck, Muššu'u, 261-313 and pl. XLVIII.
34458	Sp.582	Joined to Rm.705.
34459	Sp.583	Omens; extispicy?
34460	Sp.584	Astronomical Diary. LBAT 567.
34461	Sp.585	Ritual; namburbû?
34462	Sp.586	Promissory note for silver.
34463	Sp.587	Promissory note for dates. Dar 6/7/29. Wunsch, CM 20A-B, no. 163.
34464	Sp.588	Promissory note for silver; Egibi archive. Cam -/2/-. Babylon.
34465	Sp.589	Omens.
34466	Sp.590	Astronomical Diary. LBAT 559.
34467	Sp.591	Contract; sale of fields. + 37016.
34468	Sp.592	Promissory note for onions; Egibi archive. Nbn 26/2/4. Šaḫrīn.
34469	Sp.593	Astronomical; Normal Star Almanac. LBAT 1072; Hunger and Sachs, ADART VII, no. 118.
34470	Sp.594	Astronomical; Almanac for SE 157. LBAT 1126; Hunger and Sachs, ADART VII, no. 161.
34471	Sp.595	Astrological; groups of days associated with zodiac and planets. LBAT 1585.
34472	Sp.596	Omens; Šumma ālu.
34473	Sp.597	Astronomical.
34474	Sp.598	Omens; Šumma ālu.
34475	Sp.599	Commentary.
34476	Sp.600	Astrological omens.
34477	Sp.601	Astronomical; ibarruṣ. LBAT 1568; Reiner, Fs Borger (CM 10), 293.
34478	Sp.602	Literary.
34479	Sp.603	Omens.
34480	Sp.604	Promissory note for barley.
34481	Sp.605	Contract; mentions Ḫaḫḫaru; sealed. (+) 34281 + 35443. Nisaba 28, no. 543.
34482	Sp.606	Incantation, possibly medical.

34483	Sp.607	Receipt.
34484	Sp.608	Promissory note for silver; Egibi archive.
34485	Sp.609	Astronomical Diary. LBAT 563.
34486	Sp.610	Contract; only witnesses preserved. 3/7/6. Babylon.
34487	Sp.611	Letter?
34488	Sp.612	Joined to 34066.
34489	Sp.613	Promissory note for dates.
34490	Sp.614	Contract; sealed. Nisaba 28, no. 614.
34491	Sp.615	Letter order; sealed. Nisaba 28, no. 673.
34492	Sp.616	Astronomical Diary. LBAT 583; Sachs, PTRSL A.276, 49, fig. 14.
34493	Sp.617	Joined to 34088.
34494	Sp.618	Promissory note for silver. Dar 6/12/19. Babylon. Dar 493.
34495	Sp.619	Contract.
34496	Sp.620	Lexical.
34497	Sp.621	Astronomical procedure text for the moon; System A. ACT 1005; LBAT 156; Aaboe, KDVSMM 40/6 (1979) 10; Ossendrijver, BMAPT, no. 90.
34498	Sp.622	Astronomical; Goal Year Text for SE 155. LBAT 1363; Hunger and Sachs, ADART VI, no. 43.
34499	Sp.623	Omens.
34500	Sp.624	Contract; upper right corner. Cam 5/3/[].
34501	Sp.625	Debt note? Wunsch, CM 20A-B, no. 123.
34502	Sp.626	Joined to 34101.
34503	Sp.627	Contract; witnesses.
34504	Sp.628	Astronomical Diary. LBAT 566; Sachs, PTRSL A.276, 49, fig. 14.
34505	Sp.629	Economic. []/1/6.
34506	Sp.630	Astronomical; Goal Year Text; not datable. LBAT 1326; Hunger and Sachs, ADART VI, no. 129.
34507	Sp.631	Astronomical; System A lunar ephemeris. ACT 8a; LBAT 20.
34508	Sp.632	Literary.
34509	Sp.633	Astronomical; Goal Year Text for SE 201 and 202. (+) 34405 (+) 35453 (+) 41958 + 132275. LBAT 1327; Hunger and Sachs, ADART VI, no. 73.
34510	Sp.634	Economic.
34511	Sp.635	Ritual.
34512	Sp.636	Promissory note for barley.
34513	Sp.637	Astronomical.
34514	Sp.638	Namburbû incantation and ritual.
34515	Sp.639	Economic.
34516	Sp.640	School text; lexical.

34517	Sp.641	Mathematical table. LBAT 1646; Ossendrijver, JCS 66, 149-165 and pls.; Friberg and Al-Rawi, NMCT, Sec. 2.3.1.
34518	Sp.642	Contract; the witnesses include a judge; sealed. Nisaba 28, no. 50a.
	Sp.643	Joined to 34181.
34519	Sp.644	Economic. []/12/4.
34520	Sp.645	Astronomical Diary. LBAT 572; Sachs, PTRSL A.276, 49, fig. 14.
34521	Sp.646	Astronomical Diary. LBAT 568; Sachs, PTRSL A.276, 49, fig. 14.
34522	Sp.647	Economic.
34523	Sp.648	Literary?
34524	Sp.649	Contract.
34525	Sp.650	Receipt for sesame; Egibi archive. Cyr -/12/1. Babylon.
34526	Sp.651	Promissory note for silver. RN lost 10/5/10.
34527	Sp.652	Administrative note about a payment of silver; sealed. n.d. Nisaba 28, no. 195.
34528	Sp.653	Astrological omens; Enūma Anu Enlil 19-20. Rochberg-Halton, AfO Beih. 22, Enūma Anu Enlil 19-20; Reiner, Fs Borger (CM 10), 293.
34528a	Sp.654	Contract for a partnership.
141866	Sp.655	Contract; sale of land; fragment of left edge; sealed. Cyr []/[]/[4?].
141867	Sp.656	Joined to 32165.
141868	Sp.657	Court record; fragment of reverse and upper edge; sealed. Nbn []/[]/12.
141869	Sp.658	Contract or court record; fragment of right edge; sealed.
141870	Sp.659	Fragment of a sealing.

Sp-II collection

The Sp-II collection was purchased from Messrs. Spartali & Co., London, in December 1879. The register gives the provenance Babylon to nos. 1-32 and nos. 65-1000 and the provenance Babylonia to nos. 33-64 and nos. 1001-1086. T. G. Pinches's catalogue of the first part of this collection (nos. 1-315) is preserved in the Middle East department's archives as a bound volume marked "Catalogue slips of the Sp.II collection".

34529	Sp-II.1	Promissory note for barley. Nbk 2/2/39. Babylon. Nbk 343; CT 51, 42; Bertin 1129.
34530	Sp-II.2	Contract; sale of a house in Ḫursagkalama. AM 29?/5/1. Babylon. Sack, AOATS 4, no. 75; CT 51, 43; Bertin 1175-1176.

34531	Sp-II.3	Promissory note for dates. Nbn 5/10/8. Babylon. Nbn 309; CT 51, 44; Bertin 1341.
34532	Sp-II.4	Sale of a slave girl. Nbn 8/12/9. Babylon. Nbn 388; Bertin 1361.
34533	Sp-II.5	Promissory note for barley. Nbn 13/8/12. Babylon. Nbn 634; CT 51, 45; Bertin 1476.
34534	Sp-II.6	Receipt for silver payment. Cyr 30/5/8. Babylon. Cyr 315; CT 51, 46; Bertin 1716.
34535	Sp-II.7	Promissory note for silver. Cam 14/5/2. Babylon. Cam 116; Bertin 3003.
34536	Sp-II.8	Promissory note for silver. Bardija -/2/acc. Babylon. Strassmaier, ZA 4, 147, Sm 1; Bertin 1920.
34537	Sp-II.9	Promissory note for silver. Dar 17/12/4. Babylon. Dar 147; Bertin 1997.
34538	Sp-II.10	Promissory note for silver. Dar 10/1/10. Babylon. Dar 266; CT 51, 48; Bertin 2180.
34539	Sp-II.11	Promissory note for silver. Dar 26/11/11. Borsippa. Dar 311; CT 51, 49; Bertin 2206.
34540	Sp-II.12	Receipt for dates provisions. Dar 18/12/11. Babylon. Dar 314; CT 51, 50; Bertin 2214.
34541	Sp-II.13	Promissory note for silver as final payment on the purchase of a slave. Dar 21/7/14. Babylon. Dar 376; CT 51, 51; Bertin 2307.
34542	Sp-II.14	Receipt for silver payment. Dar 11/6/25. Babylon. CT 51, 52; Bertin 2552.
34543	Sp-II.15	Receipt for a dowry. Dar 5/8/25. Babylon. CT 51, 53; Bertin 2550.
34544	Sp-II.16	Contract; lease of a house. Dar 7/5/36. Babylon. CT 51, 54; Bertin 2713.
34545	Sp-II.17	Sale of a prebend; sealed. Dar 11/7/[]. Mar(a)da. CT 51, 56; Bertin 2819; Nisaba 28, no. 178.
34546	Sp-II.18	Dates payable as rent due on a field promised as a dowry. Dar 4/7/(26). [Alu]-ša-Mušētiq. CT 51, 55; Bertin 2596; Roth, JAOS 111, 30.
34547	Sp-II.19	Contract; lease of a house. Šamaš-eriba 22/7/acc. Babylon. Strassmaier, ZA 3, 157; Bertin 1013.
34548	Sp-II.20	Contract; lease of a house. [Art II/III] 6/8/14. Babylon. Strassmaier, ZA 3, 152; Bertin 3049.
34549	Sp-II.21	Field plan. Nemet-Nejat, LB Field Plans, no. 23; CT 51, 70; Bertin 3015.
34550	Sp-II.22	Letter to Ea-tabtanâ-bulliṭ / Murānu. SE Antiochus II 10/9/59. CT 49, 27, no. 128; van der Spek, BiOr 42, 555; Jursa, Persika 9, 156, 196-197; Bertin 2896.
34551	Sp-II.23	Account of wheat. Cyr 378; CT 51, 58; Bertin 3002.

34552	Sp-II.24	Account of grain. -/-/18. Dar 480; CT 51, 59; Bertin 3011.
34553	Sp-II.25	Letter from Remut to Iddin-Marduk. CT 22, 36, no. 195; Bertin 3010; Hackl et al., AOAT 414/1, no. 15.
34554	Sp-II.26	Letter from Nabû-ittannu to Iddin-Marduk. Cyr 375; CT 51, 71; Bertin 2979; Hackl et al., AOAT 414/1, no. 13.
34555	Sp-II.27	Letter from Lâbâši to Iddin-Bēl. SE 16/9/164. CT 51, 72; Strassmaier, 8th Orientalist Congress, no. 32; Ebeling, Glossar, 262-263; Bertin 3009; Jursa, TUAT NF 3, 171-172.
34556	Sp-II.28	Letter from Nergal-aḫu-iddin to Iddin-Marduk. Cyr 376; CT 22, 33, no. 182; Bertin 3014; Hackl et al., AOAT 414/1, no. 14.
34557	Sp-II.29	Letter from Iddin-Marduk to Marduk-rēmanni, Nergal-rēṣū'a and Ina-ṣilli-Bēl. Cyr 377; CT 22, 3, no. 9; Bertin 3013; Hackl et al., AOAT 414/1, no. 2.
34558	Sp-II.30	Promissory note for silver. CT 51, 60.
34559	Sp-II.31	List of bronze tools. CT 51, 61.
34560	Sp-II.32	Astronomical procedure text; planetary periods. LBAT 1515.
34561	Sp-II.33	Astronomical; Jupiter observations for SE 97-98. LBAT 1407; Hunger and Sachs, ADART V, no. 77.
34562	Sp-II.34	Astronomical Diary for SE 141. LBAT 367; Sachs, PTRSL A.276, 49, fig. 11; Sachs and Hunger, ADART II, no. -170 E.
34563	Sp-II.35	Astronomical Diary for SE 108. LBAT 304; Sachs and Hunger, ADART II, no. -203.
34564	Sp-II.36	Astronomical Diary for SE 116. LBAT 318; Sachs and Hunger, ADART II, no. -195 B.
34565	Sp-II.37	Promissory note. Cyr 24/3/[]. Borsippa. Cyr 17; Bertin 1715.
34566	Sp-II.38	Astrological; prayer on upper edge. LBAT 1591; Kugler, SSB I pl. II, no. 2; Ungnad, AfO 14, 261-262.
34567	Sp-II.39	Horoscope; birth notes for three children. SE 9/4/197. LBAT 1469; Rochberg, Babylonian Horoscopes, no. 32; Sachs, JCS 6, 65, pl. IV.
34568	Sp-II.40	Mathematical; problem text. + Sp-II.85 + 990 + Sp-III.137 + 252 + 645. Thureau-Dangin, TMB 57-63; Neugebauer, MKT III, 14-22.
34569	Sp-II.41	Astronomical; Jupiter, second stationary points and last visibility for (at least) SE 203 to 274; System A. LBAT 122; ACT 613a.
34570	Sp-II.42	Astronomical procedure text for Jupiter from first visibility to second stationary point, for SE 180 to 252;

		prayer on upper edge. + Sp-II.68 + 107 + 574 + 876 (+)VAT 1753 + 1755. LBAT 119; ACT 611 and 822, colophon Zm; Ossendrijver, BMAPT, no. 35.
34571	Sp-II.43	Astronomical; Jupiter ephemeris for SE 147-218 and procedure; System A. LBAT 118; ACT 603 and 821, colophon Zl; Ossendrijver, BMAPT, no. 28.
34572	Sp-II.44	Astrological; microzodiac; tabulated; cf. 32517. + Sp-II.253 + 1881,0706.705 + 78831. LBAT 1580; Weidner, Gestirn-Darstellungen, 34-38; 78831 is unpublished.
34573	Sp-II.45	Astronomical; new moons for (at least) SE 185 to 188. LBAT 65; ACT 121a.
34574	Sp-II.46	Astronomical procedure text for Jupiter, second stationary point and last visibility for SE 190 to 231; System B. LBAT 126; ACT 622 and 823, colophon Zma; Ossendrijver, BMAPT, no. 24.
34575	Sp-II.47	Astronomical; System A lunar ephemeris; several columns, for SE 144-149. + 1882,0704.164 + 189 + 34687 + 65831 (+) 32762 (+) 132282. LBAT 5-6; ACT 4; Kugler, Mondrechnung, pl. X; Steele, Fs Walker, 293-318, text C; Steele, AHES 60 (2006) 123-153, text D.
34576	Sp-II.48	Astronomical; Saros periods, ending with an undated eclipse report; the "Saros Tablet". + Sp-II.955. Strassmaier, ZA 7, 197-204 (Sp-II.48) and ZA 8,106-113 (Sp-II.955); Pinches PSBA 6 (1884) 204; Kugler, SSB II 364 n. 1; Hunger and Sachs, ADART V, no. 34.
34577	Sp-II.49	Mathematical; table of reciprocals. LBAT 1635.
34578	Sp-II.50	Mathematical; table of squares of regular numbers. LBAT 1641; Aaboe, JCS 19, 86.
34579	Sp-II.51	Astronomical; Goal Year text for SE 140. + 36006. LBAT 1251-1252; Stephenson, HEER, 170, 201-202, 209; Hunger and Sachs, ADART VI, no. 35; Hunger in Swerdlow, Astronomy, 88-94.
34580	Sp-II.52	Astronomical; new moons for SE 208 to 210; prayer on upper edge. + Sp-II.75 + 1881,0706.272 + 277 + 331 + 333 + 386 + 589 + 42690 + 42869 + 42902 + 43000 + 43030. ACT 122, colophon Zo; Aaboe, PTRSL A.276, 23-30, pl. 1; LBAT 66 (not 42690); Kugler, Mondrechnung, 9-40 (1881,0706.272 only); Aaboe, Episodes, 60-62; Steele, SCIAMVS 11 (2010), 211-239, text G.
34581	Sp-II.53	Astronomical; full moons for (at least) two years. + 34610. ACT 92; LBAT 58 + 59.

34582	Sp-II.54	Astronomical; System A lunar ephemeris. ACT 7; LBAT 18.
34583	Sp-II.55	Astronomical observations; Lunar Six and prices. + Sp-III.275 + 35698. LBAT 1347 + 1487; Hunger and Sachs, ADART V, no. 43.
34584	Sp-II.56	Hemerology for several months; colophon. + Sp-II.151 + 647 + 1882,0704.81 + 146 + 182 (+) 35349. Jiménez, JCS 68, 197-227.
34585	Sp-II.57	Astronomical; Mercury, evening and morning star, for SE 166 to 189; System A1. + Sp-II.59 + 97. ACT 302; LBAT 105.
34586	Sp-II.58	Astronomical; Jupiter, second stationary point and last visibility, for (at least) SE 185 to 221; System B. ACT 621a; LBAT 127.
	Sp-II.59	Joined to 34585.
34587	Sp-II.60	Astronomical; Jupiter, opposition and second station, from (at least) SE 200 to 232; System B. + Sp-II.81 + 34611. ACT 623, colophon Zp; LBAT 128-129.
34588	Sp-II.61	Astronomical; Normal Star Almanac for SE 188. + Sp-II.782 (+) 34078. LBAT 1052; Hunger and Sachs, ADART VII, no. 86.
34589	Sp-II.62	Astronomical; Saturn, oppositions, for SE 155 to 243; System B. + 35745 (+) 40620. ACT 704, colophon Zla (not 40620); LBAT 134-135 (not 40620).
34590	Sp-II.63	Astronomical; System A ephemeris; excerpts for SE 204 to 221. + 34749. ACT 76; LBAT 52-53.
34591	Sp-II.64	Astronomical Diary for SE 133. + 55532 + 1882,0704.144. LBAT 353-354; Sachs and Hunger, ADART II, no. -178 C.
34592	Sp-II.65	Mathematical; standard table of reciprocals, and table of squares of regular numbers. + Sp-II.77 + 188. LBAT 1637; Aaboe, JCS 19, 81-84.
34593	Sp-II.66	Astronomical; Venus, evening and morning star, for SE 246 to (at least) 256. System A1 or A2? + 42758. ACT 411; LBAT 108; Steele, SCIAMVS 11 (2010), 211-239, text J.
34594	Sp-II.67	Astronomical; Jupiter, first visibility, for (at least) SE 182 to 205. System B. ACT 621; LBAT 136.
	Sp-II.68	Joined to 34570.
34595	Sp-II.69	Astronomical; Goal Year Text for SE 168. LBAT 1267; Hunger and Sachs, ADART VI, no. 49.
34596	Sp-II.70	Mathematical; table of reciprocals. + 1882,0704.128. LBAT 1633.
34597	Sp-II.71	Astronomical; the "Saros Canon". Epping and Strassmaier, ZA 8, 176; Strassmaier, ZA 10, 66; LBAT

		1428; see ACT, p. 107 n. 2; Aaboe, JHA 3 (1972) 114-115; Aaboe, et al., TAPS 81/6 (1991), 12-22, text C.
34598	Sp-II.72	List of market prices for years 178-185 SE. Slotsky and Wallenfels, Tallies and Trends, text 7.
34599	Sp-II.73	God list; commentary. + 34811.
34600	Sp-II.74	Astronomical; System A lunar ephemeris. + 34751 (+) 77237. ACT 15; LBAT 37-38.
	Sp-II.75	Joined to 34580.
34601	Sp-II.76	Mathematical; table; analysis of reciprocals? + Sp-II.759. LBAT 1644.
	Sp-II.77	Joined to 34592.
34602	Sp-II.78	Hemerology for Tašrītu, including names of diseases. MSL 9, 107-108; Labat, Iraq 23, 88-93; Casaburi, SEL 17 (2000), 13-29; Livingstone, CUSAS 25, p. 161.
34603	Sp-II.79	Astronomical; Goal Year Text for SE 160. + 1881,0625.89. LBAT 1263; Hunger and Sachs, ADART VI, no. 46.
34604	Sp-II.80	Astronomical; System A lunar ephemeris; prayer on upper edge. + 34628 + 35661. ACT 13, colophon Zn; LBAT 33 + 34 + 36.
	Sp-II.81	Joined to 34587.
	Sp-II.82	Joined to 34094.
34605	Sp-II.83	Omens from the intestines; šà.nigin.
34606	Sp-II.84	Astronomical; daily motion of the moon for SE 178 month I; prayer on upper edge. ACT 80, colophon Zlc; LBAT 54.
	Sp-II.85	Joined to 34568.
34607	Sp-II.86	Astronomical; Normal Star Almanac for SE 210. LBAT 1061; Hunger and Sachs, ADART VII, no. 96.
34608	Sp-II.87	Astronomical; System A ephemeris; solar eclipses from (at least) SE 199 to 206. ACT 51; LBAT 46.
34609	Sp-II.88	Astronomical Diary for SE 167. (+) 34788. Sachs and Hunger, ADART III, no. -144.
34610	Sp-II.89	Joined to 34581.
34611	Sp-II.90	Joined to 34587.
34612	Sp-II.91	Mathematical; table of reciprocals. LBAT 1631.
34613	Sp-II.92	Mathematical; table of measures of length and weight (GÍN); rather illegible.
34614	Sp-II.93	Astronomical; Almanac for SE 305. LBAT 1193; Sachs and Walker, Iraq 46, 43-55, pl. II; Hunger and Sachs, ADART VII, no. 211.
34615	Sp-II.94	Astronomical; Goal Year Text for SE 168. + Sp-II.751. LBAT 1266; Hunger and Sachs, ADART VI, no. 50.

34616	Sp-II.95	Astronomical Diary for SE 9-10. + 45901. LBAT 219 + 220; Sachs and Hunger, ADART I, no. -302/301.
34617	Sp-II.96	Astronomical; System A lunar ephemeris. + 34807. ACT 16; LBAT 39-40.
	Sp-II.97	Joined to 34585.
34618	Sp-II.98	Medical astrology; joins A.1670 in Chicago. LBAT 1596; Geller, Melosthesia, 89.
34619	Sp-II.99	Astronomical; System A lunar ephemeris. (+) 34185. LBAT 26; ACT 10.
34620	Sp-II.100	Astronomical; Normal Star Almanac for SE 184. + Sp-III.62. LBAT 1048; Hunger and Sachs, ADART VII, no. 84.
34621	Sp-II.101	Astronomical procedure text; Jupiter, second stationary point and last visibility for (at least) SE 130 to 205; System A. ACT 602 and 820aa; LBAT 112; Ossendrijver, BMAPT, no. 17.
34622	Sp-II.102	Joined to 34081.
34623	Sp-II.103	Astronomical; daily positions of the moon for (at least) 5 months. ACT 194b; Jones, AHES 29 (1983) 1-11; LBAT 83.
34624	Sp-II.104	Astronomical; Mercury observations for SE 138-142. + 34877 + 35255. LBAT 1378 + 1380-1381; Hunger and Sachs, ADART V, no. 81.
	Sp-II.105	Joined to 34088.
34625	Sp-II.106	Astronomical; Goal Year Text for SE 91. + Sp-II.112 + Sp-III.328 + 1882,0704.181 + 34741 + 55543. LBAT 1219-1221; Kugler, Or NS 2, 107-112, 115-116 (part); Schaumberger, AnOr 6, 1-12; Hunger and Sachs, ADART VI, no. 7.
	Sp-II.107	Joined to 34570.
34626	Sp-II.108	Astrological omens; Enūma Anu Enlil, Sin; commentary. + Sp-II.420 + Sp-III.420 + 34922. LBAT 1535-1536; Reiner, Fs Borger (CM 10), 293-294.
34627	Sp-II.109	Astronomical; new and full moons for SE 236; prayer on upper edge. + Sp-II.403 + 1881,0201.91. ACT 123aa, colophon Zkb; LBAT 69.
34628	Sp-II.110	Joined to 34604.
34629	Sp-II.111	Astronomical; Jupiter, daily motion, for SE 147 IX to 148 V. + 45707 + 45992 + 1881,0706.155. ACT 654 + 655; LBAT 133 (34629 only).
	Sp-II.112	Joined to 34625.
34630	Sp-II.113	Astronomical; System A lunar ephemeris. (+) 35048. ACT 11; LBAT 29.
34631	Sp-II.114	Astronomical; Goal Year Text; not datable. LBAT 1305; Hunger and Sachs, ADART VI, no. 130.

34632	Sp-II.115	Astronomical Diary for SE 162. LBAT 400; Sachs and Hunger, ADART III, no. -149 A. Stephenson, HEER, 187, 203.
34633	Sp-II.116	Literary; Theodicy. Lambert, BWL 63-89, pls. 19, 25.
34634	Sp-II.117	Astronomical Diary. LBAT 165; Sachs and Hunger, ADART I, no. -384.
34635	Sp-II.118	Mathematical; table of reciprocals. LBAT 1634.
34636	Sp-II.119	Astronomical Diary for SE 170. LBAT 409; Sachs and Hunger, ADART III, no. -141 C.
34637	Sp-II.120	Historical-literary text (of Nebuchadnezzar I?). CT 51, 73; Frame, RIMB 2.4.1001 (p. 35).
34638	Sp-II.121	Astronomical Diary. LBAT 166; Sachs and Hunger, ADART I, no. -382.
34639	Sp-II.122	Astronomical procedure text; lunar latitude; ziqpu stars; rising time scheme; the path of the moon. LBAT 1501; Neugebauer, JCS 21, 202; Steele, JHA 34 (2003) 269-289; Steele, Annals of Science 64 (2007) 293-325; Steele, Rising time schemes, 22-26; Fincke and Horowitz, JNES 77, 249-261.
34640	Sp-II.123	Astronomical Diary. LBAT 574.
34641	Sp-II.124	Promissory note; Murānu archive; sealed. SE Antiochus II []/[]/54. + Sp-II.528. CT 49, 25, no. 121; Stolper, Annali Supp. 77, 45-46, no. 14; Jursa, Persika 9, 175, 190-191; Nisaba 28, no. 577.
34642	Sp-II.125	Astronomical Diary. + 35417 + 78829. LBAT 174 + 580 + 731; Sachs, PTRSL A.276 48, fig. 4; Sachs and Hunger, ADART I, no. -375 B.
34643	Sp-II.126	Ritual. CT 51, 94; Linssen, CM 25, 324.
34644	Sp-II.127	Joined to 34104.
34645	Sp-II.128	Astronomical Diary for SE 162. + Sp-III.165. LBAT 402; Sachs and Hunger, ADART III, no. -149 B.
34646	Sp-II.129	Astronomical; Goal Year Text for SE 187. + Sp-II.441 + 35026. LBAT 1280-1281; Hunger and Sachs, ADART VI, no. 63.
34647	Sp-II.130	Astrological medicine. LBAT 1601; Biggs, RA 62, 53, 57-58.
34648	Sp-II.131	Joined to 33649.
34649	Sp-II.132	Astronomical; Goal Year Text; not datable. LBAT 1365; Hunger and Sachs, ADART VI, no. 131.
34650	Sp-II.133	Literary; Ludlul V; colophon; dupl. 77253. Oshima, BPPS, 429-430; Lambert, MC 24, no. 163.
34651	Sp-II.134	Astronomical Diary. + Sp-II.249 + 77245. LBAT 190 (34651 only); Sachs and Hunger, ADART I, no. -342 A.
34652	Sp-II.135	Astronomical Diary. LBAT 584.

34653	Sp-II.136	Astrological omens; Enūma Anu Enlil 56. LBAT 1554; Reiner, Fs Borger (CM 10), 294.
34654	Sp-II.137	Literary; fable of the duqduqqu bird (wren); colophon. SE Arsaces 22/12/242. Babylon. CT 51, 93; Jiménez, BDP, 333-341; Lambert, MC 24, no. 276.
34655	Sp-II.138	Gula hymn of Bulluṭsa-rabi. + 45718. Lambert, Or NS 36, 115.
34656	Sp-II.139	Historiographic. CT 46, 45, no. 47.
34657	Sp-II.140	Joined to 34104.
34658	Sp-II.141	Astronomical; Goal Year Text for SE 186. + Sp-II.157 + 35787 (+) 35341. LBAT 1277-1278. Stephenson, HEER, 157-159 (Figs. 6.3, 6.4), 182, 187 (all as 35787); Hunger and Sachs, ADART VI, no. 62.
34659	Sp-II.142	Astronomical; Almanac for SE 305. + Sp-II.795 + Sp-III.172. LBAT 1194; Sachs and Walker, Iraq 46, 43-55, pl. II; Schaumberger, AnOr 12, 279-287; Hunger and Sachs, ADART VII, no. 211.
34660	Sp-II.143	Chronicle about the Diadochi. + 36313 (the two fragments are now joined). S. Smith, BHT, 124-149; Grayson, TCS 5, Chronicle 10; BCHP 3.
34661	Sp-II.144	Lexical; Ḫḫ IX. CT 51, 79.
34662	Sp-II.145	Omens; extispicy. CT 51, 120.
34663	Sp-II.146	Astronomical Diary for SE 104. + 36010. LBAT 577 + 857; Sachs and Hunger, ADART II, no. -204 B.
34664	Sp-II.147	Astronomical; ziqpu stars; microzodiac rising time scheme. + Sp-III.551. LBAT 1503; Steele, Rising time schemes, 57-61.
34665	Sp-II.148	Astrological omens; Enūma Anu Enlil 17. LBAT 1535a; Rochberg-Halton, AfO Beih. 22, Enūma Anu Enlil 17; Reiner, Fs Borger (CM 10), 29.
34666	Sp-II.149	Astronomical; ziqpu stars; constellational iconography. LBAT 1510.
34667	Sp-II.150	Astronomical; Almanac for SE 234; colophon. + 34668 + 55595. LBAT 1164-1166; Hunger and Sachs, ADART VII, no. 190.
	Sp-II.151	Joined to 34584.
34668	Sp-II.152	Joined to 34667. + Sp-II.687.
	Sp-II.153	Joined to 34275.
34669	Sp-II.154	Astronomical Diary for SE 177. + Sp-II.298 + 700 + 35740 (+) 34918 + 35170. LBAT 432-433; Sachs and Hunger, ADART III, no. -134 B; Stephenson, HEER, 157-158.
	Sp-II.155	Joined to 34211.
34670	Sp-II.156	Astronomical Diary. LBAT 582; Sachs, PTRSL A.276, 49, fig. 14.

	Sp-II.157	Joined to 34658.
34671	Sp-II.158	Astronomical Diary for SE 104. + 35057 + 35433 + 35540 + 35837 + 47821. LBAT 384 + 576 + 739 + 747 + 818 (not 47821); Pinches, JTVI 29 (1897) 86; Sachs and Hunger, ADART II, no. -207 A.
34672	Sp-II.159	Astronomical Diary for SE 218. LBAT 493; Sachs and Hunger, ADART III, no. -93 B.
34673	Sp-II.160	Astrological procedure text. LBAT 1602.
34674	Sp-II.161	Promissory note for silver. CT 51, 62.
34675	Sp-II.162	Astronomical; Goal Year Text; not datable. LBAT 1328; Hunger and Sachs, ADART VI, no. 132.
34676	Sp-II.163	Astronomical procedure text; Mars. + Sp-II.304 + 396 + 491 + 895. ACT 811a; LBAT 138; Ossendrijver, BMAPT, no. 13.
34677	Sp-II.164	Contract; division of property. Cam 15/4/[]. Babylon. + Sp-II.769 + 925 + Sp-III.576. CT 51, 57.
34678	Sp-II.165	Horoscopic astrology; conception of a child. LBAT 1588.
34679	Sp-II.166	Ritual; two columns. + 1882,0704.62. CT 51, 101; Linssen, CM 25, 120 n. 746, 324; George, Fs Lambert, 260 n. 6, 270 n. 21; Da Riva, WdO 47, 259-264 and WdO 48, 96-98 (wrongly as 36479).
34680	Sp-II.167	Ritual. CT 51, 125.
34681	Sp-II.168	Astronomical Diary. LBAT 581.
34682	Sp-II.169	Astronomical Diary. LBAT 585.
34683	Sp-II.170	Astrological omens; Enūma Anu Enlil 20. LBAT 1534; Rochberg-Halton, AfO Beih. 22, Enūma Anu Enlil 20; Reiner, Fs Borger (CM 10), 294.
34684	Sp-II.171	Astronomical; lunar eclipse table for at least 442-406 BC. (+) 34787. LBAT 1427; Stephenson, HEER, 149, 153, 169 174-175; Hunger and Sachs, ADART V, no. 9.
34685	Sp-II.172	Astrological; fixed star names of Venus and Jupiter; Rikis gerri Enūma Anu Enlil. + Sp-II.361. LBAT 1556; Reiner, Fs Borger (CM 10), 294; Gehlken, CM 43, p. 213.
34686	Sp-II.173	List of market prices for years 186-187 SE. + Sp-II.956 + 35604. Slotsky and Wallenfels, Tallies and Trends, text 9.
34687	Sp-II.174	Joined to 34575.
34688	Sp-II.175	Astronomical Diary. LBAT 579.
34689	Sp-II.176	Ritual; two columns. + Sp-II.300. CT 51, 95; Linssen, CM 25, 195, 324.
34690	Sp-II.177	Astrological or astronomical? LBAT 1567; Reiner, Fs Borger (CM 10), 294.

34691	Sp-II.178	Astronomical; Goal Year Text for SE 95; note that LBAT 1224 obv. line 9 referring back to SE 49 anomalously attributes this year to Antiochus and Seleucus; cf. also LBAT 1225 rev. 3. + Sp-II.989 + 45809. LBAT 1223-1224; Hunger and Sachs, ADART VI, no. 9.
34692	Sp-II.179	Astrological omens.
34693	Sp-II.180	Horoscope; birth note. SE -/-/98. LBAT 1465; Rochberg, Babylonian Horoscopes, no. 31.
34694	Sp-II.181	Astronomical Diary. LBAT 578; Sachs, PTRSL A.276, 49, fig. 14.
34695	Sp-II.182	Astronomical.
34696	Sp-II.183	Ritual. CT 51, 98.
34697	Sp-II.184	Astronomical Diary. LBAT 590; Sachs, PTRSL A.276, 49, fig. 14.
34698	Sp-II.185	Astronomical; Goal Year Text; not datable. LBAT 1329; Hunger and Sachs, ADART VI, no. 133.
34699	Sp-II.186	Astronomical Diary. LBAT 593; Sachs, PTRSL A.276, 49, fig. 14.
34700	Sp-II.187	Astronomical Diary. LBAT 587; Sachs, PTRSL A.276, 49, fig. 14.
	Sp-II.188	Joined to 34592.
34701	Sp-II.189	Astronomical Diary for SE 212. Sachs and Hunger, ADART III, no. -99 B.
34702	Sp-II.190	Astronomical Diary for SE 131. LBAT 347; Sachs and Hunger, ADART II, no. -180 D.
34703	Sp-II.191	Liver omens; kakku; two columns; colophon. CT 51, 115.
34704	Sp-II.192	List of people and regular offerings brought to the temple. CT 51, 64.
34705	Sp-II.193	Astronomical; latitudes(?) and eclipse magnitudes for (at least) 7 years. + Sp-II.482. ACT 93; Aaboe, JHA 3 (1972) 110-111; LBAT 57 (Sp-II.482 is not 34960 as stated in LBAT).
34706	Sp-II.194	Historical inscription of Nabonidus. CT 51, 75; Schaudig, AOAT 256, 474-475.
34707	Sp-II.195	Astronomical Diary for SE 204. (+) 45771 (+) 45961. Sachs and Hunger, ADART III, no. -107 D.
34708	Sp-II.196	Astrological omens; Enūma Anu Enlil, Sin. LBAT 1530; Reiner, Fs Borger (CM 10), 294.
34709	Sp-II.197	Astrological omens; Enūma Anu Enlil 29 (30). + Sp-III.352 + 1881,0706.696. LBAT 1552; Weidner, AfO 22, 70; van Soldt, Solar omens, 114-133 (A); Reiner, Fs Borger (CM 10), 294.
	Sp-II.198	Joined to 34428.

34710	Sp-II.199	Literary cylinder; hymn to Nabû. + Sp-II.794 + 35047. Lambert, Fs Matouš II, 75-111. Gesche, AOAT 275, 670.
34711	Sp-II.200	Astronomical Diary for SE 124. + Sp-III.249 + 1882,0704.131. LBAT 329; Sachs and Hunger, ADART II, no. -187 A.
34712	Sp-II.201	List of market prices for years 11-15. + Sp-II.785. Slotsky and Wallenfels, Tallies and Trends, text 1.
34713	Sp-II.202	Astronomical; Astrolabe A; microzodiac rising time scheme. + 1881,0625.140 + 1882,0704.87 + 1881, 0706.703. LBAT 1499; Steele, Rising time schemes, 49-57.
34714	Sp-II.203	Mathematical; table of squares of regular numbers. LBAT 1639; Aaboe, JCS 19, 85-86.
34715	Sp-II.204	Astronomical Diary for SE 175. Sachs and Hunger, ADART III, no. -136 C.
34716	Sp-II.205	Historical-literary text. CT 51, 74; Grayson, BHLT 101-104.
34717	Sp-II.206	Astronomical; Goal Year Text for SE 129. LBAT 1243; Hunger and Sachs, ADART VI, no. 26.
34718	Sp-II.207	Physiognomic omens; three columns. + Sp-II.313. CT 51, 124; Böck, AfO Beih. 27, 184.
34719	Sp-II.208	Astronomical; instructions for construction of a gnomon-like instrument. + Sp-II.209. LBAT 1494.
	Sp-II.209	Joined to 34719.
34720	Sp-II.210	Lexical; Syllabary B. + Sp-II.281 + 534 + 954. MSL 3, 95, 131; CT 51, 82.
34721	Sp-II.211	Astronomical procedure text; Mars. (+) 35857. ACT 811b; LBAT 139; Ossendrijver, BMAPT, no. 16.
34722	Sp-II.212	Astronomical; Almanac for SE 236. LBAT 1169; Hunger and Sachs, ADART VII, no. 191.
34723	Sp-II.213	Joined to 32206.
34724	Sp-II.214	Mathematical; problem text; the problems on the obverse deal with inheritance. LBAT 1648.
34725	Sp-II.215	Astronomical Diary for SE 34. LBAT 600; Sachs and Hunger, ADART I, no. -277 B.
34726	Sp-II.216	Astrological; prayer on upper edge; colophon. LBAT 1607.
34727	Sp-II.217	Astronomical Diary for SE 201 + Sp-II.267. Sachs and Hunger, ADART III, no. -110; Da Riva, WdO 47, 259-264 and WdO 48, 96-98.
34728	Sp-II.218	Astronomical Diary for SE 57. + 35418. LBAT 258 + 596; Sachs and Hunger, ADART II, no. -254; Stephenson, HEER, 133.
34729	Sp-II.219	Astronomical Diary. LBAT 597.

34730	Sp-II.220	Astronomical Diary. LBAT 592.
34731	Sp-II.221	Medical astrology. + Sp-II.799. LBAT 1597; Geller, Melosthesia, 80-82.
34732	Sp-II.222	Liver omens. CT 51, 116.
34733	Sp-II.223	Bilingual litany; two columns. + Sp-II.655. CT 51, 106.
34734	Sp-II.224	Joined to 32414.
	Sp-II.225	Joined to 34275.
34735	Sp-II.226	Bilingual religious. CT 51, 109.
34736	Sp-II.227	Astronomical Diary.
34737	Sp-II.228	Astronomical procedure text for the moon; System A. ACT 207c; LBAT 99; Ossendrijver, BMAPT, no. 71.
34738	Sp-II.229	Joined to 34452.
34739	Sp-II.230	Joined to 34274.
34740	Sp-II.231	Sumerian religious.
34741	Sp-II.232	Joined to 34625.
34742	Sp-II.233	Astronomical Diary. LBAT 595.
34743	Sp-II.234	Astronomical Diary. LBAT 599.
34744	Sp-II.235	Astrological omens; Enūma Anu Enlil 64; possibly continues obv. of 46236. LBAT 1559; Reiner, Fs Borger (CM 10), 294.
34745	Sp-II.236	Horoscopic astrology; conception of a child. + Sp-II.623. LBAT 1589.
34746	Sp-II.237	Sumerian incantation. CT 51, 107; Schramm, GBAO 2, p. 90, text B7.
34747	Sp-II.238	Bilingual religious. CT 51, 110; Schramm, GBAO 2, p. 90, text B6.
34748	Sp-II.239	Astronomical Diary. LBAT 586.
34749	Sp-II.240	Joined to 34590.
34750	Sp-II.241	Astronomical; Jupiter observations from year 18 of Artaxerxes II to year 13 of Artaxerxes III (387-345 BC). + 34832 + 35117 (+) 35328. LBAT 1395 and 1399-1400; Hunger and Sachs, ADART V, no. 60.
34751	Sp-II.242	Joined to 34600.
34752	Sp-II.243	Astronomical Diary.
34753	Sp-II.244	Astronomical Diary for SE 249. LBAT 520; Sachs and Hunger, ADART III, no. -62.
34754	Sp-II.245	Astronomical Diary for SE 216. LBAT 401; Sachs and Hunger, ADART III, no. -95 F.
34755	Sp-II.246	Astronomical Diary. + 45933.
34756	Sp-II.247	Astronomical Diary for SE 140. LBAT 225; Sachs and Hunger, ADART II, no. -171 A.
34757	Sp-II.248	Astronomical procedure text for Jupiter; mathematical rules for the area of a trapezoid. ACT 817; LBAT 151; Ossendrijver, BMAPT, no. 38; Ossendrijver,

		Science 351 (2016) 482-484, text B (and Supplementary Materials).
	Sp-II.249	Joined to 34651.
34758	Sp-II.250	Astronomical; Normal Star Almanac for SE 194; prayer on upper edge. + Sp-II.353 + 410 + 1882,0704.101. LBAT 1057; Hunger and Sachs, ADART VII, no. 90.
34759	Sp-II.251	Astronomical; Goal Year Text for SE 79. LBAT 1366; Hunger and Sachs, ADART VI, no. 4.
34760	Sp-II.252	Lexical; Ṭup abni; colophon; perhaps part of the same tablet as 34211 (+) 34211. CT 51, 88; Schuster-Brandis, AOAT 46, p. 333-340, Text 12; Simkó, NABU 2017, 185-188, no. 105.
	Sp-II.253	Joined to 34572.
34761	Sp-II.254	Astronomical Diary. LBAT 606.
34762	Sp-II.255	Mathematical; table of reciprocals. LBAT 1632.
34763	Sp-II.256	Astronomical Diary for SE 191. + 34825. LBAT 455 + 594; Sachs and Hunger, ADART III, no. -120.
34764	Sp-II.257	Mathematical; table of squares? LBAT 1640.
34765	Sp-II.258	Astronomical; synodic table for one or more planets and procedure text for Saturn; colophon. ACT 819c; LBAT 154; Ossendrijver, BMAPT, no. 45.
34766	Sp-II.259	Astronomical Diary. + 35037. LBAT 589 + 653.
34767	Sp-II.260	Omens; Šumma izbu 5. + Sp-II.467 + 35961. CT 51, 118 (34767 only); De Zorzi, Šumma izbu, 463.
34768	Sp-II.261	Ritual. CT 51, 99; Linssen, CM 25, 324.
34769	Sp-II.262	Bilingual religious. CT 51, 111.
34770	Sp-II.263	Lexical; Ḫḫ I (also registered in duplicate as Sp-II.963). + Sp-II.302 + 347 + 796. MSL 5, 5 (but add lines 336-348).
34771	Sp-II.263a	Astronomical; Jupiter, first stationary point and opposition, for (at least) SE 209 to 218; System A. ACT 607; LBAT 117.
34772	Sp-II.264	Astronomical Diary. LBAT 598.
34773	Sp-II.265	Literary; Theodicy. Lambert, BWL 63-89, pls. 19, 24.
34773a	Sp-II.265a	Astronomical Diary for SE 132. LBAT 348; Sachs and Hunger, ADART II, no. -179 B.
34774	Sp-II.266	Lexical; Diri IV. + Sp-II.568. CT 51, 80; S. A. Smith, MAT 12-14, pls. 25-26 (composite copy of 1882,0816.1 and of that part of 34774 which duplicates it); MSL 15 148.
34775	Sp-II.266a	Omens.
	Sp-II.267	Joined to 34727.
34776	Sp-II.268	Astrological; planets, zodiac, eclipses, locusts and earthquakes. + Sp-II.418 + 554. LBAT 1605.

34777	Sp-II.269	Contract. CT 51, 63.
34778	Sp-II.270	Joined to 32414.
34779	Sp-II.271	Chronicle. Grayson, TCS 5, Babylonian Chronicle Fragment 3.
34780	Sp-II.272	Astrological. CT 51, 126; Reiner, Fs Borger (CM 10), 294.
34781	Sp-II.273	Graeco-Babyloniaca; lexical, Syllabary B. + 35154. Sollberger, Iraq 24, 64, 72 and pls. XXV-XXVI, A1 +C5; Geller, ZA 87, 74-75 and 90, no. 7 (copy); Westenholz, ZA 97, 267-268.
34782	Sp-II.274	Astrological; Enūma Anu Enlil, Sin, eclipse. LBAT 1544; Reiner, Fs Borger (CM 10), 294.
34783	Sp-II.275	Astronomical; historical section.
34784	Sp-II.276	Unidentified. CT 51, 127.
34785	Sp-II.277	Astronomical Diary for SE 206. LBAT 591; Sachs and Hunger, ADART III, no. -105 C.
34786	Sp-II.278	Astronomical Diary. LBAT 588.
34787	Sp-II.279	Astronomical; lunar eclipse table for at least 442-406 BC. (+) 34684. LBAT 1426; Stephenson, HEER, 149, 153, 168-169, 181, 198-199; Hunger and Sachs, ADART V, no. 9.
34788	Sp-II.280	Astronomical Diary for SE 167. + Sp-II.1003 + 77617 + 78958 (+) 34609. LBAT 403-405; Sachs and Hunger, ADART III, no. -144.
	Sp-II.281	Joined to 34720.
34789	Sp-II.282	Astronomical procedure text for Jupiter, opposition to last visibility, for SE 171 to 243. System B. + 1881, 0706.293 + 297 + 35855. ACT 620a and 821a, colophon Zlb; LBAT 124-125; Ossendrijver, BMAPT, no. 36.
34790	Sp-II.283	Astronomical procedure text; lunar latitude; ziqpu stars; partly defining the path of the moon. LBAT 1502; Neugebauer, JCS 21, 202; Steele, Annals of Science 64 (2007) 293-325.
34791	Sp-II.284	Astronomical Diary for SE 216. LBAT 512; Sachs and Hunger, ADART III, no. -95 D.
34792	Sp-II.285	Astronomical Diary. LBAT 601; Sachs and Hunger, ADART I, no. -373 B.
34793	Sp-II.286	Historical-literary text; Nabopolassar epic. + Sp-II.525. Grayson, BHLT 78-86; Da Riva, JNES 76, 75-92.
34794	Sp-II.287	Astronomical Diary. + 34919 + 34990 + 35071 + 35329 + Sp-II.904. Sachs, PTRSL A.276, 48, fig. 6; LBAT 201-205; Sachs and Hunger, ADART I, no. -324 B.

34795	Sp-II.288	Astrological omens; Enūma Anu Enlil, Sin. + Sp-II.440. LBAT 1533; Reiner, Fs Borger (CM 10), 294.
34796	Sp-II.289	Ritual; two columns. CT 51, 100; Linssen, CM 25, 324.
34797	Sp-II.290	Graeco-Babyloniaca; lexical; Ḫḫ II. + Sp-III.247. Sollberger, Iraq 24, 64, A2; Pinches, PSBA 24 (1902) 111-112 and pl. II; MSL 5, 47; Geller, ZA 87, 68-69 and 87, no. 1 (copy); Westenholz, ZA 97, 263.
34798	Sp-II.291	Graeco-Babyloniaca; Tintir I. + Sp-III.311. Sollberger, Iraq 24, 67, B1; Pinches, PSBA 24 (1902) 117, pl. III; van der Meer, AfO 13, 124-126; George, BTT, pl. 6; Geller, ZA 87, 82-83, no. 16; Westenholz, ZA 97, 273.
34799	Sp-II.292	Graeco-Babyloniaca; lexical; Ḫḫ III. + 1881.0706. 142. Sollberger, Iraq 24, 66, and pl. XXV, A4; Geller, ZA 87, 70-71 and 88, no. 3 (copy); Westenholz, ZA 97, 264-265.
34800	Sp-II.293	Mathematical; problem text. LBAT 1647.
34801	Sp-II.294	Lexical; Syllabary B II. CT 51, 83.
34802	Sp-II.295	Joined to 34116.
34803	Sp-II.296	Astronomical; daily motion of the moon for SE 178 month VII. + 34815. ACT 81; LBAT 55-56.
34804	Sp-II.297	Ritual. CT 51, 97; Linssen, CM 25, 324.
	Sp-II.298	Joined to 34669.
34805	Sp-II.299	Astronomical Diary. LBAT 604.
	Sp-II.300	Joined to 34689.
34806	Sp-II.301	Astronomical Diary for SE 138. + 35610 + 35812 + 55569. LBAT 358 + 361 + 608 + 756; Sachs and Hunger, ADART II, no. -173 A.
	Sp-II.302	Joined to 34770.
	Sp-II.303	Joined to 34275.
	Sp-II.304	Joined to 34676.
34807	Sp-II.305	Joined to 34617.
34808	Sp-II.306	Astronomical Diary. LBAT 602.
34809	Sp-II.307	Omens; Iqqur īpuš, Nisannu. + 45820 + 55503 + 55505.
34810	Sp-II.308	Astronomical observations; Lunar Six for several years. LBAT 1453; Hunger and Sachs, ADART V, no. 44.
34811	Sp-II.309	Joined to 34599.
34812	Sp-II.310	Astronomical; Venus observations. LBAT 1490; Hunger and Sachs, ADART V, no. 89.
34813	Sp-II.311	Bilingual Šu'illa to Marduk; two columns. + Sp-II.600 + 35731. CT 51, 105 (34813 only); Cooper, Gs Sachs, 83-93.

34814	Sp-II.312	Astronomical; MUL.APIN. + 35708. LBAT 1496-1497; Hunger and Pingree, AfO Beih. 24, 3; Hunger and Steele, MUL.APIN, 20.
	Sp-II.313	Joined to 34718.
34815	Sp-II.314	Joined to 34803.
34816	Sp-II.315	Graeco-Babyloniaca; bilingual incantation, Udug-ḫul 9. 30/[]/-. + 1882,0704.139. Sollberger, Iraq 24, 69 and pl. XXVI, B2; Pinches and Sayce, PSBA 24 (1902) 116, 124; Gesche, AOAT 275, 670 (under wrong number 34916); Geller, ZA 87, 76-77 and 91, no. 11 (copy); Westenholz, ZA 97, 269-70; Geller, BAM 8, 302-322.
34817	Sp-II.316	Ritual. CT 51, 96; Linssen, CM 25, 324.
34818	Sp-II.317	Omens; Šumma izbu 10. CT 51, 119; De Zorzi, Šumma izbu, 608.
34819	Sp-II.318	Astronomical; Almanac. LBAT 1204; Hunger and Sachs, ADART VII, no. 167.
34820	Sp-II.318a	Lexical. CT 51, 85.
34821	Sp-II.319	Astronomical Diary for SE 170. LBAT 410; Sachs and Hunger, ADART III, no. -141 B.
34822	Sp-II.320	Contract; sale of land; mentions staters of Antiochus. SE. (+) 34856 (+) 35888. CT 51, 65; Kessler, RA 79, 87.
34823	Sp-II.321	Astronomical Diary for SE 138. + 55579 (+) 35166. LBAT 359 (34823 only); Sachs and Hunger, ADART II, no. -173 B.
34824	Sp-II.322	Ritual for 6th day of the month Nisannu. + 34842.
	Sp-II.323	Joined to 34085.
34825	Sp-II.324	Joined to 34763.
34826	Sp-II.325	Lexical; plants. CT 51, 86.
34827	Sp-II.326	Astronomical Diary for SE 190. (+) 35635. LBAT 603; Sachs and Hunger, ADART III, no. -121.
34828	Sp-II.327	Bilingual incantation; mīs pî IV; two columns. CT 51, 108; Walker and Dick, SAALT I, 156-188.
	Sp-II.328	Joined to 34211.
34829	Sp-II.329	Ritual; two columns. CT 51, 104; Linssen, CM 25, 324.
34830	Sp-II.330	Astronomical Diary. LBAT 609.
34831	Sp-II.331	Historical cylinder; duplicate not identified. CT 51, 76.
34832	Sp-II.332	Joined to 34750.
34833	Sp-II.333	Astronomical procedure text for the moon; System A. ACT 200a; Aaboe, AIHS 25/97 (1975), 191; LBAT 84; Ossendrijver, BMAPT, no. 55.

34834	Sp-II.334	Astronomical; Normal Star Almanac. LBAT 1073; Hunger and Sachs, ADART VII, no. 119.
34835	Sp-II.335	Promissory note for silver. CT 51, 66.
	Sp-II.336	Joined to 34275.
34836	Sp-II.337	Astronomical Diary. LBAT 605.
34837	Sp-II.338	Unidentified. CT 51, 128.
34838	Sp-II.339	Astronomical Diary. LBAT 615.
34839	Sp-II.340	Lexical. CT 51, 87.
34840	Sp-II.341	Contract; sale of a slave-girl; sealed. Art II/III 1/[]/9. Bi-ḫu.KI. + 34869 + 35280 + 35393 (+) 34183 + 34374 + 35192. CT 51, 67 (34840); CT 51, 68 (34869); Nisaba 28, no. 537.
34841	Sp-II.342	Astronomical Diary. LBAT 618.
34842	Sp-II.343	Joined to 34824.
34843	Sp-II.344	Astronomical Diary. LBAT 619.
34844	Sp-II.345	Literary cylinder; hymn to Nabû. Lambert, Fs Matouš II, 75-111. Gesche, AOAT 275, 670.
34845	Sp-II.346	Bilingual religious. CT 51, 112.
	Sp-II.347	Joined to 34770.
	Sp-II.348	Joined to 34428.
34846	Sp-II.349	Joined to 34081.
34847	Sp-II.350	Astronomical; System A lunar ephemeris. + 35127. ACT 12; LBAT 30-31.
34848	Sp-II.351	Liver omens; Pān tākalti Tablet 10. + Sp-II.502 + 35178. CT 51, 114; Neugebauer, Exact Sciences, pl. 14 (Sp-II.502 only); U. S. Koch-Westenholz, Babylonian Liver Omens, 377, no. 70.
34849	Sp-II.352	Astronomical; Goal Year Text for SE 107 or 108 or both. LBAT 1367; Hunger and Sachs, ADART VI, no. 19.
	Sp-II.353	Joined to 34758.
34850	Sp-II.354	Explanation of temple names. CT 51, 90; George, BTT, pl. 19.
34851	Sp-II.355	Astrological; fixed star names of planets; Dilbat (Venus); omens. LBAT 1576; Reiner, Fs Borger (CM 10), 294.
34852	Sp-II.356	Astronomical Diary for SE 212. LBAT 484; Sachs and Hunger, ADART III, no. -99 A.
34853	Sp-II.357	Joined to Rm.751.
34854	Sp-II.358	Astronomical; Normal Star Almanac for SE 66. + 55542. LBAT 1075 (34854 only); Hunger and Sachs, ADART VII, no. 16.
34855	Sp-II.359	Astronomical; Saturn for (at least) SE 201 to 224; System B. ACT 705; LBAT 137.

34856	Sp-II.360	Contract; sale of land. SE (+) 34822 (+) 35888. CT 49, 46, no. 178.
	Sp-II.361	Joined to 34685.
34857	Sp-II.362	Astronomical Diary. LBAT 620.
34858	Sp-II.363	Astronomical; full moons for (at least) one year. ACT 126a; LBAT 77.
34859	Sp-II.364	Lexical; Ḫḫ I. + Sp-II.376 + 571 + 635 + 46097 + 1881, 0706.556. MSL 5, 7.
	Sp-II.365	Joined to 34208.
34860	Sp-II.366	Physiognomic omens. CT 51, 121.
34861	Sp-II.367	Lexical; Nabnītu I. CT 51, 129; MSL 16, 339.
34862	Sp-II.368	Astronomical Diary. LBAT 612.
34863	Sp-II.369	Astronomical Diary. LBAT 617.
34864	Sp-II.370	Astronomical.
34865	Sp-II.371	Unidentified. CT 51, 130.
34866	Sp-II.372	Astronomical; Normal Star Almanac. LBAT 1074; Hunger and Sachs, ADART VII, no. 120.
34867	Sp-II.373	Astronomical; Goal Year Text for SE 182. LBAT 1273; Hunger and Sachs, ADART VI, no. 58.
34868	Sp-II.374	Astronomical; Normal Star Almanac for SE 187. + 34953. LBAT 1049-1050; Hunger and Sachs, ADART VII, no. 85.
34869	Sp-II.375	Joined to 34840. CT 51, 68.
	Sp-II.376	Joined to 34859.
34870	Sp-II.377	Astronomical Diary. LBAT 610.
34871	Sp-II.378	Astronomical Diary. LBAT 611.
34872	Sp-II.379	Astronomical Diary for SE 204. LBAT 471; Sachs and Hunger, ADART III, no. -107 A.
34873	Sp-II.380	Literary; Gilgameš VII. CT 46, 31, no. 25; Landsberger, RA 62, 123; George, Gilgamesh II, pl. 77.
34874	Sp-II.381	Astronomical; star list. Pinches, PSBA 34 (1912) 292-295 (col. i only); Weidner, AfO 19, 105-113.
34875	Sp-II.382	Mathematical; table of squares of regular numbers. LBAT 1638; Aaboe, JCS 19, 85-86.
34876	Sp-II.383	God list. CT 51, 91.
34877	Sp-II.384	Joined to 34624.
34878	Sp-II.385	Tintir V and Locations of cultic daises. CT 51, 92; Gurney, Iraq 36, 40; Unger, Babylon, 233-236, pls. 46-47; Wetzel and Unger, WVDOG 48, pl. 82; George, BTT, pl. 18; Oelsner, Materialien, 205; Linssen, CM 25, 324.
34879	Sp-II.386	Astrological omens; Enūma Anu Enlil 1. LBAT 1527; Reiner, Fs Borger (CM 10), 294; Verderame, Nisaba 2, 48-49.
34880	Sp-II.387	Astronomical Diary. LBAT 621.

34881	Sp-II.388	Astronomical; System A lunar ephemeris. ACT 8b; LBAT 21.
	Sp-II.389	Joined to 34095.
34882	Sp-II.390	Mathematical; geometrical problems with diagrams. + 34941 (+) 35381.
34883	Sp-II.391	Liver omens. CT 51, 113.
34884	Sp-II.392	Lexical. CT 51, 131.
34885	Sp-II.393	Astronomical Diary. LBAT 614.
34886	Sp-II.394	Liver omens. CT 51, 117.
34887	Sp-II.395	Astronomical Diary for SE 33. + 35400 + 45866. LBAT 235 + 500 + 616; Sachs and Hunger, ADART I, no. -278 B (not 34887).
	Sp-II.396	Joined to 34676.
34888	Sp-II.397	Astronomical; Normal Star Almanac for SE 157-158. + 35457 + 35788 + 35811 + 77269 + 99679 + Sp 3, 124. LBAT 1034-1037 + 1093; Hunger and Sachs, ADART VII, no. 71.
34889	Sp-II.398	Astronomical; Goal Year Text; not datable. LBAT 1364; Hunger and Sachs, ADART VI, no. 134.
34890	Sp-II.399	Astronomical; full moons for (at least) two years. + 34973 (+) 35120. ACT 129; LBAT 79-80; Neugebauer, Exact Sciences, pl. 14 (34973 = Sp-II.496 only).
34891	Sp-II.400	Astronomical Diary. LBAT 613.
34892	Sp-II.401	Astronomical Diary for SE 203. + 45646 + 45710 + 45985. LBAT 466 (45646) + 467 (45710) + 470 (34892); Sachs and Hunger, ADART III, no. -108 A.
34893	Sp-II.402	Astronomical Diary. LBAT 631.
	Sp-II.403	Joined to 34627.
	Sp-II.404	Joined to 34275.
34894	Sp-II.405	Joined to 32443.
34895	Sp-II.406	Theological list; series sa-a níg-gig an-šár, tablet 1; related to CBS 16.
34896	Sp-II.407	Joined to 34176.
34897	Sp-II.408	Astronomical Diary for SE 129. + 55575. LBAT 629 (34897 only); Sachs and Hunger, ADART II, no. -182 B.
34898	Sp-II.409	Contract; sale of land; sealed. CT 51, 69; Nisaba 28, no. 637.
	Sp-II.410	Joined to 34758.
34899	Sp-II.411	Prism; royal inscription of Esarhaddon; two columns. CT 51, 78; Brinkman, JAOS 103, 38; Leichty, RINAP 4.106.4.
34900	Sp-II.412	Joined to 34069.

34901	Sp-II.413	Mathematical; table; analysis of reciprocals? LBAT 1645.
34902	Sp-II.414	Ritual; two columns. CT 51, 102.
34903	Sp-II.415	Prophecy? CT 51, 122; cf. Grayson, BHLT 22, 24; Reiner, Fs Borger (CM 10), 294.
34904	Sp-II.416	Lexical. CT 51, 132.
34905	Sp-II.417	Promissory note for silver. Cam 7/3/2. Babylon. CT 51, 47.
	Sp-II.418	Joined to 34776.
34906	Sp-II.419	Astronomical; Goal Year Text; not datable. LBAT 1330; Hunger and Sachs, ADART VI, no. 135.
	Sp-II.420	Joined to 34626.
34907	Sp-II.421	Mathematical; table. LBAT 1643; Friberg and Al-Rawi, NMCT, Sec. 2.3.3.
34908	Sp-II.422	Literary. CT 51, 133.
34909	Sp-II.423	Unidentified. CT 51, 134.
34910	Sp-II.424	Astronomical Diary. LBAT 206.
	Sp-II.425	Joined to 34061.
34911	Sp-II.426	School text; lexical; Syllabary B. CT 51, 84.
34912	Sp-II.427	Lexical; Syllabary B. + Sp-II.857 + 900 + 982 + 1067 + Sp-III.393 + 745. CT 11, 21; MSL 3, 130.
34913	Sp-II.428	Astrological. LBAT 1621.
34914	Sp-II.429	Late Babylonian copy of the prologue to the Laws of Hammurabi. + 35051. Wiseman, Journal of Semitic Studies 7 (1962) 161-172.
34915	Sp-II.430	Astronomical Diary for SE 136. LBAT 357; Sachs and Hunger, ADART II, no. -175 B.
34916	Sp-II.431	Gilgameš I. + 35499. CT 46, 29, no. 17; Landsberger, RA 62, 117 n. 71; George, Gilgamesh II, pls. 48-49.
34917	Sp-II.432	Lexical; Hg. MSL 9, 185.
34918	Sp-II.433	Astronomical Diary for SE 177. + 35170 (+) 34669. LBAT 434 (34918); LBAT 683 (35170); Sachs and Hunger, ADART III, no. -134 B (not 35170)
34919	Sp-II.434	Joined to 34794.
34920	Sp-II.435	Astronomical Diary for SE 69. + 35786. LBAT 625 + 805; Sachs and Hunger, ADART II, no. -242.
34921	Sp-II.436	Astronomical.
34922	Sp-II.437	Joined to 34626.
34923	Sp-II.438	Astronomical Diary for SE 153. + 35624. LBAT 388 + 763; Sachs and Hunger, ADART III, no. -158 C.
34924	Sp-II.439	Astronomical.
	Sp-II.440	Joined to 34795.
	Sp-II.441	Joined to 34646.
34925	Sp-II.442	Literary.

34926	Sp-II.443	Astronomical Diary for SE 206. + 34937 + 34957 + 35558 + 35662 + 35776 + 45647 + 45700 + 46033 + 1881,0706.165. LBAT 477 + 479 + 480 + 481 + 622 + 627 + 749 + 777 + 809. Sachs and Hunger, ADART III, no. -105 A (but not 34926).
34927	Sp-II.444	Tintir IV and Explanations of temple names. George, BTT, pl. 10.
34928	Sp-II.445	Sumerian literary.
34929	Sp-II.446	Astronomical; lunar observations? LBAT 1331.
	Sp-II.447	Nothing registered.
34930	Sp-II.448	Astronomical Diary. LBAT 624.
34931	Sp-II.449	Joined to 34362.
	Sp-II.450	Joined to 34428.
34932	Sp-II.451	Astronomical; Goal Year Text for SE 158; prayer on upper edge. (+) 40866 + 41130 (+) 132286. LBAT 1262; Hunger and Sachs, ADART VI, no. 45.
34933	Sp-II.452	Lexical.
34934	Sp-II.453	Astronomical; System A ephemeris; auxiliary table for full moons for (at least) SE 49 to 60. + Sp-II.604. ACT 70; LBAT 51.
34935	Sp-II.454	Field plan.
34936	Sp-II.455	Astronomical Diary for SE 181. LBAT 444; Sachs and Hunger, ADART III, no. -130 D.
34937	Sp-II.456	Joined to 34926.
34938	Sp-II.457	Astronomical Diary for SE 114. + 45701. LBAT 275 + 315; Sachs and Hunger, ADART II, no. -197 C.
34939	Sp-II.458	Astronomical Diary for SE 131. LBAT 346; Sachs and Hunger, ADART II, no. -180 C.
34940	Sp-II.459	Astronomical; lunar eclipse report for eclipse of 8 January 66 BC. LBAT 1449; Hunger and Sachs, ADART V, no. 29.
34941	Sp-II.460	Joined to 34882.
34942	Sp-II.461	Astronomical. LBAT 1383.
34943	Sp-II.462	Astrological omens; Enūma Anu Enlil 57. Reiner, Fs Borger (CM 10), 294.
34944	Sp-II.463	Astronomical; Mars observations for SE 122-123. LBAT 1391; ADART V, no. 83.
34945	Sp-II.464	Sumerian literary; Dumuzi lament and rituals; Late Babylonian copy. Alster, Acta Sumerologica 7 (1985) 1-9.
34946	Sp-II.465	Astronomical; Goal Year Text for SE 231 and 232? LBAT 1258; Hunger and Sachs, ADART VI, no. 83.
34947	Sp-II.466	Astronomical Diary for SE 159. LBAT 399; Sachs and Hunger, ADART III, no. -152.
	Sp-II.467	Joined to 34767.

34948	Sp-II.468	Astronomical Diary. LBAT 623.
34949	Sp-II.469	Astronomical; Almanac for SE 185. LBAT 1139; Hunger and Sachs, ADART VII, no. 174.
34950	Sp-II.470	Lexical; Ea III. + Sp-III.178. CT 12, 30; MSL 14, 301; Landsberger, Gs Speiser, 133.
34951	Sp-II.471	Lexical; Diri IV. King, ZA 25, 302 (obv. only); MSL 15 148.
90694	Sp-II.472	Brick of Nebuchadnezzar II. CBI, no. 95.
34952	Sp-II.473	Omens.
34953	Sp-II.474	Joined to 34868.
34954	Sp-II.475	Astronomical Diary. LBAT 630.
34955	Sp-II.476	Astronomical Diary for SE 132. + 35032 + 35177. LBAT 349 + 626 + 644; Sachs and Hunger, ADART II, no. -179 C.
34956	Sp-II.477	Astronomical; Goal Year Text; not datable. LBAT 1332; Hunger and Sachs, ADART VI, no. 136.
34957	Sp-II.478	Joined to 34937.
34958	Sp-II.479	Mathematical table. + 42792. LBAT 1642; Ossendrijver, JCS 66, 149-165 and pls.; Friberg and Al-Rawi, NMCT, Sec. 2.3.2; 42792 is unpublished.
34959	Sp-II.480	Astronomical Diary for SE 158. + 35612. LBAT 633 + 760; Sachs and Hunger, ADART III, no. -153.
34960	Sp-II.481	Lexical.
	Sp-II.482	Joined to 34705.
34961	Sp-II.483	Literary.
34962	Sp-II.484	Astronomical Diary for SE 188. + 35190. LBAT 453 + 681; Sachs and Hunger, ADART III, no. -123 B.
34963	Sp-II.485	Astronomical; lunar eclipse table for at least 89-87 BC. + 35198 + 35238 + Sp-II unnum. LBAT 1334 + 1435 + 1443; Hunger and Sachs, ADART V, no. 23.
34964	Sp-II.486	Astronomical.
34965	Sp-II.487	Astronomical Diary.
34966	Sp-II.488	Astronomical; System A lunar ephemeris. + 35455. ACT 6b; LBAT 16-17.
34967	Sp-II.489	Astronomical Diary for SE 189. LBAT 637; Sachs and Hunger, ADART III, no. -122 E.
34968	Sp-II.490	Astronomical; Goal Year Text for SE 171. + Sp-II.579 + 35040. LBAT 1269-1270; Hunger and Sachs, ADART VI, no. 53.
	Sp-II.491	Joined to 34676.
34969	Sp-II.492	Astronomical; Goal Year Text for SE 185. + 35467. LBAT 1335 + 1344; Hunger and Sachs, ADART VI, no. 61.
34970	Sp-II.493	Literary cylinder; hymn to Nabû; dupl. Ebeling, Handerhebung, 110 (VAT 13649). Gesche, AOAT

		275, 670; cf. Lambert, Fs Matouš II, 75-111; Mayer, Or NS 59, 459-466, 480.
34971	Sp-II.494	Liver omens. Neugebauer, Exact Sciences, pl. 14 (Strassmaier copy).
34972	Sp-II.495	Astronomical Diary. LBAT 641.
34973	Sp-II.496	Joined to 34890.
34974	Sp-II.497	Contract; date in text. RN lost []/[]/14. Neugebauer, Exact Sciences, pl. 14 (Strassmaier copy).
34975	Sp-II.498	Astronomical Diary. LBAT 628; Neugebauer, Exact Sciences, pl. 14 (Strassmaier copy).
34976	Sp-II.499	Astronomical. Neugebauer, Exact Sciences, pl. 14 (Strassmaier copy).
34977	Sp-II.500	God list. + 35571. Neugebauer, Exact Sciences, pl. 14 (34977 only; Strassmaier copy).
34978	Sp-II.501	Astrological omens; Enūma Anu Enlil, Sin?; apodoses; eclipse. LBAT 1540; Neugebauer, Exact Sciences, pl. 14 (Strassmaier copy); Reiner, Fs Borger (CM 10), 294.
	Sp-II.502	Joined to 34848.
34979	Sp-II.503	Astronomical Diary for SE 216. LBAT 636; Sachs and Hunger, ADART III, no. -95 B.
34980	Sp-II.504	Astronomical Diary. LBAT 632.
34981	Sp-II.505	Astronomical Diary. LBAT 634.
34982	Sp-II.506	Ritual.
34983	Sp-II.507	Astronomical.
34984	Sp-II.508	Prayers; Šu'illa to Nusku no. 3, dupl. King, BMS 6: 28-35, etc.; Šu'illa to Ninurta-Sirius (Kaksisa) no. 1, dupl. BMS 49 1'-4'. Abusch and Schwemer, AMD 8/2 text 8.41 a; Mayer, Or NS 59, 466-469, 483.
34985	Sp-II.509	Astrological commentary (procedure). LBAT 1629.
34986	Sp-II.510	Astronomical Diary for SE 202. LBAT 635; Sachs and Hunger, ADART III, no. -109 B.
34987	Sp-II.511	Astronomical Diary. + 35131 + 35233. LBAT 167 + 639 + 670; Sachs and Hunger, ADART I, no. -381 A.
34988	Sp-II.512	Astronomical Diary for SE 113. LBAT 638; Sachs and Hunger, ADART II, no. -198 D.
34989	Sp-II.513	Commentary on a lexical or medical text.
34990	Sp-II.514	Joined to 34794.
34991	Sp-II.515	Astronomical; Almanac for SE 209; prayer on upper edge. + 35335 + 35988. LBAT 1154-1156; Hunger and Sachs, ADART VII, no. 185.
34992	Sp-II.516	Astronomical.
34993	Sp-II.517	Astronomical; fragment of ephemeris for (at least) one year. ACT 125c; LBAT 73.
34994	Sp-II.518	Lexical; Syllabary A. CT 11, 8; MSL 3, 7.

34995	Sp-II.519	Joined to 34176.
34996	Sp-II.520	Astronomical; Goal Year Text. LBAT 1484; Hunger and Sachs, ADART VI, no. 137.
34997	Sp-II.521	Astronomical.
34998	Sp-II.522	Astronomical.
34999	Sp-II.523	Omens; Šumma ālu, tablet 1.
35000	Sp-II.524	Bilingual historical-literary text of Nebuchadnezzar I. Frame, RIMB 2.4.9.4; Lambert, MC 24, no. 24.
	Sp-II.525	Joined to 34793.
35001	Sp-II.526	Astronomical; eclipse magnitudes for (at least) two years. ACT 125f; LBAT 74.
35002	Sp-II.527	Astronomical Diary. LBAT 642.
	Sp-II.528	Joined to 34641.
35003	Sp-II.529	Astrological; birīt SI.MEŠ / umāšišu adir. Reiner, Fs Borger (CM 10), 294.
35004	Sp-II.530	Bilingual incantation for the inauguration of a priest of Enlil. Borger, BiOr 30, 163-176.
35005	Sp-II.531	Astronomical Diary. LBAT 640.
35006	Sp-II.532	Astronomical; prices.
35007	Sp-II.533	Hemerology.
	Sp-II.534	Joined to 34720.
35008	Sp-II.535	Astronomical.
35009	Sp-II.536	Astronomical Diary. LBAT 648.
35010	Sp-II.537	Joined to 34067.
35011	Sp-II.538	Astronomical Diary for SE 135; prayer on upper edge. LBAT 188; Sachs and Hunger, ADART II, no. -176 A.
35012	Sp-II.539	Astronomical.
35013	Sp-II.540	Astronomical Diary. LBAT 651.
35014	Sp-II.541	Astronomical Diary. LBAT 643.
35015	Sp-II.542	Astronomical Diary for SE 147. + 35332 + 55531. LBAT 377 + 645; Sachs and Hunger, ADART II, no. -164 B.
35016	Sp-II.543	Astronomical Diary. LBAT 650.
35017	Sp-II.544	Contract; sale of land; finger-nail marks.
35018	Sp-II.545	Astrological; earthquake. Reiner, Fs Borger (CM 10), 294.
35019	Sp-II.546	Ritual. George, BTT, pl. 51; Linssen, CM 25, 324.
35020	Sp-II.547	Astronomical. + 35251.
35021	Sp-II.548	Sumerian religious; balag; Uruḫulake of Gula. Cohen, Canonical Lamentations pp. 796 and 837.
35022	Sp-II.549	Omens; Šumma izbu 16. De Zorzi, Šumma izbu, 726.
35023	Sp-II.550	Astronomical Diary for SE 23. LBAT 226; Sachs and Hunger, ADART I, no. -288.

35024	Sp-II.551	Astronomical Diary. + 35064 + 35087 + 35618 + 35632 + 45955. LBAT 198-200 + 625 + 764 (not 45955); Sachs and Hunger, ADART I, no. -324 A.
35025	Sp-II.552	Astronomical Diary.
35026	Sp-II.553	Joined to 34646.
	Sp-II.554	Joined to 34776.
35027	Sp-II.555	Astronomical.
35028	Sp-II.556	Contract; sale of fields. Wunsch, CM 20A-B, no. 96.
35029	Sp-II.557	Literary?
35030	Sp-II.558	Astronomical Diary for SE 102. LBAT 298; Sachs and Hunger, ADART II, no. -209 A.
35031	Sp-II.559	Chronicle about the digging of the Euphrates. SE. BCHP 20.
35032	Sp-II.560	Joined to 34955.
35033	Sp-II.561	Lexical; Ḫḫ VIII. MSL 7, 3.
35034	Sp-II.562	Astronomical Diary.
35035	Sp-II.563	Bilingual hymn to Nanâ; dupl. Reiner, JNES 33 (1974) 221-236.
35036	Sp-II.564	Astronomical; Goal Year Text for SE 181. (+) 35334. LBAT 1272; Hunger and Sachs, ADART VI, no. 57.
35037	Sp-II.565	Joined to 34766.
35038	Sp-II.566	Bilingual incantation.
35039	Sp-II.567	Astronomical; Almanac for SE 220. Strassmaier, ZA 3, 143; LBAT 1158; Hunger and Sachs, ADART VII, no. 186.
	Sp-II.568	Joined to 34774.
35040	Sp-II.569	Joined to 34968.
35041	Sp-II.570	Lexical.
	Sp-II.571	Joined to 34859.
35042	Sp-II.572	Astronomical Diary. LBAT 652.
35043	Sp-II.573	Astronomical Diary for SE 118. + 35211 (+) 41560 + 41632. LBAT 323 + 679; Sachs and Hunger, ADART II, no. -193 D.
	Sp-II.574	Joined to 34570.
35044	Sp-II.575	Astronomical observations; Lunar Six for several years. LBAT 1454; Hunger and Sachs, ADART V, no. 45.
	Sp-II.576	Joined to 34211.
35045	Sp-II.577	Astrological omens; Enūma Anu Enlil 64; colophon. + 46236. LBAT 1557 (35045 only); Reiner, Fs Borger (CM 10), 294, 299; Reiner and Pingree, BPO 4, 1-6, 8, 15-16, 40-45.
35046	Sp-II.578	Gates of Esangila. George, BTT, pl. 21; Linssen, CM 25, 324.
	Sp-II.579	Joined to 34968.

35047	Sp-II.580	Joined to 34710.
35048	Sp-II.581	Astronomical; System A lunar ephemeris. (+) 34630. ACT 11; LBAT 28.
35049	Sp-II.582	Astrological. LBAT 1608.
35050	Sp-II.583	Account of prebends.
35051	Sp-II.584	Joined to 34914.
35052	Sp-II.585	Literary?
35053	Sp-II.586	Astronomical Diary for SE 171. + 35815. LBAT 419 + 820; Sachs and Hunger, ADART III, no. -140 B.
35054	Sp-II.587	Astronomical Diary for SE 128. LBAT 339; Sachs and Hunger, ADART II, no. -183 E.
35055	Sp-II.588	Astrological omens.
35056	Sp-II.589	Bilingual incantation, Udug-ḫul 8. + 35191 + 35193 + Sp-II.746. CT 16, 27-29; Thompson, Devils I, 128-139; Geller, BAM 8, 288-301, pl. 66.
35057	Sp-II.590	Joined to 34671.
35058	Sp-II.591	Astronomical Diary for SE 125. LBAT 333; Sachs and Hunger, ADART II, no. -186 D.
35059	Sp-II.592	Astronomical; Normal Star Almanac for SE 212. + 35636 + 35638 + 35820. LBAT 1062-1065; Hunger and Sachs, ADART VII, no. 98.
35060	Sp-II.593	Astronomical Diary for SE 131. LBAT 345; Sachs and Hunger, ADART II, no. -180 A.
35061	Sp-II.594	Astrological; prophecy text; astrological protases. LBAT 1543; Biggs, Iraq 29, 128-132; Reiner, Fs Borger (CM 10), 294.
35062	Sp-II.595	Astronomical Diary. LBAT 649.
35063	Sp-II.596	Astronomical Diary for SE 108 or 238. LBAT 303.
35064	Sp-II.597	Joined to 35024.
35065	Sp-II.598	Astronomical Diary.
	Sp-II.599	Joined to 34208.
	Sp-II.600	Joined to 34813.
35066	Sp-II.601	Astronomical; Mercury observations, possibly for SE 258-259. LBAT 1379; Hunger and Sachs, ADART V, no. 84.
35067	Sp-II.602	Ritual?
35068	Sp-II.603	Literary. + 35116.
	Sp-II.604	Joined to 34934.
35069	Sp-II.605	Omens.
35070	Sp-II.606	Astronomical Diary for SE 179. + 45699. LBAT 438-439; Sachs and Hunger, ADART III, no. -132 B.
35071	Sp-II.607	Joined to 34794.
35072	Sp-II.608	Astrological medicine. (+) 47755 (+) 47913. LBAT 1622.
35073	Sp-II.609	Astrological. LBAT 1610.

35074	Sp-II.610	Astronomical.
35075	Sp-II.611	Astronomical Diary. LBAT 647.
35076	Sp-II.612	Astronomical; procedure text for the moon; System A s. LBAT 92; ACT 201a; Ossendrijver, BMAPT, no. 61E.
35077	Sp-II.613	School text; Šamaš hymn. Lambert, MC 24, no. 138.
35078	Sp-II.614	Astronomical procedure text for Jupiter, with data for SE 61-62. ACT 818; LBAT 152; Ossendrijver, BMAPT, no. 34.
35079	Sp-II.615	Literary; Gilgameš III. + Sp-II.621 + 35103. George, Gilgamesh II, pl. 68.
35080	Sp-II.616	Joined to 34216.
35081	Sp-II.617	Astronomical.
35082	Sp-II.618	Astronomical Diary. LBAT 654.
35083	Sp-II.619	Astronomical Diary. LBAT 663.
35084	Sp-II.620	Astronomical Diary. LBAT 657.
	Sp-II.621	Joined to 35079.
35085	Sp-II.622	Astronomical Diary. LBAT 656.
	Sp-II.623	Joined to 34745.
35086	Sp-II.624	Astronomical Diary for SE 202. + 46149 + 77619. LBAT 658 (35086 only); Sachs and Hunger, ADART III, no. -109 A.
35087	Sp-II.625	Joined to 35024.
35088	Sp-II.626	Astrological omens; Enūma Anu Enlil, Sin; eclipse. LBAT 1539; Reiner, Fs Borger (CM 10), 294.
35089	Sp-II.627	List of market prices for years 142-143 SE. + 45724. Slotsky and Wallenfels, Tallies and Trends, text 5.
35090	Sp-II.628	Astronomical; Normal Star Almanac for SE 177. LBAT 1076; Hunger and Sachs, ADART VII, no. 78.
35091	Sp-II.629	Astronomical Diary. LBAT 655.
35092	Sp-II.630	Astronomical; Normal Star Almanac. LBAT 1078; Hunger and Sachs, ADART VII, no. 121.
35093	Sp-II.631	Astronomical; Almanac for SE 168? + 77240. LBAT 1131 (35093 only); Hunger and Sachs, ADART VII, no. 168.
35094	Sp-II.632	Omens; Šumma ālu.
	Sp-II.633	Joined to 34428.
35095	Sp-II.634	Astronomical.
	Sp-II.635	Joined to 34859.
35096	Sp-II.636	Unidentified; 3 lines only.
35097	Sp-II.637	Astronomical.
	Sp-II.638	Joined to 34428.
35098	Sp-II.639	Astronomical; Almanac for SE 236. LBAT 1170; Hunger and Sachs, ADART VII, no. 191.
35099	Sp-II.640	Astronomical.

	Sp-II.641	Joined to 34061.
35100	Sp-II.642	Lexical.
35101	Sp-II.643	Astronomical.
35102	Sp-II.644	Astronomical. LBAT 1488.
35103	Sp-II.645	Joined to 35079.
35104	Sp-II.646	Astronomical.
	Sp-II.647	Joined to 34584.
35105	Sp-II.648	Astronomical Diary. LBAT 660.
35106	Sp-II.649	Lexical.
35107	Sp-II.650	Contract; sale of a house.
35108	Sp-II.651	Astronomical Diary. LBAT 662.
35109	Sp-II.652	Bilingual hymn to Nanâ. Reiner, JNES 33, 221-236.
	Sp-II.653	Joined to 34073.
35110	Sp-II.654	Astronomical Diary for SE 93. + 45725 + 45995 + 46133 + 46145 + 46169 + 46189. LBAT 238 + 292 + 293 (35110 + 45725 + 45995 only); Sachs and Hunger, ADART II, no. -218.
	Sp-II.655	Joined to 34733.
35111	Sp-II.656	Astronomical Diary for SE 141. LBAT 368; Sachs and Hunger, ADART II, no. -179 F.
35112	Sp-II.657	Astronomical Diary. + 35124. LBAT 661 + 664.
35113	Sp-II.658	Historical; mentions Ashurbanipal; tablet fragment.
35114	Sp-II.659	Egibi archive. + 36559.
35115	Sp-II.660	Astronomical; lunar eclipse table for at least 703-360 BC. + 35789 + 45640. LBAT 1415-1417; Stephenson, HEER, 88, 122, 149, 151, 162-164, 169-170, 175 (as 45640), 194-196 (as 45640), 206 (as 45640); Hunger and Sachs, ADART V, no. 3.
35116	Sp-II.661	Joined to 35068.
35117	Sp-II.662	Joined to 34750.
35118	Sp-II.663	Astronomical; Venus, evening star, for (at least) SE 187 to 204; System A2? ACT 421; LBAT 113.
35119	Sp-II.664	Joined to 34221.
35120	Sp-II.665	Astronomical; full moons for (at least) two years. (+) 34890 + 34973. ACT 129; LBAT 81.
	Sp-II.666	Joined to 34073.
35121	Sp-II.667	Astronomical; Goal Year Text; datable only to Arsaces. LBAT 1333; Hunger and Sachs, ADART VI, no. 138.
35122	Sp-II.668	Astrological omens; Enūma Anu Enlil 64. + Sp-II.755. Reiner, Fs Borger (CM 10), 294; Reiner and Pingree, BPO 4, 3, 82-85.
35123	Sp-II.669	Joined to 34073.
35124	Sp-II.670	Joined to 35112.

35125	Sp-II.671	Astronomical; procedure text for the moon; System A. ACT 201aa; LBAT 93; Ossendrijver, BMAPT, no. 61F.
35126	Sp-II.672	Astronomical Diary. + 35722. LBAT 675 + 795.
35127	Sp-II.673	Joined to 34847.
35128	Sp-II.674	Astronomical.
35129	Sp-II.675	Astronomical Diary. LBAT 667.
35130	Sp-II.676	Astronomical Diary. LBAT 668.
35131	Sp-II.677	Joined to 34847.
35132	Sp-II.678	Astronomical Diary. LBAT 669.
35133	Sp-II.679	Astronomical Diary. LBAT 666.
35134	Sp-II.680	Literary; Enūma eliš I. King, STC pl. VII; Lambert, BCM, p. 47.
35135	Sp-II.681	Astronomical Diary for SE 186. LBAT 448; Sachs and Hunger, ADART III, no. -125 B.
35136	Sp-II.682	Hemerology.
	Sp-II.683	Joined to 34428.
35137	Sp-II.684	Promissory note for silver. Dar -/4/28. Babylon.
35138	Sp-II.685	Fable of the fox.
35139	Sp-II.686	School text; personal names.
	Sp-II.687	Joined to 34668.
35140	Sp-II.688	Receipt for silver and vats.
35141	Sp-II.689	Astronomical.
	Sp-II.690	Joined to 34428.
35142	Sp-II.691	Astronomical; Normal Star Almanac. LBAT 1079; Hunger and Sachs, ADART VII, no. 122.
35143	Sp-II.692	Joined to 34362.
35144	Sp-II.693	Economic.
35145	Sp-II.694	Astronomical Diary for SE 248. LBAT 519; Sachs and Hunger, ADART III, no. -63.
	Sp-II.695	Joined to 34208.
35146	Sp-II.696	Astronomical Diary. LBAT 672.
35147	Sp-II.697	Contract; sealed. d.l. Nisaba 28, no. 638.
35148	Sp-II.698	School text.
35149	Sp-II.699	Astronomical; Almanac for SE 220. LBAT 1157; Hunger and Sachs, ADART VII, no. 187.
	Sp-II.700	Joined to 34669.
	Sp-II.701	Joined to 34208.
35150	Sp-II.702	Astronomical; System A lunar ephemeris. ACT 14; LBAT 35.
35151	Sp-II.703	Astronomical.
35152	Sp-II.704	Joined to 34079.
35153	Sp-II.705	Astronomical Diary. + 35158. LBAT 671 + 676.
35154	Sp-II.706	Joined to 34781.
35155	Sp-II.707	Astronomical Diary. LBAT 673.

35156	Sp-II.708	Joined to 34223.
35157	Sp-II.709	Promissory note for dates. Cam []/2?/[]. Araḫtu.
35158	Sp-II.710	Joined to 35153.
35159	Sp-II.711	Astronomical; Normal Star Almanac for SE 71. (+) 35167. LBAT 1086; Hunger and Sachs, ADART VII, no. 21.
35160	Sp-II.712	Medical; same as 35205.
35161	Sp-II.713	Astronomical; ziqpu stars? LBAT 1508.
35162	Sp-II.714	Astronomical procedure text for the moon; System A; colophon? ACT 203; LBAT 94; Ossendrijver, BMAPT, no. 63.
35163	Sp-II.715	Joined to 34110.
35164	Sp-II.716	Lexical; GI.
35165	Sp-II.717	Astronomical Diary for SE 81. LBAT 665; Sachs and Hunger, ADART II, no. -230 D.
35166	Sp-II.718	Astronomical Diary for SE 138. (+) 34823 + 55579. LBAT 360; Sachs and Hunger, ADART II, no. -173 B.
35167	Sp-II.719	Astronomical; Normal Star Almanac for SE 71. (+) 35159. LBAT 1081; Hunger and Sachs, ADART VII, no. 21.
35168	Sp-II.720	Astronomical; Goal Year Text; not datable. LBAT 1336; Hunger and Sachs, ADART VI, no. 139.
35169	Sp-II.721	Economic. 10/11/11.
35170	Sp-II.722	Joined to 34918.
35171	Sp-II.723	Incantation.
35172	Sp-II.724	Astrological; perhaps Enūma Anu Enlil. LBAT 1625.
35173	Sp-II.725	Liver omens.
35174	Sp-II.726	Joined to 34160.
35175	Sp-II.727	Astronomical.
	Sp-II.728	Joined to 34066.
35176	Sp-II.729	Lexical.
35177	Sp-II.730	Joined to 34955.
35178	Sp-II.731	Joined to 34848.
35179	Sp-II.732	Astronomical Diary. LBAT 680.
35180	Sp-II.733	Contract; sale of a house.
35181	Sp-II.734	Astronomical; Goal Year Text for SE 107. LBAT 1235; Hunger and Sachs, ADART VI, no. 17.
35182	Sp-II.735	Ritual. CT 51, 103.
35183	Sp-II.736	Astronomical Diary. Mitsuma, Orient 53 (1983) 55-68.
35184	Sp-II.737	Astronomical Diary. LBAT 186; Sachs and Hunger, ADART I, no. -366 B; Stephenson, HEER, 154.
35185	Sp-II.738	Astronomical Diary. LBAT 684.
35186	Sp-II.739	Literary.

35187	Sp-II.740	Astronomical; Almanac for SE 198. + 35737. LBAT 1148-1149; Hunger and Sachs, ADART VII, no. 182.
35188	Sp-II.741	Mythological-calendrical text; colophon. Partial duplicate to the astral-mythological text 55466+. + 55484 + 55551 + 55633. Reynolds, Fs Walker, 215-227 (on part of 55551 only); Finkel, Board Games, 30 (on the colophon); J. Koch, JCS 58, 123-135 (on the duplicate).
35189	Sp-II.742	Chronicle about Bagayasha. SE (Arsaces). + Sp-III.295 + 46018 + 46216 (+) 35229 + 35518 + 35621. BCHP 18a.
35190	Sp-II.743	Joined to 34962.
35191	Sp-II.744	Joined to 35056 + Sp-II.746.
35192	Sp-II.745	Joined to 34183. Nisaba 28, no. 537.
	Sp-II.746	Joined to 35056.
35193	Sp-II.747	Literary; catalogue of songs?
35194	Sp-II.748	Administrative; involves the assembly of Esangila. SE + Sp-II.1056.
35195	Sp-II.749	Astronomical Diary. LBAT 171; Sachs and Hunger, ADART I, no. -378.
35196	Sp-II.750	Astronomical; planetary observations (Mercury and Venus). LBAT 1386; Hunger and Sachs, ADART V, no. 53.
	Sp-II.751	Joined to 34615.
35197	Sp-II.752	Ritual.
35198	Sp-II.753	Joined to 34963.
35199	Sp-II.754	Astronomical Diary for SE 116. + 35845 + 35919. LBAT 317 + 819; Sachs and Hunger, ADART II, no. -195 A.
	Sp-II.755	Joined to 35122.
35200	Sp-II.756	Astronomical Diary. LBAT 682.
35201	Sp-II.757	Astronomical Diary for SE 180. LBAT 442; Sachs and Hunger, ADART III, no. -131 A.
35202	Sp-II.758	Contract?; sealed. SE d.l. CT 49, 48, no. 185; Nisaba 28, no. 615.
	Sp-II.759	Joined to 34601.
35203	Sp-II.760	Astronomical procedure for the moon, eclipses and ephemeris for the years SE 60 and 61. ACT 200h; LBAT 90; Ossendrijver, BMAPT, no. 98.
35204	Sp-II.761	Ritual.
35205	Sp-II.762	Medical; same as 35160.
35206	Sp-II.763	Joined to 34221.
35207	Sp-II.764	Astronomical; MUL.APIN. LBAT 1498; Hunger and Pingree, AfO Beih. 24, 3; Hunger and Steele, MUL.APIN, 21.

35208	Sp-II.765	Astronomical Diary for SE 203. LBAT 468; Sachs and Hunger, ADART III, no. -108 C.
35209	Sp-II.766	Omens; Iqqur īpuš, Nisannu. LBAT 1590.
35210	Sp-II.767	School text.
35211	Sp-II.768	Joined to 35043.
	Sp-II.769	Joined to 34677.
35212	Sp-II.770	Astronomical Diary. + Sp-II.923 + Sp-III.304 + 77235. LBAT 179-180; Sachs and Hunger, ADART I, no. -372 E.
35213	Sp-II.771	Literary.
35214	Sp-II.772	Account of dates or grain.
35215	Sp-II.773	Omens; Šumma ālu 41; dupl. CT 28, 38. Freedman, If a city, vol. 3, 3, 253.
35216	Sp-II.774	Astronomical Diary. LBAT 678.
35217	Sp-II.775	Contract. 18/5/-. Babylon.
35218	Sp-II.776	Astronomical.
	Sp-II.777	Joined to 34078.
35219	Sp-II.778	Prophecy?
35220	Sp-II.779	Astronomical Diary for SE 135. LBAT 356; Sachs and Hunger, ADART II, no. -176 B.
35221	Sp-II.780	Astronomical; Goal Year Text for SE 135 (date corrected by Hunger). LBAT 1247; Hunger and Sachs, ADART VI, no. 30.
35222	Sp-II.781	Astronomical Diary. LBAT 685.
	Sp-II.782	Joined to 34588.
	Sp-II.783	Joined to 34428.
35223	Sp-II.784	Astronomical; Goal Year Text; not datable. LBAT 1337; Hunger and Sachs, ADART VI, no. 140.
	Sp-II.785	Joined to 34712.
35224	Sp-II.786	Literary; colophon. SE 7/3/213 (= AE 149). Babylon. + Sp-II.791.
35225	Sp-II.787	Account of dates income.
35226	Sp-II.788	Astronomical Diary. LBAT 689.
35227	Sp-II.789	Literary.
35228	Sp-II.790	Astronomical; Goal Year Text for SE 122. LBAT 1241.
	Sp-II.791	Joined to 35224.
35229	Sp-II.792	Chronicle about Bagayasha. SE (Arsaces). + 35518 + 35621 (+) 35189 + 46018 + 46216. BCHP 18b.
35230	Sp-II.793	Astronomical; observations; Venus for SE 80-81. LBAT 1480; Hunger and Sachs, ADART V, no. 75.
	Sp-II.794	Joined to 34710.
	Sp-II.795	Joined to 34659.
	Sp-II.796	Joined to 34770.

35231	Sp-II.797	Astronomical; System A ephemeris; eclipses for (at least) 7 years. + 35355. ACT 54; LBAT 47-48; Aaboe, KDVSMM 40/6 (1979) 16-18.
35232	Sp-II.798	Astronomical Diary. LBAT 688.
	Sp-II.799	Joined to 34731.
35233	Sp-II.800	Joined to 34977.
35234	Sp-II.801	Omens; Šumma ālu? CT 51, 123
35235	Sp-II.802	Joined to 31722.
35236	Sp-II.803	Administrative list of writing boards (GIŠ.DA); cf. 38216.
35237	Sp-II.804	Astrological. LBAT 1613.
35238	Sp-II.805	Joined to 34963.
35239	Sp-II.806	Astronomical Diary. LBAT 686.
35240	Sp-II.807	Astronomical Diary. LBAT 698.
35241	Sp-II.808	Astronomical procedure text for Jupiter. ACT 819b; LBAT 153; Ossendrijver, BMAPT, no. 27.
35242	Sp-II.809	Astrological; Enūma Anu Enlil, Sin. LBAT 1548; Reiner, Fs Borger (CM 10), 294.
35243	Sp-II.810	Astronomical Diary. LBAT 687.
35244	Sp-II.811	Astronomical Diary. LBAT 690.
35245	Sp-II.812	Literary; Gilgameš VII. CT 46, 31, no. 24; Landsberger, RA 62, 128; George, Gilgamesh II, pl. 77.
35246	Sp-II.813	Omens; extispicy.
35247	Sp-II.814	Lexical.
35248	Sp-II.815	Unidentified; 2 lines only.
35249	Sp-II.816	Astronomical.
35250	Sp-II.817	Administrative; two-column list of names.
35251	Sp-II.818	Joined to 35020.
35252	Sp II.819	Unidentified.
35253	Sp-II.820	Astronomical procedure text for the moon; System A. ACT 206; LBAT 97; Ossendrijver, BMAPT, no. 68.
35254	Sp-II.821	Astronomical.
35255	Sp-II.822	Joined to 34624.
35256	Sp-II.823	Receipt for barley.
	Sp-II.824	Joined to 34452.
35257	Sp-II.825	Astronomical Diary. LBAT 691.
35258	Sp-II.826	Astronomical; Mars, stationary points, System A. ACT 503; LBAT 114.
35259	Sp-II.827	Lexical.
35260	Sp-II.828	Astronomical; ziqpu stars? LBAT 1511.
35261	Sp-II.829	Astronomical Diary. LBAT 692.
35262	Sp-II.830	Astronomical Diary. LBAT 697.
35263	Sp-II.831	Unidentified. CT 51, 135.
35264	Sp-II.832	Mathematical; tables.
35265	Sp-II.833	Astronomical Diary. LBAT 696.

35266	Sp-II.834	Astronomical Diary. LBAT 695.
35267	Sp-II.835	Astronomical.
35268	Sp-II.836	Mathematical; two columns.
35269	Sp-II.837	Astronomical Diary. + 35347 + 35358. LBAT 700 + 720 (35269 + 35358 only).
35270	Sp-II.838	Astronomical Diary. LBAT 701.
35271	Sp-II.839	Astronomical; observations of an outer planet. LBAT 1492; Hunger and Sachs, ADART V, no. 90.
35272	Sp-II.840	Lexical.
35273	Sp-II.841	Colophon of a two-column tablet; dated by [A]-lik-sa-an-dar LUGAL. Alex III.
35274	Sp-II.842	Astronomical Diary. LBAT 699.
35275	Sp-II.843	Astronomical Diary. + Sp-II.844. LBAT 694.
	Sp-II.844	Joined to 35275.
35276	Sp-II.845	Astronomical Diary. LBAT 693.
35277	Sp-II.846	Astronomical; Mercury, evening star, for (at least) SE 224 to 226; System A1. ACT 304; LBAT 103.
35278	Sp-II.847	Astronomical; Goal Year Text; not datable. LBAT 1338; Hunger and Sachs, ADART VI, no. 141.
35279	Sp-II.848	Astronomical Diary. LBAT 703.
35280	Sp-II.849	Joined to 34840.
35281	Sp-II.850	Omens or lexical.
35282	Sp-II.851	Astronomical; System A lunar ephemeris. LBAT 22; ACT 9.
35283	Sp-II.852	Astronomical Diary. LBAT 702.
35284	Sp-II.853	Astronomical.
35285	Sp-II.854	Prayer to Marduk no. 2. Lambert, MC 24, no. 109.
35286	Sp-II.855	Ritual.
35287	Sp-II.856	Astronomical Diary. LBAT 704.
	Sp-II.857	Joined to 34912.
35288	Sp-II.858	Astronomical; System A lunar ephemeris. ACT 8; LBAT 19.
35289	Sp-II.859	Astronomical Diary. LBAT 705.
35290	Sp-II.860	Astronomical Diary. LBAT 706.
35291	Sp-II.861	Astronomical Diary. LBAT 707.
35292	Sp-II.862	Astronomical Diary. LBAT 708.
35293	Sp-II.863	Astronomical.
35294	Sp-II.864	Astronomical Diary. LBAT 709.
35295	Sp-II.865	Astronomical; Goal Year Text; not datable. LBAT 1341; Hunger and Sachs, ADART VI, no. 142.
35296	Sp-II.866	Astronomical Diary. LBAT 710.
35297	Sp-II.867	Astronomical Diary. LBAT 713.
35298	Sp-II.868	Lexical.
35299	Sp-II.869	Contract; ú-il-tim.
35300	Sp-II.870	Astronomical Diary. LBAT 711.

35301	Sp-II.871	Astronomical; System A lunar ephemeris. LBAT 32; ACT 12.
35302	Sp-II.872	Astronomical.
35303	Sp-II.873	Astronomical Diary; historical section; mentions Alexander.
35304	Sp-II.874	Astronomical.
35305	Sp-II.875	Astronomical Diary. LBAT 715.
	Sp-II.876	Joined to 34570.
35306	Sp-II.877	Astronomical; Jupiter, opposition, for (at least) SE 239 to 247; System A'? ACT 614; LBAT 123.
35307	Sp-II.878	Astronomical Diary. LBAT 712.
35308	Sp-II.879	Astronomical Diary. LBAT 716.
35309	Sp-II.880	Lexical.
35310	Sp-II.881	Astronomical.
35311	Sp-II.882	Astronomical; Jupiter, for (at least) 14 years; System B. + 35783. ACT 625a; LBAT 131-132.
35312	Sp-II.883	Astronomical Diary. LBAT 714.
35313	Sp-II.884	Astronomical Diary. LBAT 717.
35314	Sp-II.885	Astronomical; Almanac for SE 236. + 35484 + 35755 (+) 35687. LBAT 1171 + 1205 + 1209 (+) 1173; Hunger and Sachs, ADART VII, no. 191.
35315	Sp-II.886	Prayer; colophon.
35316	Sp-II.887	Contract; sale of land.
35317	Sp-II.888	Astronomical; Goal Year Text for SE 245. LBAT 1300; Hunger and Sachs, ADART VI, no. 88.
35318	Sp-II.889	Astronomical; Jupiter from opposition to last visibility, for (at least) SE 187 to 230; System A'. + 35426. ACT 612; LBAT 120-121.
35319	Sp-II.890	Prayers.
35320	Sp-II.891	Liver omens. + 45612. Duplicates Clay, BRM.4 13.
35321	Sp-II.892	Bilingual incantations; unidentified, Udug-ḫul 9. Geller, BAM 8, 302-322, pl. 71.
35322	Sp-II.893	Historical-literary text about the Kassite period. Grayson, BHLT 47-55.
35323	Sp-II.894	Astronomical Diary for SE 124. LBAT 330; Sachs and Hunger, ADART II, no. -187 B.
	Sp-II.895	Joined to 34676.
35324	Sp-II.896	Joined to 34079.
35325	Sp-II.897	Astrological. LBAT 1600.
35326	Sp-II.898	Astrological; Enūma Anu Enlil, Sin. LBAT 1529; Reiner, Fs Borger (CM 10), 294.
35327	Sp-II.899	Astrological omens; Šamaš; commentary.
	Sp-II.900	Joined to 34912.
35328	Sp-II.901	Astronomical; Jupiter observations from year 18 of Artaxerxes II to year 13 of Artaxerxes III (387-345

		BC); colophon. (+) 34750. LBAT 1394; Hunger and Sachs, ADART V, no. 60.
35329	Sp-II.902	Joined to 34794 + Sp-II.904.
35330	Sp-II.903	Astronomical Diary for SE 127. LBAT 336; Sachs and Hunger, ADART II, no. -184 B. Stephenson, HEER, 185.
	Sp-II.904	Joined to 34794.
35331	Sp-II.905	Astronomical Diary for SE 118. LBAT 324; Sachs and Hunger, ADART II, no. -193 B. Stephenson, HEER, 156-157.
35332	Sp-II.906	Joined to 35015.
35333	Sp-II.907	Astronomical Diary. LBAT 181; Sachs and Hunger, ADART I, no. -370.
35334	Sp-II.908	Astronomical; Goal Year Text for SE 181. + 35696 (+) 35036. LBAT 1298 + 1345; Hunger and Sachs, ADART VI, no. 57.
35335	Sp-II.909	Joined to 34991.
35336	Sp-II.910	Astronomical Diary?
35337	Sp-II.911	Astrological; Enūma Anu Enlil, Sin; commentary. LBAT 1541; Reiner, Fs Borger (CM 10), 294.
35338	Sp-II.912	Promissory note for silver. Dar []/[]/17. Babylon. Dar 462.
35339	Sp-II.913	Astronomical; observations; Mercury for SE 83-85; Mars for SE 82-84 and SE 50-52; the Goal Years are SE 129-131. + Sp-II.1047 + 46235 + 46242. LBAT 1374-1376; Hunger and Sachs, ADART V, no. 76; Roughton, AOAT 297, 367-378 (as BM 46235+).
35340	Sp-II.914	Astronomical; Normal Star Almanac for SE 203. LBAT 1060; Hunger and Sachs, ADART VII, no. 94.
35341	Sp-II.915	Astronomical; Goal Year Text for SE 186. (+) 34658. LBAT 1279; Hunger and Sachs, ADART VI, no. 62.
35342	Sp-II.916	Astronomical; Goal Year Text for SE 188. LBAT 1282; Hunger and Sachs, ADART VI, no. 64.
35343	Sp-II.917	Astronomical Diary for SE 128. + 41008. LBAT 337 (35343 only); Sachs and Hunger, ADART II, no. -183 A.
35344	Sp-II.918	Astronomical Diary. LBAT 719.
35345	Sp-II.919	Promissory note for onions; Egibi archive. Nbn 18/9/-.
35346	Sp-II.920	Astronomical Diary. LBAT 718.
35347	Sp-II.921	Joined to 35269.
35348	Sp-II.922	Joined to 34160.
	Sp-II.923	Joined to 35212.
35349	Sp-II.924	Hemerology for several months. Jiménez, JCS 68, 197-227. (+) 34584.

	Sp-II.925	Joined to 34677.
35350	Sp-II.926	Liver omens.
35351	Sp-II.927	Astronomical; Mars observations. LBAT 1392; Hunger and Sachs, ADART V, no. 91.
35352	Sp-II.928	Liver omens; commentary; martu. + 35412.
35353	Sp-II.929	Astrological; UDUN ana Sin TE/DAR-ma DU. LBAT 1566; Reiner, Fs Borger (CM 10), 294.
35354	Sp-II.930	Astronomical. SE -/-/128.
35355	Sp-II.931	Joined to 35231.
35356	Sp-II.932	Astronomical; System A lunar ephemeris. LBAT 24; ACT 9.
35357	Sp-II.933	Astronomical Diary. LBAT 721.
35358	Sp-II.934	Joined to 35269.
35359	Sp-II.935	Astronomical Diary. LBAT 722.
	Sp-II.936	Joined to 34095.
35360	Sp-II.937	Literary.
35361	Sp-II.938	Astronomical Diary. LBAT 724.
35362	Sp-II.939	Sumerian literary; balag; d.utu-gin7 è-ta. Gabbay and Mirelman, ZA 101, 281 and n. 14.
35363	Sp-II.940	Promissory note for barley. 6/4/11. Babylon.
35364	Sp-II.941	Astrological. LBAT 1609.
35365	Sp-II.942	Economic.
35366	Sp-II.943	Astronomical; Almanac for SE 175. + 36020. LBAT 1132-1133; Hunger and Sachs, ADART VII, no. 169.
35367	Sp-II.944	Astrological omens.
35368	Sp-II.945	Astronomical.
35369	Sp-II.946	Astronomical; daylight and shadow scheme.
35370	Sp-II.947	Omens; Šumma ālu or dream omens.
35371	Sp-II.948	Astronomical.
35372	Sp-II.949	Astronomical; Normal Star Almanac for SE 188. (+) 35623 + 35904 + 55582. LBAT 1082; Hunger and Sachs, ADART VII, no. 86.
35373	Sp-II.950	Astronomical Diary. LBAT 732.
35374	Sp-II.951	Astronomical Diary. LBAT 725.
35375	Sp-II.952	Astronomical Diary. LBAT 726.
35376	Sp-II.953	Astronomical; Almanac. LBAT 1206; Hunger and Sachs, ADART VII, no. 222.
	Sp-II.954	Joined to 34720.
	Sp-II.955	Joined to 34576.
	Sp-II.956	Joined to 34686.
35377	Sp-II.957	Astronomical Diary. LBAT 169; Sachs and Hunger, ADART I, no. -380 A.
35378	Sp-II.958	Promissory note for sesame.
35379	Sp-II.959	Literary cylinder; hymn to Nabû. Gesche, AOAT 275, 670.

35380	Sp-II.960	Literary; Gilgameš XI. CT 46, 35-36, no. 35; George, Gilgamesh II, pls. 140-141.
35381	Sp-II.961	Mathematical; geometrical problems with diagrams. (+) 34882 + 34941.
	Sp-II.962	Joined to 34062.
	Sp-II.963	L. W. King's note in the register says that 963 was a re-registration of 263.
35382	Sp-II.964	The Nabonidus Chronicle. S. Smith, BHT, 98-123, pls. XI-XIV; Grayson, TCS 5, Chronicle 7; George, BiOr 53, 379 (new copy of col. iii 24-28).
35383	Sp-II.965	Missing.
35384	Sp-II.966	Missing.
35385	Sp-II.967	Plan of part of Babylon, with metrological commentary; similar to 36780 reverse. CT 22, 49; George, BTT, pl. 28.
35386	Sp-II.968	Joined to 32443.
35387	Sp-II.969	Astronomical; Goal Year Text for SE 142. LBAT 1253. Stephenson, HEER, 136, 140; Hunger and Sachs, ADART VI, no. 36.
35388	Sp-II.970	Astronomical; Goal Year Text for SE 96; note that LBAT 1225 rev. line 3 referring back to SE 49 anomalously attributes this year to Antiochus and Seleucus; cf. also LBAT 1224 obv. 9. LBAT 1225; Hunger and Sachs, ADART VI, no. 10.
35389	Sp-II.971	Late Babylonian copy of an inscription of Šulgi about the building of a temple of Meslamtaea. CT 9, 3; Steible, FAOS 9/2 Šulgi A 4b; Frayne, RIME 3/2.1.2.24.
35390	Sp-II.972	Astronomical observations; Lunar Six for three years. LBAT 1455; Hunger and Sachs, ADART V, no. 46.
35391	Sp-II.973	Lexical; Syllabary B. + Sp-III.430. CT 51, 81.
35392	Sp-II.974	Astronomical Diary. LBAT 723.
35393	Sp-II.975	Joined to 34840. Nisaba 28, no. 537.
35394	Sp-II.976	Šà-zi-ga incantation; four columns.
35395	Sp-II.977	Astronomical.
35396	Sp-II.978	Astronomical Diary.
35397	Sp-II.979	Joined to 34223.
35398	Sp-II.980	Joined to 34455.
35399	Sp-II.981	Astronomical; procedure text for the moon; System A; prayer on upper edge. ACT 201, colophon Zr; Neugebauer, JCS 7, 100-102; LBAT 91; Ossendrijver, BMAPT, no. 61A.
	Sp-II.982	Joined to 34912.
35400	Sp-II.983	Joined to 34887.

35401	Sp-II.984	Commentary; cf. CBS 16 and LKU 45; see Civil, AfO 25, 67; cf. 35686, 40130 and 45733. + 55485 + 99685 + 99669.
35402	Sp-II.985	Horoscopic astrology; zodiologia and list of planetary periods; part dupl. Rm.832 and 40113. LBAT 1593; Reiner, Fs Lambert, 421-427.
35403	Sp-II.986	Omens; Iqqur īpuš; obv. I = paragraphs 8, 9 of the series.
35404	Sp-II.987	Historical-literary text; one of the "Chedorlaomer" texts. Pinches, JTVI 29 (1897) 43-89; Jeremias, MVAG 21 (1916) 69-97; Brinkman, PHPKB, 80-81, 361, 396; Lambert, MC 24, no. 30.
35405	Sp-II.988	Literary; Theodicy. + Sp-II.1001. Lambert, BWL 63-89, pl. 20.
	Sp-II.989	Joined to 34691.
	Sp-II.990	Joined to 34568.
35406	Sp-II.991	Astronomical Diary for SE 110. LBAT 729.
35407	Sp-II.992	Literary. + 35644 + 55507.
35408	Sp-II.993	Astrological; commentary; DAR-ma DU; astronomical procedure text for the moon; colophon. LBAT 1571a; Reiner, Fs Borger (CM 10), 294.
35409	Sp-II.994	Astrological omens.
35410	Sp-II.995	Astronomical Diary. LBAT 727.
35411	Sp-II.996	Astronomical Diary for SE 181. LBAT 728; Sachs and Hunger, ADART III, no. -130 A.
35412	Sp-II.997	Joined to 35352.
35413	Sp-II.998	Joined to 34160.
35414	Sp-II.999	Astronomical Diary. LBAT 734.
35415	Sp-II.1000	Astronomical Diary. LBAT 735.
	Sp-II.1001	Joined to 35405.
35416	Sp-II.1002	Astronomical Diary. LBAT 733.
	Sp-II.1003	Joined to 34788.
35417	Sp-II.1004	Joined to 34642.
35418	Sp-II.1005	Joined to 34728.
35419	Sp-II.1006	Joined to 34916.
35420	Sp-II.1007	Astronomical; Goal year Text for SE 207. LBAT 1291; Stephenson and Walker, Halley's Comet 35-36; Hunger and Sachs, ADART VI, no. 77.
35421	Sp-II.1008	Chronicle about Seleucus III. Grayson, TCS 5, Chronicle 13b; Pinches, BOR 6, 36; BCHP 12; Linssen, CM 25, 84 n. 445.
35422	Sp-II.1009	Joined to 34362 + Sp-III.89.
35423	Sp-II.1010	Late Babylonian copy of an Old Babylonian inscription.

35424	Sp-II.1011	Astronomical Diary for SE 107. Sachs and Hunger, ADART II, no. -204 C; Linssen, CM 25, 84.
	Sp-II.1012	Joined to 35331.
35425	Sp-II.1013	Hemerology.
35426	Sp-II.1014	Joined to 35318.
35427	Sp-II.1015	Bilingual incantation, Udug-ḫul 10 + 35428. Geller, BAM 8, 323-339, pl. 83.
35428	Sp-II.1016	Joined to 35427.
35429	Sp-II.1017	Astronomical; Almanac for SE 305. LBAT 1195; Sachs and Walker, Iraq 46, 43-55, pl. I; Hunger and Sachs, ADART VII, no. 211.
35430	Sp-II.1018	Literary cylinder; hymn to Nabû. Gesche, AOAT 275, 671.
35431	Sp-II.1019	Astronomical Diary.
35432	Sp-II.1020	Ritual and incantation to procure a dream oracle.
35433	Sp-II.1021	Joined to 34671.
35434	Sp-II.1022	Sumerian literary; colophon, DUB 2.
35435	Sp-II.1023	Contract.
35436	Sp-II.1024	Contract; sale of land.
35437	Sp-II.1025	Contract.
35438	Sp-II.1026	Omens; terrestrial.
35439	Sp-II.1027	Sumerian literary.
35440	Sp-II.1028	Literary.
	Sp-II.1029	Joined to 34275.
35441	Sp-II.1030	Sale of a slave girl by Lâbâši; sealed. Nisaba 28, no. 543a.
35442	Sp-II.1031	Astronomical.
35443	Sp-II.1032	Joined to 34281.
35444	Sp-II.1033	Promissory note for silver.
35445	Sp-II.1034	Joined to 34221.
35446	Sp-II.1035	Sumerian literary.
35447	Sp-II.1036	Astronomical Diary.
35448	Sp-II.1037	School text; practice wedges.
35449	Sp-II.1038	Incantation.
35450	Sp-II.1039	Liver omens.
35451	Sp-II.1040	Incantation.
35452	Sp-II.1041	Promissory note for silver.
35453	Sp-II.1042	Astronomical; Goal Year Text for SE 201 and 202. (+) 34405 (+) 34509 (+) 41958 + 132275. LBAT 1339; Hunger and Sachs, ADART VI, no. 73.
35454	Sp-II.1043	Astronomical; lunar or planetary table.
35455	Sp-II.1044	Joined to 34966.
35456	Sp-II.1045	Astronomical; microzodiac rising time scheme. LBAT 1505; Steele, Rising time schemes, 69-73.
35457	Sp-II.1046	Joined to 34888.

	Sp-II.1047	Joined to 35339.
35458	Sp-II.1048	Graeco-Babyloniaca; lexical, Syllabary A. + 77807 + unnum. Sollberger, Iraq 24, 71, and pl. XXVI, C2; Geller, ZA 87, 72-73 and 89, no. 5 (copy); Westenholz, ZA 97, 265-266.
35459	Sp-II.1049	Graeco-Babyloniaca; lexical, Syllabary A. + unnum. Sollberger, Iraq 24, 71, and pl. XXVI, C3; Geller, ZA 87, 72-73 and 89 (copy).
35460	Sp-II.1050	Unidentified.
35461	Sp-II.1051	Physiognomic omens.
35462	Sp-II.1052	Literary.
35463	Sp-II.1053	Astronomical; Mercury observations for SE 13. LBAT 1382; Hunger and Sachs, ADART V, no. 92.
35464	Sp-II.1054	Astronomical; Normal Star Almanac for SE 200. LBAT 1207; Hunger and Sachs, ADART VII, no. 92.
35465	Sp-II.1055	Astronomical; Normal Star Almanac. LBAT 1083; Hunger and Sachs, ADART VII, no. 123.
	Sp-II.1056	Joined to 35194.
35466	Sp-II.1057	Incantation.
35467	Sp-II.1058	Joined to 34969.
35468	Sp-II.1059	Astronomical; Normal Star Almanac. LBAT 1084; Hunger and Sachs, ADART VII, no. 124.
35469	Sp-II.1060	Astronomical.
35470	Sp-II.1061	Astronomical.
35471	Sp-II.1062	Astronomical Diary? LBAT 1489.
35472	Sp-II.1063	Astronomical.
35473	Sp-II.1064	Astronomical Diary. LBAT 737.
35474	Sp-II.1065	Literary cylinder; hymn to Nabû.
35475	Sp-II.1066	Astronomical; Goal Year Text for SE 236. + 35879 + 47874. LBAT 1340 + 1343 (35475 and 35879 only); Hunger and Sachs, ADART VI, no. 85.
	Sp-II.1067	Joined to 34912.
35476	Sp-II.1068	Astronomical; Normal Star Almanac. LBAT 1080; Hunger and Sachs, ADART VII, no. 125.
35477	Sp-II.1069	Astronomical Diary. LBAT 738.
35478	Sp-II.1070	Astronomical Diary. LBAT 736.
35479	Sp-II.1071	Astronomical Diary. + 35573. LBAT 730 + 748.
35480	Sp-II.1072	Joined to 33057.
35481	Sp-II.1073	Astronomical; Normal Star Almanac. LBAT 1085; Hunger and Sachs, ADART VII, no. 126.
35482	Sp-II.1074	Astronomical Diary. LBAT 741.
35483	Sp-II.1075	Astronomical.
35484	Sp-II.1076	Joined to 35314.
35485	Sp-II.1077	Astronomical.
35486	Sp-II.1078	Astronomical Diary. LBAT 740.

35487	Sp-II.1079	Astronomical Diary. LBAT 742.
35488	Sp-II.1080	Lexical.
35489	Sp-II.1081	Astronomical.
35490	Sp-II.1082	Astronomical Diary. LBAT 744.
35491	Sp-II.1083	Astrological. LBAT 1623.
35492	Sp-II.1084	Contract; sale of land. Wunsch, AfO 42/43, 54-55, no. 4b.
35493	Sp-II.1085	Astronomical Diary. LBAT 743.
35494	Sp-II.1086	Omens.

Sp-III collection

The Sp-III collection was purchased from Messrs. Spartali & Co., London, in May 1880. The register gives the provenance Babylon to nos. 1-615 and the provenance Babylonia to nos. 616-831.

35495	Sp-III.1	Astronomical procedure text; Venus, evening and morning star, for SE 180 to 242; System A1 and A2. + 40102 + 42819 + 42873 + 46176 + 1881,0201.77. ACT 420 and 821b, colophon Zld: LBAT 106; Steele, SCIAMVS 11 (2010), 211-239, text I; Ossendrijver, BMAPT, no. 7; 42819 and 42873 are unpublished.
35496	Sp-III.2	Historical-literary text; one of the "Chedorlaomer" texts. Pinches, JTVI 29 (1897) 43-89; Jeremias, MVAG 21 (1916) 69-97; Brinkman, PHPKB, 361, 396; Lambert, MC 24, no. 29.
35497	Sp-III.3	Omens; terrestrial.
35498	Sp-III.4	Bilingual hymn (so register); missing.
35499	Sp-III.5	Omens; terrestrial.
35500	Sp-III.6	Lexical; Ḫḫ VIII. + 45899 + 1881,0706.739. MSL 7, 3; Pinches, PSBA 16 (1894), 308-311; Oelsner, Materialien, 223.
35501	Sp-III.7	Astronomical; observations; Jupiter for SE 11-16, 20-25, 47-50; Mars for SE 46, 48-50. + Sp-III.98 + 35532 + 35713. LBAT 1402 + 1403 + 1410; Hunger and Sachs, ADART V, no. 70.
35502	Sp-III.8	Astrological omens; Enūma Anu Enlil, Sin; colophon. LBAT 1532; Reiner, Fs Borger (CM 10), 294.
35503	Sp-III.9	Lexical; Ḫḫ IX-XI. CT 14, 47; MSL 7, 34, 73, 122.
35504	Sp-III.10	Astrological omens; Enūma Anu Enlil, Sin; commentary. LBAT 1531; Reiner, Fs Borger (CM 10), 294.
35505	Sp-III.11	List of gods' names.
35506	Sp-III.12	Literary; Enūma eliš VII. + 99642. King, STC pl. XLVI-XLVIII; Lambert, BCM, p. 123, pl. 27.
35507	Sp-III.13	Astronomical; System A lunar ephemeris; new and full moons for (at least) one year. ACT 22, colophon

		Zkd; Aaboe, KDVSMM 40/6 (1979) 33-35; LBAT 43.
35508	Sp-III.14	Court record about division of an inheritance; sealed; the year number is on Bertin's copy but is now lost on the tablet. Nbk []/[]/12. [Babylon]. (+) 38259. Bertin 1068-1069; Wunsch, Bab Arch 2, 138-145, no. 42; Nisaba 28, no. 1a.
35509	Sp-III.15	Astrological; commentary. LBAT 1577; Reiner, Fs Borger (CM 10), 294.
35510	Sp-III.16	Astronomical Diary. LBAT 745.
35511	Sp-III.17	Astronomical; ziqpu stars? LBAT 1513.
35512	Sp-III.18	Medical prescriptions; colophon. + Sp-III.77.
35513	Sp-III.19	Promissory note for barley. Dar 6/5/26. Babylon. Bertin 2598.
35514	Sp-III.20	Astronomical Diary for SE 180. LBAT 443; Bertin 2980; Sachs and Hunger, ADART III, no. -131.
35515	Sp-III.21	Horoscope; prayer on upper edge. SE (Arsaces) 25/5/236. LBAT 1474; Rochberg, Babylonian Horoscopes, no. 26; Bertin 2922; Rochberg-Halton, Or NS 58, 117-119 and pl. II.
35516	Sp-III.22	Horoscope. SE Demetrius II 6/12/169. LBAT 1467; Rochberg, Babylonian Horoscopes, no. 18; Strassmaier, ZA 3, 149, no. 11; Sachs, JCS 6, 62-64; Kugler, SSB, 555.
35517	Sp-III.23	Receipt for delivery of dates.
35518	Sp-III.24	Joined to 35229.
35519	Sp-III.25	Account of issues of silver. SE Arsaces 10/5?/218. CT 49, 39, no. 158; van der Spek, Raḫimesu, 220-221, no. 11; Bertin 2926.
35520	Sp-III.26	Letter.
35521	Sp-III.27	School text; practice dictation.
35522	Sp-III.28	Lexical.
35523	Sp-III.29	Contract.
35524	Sp-III.30	Lexical; list of verbal forms.
35525	Sp-III.31	Astronomical Diary for SE 143. LBAT 373; Sachs and Hunger, ADART II, no. -168 D.
35526	Sp-III.32	Sale of a slave. Xerxes 15/6/5. Babylon. Bertin 2849.
35527	Sp-III.33	Promissory note for silver. Cam 1/4/1. Babylon. Bertin 1773.
35528	Sp-III.34	Promissory note for silver. Nbn 28/9/2. Nbn 82; Bertin 1242; Wunsch, CM 3, no. 108.
35529	Sp-III.35	Receipt for payment of silver. Cam 23/5/2. Bertin 1799; Wunsch, CM 3, no. 325.
35530	Sp-III.36	Ritual.

35531	Sp-III.37	Astronomical; Jupiter observations from Artaxerxes II year 43 to Alexander year 13. + 45706 + 46031 + 1881,0706.344 (+) 45740. LBAT 1397 + 1401; Hunger and Sachs, ADART V, no. 66.
35532	Sp-III.38	Joined to 35501.
35533	Sp-III.39	Astronomical procedure text for Jupiter. Ossendrijver, JNES 76, 231-247, text B.
35534	Sp-III.40	Astronomical; Goal Year Text for SE 216. LBAT 1342; Hunger and Sachs, ADART VI, no. 80.
35535	Sp-III.41	Liver omens.
35536	Sp-III.42	Astronomical Diary. LBAT 191; Sachs and Hunger, ADART I, no. -342 B.
35537	Sp-III.43	Astrological. LBAT 1626; Geller, Melosthesia, 58-59.
35538	Sp-III.44	Astrological omens; Enūma Anu Enlil 5. LBAT 1525; Reiner, Fs Borger (CM 10), 294; Verderame, Nisaba 2, 158-159.
35539	Sp-III.45	Contract; sale of a house. Nbn 22/1/9. Babylon. Nbn 323; Bertin 1352.
35540	Sp-III.46	Joined to 34671.
35541	Sp-III.47	Astronomical Diary. LBAT 750.
35542	Sp-III.48	Astronomical; Normal Star Almanac for SE 116. + 35577 + 35608. LBAT 1021 + 1087 + 1090; Hunger and Sachs, ADART VII, no. 50.
35543	Sp-III.49	Astronomical; small fragment only; remainder of tablet apparently missing in 1976.
35544	Sp-III.50	Bilingual incantation, Udug-ḫul 1. Geller, BAM 8, 44-58, pl. 6.
35545	Sp-III.51	Astronomical.
35546	Sp-III.52	Joined to Rm.751.
35547	Sp-III.53	Astrological omens; Enūma Anu Enlil 5. LBAT 1521; Reiner, Fs Borger (CM 10), 294; Verderame, Nisaba 2, 160-163.
35548	Sp-III.54	List of grain disbursements.
35549	Sp-III.55	Astronomical.
35550	Sp-III.56	Astronomical; Normal Star Almanac. LBAT 1088; Hunger and Sachs, ADART VII, no. 127.
35551	Sp-III.57	Astronomical; Almanac for SE 183. LBAT 1137; Hunger and Sachs, ADART VII, no. 173.
35552	Sp-III.58	Incantations; Maqlu I. Abusch, AMD 10, 23-49.
35553	Sp-III.59	Ṣâtu commentary on Šumma izbu; cf. 38588.
35554	Sp-III.60	School text; practice signs.
35555	Sp-III.61	List of persons who guard the Adad gate; Egibi archive?
	Sp-III.62	Joined to 34620.

35556	Sp-III.63	Omens; extispicy; isru 3rd tablet; compare 32207. Babylon.
35557	Sp-III.64	"Aluzinnu text"; dupl. 2R 60, no. 1. (+) 77251 (not joining as said in CBTBM VIII).
35558	Sp-III.65	Joined to 34937.
35559	Sp-III.66	Administrative decision (date lost) about employment of astronomers, referring to an earlier contract dated 15/10/193 SE. CT 49, 33, no. 144; van der Spek, BiOr 42, 551-552; Rochberg, Fs Oelsner, 359-375.
35560	Sp-III.67	Letter; names of sender and addressee lost. Hackl et al., AOAT 414/1, no. 84.
35561	Sp-III.68	Astronomical Diary. LBAT 176; Sachs and Hunger, ADART I, no. -372 C.
35562	Sp-III.69	Astronomical; Almanac for SE 201; colophon; prayer on upper edge. LBAT 1151; Hunger and Sachs, ADART VII, no. 184.
35563	Sp-III.70	Account of disbursements on specific days to prebend holders. Npl 4/11/1.
35564	Sp-III.71	Astronomical procedure text for the moon; System A. + 40081 (+) 77256. ACT 207d; Ossendrijver, BMAPT, no. 79.
35565	Sp-III.72	Promissory note for dates.
35566	Sp-III.73	Astronomical Diary for SE 207. Sachs and Hunger, ADART III, no. -104.
35567	Sp-III.74	Literary; Gilgameš II. George, Gilgamesh II, pl. 53.
35568	Sp-III.75	Mathematical; table of squares of six place numbers, starting with 1,0,45 ending with 1,58,31,6,40; followed by catch-line of the square of 2,1,4,8,3,0,27. Friberg and Al-Rawi, NMCT, Sec. 1.2.1.
35569	Sp-III.76	Astronomical Diary. LBAT 746.
	Sp-III.77	Joined to 35512.
35570	Sp-III.78	Astronomical; Almanac for SE 300; prayer on upper edge. + 1881,0706.205 + 35602. LBAT 1188-1189; Hunger and Sachs, ADART VII, no. 208.
35571	Sp-III.79	Joined to 34977.
35572	Sp-III.80	Bilingual chronicle. Duplicates the Dynastic Chronicle (Grayson, TCS 5, Chronicle 18). Finkel, JCS 32, 65-72, 76.
35573	Sp-III.81	Joined to 35479.
35574	Sp-III.82	Lexical; Nabnītu XVIII. MSL 16, 169, 313.
35575	Sp-III.83	Contract; sale of land.
35576	Sp-III.84	Astronomical Diary for SE 132. LBAT 751; Sachs and Hunger, ADART II, no. -179 A.
35577	Sp-III.85	Joined to 35542.

35578	Sp-III.86	Commentary. + 35683.
35579	Sp-III.87	Contract; sale of fields, houses and slaves; sealed. Dupl 30122 etc. Babylon. [Cyr] [6]/[3]/[4]. Babylon. Wunsch, CM 20A-B, no. 125 E; Nisaba 28, no. 89.
35580	Sp-III.88	Sumerian literary.
	Sp-III.89	Joined to 35422.
35581	Sp-III.90	Astronomical; Normal Star Almanac for SE 137. + 35650 + 35714 + 35725 + 35984 + 36035. LBAT 1027 + 1028 + 1091 + 1092 + 1094 + 1101; Hunger and Sachs, ADART VII, no. 59.
35582	Sp-III.91	Omens; Šumma ālu, tablet 1. + Sp-III.180 + 188 + 338. CT 38, 2-6; Freedman, If a city, vol. 1, 25.
35583	Sp-III.92	Missing.
35584	Sp-III.93	Astronomical; Normal Star Almanac for SE 42. LBAT 1089; Hunger and Sachs, ADART VII, no. 8.
35585	Sp-III.94	Astronomical; Jupiter for (at least) SE 217 to 237; System A? ACT 608; LBAT 115.
35586	Sp-III.95	Lexical; Syllabary B. + 93030. CT 12, 31 (35586); CT 11 19 (93030); MSL 3, 1330-1331.
35587	Sp-III.96	Astronomical; Goal Year Text for SE 150? LBAT 1346; Hunger and Sachs, ADART VI, no. 42.
35588	Sp-III.97	Bilingual incantation.
	Sp-III.98	Joined to 35501.
35589	Sp-III.99	Bilingual eršema prayer. Gabbay, HES 2, 43-55, no. 3.
35590	Sp-III.100	Lexical.
35591	Sp-III.101	Astronomical Diary. LBAT 752.
35592	Sp-III.102	Promissory note for barley. Nbn 27/9/10. Babylon. Nbn 459; Bertin 1383.
35593	Sp-III.103	Incantation.
35594	Sp-III.104	Ritual.
35595	Sp-III.105	Ritual.
35596	Sp-III.106	Astronomical Diary. LBAT 753.
35597	Sp-III.107	Astronomical Diary. LBAT 757.
35598	Sp-III.108	Astronomical Diary. LBAT 755.
35599	Sp-III.109	Astronomical Diary. LBAT 758.
35600	Sp-III.110	Contract; sale of land.
35601	Sp-III.111	Astronomical Diary for SE 204. LBAT 754; Sachs and Hunger, ADART III, no. -107 B.
35602	Sp-III.112	Joined to 35570.
35603	Sp-III.113	The Hellenistic King List. Sachs and Wiseman, Iraq 16, 202-241; Grayson, RlA 7, 98-100.
35604	Sp-III.114	Joined to 34686.
35605	Sp-III.115	Astronomical Diary for SE 143. LBAT 372; Sachs and Hunger, ADART II, no. -168 B.

35606	Sp-III.116	Astronomical; solar eclipse report for eclipse of 30 January 10 BC. LBAT 1456; Hunger and Sachs, ADART V, no. 31; Steele, Archaeological Sciences '97 (BAR International Series 939 2001), 208-211.
35607	Sp-III.117	Omens.
35608	Sp-III.118	Joined to 35542.
35609	Sp-III.119	Ritual.
35610	Sp-III.120	Joined to 34806.
35611	Sp-III.121	Bilingual incantation, Udug-ḫul 3. + Sp-III.315. CT 16, 1-8; Thompson, Devils I, 1-29; Geller, BAM 8, 89-132.
35612	Sp-III.122	Joined to 34959.
35613	Sp-III.123	Measurements of the sides and area of a plot of land.
	Sp-III.124	Joined to 34888.
35614	Sp-III.125	Astrological; commentary. LBAT 1570.
35615	Sp-III.126	Ritual?
35616	Sp-III.127	Astronomical Diary. LBAT 767.
35617	Sp-III.128	Omens.
35618	Sp-III.129	Joined to 35024.
35619	Sp-III.130	Astronomical; Goal Year Text.
35620	Sp-III.131	Astronomical; Almanac for SE 195. LBAT 1145; Hunger and Sachs, ADART VII, no. 179.
35621	Sp-III.132	Joined to 35229.
35622	Sp-III.133	Literary; fable of the duqduqqu-bird (wren); colophon. Jiménez, BDP, 334, 338-341; Lambert, MC 24, no. 277.
35623	Sp-III.134	Astronomical; Normal Star Almanac for SE 188. + 35904 + 55582 (+) 35372. LBAT 1054 + 1097 (35623 + 35904 only); Hunger and Sachs, ADART VII, no. 86.
35624	Sp-III.135	Joined to 34923.
35625	Sp-III.136	Ritual.
	Sp-III.137	Joined to 34568.
35626	Sp-III.138	Astronomical Diary. LBAT 759.
35627	Sp-III.139	Contract.
35628	Sp-III.140	Joined to 34160.
35629	Sp-III.141	Astronomical Diary for SE 20. + 45734 + 46016. LBAT 221-223; Sachs and Hunger, ADART I, no. -291 A.
35630	Sp-III.142	Promissory note for barley.
35631	Sp-III.143	Medical.
35632	Sp-III.144	Joined to 35024.
35633	Sp-III.145	Astronomical Diary. LBAT 762.
35634	Sp-III.146	Astronomical Diary. LBAT 761.

35635	Sp-III.147	Astronomical Diary for SE 190. (+) 34827. LBAT 769; Sachs and Hunger, ADART III, no. -121.
35636	Sp-III.148	Joined to 35059. Bertin 2923.
35637	Sp-III.149	Astronomical; Normal Star Almanac for SE 192. + 35640. LBAT 1056; Hunger and Sachs, ADART VII, no. 89.
35638	Sp-III.150	Joined to 35059.
35639	Sp-III.151	Astronomical Diary. LBAT 766.
35640	Sp-III.152	Joined to 35637.
35641	Sp-III.153	Astrological omens.
35642	Sp-III.154	Astronomical Diary. LBAT 765.
35643	Sp-III.155	Astronomical Diary.
35644	Sp-III.156	Joined to 35407.
35645	Sp-III.157	Astronomical Diary. LBAT 771.
35646	Sp-III.158	Astronomical Diary. LBAT 773.
35647	Sp-III.159	Astronomical Diary. LBAT 775.
35648	Sp-III.160	Ritual.
35649	Sp-III.161	Astronomical.
35650	Sp-III.162	Joined to 35581.
35651	Sp-III.163	Astronomical Diary for SE 145. LBAT 770; Sachs and Hunger, ADART II, no. -166 B.
35652	Sp-III.164	Astronomical Diary. LBAT 772.
	Sp-III.165	Joined to 34645.
35653	Sp-III.166	Astronomical Diary.
35654	Sp-III.167	Astronomical.
35655	Sp-III.168	Astronomical.
35656	Sp-III.169	Astronomical.
35657	Sp-III.170	Astronomical Diary. LBAT 768.
35658	Sp-III.171	Astronomical Diary. LBAT 774.
	Sp-III.172	Joined to 34659.
35659	Sp-III.173	Astronomical; System A lunar ephemeris. + 35951. ACT 24; LBAT 44-45.
35660	Sp-III.174	Astronomical Diary for SE 45. LBAT 776.
35661	Sp-III.175	Joined to 34604.
35662	Sp-III.176	Joined to 34937.
35663	Sp-III.177	Ritual.
	Sp-III.178	Joined to 34950.
35664	Sp-III.179	Ledger.
	Sp-III.180	Joined to 35582.
35665	Sp-III.181	Astronomical.
35666	Sp-III.182	Lexical; Nabnītu I. MSL 16, 339, 345.
35667	Sp-III.183	Grain ledger.
35668	Sp-III.184	Astronomical.
35669	Sp-III.185	Astronomical; Jupiter for (at least) SE 185 to 197; System A. ACT 604a; LBAT 116.

35670	Sp-III.186	Omens; Šumma ālu; opening of a well.
35671	Sp-III.187	Historical inscription of Nebuchadnezzar II. Berger, AOAT 4/1, Nebukadnezar Tontafel-Fragment I,2.
	Sp-III.188	Joined to 35582.
35672	Sp-III.189	Incantation against witchcraft. Abusch and Schwemer, AMD 8/2 text 7.23 a, pl. 20; Schwemer, WO 41, 184-187.
35673	Sp-III.190	Astronomical Diary for SE 113. + 46185. LBAT 780 (35673 only); Sachs and Hunger, ADART II, no. -198 C.
	Sp-III.191	Joined to 34223.
35674	Sp-III.192	Promissory note for silver. Cyr 1/2/4. Babylon.
35675	Sp-III.193	Contract; transfer of property. Wunsch, Bab Arch 2, 86, no. 24.
35676	Sp-III.194	Astronomical; Jupiter, last visibility, for SE 171 to (at least) 180. ACT 620b.
35677	Sp-III.195	Astronomical Diary for SE 192. + 35684 + 36009 (+) 35810. LBAT 782 + 785 (35677 and 35684); Sachs and Hunger, ADART III, no. -119 A.
35678	Sp-III.196	Astronomical.
35679	Sp-III.197	Joined to 34362.
35680	Sp-III.198	Astronomical Diary. LBAT 781.
35681	Sp-III.199	Promissory note for dates. Cam 28/-/-.
35682	Sp-III.200	Astronomical Diary. LBAT 779.
35683	Sp-III.201	Joined to 35578.
35684	Sp-III.202	Joined to 35677.
35685	Sp-III.203	Astronomical Diary. LBAT 786.
35686	Sp-III.204	Commentary; cf. 35401.
35687	Sp-III.205	Astronomical; Almanac for SE 236. (+) 35314. LBAT 1173 (+) 1171 + 1205 + 1209; Hunger and Sachs, ADART VII, no. 191.
35688	Sp-III.206	Incantation.
35689	Sp-III.207	Astronomical Diary. LBAT 787.
35690	Sp-III.208	Contract. + Sp-III.444.
35691	Sp-III.209	Astronomical; Normal Star Almanac for SE 215. LBAT 1208; Hunger and Sachs, ADART VII, no. 100.
35692	Sp-III.210	Astrological omens, Enūma Anu Enlil, 20. LBAT 1538; Rochberg-Halton, AfO Beih. 22, Enūma Anu Enlil 20; Reiner, Fs Borger (CM 10), 294.
35693	Sp-III.211	Astronomical Diary. + Sp-III.382. LBAT 784.
35694	Sp-III.212	Astronomical Diary. LBAT 783.
35695	Sp-III.213	Astrological omens; Enūma Anu Enlil 6. LBAT 1522; Reiner, Fs Borger (CM 10), 294; Verderame, Nisaba 2, 191-192.
35696	Sp-III.214	Joined to 35334.

35697	Sp-III.215	Astrological; fixed star names of planets; Mars. LBAT 1573; Reiner, Fs Borger (CM 10), 295.
35698	Sp-III.216	Joined to 34583.
35699	Sp-III.217	Astronomical Diary; prayer on upper edge. LBAT 791.
35700	Sp-III.218	Astronomical Diary for SE 194. LBAT 460; Sachs and Hunger, ADART III, no. -117 B.
35701	Sp-III.219	Astronomical Diary.
35702	Sp-III.220	Astrological; fixed star names of planets. LBAT 1574; Reiner, Fs Borger (CM 10), 295.
35703	Sp-III.221	Joined to 34170.
	Sp-III.222	Joined to 34170.
35704	Sp-III.223	Astronomical Diary. LBAT 794.
35705	Sp-III.224	Mantic dream ritual.
35706	Sp-III.225	Omens; terrestrial.
35707	Sp-III.226	Astronomical; Almanac for SE 234. + 36077. LBAT 1162-1163; Hunger and Sachs, ADART VII, no. 190.
35708	Sp-III.227	Joined to 34814.
35709	Sp-III.228	Astronomical Diary. LBAT 78.
35710	Sp-III.229	List of market prices for years 208-209 SE. Slotsky and Wallenfels, Tallies and Trends, text 11.
35711	Sp-III.230	Astrological omens.
35712	Sp-III.231	Astronomical.
35713	Sp-III.232	Joined to 35501.
35714	Sp-III.233	Joined to 35581.
35715	Sp-III.234	Astronomical Diary.
35716	Sp-III.235	Astronomical Diary. LBAT 792.
35717	Sp-III.236	Literary.
35718	Sp-III.237	Astronomical Diary. LBAT 207.
35719	Sp-III.238	Astronomical; Goal Year Text for SE 222. LBAT 1294; Hunger and Sachs, ADART VI, no. 81.
35720	Sp-III.239	Astronomical; Almanac for SE 233. LBAT 1160; Hunger and Sachs, ADART VII, no. 189.
35721	Sp-III.240	Astronomical Diary for SE 217. LBAT 790; Sachs and Hunger, ADART III, no. -94.
35722	Sp-III.241	Joined to 35126.
35723	Sp-III.242	Astronomical Diary. LBAT 788.
35724	Sp-III.243	Astronomical Diary. LBAT 793.
35725	Sp-III.244	Joined to 35581.
35726	Sp-III.245	Graeco-Babyloniaca; lexical, Ḫḫ III 290-295. + 1881, 0706.141. Sollberger, Iraq 24, 66, A5; Pinches, PSBA 24 (1902) 109 and pl. I; MSL 5, 89; Geller, ZA 87, 70-71 and 88, no. 4 (copy); Westenholz, ZA 97, 265.
35727	Sp-III.246	Graeco-Babyloniaca; lexical, Ḫḫ II 229-234. Sollberger, Iraq 24, 65, A3; Pinches, PSBA 24 (1902) 118;

		Geller, ZA 87, 69-70 and 87, no. 2 (copy); Westenholz, ZA 97, 264.
	Sp-III.247	Joined to 34797.
35728	Sp-III.248	Astronomical.
	Sp-III.249	Joined to 34711.
35729	Sp-III.250	Astronomical; Almanac for SE 162. LBAT 1130; Hunger and Sachs, ADART VII, no. 166.
35730	Sp-III.251	Astronomical Diary for SE 125. LBAT 331; Sachs and Hunger, ADART II, no. -186 A.
	Sp-III.252	Joined to 34568.
35731	Sp-III.253	Joined to 34813.
35732	Sp-III.254	Astronomical.
35733	Sp-III.255	Bilingual incantations, Udug-ḫul 1. Cf. Finkel, AuOr 9 (1991) 102; Geller, BAM 8, 44-58, pl. 7.
35734	Sp-III.256	Account of barley and dates.
35735	Sp-III.257	Astronomical Diary. LBAT 801.
35736	Sp-III.258	Contract; record of deposit; Murānu archive; sealed. SE Antiochus II []/2/52?. CT 49, 25, no. 120; Stolper, Annali Supp. 77, 63; Jursa, Persika 9, 175, 189-190; Nisaba 28, no. 575.
35737	Sp-III.259	Joined to 35187.
35738	Sp-III.260	Omens.
35739	Sp-III.261	Astronomical procedure text for the moon. ACT 200g; LBAT 89; Ossendrijver, BMAPT, no. 99.
35740	Sp-III.262	Joined to 34669.
35741	Sp-III.263	Mathematical; problem text.
35742	Sp-III.264	Commentary.
35743	Sp-III.265	Ritual.
35744	Sp-III.266	Astronomical Diary.
35745	Sp-III.267	Joined to 34589.
35746	Sp-III.268	Astronomical.
35747	Sp-III.269	Astronomical Diary. LBAT 796.
35748	Sp-III.270	Astronomical.
35749	Sp-III.271	Astronomical Diary. LBAT 803.
35750	Sp-III.272	Mathematical; table of reciprocals
35751	Sp-III.273	Astronomical Diary. LBAT 797.
35752	Sp-III.274	Astronomical Diary. LBAT 798.
	Sp-III.275	Joined to 34583
35753	Sp-III.276	Astronomical; new moons for (at least) SE 221. ACT 122a; LBAT 67.
35754	Sp-III.277	Omens; Šumma izbu 1. De Zorzi, Šumma izbu, 339.
35755	Sp-III.278	Joined to 35314.
35756	Sp-III.279	Omens; Šumma izbu 12. De Zorzi, Šumma izbu, 671.
35757	Sp-III.280	Literary cylinder; hymn to Nabû?
35758	Sp-III.281	Joined to 34093.

35759	Sp-III.282	Astronomical Diary for SE 192. + 45621. Sachs and Hunger, ADART III, no. -119 C.
35760	Sp-III.283	Literary.
35761	Sp-III.284	Astronomical Diary. LBAT 802.
35762	Sp-III.285	Astronomical.
35763	Sp-III.286	Incantation.
35764	Sp-III.287	Astronomical Diary. LBAT 800.
35765	Sp-III.288	Astronomical Diary. LBAT 799.
35766	Sp-III.289	Astronomical Diary for SE 236. LBAT 517; Sachs and Hunger, ADART III, no. -73.
35767	Sp-III.290	Astrological commentary (procedure). LBAT 1628.
35768	Sp-III.291	Astrological omens; Enūma Anu Enlil 15. + 35770. LBAT 1537; Rochberg-Halton, AfO Beih. 22, Enūma Anu Enlil 15; Reiner, Fs Borger (CM 10), 295.
35769	Sp-III.292	Astronomical Diary; mentions Arsaces.
35770	Sp-III.293	Joined to 35768.
35771	Sp-III.294	Astronomical Diary. LBAT 804.
	Sp-III.295	Joined to 35189.
35772	Sp-III.296	Literary.
35773	Sp-III.297	Astronomical Diary.
35774	Sp-III.298	Astronomical.
35775	Sp-III.299	Promissory note for dates. 11/[]/6. Babylon.
35776	Sp-III.300	Joined to 34937.
35777	Sp-III.301	Liver omens; commentary.
35778	Sp-III.302	School text.
35779	Sp-III.303	Astronomical.
	Sp-III.304	Joined to 35212.
35780	Sp-III.305	Oral contract. SE []/[]/158. Babylon. CT 49, 32, no. 141.
35781	Sp-III.306	Astronomical.
35782	Sp-III.307	Incantation.
35783	Sp-III.308	Joined to 35311.
35784	Sp-III.309	Astrological; tabulated; microzodiac; cf. 32517. LBAT 1578; Weidner, Gestirn-Darstellungen, 38.
35785	Sp-III.310	Astronomical.
	Sp-III.311	Joined to 34798.
35786	Sp-III.312	Joined to 34920.
35787	Sp-III.313	Joined to 34658.
35788	Sp-III.314	Joined to 34888.
	Sp-III.315	Joined to 35611.
35789	Sp-III.316	Joined to 35115.
35790	Sp-III.317	Incantation.
35791	Sp-III.318	Astronomical Diary.
35792	Sp-III.319	Historical-literary(?) text. Grayson, BHLT 106.

35793	Sp-III.320	Astronomical; Normal Star Almanac. LBAT 1096; Hunger and Sachs, ADART VII, no. 128.
35794	Sp-III.321	Astronomical Diary for SE 139. LBAT 807.
35795	Sp-III.322	Astronomical; Normal Star Almanac for SE 51. LBAT 1095; Hunger and Sachs, ADART VII, no. 11.
35796	Sp-III.323	Commentary.
35797	Sp-III.324	Astronomical.
35798	Sp-III.325	Lexical.
35799	Sp-III.326	Astronomical Diary. LBAT 808.
35800	Sp-III.327	Astronomical Diary. LBAT 806.
	Sp-III.328	Joined to 34625.
35801	Sp-III.329	Astronomical Diary. LBAT 810.
35802	Sp-III.330	Astronomical Diary. LBAT 811.
35803	Sp-III.331	Contract; sale of land. Dar 17/1/13.
35804	Sp-III.332	Astronomical.
35805	Sp-III.333	Contract about a tithe (uš-ru-ú); sealed; finger-nail mark. Dar II 9/9/17. Nisaba 28, no. 534.
35806	Sp-III.334	Promissory note; Murānu archive; prayer on upper edge; sealed. SE Ant I and Sel. Babylon. + Sp-III.431. CT 49, 45, no. 172; Jursa, Persika 9, 175, 199-200; Nisaba 28, no. 554.
35807	Sp-III.335	Astrological omens; Enūma Anu Enlil, Sin. LBAT 1523; Reiner, Fs Borger (CM 10), 295.
35808	Sp-III.336	Astronomical.
35809	Sp-III.337	Astronomical Diary. LBAT 815.
	Sp-III.338	Joined to 35582.
35810	Sp-III.339	Astronomical Diary for SE 192. + Sp-III.539 (+) 35677. LBAT 456; Sachs and Hunger, ADART III, no. -119 A.
35811	Sp-III.340	Joined to 34888.
35812	Sp-III.341	Joined to 34806.
35813	Sp-III.342	Astronomical.
35814	Sp-III.343	Astrological omens; Enūma Anu Enlil, Sin. LBAT 1524; Reiner, Fs Borger (CM 10), 295.
35815	Sp-III.344	Joined to 35053.
35816	Sp-III.345	Ritual.
35817	Sp-III.346	Astronomical; Normal Star Almanac for SE 125. LBAT 1024; Hunger and Sachs, ADART VII, no. 53.
35818	Sp-III.347	Mathematical.
35819	Sp-III.348	Astronomical Diary. LBAT 813.
35820	Sp-III.349	Joined to 35059.
35821	Sp-III.350	Contract; sale of land.
35822	Sp-III.351	Astronomical Diary.
	Sp-III.352	Joined to 34709.
35823	Sp-III.353	Astronomical.

35824	Sp-III.354	School text.
35825	Sp-III.355	Astronomical Diary. LBAT 821.
35826	Sp-III.356	Astronomical; eclipses? ACT 1003; LBAT 155.
35827	Sp-III.357	Contract; sale of land.
35828	Sp-III.358	Promissory note for silver. Npl 20+/-/-.
35829	Sp-III.359	Incantation; Late Babylonian copy of an earlier tablet in archaic script. + 35970.
35830	Sp-III.360	Astronomical Diary or related text.
35831	Sp-III.361	Astronomical.
35832	Sp-III.362	Lexical; syllabary.
35833	Sp-III.363	Astronomical Diary for SE 99. LBAT 295; Sachs and Hunger, ADART II, no. -212 B.
35834	Sp-III.364	School text; lexical and literary extracts.
35835	Sp-III.365	Astronomical Diary. LBAT 817.
35836	Sp-III.366	Incantation.
35837	Sp-III.367	Joined to 34671.
35838	Sp-III.368	Tintir II. (+) 36017. George, BTT, pl. 7.
35839	Sp-III.369	Astronomical Diary. LBAT 814.
35840	Sp-III.370	Lexical.
35841	Sp-III.371	Astronomical Diary. LBAT 812.
35842	Sp-III.372	Astronomical.
35843	Sp-III.373	Medical astrology. + 1881,0706.571. LBAT 1598; Geller, Melosthesia, 73-75.
35844	Sp-III.374	Lexical.
35845	Sp-III.375	Joined to 35199.
35846	Sp-III.376	Astronomical.
35847	Sp-III.377	Incantations; Maqlu I 80-86.
35848	Sp-III.378	Contract; sale of land. 25/9/-. Babylon.
35849	Sp-III.379	Astronomical Diary. LBAT 822.
35850	Sp-III.380	Astronomical Diary. LBAT 816.
35851	Sp-III.381	Astronomical Diary. LBAT 823.
	Sp-III.382	Joined to 35693.
35852	Sp-III.383	Lexical.
35853	Sp-III.384	Astronomical; Venus, evening star, for (at least) SE 265 to 281. ACT 412; LBAT 109.
35854	Sp-III.385	Astronomical; Jupiter, second station and last visibility, for SE 202 to 267; System B. ACT 623; LBAT 130.
35855	Sp-III.386	Joined to 34789.
35856	Sp-III.387	Astronomical.
35857	Sp-III.388	Astronomical procedure text; Mars. (+) 34271. Ossendrijver, BMAPT, no. 16.
35858	Sp-III.389	Astronomical.
35859	Sp-III.390	Ritual. + Sp-III.541.

35860	Sp-III.391	Astronomical; Almanac. LBAT 1210; Hunger and Sachs, ADART VII, no. 223.
35861	Sp-III.392	Astronomical Diary?
	Sp-III.393	Joined to 34912.
35862	Sp-III.394	Literary.
35863	Sp-III.395	Astronomical Diary. LBAT 824.
35864	Sp-III.396	Sumerian incantation?
35865	Sp-III.397	Mythological, or dispute poem; Arsacid colophon. Lambert, MC 24, no. 50.
35866	Sp-III.398	Astronomical.
35867	Sp-III.399	Incantation.
35868	Sp-III.400	Astronomical.
35869	Sp-III.401	Astronomical; full moons? ACT 1008; LBAT 159.
35870	Sp-III.402	Astronomical Diary. LBAT 825.
35871	Sp-III.403	Liver omens.
35872	Sp-III.404	Astronomical.
35873	Sp-III.405	Omens.
35874	Sp-III.406	Contract.
35875	Sp-III.407	Astronomical.
35876	Sp-III.408	Incantation.
35877	Sp-III.409	Incantation.
35878	Sp-III.410	Astronomical Diary. LBAT 826.
35879	Sp-III.411	Joined to 35475.
35880	Sp-III.412	Astronomical Diary. LBAT 835.
35881	Sp-III.413	Astronomical.
35882	Sp-III.414	Sumerian incantation.
35883	Sp-III.415	Astronomical Diary. LBAT 828.
35884	Sp-III.416	Promissory note for silver. Dar 25/12/-. Babylon.
35885	Sp-III.417	Astrological omens.
35886	Sp-III.418	Astrological omens.
35887	Sp-III.419	Promissory note for silver.
	Sp-III.420	Joined to 34626.
35888	Sp-III.421	Contract; sale of land. SE. (+) 34822 (+) 34856.
35889	Sp-III.422	Omens; Iqqur īpuš.
35890	Sp-III.423	Astronomical Diary. LBAT 827.
35891	Sp-III.424	Astronomical.
35892	Sp-III.425	School text; extracts.
35893	Sp-III.426	Astrological.
35894	Sp-III.427	Astronomical; Almanac for SE 157. LBAT 1125; Hunger and Sachs, ADART VII, no. 162.
35895	Sp-III.428	Astronomical.
35896	Sp-III.429	Administrative; list of names.
	Sp-III.430	Joined to 35391.
	Sp-III.431	Joined to 35806.
35897	Sp-III.432	Astronomical Diary. LBAT 833.

35898	Sp-III.433	Astronomical Diary. LBAT 829.
35899	Sp-III.434	Astronomical Diary. LBAT 834.
35900	Sp-III.435	Astronomical; Normal Star Almanac for SE 51. + 36021. LBAT 996; Hunger and Sachs, ADART VII, no. 9.
35901	Sp-III.436	Lexical.
35902	Sp-III.437	Astronomical; Goal Year Text; not datable. LBAT 1348; Hunger and Sachs, ADART VI, no. 143.
35903	Sp-III.438	Sumerian literary.
35904	Sp-III.439	Joined to 35623.
35905	Sp-III.440	Astronomical Diary. LBAT 830.
35906	Sp-III.441	Astrological omens.
35907	Sp-III.442	Medical. + 36164.
35908	Sp-III.443	Astronomical.
	Sp-III.444	Joined to 35690.
35909	Sp-III.445	Literary.
35910	Sp-III.446	Incantation.
35911	Sp-III.447	Astronomical Diary. LBAT 832.
35912	Sp-III.448	Astronomical Diary. LBAT 836.
35913	Sp-III.449	Omens.
35914	Sp-III.450	Incantation.
35915	Sp-III.451	Astronomical procedure text for Jupiter. Ossendrijver, Science 351 (2016) 482-484, text D (and Supplementary Materials)
35916	Sp-III.452	Promissory note for silver. Cam -/8/-. Babylon.
35917	Sp-III.453	Astronomical; Goal Year Text; not datable. LBAT 1355; Hunger and Sachs, ADART VI, no. 144
35918	Sp-III.454	Unidentified.
35919	Sp-III.455	Joined to 35199.
35920	Sp-III.456	Astronomical Diary?; historical section?
35921	Sp-III.457	Astronomical; Goal Year Text for SE 245? LBAT 1349; Hunger and Sachs, ADART VI, no. 89.
35922	Sp-III.458	Joined to 34362.
35923	Sp-III.459	Incantation.
35924	Sp-III.460	Astronomical Diary. LBAT 837.
35925	Sp-III.461	Astronomical Diary. LBAT 846.
35926	Sp-III.462	Literary.
35927	Sp-III.463	Omens; Šumma ālu excerpt?; two columns.
35928	Sp-III.464	Astronomical.
35929	Sp-III.465	Astronomical.
35930	Sp-III.466	Contract; sale of land.
35931	Sp-III.467	Contract; giving or selling of a daughter.
35932	Sp-III.468	Astronomical; eclipses? ACT 1004; LBAT 158.
35933	Sp-III.469	Astronomical; System A lunar ephemeris. ACT 20; LBAT 42; Aaboe, PTRSL A.276, 30-31, pl. 2.

35934	Sp-III.470	Astronomical.
35935	Sp-III.471	Omens; terrestrial.
35936	Sp-III.472	Prayer.
35937	Sp-III.473	Astronomical Diary. LBAT 844.
35938	Sp-III.474	Field plan.
35939	Sp-III.475	Astronomical.
35940	Sp-III.476	Astronomical Diary. LBAT 851.
35941	Sp-III.477	Astronomical Diary. LBAT 843.
35942	Sp-III.478	Administrative; mentions Murānu.
35943	Sp-III.479	Astronomical procedure text for Jupiter. ACT 813a; LBAT 149; Ossendrijver, BMAPT, no. 19.
35944	Sp-III.480	Literary.
35945	Sp-III.481	Astronomical.
35946	Sp-III.482	Astrological; commentary.
35947	Sp-III.483	Astronomical Diary. LBAT 840.
35948	Sp-III.484	Sumerian literary.
35949	Sp-III.485	Astronomical Diary.
35950	Sp-III.486	Astrological; Jupiter; Sagmegar, MAN-ma. LBAT 1558; Reiner, Fs Borger (CM 10), 295.
35951	Sp-III.487	Joined to 35659.
35952	Sp-III.488	Contract; sale of fields.
35953	Sp-III.489	Astronomical.
35954	Sp-III.490	Astronomical; Mercury, evening star, for (at least) SE 214 to 220; System A1. ACT 303a; LBAT 102.
35955	Sp-III.491	Ritual.
35956	Sp-III.492	Astronomical; Goal Year Text for SE 240. LBAT 1299; Hunger and Sachs, ADART VI, no. 87.
35957	Sp-III.493	Astronomical.
35958	Sp-III.494	Incantation.
35959	Sp-III.495	Astronomical.
35960	Sp-III.496	Astronomical Diary.
35961	Sp-III.497	Joined to 34767.
35962	Sp-III.498	Astronomical; fragment of ephemeris for two years. ACT 125d.
35963	Sp-III.499	Economic. 13/[]/28.
35964	Sp-III.500	Astronomical.
35965	Sp-III.501	Mathematical; table of squares.
35966	Sp-III.502	Bilingual balag hymn.
35967	Sp-III.503	Account of silver.
35968	Sp-III.504	Chronicle; the Religious Chronicle. Grayson, TCS 5, Chronicle 17.
35969	Sp-III.505	Late Babylonian copy of a Naram-Sin inscription; colophon.
35970	Sp-III.506	Joined to 35829.
120372	Sp-III.507	Seal ring; Islamic (Timurid).

120374	Sp-III.508	Seal ring; Sasanian.
120371	Sp-III.509	Seal ring; Sasanian.
120375	Sp-III.510	Coin of Alexander.
120373	Sp-III.511	Coin; Kufic.
35971	Sp-III.511a	School text.
35972	Sp-III.512	Astronomical Diary.
35972a	Sp-III.512a	Astronomical; Normal Star Almanac. LBAT 1098; Hunger and Sachs, ADART VII, no. 10.
	Sp-III.513	Nothing registered.
35973	Sp-III.514	Astronomical; ziqpu stars? LBAT 1506.
35974	Sp-III.515	Astronomical Diary. LBAT 848.
35975	Sp-III.516	Lexical; god list.
35976	Sp-III.517	Astronomical Diary. LBAT 841.
35977	Sp-III.518	Omens.
35978	Sp-III.519	Bilingual incantation.
35979	Sp-III.520	Astronomical Diary for SE 154. LBAT 391; Sachs and Hunger, ADART III, no. -157 B.
35980	Sp-III.521	Astronomical Diary. LBAT 847.
35981	Sp-III.522	Contract; right edge.
35982	Sp-III.523	Astronomical Diary. LBAT 838.
35983	Sp-III.524	Astronomical Diary. LBAT 842.
35984	Sp-III.525	Joined to 35581.
35985	Sp-III.526	Astronomical; Goal Year Text; not datable. LBAT 1350; Hunger and Sachs, ADART VI, no. 145.
35986	Sp-III.527	Astronomical Diary. LBAT 839.
35987	Sp-III.528	Astronomical Diary. LBAT 845.
35988	Sp-III.529	Joined to 34991.
35989	Sp-III.530	Astrological omens.
35990	Sp-III.531	Astronomical; Goal Year Text; not datable. LBAT 1351; Hunger and Sachs, ADART VI, no. 146.
35991	Sp-III.532	Astronomical Diary. LBAT 850.
35992	Sp-III.533	Incantation.
35993	Sp-III.534	Astronomical; Normal Star Almanac. LBAT 1099; Hunger and Sachs, ADART VII, no. 129.
35994	Sp-III.535	Astronomical; Normal Star Almanac. LBAT 1100; Hunger and Sachs, ADART VII, no. 130.
35995	Sp-III.536	Literary.
35996	Sp-III.537	Astronomical Diary. LBAT 849.
35997	Sp-III.538	Astronomical Diary.
	Sp-III.539	Joined to 35810.
35998	Sp-III.540	Astronomical; numerical table or ephemeris.
	Sp-III.541	Joined to 35859.
35999	Sp-III.542	Note; 3 lines; complete.
36000	Sp-III.543	Letter.
36001	Sp-III.544	Omens or prophecies.

36002	Sp-III.545	Receipt; sealed.
36003	Sp-III.546	Literary.
36004	Sp-III.547	Astronomical procedure text for the moon; System A. Colophon mentions Jupiter and the scribe Marduk-šāpik-zēri. + 1882,0704.107 + 40611. ACT 207ca, colophon Zrb; LBAT 100; Ossendrijver, BMAPT, no. 72.
36005	Sp-III.548	Contract; sale of fields.
36006	Sp-III.549	Joined to 34579.
36007	Sp-III.550	Astronomical; System A lunar ephemeris. ACT 11a.
	Sp-III.551	Joined to 34664.
36008	Sp-III.552	Astronomical; ACT ephemeris?; lunar sixes?
36009	Sp-III.553	Joined to 35677.
36010	Sp-III.554	Joined to 34663.
36011	Sp-III.555	Ritual.
36012	Sp-III.556	Astronomical; Goal Year Text; not datable. LBAT 1352; Hunger and Sachs, ADART VI, no. 147.
36013	Sp-III.557	Lexical; list of months.
36014	Sp-III.558	Astronomical Diary.
36015	Sp-III.559	Lexical.
36016	Sp-III.560	Astronomical; Almanac for SE 226. + 36060. LBAT 1159; Hunger and Sachs, ADART VII, no. 188.
36017	Sp-III.561	Tintir II. (+) 35838. George, BTT, pl. 7.
36018	Sp-III.562	Bilingual.
36019	Sp-III.563	List of workmen.
36020	Sp-III.564	Joined to 35366.
36021	Sp-III.565	Joined to 35900.
36022	Sp-III.566	Astrological omens; Enūma Anu Enlil 17. LBAT 1516; Rochberg-Halton, AfO Beih. 22, EAE 17; Reiner, Fs Borger (CM 10), 295.
36023	Sp-III.567	Astronomical; Goal Year Text; not datable. LBAT 1353; Hunger and Sachs, ADART VI, no. 148.
36024	Sp-III.568	Astronomical Diary. LBAT 856.
36025	Sp-III.569	Astronomical Diary. LBAT 852.
36026	Sp-III.570	Astronomical; Almanac. LBAT 1211; Hunger and Sachs, ADART VII, no. 224.
36027	Sp-III.571	Astronomical Diary. LBAT 858.
36028	Sp-III.572	Astronomical Diary for SE 102; prayer on upper edge. LBAT 301; Sachs and Hunger, ADART II, no. -209 E.
36029	Sp-III.573	Astronomical.
36030	Sp-III.574	Commentary.
36031	Sp-III.575	Literary(?) cylinder.
	Sp-III.576	Joined to 34677.
36032	Sp-III.577	Lexical; Ea VIII. MSL 14, 473.

36033	Sp-III.578	Astronomical Diary or related text.
36034	Sp-III.579	Astronomical; Mercury, evening star, for (at least) SE 216 to 229; System A1. ACT 303b; LBAT 104.
36035	Sp-III.580	Joined to 35581.
36036	Sp-III.581	Astronomical Diary. LBAT 175; Sachs and Hunger, ADART I, no. -372 B.
36037	Sp-III.582	Contract; sale of land.
36038	Sp-III.583	Lexical; uzu.
36039	Sp-III.584	Letter; names of sender and addressee lost. Hackl et al., AOAT 414/1, no. 85.
36040	Sp-III.585	Astronomical Diary.
36041	Sp-III.586	Bilingual hymn to Šamaš; dupl. 33328. Abel and Winckler, KGV, 59-60.
36042	Sp-III.587	Late Babylonian copy of an inscription of Adad-šuma-uṣur; colophon: GABA.RI ṣa-lam UD.KA. BAR [] / LIBIR.RA ba-ár []. Winckler, MAOV I, 19, no. 6; cf. Grayson, BHLT 44 n. 17.
36043	Sp-III.588	Lexical; syllabary.
36044	Sp-III.589	Astronomical Diary.
36045	Sp-III.590	Astronomical.
36046	Sp-III.591	Astronomical.
	Sp-III.592	Missing; possibly written off in the 1890s.
36047	Sp-III.593	Astronomical Diary.
36048	Sp-III.594	Astronomical Diary. LBAT 854.
36049	Sp-III.595	Astronomical Diary. LBAT 863.
36050	Sp-III.596	Economic; drawing on the reverse.
36051	Sp-III.597	Astronomical.
36052	Sp-III.598	Astronomical.
36053	Sp-III.599	Promissory note for dates. 10/6/-.
36054	Sp-III.600	Omens; Šumma izbu 1. + 36087. De Zorzi, Šumma izbu, 339.
36055	Sp-III.601	Unidentified.
36056	Sp-III.602	Unidentified.
36057	Sp-III.603	Unidentified.
36058	Sp-III.604	Astronomical.
36059	Sp-III.605	Unidentified.
36060	Sp-III.606	Joined to 36016.
36061	Sp-III.607	Omens; extispicy; lung omens.
36062	Sp-III.608	Astronomical.
36063	Sp-III.609	Astronomical Diary. LBAT 862.
36064	Sp-III.610	Sumerian incantation.
36065	Sp-III.611	Mathematical table. Ossendrijver, JCS 66, 149-165 and pls.
36066	Sp-III.612	Astrological; fixed star names of planets. LBAT 1575; Reiner, Fs Borger (CM 10), 295.

36067	Sp-III.613	Astronomical Diary.
36068	Sp-III.614	Astronomical.
36069	Sp-III.615	Astronomical Diary for SE 192. LBAT 860; Sachs and Hunger, ADART III, no. -119 D.
36070	Sp-III.616	Astronomical Diary.
36071	Sp-III.617	Sumerian literary.
36072	Sp-III.618	Sumerian literary.
36073	Sp-III.619	Astronomical.
36074	Sp-III.620	Astronomical.
36075	Sp-III.621	Mathematical.
36076	Sp-III.622	Astronomical; Goal Year Text.
36077	Sp-III.623	Joined to 35707.
36078	Sp-III.624	Unidentified.
36079	Sp-III.625	Ledger.
36080	Sp-III.626	Lexical.
36081	Sp-III.627	School text; personal names only. + Sp-III.648. Gesche, AOAT 275, 671.
36082	Sp-III.628	Astronomical Diary.
36083	Sp-III.629	Unidentified.
36084	Sp-III.630	Omens.
36085	Sp-III.631	Astronomical Diary. LBAT 861.
36086	Sp-III.632	Lexical.
36087	Sp-III.633	Joined to 36054.
36088	Sp-III.634	Bilingual literary.
36089	Sp-III.635	Administrative.
36090	Sp-III.636	Unidentified; drawing on the reverse.
36091	Sp-III.637	Astronomical Diary. LBAT 865.
36092	Sp-III.638	Contract; sale of land; right edge.
36093	Sp-III.639	Astronomical.
36094	Sp-III.640	Written off.
36095	Sp-III.641	Astronomical Diary. LBAT 853.
36096	Sp-III.642	Astronomical.
36097	Sp-III.643	Astronomical.
36098	Sp-III.644	Incantation.
	Sp-III.645	Joined to 34568.
36099	Sp-III.646	Astronomical.
36100	Sp-III.647	Astronomical.
	Sp-III.648	Joined to 36081.
36101	Sp-III.649	Astronomical Diary.
36102	Sp-III.650	Astronomical Diary.
36103	Sp-III.651	Astronomical.
36104	Sp-III.652	Mathematical.
36105	Sp-III.653	Astronomical.
36106	Sp-III.654	Astronomical.
36107	Sp-III.655	Unidentified.

36108	Sp-III.656	Court record; sealed.
36109	Sp-III.657	Astronomical Diary or related text; Lunar Six data.
36110	Sp-III.658	Astronomical Diary.
36111	Sp-III.659	Incantation.
36112	Sp-III.660	Lexical; geographical names.
36113	Sp-III.661	Lexical.
36114	Sp-III.662	Astronomical.
36115	Sp-III.663	Astronomical Diary?
36116	Sp-III.664	Incantation.
36117	Sp-III.665	Sumerian literary.
36118	Sp-III.666	Economic.
36119	Sp-III.667	Unidentified.
36120	Sp-III.668	Account.
36121	Sp-III.669	Astronomical.
36122	Sp-III.670	Astronomical.
36123	Sp-III.671	Astronomical.
36124	Sp-III.672	Astronomical.
36125	Sp-III.673	Astronomical.
36126	Sp-III.674	Promissory note for grain.
36127	Sp-III.675	Astronomical Diary.
36128	Sp-III.676	School text; practice signs.
36129	Sp-III.677	Astronomical Diary.
36130	Sp-III.678	Astronomical.
36131	Sp-III.679	Astronomical.
36132	Sp-III.680	Astronomical.
36133	Sp-III.681	Astronomical.
36134	Sp-III.682	Astronomical.
36135	Sp-III.683	Astronomical.
36136	Sp-III.684	Astronomical.
36137	Sp-III.685	Omens?
36138	Sp-III.686	Astronomical.
36139	Sp-III.687	Astronomical.
36140	Sp-III.688	Unidentified.
36141	Sp-III.689	Astronomical Diary or related text.
36142	Sp-III.690	Astronomical.
36143	Sp-III.691	Contract; sale of land.
36144	Sp-III.692	Astronomical Diary.
36145	Sp-III.693	Astronomical.
36146	Sp-III.694	Unidentified.
36147	Sp-III.695	Astronomical.
36148	Sp-III.696	Sumerian literary.
36149	Sp-III.697	Economic.
36150	Sp-III.698	Astronomical.
36151	Sp-III.699	Astronomical.
36152	Sp-III.700	Astronomical Diary.

36153	Sp-III.701	Astrological omens.
36154	Sp-III.702	Astronomical Diary; fragment; Alexander mentioned in line 1.
36155	Sp-III.703	Economic.
36156	Sp-III.704	Omens; terrestrial.
36157	Sp-III.705	Unidentified.
36158	Sp-III.706	Omens; colophon mentions Bēlšunu.
36159	Sp-III.707	Omens; two columns.
36160	Sp-III.708	Astronomical.
36161	Sp-III.709	Contract; witnesses; sealed. d.l. Nisaba 28, no. 639.
36162	Sp-III.710	Astronomical Diary.
36163	Sp-III.711	Unidentified.
36164	Sp-III.712	Joined to 35907.
36165	Sp-III.713	Omens; Šumma ālu.
36166	Sp-III.714	Astronomical; lunar six.
36167	Sp-III.715	Unidentified.
36168	Sp-III.716	Omens; Šumma izbu.
36169	Sp-III.717	Astronomical.
36170	Sp-III.718	Astronomical Diary.
36171	Sp-III.719	Astronomical.
36172	Sp-III.720	Astronomical.
	Sp-III.721	Missing; possibly written off in the 1890s.
36173	Sp-III.722	Literary.
36174	Sp-III.723	Lexical.
36175	Sp-III.724	Astronomical; ziqpu star list, and lunar latitudes.
36176	Sp-III.725	Astronomical.
36177	Sp-III.726	Lexical; Hg. MSL 8/2, 45; MSL 9, 185.
36178	Sp-III.727	Astronomical Diary.
36179	Sp-III.728	Astronomical.
36180	Sp-III.729	Astronomical.
36181	Sp-III.730	Lexical.
36182	Sp-III.731	Astronomical.
36183	Sp-III.732	Lexical.
36183 a	Sp-III.733	Lexical.
36184	Sp-III.734	Astronomical.
36185	Sp-III.735	Astronomical Diary.
36186	Sp-III.736	Astronomical Diary.
36187	Sp-III.737	Astronomical.
36188	Sp-III.738	Omens.
36189	Sp-III.739	Astronomical.
36190	Sp-III.740	Astronomical.
36191	Sp-III.741	Unidentified.
36192	Sp-III.742	Astronomical Diary.
36193	Sp-III.743	Astronomical.
36194	Sp-III.744	Unidentified.

	Sp-III.745	Joined to 34912.
36195	Sp-III.746	Unidentified.
36196	Sp-III.747	Astronomical.
	Sp-III.748	Missing; possibly written off in the 1890s.
36197	Sp-III.749	Literary; Erra I, 5-19 and colophon.
36198	Sp-III.750	Incantation.
36199	Sp-III.751	Contract; Egibi archive.
36200	Sp-III.752	Astronomical.
36201	Sp-III.753	Astronomical.
36202	Sp-III.754	Unidentified.
36203	Sp-III.755	Ritual.
36204	Sp-III.756	Lexical.
36205	Sp-III.757	Commentary. + 36217.
36206	Sp-III.758	Astronomical.
36207	Sp-III.759	Unidentified.
36208	Sp-III.760	Astronomical Diary or related text.
36209	Sp-III.761	Medical.
36210	Sp-III.762	School text.
36211	Sp-III.763	Unidentified.
36212	Sp-III.764	Astronomical.
36213	Sp-III.765	Astrological omens; Sin.
36214	Sp-III.766	Unidentified.
36215	Sp-III.767	Astronomical; lunar table.
36216	Sp-III.768	Medical.
	Sp-III.769	Missing; possibly written off in the 1890s.
36217	Sp-III.770	Joined to 36205.
36218	Sp-III.771	Lexical; syllabary.
36219	Sp-III.772	Astronomical Diary.
36220	Sp-III.773	Astrological; mukallimtu commentary.
36221	Sp-III.774	Ritual.
36222	Sp-III.775	Contract; witnesses.
36223	Sp-III.776	Unidentified.
36224	Sp-III.777	Astronomical Diary?
36225	Sp-III.778	Astronomical.
36226	Sp-III.779	Incantation.
36227	Sp-III.780	Astronomical Diary.
36228	Sp-III.781	Astronomical.
36229	Sp-III.782	Unidentified.
36230	Sp-III.783	Astronomical.
36231	Sp-III.784	Unidentified.
36232	Sp-III.785	Astronomical Diary for SE 108; planetary.
36233	Sp-III.786	Astronomical Diary or related text.
36234	Sp-III.787	Unidentified.
36235	Sp-III.788	Astronomical Diary or related text.
36236	Sp-III.789	Astronomical.

	Sp-III.790	Missing; possibly written off in the 1890s.
36237	Sp-III.791	Astronomical.
36238	Sp-III.792	Written off.
36239	Sp-III.793	Unidentified.
36240	Sp-III.794	Astronomical.
36241	Sp-III.795	Lexical.
36242	Sp-III.796	Astronomical Diary.
36243	Sp-III.797	Omens?
	Sp-III.798	Missing; possibly written off in the 1890s.
36244	Sp-III.799	Mathematical.
36245	Sp-III.800	Astronomical.
36246	Sp-III.801	Commentary.
36247	Sp-III.802	Astronomical Diary.
36248	Sp-III.803	Astronomical Diary.
36249	Sp-III.804	Unidentified.
36250	Sp-III.805	Unidentified.
36251	Sp-III.806	Literary.
36252	Sp-III.807	School text.
36253	Sp-III.808	Ritual.
36254	Sp-III.809	Astronomical Diary.
36255	Sp-III.810	Late Babylonian copy of an Old Babylonian historical inscription of Hammurabi. Frayne, RIME 4.3.6.19.
36256	Sp-III.811	Astronomical.
36257	Sp-III.812	Unidentified.
36258	Sp-III.813	Ritual.
36259	Sp-III.814	Astronomical.
36260	Sp-III.815	Astronomical.
36261	Sp-III.816	Astronomical Diary.
36262	Sp-III.817	Promissory note for silver. Nabû-[] -/-/34. Alu-ša-Iddin-x.
36263	Sp-III.818	Incantation.
36264	Sp-III.819	Contract; sale of a house. Nbn? Babylon.
	Sp-III.820	Missing; possibly written off in the 1890s.
36265	Sp-III.821	Astronomical.
36266	Sp-III.822	Economic.
36267	Sp-III.823	Astronomical Diary.
36268	Sp-III.824	Astronomical.
36269	Sp-III.825	Astronomical.
36270	Sp-III.826	Astronomical.
36271	Sp-III.827	Astronomical.
36272	Sp-III.828	Economic.
36273	Sp-III.829	Letter; names of sender and addressee lost. Hackl et al., AOAT 414/1, no. 86.
36274	Sp-III.830	Astronomical.

36275	Sp-III.831	Astronomical Diary.
	Sp-III.832	Terracotta figurine.
141833	Sp-III.833	Cast of a contract dated at Babylon, Dar 24/1/18.
141834	Sp-III.834	Cast of a contract; date lost.
141835	Sp-III.835	Cast of the same contract as 141834.

1880,0126 collection

The 1880,0126 collection was purchased from Joseph M. Shemtob, London. The register gives its provenance as Babylonia.

36276	1880,0126.1	Account of issues of silver. SE []/4/218. Hackl, Fs van der Spek, 87-106, no. 9.

1880,0130 collection

The 1880,0130 collection was transferred to the British Museum from the India Museum (London)

90107	1880,0130.10	Brick of Nebuchadnezzar II. CBI, no. 102.
90108	1880,0130.11	Brick of Nebuchadnezzar II. CBI, no. 102.
30134	1880,0130.13	Receipt of barley paid as rent for a field. Previously East India House no. 1021. Dar II 21/5/10. Borsippa. Dar 274; Stolper, Fs Reiner, 393; Bertin 2171. Note that this tablet is numbered 30134 out of sequence with the rest of the collection.

1880,0617 collection

The 1880,0617 collection comes from the excavations of Hormuzd Rassam. See J. E. Reade in CBTBM VI, p. xxx. The register gives the provenance Babylon to the whole collection except for nos. 1-3 (Borsippa), nos. 175, 270 and 443 (Kouyunjik), nos. 4 and 1942-1944 (no provenance).

36277	1880,0617.1	Cylinder; inscription of Antiochus Soter. Borsippa. 5R 66; Strassmaier, Warka, no. 111; Weissbach, VAB 3, 132-135; Reade, Iraq 48, 109.
90865	1880,0617.2	Historical; inscribed stele of Ashurbanipal. Borsippa. Lehmann-Haupt, AB 8, pls. 13-16; Streck, VAB 7/1, p. xliv, and 7/2, 240-244; Reade, Iraq 48, 109.
90866	1880,0617.3	Historical; inscribed stele of Šamaš-šum-ukin. Borsippa. Lehmann-Haupt, AB 8, 10-12, pls. 5-7; Reade, Iraq 48, 109.
36278	1880,0617.4	School text; lexical, Ḫḫ V and VII. MSL 9, 173; Gesche, AOAT 275, 671.
36279	1880,0617.5	Contract; sale of land. Nbk 5/1/36. Babylon.
36280	1880,0617.6	School text; lexical; Syllabary A, acrographic list. Gesche, AOAT 275, 228-229, 671.

36281	1880,0617.7	School text; lexical; Diri II. MSL 15 121.
36282	1880,0617.8	School text; lexical; Ḫḫ VI. 5/12b/-. + unnum. Gesche, AOAT 275, 229-230, 671.
36283	1880,0617.9	School text; lexical, Ḫḫ XIX. 18/12/-. MSL 10, 127; Gesche, AOAT 275, 230-231, 671.
36284	1880,0617.10	School text; lexical, Ḫḫ VIII-IX; bilingual incantation, Šurpu II 187-192, Udug-ḫul 2; Tintir II 24'. Gesche, AOAT 275, 231-233, 671; MSL 9, 173, 181; George, NABU 2004, 21, no. 20; George, AfO 50, 404; Geller, BAM 8, 59-88.
36285	1880,0617.11	Ritual.
36286	1880,0617.12	School text; lexical, names, acrographic list. + 36317. Gesche, AOAT 275, 234, 671.
36287	1880,0617.13	Historical?; chronicle?; ruled after every line.
36288	1880,0617.14	School text; lexical, Syllabary B; colophon. Gesche, AOAT 275, 671.
36289	1880,0617.15	Unidentified.
36290	1880,0617.16	School text; lexical, Ḫḫ XVI; literary, unidentified. Gesche, AOAT 275, 671.
36291	1880,0617.17	Lexical; Ḫḫ VIII. MSL 9, 173.
36292	1880,0617.18	Astrological; tabulated; microzodiac; cf. 32517. + 37355.
36293	1880,0617.19	Contract; sale of fields. Šamaš-šum-ukin 26/7/[]. Babylon. Brinkman and Kennedy, JCS 35, 37, K.158.
36294	1880,0617.20	Physiognomic omens.
36295	1880,0617.21	Contract. Dar -/-/30.
36296	1880,0617.22	School text; bilingual incantation, Udug-ḫul 13-15; literary, Šamaš Hymn, lines 1-7; lexical, Ḫḫ XV. +38070. Geller, Iraq 42, 27, 47; MSL 9, 5; Gesche, AOAT 275, 671; Charpin, NABU 1987, 1, no. 2; Geller, BAM 8, 434-498, pl. 121; Lambert, MC 24, no. 135.
36297	1880,0617.23	School text; lexical, Syllabary B. Gesche, AOAT 275, 671.
36298	1880,0617.24	School text; lexical; Ḫḫ III-IV; incantation, unidentified, and Sag-gig. 28/[]/-. Gesche, AOAT 275, 234, 671; MSL 9, 168.
36299	1880,0617.25	Contract; sale of a house; finger-nail marks; dupl. 37448+. Cyr 24/[]/4.
36300	1880,0617.26	Astronomical; tables for Saturn. + 36753 + 37156 + 37210 + 37336. Aaboe, JCS 20, 3-4, 13-15, 26-27; see ACT, p. 315; Aaboe, Episodes, 48-49.
36301	1880,0617.27	Astronomical; Mars, Venus and lunar column phi. Neugebauer, JCS 21, 192-199, 216 text C.
36302	1880,0617.28	Liver omens.

36303	1880,0617.29	Compendium of calendrical and stellar astrology; prayer on upper edge. + 36326 (+) 36628 + ... (+) 36988. Reiner, Fs Borger (CM 10), 295; Brack-Bernsen and Steele, Fs Pingree, 103; Steele, JCS 67, 187-215.
36304	1880,0617.30	Chronicle of the Achaemenid period. CT 37, 22; Grayson, TCS 5, Chronicle 8; BCHP 1.
36305	1880,0617.31	Astrological omens; Enūma Anu Enlil, Sin?; DAR-ma DU; commentary. Reiner, Fs Borger (CM 10), 295.
36306	1880,0617.32	Dream ritual and incantation. + 36952.
36307	1880,0617.33	Late Babylonian copy of an inscription of Warad-Sin; cf. UET I 129 and Frayne, RIME 4.2.13.19.
36308	1880,0617.34	Astronomical; Jupiter observations for SE 22-46. + 1880,0617.493 + 36743 + 45855. LBAT 1404-1406; Hunger and Sachs, ADART V, no. 72.
36309	1880,0617.35	Lexical.
36310	1880,0617.36	Ritual and incantations against slanderers; dupl. CTN 4, 121 and UET 6/2, 410 (ed. Gurney, Iraq 22, 221-227). + 36468 + unnum. Abusch and Schwemer, AMD 8/2 text 8.23 a, pl. 28.
36311	1880,0617.37	Astronomical; lunar table. + 36593 + 1880,0617.143 + 322 + 514 + 706 + 826 + 830 + 925 + 933 + 1083. Aaboe, KDVSMM 36/12 (1968) 16-30, pls. II-III.
36312	1880,0617.38	Contract; sale of fields. Nbn 5/4/17. Babylon.
36313	1880,0617.39	Joined to 34660.
36314	1880,0617.40	New Year ritual.
36315	1880,0617.41	Astrological omens (Jupiter), and astronomical procedure, based on MUL.APIN. + 37517. Reiner, Fs Borger (CM 10), 297; Reiner and Pingree, BPO 4, 1-6, 16, 22, 56-57 (obverse only).
36316	1880,0617.42	School text; lexical; Ḫḫ XVII (plants). MSL 10, 81; Gesche, AOAT 275, 235, 671.
36317	1880,0617.43	Joined to 36286.
36318	1880,0617.44	Astrological omens; Enūma Anu Enlil 1; colophon of Iddin-Bēl. SE Ant & Ant []/[]/142. + 36372. Reiner, Fs Borger (CM 10), 295; Verderame, Nisaba 2, 49 and Fol. IV 5-6; Finkel, Board Games, 30 (on the colophon).
36319	1880,0617.45	Astrological omens; Enūma Anu Enlil 24 (25). van Soldt, Solar omens, 16-40 (G); Reiner, Fs Borger (CM 10), 295.
36320	1880,0617.46	Astrological omens?
36321	1880,0617.47	Astronomical procedure text; Mercury. ACT 816, colophon Zu; Ossendrijver, BMAPT, no. 5.

36322	1880,0617.48	Contract; lease of a house; sealed; finger-nail marks. Art 3/10/1. Mitchell and Searight, no. 477 Nisaba 28, no. 258.
36323	1880,0617.49	Astronomical; longitudes and latitudes of the moon in four separate years. + 1880,0617.371 + 36700 + 37453. ACT 92a (not 37453); Steele, AHES 60 (2006) 123-135, text H.
36324	1880,0617.50	Medical; incantation.
36325	1880,0617.51	School text; lexical, Ḫḫ VII B, giš. Gesche, AOAT 275, 671.
36326	1880,0617.52	Joined to 36303.
36327	1880,0617.53	Medical astrology.
36328	1880,0617.54	Account of sheep. 23/9/10+.
36329	1880,0617.55	School text; lexical; Syllabary A. CT 12, 32; MSL 3, 7 Sa; Gesche, AOAT 275, 671.
36330	1880,0617.56	Prescriptions and rituals. Abusch and Schwemer, AMD 8/2 text 10.18 a, pl. 84.
36331	1880,0617.57	School text; lexical; Ḫḫ VII-X; bilingual incantation; list of shrines. CT 14, 48; MSL 7, 4, 34, 73; Gesche, AOAT 275, 236-238, 672; George, AfO 50, 404.
36332	1880,0617.58	Ritual.
36333	1880,0617.59	School text; lexical, Ea VI-VIII; bilingual incantation, Udug-ḫul 13-15, 60-62; hymn to Gula. CT 12, 30; MSL 14, 431, 447, 473; Gesche, AOAT 275, 238-240, 672; Geller, BAM 8, 434-498; Lambert, MC 24, no. 68.
36334	1880,0617.60	Economic. 28/12/-. Babylon.
36335	1880,0617.61	Contract; guarantee for debt of silver; finger-nail mark. Art I? 20/1/23. Babylon.
36336	1880,0617.62	Receipt of silver as final payment for a harvest of onions. Nbn 22/7/3. Šaḫrīn ālu ša Nabû. Wunsch, CM 3, no. 214.
36337	1880,0617.63	Account of dates or grain.
36338	1880,0617.64	School text; god-list, An = Anum. 14/7/-. Gesche, AOAT 275, 241, 672.
36339	1880,0617.65	Ritual.
36340	1880,0617.66	Contract. Dar 5/2/36. Dūru.
36341	1880,0617.67	Contract; sale of land. Nbk 13/10/40+. Babylon.
36342	1880,0617.68	Economic.
36343	1880,0617.69	Ritual and incantation.
36344	1880,0617.70	School text; lexical, Syllabary B. Gesche, AOAT 275, 672.
36345	1880,0617.71	Economic.
36346	1880,0617.72	Contract for building materials.

36347	1880,0617.73	Contract; sale of fields. Kandalanu 21/9/2+. Babylon. Brinkman and Kennedy, JCS 35, 50, L.177.
36348	1880,0617.74	Contract; sale of a house; finger-nail marks. Babylon.
36349	1880,0617.75	Contract; sale of a house, finger-nail marks.
36350	1880,0617.76	Contract.
36351	1880,0617.77	Contract; lease of a house. Dar 8/[]/10. Babylon.
36352	1880,0617.78	Account of deliveries.
36353	1880,0617.79	Astrological.
36354	1880,0617.80	School text; lexical; Ḫḫ I-II. Gesche, AOAT 275, 241, 672.
36355	1880,0617.81	Economic. Šamaš-šum-ukin.
36356	1880,0617.82	Promissory note for silver. Dar.
36357	1880,0617.83	Lexical.
36358	1880,0617.84	Account of barley. 15/10/24.
36359	1880,0617.85	Promissory note for silver. Art 5/1/15. Babylon.
36360	1880,0617.86	School text; lexical, Syllabary A. Gesche, AOAT 275, 672.
36361	1880,0617.87	School text; Malku II. Gesche, AOAT 275, 672.
36362	1880,0617.88	Contract.
36363	1880,0617.89	Contract. 3/[]/25.
36364	1880,0617.90	Astrological omens; Enūma Anu Enlil, Sin; horns; 3 + narrow columns. Reiner, Fs Borger (CM 10), 295.
36365	1880,0617.91	Letter from Rēmūt-Bēl to Nādin. Hackl et al., AOAT 414/1, no. 87.
36366	1880,0617.92	School text; lexical; Ḫḫ XIV. 26/7/-. Gesche, AOAT 275, 242, 672.
36367	1880,0617.93	Promissory note for silver. Dar -/-/5+.
36368	1880,0617.94	Account of disbursements.
36369	1880,0617.95	School text; lexical; Syllabary A; unidentified. Gesche, AOAT 275, 672.
36370	1880,0617.96	Promissory note for dates. Xerxes 20/5/[].
36371	1880,0617.97	School text; unidentified. Gesche, AOAT 275, 672.
36372	1880,0617.98	Joined to 36318.
36373	1880,0617.99	List of workmen.
36374	1880,0617.100	Account. 2/8/-.
36375	1880,0617.101	Account. 5/8/-.
36376	1880,0617.102	School text; lexical; Syllabary B. 1/9/-. Gesche, AOAT 275, 243, 672.
36377	1880,0617.103	Contract. Cam -/-/3.
36378	1880,0617.104	School text; lexical, Syllabary B, acrographic list. Gesche, AOAT 275, 243, 672.
36379	1880,0617.105	Promissory note for silver. Dar 12/8/20+.
36380	1880,0617.106	Work roster.
36381	1880,0617.107	Economic.

36382	1880,0617.108	Astronomical; based on MUL.APIN. Reiner, Fs Borger (CM 10), 295.
36383	1880,0617.109	Economic.
36384	1880,0617.110	School text; lexical; Ḫḫ XIII-XIV; bilingual incantations, Udug-ḫul 16, and against headache. Gesche, AOAT 275, 244-245, 672; Geller, BAM 8, 499-541, pl. 131.
36385	1880,0617.111	Incantation.
36386	1880,0617.112	School text; lexical, Ea III-V and Ḫḫ V; bilingual incantation, Muššu'u tablet II; literary, Ludlul I 74-78. + 36716. Gesche, AOAT 275, 246-248, 673; MSL 14, 301, 354, 394; Böck, NABU 2001, 80-81, no. 86; Böck, Muššu'u, 113-131.
36387	1880,0617.113	School text; lexical, Malku IV-V; bilingual incantation, Udug-ḫul 5; literary, Enūma eliš IV. 2/10/-. Gesche, AOAT 275, 248-250, 673; Lambert, BCM, p. 85, pl. 18; Geller, BAM 8, 174-216.
36388	1880,0617.114	Astronomical Diary; prayer on upper edge. + 36738. LBAT 193-194; Sachs and Hunger, ADART I, no. -332 A.
36389	1880,0617.115	Omens; Šumma ālu, tablet 2. + 36866. Freedman, If a city, vol. 2, 4.
36390	1880,0617.116	Astronomical Diary. Sachs and Hunger, ADART I, no. -330 B; Wiseman, Nebuchadrezzar and Babylon, 119-121.
36391	1880,0617.117	School text; lexical; Ḫḫ XXI; Sumerian literary, dupl. Cooper, AnOr 52, pls. VIII-IX, K.9336 + 13558. 1/[]/-. Gesche, AOAT 275, 251-253, 673.
36392	1880,0617.118	Lexical; Ḫḫ I. MSL 9, 157.
36393	1880,0617.119	Lexical; Akkadian synonym list. Pinches, BOR 6, 168; von Soden, LTBA II, p. 3 and pls. 15-16.
36394	1880,0617.120	Astronomical procedure?; colophon, written by Bēl-aḫḫē-[uṣur]. SE Ant I [and Sel] []/[]/44.
36395	1880,0617.121	Astrological omens; Enūma Anu Enlil 63. + 36806 + 36853 (+) 37010 (+) 36758 + 37496 (+) 37121 + 37432. Reiner and Pingree, BPO 1, source J; Reiner, Fs Borger (CM 10), 295.
36396	1880,0617.122	School text; lexical, Ḫḫ XIV-XV; bilingual incantation. MSL 9, 5; Walker, BiOr 26 76; Gesche, AOAT 275, 673.
36397	1880,0617.123	Historical.
36398	1880,0617.124	Bilingual hymn.
36399	1880,0617.125	Astronomical Diary for SE 9. Sachs and Hunger, ADART I, no. -302.

36400	1880,0617.126	Astronomical, lunar longitudes for SE 46 to 51. Aaboe, et al., TAPS 81/6 (1991), 63-67, text F.
36401	1880,0617.127	Economic.
36402	1880,0617.128	Astronomical Diary for SE 9. + 36865. LBAT 294 (36402 only); Sachs and Hunger, ADART II, no. -214. Stephenson, HEER, 178, 186.
36403	1880,0617.129	Account of oil.
36404	1880,0617.130	Account of dead sheep.
36405	1880,0617.131	Contract; ḫarrānu. Xerxes 23/3/2.
36406	1880,0617.132	Mathematical; metrological table. Steele, SCIAMVS 16 (2015) 75-90.
36407	1880,0617.133	School text; lexical, Syllabary A and B. Gesche, AOAT 275, 673.
36408	1880,0617.134	Economic.
36409	1880,0617.135	Promissory note for silver. Dar -/-/16.
36410	1880,0617.136	Contract.
36411	1880,0617.137	School text; lexical, Syllabary B. Gesche, AOAT 275, 673.
36412	1880,0617.138	Astronomical Diary.
36413	1880,0617.139	School text; unidentified. Gesche, AOAT 275, 253, 673.
36414	1880,0617.140	Astronomical procedure?; mi-šil u4-mu; rev. blank or erased. + 36977.
36415	1880,0617.141	Omens; terrestrial.
36416	1880,0617.142	Astrological; catch line: AN.MI.MEŠ MU.MEŠ. Reiner, Fs Borger (CM 10), 295.
	1880,0617.143	Joined to 36311.
36417	1880,0617.144	School text; lexical; Ḫḫ XXIII-XXIV; Lú = ša I; literary, Enūma eliš II; god-list, dupl. 2R 60, 17-22. MSL 11, 78 and 12, 91; Gesche, AOAT 275, 254-255, 673; Lambert, BCM, p. 63, pl. 14.
36418	1880,0617.145	Account of deliveries.
36419	1880,0617.146	Contract. 6/8/19. Mar(a)da.
36420	1880,0617.147	Contract; lease of a house at the Great Gate of Uraš; sealed. RN lost 2/10/[]. Nisaba 28, no. 303.
36421	1880,0617.148	School text; lexical, Ḫḫ, giš. Gesche, AOAT 275, 673.
36422	1880,0617.149	School text; lexical, gi, verbal forms. 11/12 /-. Gesche, AOAT 275, 256, 673.
36423	1880,0617.150	Ritual?
36424	1880,0617.151	Account of disbursements.
36425	1880,0617.152	Account of disbursements.
36426	1880,0617.153	School text; lexical, syllabary, acrographic list; unidentified. Gesche, AOAT 275, 257, 673.
36427	1880,0617.154	Lexical?

36428	1880,0617.155	Promissory note for barley, etc., to be delivered in Babylon. Dar 8/[]/16. Uruk.
36429	1880,0617.156	Lexical.
36430	1880,0617.157	Contract; sale of a house at Babylon; sealed. SE Antiochus I and Seleucus 8/4/42. Babylon. Nisaba 28, no. 562.
36431	1880,0617.158	Astrological; commentary; small script. + 37223 + 44213. Reiner, Fs Borger (CM 10), 296 (37223 only).
36432	1880,0617.159	Contract; lease of a house. Cam 16/6/2. Babylon. Wunsch, CM 3, no. 326.
36433	1880,0617.160	Astronomical Diary.
36434	1880,0617.161	Astronomical; procedure for Jupiter, mentioning 27 and 32 days as duration of invisibility. Steele, SCIAMVS 6 (2005), 33-51; see ACT, p. 429; Ossendrijver, BMAPT, no. 29.
36435	1880,0617.162	Promissory note; Murānu archive; sealed. SE Antiochus II 28/[]/51. CT 49, 24, no. 119; Jursa, Persika 9, 175, 188; Nisaba 28, no. 574.
36436	1880,0617.163	Astronomical procedure text; Mercury. Ossendrijver, BMAPT, no. 2.
36437	1880,0617.164	School text; lexical; unidentified; Prayer to Marduk no. 1, 12-16. Gesche, AOAT 275, 257-259, 674; Oshima, BPM, 143; Lambert, MC 24, no. 91.
36438	1880,0617.165	Astronomical procedure text for the moon; System. + 37012 + 37026 + 37274 + 37319. ACT 207cc (36438 only); Aaboe, KDVSMM 40/6 (1979) 18-23 (new joins); Ossendrijver, BMAPT, no. 74.
36439	1880,0617.166	School text; lexical, Ḫḫ XIII; bilingual incantation, Udug-ḫul 10; unidentified. 6/3/-. Gesche, AOAT 275, 259-260, 674; Geller, BAM 8, 323-329.
36440	1880,0617.167	Astronomical Diary for SE 12. + 36787 + 36964.
36441	1880,0617.168	School text; lexical; bilingual extract. 7/10/-. Gesche, AOAT 275, 261, 674.
36442	1880,0617.169	School text; lexical, Syllabary A. Gesche, AOAT 275, 674.
36443	1880,0617.170	School text; lexical, Syllabary A. Gesche, AOAT 275, 674.
36444	1880,0617.171	Omens; Iqqur īpuš, table of months; Babylonian Almanac, table of days; colophon mentions Nippur and Babylon and barūtu.
36445	1880,0617.172	Astronomical; star-list. + 1880,0617.882.
36446	1880,0617.173	School text; lexical; literary; Counsels of Wisdom 99-105. Gesche, AOAT 275, 261, 674.
36447	1880,0617.174	Promissory note for baskets of dates. Cam.
36448	1880,0617.175	Neo-Assyrian. Letter(?).

36449	1880,0617.176	Promissory note for dates.
36450	1880,0617.177	Ledger.
36451	1880,0617.178	Economic. 6/[]/24.
36452	1880,0617.179	School text; lexical, Ḫḫ IV. MSL 9, 168; Gesche, AOAT 275, 674.
36453	1880,0617.180	Promissory note for barley.
36454	1880,0617.181	Astrological omens; Enūma Anu Enlil.
36455	1880,0617.182	Unidentified.
36456	1880,0617.183	God list.
36457	1880,0617.184	Contract; sale of land.
36458	1880,0617.185	School text; lexical, acrographic list, personal names; colophon. Gesche, AOAT 275, 262, 674.
36459	1880,0617.186	Incantation.
36460	1880,0617.187	Liver omens.
36461	1880,0617.188	Incantation.
36462	1880,0617.189	Lexical; Ḫḫ XV. MSL 9, 4.
36463	1880,0617.190	Contract; transfer of property? 16/-/-. Wunsch, Bab Arch 2, 80-81, no. 21.
36464	1880,0617.191	Promissory note for silver.
36465	1880,0617.192	Liver omens.
36466	1880,0617.193	Inheritance contract. URU Aqabi-[]. Wunsch, Bab Arch 2, 122-123, no. 37.
36467	1880,0617.194	Contract; sale of land.
36468	1880,0617.195	Joined to 36310.
36469	1880,0617.196	Contract for bitumen.
36470	1880,0617.197	Contract; sale of fields?
36471	1880,0617.198	Sale of a slave. Dar -/9/4. Babylon.
36472	1880,0617.199	School text; lexical, Erimḫuš II; drawing(?) on the reverse. Gesche, AOAT 275, 263, 674.
36473	1880,0617.200	Promissory note for barley and dates; sealed. Dar II 20/11/13. Babylon. Nisaba 28, no. 250.
36474	1880,0617.201	Lexical.
36475	1880,0617.202	Unidentified.
36476	1880,0617.203	Promissory note for silver and barley; Egibi archive. Dar 20/1/9. Babylon.
36477	1880,0617.204	Promissory note for silver. Cam 22/[]/3. Babylon.
36478	1880,0617.205	School text; lexical, Syllabary A. 26/5/-. Gesche, AOAT 275, 264, 674.
36479	1880,0617.206	Contract; exchange of fields; dupl. 36532. Šamaš-šum-ukin 11/4/13. Babylon. + 1881,0727.213. Brinkman and Kennedy, JCS 35, 30, K.89.
36480	1880,0617.207	List of prices; a-na 1/2 or 1 or 2 GÍN; probably of Arsacid date.

36481	1880,0617.208	School text; lexical, Ḫḫ VIII; incantation, Šurpu IV 35-43. 16?/2/-. CT 14, 49 (part); MSL 7, 4; Gesche, AOAT 275, 264, 674.
36482	1880,0617.209	Account of disbursements.
36483	1880,0617.210	Account of disbursements.
36484	1880,0617.211	List of expenses; Egibi archive; month 12b of Cambyses year 5 is mentioned. Cam -/-/5. Šaḫrīn.
36485	1880,0617.212	School text; lexical, Ḫḫ, giš; incantation. 30/2/-. Gesche, AOAT 275, 674.
36486	1880,0617.213	Medical. (+) 36497 (+) 36515.
36487	1880,0617.214	Astronomical?; mentions consecutive days; lal.
36488	1880,0617.215	Astronomical Diary.
36489	1880,0617.216	School text; lexical; Malku III. Gesche, AOAT 275, 674.
36490	1880,0617.217	Promissory note for silver. Dar 27/4/10.
36491	1880,0617.218	Contract.
36492	1880,0617.219	Receipt for sheep.
36493	1880,0617.220	Horoscope. SE 8/9/61. Rochberg, Babylonian Horoscopes, no. 8.
36494	1880,0617.221	Promissory note for silver.
36495	1880,0617.222	Promissory note for silver. Npl -/-/20. Babylon.
36496	1880,0617.223	Personal names.
36497	1880,0617.224	Medical. (+) 36486 (+) 36515.
36498	1880,0617.225	Economic.
36499	1880,0617.226	Promissory note for silver. Nbn 20/[]/5. Babylon.
36500	1880,0617.227	Promissory note for barley.
36501	1880,0617.228	Letter from Šāpik-zēri to Nergal-uballiṭ. CT 22, 40, no. 216.
36502	1880,0617.229	Promissory note for silver. Dar 5/5/16. Babylon.
36503	1880,0617.230	Contract for silver purchase. Dar 5/8/9. Babylon.
36504	1880,0617.231	Promissory note for dates and date products.
36505	1880,0617.232	School text; lexical, Ḫḫ XVII (plants); literary. MSL 10, 80; Gesche, AOAT 275, 674.
36506	1880,0617.233	School text; lexical, Syllabary B. Gesche, AOAT 275, 674.
36507	1880,0617.234	Letter to Murānu; the envelope is 37009. SE Ant I and Ant 4/7/50. CT 49, 24, no. 118; van der Spek, BiOr 42, 555; Jursa, Persika 9, 156, 186-187.
36508	1880,0617.235	Contract. Dar 18/5/-.
36509	1880,0617.236	Receipt for baked bricks.
36510	1880,0617.237	Account of disbursements.
36511	1880,0617.238	Receipt for sale of sheep. 3/8/-.
36512	1880,0617.239	Promissory note for silver. Nbn.
36513	1880,0617.240	Incantation; colophon on edge.

36514	1880,0617.241	Promissory note for silver; dated arki Kandalanu. Kandalanu 1+/8/21. Babylon. Wiseman, Chronicles, 89-90 and pls. xx-xxi; Brinkman and Kennedy, JCS 35, 49, L.160.
36515	1880,0617.242	Medical; incantation. (+) 36486 (+) 36497.
36516	1880,0617.243	Contract; sale of fields.
36517	1880,0617.244	Religious text mentioning favourable and unfavourable gods.
36518	1880,0617.245	Letter from f.Qutnānu to f.Inṣabtu. CT 22, 41, no. 226; Hackl et al., AOAT 414/1, no. 88.
36519	1880,0617.246	Account of disbursements.
36520	1880,0617.247	Prescriptions for salves against witchcraft. (+) 37589. Abusch and Schwemer, AMD 8/2 texts 10.6 g and 10.14 d, pl. 76.
36521	1880,0617.248	Promissory note for beer and vats. Nbk 1/10/30. Babylon.
36522	1880,0617.249	School text; lexical, place names. Gesche, AOAT 275, 266, 674.
36523	1880,0617.250	Contract; on the reverse two drawings of a bird. 10/1/-.
36524	1880,0617.251	Promissory note for dates. Nabû-[] 1/4/15.
36525	1880,0617.252	Letter from Iddin-Bēl to Ubār. CT 22, 3, no. 7; Hackl et al., AOAT 414/1, no. 89.
36526	1880,0617.253	Note about tablets.
36527	1880,0617.254	Promissory note for silver. Dar 21/-/-.
36528	1880,0617.255	Receipt for barley. Cyr 25/6/3.
36529	1880,0617.256	Incantations; Maqlu I. Abusch, AMD 10, 23-49.
36530	1880,0617.257	Contract; sale of fields. Šamaš-šum-ukin []/10/9+. Babylon. Brinkman and Kennedy, JCS 35, 37, K.164.
36531	1880,0617.258	Receipt.
36532	1880,0617.259	Contract; exchange of fields; dupl. 36479. Šamaš-šum-ukin 11+/[4]/13. Babylon. Brinkman and Kennedy, JCS 35, 30, K.70.
36533	1880,0617.260	Contract. Dar 20/-/-.
36534	1880,0617.261	Account of disbursements.
36535	1880,0617.262	Contract; division of property. Dar 7/8/2.
36536	1880,0617.263	Promissory note for dates.
36537	1880,0617.264	Deposition. Cam 28/6b/acc.
36538	1880,0617.265	Receipt for provisions. Dar 15/4/35. Babylon.
36539	1880,0617.266	Promissory note for silver. Dar -/-/13.
36540	1880,0617.267	Promissory note for dates. -/-/29.
36541	1880,0617.268	Account of disbursements.
36542	1880,0617.269	School text; bilingual incantation, Sag-ba 36-38. Gesche, AOAT 275, 266, 674; cf. Römer in Fs Sjöberg, 465-479.

36543	1880,0617.270	Neo-Assyrian. Letter to the king. van Buylaere, Fs Postgate, 659-661.
36544	1880,0617.271	Contract. 23/11/-.
36545	1880,0617.272	Personal names.
36546	1880,0617.273	Account of wheat.
36547	1880,0617.274	Promissory note for dates. Art I? 15/5/25.
36548	1880,0617.275	Contract.
36549	1880,0617.276	Contract.
36550	1880,0617.277	Receipt. Nbn 4/1/17.
36551	1880,0617.278	Contract. Dar 27/4/-.
36552	1880,0617.279	Contract. Dar 11/6/-.
36553	1880,0617.280	Promissory note for silver. Cyr 24/7/8. Babylon.
36554	1880,0617.281	Memorandum; Bēl-iddina BE-eš. 24/3/no year.
36555	1880,0617.282	Account of sesame.
36556	1880,0617.283	Receipt.
36557	1880,0617.284	Receipt. 15/6/25.
36558	1880,0617.285	Contract. Dar. Babylon.
36559	1880,0617.286	Joined to 35114.
36560	1880,0617.287	Contract for final payment on a house. Dar 25/[]/4.
36561	1880,0617.288	Receipt.
36562	1880,0617.289	Contract. 29/12/30.
36563	1880,0617.290	Letter; names of sender and addressee lost. Hackl et al., AOAT 414/1, no. 90.
36564	1880,0617.291	Promissory note. 15/12/30+.
36565	1880,0617.292	Promissory note for dates. Nbk 18/6/-.
36566	1880,0617.293	Account of sheep. 10/7/-.
36567	1880,0617.294	Sale of a slave; Aramaic note. Dar 10/6/7. Bītu-<ša>-pāni-ekalli.
36568	1880,0617.295	Account of silver.
36569	1880,0617.296	Account of wool. 15/6/3.
36570	1880,0617.297	Receipt for dead sheep. 12/2/26.
36571	1880,0617.298	Account of flour.
36572	1880,0617.299	Receipt for animals. 5/1/24.
36573	1880,0617.300	Account of barley. 19/6/-.
36574	1880,0617.301	Account of purchases. 1/5/-.
36575	1880,0617.302	Promissory note for silver. Dar 9?/12b/13. URU Bīt eš-bar.
36576	1880,0617.303	School text; lexical, Ḫḫ II. MSL 9, 157; Gesche, AOAT 275, 674.
36577	1880,0617.304	Promissory note for silver.
36578	1880,0617.305	Account of dates.
36579	1880,0617.306	Promissory note for barley. Nbk -/9/35.
36580	1880,0617.307	Contract. Cyr 7/5/8. Babylon.
36581	1880,0617.308	Account of wool.
36582	1880,0617.309	Deposition. Dar 2/2/5. Babylon.

36583	1880,0617.310	Promissory note for silver; dated by both Darius year 36 and Xerxes accession year. Dar 3+/9/36. Babylon.
36584	1880,0617.311	Incantation and ritual against witchcraft. + 1880, 0617.312. Abusch and Schwemer, AMD 8/2 text 7.25 a, pl. 22; Schwemer, WO 41, 177-184.
	1880,0617.312	Joined to 36584.
36585	1880,0617.313	Contract.
36586	1880,0617.314	School text; lexical, Syllabary B. Gesche, AOAT 275, 674.
36587	1880,0617.315	Account of pots. 23/9/-.
36588	1880,0617.316	Contract. Dar -/3/-. Babylon.
36589	1880,0617.317	Bilingual incantation; Udug-ḫul 4. CT 17, 46; Geller, BAM 8, 133-173, pl. 37.
36590	1880,0617.318	Promissory note for barley. Cam 2/2/1. Babylon.
36591	1880,0617.319	Astronomical Diary for SE 110. Sachs and Hunger, ADART II, no. -201 D.
36592	1880,0617.320	Promissory note for silver. Dar 27/4/-. Babylon.
36593	1880,0617.321	Joined to 36311.
	1880,0617.322	Joined to 36311.
36594	1880,0617.323	Contract.
36595	1880,0617.324	Ritual commentary. Antigonus. + 37055. Livingstone, MMEWABS, 68-70, pl. VII (37055 only); Reiner, Fs Borger (CM 10), 295.
36596	1880,0617.325	Contract; sale of land in Babylon; sealed. Darius II/III. Babylon. + 37091. Nisaba 28, no. 256.
36597	1880,0617.326	Lexical; Ḫḫ IV. MSL 9, 168.
36598	1880,0617.327	Astronomical; table of lunar or planetary positions(?); six columns of 1 or 2 numbers, then 1 or 2 word signs, often KI, then 1 or 2 numbers; some totals at bottom of rev. + 1880,0617.359.
36599	1880,0617.328	Astronomical; lunar functions relating to solar eclipses; Xerxes 11 to Artaxerxes I 8; colophon. + 1880, 0617.444 + 36941. Aaboe and Sachs, Centaurus 14 (1969) 11-20 and pls. II-III, text B; cf. ACT, p. 10 n. 44; Britton, Centaurus 32(1989) 1-52 (as Text S).
36600	1880,0617.329	Astronomical; planetary observations; Mars and Mercury for at least 398-388 and 390-375 respectively. + 1880,0617.332 + 36771 + 36839 + 37908. Sachs, PTRSL A.276, 49, fig. 15; Hunger and Sachs, ADART V, no. 59.
36601	1880,0617.330	Astronomical Diary.
36602	1880,0617.331	Astrological omens; Adad. NIM.GÍR šá GIM SAG.KUL.LA.
	1880,0617.332	Joined to 36600.

36603	1880,0617.333	School text; lexical, Syllabary B. Gesche, AOAT 275, 674.
36604	1880,0617.334	Unidentified.
36605	1880,0617.335	Astronomical Diary.
36606	1880,0617.336	Hymn; colophon.
36607	1880,0617.337	Promissory note for silver. Dar 14/3/27. Babylon.
36608	1880,0617.338	Promissory note for silver. Dar 26/12/-.
36609	1880,0617.339	Astronomical; compendium of texts dealing with Normal Stars and ziqpu stars. + 36664 + 37030 + 37047 + 37048 + 37076 + 37342 + 37356. Roughton et al., AHES 58 (2004) 537-572; Steele, Annals of Science 64 (2007) 293-325 (but wrongly + 37379 for + 37047); Steele, Rising time schemes, 77-87, 91-95.
36610	1880,0617.340	Astronomical Diary; mentions Antiochus and Seleucus.
36611	1880,0617.341	Astronomical; System A lunar ephemeris. (+) 36831. ACT 18a.
36612	1880,0617.342	Astronomical; lunar eclipse table for at least 328-326 BC; perhaps part of same tablet as 37276. + 37043 + 37107. Hunger and Sachs, ADART V, no. 12.
36613	1880,0617.343	Historical; mentioning Arses and Alexander. Sachs, American Journal of Ancient History 2/2 (1977), 144-147; BCHP 4.
36614	1880,0617.344	Astrological omens; Enūma Anu Enlil 9. Reiner, Fs Borger (CM 10), 295.
36615	1880,0617.345	Incantation.
36616	1880,0617.346	Astronomical Diary.
36617	1880,0617.347	Historical? Mentions Darius the king, and day 24 of month ii; reverse blank; fragment of a large tablet.
36618	1880,0617.348	School text; incantation, Maqlu IV 60-65. []/8/-. Gesche, AOAT 275, 267-268, 674; Abusch, AMD 10, 113-129.
36619	1880,0617.349	Contract; sale of fields.
36620	1880,0617.350	Horoscope; prayer on upper edge. SE 12?/7/92. LBAT 1464; Rochberg, Babylonian Horoscopes, no. 14; Rochberg, in Swerdlow, Astronomy, 39-59.
36621	1880,0617.351	Contract; lease of a house.
36622	1880,0617.352	Astronomical Diary. + 37169. LBAT 233 (36622 only); Sachs and Hunger, ADART I, no. -373 A.
36623	1880,0617.353	School text; literary; unidentified. Gesche, AOAT 275, 675.
36624	1880,0617.354	Promissory note for silver.
36625	1880,0617.355	School text; lexical; bilingual incantation, Udug-ḫul 6. Gesche, AOAT 275, 268, 675; Geller, BAM 8, 217-248.

36626	1880,0617.356	Omens; Iqqur īpuš, Du'ūzu.
36627	1880,0617.357	Astronomical; MUL.APIN. + 37112 + 37144 + 37473. Hunger and Pingree, AfO Beih. 24, 3 (36627 only); Reiner, Fs Borger (CM 10), 295; Fincke, JCS 69, 247-260; Hunger and Steele, MUL.APIN, 21.
36628	1880,0617.358	Compendium of calendrical and stellar astrology; prayer on upper edge. + 36786 + 36817 + 37178 + 37197 (+) 36303 + 36326 (+) 36988. Steele, JCS 67, 187-215.
	1880,0617.359	Joined to 36598.
36629	1880,0617.360	Mathematical problem text; two columns. + 36691 + 37046 + 37507.
36630	1880,0617.361	Lexical.
36631	1880,0617.362	School text; lexical, Ḫḫ XI. MSL 9, 195; Gesche, AOAT 275, 675.
36632	1880,0617.363	Bilingual religious.
36633	1880,0617.364	Omens.
36634	1880,0617.365	Literary.
36635	1880,0617.366	School text; literary?; lexical? Gesche, AOAT 275, 675.
36636	1880,0617.367	Astronomical; new moons(?) for (at least) three years. ACT 90.
36637	1880,0617.368	School text; lexical, Syllabary A and B. Gesche, AOAT 275, 675.
36638	1880,0617.369	Astronomical Diary.
36639	1880,0617.370	Contract; hire of a boat; Egibi archive.
	1880,0617.371	Joined to 36323.
36640	1880,0617.372	Dowry contract. + 37339.
36641	1880,0617.373	Contract; sale of fields.
36642	1880,0617.374	School text; lexical, Ḫḫ II-III. MSL 9, 157, 159; Gesche, AOAT 275, 675.
36643	1880,0617.375	School text; lexical, Ḫḫ IX-X; incantation, Maqlu IV-VI (excerpts). + 37527. MSL 9, 188; Gesche, AOAT 275, 269-272, 675; Abusch, AMD 10, 113-164.
36644	1880,0617.376	Astronomical; obv. zodiac signs and multiplication; rev. astronomical procedure(?) about eclipses; tabulated.
36645	1880,0617.377	Astronomical Diary.
36646	1880,0617.378	School text; lexical, Ḫḫ XXII-XXIII, star names; incantation, Marduk's Address (Udug-ḫul 11), and Praise of Babylon; cf. 45986. MSL 11, 22, 68; George, BTT, pl. 52; Gesche, AOAT 275, 675; Geller, BAM 8, 340-392, pl. 46; Lambert, MC 24, no. 108.

36647	1880,0617.379	Astrological; weather predictions and comet observations; three columns. + 1880,0617.1020. Schreiber, Fs Neumann, 739-756.
36648	1880,0617.380	Astronomical; planetary observations; Mercury from year 43 of Artaxerxes II to year 16 of Artaxerxes III; Mars from year 17 of Artaxerxes III to year 2 of Darius III. + 1880,0617.545 + 41687 (+) 36837 + 37067 (+) 36896. LBAT 1368 + 1371; Hunger and Sachs, ADART V, no. 65.
36649	1880,0617.381	Astrological omens; Enūma Anu Enlil. Cf. Reiner, Fs Borger (CM 10), 295 (but no join to 36781).
36650	1880,0617.382	School text; literary. Gesche, AOAT 275, 675.
36651	1880,0617.383	Astronomical; obv. Mercury phenomena from Artaxerxes I year 41 to Artaxerxes II year 2; rev. inscribed at right angles, lunar eclipses from Darius II year 7 to Artaxerxes II year 24. + 36719 + 37032 + 37053 (+) 37162. Aaboe, et al., TAPS 81/6 (1991), 34-62, Text E1.
36652	1880,0617.384	Religious; measurements in cubits and fingers; mentions ṣupur and NA4.KIŠIB. Cf. Reiner, Fs Borger (CM 10), 295.
36653	1880,0617.385	Astronomical Diary.
36654	1880,0617.386	Mathematical; arithmetic progressions of second order. Neugebauer, JCS 21, 210-212, 218 text G.
36655	1880,0617.387	Astronomical; numbers and Normal Stars.
36656	1880,0617.388	School text; unidentified; Prayer to Marduk no. 1. Lambert, MC 24, no. 95.
36657	1880,0617.389	Astronomical Diary.
36658	1880,0617.390	Bilingual incantation; mentions Asalluḫi.
36659	1880,0617.391	Astronomical Diary?
36660	1880,0617.392	Lexical; Ḫḫ XV. MSL 9, 4.
36661	1880,0617.393	School text; lexical; Ḫḫ XIX; star names; unidentified. + unnum. Gesche, AOAT 275, 675.
36662	1880,0617.394	Economic.
36663	1880,0617.395	Astrological omens; Enūma Anu Enlil, Sin? Reiner, Fs Borger (CM 10), 295.
36664	1880,0617.396	Joined to 36609.
36665	1880,0617.397	Astronomical procedure text for the moon; uddazallu and eclipses; colophon. Ossendrijver, BMAPT, no. 100.
36666	1880,0617.398	Literary; Enūma eliš I. Lambert, BCM, p. 47, pl. 7.
36667	1880,0617.399	School text; lexical; literary, Enūma eliš IV; unidentified. Gesche, AOAT 275, 675; Kämmerer and Metzler, AOAT 375, 95, Tafel IV U, pl. XXVI; Lambert, BCM, p. 85, pl. 18.

36668	1880,0617.400	School text; Lamaštu incantation, and unidentified; reverse blank. Farber, Lamaštu, 48, 57, pl. 61.
36669	1880,0617.401	Lexical. + 37958. CT 14, 12 (36669 only); Pinches, JRAS 1911, 1057-1061; MSL 8/2 95.
36670	1880,0617.402	Religious(?); mentions ox and sheep; flake from left side.
36671	1880,0617.403	Astrological omens; Enūma Anu Enlil 48; catch-line and colophon. Cf. Reiner, Fs Borger (CM 10), 295; Gehlken, CM 43, p. 166, pl. 34.
36672	1880,0617.404	Commentary.
36673	1880,0617.405	Literary.
36674	1880,0617.406	School text; lexical, Ḫḫ XI. MSL 9, 195; Gesche, AOAT 275, 675.
36675	1880,0617.407	School text; lexical; literary. Gesche, AOAT 275, 272, 675.
36676	1880,0617.408	School text; lexical, Ḫḫ XV; bilingual incantation, Udug-ḫul 3; Prayer to Marduk no. 1. MSL 9, 5: Gesche, AOAT 275, 272, 675; Geller, BAM 8, 89-132, pl. 27.
36677	1880,0617.409	Hemerology.
36678	1880,0617.410	Historical?
36679	1880,0617.411	Contract; division of property. + 36820.
36680	1880,0617.412	Astronomical procedure text for Jupiter. Steele, JHA 34 (2003) 269-289; Steele, SCIAMVS 6 (2005) 33-51; Ossendrijver, BMAPT, no. 25; Ossendrijver, JNES 76, 231-247, text C.
36681	1880,0617.413	School text; lexical; literary, Enūma eliš I; bilingual incantation, Udug-ḫul 2. + 37849. Gesche, AOAT 275, 274, 675; Lambert, BCM, p. 47. pl. 7; Geller, BAM 8, 59-88.
36682	1880,0617.414	Memorandum: ka-ap-pu Marduk-šum-uṣur A Marduk-ibni; elongated tablet.
36683	1880,0617.415	Lexical; plants.
36684	1880,0617.416	Astronomical Diary.
36685	1880,0617.417	Astronomical; Vorläufer; star list; two columns. + 36876.
36686	1880,0617.418	School text; lexical. Gesche, AOAT 275, 675.
36687	1880,0617.419	School text; unidentified. Gesche, AOAT 275, 675.
36688	1880,0617.420	School text; literary; Enūma eliš I. King, STC pl. VII; Lambert, BCM, p. 47.
36689	1880,0617.421	Incantation. + 36697.
36690	1880,0617.422	Bilingual incantation; Udug-ḫul 13-15, 16. CT 16, 19-23, 42-49; Geller, BAM 8, 434-498, 499-541.
36691	1880,0617.423	Joined to 36629.

36692	1880,0617.424	Historical-literary text about the Isin II period. Grayson, BHLT 105.
36693	1880,0617.425	School text; lexical, Ḫḫ XVIII-XX; literary. MSL 10, 127 and 11, 3; Gesche, AOAT 275, 276, 675.
36694	1880,0617.426	School text; lexical, Ḫḫ XIX-XXI. MSL 11, 10; Gesche, AOAT 275, 276, 675.
36695	1880,0617.427	Bilingual incantation.
36696	1880,0617.428	Bilingual incantation. + 36897.
36697	1880,0617.429	Joined to 36689.
36698	1880,0617.430	Astronomical procedure text for the moon; System A. Ossendrijver, BMAPT, no. 84.
36699	1880,0617.431	Astronomical table for the moon; System A. + 36846 + 37079 + 37886 + 51261. ACT 207cd (36846 only); Aaboe, KDVSMM 38/6 (1971) 6-11, pl. I.
36700	1880,0617.432	Joined to 36323.
36701	1880,0617.433	Astrological; upper right corner. + 37264. Reiner, Fs Borger (CM 10), 295, 297.
36702	1880,0617.434	Lexical.
36703	1880,0617.435	Necromancer's manual; ritual and incantation; dupl. K.2779.
36704	1880,0617.436	Literary; Theodicy.
36705	1880,0617.437	Astronomical procedure text for the moon; System A; the "Saros text". + 36725 + 37475 + 37484. Neugebauer, KDVSMM 31/4 (1957) 3-21; Aaboe, KDVSMM 36/12 (1968) 35-38 and pl. V (includes 37484); Ossendrijver, BMAPT, no. 82.
36706	1880,0617.438	Account of disbursements.
36707	1880,0617.439	Astronomical Diary.
36708	1880,0617.440	Literary; about Ninšubur and Anzu. Lambert, MC 24, no. 41.
36709	1880,0617.441	Astronomical; Vorläufer; bottom right corner; last part of obv. and all rev. uninscribed.
36710	1880,0617.442	Astronomical Diary for SE 38; colophon. + 92688 + 92689. LBAT 242-244; S. Smith, BHT, 150-159, pl. xviii (92688 + 92689 only); Sachs and Hunger, ADART I, no. -273 B.
36711	1880,0617.443	Neo-Assyrian. Edict appointing Nergal-apil-kumu'a; (+) K.3374. Kataja and Whiting, SAA XII, no. 83.
	1880,0617.444	Joined to 36599.
36712	1880,0617.445	Astronomical procedure text for the moon and sun. + 1880,0617.820 + 919. Sachs and Neugebauer, JCS 10, 131-136; J. Koch, NABU 1998, 112-114, no. 121; Britton, AOAT 297, 28-29; Ossendrijver, BMAPT, no. 102.
36713	1880,0617.446	Omens; Šumma izbu 22. De Zorzi, Šumma izbu, 856.

36714	1880,0617.447	School text; lexical, Ḫḫ XIII-XIV; bilingual incantation, Udug-ḫul 13-15, 16. Geller, Iraq 42, 27, 50; Gesche, AOAT 275, 277, 675; Geller, BAM 8, 434-498, 499-541, pl. 124.
36715	1880,0617.448	Astrological omens; Enūma Anu Enlil, Sin; in three columns; colophon. SE [Ant I & Sel] []/[]/44. Reiner, Fs Borger (CM 10), 295.
36716	1880,0617.449	Joined to 36386.
36717	1880,0617.450	Lexical; Erimḫuš IV. MSL 17, 56.
36718	1880,0617.451	Prayer; Šu'illa type; colophon. Dar I 3/[]/32. Babylon.
36719	1880,0617.452	Joined to 36651.
36720	1880,0617.453	School text; lexical, A and BAD. Gesche, AOAT 275, 675.
36721	1880,0617.454	Astronomical; Venus observations from the reigns of Artaxerxes II and III; three columns. Hunger and Sachs, ADART V, no. 64.
36722	1880,0617.455	Astronomical procedure text for the moon; first and last visibility; lunar velocity; phi; System K; colophon; prayer on upper edge. + 37205 (+) 40082. Neugebauer, JCS 22, 96-111, 113 text K; Brown, CM 18, 305; Ossendrijver, BMAPT, no. 52.
36723	1880,0617.456	Astronomical; System A2; Mercury, for (at least) SE 4 to 22. + 37234. ACT 300a.
36724	1880,0617.457	Astronomical Diary for SE 155. + 36792 + 36920. LBAT 396 (36724 only); Sachs and Hunger, ADART III, no. -156 A.
36725	1880,0617.458	Joined to 36705.
36726	1880,0617.459	School text; lexical, Ḫḫ VIIB-XI; literary, Enūma eliš I; Prayer to Marduk no. 2. 24/12/-. King, STC pl. VIII; MSL 7 35, 74, 122; Gesche, AOAT 275, 278-282, 676; Oshima, BPM, 231-232; Lambert, BCM, p. 47; Lambert, MC 24, no. 119.
36727	1880,0617.460	List of eight incantations and eight corresponding personal names. Art 10/5/28.
36728	1880,0617.461	School text; unidentified. Gesche, AOAT 275, 676.
36729	1880,0617.462	Astronomical Diary. Sachs and Hunger, ADART I, no. -343.
36730	1880,0617.463	List of market prices for years 69-71 SE. Wiseman, Gs Sachs, 363-373; Vargyas, Fs Hunger, 531-540; Slotsky and Wallenfels, Tallies and Trends, text 4.
36731	1880,0617.464	Astronomical; table of solstices, equinoxes and Sirius. Neugebauer, JCS 21, 183-190, 215 text A; cf. ACT, p. 200 on no. 200 Section 11; Brown, CM 18,

		305; J. Koch, NABU 1998, 112-114, no. 121; Britton, AOAT 297, 21, 29-30.
36732	1880,0617.465	Astronomical; System A lunar ephemeris. + 37147. ACT 23; Aaboe, KDVSMM 40/6 (1979) 33-35.
36733	1880,0617.466	Astronomical Diary for SE 114. Sachs and Hunger, ADART II, no. -197 A.
36734	1880,0617.467	Literary; Erra V; amulet format with suspension loop. Lambert, MC 24, no. 45.
36735	1880,0617.468	Astrological omens; Enūma Anu Enlil, Jupiter; commentary(?); upper or lower left corner; two columns. Reiner, Fs Borger (CM 10), 295; Reiner and Pingree, BPO 4, 18, 20, 132-133.
36736	1880,0617.469	Ritual; libations to be made at various sacred points in Esangila. + 36835.
36737	1880,0617.470	Astronomical; lunar functions related to solar eclipses; Xerxes 11 to Artaxerxes I 8. + 36850 (+) 47912. Aaboe and Sachs, Centaurus 14 (1969) 11-20 and pl. IV-V (36737 only), text C; cf. ACT, p. 10 n. 44; Aaboe, et al., TAPS 81/6 (1991), 68-71, text G; Britton, Centaurus 32 (1989) 1-52 (as Text S).
36738	1880,0617.471	Joined to 36388.
36739	1880,0617.472	School text; lexical, Syllabary B. Gesche, AOAT 275, 676.
36740	1880,0617.473	Literary.
36741	1880,0617.474	Astrological omens; Enūma Anu Enlil. Reiner, Fs Borger (CM 10), 295.
36742	1880,0617.475	Astronomical Diary for 363/2 BC (Art II year 42) with historical section. + 37478.
36743	1880,0617.476	Joined to 36308.
36744	1880,0617.477	Astronomical procedure text for the moon; System A; Saros and phi. + 37031. Neugebauer, JCS 22, 94-96, 112 text J; Ossendrijver, BMAPT, no. 92.
36745	1880,0617.478	Historical or literary?
36746	1880,0617.479	Astrological omens; Enūma Anu Enlil, unassigned, lower left corner; + 36842 + 37173. Rochberg-Halton, JNES 43, 115-140; Reiner, Fs Borger (CM 10), 295; Brown, CM 18, 305; see Rochberg-Halton, AfO Beih. 22, 293 (37173).
36747	1880,0617.480	Astronomical procedure text; lunar sixes; partly dupl. TCL 6, no. 11. + 37018. Brack-Bernsen, AOAT 297, 12-13.
36748	1880,0617.481	Astrological omens; Enūma Anu Enlil; ziqpu; two columns.
36749	1880,0617.482	Contract; sealed. d.l. Nisaba 28, no. 616.
36750	1880,0617.483	Astronomical Diary; historical section.

36751	1880,0617.484	Astronomical; planetary observations (Mars and Venus), in the reigns of Artaxerxes II and III and in Philip year 1. + 1880,0617.487 + 36918 + 37335. Hunger and Sachs, ADART V, no. 61.
36752	1880,0617.485	Economic; personal names.
36753	1880,0617.486	Joined to 36300.
	1880,0617.487	Joined to 36751.
36754	1880,0617.488	Astronomical; the "Solar Saros". + 1880,0617.564. Aaboe, JHA 3 (1972) 116, n. 22; LBAT 1430; Aaboe, et al., TAPS 81/6 (1991), 24-31, text D.
36755	1880,0617.489	School text; literary; lexical; Bīt mēseri II. + 36844. Gesche, AOAT 275, 676; Ambos, Baurituale, p. 81 (on 36844).
36756	1880,0617.490	Loan?; sealed. d.l. Nisaba 28, no. 617.
36757	1880,0617.491	Astronomical Diary for SE 28. LBAT 231; Sachs and Hunger, ADART I, no. -283 B.
36758	1880,0617.492	Astrological omens; Enūma Anu Enlil 63. + 37496 (+) 36395 + 36086 + 36853 (+) 37010 (+) 37121 + 37432. Reiner and Pingree, BPO 1, source H; Reiner, Fs Borger (CM 10), 295, 297.
	1880,0617.493	Joined to 36308.
36759	1880,0617.494	Astronomical Diary.
36760	1880,0617.495	Astronomical procedure text; cf. TCL 6, no. 11.
36761	1880,0617.496	Astronomical Diary; mentions Alexander's entry to Babylon. LBAT 196; Wiseman, Nebuchadrezzar and Babylon, 119-121; Sachs and Hunger, ADART I, no. -330 A; Brinkman, NABU 1987, 34, no. 63.
36762	1880,0617.497	Astronomical; table of longitudes of Jupiter phenomena. + 1880,0617.506 + 36813 (+) 36779 (+) 37070 (+) 37082 + 37125 (+) 37174. Aaboe, JCS 20, 7-8, 16-21, 29-30.
36763	1880,0617.498	Astronomical Diary for SE 150. + 36891. Sachs and Hunger, ADART III, no. -161 B.
36764	1880,0617.499	Bilingual incantation.
36765	1880,0617.500	School text?
36766	1880,0617.501	Astronomical procedure text; intercalations. (+) 37110.
	1880,0617.502	Joined to 34173.
36767	1880,0617.503	Astronomical Diary.
36768	1880,0617.504	Astronomical; Vorläufer; right edge; Saturn and Mars.
36769	1880,0617.505	Religious; šá ina šip-ti-šú mim-ma MU-šú.
	1880,0617.506	Joined to 36762.
36770	1880,0617.507	Astronomical Diary.
36771	1880,0617.508	Joined to 36600.

36772	1880,0617.509	Astronomical; Goal Year Text for SE 97. LBAT 1227; Hunger and Sachs, ADART VI, no. 11.
36773	1880,0617.510	Lexical; Ḫḫ I. + 37230. MSL 9, 157.
36774	1880,0617.511	Astronomical Diary.
36775	1880,0617.512	Astronomical procedure text for the moon; System A. Aaboe, KDVSMM 36/12 (1968) 30-34, pl. IV; Ossendrijver, BMAPT, no. 83.
36776	1880,0617.513	Mathematical; coefficient list; weights of bricks of various types. Robson, OECT XIV, 206-207, List L; Friberg and Al-Rawi, NMCT, Fig. 8.1.2.
	1880,0617.514	Joined to 36311.
36777	1880,0617.515	Astronomical Diary. Sachs and Hunger, ADART I, no. -329 A.
36778	1880,0617.516	Astronomical Diary.
36779	1880,0617.517	Astronomical; table of longitudes of Jupiter phenomena. (+) 36762 (+) 37070 (+) 37082 + 37125 (+) 37174. Aaboe, JCS 20, 7-8, 16-21, 29-30.
36780	1880,0617.518	Obv. theology; rev. metrological commentary on walls of Babylon; similar to the text on the reverse of 35385.
36781	1880,0617.519	Astrological omens; commentary. + 37100 + 37412. Cf. Reiner, Fs Borger (CM 10), 295 (but no join to 36649) and 297.
36782	1880,0617.520	Astronomical procedure text; lunar sixes; partly dupl. TCL 6, no. 11. Reiner, Fs Borger (CM 10), 295; Brack-Bernsen, AOAT 297, 12-13.
36783	1880,0617.521	Incantation; Marduk's Address (Udug-ḫul 11). Geller, BAM 8, 340-392, pl. 31; Lambert, MC 24, no. 187.
36784	1880,0617.522	Lexical.
36785	1880,0617.523	School text; lexical, Ḫḫ XVIII-XIX. CT 14, 12; MSL 8/2, 95 and 10, 127: Gesche, AOAT 275, 676.
36786	1880,0617.524	Joined to 36628.
36787	1880,0617.525	Joined to 36440.
36788	1880,0617.526	Astronomical; observations; Mercury observations; two columns. Hunger and Sachs, ADART V, no. 93.
36789	1880,0617.527	Astronomical Diary; prices.
36790	1880,0617.528	Astrological omens; commentary. Reiner, Fs Borger (CM 10), 295.
36791	1880,0617.529	Omens; terrestrial.
36792	1880,0617.530	Joined to 36724.
36793	1880,0617.531	Astronomical; lunar table. Aaboe, KDVSMM 38/6 (1971) 11-12, pl. I.
36794	1880,0617.532	Brick of Nebuchadnezzar II. CBI, no. 102.
36795	1880,0617.533	School text; horizontal wedges. Gesche, AOAT 275, 676.

36796	1880,0617.534	Horoscope. SE 9/11/109. LBAT 1466; Rochberg, Babylonian Horoscopes, no. 15; Rochberg-Halton, Or NS 58 (1989) 114-117 and pl. II.
36797	1880,0617.535	Astronomical Diary.
36798	1880,0617.536	Astronomical; lunar data for SE 59 and 60. LBAT 1432a; Hunger and Sachs, ADART V, no. 38.
36799	1880,0617.537	Divorce contract. Dar 9/1?/5. Babylon. (+) 31425. Wunsch, Bab Arch 2, 32-39, no. 8.
36800	1880,0617.538	Account of provisions.
36801	1880,0617.539	Astronomical procedure text for Jupiter; prayer on upper edge. ACT 813b, colophon Zt; Ossendrijver, BMAPT, no. 21; Ossendrijver, Science 351 (2016) 482-484 (and Supplementary Materials); Ossendrijver, JNES 76, 231-247, text E.
36802	1880,0617.540	Astrological omens; commentary. Reiner, Fs Borger (CM 10), 295.
36803	1880,0617.541	Astronomical Diary.
36804	1880,0617.542	Cylinder; inscription of Nebuchadnezzar II on building at Borsippa; dupl. Langdon, VAB 4, 98-99, Neb. no. 11. Borsippa. Reade, Iraq 48, 109.
36805	1880,0617.543	Lexical; Ḫḫ XV. + 37213. MSL 9, 4.
36806	1880,0617.544	Joined to 36395.
	1880,0617.545	Joined to 36648.
36807	1880,0617.546	Astronomical Diary for SE 111. LBAT 308; Sachs and Hunger, ADART II, no. -200 A.
36808	1880,0617.547	Hemerology; dupl. KAR 212 ii 19-30.
36809	1880,0617.548	Economic.
36810	1880,0617.549	Astronomical; tables for Mars. + 36947. Aaboe, JCS 20, 9, 12, 24-25, 32; see ACT pp. 305-306 and 337 on no. 504.
36811	1880,0617.550	Astronomical; tables for Mars. Aaboe, JCS 20, 9-10, 12, 24-25, 32; see ACT, p. 337 on no. 504
36812	1880,0617.551	Lexical.
36813	1880,0617.552	Joined to 36762.
36814	1880,0617.553	Astronomical; table of longitudes of Saturn phenomena. Aaboe, JCS 20, 4-5, 28.
36815	1880,0617.554	Astrological?
36816	1880,0617.555	Dialogue contract about employment of astronomers. CT 49, 49, no. 192.
36817	1880,0617.556	Joined to 36628.
36818	1880,0617.557	Bilingual incantations; Muššu'u tablets I and III; Sag-gig. Böck, Muššu'u, 93-111 and 133-146.
36819	1880,0617.558	Joined to 32259.
36820	1880,0617.559	Joined to 36679.
36821	1880,0617.560	Religious?

36822	1880,0617.561	Astronomical; lunar functions and solar table. + 37022. Aaboe, Centaurus 11 (1966) 302-303; Aaboe and Sachs, Centaurus 14 (1969) 3-11 and pl. I, text A; Britton, AOAT 297, 39-40.
36823	1880,0617.562	Astronomical; planetary observations (Jupiter), perhaps when complete recording the years 536-498 BC. LBAT 1393; Hunger and Sachs, ADART V, no. 54.
36824	1880,0617.563	Astronomical; lunar table. + 37222. Aaboe, KDVSMM 36/12 (1968) 12-14, pl. I.
	1880,0617.564	Joined to 36754.
36825	1880,0617.565	Ritual for Esangila.
36826	1880,0617.566	Astronomical Diary.
36827	1880,0617.567	Incantation; Ḫulbazizi.
36828	1880,0617.568	Astrological omens; Enūma Anu Enlil 1. (+) 36828a (1880,0617.618) (+) 36921 + 37377. Reiner, Fs Borger (CM 10), 295; Verderame, Nisaba 2, 49-50 and Fol. III 1-2.
36829	1880,0617.569	Astronomical; planetary observations; abbreviated star names. Hunger and Sachs, ADART V, no. 94.
36830	1880,0617.570	Astronomical Diary.
36831	1880,0617.571	Astronomical; System A lunar ephemeris. (+) 36611. ACT 18a.
36832	1880,0617.572	Astronomical Diary. Sachs and Hunger, ADART I, no. -368.
36833	1880,0617.573	Astronomical.
36834	1880,0617.574	Astrological omens?
36835	1880,0617.575	Joined to 36736.
36836	1880,0617.576	Astrological omens; Enūma Anu Enlil, Adad. (+) 36840. Reiner, Fs Borger (CM 10), 295.
36837	1880,0617.577	Astronomical; planetary observations; Mercury from year 43 of Artaxerxes II to year 16 of Artaxerxes III; Mars from year 17 of Artaxerxes III to year 2 of Darius III. + 37067 (+) 36648 + 41687 (+) 36896. LBAT 1369 + 1370; Hunger and Sachs, ADART V, no. 65.
36838	1880,0617.578	Astronomical; heliacal risings. Neugebauer, JCS 21, 190-192, 215 text B.
36839	1880,0617.579	Joined to 36600.
36840	1880,0617.580	Astrological omens; Enūma Anu Enlil, Adad; colophon. (+) 36836.
36841	1880,0617.581	Mathematical; table of reciprocals, and decimal equivalents of sexagesimal integers; small two column tablet.
36842	1880,0617.582	Joined to 36746.
36843	1880,0617.583	School text; Tintir II; lexical. George, BTT, pl. 57; Gesche, AOAT 275, 676.

36844	1880,0617.584	Joined to 36755.
36845	1880,0617.585	Astronomical; Vorläufer; eclipse, AN-MI Sin.
36846	1880,0617.586	Joined to 36699.
36847	1880,0617.587	List of market prices for years 23-26 SE. (+) 37353. Wiseman, Gs Sachs, 363-373; Vargyas, Fs Hunger, 531-540; Slotsky and Wallenfels, Tallies and Trends, text 2.
36848	1880,0617.588	Prayer (to Marduk?).
36849	1880,0617.589	Mathematical; combined multiplication table. + 37362. Aaboe in Swerdlow, Astronomy, 179-186; cf. Aaboe, JCS 22, 88-90 (U. 91).
36850	1880,0617.590	Joined to 36737.
36851	1880,0617.591	Astronomical; MUL.APIN. Hunger and Pingree, AfO Beih. 24, 3; Reiner, Fs Borger (CM 10), 296; Hunger and Steele, MUL.APIN, 21.
36852	1880,0617.592	Astrological omens; Enūma Anu Enlil. Reiner, Fs Borger (CM 10), 296.
36853	1880,0617.593	Joined to 36395.
36854	1880,0617.594	Astronomical procedure text; moon, planets, periods.
36855	1880,0617.595	Astronomical procedure text; lunar sixes; cf. TCL 6, no. 11.
36856	1880,0617.596	Administrative; receipt; Murānu archive; sealed. SE []/12/[]. CT 49, 44, no. 170; Jursa, Persika 9, 198-199; Nisaba 28, no. 654.
36857	1880,0617.597	Astronomical Diary for SE 121. + 37829 (+) 37148. Sachs and Hunger, ADART II, no. -190 D.
36858	1880,0617.598	Unidentified; flake.
36859	1880,0617.599	Unidentified.
36860	1880,0617.600	Astronomical or astrological table; copy; ḫe-pí repeated; two columns; flake from one side (reverse?).
36861	1880,0617.601	Astronomical.
36862	1880,0617.602	Economic. Dar 29/7/11.
36863	1880,0617.603	Astronomical Diary.
36864	1880,0617.604	Mathematical; table of reciprocals(?); colophon(?) on upper edge.
36865	1880,0617.605	Joined to 36402.
36866	1880,0617.606	Joined to 36389.
36867	1880,0617.607	Omens; apodoses; mentioning a series of months and wind directions.
36868	1880,0617.608	Astronomical Diary.
36869	1880,0617.609	Historical.
36870	1880,0617.610	Astronomical Diary(?); fragment from centre.
36871	1880,0617.611	School text; unidentified. Gesche, AOAT 275, 676
36872	1880,0617.612	Bilingual hymn; colophon: [...] x IM 4-KAM ÉŠ-GÀR ZÀ-MÍ [...].

36873	1880,0617.613	School text; lexical, Syllabary A. Gesche, AOAT 275, 676.
36874	1880,0617.614	Astronomical; Vorläufer; left edge; 5 UŠ repeated; dupl. 41004 (JCS 21, 201), lines 4-7. Steele, NABU 2012, 71-72, no. 54.
36875	1880,0617.615	Astronomical or astrological; mentions Venus, Mercury and Adad; fragment from right edge.
36876	1880,0617.616	Joined to 36685.
36877	1880,0617.617	Astronomical; Normal Star Almanac for SE 37; upper edge. Hunger and Sachs, ADART VII, no. 5.
36828a	1880,0617.618	Astrological omens; Enūma Anu Enlil 1. (+) 36828 (+) 36921 + 37377. Reiner, Fs Borger (CM 10), 295; Verderame, Nisaba 2, 49-100 and Fol. III 1-2. The tablet is numbered 36828a out of sequence because L. W. King recognised that it was part of the same tablet as 1880,0617.568.
36878	1880,0617.619	Historical copy? Mentions [...-t]i-ia-áš LUGAL LUGAL.LUGAL; colophon.
36879	1880,0617.620	Astronomical; table of lunar eclipse reports for at least 529-526 BC. Hunger and Sachs, ADART V, no. 8.
36880	1880,0617.621	Astrological omens; Enūma Anu Enlil, Sin; dupl. to ACh Sin 16 and K.3135. Reiner, Fs Borger (CM 10), 296.
36881	1880,0617.622	Astronomical Diary.
36882	1880,0617.623	Medical.
36883	1880,0617.624	Astronomical Diary for SE 182. Sachs and Hunger, ADART III, no. -129 B.
36884	1880,0617.625	Astronomical Diary; flake from centre of one side.
36885	1880,0617.626	Medical; ap-pi-šú-nu ṣu-up-pu-ru.
36886	1880,0617.627	Astronomical Diary.
36887	1880,0617.628	Astronomical procedure text for the moon; System A. Ossendrijver, BMAPT, no. 80.
36888	1880,0617.629	Astronomical Diary.
36889	1880,0617.630	Astronomical Diary for SE 84. Sachs and Hunger, ADART II, no. -227.
36890	1880,0617.631	Astronomical; ACT lunar ephemeris; lower edge. Steele, Fs Walker, 293-318, text A.
36891	1880,0617.632	Joined to 36763.
36892	1880,0617.633	Account of silver paid for garments; two columns; fragment of reverse only. Art.
36893	1880,0617.634	Stone list (from medical prescriptions).
36894	1880,0617.635	Astronomical Diary. + 37398.
36895	1880,0617.636	Astronomical; longitudes. ACT 1011.

36896	1880,0617.637	Astronomical; planetary observations; Mercury from year 43 of Artaxerxes II to year 16 of Artaxerxes III; Mars from year 17 of Artaxerxes III to year 2 of Darius III. (+) 36648 (+) 36837. Hunger and Sachs, ADART V, no. 65.
36897	1880,0617.638	Joined to 36696.
36898	1880,0617.639	Omens; extispicy?.
36899	1880,0617.640	Chronicle.
36900	1880,0617.641	Contract; Murānu archive; sealed. SE Antiochus II 10/12/58. CT 49, 26, no. 127; Jursa, Persika 9, 195; Nisaba 28, no. 580.
36901	1880,0617.642	Medical.
36902	1880,0617.643	Astronomical; Vorläufer; BE-ma ina NE lu ina GAN lu UD 12 13 14.
36903	1880,0617.644	Mathematical; numbers; fragment of right edge.
36904	1880,0617.645	Astrological omens; Enūma Anu Enlil. Reiner, Fs Borger (CM 10), 296.
36905	1880,0617.646	Astrological omens; Enūma Anu Enlil.
36906	1880,0617.647	Astronomical Diary.
36907	1880,0617.648	Astrological omens; Enūma Anu Enlil. Reiner, Fs Borger (CM 10), 296.
36908	1880,0617.649	Astronomical; lunar table. Aaboe, KDVSMM 38/6 (1971) 6-11 and pl. I.
36909	1880,0617.650	Literary; Gilgameš VIII. + 37023 + F.235. George, Gilgamesh II, pls. 104-105.
36910	1880,0617.651	Astronomical; Saros cycle text. + 36998 + 37036. LBAT 1422-1424; Aaboe, JHA 3 (1972) 115, n. 22; Aaboe, et al., TAPS 81/6 (1991), 4-8, text A.
36911	1880,0617.652	Astronomical Diary.
36912	1880,0617.653	Account of silver payments.
36913	1880,0617.654	Astronomical Diary. Sachs and Hunger, ADART I, no. -357.
36914	1880,0617.655	Astrological omens; Enūma Anu Enlil; star UD.30. KAM IGI, apodoses; right edge. Reiner, Fs Borger (CM 10), 296.
36915	1880,0617.656	School text; only ḫe-pí repeated.
36916	1880,0617.657	School text; lexical, Ḫḫ IX-XI; Tintir II 33-37; literary. MSL 9, 189, 195; Gesche, AOAT 275, 282, 676; George, AfO 50, 404.
36917	1880,0617.658	Mathematical table. Ossendrijver, JCS 66, 149-165 and pls.
36918	1880,0617.659	Joined to 36751.
36919	1880,0617.660	Astronomical; watches (EN.NUN).
36920	1880,0617.661	Joined to 36724.

36921	1880,0617.662	Astrological omens; Enūma Anu Enlil, Sin. + 37377 (+) 36828 (+) 36828a. Reiner, Fs Borger (CM 10), 296-297; Verderame, Nisaba 2, 50 (37377 only).
36922	1880,0617.663	Astronomical; Mercury for (at least) SE 10 to 18; System A2. ACT 300b.
36923	1880,0617.664	Astronomical Diary.
36924	1880,0617.665	Astronomical; lower right corner.
36925	1880,0617.666	Bilingual incantation.
36926	1880,0617.667	Astronomical Diary.
36927	1880,0617.668	Astrological omens; ziqpu.
36928	1880,0617.669	Astrological; MÚL NN ...; astronomical?; lower right corner. Reiner, Fs Borger (CM 10), 296.
36929	1880,0617.670	Economic or religious; mentions gods (Ninlil and Enlil) and quantities of silver; copy (ḫe-pí); fragment from left side.
36930	1880,0617.671	Astronomical procedure text for the moon; System A. Ossendrijver, BMAPT, no. 78.
36931	1880,0617.672	Incantation.
36932	1880,0617.673	Sale of real estate.
36933	1880,0617.674	Economic?
36934	1880,0617.675	Astronomical Diary.
36935	1880,0617.676	School text; literary?; lexical? Gesche, AOAT 275, 676.
36936	1880,0617.677	School text; lexical, Ḫḫ VIII-IX. MSL 9, 173, 181; Gesche, AOAT 275, 676.
36937	1880,0617.678	Astronomical; Goal Year Text. + 1881,0428.750.
36938	1880,0617.679	Astrological; births?; Mars and Saturn.
36939	1880,0617.680	Astrological omens; Enūma Anu Enlil, Sin; lower left corner. Reiner, Fs Borger (CM 10), 296.
36940	1880,0617.681	School text; lexical, syllabary. Gesche, AOAT 275, 676.
36941	1880,0617.682	Joined to 36599.
36942	1880,0617.683	Astronomical Diary.
36943	1880,0617.684	Horoscope?
36944	1880,0617.685	Astronomical; lunar table.
36945	1880,0617.686	Astronomical Diary.
36946	1880,0617.687	Astronomical Diary.
36947	1880,0617.688	Joined to 36810.
36948	1880,0617.689	Astronomical; Saturn ephemeris, System A. Steele, JHA 33 (2002) 261-264
36949	1880,0617.690	Omens; Šumma ālu, tablet 22; colophon. + 37028. Freedman, If a city, vols. 1, 330 and 2, 6.
36950	1880,0617.691	Astronomical; Mercury? procedure.
36951	1880,0617.692	Contract; sealed. d.l. Nisaba 28, no. 640.
36952	1880,0617.693	Joined to 36306.

36953	1880,0617.694	Bilingual incantation.
36954	1880,0617.695	Mathematical; metrological table. Steele, SCIAMVS 16 (2015) 75-90.
36955	1880,0617.696	Astronomical.
36956	1880,0617.697	Astronomical; Mercury observations; two columns. Hunger and Sachs, ADART V, no. 95.
36957	1880,0617.698	Astronomical; tables for Mars. Aaboe, JCS 20, 10, 24-25, 33.
36958	1880,0617.699	Contract.
36959	1880,0617.700	School text; lexical. Gesche, AOAT 275, 676.
36960	1880,0617.701	List of market prices, perhaps for years 65-66 SE. Wiseman, Gs Sachs, 363-373; Vargyas, Fs Hunger, 531-540; Slotsky and Wallenfels, Tallies and Trends, text 13.
36961	1880,0617.702	Astronomical; lunar System A, columns Phi, F, B. Aaboe, KDVSMM 36/12 (1968) 39; Steele, AHES 60 (2006) 123-135, text G.
36962	1880,0617.703	Astronomical; Normal Star Almanac. Hunger and Sachs, ADART VII, no. 131.
	1880,0617.704	Astrological (so register); missing or joined already in the 1890s.
36963	1880,0617.705	Omen commentary.
	1880,0617.706	Joined to 36311.
36964	1880,0617.707	Joined to 36440.
36965	1880,0617.708	School text; unidentified. Gesche, AOAT 275, 676.
36966	1880,0617.709	Astrological.
36967	1880,0617.710	Astronomical Diary. + 37013.
36968	1880,0617.711	Astrological. Reiner, Fs Borger (CM 10), 296.
36969	1880,0617.712	School text; lexical, Ḫḫ IV-V. + 37019. MSL 9, 168 (37019 only); Gesche, AOAT 275, 676.
36970	1880,0617.713	School text; lexical. Gesche, AOAT 275, 676.
36971	1880,0617.714	Astronomical Diary.
	1880,0617.715	Joined to 36323.
36972	1880,0617.716	Mathematical; metrological table. Steele, SCIAMVS 16 (2015) 75-90.
36973	1880,0617.717	School text; lexical, Syllabary A. Gesche, AOAT 275, 676.
36974	1880,0617.718	Literary; Erra I. Lambert, MC 24, no. 42.
36975	1880,0617.719	Astronomical.
36976	1880,0617.720	Astronomical; mentions years 16-20; left edge.
36977	1880,0617.721	Joined to 36414.
36978	1880,0617.722	Omens; extispicy.
36979	1880,0617.723	Lexical; Aa IV/4 = 25. + 36991 + 37268. CT 12, 22; MSL 14, 384 (36991 + 37268).
36980	1880,0617.724	Lexical.

36981	1880,0617.725	School text.
36982	1880,0617.726	Mathematical problem text; reverse lexicographical?
36983	1880,0617.727	Medical. (+) 37119.
36984	1880,0617.728	School text; lexical. Gesche, AOAT 275, 676.
36985	1880,0617.729	Astronomical; upper right corner of a very thin tablet.
36986	1880,0617.730	Contract; division of property.
36987	1880,0617.731	Astronomical; Normal Star Almanac for SE 142. Hunger and Sachs, ADART VII, no. 60.
36988	1880,0617.732	Compendium of calendrical and stellar astrology; prayer on upper edge. (+) 36303 + 36326 (+) 36628 + ... Steele, JCS 67, 187-215.
36989	1880,0617.733	List of market prices, perhaps for years 55-60 SE. Wiseman, Gs Sachs, 363-373; Vargyas, Fs Hunger, 531-540; Slotsky and Wallenfels, Tallies and Trends, text 14.
36990	1880,0617.734	Astronomical.
36991	1880,0617.735	Joined to 36979.
36992	1880,0617.736	School text; unidentified. Gesche, AOAT 275, 676.
36993	1880,0617.737	Astronomical Diary.
36994	1880,0617.738	Astronomical; lunar table. Aaboe, KDVSMM 36/12 (1968) 12, pl. I.
36995	1880,0617.739	Astronomical; calendar text for months ii and viii; fragment. Brack-Bernsen and Steele, Fs Pingree (2004), 98 n. 3.
36996	1880,0617.740	Ritual.
36997	1880,0617.741	Astronomical procedure?; fragment of upper or lower edge; DIŠ ina ITU.DU6 9 [...] sin a-na 1 ad [...] / DIŠ ina ITU.APIN 1 kùš x[...] sin a-na 1 ad 1,10 [...].
36998	1880,0617.742	Joined to 36909.
36999	1880,0617.743	Astronomical.
37000	1880,0617.744	Astronomical.
37001	1880,0617.745	Incantation?
37002	1880,0617.746	Incantation?
37003	1880,0617.747	Receipt for interest payment; sealed. SE Antiochus III 25/[7?]/96. Kuzbu-ša-Bēl-damiq. CT 49, 29, no. 133; Stolper, Annali Supp. 77, 33-34, no. 10; Nisaba 28, no. 589.
37004	1880,0617.748	Astronomical Diary.
37005	1880,0617.749	Astronomical; Goal Year Text; not datable. Hunger and Sachs, ADART VI, no. 149.
37006	1880,0617.750	Astronomical Diary.
37007	1880,0617.751	Astronomical; lunar six table. Huber and Steele, SCIAMVS 8 (2007) 3-36, text I.
37008	1880,0617.752	Omens; Šumma ālu?

37009	1880,0617.753	Envelope of 36507 (letter); sealed. SE Ant I and Ant 4/7/50. CT 49, 24, no. 118a; Jursa, Persika 9, 156, 186-187; Nisaba 28, no. 668.
37010	1880,0617.754	Astrological omens; Enūma Anu Enlil 63. (+) 36395 + 36086 + 36853 (+) 36758 + 37496 (+) 37121 + 37432. Reiner and Pingree, BPO 1, source F; Reiner, Fs Borger (CM 10), 296.
37011	1880,0617.755	Astronomical.
37012	1880,0617.756	Joined to 36438.
37013	1880,0617.757	Joined to 36967.
37014	1880,0617.758	Horoscope? or medical.
37015	1880,0617.759	Letter to Murānu. SE 11/9/[54?]. CT 49, 47, no. 182; Jursa, Persika 9, 156, 191-192.
37016	1880,0617.760	Joined to 34467.
37017	1880,0617.761	Mathematical; numerical tables; fragment.
37018	1880,0617.762	Joined to 36747.
37019	1880,0617.763	Joined to 36969.
37020	1880,0617.764	Mathematical table. Ossendrijver, JCS 66, 149-165 and pls.
37021	1880,0617.765	Astronomical; lunar System A columns K1 and M1 for SE 45 II to SE 48 XI. Aaboe, KDVSMM 40/6 (1979) 33-34; Steele, AHES 60 (2006) 123-135, text B.
37022	1880,0617.766	Joined to 36822.
37023	1880,0617.767	Joined to 36909.
37024	1880,0617.768	Astronomical procedure text; Mars; System A. Aaboe, Fs E. S. Kennedy, 1-14; Ossendrijver, BMAPT, no. 14.
37025	1880,0617.769	Hemerology.
37026	1880,0617.770	Joined to 36438.
37027	1880,0617.771	Astronomical Diary.
37028	1880,0617.772	Joined to 36949.
37029	1880,0617.773	Astronomical Diary.
37030	1880,0617.774	Joined to 36609.
37031	1880,0617.775	Joined to 36744.
37032	1880,0617.776	Joined to 36651.
37033	1880,0617.777	Contract; sealed. d.l. Nisaba 28, no. 304.
37034	1880,0617.778	List of market prices. Wiseman, Gs Sachs, 363-373; Vargyas, Fs Hunger, 531-540; Slotsky and Wallenfels, Tallies and Trends, text 15.
37035	1880,0617.779	Astronomical.
37036	1880,0617.780	Joined to 36909.
37037	1880,0617.781	Astronomical Diary. + 37109.
37038	1880,0617.782	Astronomical.
37039	1880,0617.783	Astronomical Diary.

37040	1880,0617.784	School text; lexical, Syllabary A. + 37057. Gesche, AOAT 275, 676.
37041	1880,0617.785	Astronomical Diary.
37042	1880,0617.786	Astronomical Diary.
37043	1880,0617.787	Joined to 36612.
37044	1880,0617.788	Astronomical; Saros cycle text. LBAT 1425; Aaboe, et al., TAPS 81/6 (1991), 10-11, text B.
37045	1880,0617.789	Astronomical. + 37060.
37046	1880,0617.790	Joined to 36629.
37047	1880,0617.791	Joined to 36609.
37048	1880,0617.792	Joined to 36609.
37049	1880,0617.793	Economic.
37050	1880,0617.794	Astronomical observations; lunar data for SE 104 and other years. + 1880,0617.799 + 839. LBAT 1434; Hunger and Sachs, ADART V, no. 41.
37051	1880,0617.795	Astronomical; Mercury observations; mentions year 55; two columns. Hunger and Sachs, ADART V, no. 96.
37052	1880,0617.796	Astronomical; lunar System A, column G2 for SE 37-38. Steele, AHES 60 (2006) 123-135, text A.
37053	1880,0617.797	Joined to 36651.
37054	1880,0617.798	List of market prices. + 40100. Wiseman, Gs Sachs, 363-373; Vargyas, Fs Hunger, 531-540; Slotsky and Wallenfels, Tallies and Trends, text 16.
	1880,0617.799	Joined to 37050.
37055	1880,0617.800	Joined to 36595.
37056	1880,0617.801	Astronomical procedure text for planets; also astrology? + 37074.
37057	1880,0617.802	Joined to 37040.
37058	1880,0617.803	Lexical.
37059	1880,0617.804	Commentary.
37060	1880,0617.805	Joined to 37045.
37061	1880,0617.806	Astronomical; mentions Gemini; ruled.
37062	1880,0617.807	Astronomical; System A ephemeris; lunar eclipses(?) from SE 206 to 220. ACT 51a.
37063	1880,0617.808	Medical. + 37154.
37064	1880,0617.809	Literary.
37065	1880,0617.810	Ritual; astrological. Reiner, Fs Borger (CM 10), 296.
37066	1880,0617.811	Incantation; Marduk's Address (Udug-ḫul 11).
37067	1880,0617.812	Joined to 36837.
37068	1880,0617.813	Astronomical.
37069	1880,0617.814	Astronomical Diary.
37070	1880,0617.815	Astronomical; table of longitudes of Jupiter phenomena. (+) 36762 (+) 36779 (+) 37082 + 37125 (+) 37174. Aaboe, JCS 20, 7-8, 16-21, 29-30.

37071	1880,0617.816	Astronomical Diary.
37072	1880,0617.817	Astronomical.
37073	1880,0617.818	Astronomical Diary; prayer on upper edge. LBAT 187; Sachs and Hunger, ADART I, no. -361; Grasshoff in Swerdlow, Astronomy, 100.
37074	1880,0617.819	Joined to 37056.
	1880,0617.820	Joined to 36712.
37075	1880,0617.821	School text; lexical, Syllabary A. Gesche, AOAT 275, 676.
37076	1880,0617.822	Joined to 36609.
37077	1880,0617.823	Contract; sale of fields, houses and slaves; sealed; finger-nail marks. Dupl. 30122 etc. [Cyr] [6]/[3]/[4]. Babylon. + 41909 + 41974. Wunsch, CM 3, no. 292 (37077 only); Wunsch, CM 20A, 253, no. 125D (41909 + 41974 only), and CM 20B, 150-158; Nisaba 28, no. 90.
37078	1880,0617.824	Omens; Šumma ālu; scorpions; colophon with catch line.
37079	1880,0617.825	Joined to 36699.
	1880,0617.826	Joined to 36311.
37080	1880,0617.827	Medical.
37081	1880,0617.828	Astronomical Diary.
37082	1880,0617.829	Astronomical; table of longitudes of Jupiter phenomena. + 37125 (+) 36762 (+) 36779 (+) 37070 (+) 37174. Aaboe, JCS 20, 7-8, 16-21, 29-30.
	1880,0617.830	Joined to 36311.
37083	1880,0617.831	Promissory note for silver.
37084	1880,0617.832	Astronomical Diary?
37085	1880,0617.833	Astronomical; ACT procedure.
37086	1880,0617.834	Astronomical Diary.
37087	1880,0617.835	Astronomical; longitudes. ACT 1010.
37088	1880,0617.836	Astronomical; lunar eclipse table for at least 383-362 BC. + 37652. LBAT 1429; Hunger and Sachs, ADART V, no. 10.
37089	1880,0617.837	Astronomical; Seleucid table of daily solar positions. Aaboe, JCS 18, 31-34.
37090	1880,0617.838	Astronomical; Vorläufer? or astrological?; star/zodiac positions?
	1880,0617.839	Joined to 37050.
37091	1880,0617.840	Joined to 36596.
37092	1880,0617.841	Letter order; sealed; probably Seleucid. CT 49, 48, no. 184; Mitchell and Searight, no. 758; Nisaba 28, no. 678.
37093	1880,0617.842	Astrological; commentary. + 37279. Reiner, Fs Borger (CM 10), 296-297.

37094	1880,0617.843	Astronomical; zodiac signs, months and numbers. ACT 1051.
37095	1880,0617.844	Mathematical table. Ossendrijver, JCS 66, 149-165 and pls.
37096	1880,0617.845	Mathematical; coefficient list; bricks and materials. Robson, OECT XIV, 205-207, List K.
37097	1880,0617.846	Astronomical Diary. + 37211. Sachs and Hunger, ADART I, no. -369; Stephenson, HEER, 138.
37098	1880,0617.847	Bilingual incantation; colophon.
37099	1880,0617.848	Astronomical.
37100	1880,0617.849	Joined to 36781.
37101	1880,0617.850	Astronomical; MUL.APIN?; small script. Reiner, Fs Borger (CM 10), 296.
37102	1880,0617.851	Astrological.
37103	1880,0617.852	Incantation.
37104	1880,0617.853	Astronomical Diary.
37105	1880,0617.854	Astronomical; Goal Year Text; not datable. Hunger and Sachs, ADART VI, no. 150.
37106	1880,0617.855	School text; unidentified. Gesche, AOAT 275, 677.
37107	1880,0617.856	Joined to 36612.
37108	1880,0617.857	Promissory note for silver.
37109	1880,0617.858	Joined to 37037.
37110	1880,0617.859	Astronomical procedure text; the Goal Year method for calculating KUR. + unnum. (+) 36766. Brack-Bernsen et al., Fs Slotsky, 1-6.
37111	1880,0617.860	Astronomical; lunar table.
37112	1880,0617.861	Joined to 36627.
37113	1880,0617.862	Astrological omens.
37114	1880,0617.863	Astronomical procedure text for the moon; System A. Ossendrijver, BMAPT, no. 85.
37115	1880,0617.864	Astronomical; Mercury for (at least) SE 10 to 18; System A2. + 1880,0617.975. ACT 300b.
37116	1880,0617.865	Ritual?
37117	1880,0617.866	Astronomical Diary.
37118	1880,0617.867	Astronomical Diary?
37119	1880,0617.868	Medical. (+) 36983.
37120	1880,0617.869	Astronomical Diary.
37121	1880,0617.870	Astrological omens; Enūma Anu Enlil 63; ruled. + 37432 (+) 36395 + 36086 + 36853 (+) 36758 + 37496 (+) 37010. Reiner and Pingree, BPO 1, source O; Reiner, Fs Borger (CM 10), 296-297.
37122	1880,0617.871	School text; Šamaš Hymn; lexical. Lambert, MC 24, no. 136.
37123	1880,0617.872	Astronomical procedure text for the moon. Ossendrijver, BMAPT, no. 101.

37124	1880,0617.873	Astronomical.
37125	1880,0617.874	Joined to 37082.
37126	1880,0617.875	School text; lexical; incantation, Šurpu IV 42-48; literary. 11/[]/-. + 37146. Gesche, AOAT 275, 282, 677.
37127	1880,0617.876	Astronomical; table of lunar visibility; small script; ruled; cf. Enūma Anu Enlil 14. George and ar-Rawi, AfO 38-39, 52-73; Reiner, Fs Borger (CM 10), 296.
37128	1880,0617.877	School text; lexical, Ḫḫ, place names. Gesche, AOAT 275, 677.
37129	1880,0617.878	Astronomical Diary.
37130	1880,0617.879	Astronomical or astrological; numbers and months.
37131	1880,0617.880	Account of bitumen.
37132	1880,0617.881	Account of offerings?
	1880,0617.882	Joined to 36445.
37133	1880,0617.883	Contract. Xerxes []/6/9. Babylon.
37134	1880,0617.884	Mathematical; numerical table.
37135	1880,0617.885	Lexical.
37136	1880,0617.886	Astrological; small script. Reiner, Fs Borger (CM 10), 296.
37137	1880,0617.887	Astronomical Diary.
37138	1880,0617.888	Economic.
37139	1880,0617.889	Astrological omens?; eclipses?; fragment from centre of one side only. Reiner, Fs Borger (CM 10), 296.
37140	1880,0617.890	Incantation.
37141	1880,0617.891	Astrological omens; Enūma Anu Enlil, Venus. Reiner, Fs Borger (CM 10), 296.
37142	1880,0617.892	Copy (ḫe-pí), perhaps of a contract; colophon.
37143	1880,0617.893	Religious.
37144	1880,0617.894	Joined to 36627.
37145	1880,0617.895	Economic.
37146	1880,0617.896	Joined to 37126.
37147	1880,0617.897	Joined to 36732.
37148	1880,0617.898	Astronomical Diary for SE 121. (+) 36857. Sachs and Hunger, ADART II, no. -190 D.
37149	1880,0617.899	Astronomical; velocity (ZI). Neugebauer, JCS 21, 199-200, 215 text D.
37150	1880,0617.900	Astronomical; obv. numbers; rev. culminating points for the signs of the zodiac. Steele, Rising time schemes, 101-104.
37151	1880,0617.901	Astronomical; tables for Venus. + 37249. Aaboe, Fs Finkelstein, 1-4.
37152	1880,0617.902	Astronomical procedure; eclipse calculations: ... a-rá 18 ... GE6 d.Sin u d.Šamaš ... Reiner, Fs Borger (CM 10), 296.
37153	1880,0617.903	Astronomical procedure; Goal Year rules.

37154	1880,0617.904	Joined to 37063.
37155	1880,0617.905	Astrological.
37156	1880,0617.906	Joined to 36300.
37157	1880,0617.907	Astrological omens; Enūma Anu Enlil, Adad; rainbows; left edge. + 37160. Reiner, Fs Borger (CM 10), 296.
37158	1880,0617.908	Astronomical Diary?; weather reports only.
37159	1880,0617.909	Bilingual incantation.
37160	1880,0617.910	Joined to 37157.
37161	1880,0617.911	Astronomical Diary.
37162	1880,0617.912	Astronomical; Mercury phenomena; reverse inscribed at right angles. (+) 36651. Aaboe, et al., TAPS 81/6 (1991), 34-62, Text E2.
37163	1880,0617.913	Literary; Gilgameš I. + F.234. CT 46, 30, no. 20; Garelli, Gilgameš 124-125 (copy by Wiseman); George, Gilgamesh II, pl. 50.
37164	1880,0617.914	Literary.
37165	1880,0617.915	Incantation; copy.
37166	1880,0617.916	Astronomical; ACT procedure.
37167	1880,0617.917	Medical.
37168	1880,0617.918	Astrological; ruled. Reiner, Fs Borger (CM 10), 296.
	1880,0617.919	Joined to 36712.
37169	1880,0617.920	Joined to 36622.
37170	1880,0617.921	Contract; sale of a house; sealed. Art 15+/9/[]. Babylon. + 37191. Nisaba 28, no. 267.
37171	1880,0617.922	Astronomical; numbers (eclipse table?) and diagram (for the diagram cf. 33333B, 39198, 40680 and 47890).
37172	1880,0617.923	Contract; sealed. d.l. CT 49, 46, no. 177; Nisaba 28, no. 618.
37173	1880,0617.924	Joined to 36746.
	1880,0617.925	Joined to 36311.
37174	1880,0617.926	Astronomical; table of longitudes of Jupiter phenomena. (+) 36762 (+) 36779 (+) 37070 (+) 37082 + 37125. Aaboe, JCS 20, 7-8, 16-21, 29-30.
37175	1880,0617.927	Astronomical; based on MUL.APIN; two columns. Reiner, Fs Borger (CM 10), 296.
37176	1880,0617.928	Astrological omens; Adad; earthquakes. Reiner, Fs Borger (CM 10), 296.
37177	1880,0617.929	Contract; sale of fields. -/12b/-.
37178	1880,0617.930	Joined to 36628.
37179	1880,0617.931	Astronomical; table for Mercury; System A2.
37180	1880,0617.932	School text; lexical, Ḫḫ I, acrographic list; colophon? Gesche, AOAT 275, 284, 677.
	1880,0617.933	Joined to 36311.

37181	1880,0617.934	Bilingual incantation.
37182	1880,0617.935	Unidentified.
37183	1880,0617.936	Astronomical Diary.
37184	1880,0617.937	Astronomical; observations; Normal Stars? Fragment from centre; two columns; rev. lost
37185	1880,0617.938	Literary.
37186	1880,0617.939	Astronomical; System A lunar ephemeris. (+) 37375. ACT 3b.
37187	1880,0617.940	School text; lexical, Ḫḫ XX-XXI; literary. MSL 11, 4, 10; Gesche, AOAT 275, 285, 677.
37188	1880,0617.941	Astronomical Diary for SE 107. LBAT 302; Sachs and Hunger, ADART II, no. -204 A.
37189	1880,0617.942	Literary; Gilgameš VIII. CT 46, 31, no. 27; Garelli, Gilgameš 124 (copy by Wiseman), 135; George, Gilgamesh II, pl. 104.
37190	1880,0617.943	School text; lexical, Ḫḫ. Gesche, AOAT 275, 677.
37191	1880,0617.944	Joined to 37170.
37192	1880,0617.945	Commentary.
37193	1880,0617.946	School text; literary; lexical. Gesche, AOAT 275, 677.
37194	1880,0617.947	Astronomical; lunar six.
37195	1880,0617.948	Astrological omens.
37196	1880,0617.949	Astronomical; tables for Mars. Aaboe, JCS 20, 11, 33.
37197	1880,0617.950	Joined to 36628.
37198	1880,0617.951	Astrological omens; Enūma Anu Enlil, planets, stars. Reiner, Fs Borger (CM 10), 296.
37199	1880,0617.952	Astrological omens; Enūma Anu Enlil. Reiner, Fs Borger (CM 10), 296.
37200	1880,0617.953	Astronomical; based on MUL.APIN. Reiner, Fs Borger (CM 10), 296.
37201	1880,0617.954	Astrological omens; Enūma Anu Enlil, Sin; lower edge.
37202	1880,0617.955	Mathematical; combined multiplication table; fragment.
37203	1880,0617.956	Astronomical; lunar table. Aaboe, KDVSMM 36/12 (1968) 14-15, pl. I.
37204	1880,0617.957	Lexical; Diri VI A. MSL 15 181.
37205	1880,0617.958	Joined to 36722.
37206	1880,0617.959	Lexical; uzu.
37207	1880,0617.960	Joined to 36939.
37208	1880,0617.961	Incantation.
37209	1880,0617.962	Bilingual incantation.
37210	1880,0617.963	Joined to 36300.
37211	1880,0617.964	Joined to 37097.
37212	1880,0617.965	Commentary.
37213	1880,0617.966	Joined to 36805.

37214	1880,0617.967	Astronomical; Vorläufer?; danna.
37215	1880,0617.968	Liver omens.
37216	1880,0617.969	Economic; upper left corner only; Egibi archive. Dar -/-/8.
37217	1880,0617.970	Literary; Erra I.
37218	1880,0617.971	Medical.
37219	1880,0617.972	Astrological omens; planets; ruled. Reiner, Fs Borger (CM 10), 296.
37220	1880,0617.973	Astronomical; Vorläufer or ACT procedure; line 2: GUB u ŠÚ: 2,30 DI-pi u LAL šá ITU; lines 3-4: n UD-mu GUB u ŠÚ.
37221	1880,0617.974	Astronomical.
	1880,0617.975	Joined to 37115.
37222	1880,0617.976	Joined to 36824.
37223	1880,0617.977	Joined to 36431.
37224	1880,0617.978	Literary; mythological; mentions Nergal and the gods of Kūtû.
37225	1880,0617.979	School text; colophon? Gesche, AOAT 275, 677.
37226	1880,0617.980	Address of a person.
37227	1880,0617.981	Account of silver.
37228	1880,0617.982	Receipt for grain; sealed. Art 15/5/12. Mitchell and Searight, no. 493; Nisaba 28, no. 272.
37229	1880,0617.983	Astrological report. Cf. Reiner, Fs Borger (CM 10), 297.
37230	1880,0617.984	Joined to 36773.
37231	1880,0617.985	Astronomical Diary. Sachs and Hunger, ADART I, no. -333.
37232	1880,0617.986	Economic.
37233	1880,0617.987	Incantation. + 1880,0617.1009.
37234	1880,0617.988	Joined to 36723.
37235	1880,0617.989	School text; lexical, syllabary?; unidentified. Gesche, AOAT 275, 677.
37236	1880,0617.990	Astronomical; longitudes of Mars for (at least) 102 years; System A. ACT 504; Aaboe, JCS 20, 10, 24-25, 33.
37237	1880,0617.991	School text; unidentified. Gesche, AOAT 275, 677.
37238	1880,0617.992	Contract; sale of fields.
37239	1880,0617.993	School text; lexical, Syllabary A; unidentified. Gesche, AOAT 275, 677.
37240	1880,0617.994	Lexical, commentary on Diri V.
37241	1880,0617.995	Lexical.
37242	1880,0617.996	School text; lexical, Syllabary A. Gesche, AOAT 275, 677.
37243	1880,0617.997	Muššu'u tablet I. Jiménez, Iraq 76, 118.
37244	1880,0617.998	Chronicle.

37245	1880,0617.999	Sale of a donkey.
37246	1880,0617.1000	Contract; sale of land. Sandowicz, AOAT 398, 452, C.133.
37247	1880,0617.1001	Administrative. Art.
37248	1880,0617.1002	School text; lexical, Syllabary A. Gesche, AOAT 275, 677.
37249	1880,0617.1003	Joined to 37151.
37250	1880,0617.1004	Incantation.
37251	1880,0617.1005	Promissory note for dates.
37252	1880,0617.1006	Lexical; god list.
37253	1880,0617.1007	School text; lexical. Gesche, AOAT 275, 677.
37254	1880,0617.1008	Literary cylinder.
	1880,0617.1009	Joined to 37233.
37255	1880,0617.1010	School text; lexical, syllabary?; colophon? Gesche, AOAT 275, 677.
37256	1880,0617.1011	School text; lexical, Syllabary B. Gesche, AOAT 275, 677.
37257	1880,0617.1012	Omens?
37258	1880,0617.1013	Literary.
37259	1880,0617.1014	Astronomical.
37260	1880,0617.1015	Economic.
37261	1880,0617.1016	Astronomical.
37262	1880,0617.1017	School text; unidentified. Gesche, AOAT 275, 677.
37263	1880,0617.1018	Astronomical.
37264	1880,0617.1019	Joined to 36701.
	1880,0617.1020	Joined to 36647.
37265	1880,0617.1021	School text; unidentified. Gesche, AOAT 275, 677.
37266	1880,0617.1022	Astronomical procedure text for Jupiter, Saturn and Mars. Colophon: "[Tablet of Mard]uk-šāpik-zēri son of Bēl-apla-idinna descendant of Mušēzib; (written by) the hand of Iddin-Bēl his son". Neugebauer, JCS 21, 208-210, 215 text F; Brown, CM 18, 305; Steele, JHA 34 (2003) 269-289; Ossendrijver, BMAPT, no. 47.
37267	1880,0617.1023	School text; unidentified. Gesche, AOAT 275, 677.
37268	1880,0617.1024	Joined to 36979.
37269	1880,0617.1025	Unidentified.
37270	1880,0617.1026	School text; lexical; literary; unidentified. Gesche, AOAT 275, 286, 677.
37271	1880,0617.1027	Historical?
37272	1880,0617.1028	Account of disbursements.
37273	1880,0617.1029	Omens.
37274	1880,0617.1030	Joined to 36438.
37275	1880,0617.1031	Literary.

37276	1880,0617.1032	Astronomical; lunar eclipse table; mentions years 9-11 of Alexander III; probably part of same tablet as 36612. Hunger and Sachs, ADART V, no. 13.
37277	1880,0617.1033	Astronomical.
37278	1880,0617.1034	School text; lexical, Syllabary A. Gesche, AOAT 275, 677.
37279	1880,0617.1035	Joined to 37093.
37280	1880,0617.1036	School text; lexical; unidentified. 23/7/-. Gesche, AOAT 275, 677.
37281	1880,0617.1037	Literary.
37282	1880,0617.1038	Astronomical or astrological; colophon. Reiner, Fs Borger (CM 10), 297.
37283	1880,0617.1039	Astronomical; Vorläufer; lower left corner; line 2: 1 danna ud-da-zal.
37284	1880,0617.1040	Astronomical Diary for SE 141. LBAT 364; Sachs and Hunger, ADART II, no. -170 B.
37285	1880,0617.1041	Incantation.
37286	1880,0617.1042	School text; lexical; unidentified. Gesche, AOAT 275, 677.
37287	1880,0617.1043	Unidentified.
37288	1880,0617.1044	School text; lexical. Gesche, AOAT 275, 677.
37289	1880,0617.1045	Unidentified.
37290	1880,0617.1046	School text; lexical. Gesche, AOAT 275, 677.
37291	1880,0617.1047	School text; lexical, Syllabary A. Gesche, AOAT 275, 677.
37292	1880,0617.1048	Address of a person.
37293	1880,0617.1049	School text; lexical; bilingual incantation, Muššu'u tablet I. Gesche, AOAT 275, 286, 678; Böck, Muššu-'u, 93-111.
37294	1880,0617.1050	Lexical; stones.
37295	1880,0617.1051	School text; lexical; Ḫḫ XXI. MSL 11, 10; Gesche, AOAT 275, 678.
37296	1880,0617.1052	Astronomical Diary.
37297	1880,0617.1053	School text; unidentified. Gesche, AOAT 275, 678.
37298	1880,0617.1054	School text; unidentified. Gesche, AOAT 275, 678.
37299	1880,0617.1055	Deposition.
37300	1880,0617.1056	Account of disbursements.
37301	1880,0617.1057	Astronomical.
37302	1880,0617.1058	School text; literary; unidentified. Gesche, AOAT 275, 678.
37303	1880,0617.1059	School text; lexical, Syllabary A. Gesche, AOAT 275, 678.
37304	1880,0617.1060	School text; lexical, Syllabary B. Gesche, AOAT 275, 678.
37305	1880,0617.1061	Medical ritual.

37306	1880,0617.1062	Religious.
37307	1880,0617.1063	School text; literary; lexical? Gesche, AOAT 275, 678.
37308	1880,0617.1064	Commentary?
37309	1880,0617.1065	Economic.
37310	1880,0617.1066	School text; lexical, personal names. Gesche, AOAT 275, 678.
37311	1880,0617.1067	School text; lexical? Gesche, AOAT 275, 678.
37312	1880,0617.1068	School text; lexical, Ḫḫ III. MSL 9, 159; Gesche, AOAT 275, 678.
37313	1880,0617.1069	Astrological or Vorläufer; two columns, Saturn (SAG.UŠ).
37314	1880,0617.1070	School text.
37315	1880,0617.1071	Astrological, omens from eclipses. Cf. Reiner, Fs Borger (CM 10), 297.
37316	1880,0617.1072	School text; lexical, Syllabary A, personal names. Gesche, AOAT 275, 678.
37317	1880,0617.1073	Astronomical Diary.
37318	1880,0617.1074	Economic.
37319	1880,0617.1075	Joined to 36438.
37320	1880,0617.1076	Astrological omens; Enūma Anu Enlil; colophon. Cf. Reiner, Fs Borger (CM 10), 297.
37321	1880,0617.1077	Ritual; mentions KA LUḪ.
37322	1880,0617.1078	Incantation.
37323	1880,0617.1079	Court record; about land; captions for seals but not sealed. [Nbn] []/[]/13. Babylon. Wunsch, AfO 44/45, 93, no. 24.
37324	1880,0617.1080	Mathematical; metrological table. Steele, SCIAMVS 16 (2015) 75-90.
37325	1880,0617.1081	Astronomical; MUL.APIN. Hunger and Pingree, AfO Beih. 24, 3; Reiner, Fs Borger (CM 10), 297; Hunger and Steele, MUL.APIN, 21.
37326	1880,0617.1082	Astronomical Diary.
	1880,0617.1083	Joined to 36311.
37327	1880,0617.1084	God list. König, RlA 1, 96a “Amman-kasipar”.
37328	1880,0617.1085	Receipt of silver; Egibi archive. Nbk 12/6/43. Upija.
37329	1880,0617.1086	Astrological omens; Enūma Anu Enlil, Sin, planets.
37330	1880,0617.1087	Medical ritual.
37331	1880,0617.1088	Ritual.
37332	1880,0617.1089	Astronomical procedure text about lunar sixes; cf. TCL 6, no. 11; rev. unfinished.
37333	1880,0617.1090	Astronomical; ACT ephemeris; šú, me, na; cf. 37341.
37334	1880,0617.1091	Economic.
37335	1880,0617.1092	Joined to 36751.
37336	1880,0617.1093	Joined to 36300.

37337	1880,0617.1094	School text; lexical, Syllabary A. Gesche, AOAT 275, 678.
37338	1880,0617.1095	Mathematical table. Ossendrijver, JCS 66, 149-165 and pls.
37339	1880,0617.1096	Joined to 36640.
37340	1880,0617.1097	Topographical; dupl. 35385 (George, Babylonian Topographical Texts, no. 16) i 1'-10'.
37341	1880,0617.1098	Astronomical; ACT ephemeris; šú, me, na; cf. 37333.
37342	1880,0617.1099	Joined to 36609.
37343	1880,0617.1100	Lexical; Ḫḫ VIII. MSL 9, 173
37344	1880,0617.1101	Promissory note for silver; sealed; finger-nail marks. Dar I []/[]/33. Šušan. Nisaba 28, no. 42a.
37345	1880,0617.1102	School text; lexical, syllabary. Gesche, AOAT 275, 678.
37346	1880,0617.1103	Economic.
37347	1880,0617.1104	Astronomical Diary.
37348	1880,0617.1105	Astrological omens; Enuma Anu Enlil, Sin; colophon.
37349	1880,0617.1106	Astronomical Diary for SE 111.
37350	1880,0617.1107	School text; lexical, practice wedges. Gesche, AOAT 275, 678.
37351	1880,0617.1108	School text; god list. Gesche, AOAT 275, 678.
37352	1880,0617.1109	Astrological; right edge. Reiner, Fs Borger (CM 10), 297.
37353	1880,0617.1110	List of market prices for years 23-26 SE. (+) 36847. Wiseman, Gs Sachs, 363-373; Vargyas, Fs Hunger, 531-540; Slotsky and Wallenfels, Tallies and Trends, text 2.
37354	1880,0617.1111	Prayer to Marduk no. 2. Lambert, MC 24, no. 111.
37355	1880,0617.1112	Joined to 36292.
37356	1880,0617.1113	Joined to 36609.
37357	1880,0617.1114	Economic.
37358	1880,0617.1115	School text; incantation, Maqlu V 138-146. Gesche, AOAT 275, 287, 678; Abusch, AMD 10, 131-150.
37359	1880,0617.1116	Astronomical; observations; Mars and Mercury. Hunger and Sachs, ADART V, no. 97.
37360	1880,0617.1117	Astronomical; ACT ephemeris?
37361	1880,0617.1118	Astronomical; star catalogue? Britton, Fs Walker, p. 35.
37362	1880,0617.1119	Joined to 36849.
37363	1880,0617.1120	Unidentified.
37364	1880,0617.1121	Astronomical? or late astrological?; zodiacal signs; left edge.
37365	1880,0617.1122	Promissory note for dates.
37366	1880,0617.1123	School text; lexical, syllabary. Gesche, AOAT 275, 678.

37367	1880,0617.1124	Astronomical Diary.
37368	1880,0617.1125	Literary.
37369	1880,0617.1126	Account of silver.
37370	1880,0617.1127	School text; incantation; unidentified. Gesche, AOAT 275, 678.
37371	1880,0617.1128	Receipt for sheep. 20/11/29.
37372	1880,0617.1129	Incantation.
37373	1880,0617.1130	Astronomical; ziqpu stars. Reiner, Fs Borger (CM 10), 297; Fincke and Horowitz, JNES 77, 249-261.
37374	1880,0617.1131	Horoscope. Rochberg, Babylonian Horoscopes, no. 28.
37375	1880,0617.1132	Astronomical. (+) 37186. Aaboe, KDVSMM 40/6 (1979) 28.
37376	1880,0617.1133	Economic.
37377	1880,0617.1134	Joined to 36921.
37378	1880,0617.1135	Contract.
37379	1880,0617.1136	Literary; Enūma eliš VII. Kämmerer and Metzler, AOAT 375, 105, Tafel VII V, pl. XLIII; Lambert, BCM, p. 123, pl. 34.
37380	1880,0617.1137	Astronomical procedure text for a planet. Ossendrijver, BMAPT, no. 51.
37381	1880,0617.1138	Unidentified.
37382	1880,0617.1139	Astrological. Reiner, Fs Borger (CM 10), 297.
37383	1880,0617.1140	Astrological omens.
37384	1880,0617.1141	Account.
37385	1880,0617.1142	Incantation.
37386	1880,0617.1143	School text; unidentified. Gesche, AOAT 275, 678.
37387	1880,0617.1144	Astronomical.
37388	1880,0617.1145	Astronomical Diary.
37389	1880,0617.1146	Administrative. Art.
37390	1880,0617.1147	School text; lexical, Ḫḫ? Gesche, AOAT 275, 678.
37391	1880,0617.1148	Astrological omens; Enūma Anu Enlil, Dilbat (Venus); small script. Reiner, Fs Borger (CM 10), 297.
37392	1880,0617.1149	School text; unidentified; Prayer to Marduk no. 2. Gesche, AOAT 275, 678; Lambert, MC 24, no. 121.
37393	1880,0617.1150	Astronomical.
37394	1880,0617.1151	Contract; lease of a house. 5/-/-.
37395	1880,0617.1152	School text; literary, Enūma eliš IV; lexical, Ḫḫ XIV? (+) 37573. Gesche, AOAT 275, 678; Kämmerer and Metzler, AOAT 375, 95, Tafel IV V, pl. XXVI; Lambert, BCM, p. 85, pl. 18.
37396	1880,0617.1153	Astronomical.
37397	1880,0617.1154	Astrological omens?
37398	1880,0617.1155	Joined to 36894.
37399	1880,0617.1156	Astronomical Diary.

37400	1880,0617.1157	Astronomical; Normal Star Almanac. Hunger and Sachs, ADART VII, no. 132.
37401	1880,0617.1158	Astronomical; Mercury. Reiner, Fs Borger (CM 10), 297.
37402	1880,0617.1159	School text; incantation, dupl. LKA 77 obv. i; and lexical, Ḫḫ XXIV. MSL 11 78; Lambert, MC 24, no. 216.
37403	1880,0617.1160	School text; lexical; bilingual incantation. Gesche, AOAT 275, 288, 678.
37404	1880,0617.1161	School text; literary. Gesche, AOAT 275, 678.
37405	1880,0617.1162	Astronomical; ACT procedure or Vorläufer; fragment of small rounded tablet; reused with numbers in two directions on Rev.
37406	1880,0617.1163	Astrological; zodiac; parts of body.
37407	1880,0617.1164	Astronomical Diary.
37408	1880,0617.1165	Promissory note for dates and date products. Nabû-[] -/-/18.
37409	1880,0617.1166	School text; lexical. Gesche, AOAT 275, 678.
37410	1880,0617.1167	Astronomical Diary or related text.
37411	1880,0617.1168	Unidentified.
37412	1880,0617.1169	Joined to 36781. Reiner, Fs Borger (CM 10), 297.
37413	1880,0617.1170	Mathematical problem text? (mi-nu-ú), or astronomical procedure? or Vorläufer?; large crude script; rev. unfinished.
37414	1880,0617.1171	Mathematical procedure.
37415	1880,0617.1172	Commentary; medical.
37416	1880,0617.1173	School text; lexical, Ḫḫ, giš; bilingual incantation. 20+/9/-. Gesche, AOAT 275, 288, 678; Schramm, GBAO 2, text B15.
37417	1880,0617.1174	Astronomical.
37418	1880,0617.1175	Account of offerings.
37419	1880,0617.1176	School text; incantation, Sag-gig / Muššu'u tablet I; lexical. Gesche, AOAT 275, 289, 678; Böck, NABU 2001, 80-81, no. 86; Böck, Muššu'u, 93-111.
37420	1880,0617.1177	Ritual and incantation.
37421	1880,0617.1178	School text; lexical; Ḫḫ XI. MSL 9, 195.
37422	1880,0617.1179	Economic.
37423	1880,0617.1180	Astrological omens; eclipse; AN-MI GAR-an. Reiner, Fs Borger (CM 10), 297.
37424	1880,0617.1181	School text; unidentified. Gesche, AOAT 275, 678.
37425	1880,0617.1182	Astronomical.
37426	1880,0617.1183	Astrological; eclipse (AN.MI); MÚL x u MÚL y repeated; prayer on upper edge. Reiner, Fs Borger (CM 10), 297.
37427	1880,0617.1184	School text; lexical; literary. Gesche, AOAT 275, 678.

37428	1880,0617.1185	School text.
37429	1880,0617.1186	Unidentified.
37430	1880,0617.1187	Contract.
37431	1880,0617.1188	Incantation.
37432	1880,0617.1189	Joined to 37121.
37433	1880,0617.1190	Astrological omens; Enūma Anu Enlil, Venus, group G; commentary(?). Reiner and Pingree, BPO 3, 273; Reiner, Fs Borger (CM 10), 297.
37434	1880,0617.1191	School text; lexical; literary. Gesche, AOAT 275, 678.
37435	1880,0617.1192	Promissory note for dates or grain. Nbn -/1/11. Babylon.
37436	1880,0617.1193	Mathematical; tabular; numbers and words; two columns; fragment.
37437	1880,0617.1194	Mathematical; metrological table. Steele, SCIAMVS 16 (2015) 75-90.
37438	1880,0617.1195	Astronomical; observations. Hunger and Sachs, ADART V, no. 98.
37439	1880,0617.1196	Astrological omens.
37440	1880,0617.1197	Astronomical Diary.
37441	1880,0617.1198	Account of deliveries of silver.
37442	1880,0617.1199	Contract.
37443	1880,0617.1200	School text; lexical; literary. Gesche, AOAT 275, 678.
37444	1880,0617.1201	Promissory note for dates. Cam 12/[]/2.
37445	1880,0617.1202	Astrological omens. Reiner, Fs Borger (CM 10), 297.
37446	1880,0617.1203	Ritual and incantation.
37447	1880,0617.1204	Astronomical Diary.
37448	1880,0617.1205	Contract; sale of a house; finger-nail marks; dupl. 36299+. Cyr [24]/[]/4. Babylon. + 37676 (+) 37553 + 37662 + 37843 (+) 37890.
37449	1880,0617.1206	Astronomical Diary.
37450	1880,0617.1207	Astronomical Diary.
37451	1880,0617.1208	Astronomical Diary.
37452	1880,0617.1209	Unidentified.
37453	1880,0617.1210	Joined to 36323.
37454	1880,0617.1211	Astrological omens. Reiner, Fs Borger (CM 10), 297.
37455	1880,0617.1212	Incantation.
37456	1880,0617.1213	Astronomical Diary.
37457	1880,0617.1214	Unidentified.
37458	1880,0617.1215	Incantation.
37459	1880,0617.1216	School text; literary? Gesche, AOAT 275, 679.
37460	1880,0617.1217	School text; literary, Enūma eliš I; unidentified. Kämmerer and Metzler, AOAT 375, 86, Tafel I QQ, pl. X; Lambert, BCM, p. 48, pl. 8.
37461	1880,0617.1218	School text; lexical, syllabary. Gesche, AOAT 275, 679.

37462	1880,0617.1219	School text; lexical, Ḫḫ XXIV. MSL 11, 78; Gesche, AOAT 275, 679.
37463	1880,0617.1220	School text; lexical; literary. + unnum. Gesche, AOAT 275, 290, 679.
37464	1880,0617.1221	Incantation.
37465	1880,0617.1222	Letter of Sin-šarra-iškun to Nabopolassar; dupl. Lambert in CTMMA II, 207, no. 44.
37466	1880,0617.1223	Economic.
37467	1880,0617.1224	Astronomical; Mercury observations. Pingree and Reiner, RA 69, 175-180; Brown, CM 18, 305.
37468	1880,0617.1225	School text; unidentified. Gesche, AOAT 275, 679.
37469	1880,0617.1226	School text; bilingual incantation. Gesche, AOAT 275, 679.
37470	1880,0617.1227	Astronomical?; unusual format; upper or lower left corner.
37471	1880,0617.1228	School text; lexical; bilingual incantation; literary. 23/[]/-. Gesche, AOAT 275, 291, 679.
37472	1880,0617.1229	Account of disbursements.
37473	1880,0617.1230	Joined to 36627.
37474	1880,0617.1231	Astronomical; tables for Jupiter? Aaboe, JCS 20, 8-9, 31.
37475	1880,0617.1232	Joined to 36705.
37476	1880,0617.1233	Lexical.
37477	1880,0617.1234	Astronomical Diary for SE 12. Sachs and Hunger, ADART I, no. -299.
37478	1880,0617.1235	Joined to 36742.
37479	1880,0617.1236	Astronomical?; peculiar; stars, šumma ud 1-kam; left edge.
37480	1880,0617.1237	School text; lexical. Gesche, AOAT 275, 679.
37481	1880,0617.1238	Astronomical?; numbers, zi (=velocity?).
37482	1880,0617.1239	School text; bilingual incantation, Udug-ḫul 5; lexical. Gesche, AOAT 275, 291, 679; Geller, BAM 8, 174-216.
37483	1880,0617.1240	Unidentified.
37484	1880,0617.1241	Joined to 36705.
37485	1880,0617.1242	Lexical; Aa IV/4 = 25. CT 12, 21; MSL 14, 384.
37486	1880,0617.1243	Astrological; stars, wind, rapādu.
37487	1880,0617.1244	Mathematical; metrological table; unidentified. Steele, SCIAMVS 16 (2015) 75-90.
37488	1880,0617.1245	School text; lexical; bilingual incantation. Gesche, AOAT 275, 292, 679.
37489	1880,0617.1246	Lexical.
37490	1880,0617.1247	Ritual.
37491	1880,0617.1248	School text; lexical, personal names? Gesche, AOAT 275, 679.

37492	1880,0617.1249	Lexical.
37493	1880,0617.1250	Astronomical Diary or related text; Lunar Six data. SE -/-/203?
37494	1880,0617.1251	Astronomical.
37495	1880,0617.1252	Contract; lease of a house.
37496	1880,0617.1253	Joined to 36758.
37497	1880,0617.1254	Lexical.
37498	1880,0617.1255	Missing.
37499	1880,0617.1256	Medical.
37500	1880,0617.1257	Lexical; giš.
37501	1880,0617.1258	School text; literary; Enūma eliš II; Prayer to Marduk no. 2. Kämmerer and Metzler, AOAT 375, 90, Tafel II V, pl. XVIII; Lambert, BCM, p. 63, pl. 14.
37502	1880,0617.1259	School text; Šamaš Hymn; unidentified. Gesche, AOAT 275, 679; Lambert, MC 24, no. 139.
37503	1880,0617.1260	Astronomical.
37504	1880,0617.1261	Stone list; medical prescriptions.
37505	1880,0617.1262	Mantic dream ritual.
37506	1880,0617.1263	School text; lexical. Gesche, AOAT 275, 679.
37507	1880,0617.1264	Joined to 36629.
37508	1880,0617.1265	School text; lexical, Ḫḫ, giš; bilingual incantation. Gesche, AOAT 275, 679.
37509	1880,0617.1266	Incantation.
37510	1880,0617.1267	Lexical.
37511	1880,0617.1268	School text; lexical. Gesche, AOAT 275, 679.
37512	1880,0617.1269	Astrological; ṣīt Šamaš.
37513	1880,0617.1270	Commentary.
37514	1880,0617.1271	School text; literary; lexical, Diri II. Gesche, AOAT 275, 679; MSL 15 121.
37515	1880,0617.1272	Promissory note for barley.
37516	1880,0617.1273	Economic.
37517	1880,0617.1274	Joined to 36315.
37518	1880,0617.1275	Bilingual incantation.
37519	1880,0617.1276	Astronomical.
37520	1880,0617.1277	Astronomical.
37521	1880,0617.1278	Ritual.
37522	1880,0617.1279	School text; lexical, Ḫḫ VI; incantation, Maqlu V 143-151. + 37567 + 37824. Gesche, AOAT 275, 292, 679; Abusch, AMD 10, 131-150.
37523	1880,0617.1280	Ritual?
37524	1880,0617.1281	School text; lexical. Gesche, AOAT 275, 679.
37525	1880,0617.1282	School text; lexical, Ḫḫ XVII (plants). MSL 10, 81; Gesche, AOAT 275, 679.
37526	1880,0617.1283	School text; lexical, Lú = ša I. MSL 12, 91 (under wrong number 37256); Gesche, AOAT 275, 679.

37527	1880,0617.1284	Joined to 36643.
37528	1880,0617.1285	Astrological omens. Reiner, Fs Borger (CM 10), 297.
37529	1880,0617.1286	Unfinished ledger. Art 3/2/30.
37530	1880,0617.1287	School text; lexical, Syllabary B; unidentified. Gesche, AOAT 275, 679.
37531	1880,0617.1288	School text; lexical, Ḫḫ XIII; bilingual incantation, Udug-ḫul. 10[]/2/-. Gesche, AOAT 275, 294, 679; Geller, BAM 8, 323-339.
37532	1880,0617.1289	School text; bilingual incantation. 10/[]/-. Gesche, AOAT 275, 295, 679.
37533	1880,0617.1290	Account of disbursements.
37534	1880,0617.1291	Account of disbursements.
37535	1880,0617.1292	Promissory note for onions.
37536	1880,0617.1293	School text; lexical, Ḫḫ I; bilingual incantation, Sagba 57. 7/3/-. Gesche, AOAT 275, 295, 679; cf. Römer in Fs Sjöberg, 465-479.
37537	1880,0617.1294	Contract.
37538	1880,0617.1295	School text; literary; bilingual incantation, Ḫulbazizi; lexical, Ḫḫ XVI-XVII. Gesche, AOAT 275, 296, 679.
37539	1880,0617.1296	School text; lexical, Ḫḫ X. MSL 9, 188; Gesche, AOAT 275, 679.
37540	1880,0617.1297	Contract.
37541	1880,0617.1298	Lexical; Ea IV. MSL 14, 354.
37542	1880,0617.1299	Economic.
37543	1880,0617.1300	School text; lexical, Ḫḫ XIV; literary. + unnum. Gesche, AOAT 275, 679.
37544	1880,0617.1301	Lexical and literary extract.
37545	1880,0617.1302	Contract.
37546	1880,0617.1303	Astronomical Diary.
37547	1880,0617.1304	Astronomical.
37548	1880,0617.1305	Contract; sale of fields.
37549	1880,0617.1306	Lexical; god list.
37550	1880,0617.1307	School text; lexical. Gesche, AOAT 275, 680.
37551	1880,0617.1308	Economic.
37552	1880,0617.1309	Unidentified.
37553	1880,0617.1310	Lexical or economic; right edge only.
37554	1880,0617.1311	Astronomical.
37555	1880,0617.1312	Contract; sale of a house. + 37662 + 37843 (+) 37448 + 37676 (+) 37890.
37556	1880,0617.1313	Bilingual incantation. + 37815.
37557	1880,0617.1314	School text; lexical, Ḫḫ X. MSL 9, 188; Gesche, AOAT 275, 680.
37558	1880,0617.1315	Economic. -/-/3.
37559	1880,0617.1316	School text; lexical, Ḫḫ XVII (plants); ritual? MSL 10, 81; Gesche, AOAT 275, 680.

37560	1880,0617.1317	Omens; terrestrial.
37561	1880,0617.1318	School text; lexical; literary; on the lower edge is [...].NE UD (blank) [...]. -/5/-. Gesche, AOAT 275, 680.
37562	1880,0617.1319	Literary; Enūma eliš VII. Lambert, BCM, p. 123, pl. 34.
37563	1880,0617.1320	Contract; witnesses; sealed. d.l. Nisaba 28, no. 619.
37564	1880,0617.1321	School text; lexical; "aluzinnu text", dupl. 2R 60, no. 1. Gesche, AOAT 275, 298-299, 680.
37565	1880,0617.1322	Astronomical.
37566	1880,0617.1323	Sumerian literary.
37567	1880,0617.1324	Joined to 37522.
37568	1880,0617.1325	School text; lexical; Ḫḫ IX-X. MSL 9, 181, 189; Gesche, AOAT 275, 680.
37569	1880,0617.1326	Contract; sale of a house.
37570	1880,0617.1327	School text; lexical; Ḫḫ XIX. MSL 10, 127; Gesche, AOAT 275, 680.
37571	1880,0617.1328	School text; lexical, Ḫḫ IX-XI; bilingual incantation, Udug-ḫul 10; Prayer to Marduk no. 1, 127-132. + 37931. MSL 9, 181, 188, 195 (37931 only); Gesche, AOAT 275, 299, 680; Geller, BAM 8, 323-339; Oshima, BPM, 151-152; Lambert, MC 24, no. 96.
37572	1880,0617.1329	Economic. 8/-/-.
37573	1880,0617.1330	School text; lexical; literary, Enūma eliš IV. (+) 37395. Gesche, AOAT 275, 680; Kämmerer and Metzler, AOAT 375, 95, Tafel IV W, pl. XXVI; Lambert, BCM, p. 85, pl. 18.
37574	1880,0617.1331	School text; lexical; literary? Gesche, AOAT 275, 680.
37575	1880,0617.1332	Letter. 11/5/-.
37576	1880,0617.1333	School text; Ludlul II; unidentified. Oshima, BPPS, 400; Lambert, MC 24, no. 154.
37577	1880,0617.1334	Contract; sale of land; sealed. d.l. Nisaba 28, no. 139.
37578	1880,0617.1335	School text; lexical, Ḫḫ, uzu, na4; literary. Gesche, AOAT 275, 680.
37579	1880,0617.1336	Letter.
37580	1880,0617.1337	School text; lexical, Ḫḫ IV. MSL 9, 168; Gesche, AOAT 275, 680.
37581	1880,0617.1338	School text; lexical. Gesche, AOAT 275, 680.
37582	1880,0617.1339	Historical or literary?
37583	1880,0617.1340	School text; lexical; incantation. Gesche, AOAT 275, 680.
37584	1880,0617.1341	School text; lexical? Gesche, AOAT 275, 680.
37585	1880,0617.1342	School text; unidentified. Gesche, AOAT 275, 680.
37586	1880,0617.1343	Economic.

37587	1880,0617.1344	Lexical.
37588	1880,0617.1345	Unidentified.
37589	1880,0617.1346	Prescriptions for salves against witchcraft. (+) 36520. Abusch and Schwemer, AMD 8/2 texts 10.6 g and 10.14 d, pl. 76.
37590	1880,0617.1347	Receipt for dead sheep. 28/6/24.
37591	1880,0617.1348	Economic.
37592	1880,0617.1349	School text; lexical, Ḫḫ V 55?-57; Tintir I. 20/2/-. George, BTT, pl. 57; Gesche, AOAT 275, 680.
37593	1880,0617.1350	School text; lexical, Syllabary A. Gesche, AOAT 275, 680.
37594	1880,0617.1351	Literary?
37595	1880,0617.1352	Account of dates.
37596	1880,0617.1353	School text; lexical; literary, Ludlul. Gesche, AOAT 275, 680.
37597	1880,0617.1354	Economic.
37598	1880,0617.1355	Lexical.
37599	1880,0617.1356	Hymn or prayer.
37600	1880,0617.1357	Astronomical; lunar table. Aaboe, KDVSMM 36/12 (1968) 15-16, pl. I.
37601	1880,0617.1358	School text; lexical, syllabary. Gesche, AOAT 275, 680.
37602	1880,0617.1359	Contract.
37603	1880,0617.1360	Contract; transfer of property. + 37620. Wunsch, Bab Arch 2, 78-80, no. 20.
37604	1880,0617.1361	School practice text.
37605	1880,0617.1362	Unidentified.
37606	1880,0617.1363	Hemerology.
37607	1880,0617.1364	Bilingual incantation.
37608	1880,0617.1365	School text; lexical, Syllabary A. Gesche, AOAT 275, 608.
37609	1880,0617.1366	Contract; lease of a house.
37610	1880,0617.1367	Economic.
37611	1880,0617.1368	Literary.
37612	1880,0617.1369	Economic. 8/8/-.
37613	1880,0617.1370	Lexical; Ḫḫ VIII. + 37644. MSL 9, 173.
37614	1880,0617.1371	Medical.
37615	1880,0617.1372	Lexical; Ḫḫ XI. MSL 9, 195.
37616	1880,0617.1373	Hymn to Gula; dupl. Ebeling, KAR 109+343. Lambert, MC 24, no. 67.
37617	1880,0617.1374	Lexical; Ḫḫ III. MSL 9, 159.
37618	1880,0617.1375	Contract; sale of fields. Cyr 5/10/-. Babylon. + 37643 + 37696.
37619	1880,0617.1376	Economic.
37620	1880,0617.1377	Joined to 37603.

37621	1880,0617.1378	Bilingual incantation, Udug-ḫul 3; rev. unidentified. Geller, BAM 8, 89-132, pl. 27.
37622	1880,0617.1379	School text; lexical, Ḫḫ XI. MSL 9, 195; Gesche, AOAT 275, 680.
37623	1880,0617.1380	Economic.
37624	1880,0617.1381	Economic.
37625	1880,0617.1382	School text; lexical; Syllabary A. Gesche, AOAT 275, 680.
37626	1880,0617.1383	Economic.
37627	1880,0617.1384	Promissory note for silver. Nabû-[] 13/-/-.
37628	1880,0617.1385	Promissory note for silver. Dar 5/12/12.
37629	1880,0617.1386	Receipt.
37630	1880,0617.1387	Astrological; MUL.IKU u MUL lu-lim IGI.MEŠ; right edge.
37631	1880,0617.1388	Contract.
37632	1880,0617.1389	School text; god list. Gesche, AOAT 275, 680.
37633	1880,0617.1390	Promissory note for barley. Cyr 6/-/-. Babylon.
37634	1880,0617.1391	School text; lexical, syllabary; unidentified. Gesche, AOAT 275, 680.
37635	1880,0617.1392	Largely illegible; fragment.
37636	1880,0617.1393	Literary.
37637	1880,0617.1394	Astronomical.
37638	1880,0617.1395	School text; lexical. Gesche, AOAT 275, 680.
37639	1880,0617.1396	Receipt for silver. -/4/10.
37640	1880,0617.1397	Promissory note for silver. Dar -/-/7. Babylon.
37641	1880,0617.1398	School text; incantation, Šurpu II 94-100; literary; lexical, Ḫḫ X. + unnum. Gesche, AOAT 275, 301, 680; Lambert, MC 24, no. 245.
37642	1880,0617.1399	Contract. Dar -/5/11.
37643	1880,0617.1400	Joined to 37618.
37644	1880,0617.1401	Joined to 37613.
37645	1880,0617.1402	School text; lexical. Gesche, AOAT 275, 680.
37646	1880,0617.1403	Economic.
37647	1880,0617.1404	Bilingual religious; commentary.
37648	1880,0617.1405	Contract. Nbn 1/2/-.
37649	1880,0617.1406	Promissory note for dates. Dar 6/[]/4. Babylon.
37650	1880,0617.1407	Economic. -/-/acc.
37651	1880,0617.1408	Letter from Kalbūtu to Bulluṭāya; sealed. 25/7/6+. Nisaba 28, no. 204.
37652	1880,0617.1409	Joined to 37088.
37653	1880,0617.1410	School text; lexical. Gesche, AOAT 275, 680
37654	1880,0617.1411	Late Babylonian copy of the prologue to Laws of Hammurabi. + 37665.
37655	1880,0617.1412	School text; lexical; literary; unidentified. Gesche, AOAT 275, 681.

37656	1880,0617.1413	Contract.
37657	1880,0617.1414	School text; lexical. Gesche, AOAT 275, 681.
37658	1880,0617.1415	School text; Šu'illa prayer to Nabû. Gesche, AOAT 275, 303, 681; Mayer, Or NS 59, 459-466, 483.
37659	1880,0617.1416	Prayer to Marduk no. 2. Lambert, MC 24, no. 110.
37660	1880,0617.1417	Contract; lease of a house. Dar 24/1/-.
37661	1880,0617.1418	School text; Tintir II 28-31; Ḫḫ III 490-491. Gesche, AOAT 275, 304, 681; George, AfO 50, 404-405.
37662	1880,0617.1419	Joined to 37555.
37663	1880,0617.1420	Lexical and literary extract.
37664	1880,0617.1421	Contract; ḫarrānu.
37665	1880,0617.1422	Joined to 37654.
37666	1880,0617.1423	Letter.
37667	1880,0617.1424	Economic.
37668	1880,0617.1425	Lexical.
37669	1880,0617.1426	School text; unidentified. Gesche, AOAT 275, 304, 681.
37670	1880,0617.1427	Economic.
37671	1880,0617.1428	Lexical; literary extract.
37672	1880,0617.1429	Economic.
37673	1880,0617.1430	Lexical.
37674	1880,0617.1431	Economic.
37675	1880,0617.1432	Astronomical.
37676	1880,0617.1433	Joined to 37448.
37677	1880,0617.1434	Contract.
37678	1880,0617.1435	School text; lexical, Ḫḫ XXIII?. []/9/-. Gesche, AOAT 275, 304, 681.
37679	1880,0617.1436	Astronomical.
37680	1880,0617.1437	Economic.
37681	1880,0617.1438	Promissory note for silver. 18/7/4.
37682	1880,0617.1439	School practice text.
37683	1880,0617.1440	School text; lexical, Ḫḫ X. MSL 9, 188; Gesche, AOAT 275, 681.
37684	1880,0617.1441	Contract; sale of a house. Nbn 24/-/-.
37685	1880,0617.1442	School text; bilingual incantation. Gesche, AOAT 275, 681; Schramm, GBAO 2, p. 91, pl. 46, text B14.
37686	1880,0617.1443	Economic. Dar 19/[]/2.
37687	1880,0617.1444	Economic.
37688	1880,0617.1445	Economic.
37689	1880,0617.1446	Account of disbursements.
37690	1880,0617.1447	Sumerian literary.
37691	1880,0617.1448	Promissory note for silver. Dar 28/9/23.
37692	1880,0617.1449	School text; Prayer to Marduk no. 2; lexical. Lambert, MC 24, no. 125.

37693	1880,0617.1450	School text; lexical; bilingual incantation, Udug-ḫul 6. Gesche, AOAT 275, 305, 681; Geller, BAM 8, 217-248.
37694	1880,0617.1451	School text; lexical. Gesche, AOAT 275, 681.
37695	1880,0617.1452	Literary; Ludlul I. Cf. Lambert, Or NS 40, 95. Oshima, BPPS, 381-382, 393-394; Lambert, MC 24, no. 147.
37696	1880,0617.1453	Joined to 37618.
37697	1880,0617.1454	School text; incantations, Muššu'u V, unidentified. Gesche, AOAT 275, 681; Böck, AuOr 36, 6-7
37698	1880,0617.1455	Bilingual incantation. Schramm, GBAO 2, p. 91, pl. 46 text B11.
37699	1880,0617.1456	School text; lexical, Syllabary B. Gesche, AOAT 275, 681.
37700	1880,0617.1457	School text; lexical. Gesche, AOAT 275, 681.
37701	1880,0617.1458	Astronomical.
37702	1880,0617.1459	Economic.
37703	1880,0617.1460	Contract; sale of fields.
37704	1880,0617.1461	School text; lexical, Syllabary B. Gesche, AOAT 275, 681.
37705	1880,0617.1462	Lexical and literary extract; Diri VI. MSL 15 181.
37706	1880,0617.1463	Sumerian literary.
37707	1880,0617.1464	Literary.
37708	1880,0617.1465	School text; lexical, Ḫḫ I; personal names. Gesche, AOAT 275, 681.
37709	1880,0617.1466	Economic.
37710	1880,0617.1467	Literary.
37711	1880,0617.1468	Account of dates.
37712	1880,0617.1469	Economic.
37713	1880,0617.1470	Lexical.
37714	1880,0617.1471	School text; lexical, acrographic list. Gesche, AOAT 275, 305, 681.
37715	1880,0617.1472	School text; lexical, Ḫḫ XII; literary. MSL 9, 203; Gesche, AOAT 275, 681.
37716	1880,0617.1473	School text; lexical. Gesche, AOAT 275, 681.
37717	1880,0617.1474	Receipt. Dar -/8/4. Babylon.
37718	1880,0617.1475	Promissory note for silver.
37719	1880,0617.1476	Contract.
37720	1880,0617.1477	School text; literary (gods). Gesche, AOAT 275, 681.
37721	1880,0617.1478	Economic.
37722	1880,0617.1479	Contract; transfer of property. Wunsch, Bab Arch 2, 87, no. 25.
37723	1880,0617.1480	School text; lexical; Ḫḫ XI. MSL 9, 195.
37724	1880,0617.1481	Literary extracts.

37725	1880,0617.1482	School text; lexical, Ḫḫ X. MSL 9, 188; Gesche, AOAT 275, 681.
37726	1880,0617.1483	Medical.
37727	1880,0617.1484	School text; lexical? Gesche, AOAT 275, 681.
37728	1880,0617.1485	Promissory note for silver.
37729	1880,0617.1486	Incantation; copy. Cf. 65531.
37730	1880,0617.1487	Economic.
37731	1880,0617.1488	School text; lexical, practice signs. Gesche, AOAT 275, 681.
37732	1880,0617.1489	Economic.
37733	1880,0617.1490	School text; lexical, Syllabary A. Gesche, AOAT 275, 681.
37734	1880,0617.1491	Colophon.
37735	1880,0617.1492	School text; lexical? Gesche, AOAT 275, 681.
37736	1880,0617.1493	School text; lexical, Ḫḫ VIII. MSL 9, 173; Gesche, AOAT 275, 681.
37737	1880,0617.1494	Economic.
37738	1880,0617.1495	Economic. 3/[]/6.
37739	1880,0617.1496	Economic.
37740	1880,0617.1497	Medical.
37741	1880,0617.1498	Economic. Dar 10/[]/12.
37742	1880,0617.1499	Economic.
37743	1880,0617.1500	Contract. Dar -/8/2. Babylon.
37744	1880,0617.1501	Promissory note for silver.
37745	1880,0617.1502	Contract. Dar -/10/-.
37746	1880,0617.1503	Ritual.
37747	1880,0617.1504	Economic.
37748	1880,0617.1505	Bilingual incantation, Udug-ḫul 13-15. Geller, BAM 8, 434-498, pl. 108.
37749	1880,0617.1506	Astrological omens; Enūma Anu Enlil, Sin. Cf. Reiner, Fs Borger (CM 10), 297.
37750	1880,0617.1507	Receipt. -/3/10.
37751	1880,0617.1508	Receipt for dead sheep.
37752	1880,0617.1509	Economic.
37753	1880,0617.1510	Administrative; sealed. d.l. Nisaba 28, no. 188.
37754	1880,0617.1511	Literary.
37755	1880,0617.1512	Economic.
37756	1880,0617.1513	Contract; sale of fields.
37757	1880,0617.1514	Economic. -/-/4.
37758	1880,0617.1515	Economic. 22/-/-.
37759	1880,0617.1516	Economic. -/-/4.
37760	1880,0617.1517	Economic. Ner.
37761	1880,0617.1518	School text; unidentified. Gesche, AOAT 275, 681.
37762	1880,0617.1519	School text; lexical. Gesche, AOAT 275, 681.
37763	1880,0617.1520	Economic.

37764	1880,0617.1521	God list.
37765	1880,0617.1522	Contract.
37766	1880,0617.1523	Astronomical.
37767	1880,0617.1524	Hemerology.
37768	1880,0617.1525	Economic.
37769	1880,0617.1526	School text; illegible.
37770	1880,0617.1527	Contract for ewes. Cam 16/[]/6.
37771	1880,0617.1528	Contract. 18/6/1.
37772	1880,0617.1529	Omens.
37773	1880,0617.1530	Commentary.
37774	1880,0617.1531	Memorandum.
37775	1880,0617.1532	School text; lexical, Ḫḫ, giš. Gesche, AOAT 275, 682.
37776	1880,0617.1533	School text; lexical, Syllabary A; unidentified. Gesche, AOAT 275, 682.
37777	1880,0617.1534	Promissory note for dates.
37778	1880,0617.1535	School text; lexical, Syllabary A. Gesche, AOAT 275, 682.
37779	1880,0617.1536	Erra V. Lambert, MC 24, no. 44.
37780	1880,0617.1537	Economic.
37781	1880,0617.1538	Ritual; copy.
37782	1880,0617.1539	Economic.
37783	1880,0617.1540	Bilingual incantation.
37784	1880,0617.1541	Contract. Dar -/2/-. Babylon.
37785	1880,0617.1542	Contract. Dar 3/6/17.
37786	1880,0617.1543	Contract.
37787	1880,0617.1544	Economic.
37788	1880,0617.1545	Contract; Aramaic note.
37789	1880,0617.1546	Astronomical Diary.
37790	1880,0617.1547	Account.
37791	1880,0617.1548	Deposition. Xerxes []/[]/1.
37792	1880,0617.1549	Promissory note for silver.
37793	1880,0617.1550	School text; lexical; literary. Gesche, AOAT 275, 306, 682.
37794	1880,0617.1551	Administrative note. 11/9/no year.
37795	1880,0617.1552	Sumerian incantation.
37796	1880,0617.1553	Economic.
37797	1880,0617.1554	Contract; lease of a house.
37798	1880,0617.1555	Ritual; Lamaštu II 20-22.
37799	1880,0617.1556	Economic.
37800	1880,0617.1557	School text; lexical, Syllabary B. Gesche, AOAT 275, 682.
37801	1880,0617.1558	Promissory note for silver. Dar 18/[]/4.
37802	1880,0617.1559	School text; lexical? Gesche, AOAT 275, 682.
37803	1880,0617.1560	Ritual.

37804	1880,0617.1561	School text; lexical, Syllabary B. Gesche, AOAT 275, 306, 682.
37805	1880,0617.1562	Economic.
37806	1880,0617.1563	Colophon.
37807	1880,0617.1564	School text; lexical? Gesche, AOAT 275, 682.
37808	1880,0617.1565	Economic.
37809	1880,0617.1566	School text; lexical, practice signs. Gesche, AOAT 275, 682.
37810	1880,0617.1567	Economic.
37811	1880,0617.1568	Liver omens.
37812	1880,0617.1569	Promissory note for dates. Nbn -/6/4.
37813	1880,0617.1570	School text; lexical, Diri II. Gesche, AOAT 275, 682; MSL 15 121.
37814	1880,0617.1571	Letter from Sîn-erība to Iddināya. Hackl et al., AOAT 414/1, no. 25.
37815	1880,0617.1572	Joined to 37556.
37816	1880,0617.1573	School text; lexical, Ḫḫ, giš. Gesche, AOAT 275, 682.
37817	1880,0617.1574	School text; lexical?; literary? Gesche, AOAT 275, 682.
37818	1880,0617.1575	School text; lexical; bilingual incantation, Udug-ḫul 10. Gesche, AOAT 275, 306, 682; Geller, BAM 8, 323-339.
37819	1880,0617.1576	School text; unidentified. Gesche, AOAT 275, 682.
37820	1880,0617.1577	Contract; lease of a house. Cyr 9/12/5. Babylon.
37821	1880,0617.1578	Contract; sale of fields.
37822	1880,0617.1579	Sumerian incantation.
37823	1880,0617.1580	School text; lexical; bilingual incantation? Gesche, AOAT 275, 307, 682.
37824	1880,0617.1581	Joined to 37522.
37825	1880,0617.1582	Economic.
37826	1880,0617.1583	Sumerian incantation.
37827	1880,0617.1584	School text; lexical; incantation. Gesche, AOAT 275, 308, 682.
37828	1880,0617.1585	Contract.
37829	1880,0617.1586	Joined to 36857.
37830	1880,0617.1587	Economic. 1/[]/2.
37831	1880,0617.1588	Astronomical.
37832	1880,0617.1589	Contract. -/-/2.
37833	1880,0617.1590	Promissory note for dates.
37834	1880,0617.1591	School text; lexical, Syllabary A, acrographic list. Gesche, AOAT 275, 309, 682.
37835	1880,0617.1592	Incantation.
37836	1880,0617.1593	School text; lexical; literary (houses). Gesche, AOAT 275, 682.
37837	1880,0617.1594	Economic.

37838	1880,0617.1595	School text; lexical. Gesche, AOAT 275, 682.
37839	1880,0617.1596	Incantation.
37840	1880,0617.1597	Astronomical Diary for SE 25; prayer on upper edge. LBAT 227; Sachs and Hunger, ADART I, no. -286 B.
37841	1880,0617.1598	Contract.
37842	1880,0617.1599	Astronomical Diary.
37843	1880,0617.1600	Joined to 37555.
37844	1880,0617.1601	Bilingual incantation; cf. CT 17, 34.
37845	1880,0617.1602	School text; literary, Enūma eliš I; unidentified. Kämmerer and Metzler, AOAT 375, 87, Tafel I RR, pl. X.
37846	1880,0617.1603	Contract; sale of fields.
37847	1880,0617.1604	Letter.
37848	1880,0617.1605	Economic.
37849	1880,0617.1606	Joined to 36681.
37850	1880,0617.1607	Contract.
37851	1880,0617.1608	Incantation; colophon.
37852	1880,0617.1609	School text; unidentified. Gesche, AOAT 275, 682.
37853	1880,0617.1610	Contract; sale of fields.
37854	1880,0617.1611	Economic. Ner 23/1/-.
37855	1880,0617.1612	School text; lexical; Erimḫuš III-IV. MSL 17, 46; Gesche, AOAT 275, 682.
37856	1880,0617.1613	School text; lexical? Gesche, AOAT 275, 682.
37857	1880,0617.1614	School text; lexical; Nabnītu IV-IVa. MSL 16, 75; Gesche, AOAT 275, 682.
37858	1880,0617.1615	Medical.
37859	1880,0617.1616	Astronomical.
37860	1880,0617.1617	Economic.
37861	1880,0617.1618	School text; lexical; literary. Gesche, AOAT 275, 682.
37862	1880,0617.1619	Economic.
37863	1880,0617.1620	Missing.
37864	1880,0617.1621	School text; lexical; Ḫḫ XXI. MSL 11, 9; Gesche, AOAT 275, 862.
37865	1880,0617.1622	Astronomical; ACT ephemeris or auxiliary table; two columns.
37866	1880,0617.1623	Bilingual incantation, Udug-ḫul 11; colophon. Cf. Wiggermann, CM 1, 224; Geller, BAM 8, 340-392, pl. 52; Lambert, MC 24, no. 198.
37867	1880,0617.1624	School text; literary?; bilingual? Gesche, AOAT 275, 682.
37868	1880,0617.1625	Joined to 37675.
37869	1880,0617.1626	School text; lexical? Gesche, AOAT 275, 682.
37870	1880,0617.1627	Economic.
37871	1880,0617.1628	Contract.
37872	1880,0617.1629	Literary; centres on Marduk.
37873	1880,0617.1630	Economic.

37874	1880,0617.1631	Promissory note for barley. -/-/acc.
37875	1880,0617.1632	Economic.
37876	1880,0617.1633	Incantation?; ṣi-it pi-i.
37877	1880,0617.1634	School text; lexical? Gesche, AOAT 275, 682.
37878	1880,0617.1635	Astrological omens.
37879	1880,0617.1636	School text; lexical. Gesche, AOAT 275, 682.
37880	1880,0617.1637	Economic. 16/-/-.
37881	1880,0617.1638	Literary.
37882	1880,0617.1639	School text; lexical; literary. Gesche, AOAT 275, 682.
37883	1880,0617.1640	Economic. Dar -/3/2.
37884	1880,0617.1641	Deposition. Kandalanu 20+/7/14. Babylon. Brinkman and Kennedy, JCS 35, 44, L.81.
37885	1880,0617.1642	Bilingual incantation, Udug-ḫul 13-15. Geller, BAM 8, 434-498, pl. 110.
37886	1880,0617.1643	Joined to 36699.
37887	1880,0617.1644	Contract; lease.
37888	1880,0617.1645	Economic. 26/[]/2.
37889	1880,0617.1646	Economic.
37890	1880,0617.1647	Contract; sale of a house. [Cyrus] [24]/[]/[4]. (+) 37448 + 37676 (+) 37555 + 37662 + 37843.
37891	1880,0617.1648	Economic.
37892	1880,0617.1649	Economic.
37893	1880,0617.1650	Promissory note for dates.
37894	1880,0617.1651	Economic. Dar 28/2/-.
37895	1880,0617.1652	Sumerian literary.
37896	1880,0617.1653	Astronomical; based on MUL.APIN; small script.
37897	1880,0617.1654	Economic. Dar. Babylon.
37898	1880,0617.1655	Sumerian literary.
37899	1880,0617.1656	Economic.
37900	1880,0617.1657	Contract.
37901	1880,0617.1658	Promissory note for silver. Dar 3/-/-.
37902	1880,0617.1659	Promissory note for barley or grain.
37903	1880,0617.1660	Economic.
37904	1880,0617.1661	Economic.
37905	1880,0617.1662	Promissory note for barley. -/-/4.
37906	1880,0617.1663	Promissory note for silver. Dar 2/[]/11.
37907	1880,0617.1664	Sumerian literary.
37908	1880,0617.1665	Joined to 36600.
37909	1880,0617.1666	Receipt.
37910	1880,0617.1667	Letter.
37911	1880,0617.1668	Promissory note for wheat.
37912	1880,0617.1669	Small olive shaped tablet; economic.
37913	1880,0617.1670	Omens.
37914	1880,0617.1671	Account. 25/11/10.
37915	1880,0617.1672	Incantation; attî kilîli. Lambert, AfO 26, 108.

37916	1880,0617.1673	Economic.
37917	1880,0617.1674	Economic. 22/-/-.
37918	1880,0617.1675	School text; lexical, sign practice. Gesche, AOAT 275, 682.
37919	1880,0617.1676	Incantation and ritual; namburbû?
37920	1880,0617.1677	Literary.
37921	1880,0617.1678	School text; lexical, Syllabary B. Gesche, AOAT 275, 682.
37922	1880,0617.1679	School text; lexical, Syllabary B. Gesche, AOAT 275, 682.
37923	1880,0617.1680	Economic.
37924	1880,0617.1681	Medical.
	1880,0617.1682ff.	Nos. 1682-1689 are sealings except for 1686.
37924a	1880,0617.1686	Administrative; sealed. Nisaba 28, no. 666.
104407	1880,0617.1690	Fragment of a boundary-stone (kudurru); inscription lost. King, BBSt, pp. 87, pl. 14, no. XVII.
	1880,0617.1691ff.	Nos. 1691-1724 are uninscribed objects.
	1880,0617.1725	Fragment of a clay envelope with on the inside the impression of a clay tablet which has seal impressions and a finger-nail mark.
	1880,0617.1726ff.	Nos. 1726-1730 are uninscribed objects.
137497	1880,0617.1731	Fragmcnt of tablet cut down to an unusual shape; inscribed na id nu on the back.
	1880,0617.1732ff.	Nos. 1732-1753 are uninscribed objects.
37925	1880,0617.1754	Lexical; Erimḫuš V. MSL 17, 66.
37926	1880,0617.1755	School text; lexical; literary? Gesche, AOAT 275, 682.
37927	1880,0617.1756	School text; literary, Enūma eliš VI; incantation, Marduk's Address (Udug-ḫul 11); unidentified. Gesche, AOAT 275, 683; Kämmerer and Metzler, AOAT 375, 102, Tafel VI X, pl. XL; Lambert, BCM, p. 109, pl. 26; Geller, BAM 8 340-392.
37928	1880,0617.1757	School text; lexical, Ḫḫ, giš; bilingual incantation, Udug-ḫul 6. []/8/-. Gesche, AOAT 275, 309, 683; Geller, BAM 8, 217-248.
37929	1880,0617.1758	List of people.
37930	1880,0617.1759	School text; lexical, Ḫḫ XVI-XVII (stones and plants). MSL 10, 4, 81; Gesche, AOAT 275, 683.
37931	1880,0617.1760	Joined to 37571.
37932	1880,0617.1761	School text; lexical, Ḫḫ XVI (stones). Gesche, AOAT 275, 311, 683; Schuster-Brandis, NABU 2001, 44, no. 39.
37933	1880,0617.1762	Incantation.
37934	1880,0617.1763	School text; lexical, Syllabary A. Gesche, AOAT 275, 683.

37935	1880,0617.1764	School text; lexical, Syllabary A. Gesche, AOAT 275, 683.
37936	1880,0617.1765	School text; lexical, Ḫḫ, dug; incantation, Maqlu VI 126-133. []/7/-. Gesche, AOAT 275, 312, 683; Abusch, AMD 10, 151-164.
37937	1880,0617.1766	School text; literary, Enūma eliš I; Prayer to Marduk no. 2; star list. +38060. Gesche, AOAT 275, 683; Kämmerer and Metzler, AOAT 375, 86, Tafel I Jjbis, pl. IX; Lambert, BCM, p. 48, pl. 8; Lambert, MC 24, no. 127.
37938	1880,0617.1767	School text; lexical, Syllabary A. Gesche, AOAT 275, 683.
37939	1880,0617.1768	School text; draft of an apprenticeship contract dated in the 7th year of Artaxerxes; personal names; lexical (DUG); colophon in unusual format. + 37947. Hackl, AfO 52, 90-91, no. 11.
37940	1880,0617.1769	School text; lexical, Diri III-V. MSL 15 135, 149, 167.
37941	1880,0617.1770	School text. 12/5/-. Gesche, AOAT 275, 683.
37942	1880,0617.1771	School text; lexical. Gesche, AOAT 275, 683.
37943	1880,0617.1772	School text; lexical; incantation, Šurpu III 112-115; bilingual literary. Gesche, AOAT 275, 683.
37944	1880,0617.1773	Lexical.
37945	1880,0617.1774	Bilingual literary.
37946	1880,0617.1775	School text; lexical; literary; unidentified. Gesche, AOAT 275, 683.
37947	1880,0617.1776	Joined to 37939.
37948	1880,0617.1777	School text.
37949	1880,0617.1778	School text.
37950	1880,0617.1779	School text.
37951	1880,0617.1780	School text; lexical. Gesche, AOAT 275, 683.
37952	1880,0617.1781	School text; lexical, Ḫḫ IX. MSL 9, 181; Gesche, AOAT 275, 683.
37953	1880,0617.1782	School text; lexical. Gesche, AOAT 275, 683.
37954	1880,0617.1783	Lexical.
37955	1880,0617.1784	School text; lexical. Gesche, AOAT 275, 683.
37956	1880,0617.1785	School text; lexical, Ḫḫ II-III. MSL 9, 157, 159; Gesche, AOAT 275, 683.
37957	1880,0617.1786	School text; lexical; Syllabary B, archaising signs. Gesche, AOAT 275, 683.
37958	1880,0617.1787	Joined to 36669.
37959	1880,0617.1788	School text; bilingual incantation, Udug-ḫul 10; Prayer to Marduk no. 2 iii 14-16; unidentified; lexical. +38018. Gesche, AOAT 275, 313, 683; Geller, BAM 8, 323-339; Oshima, BPM, 236; Lambert, MC 24, no. 124.

37960	1880,0617.1789	Literary; Enūma eliš III. Lambert, BCM, p. 75, pl. 16.
37961	1880,0617.1790	School text.
37962	1880,0617.1791	Lexical.
37963	1880,0617.1792	Administrative; list of names. Art 5/[]/22.
37964	1880,0617.1793	Literary.
37965	1880,0617.1794	School text; lexical, Syllabary A. Gesche, AOAT 275, 684.
37966	1880,0617.1795	School text; lexical; Diri II. CT 11, 43; Gesche, AOAT 275, 684; MSL 15 120.
37967	1880,0617.1796	School text; literary. Gesche, AOAT 275, 684.
37968	1880,0617.1797	School text; lexical. Gesche, AOAT 275, 684.
37969	1880,0617.1798	School text; lexical, Ḫḫ XI; literary, Enūma eliš I; bilingual incantation, Udug-ḫul 13-15. MSL 9, 195; Gesche, AOAT 275, 684; Kämmerer and Metzler, AOAT 375, 86, Tafel I JJ, pl. VIII; Lambert, BCM, 48, pl. 8; Geller, BAM 8, 434-498.
37970	1880,0617.1799	School text; lexical. Gesche, AOAT 275, 684.
37971	1880,0617.1800	School text; lexical; Ea V. MSL 14, 393; Gesche, AOAT 275, 684.
37972	1880,0617.1801	School text; lexical; Ḫḫ X. MSL 9, 189; Gesche, AOAT 275, 684.
37973	1880,0617.1802	School text; lexical, Syllabary A. Gesche, AOAT 275, 684.
37974	1880,0617.1803	School text; lexical; bilingual incantation, Udug-ḫul 2. 23/2/-. Gesche, AOAT 275, 684; Geller, BAM 8,59-88.
37975	1880,0617.1804	Lexical.
37976	1880,0617.1805	School text; literary? Gesche, AOAT 275, 684.
37977	1880,0617.1806	School text; lexical, Ḫḫ XII; literary? 14/-/-. MSL 9, 203; Gesche, AOAT 275, 684.
37978	1880,0617.1807	Lexical; names of rivers.
37979	1880,0617.1808	Contract.
37980	1880,0617.1809	God list and literary extract.
37981	1880,0617.1810	School text; lexical; literary? Gesche, AOAT 275, 684.
37982	1880,0617.1811	Lexical; Ḫḫ X. MSL 9, 188 (as 37892).
37983	1880,0617.1812	School text; lexical; Diri IV. MSL 15, 149.
37984	1880,0617.1813	School text; lexical, Ḫḫ VIII. MSL 9, 173; Gesche, AOAT 275, 684.
37985	1880,0617.1814	School text; lexical, Ḫḫ, giš; literary? Gesche, AOAT 275, 684.
37986	1880,0617.1815	Literary.
37987	1880,0617.1816	School text; lexical; bilingual incantation; unidentified. Gesche, AOAT 275, 684.

37988	1880,0617.1817	School text; lexical, Syllabary B; unidentified. Gesche, AOAT 275, 684.
37989	1880,0617.1818	Ritual.
37990	1880,0617.1819	Ritual.
37991	1880,0617.1820	School text; lexical; literary, Enūma eliš VI; Marduk's Address (Udug-ḫul 11). Gesche, AOAT 275, 314, 684; Lambert, BCM, p. 109, pl. 26; Geller, BAM 8, 340-392.
37992	1880,0617.1821	School text; lexical; bilingual incantation, Udug-ḫul 10. 10/4/-. Gesche, AOAT 275, 316, 684; Geller, BAM 8, 323-339.
37993	1880,0617.1822	School text; literary; bilingual incantation, Udug-ḫul 13-15. Gesche, AOAT 275, 684; Geller, BAM 8, 434-498, pl. 108.
37994	1880,0617.1823	Bilingual religious.
37995	1880,0617.1824	School text; lexical?; literary. Gesche, AOAT 275, 684.
37996	1880,0617.1825	Lexical; Diri II. MSL 15 121.
37997	1880,0617.1826	Bilingual incantation, Udug-ḫul 2. Geller, BAM 8, 59-88.
37998	1880,0617.1827	Lexical; Diri VI. MSL 15 182.
37999	1880,0617.1828	Literary.
38000	1880,0617.1829	School text; literary. Gesche, AOAT 275, 684.
38001	1880,0617.1830	School text; lexical; bilingual incantation, Udug-ḫul; literary, Enūma eliš II. Gesche, AOAT 275, 684; Kämmerer and Metzler, AOAT 375, 90, Tafel II S, pl. XV; Lambert, BCM, p. 63, pl. 14.
38002	1880,0617.1831	School text; unidentified; Ludlul IV/V. Oshima, BPPS, 430-431; Lambert, MC 24, no. 161.
38003	1880,0617.1832	School text; lexical, Ḫḫ VI, giš; Tintir V. Gesche, AOAT 275, 684; George, BTT, pl. 57.
38004	1880,0617.1833	Lexical; Ea unplaced fragment. MSL 14, 518.
38005	1880,0617.1834	Literary; Enūma eliš II. Lambert, BCM, p. 62, pl. 13.
38006	1880,0617.1835	School text; bilingual literary. Gesche, AOAT 275, 684.
38007	1880,0617.1836	Lexical.
38008	1880,0617.1837	School text; lexical, Ḫḫ IV-V; incantation, Maqlu III. MSL 9, 168; Gesche, AOAT 275, 317, 684; Civil, RA 61, 66 n. 3L; Abusch, AMD 10, 79-112.
38009	1880,0617.1838	Incantation.
38010	1880,0617.1839	School text; incantations, Maqlu II and IV. Abusch, AMD 10, 51-77 and 113-129.
38011	1880,0617.1840	Literary; bilingual.
38012	1880,0617.1841	School text; lexical. Gesche, AOAT 275, 684.

38013	1880,0617.1842	Ritual and incantation; ušburruda ritual. Abusch and Schwemer, AMD 8/1 text 7.8 u, pl. 45.
38014	1880,0617.1843	Incantation.
38015	1880,0617.1844	Religious; mentions Marduk, Nabû, mīs pî.
38016	1880,0617.1845	Lexical.
38017	1880,0617.1846	Incantation.
38018	1880,0617.1847	Joined to 37959.
38019	1880,0617.1848	School text; unidentified. Gesche, AOAT 275, 685.
38020	1880,0617.1849	Incantations; Maqlu II 46-51.
38021	1880,0617.1850	Literary.
38022	1880,0617.1851	School text; lexical, Ḫḫ XXIV. MSL 11, 77; Gesche, AOAT 275, 685.
38023	1880,0617.1852	School text; lexical; literary. Gesche, AOAT 275, 685.
38024	1880,0617.1853	Bilingual incantation.
38025	1880,0617.1854	School text; bilingual incantation; Prayer to Marduk no. 1; unidentified. Gesche, AOAT 275, 685; Lambert, MC 24, no. 94.
38026	1880,0617.1855	Astronomical.
38027	1880,0617.1856	School text; lexical, Ḫḫ XII; bilingual incantation, Udug-ḫul 2. 6/12b/-. Gesche, AOAT 275, 317, 685; Geller, BAM 8, 59-88.
38028	1880,0617.1857	Commentary.
38029	1880,0617.1858	School text; lexical. Gesche, AOAT 275, 685.
38030	1880,0617.1859	School text; lexical, Ḫḫ XXIII. MSL 11, 68; Gesche, AOAT 275, 685.
38031	1880,0617.1860	School text; lexical. Gesche, AOAT 275, 685.
38032	1880,0617.1861	Astrological omens.
38033	1880,0617.1862	School text; lexical. Gesche, AOAT 275, 685.
38034	1880,0617.1863	Literary; Enūma eliš I. Kämmerer and Metzler, AOAT 375, 90, Tafel II W, pl. XVIII; Lambert, BCM, p. 47, pl. 6.
38035	1880,0617.1864	Lexical; Diri I. MSL 15 104.
38036	1880,0617.1865	Economic.
38037	1880,0617.1866	School text; lexical, Ḫḫ I. Gesche, AOAT 275, 685.
38038	1880,0617.1867	School text; lexical. Gesche, AOAT 275, 685.
38039	1880,0617.1868	School text; lexical. Gesche, AOAT 275, 685.
38040	1880,0617.1869	School text; lexical. Gesche, AOAT 275, 685.
38041	1880,0617.1870	Ritual.
38042	1880,0617.1871	Ritual.
38043	1880,0617.1872	School text; lexical; bilingual incantation, Udug-ḫul 13-15; literary, Enūma eliš VI. Gesche, AOAT 275, 685; Kämmerer and Metzler, AOAT 375, 102, Tafel II W, pl. XXXIX; Lambert, BCM, p. 109, pl. 26; Geller, BAM 8, 434-498.
38044	1880,0617.1873	Personal name only; small irregular shaped tablet.

38045	1880,0617.1874	Literary.
38046	1880,0617.1875	School text; lexical; Ḫḫ XI. MSL 9, 195; Gesche, AOAT 275, 685.
38047	1880,0617.1876	School text; lexical. Gesche, AOAT 275, 685.
38048	1880,0617.1877	Economic.
38049	1880,0617.1878	Literary.
38050	1880,0617.1879	Medical ritual.
38051	1880,0617.1880	School text; literary; Enūma eliš I. Lambert, BCM, p. 48, pl. 8.
38052	1880,0617.1881	Incantation.
38053	1880,0617.1882	Incantation.
38054	1880,0617.1883	Religious.
38055	1880,0617.1884	Prayer.
38056	1880,0617.1885	School text; lexical; Šurpu II. Gesche, AOAT 275, 685.
38057	1880,0617.1886	School text; lexical; literary, dupl. CT 17, 19. Gesche, AOAT 275, 685.
38058	1880,0617.1887	School text; lexical, Ḫḫ XII; literary. -/7/-. MSL 9, 203; Gesche, AOAT 275, 685.
38059	1880,0617.1888	School text; lexical, Ḫḫ X-XI. MSL 9, 189, 195; Gesche, AOAT 275, 685.
38060	1880,0617.1889	Joined to 37937.
38061	1880,0617.1890	School text; lexical; literary, Šamaš hymn. Gesche, AOAT 275, 685.
38062	1880,0617.1891	School text; lexical; unidentified. Gesche, AOAT 275, 685.
38063	1880,0617.1892	Lexical.
38064	1880,0617.1893	School text; lexical; Ḫḫ VIII. MSL 9, 173; Gesche, AOAT 275, 685.
38065	1880,0617.1894	Lexical; Diri I. MSL 15 104.
38066	1880,0617.1895	Muššu'u tablet V. Jiménez, Iraq 76, 118; Böck, AuOr 36, 7-8.
38067	1880,0617.1896	Literary; Ludlul II. Oshima, BPPS, 400-403; Lambert, MC 24, no. 152.
38068	1880,0617.1897	Lexical.
38069	1880,0617.1898	Lexical; Ḫḫ II. MSL 9, 157.
38070	1880,0617.1899	Joined to 36296.
38071	1880,0617.1900	School text; literary. Gesche, AOAT 275, 685.
38072	1880,0617.1901	School text; lexical, Ḫḫ, giš. Gesche, AOAT 275, 685.
38073	1880,0617.1902	Economic.
38074	1880,0617.1903	School text; lexical, Ḫḫ I. 13/[]/-. MSL 9, 157; Gesche, AOAT 275, 319, 685.
38075	1880,0617.1904	School text; lexical, Ḫḫ XV. MSL 9, 5; Gesche, AOAT 275, 685.
38076	1880,0617.1905	Incantation.

38077	1880,0617.1906	Unidentified.
38078	1880,0617.1907	Astronomical.
38079	1880,0617.1908	School text; lexical. Gesche, AOAT 275, 685.
38080	1880,0617.1909	Lexical; god-list, An = Anum VI.
38081	1880,0617.1910	Lexical.
38082	1880,0617.1911	Astronomical.
38083	1880,0617.1912	School text; lexical; literary. Gesche, AOAT 275, 685.
38084	1880,0617.1913	Literary.
38085	1880,0617.1914	School text; lexical. Gesche, AOAT 275, 686.
38086	1880,0617.1915	School text; lexical, giš. Gesche, AOAT 275, 686.
38087	1880,0617.1916	Economic. Cyr 20/[]/6.
38088	1880,0617.1917	God list.
38089	1880,0617.1918	Astronomical.
38090	1880,0617.1919	Astronomical.
38091	1880,0617.1920	Sealing, inscribed, with two stamp-seal impressions.
38092	1880,0617.1921	School text; god list. Gesche, AOAT 275, 686.
38093	1880,0617.1922	Lexical.
38094	1880,0617.1923	School text; lexical; Erimḫuš III. MSL 17, 45; Gesche, AOAT 275, 686.
38095	1880,0617.1924	Lexical; Ḫḫ IV 294-305.
38096	1880,0617.1925	School text; lexical. Gesche, AOAT 275, 686.
38097	1880,0617.1926	Counsels of Wisdom. Lambert, MC 24, no. 258.
38098	1880,0617.1927	Lexical.
	1880,0617.1928ff.	Nos. 1928-1930 are uninscribed objects
92494	1880,0617.1931	Inscribed qutāru pot. Walker, Iraq 42, 84-86.
92348	1880,0617.1932	Inscribed qutāru pot. Walker, Iraq 42, 84-86.
	1880,0617.1933ff.	Nos. 1933-1940 are uninscribed objects.
90920	1880,0617.1941	Cylinder; the Cyrus Cylinder; also once numbered 12049; a fragment from the Yale Babylonian collection, NBC 2504 (BIN 2, no. 32), is part of the same cylinder. Cyr. 5R 35; Schaudig, AOAT 256, 550-556; Finkel, The Cyrus Cylinder (2015).
90302	1880,0617.1942	Brick of Nebuchadnezzar II. CBI, no. 100.
90303	1880,0617.1943	Brick of Nebuchadnezzar II. CBI, no. 100.
90604	1880,0617.1944	Brick of Nebuchadnezzar II. CBI, no. 100.
	1880,0617.1945ff.	Nos. 1945-1948 are uninscribed objects.
92388	1880,0617.1949	Inscribed qutāru pot. Walker, Iraq 42, 84-86.

1880,1012 collection

The 1880,1012 collection was purchased from Messrs. Spartali & Co, London. The register gives the provenance Babylonia to nos. 1-18 and the provenance Babylon to nos. 19-21.

38099	1880,1012.1	Old Babylonian, Sumerian literary; love song. CT 58, no. 22.

38100	1880,1012.2	Old Babylonian, letter. van Soldt, AbB 12, 179.
38101	1880,1012.3	Old Babylonian, letter. van Soldt, AbB 12, 180.
38102	1880,1012.4	Memorandum; Old Babylonian or earlier; crude script.
38103	1880,1012.5	Old Babylonian, letter. van Soldt, AbB 12, 181.
38104	1880,1012.6	Horoscope. SE 20/1/243. LBAT 1475; Rochberg, Babylonian Horoscopes, no. 27; Rochberg, Centaurus 32 (1989) 160-162.
38105	1880,1012.7	Lexical; Ḫḫ III. MSL 9, 159.
38106	1880,1012.8	Lexical; Ḫḫ IV. + 38108. MSL 9, 168.
38107	1880,1012.9	Administrative note(?).
38108	1880,1012.10	Joined to 38106.
38109	1880,1012.11	Account of disbursements. + 38119.
38110	1880,1012.12	Lexical; syllabary.
38111	1880,1012.13	Joined to 32188.
38112	1880,1012.14	Joined to 33057.
38113	1880,1012.15	Joined to 34386.
38114	1880,1012.16	Court record about land; finger-nail marks. Nabû-naṣir 9?/[]/2. Babylon. Bertin 1002; cf. Brinkman, PHPKB pp. 272 and 356; Brinkman and Kennedy, JCS 35, 63, AF.2.
38115	1880,1012.17	Promissory note for dates. Xerxes 2/2/3. Babylon. Strassmaier, 8th Orientalist Congress, no. 20.
38116	1880,1012.18	Bilingual eršema prayer. Gabbay, HES 2, 43-55, no. 3.
38117	1880,1012.19	Astronomical Diary for SE 226. Sachs and Hunger, ADART III, no. -85 B.
38118	1880,1012.20	Fragment of a stone tablet with inscription of Gudea, dedication to Šul-šaga; dupl. RIME 3/1.1.7.73 (lines 6-9). Registered as from Babylon; but de Sarzec's duplicates come from Girsu. Perhaps a later copy.
38119	1880,1012.21	Joined to 38109.

1880,1112 collection

The 1880,1112 collection comes from the excavations of Hormuzd Rassam. See J. E. Reade in CBTBM VI, p. xxx. The register gives the provenance Birs Nimroud to nos. 1-32, 447, 526-528, 529b, 530, 534, 535, 574, 580, 663, 664, 708-710, 956, 1047, 1077, 1783, 1784, 1786, 1790, 1793, 1795, 1796, 1801, 1802, 1805, 1808, 1816, 1827, 1830, 1839, 1841, 1867, 1871, 1889, 1895, 2081, 2134, 2146, 2147, 2166, 2167, 2171, 2173 (these last four listed as Borsippa); it gives the provenance Nippur (bought in Hillah) to no. 2172; the rest of the collection is given the provenance Babylon, except that nos. 65-96, 225-288, and 417-446 are given the provenance Babylonia.

38120	1880,1112.1	Lexical; Nabnītu IV-IVa; colophon. Cyr -/-/1. CT 12, 36-37; MSL 16, 73; Hunger, AOAT 2, no. 426; Reade, Iraq 48, 110.
38121	1880,1112.2	Commentary. 5R 39, 4.
38122	1880,1112.3	Babylonian King List B. Pinches, PSBA 3 (1881) 21-22; Grayson, RlA 7, 100.
38123	1880,1112.4	Commentary on Šumma ālu.
38124	1880,1112.5	Contract; division of property. -/1/2. Babylon.
38125	1880,1112.6	Adoption contract. []/[]/38. Babylon. Wunsch, Bab Arch 2, 146-149, no. 43; Wunsch, CM 20A, n. 265.
38126	1880,1112.7	Ritual and incantation against mūtānu; colophon of Nabû-balāssu-iqbi.
38127	1880,1112.8	List of gods and offerings; colophon.
38128	1880,1112.9	Lexical; Aa I/2 = 2. CT 12, 25-26; Pinches, JRAS 1894, 830; Dossin, Iraq 31, 1; MSL 14, 207.
38129	1880,1112.10	Lexical; Ea V. + 38894. CT 12, 24; MSL 14, 393; Hallock, AS 7, 36-38.
38130	1880,1112.11	Lexical; Aa VIII/2 = 40. + 38744. CT 12, 12-13 and 30; MSL 14, 497.
38131	1880,1112.12	Bilingual incantation, Udug-ḫul 15. Geller, Iraq 42, 27 and 46; Geller, BAM 8, 434-498, pl. 122.
38132	1880,1112.13	School text; lexical, Ḫḫ XXIII. 25/12/-. Gesche, AOAT 275, 686.
38133	1880,1112.14	Promissory note for silver. Dar 25/[]/13. Babylon.
38134	1880,1112.15	Letter; names of sender and addressee lost. Hackl et al., AOAT 414/1, no. 91.
38135	1880,1112.16	Deposition. Ner 10/10/2. Sippar. Evetts, Ner 47; Sack, AOAT 236, no. 47.
38136	1880,1112.17	Promissory note for dates. Dar 16/6/28. Alu-ša-mārê-ša-Nūrea.
38137	1880,1112.18	Lexical, commentary on Aa III/1 = 16. MSL 14, 323 and pl. 11.
	1880,1112.19	Contract, Nabonidus 7th year (so register, but subsequently recorded as "Illegible; smashed"); now missing; possibly written off in the 1890s.
38138	1880,1112.20	Receipt for travel provisions. Dar 22/1/25.
38139	1880,1112.21	Medical.
38140	1880,1112.22	Promissory note for silver. Dar 23/5/13. Babylon.
38141	1880,1112.23	Contract. Dar 17/11/14. Babylon.
38142	1880,1112.24	Promissory note for dates. Dar 24/10/30.
38143	1880,1112.25	Letter order; sealed. (Artaxerxes) 6/10/12. Nisaba 28, no. 273a.
38144	1880,1112.26	Contract; sale of a house. Nbn -/3/13.
38145	1880,1112.27	Contract; sale of a house. Nbn -/-/14.

38146	1880,1112.28	Contract; sale of land; finger-nail marks. Cyr []/12/7. Babylon.
38147	1880,1112.29	Contract; sale of fields. 3/[]/3. Babylon.
38148	1880,1112.30	Contract for services. Dar -/11/20.
38149	1880,1112.31	Contract; lease of a house. Dar 8/12/27. Babylon.
38150	1880,1112.32	Economic.
38151	1880,1112.33	Contract; sale of fields. Nbk 16/4/-.
38152	1880,1112.34	Payment of debt. 28/[]/29?
38153	1880,1112.35	Sumerian religious.
38154	1880,1112.36	Dream omens; Zaqīqu.
38155	1880,1112.37	Bilingual epic; Lugal-e II, 53-66 and 75-87; bilingual version. van Dijk, Lugal, text j.
38156	1880,1112.38	Sumerian hymn; same tablet as 38166.
38157	1880,1112.39	Ritual.
38158	1880,1112.40	Omens; Šumma ālu; birds. CT 41, 6-8.
38159	1880,1112.41	Ritual; Bīt rimki III; colophon.
38160	1880,1112.42	Omens; Iqqur īpuš, Ayyaru. Cf. Reiner, Fs Borger (CM 10), 297.
38161	1880,1112.43	Hemerology.
38162	1880,1112.44	Late Babylonian copy of brick inscriptions of Amar-Suen and Ur-Nammu; colophon.
38163	1880,1112.45	Omens; extispicy.
38164	1880,1112.46	Astrological omens; Enūma Anu Enlil 20. Rochberg-Halton, AfO Beih. 22, EAE 20; Reiner, Fs Borger (CM 10), 297; Fincke, Kaskal 14, 55-74. (+) 39164.
38165	1880,1112.47	Medical ritual; two columns.
38166	1880,1112.48	Sumerian hymn; same tablet as 38156.
38167	1880,1112.49	School text; lexical; literary, Šamaš hymn 50-54. Gesche, AOAT 275, 686.
38168	1880,1112.50	Omens; Šumma izbu 11. + 38202 + 39365 + 39549 + 39752 (+) 39072 (+) 39607. De Zorzi, Šumma izbu, 638.
38169	1880,1112.51	Hymn.
38170	1880,1112.52	Letter from Nabû-nūru to Mušēzib-Marduk. CT 22, 29-30, no. 159.
38171	1880,1112.53	Letter from the judges to the šangû of Sippar. CT 22, 42, no. 229.
38172	1880,1112.54	Letter.
38173	1880,1112.55	Lexical; Aa V/2 = 27 and V/3 = 28. CT 12, 20; MSL 14, 415, 421.
38174	1880,1112.56	Lexical; Erimḫuš IV. MSL 17, 56.
38175	1880,1112.57	Lexical.
38176	1880,1112.58	Incantation.
38177	1880,1112.59	Lexical; Aa VI/3 = 32. CT 12, 31; MSL 14, 440.
38178	1880,1112.60	Lexical; Ea V. CT 12, 30; MSL 14, 393.

38179	1880,1112.61	Lexical. CT 12, 30.
38180	1880,1112.62	Lexical; Aa I/7 = 7. CT 12, 22; MSL 14, 236.
38181	1880,1112.63	Lexical. CT 12, 32.
38182	1880,1112.64	School text; lexical; Ḫḫ XVIII. CT 12, 31; MSL 8/2 95.
38183	1880,1112.65	Lexical.
38184	1880,1112.66	Lexical.
38185	1880,1112.67	School text; lexical; Ḫḫ XI. MSL 9, 195.
38186	1880,1112.68	Lexical. CT 12, 26.
38187	1880,1112.69	Incantation.
38188	1880,1112.70	Lexical.
38189	1880,1112.71	Lexical; Aa I/2 = 2; I/3 =3. (+) 38190. CT 12, 20; MSL 14, 207; 219.
38190	1880,1112.72	Lexical; Aa I/2 = 2; I/3 =3. (+) 38189. CT 12, 20; MSL 14, 207; 219.
38191	1880,1112.73	Lexical.
38192	1880,1112.74	God list, An = Anum I; colophon. + 38839.
38193	1880,1112.75	Joined to 32654.
38194	1880,1112.76	Omens; extispicy.
38195	1880,1112.77	Bilingual incantation.
38196	1880,1112.78	Hymn.
38197	1880,1112.79	Commentary; mentions ritual for the month Ṭebētu, Ninurta and Allatum.
38198	1880,1112.80	Incantation; magic?
38199	1880,1112.81	Astrological.
38200	1880,1112.82	Cylinder; inscription of Nebuchadnezzar II(?); duplicate not identified.
38201	1880,1112.83	Sale of a slave. Cam -/1/7. Babylon.
38202	1880,1112.84	Joined to 38168.
38203	1880,1112.85	Promissory note for barley. Nbn 28/12/7.
38204	1880,1112.86	Promissory note for silver. 12/[]/11. Babylon.
38205	1880,1112.87	Inheritance contract drafted as a transfer of property. Nbn 20/7/5. Babylon. Wunsch, Bab Arch 2, 120-121, no. 36.
38206	1880,1112.88	Promissory note for silver. Dar 10/[]/30. Babylon.
38207	1880,1112.89	Promissory note for barley.
38208	1880,1112.90	Economic.
38209	1880,1112.91	Receipt for payment of silver.
38210	1880,1112.92	Economic.
38211	1880,1112.93	Sale of a slave. Dar -/-/13. Babylon.
38212	1880,1112.94	Astronomical; Almanac for SE 200. LBAT 1150; Hunger and Sachs, ADART VII, no. 183.
38213	1880,1112.95	Promissory note for silver.
38214	1880,1112.96	Inventory of objects in the temple of Borsippa.

38215	1880,1112.97	Contract; transfer of property. Wunsch, Bab Arch 2, 76-77, no. 19.
38216	1880,1112.98	Administrative list of writing boards (GIŠ.DA); cf. 35236.
38217	1880,1112.99	Plan of the ziggurat of Ashur; colophon. Wiseman, AnSt 22, 141-145.
38218	1880,1112.100	Economic.
38219	1880,1112.101	Contract; sale of land. Nbn 20+/11/5. Babylon.
38220	1880,1112.102	Contract about rubble and bricks; sealed. SE A[nt & Sel] []/[]/33. CT 49, 19, no. 104; Nisaba 28, no. 555.
38221	1880,1112.103	List of days.
38222	1880,1112.104	Promissory note for silver. Dar -/12b/-.
38223	1880,1112.105	Promissory note for dates. 8/-/-.
38224	1880,1112.106	Contract; sale of fields. Dar 23/7/-.
38225	1880,1112.107	Commentary. + 39450.
38226	1880,1112.108	Record of tax obligation.
38227	1880,1112.109	Contract; ḫarrānu. -/6b/-.
38228	1880,1112.110	Receipt for barley and sesame. Dar 14/[]/28. Borsippa. Zadok, Nisaba 21, 235.
38229	1880,1112.111	Contract. Dar 16/[]/26.
38230	1880,1112.112	Promissory note for silver. 1/3/-.
38231	1880,1112.113	Deposition. Nbk 18/12/39.
38232	1880,1112.114	Sale of a slave. Dar -/12/22. Babylon.
38233	1880,1112.115	Marriage contract. Nbn 4/7/8. Babylon.
38234	1880,1112.116	Account of barley or grain disbursements.
38235	1880,1112.117	Promissory note for silver. Nbk 16/2/6. Babylon.
38236	1880,1112.118	Letter from Nabû-silim to the šatammu. CT 22, 30, no. 160; Levavi, dubsar 3, 491-493, Appendix B.
38237	1880,1112.119	Promissory note for barley. Dar 2/2/10. Babylon.
38238	1880,1112.120	Receipt of payment in silver. Cam 11/4/[1]. Babylon.
38239	1880,1112.121	Account. Shalmaneser V []/6/3. Babylon. Brinkman and Kennedy, JCS 35, 65, AK.1.
38240	1880,1112.122	Promissory note for silver. Nbn 13/3/5. Babylon.
38241	1880,1112.123	Account of dates or grain.
38242	1880,1112.124	Promissory note for silver. Cam 24/10/1. Babylon.
38243	1880,1112.125	Promissory note for sesame. Cam 25/7/7.
38244	1880,1112.126	Contract. 11/8/6. Babylon.
38245	1880,1112.127	Promissory note for barley. Cyr 23/11/8. Babylon.
38246	1880,1112.128	Promissory note for silver. Kandalanu 20/12/13. Babylon. Weidner, AfO 16, 40-41 and pl. IV; Brinkman and Kennedy, JCS 35, 44, L.74.
38247	1880,1112.129	Contract; sale of fields. Cam -/1/5.
38248	1880,1112.130	Legal record of alternative dispute resolution proceedings. Kandalanu 6/12/13. Babylon. Brinkman

		and Kennedy, JCS 35, 44, L.72; Sandowicz, dubsar 11, no. 1.
38249	1880,1112.131	Contract for garments. Nbk 20/1/32. Babylon.
38250	1880,1112.132	Letter from Marduk-zēru-[] to f.Ṭuḫpu-[]. Hackl et al., AOAT 414/1, no. 92.
38251	1880,1112.133	Promissory note for dates. Dar 9/8/13. GÚ.URU.A.GAL.MEŠ.
38252	1880,1112.134	Receipt for barley. -/8/16.
38253	1880,1112.135	Promissory note for silver.
38254	1880,1112.136	Contract; quitclaim about land. Cyr 22/3/8. Borsippa. Zadok, Nisaba 21, 235.
38255	1880,1112.137	Promissory note for silver. 16/6/2.
38256	1880,1112.138	Deposition. -/7/-. Babylon.
38257	1880,1112.139	Contract for hire of a slave. Artaxerxes II/III 14/8/10. Babylon. Nisaba 28, no. 271.
38258	1880,1112.140	Contract; sale of a house; finger-nail marks.
38259	1880,1112.141	Court record, about division of an inheritance; sealed. [Nbk] []/[]/[12]. [Babylon]. (+) 35508. Wunsch, Bab Arch 2, 138-145, no. 42; Nisaba 28, no. 1b.
38260	1880,1112.142	Promissory note for dates. Dar 25/1/-. Ḫallatu.
38261	1880,1112.143	Account of silver.
38262	1880,1112.144	Promissory note for dates. Nbn 12/3/7. Mar(a)da.
38263	1880,1112.145	Astronomical?
38264	1880,1112.146	Sale of a slave girl. Nbk 14/7/1. Babylon.
38265	1880,1112.147	Sale of a slave. 5/[]/21. Babylon.
38266	1880,1112.148	Lexical. CT 12, 29.
38267	1880,1112.149	Lexical; Lú =ša.
38268	1880,1112.150	God list, An = Anum II. + 39046.
38269	1880,1112.151	God list.
38270	1880,1112.152	Lexical; Ḫḫ I.
38271	1880,1112.153	Namburbû commentary.
38272	1880,1112.154	List of gods and stars but with ritual at the end; beginning of reverse obscured by the impression of another tablet; colophon.
38273	1880,1112.155	Commentary.
38274	1880,1112.156	Bilingual proverbs; dupl. Lambert, BWL 240. Lambert, MC 24, no. 293.
38275	1880,1112.157	Lexical.
38276	1880,1112.158	Lexical; Aa VI/1 = 30. CT 12, 20; MSL 14, 437.
38277	1880,1112.159	Lexical; syllabary.
38278	1880,1112.160	Lexical; giš.
38279	1880,1112.161	Lexical.
38280	1880,1112.162	Bilingual Šu'illa prayer to Marduk; dupl. Weissbach, Miscellen, pl. 13-14.
38281	1880,1112.163	Hymn.

38282	1880,1112.164	Bilingual incantation; dupl. 52084.
38283	1880,1112.165	Literary; bilingual proverbs. Lambert, BWL 262-264, pl. 66.
38284	1880,1112.166	Chronicle. CT 37, 21; Grayson, TCS 5, Babylonian Chronicle Fragment 2.
38285	1880,1112.167	Astrological omens; colophon. Reiner, Fs Borger (CM 10), 297.
38286	1880,1112.168	Astrological omens.
38287	1880,1112.169	Copy of an account of oil in the stores of temples in the 18th year of Nazimaruttash. Nbk 20/5/16.
38288	1880,1112.170	Astrological omens; Enūma Anu Enlil 11?; Sin. Reiner, Fs Borger (CM 10), 297.
38289	1880,1112.171	Astrological omens; Enūma Anu Enlil 5. + 38762. Reiner, Fs Borger (CM 10), 297; Verderame, Nisaba 2, 143-147 and Fol. VIII 1-2.
38290	1880,1112.172	Astronomical.
38291	1880,1112.173	Incantation.
38292	1880,1112.174	Historical; Nebuchadnezzar II?
38293	1880,1112.175	Ritual. George, BTT, pl. 50; Linssen, CM 25, 324.
38294	1880,1112.176	Incantation against witchcraft. Abusch and Schwemer, AMD 8/2 text 8.20 e, pl. 29.
38295	1880,1112.177	Astrological omens; Enūma Anu Enlil, Sin. Reiner, Fs Borger (CM 10), 297.
38296	1880,1112.178	Astrological omens; Enūma Anu Enlil 17. Rochberg-Halton, AfO Beih. 22, EAE 17; Reiner, Fs Borger (CM 10), 297.
38297	1880,1112.179	Literary; bilingual proverbs. + 38596 + 38743 + 38853 + 39254. Lambert, BWL 267-269 (38596 only).
38298	1880,1112.180	Prophecy text; mentions Kurigalzu; dupl. 38801 and 42546.
38299	1880,1112.181	Historical; the Verse Account of Nabonidus. S. Smith, BHT, 27-97 and pls. V-X; Schaudig, AOAT 256, pp. 563-578.
38300	1880,1112.182	Mathematical; measurements of a building reckoned in bricks; copy (ḫe-pí eš-šú).
38301	1880,1112.183	Astrological omens; Enūma Anu Enlil 51 and 55. Reiner and Pingree, BPO 2, 78-79, text XVIII; Reiner, Fs Borger (CM 10), 297.
38302	1880,1112.184	Late Babylonian copy of an inscription of Šar-kali-šarri. Sollberger, Fs Diakonoff, 345-348; Frayne, RIME 2.1.5.5; Westenholz, Fs Oelsner, 545.
38303	1880,1112.185	Late Babylonian copy of an Old Babylonian inscription of Ammi-ditana. King, LIH, no. 100; Frayne, RIME 4.3.9.1.1.

38304	1880,1112.186	Old Babylonian, Sumerian literary; Dialogue 1, "Two scribes". CT 58, no. 56.
38305	1880,1112.187	Late Babylonian copy of a pre-Sargonic votive inscription from Mari. Sollberger, RAI XV, 103-105 and pl. I.
38306	1880,1112.188	Promissory note for silver.
38307	1880,1112.189	Medical; foot or leg disease; very late script.
38308	1880,1112.190	List of three personal names; continuation partly erased.
38309	1880,1112.191	Promissory note for dates. Dar -/6/24. Ḫallatu.
38310	1880,1112.192	Economic.
38311	1880,1112.193	Deposition.
38312	1880,1112.194	Receipt for purchase of barley. Nbn 7/[]/2. Babylon.
38313	1880,1112.195	Omens; Šumma ālu, tablet 37. Freedman, If a city, vol. 2, 243.
38314	1880,1112.196	Economic.
38315	1880,1112.197	Prayer to the star Dilbat (Venus).
38316	1880,1112.198	Promissory note for dates. Cyr 24/-/-.
38317	1880,1112.199	Contract; division of property. Dar 12/3/13. Babylon.
38318	1880,1112.200	Promissory note for silver.
38319	1880,1112.201	Contract; sale of fields.
38320	1880,1112.202	Account of seed.
38321	1880,1112.203	Contract. Nbn? 27/12/1.
38322	1880,1112.204	Promissory note for silver. Dar 20/12a/24. Babylon.
38323	1880,1112.205	Contract; sale of fields. Dar 3/10/17. URU Bīt-1.MU-MU.
38324	1880,1112.206	Promissory note for dates or grain. Dar 5/6/22.
38325	1880,1112.207	Old Babylonian, economic: barley and silver received by Mu-ti-e-x-x and Be-le-tum from Sin-im-ma-tim son of E-te-lum; 4 witnesses; tablet in unopened envelope; sealed. 30/Tamhirim/mu ma-da ma-ḫa-zum (Išcali year name).
38326	1880,1112.208	Memorandum.
38327	1880,1112.209	Memorandum.
38328	1880,1112.210	Contract; sale of fields; sealed; finger-nail marks. d.l. Mitchell and Searight, no. 329; Nisaba 28, no. 61.
38329	1880,1112.211	Contract; sale of fields.
38330	1880,1112.212	Omens; terrestrial.
38331	1880,1112.213	Contract; sale of fields.
38332	1880,1112.214	Omens; terrestrial.
38333	1880,1112.215	Letter.
38334	1880,1112.216	Omens; physiognomic.
38335	1880,1112.217	Omens; Šumma izbu 14. De Zorzi, Šumma izbu, 698.
38336	1880,1112.218	Literary; Mami myth or incantation.
38337	1880,1112.219	Literary.

38338	1880,1112.220	Omens; extispicy.
38339	1880,1112.221	Astronomical.
38340	1880,1112.222	Sumerian literary.
38341	1880,1112.223	Omens; Šumma ālu; birds. CT 39, 25.
38342	1880,1112.224	Commentary.
38343	1880,1112.225	Prayer to Marduk no. 1. Lambert, MC 24, no. 89.
38344	1880,1112.226	Letter; names of sender and addressee lost. Hackl et al., AOAT 414/1, no. 93.
38345	1880,1112.227	Cylinder; inscription of Esarhaddon on restoration of the temple of Gula at Borsippa. CT 37, 23; Borger, AfO Beih. 9, 32, Borsippa A; Frame, RIMB 2.6.31.10; Leichty, RINAP 4.127.
38346	1880,1112.228	Cylinder; inscription of Nabonidus. CT 37, 21; Schaudig, AOAT 256, 483-484.
38347	1880,1112.229	Economic.
38348	1880,1112.230	Account of bricks.
38349	1880,1112.231	Letter.
38350	1880,1112.232	Contract; witnesses. Art []/[]/6. Babylon?
38351	1880,1112.233	Contract; sale of a house.
38352	1880,1112.234	List of people.
38353	1880,1112.235	Memorandum.
38354	1880,1112.236	Account of disbursements.
38355	1880,1112.237	Unidentified.
38356	1880,1112.238	Astrological omens.
38357	1880,1112.239	Astronomical observations; eclipses and other events from at least 612-608 BC; late copy (ḫe-pí eš-šú). Hunger and Sachs, ADART V, no. 5.
38358	1880,1112.240	Medical; mentions mišittu disease.
38359	1880,1112.241	Astrological; commentary on Enūma Anu Enlil 24 (25). + 38757 + 39214 + 46241. van Soldt, Solar omens, 16, 44-46, pl. VI; Fincke, Kaskal 11, 103-139; Reiner, Fs Borger (CM 10), 298.
38360	1880,1112.242	Sumerian literary.
38361	1880,1112.243	Astrological omens; Mars.
38362	1880,1112.244	Medical omens; Sa-gig I. Heeßel, AOAT 43, 139; George, RA 85, 137-164.
38363	1880,1112.245	Astrological omens; Venus.
38364	1880,1112.246	Astrological omens; Sin.
38365	1880,1112.247	Omens.
38366	1880,1112.248	Medical.
38367	1880,1112.249	Incantation. Lambert, MC 24, no. 218.
38368	1880,1112.250	Bilingual incantation. + 38672 + 39243 + 39251 + 39544.

38369	1880,1112.251	Astronomical; stellar distances. + 38694. Reiner, Fs Borger (CM 10), 298; Horowitz, JCS 46, 89-98; J. Koch, NABU 2002, 4-6, no. 5.
38370	1880,1112.252	Literary; colophon of [Kabti?]-ilāni-Marduk.
38371	1880,1112.253	Lexical and literary extracts: Ḫḫ XIX; Lú = ša I and Short Recension Excerpt II (cf. MSL XII 91-110).
38372	1880,1112.254	Lexical; Aa II/1 = 9. CT 12, 23; MSL 14, 265.
38373	1880,1112.255	Late Babylonian copy of an inscription of [Kurigal-z]u.
38374	1880,1112.256	Lexical; Aa VIII/4 = 42; colophon. + 39015. CT 12, 18-19; MSL 14, 508.
38375	1880,1112.257	Commentary on medical omens, Sa-gig XXIX. Cf. Finkel in Gs Sachs 147 n. 29; Heeßel, AOAT 43, 318, 323 and 465; Finkel, JCS 46, 87.
38376	1880,1112.258	Lexical.
38377	1880,1112.259	Bilingual incantation.
38378	1880,1112.260	Late Babylonian copy of an Old Babylonian field sale; no witnesses; no seal; complete year formula. Samsu-ditana 11/2/12.
38379	1880,1112.261	Omens; extispicy; right side of a large tablet.
38380	1880,1112.262	Astronomical Diary.
38381	1880,1112.263	Economic. -/11/-. Babylon.
38382	1880,1112.264	Lexical.
38383	1880,1112.265	Lexical.
38384	1880,1112.266	Extract of the Weidner god list.
38385	1880,1112.267	Lexical; list of stones; series Kunuk ḫalti. MSL 10, 65-68; Schuster-Brandis, AOAT 46, pp. 22, 192.
38386	1880,1112.268	Lexical; giš.
38387	1880,1112.269	Lexical and literary extracts.
38388	1880,1112.270	Lexical.
38389	1880,1112.271	Lexical; Ḫḫ XVII (plants). MSL 10, 79.
38390	1880,1112.272	Omens; Šumma ālu?
38391	1880,1112.273	Legend; colophon. SE Arsaces []/[]/24+. + 38399.
38392	1880,1112.274	Astrological; 1 MUL GAL … + 38416. Reiner, Fs Borger (CM 10), 297.
38393	1880,1112.275	Astronomical; stars.
38394	1880,1112.276	Literary; colophon.
38395	1880,1112.277	Incantation.
38396	1880,1112.278	Literary; Enūma eliš II. CT 13, 4; Lambert, BCM, p. 62.
38397	1880,1112.279	Sumerian literary.
38398	1880,1112.280	Astronomical.
38399	1880,1112.281	Joined to 38391.
38400	1880,1112.282	Lexical. + 1880.1112.284.
38401	1880,1112.283	Medical; incantation?

	1880,1112.284	Joined to 38400.
38402	1880,1112.285	Late Babylonian copy of an Old Babylonian inscription of Samsu-iluna, Akkadian version. King, LIH, no. 97; Frayne, RIME 4.3.7.5.2a.
38403	1880,1112.286	Cylinder; inscription of Nebuchadnezzar II(?); duplicate not identified.
38404	1880,1112.287	Late Babylonian copy of an Old Babylonian inscription in Akkadian.
38405	1880,1112.288	Astronomical; Goal Year Text for SE 192; colophon. LBAT 1284; Hunger and Sachs, ADART VI, no. 68.
38406	1880,1112.289	Description of a field.
38407	1880,1112.290	Contract; sale of fields. Nbk -/11/26. Babylon.
38408	1880,1112.291	Memorandum of silver debt.
38409	1880,1112.292	Contract; sale of a house. Cyr 25/9/8. Babylon.
38410	1880,1112.293	Contract; sale of fields; sealed; finger-nail marks. Dar 10+/8/[]. Babylon. + 38424. Nisaba 28, no. 113.
38411	1880,1112.294	Commentary.
38412	1880,1112.295	Bilingual incantation.
38413	1880,1112.296	Nippur Compendium. George, BTT, pl. 29.
38414	1880,1112.297	Astronomical; lunar six table for -642 to -640. Huber and Steele, SCIAMVS 8 (2007) 3-36, text A; Britton and Huber, Fs Hunger, 217.
38415	1880,1112.298	Tabulated account of barley; perhaps copy of an earlier text? GIŠ.BAN d.UTU.
38416	1880,1112.299	Joined to 38392.
38417	1880,1112.300	Bilingual incantation.
38418	1880,1112.301	Omens; Šumma ālu, tablet 33. CT 38, 41-43; Freedman, If a city, vols. 1, 332 and 2, 202.
38419	1880,1112.302	Contract; sale of fields; sealed; finger-nail marks. d.l. Nisaba 28, no. 62.
38420	1880,1112.303	Medical.
38421	1880,1112.304	Commentary.
38422	1880,1112.305	Bilingual incantation.
38423	1880,1112.306	Receipt for dates or grain. Dar 23/-/-.
38424	1880,1112.307	Joined to 38410.
38425	1880,1112.308	Literary; Love Lyrics.
38426	1880,1112.309	Contract; sale of fields.
38427	1880,1112.310	Promissory note for silver. Nbk 12/1/18. Babylon.
38428	1880,1112.311	Contract; transfer of property. 16/8/6. Wunsch, Bab Arch 2, 88-92, no. 26.
38429	1880,1112.312	Lexical.
38430	1880,1112.313	Late Babylonian copy of an Old Babylonian or Ur III inscription; cf. 39720.
38431	1880,1112.314	Astronomical.
38432	1880,1112.315	God list; colophon.

38433	1880,1112.316	Bilingual epic; Lugal-e V 182-195 and 225-236; colophon. van Dijk, Lugal, text x.
38434	1880,1112.317	Astronomical. + 38465.
38435	1880,1112.318	Omens; terrestrial. + 38781.
38436	1880,1112.319	Sumerian literary.
38437	1880,1112.320	Literary; bilingual proverbs?; perhaps part of same tablet as 38539 (Lambert, BWL pl. 67).
38438	1880,1112.321	Medical; includes a prescription for KÙ.GI UD.UD.MEŠ. Cf. Finkel, AuOr 9 (1991) 103 (under wrong number 33438).
38439	1880,1112.322	Lexical.
38440	1880,1112.323	Account of garments. Marduk-apla-iddina I 11/4/acc. Brinkman, MSKH I, 250, pl. 3, no. 3.
38441	1880,1112.324	Omens; terrestrial; three columns. + 38498 + 38625.
38442	1880,1112.325	Tintir I, IV. George, BTT, pl. 2.
38443	1880,1112.326	Omens; Šumma izbu 11. De Zorzi, Šumma izbu, 638.
38444	1880,1112.327	Namburbû ritual and incantation against evil birds.
38445	1880,1112.328	Dream omens; cf. Oppenheim, Dreams, 322-326.
38446	1880,1112.329	Late Babylonian copy of an Old Babylonian historical inscription of Abi-ešuḫ. King, LIH, no. 68; Frayne, RIME 4.3.8.1.1.
38447	1880,1112.330	Bilingual incantation, Udug-ḫul 2, colophon. CT 16, 40; Geller, BAM 8, 59-88.
38448	1880,1112.331	Late Babylonian copy of the Laws of Hammurabi.
38449	1880,1112.332	Mentions four wind directions.
38450	1880,1112.333	Lexical.
38451	1880,1112.334	Contract; sale of fields.
38452	1880,1112.335	Astrological; tabulated; cf. 32517. (+) 39680.
38453	1880,1112.336	Contract; lease of a house.
38454	1880,1112.337	Promissory note for barley.
38455	1880,1112.338	Promissory note for dates.
38456	1880,1112.339	List of people.
38457	1880,1112.340	Promissory note for dates or grain. Nbk 4/[]/31.
38458	1880,1112.341	Economic.
38459	1880,1112.342	Account of grain.
38460	1880,1112.343	Letter.
38461	1880,1112.344	Graeco-Babyloniaca; colophon. Geller, ZA 87, 79-80 and 94, no. 14 (copy); Westenholz, ZA 97, 272-273.
38462	1880,1112.345	Astronomical; lunar eclipse table for years 1-29 of Nebuchadnezzar II (604-576 BC). LBAT 1420; Stephenson, HEER, 149, 164-165, 196-197, 205; Hunger and Sachs, ADART V, no. 6.
38463	1880,1112.346	Liver omens. + 1880,1112.354.
38464	1880,1112.347	Receipt for wool?
38465	1880,1112.348	Joined to 38434.

38466	1880,1112.349	Lexical; list of plants.
38467	1880,1112.350	Promissory note for silver. -/-/9.
38468	1880,1112.351	Incantation.
38469	1880,1112.352	Incantation.
38470	1880,1112.353	Sumerian literary.
	1880,1112.354	Joined to 38463.
38471	1880,1112.355	Letter.
38472	1880,1112.356	Astronomical; lunar six table for -513 to -511. Huber and Steele, SCIAMVS 8 (2007) 3-36, text F.
38473	1880,1112.357	Astrological.
38474	1880,1112.358	Historical cylinder; duplicate not identified; perhaps a copy of an earlier cylinder.
38475	1880,1112.359	Liver omens.
38476	1880,1112.360	Literary; myth about Marduk.
38477	1880,1112.361	Medical.
38478	1880,1112.362	Incantations.
38479	1880,1112.363	Incantation.
38480	1880,1112.364	Contract; sale of fields.
38481	1880,1112.365	Bilingual incantation.
38482	1880,1112.366	Astronomical.
38483	1880,1112.367	Medical.
38484	1880,1112.368	Literary; Counsels of Wisdom; four columns; dupl. 73873. + 38488. Lambert, MC 24, no. 262.
38485	1880,1112.369	Medical.
38486	1880,1112.370	Literary; bilingual proverbs. Lambert, BWL 264-266, pl. 66.
38487	1880,1112.371	Literary; Erra III.
38488	1880,1112.372	Joined to 38484.
38489	1880,1112.373	Medical omens; TDP 38 (38-am). + 39428.
38490	1880,1112.374	Lexical.
38491	1880,1112.375	Bilingual incantation.
38492	1880,1112.376	Literary.
38493	1880,1112.377	Later copy of a letter to the king. + 38852. CT 22, 46, no. 247.
38494	1880,1112.378	Late Babylonian copy of a Kassite inscription; two columns.
38495	1880,1112.379	Literary.
38496	1880,1112.380	Lexical; similar to Idu; two columns.
38497	1880,1112.381	Contract; sale of a house; month iv or vii. [Cyr?] 1/4?/1+. [Babylon].
38498	1880,1112.382	Joined to 38441.
38499	1880,1112.383	Medical.
38500	1880,1112.384	Account of seed. Nbn 25/6/-.
38501	1880,1112.385	Account of disbursements.
38502	1880,1112.386	Account of grain?; bead-shaped.

38503	1880,1112.387	Memorandum.
38504	1880,1112.388	Receipt for sesame.
38505	1880,1112.389	Medical.
38506	1880,1112.390	Contract; sale of fields?
38507	1880,1112.391	Sumerian literary.
38508	1880,1112.392	Contract; sale of fields.
38509	1880,1112.393	Weidner god list.
38510	1880,1112.394	Oracle question (tamītu) to Šamaš. Lambert, BOQ, pp. 134-135, Frg. A, pl. 56.
38511	1880,1112.395	Incantation.
38512	1880,1112.396	Incantation.
38513	1880,1112.397	Lexical.
38514	1880,1112.398	Late Babylonian copy of a Kassite or earlier inscription.
38515	1880,1112.399	Sumerian literary.
38516	1880,1112.400	Dream omens.
38517	1880,1112.401	Lexical.
38518	1880,1112.402	Medical.
38519	1880,1112.403	Lexical, commentary on Aa VI.
38520	1880,1112.404	Account of dates or grain.
38521	1880,1112.405	Contract; sale of fields; sealed. d.l. Nisaba 28, no. 85.
38522	1880,1112.406	Economic.
38523	1880,1112.407	Contract; sale of a house. 3/2/2.
38524	1880,1112.408	Astronomical.
38525	1880,1112.409	Lexical, commentary on Aa II/4 (pirsu 12).
38526	1880,1112.410	Promissory note for sesame. Dar 4/6/16.
38527	1880,1112.411	Contract; sale of fields.
38528	1880,1112.412	Literary.
38529	1880,1112.413	Dream omens.
38530	1880,1112.414	Medical omens; Sa-gig XXXI. Heeßel, AOAT 43, 342 and 466-467; Finkel, JCS 46, 88.
38531	1880,1112.415	Liver omens; Šumma isru.
38532	1880,1112.416	Astrological omens; Enūma Anu Enlil 10; Sin. Reiner, Fs Borger (CM 10), 297.
38533	1880,1112.417	Omens; Šumma izbu 8. Leichty, TCS 4, 23; De Zorzi, Šumma izbu, 562.
38534	1880,1112.418	Astrological omens; Enūma Anu Enlil 8/9; Sin. Reiner, Fs Borger (CM 10), 297.
38535	1880,1112.419	Fable of the fox. Jiménez, BDP, 378-380; Lambert, MC 24, no. 270.
38536	1880,1112.420	Astrological omens; Enūma Anu Enlil.
38537	1880,1112.421	Šu'illa prayer; Bīt salā' mê III; colophon. Ambos, Der König, 296; Lenzi, Or NS 82, 1-10.

38538	1880,1112.422	Literary; Gilgameš I. CT 46, 29, no. 18; Garelli, Gilgameš, 125-127 (copy by Wiseman); George, Gilgamesh II, pl. 50.
38539	1880,1112.423	Literary; bilingual proverbs. Lambert, BWL 266-267, pl. 67.
38540	1880,1112.424	School text; lexical, Syllabary A. Gesche, AOAT 275, 686.
38541	1880,1112.425	School text; lexical, Syllabary A. Gesche, AOAT 275, 686.
38542	1880,1112.426	School text; lexical, Syllabary A. Gesche, AOAT 275, 686.
38543	1880,1112.427	Lexical.
38544	1880,1112.428	Late Babylonian copy of an Old Babylonian inscription.
38545	1880,1112.429	Late Babylonian copy of an inscription of Burnaburiaš.
38546	1880,1112.430	Impression from a stele inscription, with "colophon" on the back. Cf. Clay, Museum Journal 3 (1912) 23ff. + 39737.
38547	1880,1112.431	Contract; sale of fields. Dar 22/8/-.
38548	1880,1112.432	Contract for bricks; mentions year 19.
38549	1880,1112.433	Contract.
38550	1880,1112.434	Contract; sale of a field; plan on the reverse.
38551	1880,1112.435	Deposition.
38552	1880,1112.436	Sumerian balag to Marduk; dupl. K.5168+.
38553	1880,1112.437	Incantation against bad dreams. Near duplicate to Oppenheim, Dreams, 301.
38554a	1880,1112.438a	Astrological omens; MN/UD ... šá DN – lipšur? Reiner, Fs Borger (CM 10), 297.
38554b	1880,1112.438b	Bilingual proverbs. (+) 38283. Lambert, MC 24, no. 296.
38555	1880,1112.439	Astrological omens.
38556	1880,1112.440	Medical.
38557	1880,1112.441	Historical-literary.
38558	1880,1112.442	Late Babylonian copy of the Laws of Hammurabi.
38559	1880,1112.443	Omens; Šumma izbu 18. De Zorzi, Šumma izbu, 763.
38560	1880,1112.444	Literary.
38561	1880,1112.445	Incantation; exorcistic.
38562	1880,1112.446	Historical-literary.
38563	1880,1112.447	School text; lexical, Syllabary A. Gesche, AOAT 275, 686.
38564	1880,1112.448	God list.
38565	1880,1112.449	Lexical.
38566	1880,1112.450	Lexical.
38567	1880,1112.451	Lexical.

38568	1880,1112.452	Lexical.
38569	1880,1112.453	Lexical.
38570	1880,1112.454	Lexical.
38571	1880,1112.455	Lexical.
38572	1880,1112.456	Contract.
38573	1880,1112.457	Promissory note for barley. Dar 6/2/-. Babylon.
38574	1880,1112.458	Receipt. Cyr -/5/-. Babylon.
38575	1880,1112.459	Contract. 21/9/-. Babylon.
38576	1880,1112.460	Promissory note for dates.
38577	1880,1112.461	Promissory note for barley. Cam 23/8/3.
38578	1880,1112.462	Lexical; Diri II.
38579	1880,1112.463	Economic. Babylon.
38580	1880,1112.464	Contract.
38581	1880,1112.465	Promissory note for barley. Cam 10/6/1. Babylon.
38582	1880,1112.466	Stones identified with cities, temples and gods.
38583	1880,1112.467	Excerpts with medical prescriptions against diseases. Finkel, Fs Borger (CM 10), 80, n. 9.
38584	1880,1112.468	Lexical.
38585	1880,1112.469	Physiognomic omens. CT 41, 20-21; cf. Kraus, AfO Bh. 3, p. 58; cf. Reiner, Fs Borger (CM 10), 297.
38586	1880,1112.470	Akkadian én é-nu-ru incantation, Udug-ḫul 1, colophon. CT 51, 142; Geller, BAM 8, 44-58.
38587	1880,1112.471	Omens; extispicy; tīrānu 7th tablet. Colophon: copied from an original from Borsippa. Reade, Iraq 48, 110.
38588	1880,1112.472	Commentary on Šumma izbu; colophon; cf. 35553. CT 41, 35-38; Leichty, TCS 4, 238; De Zorzi, Šumma izbu, 937.
38589	1880,1112.473	Lexical.
38590	1880,1112.474	Lexical; vocabulary of an unknown language. Lambert, MARI 5 (1987), 409-413.
38591	1880,1112.475	School text; lexical; Ḫḫ II; dated SIG4 13 MU 1(sic!). 13/3/1. MSL 5, 47; Langdon, RA 14, 12 (date not copied); Gesche, AOAT 275, 686.
38592	1880,1112.476	Lexical; Diri I. + 64190. CT 12, 29; MSL 15 104.
38593	1880,1112.477	Sumerian religious; balag; Uruamirabi tablet 19; colophon. Nbk II []/[]/11. + 38606. Cohen, Canonical Lamentations, p. 796; Volk, FAOS 18, 9, 56-131 and pls. Ia-III.
38594	1880,1112.478	Bilingual incantation, Udug-ḫul 3. CT 16, 1-8; Geller, BAM 8, 89-132.
38595	1880,1112.479	Literary.
38596	1880,1112.480	Joined to 38297.
38597	1880,1112.481	Commentary; physiognomic omens; Alamdimmu; colophon. Böck, AfO Beih. 27, 264, pl. 28-29.

38598	1880,1112.482	School text; lexical, Syllabary A. Gesche, AOAT 275, 686.
38599	1880,1112.483	Incantations and rituals before astral deities. Schwemer, StBoT 58, 211-228.
38600	1880,1112.484	Bilingual text; "Enlil and Ninlil: the birth of Nanna". Pinches, JRAS 1919, 190 and 575; Pinches, PSBA 33 (1911) 77-93; Langdon, RA 19, 67-77.
38601	1880,1112.485	Lexical; Ana ittišu I.
38602	1880,1112.486	Literary compendium; i: Gates of Esangila; ii: Locations of Cultic Daises; iii: literary and scholarly extracts. George, BTT, pl. 22.
38603	1880,1112.487	Lexical.
38604	1880,1112.488	Astrological omens; Enūma Anu Enlil 25.
38605	1880,1112.489	Bilingual incantation.
38606	1880,1112.490	Joined to 38593.
38607	1880,1112.491	Astrological omens; Enūma Anu Enlil?
38608	1880,1112.492	Contract; sale of land; sealed; finger-nail marks. Nbk 15/10/24. Nisaba 28, no. 51.
38609	1880,1112.493	Incantations; Maqlu I.
38610	1880,1112.494	Literary; copy (ḫe-pí eš-šú); colophon.
38611	1880,1112.495	Late Babylonian copy of an historical epic about successive Kassite kings. Dupl. K.9952.
38612	1880,1112.496	Fragment of a boundary stone; inscribed; lower part of a human figure holding a bucket. Eriba-Marduk. Paulus, AOAT 51, 678-679, pl. 58, EM I; Reade, ARRIM 5, 47.
38613	1880,1112.497	Contract; sale of fields; finger-nail marks. [Nbk] 23/[]/42+. Wunsch, CM 20A-B, p. 36, n. 102.
38614	1880,1112.498	School text; lexical, Syllabary A. Gesche, AOAT 275, 686.
38615	1880,1112.499	School text; lexical, Syllabary A, Lú list, personal names, acrographic list. Gesche, AOAT 275, 319, 687.
38616	1880,1112.500	Astronomical. (+) 39426.
38617	1880,1112.501	Bilingual incantation.
38618	1880,1112.502	School text; lexical, Syllabary A. Gesche, AOAT 275, 687.
38619	1880,1112.503	Šu'illa prayer.
38620	1880,1112.504	Lexical; Ḫḫ XXI. MSL 11, 10.
38621	1880,1112.505	Astronomical.
38622	1880,1112.506	Lexical; Nabnītu XIV (= S). CT 41, 49; MSL 16, 133.
38623	1880,1112.507	School text.
38624	1880,1112.508	Medical omens; Šumma ana bīt amēl marṣi; gynaecological prescriptions. + 38828 + 45414.
38625	1880,1112.509	Joined to 38441.

38626	1880,1112.510	Ritual with incantation to Šamaš.
38627	1880,1112.511	Contract; sale of fields.
38628	1880,1112.512	Contract; sale of a house. Dar 22/1/6. URU Dūru-šá-Bal-da-du.
38629	1880,1112.513	Lexical.
38630	1880,1112.514	Literary letter; colophon. Grayson, JAOS 103, 143-146.
38631	1880,1112.515	Medical.
38632	1880,1112.516	Sumerian hymn.
38633	1880,1112.517	Lexical and literary extracts.
38634	1880,1112.518	Contract; sale of fields.
38635	1880,1112.519	Ritual and incantation; ušburruda ritual; ḫe-pí eš-šú. Abusch and Schwemer, AMD 8/1 text 7.8 t, pls. 44-45.
38636	1880,1112.520	Lexical. 5R 39, 2.
38637	1880,1112.521	Medical; duplicate to TDP 3.
38638	1880,1112.522	Promissory note for dates.
38639	1880,1112.523	Astrological omens; Enūma Anu Enlil 18?; colophon. Fincke, Kaskal 13, 101-105, Text I, 117-18 figure 7.
38640	1880,1112.524	Literary.
38641	1880,1112.525	Contract for wine; sealed. Darius II/III 22/[]/3. Babylon? Nisaba 28, no. 244a.
38642	1880,1112.526	School text; lexical; sign-list; colophon of Nabû-balāssu-iqbi. + 38644.
38643	1880,1112.527	Lexical; practice wedges.
38644	1880,1112.528	Joined to 38642.
38645	1880,1112.529a	Literary.
38646	1880,1112.529b	Fragment of a boundary stone; inscribed; recording a sale of land. Middle Babylonian. Borsippa. (+) 40590. King, BBSt, 90-95 and pl. 19, no. XXII; Seidl, Bagh Mitt 4, 65 G 16; Reade, Iraq 48, 109; Reade, ARRIM 5, 47; Paulus, AOAT 51, 829-834, U 33.
38647	1880,1112.530	Contract; exchange of slaves. Nbk 1?/5/39. Borsippa. Zadok, Nisaba 21, 235.
38648	1880,1112.531	Commentary.
38649	1880,1112.532	God-list and literary extracts. + 38665.
38650	1880,1112.533	Bilingual hymn to Marduk.
38651	1880,1112.534	Contract; sale of land. (Borsippa). Zadok, Nisaba 21, 235.
38652	1880,1112.535	Contract; sale of fields.
38653	1880,1112.536	Promissory note for dates; sealed; finger-nail marks. Artaxerxes 12/7?/5. Babylon. Nisaba 28, no. 262.
38654	1880,1112.537	Medical.
38655	1880,1112.538	Medical omens; Sa-gig XIV. Geller, BAM 7, 248-257, no. 49, pls. 31-35; cf. Heeßel, AOAT 43, 145.

38656	1880,1112.539	Medical.
38657	1880,1112.540	School text; namburbû-like ritual with examination of ingredients; lexical. 7/5/-.
38658	1880,1112.541	Literary.
38659	1880,1112.542	Bilingual incantation.
38660	1880,1112.543	Bilingual incantation, Udug-ḫul 16, colophon. Geller, BAM 8, 499-541, pl. 132.
38661	1880,1112.544	Bilingual incantation.
38662	1880,1112.545	Sumerian incantation.
38663	1880,1112.546	Animal ledger.
38664	1880,1112.547	Contract. Dar 10/4/4.
38665	1880,1112.548	Joined to 38649.
38666	1880,1112.549	Medical; list of stones and their properties; series Kunuk ḫalti tablet V; three columns. + 39447 + 1880,1112.562. Schuster-Brandis, AOAT 46, p. 487, pl. 38; Abusch and Schwemer, AMD 8/2 text 3.4 c, pls. 1-2.
38667	1880,1112.550	Medical; materia medica with amounts.
38668	1880,1112.551	Medical; SAG.KI.DAB.BA.
38669	1880,1112.552	Omens; extispicy.
38670	1880,1112.553	Contract; sale of fields.
38671	1880,1112.554	Lexical.
38672	1880,1112.555	Joined to 38368.
38673	1880,1112.556	Medical prescriptions for afflictions of GÌŠ, the penis.
38674	1880,1112.557	Literary; colophon.
38675	1880,1112.558	Contract; sale of fields. 22/7/39.
38676	1880,1112.559	Incantation.
38677	1880,1112.560	Omens; extispicy; lung omens.
38678	1880,1112.561	Sumerian literary.
	1880,1112.562	Joined to 38666.
38679	1880,1112.563	Medical.
38680	1880,1112.564	Omens; Šumma ālu.
38681	1880,1112.565	Commentary or explanatory text probably concerned with a divination text; rev. lists different styluses of the priestly classes: qan ṭuppi šulḫû, barû, kalû.
38682	1880,1112.566	God list. Pinches, Fs Haupt, 212-216.
38683	1880,1112.567	Astrological omens.
38684	1880,1112.568	Commentary.
38685	1880,1112.569	Bilingual incantation.
38686	1880,1112.570	Contract; sale of fields.
38687	1880,1112.571	School text; lexical, Syllabary A. Gesche, AOAT 275, 687.
38688	1880,1112.572	Promissory note for dates.
38689	1880,1112.573	Lexical; syllabary.

38690	1880,1112.574	School text; lexical, Syllabary A, Lú list, personal names, acrographic list; colophon. + 40007. Gesche, AOAT 275, 321, 687.
38691	1880,1112.575	Late Babylonian copy of the Laws of Hammurabi.
38692	1880,1112.576	Astrological; commentary. Reiner, Fs Borger (CM 10), 298.
38693	1880,1112.577	Literary.
38694	1880,1112.578	Joined to 38369.
38695	1880,1112.579	School text; lexical; Ḫḫ IV. MSL 9, 168.
38696	1880,1112.580	Cylinder; inscription of Nebuchadnezzar II(?); duplicate not identified.
38697	1880,1112.581	Lexical; syllabary.
38698	1880,1112.582	Economic.
38699	1880,1112.583	Account of offerings.
38700	1880,1112.584	Economic. Nbk 23/[]/6.
38701	1880,1112.585	Contract; lease of fields; sealed; finger-nail marks. Artaxerxes II/III 3?/6?/8+? Nisaba 28, no. 295.
38702	1880,1112.586	School text.
38703	1880,1112.587	Sumerian literary; "Examination text D". CT 58, no. 66.
38704	1880,1112.588	Astronomical; list of ziqpu stars; cf. LBAT 1501; monthly rising time sheme. Steele, Rising time schemes, 26-28; Fincke and Horowitz, JNES 77, 249-261.
38705	1880,1112.589	Astronomical.
38706	1880,1112.590	God list; names of Marduk. + 39843. George, BTT, pl. 55 (39843); Lambert, BCM, pp. 106 and 134, pl. 41.
38707	1880,1112.591	Literary.
38708	1880,1112.592	Lexical.
38709	1880,1112.593	Incantation. + 38898.
38710	1880,1112.594	Lexical.
38711	1880,1112.595	Šu'illa prayer. + 39814.
38712	1880,1112.596	Promissory note for barley.
38713	1880,1112.597	Letter from Dummuqu to Sūqāya. CT 22, 18, no. 87; Hackl et al., AOAT 414/1, no. 94.
38714	1880,1112.598	Account of silver withdrawn from capital.
38715	1880,1112.599	Incantation.
38716	1880,1112.600	Omens?
38717	1880,1112.601	Bilingual.
38718	1880,1112.602	Omens; extispicy.
38719	1880,1112.603	Old Babylonian; field sale; sealed; upper right corner. [...]-ditana 8/10/?
38720	1880,1112.604	Chronicle. + 38721 + 38775 + 38778 + 38999 + 39036 + 39256 + 39599.

38721	1880,1112.605	Joined to 38720.
38722	1880,1112.606	Unidentified.
38723	1880,1112.607	Lexical; syllabary.
38724	1880,1112.608	Account of dates.
38725	1880,1112.609	Contract; sale of fields. -/-/20.
38726	1880,1112.610	Omens; Šumma izbu 1. + 39089. De Zorzi, Šumma izbu, 339.
38727	1880,1112.611	vale of fields. 10/1/18.
38728	1880,1112.612	Contract; sale of a house; sealed. d.l. Nisaba 28, no. 137.
38729	1880,1112.613	Liver omens.
38730	1880,1112.614	Bilingual incantation.
38731	1880,1112.615	Promissory note for silver. Nbn -/5/12. Babylon.
38732	1880,1112.616	Astrological; mukallimtu commentary.
38733	1880,1112.617	Lexical; stars.
38734	1880,1112.618	Contract; sale of fields.
38735	1880,1112.619	Ledger.
38736	1880,1112.620	Literary.
38737	1880,1112.621	Lexical; syllabary.
38738	1880,1112.622	Omens; Šumma ālu.
38739	1880,1112.623	Incantation; namburbû.
38740	1880,1112.624	Lexical.
38741	1880,1112.625	Astronomical.
38742	1880,1112.626	Emesal bilingual balag. + 38747.
38743	1880,1112.627	Joined to 38297.
38744	1880,1112.628	Joined to 38130.
38745	1880,1112.629	Explanatory text.
38746	1880,1112.630	Lexical.
38747	1880,1112.631	Joined to 38742.
38748	1880,1112.632	Literary.
38749	1880,1112.633	Astronomical; lunar six table for -523 to -521. Huber and Steele, SCIAMVS 8 (2007) 3-36, text C.
38750	1880,1112.634	Astronomical. + 38806.
38751	1880,1112.635	Joined to 38359.
38752	1880,1112.636	Physiognomic omens.
38753	1880,1112.637	Omens; Šumma izbu 5. De Zorzi, Šumma izbu, 937.
38754	1880,1112.638	Incantation.
38755	1880,1112.639	Literary.
38756	1880,1112.640	Bilingual eršema prayer. Gabbay, HES 2, 34-43, no. 2.
38757	1880,1112.641	Joined to 38359.
38758	1880,1112.642	Incantations; Maqlu VIII. Abusch, AMD 10, 193-203.
38759	1880,1112.643	Incantation.
38760	1880,1112.644	Bilingual incantation.
38761	1880,1112.645	Literary. + 38784.

38762	1880,1112.646	Joined to 38289.
38763	1880,1112.647	Omens; Šumma ālu 41. Freedman, If a city, vol. 3, 3, 253.
38764	1880,1112.648	Literary; Erra V.
38765	1880,1112.649	Unidentified.
38766	1880,1112.650	Receipt for dates.
38767	1880,1112.651	Inventory. + 1880,1112.699.
38768	1880,1112.652	Bilingual incantation.
38769	1880,1112.653	Bilingual incantation.
38770	1880,1112.654	Dedication of a table to Ishtar by Nabonidus. Lee, Journal of Ancient Civilizations 10 (1995) 65-69; Schaudig, AOAT 256, 476.
38771	1880,1112.655	Incantation.
38772	1880,1112.656	Bilingual incantation.
38773	1880,1112.657	Hymn.
38774	1880,1112.658	Bilingual incantation.
38775	1880,1112.659	Joined to 38720.
38776	1880,1112.660	Promissory note for dates. Dar 19/6/[]. Borsippa. Zadok, Nisaba 21, 235.
38777	1880,1112.661	Letter from Nabû-šāpik-zēri to Bēl-rēṣū'a. Hackl et al., AOAT 414/1, no. 95.
38778	1880,1112.662	Joined to 38720.
38779	1880,1112.663	Hymn.
38780	1880,1112.664	Economic.
38781	1880,1112.665	Joined to 38435.
38782	1880,1112.666	Promissory note for dates or grain. -/-/22.
38783	1880,1112.667	Incantation.
38784	1880,1112.668	Joined to 38761.
38785	1880,1112.669	Literary.
38786	1880,1112.670	Bilingual incantations, Muššu'u VIII; colophon. + 38857 + 39660. Cf. Finkel, AuOr 9 (1991) 99; Böck, Muššu'u, 261-313 and pls. XLI-XLII.
38787	1880,1112.671	Physiognomic omens?
38788	1880,1112.672	Commentary; physiognomic omens; Alamdimmu.
38789	1880,1112.673	Lexical.
38790	1880,1112.674	Letter.
38791	1880,1112.675	Lexical; Izi; two columns.
38792	1880,1112.676	Lexical.
38793	1880,1112.677	Lexical.
38794	1880,1112.678	Literary.
38795	1880,1112.679	Economic.
38796	1880,1112.680	Memorandum.
38797	1880,1112.681	Incantation.
38798	1880,1112.682	Bilingual incantation, Udug-ḫul 5. CT 16, 12-16; Geller, BAM 8, 174-216, pl. 43.

38799	1880,1112.683	Medical.
38800	1880,1112.684	Commentary.
38801	1880,1112.685	Prophecy; dupl. 38298 and 42546.
38802	1880,1112.686	Astronomical; lunar six table for -518 to -516. Huber and Steele, SCIAMVS 8 (2007) 3-36, text D.
38803	1880,1112.687	Bilingual incantation, Udug-ḫul 7. Geller, BAM 8, 249-2287, pl. 55.
38804	1880,1112.688	Lexical.
38805	1880,1112.689	Bilingual incantation, Udug-ḫul 4. Geller, BAM 8, 133-173, pl. 35.
38806	1880,1112.690	Joined to 38750.
38807	1880,1112.691	Bilingual incantation.
38808	1880,1112.692	Medical.
38809	1880,1112.693	Literary; Love Lyrics; dupl. Lambert in Unity and Diversity, p. 118.
38810	1880,1112.694	Literary.
38811	1880,1112.695	Literary.
38812	1880,1112.696	Late Babylonian copy of the Laws of Hammurabi.
38813	1880,1112.697	Bilingual hymn to a goddess of Nippur celebrated for writing. + 39594.
38814	1880,1112.698	Lexical.
	1880,1112.699	Joined to 38767.
38815	1880,1112.700	Lexical.
38816	1880,1112.701	Lexical; syllabary.
38817	1880,1112.702	Economic. Dar 17/[]/18. Babylon.
38818	1880,1112.703	Fragment of a baked clay amulet(?) with carefully incised decoration in a pattern of squares and dots; date unknown.
38819	1880,1112.704	Promissory note for silver. Šamaš-šum-ukin 1/9/-.
38820	1880,1112.705	Astrological.
38821	1880,1112.706	Incantation.
38822	1880,1112.707	Lexical; temple list.
38823	1880,1112.708	Promissory note for dates. Dar 22/5/16. Borsippa. Zadok, Nisaba 21, 235.
38824	1880,1112.709	Late copy of a contract. Artaxerxes []/4/[]. Borsippa.
38825	1880,1112.710	Aramaic text; marked B.N.
38826	1880,1112.711	Hemerology.
38827	1880,1112.712	Old Babylonian, record of textiles delivered by the overseers of weavers; two scribes as witnesses; year formula mentions Dur-Ammiditana. Ammiditana 27/[]/?
38828	1880,1112.713	Joined to 38624.
38829	1880,1112.714	Lexical and literary extracts
38830	1880,1112.715	Astronomical Diary?
38831	1880,1112.716	Astronomical.

38832	1880,1112.717	Bilingual incantation.
38833	1880,1112.718	Literary; Gilgameš II. George, Gilgamesh II, pl. 53.
38834	1880,1112.719	Oracle question (tamītu) to Šamaš; dupl. Lambert, Babylonian Oracle Questions, pp. 80-83, no. 9.
38835	1880,1112.720	Omens; Šumma izbu 9. De Zorzi, Šumma izbu, 592.
38836	1880,1112.721	Lexical; syllabary.
38837	1880,1112.722	Medical.
38838	1880,1112.723	Bilingual epic; Lugal-e IV 136-144 and 175-181; colophon. van Dijk, Lugal, text i2.
38839	1880,1112.724	Joined to 38192.
38840	1880,1112.725	Astrological omens; Enūma Anu Enlil 47.
38841	1880,1112.726	Lexical.
38842	1880,1112.727	Lexical; syllabary.
38843	1880,1112.728	Receipt for silver payment. Nbn -/-/3. Babylon.
38844	1880,1112.729	Lexical.
38845	1880,1112.730	Incantation.
38846	1880,1112.731	Commentary.
38847	1880,1112.732	Incantation.
38848	1880,1112.733	Late Babylonian copy of an Old Babylonian royal inscription; colophon.
38849	1880,1112.734	Bilingual incantation.
38850	1880,1112.735	Sumerian literary.
38851	1880,1112.736	Astrological omens; moon.
38852	1880,1112.737	Joined to 38493.
38853	1880,1112.738	Joined to 38297.
38854	1880,1112.739	Omens; Šumma izbu 19. (+) 39081. De Zorzi, Šumma izbu, 937.
38855	1880,1112.740	Lexical.
38856	1880,1112.741	Astronomical; lunar six table for -516 to -515. Huber and Steele, SCIAMVS 8 (2007) 3-36, text E.
38857	1880,1112.742	Joined to 38786.
38858	1880,1112.743	Omens; Šumma izbu 6. De Zorzi, Šumma izbu, 503.
38859	1880,1112.744	Incantation.
38860	1880,1112.745	Hymn.
38861	1880,1112.746	Omens; Šumma izbu 8. De Zorzi, Šumma izbu, 562.
38862	1880,1112.747	Memorandum.
38863	1880,1112.748	Receipt. -/-/40.
38864	1880,1112.749	School text; lexical, Ḫḫ XVI (stones); literary; Enūma eliš II. Gesche, AOAT 275, 323, 687; Lambert, BCM, p. 63, pl. 14.
38865	1880,1112.750	Incantations.
38866	1880,1112.751	Late Babylonian copy of an Ur III royal inscription.
38867	1880,1112.752	Commentary; medical.
38868	1880,1112.753	Bilingual incantation.
38869	1880,1112.754	Astronomical. + 1880,1112.767.

38870	1880,1112.755	Literary.
38871	1880,1112.756	Incantation; namburbû? + 38878.
38872	1880,1112.757	Literary.
38873	1880,1112.758	Bilingual incantation.
38874	1880,1112.759	Astronomical.
38875	1880,1112.760	Literary; Love Lyrics.
38876	1880,1112.761	Omens; Šumma ālu, tablet 30. Freedman, If a city, vol. 2, 132.
38877	1880,1112.762	Bilingual incantation.
38878	1880,1112.763	Joined to 38871.
38879	1880,1112.764	Literary.
38880	1880,1112.765	Omens; terrestrial.
38881	1880,1112.766	Incantation. + 39152.
	1880,1112.767	Joined to 38869.
38882	1880,1112.768	Bilingual epic; Lugal-e II 89; colophon. van Dijk, Lugal, text 12.
38883	1880,1112.769	Astrological omens.
38884	1880,1112.770	Account of silver expenditures. 2/2/-.
38885	1880,1112.771	Lexical; Aa VII/4 = 38. CT 12, 31; MSL 14, 466.
38886	1880,1112.772	Incantation; hul.zi.[].
38887	1880,1112.773	Literary.
38888	1880,1112.774	Incantation.
38889	1880,1112.775	Commentary.
38890	1880,1112.776	Lexical.
38891	1880,1112.777	Memorandum.
38892	1880,1112.778	Late Babylonian copy of one or more Old Babylonian letters. Lambert, BOQ, p. 156, appendix, pl. 57.
38893	1880,1112.779	Letter.
38894	1880,1112.780	Joined to 38129.
38895	1880,1112.781	Obv. school text; lexical, syllabary; rev. astronomical, perhaps stellar geography. Gesche, AOAT 275, 325, 687.
38896	1880,1112.782	Bilingual epic; Lugal-e II. Geller, Fs Black, 93-101.
38897	1880,1112.783	Sale of a slave.
38898	1880,1112.784	Joined to 38709.
38899	1880,1112.785	Medical.
38900	1880,1112.786	Unidentified.
38901	1880,1112.787	Incantation.
38902	1880,1112.788	Commentary.
38903	1880,1112.789	Incantation.
38904	1880,1112.790	Lexical.
38905	1880,1112.791	Lexical.
38906	1880,1112.792	Bilingual incantation.
38907	1880,1112.793	Medical.
38908	1880,1112.794	Medical.

38909	1880,1112.795	Literary; Erra IV.
38910	1880,1112.796	Medical; diarrhoea.
38911	1880,1112.797	Lexical.
38912	1880,1112.798	Medical.
38913	1880,1112.799	Medical.
38914	1880,1112.800	Contract; sale of fields.
38915	1880,1112.801	Omens.
38916	1880,1112.802	Contract; sale of fields.
38917	1880,1112.803	Incantation.
38918	1880,1112.804	Unidentified.
38919	1880,1112.805	Omens; extispicy.
38920	1880,1112.806	Lexical.
38921	1880,1112.807	Unidentified.
38922	1880,1112.808	Incantation.
38923	1880,1112.809	Incantation.
38924	1880,1112.810	Incantations.
38925	1880,1112.811	Incantation.
38926	1880,1112.812	Late Babylonian copy of an Ur III building inscription.
38927	1880,1112.813	Literary.
38928	1880,1112.814	Promissory note for dates and date products. Artaxerxes []/8/5?
38929	1880,1112.815	Contract.
38930	1880,1112.816	Promissory note for dates. Dar -/-/13.
38931	1880,1112.817	Bilingual incantation.
38932	1880,1112.818	School text; bilingual.
38933	1880,1112.819	Unidentified.
38934	1880,1112.820	School text.
38935	1880,1112.821	Contract; sale of fields. Dar -/-/14.
38936	1880,1112.822	Bilingual incantation.
38937	1880,1112.823	Bilingual incantation.
38938	1880,1112.824	Unidentified.
38939	1880,1112.825	Bilingual incantation.
38940	1880,1112.826	Astronomical.
38941	1880,1112.827	Promissory note.
38942	1880,1112.828	Commentary.
38943	1880,1112.829	Contract; division of an inheritance. Wunsch, Bab Arch 2, 134-135, no. 40.
38944	1880,1112.830	Lexical; stars.
38945	1880,1112.831	Lexical.
38946	1880,1112.832	Bilingual incantation.
38947	1880,1112.833	Late Babylonian copy of an inscription of the son of Puzur-Eštar of Mari. Sollberger, RAI XV, 104-107; Frayne, RIME 3/2.4.6.1.
38948	1880,1112.834	Manumission of a slave woman.

38949	1880,1112.835	Promissory note for silver.
38950	1880,1112.836	Astrological omens; Enūma Anu Enlil.
38951	1880,1112.837	Omens; terrestrial.
38952	1880,1112.838	Lexical.
38953	1880,1112.839	Astronomical.
38954	1880,1112.840	Promissory note for dates.
38955	1880,1112.841	Commentary.
38956	1880,1112.842	Lexical.
38957	1880,1112.843	Astronomical.
38958	1880,1112.844	Unidentified.
38959	1880,1112.845	Bilingual incantation.
38960	1880,1112.846	Astronomical.
38961	1880,1112.847	Contract; sale of fields. Dar -/11/-. Babylon.
38962	1880,1112.848	Unidentified.
38963	1880,1112.849	Bilingual incantation.
38964	1880,1112.850	Contract.
38965	1880,1112.851	Astrological omens; Enūma Anu Enlil.
38966	1880,1112.852	Incantation.
38967	1880,1112.853	Unidentified.
38968	1880,1112.854	Contract.
38969	1880,1112.855	Astronomical.
38970	1880,1112.856	Lexical; syllabary; personal names.
38971	1880,1112.857	Economic.
38972	1880,1112.858	Contract; sale of fields. Nbk -/5/19. Babylon.
38973	1880,1112.859	Economic.
38974	1880,1112.860	Ritual? Mentions ardat-lilî.
38975	1880,1112.861	Astronomical.
38976	1880,1112.862	Lexical.
38977	1880,1112.863	Astronomical.
38978	1880,1112.864	Unidentified.
38979	1880,1112.865	Astronomical.
38980	1880,1112.866	Bilingual incantation.
38981	1880,1112.867	Field plan. Nemet-Nejat, LB Field Plans, no. 49.
38982	1880,1112.868	Contract; sale of fields.
38983	1880,1112.869	Astronomical.
38984	1880,1112.870	Bilingual incantation.
38985	1880,1112.871	School text.
38986	1880,1112.872	Unidentified.
38987	1880,1112.873	Unidentified.
38988	1880,1112.874	Astronomical.
38989	1880,1112.875	Bilingual incantation.
38990	1880,1112.876	Economic. -/-/33.
38991	1880,1112.877	Astronomical.
38992	1880,1112.878	Medical; two columns; colophon. + 39443.
38993	1880,1112.879	Bilingual incantation.

38994	1880,1112.880	Bilingual incantation.
38995	1880,1112.881	Lexical.
38996	1880,1112.882	Bilingual incantation.
38997	1880,1112.883	Bilingual incantation.
38998	1880,1112.884	Letter from Mūrānu to []-Bēl. CT 22, 25, no. 130; Hackl et al., AOAT 414/1, no. 96.
38999	1880,1112.885	Joined to 38720.
39000	1880,1112.886	Commentary.
39001	1880,1112.887	Account of dates or grain.
39002	1880,1112.888	Commentary.
39003	1880,1112.889	Astronomical; normal stars.
39004	1880,1112.890	Lexical; temple list.
39005	1880,1112.891	Commentary.
39006	1880,1112.892	Bilingual incantation.
39007	1880,1112.893	School text; lexical? Gesche, AOAT 275, 687.
39008	1880,1112.894	Bilingual incantation.
39009	1880,1112.895	Contract; sale of fields.
39010	1880,1112.896	Omens.
39011	1880,1112.897	Lexical.
39012	1880,1112.898	Bilingual incantation.
39013	1880,1112.899	Astronomical.
39014	1880,1112.900	List of people.
39015	1880,1112.901	Joined to 38374.
39016	1880,1112.902	Contract; sale of fields.
39017	1880,1112.903	Bilingual incantation.
39018	1880,1112.904	Lexical.
39019	1880,1112.905	Bilingual incantation.
39020	1880,1112.906	Medical.
39021	1880,1112.907	Ritual.
39022	1880,1112.908	Account.
39023	1880,1112.909	Ritual.
39024	1880,1112.910	Archaic script; ritual?; copy?
39025	1880,1112.911	Lexical; giš.
39026	1880,1112.912	Economic.
39027	1880,1112.913	Economic.
39028	1880,1112.914	Unidentified.
39029	1880,1112.915	Astronomical.
39030	1880,1112.916	Lexical; stars. + 39093 + 39474 + 39591 + 39648.
39031	1880,1112.917	Commentary.
39032	1880,1112.918	Bilingual incantation.
39033	1880,1112.919	Lexical.
39034	1880,1112.920	Bilingual incantation.
39035	1880,1112.921	Unidentified.
39036	1880,1112.922	Joined to 38720.
39037	1880,1112.923	Lexical.

39038	1880,1112.924	Bilingual incantation.
39039	1880,1112.925	Receipt for payment of silver.
39040	1880,1112.926	Lexical and literary extracts; god list, etc.
39041	1880,1112.927	Lexical; GU4.
39042	1880,1112.928	Bilingual incantation.
39043	1880,1112.929	List of days and activities.
39044	1880,1112.930	Unidentified.
39045	1880,1112.931	Receipt.
39046	1880,1112.932	Joined to 38268.
39047	1880,1112.933	Bilingual incantation.
39048	1880,1112.934	Economic.
39049	1880,1112.935	Astronomical.
39050	1880,1112.936	Omens; Šumma izbu 8. De Zorzi, Šumma izbu, 937.
39051	1880,1112.937	Astronomical.
39052	1880,1112.938	Bilingual incantation.
39053	1880,1112.939	Bilingual incantation.
39054	1880,1112.940	Bilingual incantation.
39055	1880,1112.941	Bilingual incantation.
39056	1880,1112.942	Bilingual incantation.
39057	1880,1112.943	Unidentified.
39058	1880,1112.944	Medical.
39059	1880,1112.945	Unidentified.
39060	1880,1112.946	Literary.
39061	1880,1112.947	Unidentified.
39062	1880,1112.948	Lexical; syllabary; literary extract.
39063	1880,1112.949	Medical.
39064	1880,1112.950	Unidentified.
39065	1880,1112.951	Economic.
39066	1880,1112.952	Medical prescription.
39067	1880,1112.953	Commentary.
39068	1880,1112.954	Unidentified.
39069	1880,1112.955	Lexical.
39070	1880,1112.956	Lexical; god list.
39071	1880,1112.957	Unidentified.
39072	1880,1112.958	Omens; Šumma izbu 11. (+) 38168 (+) 39607. De Zorzi, Šumma izbu, 638.
39073	1880,1112.959	Economic.
39074	1880,1112.960	Lexical.
39075	1880,1112.961	Lexical.
39076	1880,1112.962	Lexical.
39077	1880,1112.963	Lexical.
39078	1880,1112.964	Astronomical.
39079	1880,1112.965	Bilingual incantation.
39080	1880,1112.966	Promissory note for silver. -/-/8. Babylon.

39081	1880,1112.967	Omens; Šumma izbu 19. (+) 38854. De Zorzi, Šumma izbu, 937.
39082	1880,1112.968	Bilingual incantation.
39083	1880,1112.969	Bilingual incantation.
39084	1880,1112.970	Unidentified.
39085	1880,1112.971	Bilingual incantation.
39086	1880,1112.972	Late Babylonian copy of an earlier inscription.
39087	1880,1112.973	Bilingual incantation.
39088	1880,1112.974	Bilingual incantation.
39089	1880,1112.975	Joined to 38726.
39090	1880,1112.976	Letter.
39091	1880,1112.977	School text.
39092	1880,1112.978	Astronomical.
39093	1880,1112.979	Joined to 39030.
39094	1880,1112.980	Contract; sale of fields.
39095	1880,1112.981	Bilingual incantation.
39096	1880,1112.982	Unidentified.
39097	1880,1112.983	Astronomical.
39098	1880,1112.984	Contract.
39099	1880,1112.985	Contract.
39100	1880,1112.986	Lexical; IM.
39101	1880,1112.987	Bilingual incantation.
39102	1880,1112.988	School text.
39103	1880,1112.989	Contract.
39104	1880,1112.990	Astronomical Diary?
39105	1880,1112.991	Unidentified.
39106	1880,1112.992	Sale of a slave; mentions the mašennu Balāṭu; Egibi archive. [Dar I] 7/2/24. Jursa, AfO Beih. 25, 181.
39107	1880,1112.993	Bilingual incantation.
39108	1880,1112.994	Astronomical.
39109	1880,1112.995	Economic.
39110	1880,1112.996	Unidentified.
39111	1880,1112.997	Receipt.
39112	1880,1112.998	Unidentified.
39113	1880,1112.999	Unidentified.
39114	1880,1112.1000	Lexical.
39115	1880,1112.1001	Unidentified.
39116	1880,1112.1002	Bilingual incantation.
39117	1880,1112.1003	Unidentified.
39118	1880,1112.1004	Lexical.
39119	1880,1112.1005	Medical.
39120	1880,1112.1006	Lexical.
39121	1880,1112.1007	Unidentified.
39122	1880,1112.1008	Unidentified.
39123	1880,1112.1009	Omens; Šumma izbu. De Zorzi, Šumma izbu, 926.

39124	1880,1112.1010	Unidentified.
39125	1880,1112.1011	Bilingual incantation.
39126	1880,1112.1012	Unidentified.
39127	1880,1112.1013	Lexical.
39128	1880,1112.1014	Bilingual incantation.
39129	1880,1112.1015	Astronomical.
39130	1880,1112.1016	Receipt.
39131	1880,1112.1017	Astrological omens.
39132	1880,1112.1018	Commentary.
39133	1880,1112.1019	Astronomical.
39134	1880,1112.1020	Lexical.
39135	1880,1112.1021	Economic.
39136	1880,1112.1022	Lexical.
39137	1880,1112.1023	Lexical; syllabary.
39138	1880,1112.1024	Contract; sale of fields.
39139	1880,1112.1025	Bilingual incantation.
39140	1880,1112.1026	Contract; sale of fields.
39141	1880,1112.1027	Bilingual incantation.
39142	1880,1112.1028	Unidentified.
39143	1880,1112.1029	Astrological omens.
39144	1880,1112.1030	Astronomical.
39145	1880,1112.1031	Bilingual incantation.
39146	1880,1112.1032	Unidentified.
39147	1880,1112.1033	Bilingual incantation.
39148	1880,1112.1034	Economic.
39149	1880,1112.1035	Astronomical Diary or related text.
39150	1880,1112.1036	Contract; sale of fields.
39151	1880,1112.1037	Astrological omens?
39152	1880,1112.1038	Joined to 38881.
39153	1880,1112.1039	Unidentified.
39154	1880,1112.1040	Unidentified.
39155	1880,1112.1041	Astronomical Diary or related text.
39156	1880,1112.1042	Astronomical.
39157	1880,1112.1043	Astronomical.
39158	1880,1112.1044	Incantation.
39159	1880,1112.1045	Astronomical.
39160	1880,1112.1046	Bilingual incantation.
39161	1880,1112.1047	Literary. + 39392.
39162	1880,1112.1048	Bilingual incantation; balag composition.
39163	1880,1112.1049	Astronomical.
39164	1880,1112.1050	Astrological omens; Enūma Anu Enlil 20. Fincke, Kaskal 14, 55-74. (+) 38164.
39165	1880,1112.1051	Late Babylonian copy of the Laws of Hammurabi.
39166	1880,1112.1052	Omens; physiognomic; Šumma tirku. Fincke, Fs Geller, 203-231.

39167	1880,1112.1053	Unidentified.
39168	1880,1112.1054	Sumerian literary.
39169	1880,1112.1055	Deposition. -/-/10. Babylon.
39170	1880,1112.1056	Astrological omens.
39171	1880,1112.1057	Unidentified.
39172	1880,1112.1058	Omens; physiognomic; Šumma tirku. Böck, AfO Beih. 27, 206; Fincke, Fs Geller, 203-231.
39173	1880,1112.1059	Unidentified.
39174	1880,1112.1060	Unidentified.
39175	1880,1112.1061	Unidentified.
39176	1880,1112.1062	Commentary.
39177	1880,1112.1063	Lexical.
39178	1880,1112.1064	Bilingual incantation.
39179	1880,1112.1065	Letter order; names of sender and addressee lost.
39180	1880,1112.1066	Lexical.
39181	1880,1112.1067	Incantation.
39182	1880,1112.1068	Omens.
39183	1880,1112.1069	Account.
39184	1880,1112.1070	Bilingual incantation; two columns; Udug-ḫul 3. Geller, BAM 8, 89-132, pl. 159.
39185	1880,1112.1071	Promissory note.
39186	1880,1112.1072	Field plan?
39187	1880,1112.1073	Lexical?
39188	1880,1112.1074	Astronomical.
39189	1880,1112.1075	Lexical.
39190	1880,1112.1076	Account.
39191	1880,1112.1077	Lexical.
39192	1880,1112.1078	Lexical.
39193	1880,1112.1079	Astronomical; lunar six table. Huber and Steele, SCIAMVS 8 (2007) 3-36, text J.
39194	1880,1112.1080	Astronomical Diary.
39195	1880,1112.1081	Unidentified.
39196	1880,1112.1082	Bilingual incantation.
39197	1880,1112.1083	Bilingual incantation.
39198	1880,1112.1084	Mathematical problem about še-numun; geometric diagram on reverse with numbers (for the diagram cf. 33333B, 37171, 40680 and 47890).
39199	1880,1112.1085	Astronomical.
39200	1880,1112.1086	Economic.
39201	1880,1112.1087	Economic.
39202	1880,1112.1088	Bilingual copy of the Weidner Chronicle (Grayson, TCS 5, Chronicle 19). Finkel, JCS 32, 72-74, 78.
39203	1880,1112.1089	Contract.
39204	1880,1112.1090	Bilingual incantation.
39205	1880,1112.1091	Astronomical.

39206	1880,1112.1092	Astronomical.
39207	1880,1112.1093	Astronomical.
39208	1880,1112.1094	Lexical; syllabary.
39209	1880,1112.1095	Bilingual incantation.
39210	1880,1112.1096	Bilingual incantation.
39211	1880,1112.1097	Astronomical procedure text.
39212	1880,1112.1098	Bilingual incantation.
39213	1880,1112.1099	Bilingual incantation.
39214	1880,1112.1100	Joined to 38359.
39215	1880,1112.1101	Bilingual incantation.
39216	1880,1112.1102	Omens; Šumma ālu 42; oxen. Freedman, If a city, vol. 3, 10, 254.
39217	1880,1112.1103	Astronomical.
39218	1880,1112.1104	Unidentified.
39219	1880,1112.1105	Lexical; syllabary.
39220	1880,1112.1106	Bilingual incantation.
39221	1880,1112.1107	Unidentified.
39222	1880,1112.1108	Bilingual incantation.
39223	1880,1112.1109	Lexical; syllabary.
39224	1880,1112.1110	Unidentified.
39225	1880,1112.1111	Unidentified.
39226	1880,1112.1112	Bilingual incantation.
39227	1880,1112.1113	Astronomical.
39228	1880,1112.1114	Lexical.
39229	1880,1112.1115	Unidentified.
39230	1880,1112.1116	Astronomical.
39231	1880,1112.1117	Economic.
39232	1880,1112.1118	Lexical.
39233	1880,1112.1119	Unidentified.
39234	1880,1112.1120	Astronomical.
39235	1880,1112.1121	Account of issues of silver. SE []/[]/210+. (Babylon, Rahimesu archive). Hackl, Fs van der Spek, 87-106, no. 10.
39236	1880,1112.1122	Lexical.
39237	1880,1112.1123	Astronomical.
39238	1880,1112.1124	Bilingual incantation.
39239	1880,1112.1125	Unidentified.
39240	1880,1112.1126	Omens; Šumma ālu?
39241	1880,1112.1127	Unidentified.
39242	1880,1112.1128	Omens.
39243	1880,1112.1129	Joined to 38368.
39244	1880,1112.1130	Contract.
39245	1880,1112.1131	Unidentified.
39246	1880,1112.1132	Bilingual incantation.
39247	1880,1112.1133	Lexical.

39248	1880,1112.1134	Economic.
39249	1880,1112.1135	Bilingual incantation.
39250	1880,1112.1136	Unidentified.
39251	1880,1112.1137	Joined to 38368.
39252	1880,1112.1138	Bilingual incantation.
39253	1880,1112.1139	Commentary.
39254	1880,1112.1140	Joined to 38297.
39255	1880,1112.1141	Unidentified.
39256	1880,1112.1142	Joined to 38720.
39257	1880,1112.1143	Lexical.
39258	1880,1112.1144	Unidentified.
39259	1880,1112.1145	Account of dates and date products.
39260	1880,1112.1146	Unidentified.
39261	1880,1112.1147	Deposition.
39262	1880,1112.1148	Astronomical.
39263	1880,1112.1149	Bilingual incantation.
39264	1880,1112.1150	Clay fragment with curious marks, not cuneiform script but perhaps worm tracks; compare 33022 and 49083.
39265	1880,1112.1151	Bilingual incantation.
39266	1880,1112.1152	Literary.
39267	1880,1112.1153	Bilingual incantation.
39268	1880,1112.1154	Astronomical Diary.
39269	1880,1112.1155	Bilingual incantation.
39270	1880,1112.1156	Bilingual incantation.
39271	1880,1112.1157	Economic.
39272	1880,1112.1158	Bilingual incantation.
39273	1880,1112.1159	Astronomical.
39274	1880,1112.1160	Incantation.
39275	1880,1112.1161	Promissory note for dates.
39276	1880,1112.1162	Bilingual incantation.
39277	1880,1112.1163	Astronomical Diary or related text.
39278	1880,1112.1164	Bilingual incantation.
39279	1880,1112.1165	Lexical.
39280	1880,1112.1166	Account.
39281	1880,1112.1167	Unidentified.
39282	1880,1112.1168	Astronomical Diary or related text.
39283	1880,1112.1169	Medical.
39284	1880,1112.1170	Literary?
39285	1880,1112.1171	Economic.
39286	1880,1112.1172	Economic. 25/-/-.
39287	1880,1112.1173	Economic.
39288	1880,1112.1174	Economic.
39289	1880,1112.1175	Astrological omens.
39290	1880,1112.1176	Account.

39291	1880,1112.1177	Astronomical; lunar six table. Huber and Steele, SCIAMVS 8 (2007) 3-36, text K.
39292	1880,1112.1178	Promissory note. -/11/12.
39293	1880,1112.1179	Unidentified.
39294	1880,1112.1180	Literary.
39295	1880,1112.1181	Lexical; god list, equivalents to Nabû.
39296	1880,1112.1182	Omens; Šumma izbu 22. De Zorzi, Šumma izbu, 937.
39297	1880,1112.1183	Bilingual incantation.
39298	1880,1112.1184	Contract. Nbk 7/4/8. Babylon.
39299	1880,1112.1185	Bilingual incantation; colophon.
39300	1880,1112.1186	Contract; sale of fields.
39301	1880,1112.1187	Unidentified.
39302	1880,1112.1188	Economic.
39303	1880,1112.1189	School text; lexical, Syllabary A. Gesche, AOAT 275, 687.
39304	1880,1112.1190	Bilingual incantation.
39305	1880,1112.1191	Economic.
39306	1880,1112.1192	Lexical.
39307	1880,1112.1193	Memorandum.
39308	1880,1112.1194	Medical.
39309	1880,1112.1195	Contract; sale of fields.
39310	1880,1112.1196	Account of issues of silver. SE Arsaces 5/[]/218. Hackl, Fs van der Spek, 87-106, no. 4.
39311	1880,1112.1197	Late Babylonian copy of an Old Akkadian royal inscription.
39312	1880,1112.1198	Lexical; god list.
39313	1880,1112.1199	Literary.
39314	1880,1112.1200	Joined to 34137.
39315	1880,1112.1201	Unidentified.
39316	1880,1112.1202	Omens; Šumma izbu 3. De Zorzi, Šumma izbu, 408.
39317	1880,1112.1203	Astrological omens.
39318	1880,1112.1204	Astrological omens.
39319	1880,1112.1205	Bilingual incantation.
39320	1880,1112.1206	Prayer.
39321	1880,1112.1207	Astronomical.
39322	1880,1112.1208	Letter.
39323	1880,1112.1209	Economic.
39324	1880,1112.1210	Bilingual incantation.
39325	1880,1112.1211	Unidentified.
39326	1880,1112.1212	Lexical.
39327	1880,1112.1213	Astronomical.
39328	1880,1112.1214	Economic.
39329	1880,1112.1215	Astronomical table.
39330	1880,1112.1216	Lexical.
39331	1880,1112.1217	Unidentified.

39332	1880,1112.1218	Omens.
39333	1880,1112.1219	Bilingual incantation.
39334	1880,1112.1220	Contract.
39335	1880,1112.1221	Economic.
39336	1880,1112.1222	Literary; Erra IV. + 39457. Lambert, MC 24, no. 43.
39337	1880,1112.1223	Unidentified.
39338	1880,1112.1224	Bilingual incantation.
39339	1880,1112.1225	Astrological omens; Sin.
39340	1880,1112.1226	Hemerology.
39341	1880,1112.1227	Sumerian literary. CT 58, no. 72.
39342	1880,1112.1228	Literary.
39343	1880,1112.1229	Liver omens.
39344	1880,1112.1230	Contract.
39345	1880,1112.1231	Astronomical.
39346	1880,1112.1232	Medical.
39347	1880,1112.1233	Lexical; verbal paradigms.
39348	1880,1112.1234	Economic.
39349	1880,1112.1235	Promissory note.
39350	1880,1112.1236	Contract; sale of fields.
39351	1880,1112.1237	Contract; sale of fields.
39352	1880,1112.1238	Contract; sale of a house.
39353	1880,1112.1239	Prayer.
39354	1880,1112.1240	Medical.
39355	1880,1112.1241	Bilingual litany (é-zi-da, é bád.si.a[ba.ba]).
39356	1880,1112.1242	Bilingual epic; Lugal-e VII 371-374. van Dijk, Lugal, text j2.
39357	1880,1112.1243	Incantation.
39358	1880,1112.1244	Economic.
39359	1880,1112.1245	Literary.
39360	1880,1112.1246	Economic.
39361	1880,1112.1247	Astronomical Diary.
39362	1880,1112.1248	Lexical.
39363	1880,1112.1249	Contract; sale of fields.
39364	1880,1112.1250	Bilingual incantation.
39365	1880,1112.1251	Joined to 38168.
39366	1880,1112.1252	Bilingual incantation.
39367	1880,1112.1253	Sumerian lament, Abzu pelam; dupl. Cohen, Lamentations, pp. 53, 67-78.
39368	1880,1112.1254	Unidentified.
39369	1880,1112.1255	Field plan.
39370	1880,1112.1256	Missing.
39371	1880,1112.1257	Astronomical?
39372	1880,1112.1258	Astronomical.
39373	1880,1112.1259	Unidentified.
39374	1880,1112.1260	Late Babylonian copy of an Ur III royal inscription.

39375	1880,1112.1261	Unidentified.
39376	1880,1112.1262	Economic; mentions a prebend (isqu).
39377	1880,1112.1263	Unidentified.
39378	1880,1112.1264	Unidentified.
39379	1880,1112.1265	Unidentified.
39380	1880,1112.1266	Economic.
39381	1880,1112.1267	Economic.
39382	1880,1112.1268	Omens; terrestrial.
39383	1880,1112.1269	School text; lexical, Syllabary A. Gesche, AOAT 275, 687.
39384	1880,1112.1270	Hemerology.
39385	1880,1112.1271	Medical.
39386	1880,1112.1272	Unidentified.
39387	1880,1112.1273	Astronomical.
39388	1880,1112.1274	Lexical.
39389	1880,1112.1275	Ritual?
39390	1880,1112.1276	Bilingual incantation.
39391	1880,1112.1277	Contract; seal caption.
39392	1880,1112.1278	Joined to 39161.
39393	1880,1112.1279	Lexical.
39394	1880,1112.1280	Bilingual incantation.
39395	1880,1112.1281	Unidentified.
39396	1880,1112.1282	Bilingual incantation.
39397	1880,1112.1283	Lexical.
39398	1880,1112.1284	Unidentified.
39399	1880,1112.1285	Lexical; god list.
39400	1880,1112.1286	Bilingual incantation.
39401	1880,1112.1287	Sumerian literary.
39402	1880,1112.1288	Bilingual incantation.
39403	1880,1112.1289	Sumerian literary.
39404	1880,1112.1290	Sale of a slave?; Aramaic note; sealed. Artaxerxes II/III 11/6/[]. Babylon. Stevenson, Ass.-Bab. Contracts, no. 45 (Aramaic note only); Nisaba 28, no. 296.
39405	1880,1112.1291	Sumerian incantation; Sag-gig; dupl. Schramm, GBAO 2, 68-69, Beschwörung 12.
39406	1880,1112.1292	Medical; stricture (ḫiniqtu). + 39456.
39407	1880,1112.1293	Lexical; geographical list.
39408	1880,1112.1294	Late Babylonian copy of an Old Akkadian royal inscription.
39409	1880,1112.1295	Unidentified.
39410	1880,1112.1296	Astronomical; lunar six table. Huber and Steele, SCIAMVS 8 (2007) 3-36, text L.
39411	1880,1112.1297	Medical.

39412	1880,1112.1298	Late Babylonian copy of an Old Akkadian royal inscription.
39413	1880,1112.1299	Bilingual incantation.
39414	1880,1112.1300	Astronomical.
39415	1880,1112.1301	Unidentified.
39416	1880,1112.1302	Bilingual incantation.
39417	1880,1112.1303	Lexical.
39418	1880,1112.1304	Bilingual incantation.
39419	1880,1112.1305	Literary.
39420	1880,1112.1306	Bilingual incantation.
39421	1880,1112.1307	Lexical.
39422	1880,1112.1308	Astronomical Diary or related text.
39423	1880,1112.1309	Unidentified.
39424	1880,1112.1310	Economic.
39425	1880,1112.1311	Economic. 8/3/-.
39426	1880,1112.1312	Astronomical. (+) 38616.
39427	1880,1112.1313	Medical.
39428	1880,1112.1314	Joined to 38489.
39429	1880,1112.1315	Bilingual incantation.
39430	1880,1112.1316	Omens; diagnostic. + 1880,1112.1496.
39431	1880,1112.1317	Unidentified.
39432	1880,1112.1318	Bilingual incantation.
39433	1880,1112.1319	Liver omens.
39434	1880,1112.1320	Omens; Šumma izbu. + 39754. De Zorzi, Šumma izbu, 926.
39435	1880,1112.1321	Memorandum; personal names.
39436	1880,1112.1322	Astronomical?
39437	1880,1112.1323	List of temples.
39438	1880,1112.1324	Promissory note. Cam -/10/-. Babylon.
39439	1880,1112.1325	Bilingual incantation.
39440	1880,1112.1326	Commentary; medical.
39441	1880,1112.1327	Late Babylonian copy of an Ur III royal inscription.
39442	1880,1112.1328	Lexical.
39443	1880,1112.1329	Joined to 38992.
39444	1880,1112.1330	Unidentified.
39445	1880,1112.1331	Lexical; syllabary.
39446	1880,1112.1332	Unidentified.
39447	1880,1112.1333	Joined to 38666.
39448	1880,1112.1334	Unidentified; colophon.
39449	1880,1112.1335	Bilingual incantation.
39450	1880,1112.1336	Joined to 38225.
39451	1880,1112.1337	Bilingual incantation.
39452	1880,1112.1338	Contract; sale of fields.
39453	1880,1112.1339	Unidentified.
39454	1880,1112.1340	Literary.

39455	1880,1112.1341	Lexical.
39456	1880,1112.1342	Joined to 39406.
39457	1880,1112.1343	Joined to 39336.
39458	1880,1112.1344	Hemerology.
39459	1880,1112.1345	Bilingual incantation.
39460	1880,1112.1346	Unidentified.
39461	1880,1112.1347	Medical.
39462	1880,1112.1348	Economic.
39463	1880,1112.1349	Lexical.
39464	1880,1112.1350	Economic.
39465	1880,1112.1351	Bilingual incantation.
39466	1880,1112.1352	Unidentified.
39467	1880,1112.1353	Unidentified.
39468	1880,1112.1354	Economic.
39469	1880,1112.1355	Economic.
39470	1880,1112.1356	Bilingual incantation.
39471	1880,1112.1357	Economic.
39472	1880,1112.1358	Lexical.
39473	1880,1112.1359	Economic.
39474	1880,1112.1360	Joined to 39030.
39475	1880,1112.1361	Lexical.
39476	1880,1112.1362	Bilingual incantation.
39477	1880,1112.1363	Bilingual incantation.
39478	1880,1112.1364	Astronomical Diary; left edge.
39479	1880,1112.1365	Unidentified.
39480	1880,1112.1366	Astronomical.
39481	1880,1112.1367	Economic. Cam -/2/-.
39482	1880,1112.1368	Late Babylonian copy of an Ur III or Old Babylonian inscription.
39483	1880,1112.1369	Unidentified.
39484	1880,1112.1370	Incantations; Maqlu I. Abusch, AMD 10, 23-49.
39485	1880,1112.1371	Lexical.
39486	1880,1112.1372	Bilingual incantation.
39487	1880,1112.1373	Economic.
39488	1880,1112.1374	Letter; names of sender and addressee lost. Hackl et al., AOAT 414/1, no. 97.
39489	1880,1112.1375	Bilingual incantation.
39490	1880,1112.1376	Bilingual incantation.
39491	1880,1112.1377	Omens.
39492	1880,1112.1378	Unidentified.
39493	1880,1112.1379	Astronomical.
39494	1880,1112.1380	Bilingual incantation.
39495	1880,1112.1381	Bilingual incantation.
39496	1880,1112.1382	Unidentified.
39497	1880,1112.1383	Unidentified.

39498	1880,1112.1384	Liver omens.
39499	1880,1112.1385	Unidentified.
39500	1880,1112.1386	Economic.
39501	1880,1112.1387	Economic.
39502	1880,1112.1388	Astronomical.
39503	1880,1112.1389	Lexical; god list.
39504	1880,1112.1390	Astronomical.
39505	1880,1112.1391	Astronomical.
39506	1880,1112.1392	Lexical; IM.
39507	1880,1112.1393	Bilingual incantation.
39508	1880,1112.1394	Omens; terrestrial.
39509	1880,1112.1395	Lexical.
39510	1880,1112.1396	Medical.
39511	1880,1112.1397	Late Babylonian copy of an Ur III royal inscription.
39512	1880,1112.1398	Bilingual incantation.
39513	1880,1112.1399	Contract; sale of fields.
39514	1880,1112.1400	Medical.
39515	1880,1112.1401	Bilingual incantation.
39516	1880,1112.1402	Lexical.
39517	1880,1112.1403	Unidentified.
39518	1880,1112.1404	Omens.
39519	1880,1112.1405	Unidentified.
39520	1880,1112.1406	Astronomical.
39521	1880,1112.1407	Economic.
39522	1880,1112.1408	Economic.
39523	1880,1112.1409	Bilingual incantation.
39524	1880,1112.1410	Unidentified.
39525	1880,1112.1411	Lexical; uzu.
39526	1880,1112.1412	Literary.
39527	1880,1112.1413	Bilingual incantation.
39528	1880,1112.1414	Unidentified.
39529	1880,1112.1415	Unidentified.
39530	1880,1112.1416	Receipt for delivery.
39531	1880,1112.1417	Astronomical.
39532	1880,1112.1418	Astronomical.
39533	1880,1112.1419	Bilingual incantation.
39534	1880,1112.1420	Astronomical.
39535	1880,1112.1421	Bilingual incantation.
39536	1880,1112.1422	Economic.
39537	1880,1112.1423	Commentary.
39538	1880,1112.1424	Astronomical.
39539	1880,1112.1425	Literary.
39540	1880,1112.1426	Medical omens; Sa-gig XXXIII.
39541	1880,1112.1427	Promissory note for barley. 13/[]/2.
39542	1880,1112.1428	Economic.

39543	1880,1112.1429	Astronomical.
39544	1880,1112.1430	Joined to 38368.
39545	1880,1112.1431	Unidentified.
39546	1880,1112.1432	School text; personal names.
39547	1880,1112.1433	Economic.
39548	1880,1112.1434	Astrological omens?
39549	1880,1112.1435	Joined to 38168.
39550	1880,1112.1436	Bilingual incantation.
39551	1880,1112.1437	Economic.
39552	1880,1112.1438	Mathematical; factorization table (decreasing powers of 3).
39553	1880,1112.1439	Astronomical; lunar six table. Huber and Steele, SCIAMVS 8 (2007) 3-36, text M.
39554	1880,1112.1440	Unidentified.
39555	1880,1112.1441	Incantation.
39556	1880,1112.1442	Unidentified.
39557	1880,1112.1443	Bilingual incantation.
39558	1880,1112.1444	Incantation; namburbû?
39559	1880,1112.1445	Astronomical.
39560	1880,1112.1446	Economic.
39561	1880,1112.1447	Lexical.
39562	1880,1112.1448	Ritual.
39563	1880,1112.1449	Economic.
39564	1880,1112.1450	Astronomical.
39565	1880,1112.1451	School text.
39566	1880,1112.1452	Economic.
39567	1880,1112.1453	Lexical; syllabary.
39568	1880,1112.1454	Sealing, inscribed but not sealed; 32,30 NU TIL / 32,30 NU TIL / 32,30 TIL / 32,30 NU TIL / 32,30 TIL.
39569	1880,1112.1455	Economic.
39570	1880,1112.1456	Economic. -/11/4.
39571	1880,1112.1457	Unidentified; mentions DAM LUGAL and DUMU LUGAL.
39572	1880,1112.1458	Letter; names of sender and addressee lost. Hackl et al., AOAT 414/1, no. 98.
39573	1880,1112.1459	Bilingual incantation.
39574	1880,1112.1460	Economic.
39575	1880,1112.1461	Omens; Šumma izbu 14. De Zorzi, Šumma izbu, 937.
39576	1880,1112.1462	Astronomical.
39577	1880,1112.1463	Economic.
39578	1880,1112.1464	Astronomical.
39579	1880,1112.1465	Unidentified.
39580	1880,1112.1466	Bilingual incantation.
39581	1880,1112.1467	Economic.

39582	1880,1112.1468	Incantation.
39583	1880,1112.1469	Bilingual incantation.
39584	1880,1112.1470	Sumerian literary.
39585	1880,1112.1471	Astronomical.
39586	1880,1112.1472	Field plan.
39587	1880,1112.1473	Bilingual incantation.
39588	1880,1112.1474	Memorandum.
39589	1880,1112.1475	Bilingual incantation.
39590	1880,1112.1476	Account of silver.
39591	1880,1112.1477	Joined to 39030.
39592	1880,1112.1478	Unidentified.
39593	1880,1112.1479	Unidentified.
39594	1880,1112.1480	Joined to 38813.
39595	1880,1112.1481	Incantation.
39596	1880,1112.1482	Promissory note for barley. Nabû-[] 26/[]/2.
39597	1880,1112.1483	Astronomical?
39598	1880,1112.1484	Commentary.
39599	1880,1112.1485	Joined to 38720.
39600	1880,1112.1486	Field plan.
39601	1880,1112.1487	Economic.
39602	1880,1112.1488	Lexical.
39603	1880,1112.1489	Economic.
39604	1880,1112.1490	Unidentified; mentions the Anunnaki.
39605	1880,1112.1491	Economic.
39606	1880,1112.1492	Economic.
39607	1880,1112.1493	Omens; Šumma izbu 11. (+) 38168 (+) 39072. De Zorzi, Šumma izbu, 638.
39608	1880,1112.1494	Bilingual incantation.
39609	1880,1112.1495	Omens?
	1880,1112.1496	Joined to 39430.
39610	1880,1112.1497	Literary?; colophon of Na'id-Marduk.
39611	1880,1112.1498	Lexical.
39612	1880,1112.1499	Commentary.
39613	1880,1112.1500	Economic.
39614	1880,1112.1501	Lexical.
39615	1880,1112.1502	Contract for bricks. Artaxerxes I 3/1/19.
39616	1880,1112.1503	Mathematical.
39617	1880,1112.1504	Astronomical.
39618	1880,1112.1505	Hymn to Ningirsu; dupl. Ebeling, KAR 97 rev.
39619	1880,1112.1506	Incantation?
39620	1880,1112.1507	Literary; Lugalbanda Epic, bilingual version; dupl. Wilcke, LE 100-104 and 139-141.
39621	1880,1112.1508	Astronomical.
39622	1880,1112.1509	Unidentified.
39623	1880,1112.1510	Unidentified.

39624	1880,1112.1511	Economic.
39625	1880,1112.1512	Astronomical.
39626	1880,1112.1513	Astrological omens; Venus. Fincke, Kaskal 10, 90-92, pl. 106.
39627	1880,1112.1514	Unidenitified.
39628	1880,1112.1515	Astronomical.
39629	1880,1112.1516	Astrological; tabulated; cf. 32517.
39630	1880,1112.1517	Astronomical.
39631	1880,1112.1518	Commentary.
39632	1880,1112.1519	Unidentified.
39633	1880,1112.1520	Unidentified.
39634	1880,1112.1521	Bilingual incantation.
39635	1880,1112.1522	Letter.
39636	1880,1112.1523	Commentary.
39637	1880,1112.1524	Astronomical.
39638	1880,1112.1525	Astronomical Diary.
39639	1880,1112.1526	Bilingual incantation.
39640	1880,1112.1527	Sumerian literary.
39641	1880,1112.1528	Bilingual incantation.
39642	1880,1112.1529	Unidentified.
39643	1880,1112.1530	Medical.
39644	1880,1112.1531	Bilingual incantation.
39645	1880,1112.1532	Obverse: prayer to Sîn, dupl. Mayer, Untersuchungen, 493-494, Sin 1, lines 18-24. Reverse: ritual naming Sîn and Zaqīqu; cf. Kunstmann, Gebetsbeschwörung, 69.
39646	1880,1112.1533	Economic.
39647	1880,1112.1534	School text.
39648	1880,1112.1535	Joined to 39030.
39649	1880,1112.1536	Astronomical.
39650	1880,1112.1537	Economic. Dar -/3/-.
39651	1880,1112.1538	Contract; sale of fields.
39652	1880,1112.1539	Economic.
39653	1880,1112.1540	Unidentified.
39654	1880,1112.1541	Contract; sale of a house.
39655	1880,1112.1542	Letter.
39656	1880,1112.1543	Unidentified.
39657	1880,1112.1544	Economic.
39658	1880,1112.1545	Missing.
39659	1880,1112.1546	Receipt for grain.
39660	1880,1112.1547	Joined to 38786.
39661	1880,1112.1548	School text; four archaic fish signs.
39662	1880,1112.1549	Ritual.
39663	1880,1112.1550	Economic.
39664	1880,1112.1551	Unidentified.

39665	1880,1112.1552	Sumerian literary.
39666	1880,1112.1553	Omens. + 39877.
39667	1880,1112.1554	Economic.
39668	1880,1112.1555	Economic.
39669	1880,1112.1556	Commentary.
39670	1880,1112.1557	Balag lamentation or other liturgical text. Lambert, MC 24, no. 39.
39671	1880,1112.1558	Lexical; birds.
39672	1880,1112.1559	Economic.
39673	1880,1112.1560	Contract; sale of fields.
39674	1880,1112.1561	Inventory; mentions plants.
39675	1880,1112.1562	Economic.
39676	1880,1112.1563	Incantation.
39677	1880,1112.1564	Lexical.
39678	1880,1112.1565	Unidentified.
39679	1880,1112.1566	Unidentified.
39680	1880,1112.1567	Astrological; tabulated; cf. 32517. (+) 38452.
39681	1880,1112.1568	Promissory note for silver
39682	1880,1112.1569	Ritual.
39683	1880,1112.1570	Medical.
39684	1880,1112.1571	Commentary.
39685	1880,1112.1572	Ritual.
39686	1880,1112.1573	Astronomical omens; mentions Ninsianna and calendar dates.
39687	1880,1112.1574	Unidentified.
39688	1880,1112.1575	Unidentified.
39689	1880,1112.1576	Receipt for barley. Dar -/4/27.
39690	1880,1112.1577	Astronomical.
39691	1880,1112.1578	Lexical.
39692	1880,1112.1579	Unidentified.
39693	1880,1112.1580	Medical.
39694	1880,1112.1581	Unidentified; mentions Babylon.
39695	1880,1112.1582	Unidentified.
39696	1880,1112.1583	Omens; extispicy; lung omens.
39697	1880,1112.1584	Astrological omens; Venus. Fincke, Kaskal 10, 92-99, pl. 106.
39698	1880,1112.1585	Astrological omens.
39699	1880,1112.1586	Lexical.
39700	1880,1112.1587	Omens; terrestrial.
39701	1880,1112.1588	Unidentified.
39702	1880,1112.1589	Unidentified.
39703	1880,1112.1590	Lexical.
39704	1880,1112.1591	Astrological.
39705	1880,1112.1592	Economic.

39706	1880,1112.1593	Tablet in shape like a part of a sealing, but with the formula of a land-sale contract.
39707	1880,1112.1594	Sumerian literary.
39708	1880,1112.1595	Unidentified.
39709	1880,1112.1596	Unidentified.
39710	1880,1112.1597	Economic.
39711	1880,1112.1598	Receipt.
39712	1880,1112.1599	Unidentified.
39713	1880,1112.1600	Field plan.
39714	1880,1112.1601	Late Babylonian copy of an earlier inscription; archaic LÚ; colophon.
39715	1880,1112.1602	Economic.
39716	1880,1112.1603	Bilingual incantation.
39717	1880,1112.1604	Incantation.
39718	1880,1112.1605	Lexical; GU4.
39719	1880,1112.1606	Lexical; A.LÁ.
39720	1880,1112.1607	Late Babylonian copy of an Old Babylonian or Ur III inscription; cf. 38430.
39721	1880,1112.1608	Unidentified.
39722	1880,1112.1609	Late Babylonian copy of an Ur III royal inscription.
39723	1880,1112.1610	Economic.
39724	1880,1112.1611	Medical.
39725	1880,1112.1612	Medical.
39726	1880,1112.1613	Unidentified.
39727	1880,1112.1614	Astronomical.
39728	1880,1112.1615	Unidentified.
39729	1880,1112.1616	Unidentified.
39730	1880,1112.1617	Lexical.
39731	1880,1112.1618	Lexical; syllabary.
39732	1880,1112.1619	Unidentified.
39733	1880,1112.1620	Lexical.
39734	1880,1112.1621	Medical.
39735	1880,1112.1622	Unidentified.
39736	1880,1112.1623	Unidentified.
39737	1880,1112.1624	Joined to 38546.
39738	1880,1112.1625	Unidentified.
39739	1880,1112.1626	Lexical?
39740	1880,1112.1627	Economic.
39741	1880,1112.1628	Ritual.
39742	1880,1112.1629	Unidentified.
39743	1880,1112.1630	Economic.
39744	1880,1112.1631	Ritual.
39745	1880,1112.1632	Hymn.
39746	1880,1112.1633	Astronomical Diary.
39747	1880,1112.1634	Bilingual incantation.

39748	1880,1112.1635	Unidentified.
39749	1880,1112.1636	Astronomical.
39750	1880,1112.1637	Astronomical.
39751	1880,1112.1638	Unidentified.
39752	1880,1112.1639	Joined to 38168.
39753	1880,1112.1640	Economic.
39754	1880,1112.1641	Joined to 39434.
39755	1880,1112.1642	Bilingual incantation. + 39846.
39756	1880,1112.1643	Astronomical.
39757	1880,1112.1644	Astronomical.
39758	1880,1112.1645	Contract.
39759	1880,1112.1646	Contract. Nbk 36(sic!)/1/[].
39760	1880,1112.1647	Ritual.
39761	1880,1112.1648	Receipt.
39762	1880,1112.1649	Ritual.
39763	1880,1112.1650	Lexical; god list.
39764	1880,1112.1651	Ritual.
39765	1880,1112.1652	Literary.
39766	1880,1112.1653	Medical; list of plants.
39767	1880,1112.1654	Ritual.
39768	1880,1112.1655	Bilingual incantation.
39769	1880,1112.1656	Contract; division of property.
39770	1880,1112.1657	Medical; GIG d.NAM.TAR.GIG.
39771	1880,1112.1658	Literary cylinder.
39772	1880,1112.1659	Unidentified.
39773	1880,1112.1660	Unidentified.
39774	1880,1112.1661	Medical prescription; landscape format; mentions iniqtu.
39775	1880,1112.1662	Unidentified.
39776	1880,1112.1663	Commentary.
39777	1880,1112.1664	Ritual.
39778	1880,1112.1665	Omens; the colophon mentions Borsippa.
39779	1880,1112.1666	Astronomical?
39780	1880,1112.1667	Economic.
39781	1880,1112.1668	Astronomical Diary.
39782	1880,1112.1669	Commentary; medical?
39783	1880,1112.1670	Ritual.
39784	1880,1112.1671	Incantation.
39785	1880,1112.1672	Economic.
39786	1880,1112.1673	Unidentified.
39787	1880,1112.1674	Letter.
39788	1880,1112.1675	Astrological; microzodiac text; rectangular table.
39789	1880,1112.1676	Unidentified.
39790	1880,1112.1677	Liver omens.
39791	1880,1112.1678	Astronomical.

39792	1880,1112.1679	Astronomical.
39793	1880,1112.1680	Ritual.
39794	1880,1112.1681	Commentary.
39794a	1880,1112.1681a	Economic.
39795	1880,1112.1682	Unidentified.
39796	1880,1112.1683	Unidentified.
39797	1880,1112.1684	Lexical.
39798	1880,1112.1685	Literary; Enūma eliš VII. Lambert, BCM, p. 123, pl. 34.
39799	1880,1112.1686	Unidentified.
39800	1880,1112.1687	Unidentified.
39801	1880,1112.1688	Lexical.
39802	1880,1112.1689	Lexical.
39803	1880,1112.1690	Unidentified.
39804	1880,1112.1691	Incantation.
39805	1880,1112.1692	Astronomical.
39806	1880,1112.1693	Lexical; nail marks.
39807	1880,1112.1694	Bilingual incantation.
39808	1880,1112.1695	Lexical.
39809	1880,1112.1696	Economic. -/2/-.
39810	1880,1112.1697	Unidentified.
39811	1880,1112.1698	Letter.
39812	1880,1112.1699	Unidentified.
39813	1880,1112.1700	Astronomical.
39814	1880,1112.1701	Joined to 38711.
39815	1880,1112.1702	Unidentified.
39816	1880,1112.1703	Unidentified.
39817	1880,1112.1704	Economic.
39818	1880,1112.1705	Economic.
39819	1880,1112.1706	Astronomical.
39820	1880,1112.1707	Astronomical.
39821	1880,1112.1708	Unidentified.
39822	1880,1112.1709	Lexical.
39823	1880,1112.1710	Contract.
39824	1880,1112.1711	Astronomical.
39825	1880,1112.1712	Astronomical.
39826	1880,1112.1713	Account of payments.
39827	1880,1112.1714	Medical; list of diseases; list of ŠU+EN.
39828	1880,1112.1715	Commentary.
39829	1880,1112.1716	Sumerian literary.
39830	1880,1112.1717	Incantation.
39831	1880,1112.1718	Hemerology.
39832	1880,1112.1719	Sumerian literary.
39833	1880,1112.1720	Unidentified.
39834	1880,1112.1721	Economic.

39835	1880,1112.1722	Lexical.
39836	1880,1112.1723	Unidentified; mentions agrig and la-ḫa-an.
39837	1880,1112.1724	Hemerology: Babylonian Almanac.
39838	1880,1112.1725	Omens.
39839	1880,1112.1726	Unidentified.
39840	1880,1112.1727	Unidentified.
39841	1880,1112.1728	Astronomical.
39842	1880,1112.1729	Bilingual incantation.
39843	1880,1112.1730	Joined to 38706.
39844	1880,1112.1731	Lexical.
39845	1880,1112.1732	Commentary.
39846	1880,1112.1733	Joined to 39755.
39847	1880,1112.1734	Bilingual incantation.
39848	1880,1112.1735	Economic.
39849	1880,1112.1736	Sumerian literary.
39850	1880,1112.1737	Astronomical.
39851	1880,1112.1738	Lexical.
39852	1880,1112.1739	Lexical.
39853	1880,1112.1740	Ritual.
39854	1880,1112.1741	Omens.
39855	1880,1112.1742	Unidentified.
39856	1880,1112.1743	School text.
39857	1880,1112.1744	Sumerian literary.
39858	1880,1112.1745	Unidentified.
39859	1880,1112.1746	Unidentified.
39860	1880,1112.1747	Commentary.
39861	1880,1112.1748	Unidentified.
39862	1880,1112.1749	Economic.
39863	1880,1112.1750	Unidentified.
39864	1880,1112.1751	Commentary.
39865	1880,1112.1752	Astronomical Diary or related text.
39866	1880,1112.1753	Ritual.
39867	1880,1112.1754	Economic.
39868	1880,1112.1755	Unidentified.
39869	1880,1112.1756	Economic.
39870	1880,1112.1757	Medical.
39871	1880,1112.1758	God list.
39872	1880,1112.1759	Medical.
39873	1880,1112.1760	Incantation.
39874	1880,1112.1761	Astronomical Diary; solstice on day 19, KI GU4-AN ...
39875	1880,1112.1762	Memorandum.
39876	1880,1112.1763	Omens; Šumma izbu 19. De Zorzi, Šumma izbu, 937.
39877	1880,1112.1764	Joined to 39666.
39878	1880,1112.1765	Unidentified.

39879	1880,1112.1766	Bilingual.
39880	1880,1112.1767	Omens; extispicy.
39881	1880,1112.1768	Omens? Colophon.
39882	1880,1112.1769	Astronomical.
39883	1880,1112.1770	Unidentified.
39884	1880,1112.1771	Late Babylonian copy of an Old Babylonian royal inscription of Sumu-la-el.
39885	1880,1112.1772	Lexical; god list.
39886	1880,1112.1773	Bilingual incantation.
39887	1880,1112.1774	Economic.
39888	1880,1112.1775	Late Babylonian copy of an earlier administrative tablet; colophon on left edge.
39889	1880,1112.1776	Economic.
39890	1880,1112.1777	Lexical.
39891	1880,1112.1778	God list.
39892	1880,1112.1779	Bilingual incantation.
39893	1880,1112.1780	Commentary.
39894	1880,1112.1781	Lexical.
39895	1880,1112.1782	Lexical.
39896	1880,1112.1783	Lexical; syllabary.
39897	1880,1112.1784	Lexical; syllabary. + 39927.
137448	1880,1112.1785	Brick of Nebuchadnezzar II. CBI, no. 100.
39898	1880,1112.1786	School text; lexical, Syllabary A; colophon. Gesche, AOAT 275, 326, 687.
39899	1880,1112.1787	Lexical; syllabary.
39899a	1880,1112.1788	Uninscribed, but ruled as if for a lexical text.
39900	1880,1112.1789	Lexical; syllabary.
39901	1880,1112.1790	School text; lexical, Syllabary A. Gesche, AOAT 275, 687.
39902	1880,1112.1791	Lexical; syllabary.
39903	1880,1112.1792	School text; lexical, Syllabary A. Gesche, AOAT 275, 687.
39904	1880,1112.1793	School text; lexical, Syllabary A. Gesche, AOAT 275, 688.
39905	1880,1112.1794	Lexical; syllabary.
39906	1880,1112.1795	Lexical; syllabary.
39907	1880,1112.1796	Lexical; syllabary.
39908	1880,1112.1797	School text; lexical, Syllabary A. Gesche, AOAT 275, 688.
39909	1880,1112.1798	Lexical; syllabary; feminine names.
39910	1880,1112.1799	Lexical; syllabary.
39911	1880,1112.1800	Lexical; syllabary.
39912	1880,1112.1801	Lexical.
39913	1880,1112.1802	Lexical; syllabary.
39914	1880,1112.1803	Lexical; syllabary.

39915	1880,1112.1804	Lexical; syllabary; literary extract.
39916	1880,1112.1805	Lexical; syllabary.
39917	1880,1112.1806	Lexical; syllabary.
39918	1880,1112.1807	School text.
39919	1880,1112.1808	Lexical; syllabary.
39920	1880,1112.1809	Lexical; syllabary.
39921	1880,1112.1810	Lexical; syllabary.
39922	1880,1112.1811	Lexical; syllabary.
39923	1880,1112.1812	Lexical; syllabary.
39924	1880,1112.1813	Lexical; syllabary.
39925	1880,1112.1814	Lexical; syllabary.
39926	1880,1112.1815	Lexical; syllabary.
39927	1880,1112.1816	Joined to 39897.
39928	1880,1112.1817	Lexical; syllabary.
39929	1880,1112.1818	Lexical; syllabary.
39930	1880,1112.1819	Lexical; syllabary.
39931	1880,1112.1820	Lexical.
39932	1880,1112.1821	Lexical; syllabary.
39933	1880,1112.1822	Lexical.
39934	1880,1112.1823	Lexical; syllabary.
39935	1880,1112.1824	Lexical; syllabary.
39936	1880,1112.1825	Lexical; syllabary.
39937	1880,1112.1826	Lexical; syllabary.
39938	1880,1112.1827	Lexical; syllabary.
39939	1880,1112.1828	Lexical; syllabary.
39940	1880,1112.1829	Lexical; syllabary; literary extract.
39941	1880,1112.1830	Lexical; practice signs.
39942	1880,1112.1831	Lexical; syllabary.
39943	1880,1112.1832	School text; lexical, Syllabary A. Gesche, AOAT 275, 688.
39944	1880,1112.1833	Unidentified.
39945	1880,1112.1834	Lexical; syllabary.
39946	1880,1112.1835	Lexical; syllabary.
39947	1880,1112.1836	Lexical; syllabary.
39948	1880,1112.1837	Lexical; syllabary.
39949	1880,1112.1838	Lexical.
39950	1880,1112.1839	Lexical; syllabary.
39951	1880,1112.1840	Lexical; syllabary.
39952	1880,1112.1841	Lexical.
39953	1880,1112.1842	Lexical; syllabary.
39954	1880,1112.1843	Lexical; syllabary.
39955	1880,1112.1844	Lexical; syllabary.
39956	1880,1112.1845	Lexical; syllabary.
39957	1880,1112.1846	Lexical; syllabary.
39958	1880,1112.1847	Lexical; syllabary.

39959	1880,1112.1848	Lexical; syllabary.
39960	1880,1112.1849	Lexical; syllabary.
39961	1880,1112.1850	Lexical; practice signs.
39962	1880,1112.1851	Lexical; syllabary.
39963	1880,1112.1852	Lexical; syllabary.
39964	1880,1112.1853	Lexical; syllabary.
39965	1880,1112.1854	Lexical; syllabary; personal names.
39966	1880,1112.1855	Lexical; syllabary.
39967	1880,1112.1856	Lexical; syllabary.
39968	1880,1112.1857	Lexical; syllabary.
39969	1880,1112.1858	Lexical; syllabary.
39970	1880,1112.1859	Lexical; syllabary; literary extract.
39971	1880,1112.1860	Lexical; syllabary.
39972	1880,1112.1861	Lexical; syllabary.
39973	1880,1112.1862	Lexical; syllabary.
39974	1880,1112.1863	Lexical; syllabary.
39975	1880,1112.1864	Lexical.
39976	1880,1112.1865	Lexical; syllabary.
39977	1880,1112.1866	Lexical; syllabary.
39978	1880,1112.1867	Lexical; syllabary.
39979	1880,1112.1868	Lexical; syllabary.
39980	1880,1112.1869	Lexical; syllabary.
39981	1880,1112.1870	Lexical; syllabary.
39982	1880,1112.1871	School text; lexical, Syllabary A. Gesche, AOAT 275, 688.
39983	1880,1112.1872	Lexical; syllabary.
39984	1880,1112.1873	Lexical; practice signs.
39985	1880,1112.1874	Lexical; syllabary.
39986	1880,1112.1875	School text; lexical, Syllabary A. Gesche, AOAT 275, 688.
39987	1880,1112.1876	Lexical; syllabary.
39988	1880,1112.1877	Lexical; syllabary.
39989	1880,1112.1878	Lexical; syllabary.
39990	1880,1112.1879	Lexical; syllabary.
39991	1880,1112.1880	Lexical; syllabary.
39992	1880,1112.1881	Lexical; syllabary.
39993	1880,1112.1882	Lexical; syllabary.
39994	1880,1112.1883	Lexical; syllabary; personal names.
39995	1880,1112.1884	Lexical.
39996	1880,1112.1885	Lexical; syllabary.
39997	1880,1112.1886	Lexical; syllabary.
39998	1880,1112.1887	Lexical; syllabary.
39999	1880,1112.1888	Lexical; syllabary.
40000	1880,1112.1889	Lexical; syllabary.
40001	1880,1112.1890	Lexical; stones.

40002	1880,1112.1891	Lexical; syllabary.
40003	1880,1112.1892	School text; lexical, Syllabary A. Gesche, AOAT 275, 688.
40004	1880,1112.1893	Lexical; syllabary.
40005	1880,1112.1894	Lexical.
40006	1880,1112.1895	Fragment of a stone tablet, recording temple prebends. Marduk-apla-iddina II. (Borsippa). King, BBSt, 116-119 and pls. 25-26, no. XXXV; Seux, RA 54, 206-208; Brinkman, Fs Oppenheim, 52; Seidl, Bagh Mitt 4, 59; Brinkman and Kennedy, JCS 35, 12, A.36; Reade, Iraq 48, 110; Paulus, AOAT 51, 704-708, MAI II 2.
104408	1880,1112.1896	Fragment of a boundary-stone (kudurru), recording a land sale. (Borsippa). King, BBSt, pp. 90-95, pl. 19, no. XXIII; Seidl, Bagh Mitt 4, 65 G 17; Reade, Iraq 48, 110
	1880,1112.1897ff.	Nos. 1897-2080 are uninscribed objects.
	1880,1112.2081	Stone inscription of Nebuchadnezzar II; marked as from Birs Nimroud. (Borsippa). Reade, Iraq 48, 109, 114.
	1880,1112.2082ff.	Nos. 2082-2133 are uninscribed objects.
40007	1880,1112.2134	Joined to 38690.
40008	1880,1112.2135	Lexical; syllabary.
40009	1880,1112.2136	Literary; mentions Esangila and Babylon.
40010a	1880,1112.2137a	Liver omens.
40010b	1880,1112.2137b	Liver omens.
40010c	1880,1112.2137c	Liver omens.
40011	1880,1112.2138	Letter?
40012	1880,1112.2139	Sumerian literary.
40013	1880,1112.2140	Bilingual incantation.
40014	1880,1112.2141	Lexical; syllabary.
40015	1880,1112.2142	Unidentified.
40016	1880,1112.2143	Sumerian literary.
40017	1880,1112.2144	Sumerian literary.
40018	1880,1112.2145	Astrological omens.
40018a	1880,1112.2147	Sealing, uninscribed with impression of a scaraboid seal.
89560	1880,1112.2146	Cylinder seal; Kassite.
40019	1880,1112.2148	Astronomical; lunar six table. Huber and Steele, SCIAMVS 8 (2007) 3-36, text N.
40020	1880,1112.2149	Economic.
40021	1880,1112.2150	Astrological omens.
40022	1880,1112.2151	Medical.
40023	1880,1112.2152	Literary.
40024	1880,1112.2153	Historical.

40025	1880,1112.2154	Lexical.
40026	1880,1112.2155	Economic.
40027	1880,1112.2156	Unidentified.
40028	1880,1112.2157	Astronomical.
40029	1880,1112.2158	Astronomical.
40030	1880,1112.2159	Contract; division of an inheritance; sealed. d.l. Wunsch, Bab Arch 2, 136-137, no. 41; Nisaba 28, no. 63.
40031	1880,1112.2160	Contract; sale of fields; finger-nail marks. 5/[]/18.
40032	1880,1112.2161	Contract; sale of fields.
40033	1880,1112.2162	Prophecy.
40034	1880,1112.2163	Economic.
40035	1880,1112.2164	Incantation.
40036	1880,1112.2165	Economic.
90851	1880,1112.2166	Bronze door-sill with inscription of Nebuchadnezzar II. Borsippa. Rassam, TSBA 8 (1885) 188-190 and pl.; Langdon, VAB 4, 200-201, Neb. no. 34; Reade, Iraq 48, 111, 115 and pl. XVI.
	1880,1112.2167	Stone inscription of Nebuchadnezzar II. (Borsippa). Reade, Iraq 48, 109, 114 and pl. XIVd.
	1880,1112.2168ff.	Nos. 2168-2170 are uninscribed objects.
91445	1880,1112.2171	Brown stone with alphabetic inscription; marked Birs Nimroud.
90826	1880,1112.2172	Stone door-socket with inscription of Ur-Nammu; previously numbered 12069. Nippur. 1R 1, 8; CT 21, 6; Frayne, RIME 3/2.1.1.37.1.
104414	1880,1112.2173	Stone tablet; probably recording a gift of land, but inscription lost. Borsippa. King, BBSt, p. 111, pl. 23, no. XXXI; Reade, Iraq 48, 110.

1881,0201 collection

The 1881,0201 collection comes from Messrs. Spartali & Co., London. The register gives Babylonia as the provenance of the whole collection.

40037	1881,0201.1	Old Babylonian; letter. CT 29, 22.
40038	1881,0201.2	Contract; sale of fields; possibly a siege text. Šamaš-šum-ukin 15/12/18. Babylon. Brinkman and Kennedy, JCS 35, 35, K.135; Frame, JCS 51, 105.
40039	1881,0201.3	Receipt for sale of seed; dated arki Kandalanu. Kandalanu 2/8/22. Babylon. Wiseman, Chronicles, 89f and pls. xix-xx; Brinkman and Kennedy, JCS 35, 49, L.163.
40040	1881,0201.4	Promissory note for silver with garden given as pledge. Kandalanu 13/1/10. Babylon. Weidner, AfO

		16, 39-40 and pl. IV; Petschow, Eos 48/2 (1957) 22-23; Brinkman and Kennedy, JCS 35, 42, L.42.
40041	1881,0201.5	Promissory note for silver. Cyr 21/3/8.
40042	1881,0201.6	Promissory note for silver. Cam []/5/1.
40043	1881,0201.7	Promissory note for onions. Dar.
40044	1881,0201.8	Receipt for payment of silver; finger-nail mark. Dar []/10/24. Babylon.
40045	1881,0201.9	Promissory note for silver. Cam 8/1/2. Babylon.
40046	1881,0201.10	Promissory note for silver. Kandalanu 26/1/21. Babylon. Brinkman and Kennedy, JCS 35, 49, L.154.
40047	1881,0201.11	Field sale(?).
40048	1881,0201.12	Promissory note for silver. Dar 22/12/6. Šušan.
40049	1881,0201.13	Account of issues of silver to the creditors of Nadnaya.
40050	1881,0201.14	Incantation.
40051	1881,0201.15	Medical; prescriptions for the nose; būšānu disease. Geller, Fs Fales (2012) 325-328.
40052	1881,0201.16	Promissory note for silver. Nbn 28/5/11. Babylon.
40053	1881,0201.17	Astronomical Diary.
40054	1881,0201.18	Astronomical; procedure text for Jupiter. Ossendrijver, Science 351 (2016) 482-484, text A (and Supplementary Materials); Ossendrijver, JNES 76, 231-247, text A.
40055	1881,0201.19	Promissory note for sesame for ḫarrānu. Nbk 20/3/36. Babylon.
40056	1881,0201.20	Promissory note for dates.
40057	1881,0201.21	Astronomical Diary for SE 141. Sachs and Hunger, ADART II, no. -170 C.
40058	1881,0201.22	Astronomical.
40059	1881,0201.23	Contract for farming. Dar -/5/-. Babylon.
40060	1881,0201.24	Contract; sale of land.
40061	1881,0201.25	Contract; quitclaim; sealed; Aramaic note. Art II/III 12/[]/14. [Babylon]. Mitchell and Searight, no. 496; Nisaba 28, no. 538.
40062	1881,0201.26	Sale of dates. Nbn 26/12/11. Babylon.
40063	1881,0201.27	Sale of dates. Dar 25/7/14. x-x.KI.
40064	1881,0201.28	Sale of a slave? Cyr 18/-/-. Babylon.
40065	1881,0201.29	Contract for bricks. Nbn 21/11/5. Babylon.
40066	1881,0201.30	Contract; obverse vitrified; witnesses. Probably from the Kasr archive. Dar II 11/8/1. URU Ḫalpattu.
40067	1881,0201.31	Astronomical Diary for SE 123. Sachs and Hunger, ADART II, no. -188.
40068	1881,0201.32	Account of issues of silver; SE Arsaces []/[]/219 (= AE 155). Hackl, Fs van der Spek, 87-106, no. 5.

40069	1881,0201.33	Astronomical Diary for SE 157. Sachs and Hunger, ADART III, no. -154 B.
40070	1881,0201.34	List of names and numbers; circular tablet.
40071	1881,0201.35	Ritual against evil demons; colophon. Maul, Bagh Forsch 18, 96-97; 167; 373ff.
40072	1881,0201.36	Lexical; Ḫḫ I. MSL 9, 157.
40073	1881,0201.37	Cylinder; inscription of Neriglissar. 1R, 67; Langdon, VAB 4, 208-214, Neb. no. 1; Berger, AOAT 4/1, Neriglissar Zylinder II, 3, no. 2.
40074	1881,0201.38	Cylinder, inscription of Ashurbanipal on the rebuilding of the temple of Ištar at Babylon. Frame, RIMB 2.6.32.4.2.
40075	1881,0201.39	Cylinder; inscription of Nebuchadnezzar II. Mar(a)-da. + 40135. Winckler, ZA 2, 137-140; Langdon, VAB 4, 78-79, Neb. no. 3; Berger, AOAT 4/1, Nebukadnezar Zylinder II,10, no. 2.
40076	1881,0201.40	Cylinder; historical; begins ì-nu-um d.Marduk ... d.Enlil ...
40077	1881,0201.41	Joined to 32467.
40078	1881,0201.42	Astronomical Diary. Alexander IV. + 40105. LBAT 216 (40078 only); Sachs and Hunger, ADART I, no. -308; Reiner, Fs Borger (CM 10), 298.
40079	1881,0201.43	Astronomical Diary for SE 11. Sachs and Hunger, ADART I, no. -300.
40080	1881,0201.44	School text; bilingual incantation; Šamaš hymn; lexical, Ḫḫ VII/B. Pinches, PSBA 23 (1901) pl. I after p. 188; Lambert, MC 24, no. 134.
40081	1881,0201.45	Joined to 35564.
	1881,0201.46	Joined to 34070.
40082	1881,0201.47	Astronomical; first and last visibility of the moon; lunar velocity; column phi; colophon of Iddin-Bēl. (+) 36722. Neugebauer, JCS 22, 96-111, 113, Atypical text K.
40083	1881,0201.48	Astronomical; Almanac for SE 372. LBAT 1199; Sachs, AOAT 25, 389-392, pl. XVII; Hunger and Sachs, ADART VII, no. 216.
40084	1881,0201.49	Astronomical; Almanac for SE 372. LBAT 1200; Sachs, AOAT 25, 392-393, pl. XVIII; Hunger and Sachs, ADART VII, no. 217.
40085	1881,0201.50	Astrological; Enūma Anu Enlil 28 (29); colophon. van Soldt, Solar Omens, 92-109 (A), pls. XII-XIII; Reiner, Fs Borger (CM 10), 298.
40086	1881,0201.51	Astronomical; Goal Year Text for SE 202. + 40110. LBAT 1288 (40086 only); Hunger and Sachs, ADART VI, no. 74.

40087	1881,0201.52	Literary.
40088	1881,0201.53	Medical.
40089	1881,0201.54	Omens; extispicy.
40090	1881,0201.55	Ritual for the 4th day, for the temple É-túr-kalam-ma at Babylon; colophon. + 41005 + 41107. Lambert, Unity and Diversity, 98-135 (41005 and 41107 only).
40091	1881,0201.56	Astronomical observations; lunar data for SE 69-72. + 1881,0706.116. LBAT 1433; Hunger and Sachs, ADART V, no. 40.
40092	1881,0201.57	Astronomical Diary for SE 141. Sachs and Hunger, ADART II, no. -170 J.
40093	1881,0201.58	Astronomical Diary.
40094	1881,0201.59	Astronomical; lunar ephemeris; computed list of new moons, 319-316 BC. + 45662. LBAT 78 (45662 only); ACT 128 (45662 only); Aaboe, KDVSMM 36/12 (1968) 39 (40094 only) and 37/3 (1969) 3-25 (40094 only) and 40/6 (1979) 23-28 (both fragments); Brown, CM 18, 305.
40095	1881,0201.60	Astronomical Diary for SE 130. + 55572. LBAT 343-344; Sachs, PTRSL A.276, 49, fig. 12; Sachs and Hunger, ADART II, no. -181.
40096	1881,0201.61	Astronomical Diary for SE 120. Sachs and Hunger, ADART II, no. -191 B.
40097	1881,0201.62	Astronomical Diary fragment?
40098	1881,0201.63	Theodicy. (+) 40124 + 77255. Lambert, BWL 63-89, pls. 21, 23; Lambert, MC 24, no. 254.
40099	1881,0201.64	Astronomical Diary. LBAT 195; Sachs and Hunger, ADART I, no. -332 B.
40100	1881,0201.65	Joined to 37054.
40101	1881,0201.66	Astronomical; Almanac for SE 92. + 55536. LBAT 1118-1119; Reiner, Fs Borger (CM 10), 298; Hunger and Sachs, ADART VII, no. 153.
40102	1881,0201.67	Joined to 35495.
40103	1881,0201.68	Literary. MB.
40104	1881,0201.69	Bilingual incantation, Udug-ḫul 5. + 1881,0625.743.
40105	1881,0201.70	Joined to 40078.
40106	1881,0201.71	Astronomical Diary for SE 89. Sachs and Hunger, ADART II, no. -222.
40107	1881,0201.72	Mathematical; table of squares of regular numbers. Neugebauer, MKT I pp. 68, no. 4, 69, no. 4.
40108	1881,0201.73	Astrological omens.
40109	1881,0201.74	Ritual for Esangila.
40110	1881,0201.75	Joined to 40086.

40111	1881,0201.76	Astrological; Enūma Anu Enlil, Venus, group A. Reiner and Pingree, BPO 3, 29, 72-74; Reiner, Fs Borger (CM 10), 298.
	1881,0201.77	Joined to 40102.
40112	1881,0201.78	Astronomical Diary.
40113	1881,0201.79	Astronomical; list of planetary periods; dupl. 35402. Neugebauer and Sachs, JCS 21, 206.
40114	1881,0201.80	Astronomical; Goal Year Text; not datable. Hunger and Sachs, ADART VI, no. 151; Reiner, Fs Borger (CM 10), 298.
40115	1881,0201.81	Lexical.
40116	1881,0201.82	Astronomical Diary for SE 102. Sachs and Hunger, ADART II, no. -209 B.
40117	1881,0201.83	"Aluzinnu text"; dupl. 2R 60, no. 1. (+) 77264.
40118	1881,0201.84	Astronomical Diary fragment?
40119	1881,0201.85	Astronomical Diary for SE 140. LBAT 362; Sachs and Hunger, ADART II, no. -171 B.
40120	1881,0201.86	Late Babylonian copy of an inscription of Karaindash; cf. 4R, 36, no. 3.
40121	1881,0201.87	Lexical, commentary on Aa 1/2.
40122	1881,0201.88	Astronomical Diary for SE 7. LBAT 218; J. Koch, AfO 38/39, 103-107; Sachs and Hunger, ADART I, no. -304; Reiner, Fs Borger (CM 10), 298.
40123	1881,0201.89	Astronomical; lunar ephemeris; System A. ACT 21.
40124	1881,0201.90	Theodicy. + 77255 (+) 40098. Lambert, BWL 63-89, pl. 20 (40124 only); Lambert, MC 24, no. 254.
	1881,0201.91	Joined to 34627.
40125	1881,0201.92	Late Babylonian copy of an historical inscription of Abiešuḫ. + 55472. Sollberger, Fs Finkelstein, 198-200 (55472 only); Frayne, RIME 4.3.8.1.2.
40126	1881,0201.93	Astrological; ziqpu settings; MUL.APIN type or later. Reiner, Fs Borger (CM 10), 298.
40127	1881,0201.94	Lexical; Nabnītu I. MSL 16, 49, 339, 345.
40128	1881,0201.95	Lexical; Aa V/4 = 29. MSL 14, 426.
40129	1881,0201.96	Incantation.
40130	1881,0201.97	Commentary; cf. 35401.
40131	1881,0201.98	Ritual.
40132	1881,0201.99	Literary.
40133	1881,0201.100	Literary; prayer to the gods of the night; colophon: Bēl-uballiṭ son of Utul-Marduk.
40134	1881,0201.101	Literary cylinder; hymn to Nabû; two columns inscribed in opposite directions. The sign ú is repeated along the left edge. Gesche, AOAT 275, 688.
40135	1881,0201.102	Joined to 40075.

90935	1881,0201.103	Cylinder, inscription of Ashurbanipal on the rebuilding of the temple of Ištar at Babylon; also once numbered as 12064. Frame, RIMB 2.6.32.4.1.

1881,0324 collection

The 1881,0324 collection comes from the excavations of Hormuzd Rassam. See J. E. Reade in CBTBM VI, p. xxx. The register gives Babylon (Ibrahim al-Halil) as the provenance of the whole collection.

40136	1881,0324.1	Lexical.
40137	1881,0324.2	Lexical; Ea; sign list; literary extracts.
40138	1881,0324.3	Lexical; Ea; sign list; literary extracts.
40139	1881,0324.4	Lexical; god-list and writing exercise.
40140	1881,0324.5	Lexical; Ea; sign list.
40141	1881,0324.6	School text; lexical. 13/8/-.
40142	1881,0324.7	Account of disbursements.
40143	1881,0324.8	Lexical; Ea; sign list and personal names.
40144	1881,0324.9	Lexical; Ea; sign list.
40145	1881,0324.10	Lexical; Ea; sign list; personal names and colophon.
40146	1881,0324.11	Lexical; Ḫḫ I. + 40438.
40147	1881,0324.12	Bilingual incantation.
40148	1881,0324.13	Incantation.
40149	1881,0324.14	Astrological.
40150	1881,0324.15	Lexical; syllabary; literary extracts.
40151	1881,0324.16	Tintir II. George, BTT, pl. 7.
40152	1881,0324.17	Medical ritual; gynaecology.
40153	1881,0324.18	Astronomical.
40154	1881,0324.19	Lexical; syllabary.
40155	1881,0324.20	Medical. + 40331 (+) 40218.
40156	1881,0324.21	Field sale; sealed. Dar II 16/12/11. Babylon. (+) 40198. Mitchell and Searight, no. 407; Nisaba 28, no. 247.
40157	1881,0324.22	Contract; sealed. Art 30/[]/8. Nisaba 28, no. 268.
40158	1881,0324.23	Promissory note for silver; sealed. Dar II 18/[]/15. Nisaba 28, no. 251.
40159	1881,0324.24	Lexical; syllabary.
40160	1881,0324.25	Lexical; syllabary; literary extract.
40161	1881,0324.26	Receipt for silver; sealed. SE -/7/90. Nisaba 28, no. 656.
40162	1881,0324.27	Lexical.
40163	1881,0324.28	Oracle questions (tamītu) to Šamaš; colophon. + 1881,0324.29. Lambert, BOQ, no. 23, pls. 53-54.
	1881,0324.29	Joined to 40163.
40164	1881,0324.30	Lexical; syllabary.
40165	1881,0324.31	Lexical.

40166	1881,0324.32	Lexical; syllabary.
40167	1881,0324.33	Lexical; syllabary
40168	1881,0324.34	Contract; lease of a field; sealed; prayer on upper edge. Art II 28/5/[]. Borsippa. Mitchell and Searight, no. 504; Nisaba 28, no. 297.
40169	1881,0324.35	Religious list; linking professions (e.g. BUR.GUL, AD.KID) and deities.
40170	1881,0324.36	Astrological omens.
40171	1881,0324.37	Deposition.
40172	1881,0324.38	Promissory note for grain. Nbn 7/5/11. Babylon.
40173	1881,0324.39	Contract for payment of silver. Dar 17/4/-.
40174	1881,0324.40	Ritual.
40175	1881,0324.41	Medical.
40176	1881,0324.42	Oracle questions (tamītu) to Šamaš and Adad; colophon. Lambert, BOQ, no. 24, pl. 55.
40177	1881,0324.43	School text; bilingual incantations; Muššu'u tablets VII-VIII; also Udug-ḫul 5. Cf. Finkel, AuOr 9 (1991), 99; Böck, Muššu'u, 261-313 and pls. XXXVI-XXXVII; Geller, BAM 8, 174-216.
40178	1881,0324.44	Lexical; Ea; sign list.
40179	1881,0324.45	Lexical; syllabary; personal names.
40180	1881,0324.46	Astronomical Diary; weather reports only. van der Spek, AchHist 13, 310-311.
40181	1881,0324.47	Lexical; syllabary; personal names.
40182	1881,0324.48	Administrative; list of distributions; two columns. + 40192 + 40221 + 40315 + 40316 + 40317 + 40326 + 40330 + 40434.
40183	1881,0324.49	Magico-medical prescriptions against demons and sickness, with drawings. + 1881,0324.58 + 40333 + 40352 + 40443 + 40444 + 5 unnum. frags. Finkel, Scienze dell'Antichita 17, 340, fig. 4; Steinert, ABSTC, 378.
40184	1881,0324.50	Astronomical Diary or related text.
40185	1881,0324.51	Contract; sealed. Art II 13/11/23. Borsippa. + 40194. Nisaba 28, no. 282.
40186	1881,0324.52	Contract; sale of a field. Nbk 19/11/22. Borsippa. Zadok, Nisaba 21, 235.
40187	1881,0324.53	Birth note for two girls born in year 41 of Artaxerxes II and year 1 of Artaxerxes III; prayer on upper edge. Art III -/-/1.
40188	1881,0324.54	Promissory note for barley. Dar 8/2/25.
40189	1881,0324.55	Medical; list of stones only.
40190	1881,0324.56	Physiognomic omens. (+) 40286.
40191	1881,0324.57	Omens; physiognomic.
	1881,0324.58	Joined to 40183.

40192	1881,0324.59	Joined to 40182.
40193	1881,0324.60	Ritual.
40194	1881,0324.61	Joined to 40185.
40195	1881,0324.62	Astronomical.
40196	1881,0324.63	Ritual; namburbû.
40197	1881,0324.64	Economic.
40198	1881,0324.65	Field sale; sealed. (+) 40156. Nisaba 28, no. 248.
40199	1881,0324.66	Economic.
40200	1881,0324.67	Promissory note for dates. Nbn 18/6/15. Šaṭeru.
40201	1881,0324.68	Astrological.
40202	1881,0324.69	Contract; transfer of property.
40203	1881,0324.70	Field sale; sealed. Nisaba 28, no. 120.
40204	1881,0324.71	Fragment of a boundary stone; inscribed; measurement of an estate. Middle Babylonian. Paulus, AOAT 51, 860-861, pl. 89, U 44; Reade, ARRIM 9, 47.
40205	1881,0324.72	School text, lexical; giš list, etc.; colophon.
40206	1881,0324.73	Lexical; Aa.
40207	1881,0324.74	Promissory note for silver. Bardija -/5/-. Babylon.
40208	1881,0324.75	Economic.
40209	1881,0324.76	Geographical; temples?
40210	1881,0324.77	Promissory note for dates. 14/1/-.
40211	1881,0324.78	Promissory note for silver. Npl 2/10/-.
40212	1881,0324.79	Deposition.
40213	1881,0324.80	Incantation.
40214	1881,0324.81	Incantation.
40215	1881,0324.82	Economic.
40216	1881,0324.83	Oracle questions (tamītu) to Šamaš and Adad; colophon. Lambert, BOQ, no. 25, pl. 56
40217	1881,0324.84	Incantation.
40218	1881,0324.85	Medical. (+) 40155 + 40331.
40219	1881,0324.86	Lexical; Ea; sign list.
40220	1881,0324.87	Economic.
40221	1881,0324.88	Joined to 40182.
40222	1881,0324.89	Ritual.
40223	1881,0324.90	Memorandum. 8/10/-. Babylon.
40224	1881,0324.91	Contract.
40225	1881,0324.92	Receipt.
40226	1881,0324.93	Bilingual incantation.
40227	1881,0324.94	Lexical; syllabary. + 40337.
40228	1881,0324.95	Bilingual incantation.
40229	1881,0324.96	Omens; Šumma izbu 20. De Zorzi, Šumma izbu, 824.
40230	1881,0324.97	Economic.
40231	1881,0324.98	Contract.
40232	1881,0324.99	Astrological omens.
40233	1881,0324.100	Economic. Cyr 17/8/3.

40234	1881,0324.101	Astronomical Diary?
40235	1881,0324.102	Economic. 5/[]/12.
40236	1881,0324.103	Promissory note.
40237	1881,0324.104	Promissory note for silver with house pledged. Cam 15/8/1. Babylon.
40238	1881,0324.105	Promissory note for dates. Nbn 20/9/-.
40239	1881,0324.106	Promissory note for silver. Nbk 22/[]/16. Babylon.
40240	1881,0324.107	Contract for gardening. 3/[]/7.
40241	1881,0324.108	Sale of fields.
40242	1881,0324.109	Contract; transfer of property. No RN 3/6b/19. Borsippa. Zadok, Nisaba 21, 235-236.
40243	1881,0324.110	Economic.
40244	1881,0324.111	Contract for farming. Nbn 8/4/11.
40245	1881,0324.112	Promissory note for dates. Nbn 7/7/6. Babylon.
40246	1881,0324.113	Promissory note for silver. Nbn 15/10/-.
40247	1881,0324.114	Promissory note for dates. Nbn 9/1/-.
40248	1881,0324.115	School text; topographical.
40249	1881,0324.116	Lexical; syllabary.
40250	1881,0324.117	Contract. Nbn 7/6/-. Babylon.
40251	1881,0324.118	Economic.
40252	1881,0324.119	Contract; mentions URU É-1.d.AG-x-x; sealed. Dar II []/1/18. Babylon. Nisaba 28, no. 255.
40253	1881,0324.120	Lexical; gi.
40254	1881,0324.121	Astronomical?
40255	1881,0324.122	Astronomical; star list.
40256	1881,0324.123	Lexical.
40257	1881,0324.124	Incantation.
40258	1881,0324.125	Economic.
40259	1881,0324.126	Economic. Babylon
40260	1881,0324.127	Economic.
40261	1881,0324.128	Sale of a bed. 24/[]/14.
40262	1881,0324.129	Economic. 10/7/-.
40263	1881,0324.130	Court record; sealed. [Nbn]. [Babylon]. Wunsch, AfO 44/45, 94, no. 25; Nisaba 28, no. 27.
40264	1881,0324.131	Economic.
40265	1881,0324.132	Memorandum.
40266	1881,0324.133	Receipt for onions.
40267	1881,0324.134	Economic.
40268	1881,0324.135	Receipt of silver for the rations of brewers; sealed by Bulluṭ. Philip []/10/1. (Borsippa). Nisaba 28, no. 440.
40269	1881,0324.136	Economic.
40270	1881,0324.137	Astronomical?
40271	1881,0324.138	Promissory note for dates. -/5/-.
40272	1881,0324.139	Economic.
40273	1881,0324.140	Ledger.

40274	1881,0324.141	Promissory note for dates. Nbn 16/6/-. Babylon.
40275	1881,0324.142	Economic. Dar -/ 6/33.
40276	1881,0324.143	Economic.
40277	1881,0324.144	Astronomical; lunar six table. Huber and Steele, SCIAMVS 8 (2007) 3-36, text O.
40278	1881,0324.145	Incantation.
40279	1881,0324.146	Economic. 30/[]/12. Babylon.
40280	1881,0324.147	Astronomical?
40281	1881,0324.148	Unidentified; two columns.
40282	1881,0324.149	Astronomical?
40283	1881,0324.150	Unidentified.
40284	1881,0324.151	Unidentified.
40285	1881,0324.152	Medical; TDP tablet IV.
40286	1881,0324.153	Physiognomic omens. (+) 40190.
40287	1881,0324.154	Economic. 12/-/-.
40288	1881,0324.155	Lexical; syllabary.
40289	1881,0324.156	Economic.
40290	1881,0324.157	Unidentified.
40291	1881,0324.158	Economic.
40292	1881,0324.159	Omens; Iqqur īpuš, Ayyaru. + 40334.
40293	1881,0324.160	Incantation.
40294	1881,0324.161	Incantation.
40295	1881,0324.162	Ritual.
40296	1881,0324.163	Economic.
40297	1881,0324.164	Economic.
40298	1881,0324.165	Bilingual incantation.
40299	1881,0324.166	Ritual. + 40327 + unnum.
40300	1881,0324.167	Economic. Babylon.
40301	1881,0324.168	Bilingual incantation.
40302	1881,0324.169	Economic. Cam -/-/2.
40302a	1881,0324.169a	Unidentified; Marked T.I.
40303	1881,0324.170	Incantation; lines end MU.NE.
40304	1881,0324.171	Promissory note for barley.
40305	1881,0324.172	Economic. Nbk -/6/-.
40306	1881,0324.173	Promissory note for silver. Dar 18/4/2. Babylon.
40307	1881,0324.174	Unidentified.
40308	1881,0324.175	Omens; terrestrial. + 40324.
40309	1881,0324.176	Unidentified.
40310	1881,0324.177	Bilingual incantation; cf. CT 17, 3:23-26
40311	1881,0324.178	Unidentified.
40312	1881,0324.179	Bilingual incantation.
40313	1881,0324.180	Astronomical?
40314	1881,0324.181	Unidentified.
40315	1881,0324.182	Joined to 40182.
40316	1881,0324.183	Joined to 40182.

40317	1881,0324.184	Joined to 40182.
40318	1881,0324.185	Unidentified.
40319	1881,0324.186	Promissory note for silver. Nbn -/5/-. Babylon.
40320	1881,0324.187	Economic.
40321	1881,0324.188	Incantation.
40322	1881,0324.189	Economic.
40323	1881,0324.190	Sumerian literary.
40324	1881,0324.191	Joined to 40308.
40325	1881,0324.192	Promissory note for silver. Babylon.
40326	1881,0324.193	Joined to 40182.
40327	1881,0324.194	Joined to 40299.
40328	1881,0324.195	Incantation.
40329	1881,0324.196	Economic.
40330	1881,0324.197	Joined to 40182.
40331	1881,0324.198	Joined to 40155.
40332	1881,0324.199	Incantation.
40333	1881,0324.200	Joined to 40183.
40334	1881,0324.201	Joined to 40292.
40335	1881,0324.202	Omens; terrestrial.
40336	1881,0324.203	Unidentified.
40337	1881,0324.204	Joined to 40227.
40338	1881,0324.205	Astronomical Diary or related text.
40339	1881,0324.206	Astronomical?
40340	1881,0324.207	Incantation.
40341	1881,0324.208	Incantation.
40342	1881,0324.209	Incantation.
40343	1881,0324.210	Economic. Ner -/ 1/-.
40344	1881,0324.211	Contract. Art 22/[]/[].
40345	1881,0324.212	Lexical.
40346	1881,0324.213	Promissory note for silver. Cam.
40347	1881,0324.214	Promissory note for silver.
40348	1881,0324.215	Field sale.
40349	1881,0324.216	Medical.
40350	1881,0324.217	Lexical, commentary on Aa.
40351	1881,0324.218	Ritual.
40352	1881,0324.219	Joined to 40183.
40353	1881,0324.220	Bilingual incantation.
40354	1881,0324.221	Unidentified.
40355	1881,0324.222	Bilingual incantation.
40356	1881,0324.223	Lexical; stones. + 44159. Schuster-Brandis, AOAT 46, p. 487 (44159 only).
40357	1881,0324.224	Incantation.
40358	1881,0324.225	Lexical.
40360	1881,0324.227	Incantation.
40361	1881,0324.228	Lexical; Ea; sign list.

40362	1881,0324.229	Astronomical?
40363	1881,0324.230	Medical; TDP.
40364	1881,0324.231	Economic.
40365	1881,0324.232	Medical.
40366	1881,0324.233	Omens; Iqqur īpuš, Ayyaru.
40367	1881,0324.234	Promissory note for silver. Nbn -/1/1. Babylon.
40368	1881,0324.235	Economic. Dar 25/[]/30+. Babylon.
40369	1881,0324.236	Promissory note for silver. Nbk 8/[]/21.
40370	1881,0324.237	Promissory note for dates. Nbn.
40371	1881,0324.238	Promissory note for dates. Nbn 19/5/-.
40372	1881,0324.239	Promissory note for dates. Nabû-[] -/1/-.
40373	1881,0324.240	Economic.
40374	1881,0324.241	Promissory note for silver. Nbn -/1/-.
40375	1881,0324.242	Lexical; syllabary.
40376	1881,0324.243	Contract.
40377	1881,0324.244	Contract; sealed; finger-nail marks. Art. Babylon. Nisaba 28, no. 239.
40378	1881,0324.245	Astronomical?
40379	1881,0324.246	Incantations; Maqlu II. Abusch, AMD 10, 51-77.
40380	1881,0324.247	Medical; a-ḫa-an GIG.
40381	1881,0324.248	Promissory note for silver. 11/-/-.
40382	1881,0324.249	Lexical; stones.
40383	1881,0324.250	Lexical; stones.
40384	1881,0324.251	Astronomical?
40385	1881,0324.252	Unidentified.
40386	1881,0324.253	Account of tax payments.
40387	1881,0324.254	Maqlu tablet IX (ritual tablet). Schwemer, JCS 63, 108-109; Abusch, AMD 10, 205-225.
40388	1881,0324.255	Economic. Nbk 13/8/-.
40389	1881,0324.256	Omens.
40390	1881,0324.257	Medical omens.
40391	1881,0324.258	Unidentified.
40392	1881,0324.259	Lexical; stones.
40393	1881,0324.260	Medical.
40394	1881,0324.261	Economic.
40395	1881,0324.262	Promissory note for dates.
40396	1881,0324.263	Unidentified.
40397	1881,0324.264	Commentary on Venus omens.
40398	1881,0324.265	Astrological omens.
40399	1881,0324.266	Bilingual incantation.
40400	1881,0324.267	Lexical; plants.
40401	1881,0324.268	Incantation.
40402	1881,0324.269	Economic. Nbn 9/8/-.
40403	1881,0324.270	Incantation.
40404	1881,0324.271	Unidentified.

40405	1881,0324.272	Promissory note for dates.
40406	1881,0324.273	School text; literary; lexical. []/1/-.
40407	1881,0324.274	Literary; list of ikkibs (taboos).
40408	1881,0324.275	Unidentified.
40409	1881,0324.276	Lexical?
40410	1881,0324.277	Lexical; colophon.
40411	1881,0324.278	Economic.
40412	1881,0324.279	Unidentified.
40413	1881,0324.280	Astronomical?
40414	1881,0324.281	Economic.
40415	1881,0324.282	Unidentified.
40416	1881,0324.283	Literary; colophon.
40417	1881,0324.284	Astronomical?
40418	1881,0324.285	Lexical; giš.
40419	1881,0324.286	Astronomical?
40420	1881,0324.287	Economic.
40421	1881,0324.288	Economic.
40422	1881,0324.289	Unidentified.
40423	1881,0324.290	Economic.
40424	1881,0324.291	Lexical; giš.
40425	1881,0324.292	School text; practice wedges.
40426	1881,0324.293	Lexical.
40427	1881,0324.294	Lexical; ì (oil).
40428	1881,0324.295	Unidentified.
40429	1881,0324.296	Ritual.
40430	1881,0324.297	Unidentified.
40431	1881,0324.298	Incantation.
40432	1881,0324.299	Unidentified; two columns.
40433	1881,0324.300	Late Babylonian copy of an Old Babylonian? inscription.
40434	1881,0324.301	Joined to 40182.
40435	1881,0324.302	Sumerian literary.
40436	1881,0324.303	Astronomical Diary?
40437	1881,0324.304	Late Babylonian copy of an Old Babylonian? inscription.
40438	1881,0324.305	Joined to 40146.
40439	1881,0324.306	Literary.
40440	1881,0324.307	Lexical; plants.
40441	1881,0324.308	Lexical.
40442	1881,0324.309	Unidentified.
40443	1881,0324.310	Joined to 40183.
40444	1881,0324.311	Joined to 40183.
40445	1881,0324.312	Lexical. + 40460.
40446	1881,0324.313	Lexical; Ea; sign list.
40447	1881,0324.314	Lexical; Ea; sign list.

40448	1881,0324.315	Lexical; Ea; sign list.
40449	1881,0324.316	Lexical; Ea; sign list; personal names.
40450	1881,0324.317	Lexical; Ea; sign list.
40451	1881,0324.318	Lexical; Ea; sign list.
40452	1881,0324.319	Lexical; syllabary.
40453	1881,0324.320	Unidentified.
40454	1881,0324.321	Lexical; Ea; sign list.
40455	1881,0324.322	Lexical; Ea; sign list.
40456	1881,0324.323	Lexical; Ea; sign list.
40457	1881,0324.324	Lexical; Ea; sign list.
40458	1881,0324.325	Lexical and literary extracts.
40459	1881,0324.326	Lexical; Ea; sign list; literary extracts; colophon.
40460	1881,0324.327	Joined to 40445.
40461	1881,0324.328	Lexical (so register); now missing.
	1881,0324.329ff.	Nos. 329-366 are uninscribed items except as listed below.
117873	1881,0324.350	Incantation bowl. Segal, Incantation Bowls, no. 130P, pl. 147.
117869	1881,0324.351	Incantation bowl. Segal, Incantation Bowls, no. 071A, pl. 75
	1881,0324.354	Fragment of stone with cuneiform inscription.
90864	1881,0324.367	Stele of Ashurbanipal; previously numbered 12110. Lehmann-Haupt, AB 8, 14-19, pls. 17-22; Streck, VAB 7/1, p. xlv, and 7/2, 244-249; Frame, RIMB 2.6.32.2.1.
90827	1881,0324.368	Boundary-stone (kudurru) recording ownership of land. Melišipak. King, BBSt, pp. 7-18, pls. V-XXII, no. III.

1881,0428 collection

The 1881,0428 collection comes from the excavations of Hormuzd Rassam. See J. E. Reade in CBTBM VI pp. xxx-xxxi. The register gives the provenance

as Abu Habbah for nos. 3a, 22, 34a, 74, 100, 118b, 124-128, 656, 683, 1085,
as Babylon (B.N.) for nos. 1-3, 4-21, 24-32, 35b, 36-67,
as Babylon (B.N.?) for nos. 23, 101-118a, 119-123,
as Babylon for nos. 68-73, 75-78, 80-96, 98-99, 131, 756-1084,
as Babylon or Abu-Habbah for no. 79,
as Babylon Birs Nimroud for no. 97,
as Birs Nimroud for nos. 129-130, 132-134, 136-165,
as Birs Nimroud or Babylon for no. 135,
as Borsippa for no. 1086,
as Jimjima for nos. 166-286, 288-530,
as Omran for nos. 287, 531-655, 657-682, 684-755,
and gives no provenance for nos. 4a, 33, 34b, 35a.

40462	1881,0428.1	Letter order from Bulluṭ; sealed. Antig -/7/5. (Borsippa). CT 49, 10, no. 43; Nisaba 28, no. 452.
40463	1881,0428.2	Receipt of barley; sealed. Alex IV 4/3/6. CT 49, 4, no. 19; Strassmaier, ZA 3, 150, no. 12; Nisaba 28, no. 516.
40464	1881,0428.3	Letter order from Nabû-kuṣuršu; sealed. Alex IV 15/5/6. (Borsippa). CT 49, 5, no. 22; Nisaba 28, no. 475.
91140	1881,0428.3a	Cylinder; inscription of Nabonidus. Sippar. 5R, 65; Berger, AOAT 4/1, Nabonid Zylinder II, 9, no. 1; Walker and Collon, Tell ed-Dēr 3, 94-95; Schaudig, AOAT 256, 384-394.
	1881,0428.4a	Cylinder; inscription of Nabonidus. Presented to the Sultan in 1882, and now in Istanbul. Sippar. 5R, 65; Berger, AOAT 4/1, Nabonid Zylinder II, 9, no. 2; Sollberger, JEOL 20, 53 n. 22; Walker and Collon, Tell ed-Dēr 3, 94; Schaudig, AOAT 256, 384-394.
40465	1881,0428.4	Letter order from Bulluṭ; sealed. Antig 18/7/4. (Borsippa). CT 49, 8, no. 33; Nisaba 28, no. 444.
40466	1881,0428.5	Letter order from Bulluṭ; sealed. Antig 4/10/5. CT 49, 9, no. 42; Nisaba 28, no. 451
40467	1881,0428.6	Letter from Nabû-kuṣuršu; sealed. n.d. CT 49, 14, no. 73; Nisaba 28, no. 490.
40468	1881,0428.7	Receipt for silver; sealed. Alex IV 4/6/6. (Borsippa). CT 49, 5, no. 21; Nisaba 28, no. 517.
40469	1881,0428.8	Omens; Šumma ālu, tablet 21; colophon. CT 38, 30-31; Freedman, If a city, vol. 1, 307, 329.
40470	1881,0428.9	Lexical; ṭup abni.
40471	1881,0428.10	Field sale; sealed; finger-nail marks. Dar I 21/11/25 Babylon. Nisaba 28, no. 134.
40472	1881,0428.11	Field sale. Esarhaddon 11/8/-.
40473	1881,0428.12	Economic.
40474	1881,0428.13	Prayer to Marduk for release from prison; colophon: scribe Nabû-šum-ukīn / Nebuchadnezzar. Finkel in Renger, Babylon, 323-342 (giving wrong registration 81-4-28, 9 on p. 324 and wrong number 40475 on pp. 339-342); Oshima, BPM, 95-96, P 16 (giving wrong number 40475).
40475	1881,0428.14	Astrological omens; eclipses and planets; unusual type; colophon; cf. 30336, 30432, etc.
40476	1881,0428.15	Economic.
40477	1881,0428.16	Promissory note for dates. -/-/16.
40478	1881,0428.17	Ledger.
40479	1881,0428.18	Ritual.
40480	1881,0428.19	Tintir IV; colophon. George, BTT, pl. 12.

40481	1881,0428.20	Lexical; Ḫḫ XXI. MSL 11, 10.
40482	1881,0428.21	Incantation and ritual, partly duplicating Ebeling, LKA 135 (to recapture a runaway slave); colophon. Babylon. + 40535 + 41299.
40483	1881,0428.22	Cylinder; inscription of Nebuchadnezzar II; no. 14 i 1-4.
40484	1881,0428.23	Court record?
40485	1881,0428.24	Lexical; synonym list or commentary in vocabulary form.
40486	1881,0428.25	Medical. + 40784 (+) 40843.
40487	1881,0428.26	Lexical; syllabary. CT 11, 11.
40488	1881,0428.27	Medical; two columns.
40489	1881,0428.28	Lexical; Malku I. + 40782 CT 18, 27 (40782 only).
40490	1881,0428.29	Astronomical; procedure or Vorläufer; begins a-na tar-ṣi ša ... Rev. unfinished; left edge almost complete; defaced.
40491	1881,0428.30	Lexical; Ḫḫ XIX. + 40724 MSL 10, 127.
40492	1881,0428.31	Contract; sealed. Art II/III ? []/3/4. Babylon. Mitchell and Searight, no. 482; Nisaba 28, no. 260.
40493	1881,0428.32	Astronomical; lunar data for SE 27 and 28 (284/3 BC). LBAT 1431a; Hunger and Sachs, ADART V, no. 37.
91002	1881,0428.33	Clay cover for the "Sun-God tablet" of Nabû-apla-iddina, with inscription of Nabopolassar; also numbered 12137b. A modern cast of the inscription on the back of this cover is numbered 91003. For the older original cast see 91001 (1881,0701.3422). Sippar. King, BBSt, 120-129 and pls. C-CI, no. XXXVI; Berger, AOAT 4/1, p. 144; Walker and Collon, Tell ed-Dēr 3, 102-103, no. 62.
91000	1881,0428.34a	The "Sun-god tablet" of Nabû-apla-iddina; also numbered 12137; see also 91001 (1881,0701.3422), 91002 and 91004. Sippar. King, BBSt, 120-129 and pls. XCVIII-XCIX, no. XXXVI; Walker and Collon, Tell ed-Dēr 3, 102-103, no. 60.
91004	1881,0428.34b	Clay box for the "Sun-god tablet" of Nabû-apla-iddina; also numbered 12137d. Sippar. King, BBSt, 120-129 and pls. CI-CII, no. XXXVI; Walker and Collon, Tell ed-Dēr 3, 102-103, no. 63.
40494a	1881,0428.35a	Upper part of a boundary-stone with divine symbols in relief. MB? Paulus, AOAT 51, 879, OI 43; Reade, ARRIM 9, 47.
40494b	1881,0428.35b	Field sale.
40495	1881,0428.36	Promissory note for dates. Xerxes 25/12/12.

40496	1881,0428.37	Astronomical; Almanac for SE 242. Hunger and Sachs, ADART VII, no. 195.
40497	1881,0428.38	Medical.
40498	1881,0428.39	Promissory note for silver; sealed. Art II/III ? []/[]/4. URU Maškattu. Mitchell and Searight, no. 505; Nisaba 28, no. 261.
40499	1881,0428.40	Medical; stones.
40500	1881,0428.41	Unidentified.
40501	1881,0428.42	Lexical; plants; medical. + 40809 + 41302 + 41371.
40502	1881,0428.43	Memorandum, mentions day 2 month Abu. Npl -/-/1
40503	1881,0428.44	Promissory note for silver. Nbk 2/12/16. Babylon.
40504	1881,0428.45	Memorandum about wool. -/-/28.
40505	1881,0428.46	Legal declaration. Kandalanu 22?/12/13. Babylon. Brinkman and Kennedy, JCS 35, 44, L.75.
40506	1881,0428.47	Legal declaration. Dar 23/[]/24.
40507	1881,0428.48	Apprenticeship contract. Dar 7/10/7.
40508	1881,0428.49	Note about silver. Nbk 27/1/35.
40509	1881,0428.50	Promissory note for silver. Dar 13/2/-.
40510	1881,0428.51	Contract about real estate. Nbk 26/5/38. Babylon.
40511	1881,0428.52	Bilingual incantation; dupl. CT 17, 23.
40512	1881,0428.53	Account of disbursements.
40513	1881,0428.54	Medical; mentions stones. Schuster-Brandis, AOAT 46, p. 127, Kette 105, 106, 107.
40514	1881,0428.55	Ritual and incantation; dug-a-gub-ba. + 40770.
40515	1881,0428.56	Promissory note for dates. Nbn 15/6/15. Alu-ša-itbarāti.
40516	1881,0428.57	Medical; colophon.
40517	1881,0428.58	Literary; Šu'illa?
40518	1881,0428.59	Historical? Mentions URU Ḫa-ri-... and Ur.
40519	1881,0428.60	Contract. Nbn 20/12/12. Babylon.
40520	1881,0428.61	Contract; sealed. d.l. Nisaba 28, no. 641.
40521	1881,0428.62	Promissory note for silver. Dar 7/2/8. Babylon.
40522	1881,0428.63	Incantation; kima immeri liṭbuḫu.
40523	1881,0428.64	Contract; transfer of property. Nbk. Babylon. Wunsch, Bab Arch 2, no. 13.
40524	1881,0428.65	Promissory note for silver. Dar 18/2/11. Babylon.
40525	1881,0428.66	Letter from Mušēzibtu to Balāssu. CT 22, 41, no. 224; Hackl et al., AOAT 414/1, no. 99.
40526	1881,0428.67	Bilingual incantation.
40527	1881,0428.68	Letter from Šamaš-[] and Sîn-aḫu-[] to Bēl-ibni. CT 22, 39, no. 313; Hackl et al., AOAT 414/1, no. 100.
40528	1881,0428.69	Letter.
40529	1881,0428.70	Receipt for sale of a field. Nbk 6/[]/26.
40530	1881,0428.71	Memorandum; mentions 12/xi/36.
40531	1881,0428.72	Sumerian incantation.

40532	1881,0428.73	Cylinder; Nabonidus. Sippar. + 40581 + 40582 + 40583 + 41109 + 41136. See Da Riva, GMTR 4, 126, 155.
40533	1881,0428.74	Historical? Mentions 10 DANNA qaqqaru; māt Aššur; copy (ḫepi).
40534	1881,0428.75	Unidentified.
40535	1881,0428.76	Joined to 40482.
40536	1881,0428.77	Sumerian literary.
40537	1881,0428.78	Economic.
40538	1881,0428.79	Promissory note for silver. Nbk 8+/[]/31. Sippar.
40538a	1881,0428.80	Lexical; Ea; sign list.
40539	1881,0428.81	Lexical; god-list.
40540	1881,0428.82	Unidentified.
40541	1881,0428.83	Contract; sale of a house. Nbk 25/1/15. Borsippa. Zadok, Nisaba 21, 236.
40542	1881,0428.84	Promissory note for silver. Kandalanu 19/12/[]. Babylon. Brinkman and Kennedy, JCS 35, 51, L.185.
40543	1881,0428.85	Contract; sale of a girl. Xerxes []/4/[]. Babylon.
40544	1881,0428.86	Hemerology.
40545	1881,0428.87	Medical; mentions stones.
40546	1881,0428.88	Contract for sale of cows by Aia to Iški-idiri; mentions governor of URU ki-di-iṣ (Kadesh). Nbk 22/4/40. Ṣūru. Wiseman, Chronicles, 31 n. 6; Pinches, Records of the Past, NS 4, 99-101; Pinches, JTVI 49 (1917) 128-130.
40547	1881,0428.89	Receipt for a jenny; dupl. 40556. Dar 4/12/34. Babylon. Weszeli, WZKM 86, 468-469 and 478; Weszeli and Baker, WZKM 87, 231-236 and 244; Bertin 2754.
40548	1881,0428.90	Land sale; finger-nail marks. Eriba-Marduk 15/3/9. Babylon. Brinkman and Kennedy, JCS 35, 63, AD.1; Brinkman, Fs Sjöberg, 37-47; Paulus, AOAT 51, 680-682, EM-RU 1.
40549	1881,0428.91	Contract about real estate; finger-nail marks.
40550	1881,0428.92	Promissory note for silver; sealed. Dar II/III []+4/[]/2. Babylon. Nisaba 28, no. 242.
40551	1881,0428.93	Promissory note for silver. Dar 2/2/35. Babylon.
40552	1881,0428.94	Medical.
40553	1881,0428.95	Field sale. Nbk 24/[]/24. Babylon.
40554	1881,0428.96	Receipt for house rent; sealed. Art II 22/6/33. Babylon. Nisaba 28, no. 290.
40555	1881,0428.97	Promissory note for barley. Ner 26/12?/3. Babylon.
40556	1881,0428.98	Receipt for a jenny; dupl. 40547. Dar 5/12/34. Babylon. Weszeli, WZKM 86, 468-469 and 477; Weszeli and Baker, WZKM 87, 236-237; Bertin 2754.
40557	1881,0428.99	Promissory note for silver. Dar 1/3/-.

40558	1881,0428.100	Old Babylonian. Year formula for Samsuiluna year 8; mu ki-lugal-gub ḫur-sag i7-didli-bi-ta. Sippar. Walker and Collon, Tell ed-Dēr 3, 95.
40559	1881,0428.101	Literary; Enūma eliš II. King, STC pl. XIV; Oshima, NABU 2003, 109-111, no. 99; Lambert, BCM, p. 62.
40560	1881,0428.102	Contract about real estate. Šamaš-šum-ukin 19/7/[]. Babylon. Brinkman and Kennedy, JCS 35, 13, B.5.
40561	1881,0428.103	Promissory note for dates. Dar 18/11/34?. Babylon.
40562	1881,0428.104	Receipt. Nbn -/-/6.
40563	1881,0428.105	Field sale.
40564	1881,0428.106	Unidentified.
40565	1881,0428.107	The Dynastic Chronicle. Finkel, JCS 32, 65-72, 76.
40566	1881,0428.108	Contract for a dowry. Babylon. Wunsch, Bab Arch 2, no. 12.
40567	1881,0428.109	Economic.
40568	1881,0428.110	Bilingual incantation and ritual against witchcraft. Geller, AfO 42/43, 247-248; Schwemer, Or NS 78, 58-66; Abusch and Schwemer, AMD 8/2 text 8.18 a, pl. 26.
40569	1881,0428.111	Contract. Nbn 21/11?/-.
40570	1881,0428.112	Promissory note for silver. Šamaš-šum-ukin 18/9/12. Borsippa. Brinkman and Kennedy, JCS 35, 29, K.57; Zadok, Nisaba 21, 236.
40571	1881,0428.113	Sale of fields. Nbn 9/7/16.
40572	1881,0428.114	Promissory note for silver. Ner 19/5/1. Babylon.
40573	1881,0428.115	Sale of a slave. Nbn 22/1/2. Babylon.
40574	1881,0428.116	Astronomical Diary for SE 140. LBAT 363; Sachs and Hunger, ADART II, no. -171 E.
40575	1881,0428.117	Sale of a field. Cam -/-/2.
40576	1881,0428.118a	Field sale.
91022	1881,0428.118b	Cruciform monument of Maništusu; also numbered 12164. Sippar. CT 32, 1-4; Sollberger, JEOL 20, 50-70; Walker and Collon, Tell ed-Dēr 3, 103, no. 65.
40577	1881,0428.119	Legal declaration. Šamaš-šum-ukin 30/5/20. Babylon. Brinkman and Kennedy, JCS 35, 36, K.143.
89567	1881,0428.120	Cylinder seal. Collon, CS V, p. 159, pl. XXV, no. 301.
89561	1881,0428.121	Cylinder seal.
40578	1881,0428.122	Cylinder; inscription of Nebuchadnezzar II; no. 23 ii 2-5, 19.
40579	1881,0428.123	Medical omens.
40580	1881,0428.124	Cylinder; inscription of Nebuchadnezzar II; no. 23 ii 2-5.
40581	1881,0428.125	Joined to 40532.
40582	1881,0428.126	Joined to 40532.
40583	1881,0428.127	Joined to 40532.

40584	1881,0428.128	Promissory note for dates. Dar 3/[]/22.
40585	1881,0428.129	Letter order from Bulluṭ; sealed. Antig 13+/[]/5. (Borsippa). CT 49, 9, no. 38; Nisaba 28, no. 447.
40586	1881,0428.130	Letter order from Bulluṭ; sealed. Antig 5/9/5. (Borsippa). CT 49, 9, no. 40; Mitchell and Searight, no. 614; Nisaba 28, no. 449.
40586 a	1881,0428.131	Omens; extispicy. Fragment of a two column tablet with drawings of the entrails of a sheep.
40587	1881,0428.132	Letter order from Nabû-kuṣuršu; sealed. Antig 9/[]/6. (Borsippa). CT 49, 10, no. 45; Nisaba 28, no. 476.
40588	1881,0428.133	Letter order from Bulluṭ; sealed. Antig 4?/6/[]. (Borsippa). CT 49, 11, no. 51; Nisaba 28, no. 455.
40589	1881,0428.134	List of personal names.
40590	1881,0428.135	Fragment of a boundary stone; inscribed; recording a sale of land. Middle Babylonian. (+) 38646. King, BBSt, 90-95 and pl. 18, no. XXI; Seidl, Bagh Mitt 4, 65 G 15; Paulus, AOAT 51, 829-834, U 33; Reade, ARRIM 5, 48.
40591	1881,0428.136	Astronomical Diary for SE 2. LBAT 215; Sachs and Hunger, ADART I, no. -309.
40592	1881,0428.137	Astronomical; Enūma Anu Enlil 14; lengths of day and night watches; also re-registered as 139426 (1981,0101.1) when found unnumbered after firing. George and ar-Rawi, AfO 38-39, 52-73; Reiner, Fs Borger (CM 10), 298.
40593	1881,0428.138	Astronomical Diary. + 40614.
40594	1881,0428.139	Cylinder; inscription of Nebuchadnezzar II. Berger, AOAT 4/1, Nebukadnezar Zylinder-Fragment IV,1, no. 2.
40595	1881,0428.140	Astronomical Diary.
40596	1881,0428.141	Astronomical; Normal Star Almanac for SE 87. Hunger and Sachs, ADART VII, no. 25.
40597	1881,0428.142	Contract; lease(?); sealed; finger-nail marks. Alex IV []/9/6. Babylon. Nisaba 28, no. 340.
40598	1881,0428.143	Historical? mentions Darius.
40599	1881,0428.144	Astronomical Diary.
40600	1881,0428.145	Bilingual emesal prayer to Marduk. Dupl. Maul, Fs Borger (CM 10), 160-170.
40601	1881,0428.146	Field sale.
40602	1881,0428.147	Astronomical Diary.
40603	1881,0428.148	Medical(?).
40604	1881,0428.149	Astronomical; Normal Star Almanac for SE 179. Hunger and Sachs, ADART VII, no. 81.
40605	1881,0428.150	Astronomical?

40606	1881,0428.151	Astronomical; Goal Year Text; not datable. Hunger and Sachs, ADART VI, no. 152.
40607	1881,0428.152	Astronomical Diary.
40608	1881,0428.153	Astronomical.
40609	1881,0428.154	Astronomical Diary.
40610	1881,0428.155	Astronomical?
40611	1881,0428.156	Joined to 36004.
40612	1881,0428.157	Literary cylinder; hymn to Nabû; two columns.
40613	1881,0428.158	Astronomical; Normal Star Almanac. SE. Hunger and Sachs, ADART VII, no. 133.
40614	1881,0428.159	Joined to 40593.
40615	1881,0428.160	Astronomical?
40616	1881,0428.161	Astronomical Diary.
40617	1881,0428.162	Bilingual incantation.
40618	1881,0428.163	Pottery jar fragment with stamped impression; early Islamic.
40619	1881,0428.164	Astronomical; lunar ephemeris; System A, columns C'a, K1, M1, for SE 189. Steele, AHES 60 (2006) 123-135, text F.
40620	1881,0428.165	Astronomical; Saturn, oppositions, for SE 155 to 243; System B. (+) 34589 + 35745
40621	1881,0428.166	Ritual for the baru-priest and instruction with commentary; e-nu-ru; bīt mēseri II-III; prayer on upper edge.
40622	1881,0428.167	Astronomical Diary for SE 203. LBAT 469; Sachs and Hunger, ADART III, no. -108 B; Stephenson, HEER, 158-159.
40623	1881,0428.168	Historical-literary text; the Dynastic Prophecy. Grayson, BHLT, 24-37; van der Spek, AchHist 13, 311-324; Glassner, NABU 2016, 170-172, no. 105.
40624	1881,0428.169	Astrological omens; commentary.
40625	1881,0428.170	Astronomical; Normal Star Almanac for SE 105. LBAT 1011; Hunger and Sachs, ADART VII, no. 41.
40626	1881,0428.171	Astronomical; Normal Star Almanac for SE 68; two columns. Hunger and Sachs, ADART VII, no. 17.
40627	1881,0428.172	Astronomical Diary; historical references.
40628	1881,0428.173	Astronomical Diary for SE 112. LBAT 309; Sachs and Hunger, ADART II, no. -199 A.
40629	1881,0428.174	Literary.
40630	1881,0428.175	Bilingual incantation.
40631	1881,0428.176	Old Babylonian cone; historical inscription of Hammurabi, Akkadian version. Sippar. Frayne, RIME 4.3.6.12.7a.
40632	1881,0428.177	Unidentified

40633	1881,0428.178	Ritual and incantation against witchcraft addressed to Šamaš. Fincke, NABU 2018, 45-49, no. 28.
40634	1881,0428.179	Field sale; landscape format. RN lost (king of Babylon) 3/[]/6.
40635	1881,0428.180	Medical ritual.
40636	1881,0428.181	Astronomical?
40637	1881,0428.182	Lexical; god-list. + 40839.
40638	1881,0428.183	Astronomical?
40639	1881,0428.184	Bilingual incantation; late script.
40640	1881,0428.185	Unidentified.
40641	1881,0428.186	Lexical; Ea; sign list; literary extracts.
40642	1881,0428.187	Lexical.
40643	1881,0428.188	Medical.
40644	1881,0428.189	Astronomical?
40645	1881,0428.190	Commentary.
40646	1881,0428.191	Astronomical Diary.
40647	1881,0428.192	Ritual.
40648	1881,0428.193	Omens; physiognomic.
40649	1881,0428.194	Promissory note for dates.
40650	1881,0428.195	Astronomical?
40651	1881,0428.196	Lexical; god list.
40652	1881,0428.197	Astronomical Diary?; prices?
40653	1881,0428.198	Bilingual incantation; Udug-ḫul 4. Geller, BAM 8, 133-173, pl. 35.
40654	1881,0428.199	Omens; extispicy.
40655	1881,0428.200	Unidentified.
40656	1881,0428.201	Lexical; Ḫḫ IX. MSL 9, 181.
40657	1881,0428.202	Incantation to Šamaš. + 40686. Abusch and Schwemer, AMD 8/2 text A.4 d, pl. 88.
40658	1881,0428.203	Astronomical; Almanac. SE Arsaces. Hunger and Sachs, ADART VII, no. 225.
40659	1881,0428.204	Astronomical procedure text for Jupiter. Steele, JHA 34 (2003) 269-289; Steele, SCIAMVS 6 (2005), 33-51; Ossendrijver, BMAPT, no. 30.
40660	1881,0428.205	Literary cylinder.
40661	1881,0428.206	Astronomical procedure text for Jupiter. Steele, SCIAMVS 6 (2005), 33-51; Ossendrijver, BMAPT, no. 26; Ossendrijver, JNES 76, 231-247, text H.
40662	1881,0428.207	Astronomical Diary.
40663	1881,0428.208	Lexical, Lú = ša I. + 40670 + 40690. MSL 12, 92.
40664	1881,0428.209	Lexical; cf. 40685.
40665	1881,0428.210	Bilingual incantation.
40666	1881,0428.211	Unidentified.
40667	1881,0428.212	Hymn or prayer.
40668	1881,0428.213	Unidentified.

40669	1881,0428.214	School text; fragment from left edge.
40670	1881,0428.215	Joined to 40663.
40671	1881,0428.216	Ritual.
40672	1881,0428.217	Lexical; Ea; sign list.
40673	1881,0428.218	Medical.
40674	1881,0428.219	Astronomical Diary; eclipse.
40675	1881,0428.220	Bilingual incantation; Udug-ḫul 12 . + 40987. Geller, BAM 8, 399-433, pl. 95.
40676	1881,0428.221	Ritual.
40677	1881,0428.222	Astronomical; Normal Star Almanac for SE 166. Hunger and Sachs, ADART VII, no. 73.
40678	1881,0428.223	Astronomical Diary.
40679	1881,0428.224	Lexical; syllabary.
40680	1881,0428.225	Astrological; microzodiac table; diagram; partly duplicate to 56605; for the diagram cf. 33333B, 37171, 39198 and 47890. Heeßel, AOAT 43, 117 (and n. 106), 470.
40681	1881,0428.226	Promissory note for silver. Nbk 19/[]/18?
40682	1881,0428.227	Bilingual incantation.
40683	1881,0428.228	Unidentified.
40684	1881,0428.229	Medical incantation.
40685	1881,0428.230	Lexical; cf. 40664.
40686	1881,0428.231	Joined to 40657.
40687	1881,0428.232	Bilingual incantation. Schramm, GBAO 2, p. 91, text B16.
40688	1881,0428.233	Lexical.
40689	1881,0428.234	Contract.
40690	1881,0428.235	Joined to 40663.
40691	1881,0428.236	Hemerology: Babylonian Almanac.
40692	1881,0428.237	Astronomical; table for a planet
40693	1881,0428.238	Ritual.
40694	1881,0428.239	Astronomical; eclipse report or short Diary?
40695	1881,0428.240	Contract. Cam 18/-/-.
40696	1881,0428.241	Medical.
40697	1881,0428.242	Lexical; Ea; sign list.
40698	1881,0428.243	Account. Nbk 30/6/23. Ḫu-ṣu-šá-d.x-x-DÙ.
40699	1881,0428.244	Mathematical; metrological table. Steele, SCIAMVS 16 (2015) 75-90.
40700	1881,0428.245	Copy of a legal text; ḫe-pí eš-šú.
40701	1881,0428.246	Promissory note for silver. Art II 10/[]/31. Babylon.
40702	1881,0428.247	Promissory note for silver. Nabû-[] 4/[]/22.
40703	1881,0428.248	Contract; sealed. d.l. Nisaba 28, no. 620.
40704	1881,0428.249	Promissory note for silver. Cam 20/3/-.
40705	1881,0428.250	Contract.

40706	1881,0428.251	Promissory note for barley; mentions Nidintu; sealed. []/[]/5. Ḫursag-kalamma. Nisaba 28, no. 305.
40707	1881,0428.252	Lexical; Ea; sign list.
40708	1881,0428.253	School text; lexical; Ḫḫ XV. MSL 9, 5.
40709	1881,0428.254	Lexical; syllabary; literary extract.
40710	1881,0428.255	Contract. Dar -/12/-. Babylon.
40711	1881,0428.256	Bilingual incantation.
40712	1881,0428.257	Omens; extispicy?
40713	1881,0428.258	Oracle question (tamītu) to Šamaš and Adad. Lambert, BOQ, no. 2c, pl. 21.
40714	1881,0428.259	Promissory note for silver.
40715	1881,0428.260	Lexical.
40716	1881,0428.261	Prayer.
40717	1881,0428.262	Court record; dispute over inheritance; later copy (ḫepí); finger-nail marks; dupl. 78156. Tiglath-pileser III [25]/4/2. Babylon. Thureau-Dangin, RA 6, 37; Brinkman and Kennedy, JCS 35, 65, AJ.5; Leichty, Fs Reiner, 227-228.
40718	1881,0428.263	Contract.
40719	1881,0428.264	School text; lexical; god-list. 2/6/-.
40720	1881,0428.265	Lexical; Ḫḫ X. MSL 9, 188.
40721	1881,0428.266	Contract.
40722	1881,0428.267	Letter.
40723	1881,0428.268	List of names.
40724	1881,0428.269	Joined to 40491.
40725	1881,0428.270	Field sale.
40726	1881,0428.271	Incantations; Maqlu IV 29-37. Abusch, AMD 10, 113-129.
40727	1881,0428.272	Lexical; Malku I.
40728	1881,0428.273	Economic.
40729	1881,0428.274	Contract. -/2/-.
40730	1881,0428.275	Economic.
40731	1881,0428.276	Prayer.
40732	1881,0428.277	Lexical.
40733	1881,0428.278	Unidentified.
40734	1881,0428.279	Medical; stones; cf. 40875.
40735	1881,0428.280	Contract.
40736	1881,0428.281	Building ritual; emesal litanies. Dupl. Thureau-Dangin, RAcc, 44-47.
40737	1881,0428.282	Medical; prescriptions for eye diseases; colophon. Fincke, CM 37, 79-104.
40738	1881,0428.283	Account of barley.
40739	1881,0428.284	Lexical; Ḫḫ XXI. MSL 11, 9.
40740	1881,0428.285	Lexical; Ḫḫ XXI. MSL 11, 9.

40741	1881,0428.286	Sale of land in Šuppatu. []/[]/4. Babylon. Wunsch, CM 20A-B, no. 352.
40742	1881,0428.287	Account of income.
40743	1881,0428.288	Apprenticeship contract. Xerxes 5/11/4. Babylon. Hackl, AfO 52, 86-87, no. 8.
40744	1881,0428.289	Medical; TDP tablet III.
40745	1881,0428.290	Lexical, commentary on Aa III/2 = 17. MSL 14, 331 and pl. 11; Landsberger, Gs Speiser, 134.
40746	1881,0428.291	Contract. AM 30/4/1. Babylon
40747	1881,0428.292	Commentary on god-list.
40748	1881,0428.293	Lexical; Ḫḫ IV 303-307.
40749	1881,0428.294	Commentary on Šumma ālu.
40750	1881,0428.295	Omens.
40751	1881,0428.296	Contract; finger-nail marks with caption. Art 7/3/32+. [] Mār-bīti.
40752	1881,0428.297	Lexical; syllabary.
40753	1881,0428.298	Unidentified.
40754	1881,0428.299	Astronomical; lunar ephemeris; System A, for (at least) SE 180. + 44196. Aaboe, AIHS 25/97 (1975) 182-183, 204, 220-221 (40754 only); Steele, SCIAMVS 11 (2010), 211-239, text B.
40755	1881,0428.300	Ritual.
40756	1881,0428.301	School text; lexical, Lú list; metrological table, acrographic list; unidentified. Gesche, AOAT 275, 688.
40757	1881,0428.302	Ritual.
40758	1881,0428.303	Ritual.
40759	1881,0428.304	Omens; Šumma ālu; dupl. K.2372+. + 40780.
40760	1881,0428.305	Lexical; dupl. 5R 41,1.
40761	1881,0428.306	Astronomical Diary.
40762	1881,0428.307	Astronomical Diary or related text.
40763	1881,0428.308	Medical; copy. + 40775 (+) 40769+.
40764	1881,0428.309	Unidentified.
40765	1881,0428.310	Contract. 15/[]/15. Babylon.
40766	1881,0428.311	Incantation; dupl. Farber, Beschwörungsrituale, 57-58, ll. ca. 23-39.
40767	1881,0428.312	Lexical, commentary on Aa.
40768	1881,0428.313	Astrological; eclipses. Reiner, Fs Borger (CM 10), 298.
40769	1881,0428.314	Medical. + 41269 + 41310 (+) 40763 + 40775.
40770	1881,0428.315	Joined to 40514.
40771	1881,0428.316	Lexical; syllabary.
40772	1881,0428.317	Contract.
40773	1881,0428.318	Lexical.
40774	1881,0428.319	Nergal god-list; three columns. + 41255b+j+m + 41363.

40775	1881,0428.320	Joined to 40763.
40776	1881,0428.321	Lexical; syllabary.
40777	1881,0428.322	List of names.
40778	1881,0428.323	Field sale. -/-/25.
40779	1881,0428.324	Account of barley or grain.
40780	1881,0428.325	Joined to 40759.
40781	1881,0428.326	Lexical; syllabary.
40782	1881,0428.327	Joined to 40489.
40783	1881,0428.328	Cylinder; inscription of Nebuchadnezzar II. Berger, AOAT 4/1, Nebukadnezar Zylinder-Fragment IV,1, no. 5.
40784	1881,0428.329	Joined to 40486.
40785	1881,0428.330	Literary.
40786	1881,0428.331	Field sale. Art []/[]/10?
40787	1881,0428.332	Account of wool.
40788	1881,0428.333	Legal record of alternative dispute resolution proceedings; mentions an ērib bīti of Uraš. Nbn []/[]/1+. [Dilbat?]. + 40823. Sandowicz, dubsar 11, no. 4.
40789	1881,0428.334	Account of barley.
40790	1881,0428.335	Ritual for Esangila; two columns. Da Riva and Galetti, JCS 70, 189-227.
40791	1881,0428.336	Medical ritual.
40792	1881,0428.337	Omens; extispicy.
40793	1881,0428.338	Lexical; syllabary.
40794	1881,0428.339	Field sale.
40795	1881,0428.340	Literary; tamītu. + 40806 + 41256a.
40796	1881,0428.341	Account of disbursements.
40797	1881,0428.342	Lexical; syllabary.
40798	1881,0428.343	Omens; extispicy.
	1881,0428.344	Recorded by L. W. King as "Said to be lost by Mr Ready Ap(ril 18)96".
40799	1881,0428.345	Lexical.
40800	1881,0428.346	Lexical.
40801	1881,0428.347	Lexical; syllabary. CT 11, 12.
40802	1881,0428.348	Hymn to Ninurta; dupl. Gurney, STT 70 (Lambert, RA 53, 131-134) and 32467 + and 95480 and 113241.
40803	1881,0428.349	Lexical; syllabary.
40804	1881,0428.350	Ritual; mentions Annunaki and Ishtar.
40805	1881,0428.351	Bilingual incantation. + 40850 + 44195 + 44241. Lambert, MC 24, no. 224 (40805 only).
40806	1881,0428.352	Joined to 40795.
40807	1881,0428.353	Incantations, Bīt rimki III; colophon; sealed. Dar []/[]/14. Borger, JCS 21, 2; Nisaba 28, no. 217a.
40808	1881,0428.354	Account.
40809	1881,0428.355	Joined to 40501.

40810	1881,0428.356	Lexical; Ea; sign list.
40811	1881,0428.357	Medical.
40812	1881,0428.358	Account of wool.
40813	1881,0428.359	Esangila tablet. George, BTT, pl. 23.
40814	1881,0428.360	Literary extracts.
40815	1881,0428.361	List of personal names. + 1881,0428.367.
40816	1881,0428.362	Deposition.
40817	1881,0428.363	Lexical.
40818	1881,0428.364	Hymn (to Ninurta?).
40819	1881,0428.365	Lexical; Nabnītu VI (= D). MSL 16, 99.
40820	1881,0428.366	Account of barley. CT 49, 46, no. 176.
	1881,0428.367	Joined to 40815.
40821	1881,0428.368	Document about irrigation matters; reminiscent of MB Nippur; literary forms and expressions; mentions Patti-Enlil; chief character is Murānu; mentions horses; scribe Ninurta-MU son of Taddannu; small difficult script; colophon.
40822	1881,0428.369	Account of grain. Nbn 6/5 /17.
40823	1881,0428.370	Joined to 40788.
40824	1881,0428.371	Letter order from Nabû-kuṣuršu; sealed. Alex IV 25/6/6. (Borsippa). CT 49, 4, no. 18; Nisaba 28, no. 473.
40825	1881,0428.372	Letter order from Nabû-kuṣuršu; sealed. Alex IV -/-/6. (Borsippa). CT 49, 5, no. 20; Nisaba 28, no. 474.
40826	1881,0428.373	Contract; sale of cattle. Nbn 19/3/11. Borsippa. Zadok, Nisaba 21, 236.
40827	1881,0428.374	Contract; lease; mentions Artaxerxes; sealed. Art II 1/8/[]. Nisaba 28, no. 298.
40828	1881,0428.375	Memorandum; spherical, one line inscription: ... mār bīti son of Nabium-iqṣur … lišpuru.
40829	1881,0428.376	Kufic inscription.
40830	1881,0428.377	Kufic inscription.
40831	1881,0428.378	Contract. 9/[]/4.
40832	1881,0428.379	Unidentified.
40833	1881,0428.380	Lexical; Ea; sign list; literary extracts.
40834	1881,0428.381	List of names. (+) 40859.
40835	1881,0428.382	Late Babylonian copy of an earlier inscription.
40836	1881,0428.383	Account of dates or grain.
40837	1881,0428.384	Commentary; medical; Sa-gig IV.
40838	1881,0428.385	Economic.
40839	1881,0428.386	Joined to 40637.
40840	1881,0428.387	Account of wool payments.
40841	1881,0428.388	Lexical and personal names.
40842	1881,0428.389	Receipt for barley.
40843	1881,0428.390	Medical. (+) 40486 + 40784.

40844	1881,0428.391	Literary cylinder.
40845	1881,0428.392	Bilingual incantation.
40846	1881,0428.393	Bilingual incantation; balag to Enlil; cf. Cohen, Lamentations, p. 103-104.
40847	1881,0428.394	Unidentified.
40848	1881,0428.395	Lexical; Ea; sign list.
40849	1881,0428.396	Unidentified.
40850	1881,0428.397	Joined to 40805.
40851	1881,0428.398	Incantation.
40852	1881,0428.399	List of workmen; 50-ú šá PN.
40853	1881,0428.400	Account of purchases.
40854	1881,0428.401	Ritual for Esangila; two columns. + 41208. Da Riva and Galetti, JCS 70, 189-227.
40855	1881,0428.402	Lexical; catalogue of Nabnītu; dupl. 65529 (MSL XVI 12).
40856	1881,0428.403	Lexical.
40857	1881,0428.404	Medical omens; Sa-gig XIII? + 41180.
40858	1881,0428.405	Lexical; personal names.
40859	1881,0428.406	List of personal names. (+) 40834.
40860	1881,0428.407	Astronomical Diary for SE 226. Sachs and Hunger, ADART III, no. -85 A.
40861	1881,0428.408	Astronomical; Vorläufer; obv.: 6 ME 6 GE6 GAR-GAR-ma; rev.: x TA UD-NÁ-A ŠÚ ŠÚ.
40862	1881,0428.409	Contract; adoption? 11/7/2. Babylon.
40863	1881,0428.410	Astronomical Diary.
40864	1881,0428.411	Astronomical; Goal Year Text; not datable. Hunger and Sachs, ADART VI, no. 153.
40865	1881,0428.412	Joined to 32511.
40866	1881,0428.413	Astronomical; Goal Year Text for SE 158. + 41130 (+) 34932 (+) 132286. Hunger and Sachs, ADART VI, no. 45.
40867	1881,0428.414	Letter order from Nabû-kuṣuršu; sealed. No RN 16/11/6. (Borsippa). CT 49, 12, no. 57; Nisaba 28, no. 478.
40868	1881,0428.415	Letter order from Nabû-kuṣuršu; sealed. n.d. (Borsippa). CT 49, 13, no. 62; Nisaba 28, no. 480.
40869	1881,0428.416	Letter order from Nabû-kuṣuršu; sealed. n.d. (Borsippa). CT 49, 13, no. 61; Nisaba 28, no. 479.
40870	1881,0428.417	Receipt of silver. Alex IV []/[]/8. CT 49, 5, no. 23.
40871	1881,0428.418	Letter order from Nabû-kuṣuršu; sealed. n.d. (Borsippa). CT 49, 13, no. 63; Nisaba 28, no. 481.
40872	1881,0428.419	Account of barley.
40873	1881,0428.420	Receipt for barley. No RN 13/5/6. CT 49, 12, no. 58.
40874	1881,0428.421	Administrative. CT 49, 48, no. 183.

40875	1881,0428.422	Medical; magical? ingredients; mentions EN.GI. SAR6, scorpion, eye of fish; stone list; cf. 40734.
40876	1881,0428.423	Letter.
40877	1881,0428.424	Letter order order from Bēl-ibni to Nabû-kuṣuršu; sealed. [Alex IV?] []/[]/4+. (Borsippa). CT 49, 4, no. 14; Nisaba 28, no. 515.
40878	1881,0428.425	Letter order from Nabû-kuṣuršu; sealed. n.d. (Borsippa). CT 49, 13, no. 64; Nisaba 28, no. 482.
40879	1881,0428.426	Letter order from Bulluṭ; sealed. No RN 9/1/5. (Borsippa). CT 49, 12, no. 56; Nisaba 28, no. 458.
40880	1881,0428.427	Letter order from Nabû-kuṣuršu; sealed. n.d. (Borsippa). CT 49, 13, no. 66; Nisaba 28, no. 484.
40881	1881,0428.428	Letter order from Nabû-kuṣuršu; sealed. Antig []/9/6. (Borsippa). CT 49, 11, no. 49; Nisaba 28, no. 467.
40882	1881,0428.429	Receipt for silver; sealed. Antig 12/2/7. (Borsippa). CT 49, 11, no. 50; Mitchell and Searight, no. 625; Nisaba 28, no. 514.
40883	1881,0428.430	Receipt?; sealed. (Borsippa?). Nisaba 28, no. 522.
40884	1881,0428.431	Letter order from Nabû-kuṣuršu; sealed. n.d. (Borsippa). CT 49, 13, no. 65; Nisaba 28, no. 483.
40885	1881,0428.432	Letter order from Nabû-kuṣuršu; sealed. n.d. (Borsippa). CT 49, 15, no. 78; Nisaba 28, no. 470.
40886	1881,0428.433	Letter order from Nabû-kuṣuršu; sealed. n.d. (Borsippa). CT 49, 15, no. 79; Nisaba 28, no. 494.
40887	1881,0428.434	Receipt for wool; sealed. Antig 8/7/6. (Borsippa). CT 49, 10, no. 47; Nisaba 28, no. 454.
40888	1881,0428.435	Letter order from Nabû-kuṣuršu; sealed. n.d. (Borsippa). CT 49, 14, no. 71; Nisaba 28, no. 489.
40889	1881,0428.436	Letter order from Nabû-kuṣuršu; sealed. n.d. (Borsippa). CT 49, 14, no. 72; Nisaba 28, no. 469.
40890	1881,0428.437	Letter order from Bulluṭ; sealed. Antig []/[]/5. (Borsippa). CT 49, 9, no. 39; Nisaba 28, no. 448.
40891	1881,0428.438	Letter order from Nabû-kuṣuršu; sealed. No RN 26/11?/no year. (Borsippa). CT 49, 12, no. 54; Nisaba 28, no. 477.
40892	1881,0428.439	Letter order from Bulluṭ; sealed. RN lost 3/[]/[] (Borsippa). CT 49, 11, no. 53; Nisaba 28, no. 457.
40893	1881,0428.440	Letter order from Nabû-kuṣuršu; sealed. n.d. (Borsippa). CT 49, 15, no. 80; Nisaba 28, no. 495.
40894	1881,0428.441	Letter order. Alex IV 2+/3/7.
40895	1881,0428.442	Economic; fragment of a circular(?) tablet.
40896	1881,0428.443	Receipt or Letter order; sealed by Bulluṭ. n.d. (Borsippa). CT 49, 17, no. 100; Nisaba 28, no. 460.
40897	1881,0428.444	Incantation.

40898	1881,0428.445	Letter order from Bulluṭ; sealed. n.d. (Borsippa). CT 49, 17, no. 96; Mitchell and Searight, no. 629; Nisaba 28, no. 464.
40899	1881,0428.446	Letter order from Nabû-kuṣuršu; sealed. Antig -/-/6. (Borsippa). CT 49, 11, no. 48; Mitchell and Searight, no. 621; Nisaba 28, no. 466.
40900	1881,0428.447	Note about smiths (simug). Nbn 1/12/1.
40901	1881,0428.448	Letter order from Bulluṭ; Antigonus mentioned in line 6; sealed. Antig 30/[]/[]. (Borsippa). CT 49, 11, no. 52; Nisaba 28, no. 456.
40902	1881,0428.449	Letter order from Nabû-kuṣuršu; sealed. n.d. (Borsippa). CT 49, 14, no. 77; Nisaba 28, no. 493.
40903	1881,0428.450	Letter order from Nabû-kuṣuršu; sealed. n.d. (Borsippa). CT 49, 13, no. 68; Nisaba 28, no. 486.
40904	1881,0428.451	Letter order from Nabû-kuṣuršu; sealed. n.d. (Borsippa). CT 49, 16, no. 90; Nisaba 28, no. 504.
40905	1881,0428.452	Letter order from Nabû-kuṣuršu. n.d. CT 49, 14, no. 75.
40906	1881,0428.453	Letter from Nabû-apla-uṣur; sealed. n.d. Nisaba 28, no. 523
40907	1881,0428.454	Letter order from Nabû-kuṣuršu; sealed. n.d. (Borsippa). CT 49, 13, no. 69; Nisaba 28, no. 487.
40908	1881,0428.455	Letter order from Nabû-kuṣuršu; sealed. n.d. (Borsippa). CT 49, 15, no. 81; Nisaba 28, no. 496.
40909	1881,0428.456	Letter order from Nabû-kuṣuršu; sealed. n.d. (Borsippa). CT 49, 14, no. 70; Nisaba 28, no. 488.
40910	1881,0428.457	Letter order from Nabû-kuṣuršu; sealed. n.d. (Borsippa). CT 49, 14, no. 76; Nisaba 28, no. 492.
40911	1881,0428.458	Letter order from Nabû-kuṣuršu; sealed. n.d. (Borsippa). CT 49, 14, no. 74; Nisaba 28, no. 491.
40912	1881,0428.459	Letter order from Nabû-kuṣuršu; sealed. n.d. (Borsippa). CT 49, 15, no. 83; Nisaba 28, no. 498.
40913	1881,0428.460	Letter order from Nabû-kuṣuršu; sealed. n.d. (Borsippa). CT 49, 15, no. 82; Nisaba 28, no. 497.
40914	1881,0428.461	Letter order from Nabû-kuṣuršu; sealed. n.d. (Borsippa). CT 49, 13, no. 67; Nisaba 28, no. 485.
40915	1881,0428.462	Economic; upper left corner.
40916	1881,0428.463	Memorandum.
40917	1881,0428.464	Letter order or receipt. CT 49, 16, no. 88.
40918	1881,0428.465	Letter order from Nabû-kuṣuršu; sealed. n.d. (Borsippa). CT 49, 16, no. 87; Nisaba 28, no. 502.
40919	1881,0428.466	Letter order from Bulluṭ; sealed. RN lost 14+/[]/6. (Borsippa). CT 49, 12, no. 60; Mitchell and Searight, no. 622; Nisaba 28, no. 459.
40920	1881,0428.467	Note about 18 shekels of silver.

40921	1881,0428.468	Receipt; sealed. Alex IV. (Borsippa?). CT 49, 6, no. 28; Nisaba 28, no. 520.
40922	1881,0428.469	Letter order from Nabû-kuṣuršu; sealed. n.d. (Borsippa). CT 49, 16, no. 92; Nisaba 28, no. 506.
40923	1881,0428.470	Letter order or receipt. CT 49, 17, no. 99.
40924	1881,0428.471	Letter order from Nabû-kuṣuršu; sealed. n.d. (Borsippa). CT 49, 16, no. 94; Nisaba 28, no. 508.
40925	1881,0428.472	Economic; upper right corner.
40926	1881,0428.473	Receipt for barley; sealed by Nabû-kuṣuršu. n.d. (Borsippa). CT 49, 17, no. 95; Nisaba 28, no. 524.
40927	1881,0428.474	Letter order from Nabû-kuṣuršu; sealed. n.d. (Borsippa). CT 49, 16, no. 93; Nisaba 28, no. 507.
40928	1881,0428.475	Letter order from Nabû-kuṣuršu; sealed. n.d. (Borsippa). CT 49, 15, no. 84; Nisaba 28, no. 499.
40929	1881,0428.476	Letter order from Nabû-kuṣuršu; sealed. n.d. (Borsippa). CT 49, 16, no. 89; Nisaba 28, no. 503.
40930	1881,0428.477	Letter order from Nabû-kuṣuršu; sealed. n.d. (Borsippa). CT 49, 15, no. 86; Nisaba 28, no. 501.
40931	1881,0428.478	Letter order from Nabû-kuṣuršu; sealed. n.d. (Borsippa). CT 49, 15, no. 85; Nisaba 28, no. 500.
40932	1881,0428.479	Letter order from Nabû-kuṣuršu; sealed. RN lost []/[]/5. (Borsippa). CT 49, 12, no. 55; Nisaba 28, no. 468.
40933	1881,0428.480	Lexical; Ea; sign list.
40934	1881,0428.481	Memorandum.
40935	1881,0428.482	Astronomical?
40936	1881,0428.483	Bilingual incantation.
40937	1881,0428.484	Lexical; Ea IV. MSL 14, 354.
40938	1881,0428.485	Bilingual incantation.
40939	1881,0428.486	Commentary.
40940	1881,0428.487	Economic.
40941	1881,0428.488	Lexical; Ea; sign list.
40942	1881,0428.489	Contract; obv. Illegible. Antig []/[]/3?
40943	1881,0428.490	Mathematical; problem text about bricks; fragment.
40944	1881,0428.491	Promissory note for barley.
40945	1881,0428.492	Economic.
40946	1881,0428.493	Lexical; Ea; sign list.
40947	1881,0428.494	Contract.
40948	1881,0428.495	Field sale.
40949	1881,0428.496	Lexical.
40950	1881,0428.497	Lexical; syllabary.
40951	1881,0428.498	Promissory note for silver.
40952	1881,0428.499	List of witnesses.
40953	1881,0428.500	Contract; sale of orchards, fields, and meadows.
40954	1881,0428.501	Unidentified.

40955	1881,0428.502	Old Babylonian; ration list.
40956	1881,0428.503	Contract.
40957	1881,0428.504	Contract; sealed; prayer on upper edge. Art II/III []/[]/9+. Nisaba 28, no. 270.
40958	1881,0428.505	Astronomical; lunar ephemeris; System A.
40959	1881,0428.506	Astrological; commentary. King, STC I, 215-216.
40960	1881,0428.507	Prayer; line 2: ina za-ba-li-ia.
40961	1881,0428.508	Astronomical?
40962	1881,0428.509	Lexical; sign list.
40963	1881,0428.510	Contract; witnesses.
40964	1881,0428.511	Promissory note for dates; sealed. d.l. Nisaba 28, no. 306.
40965	1881,0428.512	Medical.
40966	1881,0428.513	Promissory note for onions.
40967	1881,0428.514	Sumerian literary; cf. 40970 + 40974.
40968	1881,0428.515	Account of dates.
40969	1881,0428.516	List of measures and personal names.
40970	1881,0428.517	Bilingual incantation; liḫalliqu; cf. 40967. + 40974.
40971	1881,0428.518	Sumerian literary .
40972	1881,0428.519	Economic.
40973	1881,0428.520	Sealing, inscribed NÍG.GA [...], and sealed.
40974	1881,0428.521	Joined to 40970.
40975	1881,0428.522	Hymn to a god.
40976	1881,0428.523	Promissory note for silver.
40977	1881,0428.524	Account of months and sums of money.
40978	1881,0428.525	Commentary; literary, Theodicy.
40979	1881,0428.526	Literary; mentions māt Aššur.KI.
40980	1881,0428.527	Personal names.
40981	1881,0428.528	Unidentified.
40982	1881,0428.529	Contract.
40983	1881,0428.530	Unidentified.
40984	1881,0428.531	Bilingual incantation; mentions tu.mušen.
40985	1881,0428.532	Omens.
40986	1881,0428.533	Field sale.
40987	1881,0428.534	Joined to 40675.
40988	1881,0428.535	Colophon. [] 3/5/32.
40989	1881,0428.536	Unidentified.
40990	1881,0428.537	Record of 1020 ox-hides.
40991	1881,0428.538	Lexical; sign list.
40992	1881,0428.539	Astronomical Diary.
40993	1881,0428.540	Astronomical; Goal Year Text for SE 130+. Hunger and Sachs, ADART VI, no. 154.
40994	1881,0428.541	Unidentified.
40995	1881,0428.542	Unidentified.

40996	1881,0428.543	Letter; names of sender and addressee lost. Hackl et al., AOAT 414/1, no. 101.
40997	1881,0428.544	Astrological omens.
40998	1881,0428.545	Receipt.
40999	1881,0428.546	Lexical.
41000	1881,0428.547	Building ritual; dupl. K.3664+ (Borger, Fs Böhl, 550-555; Ambos, Baurituale, 136-137); Ambos, NABU 2016, 51-52, no. 30.
41001	1881,0428.548	Astronomical?
41002	1881,0428.549	Memorandum. Nbk 13/4/-.
41003	1881,0428.550	Astronomical?
41004	1881,0428.551	Astronomical procedure text; lunar latitude; planetary periods; colophon; partial duplicates: 33739, 34639. Neugebauer, JCS 21, 200-208, 217 text E; Brown, CM 18, 305; Steele, JHA 34 (2003) 269-289.
41005	1881,0428.552	Joined to 40090.
41006	1881,0428.553	Astrological; Enūma Anu Enlil tablet 49. Reiner, Fs Borger (CM 10), 298; Gehlken, CM 43, p. 201, pl. 41.
41007	1881,0428.554	Astronomical Diary for SE 85. Sachs and Hunger, ADART II, no. -226 B.
41008	1881,0428.555	Joined to 35343.
41009	1881,0428.556	Liver omens; martu 4th table.
41010	1881,0428.557	Astronomical; Almanac for SE 159 . SE Demetrius I -/-/159. LBAT 1128; Hunger and Sachs, ADART VII, no. 164.
41011	1881,0428.558	School text; lexical; syllabary.
41012	1881,0428.559	Astronomical Diary for SE 48. Sachs and Hunger, ADART I, no. -263.
41013	1881,0428.560	Lexical; sign list.
41014	1881,0428.561	Astronomical Diary for SE 233. Sachs and Hunger, ADART III, no. -78.
41015	1881,0428.562	Contract.
41016	1881,0428.563	Incantation.
41017	1881,0428.564	School text; extracts.
41018	1881,0428.565	Astronomical Diary for SE 225. Stephenson and Walker, Halley's Comet 39-40; Sachs and Hunger, ADART III, no. -86 A.
41019	1881,0428.566	Sale of fields; 53 GI.MEŠ.
41020	1881,0428.567	Astronomical Diary for SE 167; dated by Demetrius.
41021	1881,0428.568	Astronomical Diary.
41022	1881,0428.569	Astronomical; Normal Star Almanac for SE 106. + 41079. LBAT 1013-1014; Hunger and Sachs, ADART VII, no. 43.
41023	1881,0428.570	School text; lexical and literary extracts.

41024	1881,0428.571	Astronomical; compendium of texts dealing with Normal Stars and ziqpu stars; two columns; partial dupl. 36609+.
41025	1881,0428.572	School text; lexical; syllabary and numbers.
41026	1881,0428.573	Astrological omens.
41027	1881,0428.574	Practice wedges.
41028	1881,0428.575	Astronomical Diary; early.
41029	1881,0428.576	Astronomical; lunar ephemeris; System A. (+) 41153 (+) 41075. ACT 6a.
41030	1881,0428.577	Medical; copy; colophon.
41031	1881,0428.578	Astrological; Enūma Anu Enlil 56. Fincke, Kaskal 12, 267-279.
41032	1881,0428.579	Receipt by Bēl-šuma-uṣur / Bēl-aba-uṣur; sealed. SE 12/[]/182+. Babylon. Nisaba 28, no. 662.
41033	1881,0428.580	Astronomical; procedure text or astrological number theory; colophon. SE -/-/135.
41034	1881,0428.581	Contract.
41035	1881,0428.582	Astronomical Diary.
41036	1881,0428.583	Chronicle(?); mentions gods and various places including Dur-Šarrukin; copy (ḫe-pí).
41037	1881,0428.584	Astronomical Diary for SE 128. LBAT 338*; Sachs and Hunger, ADART II, no. -183 B.
41038	1881,0428.585	Astronomical Diary; historical references.
41039	1881,0428.586	Astronomical; Mars observations. Hunger and Sachs, ADART V, no. 99.
41040	1881,0428.587	Astronomical procedure text; Vorläufer?
41041	1881,0428.588	Astronomical table in narrow columns; micro-zodiac text.
41042	1881,0428.589	Astronomical; planetary observation.; SE. (+) 41056. Hunger and Sachs, ADART V, no. 100.
41043	1881,0428.590	Astronomical procedure text for Jupiter; prayer on upper edge. Ossendrijver, BMAPT, no. 22; Ossendrijver, Science 351 (2016) 482-484 (and Supplementary Materials); Ossendrijver, JNES 76, 231-247, text D.
41044	1881,0428.591	Medical; mentions seduction of a woman; É-gal-ku4-ra. + 41112.
41045	1881,0428.592	Astronomical Diary.
41046	1881,0428.593	Personal names.
41047	1881,0428.594	Incantation; ša ina apti ṣilli apalašu, 'who in the window sees a shadow'. + 41144.
41048	1881,0428.595	Field sale.
41049	1881,0428.596	Letter.
41050	1881,0428.597	Medical.
41051	1881,0428.598	Omens; terrestrial.

41052	1881,0428.599	List of prices(?) in silver; mentions month xi(?) of year 114 SE. Babylon.
41053	1881,0428.600	Astrological omens; Enūma Anu Enlil, Jupiter and lunar eclipses; also commentary. Reiner, Fs Borger (CM 10), 298.
41054	1881,0428.601	Horoscope. SE Sel IV -/7/136. Rochberg, Babylonian Horoscopes, no. 17.
41055	1881,0428.602	Astronomical Diary for SE 132. Sachs and Hunger, ADART II, no. -179 D.
41056	1881,0428.603	Astronomical; planetary observations. SE. (+) 41042. Hunger and Sachs, ADART V, no. 100.
41057	1881,0428.604	Astronomical Diary.
41058	1881,0428.605	Mathematical; table of reciprocals.
41059	1881,0428.606	Astronomical Diary; historical references.
41060	1881,0428.607	Bilingual incantation; colophon dated in reign of Nabopolassar LUGAL NUN.KI.
41061	1881,0428.608	Omens.
41062	1881,0428.609	Astronomical Diary or related text; Lunar Six data.
41063	1881,0428.610	Astronomical Diary.
41064	1881,0428.611	Account.
41065	1881,0428.612	Contract.
41066	1881,0428.613	Astronomical Diary.
41067	1881,0428.614	Astronomical Diary or observation text; year 141.
41068	1881,0428.615	Lexical.
41069	1881,0428.616	Astrological; Enūma Anu Enlil, solar eclipses. Reiner, Fs Borger (CM 10), 298.
41070	1881,0428.617	Astronomical?
41071	1881,0428.618	Astronomical?
41072	1881,0428.619	Astronomical; Goal Year Text for SE 142? Hunger and Sachs, ADART VI, no. 38.
41073	1881,0428.620	Astronomical; Normal Star Almanac. SE. Hunger and Sachs, ADART VII, no. 134.
41074	1881,0428.621	List of witnesses
41075	1881,0428.622	Astronomical; lunar ephemeris; System A. (+) 41029 (+) 41153. ACT 6a.
41076	1881,0428.623	Lexical; synonyms or vocabulary.
41077	1881,0428.624	Astronomical Diary.
41078	1881,0428.625	Unidentified.
41079	1881,0428.626	Joined to 41022.
41080	1881,0428.627	Chronicle about Alexander in Arabia. BCHP 2.
41081	1881,0428.628	Contract.
41082	1881,0428.629	Astronomical; Jupiter, first station and opposition for (at least) SE 202 to 273. ACT 613ab.
41083	1881,0428.630	Contract.
41084	1881,0428.631	Astronomical Diary; prices.

41085	1881,0428.632	Astronomical?
41086	1881,0428.633	Mathematical; directions and numbers; details for a land survey?; west 149,20; east 4,46; etc.; rev. palimpsest.
41087	1881,0428.634	Astronomical?
41088	1881,0428.635	Literary or religious.
41089	1881,0428.636	Astronomical?
41090	1881,0428.637	Astronomical?
41091	1881,0428.638	Lexical; god-list.
41092	1881,0428.639	Unidentified.
41093	1881,0428.640	Astronomical Diary.
41094	1881,0428.641	Prayer.
41095	1881,0428.642	Incantation.
41096	1881,0428.643	Bilingual literary(?); two columns; colophon. Alex III/IV.
41097	1881,0428.644	Deposition.
41098	1881,0428.645	Astronomical; Goal Year Text for SE 124?; or perhaps only observations of Mercury. LBAT 1242; Hunger and Sachs, ADART VI, no. 24.
41099	1881,0428.646	Astronomical Diary.
41100	1881,0428.647	Lexical; syllabary.
41101	1881,0428.648	Mathematical; extended table of reciprocals; fragment. Aaboe, JCS 19, 80.
41102	1881,0428.649	Astronomical Diary
41103	1881,0428.650	Astronomical; text defining the path of the moon. Steele, Annals of Science 64 (2007) 293-325.
41104	1881,0428.651	Lexical; god-list.
41105	1881,0428.652	Mathematical; table of reciprocals.
41106	1881,0428.653	Astronomical; Normal Star Almanac for SE 142. LBAT 1028a; Hunger and Sachs, ADART VII, no. 61.
41107	1881,0428.654	Joined to 40090.
41108	1881,0428.655	Astronomical; Goal Year Text for SE 196. LBAT 1286; Hunger and Sachs, ADART VI, no. 70.
41109	1881,0428.656	Joined to 40532.
41110	1881,0428.657	Contract; dated by [Antiochus] and Seleucus SE [Ant I] and Sel 5/9/10+[]. CT 49, 46, no. 175.
41111	1881,0428.658	Astronomical Diar. SE -/-/144. Sachs and Hunger, ADART II, no. -167 B.
41112	1881,0428.659	Joined to 41044.
41113	1881,0428.660	Contract for a dowry.
41114	1881,0428.661	Cylinder; historical or literary?
41115	1881,0428.662	Medical.
41116	1881,0428.663	Lexical.
41117	1881,0428.664	Astronomical; Normal Star Almanac for SE 109? Hunger and Sachs, ADART VII, no. 46.

41118	1881,0428.665	Unidentified.
41119	1881,0428.666	Astronomical; procedure?
41120	1881,0428.667	Astronomical; lunar ephemeris; System A. Steele, Fs Walker, 293-318, text F.
41121	1881,0428.668	Astronomical Diary; mentions ašamšutu, hurricane.
41122	1881,0428.669	Bilingual incantation.
41123	1881,0428.670	Astronomical Diary for SE 119. LBAT 325; Sachs and Hunger, ADART II, no. -192.
41124	1881,0428.671	Court record; Murānu archive; sealed. SE Ant I & Ant []/12b/47. CT 49, 24, no. 117; Jursa, Persika 9, 186; Nisaba 28, no. 572.
41125	1881,0428.672	Astronomical Diary; prices.
41126	1881,0428.673	Astronomical Diary.
41127	1881,0428.674	Astronomical; Normal Star Almanac. SE. Hunger and Sachs, ADART VII, no. 135.
41128	1881,0428.675	Contract; lease of a house. Xerxes 26/1/13. Babylon.
41129	1881,0428.676	Astronomical; lunar eclipse report for eclipse of 21 March 154 BC. LBAT 1440; Stephenson, HEER, 182; Hunger and Sachs, ADART V, no. 20.
41130	1881,0428.677	Joined to 40866.
41131	1881,0428.678	Astronomical Diary for SE 192. + 41149 + 41206 (+) Rm.756 + 42110 (+) 41189. LBAT 458; Sachs and Hunger, ADART III, no. -119 B.
41132	1881,0428.679	Astronomical?
41133	1881,0428.680	Astronomical Diary.
41134	1881,0428.681	Incantation.
41135	1881,0428.682	Account.
41136	1881,0428.683	Joined to 40532.
41137	1881,0428.684	Astronomical; Normal Star Almanac. SE. Hunger and Sachs, ADART VII, no. 136.
41138	1881,0428.685	Locations of cultic daises. George, BTT, pl. 23.
41139	1881,0428.686	Astronomical; unusual type.
41140	1881,0428.687	Contract.
41141	1881,0428.688	Religious; repeated ilāni muštalu ... uri.
41142	1881,0428.689	Astronomical Diary for SE 99/100.
41143	1881,0428.690	Order for building. 4/6/1.
41144	1881,0428.691	Joined to 41047.
41145	1881,0428.692	Astronomical?
41146	1881,0428.693	Astrological; commentary. Reiner, Fs Borger (CM 10), 298.
41147	1881,0428.694	Magical; mentions a witch.
41148	1881,0428.695	Omens; extispicy.
41149	1881,0428.696	Joined to 41131.
41150	1881,0428.697	Astronomical; Normal Star Almanac. SE. Hunger and Sachs, ADART VII, no. 137.

41151	1881,0428.698	Astronomical; procedure text?; mentions months and years.
41152	1881,0428.699	Economic.
41153	1881,0428.700	Astronomical; lunar ephemeris; System A. (+) 41029 (+) 41075. ACT 6a.
41154	1881,0428.701	Astronomical; ACT? procedure; mentions 2-ta ḫab-rat; cf. 41205.
41155	1881,0428.702	Lexical.
41156	1881,0428.703	Astronomical?
41157	1881,0428.704	Astronomical Diary.
41158	1881,0428.705	Astronomical Diary; year 7[].
41159	1881,0428.706	Promissory note for silver; sealed; finger-nail marks; Murānu archive. SE (Ant & Sel) 13/9/42. Babylon. CT 49, 22, no. 111; Stolper, Annali Supp. 77, 42-44, no. 13; Jursa, Persika 9, 175, 183; Mitchell and Searight, no. 665; Nisaba 28, no. 563.
41160	1881,0428.707	Receipt for house rent; sealed. Philip []/[]/5. Nisaba 28, no. 334.
41161	1881,0428.708	Astronomical Diary for SE 110. Sachs and Hunger, ADART II, no. -201 B.
41162	1881,0428.709	Note; measures of capacity.
41163	1881,0428.710	Historical(?); or perhaps part of an Astronomical Diary; mentions é-gal; two columns.1881,0428.711 Astronomical; ACT ephemeris?; one column ends DU.
41165	1881,0428.712	Astronomical Diary for SE 111. Sachs and Hunger, ADART II, no. -200 B.
41166	1881,0428.713	Incantations.
41167	1881,0428.714	Astronomical; Goal Year Text; not datable. Hunger and Sachs, ADART VI, no. 155.
41168	1881,0428.715	Astronomical Diary; historical references. + 41182.
41169	1881,0428.716	Unidentified.
41170	1881,0428.717	Kufic inscription.
41171	1881,0428.718	Astrological; copied from a Borsippa tablet; colophon. Reiner, Fs Borger (CM 10), 298.
41172	1881,0428.719	Omens; extispicy?
41173	1881,0428.720	Medical incipits?
41174	1881,0428.721	Promissory note for silver. Kandalanu 25/3/9. URU KID-ra.ki. Brinkman and Kennedy, JCS 35, 42, L.34.
41175	1881,0428.722	Ritual; GIŠ.GU.ZA.
41176	1881,0428.723	Astrological omens. Reiner, Fs Borger (CM 10), 298.
41177	1881,0428.724	Inventory of copper vessels.
41178	1881,0428.725	Astronomical Diary.
41179	1881,0428.726	Astronomical Diary for SE 206. Sachs and Hunger, ADART III, no. -105 D.

41180	1881,0428.727	Joined to 40857.
41181	1881,0428.728	Promissory note for silver. Nbn 27/1/-.
41182	1881,0428.729	Joined to 41168.
41183	1881,0428.730	Personal names.
41184	1881,0428.731	Envelope of a letter; sealed. n.d. Nisaba 28, no. 670.
41185	1881,0428.732	Astronomical; numerical table; ACT ephemeris?; very thin (c 1 cm).
41186	1881,0428.733	Astronomical Diary?; mentions Euphrates and river god; mentions d.ṣal-bat-a-nu twice.
41187	1881,0428.734	Lexical.
41188	1881,0428.735	Astronomical?
41189	1881,0428.736	Astronomical Diary for SE 192. (+) Rm.756 + 42110 (+) 41131 + 41149 + 41206. Sachs and Hunger, ADART III, no. -119 B.
41190	1881,0428.737	Astronomical?
41191	1881,0428.738	Incantation; Udug-ḫul. Cf. Finkel, AuOr 9 (1991), 101 (partial transliteration).
41192	1881,0428.739	Unidentified.
41193	1881,0428.740	Medical.
41194	1881,0428.741	Astronomical Diary.
41195	1881,0428.742	Astrological. Reiner, Fs Borger (CM 10), 298.
41196	1881,0428.743	Bilingual literary; commentary.
41197	1881,0428.744	Astronomical Diary.
41198	1881,0428.745	Incantations; Maqlu VII. Abusch, AMD 10, 165-191.
41199	1881,0428.746	Joined to 41173.
41200	1881,0428.747	Astronomical?
41201	1881,0428.748	Astrological; meteorological; eg hurricanes. Reiner, Fs Borger (CM 10), 298.
41202	1881,0428.749	Astronomical; mentions danna 1/2 umu, šu-bi-aš-am.
	1881,0428.750	Joined to 36937.
41203	1881,0428.751	Astrological; sun. Cf. Reiner, Fs Borger (CM 10), 298.
41204	1881,0428.752	Unidentified.
41205	1881,0428.753	Astronomical; procedure; cf. 41154.
41206	1881,0428.754	Joined to 41131.
41207	1881,0428.755	Promissory note for beer.
41208	1881,0428.756	Joined to 40854.
41209	1881,0428.757	Account; personal names, silver, ox-hides.
41210	1881,0428.758	Lexical; Ea; sign list.
41211	1881,0428.759	Incantations and rituals; three columns on each side; obv. Lamaštu; rev. Qutaru. Farber, Lamaštu, 47, 57, pl. 81; Finkel, Fs Lambert, pp. 194-195.
41212	1881,0428.760	Lexical; Ea; sign list.
41213	1881,0428.761	Lexical; Ea; sign list.
41214	1881,0428.762	Account of silver ina IGI PN.

41215	1881,0428.763	Lexical; personal names.
41216	1881,0428.764	Lexical; syllabary. CT 11, 11.
41217	1881,0428.765	Account of disbursements; personal names; turns sideways.
41218	1881,0428.766	Astronomical; MUL.APIN. Hunger and Pingree, AfO Beih. 24, MUL.APIN text T; Reiner, Fs Borger (CM 10), 298; Hunger and Steele, MUL.APIN, 21.
41219	1881,0428.767	Unidentified.
41220	1881,0428.768	Personal names; account of disbursements.
41221	1881,0428.769	Account of disbursements.
41222	1881,0428.770	Astronomical; planetary observations (Saturn, Mars and Mercury); mentions year 8 of Ḫumbaḫaldašu, year 2 of Esarhaddon, year 14 of Šamaš-šum-ukin, year 1 of Kandalanu and year 7 of Nabopolassar. Hunger and Sachs, ADART V, no. 52.
41223	1881,0428.771	Field plan. + 46889. Nemet-Nejat, LB Field Plans, no. 63.
41224	1881,0428.772	Lexical; syllabary.
41225	1881,0428.773	Contract; lease of a house. Cam 10/12b/5. Babylon.
41226	1881,0428.774	Field sale.
41227	1881,0428.775	Account of purchases.
41228	1881,0428.776	Incantation.
41229	1881,0428.777	Literary.
41230	1881,0428.778	Contract. Dar -/5/11.
41231	1881,0428.779	Account.
41232	1881,0428.780	Omens; Šumma ālu, tablet 23. Freedman, If a city, vol. 2, 34.
41233	1881,0428.781	Promissory note for silver. Cyr -/6/5 Babylon.
41234	1881,0428.782	Contract.
41235	1881,0428.783	Promissory note for silver. Npl 9/10/[]. Kennedy, JCS 38, 219, T.x.81.
41236	1881,0428.784	Promissory note for dates.
41237	1881,0428.785	Catalogue of medical omens; Sa-gig; dupl. ND 4358+ (Iraq 24, 57, CTN 4, 71); colophon mentioning Adad-apla-iddina and Esagil-kīn-apli. + 46607 + 47163. Finkel, Gs Sachs, 143-153 and 156-157.
41238	1881,0428.786	Silver ina IGI PN.
41239	1881,0428.787	Ritual; about a procession of gods from E-tur-kalamma in Babylon to Kish; dupl. 32516. George, BTT, pl. 54; George, Fs Lambert, 289-299; Linssen, CM 25, 10 n. 66, 324.
41240	1881,0428.788	Incantation.
41241	1881,0428.789	Economic.
41242	1881,0428.790	Account.
41243	1881,0428.791	Receipt. 22/10/19.

41244	1881,0428.792	Sale of a person? Šamaš-šum-ukin 14/[]/acc.
41245	1881,0428.793	Contract; ḫarrānu.
41246	1881,0428.794	Lexical; Ḫḫ XXIII. MSL 11, 67.
41247	1881,0428.795	Letter order. Alex IV []/[]/8.
41248	1881,0428.796	Economic.
41249	1881,0428.797	Literary; colophon.
41250	1881,0428.798	Astronomical; procedure?; mišil UD 6 kaskal UD ITU DU6; fragment.
41251	1881,0428.799	Account.
41252	1881,0428.800	Commentary; medical; Sa-gig IV.
41253	1881,0428.801	Commentary; medical; Sa-gig IV.
41254	1881,0428.802	Incantation.
41255a	1881,0428.803a	God-list with explanations. (+) 40774 (+) 41255c.
41255b	1881,0428.803b	God-list; fragments b+m+p are all joined to 40774 + 41363.
41255c-p	1881,0428.803c-p	God list; 12 fragments probably all parts of the same tablet as 41255a and 40774+; originally 16 pieces numbered a to p; there are joins among the fragments, c+i+l and e+o. (+) 40774 (+) 41255a.
41256a	1881,0428.804a	Joined to 40795.
41256b	1881,0428.804b	Literary.
41257a	1881,0428.805a	Account; silver and personal names.
41257b	1881,0428.805b	Account; silver and personal names.
41258	1881,0428.806	Lexical; Ea; sign list.
41259	1881,0428.807	Account; mentions years 11, 12 and 1
41260	1881,0428.808	Lexical; Ea; sign list.
41261	1881,0428.809	Medical.
41262	1881,0428.810	School text; practice wedges.
41263	1881,0428.811	Memorandum. Disintegrated.
41264	1881,0428.812	Lexical; Ea; sign list.
41265	1881,0428.813	School text; practice wedges.
41266	1881,0428.814	Economic.
41268	1881,0428.816	Lexical; Ḫḫ XXI. MSL 11, 10.
41269	1881,0428.817	Joined to 40769.
41270	1881,0428.818	Economic.
41271	1881,0428.819	Bilingual incantations; Muššu'u tablet II. + 41306. Cf. Finkel, AuOr 9 (1991), 95; Böck, Muššu'u, 113-131.
41272	1881,0428.820	Field plan. Nemet-Nejat, LB Field Plans, no. 21.
41273	1881,0428.821	Contract. Babylon.
41274	1881,0428.822	Lexical; Ea; sign list.
41275	1881,0428.823	Astronomical; Goal Year Text for SE 232? Hunger and Sachs, ADART VI, no. 84
41276	1881,0428.824	Contract? Disintegrating.
41277	1881,0428.825	Economic. 23/6/[].

41278	1881,0428.826	Contract; witnesses.
41279	1881,0428.827	Medical compendium; obv. 20-25 quoted in Biggs, TCS 2, 44 (number not given there).
41280	1881,0428.828	School text; obv. literary extracts; rev. Lamaštu I, unidentified; lexical. Farber, Lamaštu, 47, 57, pl. 60.
41281	1881,0428.829	Medical; stones grouped for medical purposes; hands, etc; Kunuk ḫalti tablet N. Abusch, AMD 5, p. 311; cf. Böck, Muššu'u, p. 37; Schuster-Brandis, AOAT 46, p. 487, pls. 36-37.
41282	1881,0428.830	Medical prescriptions for skin diseases. (+) 41294. Fincke in G. J. Selz (ed.) WOO 6 (2011) 159-208.
41283a	1881,0428.831a	Account; silver and personal names. + 41283b (+) 42813c+d.
41283b	1881,0428.831b	Joined to 41283a.
41283c	1881,0428.831c	Account; silver and personal names. + 42813d (+) 41283a+b.
41283d	1881,0428.831d	Joined to 41283c.
41284	1881,0428.832	Medical prescriptions; šumma KI.MIN GIŠ NU.UR.MA.
41285	1881,0428.833	List of commodities granted by palaces to various gods.
41286	1881,0428.834	Lexical, commentary on Aa III/1 = 16. MSL 14, 322-326 and pls. 5-8.
41287	1881,0428.835	Astronomical?
41288	1881,0428.836	Literary; esoteric text; dupl. CBS 16.
41289	1881,0428.837	Medical. + 41373 + 44238.
41290	1881,0428.838	Unidentified.
41291	1881,0428.839	Incantation.
41292	1881,0428.840	Lexical; stones.
41293	1881,0428.841	Medical; prescriptions for eye diseases. + 44866. Geller, ABM, 16.
41294	1881,0428.842	Medical prescriptions for skin diseases. (+) 41282. Fincke in G. J. Selz (ed.) WOO 6 (2011) 159-208.
41295	1881,0428.843	Prayer to Marduk no. 2. Lambert, MC 24, no. 103.
41296	1881,0428.844	Hymn to Ninurta.
41297	1881,0428.845	Commentary.
41298	1881,0428.846	Medical; mentions stones. Schuster-Brandis, AOAT 46, p. 139, Kette 133.
41299	1881,0428.847	Joined to 40482.
41299a	1881,0428.847a	Box of small fragments marked 41299 but not belonging to that tablet.
41300	1881,0428.848	Medical; SAG.KI.DAB.BA.
41301	1881,0428.849	Horoscopes for two children, dated SE 195 and 197. SE 7/4/197. Rochberg, Babylonian Horoscopes, no. 22.

41302	1881,0428.850	Joined to 40501.
41303	1881,0428.851	Lexical; four columns on each side.
41304	1881,0428.852	Contract; sale of a house; sealed; finger-nail marks. d.l. Nisaba 28, no. 140.
41305	1881,0428.853	Contract. Art.
41306	1881,0428.854	Joined to 41271.
41307	1881,0428.855	Contract. RN lost 15/8/26.
41308	1881,0428.856	Lexical; god-list.
41309	1881,0428.857	Lexical; syllabary; gods names.
41310	1881,0428.858	Joined to 40769.
41311	1881,0428.859	Omens; celestial.
41312	1881,0428.860	Lexical; Šammu šikinšu.
41313	1881,0428.861	Lexical; Aa I/2 = 2. Pinches, JRAS 1894, 830; MSL 14, 207.
41314	1881,0428.862	Astronomical, observations; unusual type; two columns; four lines marked ḫe-pí; mu 28 1.Da-ri-[].
41315	1881,0428.863	Medical; plants.
41316	1881,0428.864	Deposition; dupl. 41434. Dar [5]/[3]/16. Babylon. Wunsch, AfO 42/43, 55, no. 5
41317	1881,0428.865	Contract.
41318	1881,0428.866	Field plan. Nemet-Nejat, LB Field Plans, no. 53.
41319	1881,0428.867	Field plan. Nemet-Nejat, LB Field Plans, no. 5.
41320	1881,0428.868	Promissory note for dates. 20/[]/10+.
41321	1881,0428.869	Sale of oxen. Nbk 25/12/30.
41322	1881,0428.870	Incantation; colophon.
41323	1881,0428.871	Medical.
41324	1881,0428.872	School text; lexical; Ḫḫ XX, XXI. MSL 11, 3, 11.
41325	1881,0428.873	Promissory note for silver. Šamaš-šum-ukin 3/5/[]. Babylon. Brinkman and Kennedy, JCS 35, 37, K.155.
41326	1881,0428.874	Promissory note for silver. -/-/12.
41327	1881,0428.875	Contract. Ner 6/9/-.
41328	1881,0428.876	Bilingual incantation. + 1881,0428.903.
41329	1881,0428.877	Sumerian literary. + 41374.
41330	1881,0428.878	Unidentified.
41331	1881,0428.879	Letter.
41332	1881,0428.880	Incantations; Maqlu IV. Abusch, AMD 10, 113-129.
41333	1881,0428.881	Contract.
41334	1881,0428.882	Ritual.
41335	1881,0428.883	Promissory note for silver.
41336	1881,0428.884	Contract. -/-/4.
41337	1881,0428.885	Contract.
41338	1881,0428.886	Lexical; Ea; sign list.
41339	1881,0428.887	Medical.
41340	1881,0428.888	Contract. Babylon.
41341	1881,0428.889	Economic.

41342	1881,0428.890	Contract; lease of a house. Dar 7/5/17. Babylon.
41343	1881,0428.891	Receipt.
41344	1881,0428.892	Contract about slaves.
41345	1881,0428.893	Promissory note.
41346	1881,0428.894	Contract.
41347	1881,0428.895	Unidentified.
41348	1881,0428.896	School text; lexical; Ḫḫ XX. MSL 11, 3.
41349	1881,0428.897	Literary.
41350	1881,0428.898	Prayer.
41351	1881,0428.899	Promissory note for dates. Dar 20/11/34.
41352	1881,0428.900	Contract. Babylon.
41353	1881,0428.901	Ritual.
41354	1881,0428.902	Lexical, commentary on Aa II/2 = 10. MSL 14, 273-275 and pl. 3.
	1881,0428.903	Joined to 41328.
41355	1881,0428.904	Bilingual incantation.
41356	1881,0428.905	Contract.
41357	1881,0428.906	Bilingual incantation; minute writing.
41358	1881,0428.907	Contract.
41359	1881,0428.908	Literary.
41360	1881,0428.909	Incantation.
41361	1881,0428.910	Cultic commentary; list of wooden objects equated with different gods; dupl. 47463 and a PBS tablet (Livingstone, MMEWABS, 6, etc); cf. Finkel, Fs Sachs, 154. + 44179.
41362	1881,0428.911	Contract.
41363	1881,0428.912	Joined to 40774.
41364	1881,0428.913	Medical.
41365	1881,0428.914	Unidentified.
41366	1881,0428.915	Astronomical?
41367	1881,0428.916	Field sale.
41368	1881,0428.917	Economic.
41369	1881,0428.918	Lexical; syllabary.
41370	1881,0428.919	Astronomical?
41371	1881,0428.920	Joined to 40501.
41372	1881,0428.921	Omens; extispicy.
41373	1881,0428.922	Joined to 41289.
41374	1881,0428.923	Joined to 41329.
41375	1881,0428.924	List of workmen.
41376	1881,0428.925	Bilingual incantation.
41377	1881,0428.926	Medical ritual; includes ṣaṣuntu.
41378	1881,0428.927	Lexical; Erimḫuš I. MSL 17, 9.
41379	1881,0428.928	Field plan. Nemet-Nejat, LB Field Plans, no. 39.
41380	1881,0428.929	Contract; lease of a house. Nbk -/5/acc. Babylon.
41381	1881,0428.930	Sealing, uninscribed; 4 impressions of a stamp seal.

41382	1881,0428.931	Sealing, uninscribed; 2 impressions of stamp seals.
41383	1881,0428.932	Sealing, uninscribed; 1 impression of a stamp seal.
41384	1881,0428.933	Sealing, uninscribed; 4 impressions of stamp seals.
41385	1881,0428.934	Sealing, uninscribed; 1 impression of a stamp seal.
41386	1881,0428.935	Sealing, uninscribed; 3 impressions of a stamp seal; stud behind.
41387	1881,0428.936	Sealing, uninscribed; 1 impression of a stamp seal.
41388	1881,0428.937	Sealing, uninscribed; 1 impression of a stamp seal.
41389	1881,0428.938	Sealing, uninscribed; 1 impression of a stamp seal.
	1881,0428.939ff.	Nos. 939-1074 are uninscribed objects.
	1881,0428.1075ff.	Nos. 1075-1083 are bricks of Nebuchadnezzar II. See CBI nos. 100 and 106.
90834	1881,0428.1084	Commemorative stele of Adad-ēṭir, dagger bearer (nāš patri) of Marduk. King, BBSt, pp. 115-116, pl. XCII, no. XXXIV.
91471	1881,0428.1085	Glass vessel. (Sippar). Walker and Collon, Tell ed-Dēr 3, 109, no. 131.
91593	1881,0428.1086	Alabaster figurine.

1881,0625 collection

The 1881,0625 collection comes from Messrs. Spartali & Co., London. The register gives the provenance as Babylonia for nos. 1-596, as Abu Habba for nos. 597-748, and as Babylonia for nos. 749-882.

41390	1881,0625.1	Promissory note for silver. Nbk 6/10/5. Saḫrītu. Nbk 47 (wrongly marked as 84-2-11, 65); Bertin 31.
41391	1881,0625.2	Settlement of a debt. Nbk 15/4/24. Babylon. Nbk 141; Bertin 113.
41392	1881,0625.3	Promissory note for silver. Nbk 15/5/28. Babylon. Nbk 185; Bertin 129.
41393	1881,0625.4	Promissory note for silver. Nbk 29/[]/32. Babylon. Nbk 252; Bertin 156; Wunsch, CM 3, no. 8.
41394	1881,0625.5	Division of property. Nbk 29/6/18. Ḫuṣṣeti-ša-Ḫalḫuru. Nbk 115; Bertin 89-90.
41395	1881,0625.6	Deposition. Nbk 6/1/17. Babylon. Nbk 109; Bertin 83-83.
41396	1881,0625.7	Sale of slaves. Nbk 26/11/33. Babylon. Bertin 168; Wunsch, CM 3, no. 16.
41397	1881,0625.8	Contract; partnership agreement. Nbk 1/5/36. Babylon. Nbk 300; Bertin 170.
41398	1881,0625.9	Contract; sale of a house; caption for a seal, but not sealed; dupl. 32160 and 33057+. AM [11]/8/1. Babylon. Sack, AOATS 4, no. 22; Bertin 269-270.
41399	1881,0625.10	Contract; sale of a date orchard; sealed; finger-nail marks. Dupl. Amherst no. 57A. There is a cast of this

		tablet in the Rijksmuseum, Leiden; LKA 1158. Ner 9/11/acc. Babylon. 5R 67, 1; Sack, ZA 68, 146-149; Sack, AOAT 236, no. 80; S. Maul, AoF 17, 107-112 (duplicate and collations); Wunsch, AfO 44/45, 60; Nisaba 28, no. 2.
41400	1881,0625.11	Contract; lease of a house. Ner 6/9/acc. Evetts, Ner. 5; Sack, AOAT 236, no. 5; Bertin 293.
41401	1881,0625.12	Promissory note for onions. Ner 2/1/4. Šaḫrīn. Evetts, Ner 68; Sack, AOAT 236, no. 68; Bertin 329; Wunsch, CM 3, no. 81.
41402	1881,0625.13	Court record; about payment for a slave; sealed. Nbn 12/11/acc. Babylon. Nbn 13; Bertin 338-339; Wunsch, AfO 44/45, 96-97, no. 30; Nisaba 28, no. 7.
41403	1881,0625.14	Promissory note for dates. Nbn 25/10/1. Babylon. Nbn 45; Bertin 353.
41404	1881,0625.15	Receipt for dates. Nbn 16/12b/1. Babylon. Nbn 52; Bertin 358; Wunsch, CM 3, no. 101.
41405	1881,0625.16	Promissory note for silver. Nbn 12/[]/4. Babylon. Nbn 183; Bertin 390.
41406	1881,0625.17	Contract; sale of a date orchard; sealed; finger-nail marks; dupl. 33089. Nbn 6/12/4. Babylon. Nbn 178; Bertin 409; Wunsch, CM 20A-B, no. 49; Nisaba 28, no. 67.
41407	1881,0625.18	Contract; sale of a date orchard; sealed; finger-nail marks. Nbn 8/3/8. Babylon. Nbn 293; Wunsch, CM 20A-B, no. 242; Nisaba 28, no. 70.
41408	1881,0625.19	Receipt for payment of silver. Nbn 11/12/9. Babylon. Nbn 391; Bertin 485; Wunsch, CM 3, no. 172.
41409	1881,0625.20	Promissory note for silver and vats. Nbn 7/12/11. Nbn 572; Bertin 546.
41410	1881,0625.21	Promissory note for silver. Nbn 13/3/11. Nbn 511; Bertin 525.
41411	1881,0625.22	Deposition. Nbn 17/4/12Babylon. Nbn 608; Bertin 562.
41412	1881,0625.23	Promissory note for barley. Nbn 10/12/13 Babylon. Nbn 740; Bertin 614; Wunsch, CM 3, no. 217.
41413	1881,0625.24	Promissory note for silver. Nbn 28/6/14. Babylon. Nbn 790; Bertin 629.
41414	1881,0625.25	Contract; hire of a boat. Nbn 27/12/16. Babylon. Nbn 1019; Bertin 688.
41415	1881,0625.26	Court record; sealed. Nbn 11/11/[1+]. Babylon. Nbn 1128; Wunsch, AfO 44/45, 98-99, no. 35; Mitchell and Searight, no. 298; Nisaba 28, no. 9.
41416	1881,0625.27	Promissory note for silver. Cyr 22/6b/2. Agamatānu. Cyr 60; Bertin 753.

41417	1881,0625.28	Contract. Cyr 3/5/[]. Babylon. Cyr 351; Bertin 850.
41418	1881,0625.29	Promissory note for dates. Cam 1/12/acc. Babylon. Cam 17; Bertin 862.
41419	1881,0625.30	Promissory note for dates. Cam 27/7/2. Babylon. Cam 122; Bertin 886.
41420	1881,0625.31	Promissory note for barley, silver and onions. Cam 24/11/3. Šaḫrīn. Cam 218; Bertin 911; Wunsch, CM 3, no. 337.
41421	1881,0625.32	Promissory note for dates. Cam 14/6b/3. Babylon. Cam 179; Bertin 912.
41422	1881,0625.33	Promissory note for silver. Cam 12/10/6. Babylon. Cam 338; Bertin 960-961.
41423	1881,0625.34	Promissory note for silver. Cam 16/2/6. Ḫumadēšu. Cam 310; Bertin 959.
41424	1881,0625.35	Promissory note for silver and sesame. Cam 30/10/6. Babylon. Cam 305; Bertin 958.
41425	1881,0625.36	Contract; exchange of fields; sealed. Cam 1/5/7. Babylon. Cam 375; Bertin 976-977; Wunsch, CM 20A-B, no. 176; Nisaba 28, no. 102.
41426	1881,0625.37	Receipt for silver for urāšu service Dar 21/12/2. Babylon. Dar 56; Bertin 1958; Wunsch, CM 3, no. 349.
41427	1881,0625.38	Promissory note for silver and onions. Cyr 4/11/3. Babylon. Cyr 141; Bertin 1668; Wunsch, CM 3, no. 287.
41428	1881,0625.39	Promissory note to pay a debt of silver and onions to Marduk-nāṣir-apli. Dar 1/5/5. Šaḫrīn. Dar 164; Bertin 2077; Abraham, BPPE, 381-383, no. 95.
41429	1881,0625.40	Promissory note for dates. Dar 12/10/6. Ḫursag-kalamma. Dar 214; Bertin 2122.
41430	1881,0625.41	Promissory note for dates. Dar 12/6/12. Bāb-Nār-Kūtê. Dar 332; Bertin 2229.
41431	1881,0625.42	Promissory note for dates. Dar 10/6/13. Nāru-eššu. Dar 353; Bertin 2259.
41432	1881,0625.43	Contract; lease of a field. Dar 5/8/15. Babylon. Dar 409; Bertin 2332.
41433	1881,0625.44	Field sale. Dar. 24/1/18. Babylon. Dar 466; Bertin 2389.
41434	1881,0625.45	Deposition; dupl. 41316. Dar 5/3/16. Babylon. Pinches, BOR 2, 3-4; Bertin 2343.
41435	1881,0625.46	Promissory note for silver and dates. Dar []/7/17. Babylon. Dar 447; Bertin 2383.
41436	1881,0625.47	Promissory note for silver. Dar 10/3/17. Babylon. Dar 440; Bertin 2366.
41437	1881,0625.48	Promissory note for silver. Dar 15/12/19. Babylon. Dar 494; Bertin 2366.

41438	1881,0625.49	Promissory note to deliver dates as imittu payment from land at the Rab-kāṣir canal to Marduk-nāṣir-apli; one third is due to Bagasarū (Old Iranian name). Dar 17/7/21. Bīt-Ṭāb-Bēl. Dar 527; Bertin 2490; Abraham, BPPE, 443-444, no. 130.
41439	1881,0625.50	Sale of a donkey. Dar 7/9/22. Uruk? (URU UNUG?.KI). Dar 550; Bertin 2485.
41440	1881,0625.51	Contract. Dar 22/12/23. Šušan. Bertin 2512.
41441	1881,0625.52	Promissory note for silver; caption for a seal but not sealed. Dar 18/1/24. Šušan. Bertin 2549.
41442	1881,0625.53	Apprenticeship contract to teach Marduk-nāṣir-apli's slave the baker's profession. Dar 15/12/26. Babylon. Bertin 2604; Pinches, BOR 1, 83-85, pl. facing p. 88; dupl. Holt, AJSL 27 (1911), 221; Abraham, BPPE, 360-362, no 84.
41443	1881,0625.54	Promissory note for silver. Dar 8/3/26. Babylon.
41444	1881,0625.55	Promissory note for silver. Dar 28/[]/27. Babylon. Bertin 2630.
41445	1881,0625.56	Contract; transfer of responsibility. Dar 5/12/28. Bertin 2658.
41446	1881,0625.57	Promissory note for dates. Dar 7/6/no year. Babylon. Bertin 2835; Wunsch, CM 20A-B, no. 109.
41447	1881,0625.58	Promissory note for silver. Dar []/3/1. Babylon. Dar 15; Bertin 2830.
41448	1881,0625.59	Promissory note for barley. Dar 6/5/10. Dilbat. Dar 269; Bertin 2831.
41449	1881,0625.60	Contract; undertaking to bring thieves in handcuffs to the house of Marduk-nāṣir-apli. Dar ⸢3⸣+/12a/[5?] (or year [8?]) Babylon. Bertin 2833; Abraham, BPPE, 362-364, no. 85; Baker, NABU 2004, 89-90, 89.
41450	1881,0625.61	Sale of oxen. Dar 21/9/25. Alu-ša-Nabû-[ēreš]. Bertin 2590; Wunsch, CM 20A-B, no. 197.
41451	1881,0625.62	Promissory note to pay a debt of silver and onions to Marduk-nāṣir-apli. Dar [1]/5/[5]. Šaḫrīn. Dar 167; Bertin 2103.
41452	1881,0625.63	Contract for materials. Dar 17/[]/27. Babylon. Bertin 2629.
41453	1881,0625.64	Contract; lease of a small house at the harbour and a loft by Marduk-nāṣir-apli's son until year 36. Dar 19/[]/[35?]. Abraham, BPPE, 365-366, no. 86; Bertin 2820.
41454	1881,0625.65	Record of deposit of silver in staters of Antiochus; sealed; finger-nail marks. SE Ant III 2/1/94. (Babylon). Strassmaier, ZA 3, 150, no. 13; Stolper, Annali

		Supp. 77, 28-33, no. 9; Bertin 2901-2902; Mitchell and Searight, no. 718; Nisaba 28, no. 588.
41455	1881,0625.66	Promissory note for silver. Bardija 19/1/1. Ḫumadē-šu. Strassmaier, ZA 4, 148 Sm. 2; Bertin 1932; Zadok, Iran 14 (1976) 70; Zawadzki, NABU 1995, 47, no. 54.
41456	1881,0625.67	Promissory note for dates. Dar 2/[]/14. Babylon. Dar 395; Bertin 2283.
41457	1881,0625.68	Sale of a slave. Babylon.
41458	1881,0625.69	Promissory note for silver.
41459	1881,0625.70	Court record; about the dowry and house of Bunnānī-tu daughter of Ḫāriṣāya (cf. 32871; captions for seals but not sealed; dupl. 33945. Nbn 26/6/9. [Babylon]. Nbn 356; Pinches, TSBA 8, 274-276; Wunsch, CM 3, no. 167.
41460	1881,0625.71	Account of issues of silver. SE Arsaces 22/6/218. CT 49, 36, no. 152; van der Spek, Raḫimesu, 219-220, no. 9.
41461	1881,0625.72	Promissory note for silver; sealed. SE RN lost 26+/[]/73+. Babylon. Mitchell and Searight, no. 702; Nisaba 28, no. 584.
41462	1881,0625.73	Astronomical Diary for SE 148. + 41941. LBAT 380 + 920; Stephenson and Walker, Halley's Comet 21-27; Sachs and Hunger, ADART III, no. -163 B; Stephenson, HEER, 108-110 (fig. 4.4), 170.
41463	1881,0625.74	Account; dated by [] and Seleucus. SE. CT 49, 49, no. 189.
41464	1881,0625.75	Astronomical Diary for SE 74. + 1881,0625.76 + 41465 + 41524 + 41834 + 41837 + 132277. LBAT 279-280, 855, 882; Sachs and Hunger, ADART II, no. -237.
41465	1881,0625.76	Joined to 41464.
41466	1881,0625.77	Contract. Dar 6/5/[]. Babylon.
41467	1881,0625.78	Astronomical; lunar ephemeris; System A, several columns, for SE 142; prayer on upper edge. + 41937 + 41968 (+) 41865 + 132280. LBAT 2-3; ACT 3a and colophon Zja; Aaboe, AIHS 25/97 (1975), 194; Steele, AHES 60 (2006) 123-153, text C.
41468	1881,0625.79	Astronomical; Almanac for SE 297. + 41516. LBAT 1187; Hunger and Sachs, ADART VII, no. 207.
41469	1881,0625.80	Astronomical Diary for SE 165. LBAT 859; Sachs and Hunger, ADART III, no. -146.
41470	1881,0625.81	Astronomical Diary. LBAT 866.
41471	1881,0625.82	Astronomical Diary for SE 100. LBAT 868; Sachs and Hunger, ADART II, no. -211 A.

41472	1881,0625.83	Astronomical Diary. LBAT 871.
41473	1881,0625.84	Contract.
41474	1881,0625.85	Astronomical Diary for SE 170. + 41882. LBAT 864 + 904; Sachs and Hunger, ADART III, no. -141 D.
41475	1881,0625.86	Astrological; colophon.
41476	1881,0625.87	Astronomical Diary for SE 229. LBAT 510; Sachs and Hunger, ADART III, no. -82 A.
41477	1881,0625.88	Astronomical Diary for SE 117. LBAT 320; Sachs and Hunger, ADART II, no. -194 A.
	1881,0625.89	Joined to 34603.
41478	1881,0625.90	Joined to Rm.701.
41479	1881,0625.91	Joined to Rm.710.
41480	1881,0625.92	Promissory note for barley. Nabû-[]-/12/13.
41481	1881,0625.93	Astrological commentary; Sîn ina tāmartišu. (+) 41635.
41482	1881,0625.94	Joined to 34108.
41483	1881,0625.95	Account of issues of silver. SE 1/11/218. CT 49, 35-36, no. 150; van der Spek, Raḫimesu, 222-226, no. 13.
41484	1881,0625.96	Joined to 32583.
	1881,0625.97	Joined to 32154.
41485	1881,0625.98	Astrological; similar to TCL 6, nos. 19-20. LBAT 1611 (and see p. xxxvii); Pinches, JTVI 26 (1893) 153.
41486	1881,0625.99	Astronomical Diary for SE 170. LBAT 874; Sachs and Hunger, ADART III, no. -141 E.
41487	1881,0625.100	Omens; Šumma izbu 18; the colophon states that the tablet was copied from a leather scroll from Borsippa. + 41548 + 41864 + 1881,0625.239. Leichty, TCS 4, 166, 174, 200-201 (41548 only); Frahm, NABU 2005, 43-45, no. 43 (on 41548); De Zorzi, Šumma izbu, 763.
41488	1881,0625.101	Receipt for onions. 20/4/-.
41489	1881,0625.102	Promissory note for silver. Nabû-[] 25/5/11.
41490	1881,0625.103	Astronomical Diary for SE 208. LBAT 483; Sachs and Hunger, ADART III, no. -103 B.
41491	1881,0625.104	Account of iron.
41492	1881,0625.105	Account of dates.
41493	1881,0625.106	Account of dates or grain.
41494	1881,0625.107	Contract.
41495	1881,0625.108	Memorandum.
41496	1881,0625.109	Astrological; groups of days associated with zodiac and planets. LBAT 1581.
41497	1881,0625.110	Astronomical Diary. LBAT 870.

41498	1881,0625.111	Astrological; Enūma Anu Enlil 63. LBAT 1562; Reiner and Pingree, BPO 1, source E and p. 64; Reiner, Fs Borger (CM 10), 298; Walker, JCS 36, 64-66.
41499	1881,0625.112	Lexical; Aa VII/1 = 35. + 1881,0625.299. CT 12, 23; MSL 14, 459.
41500	1881,0625.113	Account of disbursements.
41501	1881,0625.114	Astronomical.
41502	1881,0625.115	Astronomical Diary. LBAT 875.
41503	1881,0625.116	Promissory note for silver. 29/3/11. Babylon.
41504	1881,0625.117	Contract; vitrified; probably from the Kasr archive at Babylon.
41505	1881,0625.118	Field sale. Wunsch, CM 20A-B, no. 3.
41506	1881,0625.119	Account of boatloads of dates.
41507	1881,0625.120	Temple accounts. SE.
41508	1881,0625.121	Economic.
41509	1881,0625.122	Inventory of household furniture. Bertin 2975.
41510	1881,0625.123	Account of issues of silver. SE Arsaces 20/6/219. CT 49, 41, no. 162; Strassmaier, ZA 3, 146; Bertin 2921; van der Spek, Raḫimesu, 241-242, no. 29.
41511	1881,0625.124	Field sale; sealed; finger-nail marks; dupl. 32192. [Nbn] 2/12b/3. Babylon. Bertin 3042-3043; Wunsch, CM 20A-B, no. 48; Nisaba 28, no. 66.
41512	1881,0625.125	Lexical; syllabary. CT 11, 5.
41513	1881,0625.126	Promissory note for silver.
41514	1881,0625.127	Astronomical?
41515	1881,0625.128	Only personal names.
41516	1881,0625.129	Joined to 41468.
41517	1881,0625.130	Astronomical?
41518	1881,0625.131	Astronomical Diary. LBAT 872.
41519	1881,0625.132	Astronomical Diary for SE 90. + 41860. LBAT 291 and 873; Sachs and Hunger, ADART II, no. -221.
41520	1881,0625.133	Astronomical; Normal Star Almanac for SE 107. + 41532 + 41863. LBAT 1016-1018; Hunger and Sachs, ADART VII, no. 44.
41521	1881,0625.134	Account of issues of silver. SE Arsaces 6/6/219. Strassmaier, ZA 3, 147; Bertin 2919; van der Spek, Raḫimesu, 242-243, no. 30; Hackl, Fs van der Spek, 87-106, no. 6.
41522	1881,0625.135	Joined to Rm.720.
41523	1881,0625.136	Astrological omens; protases written in numbers. Gadd, JCS 21, 53-63; Hunger, AOAT 1, 133-145; cf. Hunger, ZA 64, 43-45.
41524	1881,0625.137	Joined to 41464.
41525	1881,0625.138	Tintir II. + 41914. George, BTT, pl. 7.
41526	1881,0625.139	Astronomical Diary. LBAT 867.

	1881,0625.140	Joined to 34713.
41527	1881,0625.141	Astronomical; Goal Year Text for SE 107. LBAT 1236; Hunger and Sachs, ADART VI, no. 18.
41528	1881,0625.142	Account.
41529	1881,0625.143	Astronomical Diary for SE 221. + 41546 + 132278 (+) Böhl 1332 (Leiden). LBAT 495-496; Sachs, PTRSL A.276, 49, fig. 13; Sachs and Hunger, ADART III, no. -90.
41530	1881,0625.144	Astronomical Diary. BAT 879
41531	1881,0625.145	Astronomical?
41532	1881,0625.146	Joined to 41520.
41533	1881,0625.147	Contract; sealed. [Cyr]. [Babylon]. Wunsch, CM 20A-B, no. 124; Nisaba 28, no. 95.
41534	1881,0625.148	Memorandum.
41535	1881,0625.149	Incantation.
41536	1881,0625.150	Astronomical; lunar eclipse table for at least 563-562 BC. LBAT 1421; Stephenson, HEER, 152, 197, 205; Hunger and Sachs, ADART V, no. 7.
41537	1881,0625.151	Astronomical Diary.
41538	1881,0625.152	Economic; only the date preserved. SE -/-/149.
41539	1881,0625.153	Sumerian literary.
41540	1881,0625.154	Contract(?).
41541	1881,0625.155	Medical.
41542	1881,0625.156	Joined to 32205.
41543	1881,0625.157	Joined to 34392.
41544	1881,0625.158	Receipt for dates or grain.
41545	1881,0625.159	Astronomical; Normal Star Almanac for SE 105; part of same tablet as 132283; prayer on upper edge. + 1881,0625.459. LBAT 1012; Hunger and Sachs, ADART VII, no. 40.
41546	1881,0625.160	Joined to 41529.
41547	1881,0625.161	Economic. 26/-/-.
41548	1881,0625.162	Joined to 41487.
41549	1881,0625.163	Contract.
41550	1881,0625.164	Prayer.
41551	1881,0625.165	Contract; division of an inheritance. Dar. Babylon. Wunsch, CM 20A-B, no. 10 B.
41552	1881,0625.166	Astronomical Diary. LBAT 880
41553	1881,0625.167	Memorandum involving the šatammu and assembly of Esangila. SE []/7/153. Kessler, Fs Oelsner, 225
41554	1881,0625.168	Astronomical?
41555	1881,0625.169	Astronomical Diary.
41556	1881,0625.170	Account of silver(?). SE Arsaces []/[]/218. (Babylon). Kessler, Fs Oelsner, 219, 234, no. 8; van der Spek, Raḫimesu, 221-222, no. 12.

41557	1881,0625.171	Astronomical Diary. + 42017. LBAT 878 + 945.
41558	1881,0625.172	Economic.
41559	1881,0625.173	Astronomical Diary for SE 235. LBAT 881; Sachs and Hunger, ADART III, no. -76.
41560	1881,0625.174	Astronomical Diary for SE 118. + 41632 (+) 35043 + 35211. LBAT 886 + 890; Sachs and Hunger, ADART II, no. -193 D.
41561	1881,0625.175	Joined to 32205.
41562	1881,0625.176	Contract; lease of a house. Cam 2/12/5. Babylon.
41563	1881,0625.177	Promissory note for dates. Nbn 5/7/10. Babylon. Wunsch, CM 20A-B, no. 89.
41564	1881,0625.178	Astronomical?
41565	1881,0625.179	Astronomical; lunar eclipse report for eclipse of 19 January 67 BC. SE Arsaces -/-/244. LBAT 1447; Stephenson, HEER, 161-162, 183, 204-205; Hunger and Sachs, ADART V, no. 2
41566	1881,0625.180	Astronomical Diary; historical section.
41567	1881,0625.181	Astronomical Diary. LBAT 877.
41568	1881,0625.182	Astronomical Diary. + 42072 + 42088. LBAT 876 + 962.
41569	1881,0625.183	Economic.
41570	1881,0625.184	Astronomical; ziqpu stars; turns at right angles. LBAT 1507.
41571	1881,0625.185	Joined to Rm.778.
41572	1881,0625.186	Contract. Nabû-[] -/-/21.
41573	1881,0625.187	Contract. Cam 13/6/-.
41574	1881,0625.188	Contract.
41575	1881,0625.189	Contract(?).
41576	1881,0625.190	Issue of silver. SE 5/3/219. van der Spek, Raḫimesu, 245, no. 35; Kessler, Fs Oelsner, 222, 238, no. 15.
41577	1881,0625.191	Temple ritual for Esangila for the month Nisannu; probably a three-column tablet; probably Seleucid. George, Fs Lambert 263-270; Linssen, CM 25, 9, 26 n. 26, 80 n. 414, 83, 86, 90, 324.
41578	1881,0625.192	Astronomical Diary for SE 228. LBAT 509; Sachs and Hunger, ADART III, no. -83.
41579	1881,0625.193	Astronomical Diary for SE 34. (+) 34099 + 41925 + 42003. LBAT 236; Sachs and Hunger, ADART I, no. -277 A.
41580	1881,0625.194	Astronomical Diary.
41581	1881,0625.195	Astronomical Diary for SE 143. + 1881,0625.197. LBAT 371; Sachs and Hunger, ADART II, no. -168 A.

41582	1881,0625.196	Promissory note for silver; sealed. SE Ant III & Ant 10/7/116. Mitchell and Searight, no. 728; Nisaba 28, no. 596.
	1881,0625.197	Joined to 41581.
41583	1881,0625.198	Astrological; tabulated; microzodiac; cf. 32517 etc. LBAT 1579; Weidner, Gestirn-Darstellungen, 38.
41584	1881,0625.199	Joined to 34283.
41585	1881,0625.200	Account.
41586	1881,0625.201	Omens; Šumma ālu, tablet 31 (colophon says tablet 29); commentary; colophon refers to the following tablet being written as a leather scroll at Babylon. Frahm, NABU 2005, 43-45, no. 43; Freedman, If a city, vol. 2, 149-150, 166.
41587	1881,0625.202	Astronomical Diary. LBAT 888.
41588	1881,0625.203	Astronomical; Normal Star Almanac for SE 96. + 132284. LBAT 1008 (41588 only); Hunger and Sachs, ADART VII, no. 30.
41589	1881,0625.204	Astronomical Diary. LBAT 884.
41590	1881,0625.205	Joined to 34368.
41591	1881,0625.206	Promissory note for barley; dupl. 30325. Nbk 29/2/30. Babylon. Nbk 212; Bertin 146.
41592	1881,0625.207	Joined to 32072.
41593	1881,0625.208	Promissory note for silver. Dar 20+/2/-.
41594	1881,0625.209	Division of property. Nbk 18/11/32. Babylon. Nbk 251; Bertin 157.
41595	1881,0625.210	Letter from Madān-bēlu-uṣur to Iddin-Marduk. CT 22, 16-17, no. 79; Hackl et al., AOAT 414/1, no. 6.
41596	1881,0625.211	Receipt for payment.
41597	1881,0625.212	Receipt. 18/5/-.
41598	1881,0625.213	Letter; names of sender and addressee lost. Hackl et al., AOAT 414/1, no. 102.
41599	1881,0625.214	Astronomical; Normal Star Almanac for SE 120. LBAT 1022; Bertin 2895; Hunger and Sachs, ADART VII, no. 51.
41600	1881,0625.215	Joined to 32205.
41601	1881,0625.216	Marriage contract.
41602	1881,0625.217	Joined to 32325.
41603	1881,0625.218	Receipt of onions, šibšu-tax on land; one third is due to Bagasarū (Old Iranian name). Dar 5/1/4. Bīt-rab-kāṣir. Dar 105; Bertin 2034; Abraham, BPPE, 372-373, no. 89.
41604	1881,0625.219	Contract. 25/-/-.
41605	1881,0625.220	Letter to a woman; unusually large.
41606	1881,0625.221	Contract.

41607	1881,0625.222	Receipt of ilku-tax by Marduk-nāṣir-apli. Dar 8/7/24. Abraham, BPPE, 367-368, no. 87; Bertin 2548.
41608	1881,0625.223	Joined to 34245.
41609	1881,0625.224	Receipt.
41610	1881,0625.225	Sale of an ox. Dar 6/7/10. Alu-ša-Nabû. Dar 276; Bertin 2181.
41611	1881,0625.226	Bilingual incantation.
41612	1881,0625.227	LetterLetter from Rēmūt to f.[]. CT 22, 37, no. 200; Hackl et al., AOAT 414/1, no. 47.
41613	1881,0625.228	Lexical; geographical list.
41614	1881,0625.229	+ 1881,0625.233. Joined to 32889.
41615	1881,0625.230	Joined to 32352.
41616	1881,0625.231	Astronomical Diary for SE 56. + 41636 + 41645 + 41797 + 42233. LBAT 255-256, 885, 895 and 985; Sachs and Hunger, ADART II, no. -255 A.
41617	1881,0625.232	Omens.
41618	1881,0625.233	Joined to 32889.
41619	1881,0625.234	Astrological; Enūma Anu Enlil 56. LBAT 1555; Reiner, Fs Borger (CM 10), 298; Fincke, Kaskal 12, 267-279.
41620	1881,0625.235	Mathematical table.
41621	1881,0625.236	Omens. (+) 41651 (+) 41694 (+) 41836.
41622	1881,0625.237	Apparently a royal ritual involving specific dates in the year, in which the ērib bīti priest is involved, and repeated visits to a garden (gannatu); the text mentions an Asalluḫi-mansum, possibly the apkallu-sage of the reign of Hammurabi (see Finkel in Fs Sachs, p. 145).
41623	1881,0625.238	Commentary; physiognomic omens; Alamdimmû.
	1881,0625.239	Joined to 41487.
41624	1881,0625.240	Lexical; Ea; sign list; literary extracts; prayer to Nabû; turns sideways.
41625	1881,0625.241	Obv. extracts, dupl. RA 28, 138, 37-38; rev. lexical, giš.
41626	1881,0625.242	Account of issues of silver. SE Arsaces 21/5/218. Babylon. CT 49, 39, no. 159; Strassmaier, ZA 3, 144; Bertin 2920; van der Spek, Raḫimesu, 216-217, no. 7.
41627	1881,0625.243	Astronomical; procedure text for the moon, related to System A.
41628	1881,0625.244	Astronomical Diary for SE 148. (+) 41670. LBAT 378; Stephenson and Walker, Halley's Comet 28-30; Sachs and Hunger, ADART III, no. -163 C; Stephenson, HEER, 170.
41629	1881,0625.245	Joined to 32839.
41630	1881,0625.246	Astrological. + 41664. LBAT 1614 (41630 only).

41631	1881,0625.247	Astronomical?
41632	1881,0625.248	Joined to 41560.
41633	1881,0625.249	Joined to Rm.767.
41634	1881,0625.250	Astronomical; Normal Star Almanac for SE 93; prayer on upper edge. + 1881,0625.272. LBAT 1006; Hunger and Sachs, ADART VII, no. 29.
41635	1881,0625.251	Astrological commentary; Sîn ina tāmartišu. (+) 41481.
41636	1881,0625.252	Joined to 41616.
41637	1881,0625.253	Commentary. + 41667.
41638	1881,0625.254	Astronomical Diary. LBAT 889.
41639	1881,0625.255	Lexical; Ea II.
41640	1881,0625.256	Astronomical; Normal Star Almanac for SE 229. LBAT 1102; Hunger and Sachs, ADART VII, no. 101.
41641	1881,0625.257	Joined to Rm.694.
41642	1881,0625.258	Astrological omens.
41643	1881,0625.259	Astronomical; Goal Year Text for SE 97. LBAT 1228; Hunger and Sachs, ADART VI, no. 12.
41644	1881,0625.260	Late astrological speculation. + 41695. LBAT 1612 (41644 only); LBAT 1615 (41695 only).
41645	1881,0625.261	Joined to 41616.
41646	1881,0625.262	Joined to Rm.701.
41647	1881,0625.263	Astronomical Diary for SE 81. + 41853. LBAT 285-286; Sachs and Hunger, ADART II, no. -230 A.
41648	1881,0625.264	Field sale.
41649	1881,0625.265	Cylinder; inscription of Nebuchadnezzar II. Berger, AOAT 4/1, Nebukadnezar Zylinder-Fragment IV, 1, no. 4.
41650	1881,0625.266	Cylinder; inscription of Šamaš-šum-ukin. Frame, RIMB 2.6.33.6.
41651	1881,0625.267	Omen apodoses. (+) 41621 (+) 41694 (+) 41836.
41652	1881,0625.268	Astronomical Diary. LBAT 887.
41653	1881,0625.269	Receipt for silver as payment of interest. Cyr 21/6/2. Babylon. Cyr 51; Bertin 1712; Wunsch, CM 3, no. 276.
41654	1881,0625.270	Astronomical; Goal Year Text; not datable. LBAT 1356; Hunger and Sachs, ADART VI, no. 156.
41655	1881,0625.271	Astronomical Diary. SE 85. + 41683 + 41866. LBAT 288-289; Sachs and Hunger, ADART II, no. -226 A; Pirngruber, NABU 2014, 55-56, no. 35.
	1881,0625.272	Joined to 41634.
41656	1881,0625.273	Astronomical Diary for SE 214. LBAT 485; Sachs and Hunger, ADART III, no. -97.
41657	1881,0625.274	Astrological omens; Enūma Anu Enlil.
41658	1881,0625.275	Economic; probably Seleucid.

41659	1881,0625.276	Field sale.
41660	1881,0625.277	Astronomical Diary for SE 30; colophon. LBAT 232; Sachs and Hunger, ADART I, no. -281 A.
41661	1881,0625.278	Omens.
41662	1881,0625.279	Astronomical?
41663	1881,0625.280	Court record about a deposit; caption for a seal, but not sealed. d.l. [Babylon]. + 41698 + 41905. Wunsch, Bab Arch 2, no. 45; Sandowicz, AOAT 398, 174, no. O.5.
41664	1881,0625.281	Joined to 41630.
41665	1881,0625.282	Issue of silver. SE []/[]/218. van der Spek, Raḫimesu, 231-232, no. 20; Kessler, Fs Oelsner, 220-221, 236, no. 11.
41666	1881,0625.283	Astronomical; ziqpu stars. LBAT 1504.
41667	1881,0625.284	Joined to 41637.
41668	1881,0625.285	Promissory note for dates. Dar 16/7/5. Dar 177; Bertin 2832.
41669	1881,0625.286	Contract.
41670	1881,0625.287	Astronomical Diary for SE 148. + 41840 + 41915 + 42239 (+) 41628. LBAT 379 + 891 + 911 + 993; Stephenson and Walker, Halley's Comet 31-33; Sachs and Hunger, ADART III, no. -163 C.
41671	1881,0625.288	Astrological; Enūma Anu Enlil, Sin; dupl. ACh Supp 20. LBAT 1569; Reiner, Fs Borger (CM 10), 298.
41672	1881,0625.289	Envelope of a letter; a-na 1.SUM-na-d.Marduk AD-ia; sealed. n.d. Mitchell and Searight, no. 340; Nisaba 28, no. 216.
41673	1881,0625.290	Memorandum.
41674	1881,0625.291	Joined to 32157.
41675	1881,0625.292	Field sale.
41676	1881,0625.293	Inventory?
41677	1881,0625.294	Joined to 32210.
41678	1881,0625.295	Unidentified.
41679	1881,0625.296	Astronomical; ziqpu stars. LBAT 1509.
41680	1881,0625.297	Joined to 32525.
41681	1881,0625.298	Omens; extispicy.
	1881,0625.299	Joined to 41499.
41682	1881,0625.300	Astronomical?
41683	1881,0625.301	Joined to 41655.
41684	1881,0625.302	Field sale; finger-nail marks. Šamaš-šum-ukin. Brinkman and Kennedy, JCS 35, 38, K.171; Bertin 1011.
41685	1881,0625.303	Mantic dream ritual.
41686	1881,0625.304	Astronomical?
41687	1881,0625.305	Joined to 36648.

41688	1881,0625.306	Astrological; Enūma Anu Enlil 63. LBAT 1563; Reiner and Pingree, BPO 1, source N; Reiner, Fs Borger (CM 10), 298.
41689	1881,0625.307	Astronomical Diary for SE 215. LBAT 487; Sachs and Hunger, ADART III, no. -96 B.
41690	1881,0625.308	Astronomical Diary for SE 50. LBAT 249; Sachs and Hunger, ADART I, no. -261 A.
41691	1881,0625.309	Astronomical Diary for SE 226. + 42100 (+) 32848. LBAT 507 + 970; Sachs and Hunger, ADART III, no. -85 C.
41692	1881,0625.310	Astronomical Diary. LBAT 898.
41693	1881,0625.311	Astronomical Diary for SE 193; prayer on upper edge. LBAT 459; Sachs and Hunger, ADART III, no. -118 A.
41694	1881,0625.312	Omen apodoses. (+) 41621 (+) 41651 (+) 41836.
41695	1881,0625.313	Joined to 41644.
41696	1881,0625.314	Letter from [Širku] to []. Hackl et al., AOAT 414/1, no. 43.
41697	1881,0625.315	Joined to 32163.
41698	1881,0625.316	Joined to 41663.
41699	1881,0625.317	Joined to 33922.
	1881,0625.318	Recorded by L. W. King as missing; the register describes it as a contract.
41700	1881,0625.319	Joined to 34392.
41701	1881,0625.320	Promissory note for silver. Nbk []/12/4. Saḫrītu. Nbk 39; Bertin 1061.
41702	1881,0625.321	Sale of a slave girl. Nbn 11/4/15. Babylon.
41703	1881,0625.322	Promissory note for silver. Nbk 6/10/-.
41704	1881,0625.323	Contract. Nbn 28/1/13. Babylon.
41705	1881,0625.324	Promissory note for dates. Dar 30/5/12.
41706	1881,0625.325	Promissory note for silver. Dar 30/9/[].
41707	1881,0625.326	Contract.
41708	1881,0625.327	Contract; hire of a boat.
41709	1881,0625.328	Account of disbursements.
41710	1881,0625.329	Astronomical Diary. LBAT 899.
41711	1881,0625.330	Promissory note for silver.
41712	1881,0625.331	Promissory note for dates.
41713a	1881,0625.332a	Promissory note for silver.
41713b	1881,0625.332b	Promissory note for silver. Nbn 6/[]/11. Babylon.
41714	1881,0625.333	Memorandum.
41715	1881,0625.334	Contract. 15/-/-.
41716	1881,0625.335	Contract.
41717	1881,0625.336	Astronomical?
41718	1881,0625.337	Contract.

41719	1881,0625.338	Promissory note for silver. Nbn 20/5/17. Babylon. Wunch, CM 20A-B, no. 9.
41720	1881,0625.339	Joined to 32205.
41721	1881,0625.340	Promissory note for silver. Dar 7/7/6. Babylon.
41722	1881,0625.341	Audit. Cam. Babylon.
41723	1881,0625.342	Account of silver .
41724	1881,0625.343	Sale of a donkey. -/-/6.
41725	1881,0625.344	Receipt.
41726	1881,0625.345	Promissory note for dates or grain.
41727	1881,0625.346	Economic.
41728	1881,0625.347	Account.
41729	1881,0625.348	Contract.
41730	1881,0625.349	Field sale.
41731	1881,0625.350	Contract.
41732	1881,0625.351	Field sale.
41733	1881,0625.352	Contract.
41734	1881,0625.353	Promissory note for dates or grain.
41735	1881,0625.354	Sumerian incantation.
41736	1881,0625.355	Promissory note for silver. Cam -/2/-. Babylon.
41737	1881,0625.356	Promissory note for silver.
41738	1881,0625.357	Deposition. -/2/-.
41739	1881,0625.358	Contract.
41740	1881,0625.359	Promissory note for onions.
41741	1881,0625.360	Contract.
41742	1881,0625.361	Contract. 14/5/-. Babylon.
41743	1881,0625.362	Field sale. Wunsch, CM 20A-B, no. 203.
41744	1881,0625.363	Sale of a slave? + 42216.
41745	1881,0625.364	Astronomical?
41746	1881,0625.365	Economic.
41747	1881,0625.366	Issue of silver. SE []/[]/219. van der Spek, Raḫimesu, 243-244, no. 32; Kessler, Fs Oelsner, 221, 236, no. 12
41748	1881,0625.367	Contract; lease of a house.
41749	1881,0625.368	Economic.
41750	1881,0625.369	Account of silver .
41751	1881,0625.370	Economic.
41752	1881,0625.371	Receipt. 19/6/-.
41753	1881,0625.372	Receipt. Cyr 3/4/8.
41754	1881,0625.373	Contract. Dar 28/[]/15. Babylon.
41755	1881,0625.374	Field sale. + 41765.
41756	1881,0625.375	Contract. Nbn 7/6/-. Babylon.
41757	1881,0625.376	Contract; refers to an earlier contract on parchment. SE Ant I & Sel []/2/39. CT 49, 21, no. 109.
41758	1881,0625.377	Memorandum; refers to a leather protocol. SE. Kessler, Fs Oelsner, 224-225, 240, no. 18.
41759	1881,0625.378	Contract.

41760	1881,0625.379	Contract.
41761	1881,0625.380	Account of disbursements.
41762	1881,0625.381	Contract.
41763	1881,0625.382	Economic.
41764	1881,0625.383	Contract.
41765	1881,0625.384	Joined to 41755.
41766	1881,0625.385	Astronomical?
41767	1881,0625.386	Contract. Cam 1/[]/acc.
41768	1881,0625.387	Astronomical Diary. LBAT 896.
41769	1881,0625.388	Economic.
41770	1881,0625.389	Economic.
41771	1881,0625.390	Account.
41772	1881,0625.391	Unidentified.
41773	1881,0625.392	Economic.
41774	1881,0625.393	Economic.
41775	1881,0625.394	Contract.
41776	1881,0625.395	Contract.
41777	1881,0625.396	Contract; accounts of a ḫarrānu partnership. [Cam] [22]/[6]/[5]. Wunsch, CM 20A-B, no. 60 B.
41778	1881,0625.397	Promissory note for dates.
41779	1881,0625.398	Account of disbursements.
41780	1881,0625.399	Account of issues of silver. SE 2/2/219. van der Spek, Raḫimesu, 238, no. 25; Kessler, Fs Oelsner, 219-220, 235, no. 10.
41781	1881,0625.400	Contract. 15/9/-.
41782	1881,0625.401	Contract.
41783	1881,0625.402	Contract. 16/11/-.
41784	1881,0625.403	Contract.
41785	1881,0625.404	Deposition; sealed. [Nbn] []/[]/17. [Babylon]. Wunsch, AfO 44/45, 94-95, no. 26; Mitchell and Searight, no. 322; Nisaba 28, no. 26.
41786	1881,0625.405	Contract. 1/12/-.
41787	1881,0625.406	Promissory note for silver. Nbk 24/12/23.
41788	1881,0625.407	Contract. Cam 12/10/7.
41789	1881,0625.408	Economic.
41790	1881,0625.409	Promissory note for dates or grain. 22/-/-.
41791	1881,0625.410	Promissory note for silver.
41792	1881,0625.411	Contract.
41793	1881,0625.412	Contract. AM.
41794	1881,0625.413	Economic.
41795	1881,0625.414	Economic.
41796	1881,0625.415	Astronomical Diary. LBAT 894.
41797	1881,0625.416	Joined to 41616.
41798	1881,0625.417	Economic.
41799	1881,0625.418	Economic.

41800	1881,0625.419	Astronomical; lunar eclipse report for eclipse of 17 March 284 BC. LBAT 1452; Hunger and Sachs, ADART V, no. 14.
41801	1881,0625.420	Astronomical?
41802	1881,0625.421	Deposition.
41803	1881,0625.422	Astronomical?
41804	1881,0625.423	Joined to 32097.
41805	1881,0625.424	Promissory note for barley.
41806	1881,0625.425	Sale of a slave girl.
41807	1881,0625.426	Promissory note for silver.
41808	1881,0625.427	Contract. Nbn -/12/-.
41809	1881,0625.428	Promissory note for silver. Nbn []/[]/1. Borsippa. Zadok, Nisaba 21, 236.
41810	1881,0625.429	Promissory note for silver.
41811	1881,0625.430	Economic.
41812	1881,0625.431	Deposition. Nabû-[] -/-/1. Babylon.
41813	1881,0625.432	Economic.
41814	1881,0625.433	Astronomical Diary. LBAT 900.
41815	1881,0625.434	Account.
41816	1881,0625.435	Astronomical?
41817	1881,0625.436	Medical.
41818	1881,0625.437	Economic.
41819	1881,0625.438	Promissory note for silver.
41820	1881,0625.439	Contract. 19/-/-. Babylon.
41821	1881,0625.440	Contract.
41822	1881,0625.441	Economic.
41823	1881,0625.442	Promissory note for dates. -/2/-.
41824	1881,0625.443	Receipt.
41825	1881,0625.444	Contract.
41826	1881,0625.445	Promissory note for silver. Cam 13/10/-.
41827	1881,0625.446	Economic.
41828	1881,0625.447	Contract; land sale; finger-nail marks.
41829	1881,0625.448	Promissory note for barley. 10/4/7.
41830	1881,0625.449	Deposition. Dar -/8/-.
41831	1881,0625.450	Economic.
41832	1881,0625.451	Astronomical Diary. LBAT 897.
41833	1881,0625.452	Joined to 32839.
41834	1881,0625.453	Joined to 41464.
41835	1881,0625.454	Joined to 34191.
41836	1881,0625.455	Omen apodoses. (+) 41621 (+) 41651 (+) 41694.
41837	1881,0625.456	Joined to 41464.
41838	1881,0625.457	Astronomical; Normal Star Almanac for SE 100 and 101. LBAT 1104; Hunger and Sachs, ADART VII, no. 37.

41839	1881,0625.458	Astronomical Diary for SE 223. LBAT 499; Sachs and Hunger, ADART III, no. -88 B.
	1881,0625.459	Joined to 41545.
41840	1881,0625.460	Joined to 41670.
41841	1881,0625.461	Astronomical Diary for SE 175. + 41881. LBAT 430-431; Sachs and Hunger, ADART III, no. -136 A.
41842	1881,0625.462	Joined to 32847.
41843	1881,0625.463	Omens.
41844	1881,0625.464	Contract.
41845	1881,0625.465	Field sale; sealed; finger-nail marks. RN lost 13/6/3. Babylon. Nisaba 28, no. 97
41846	1881,0625.466	Astronomical; Normal Star Almanac for SE 106. LBAT 1015; Hunger and Sachs, ADART VII, no. 42.
41847	1881,0625.467	Astronomical; Goal Year Text for SE 246. LBAT 1302; Hunger and Sachs, ADART VI, no. 90.
41848	1881,0625.468	Joined to 32490.
41849	1881,0625.469	Sale of fields; dupl. 33922. [Cam] [14]/[3]/[4]. + 42024.
41850	1881,0625.470	Astronomical Diary for SE 77. LBAT 283; Sachs and Hunger, ADART II, no. -234 B.
41851	1881,0625.471	Astronomical Diary for SE 54. LBAT 252; Sachs and Hunger, ADART II, no. -257 A.
41852	1881,0625.472	Account.
41853	1881,0625.473	Joined to 41647.
41854	1881,0625.474	Joined to 32209.
41855	1881,0625.475	Astronomical Diary. LBAT 893.
41856	1881,0625.476	Astrological omens.
41857	1881,0625.477	Astrological omens.
41858	1881,0625.478	Chronicle; parallel to 27796 (Walker, Fs Kraus, 398-417); mentions Itti-Marduk-balāṭu and Mutakkil-Nusku.
41859	1881,0625.479	Field sale; sealed; finger-nail marks. [Dar]. [Babylon]. Wunsch, CM 20A-B, no. 188; Mitchell and Searight, no. 469; Nisaba 28, no. 111.
41860	1881,0625.480	Joined to 41519.
41861	1881,0625.481	Account of silver.
41862	1881,0625.482	Literary; Gilgameš XII. George, Gilgamesh II, pl. 147.
41863	1881,0625.483	Joined to 41520.
41864	1881,0625.484	Joined to 41487.
41865	1881,0625.485	Astronomical; lunar ephemeris; System A, several columns, for SE 142. + 132280 (+) 41467+. LBAT 4; ACT 3a, colophon Zja; Steele, AHES 60 (2006) 123-153, text C.
41866	1881,0625.486	Joined to 41655.

41867	1881,0625.487	Names of gods in the court of Ea.
41868	1881,0625.488	Promissory note for silver. 2/12/-.
41869	1881,0625.489	Contract; transfer of property in lieu of part of a dowry. Wunsch, Bab Arch 2, no. 23.
41870	1881,0625.490	Omens.
41871	1881,0625.491	Astronomical Diary for SE 82. Sachs and Hunger, ADART II, no. -229 B; van der Spek, NABU 2016, 52-53, no. 27.
41872	1881,0625.492	Astrological omens.
41873	1881,0625.493	Astrological. LBAT 1620.
41874	1881,0625.494	Lexical; dupl. MSL III 19: Syllabary A 61-67.
41875	1881,0625.495	Astronomical?
41876	1881,0625.496	Contract.
41877	1881,0625.497	Astronomical Diary. LBAT 892.
41878	1881,0625.498	Astronomical Diary. LBAT 901.
41879	1881,0625.499	Joined to 34373.
41880	1881,0625.500	Astronomical; Normal Star Almanac for SE 92. LBAT 1005; Hunger and Sachs, ADART VII, no. 28.
41881	1881,0625.501	Joined to 41841.
41882	1881,0625.502	Joined to 41474.
41883	1881,0625.503	Astronomical Diary. LBAT 907.
41884	1881,0625.504	Astronomical Diary for SE 134. + 42112 + 42212. LBAT 355 + 966 + 990; Sachs and Hunger, ADART II, no. -177.
41885	1881,0625.505	Astronomical?
41886	1881,0625.506	Economic.
41887	1881,0625.507	Contract. SE []/[]/216? Kessler, Fs Oelsner, 225, 241, no. 20.
41888	1881,0625.508	Astronomical Diary for SE 178. LBAT 905; Sachs and Hunger, ADART III, no. -133 C.
41889	1881,0625.509	Astronomical Diary. LBAT 910.
41890	1881,0625.510	Joined to 34182.
41891	1881,0625.511	Unidentified.
41892	1881,0625.512	Astronomical Diary for SE 160. LBAT 906; Sachs and Hunger, ADART III, no. -151.
41893	1881,0625.513	Account of issues of silver. SE 10/9/217. CT 49, 34, no. 148; van der Spek, Raḫimesu, 214, no. 4.
41894	1881,0625.514	Account of issues of silver. SE. + 41982. van der Spek, Raḫimesu, 228-229, no. 17 (suggesting date in xii/218 SE) and 244, no. 34; Kessler, Fs Oelsner, 222-223, 239, nos. 14 and 16; Hackl, Fs van der Spek, 87-106, no. 7.
41895	1881,0625.515	Astronomical; Normal Star Almanac for SE 127. LBAT 1103; Hunger and Sachs, ADART VII, no. 54.
41896	1881,0625.516	Astronomical Diary. LBAT 903.

41897	1881,0625.517	Astronomical?
41898	1881,0625.518	Promissory note for dates.
41899	1881,0625.519	Joined to 34373.
41900	1881,0625.520	Astronomical; Almanac for SE 244; colophon. + 132285. LBAT 1177 (41900 only); Hunger and Sachs, ADART VII, no. 196
41901	1881,0625.521	Joined to 34105.
41902	1881,0625.522	Astronomical; procedure for the moon? LBAT 157; ACT 1006.
41903	1881,0625.523	Oral contract(?). + 1881,0625.584.
41904	1881,0625.524	Astronomical Diary. LBAT 908.
41905	1881,0625.525	Joined to 41663.
41906	1881,0625.526	Astronomical?
41907	1881,0625.527	Joined to 34392.
41908	1881,0625.528	Astronomical Diary. LBAT 909.
41909	1881,0625.529	Joined to 37077.
41910	1881,0625.530	Joined to 32188.
41911	1881,0625.531	Geographical list. George, BTT, pl. 53.
41912	1881,0625.532	Astrological or schematic astronomy. LBAT 1630.
41913	1881,0625.533	Joined to 32352.
41914	1881,0625.534	Joined to 41525.
41915	1881,0625.535	Joined to 41670.
41916	1881,0625.536	Joined to 34447.
	1881,0625.537	Joined to 41899.
41917	1881,0625.538	Astronomical Diary. LBAT 913
41918	1881,0625.539	Economic.
41919	1881,0625.540	Promissory note; sealed. SE Ant. Nisaba 28, no. 621.
41920	1881,0625.541	Astronomical?
41921	1881,0625.542	Astronomical Diary for SE 224. (+) Rm.695. LBAT 506; Sachs and Hunger, ADART III, no. -87 C.
41922	1881,0625.543	Contract. 8/[]/3.
41923	1881,0625.544	Astronomical Diary. LBAT 914.
41924	1881,0625.545	Medical omens.
41925	1881,0625.546	Joined to 34099.
41926	1881,0625.547	Astronomical Diary. LBAT 915.
41927	1881,0625.548	Joined to Rm.698.
41928	1881,0625.549	Astronomical Diary. LBAT 918
41929	1881,0625.550	Astrological omens.
41930	1881,0625.551	Joined to Rm.694.
41931	1881,0625.552	Literary; Counsels of Wisdom. Lambert, MC 24, no. 256.
41932	1881,0625.553	Joined to Rm.705.
41933	1881,0625.554	Contract; transfer of land. 21/9/[]. Borsippa. Wunsch, Bab Arch 2, no. 14; Zadok, Nisaba 21, 236.
41934	1881,0625.555	Astronomical Diary. LBAT 921.

41935	1881,0625.556	Sale of fields; sealed. [Nbn] [12]/[12]/[x+2]. [Babylon]. (+) 42215. Wunsch, CM 20A-B, no. 8 C; Mitchell and Searight, no. 325; Nisaba 28, no. 76a.
41936	1881,0625.557	Division of property.
41937	1881,0625.558	Joined to 41467.
41938	1881,0625.559	Astronomical Diary. LBAT 916.
41939	1881,0625.560	Astronomical; Mars, heliacal risings and first stationary points for (at least) SE 172-187. LBAT 111; ACT 501b.
41940	1881,0625.561	Astronomical observations. LBAT 1493.
41941	1881,0625.562	Joined to 41462.
41942	1881,0625.563	Astronomical Diary. LBAT 919.
41943	1881,0625.564	Astronomical Diary. LBAT 922.
41944	1881,0625.565	Prayer.
41945	1881,0625.566	Astronomical?
41946	1881,0625.567	Astronomical Diary for SE 41; colophon. LBAT 925; Sachs and Hunger, ADART I, no. -270 A.
41947	1881,0625.568	Astronomical Diary. LBAT 928
41948	1881,0625.569	Literary.
41949	1881,0625.570	Literary.
41950	1881,0625.571	Omens.
41951	1881,0625.572	Astronomical?
41952	1881,0625.573	Contract for a dowry.
41953	1881,0625.574	Astronomical Diary. LBAT 933.
41954	1881,0625.575	Astronomical; Goal Year Text; not datable. LBAT 1358; Hunger and Sachs, ADART VI, no. 157.
41955	1881,0625.576	Ritual.
41956	1881,0625.577	Astronomical; intermediate astronomy, moon; also astrology. LBAT 1520.
41957	1881,0625.578	Astronomical Diary.
41958	1881,0625.579	Astronomical; Goal Year Text for SE 201 and 202. + 132275 (+) 34405 (+) 34509 (+) 35453. LBAT 1384 (41958 only); Hunger and Sachs, ADART VI, no. 73.
41959	1881,0625.580	Astronomical Diary. LBAT 931.
41960	1881,0625.581	Medical.
41961	1881,0625.582	Omens.
41962	1881,0625.583	Astronomical Diary. LBAT 929.
	1881,0625.584	Joined to 41903.
41963	1881,0625.585	Joined to Rm.694.
41964	1881,0625.586	Astronomical Diary. LBAT 926.
41965	1881,0625.587	Astronomical; Normal Star Almanac for SE 152. LBAT 1105; Hunger and Sachs, ADART VII, no. 67.
41966	1881,0625.588	Astronomical?
41967	1881,0625.589	Astronomical Diary. LBAT 927.
41968	1881,0625.590	Joined to 41467.

41969	1881,0625.591	Astronomical?
41970	1881,0625.592	Sumerian literary.
41971	1881,0625.593	Astronomical?
41972	1881,0625.594	Astronomical?
41973	1881,0625.595	Astronomical Diary. LBAT 934.
41974	1881,0625.596	Joined to 37077.
41975	1881,0625.597	Envelope of a letter. SE Sel I 27/[]/21.
41976	1881,0625.598	Astronomical Diary. LBAT 938.
41977	1881,0625.599	Contract.
41978	1881,0625.600	Astronomical Diary. LBAT 943.
41979	1881,0625.601	Economic.
41980	1881,0625.602	Receipt.
41981	1881,0625.603	Contract.
41982	1881,0625.604	Joined to 41894.
41983	1881,0625.605	Ritual.
41984	1881,0625.606	Astronomical Diary. LBAT 940.
41985	1881,0625.607	Astronomical; lunar eclipse table, probably for the years 747-744 BC; prayer on upper edge. LBAT 1413; Hunger and Sachs, ADART V, no. 1; Britton, AOAT 297, 39.
41986	1881,0625.608	Literary cylinder.
41987	1881,0625.609	Unidentified; mentions d.iš8-tar.MEŠ.
41988	1881,0625.610	Astronomical; Normal Star Almanac; not datable. SE. LBAT 1106; Hunger and Sachs, ADART VII, no. 138.
41989	1881,0625.611	Astronomical Diary. LBAT 942.
41990	1881,0625.612	Astronomical procedure text for the moon; System A. LBAT 101; ACT 207cb; Ossendrijver, BMAPT, no. 73.
41991	1881,0625.613	Contract.
41992	1881,0625.614	Astronomical Diary for SE 215. LBAT 489; Sachs and Hunger, ADART III, no. -96 D.
41993	1881,0625.615	Physiognomic omens; Šumma liptu.
41994	1881,0625.616	Economic.
41995	1881,0625.617	Medical.
41996	1881,0625.618	Deposition.
41997	1881,0625.619	Joined to Rm.694.
41998	1881,0625.620	Contract.
41999	1881,0625.621	Dialogue contract involving the šatammu and assembly of Esangila. SE 16/12/221. Kessler, Fs Oelsner, 223-224, 240, no. 17; van der Spek, Fs Oelsner, 440.
42000	1881,0625.622	Contract; lease of a house; month 6b or 12b.
42001	1881,0625.623	Contract; sale of a house; sealed. d.l. Babylon. Nisaba 28, no. 79.
42002	1881,0625.624	Astronomical; table for Jupiter, at least SE 233-240; System B. Probably (+) 45865.

42003	1881,0625.625	Joined to 34099.
42004	1881,0625.626	Literary?
42005	1881,0625.627	Astronomical; Normal Star Almanac. SE. LBAT 1107; Hunger and Sachs, ADART VII, no. 139.
42006	1881,0625.628	Astronomical Diary. LBAT 936.
42007	1881,0625.629	Astronomical; Goal Year Text; not datable. LBAT 1359; Hunger and Sachs, ADART VI, no. 158.
42008	1881,0625.630	Astronomical Diary. LBAT 937.
42009	1881,0625.631	Omens.
42010	1881,0625.632	Offering list.
42011	1881,0625.633	Bilingual incantation.
42012	1881,0625.634	Literary(?).
42013	1881,0625.635	Astronomical Diary.
42014	1881,0625.636	Economic.
42015	1881,0625.637	Astronomical Diary for SE 58. (+) 34105. LBAT 941; Sachs and Hunger, ADART II, no. -253 B.
42016	1881,0625.638	Astronomical; Normal Star Almanac. SE. LBAT 1108; Hunger and Sachs, ADART VII, no. 140.
42017	1881,0625.639	Joined to 41557.
42018	1881,0625.640	Astronomical Diary. LBAT 939.
42019	1881,0625.641	Astronomical.
42020	1881,0625.642	Contract.
42021	1881,0625.643	Astronomical; Goal Year Text; not datable. LBAT 1354; Hunger and Sachs, ADART VI, no. 159.
42022	1881,0625.644	Astronomical; Normal Star Almanac for SE 100. LBAT 1109; Hunger and Sachs, ADART VII, no. 35.
42023	1881,0625.645	Astronomical?
42024	1881,0625.646	Joined to 41849.
42025	1881,0625.647	Horoscope. SE 30/1/231. + 42164. LBAT 1472-1473; Rochberg, Babylonian Horoscopes, no. 25.
42026	1881,0625.648	Astronomical procedure text or Vorläufer; rev. incomplete.
42027	1881,0625.649	Astronomical; Goal Year Text; not datable. LBAT 1360.
42028	1881,0625.650	Astronomical Diary. LBAT 946
42029	1881,0625.651	Astronomical?
42030	1881,0625.652	Contract.
42031	1881,0625.653	Contract.
42032	1881,0625.654	Astronomical Diary. LBAT 947.
42033	1881,0625.655	Joined to 34227.
42034	1881,0625.656	Astronomical Diary. LBAT 948.
42035	1881,0625.657	Astronomical Diary. LBAT 949.
42036	1881,0625.658	Astronomical?
42037	1881,0625.659	Astronomical Diary. LBAT 950.
42038	1881,0625.660	Astronomical Diary. LBAT 955.

42039	1881,0625.661	Astronomical?
42040	1881,0625.662	Court record; sealed. [Nbn] []/[]/[14+]. [Babylon]. Wunsch, AfO 44/45, 95, no. 27; Nisaba 28, no. 25.
42041	1881,0625.663	Joined to 34105.
42042	1881,0625.664	Contract.
42043	1881,0625.665	Account of issues of silver. SE []/[]/219? van der Spek, Raḫimesu, 244, no. 33; Kessler, Fs Oelsner, 221-222, 237, no. 13.
42044	1881,0625.666	Economic.
42045	1881,0625.667	Astronomical; Normal Star Almanac. SE. LBAT 1110; Hunger and Sachs, ADART VII, no. 141.
42046	1881,0625.668	Joined to 32383.
42047	1881,0625.669	Astronomical?
42048	1881,0625.670	Lexical.
42049	1881,0625.671	Contract.
42050	1881,0625.672	Lexical?
42051	1881,0625.673	Astronomical Diary. LBAT 959.
42052	1881,0625.674	Joined to 31728.
42053	1881,0625.675	Astronomical; lunar eclipse reports from 195 and 178 BC. LBAT 1439; Stephenson, HEER, 185; Hunger and Sachs, ADART V, no. 17.
42054	1881,0625.676	Receipt for purchase.
42055	1881,0625.677	Astronomical Diary. LBAT 956.
42056	1881,0625.678	Horoscope. SE 13/8/213. LBAT 1476.
42057	1881,0625.679	Joined to Rm.778.
42058	1881,0625.680	Astronomical Diary. LBAT 951.
42059	1881,0625.681	Astronomical Diary. LBAT 952.
42060	1881,0625.682	Astronomical Diary for SE 121. LBAT 327; Sachs and Hunger, ADART II, no. -190 C.
42061	1881,0625.683	Economic.
42062	1881,0625.684	Astronomical Diary. LBAT 961.
42063	1881,0625.685	Astronomical Diary for SE 52. + 42177. LBAT 954 and 980; Sachs and Hunger, ADART II, no. -259.
42064	1881,0625.686	Economic.
42065	1881,0625.687	Joined to 32204.
42066	1881,0625.688	Receipt.
42067	1881,0625.689	Contract.
42068	1881,0625.690	Astronomical Diary. LBAT 957.
42069	1881,0625.691	Astronomical Diary. LBAT 960.
42070	1881,0625.692	Astronomical Diary. LBAT 958.
42071	1881,0625.693	Contract.
42072	1881,0625.694	Joined to 41568.
42073	1881,0625.695	Astronomical; lunar eclipse report for eclipse of 5 October 80 BC. SE 232 (Arsaces). LBAT 1446; Stephen-

		son, HEER, 160-161; Hunger and Sachs, ADART V, no. 26.
42074	1881,0625.696	Promissory note for silver. Nbn. Babylon.
42075	1881,0625.697	Astronomical Diary. LBAT 973.
42076	1881,0625.698	Astronomical; Normal Star Almanac for SE 68. LBAT 1001; Hunger and Sachs, ADART VII, no. 18.
42077	1881,0625.699	Astronomical; Normal Star Almanac for SE 229. LBAT 1111; Hunger and Sachs, ADART VII, no. 102.
42078	1881,0625.700	Contract.
42079	1881,0625.701	Astronomical?
42080	1881,0625.702	Contract. Nbk -/-/32. Babylon.
42081	1881,0625.703	Astronomical; lunar ephemeris; System A. LBAT 15; ACT 6ab.
42082	1881,0625.704	Economic.
42083	1881,0625.705	Astronomical observations; Venus and lunar data from 463 to 392 BC. (+) 32299 (+) 45674. LBAT 1486; Hunger and Sachs, ADART V, no. 56.
42084	1881,0625.706	Astronomical?
42085	1881,0625.707	Astronomical Diary. LBAT 975.
42086	1881,0625.708	Astronomical Diary. LBAT 971.
42087	1881,0625.709	Astronomical?
42088	1881,0625.710	Joined to 41568.
42089	1881,0625.711	Promissory note for silver. -/4/-. Babylon.
42090	1881,0625.712	Astronomical?
42091	1881,0625.713	Astronomical?
42092	1881,0625.714	Astronomical Diary. LBAT 967.
42093	1881,0625.715	Astronomical?
42094	1881,0625.716	Contract.
42095	1881,0625.717	Letter from Itti-Marduk-balāṭu. SE Ant 17/6/[]. CT 49, 49, no. 191.
42096	1881,0625.718	Literary cylinder.
42097	1881,0625.719	Astronomical procedure text for the moon; System A. Ossendrijver, BMAPT, no. 86.
42098	1881,0625.720	Administrative. SE. Kessler, Fs Oelsner, 226, 241, no. 21 (copy) under wrong number 42058.
42099	1881,0625.721	Astronomical Diary. []/8/[].
42100	1881,0625.722	Joined to 41691.
42101	1881,0625.723	Astronomical?
42102	1881,0625.724	Astronomical Diary.
42103	1881,0625.725	Astronomical?
42104	1881,0625.726	Astronomical Diary. LBAT 965.
42105	1881,0625.727	Astrological omens.
42106	1881,0625.728	Astronomical; Goal Year Text; not datable. LBAT 1357; Hunger and Sachs, ADART VI, no. 160.

42107	1881,0625.729	Issue of silver. SE []/[]/218. (Babylon). van der Spek, Raḫimesu, 231, no. 19; Kessler, Fs Oelsner, 219, 234, no. 9.
42108	1881,0625.730	Joined to 34283.
42109	1881,0625.731	Lexical; Ea; sign list; literary extract.
42110	1881,0625.732	Joined to Rm.756.
42111	1881,0625.733	Incantation; Šuilla Išḫara no. 1 (prayer to Scorpius). Abusch and Schwemer, AMD 8/2 text 8.40 b, pl. 69.
42112	1881,0625.734	Joined to 41884.
42113	1881,0625.735	Promissory note for silver.
42114	1881,0625.736	Astronomical?
42115	1881,0625.737	Contract; fragment; about silver, oxen and sheep; sealed. d.l. Nisaba 28, no. 12.
42116	1881,0625.738	Field sale. -/8/-.
42117	1881,0625.739	Astronomical Diary. LBAT 968.
42118	1881,0625.740	Astronomical?
42119	1881,0625.741	Astronomical Diary. LBAT 964
42120	1881,0625.742	Astronomical?
	1881,0625.743	Joined to 40104.
42121	1881,0625.744	Astronomical?
42122	1881,0625.745	Astronomical?
42123	1881,0625.746	Literary.
42124	1881,0625.747	Literary.
42125	1881,0625.748	Astronomical?
42126	1881,0625.749	Lexical; syllabary.
42127	1881,0625.750	Astronomical?
42128	1881,0625.751	Astronomical Diary. LBAT 963.
42129	1881,0625.752	Lexical; god-list.
42130	1881,0625.753	Medical.
42131	1881,0625.754	Omens.
42132	1881,0625.755	Astronomical?
42133	1881,0625.756	Lexical; god-list.
42134	1881,0625.757	Astronomical Diary. LBAT 974.
42135	1881,0625.758	Astronomical; Normal Star Almanac for SE 80. LBAT 1002; Hunger and Sachs, ADART VII, no. 22.
42136	1881,0625.759	Astrological.
42137	1881,0625.760	Astronomical?
42138	1881,0625.761	Astronomical Diary. LBAT 969.
42139	1881,0625.762	Astronomical?
42140	1881,0625.763	Astronomical Diary. LBAT 976
42141	1881,0625.764	Astronomical; Goal Year Text; not datable. LBAT 1361; Hunger and Sachs, ADART VI, no. 161.
42142	1881,0625.765	Unidentified.
42143	1881,0625.766	Astronomical?
42144	1881,0625.767	Astronomical Diary. LBAT 977.

42145	1881,0625.768	Astronomical; lunar eclipse report for eclipse of 21 April 81 BC; prayer on upper edge. SE 231 (Arsaces). LBAT 1444; Hunger and Sachs, ADART V, no. 24.
42146	1881,0625.769	Astronomical?
42147	1881,0625.770	Astronomical; planetary observations; Greek letter phenomena for several planets. (+) 34368. LBAT 1483; Hunger and Sachs, ADART V, no. 87.
42148	1881,0625.771	Astronomical; Goal Year Text for SE 255. LBAT 1303; Hunger and Sachs, ADART VI, no. 94.
42149	1881,0625.772	Cylinder; historical?
42150	1881,0625.773	Administrative. SE.
42151	1881,0625.774	Contract.
42152	1881,0625.775	Astronomical; lunar ephemeris; System A. LBAT 1; ACT 3aa.
42153	1881,0625.776	Astronomical Diary. LBAT 978.
42154	1881,0625.777	Contract. -/-/1.
42155	1881,0625.778	Lcdgcr.
42156	1881,0625.779	Astronomical Diary. LBAT 983.
42157	1881,0625.780	Astrological. LBAT 1627.
42158	1881,0625.781	Astronomical Diary. LBAT 987.
42159	1881,0625.782	Literary; partly bilingual.
42160	1881,0625.783	Economic.
42161	1881,0625.784	Astronomical?
42162	1881,0625.785	Economic.
42163	1881,0625.786	Marriage contract.
42164	1881,0625.787	Joined to 42025.
42165	1881,0625.788	Astronomical Diary. LBAT 989.
42166	1881,0625.789	Economic.
42167	1881,0625.790	Account of wool.
42168	1881,0625.791	Astronomical?
42169	1881,0625.792	Contract.
42170	1881,0625.793	Economic.
42171	1881,0625.794	Fragment of a circular account.
42172	1881,0625.795	Receipt. 15/-/-.
42173	1881,0625.796	Contract.
42174	1881,0625.797	Colophon (widely spaced). Nbn. Babylon.
42175	1881,0625.798	Mathematical astronomy? LBAT 1491.
42176	1881,0625.799	Astronomical Diary. LBAT 979
42177	1881,0625.800	Joined to 42063.
42178	1881,0625.801	Astronomical Diary. LBAT 984.
42179	1881,0625.802	Astronomical?
42180	1881,0625.803	Unidentified.
42181	1881,0625.804	Lexical; cities.
42182	1881,0625.805	Economic; sealed.
42183	1881,0625.806	Contract.

42184	1881,0625.807	Field sale. Dar. Babylon.
42185	1881,0625.808	Contract. Nbn 5/-/-.
42186	1881,0625.809	Field sale.
42187	1881,0625.810	Astronomical?
42188	1881,0625.811	Contract; dated by Antiochus and Seleucus. SE 21/-/-.
42189	1881,0625.812	Contract(?); sealed.
42190	1881,0625.813	Promissory note.
42191	1881,0625.814	Astronomical; Normal Star Almanac. SE. LBAT 1112; Hunger and Sachs, ADART VII, no. 142.
42192	1881,0625.815	Astronomical Diary. LBAT 525.
42193	1881,0625.816	Astronomical?
42194	1881,0625.817	Astronomical?
42195	1881,0625.818	Astronomical Diary. LBAT 981.
42196	1881,0625.819	Contract.
42197	1881,0625.820	Contract. Dar 21/[]/6.
42198	1881,0625.821	Receipt.
42199	1881,0625.822	Astronomical Diary. LBAT 992.
42200	1881,0625.823	Astronomical?
42201	1881,0625.824	Astronomical Diary. LBAT 982
42202	1881,0625.825	Joined to 32169.
42203	1881,0625.826	Astronomical?
42204	1881,0625.827	Astronomical Diary. LBAT 988.
42205	1881,0625.828	Contract; refers to smiths; sealed. SE. Nisaba 28, no. 622.
42206	1881,0625.829	Sale of an ox. Dar 14/3/-. Dilbat.
42207	1881,0625.830	Contract.
42208	1881,0625.831	Economic.
42209	1881,0625.832	Literary.
42210	1881,0625.833	Joined to 31521.
42211	1881,0625.834	Astronomical; Normal Star Almanac. SE. LBAT 1113; Hunger and Sachs, ADART VII, no. 143.
42212	1881,0625.835	Joined to 41884.
42213	1881,0625.836	Economic.
42214	1881,0625.837	Medical.
42215	1881,0625.838	Sale of fields; sealed. Nbn [12]/[12]/[x]+2. Babylon. (+) 41935. Wunsch, CM 20A-B, no. 8 D; Mitchell and Searight, no. 325; Nisaba 28, no. 76b.
42216	1881,0625.839	Joined to 41744.
42217	1881,0625.840	Contract.
42218	1881,0625.841	Contract. Nbk 8/-/-.
42219	1881,0625.842	Astronomical?
42220	1881,0625.843	Economic.
42221	1881,0625.844	Economic.
42222	1881,0625.845	Economic.

42223	1881,0625.846	Astronomical?
42224	1881,0625.847	Contract.
42225	1881,0625.848	Promissory note for barley. Nbk 2/12/-.
42226	1881,0625.849	Astronomical; Normal Star Almanac for SE 129. LBAT 1114; Hunger and Sachs, ADART VII, no. 56.
42227	1881,0625.850	Sale of an ox.
42228	1881,0625.851	Contract.
42229	1881,0625.852	Contract.
42230	1881,0625.853	Astronomical?
42231	1881,0625.854	Astronomical?
42232	1881,0625.855	Astronomical; Normal Star Almanac. SE. LBAT 1115; Hunger and Sachs, ADART VII, no. 144.
42233	1881,0625.856	Joined to 41616.
42234	1881,0625.857	Astronomical?
42235	1881,0625.858	Astronomical Diary. LBAT 994.
42236	1881,0625.859	Astronomical?
42237	1881,0625.860	Astronomical Diary. LBAT 986.
42238	1881,0625.861	Economic.
42239	1881,0625.862	Joined to 41670.
42240	1881,0625.863	Astronomical Diary. LBAT 991.
42241	1881,0625.864	Contract.
42242	1881,0625.865	Economic.
42243	1881,0625.866	Astronomical; table for Jupiter; System B.
42244	1881,0625.867	Economic.
42245	1881,0625.868	Astronomical?
42246	1881,0625.869	Astronomical Diary. LBAT 528.
42247	1881,0625.870	Astronomical; Normal Star Almanac. SE. LBAT 1116; Hunger and Sachs, ADART VII, no. 145.
42248	1881,0625.871	Astronomical; lunar ephemeris; System A. LBAT 14; ACT 5a.
42249	1881,0625.872	Economic.
42250	1881,0625.873	Economic. + 1881,0625.878.
42251	1881,0625.874	Astronomical Diary. LBAT 529.
42252	1881,0625.875	Astronomical; Almanac. SE. LBAT 1212; Hunger and Sachs, ADART VII, no. 226.
42253	1881,0625.876	Astronomical?
42254	1881,0625.877	Contract.
	1881,0625.878	Joined to 42250.
42255	1881,0625.879	Contract.
42256	1881,0625.880	Contract. Dar -/12/5. Babylon.
42257	1881,0625.881	Field sale.
42258	1881,0625.882	Economic.

1881,0701 collection

The 1881,0701 collection comes from the excavations of Hormuzd Rassam at Babylon, Borsippa, Geraineh, Kutha, and Sippar. See J. E. Reade in CBTBM VI, p. xxxi. Geraineh, some 20 km north of Babylon, is almost certainly the source of all the Old Babylonian tablets in this collection, most of which are dated in the reigns of Ammiditana and Ammiṣaduqa. The Babylonian name of the site remains unknown. A few of these tablets (nos. 1-3, 5-8) are mistakenly recorded in the register as coming from Tell Ibrahim (Kutha) and two are marked as coming from Abu Habbah (nos. 136 and 138).

The register gives no provenance for most of the collection, but gives the provenance

as A.H. for nos. 72(?), 194, 200,
as Abu-habbah for nos. 31, 59, 61, 62, 70, 73-77, 100, 106-109, 111, 113, 115, 117, 119, 130, 133-138, 162, 175, 176, 178, 312-315, 319, 322, 331-334, 337, 338, 345-401 and 3422,
as B.N.(?) for no. 97,
as Birs Nimroud for no. 4,
as Kouyunjik for no. 199,
as Tell Ibrahim for nos. 1-3, 5-8, 34, 55, 68, 80, 83, 139, 140, 236, 254, 256, 402, 403, 428.

42259	1881,0701.1	Old Babylonian. Issue of wool. Ammiṣaduqa 11/3/12. Kessler, AfO 44/45, 131-133.
42260	1881,0701.2	Old Babylonian. Issue of barley rations. Ammiṣaduqa 18/3/14. Kessler, AfO 44/45, 131-133.
42261	1881,0701.3	Old Babylonian. Barley loan; sealed. Ammiditana 30/5/36. Kessler, AfO 44/45, 131-133.
42262	1881,0701.4	Astronomical; star list; colophon. 5R, 46, 1.
42263	1881,0701.5	Old Babylonian. Barley loan; sealed. Ammiditana. 30/5/36? Kessler, AfO 44/45, 131-133.
42264	1881,0701.6	Old Babylonian. Barley loan; sealed. Ammiditana 22/7/36. Kessler, AfO 44/45, 131-133.
42265	1881,0701.7	Old Babylonian. Barley loan; sealed. Ammiditana 6/12/35. Kessler, AfO 44/45, 131-133.
42266	1881,0701.8	Old Babylonian. Account of silver. Kessler, AfO 44/45, 131-133.
42267	1881,0701.9	Cylinder; inscription of Nabonidus. Sippar. Bezold, PSBA 11 (1889) 84-92 and pls. I-II; Schaudig, AOAT 256, 358-362; Berger, AOAT 4/1, Nabonid Zylinder II,4 no 1.
42268		This number is used for a cast of a Lamaštu amulet, ACa.1; comparable with BE 12003 (Weissbach, Babylonische Miscellen, 42-43 and pl. 16:1).
104415	1881,0701.10	Boundary-stone (kudurru) with divine symbols and figures of the king and the recipient of the grant; text

		obliterated and lines ruled for a new text; also sometime numbered 102486. King, BBSt, 112 and pl. 24, no. XXXII; Seidl, Bagh Mitt 4, 59, no. 102.
	1881,0701.11ff.	Nos. 11-27 are uninscribed objects.
42269	1881,0701.28	Cylinder; inscription of Nabonidus. Sippar. 5R 63; Schaudig, AOAT 256, 378-384.
42270	1881,0701.29	Old Babylonian. Account of barley. Ammiṣaduqa 1+/4/14. Kessler, AfO 44/45, 131-133.
42271	1881,0701.30	School text; excerpts: Lugal-e, 459 (Akkadian); lexical, commentary on Aa II/5 (MSL 14); dupl. 55490. van Dijk, Lugal II, 23 and 127, source o2.
42272	1881,0701.31	Ritual; ušburruda, Abusch and Schwemer, AMD 8/1 text 7.10 j, and AMD 8/2 text 7.11 n; cf. Böck, Muššu'u, 147-180 text I.
42273	1881,0701.32	Ritual and bilingual incantation; against izišubbú (lightning); colophon. Matuszak, WdO 42, 135-152.
42274	1881,0701.33	Sumerian literary; hymn to Ninurta. CT 42, 37, no. 24.
42275	1881,0701.34	Contract; cf. 42295; sealed. d.l. Kūtû. Nisaba 28, no. 623.
42276	1881,0701.35	Commentary on astrological omens.
42277	1881,0701.36	Astronomical; MUL.APIN. + 1881,0701.40. Hunger and Pingree, AfO Beih. 24, 3; Reiner, Fs Borger (CM 10), 298; Hunger and Steele, MUL.APIN, 21.
42278	1881,0701.37	Ritual against eclipses; mentions stones. + 42320 + 43363. Schuster-Brandis, AOAT 46, p. 162 Kette 203, p. 181, Kette 241tc.
42279	1881,0701.38	Old Babylonian. Ration list. Ammiṣaduqa 5/7/14. Kessler, AfO 44/45, 131-133.
42280	1881,0701.39	Old Babylonian. Ration list. Kessler, AfO 44/45, 131-133.
	1881,0701.40	Joined to 42277.
42281	1881,0701.41	School text: obv. sign forms; rev. practice contract.
42282	1881,0701.42	Astronomical procedure text about lunar sixes; dupl. TCL 6, no. 11. + 42294. Brack-Bernsen, AOAT 297, 12-13.
42283	1881,0701.43	Bilingual incantation; dupl. CT 17, 35.
42284	1881,0701.44	Lexical.
42285	1881,0701.45	Literary; Enūma eliš III. King, STC pl. XXX; Lambert, BCM, p. 74.
42286	1881,0701.46	Commentary on astrological omens; colophon; cf. 45751; prayer on upper edge. + 43343. CT 41, 39 (42286 only); Reiner, Fs Borger (CM 10), 298.
42287	1881,0701.47	Ritual involving weapons.

42288	1881,0701.48	Astrological; tabulated; cf. 32517 etc. + 42935 + 43347 + 43786.
42289	1881,0701.49	Spherical tablet, inscribed spirally with an invocation for divine aid.
42290	1881,0701.50	Receipt for barley; circular; sealed; finger-nail marks. n.d. Nisaba 28, no. 525.
42291	1881,0701.51	Clay bead; pierced; inscribed only šá d.Nabû / šá d.Nabû.
42292	1881,0701.52	Medical.
42293	1881,0701.53	Ritual; mentions Sutīli three times and Uṣur-amāssu twice.
42294	1881,0701.54	Joined to 42282.
42295	1881,0701.55	Contract; sale of a house or field; sealed; cf. 42275. RN lost 21/11/[]. Kūtû. Mitchell and Searight, no. 343; Nisaba 28, no. 624.
42296	1881,0701.56	Lexical; Erimḫuš V; colophon. Nbk -/5/9. MSL 17, 65.
42297	1881,0701.57	Omens; Iqqur īpuš, Araḫsamnu. + 43135 + 43136.
42298	1881,0701.58	Medical prescription. Finkel, Fs Lambert, 180-182, text 23 A.
42299	1881,0701.59	Legal process about a claim to prebendary income in Ebabbar. Dar 11/7/-. [Sippar]. Jursa, Bēl-rēmanni, 129, pl. I-II.
42300	1881,0701.60	Esoteric cultic text; colophon: d.na-'i-la-tu4-šú šá Uruk.KI-a. + 42614 + 42908 + unnum.
42301	1881,0701.61	Contract; lease of land with rent payable in dates. Dar 1/11/13. Sippar. Jursa, Bēl-rēmanni, 16-18, 24, 87, 92, 131, pl. III.
42302	1881,0701.62	Promissory note for silver. Dar []/[]/19. Sippar. Jursa, Bēl-rēmanni, 13, 25, 52, 66, 67, 99, 106, 116, 121, 133, pl. IV.
42303	1881,0701.63	Summary account, listing wages paid to fullers. Nbk -/-/7.
42304	1881,0701.64	Lexical; signs and their pronunciations.
42305	1881,0701.65	Field sale; finger-nail marks. 20+/8/[]. Babylon.
42306	1881,0701.66	Lexical; Ea; sign list.
42307	1881,0701.67	Astrological omens.
42308	1881,0701.68	Contract; sealed. SE Ant III and Ant []/12/104? Tell Ibrahim = Kūtû (tablet marked T.I.). + 42323 + 43160. Nisaba 28, no. 593; cf. Oelsner, Materialien, 232a, 500.
42309	1881,0701.69	Lexical; personal names.
42310	1881,0701.70	Medical omens; Sa-gig XXIX; colophon. + 42401 + 42623 + 43121 + 43231 + 43318 + 43351 + 43416 +

		43647. Cf. Finkel, Gs Sachs, 147 n. 29; Heeßel, AOAT 43, 318-327 and 462-463.
42311	1881,0701.71	Contract; lease of land with rent payable in dates. Dar 1/11/13. Sippar. + 43224. Jursa, Bēl-rēmanni, 13, 16-18, 24, 87, 91, 92, 134, pl. V.
42312	1881,0701.72	Hemerology; days of months Ayyaru and Simānu listed and annotated.
42313	1881,0701.73	Medical; gynaecological prescriptions for barrenness, haemorrhage and related matters. + 42427 + 42585 + 43174 + 43215 + 43274 + 43279 + 43281 + 43439 + 43483 + 43595 + 43766 + 43803 + 1881,0701.353 + three 1881,0701 unnum.
42314	1881,0701.74	Historical; inscription of Nabonidus. Duplicates CT 34, 26-37 (BM 104738); cf. Schaudig, AOAT 256, 445-466; Berger, AOAT 4/1, Nabonid Zylinder II,4 no 1.
42315	1881,0701.75	Incantation. Finkel, Fs Lambert, 203, text 46 A.
42316	1881,0701.76	"Aluzinnu text", šumma incipits; dupl. 2R 60, no. 1.
42317	1881,0701.77	Incantation; ušburruda.
42318	1881,0701.78	Contract.
42319	1881,0701.79	Royal inscription?; archaising script.
42320	1881,0701.80	Joined to 42278.
42321	1881,0701.81	Old Babylonian. Issue of rations. Ammiṣaduqa 2/7/? Kessler, AfO 44/45, 131-133.
42322	1881,0701.82	Commentary on extispicy; isru.
42323	1881,0701.83	Joined to 42308.
42324	1881,0701.84	Mathematical; list of talents (GUN); varying figures, rising to 16,000 talents.
42325	1881,0701.85	Incantation prayers to Ea and Nabû; two columns.
42326	1881,0701.86	Omens.
42327	1881,0701.87	Incantation to prevent miscarriage through sorcery, etc. + 42410 + 42604 + 42628 + 43474 + 43523. Farber, Lamaštu, 51, 57; Farber, SKS, pp. 26, 30-31, 112-115, pls. 14-15.
42328	1881,0701.88	Medical; incantation against ušburruda. + 43127 + 43310. Finkel, Fs Lambert, 203-206, text 48 A.
42329	1881,0701.89	Promissory note for dates. Dar 15/3/17. Sippar. Jursa, Bēl-rēmanni, 13, 89, 116, 123, 136, pl. VI.
42330	1881,0701.90	Promissory note for silver. Dar 30/10/19. Sippar. Jursa, Bēl-rēmanni, 116, 124, 137, pl. VI.
42331	1881,0701.91	Promissory note for silver. Dar 11/3/27. Sippar. Jursa, Bēl-rēmanni, 117, 120, 138, pl. VII.
42332	1881,0701.92	Field sale. Dar 10/12/19. Sippar. + 43610. Jursa, Bēl-rēmanni, 87, 93, 139, pl. VII.

42333	1881,0701.93	Medical prescription against miscarriage. + 42453 + 43602. Finkel, Fs Lambert, 171-173, text 17 A.
42334	1881,0701.94	Promissory note for dates. Dar 17/12/-. Sippar. Jursa, Bēl-rēmanni, 13, 115, 122, 140, pl. VIII.
42335	1881,0701.95	Promissory note for dates. Dar 23/6/22. Sippar. Jursa, Bēl-rēmanni, 94, 140, pl. VIII.
42336	1881,0701.96	Receipt for gift of silver, slaves and household goods as dowry; dupl. 42556. Dar 8/11/1. Sippar.+ 42606 + 43432. Jursa, Bēl-rēmanni, 13, 21, 24, 36, 141, pl. I.
42337	1881,0701.97	Lexical; god-list.
42338	1881,0701.98	Bilingual incantations against demons, including ardat-lilî; part dupl. Udug-hul 4. Pinches, JTVI 26 (1893) 153ff; Finkelstein, RA 63, 63 n. 2; Lackenbacher, RA 65, 119-154; Geller, BAM 8, 133-173.
42339	1881,0701.99	Lexical; Ḫḫ VIIB-XII. CT 14, 47; MSL 6, 114 (S3); MSL 7, 4 (S5), 34 (S4), 73 (S6), 122 (S2), and 159 (S3).
42340	1881,0701.100	Field sale; finger-nail marks with caption. Nbk 20/6/35. Sippar. Jursa, Bēl-rēmanni, 11, 19, 25, 35, 89, 142, pl. X.
42341	1881,0701.101	Account of daily and monthly temple income; dupl. 43178+. Sippar. Jursa, Bēl-rēmanni, 14, 24, 229.
42342	1881,0701.102	Medical prescription. Finkel, Fs Lambert, 163-164, text 10 A.
42343	1881,0701.103	Sale of a prebend. d.l. Sippar. + 43232 + 43469 + 43563. Jursa, Bēl-rēmanni, 11, 24, 43, 144, pl. XI.
42344	1881,0701.104	Household inventory.
42345	1881,0701.105	Promissory note for silver. Dar -/2/-. Sippar. + 43103 + 43264. Jursa, Bēl-rēmanni, 21, 114, 122, 146, pl. XII.
42346	1881,0701.106	Promissory note for dates. Dar 10/3/15. Sippar.
42347	1881,0701.107	Receipt for dates for a caravan. Cam -/11/5. Sippar. Jursa, Bēl-rēmanni, 32, 53, 100, 104, 109, 147, pl. XIV.
42348	1881,0701.108	Sale of slaves. Dar 22/4/34? [Sippar]. Jursa, Bēl-rēmanni, 11, 25, 37, 66, 83, 148, pl. XIII.
42349	1881,0701.109	Promissory note to provide 40 gur of barley rations in month xi at Sippar. Dar 1/10/19. [Sippar]. Jursa, Bēl-rēmanni, 116, 120, 149, pl. XIV.
42350	1881,0701.110	Bilingual incantation; Muššu'u tablet II. CT 17, 14; cf. Finkel, AuOr 9 (1991) 94; Böck, Muššu'u, 113-131.
42351	1881,0701.111	Letter from Bēl-iddin, Uballissu-Gula, Marduk-mukīn-apli and Tabnē'a the sepīru, to Buraqa (Biruqa) the rab sūti; sealed. Dar 5/2/28. (Sippar). Jursa,

		Bēl-rēmanni, 11, 82, 150-151, pl. XV; Nisaba 20, no. 234.
42352	1881,0701.112	Silver for share of land rent. Dar 15/[]/20. Sippar. Jursa, Bēl-rēmanni, 99, 100-102, 105, 109, 151, pl. XVI.
42353	1881,0701.113	Promissory note for payment of 86 gur of dates in month v year 26. Dar 5/[]/26. Babylon. Jursa, Bēl-rēmanni, 21, 107, 152, pl. XVI.
42354	1881,0701.114	Promissory note for silver. d.l. Sippar. Jursa, Bēl-rēmanni, 37, 52, 63, 64, 85, 114, 153, pl. XVII.
42355	1881,0701.115	Contract with pledge of a house in Sippar. Nbk 9/5/-. (Sippar).
42356	1881,0701.116	Receipt for a promised payment of barley. Dar -/-/30. Sippar. + 43115 + 43251 + 43497 + 43562 + 43626 + 43697. Jursa, Bēl-rēmanni, 25, 117, 120, 155, pl. XVIII.
42357	1881,0701.117	Receipt for a promised payment of silver. Dar 4/9/21. Sippar. Jursa, Bēl-rēmanni, 21, 116, 122, 156, pl. XVII.
42358	1881,0701.118	Promissory note for silver. Dar 24/4/14. (Sippar).
42359	1881,0701.119	Bilingual incantation; cf. CT 16-17.
42360	1881,0701.120	Promissory note for dates and barley; dupl. 43198. Dar 22/-/-. Sippar. (+) 43487. Jursa, Bēl-rēmanni, 13, 24, 115, 122, 157, pl. XI.
42361	1881,0701.121	Contract; transfer of a širku. d.l. (Sippar).
42362	1881,0701.122	Contract; lease of a field. Dar 23/6/19. Sippar. + 42485. Jursa, Bēl-rēmanni, 87, 88, 94, 158, pl. XX.
42363	1881,0701.123	Sale of a prebend. Dar -/-/30? Sippar. Jursa, Bēl-rēmanni, 21, 25 45, 46, 49, 64, 80, 159, pl. XIX.
42364	1881,0701.124	Receipt of barley owed to Marduk-rēmanni. Dar 16/7/26. Sippar. Jursa, Bēl-rēmanni, 13, 24, 117, 120, 160, pl. XX.
42365	1881,0701.125	Sale of a prebend. Dar 3/1/33? Sippar. Jursa, Bēl-rēmanni, 46, 48, 49, 62, 161, pl. XXI.
42366	1881,0701.126	Field sale; witnesses only, including an ērib bīt Marduk. d.l. (Babylon?).
42367	1881,0701.127	Fragment of a calcite vase with inscription of Rimuš. Sippar? Frayne, RIME 2.1.2.14.1; Walker and Collon, Tell-ed-Der 3, 98, no. 23; Potts, Iraq 51, 154.
42368	1881,0701.128	Receipt for a promised payment of silver. Dar 23/7/26. Sippar. + 42608. Jursa, Bēl-rēmanni, 35, 117, 124, 162, pl. XXI.
42369	1881,0701.129	Promissory note for dates; dupl. 42593. d.l. Sippar. (+) 43501. Jursa, Bēl-rēmanni, 13, 25, 109, 163, pl. XXII.

42370	1881,0701.130	Cylinder; inscription of Nebuchadnezzar II no. 23 i 1-5, ii 2-6, 19.
42371	1881,0701.131	Contract about a rab-banê prebend on royal land. [Dar] 27/6/23. Sippar. Jursa, Bēl-rēmanni, 90, 164, pl. XXIII.
42372	1881,0701.132	Field sale. Nbk 29/6/18. Babylon.
42373	1881,0701.133	Account of grain. n.d. (Sippar). Jursa, Bēl-rēmanni, 21, 88, 121, 165, pl. XXIII.
42374	1881,0701.134	Account of grain harvest. n.d. (Sippar). + 43313 + 43621 + 1881,0701 F.232. Jursa, Bēl-rēmanni, 87, 94, 107, 166, pl. XXIV.
42375	1881,0701.135	Incantation; obv. ends: urud-an-na urud-níg-kala-ga-ke4; rev. ÁBxX-bi ši-ni-pu.
42376	1881,0701.136	Old Babylonian. Account of silver; sealed. Ammiṣaduqa -/-/16. Kessler, AfO 44/45, 131-133.
42377	1881,0701.137	School practice text.
42378	1881,0701.138	Old Babylonian. List of names; two columns.
42379	1881,0701.139	Deposit agreement; perhaps Seleucid. d.l. Tell Ibrahim = Kūtû (register).
42380	1881,0701.140	Promissory note for silver; sealed. SE Sel IV []/[]/135. Kūtû. Jursa, Persika 9, 201-202, 214; Mitchell and Searight, no. 734; Nisaba 28, no. 603.
42381	1881,0701.141	Sumerian; copy of a votive inscription of the Ur III period; part of curse formula ("... be he a king, be he a priest", etc.); note rev. 2: [en] máš-e pà-da ḫ̮é-a, "be (s)he a priest(ess) chosen by the kid-(omen)".
42382	1881,0701.142	Envelope; part of one line only, ša Ezida; impression of inner text visible, with ruling after the 10th line. n.d. (Borsippa?).
42383	1881,0701.143	Promissory note for dates. d.l. [Babylon]. Jursa, Bēl-rēmanni, 13, 19, 107-109, 168, pl. XXV.
42384	1881,0701.144	Administrative. n.d. (Sippar). Jursa, Bēl-rēmanni, 34, 99, 101, 102, 107, 109, 169, pl. I.
42385	1881,0701.145	Astrological medicine. + 1881,0701.329. Finkel, Fs Lambert, 212-215, text 55 B.
42386	1881,0701.146	School text; incantations, Maqlu II; lexical. 26/4/-. Abusch, AMD 10, 51-77.
42387	1881,0701.147	Contract; probably datable to Xerxes.
42388	1881,0701.148	Promissory note for barley. 17/1/-.
42389	1881,0701.149	Promissory note for silver for trading. Dar 26?/8/19. Sippar. Jursa, Bēl-rēmanni, 116, 121, 169, pl. XXV.
42390	1881,0701.150	Promissory note for dates. Dar 3/4/10. (Sippar). Jursa, Bēl-rēmanni, 102, 115, 123, 170, pl. XXVI.
42391	1881,0701.151	Promissory note for silver. 14/-/-. (Babylon?).
42392	1881,0701.152	Promissory note for silver. Nbk 9/3/5. Babylon.

42393	1881,0701.153	Contract; lease of a house. Dar 18/4/36. Sippar.
42394	1881,0701.154	School text; lexical; Ḫḫ I 265-275. 14/6/-.
42395	1881,0701.155	Promissory note for silver. 1/9/30. Sippar. Jursa, Bēl-rēmanni, 102, 107, 109, 171, pl. XXVI.
42396	1881,0701.156	Contract for use of a reed hut. 21/12/9. [Sippar]. Jursa, Bēl-rēmanni, 35, 89, 172, pl. XXVI.
42397	1881,0701.157	Promissory note for barley. Dar 3/7/24. Sippar. Jursa, Bēl-rēmanni, 13, 19, 117, 121, 173, pl. XXVII.
42398	1881,0701.158	Medical prescription. Finkel, Fs Lambert, 162, text 9 A.
42399	1881,0701.159	Incantation to Gula. Finkel, Fs Lambert, 200-202, text 45 B.
42400	1881,0701.160	Receipt for dates. Dar []/[]/30. Til-gubbi. Jursa, Bēl-rēmanni, 95, 122, 174, pl. XXVII.
42401	1881,0701.161	Joined to 42310.
42402	1881,0701.162	Account of barley. d.l. (Sippar). Jursa, Bēl-rēmanni, 77, 175, pl. XXVII-XXVIII.
42403	1881,0701.163	Payments of silver for dates and grain. (Babylon?).
42404	1881,0701.164	Medical prescription. Finkel, Fs Lambert, 153-154, text 4 B.
42405	1881,0701.165	Prebend as pledge. Dar 13/9/-. Sippar. + 42611 + 43197. Jursa, Bēl-rēmanni, 51, 79, 175, pl. XXVIII.
42406	1881,0701.166	Medical; prescription and ritual. + 43507 + 43544. Finkel, Fs Lambert, 207-208, text 50 A.
42407	1881,0701.167	Astrological medicine. Finkel, Fs Lambert, 212-215, text 55 C.
42408	1881,0701.168	Contract about a prebend. Dar 27/12a/13. Sippar. Jursa, Bēl-rēmanni, 19, 22, 44, 72, 86, 177, pl. XXIX.
42409	1881,0701.169	Promissory note for silver. Dar 28/11/22. Sippar.
42410	1881,0701.170	Joined to 42327.
42411	1881,0701.171	Astronomical; eclipses; colophon. + 42636 + 43097.
42412	1881,0701.172	Sale of prebends, dupl. 42424. RN lost 12/12/7. Sippar. Jursa, Bēl-rēmanni, 13, 24, 180, 181, pl. XXX.
42413	1881,0701.173	School text; bilingual incantation, dupl. STT 168 and 171. 21/12/-.
42414	1881,0701.174	Promissory note for silver; dupl. 43524 and VAS 4, 135. Dar 19/8/-. Sippar. + 43660. Jursa, Bēl-rēmanni, 14, 263.
42415	1881,0701.175	Deposition; dupl. 42571. Dar 30/1/[]. Sippar. Jursa, Bēl-rēmanni, 13, 21, 115, 121, 123, 178, pl. XXIX.
42416	1881,0701.176	Receipt of silver as the price of a house, paid to the Ebabbar in the presence of the šangû, Marduk-šum-iddin; sealed. [Cyr] 11+/1/3+. [Sippar]. Nisaba 20, no. 344.
42417	1881,0701.177	Lexical.

42418	1881,0701.178	Contract; transfer of prebends; part of the Bēl-rēmanni archive. Dar [4]/[]/32. Sippar. + 42580 + 45578 + 45592. Waerzeggers, OLA 233, 66 and 166-167.
42419	1881,0701.179	Medical prescription. Finkel, Fs Lambert, 161-162, text 8 A.
42420	1881,0701.180	Lexical; Ḫḫ VI.
42421	1881,0701.181	Promissory note for barley. Dar 3/7/24. Sippar. Jursa, Bēl-rēmanni, 13, 19, 24, 173.
42422	1881,0701.182	Medical. Finkel, Fs Lambert, 219, text 63 A.
42423	1881,0701.183	Contract; lease of land. Dar 14/1/35. Sippar. Jursa, Bēl-rēmanni, 21, 87-88, 90, 95, 97, 179, pl. XXX.
42424	1881,0701.184	Sale of prebends; dupl. 42412. Dar -/3/8. Sippar. Jursa, Bēl-rēmanni, 13, 24, 46, 49, 62, 85, 180, pl. XXX.
42425	1881,0701.185	Contract about a prebend; dupl. 42595 (+) 43627. Dar -/8/-. Sippar. + 42530 + 43114 + 43129 + 43141 + 43797 Jursa, Bēl-rēmanni, 11, 13, 19, 25, 43, 67, 69, 181, pl. XXXI.
42426	1881,0701.186	Medical; incantation short catalogue. Finkel, Fs Lambert, 191-192, text 35 A.
42427	1881,0701.187	Joined to 42313.
42428	1881,0701.188	School text; incantations, Maqlu III and IV. Abusch, AMD 10, 79-112.
42429	1881,0701.189	Astronomical; figures: kur 16-kám u4 26-kám, etc. + 42586 + 43658.
42430	1881,0701.190	Medical prescription. + F.222. Finkel, Fs Lambert, 149-151, text 1 C.
42431	1881,0701.191	Medical; prescription and incantation. + 43196 + F.223. Finkel, Fs Lambert, 208-209, text 51 A.
42432	1881,0701.192	Administrative; about bow-service for Nidinti-Marduk; sealed. Dar 9/12/18. (Sippar). Jursa, Bēl-rēmanni, 11, 99, 101, 104, 109, 182-183, pl. XXXII; Nisaba 20, no. 476.
42433	1881,0701.193	Promissory note for dates. 20/-/-. Sippar. Jursa, Bēl-rēmanni, 115, 124, 183, pl. XXXII.
42434	1881,0701.194	Promissory note for silver related to a brewer's prebend; dupl. 42609; a later copy (ḫe-pí ḪI-šú). Dar 20/8/-. Sippar. Jursa, Bēl-rēmanni, 14, 49, 51, 63, 79, 184, pl. XXXII.
42435	1881,0701.195	Hemerology; ud 24 gaba-raḫ u / ud 26 dingir še.ga / ud 27 ud še.ga / itu.apin šà.ga.
42436	1881,0701.196	Promissory note for dates. Dar 2/2/10. Sippar. Jursa, Bēl-rēmanni, 14, 115, 124, 185, pl. XXXIII.
42437	1881,0701.197	Receipt for dates. Dar 4/8/31. Sippar.

42438	1881,0701.198	Promissory note for dates. d.l. [Sippar?]. Jursa, Bēl-rēmanni, 114, 124, 186, pl. XXXIII.
42439	1881,0701.199	Neo-Assyrian. Liver omens; padanu.
42440	1881,0701.200	Bilingual incantation, Udug-ḫul 2. Finkel, Fs Lambert, 197-198, text 41 A; Geller, BAM 8, 59-88.
42441	1881,0701.201	Receipt for silver payment. d.l. [Sippar]. Jursa, Bēl-rēmanni, 14, 117, 122, 187, pl. XXXIII.
42442	1881,0701.202	Promissory note. d.l. Sippar. Jursa, Bēl-rēmanni, 25-26, pl. XXXIV.
42443	1881,0701.203	Promissory note for dates or barley. Dar -/7/29. (Sippar).
42444	1881,0701.204	List of wages and persons. (Sippar). Jursa, Bēl-rēmanni, 14, 16, 103, 219-220, pl. L.
42445	1881,0701.205	Medical; stone list. Finkel, Fs Lambert, 183-184, text 25 A; Schuster-Brandis, AOAT 46, p. 137, Kette 130, p. 131, Kette 116.
42446	1881,0701.206	Receipt for Telmun dates. Cam 1?/2/2. Babylon. + 43488 + 43547. Jursa, Bēl-rēmanni, 21, 32, 188, pl. XXXIV.
42447	1881,0701.207	Bilingual incantation and ritual. Finkel, Fs Lambert, 198-199, text 42 A.
42448	1881,0701.208	Letter from Marduk-bēlu-uṣur to Marduk-nāṣir-apil. CT 22, 17, no. 83; Hackl et al., AOAT 414/1, no. 39.
42449	1881,0701.209	Promissory note for dates. Dar 6+/5/27. Babylon. Jursa, Bēl-rēmanni, 13, 25, 168.
42450	1881,0701.210	Medical prescription. + 43809. Finkel, Fs Lambert, 169-171, text 16 A.
42451	1881,0701.211	Promissory note for dates. Dar 7/5/[]. Babylon. + 43459 + 45590. Jursa, Bel-remanni, 13, 24, 168.
42452	1881,0701.212	School text; god list; incantation.
42453	1881,0701.213	Joined to 42333.
42454	1881,0701.214	Incantation to Gula. + 43271 + 43296 + 43580. Finkel, Fs Lambert, 200-202, text 45 A.
42455	1881,0701.215	Old Babylonian. Barley loan; sealed. Ammiditana 16?/9/35. Kessler, AfO 44/45, 131-133.
42456	1881,0701.216	Old Babylonian. Barley loan; sealed. Ammiditana 3/8/36. Kessler, AfO 44/45, 131-133.
42457	1881,0701.217	Contract; lease of a house.
42458	1881,0701.218	Old Babylonian. Barley loan; sealed. Ammiditana 5/5/35. Kessler, AfO 44/45, 131-133.
42459	1881,0701.219	Old Babylonian. Barley loan; sealed. Ammiditana 30/5/35. Kessler, AfO 44/45, 131-133.
42460	1881,0701.220	Memorandum.

42461	1881,0701.221	Letter order from Bulluṭ; sealed. (Antigonus). (Borsippa). Kessler, Fs Oelsner, 216, 231, no. 4; Nisaba 28, no. 461.
42462	1881,0701.222	Old Babylonian. Receipt; sealed. Ammiditana 3/8/36.
42463	1881,0701.223	Practice signs.
42464	1881,0701.224	Old Babylonian. Receipt; sealed. Ammiditana 3/8/36.
42465	1881,0701.225	Memorandum about barley. No RN -/11/7.
42466	1881,0701.226	Old Babylonian. Receipt; sealed. Ammiditana 2/10/36.
42467	1881,0701.227	Old Babylonian. Receipt; sealed. Ammiditana 30/5/36.
42468	1881,0701.228	Old Babylonian. Receipt; sealed. Ammiditana 1/9/36.
42469	1881,0701.229	Letter order from Bulluṭ; sealed. Alex III 14/12/8. (Borsippa). Kessler, Fs Oelsner, 214, 228, no. 1; Mitchell and Searight, no. 596; Nisaba 28, no. 435.
42470	1881,0701.230	Marriage contract. Cyr 26/2/9. Borsippa. Wunsch, Bab Arch 2, no. 3; Zadok, Nisaba 21, 236.
42471	1881,0701.231	Old Babylonian. Receipt for grain?; sealed. Ammiditana. 30/1/36.
42472	1881,0701.232	Old Babylonian. Contract; sealed. Ammiditana 1/9/36.
42473	1881,0701.233	Old Babylonian. Distribution list of grain, oil, etc.; round type. Ammi-[] -/2/-.
42474	1881,0701.234	Old Babylonian. Receipt for barley; sealed. Ammiṣaduqa 5/8/?
42475	1881,0701.235	Medical prescription. Finkel, Fs Lambert, 218, text 60 A.
42476	1881,0701.236	Field sale. Kūtû (register).
42477	1881,0701.237	Old Babylonian. Receipt for barley; sealed. Ammiditana 2/10/36.
42478	1881,0701.238	Receipt for dates.
42479	1881,0701.239	Receipt for house rent; alphabetic? characters on the reverse. Dar 16/3/16. Babylon.
42480	1881,0701.240	Receipt of dates; sealed. Alex III 8+/[]/8. (Borsippa). Kessler, Fs Oelsner, 215-216, 230, no. 3; Mitchell and Searight, no. 598; Nisaba 28, no. 437.
42481	1881,0701.241	Old Babylonian. Receipt for barley; sealed. Ammiditana 14/8/36.
42482	1881,0701.242	Old Babylonian. Receipt for barley; sealed. Ammiditana 13/8/36.
42483	1881,0701.243	Note of three personal names.
42484	1881,0701.244	Pledge for a loan. d.l. [Sippar?]. Jursa, Bēl-rēmanni, 52, 189, pl. XXXIV.
42485	1881,0701.245	Joined to 42362.
42486	1881,0701.246	Contract. RN lost 21/12/3.

42487	1881,0701.247	Promissory note for silver. Nbk 29/6/18. Babylon.
42488	1881,0701.248	Hymn to a god.
42489	1881,0701.249	Lexical, commentary on Aa (MSL 14).
42490	1881,0701.250	Lexical; Ḫḫ III.
42491	1881,0701.251	Old Babylonian. Issue of oil. Ammiṣaduqa 5/8/12. Kessler, AfO 44/45, 131-133.
42492	1881,0701.252	List of women (personal names only).
42493	1881,0701.253	Old Babylonian. Receipt of barley; sealed. Ammiditana 30/5/36.
42494	1881,0701.254	Contract; quit-claim; sealed; finger-nail marks. SE Ant III 14/[]/97. [Kūtû] (register, and marked T.I.). + 43461. Mitchell and Searight, no. 719; Nisaba 28, no. 590.
42495	1881,0701.255	Letter order from Bulluṭ; sealed. Alex III 27/[]/8. (Borsippa). Kessler, Fs Oelsner, 215, 229, no. 2; Nisaba 28, no. 436.
42496	1881,0701.256	Field sale. Kūtû (register).
42497	1881,0701.257	Mathematical; problems; fragment from upper edge.
42498	1881,0701.258	Ritual.
42499	1881,0701.259	Incantation; only KÙ.GA TA È repeated.
42500	1881,0701.260	Medical prescription. Finkel, Fs Lambert, 182, text 24 A.
42501	1881,0701.261	Memorandum about silver.
42502	1881,0701.262	Literary.
42503	1881,0701.263	Prayer to a goddess. + 43377.
42504	1881,0701.264	Receipt for harvest of dates and their byproducts. Dar 1/2/14. [Sippar]. + 42624 + 43741 + 43799. Jursa, Bēl-rēmanni, 17, 93, 190, pl. XXXV.
42505	1881,0701.265	Medical; drugs for fumigation. + 43495. Finkel, Fs Lambert, 190-191, text 34 A.
42506	1881,0701.266	Receipt for silver. [Sippar?]. Jursa, Bēl-rēmanni, 191, pl. XXXVI.
42507	1881,0701.267	Medical prescription. Finkel, Fs Lambert, 157-159, text 5 A.
42508	1881,0701.268	Field sale. -/12/-. Sippar. + 43325 + 43453 + 43538 + 43542 + 43555. Jursa, Bēl-rēmanni, 52, 66, 67, 83, 94, 114, 122, 191, pl. XXXVI.
42509	1881,0701.269	Ritual.
42510	1881,0701.270	Medical prescription. + F.224. Finkel, Fs Lambert, 160-161, text 7 A.
42511	1881,0701.271	Old Babylonian. Barley loan; sealed. Ammiditana 28/7/35. Kessler, AfO 44/45, 131-133.
42512	1881,0701.272	Old Babylonian. Barley loan; sealed. Ammiditana 30/5/35. Kessler, AfO 44/45, 131-133.

42513	1881,0701.273	Old Babylonian. Barley loan; sealed. Ammiditana 30/5/36. Kessler, AfO 44/45, 131-133.
42514	1881,0701.274	Old Babylonian. Barley loan. Ammiditana -/5/36. Kessler, AfO 44/45, 131-133.
42515	1881,0701.275	Old Babylonian. Barley loan; sealed. Ammiṣaduqa 1?/6/1. Kessler, AfO 44/45, 131-133.
42516	1881,0701.276a	Old Babylonian. Barley loan; sealed. Ammiditana 15?/[]/36. Kessler, AfO 44/45, 131-133.
42517	1881,0701.276b	Old Babylonian. Barley loan; sealed. Ammiditana 5/7/34. Kessler, AfO 44/45, 131-133.
42518	1881,0701.277	Old Babylonian. Barley loan; sealed. Ammiditana -/9/-. Kessler, AfO 44/45, 131-133.
42519	1881,0701.278	Old Babylonian. Barley loan; sealed. Ammiditana 20+/6/36. Kessler, AfO 44/45, 131-133.
42520	1881,0701.279	Old Babylonian. Barley loan; sealed. Ammiditana 26/7/33. Kessler, AfO 44/45, 131-133.
42521	1881,0701.280	Old Babylonian. Barley loan; sealed. Ammiditana -/12/36. Kessler, AfO 44/45, 131-133.
42522	1881,0701.281	Medical prescription. Finkel, Fs Lambert, 175-177, text 21 A.
42523	1881,0701.282	Promissory note for silver and dates for trading. Dar 24/10/[]. Sippar. + 42615. Jursa, Bēl-rēmanni, 89, 115, 192, pl. XXXVII.
42524	1881,0701.283	Promissory note for dates. Dar 3/2/2. Sippar. Jursa, Bēl-rēmanni, 14, 24, 185.
42525	1881,0701.284	Sale of prebends. Dar -/-/5. Sippar. Jursa, Bēl-rēmanni, 51, 79, 193, pl. XXXVII.
42526	1881,0701.285	Old Babylonian. Account of gugallu-rations. Ammiṣaduqa 1/6/14. Kessler, AfO 44/45, 131-133.
42527	1881,0701.286	Contract. d.l. (Sippar).
42528	1881,0701.287	Receipt of barley rations; sealed by Nabû-kuṣuršu. Alex IV -/1/8. (Borsippa). Kessler, Fs Oelsner, 217, 232, no. 5; Nisaba 28, no. 509.
42529	1881,0701.288	Old Babylonian. Barley loan; sealed. Ammiditana 22+/8/32. Kessler, AfO 44/45, 131-133.
42530	1881,0701.289	Joined to 42425.
42531	1881,0701.290	Old Babylonian. Barley loan; sealed. Ammiditana 23/5/36. Kessler, AfO 44/45, 131-133.
42532	1881,0701.291	Letter from Ea-mudammiq to Guzānu, his "brother".
42533	1881,0701.292	Contract.
42534	1881,0701.293	Old Babylonian. Barley loan; sealed. Ammiditana -/10/35? Kessler, AfO 44/45, 131-133.
42535	1881,0701.294	Old Babylonian. Barley loan; sealed. Ammiditana 21+/5/-. Kessler, AfO 44/45, 131-133.

42536	1881,0701.295	Old Babylonian. Barley loan; sealed. Ammiditana 30/5/36. Kessler, AfO 44/45, 131-133.
42537	1881,0701.296	Old Babylonian. Barley loan; sealed. Ammiditana 18/11/35. Kessler, AfO 44/45, 131-133.
42538	1881,0701.297	Lexical; Ḫḫ XI-XII.
42539	1881,0701.298	Field sale. Cyr 28/[]/9. (Babylon?).
42540	1881,0701.299	Promissory note for wheat. Dar 20+/2/24. Sippar. Jursa, Bēl-rēmanni, 21, 36, 75, 99, 100, 117, 194, pl. XXXVIII.
42541	1881,0701.300	Summary account of date harvest in years 16-21 (of Darius?). n.d. (Sippar). Jursa, Bēl-rēmanni, 87, 93, 195, pl. XXXVIII.
42542	1881,0701.301	Medical, incantation for fumigation. + 43722. Finkel, Fs Lambert, 193, text 36 A.
42543	1881,0701.302	Apprenticeship contract. Cyr 5/9/4. Borsippa. Zadok, Nisaba 21, 237; Hackl, AfO 52, 83-84, no. 6.
42544	1881,0701.303	School exercise, or memorandum.
42545	1881,0701.304	Promissory note for dates.
42546	1881,0701.305	Prophecy; dupl. 38801. + 42605.
42547	1881,0701.306	Contract; lease of a field. Dar 10+/12/24. Sippar. + 42647. Jursa, Bēl-rēmanni, 87, 88, 95, 96, 196, pl. XXXIX.
42548	1881,0701.307	Contract; lease of a field. Dar 3/6/20. Sippar. Jursa, Bēl-rēmanni, 99, 197, pl. XXXIX.
42549	1881,0701.308	Medical prescription. Finkel, Fs Lambert, 175-177, text 21 B.
42550	1881,0701.309	Medical; incantation against ušburruda. Finkel, Fs Lambert, 203-206, text 48 B.
42551	1881,0701.310	Sale of prebends. Dar 26/4/19. Sippar. + 42632 + 43303 + 43458. Jursa, Bēl-rēmanni, 56, 58, 75, 77, 198, pl. XL.
42552	1881,0701.311	List of statues of the gods in Esangila. Pinches, Fs Haupt, 216.
42553	1881,0701.312	Promissory note for dates. Cam 2/4/6. Sippar. Jursa, Bēl-rēmanni, 21, 114, 122, 123, 200, pl. XLI.
42554	1881,0701.313	Receipt for payment on a loan. Dar 13/12/13. Sippar. Jursa, Bēl-rēmanni, 25, 115, 120, 200, pl. XLI.
42555	1881,0701.314	Promissory note for dates; duplicates 79103. Dar 7/[12b]/22. Sippar. Jursa, Bēl-rēmanni, 14, 21, 24, 36, 116, 201, pl. XLII.
42556	1881,0701.315	Receipt for gift silver, slaves and household goods as dowry; dupl. 42336+. Dar [8/11/1]. Sippar. Jursa, Bēl-rēmanni, 13, 24, 142.
42557	1881,0701.316	Letter order from Lūṣi-ana-nūri; sealed. Dar 23/1/29. (Sippar). Nisaba 20, no. 248.

42558	1881,0701.317	Promissory note for dates; imittu. d.l. [Sippar?]. Jursa, Bēl-rēmanni, 92, 202, pl. XXXVII.
42559	1881,0701.318	Ritual; namburbû preparations. + 42603. Maul, Bagh Forsch 18, 192 n. 307, 297; Finkel, Fs Lambert, 206-207, text 49 B.
42560	1881,0701.319	Promissory note for dates. Cam 15/6/5. Sippar. Jursa, Bēl-rēmanni, 114, 122, 203, pl. XLII.
42561	1881,0701.320	Promissory note for dates with field as pledge. d.l. Sippar. + 43708 + 43751 + 45577. Jursa, Bēl-rēmanni, 35, 91, 116, 121, 203, pl. XLIII.
42562	1881,0701.321	Medical prescription. Finkel, Fs Lambert, 149-151, text 1 B.
42563	1881,0701.322	Promissory note for dates. Cam 26/12/6. Sippar. Jursa, Bēl-rēmanni, 34, 114, 122, 205, pl. XLIV.
42564	1881,0701.323	Sale of prebends. Dar -/-/33. Sippar. Jursa, Bēl-rēmanni, 65, 206, pl. XLIV.
42565	1881,0701.324	Incantation beginning ša Nabû anāku.
42566	1881,0701.325	Medical prescription. Finkel, Fs Lambert, 153-154, text 3 B.
42567	1881,0701.326	Receipt for dates. Xerxes 24/[]/acc. [Sippar]. Jursa, Bēl-rēmanni, 35, 77, 206, pl. XLIV.
42568	1881,0701.327	Receipt for silver. Dar 14?/4/8. Babylon. Jursa, Bēl-rēmanni, 14, 19, 35, 72, 83, 207, pl. XLV.
42569	1881,0701.328	Bilingual incantation, Udug-ḫul 2. + 43216 + 43771 + 43776. Finkel, Fs Lambert, 196-197, text 40 A; Geller, BAM 8, 59-88.
	1881,0701.329	Joined to 42385.
42570	1881,0701.330	Medical; incantation short catalogue; Lamaštu. + 43619 + 43679 + F.225. Finkel, Fs Lambert, 195-196, text 38 A; Farber, Lamaštu, 48, 57, pl. 61.
42571	1881,0701.331	Deposition; dupl. 42415. d.l. Sippar. + 43256. Jursa, Bēl-rēmanni, 13, 24, 179.
42572	1881,0701.332	Sale of prebends. Dar 22/1/4. Sippar. Jursa, Bēl-rēmanni, 46, 49, 71, 72, 82, 208-209, pl. XLV; Bertin 2753.
42573	1881,0701.333	Promissory note for barley. Sippar.
42574	1881,0701.334	Promissory note for dates. Dar 24/[]/14. Sippar. (+) 43624. Jursa, Bēl-rēmanni, 116, 209, pl. XLVI.
42575	1881,0701.335	Omen apodoses.
42576	1881,0701.336	Medical prescription. + 43546 + 43589. Finkel, Fs Lambert, 159-160, text 6 A; Geller, BAM 7, 264-265, no. 52.
42577	1881,0701.337	Receipt for ilku payment. Dar 17/5/[]. Sippar. Jursa, Bēl-rēmanni, 99, 101, 121, 210, pl. XLVI.

42578	1881,0701.338	Sale of prebends. Dar 27/9/-. Sippar. Jursa, Bēl-rēmanni, 56, 59, 76, 211, pl. XLVII.
42579	1881,0701.339	Letter from Bēl-[] to Ap-la-[a].
42580	1881,0701.340	Joined to 42418.
42581	1881,0701.341	Contract about work with bricks. Nbn 23/2/8. Kiš.
42582	1881,0701.342	Promissory note for silver. Nbn 4/[]/8. Šaḫrīn.
42583	1881,0701.343	Contract. Nbk 12/12/23. Babylon.
42584	1881,0701.344	Promissory note for silver. Nbn 5/11/12. Babylon.
42585	1881,0701.345	Joined to 42313.
42586	1881,0701.346	Joined to 42429.
42587	1881,0701.347	Medical prescription. + 42640 + 43217 + 43287 + 43475 + 43812. Finkel, Fs Lambert, 168-169, text 15 A.
42588	1881,0701.348	Economic or literary?
42589	1881,0701.349	Medical; incantation for fumigation. (+) F.234. Finkel, Fs Lambert, 193-195, text 37 A (under wrong registration number 81-7-1, 1692).
42590	1881,0701.350	Contract. (Sippar).
42591	1881,0701.351	Promissory note for dates. d.l. [Sippar?]. + 43586. Jursa, Bēl-rēmanni, 97, 212, pl. XLVII.
42592	1881,0701.352	Contract.
	1881,0701.353	Joined to 42313.
42593	1881,0701.354	Promissory note for dates; dupl. 42369. Dar -/-/[31]. Sippar. + 1881,0701 F.228. Jursa, Bēl-rēmanni, 13, 24, 164.
42594	1881,0701.355	Account of dates or grain. d.l. (Sippar). Jursa, Bēl-rēmanni, 213, pl. XLVII.
42595	1881,0701.356	Contract about a prebend; dupl. 42425, (Sippar). (+) 43627. Jursa, Bēl-rēmanni, 13, 19, 67, 182, pl. LXVIII.
42596	1881,0701.357	Medical; school tablet; im.gíd.da.
42597	1881,0701.358	Receipt for silver for trading. -/-/14. Šušan.
42598	1881,0701.359	Commentary; medical.
42599	1881,0701.360	Commentary on Enūma Anu Enlil. + 43154.
42600	1881,0701.361	Temple names explained. Nippur Compendium; dupl. George, BTT, no. 18 column I.
42601	1881,0701.362	Promissory note for dates with a field as pledge; imittu. Dar -/6/24. Sippar. + 43498 + 43719. Jursa, Bēl-rēmanni, 92, 213, pl. XLVIII.
42602	1881,0701.363	Contract; ḫarrānu.
42603	1881,0701.364	Joined to 42559.
42604	1881,0701.365	Joined to 42327.
42605	1881,0701.366	Joined to 42546.
42606	1881,0701.367	Joined to 42336.

42607	1881,0701.368	Account of tithes of dates. -/-/12. (Sippar). Jursa, NABU 1998, 72-73, no. 70.
42608	1881,0701.369	Joined to 42368.
42609	1881,0701.370	Promissory note for silver related to a brewer's prebend; dupl. 42434; a later copy (ḫe-pí eš-šú). Dar 20/8/-. Sippar. + 43783. Jursa, Bēl-rēmanni, 14, 49, 184.
42610	1881,0701.371	Medical prescription. + 43481. Finkel, Fs Lambert, 164, text 12 A.
42611	1881,0701.372	Joined to 42405.
42612	1881,0701.373	School tablet; ritual related to Lamaštu III 49-63; dupl. 1883,0118.752. + 43477 + 43525 (+) 43267. Finkel, Fs Lambert, 210-211, text 53 A; Farber, Lamaštu, 52, 57, 276-277; Stadthouders, NABU 2016, 166-167, no. 101.
42613	1881,0701.374	Sale of prebends. d.l. [Sippar]. + 43211. Jursa, Bēl-rēmanni, 49, 56, 214, pl. XLIX.
42614	1881,0701.375	Joined to 42300.
42615	1881,0701.376	Joined to 42523.
42616	1881,0701.377	Letter order from Bēl-iddin, Marduk-[rēmanni.] and Uballissu-Gula to Kāṣir ša muḫḫi ešrû; sealed. Dar []/[]/20. (Sippar). + 43740. Jursa, Bēl-rēmanni, 11, 80, 215, pl. XLIX; Jursa, NABU 1998, 72-73, no. 70; Nisaba 20, no. 194.
42617	1881,0701.378	Medical prescription. Finkel, Fs Lambert, 164, text 11 A.
42618	1881,0701.379	Account. d.l. (Sippar). Jursa, Bēl-rēmanni, 77, 215, pl. XLIX.
42619	1881,0701.380	Promissory note for barley and wheat. Dar? 2/4/-. Sippar. Jursa, Bēl-rēmanni, 114, 216, pl. L.
42620	1881,0701.381	Promissory note? Dar. Sippar. Jursa, Bēl-rēmanni, 114, 122, 216, pl. L.
42621	1881,0701.382	Medical; drugs for fumigation. + 43221 + 43508 + 43622. Finkel, Fs Lambert, 190-191, text 34 C.
42622	1881,0701.383	Promissory note for barley. Dar 10/[]/8. [Sippar]. Jursa, Bēl-rēmanni, 115, 121, 217, pl. L.
42623	1881,0701.384	Joined to 42310.
42624	1881,0701.385	Joined to 42504.
42625	1881,0701.386	Medical; plant list. + 43239 + 43248 + 43476 + 43541 + 43616 + 43705 + F.226. Finkel, Fs Lambert, 186-187, text 29 A.
42626	1881,0701.387	Receipt for silver; dupl. 79055. [Dar] [17]/3/[25]. [Babylon]. + 43165. Jursa, Bēl-rēmanni, 14, 250.
42627	1881,0701.388	Economic.
42628	1881,0701.389	Joined to 42327.

42629	1881,0701.390	Medical; plant list. + 42653 + 43435. Finkel, Fs Lambert, 185-186, text 28 A.
42630	1881,0701.391	Promissory note for dates; imittu. Dar []/6/13. Sippar. + 42631 + 43107. Jursa, Bēl-rēmanni, 92, 218, pl. L.
42631	1881,0701.392	Joined to 42630.
42632	1881,0701.393	Joined to 42551.
42633	1881,0701.394	Receipt for loan payments. Dar -/-/9. (Sippar). Jursa, Bēl-rēmanni, 14, 16, 103, 219, pl. L.
42634	1881,0701.395	Medical prescription. + 42635 + 43163. Finkel, Fs Lambert, 165-167, text 13 A.
42635	1881,0701.396	Joined to 42634.
42636	1881,0701.397	Joined to 42411.
42637	1881,0701.398	Astronomical; star names.
42638	1881,0701.399	Medical prescription. + 43262 + 43811. Finkel, Fs Lambert, 177-180, text 22 A.
42639	1881,0701.400	Incantation. Finkel, Fs Lambert, 199-200, text 43 A.
42640	1881,0701.401	Joined to 42587.
42641	1881,0701.402	Contract; sale of land. Kūtû (register).
42642	1881,0701.403	Promissory note for silver. RN lost []/[]/acc. Babylon (but marked T.I.).
42643	1881,0701.404	Old Babylonian. Barley loan; sealed. Ammiditana -/9/35. Kessler, AfO 44/45, 131-133.
42644	1881,0701.405	School text; lexical; star list.
42645	1881,0701.406	Promissory note for dates. Nbk 14/2/[]. Babylon.
42646	1881,0701.407	Letter order from Uballissu-Gula and Marduk-mukīn-apli, scribes, to Gimil-Šamaš, Bēlšunu and Biruqā, rab sūti's of Šamaš; sealed. Dar 10/11/33. (Sippar). + 43612. Jursa, Bēl-rēmanni, 221-222, pl. LII; Jursa, NABU 1998, 72-73, no. 70; Nisaba 20, no. 291.
42647	1881,0701.408	Joined to 42547.
42648	1881,0701.409	Medical; stone list. Finkel, Fs Lambert, 184, text 26 A; Schuster-Brandis, AOAT 46, pp, 10, 315.
42649	1881,0701.410	Medical; stone list. + F.227. Finkel, Fs Lambert, 183-184, text 25 B; Schuster-Brandis, AOAT 46, p. 137, Kette 130.
42650	1881,0701.411	List of personal names and details, (Sippar).
42651	1881,0701.412	Contract. Xerxes 2/[]/[].
42652	1881,0701.413	School text; Šamaš Hymn 157-163; lexical, giš. Jursa, NABU 1999, 101, no. 104; Lambert, MC 24, no. 133.
42653	1881,0701.414	Joined to 42629.
42654	1881,0701.415	Contract.
42655	1881,0701.416	Astrological; days and stones, trees, etc. + 43299 + 43752. Finkel, Fs Lambert, 216-217, text 56 A.
42656	1881,0701.417	Kufic inscription. + 1881,0701.418.

	1881,0701.418	Joined to 42656.
42657	1881,0701.419	Promissory note for dates; imittu. Art 22/6/21. Parakku ša Mār-bīti.
42658	1881,0701.420	Bilingual litany.
42659	1881,0701.421	Lexical; Ḫḫ II.
42660	1881,0701.422	Lexical; Ea; sign list.
42661	1881,0701.423	Lexical; Ea; sign list.
42662	1881,0701.424	Receipt for dates. Nbn 3/9/[].
42663	1881,0701.425	Promissory note for silver. Šamaš-šum-ukin 11/[]/15. Kūtû.
42664	1881,0701.426	Contract. AM 19/7/acc. Babylon.
42665	1881,0701.427	Omens.
42666	1881,0701.428	Sale of land in Kutha; sealed. The scribe is a LÚ Kute-e. SE Sel II 19/7/85. Kūtû (register). CT 49, 28, no. 131; Mitchell and Searight, no. 714; Nisaba 28, no. 587.
42667	1881,0701.429	Cylinder; royal inscription of Nebuchadnezzar II; rebuilding of Eurmeiminanki, the ziggurat of Borsippa; partly dupl. Neb II nos. 11 and 17; possibly (+ 40783). (Borsippa).
42668	1881,0701.430	Prism; royal inscription of Esarhaddon (Bab: Recension E). Millard, AfO 24, 118 and pl. XIII; Leichty, RINAP 4.106.3.
91463	1881,0701.431	Glass vessel.
91581	1881,0701.432	Glass vessel.
42669	1881,0701.433	Lexical; similar to OBGT II.
42670	1881,0701.434	Old Babylonian. Ration list; check-marks. + 43323 + 43385. Kessler, AfO 44/45, 131-133.
42671	1881,0701.435	Old Babylonian. Account of silver. Kessler, AfO 44/45, 131-133.
42672	1881,0701.436	Unidentified; mostly illegible.
42673	1881,0701.437	Unidentified.
42674	1881,0701.438	Economic.
42675	1881,0701.439	Lexical; syllabary.
42676	1881,0701.440	Unidentified.
42677	1881,0701.441	Astronomical; lunar procedure text.
42678	1881,0701.442	Lexical; Ḫḫ, giš.
42679	1881,0701.443	Economic.
42680	1881,0701.444	Astronomical.
42681	1881,0701.445	Astronomical Diary.
42682	1881,0701.446	Literary.
42683	1881,0701.447	Astronomical Diary.
42684	1881,0701.448	Astronomical Diary; prices.
42685	1881,0701.449	Astronomical; procedure for the moon; System A. ACT 207f; Aaboe, KDVSMM 40/6 (1979) 32.

42686	1881,0701.450	Astronomical Diary.
42687	1881,0701.451	Unidentified.
42688	1881,0701.452	Contract.
42689	1881,0701.453	Astronomical Diary.
42690	1881,0701.454	Joined to 34580.
42691	1881,0701.455	Lexical; Ḫḫ I 276-282.
42692	1881,0701.456	Astronomical Diary.
42693	1881,0701.457	Astronomical.
42694	1881,0701.458	Astronomical Diary.
42695	1881,0701.459	Astronomical.
42696	1881,0701.460	Literary cylinder.
42697	1881,0701.461	Omens?
42698	1881,0701.462	Astronomical.
42699	1881,0701.463	Astronomical Diary.
42700	1881,0701.464	Medical(?).
42701	1881,0701.465	Astronomical.
42702	1881,0701.466	Astronomical Diary.
42703	1881,0701.467	Medical(?).
42704	1881,0701.468	Astronomical Diary; floods.
42705	1881,0701.469	Astronomical; calculations?
42706	1881,0701.470	Astronomical; lunar six table.
42707	1881,0701.471	Astronomical.
42708	1881,0701.472	Astronomical Diary.
42709	1881,0701.473	Astronomical.
42710	1881,0701.474	List of market prices.
42711	1881,0701.475	Astronomical Diary; historical references.
42712	1881,0701.476	Astronomical Diary?
42713	1881,0701.477	Astronomical Diary?
42714	1881,0701.478	Astronomical Diary?
42715	1881,0701.479	Astronomical Diary.
42716	1881,0701.480	Astronomical Diary.
42717	1881,0701.481	Astrological omens or extispicy; apodoses; colophon?
42718	1881,0701.482	Unidentified.
42719	1881,0701.483	Astronomical.
42720	1881,0701.484	Medical(?).
42721	1881,0701.485	Astronomical Diary?
42722	1881,0701.486	Astronomical Diary?
42723	1881,0701.487	Astronomical.
42724	1881,0701.488	Astronomical Diary.
42725	1881,0701.489	Astronomical.
42726	1881,0701.490	Astronomical Diary.
42727	1881,0701.491	Astronomical.
42728	1881,0701.492	Astronomical Diary.
42729	1881,0701.493	Unidentified; mostly illegible.

42730	1881,0701.494	Astronomical Diary?
42731	1881,0701.495	Astronomical; ACT type?; measurements per month; two columns.
42732	1881,0701.496	Astronomical Diary.
42733	1881,0701.497	Ritual; two columns; colophon. 22/6/[].
42734	1881,0701.498	Astronomical Diary?
42735	1881,0701.499	Astronomical.
42736	1881,0701.500	Astronomical; ephemeris for Mercury. Steele, SCIAMVS 11 (2010), 211-239, text H.
42737	1881,0701.501	Astronomical.
42738	1881,0701.502	Astronomical Diary; prices.
42739	1881,0701.503	Astronomical.
42740	1881,0701.504	Ritual.
42741	1881,0701.505	Literary.
42742	1881,0701.506	Astronomical?
42743	1881,0701.507	Astronomical.
42744	1881,0701.508	Mathematical table. + 45977 + 46008. Ossendrijver, JCS 66, 149-165 and pls.
42745	1881,0701.509	Unidentified.
42746	1881,0701.510	Astronomical Diary.
42747	1881,0701.511	Astronomical procedure text for the moon; System A. Ossendrijver, BMAPT, no. 89.
42748	1881,0701.512	Astronomical Diary.
42749	1881,0701.513	Unidentified.
42750	1881,0701.514	Astronomical.
42751	1881,0701.515	Astronomical Diary.
42752	1881,0701.516	List of market prices for SE 178.
42753	1881,0701.517	Astronomical; System A lunar ephemeris for SE 223. Steele, SCIAMVS 11 (2010), 211-239, text C.
42754	1881,0701.518	Astronomical Almanac.
42755	1881,0701.519	Astronomical.
42756	1881,0701.520	Astronomical Diary.
42757	1881,0701.521	Astronomical; Almanac for SE 244. Hunger and Sachs, ADART VII, no. 198.
42758	1881,0701.522	Joined to 34593.
42759	1881,0701.523	Astronomical Diary.
42760	1881,0701.524	Astronomical Diary.
42761	1881,0701.525	Astronomical; System B ephemeris for Jupiter for (at least) SE 160-170. + 46164. ACT 624 (46164 only); Steele, SCIAMVS 11 (2010), 211-239, text M (42761 only).
42762	1881,0701.526	Astronomical Diary.
42763	1881,0701.527	Astronomical; eclipses.
42764	1881,0701.528	Astronomical.
42765	1881,0701.529	Unidentified; mostly illegible.

42766	1881,0701.530	Astronomical Diary.
42767	1881,0701.531	Omen apodoses.
42768	1881,0701.532	Literary cylinder; hymn to Nabû. + 46082. Gesche, AOAT 275, 688.
42769	1881,0701.533	Literary.
42770	1881,0701.534	Astronomical.
42771	1881,0701.535	Astronomical Diary.
42772	1881,0701.536	Astronomical Diary or related text.
42773	1881,0701.537	Astronomical.
42774	1881,0701.538	Literary.
42775	1881,0701.539	Astronomical.
42776	1881,0701.540	Contract.
42777	1881,0701.541	Astronomical; Goal Year Text for SE 190. Hunger and Sachs, ADART VI, no. 72.
42778	1881,0701.542	Astronomical.
42779	1881,0701.543	Astronomical; Goal Year Text; not datable. Hunger and Sachs, ADART VI, no. 162.
42780	1881,0701.544	Astronomical Diary.
42781	1881,0701.545	Astronomical.
42782	1881,0701.546	Literary cylinder.
42783	1881,0701.547	Unidentified.
42784	1881,0701.548	Astronomical; mentions ziqpu stars.
42785	1881,0701.549	Astronomical.
42786	1881,0701.550	Literary.
42787	1881,0701.551	Astronomical Diary.
42788	1881,0701.552	Astronomical.
42789	1881,0701.553	Astronomical Diary.
42790	1881,0701.554	Astronomical.
42791	1881,0701.555	Astronomical.
42792	1881,0701.556	Joined to 34958.
42793	1881,0701.557	Astronomical; System A lunar ephemeris for SE 248. Steele, SCIAMVS 11 (2010), 211-239, text E.
42794	1881,0701.558	Astronomical Diary.
42795	1881,0701.559	Astronomical Diary.
42796	1881,0701.560	Astronomical Diary.
42797	1881,0701.561	Astronomical; procedure?
42798	1881,0701.562	Lexical; Malku IV.
42799	1881,0701.563	Astronomical procedure text; Venus, evening and morning star for (at least) SE 183 to 242. + 45777. ACT 421a; Ossendrijver, BMAPT, no. 8.
42800	1881,0701.564	Astronomical; procedure; numbers.
42801	1881,0701.565	Medical omens; Šumma umṣatu. Fincke, Fs Geller, 203-231.
42802	1881,0701.566	Astronomical Diary.
42803	1881,0701.567	Astronomical Diary; dated Aršu year 29. + 42974.

42804	1881,0701.568	Astronomical
42805	1881,0701.569	Unidentified.
42806	1881,0701.570	Medical.
42807	1881,0701.571	Astronomical; numbers; lunar sixes?
42808	1881,0701.572	Astronomical.
42809	1881,0701.573	Unidentified.
42810	1881,0701.574	Astronomical Diary.
42811	1881,0701.575	Astronomical.
42812	1881,0701.576	Unidentified; mostly illegible.
42813	1881,0701.577	Astronomical.
42814	1881,0701.578	Mantic dream ritual; commentary.
42815	1881,0701.579	Astronomical.
42816	1881,0701.580	Joined to 34081.
42817	1881,0701.581	Astronomical Diary.
42818	1881,0701.582	Astronomical Diary.
42819	1881,0701.583	Joined to 35495.
42820	1881,0701.584	Mathematical; numerical table; fragment of upper edge, with a prayer at the top of the obverse.
42821	1881,0701.585	Unidentified.
42822	1881,0701.586	Astronomical.
42823	1881,0701.587	Astronomical.
42824	1881,0701.588	Astronomical Diary.
42825	1881,0701.589	Astronomical.
42826	1881,0701.590	Astronomical Diary.
42827	1881,0701.591	Astronomical.
42828	1881,0701.592	Astronomical Diary.
42829	1881,0701.593	Astronomical.
42830	1881,0701.594	Astronomical.
42831	1881,0701.595	Medical.
42832	1881,0701.596	Astronomical.
42833	1881,0701.597	Astronomical Diary.
42834	1881,0701.598	Sumerian literary.
42835	1881,0701.599	Astronomical Diary?
42836	1881,0701.600	Lexical.
42837	1881,0701.601	Astronomical Diary.
42838	1881,0701.602	Astronomical.
42839	1881,0701.603	Astronomical.
42840	1881,0701.604	Astronomical procedure text for the moon; System A. Ossendrijver, BMAPT, no. 91.
42841	1881,0701.605	Lexical; synonym list?
42842	1881,0701.606	Astronomical.
42843	1881,0701.607	Astrological omen apodoses.
42844	1881,0701.608	Lexical; mentions [sa]g-gil-mud.
42845	1881,0701.609	Economic.
42846	1881,0701.610	Astronomical.

42847	1881,0701.611	Lexical; Erimḫuš V.
42848	1881,0701.612	Astronomical.
42849	1881,0701.613	Astronomical.
42850	1881,0701.614	Astronomical.
42851	1881,0701.615	Practice wedges.
42852	1881,0701.616	Astronomical.
42853	1881,0701.617	Astronomical Diary; fragment.
42854	1881,0701.618	Astronomical.
42855	1881,0701.619	Astronomical.
42856	1881,0701.620	Colophon of a two column literary or lexical text. SE -/-/179.
42857	1881,0701.621	Unidentified; mostly illegible.
42858	1881,0701.622	Astronomical.
42859	1881,0701.623	Astronomical Diary or observations.
42860	1881,0701.624	Astronomical; mentions 1st year.
42861	1881,0701.625	Astronomical Diary.
42862	1881,0701.626	Astronomical; daily motion table for the moon.
42863	1881,0701.627	Lexical.
42864	1881,0701.628	Astronomical Diary or related text.
42865	1881,0701.629	Astronomical.
42866	1881,0701.630	Astronomical.
42867	1881,0701.631	Astronomical.
42868	1881,0701.632	Lexical.
42869	1881,0701.633	Joined to 34580.
42870	1881,0701.634	Astronomical.
42871	1881,0701.635	Astronomical.
42872	1881,0701.636	Astronomical.
42873	1881,0701.637	Joined to 35495.
42874	1881,0701.638	Astronomical Diary or related text.
42875	1881,0701.639	Astronomical.
42876	1881,0701.640	Astronomical; System A lunar ephemeris for SE 180. Steele, SCIAMVS 11 (2010), 211-239, text A.
42877	1881,0701.641	Unidentified.
42878	1881,0701.642	Astronomical; Greek letter phenomena of Saturn. (+) 45807. Steele, JHA 41 (2010) 261-268.
42879	1881,0701.643	Astrological omens.
42880	1881,0701.644	Unidentified.
42881	1881,0701.645	Astronomical.
42882	1881,0701.646	Ṣâtu commentary on celestial omens.
42883	1881,0701.647	Astronomical.
42884	1881,0701.648	Astronomical.
42885	1881,0701.649	Astronomical.
42886	1881,0701.650	Astronomical.
42887	1881,0701.651	Sumerian literary.
42888	1881,0701.652	Astronomical Diary or related text

42889	1881,0701.653	Astronomical.
42890	1881,0701.654	Astronomical.
42891	1881,0701.655	Astronomical Diary.
42892	1881,0701.656	Astronomical.
42893	1881,0701.657	Lexical; list of stones.
42894	1881,0701.658	Astronomical.
42895	1881,0701.659	Astronomical.
42896	1881,0701.660	Astronomical.
42897	1881,0701.661	Astronomical Diary.
42898	1881,0701.662	Astronomical Diary.
42899	1881,0701.663	Ritual?
42900	1881,0701.664	Medical.
42901	1881,0701.665	Astronomical.
42902	1881,0701.666	Joined to 34580.
42903	1881,0701.667	Astronomical Diary or related text.
42904	1881,0701.668	Astronomical Diary.
42905	1881,0701.669	Incantation.
42906	1881,0701.670	Literary cylinder.
42907	1881,0701.671	Astronomical.
42908	1881,0701.672	Joined to 42300.
42909	1881,0701.673	Astronomical.
42910	1881,0701.674	Field sale; mentions Nergal-apla-uṣur šatammu of E[meslam]; probably Seleucid. + 43814.
42911	1881,0701.675	Lexical; Ea; sign list.
42912	1881,0701.676	Promissory note for silver.
42913	1881,0701.677	Ea; sign list; practice contract; two columns.
42914	1881,0701.678	Contract. 14/9/-.
42915	1881,0701.679	Astronomical.
42916	1881,0701.680	Commentary; astrological. + 43687 + 43710 + 43712.
42917	1881,0701.681	Lexical; Ea; sign list.
42918	1881,0701.682	Ea; sign list; literary extract.
42919	1881,0701.683	Administrative; list of date rations; probably Seleucid; barely legible.
42920	1881,0701.684	Lexical; Ea; sign list.
42921	1881,0701.685	Lexical.
42922	1881,0701.686	Contract; mentions year 12 of Alexander III. + 42924.
42923	1881,0701.687	Unidentified.
42924	1881,0701.688	Joined to 42922.
42925	1881,0701.689	Unidentified.
42926	1881,0701.690	Contract.
42927	1881,0701.691	Contract.
42928	1881,0701.692	Contract.
42929	1881,0701.693	Lexical. + 42934.
42930	1881,0701.694	Literary.
42931	1881,0701.695	Lexical; Ea; sign list.

42932	1881,0701.696	Account of dates.
42933	1881,0701.697	Lexical; Ea; sign list.
42934	1881,0701.698	Joined to 42929.
42935	1881,0701.699	Joined to 42288.
42936	1881,0701.700	Lexical; giš.
42937	1881,0701.701	Economic.
42938	1881,0701.702	Lexical; Ea; sign list.
42939	1881,0701.703	Literary cylinder.
42940	1881,0701.704	Astronomical.
42941	1881,0701.705	Astrological omens.
42942	1881,0701.706	Literary.
42943	1881,0701.707	Astronomical Diary.
42944	1881,0701.708	Mathematical; table of reciprocals. + 45893.
42945	1881,0701.709	Astronomical.
42946	1881,0701.710	Astronomical.
42947	1881,0701.711	Astronomical.
42948	1881,0701.712	Literary.
42949	1881,0701.713	Astronomical Diary; prices.
42950	1881,0701.714	Astronomical.
42951	1881,0701.715	Astronomical; Venus ephemeris. Steele, SCIAMVS 11 (2010), 211-239, text K.
42952	1881,0701.716	Unidentified.
42953	1881,0701.717	Astronomical.
42954	1881,0701.718	Astronomical.
42955	1881,0701.719	Lexical.
42956	1881,0701.720	Astronomical.
42957	1881,0701.721	Astronomical.
42958	1881,0701.722	Unidentified.
42959	1881,0701.723	Astronomical.
42960	1881,0701.724	Astronomical.
42961	1881,0701.725	Astronomical; commentary on Enūma Anu Enlil 14; lengths of day and night watches. + 42964 + 43081 + 45821 + 46215 + 1881,0706.399 + 565 + 676. George and ar-Rawi, AfO 38-39, 52-73 (only 45821 + 46215); Ossendrijver, NABU 2014, 158-161, no. 101.
42962	1881,0701.726	Unidentified.
42963	1881,0701.727	Astronomical.
42964	1881,0701.728	Joined to 42961.
42965	1881,0701.729	Astronomical.
42966	1881,0701.730	Literary cylinder.
42967	1881,0701.731	Economic.
42968	1881,0701.732	Astronomical.
42969	1881,0701.733	Astronomical.
42970	1881,0701.734	Medical. + 42977.
42971	1881,0701.735	Astronomical.

42972	1881,0701.736	Astronomical.
42973	1881,0701.737	Astronomical.
42974	1881,0701.738	Astronomical.
42975	1881,0701.739	Astronomical.
42976	1881,0701.740	Astronomical.
42977	1881,0701.741	Joined to 42970.
42978	1881,0701.742	Ritual.
42979	1881,0701.743	Astronomical.
42980	1881,0701.744	Mathematical table. Ossendrijver, JCS 66, 149-165 and pls.
42981	1881,0701.745	Astronomical; Almanac. SE. Hunger and Sachs, ADART VII, no. 227.
42982	1881,0701.746	Medical.
42983	1881,0701.747	Astronomical.
42984	1881,0701.748	Astronomical.
42985	1881,0701.749	Unidentified.
42986	1881,0701.750	Astronomical table.
42987	1881,0701.751	Astronomical.
42988	1881,0701.752	Unidentified.
42989	1881,0701.753	Astronomical.
42990	1881,0701.754	Astronomical.
42991	1881,0701.755	Astronomical.
42992	1881,0701.756	Astronomical Diary.
42993	1881,0701.757	Astronomical.
42994	1881,0701.758	Astronomical.
42995	1881,0701.759	Inventory?
42996	1881,0701.760	Astronomical Diary.
42997	1881,0701.761	Astronomical.
42998	1881,0701.762	Astronomical; planetary.
42999	1881,0701.763	Astronomical.
43000	1881,0701.764	Joined to 34580.
43001	1881,0701.765	Astronomical.
43002	1881,0701.766	Astronomical.
43003	1881,0701.767	Unidentified.
43004	1881,0701.768	Astronomical Diary.
43005	1881,0701.769	Astronomical.
43006	1881,0701.770	Astronomical.
43007	1881,0701.771	Unidentified.
43008	1881,0701.772	Astronomical.
43009	1881,0701.773	Astronomical.
43010	1881,0701.774	Astronomical Diary.
43011	1881,0701.775	Astronomical Diary.
43012	1881,0701.776	Astronomical.
43013	1881,0701.777	Medical.
43014	1881,0701.778	Astronomical.

43015	1881,0701.779	Astronomical Diary or related text.
43016	1881,0701.780	Astronomical.
43017	1881,0701.781	Astronomical.
43018	1881,0701.782	Astronomical.
43019	1881,0701.783	Astronomical.
43020	1881,0701.784	Astronomical.
43021	1881,0701.785	Astronomical.
43022	1881,0701.786	Astronomical.
43023	1881,0701.787	Astronomical; Jupiter, second stationary point and last visibility, for (at least) SE 142 to 195; System A. + 45730 + 46142 (+) Columbia University Library CULC 372. ACT 610; Kugler, SSB I pl. 15; Steele, SCIAMVS 11 (2010), 211-239, text L; 43023 is unpublished.
43024	1881,0701.788	Astronomical; System A Phi-W table. Steele, SCIAMVS 11 (2010), 211-239, text F
43025	1881,0701.789	Astronomical Diary for SE 234. + 45689 + 46047. LBAT 514 (45689 only); Sachs and Hunger, ADART III, no. -77 A; Sachs, PTRSL A.276, 48, fig. 7 (45689 only).
43026	1881,0701.790	Astronomical.
43027	1881,0701.791	Astronomical Diary.
43028	1881,0701.792	Astronomical.
43029	1881,0701.793	Unidentified.
43030	1881,0701.794	Joined to 34580.
43031	1881,0701.795	Astronomical; Goal Year Text; lunar six values.
43032	1881,0701.796	Astronomical.
43033	1881,0701.797	Astronomical.
43034	1881,0701.798	Astronomical.
43035	1881,0701.799	Mathematical astronomy; synodic table, Saturn system B.
43036	1881,0701.800	Astronomical.
43037	1881,0701.801	Astronomical.
43038	1881,0701.802	Astronomical.
43039	1881,0701.803	Omens.
43040	1881,0701.804	Astronomical.
43041	1881,0701.805	Unidentified.
43042	1881,0701.806	Literary cylinder.
43043	1881,0701.807	Unidentified.
43044	1881,0701.808	Astronomical.
43045	1881,0701.809	Unidentified.
43046	1881,0701.810	Astronomical; Almanac. SE. Hunger and Sachs, ADART VII, no. 228.
43047	1881,0701.811	Astronomical.
43048	1881,0701.812	Astronomical.

43049	1881,0701.813	Astronomical Diary or related text.
43050	1881,0701.814	Astronomical Diary.
43051	1881,0701.815	Astronomical Diary.
43052	1881,0701.816	Astronomical Diary.
43053	1881,0701.817	Astronomical.
43054	1881,0701.818	Astronomical Diary or related text.
43055	1881,0701.819	School text; lexical; Ea; sign list.
43056	1881,0701.820	Astronomical Diary or related text.
43057	1881,0701.821	Astronomical.
43058	1881,0701.822	Incantation; mentions Asalluḫi; Marduk-Ea formula.
43059	1881,0701.823	Astronomical.
43060	1881,0701.824	Unidentified.
43061	1881,0701.825	Astronomical Diary.
43062	1881,0701.826	Mathematical table.
43063	1881,0701.827	Ritual.
43064	1881,0701.828	Astronomical.
43065	1881,0701.829	Unidentified.
43066	1881,0701.830	Unidentified.
43067	1881,0701.831	Astronomical; Normal Star Almanac for SE 167. Hunger and Sachs, ADART VII, no. 74.
43068	1881,0701.832	Astronomical.
43069	1881,0701.833	Mathematical table.
43070	1881,0701.834	Mathematical table.
43071	1881,0701.835	Astronomical.
43072	1881,0701.836	Astronomical.
43073	1881,0701.837	Astronomical Diary or related text.
43074	1881,0701.838	Lexical.
43075	1881,0701.839	Astronomical.
43076	1881,0701.840	Astronomical.
43077	1881,0701.841	Astronomical Diary or related text.
43078	1881,0701.842	Unidentified.
43079	1881,0701.843	Astronomical Diary or related text.
43080	1881,0701.844	Astronomical.
43081	1881,0701.845	Joined to 42961.
43082	1881,0701.846	Mathematical; table of reciprocals.
43083	1881,0701.847	Unidentified.
43084	1881,0701.848	Astronomical.
43085	1881,0701.849	Astronomical Diary.
43086	1881,0701.850	Astronomical Diary?
43087	1881,0701.851	Astronomical.
43088	1881,0701.852	Unidentified.
43089	1881,0701.853	Sumerian literary.
43090	1881,0701.854	Ritual; namburbû preparations. + 43504 + 43676 + 43773 + F.228. Maul, Bagh Forsch 18, 12 n. 91, 192 n. 307, 297; Finkel, Fs Lambert, 206-207, text 49 A.

43091	1881,0701.855	Economic.
43092	1881,0701.856	School text; lexical, Ea; bilingual incantation. + 43164.
43093	1881,0701.857	Incantation.
43094	1881,0701.858	Lexical.
43095	1881,0701.859	Sale of prebends. Dar. Sippar. + 43452 (+) 1881,0701 F 230 and F 233. Jursa, Bēl-rēmanni, 48, 68, 72, 83, 221, pl. LIII.
43096	1881,0701.860	Promissory note for silver.
43097	1881,0701.861	Joined to 42411.
43098	1881,0701.862	Promissory note for silver with prebends as pledge. 11/[]/18. Sippar. + 43260 + 1881,0701 F.229. Jursa, Bēl-rēmanni, 223-224, pl. LIV.
43099	1881,0701.863	Economic. (Sippar). Jursa, Bēl-rēmanni, 91, 224, pl. LII.
43100	1881,0701.864	Economic.
43101	1881,0701.865	Economic. Nbk.
43102	1881,0701.866	Economic.
43103	1881,0701.867	Joined to 42345.
43104	1881,0701.868	Receipt? [Sippar?] Jursa, Bēl-rēmanni, 114, 120, 224, pl. LII.
43105	1881,0701.869	Astronomical.
43106	1881,0701.870	Receipt for dates or grain.
43107	1881,0701.871	Joined to 42630.
43108	1881,0701.872	Contract.
43109	1881,0701.873	Lexical. + 43118.
43110	1881,0701.874	Medical prescription. + 43291 + 43470. Finkel, Fs Lambert, 173-174, text 18 A.
43111	1881,0701.875	Lexical; two columns.
43112	1881,0701.876	Economic
43113	1881,0701.877	Lexical.
43114	1881,0701.878	Joined to 42425.
43115	1881,0701.879	Joined to 42356.
43116	1881,0701.880	Commentary.
43117	1881,0701.881	Economic.
43118	1881,0701.882	Joined to 43109.
43119	1881,0701.883	Receipt for dates.
43120	1881,0701.884	Deposition. [Sippar?]. Jursa, Bēl-rēmanni, 224, pl. LII.
43121	1881,0701.885	Joined to 42310.
43122	1881,0701.886	Bilingual literary.
43123	1881,0701.887	Medical; incantation against ušburruda. + 43219. Finkel, Fs Lambert, 203-206, text 48 C.
43124	1881,0701.888	Ritual.
43125	1881,0701.889	List of objects.

43126	1881,0701.890	Economic.
43127	1881,0701.891	Joined to 42328.
43128	1881,0701.892	Promissory note with a prebend as pledge. [Sippar?]. Jursa, Bēl-rēmanni, 52, 225, pl. LII.
43129	1881,0701.893	Joined to 42425.
43130	1881,0701.894	Incantations; Maqlu II. Abusch, AMD 10, 51-77.
43131	1881,0701.895	Contract. Dar -/-/34.
43132	1881,0701.896	Contract.
43133	1881,0701.897	Old Babylonian. Contract. Ammiṣaduqa -/5/?.
43134	1881,0701.898	Astronomical.
43135	1881,0701.899	Joined to 42297.
43136	1881,0701.900	Joined to 42297.
43137	1881,0701.901	Economic.
43138	1881,0701.902	Ritual.
43139	1881,0701.903	Astronomical.
43140	1881,0701.904	Unidentified; mostly illegible.
43141	1881,0701.905	Joined to 42425.
43142	1881,0701.906	Contract; sealed. Art II/III 16/5/[]. Nisaba 28, no. 299.
43143	1881,0701.907	Promissory note for barley. Art I/II -/-/30.
43144	1881,0701.908	Ritual.
43145	1881,0701.909	Contract.
43146	1881,0701.910	Sale of a prebend; finger-nail marks. [Sippar]. + 43366 + 43668 + 43723 + 43798 + 43800 (+) 43695. Jursa, Bēl-rēmanni, 11, 22, 24, 35, 42, 43, 48, 69, 81, 225-227, pl. LV.
43147	1881,0701.911	Literary.
43148	1881,0701.912	Ritual.
43149	1881,0701.913	Ritual.
43150	1881,0701.914	Incantation.
43151	1881,0701.915	Lexical; Ea; sign list.
43152	1881,0701.916	Economic. (Sippar). Jursa, Bēl-rēmanni, 121, 227, pl. LII.
43153	1881,0701.917	Contract.
43154	1881,0701.918	Joined to 42599.
43155	1881,0701.919	Economic.
43156	1881,0701.920	Contract.
43157	1881,0701.921	Old Babylonian. Economic.
43158	1881,0701.922	Lexical; Ea; sign list.
43159	1881,0701.923	Literary.
43160	1881,0701.924	Joined to 42308.
43161	1881,0701.925	Literary.
43162	1881,0701.926	Economic.
43163	1881,0701.927	Joined to 42634.
43164	1881,0701.928	Joined to 43092.
43165	1881,0701.929	Joined to 42626.

43166	1881,0701.930	Lexical; Ea; sign list.
43167	1881,0701.931	Lexical.
43168	1881,0701.932	Lexical; Ḫḫ; stones; oxen.
43169	1881,0701.933	Literary.
43170	1881,0701.934	Economic.
43171	1881,0701.935	Medical prescription. + 43283 + 43294. Finkel, Fs Lambert, 152-153, text 2 A.
43172	1881,0701.936	Memorandum.
43173	1881,0701.937	Medical. + 43199. Finkel, Fs Lambert, 219, text 62 A.
43174	1881,0701.938	Joined to 42313.
43175	1881,0701.939	Lexical; Ea; sign list.
43176	1881,0701.940	Literary.
43177	1881,0701.941	Sale of slaves. (Sippar). + 43735 + 43792. Jursa, Bēl-rēmanni, 11, 36, 227, pl. LIV.
43178	1881,0701.942	Sale of prebends; dupl. 42341. Dar 26/3/-. Sippar. + 43250 + 43434 + 43445 + 43572 + 43648. Jursa, Bēl-rēmanni, 11, 14, 19, 25, 42, 43, 59, 76, 228, pl. LVI.
43179	1881,0701.943	Medical; stone list. Finkel, Fs Lambert, 184-185, text 27 A.
43180	1881,0701.944	Contract; sealed. Nbk 23/2/7+. Kūtû (marked T.I).
43181	1881,0701.945	Lexical; Ea; sign list and personal names.
43182	1881,0701.946	Mathematical.
43183	1881,0701.947	Literary; Enūma eliš I. Kämmerer and Metzler, AOAT 375, 97, Tafel I TT, pl. XI; Lambert, BCM, p. 47, pl. 4.
43184	1881,0701.948	Lexical.
43185	1881,0701.949	Contract.
43186	1881,0701.950	Economic.
43187	1881,0701.951	Lexical; Ea; sign list.
43188	1881,0701.952	Literary.
43189	1881,0701.953	Medical.
43190	1881,0701.954	Promissory note for dates; perhaps Macedonian dynasty; sealed. (Borsippa). Nisaba 28, no. 526.
43191	1881,0701.955	Incantation.
43192	1881,0701.956	Economic.
43193	1881,0701.957	Literary.
43194	1881,0701.958	Unidentified.
43195	1881,0701.959	Economic.
43196	1881,0701.960	Joined to 42431.
43197	1881,0701.961	Joined to 42405.
43198	1881,0701.962	Promissory note for dates; dupl. 42360; Aramaic note. Sippar. + 43245. Jursa, Bēl-rēmanni, 13, 24, 157, pl. XIX.
43199	1881,0701.963	Joined to 43173.

43200	1881,0701.964	Lexical.
43201	1881,0701.965	Account of dates or grain.
43202	1881,0701.966	Economic.
43203	1881,0701.967	Economic. (Sippar). Jursa, Bēl-rēmanni, 79, 230, pl. LVII.
43204	1881,0701.968	Economic.
43205	1881,0701.969	Unidentified.
43206	1881,0701.970	Old Babylonian. List of persons; check-marks. + 43269.
43207	1881,0701.971	Purchase of furnishings with silver.
43208	1881,0701.972	Economic. 30/-/-.
43209	1881,0701.973	Sumerian literary.
43210	1881,0701.974	Unidentified.
43211	1881,0701.975	Joined to 42613.
43212	1881,0701.976	Astrological medicine. Finkel, Fs Lambert, 212-215, text 55 D.
43213	1881,0701.977	Promissory note for silver.
43214	1881,0701.978	Contract.
43215	1881,0701.979	Joined to 42313.
43216	1881,0701.980	Joined to 42569.
43217	1881,0701.981	Joined to 42587.
43218	1881,0701.982	Astronomical.
43219	1881,0701.983	Joined to 43123.
43220	1881,0701.984	Contract. 5/8/2.
43221	1881,0701.985	Joined to 42621.
43222	1881,0701.986	Medical prescription. Finkel, Fs Lambert, 174-175, text 20 A.
43223	1881,0701.987	Incantation.
43224	1881,0701.988	Joined to 42311.
43225	1881,0701.989	Old Babylonian. Contract; sealed. Ammiditana 20+/5/36.
43226	1881,0701.990	Promissory note for barley. Dar I []/[]/32. Babylon.
43227	1881,0701.991	Astronomical.
43228	1881,0701.992	Old Babylonian. Contract; sealed.
43229	1881,0701.993	Medical prescription. Finkel, Fs Lambert, 157-159, text 5 C.
43230	1881,0701.994	Astronomical.
43231	1881,0701.995	Joined to 42310.
43232	1881,0701.996	Joined to 42343.
43233	1881,0701.997	Receipt. (Sippar). Jursa, Bēl-rēmanni, 230, pl. LVII.
43234	1881,0701.998	Receipt.
43235	1881,0701.999	Economic.
43236	1881,0701.1000	Economic Dar. (Sippar). Jursa, Bēl-rēmanni, 231, pl. LVII.

43237	1881,0701.1001	Medical prescription. Finkel, Fs Lambert, 174, text 19 A.
43238	1881,0701.1002	Old Babylonian. Contract.
43239	1881,0701.1003	Joined to 42625.
43240	1881,0701.1004	Economic.
43241	1881,0701.1005	Old Babylonian. Account of dates or grain; check-marks.
43242	1881,0701.1006	Deposition.
43243	1881,0701.1007	Old Babylonian. Ration list.
43244	1881,0701.1008	Account of deliveries.
43245	1881,0701.1009	Joined to 43198.
43246	1881,0701.1010	Receipt for payment of silver.
43247	1881,0701.1011	Sumerian literary.
43248	1881,0701.1012	Joined to 42625.
43249	1881,0701.1013	Economic.
43250	1881,0701.1014	Joined to 43178.
43251	1881,0701.1015	Joined to 42356.
43252	1881,0701.1016	Contract.
43253	1881,0701.1017	Sale of a prebend? (Sippar). Jursa, Bēl-rēmanni, 59, 76, 231, pl. LVII.
43254	1881,0701.1018	Old Babylonian. Economic. Ammiṣaduqa.
43255	1881,0701.1019	Old Babylonian. Receipt; sealed; mu [...] gú íd [...]. RN lost []/[]/?.
43256	1881,0701.1020	Joined to 42571.
43257	1881,0701.1021	Account of dates.
43258	1881,0701.1022	Economic.
43259	1881,0701.1023	Medical prescription; stones. Finkel, Fs Lambert, 211-212, text 54 A.
43260	1881,0701.1024	Joined to 43098.
43261	1881,0701.1025	Sumerian literary.
43262	1881,0701.1026	Joined to 42638.
43263	1881,0701.1027	Literary.
43264	1881,0701.1028	Joined to 42345.
43265	1881,0701.1029	Sumerian literary.
43266	1881,0701.1030	Economic.
43267	1881,0701.1031	School tablet; ritual related to Lamaštu III 49-63; dupl. 1883,0118.752. (+) 42612. Finkel, Fs Lambert, 210-211, text 53 B; Farber, Lamaštu, 52, 57, 276-277; Stadthouders, NABU 2016, 166-167, no. 101.
43268	1881,0701.1032	Medical prescription. (+) F.238. Finkel, Fs Lambert, 157-159, text 5 B.
43269	1881,0701.1033	Joined to 43206.
43270	1881,0701.1034	Contract.
43271	1881,0701.1035	Joined to 42454.
43272	1881,0701.1036	Economic.

43273	1881,0701.1037	Promissory note for dates or grain.
43274	1881,0701.1038	Joined to 42313.
43275	1881,0701.1039	Literary.
43276	1881,0701.1040	Promissory note for barley.
43277	1881,0701.1041	Unidentified.
43278	1881,0701.1042	Old Babylonian. Contract; sealed.
43279	1881,0701.1043	Joined to 42313.
43280	1881,0701.1044	Contract; transfer of prebends; part of the Bēl-rēmanni archive. [Dar] [4]/[]/[32] (Sippar). + 43354. Waerzeggers, OLA 233, 66 and 166-167.
43281	1881,0701.1045	Joined to 42313.
43282	1881,0701.1046	Medical prescription. + 43502. Finkel, Fs Lambert, 218, text 58 A.
43283	1881,0701.1047	Joined to 43171.
43284	1881,0701.1048	Economic.
43285	1881,0701.1049	Old Babylonian. Economic; sealed. Ammiṣaduqa 24/12/?.
43286	1881,0701.1050	Account of dates harvest. (Sippar). Jursa, Bēl-rēmanni, 87, 93, 107, 232, pl. LVII.
43287	1881,0701.1051	Joined to 42587.
43288	1881,0701.1052	Old Babylonian. Contract for barley at harvest; sealed.
43289	1881,0701.1053	Old Babylonian. Contract; mu ... bád am-mi-[...]; sealed. Ammi-[] []/5/?
43290	1881,0701.1054	Receipt of silver in payment of a dowry. Dar 27/2/33. Sippar. + 43597 + 43763. Jursa, Bēl-rēmanni, 35, 232, pl. LVIII.
43291	1881,0701.1055	Joined to 43110.
43292	1881,0701.1056	Promissory note for barley.
43293	1881,0701.1057	Promissory note for dates. Dar 3/6/27. Sippar. + 1881,0701.335.
43294	1881,0701.1058	Joined to 43171.
43295	1881,0701.1059	Medical prescription. + F.229. Finkel, Fs Lambert, 153-154, text 3 A.
43296	1881,0701.1060	Joined to 42454.
43297	1881,0701.1061	Deposition. Dar -/3/8+.
43298	1881,0701.1062	Letter order.
43299	1881,0701.1063	Joined to 42655.
43300	1881,0701.1064	Administrative; about men available for bow service; at the disposal of Nidinti-Marduk; sealed. Dar 6/3/17. (Sippar). + 43665. Jursa, Bēl-rēmanni, 233-234, pl. LVIII; Nisaba 20, no. 474.
43301	1881,0701.1065	Receipt for silver. Dar 26/4/8. Babylon. + 43441 + 43473. Jursa, Bēl-rēmanni, 14, 19, 24, 207.

43302	1881,0701.1066	Promissory note for dates. -/-/8. Sippar. + 43383 + 43598. Jursa, Bēl-rēmanni, 115, 122, 234, pl. LIX.
43303	1881,0701.1067	Joined to 42551.
43304	1881,0701.1068	Economic.
43305	1881,0701.1069	Sumerian literary.
43306	1881,0701.1070	Economic; about dates, property of Šamaš. (Sippar).
43307	1881,0701.1071	Promissory note for dates.
43308	1881,0701.1072	Account of dates.
43309	1881,0701.1073	Sale of prebends. Dar -/6/-. Sippar. + 43437 + 45585. Jursa, Bēl-rēmanni, 50, 62, 79, 234, pl. LIX.
43310	1881,0701.1074	Joined to 42328.
43311	1881,0701.1075	Astronomical.
43312	1881,0701.1076	Old Babylonian. Economic.
43313	1881,0701.1077	Joined to 42374.
43314	1881,0701.1078	Contract; transfer of prebends; part of the Bēl-rēmanni archive. Dar [4]/[]/32. (Sippar). Waerzeggers, OLA 233, 66 and 166-167.
43315	1881,0701.1079	Promissory note? (Sippar). Jursa, Bēl-rēmanni, 236, pl. LX.
43316	1881,0701.1080	Old Babylonian. Ledger. + 43424.
43317	1881,0701.1081	Old Babylonian. Barley loan; sealed. Ammiditana -/12/35 or 36. Kessler, AfO 44/45, 131-133.
43318	1881,0701.1082	Joined to 42310.
43319	1881,0701.1083	Ritual.
43320	1881,0701.1084	Letter?
43321	1881,0701.1085	Account. (Sippar?).
43322	1881,0701.1086	Deposition. Dar -/-/12.
43323	1881,0701.1087	Joined to 42670.
43324	1881,0701.1088	Incantation. + 43485.
43325	1881,0701.1089	Joined to 42508.
43326	1881,0701.1090	Old Babylonian. Ration list. Kessler, AfO 44/45, 131-133.
43327	1881,0701.1091	Old Babylonian. Account.
43328	1881,0701.1092	Old Babylonian. Barley loan. Ammiditana 30/-/-. Kessler, AfO 44/45, 131-133.
43329	1881,0701.1093	Old Babylonian. Barley loan. Ammiditana -/-/35. Kessler, AfO 44/45, 131-133.
43330	1881,0701.1094	Old Babylonian. Barley loan. Ammiditana 22?/[]/35. Kessler, AfO 44/45, 131-133.
43331	1881,0701.1095	Old Babylonian. Barley loan. Ammiditana -/8/-. Kessler, AfO 44/45, 131-133.
43332	1881,0701.1096	Old Babylonian. Account of barley, silver and stones. + 43415. Kessler, AfO 44/45, 131-133.
43333	1881,0701.1097	Old Babylonian. Administrative. Kessler, AfO 44/45, 131-133.

43334	1881,0701.1098	Old Babylonian. Silver loan. Ammiṣaduqa -/-/15. + 43395. Kessler, AfO 44/45, 131-133.
43335	1881,0701.1099	Contract.
43336	1881,0701.1100	School text; list of stones; uzu.
43337	1881,0701.1101	Economic.
43338	1881,0701.1102	Literary.
43339	1881,0701.1103	School practice.
43340	1881,0701.1104	Promissory note for dates or grain. (Sippar). Jursa, Bēl-rēmanni, 14.
43341	1881,0701.1105	Literary.
43342	1881,0701.1106	Economic.
43343	1881,0701.1107	Joined to 42286.
43344	1881,0701.1108	Medical(?).
43345	1881,0701.1109	Economic. []/[]/18.
43346	1881,0701.1110	Incantation. Finkel, Fs Lambert, 200, text 44 A.
43347	1881,0701.1111	Joined to 42288.
43348	1881,0701.1112	Contract. Nbk 22/2/-.
43349	1881,0701.1113	Medical.
43350	1881,0701.1114	Unidentified.
43351	1881,0701.1115	Joined to 42310.
43352	1881,0701.1116	Old Babylonian? Literary?
43353	1881,0701.1117	School text; extracts; lexical; Ḫḫ IV.
43354	1881,0701.1118	Joined to 43280. Waerzeggers, OLA 233, 66 n. 24.
43355	1881,0701.1119	Literary or lexical.
43356	1881,0701.1120	Literary.
43357	1881,0701.1121	Bilingual incantation.
43358	1881,0701.1122	Lexical?. + 43368.
43359	1881,0701.1123	Ritual to make clay cylinder seals inscribed with spells against fever. Duplicates 49141. + 43378 + 43567 + 2 unnum.
43360	1881,0701.1124	Lexical.
43361	1881,0701.1125	Contract. (Sippar).
43362	1881,0701.1126	Astronomical.
43363	1881,0701.1127	Joined to 42278.
43364	1881,0701.1128	Bilingual incantation.
43365	1881,0701.1129	Receipt.
43366	1881,0701.1130	Joined to 43146.
43367	1881,0701.1131	Lexical.
43368	1881,0701.1132	Joined to 43358.
43369	1881,0701.1133	Omens; terrestrial. + 43373.
43370	1881,0701.1134	Contract; perhaps Seleucid.
43371	1881,0701.1135	Literary.
43372	1881,0701.1136	Literary.
43373	1881,0701.1137	Joined to 43369.
43374	1881,0701.1138	Liver omens; kakku.

43375	1881,0701.1139	Literary.
43376	1881,0701.1140	Field sale.
43377	1881,0701.1141	Joined to 42503.
43378	1881,0701.1142	Joined to 43359.
43379	1881,0701.1143	Contract.
43380	1881,0701.1144	Account of dates or grain.
43381	1881,0701.1145	Old Babylonian. Barley rations. Kessler, AfO 44/45, 131-133.
43382	1881,0701.1146	Old Babylonian. Economic.
43383	1881,0701.1147	Joined to 43302.
43384	1881,0701.1148	Lexical.
43385	1881,0701.1149	Joined to 42670.
43386	1881,0701.1150	Old Babylonian. Barley loan. Ammiditana 20+/[]/35 or 36. Kessler, AfO 44/45, 131-133.
43387	1881,0701.1151	Economic.
43388	1881,0701.1152	Old Babylonian. Ration list. Kessler, AfO 44/45, 131-133.
43389	1881,0701.1153	Old Babylonian. Memorandum; two line of numbers only; marked T.-I.
43390	1881,0701.1154	Old Babylonian. Barley loan. Ammiditana 30/1?/35. Kessler, AfO 44/45, 131-133.
43391	1881,0701.1155	Old Babylonian. Barley loan. Ammiditana 10+/5?/35 or 36. Kessler, AfO 44/45, 131-133.
43392	1881,0701.1156	Old Babylonian. Barley loan. Kessler, AfO 44/45, 131-133.
43393	1881,0701.1157	Old Babylonian. Barley loan. Kessler, AfO 44/45, 131-133.
43394	1881,0701.1158	Old Babylonian. Barley loan. Ammiditana 1/9/36. Kessler, AfO 44/45, 131-133.
43395	1881,0701.1159	Joined to 43334.
43396	1881,0701.1160	Old Babylonian. Barley loan. Ammiditana 30/12/35 or 36. Kessler, AfO 44/45, 131-133.
43397	1881,0701.1161	Old Babylonian. Barley loan. Ammiditana 30/5/36. Kessler, AfO 44/45, 131-133.
43398	1881,0701.1162	Old Babylonian. Barley loan. Kessler, AfO 44/45, 131-133.
43399	1881,0701.1163	Old Babylonian. Barley loan. Ammiditana -/9/36. Kessler, AfO 44/45, 131-133.
43400	1881,0701.1164	Old Babylonian. Barley loan. Ammiditana 23/7/36. Kessler, AfO 44/45, 131-133.
43401	1881,0701.1165	Old Babylonian. Barley loan. -/5?/-. Kessler, AfO 44/45, 131-133.
43402	1881,0701.1166	Old Babylonian. Barley loan. Kessler, AfO 44/45, 131-133.

43403	1881,0701.1167	Old Babylonian. Barley loan. Ammiditana 14/12/-. Kessler, AfO 44/45, 131-133.
43404	1881,0701.1168	Old Babylonian. Silver loan. Ammiditana 30/7/36. Kessler, AfO 44/45, 131-133.
43405	1881,0701.1169	Old Babylonian. Barley loan. Ammiṣaduqa 30/7?/-. Kessler, AfO 44/45, 131-133.
43406	1881,0701.1170	Account of dates or grain.
43407	1881,0701.1171	Contract; lease of a house. -/6/acc. Sippar.
43408	1881,0701.1172	Bilingual incantation.
43409	1881,0701.1173	Bilingual incantation.
43410	1881,0701.1174	Incantation.
43411	1881,0701.1175	Old Babylonian. Ration list. Ammiṣaduqa 4/?/-.
43412	1881,0701.1176	School text; lexical (DUG) and literary extracts.
43413	1881,0701.1177	Unidentified; mostly illegible.
43414	1881,0701.1178	Astronomical.
43415	1881,0701.1179	Joined to 43332.
43416	1881,0701.1180	Joined to 42310.
43417	1881,0701.1181	Incantation.
43418	1881,0701.1182	Astronomical procedure text; lunar sixes and eclipses; cf. TCL 6, no. 11.
43419	1881,0701.1183	Incantation.
43420	1881,0701.1184	School text; extracts.
43421	1881,0701.1185	Contract; land sale; caption for finger-nail marks. Kandalanu? 13/10/12. (Babylon).
43422	1881,0701.1186	Incantation.
43423	1881,0701.1187	Omens; Šumma ālu.
43424	1881,0701.1188	Joined to 43316.
43425	1881,0701.1189	Old Babylonian. Ration list.
43426	1881,0701.1190	Unidentified.
43427	1881,0701.1191	Astronomical.
43428	1881,0701.1192	Old Babylonian. Account; check-marks. Ammi-[] []/5/[].
43429	1881,0701.1193	Account of silver. (Sippar). Jursa, Bēl-rēmanni, 101, 236, pl. LX.
43430	1881,0701.1194	Incantation.
43431	1881,0701.1195	Joined to 43312.
43432	1881,0701.1196	Joined to 42336.
43433	1881,0701.1197	Receipt for silver as dowry. Dar 15/2/34. Sippar. + 43591 + 43682 + 43689 + 45588. Jursa, Bēl-rēmanni, 35, 236, pl. LXI.
43434	1881,0701.1198	Joined to 43178.
43435	1881,0701.1199	Joined to 42629.
43436	1881,0701.1200	Lexical.
43437	1881,0701.1201	Joined to 43309.
43438	1881,0701.1202	Deposition. Dar 12/9/-.

43439	1881,0701.1203	Joined to 42313.
43440	1881,0701.1204	Bilingual incantation, Udug-ḫul 2. Geller, BAM 8, 59-88, pl. 15.
43441	1881,0701.1205	Joined to 43301.
43442	1881,0701.1206	Economic.
43443	1881,0701.1207	Economic.
43444	1881,0701.1208	Astronomical.
43445	1881,0701.1209	Joined to 43178.
43446	1881,0701.1210	Economic.
43447	1881,0701.1211	Promissory note for wheat.
43448	1881,0701.1212	Literary.
43449	1881,0701.1213	Incantation.
43450	1881,0701.1214	Old Babylonian. Contract. Ammi-[] -/5/?
43451	1881,0701.1215	Receipt.
43452	1881,0701.1216	Joined to 43095.
43453	1881,0701.1217	Joined to 42508.
43454	1881,0701.1218	Incantation.
43455	1881,0701.1219	Lexical; god-list.
43456	1881,0701.1220	Economic.
43457	1881,0701.1221	Unidentified.
43458	1881,0701.1222	Joined to 42551.
43459	1881,0701.1223	Joined to 42451.
43460	1881,0701.1224	Medical. Finkel, Fs Lambert, 219, text 61 A.
43461	1881,0701.1225	Joined to 42494.
43462	1881,0701.1226	Receipt(?); sealed by Marduk-erība. d.l. (Borsippa?). Nisaba 28, no. 527.
43463	1881,0701.1227	Incantation.
43464	1881,0701.1228	Contract.
43465	1881,0701.1229	Incantation.
43466	1881,0701.1230	Promissory note with prebend as pledge. (Sippar). Jursa, Bēl-rēmanni, 52, 114, 237, pl. LVII.
43467	1881,0701.1231	Promissory note for dates or grain.
43468	1881,0701.1232	Medical.
43469	1881,0701.1233	Joined to 42343.
43470	1881,0701.1234	Joined to 43110.
43471	1881,0701.1235	Letter order; sealed. n.d. (Kūtû). Nisaba 28, no. 211.
43472	1881,0701.1236	Unidentified.
43473	1881,0701.1237	Joined to 43301.
43474	1881,0701.1238	Joined to 42327.
43475	1881,0701.1239	Joined to 42587.
43476	1881,0701.1240	Joined to 42625.
43477	1881,0701.1241	Joined to 42612.
43478	1881,0701.1242	Contract. Dar 9/9/-.
43479	1881,0701.1243	Account of dates or grain.
43480	1881,0701.1244	Incantation.

43481	1881,0701.1245	Joined to 42610.
43482	1881,0701.1246	Old Babylonian. Contract; sealed. 23/8/-.
43483	1881,0701.1247	Joined to 42313.
43484	1881,0701.1248	Economic.
43485	1881,0701.1249	Joined to 43324.
43486	1881,0701.1250	Contract.
43487	1881,0701.1251	Promissory note for dates and grain. Sippar. (+) 42360. Jursa, Bēl-rēmanni, 13, 24, 115, 122, 157, pl. XIX.
43488	1881,0701.1252	Joined to 42446.
43489	1881,0701.1253	Incantation.
43490	1881,0701.1254	Promissory note. (Sippar). Jursa, Bēl-rēmanni, 114, 238, pl. LVII.
43491	1881,0701.1255	Receipt. (Sippar). Jursa, Bēl-rēmanni, 114, 122, 238, pl. LVIII.
43492	1881,0701.1256	Contract. Cyr -/-/3. Sippar.
43493	1881,0701.1257	Economic.
43494	1881,0701.1258	Economic.
43495	1881,0701.1259	Joined to 42505.
43496	1881,0701.1260	Medical prescription. + 43652. Finkel, Fs Lambert, 165-167, text 13 B.
43497	1881,0701.1261	Joined to 42356.
43498	1881,0701.1262	Joined to 42601.
43499	1881,0701.1263	Astronomical?
43500	1881,0701.1264	Contract; sealed. d.l. [Kūtû]. Nisaba 28, no. 625.
43501	1881,0701.1265	Promissory note for dates. -/-/31. Sippar. (+) 42369. Jursa, Bēl-rēmanni, 13, 25, 109, 163, pl. XXII.
43502	1881,0701.1266	Joined to 43282.
43503	1881,0701.1267	Old Babylonian. Contract.
43504	1881,0701.1268	Joined to 43090.
43505	1881,0701.1269	Economic. (Sippar). Jursa, Bēl-rēmanni, 239, pl. LX.
43506	1881,0701.1270	Incantation; ušburruda; dupl. Finkel, Fs Lambert, 204-205. + 43548 + 43625 + 43666 + 43672.
43507	1881,0701.1271	Joined to 42406.
43508	1881,0701.1272	Joined to 42621.
43509	1881,0701.1273	Contract.
43510	1881,0701.1274	Economic. (Sippar). Jursa, Bēl-rēmanni, 52, 239, pl. LX.
43511	1881,0701.1275	Economic. (Sippar). Jursa, Bēl-rēmanni, 239, pl. LX.
43512	1881,0701.1276	Promissory note for silver. -/-/6.
43513	1881,0701.1277	Medical prescription. + 43620. Finkel, Fs Lambert, 218, text 59 A.
43514	1881,0701.1278	Omens; Šumma ālu?
43515	1881,0701.1279	Economic. -/-/25. Sippar.
43516	1881,0701.1280	Unidentified.

43517	1881,0701.1281	Contract.
43518	1881,0701.1282	Economic. Dar.
43519	1881,0701.1283	Economic.
43520	1881,0701.1284	Economic.
43521	1881,0701.1285	Medical prescription. + F.236. Finkel, Fs Lambert, 217, text 57 A.
43522	1881,0701.1286	Deposition.
43523	1881,0701.1287	Joined to 42327.
43524	1881,0701.1288	Promissory note for silver; duplicate of 42414 and VS 4, 135. Dar 19/8/-. (Sippar). Jursa, Bēl-rēmanni, 14, 263.
43525	1881,0701.1289	Joined to 42612.
43526	1881,0701.1290	Field sale.
43527	1881,0701.1291	Economic.
43528	1881,0701.1292	Commentary on astrological omens.
43529	1881,0701.1293	Economic.
43530	1881,0701.1294	Unidentified.
43531	1881,0701.1295	Economic.
43532	1881,0701.1296	Old Babylonian economic; corner fragment of a contract?
43533	1881,0701.1297	Economic.
43534	1881,0701.1298	Economic.
43535	1881,0701.1299	Economic.
43536	1881,0701.1300	Economic. Dar.
43537	1881,0701.1301	Economic.
43538	1881,0701.1302	Joined to 42508.
43539	1881,0701.1303	Economic.
43540	1881,0701.1304	Economic.
43541	1881,0701.1305	Joined to 42625.
43542	1881,0701.1306	Joined to 42508.
43543	1881,0701.1307	Economic.
43544	1881,0701.1308	Joined to 42406.
43545	1881,0701.1309	Promissory note for dates. Dar -/-/31. (Sippar). Jursa, Bēl-rēmanni, 13, 163, pl. XXII.
43546	1881,0701.1310	Joined to 42576.
43547	1881,0701.1311	Joined to 42446.
43548	1881,0701.1312	Joined to 43506.
43549	1881,0701.1313	Missing.
43550	1881,0701.1314	School text; Lamaštu incantation Finkel, Fs Lambert, 196, text 39 A; Farber, Lamaštu, 47, 57, pl. 59.
43551	1881,0701.1315	Medical prescription. Finkel, Fs Lambert, 152-153, text 2 B.
43552	1881,0701.1316	Economic.
43553	1881,0701.1317	Contract.

43554	1881,0701.1318	Contract; lease of a field. (Sippar). + 43772. Jursa, Bēl-rēmanni, 87, 88, 95, 96, 240, pl. LXI.
43555	1881,0701.1319	Joined to 42508.
43556	1881,0701.1320	Incantation.
43557	1881,0701.1321	Astronomical procedure text.
43558	1881,0701.1322	Astrological medicine. + F.230. Finkel, Fs Lambert, 212-215, text 55 A.
43559	1881,0701.1323	Old Babylonian contract.
43560	1881,0701.1324	Lexical; literary extract; Malku III 190-196.
43561	1881,0701.1325	Economic.
43562	1881,0701.1326	Joined to 42356.
43563	1881,0701.1327	Joined to 42343.
43564	1881,0701.1328	Unidentified.
43565	1881,0701.1329	Economic.
43566	1881,0701.1330	Promissory note for dates.
43567	1881,0701.1331	Joined to 43359.
43568	1881,0701.1332	Medical.
43569	1881,0701.1333	Unidentified.
43570	1881,0701.1334	Incantation.
43571	1881,0701.1335	Economic.
43572	1881,0701.1336	Joined to 43178.
43573	1881,0701.1337	Contract; fragment of the left edge; sealed. d.l. [Babylon?]. Nisaba 28, no. 180.
43574	1881,0701.1338	Receipt for dates or grain. (Sippar). Jursa, Bēl-rēmanni, 240, pl. LX
43575	1881,0701.1339	Incantation.
43576	1881,0701.1340	Astronomical.
43577	1881,0701.1341	Incantation. Finkel, Fs Lambert, 203, text 47 A (under wrong number 43572).
43578	1881,0701.1342	Economic.
43579	1881,0701.1343	Economic.
43580	1881,0701.1344	Joined to 42454.
43581	1881,0701.1345	Contract. Dar. 20/6/-.
43582	1881,0701.1346	Economic.
43583	1881,0701.1347	Economic.
43584	1881,0701.1348	Economic.
43585	1881,0701.1349	Economic.
43586	1881,0701.1350	Joined to 42591.
43587	1881,0701.1351	Economic. Dar.
43588	1881,0701.1352	Economic.
43589	1881,0701.1353	Joined to 42576.
43590	1881,0701.1354	Medical; drugs for fumigation. (+) F.235. Finkel, Fs Lambert, 190-191, text 34 B.
43591	1881,0701.1355	Joined to 43433.
43592	1881,0701.1356	Economic.

43593	1881,0701.1357	Lexical and literary extracts.
43594	1881,0701.1358	Economic.
43595	1881,0701.1359	Joined to 42313.
43596	1881,0701.1360	Economic.
43597	1881,0701.1361	Joined to 43290.
43598	1881,0701.1362	Joined to 43302.
43599	1881,0701.1363	Incantation.
43600	1881,0701.1364	Promissory note for dates.
43601	1881,0701.1365	Economic. (Sippar). Jursa, Bēl-rēmanni, 114, 241, pl. LX.
43602	1881,0701.1366	Joined to 42333.
43603	1881,0701.1367	Economic. Dar.
43604	1881,0701.1368	Letter.
43605	1881,0701.1369	Economic. -/-/acc.
43606	1881,0701.1370	Economic. Sippar.
43607	1881,0701.1371	Contract.
43608	1881,0701.1372	Medical prescription. (+) F.239. Finkel, Fs Lambert, 177-180, text 22 B.
43609	1881,0701.1373	Economic.
43610	1881,0701.1374	Joined to 42332.
43611	1881,0701.1375	Promissory note for silver.
43612	1881,0701.1376	Joined to 42646.
43613	1881,0701.1377	Economic. (Sippar). Jursa, Bēl-rēmanni, 241, pl. LXI.
43614	1881,0701.1378	Astronomical.
43615	1881,0701.1379	Economic.
43616	1881,0701.1380	Joined to 42625.
43617	1881,0701.1381	Economic.
43618	1881,0701.1382	Promissory note for silver. Dar 5/[]/13. (Sippar). Jursa, Bēl-rēmanni, 241, pl. LXII.
43619	1881,0701.1383	Joined to 42570.
43620	1881,0701.1384	Joined to 43513.
43621	1881,0701.1385	Joined to 42374.
43622	1881,0701.1386	Joined to 42621.
43623	1881,0701.1387	Incantation.
43624	1881,0701.1388	Promissory note for dates. (Sippar). (+) 42574. Jursa, Bēl-rēmanni, 116, 209, pl. XLVI.
43625	1881,0701.1389	Joined to 43506.
43626	1881,0701.1390	Joined to 42356.
43627	1881,0701.1391	Contract about a prebend; dupl. 42425. (Sippar). (+) 42595. Jursa, Bēl-rēmanni, 13, 19, 67, 182.
43628	1881,0701.1392	School text; practice wedges.
43629	1881,0701.1393	Economic.
43630	1881,0701.1394	Promissory note for silver.
43631	1881,0701.1395	Omens; extispicy.
43632	1881,0701.1396	Economic.

43633	1881,0701.1397	Sumerian literary.
43634	1881,0701.1398	Economic.
43635	1881,0701.1399	Astronomical.
43636	1881,0701.1400	Economic. (Sippar). Jursa, Bēl-rēmanni, 242, pl. LXII.
43637	1881,0701.1401	Promissory note for barley.
43638	1881,0701.1402	Old Babylonian economic.
43639	1881,0701.1403	Economic.
43640	1881,0701.1404	Economic.
43641	1881,0701.1405	Economic.
43642	1881,0701.1406	Deposition.
43643	1881,0701.1407	Economic.
43644	1881,0701.1408	Economic.
43645	1881,0701.1409	Economic. (Sippar). Jursa, Bēl-rēmanni, 92, 242, pl. LXII.
43646	1881,0701.1410	Economic.
43647	1881,0701.1411	Joined to 42310.
43648	1881,0701.1412	Joined to 43178.
43649	1881,0701.1413	Economic.
43650	1881,0701.1414	Economic. (Sippar). Jursa, Bēl-rēmanni, 243, pl. LXII.
43651	1881,0701.1415	Astronomical.
43652	1881,0701.1416	Joined to 43496.
43653	1881,0701.1417	Old Babylonian contract; sealed.
43654	1881,0701.1418	Economic. Dar -/5/-. Sippar.
43655	1881,0701.1419	Promissory note for dates.
43656	1881,0701.1420	Economic.
43657	1881,0701.1421	Promissory note for dates. (Sippar).
43658	1881,0701.1422	Joined to 42429.
43659	1881,0701.1423	Economic.
43660	1881,0701.1424	Joined to 42414.
43661	1881,0701.1425	Economic.
43662	1881,0701.1426	Economic.
43663	1881,0701.1427	Economic.
43664	1881,0701.1428	Economic. Dar.
43665	1881,0701.1429	Joined to 43300.
43666	1881,0701.1430	Joined to 43506.
43667	1881,0701.1431	Economic.
43668	1881,0701.1432	Joined to 43146.
43669	1881,0701.1433	Contract; lease of land. (Sippar). Jursa, Bēl-rēmanni, 13, 18, 132.
43670	1881,0701.1434	Economic.
43671	1881,0701.1435	Receipt for dates.
43672	1881,0701.1436	Joined to 43506.

43673	1881,0701.1437	Economic. Dar ? -/11/-. (Sippar). Jursa, Bēl-rēmanni, 81, 243, pl. LXII.
43674	1881,0701.1438	Contract; sale of an orchard; sealed; perhaps Seleucid. d.l. [Babylon]. Nisaba 28, no. 642.
43675	1881,0701.1439	Economic.
43676	1881,0701.1440	Joined to 43090.
43677	1881,0701.1441	Commentary.
43678	1881,0701.1442	Commentary on liver omens; tirānu.
43679	1881,0701.1443	Joined to 42570.
43680	1881,0701.1444	Promissory note for silver. Sippar. Jursa, Bēl-rēmanni, 13, 133.
43681	1881,0701.1445	Lexical.
43682	1881,0701.1446	Joined to 43433.
43683	1881,0701.1447	Economic.
43684	1881,0701.1448	Economic. Dar -/-/9+.
43685	1881,0701.1449	Economic.
43686	1881,0701.1450	Economic.
43687	1881,0701.1451	Joined to 42916.
43688	1881,0701.1452	Unidentified.
43689	1881,0701.1453	Joined to 43433.
43690	1881,0701.1454	Promissory note for silver. (Sippar). + 43769 Jursa, Bēl-rēmanni, 114, 122, 243, pl. LXII.
43691	1881,0701.1455	Field sale.
43692	1881,0701.1456	Economic.
43693	1881,0701.1457	Economic.
43694	1881,0701.1458	Contract; sealed; perhaps Seleucid. d.l. Nisaba 28, no. 643.
43695	1881,0701.1459	Sale of a prebend; finger-nail marks. (Sippar). (+) 43146. Jursa, Bēl-rēmanni, 225-227, pl. LV.
43696	1881,0701.1460	Lexical; Ea; sign list.
43697	1881,0701.1461	Joined to 42356.
43698	1881,0701.1462	Economic.
43699	1881,0701.1463	Incantation.
43700	1881,0701.1464	Astrological medicine. + 43808. Finkel, Fs Lambert, 212-215, text 55 A.
43701	1881,0701.1465	Lexical.
43702	1881,0701.1466	Economic.
43703	1881,0701.1467	Old Babylonian contract.
43704	1881,0701.1468	Unidentified; archaic script.
43705	1881,0701.1469	Joined to 42625.
43706	1881,0701.1470	Contract; sealed; finger-nail marks. SE Alexander I Balas 14/7/166. [Kūtû?]. Mitchell and Searight, no. 749; Nisaba 28, no. 605.
43707	1881,0701.1471	Astrological omens.
43708	1881,0701.1472	Joined to 42561.

43709	1881,0701.1473	Contract; transfer of prebends; part of the Bēl-rēmanni archive. Dar 4/[]/[32]. Sippar. Waerzeggers, OLA 233, 66 and 166-167.
43710	1881,0701.1474	Joined to 42916.
43711	1881,0701.1475	Commentary on astrological omens.
43712	1881,0701.1476	Joined to 42916.
43713	1881,0701.1477	Medical.
43714	1881,0701.1478	Contract; witnesses.
43715	1881,0701.1479	Receipt for barley. Dar 3/6/28. Sippar. + 1881,0701 F.227. Jursa, Bēl-rēmanni, 80, 244, pl. LXIII.
43716	1881,0701.1480	Astronomical.
43717	1881,0701.1481	Administrative; refers to le'u and imgidda.
43718	1881,0701.1482	Account of silver Art. [] /2/16. URU Am-me-šu-ṣa.
43719	1881,0701.1483	Joined to 42601.
43720	1881,0701.1484	Economic.
43721	1881,0701.1485	Lexical; Ea; sign list.
43722	1881,0701.1486	Joined to 42542.
43723	1881,0701.1487	Joined to 43146.
43724	1881,0701.1488	School text; archaic script.
43725	1881,0701.1488a	School text; archaic script.
43726	1881,0701.1488b	Economic.
43727	1881,0701.1489	Promissory note for silver. (Sippar). (+) 43728. Jursa, Bēl-rēmanni, 25, 116, 245, pl. LXIV.
43728	1881,0701.1489a	Promissory note for silver. 24/-/-. Sippar). (+) 43727. Jursa, Bēl-rēmanni, 25, 116, 245, pl. LXIV.
43729	1881,0701.1490	Promissory note for beer. Dar -/-/1. (Sippar). Jursa, Bēl-rēmanni, 246, pl. LXIV.
43730	1881,0701.1491	Copy of an archaic text; colophon; compare 43745.
43731	1881,0701.1492	Old Babylonian literary.
43732	1881,0701.1493	Lexical; syllabary.
43733	1881,0701.1494	Astrological omens.
43734	1881,0701.1495	School text; lexical. []/9/[].
43735	1881,0701.1496	Joined to 43177.
43736	1881,0701.1497	Lexical.
43737	1881,0701.1498	Division of property; perhaps Seleucid.
43738	1881,0701.1499	Literary.
43739	1881,0701.1500	Receipt?; mentions Nabû-udammiq.
43740	1881,0701.1501	Joined to 42616.
43741	1881,0701.1502	Joined to 42504.
43742	1881,0701.1503	Astronomical.
43743	1881,0701.1504	Lexical; syllabary.
43744	1881,0701.1505	School text; lexical; temple list. 13/[]/-.
43745	1881,0701.1506	Copy of an archaic text; compare 43730.
43746	1881,0701.1507	Lexical.

43747	1881,0701.1508	Receipt?; sealed. d.l. (Borsippa?). Mitchell and Searight, no. 344; Nisaba 28, no. 528.
43748	1881,0701.1509	Incantation.
43749	1881,0701.1510	Incantation.
43750	1881,0701.1511	Astronomical.
43751	1881,0701.1512	Joined to 42561.
43752	1881,0701.1513	Joined to 42655.
43753	1881,0701.1514	Economic.
43754	1881,0701.1515	Contract; Aramaic note. Stevenson, Ass.-Bab. Contracts, no. 44.
43755	1881,0701.1516	Illegible.
43756	1881,0701.1517	Promissory note for silver. -/6/12. Babylon.
43757	1881,0701.1518	Economic.
43758	1881,0701.1519	Contract about a tithe. Dar -/2/5. Sippar.
43759	1881,0701.1520	Astrological omens; lunar eclipses.
43760	1881,0701.1521	Lexical.
43761	1881,0701.1522	Astrological; days and stones, trees and plants. + 43815. Finkel, Fs Lambert, 216-217, text 56 B.
43762	1881,0701.1523	Contract.
43763	1881,0701.1524	Joined to 43290.
43764	1881,0701.1525	Lexical; syllabary.
43765	1881,0701.1526	Letter order; sealed. Alex IV 8/[]/8. (Borsippa?). Nisaba 28, no. 518.
43766	1881,0701.1527	Joined to 42313
43767	1881,0701.1528	Incantation.
43768	1881,0701.1529	Incantation.
43769	1881,0701.1530	Joined to 43690.
43770	1881,0701.1531	Contract.
43771	1881,0701.1532	Joined to 42569.
43772	1881,0701.1533	Joined to 43554.
43773	1881,0701.1534	Joined to 43090.
43774	1881,0701.1535	Lexical.
43775	1881,0701.1536	Economic; administrative?
43776	1881,0701.1537	Joined to 42569.
43777	1881,0701.1538	Letter about barley.
43778	1881,0701.1539	Astronomical.
43779	1881,0701.1540	Incantation.
43780	1881,0701.1541	Medical. Finkel, Fs Lambert, 220, text 66 A.
43781	1881,0701.1542	Contract; witnesses. 4/3/-.
43782	1881,0701.1543	Contract about ducks.17/-/-.
43783	1881,0701.1544	Joined to 42609.
43784	1881,0701.1545	Promissory note for barley and dates.
43785	1881,0701.1546	Promissory note for dates or grain.
43786	1881,0701.1547	Joined to 42288.
43787	1881,0701.1548	Field sale.

43788	1881,0701.1549	Economic.
43789	1881,0701.1550	Old Babylonian. Contract; sealed. Ammiditana 19/6/36.
43790	1881,0701.1551	Bilingual incantation, Marduk's Address (Udug-ḫul 11). Geller, BAM 8, 340-392; Lambert, MC 24, no. 195.
43791	1881,0701.1552	Contract; right edge.
43792	1881,0701.1553	Joined to 43177.
43793	18s81,0701.1554	Field sale.
43794	1881,0701.1555	Economic. (Sippar). Jursa, Bēl-rēmanni, 246, pl. LXIII.
43795	1881,0701.1556	Old Babylonian. Contract; sealed.
43796	1881,0701.1557	Economic; administrative. (Sippar).
43797	1881,0701.1558	Joined to 42425.
43798	1881,0701.1559	Joined to 43146.
43799	1881,0701.1560	Joined to 42504.
43800	1881,0701.1561	Joined to 43146.
43801	1881,0701.1562	Medical; prescription. Finkel, Fs Lambert, 210, text 52 A.
43802	1881,0701.1563	Old Babylonian. Contract; sealed.
43803	1881,0701.1564	Joined to 42313.
43804	1881,0701.1565	Incantation.
43805	1881,0701.1566	Incantation.
43806	1881,0701.1567	Economic.
43807	1881,0701.1568	Economic. Dar.
43808	1881,0701.1569	Joined to 43700.
43809	1881,0701.1570	Joined to 42450.
43810	1881,0701.1571	Promissory note for dates. Dar 28/[]/29. Sippar. Jursa, Bēl-rēmanni, 246, pl. LXIII.
43811	1881,0701.1572	Joined to 42638.
43812	1881,0701.1573	Joined to 42587.
43813	1881,0701.1574	Incantation.
43814	1881,0701.1575	Joined to 42910.
43815	1881,0701.1576	Joined to 43761.
43816	1881,0701.1577	Economic.
43817	1881,0701.1578	Missing.
43818	1881,0701.1579	Astronomical?; mostly illegible.
43819	1881,0701.1580	Contract; sale of a field; finger-nail marks with caption. Dar []/[]/[].
43820	1881,0701.1581	Bilingual incantation.
43821	1881,0701.1582	Astronomical.
43822	1881,0701.1583	Field plan; perhaps (+) 43823.
43823	1881,0701.1584	Field plan; perhaps (+) 43822. Dar.
43824	1881,0701.1585	Sale of fields in Babylon; sealed. Dar 8/3/27+. Babylon. + 46897. Nisaba 28, no. 132.

43825	1881,0701.1586	Field sale.
43826	1881,0701.1587	Incantations; Maqlu I. + 43835 (+) 45249. Abusch, AMD 10, 23-49.
43827	1881,0701.1588	Sale of a slave. Nbk. Babylon.
43828	1881,0701.1589	Incantation?; mentions Sin.
43829	1881,0701.1590	Division of property. Cam.
43830	1881,0701.1591	Contract.
43831	1881,0701.1592	Contract; witnesses. 10/9/-.
43832	1881,0701.1593	Field sale. (Sippar).
43833	1881,0701.1594	Promissory note for dates. Dar 13/6/18. Bīt-bārî.
43834	1881,0701.1595	Receipt for a payment.
43835	1881,0701.1596	Joined to 43826.
43836	1881,0701.1597	Omens.
43837	1881,0701.1598	School text; lexical and literary extracts.
43838	1881,0701.1599	Promissory note for dates.
43839	1881,0701.1600	Ritual; dupl. Ebeling, KAR 304 (+) 337. + 43842 + 45240 + 46574.
43840	1881,0701.1601	Contract.
43841	1881,0701.1602	Medical; materia medica.
43842	1881,0701.1603	Joined to 43839.
43843	1881,0701.1604	Incantation.
43844	1881,0701.1605	Promissory note for silver. Cyr 22/12/1. Babylon.
43845	1881,0701.1606	Contract.
43846	1881,0701.1607	Astronomical.
43847	1881,0701.1608	Division of property.
43848	1881,0701.1609	Administrative; about gold, etc.
43849	1881,0701.1610	Astronomical; MUL.APIN. Hunger and Steele, MUL.APIN, 20.
43850	1881,0701.1611	Lexical; syllabary.
43851	1881,0701.1612	School text.
43852	1881,0701.1613	Literary.
43853	1881,0701.1614	Receipt for dates.
43854	1881,0701.1615	Medical; commentary on TDP III. + 43938.
43855	1881,0701.1616	Incantation.
43856	1881,0701.1617	Illegible.
43857	1881,0701.1618	Field sale. (Borsippa?).
43858	1881,0701.1619	Promissory note for dates. Cam 27/12/-.
43859	1881,0701.1620	Lexical; Ea; sign list.
43860	1881,0701.1621	Contract.
43861	1881,0701.1622	Field plan.
43862	1881,0701.1623	Contract.
43863	1881,0701.1624	Letter from [] to Aḫušunu. Hackl et al., AOAT 414/1, no. 103.
43864	1881,0701.1625	Field sale.
43865	1881,0701.1626	Economic.

43866	1881,0701.1627	Astronomical.
43867	1881,0701.1628	Lexical; Ea; sign list.
43868	1881,0701.1629	Medical.
43869	1881,0701.1630	Promissory note for dates.
43870	1881,0701.1631	Lexical; Ea; sign list.
43871	1881,0701.1632	Astronomical; MUL.APIN. Fincke, NABU 2014, 54-55, no. 34; Hunger and Steele, MUL.APIN, 20.
43872	1881,0701.1633	Economic.
43873	1881,0701.1634	Field plan.
43874	1881,0701.1635	Contract. Dar 18/10/2. Babylon.
43875	1881,0701.1636	Contract; lease of an exitway.
43876	1881,0701.1637	Contract.
43877	1881,0701.1638	Promissory note for silver; mentions Ḫarīṣānu; cf. 43881. Dar 19/7/29. Babylon.
43878	1881,0701.1639	School text; literary extracts.
43879	1881,0701.1640	Incantation.
43880	1881,0701.1641	Incantation.
43881	1881,0701.1642	Contract about land, made before judges; sealed. Dar []/[]/36. Borsippa. Zadok, Nisaba 21, 237; Nisaba 28, no. 46; Sandowicz, dubsar 11, no. 41.
43882	1881,0701.1643	Astronomical.
43883	1881,0701.1644	Literary.
43884	1881,0701.1645	Incantation.
43885	1881,0701.1646	Lexical; Ea; sign list; literary extract.
43886	1881,0701.1647	Economic.
43887	1881,0701.1648	Promissory note for silver. Dar -/-/13.
43888	1881,0701.1649	Contract; witnesses; fragment of left edge. Nbn []/2/[]. Babylon.
43889	1881,0701.1650	Astronomical; turns at right angles.
43890	1881,0701.1651	Promissory note for dates. Nbn -/-/15. Babylon.
43891	1881,0701.1652	Medical.
43892	1881,0701.1653	Incantation.
43893	1881,0701.1654	Incantation.
43894	1881,0701.1655	Contract. Esarhaddon -/-/4.
43895	1881,0701.1656	Contract. -/-/18.
43896	1881,0701.1657	Colophon; mentions eršema.
43897	1881,0701.1658	Medical prescriptions involving fumigation. + 46978 (+) 43975+ which is stored in the same box. Farber, Lamaštu, 58; Farber, SKS, pp. 25, 30, 108-111.
43898	1881,0701.1659	Lexical; Ḫḫ; giš.
43899	1881,0701.1660	Omens; Šumma ālu, tablets 71-72. + 45438 + 46598. Freedman, If a city, vol. 1, 340 (46598 only).
43900	1881,0701.1661	Lexical; Ea; sign list; literary extracts; personal names.

43901	1881,0701.1662	Field sale; later copy; ḫe-pí; colophon. Nbk []/2/36. Babylon.
43902	1881,0701.1663	Deposition. Dar 17/6/-.
43903	1881,0701.1664	Astronomical.
43904	1881,0701.1665	Mathematical problem text.
43905	1881,0701.1666	List of land measurements.
43906	1881,0701.1667	Astronomical.
43907	1881,0701.1668	Mathematical; table of coefficients, similar to 36776.
43908	1881,0701.1669	Lexical.
43909	1881,0701.1670	Field sale. Dar 22/5/12. Borsippa.
43910	1881,0701.1671	Economic.
43911	1881,0701.1672	Economic.
43912	1881,0701.1673	Astronomical.
43913	1881,0701.1674	Contract. -/-/16.
43914	1881,0701.1675	Contract; land sale; finger-nail marks.
43915	1881,0701.1676	Illegible.
43916	1881,0701.1677	Literary cylinder.
43917	1881,0701.1678	Economic.
43918	1881,0701.1679	Commentary.
43919	1881,0701.1680	Economic.
43920	1881,0701.1681	Field plan.
43921	1881,0701.1682	Economic.
43922	1881,0701.1683	Promissory note for barley.
43923	1881,0701.1684	Field sale.
43924	1881,0701.1685	Astronomical.
43925	1881,0701.1686	Economic.
43926	1881,0701.1687	Lexical; Ea.
43927	1881,0701.1688	Lexical.
43928	1881,0701.1689	Promissory note for silver. Nbn 11/2/-. Babylon.
43929	1881,0701.1690	Contract. Art 21/[]/[].
43930	1881,0701.1691	Astronomical.
43931	1881,0701.1692	Astronomical.
43932	1881,0701.1693	Lexical; personal names.
43933	1881,0701.1694	Field plan.
43934	1881,0701.1695	Contract.
43935	1881,0701.1696	Land sale; finger-nail marks. []/[]/1.
43936	1881,0701.1697	Economic.
43937	1881,0701.1698	Contract. Nbk []/1/40.
43938	1881,0701.1699	Joined to 43854.
43939	1881,0701.1700	Lexical; Ḫḫ I; literary extracts.
43940	1881,0701.1701	Economic.
43941	1881,0701.1702	Lexical; Ea; sign list.
43942	1881,0701.1703	Economic.
43943	1881,0701.1704	Economic.
43944	1881,0701.1705	Economic.

43945	1881,0701.1706	Medical prescription. Finkel, Fs Lambert, 189, text 33 A.
43946	1881,0701.1707	Economic.
43947	1881,0701.1708	Economic.
43948	1881,0701.1709	Incantation.
43949	1881,0701.1710	Letter from Bēl-bullissu to Ḫarīṣānu (cf. 43881).
43950	1881,0701.1711	Economic.
43951	1881,0701.1712	Receipt.
43952	1881,0701.1713	List of names.
43953	1881,0701.1714	Medical; colophon.
43954	1881,0701.1715	Field sale.
43955	1881,0701.1716	Economic.
43956	1881,0701.1717	Lexical; Ea; sign list.
43957	1881,0701.1718	Contract. -/-/29.
43958	1881,0701.1719	Account of silver income. (Sippar?).
43959	1881,0701.1720	Promissory note for silver. 27/-/-.
43960	1881,0701.1721	Economic.
43961	1881,0701.1722	Account.
43962	1881,0701.1723	Account of dates or grain.
43963	1881,0701.1724	Account.
43964	1881,0701.1725	Economic.
43965	1881,0701.1726	Economic.
43966	1881,0701.1727	Contract for purchase of dates.
43967	1881,0701.1728	Letter.
43968	1881,0701.1729	Economic.
43969	1881,0701.1730	School text; literary; Enūma eliš V 127-130. Lambert, BCM, p. 97, pl. 20.
43970	1881,0701.1731	Economic.
43971	1881,0701.1732	Field plan?
43972	1881,0701.1733	Account of dates or grain.
43973	1881,0701.1734	Economic.
43974	1881,0701.1735	Bilingual epic; Lugal-e, lines 182-191 and 229-237. + 46971. van Dijk, Lugal II, 23, 77-85 text n2.
43975	1881,0701.1736	Medical. + 45456 + 46766 + 46984 + 46990 + 47137 (+) 43897 + 46978. Farber, Lamaštu, 58.
43976	1881,0701.1737	Lexical; syllabary.
43977	1881,0701.1738	Astronomical.
43978	1881,0701.1739	Account of seed.
43979	1881,0701.1740	Astronomical.
43980	1881,0701.1741	Omens; Šumma ālu?
43981	1881,0701.1742	Economic.
43982	1881,0701.1743	Contract.
43983	1881,0701.1744	Sumerian literary.
43984	1881,0701.1745	Lexical; Ea?
43985	1881,0701.1746	Lexical; Ea; sign list; literary extracts.

43986	1881,0701.1747	Omens; extispicy?
43987	1881,0701.1748	Receipt.
43988	1881,0701.1749	Economic.
43989	1881,0701.1750	Economic.
43990	1881,0701.1751	Economic.
43991	1881,0701.1752	Field sale. -/-/10.
43992	1881,0701.1753	Promissory note for silver. Dar -/3/-.
43993	1881,0701.1754	Economic.
43994	1881,0701.1755	Economic.
43995	1881,0701.1756	Astronomical.
43996	1881,0701.1757	Economic.
43997	1881,0701.1758	Economic.
43998	1881,0701.1759	Economic.
43999	1881,0701.1760	Economic.
44000	1881,0701.1761	Promissory note for silver.
44001	1881,0701.1762	Economic.
44002	1881,0701.1763	Contract; lease of a house. Nbk -/12/34. Babylon.
44003	1881,0701.1764	Astronomical.
44004	1881,0701.1765	Economic.
44005	1881,0701.1766	Astronomical.
44006	1881,0701.1767	Economic.
44007	1881,0701.1768	Omens; weather.
44008	1881,0701.1769	Field plan.
44009	1881,0701.1770	Economic.
44010	1881,0701.1771	Sale of a slave girl?
44011	1881,0701.1772	Astrological omens?
44012	1881,0701.1773	Field sale.
44013	1881,0701.1774	Economic.
44014	1881,0701.1775	Contract.
44015	1881,0701.1776	Astronomical.
44016	1881,0701.1777	Astronomical.
44017	1881,0701.1778	Promissory note for silver.
44018	1881,0701.1779	Economic.
44019	1881,0701.1780	Economic.
44020	1881,0701.1781	Lexical.
44021	1881,0701.1782	Omens; terrestrial.
44022	1881,0701.1783	Contract for bitumen. -/11/-.
44023	1881,0701.1784	Contract. Dar.
44024	1881,0701.1785	Field plan.
44025	1881,0701.1786	Economic.
44026	1881,0701.1787	Deposition. Dar.
44027	1881,0701.1788	Promissory note for silver. Dar 24/[]/14. Babylon.
44028	1881,0701.1789	Letter.
44029	1881,0701.1790	Lexical; Ḫḫ III.
44030	1881,0701.1791	Economic.

44031	1881,0701.1792	Economic.
44032	1881,0701.1793	Field plan.
44033	1881,0701.1794	Economic.
44034	1881,0701.1795	Contract.
44035	1881,0701.1796	Astronomical.
44036	1881,0701.1797	Field sale.
44037	1881,0701.1798	Economic.
44038	1881,0701.1799	Contract.
44039	1881,0701.1800	Astronomical Diary or related text.
44040	1881,0701.1801	Economic.
44041	1881,0701.1802	Economic.
44042	1881,0701.1803	Letter about silver.
44043	1881,0701.1804	Incantation.
44044	1881,0701.1805	Economic.
44045	1881,0701.1806	Lexical; Ea; sign list.
44046	1881,0701.1807	Astronomical.
44047	1881,0701.1808	Promissory note for silver. Dar 2/4/6. Babylon.
44048	1881,0701.1809	Lexical; Ḫḫ VI.
44049	1881,0701.1810	Astronomical.
44050	1881,0701.1811	Economic.
44051	1881,0701.1812	Astronomical.
44052	1881,0701.1813	Lexical; syllabary.
44053	1881,0701.1814	Astronomical.
44054	1881,0701.1815	Economic.
44055	1881,0701.1816	Economic.
44056	1881,0701.1817	Field plan. Dar 23/-/-.
44057	1881,0701.1818	Promissory note for dates or grain. -/-/8.
44058	1881,0701.1819	Economic.
44059	1881,0701.1820	Economic.
44060	1881,0701.1821	Economic.
44061	1881,0701.1822	Economic.
44062	1881,0701.1823	Astronomical.
44063	1881,0701.1824	Economic.
44064	1881,0701.1825	Uninscribed ledger with horizontal and vertical rulings.
44065	1881,0701.1826	Offering ledger. Tarasewicz and Zawadzki, AOAT 451, no. 138.
44066	1881,0701.1827	Account of disbursements.
44067	1881,0701.1828	Account of disbursements.
44068	1881,0701.1829	Economic.
44069	1881,0701.1830	Incantation.
44070	1881,0701.1831	Account of dates or grain.
44071	1881,0701.1832	Economic.
44072	1881,0701.1833	Receipt for asphalt.
44073	1881,0701.1834	Receipt for flour.

44074	1881,0701.1835	Incantation.
44075	1881,0701.1836	Astronomical.
44076	1881,0701.1837	Economic.
44077	1881,0701.1838	Receipt.
44078	1881,0701.1839	Incantation.
44079	1881,0701.1840	Unidentified.
44080	1881,0701.1841	Economic.
44081	1881,0701.1842	Contract; sale of a house plot in Sippar; finger-nail marks. Neb.
44082	1881,0701.1843	Field plan.
44083	1881,0701.1844	Economic.
44084	1881,0701.1845	Field plan.
44085	1881,0701.1846	Economic.
44086	1881,0701.1847	Account of dates or grain.
44087	1881,0701.1848	Economic.
44088	1881,0701.1849	Receipt for disbursements.
44089	1881,0701.1850	Economic.
44090	1881,0701.1851	Receipt for wheat.
44091	1881,0701.1852	Economic.
44092	1881,0701.1853	Unidentified.
44093	1881,0701.1854	Account of disbursements.
44094	1881,0701.1855	Economic; mentions slaves of a sepīru. -/10/-.
44095	1881,0701.1856	Ledger.
44096	1881,0701.1857	Memorandum.
44097	1881,0701.1858	Receipt for asphalt.
44098	1881,0701.1859	Account.
44099	1881,0701.1860	Account.
44100	1881,0701.1861	Economic. Bīt-Kīnā.
44101	1881,0701.1862	Receipt for bitumen. -/7/3.
44102	1881,0701.1863	Account.
44103	1881,0701.1864	Economic. 3/[]/16.
44104	1881,0701.1865	Economic.
44105	1881,0701.1866	Account of wool.
44106	1881,0701.1867	Contract. -/8/-. Babylon.
44107	1881,0701.1868	Letter.
44108	1881,0701.1869	Account of barley.
44109	1881,0701.1870	Account of disbursements.
44110	1881,0701.1871	Account.
44111	1881,0701.1872	Field sale?; finger-nail marks.
44112	1881,0701.1873	Astronomical.
44113	1881,0701.1874	Economic.
44114	1881,0701.1875	Account.
44115	1881,0701.1876	Economic.
44116	1881,0701.1877	Astronomical.
44117	1881,0701.1878	Astronomical.

44118	1881,0701.1879	Astronomical.
44119	1881,0701.1880	Astronomical.
44120	1881,0701.1881	Astronomical.
44121	1881,0701.1882	Astronomical.
44122	1881,0701.1883	Economic.
44123	1881,0701.1884	Astronomical.
44124	1881,0701.1885	Astronomical.
44125	1881,0701.1886	Promissory note for dates. Nbk 17/[]/14.
44126	1881,0701.1887	Economic.
44127	1881,0701.1888	Ledger.
44128	1881,0701.1889	Ledger.
44129	1881,0701.1890	Economic.
44130	1881,0701.1891	Account of barley. Npl 20/4/17. (Sippar).
44131	1881,0701.1892	Ledger.
44132	1881,0701.1893	Offering ledger. Npl 13/6?/17. Tarasewicz and Zawadzki, AOAT 451, no. 134.
44133	1881,0701.1894	Economic. 6/12/-.
44134	1881,0701.1895	Economic.
44135	1881,0701.1896	Account of wool. (Sippar).
44136	1881,0701.1897	Receipt 20/12/14.
44137	1881,0701.1898	Account 20/2/-.
44138	1881,0701.1899	Economic.
44139	1881,0701.1900	Economic.
44140	1881,0701.1901	Lexical; Ea; sign list.
44141	1881,0701.1902	Promissory note for dates and barley; mentions Ezida; sealed. d.l. (Borsippa) Nisaba 28, no. 307.
44142	1881,0701.1903	Account of dates.
44143	1881,0701.1904	Economic.
44144	1881,0701.1905	Incantations; Maqlu II. Abusch, AMD 10, 51-77.
44145	1881,0701.1906	Field sale.
44146	1881,0701.1907	Astronomical.
44147	1881,0701.1908	Lexical; Ea; sign list.
44148	1881,0701.1909	Lexical; Ea; sign list.
44149	1881,0701.1910	Illegible.
44150	1881,0701.1911	Medical.
44151	1881,0701.1912	Astronomical Diary or related text.
44152	1881,0701.1913	Deposition. Babylon.
44153	1881,0701.1914	Economic.
44154	1881,0701.1915	Contract. 29/[]/27.
44155	1881,0701.1916	Lexical; Ea; sign list and literary extracts.
44156	1881,0701.1917	Economic.
44157	1881,0701.1918	Economic.
44158	1881,0701.1919	Incantation.
44159	1881,0701.1920	Joined to 40356.
44160	1881,0701.1921	Account of disbursements (Sippar?).

44161	1881,0701.1922	Astronomical.
44162	1881,0701.1923	Economic.
44163	1881,0701.1924	Astronomical.
44164	1881,0701.1925	Economic.
44165	1881,0701.1926	Incantation.
44166	1881,0701.1927	Unidentified.
44167	1881,0701.1928	Astronomical.
44168	1881,0701.1929	Astronomical.
44169	1881,0701.1930	Economic. Nbk.
44170	1881,0701.1931	Medical.
44171	1881,0701.1932	Economic.
44172	1881,0701.1933	Receipt.
44173	1881,0701.1934	Account of silver. (Sippar).
44174	1881,0701.1935	Incantation.
44175	1881,0701.1936	Receipt. Alexander IV 10/3/7. (Borsippa).
44176	1881,0701.1937	Economic.
44177	1881,0701.1938	Economic.
44178	1881,0701.1939	Economic.
44179	1881,0701.1940	Joined to 41361.
44180	1881,0701.1941	Division of property.
44181	1881,0701.1942	Illegible.
44182	1881,0701.1943	Economic.
44183	1881,0701.1944	Astronomical.
44184	1881,0701.1945	Astronomical.
44185	1881,0701.1946	Unidentified.
44186	1881,0701.1947	Economic.
44187	1881,0701.1948	Medical.
44188	1881,0701.1949	Contract.
44189	1881,0701.1950	Contract.
44190	1881,0701.1951	Economic; mostly illegible.
44191	1881,0701.1952	Economic; mostly illegible.
44192	1881,0701.1953	Illegible.
44193	1881,0701.1954	Contract. Dar 13/[ ]/4.
44194	1881,0701.1955	Economic.
44195	1881,0701.1956	Joined to 40805.
44196	1881,0701.1957	Joined to 40754.
44197	1881,0701.1958	Unidentified.
44198	1881,0701.1959	Unidentified.
44199	1881,0701.1960	Economic.
44200	1881,0701.1961	Lexical.
44201	1881,0701.1962	Economic.
44202	1881,0701.1963	Land sale with field measurements.
44203	1881,0701.1964	Astronomical.
44204	1881,0701.1965	Medical; plant list. Finkel, Fs Lambert, 187, text 30 A.

44205	1881,0701.1966	Astronomical.
44206	1881,0701.1967	Incantation.
44207	1881,0701.1968	Astronomical.
44208	1881,0701.1969	Economic.
44209	1881,0701.1970	Astronomical.
44210	1881,0701.1971	Contract. Nbk -/-/39. Babylon.
44211	1881,0701.1972	Medical.
44212	1881,0701.1973	Promissory note for barley. 3/-/-. Babylon.
44213	1881,0701.1974	Joined to 36431.
44214	1881,0701.1975	Astronomical.
44215	1881,0701.1976	Unidentified.
44216	1881,0701.1977	Incantation. Lambert, MC 24, no. 223.
44217	1881,0701.1978	Economic.
44218	1881,0701.1979	Contract. Nbn 7/11/-. Maškattu.
44219	1881,0701.1980	Contract.
44220	1881,0701.1981	Contract.
44221	1881,0701.1982	Economic.
44222	1881,0701.1983	Economic.
44223	1881,0701.1984	Account.
44224	1881,0701.1985	Astronomical.
44225	1881,0701.1986	Contract.
44226	1881,0701.1987	Omens.
44227	1881,0701.1988	Contract.
44228	1881,0701.1989	Contract. Dar 3/-/-. Babylon.
44229	1881,0701.1990	Economic.
44230	1881,0701.1991	Account.
44231	1881,0701.1992	Economic.
44232	1881,0701.1993	Contract.
44233	1881,0701.1994	Astronomical.
44234	1881,0701.1995	Medical.
44235	1881,0701.1996	Unidentified.
44236	1881,0701.1997	Unidentified; mostly illegible.
44237	1881,0701.1998	Economic.
44238	1881,0701.1999	Joined to 41289.
44239	1881,0701.2000	Memorandum.
44240	1881,0701.2001	Unidentified.
44241	1881,0701.2002	Joined to 40805.
44242	1881,0701.2003	Unidentified.
44243	1881,0701.2004	Commentary; medical.
44244	1881,0701.2005	Account.
44245	1881,0701.2006	Incantation.
44246	1881,0701.2007	Economic.
44247	1881,0701.2008	Incantation.
44248	1881,0701.2009	Medical; aromatic prescription. Finkel, Fs Lambert, 188, text 32 A.

44249	1881,0701.2010	Astronomical.
44250	1881,0701.2011	Economic.
44251	1881,0701.2012	Contract.
44252	1881,0701.2013	Contract.
44253	1881,0701.2014	Lexical; Ea; sign list.
44254	1881,0701.2015	Contract.
44255	1881,0701.2016	Lexical; Ea; sign list.
44256	1881,0701.2017	Contract.
44257	1881,0701.2018	Unidentified.
44258	1881,0701.2019	Ledger.
44259	1881,0701.2020	Economic.
44260	1881,0701.2021	Division of property.
44261	1881,0701.2022	Contract. Nbk 5/[]/8.
44262	1881,0701.2023	Economic.
44263	1881,0701.2024	Uninscribed.
44264	1881,0701.2025	Account of oxen. -/-/1.
44265	1881,0701.2026	Ledger.
44266	1881,0701.2027	Unidentified.
44267	1881,0701.2028	Account.
44268	1881,0701.2029	Offering ledger. Nbk 10+[]/2/[]. Tarasewicz and Zawadzki, AOAT 451, no. 142.
44269	1881,0701.2030	Contract.
44270	1881,0701.2031	Contract.
44271	1881,0701.2032	Astronomical.
44272	1881,0701.2033	Account of dates.
44273	1881,0701.2034	Account of sheep.
44274	1881,0701.2035	Receipt for bitumen. -/-/10.
44275	1881,0701.2036	Account.
44276	1881,0701.2037	Ledger.
44277	1881,0701.2038	Account of silver.
44278	1881,0701.2039	Account of barley.
44279	1881,0701.2040	Account of wool?
44280	1881,0701.2041	Account.
44281	1881,0701.2042	Letter from Nabû-balāṭu-ereš to the šangû of Sippar. d.l. (Sippar).
44282	1881,0701.2043	Contract.
44283	1881,0701.2044	Medical.
44284	1881,0701.2045	Medical.
44285	1881,0701.2046	Promissory note for barley. Npl 20/5/16. Sippar.
44286	1881,0701.2047	Account of dates or grain.
44287	1881,0701.2048	Economic. Nbk -/-/19.
44288	1881,0701.2049	Account.
44289	1881,0701.2050	Account of dates. 18/10/-.
44290	1881,0701.2051	Account of sheep.
44291	1881,0701.2052	Account.

44292	1881,0701.2053	Medical.
44293	1881,0701.2054	Ledger.
44294	1881,0701.2055	Account of dates or grain.
44295	1881,0701.2056	Unidentified.
44296	1881,0701.2057	Economic; mostly illegible.
44297	1881,0701.2058	Economic; mostly illegible.
44298	1881,0701.2059	Economic.
44299	1881,0701.2060	Account.
44300	1881,0701.2061	Account of jewellery of Šarrat Sippar. (Sippar).
44301	1881,0701.2062	Incantation.
44302	1881,0701.2063	Omens; Iqqur īpuš.
44303	1881,0701.2064	Unidentified.
44304	1881,0701.2065	Account.
44305	1881,0701.2066	Medical.
44306	1881,0701.2067	Incantation.
44307	1881,0701.2068	Ledger.
44308	1881,0701.2069	Account.
44309	1881,0701.2070	Account.
44310	1881,0701.2071	Account. (Sippar?).
44311	1881,0701.2072	Economic.
44312	1881,0701.2073	Account.
44313	1881,0701.2074	Letter.
44314	1881,0701.2075	Contract.
44315	1881,0701.2076	Ledger.
44316	1881,0701.2077	Economic.
44317	1881,0701.2078	Account of sheep.
44318	1881,0701.2079	Memorandum.
44319	1881,0701.2080	Account.
44320	1881,0701.2081	Contract for bitumen.
44321	1881,0701.2082	Ledger.
44322	1881,0701.2083	Account of dates or grain.
44323	1881,0701.2084	Account of dates or grain.
44324	1881,0701.2085	Field plan.
44325	1881,0701.2086	Economic.
44326	1881,0701.2087	Account.
44327	1881,0701.2088	Account.
44328	1881,0701.2089	Account.
44329	1881,0701.2090	Account.
44330	1881,0701.2091	Account.
44331	1881,0701.2092	Account of dates or grain.
44332	1881,0701.2093	Receipt. 6/8/-.
44333	1881,0701.2094	Account of sheep. Npl -/3/-. (Sippar).
44334	1881,0701.2095	Account.
44335	1881,0701.2096	Economic.
44336	1881,0701.2097	Economic.

44337	1881,0701.2098	Economic.
44338	1881,0701.2099	Account.
44339	1881,0701.2100	Economic.
44340	1881,0701.2101	Ritual.
44341	1881,0701.2102	Economic.
44342	1881,0701.2103	Economic.
44343	1881,0701.2104	Account.
44344	1881,0701.2105	Receipt. 1/5/13.
44345	1881,0701.2106	Ledger.
44346	1881,0701.2107	Medical. Finkel, Fs Lambert, 219, text 64 A.
44347	1881,0701.2108	Administrative. Npl -/-/8. (Sippar).
44348	1881,0701.2109	Account of dates or grain.
44349	1881,0701.2110	Economic.
44350	1881,0701.2111	Account of tithes.
44351	1881,0701.2112	Contract. Nabû-[] -/-/1.
44352	1881,0701.2113	Economic.
44353	1881,0701.2114	Contract.
44354	1881,0701.2115	Economic.
44355	1881,0701.2116	Ledger.
44356	1881,0701.2117	Contract. 27/[]/acc.
44357	1881,0701.2118	Account of barley.
44358	1881,0701.2119	Economic.
44359	1881,0701.2120	Economic.
44360	1881,0701.2121	Economic. -/-/16.
44361	1881,0701.2122	Economic.
44362	1881,0701.2123	Memorandum about tax.
44363	1881,0701.2124	Account of dates or grain.
44364	1881,0701.2125	Memorandum.
44365	1881,0701.2126	Economic.
44366	1881,0701.2127	Unidentified.
44367	1881,0701.2128	Receipt.
44368	1881,0701.2129	Promissory note for silver. (Sippar).
44369	1881,0701.2130	Ledger.
44370	1881,0701.2131	Account of dates. 13/6/-. (Sippar).
44371	1881,0701.2132	Receipt. Npl 18/3/[]. Borsippa? Zadok, Nisaba 21, 237.
44372	1881,0701.2133	Account of garments of gods in Ebabbar. (Sippar).
44373	1881,0701.2134	Economic.
44374	1881,0701.2135	Receipt for dates. 12/-/-.
44375	1881,0701.2136	Economic.
44376	1881,0701.2137	Economic.
44377	1881,0701.2138	Incantation.
44378	1881,0701.2139	Ledger.
44379	1881,0701.2140	Medical.
44380	1881,0701.2141	Account of dates or barley.

44381	1881,0701.2142	Unidentified.
44382	1881,0701.2143	Receipt for asphalt. -/3/2.
44383	1881,0701.2144	Account of lambs.
44384	1881,0701.2145	Receipt for jewellery.
44385	1881,0701.2146	Incantation.
44386	1881,0701.2147	Incantation.
44387	1881,0701.2148	Economic.
44388	1881,0701.2149	Receipt. -/-/acc.
44389	1881,0701.2150	Account of disbursements to hired men.
44390	1881,0701.2151	List of men.
44391	1881,0701.2152	Economic.
44392	1881,0701.2153	Economic.
44393	1881,0701.2154	Economic.
44394	1881,0701.2155	Contract.
44395	1881,0701.2156	Promissory note for dates.
44396	1881,0701.2157	Account of garments. Nbk -/4?/2.
44397	1881,0701.2158	Economic.
44398	1881,0701.2159	Economic.
44399	1881,0701.2160	Unidentified.
44400	1881,0701.2161	Receipt. Nbk 20/3/4.
44401	1881,0701.2162	Receipt.
44402	1881,0701.2163	Ledger.
44403	1881,0701.2164	Economic.
44404	1881,0701.2165	Account.
44405	1881,0701.2166	Receipt for onions.
44406	1881,0701.2167	Account.
44407	1881,0701.2168	Receipt for tools.
44408	1881,0701.2169	Economic.
44409	1881,0701.2170	Medical; amounts of ingredients. Finkel, Fs Lambert, 219, text 65 A.
44410	1881,0701.2171	Incantation.
44411	1881,0701.2172	Receipt 11/6/17. (Sippar).
44412	1881,0701.2173	Unidentified; mostly illegible.
44413	1881,0701.2174	Economic.
44414	1881,0701.2175	Incantation.
44415	1881,0701.2176	Account of dates or grain.
44416	1881,0701.2177	Astronomical.
44417	1881,0701.2178	Astronomical.
44418	1881,0701.2179	Field plan.
44419	1881,0701.2180	Economic.
44420	1881,0701.2181	Incantation.
44421	1881,0701.2182	Incantation.
44422	1881,0701.2183	Account of purchase.
44423	1881,0701.2184	Contract for bitumen.
44424	1881,0701.2185	Economic.

44425	1881,0701.2186	Ledger.
44426	1881,0701.2187	Economic.
44427	1881,0701.2188	Account.
44428	1881,0701.2189	Account of dates or grain.
44429	1881,0701.2190	Economic. Nbk.
44430	1881,0701.2191	Economic. Nbk (Sippar).
44431	1881,0701.2192	Offering ledger. Tarasewicz and Zawadzki, AOAT 451, no. 212.
44432	1881,0701.2193	Promissory note for barley. Npl 8/6/-.
44433	1881,0701.2194	Offering ledger. Tarasewicz and Zawadzki, AOAT 451, no. 173.
44434	1881,0701.2195	Economic.
44435	1881,0701.2196	Contract. Nabû-[] -/-/1.
44436	1881,0701.2197	Economic.
44437	1881,0701.2198	Incantation.
44438	1881,0701.2199	Astronomical.
44439	1881,0701.2200	Account of men.
44440	1881,0701.2201	Unidentified.
44441	1881,0701.2202	Economic.
44442	1881,0701.2203	Account.
44443	1881,0701.2204	Literary.
44444	1881,0701.2205	Receipt for payment. 1/9/20.
44445	1881,0701.2206	Economic.
44446	1881,0701.2207	Economic.
44447	1881,0701.2208	Account of disbursements.
44448	1881,0701.2209	Offering ledger. Tarasewicz and Zawadzki, AOAT 451, no. 174.
44449	1881,0701.2210	Astronomical.
44450	1881,0701.2211	Contract.
44451	1881,0701.2212	Economic.
44452	1881,0701.2213	Account of barley tax.
44453	1881,0701.2214	Astronomical.
44454	1881,0701.2215	Account of animals. -/3/8.
44455	1881,0701.2216	Account of animals.
44456	1881,0701.2217	Account.
44457	1881,0701.2218	Economic.
44458	1881,0701.2219	Account.
44459	1881,0701.2220	Ledger.
44460	1881,0701.2221	Account of dates or grain.
44461	1881,0701.2222	Economic.
44462	1881,0701.2223	Ledger.
44463	1881,0701.2224	Promissory note. 18/10/-.
44464	1881,0701.2225	Economic.
44465	1881,0701.2226	Unidentified.
44466	1881,0701.2227	Account.

44467	1881,0701.2228	Account of dates or grain.
44468	1881,0701.2229	Account of dates or grain.
44469	1881,0701.2230	Economic; fragment; three lines.
44470	1881,0701.2231	Account of dates or grain.
44471	1881,0701.2232	Account.
44472	1881,0701.2233	Receipt. 16/8/-.
44473	1881,0701.2234	Incantation.
44474	1881,0701.2235	Account of dates; mentions Dilbat.
44475	1881,0701.2236	Economic.
44476	1881,0701.2237	Economic.
44477	1881,0701.2238	Receipt for dates.
44478	1881,0701.2239	Ledger.
44479	1881,0701.2240	Account.
44480	1881,0701.2241	Memorandum; finger-nail marks.
44481	1881,0701.2242	Deposition. Nbk 21/-/-.
44482	1881,0701.2243	Receipt.
44483	1881,0701.2244	Receipt.
44484	1881,0701.2245	Deposition. Npl 10/3/13.
44485	1881,0701.2246	Economic.
44486	1881,0701.2247	Astrological omens. + 45126.
44487	1881,0701.2248	Promissory note for sesame 29/8/-. (Sippar).
44488	1881,0701.2249	Unidentified.
44489	1881,0701.2250	Economic.
44490	1881,0701.2251	Contract.
44491	1881,0701.2252	Economic. -/-/acc.
44492	1881,0701.2253	Astronomical.
44493	1881,0701.2254	Ledger.
44494	1881,0701.2255	Receipt.
44495	1881,0701.2256	Missing.
44496	1881,0701.2257	Account.
44497	1881,0701.2258	Economic.
44498	1881,0701.2259	Account of dates or grain.
44499	1881,0701.2260	Economic.
44500	1881,0701.2261	Ledger.
44501	1881,0701.2262	Ledger.
44502	1881,0701.2263	Contract.
44503	1881,0701.2264	Account of hides.
44504	1881,0701.2265	Economic.
44505	1881,0701.2266	Account.
44506	1881,0701.2267	Economic. 26/-/-.
44507	1881,0701.2268	Account.
44508	1881,0701.2269	Account.
44509	1881,0701.2270	Receipt for tools?
44510	1881,0701.2271	Astronomical.
44511	1881,0701.2272	Economic.

44512	1881,0701.2273	Economic.
44513	1881,0701.2274	Economic.
44514	1881,0701.2275	List of jewellery?
44515	1881,0701.2276	Economic.
44516	1881,0701.2277	Economic.
44517	1881,0701.2278	Incantation.
44518	1881,0701.2279	Economic. 5/2/21.
44519	1881,0701.2280	Account.
44520	1881,0701.2281	Ledger.
44521	1881,0701.2282	Account of dates or grain.
44522	1881,0701.2283	Ledger.
44523	1881,0701.2284	Economic.
44524	1881,0701.2285	Economic.
44525	1881,0701.2286	Account.
44526	1881,0701.2287	Economic. -/2/-.
44527	1881,0701.2288	Economic.
44528	1881,0701.2289	Account of tithes.
44529	1881,0701.2290	Astronomical.
44530	1881,0701.2291	Astronomical.
44531	1881,0701.2292	Receipt for copper.
44532	1881,0701.2293	Receipt for dates.
44533	1881,0701.2294	Receipt.
44534	1881,0701.2295	Account.
44535	1881,0701.2296	Economic.
44536	1881,0701.2297	Receipt for a sheep.
44537	1881,0701.2298	Account.
44538	1881,0701.2299	Account of dates or grain. -/9/-.
44539	1881,0701.2300	Account.
44540	1881,0701.2301	Receipt for iron. 18/-/-.
44541	1881,0701.2302	Account.
44542	1881,0701.2303	Account of sesame and barley.
44543	1881,0701.2304	Account.
44544	1881,0701.2305	Offering ledger. Tarasewicz and Zawadzki, AOAT 451, no. 175.
44545	1881,0701.2306	Ledger.
44546	1881,0701.2307	Account of dates or grain.
44547	1881,0701.2308	Economic.
44548	1881,0701.2309	Ledger.
44549	1881,0701.2310	Account of gold.
44550	1881,0701.2311	Ledger.
44551	1881,0701.2312	Astronomical.
44552	1881,0701.2313	Account.
44553	1881,0701.2314	Contract -/10/-. Sippar.
44554	1881,0701.2315	Economic.
44555	1881,0701.2316	Account.

44556	1881,0701.2317	Promissory note for silver.
44557	1881,0701.2318	Account.
44558	1881,0701.2319	Account of dates or grain.
44559	1881,0701.2320	Economic.
44560	1881,0701.2321	Account.
44561	1881,0701.2322	Account.
44562	1881,0701.2323	Account of barley.
44563	1881,0701.2324	Account.
44564	1881,0701.2325	Account.
44565	1881,0701.2326	Account.
44566	1881,0701.2327	Offering ledger. 16/[]/[]. Tarasewicz and Zawadzki, AOAT 451, no. 167.
44567	1881,0701.2328	Receipt.
44568	1881,0701.2329	Account.
44569	1881,0701.2330	Contract.
44570	1881,0701.2331	Account.
44571	1881,0701.2332	Account.
44572	1881,0701.2333	Contract; lease. Sippar.
44573	1881,0701.2334	Account.
44574	1881,0701.2335	Account of copper.
44575	1881,0701.2336	Receipt.
44576	1881,0701.2337	Economic.
44577	1881,0701.2338	Economic.
44578	1881,0701.2339	Account.
44579	1881,0701.2340	Economic.
44580	1881,0701.2341	Economic. -/-/12.
44581	1881,0701.2342	Offering ledger. 20+[]/2/[]. Tarasewicz and Zawadzki, AOAT 451, no. 168.
44582	1881,0701.2343	Account.
44583	1881,0701.2344	Account.
44584	1881,0701.2345	Account of dates or grain.
44585	1881,0701.2346	Account.
44586	1881,0701.2347	Account.
44587	1881,0701.2348	Economic.
44588	1881,0701.2349	Account.
44589	1881,0701.2350	Receipt for sale of bird?
44590	1881,0701.2351	Economic.
44591	1881,0701.2352	Economic.
44592	1881,0701.2353	Economic.
44593	1881,0701.2354	Account.
44594	1881,0701.2355	Account.
44595	1881,0701.2356	Economic.
44596	1881,0701.2357	Account.
44597	1881,0701.2358	Economic.
44598	1881,0701.2359	Receipt.

44599	1881,0701.2360	Economic.
44600	1881,0701.2361	Promissory note for silver. Npl.
44601	1881,0701.2362	Letter. (Sippar).
44602	1881,0701.2363	Account of dates or grain.
44603	1881,0701.2364	Account of dates or grain.
44604	1881,0701.2365	Promissory note for silver.
44605	1881,0701.2366	Economic.
44606	1881,0701.2367	Economic.
44607	1881,0701.2368	Account of dates or grain.
44608	1881,0701.2369	Account.
44609	1881,0701.2370	Medical.
44610	1881,0701.2371	Account.
44611	1881,0701.2372	Account.
44612	1881,0701.2373	Economic.
44613	1881,0701.2374	Contract.
44614	1881,0701.2375	Medical.
44615	1881,0701.2376	Administrative. (Sippar).
44616	1881,0701.2377	Unidentified.
44617	1881,0701.2378	Account of dates or grain.
44618	1881,0701.2379	Account of dates or grain.
44619	1881,0701.2380	Ledger.
44620	1881,0701.2381	Medical(?).
44621	1881,0701.2382	Astronomical.
44622	1881,0701.2383	Account.
44623	1881,0701.2384	Economic.
44624	1881,0701.2385	Account.
44625	1881,0701.2386	Economic. Sippar.
44626	1881,0701.2387	Account.
44627	1881,0701.2388	Account of dates or grain.
44628	1881,0701.2389	Economic.
44629	1881,0701.2390	Economic.
44630	1881,0701.2391	Account.
44631	1881,0701.2392	Ledger.
44632	1881,0701.2393	Ledger.
44633	1881,0701.2394	Economic. -/-/1.
44634	1881,0701.2395	Receipt.
44635	1881,0701.2396	Economic.
44636	1881,0701.2397	Economic.
44637	1881,0701.2398	Account.
44638	1881,0701.2399	Economic.
44639	1881,0701.2400	Economic. 15/12/-.
44640	1881,0701.2401	Account.
44641	1881,0701.2402	Account. -/-/16.
44642	1881,0701.2403	Account.
44643	1881,0701.2404	Contract. Npl -/2/16.

44644	1881,0701.2405	Economic.
44645	1881,0701.2406	Economic.
44646	1881,0701.2407	Ledger.
44647	1881,0701.2408	Contract. Npl 4/3/11. Dūr-Šamaš (Sippar).
44648	1881,0701.2409	Economic. -/-/13.
44649	1881,0701.2410	Account of dates or grain.
44650	1881,0701.2411	Account.
44651	1881,0701.2412	Contract about garments. (Sippar).
44652	1881,0701.2413	Medical. + 44826.
44653	1881,0701.2414	Promissory note for dates or grain. -/4/-.
44654	1881,0701.2415	Promissory note for silver.
44655	1881,0701.2416	Receipt. 17/10/-.
44656	1881,0701.2417	Economic.
44657	1881,0701.2418	Promissory note for barley.
44658	1881,0701.2419	Account of barley. Npl -/-/14.
44659	1881,0701.2420	Account of silver. 7/3/-.
44660	1881,0701.2421	Contract.
44661	1881,0701.2422	Memorandum.
44662	1881,0701.2423	Account.
44663	1881,0701.2424	Account of dates or grain.
44664	1881,0701.2425	Account.
44665	1881,0701.2426	Incantation.
44666	1881,0701.2427	Account.
44667	1881,0701.2428	Account of dates or grain.
44668	1881,0701.2429	Account.
44669	1881,0701.2430	Ledger.
44670	1881,0701.2431	Receipt for gold.
44671	1881,0701.2432	Receipt. Nbk -/12/26.
44672	1881,0701.2433	Economic.
44673	1881,0701.2434	Account.
44674	1881,0701.2435	Receipt for purchase of sheep.
44675	1881,0701.2436	Ledger.
44676	1881,0701.2437	Unidentified.
44677	1881,0701.2438	Economic.
44678	1881,0701.2439	Ledger.
44679	1881,0701.2440	Account.
44680	1881,0701.2441	Account.
44681	1881,0701.2442	Economic.
44682	1881,0701.2443	Economic.
44683	1881,0701.2444	Account. Npl 1/[]/20.
44684	1881,0701.2445	Receipt for dates or grain. Npl -/7/-.
44685	1881,0701.2446	Economic. 19/6/13.
44686	1881,0701.2447	Economic.
44687	1881,0701.2448	Account of dates or grain.
44688	1881,0701.2449	Account.

44689	1881,0701.2450	Economic.
44690	1881,0701.2451	Receipt. 27/-/-.
44691	1881,0701.2452	Receipt for dates.
44692	1881,0701.2453	Mathematical.
44693	1881,0701.2454	Receipt for a lamb.
44694	1881,0701.2455	Account of silver.
44695	1881,0701.2456	Economic.
44696	1881,0701.2457	Economic.
44697	1881,0701.2458	Ledger.
44698	1881,0701.2459	Account of silver.
44699	1881,0701.2460	Economic.
44700	1881,0701.2461	Economic.
44701	1881,0701.2462	Ledger.
44702	1881,0701.2463	Account.
44703	1881,0701.2464	Account of animals; qabuttu. Npl 1/9/20.
44704	1881,0701.2465	Account.
44705	1881,0701.2466	Promissory note for dates or grain. 18/9/-.
44706	1881,0701.2467	Receipt.
44707	1881,0701.2468	Economic.
44708	1881,0701.2469	Unidentified.
44709	1881,0701.2470	Memorandum.
44710	1881,0701.2471	Account.
44711	1881,0701.2472	Account.
44712	1881,0701.2473	Account of barley.
44713	1881,0701.2474	Contract.
44714	1881,0701.2475	Contract. Nbk.
44715	1881,0701.2476	Economic.
44716	1881,0701.2477	Account.
44717	1881,0701.2478	Account.
44718	1881,0701.2479	Economic.
44719	1881,0701.2480	Unidentified.
44720	1881,0701.2481	Receipt for oxen. Nbk 21/[]/4. (Sippar).
44721	1881,0701.2482	Account.
44722	1881,0701.2483	Economic.
44723	1881,0701.2484	Economic.
44724	1881,0701.2485	Account.
44725	1881,0701.2486	Account.
44726	1881,0701.2487	Account.
44727	1881,0701.2488	Economic. 16/-/-.
44728	1881,0701.2489	Account.
44729	1881,0701.2490	Account of dates.
44730	1881,0701.2491	About garments of the gods. Npl -/2/17. (Sippar).
44731	1881,0701.2492	Old Babylonian. Contract.
44732	1881,0701.2493	Ledger.
44733	1881,0701.2494	List of names.

44734	1881,0701.2495	Field sale.
44735	1881,0701.2496	Ledger.
44736	1881,0701.2497	Economic.
44737	1881,0701.2498	Account of dates or grain.
44738	1881,0701.2499	Account.
44739	1881,0701.2500	Account.
44740	1881,0701.2501	Economic.
44741	1881,0701.2502	Administrative.
44742	1881,0701.2503	Economic. -/-/20.
44743	1881,0701.2504	Economic.
44744	1881,0701.2505	Astronomical.
44745	1881,0701.2506	Account. Nbk (Sippar).
44746	1881,0701.2507	Astronomical.
44747	1881,0701.2508	Field sale. Npl 8/6/[]. Bēl-iqbi ālu [ša Šamaš]. Da Riva, AOAT 291, 111, pl. 1; Kennedy, JCS 38, 219, T.x.59.
44748	1881,0701.2509	Economic.
44749	1881,0701.2510	Economic.
44750	1881,0701.2511	Account.
44751	1881,0701.2512	Contract for work on garments of the gods. Nbk -/7/3. (Sippar).
44752	1881,0701.2513	Astronomical.
44753	1881,0701.2514	Bilingual incantation.
44754	1881,0701.2515	Contract.
44755	1881,0701.2516	Measurements of fields.
44756	1881,0701.2517	Economic.
44757	1881,0701.2518	Economic.
44758	1881,0701.2519	Memorandum about barley. -/4/-.
44759	1881,0701.2520	Receipt.
44760	1881,0701.2521	Ledger.
44761	1881,0701.2522	Economic.
44762	1881,0701.2523	Economic.
44763	1881,0701.2524	Measurements of fields. (Sippar).
44764	1881,0701.2525	Ledger.
44765	1881,0701.2526	Economic; unusually shaped small tablet.
44766	1881,0701.2527	Ledger.
44767	1881,0701.2528	Account of silver. Kandalanu 2/6/[13]. Brinkman and Kennedy, JCS 35, 50, L.169.
44768	1881,0701.2529	Economic. []-uṣur -/-/1.
44769	1881,0701.2530	Incantation.
44770	1881,0701.2531	Economic; drawing of a bird. (Sippar).
44771	1881,0701.2532	Receipt for bitumen. 6/11/-.
44772	1881,0701.2533	Economic. Npl 20/8/-.
44773	1881,0701.2534	Promissory note for flour.
44774	1881,0701.2535	Ledger.

44775	1881,0701.2536	Account.
44776	1881,0701.2537	Account.
44777	1881,0701.2538	Account.
44778	1881,0701.2539	Economic.
44779	1881,0701.2540	Account.
44780	1881,0701.2541	Account.
44781	1881,0701.2542	Economic.
44782	1881,0701.2543	Account of dates or grain.
44783	1881,0701.2544	Receipt.
44784	1881,0701.2545	Ledger.
44785	1881,0701.2546	Economic.
44786	1881,0701.2547	Economic.
44787	1881,0701.2548	Economic.
44788	1881,0701.2549	Economic.
44789	1881,0701.2550	Medical.
44790	1881,0701.2551	Memorandum.
44791	1881,0701.2552	Receipt.
44792	1881,0701.2553	Account of dates or grain.
44793	1881,0701.2554	Ledger.
44794	1881,0701.2555	Economic.
44795	1881,0701.2556	Economic.
44796	1881,0701.2557	Account of temple objects.
44797	1881,0701.2558	Account.
44798	1881,0701.2559	Economic.
44799	1881,0701.2560	Account of dates.
44800	1881,0701.2561	Receipt.
44801	1881,0701.2562	Receipt.
44802	1881,0701.2563	Account.
44803	1881,0701.2564	Economic.
44804	1881,0701.2565	Unidentified.
44805	1881,0701.2566	Incantation.
44806	1881,0701.2567	Memorandum.
44807	1881,0701.2568	Receipt for sheep.
44808	1881,0701.2569	Medical.
44809	1881,0701.2570	Economic. -/-/acc.
44810	1881,0701.2571	Economic.
44811	1881,0701.2572	Account of gold?
44812	1881,0701.2573	Economic.
44813	1881,0701.2574	Account.
44814	1881,0701.2575	Economic.
44815	1881,0701.2576	Economic.
44816	1881,0701.2577	Promissory note for dates or grain.
44817	1881,0701.2578	Economic.
44818	1881,0701.2579	Promissory note for barley. Npl.
44819	1881,0701.2580	Receipt.

44820	1881,0701.2581	Ledger.
44821	1881,0701.2582	Account.
44822	1881,0701.2583	Economic.
44823	1881,0701.2584	Account.
44824	1881,0701.2585	Unidentified.
44825	1881,0701.2586	Letter.
44826	1881,0701.2587	Joined to 44652.
44827	1881,0701.2588	Account of inspection of cattle. RN lost 12/3/17. (Sippar).
44828	1881,0701.2589	Economic.
44829	1881,0701.2590	Receipt.
44830	1881,0701.2591	Personal names.
44831	1881,0701.2592	Account.
44832	1881,0701.2593	Account.
44833	1881,0701.2594	Account.
44834	1881,0701.2595	Ledger.
44835	1881,0701.2596	Account.
44836	1881,0701.2597	Account.
44837	1881,0701.2598	Account of dates.
44838	1881,0701.2599	Ledger.
44839	1881,0701.2600	Account of dates or grain.
44840	1881,0701.2601	Account.
44841	1881,0701.2602	Account. 18/12b/20.
44842	1881,0701.2603	Account of barley. 3/[]/17.
44843	1881,0701.2604	Account.
44844	1881,0701.2605	Receipt. 1/[]/18.
44845	1881,0701.2606	Ledger.
44846	1881,0701.2607	Account.
44847	1881,0701.2608	Economic.
44848	1881,0701.2609	Account.
44849	1881,0701.2610	Account.
44850	1881,0701.2611	Account.
44851	1881,0701.2612	Incantation.
44852	1881,0701.2613	Economic.
44853	1881,0701.2614	Account.
44854	1881,0701.2615	Account.
44855	1881,0701.2616	Economic.
44856	1881,0701.2617	Economic.
44857	1881,0701.2618	Offering ledger.
44858	1881,0701.2619	Economic.
44859	1881,0701.2620	Account.
44860	1881,0701.2621	Account of animals.
44861	1881,0701.2622	Ledger.
44862	1881,0701.2623	Account.
44863	1881,0701.2624	Economic.

44864	1881,0701.2625	Medical.
44865	1881,0701.2626	Offering ledger. Tarasewicz and Zawadzki, AOAT 451, no. 177.
44866	1881,0701.2627	Joined to 41293.
44867	1881,0701.2628	Astronomical.
44868	1881,0701.2629	Account of dates.
44869	1881,0701.2630	Account of dates or grain.
44870	1881,0701.2631	Economic.
44871	1881,0701.2632	Ledger.
44872	1881,0701.2633	Economic.
44873	1881,0701.2634	Account.
44874	1881,0701.2635	Economic.
44875	1881,0701.2636	Economic.
44876	1881,0701.2637	List of stones; medical?
44877	1881,0701.2638	Economic.
44878	1881,0701.2639	Economic.
44879	1881,0701.2640	Economic.
44880	1881,0701.2641	Ledger.
44881	1881,0701.2642	Incantation.
44882	1881,0701.2643	Unidentified.
44883	1881,0701.2644	Economic.
44884	1881,0701.2645	Account.
44885	1881,0701.2646	Account.
44886	1881,0701.2647	Account.
44887	1881,0701.2648	Economic.
44888	1881,0701.2649	Economic.
44889	1881,0701.2650	Offering ledger. 17/6/2. Tarasewicz and Zawadzki, AOAT 451, no. 164.
44890	1881,0701.2651	Receipt for bitumen. 24/-/-.
44891	1881,0701.2652	Account of dates or grain.
44892	1881,0701.2653	Receipt.
44893	1881,0701.2654	Economic.
44894	1881,0701.2655	Account of barley.
44895	1881,0701.2656	Offering ledger. Tarasewicz and Zawadzki, AOAT 451, no. 176.
44896	1881,0701.2657	Receipt.
44897	1881,0701.2658	Economic.
44898	1881,0701.2659	Economic.
44899	1881,0701.2660	Receipt for silver.
44900	1881,0701.2661	Receipt.
44901	1881,0701.2662	Receipt. Nbk.
44902	1881,0701.2663	Account.
44903	1881,0701.2664	Account.
44904	1881,0701.2665	Economic.
44905	1881,0701.2666	Measurements of fields. 6+/12b/[]. (Sippar).

44906	1881,0701.2667	Receipt. Nabû-[] 21/7/16.
44907	1881,0701.2668	Economic.
44908	1881,0701.2669	Account.
44909	1881,0701.2670	Account of animals. Nbk 22+/8/6. (Sippar).
44910	1881,0701.2671	Land sale with field measurements. (Sippar).
44911	1881,0701.2672	Account.
44912	1881,0701.2673	Memorandum.
44913	1881,0701.2674	Account.
44914	1881,0701.2675	Ledger.
44915	1881,0701.2676	Account.
44916	1881,0701.2677	Account.
44917	1881,0701.2678	Account.
44918	1881,0701.2679	Account.
44919	1881,0701.2680	Economic.
44920	1881,0701.2681	Economic.
44921	1881,0701.2682	Promissory note for dates. Npl 12/9/-. (Sippar).
44922	1881,0701.2683	Ledger.
44923	1881,0701.2684	Account.
44924	1881,0701.2685	Offering ledger. Tarasewicz and Zawadzki, AOAT 451, no. 178.
44925	1881,0701.2686	Economic.
44926	1881,0701.2687	Ledger.
44927	1881,0701.2688	Economic.
44928	1881,0701.2689	Economic.
44929	1881,0701.2690	Economic.
44930	1881,0701.2691	Offering ledger. Tarasewicz and Zawadzki, AOAT 451, no. 213.
44931	1881,0701.2692	Economic.
44932	1881,0701.2693	Account. 16/-/-.
44933	1881,0701.2694	Economic.
44934	1881,0701.2695	Economic.
44935	1881,0701.2696	Account of animals. Npl -/-/10.
44936	1881,0701.2697	Account.
44937	1881,0701.2698	Account.
44938	1881,0701.2699	Ledger.
44939	1881,0701.2700	Account of cows.
44940	1881,0701.2701	Economic.
44941	1881,0701.2702	Memorandum.
44942	1881,0701.2703	Account of oil for offerings. (Sippar).
44943	1881,0701.2704	Account.
44944	1881,0701.2705	Economic.
44945	1881,0701.2706	Account.
44946	1881,0701.2707	Account. (Sippar).
44947	1881,0701.2708	Offering ledger. Tarasewicz and Zawadzki, AOAT 451, no. 214.

44948	1881,0701.2709	Economic.
44949	1881,0701.2710	Ledger.
44950	1881,0701.2711	Purchase of bitumen. Nbk 18/12/2. (Sippar).
44951	1881,0701.2712	Receipt for dates or grain.
44952	1881,0701.2713	Contract. Nbk 5/[]/9.
44953	1881,0701.2714	Receipt. 1/8/16.
44954	1881,0701.2715	Economic.
44955	1881,0701.2716	Receipt.
44956	1881,0701.2717	Economic.
44957	1881,0701.2718	Ledger. (Sippar).
44958	1881,0701.2719	Account.
44959	1881,0701.2720	Account? Nbk []/[]/15.
44960	1881,0701.2721	Ledger.
44961	1881,0701.2722	Account. Npl.
44962	1881,0701.2723	Account of garments.
44963	1881,0701.2724	Economic.
44964	1881,0701.2725	Astronomical.
44965	1881,0701.2726	Account.
44966	1881,0701.2727	Economic. 13/4/-.
44967	1881,0701.2728	Economic.
44968	1881,0701.2729	Economic.
44969	1881,0701.2730	Account.
44970	1881,0701.2731	Account.
44971	1881,0701.2732	Receipt. Nbk -/4/17.
44972	1881,0701.2733	Account.
44973	1881,0701.2734	Account.
44974	1881,0701.2735	Account.
44975	1881,0701.2736	Economic.
44976	1881,0701.2737	Economic.
44977	1881,0701.2738	Account.
44978	1881,0701.2739	Economic.
44979	1881,0701.2740	Economic.
44980	1881,0701.2741	Account of barley.
44981	1881,0701.2742	Ledger.
44982	1881,0701.2743	Receipt for dates or grain. -/9/-.
44983	1881,0701.2744	Economic.
44984	1881,0701.2745	Account of dates or grain.
44985	1881,0701.2746	Receipt.
44986	1881,0701.2747	Economic.
44987	1881,0701.2748	Contract.
44988	1881,0701.2749	Account of dates or grain.
44989	1881,0701.2750	Account.
44990	1881,0701.2751	Ledger.
44991	1881,0701.2752	Account of dates or grain.
44992	1881,0701.2753	Receipt.

44993	1881,0701.2754	Receipt for barley. Npl -/-/13.
44994	1881,0701.2755	Receipt for bitumen.
44995	1881,0701.2756	Account of days of work for various craftsmen.
44996	1881,0701.2757	Account.
44997	1881,0701.2758	Offering ledger.
44998	1881,0701.2759	Measurements of fields.
44999	1881,0701.2760	Account of dates and grain.
45000	1881,0701.2761	Economic.
45001	1881,0701.2762	Economic.
45002	1881,0701.2763	Account.
45003	1881,0701.2764	Account.
45004	1881,0701.2765	Letter.
45005	1881,0701.2766	Account of dates and grain.
45006	1881,0701.2767	Economic.
45007	1881,0701.2768	Economic.
45008	1881,0701.2769	Receipt for tools.
45009	1881,0701.2770	Ledger; RN = []-uṣur. Nbk?
45010	1881,0701.2771	Account of silver.
45011	1881,0701.2772	Receipt for dates or grain.
45012	1881,0701.2773	Measurements of fields.
45013	1881,0701.2774	Economic.
45014	1881,0701.2775	Account of barley.
45015	1881,0701.2776	Promissory note for dates. -/-/37. Sippar.
45016	1881,0701.2777	Account of dates or grain.
45017	1881,0701.2778	Account of animals.
45018	1881,0701.2779	Account of oxen.
45019	1881,0701.2780	Account of dates or grain.
45020	1881,0701.2781	Economic.
45021	1881,0701.2782	Economic. 21/-/-.
45022	1881,0701.2783	Account.
45023	1881,0701.2784	Account of silver. 7/11/8.
45024	1881,0701.2785	Medical.
45025	1881,0701.2786	Economic.
45026	1881,0701.2787	Receipt for dates or grain. -/-/16. Sippar.
45027	1881,0701.2788	Account. 11/[]/6.
45028	1881,0701.2789	Economic -/-/21. Akkadu.
45029	1881,0701.2790	Account.
45030	1881,0701.2791	Memorandum.
45031	1881,0701.2792	Economic. Nbk.
45032	1881,0701.2793	Promissory note for barley.
45033	1881,0701.2794	Ledger.
45034	1881,0701.2795	Receipt.
45035	1881,0701.2796	Economic.
45036	1881,0701.2797	Economic.
45037	1881,0701.2798	Incantation.

45038	1881,0701.2799	Account of bricks.
45039	1881,0701.2800	Memorandum.
45040	1881,0701.2801	Account of sheep.
45041	1881,0701.2802	Ledger. Npl -/-/20.
45042	1881,0701.2803	Economic.
45043	1881,0701.2804	Account of barley.
45044	1881,0701.2805	Account of jewellery.
45045	1881,0701.2806	Account of sheep.
45046	1881,0701.2807	Account of garments.
45047	1881,0701.2808	Receipt. Nbk 20/-/-.
45048	1881,0701.2809	Receipt. -/3/-.
45049	1881,0701.2810	Account.
45050	1881,0701.2811	Receipt.
45051	1881,0701.2812	Economic.
45052	1881,0701.2813	Unidentified.
45053	1881,0701.2814	Receipt for barley. 14/9/-.
45054	1881,0701.2815	Economic.
45055	1881,0701.2816	Ledger.
45056	1881,0701.2817	Receipt.
45057	1881,0701.2818	Receipt 21/[]/acc. Sippar.
45058	1881,0701.2819	Economic.
45059	1881,0701.2820	Contract.
45060	1881,0701.2821	Unidentified.
45061	1881,0701.2822	Economic.
45062	1881,0701.2823	Account of cows.
45063	1881,0701.2824	Ledger.
45064	1881,0701.2825	Account.
45065	1881,0701.2826	Account of garments. -/12b/-.
45066	1881,0701.2827	Ledger.
45067	1881,0701.2828	Account.
45068	1881,0701.2829	Economic.
45069	1881,0701.2830	Account of objects sent out for repair. 28/11/-.
45070	1881,0701.2831	Account.
45071	1881,0701.2832	Account of sheep. Nabû-[] -/-/16.
45072	1881,0701.2833	Account.
45073	1881,0701.2834	Account of dates or grain. Npl -/-/16.
45074	1881,0701.2835	Receipt. Nbk -/3/4. (Sippar).
45075	1881,0701.2836	Offering ledger. Tarasewicz and Zawadzki, AOAT 451, no. 179.
45076	1881,0701.2837	Ledger.
45077	1881,0701.2838	Economic.
45078	1881,0701.2839	Account of dates or grain.
45079	1881,0701.2840	List of names.
45080	1881,0701.2841	Account.
45081	1881,0701.2842	Economic.

45082	1881,0701.2843	Offering ledger. Tarasewicz and Zawadzki, AOAT 451, no. 180.
45083	1881,0701.2844	Economic.
45084	1881,0701.2845	Astronomical.
45085	1881,0701.2846	Audit. 10/4/-.
45086	1881,0701.2847	Account.
45087	1881,0701.2848	Economic.
45088	1881,0701.2849	Account.
45089	1881,0701.2850	Receipt.
45090	1881,0701.2851	Account of oxen.
45091	1881,0701.2852	Account.
45092	1881,0701.2853	Astronomical.
45093	1881,0701.2854	Account. -/12/-.
45094	1881,0701.2855	Economic.
45095	1881,0701.2856	Economic.
45096	1881,0701.2857	Account.
45097	1881,0701.2858	Ledger.
45098	1881,0701.2859	Receipt. 23/5/20.
45099	1881,0701.2860	Receipt. Nbk 24/2/4.
45100	1881,0701.2861	Account of barley.
45101	1881,0701.2862	Account of dates. Nabû-[] -/-/13. (Sippar).
45102	1881,0701.2863	Account of silver.
45103	1881,0701.2864	Incantation.
45104	1881,0701.2865	Account.
45105	1881,0701.2866	Commentary.
45106	1881,0701.2867	Receipt. -/12/-.
45107	1881,0701.2868	Receipt for dates or grain.
45108	1881,0701.2869	Account of dates or grain tax. 4/1/17.
45109	1881,0701.2870	Offering ledger. Nbk 16/[]/[]. Tarasewicz and Zawadzki, AOAT 451, no. 143.
45110	1881,0701.2871	Economic.
45111	1881,0701.2872	Promissory note for silver.
45112	1881,0701.2873	Account.
45113	1881,0701.2874	Account.
45114	1881,0701.2875	Account.
45115	1881,0701.2876	Unidentified.
45116	1881,0701.2877	Economic.
45117	1881,0701.2878	Field sale.
45118	1881,0701.2879	Receipt for sheep. Nbk -/-/4.
45119	1881,0701.2880	Account.
45120	1881,0701.2881	Economic.
45121	1881,0701.2882	Account.
45122	1881,0701.2883	Account.
45123	1881,0701.2884	Ledger.
45124	1881,0701.2885	Account.

45125	1881,0701.2886	Economic.
45126	1881,0701.2887	Joined to 44486.
45127	1881,0701.2888	Economic.
45128	1881,0701.2889	Receipt for a garment.
45129	1881,0701.2890	Ledger.
45130	1881,0701.2891	Promissory note for oil.
45131	1881,0701.2892	Account.
45132	1881,0701.2893	List of men.
45133	1881,0701.2894	Promissory note for silver.
45134	1881,0701.2895	Economic.
45135	1881,0701.2896	Receipt. Nbk -/4/12.
45136	1881,0701.2897	Economic.
45137	1881,0701.2898	Economic.
45138	1881,0701.2899	Account.
45139	1881,0701.2900	Account of dates or grain.
45140	1881,0701.2901	Receipt for barley. 12/[]/acc.
45141	1881,0701.2902	Account.
45142	1881,0701.2903	Receipt for dates.
45143	1881,0701.2904	Account.
45144	1881,0701.2905	Account.
45145	1881,0701.2906	Ledger.
45146	1881,0701.2907	Ritual.
45147	1881,0701.2908	Account.
45148	1881,0701.2909	Economic.
45149	1881,0701.2910	Account.
45150	1881,0701.2911	Astronomical.
45151	1881,0701.2912	Ledger.
45152	1881,0701.2913	Account.
45153	1881,0701.2914	Account.
45154	1881,0701.2915	Ledger. Nbk.
45155	1881,0701.2916	Contract.
45156	1881,0701.2917	Incantation.
45157	1881,0701.2918	Account of dates or grain.
45158	1881,0701.2919	Ledger.
45159	1881,0701.2920	Economic. 19/-/-.
45160	1881,0701.2921	Economic.
45161	1881,0701.2922	Account of animals.
45162	1881,0701.2923	Receipt.
45163	1881,0701.2924	Account of sheep.
45164	1881,0701.2925	Economic.
45165	1881,0701.2926	Unidentified.
45166	1881,0701.2927	Account.
45167	1881,0701.2928	Account.
45168	1881,0701.2929	Economic.
45169	1881,0701.2930	Account of dates or grain. 8/-/-.

45170	1881,0701.2931	Promissory note for silver. Npl 10+/9/-.
45171	1881,0701.2932	Receipt. Npl.
45172	1881,0701.2933	Receipt. 8/2/-.
45173	1881,0701.2934	Account.
45174	1881,0701.2935	Ledger.
45175	1881,0701.2936	Economic.
45176	1881,0701.2937	Receipt. Nbk.
45177	1881,0701.2938	Promissory note given by Bēl-ušēzib / Madānu-ēreš. -/4/9. Sippar.
45178	1881,0701.2939	Economic.
45179	1881,0701.2940	Account of dates or grain.
45180	1881,0701.2941	Economic. Npl.
45181	1881,0701.2942	Account.
45182	1881,0701.2943	Promissory note for dates.
45183	1881,0701.2944	Receipt. 16/6/-.
45184	1881,0701.2945	Economic.
45185	1881,0701.2946	Uninscribed.
45186	1881,0701.2947	Account.
45187	1881,0701.2948	Account.
45188	1881,0701.2949	Ledger.
45189	1881,0701.2950	Account.
45190	1881,0701.2951	Account.
45191	1881,0701.2952	Account of dates or grain.
45192	1881,0701.2953	Offering ledger. 5/[]/[]. Tarasewicz and Zawadzki, AOAT 451, no. 169.
45193	1881,0701.2954	Economic.
45194	1881,0701.2955	Receipt for deliveries to storehouse. Nbk 1/-/-.
45195	1881,0701.2956	Contract for bricks.
45196	1881,0701.2957	Account.
45197	1881,0701.2958	Economic.
45198	1881,0701.2959	Account.
45199	1881,0701.2960	Account.
45200	1881,0701.2961	Economic.
45201	1881,0701.2962	Contract for sheep.
45202	1881,0701.2963	Unidentified.
45203	1881,0701.2964	Incantation.
45204	1881,0701.2965	Economic.
45205	1881,0701.2966	Memorandum.
45206	1881,0701.2967	Economic.
45207	1881,0701.2968	Ledger.
45208	1881,0701.2969	Account.
45209	1881,0701.2970	Account of barley provisions.
45210	1881,0701.2971	Economic.
45211	1881,0701.2972	Offering ledger. []/[]/11. Tarasewicz and Zawadzki, AOAT 451, no. 165.

45212	1881,0701.2973	Account.
45213	1881,0701.2974	Receipt for dates or grain.
45214	1881,0701.2975	Account.
45215	1881,0701.2976	Receipt. 5/-/-.
45216	1881,0701.2977	Measurements of fields.
45217	1881,0701.2978	Receipt. -/10/-.
45218	1881,0701.2979	Account of dates or grain.
45219	1881,0701.2980	Account.
45220	1881,0701.2981	Receipt for garments.
45221	1881,0701.2982	Receipt.
45222	1881,0701.2983	Account.
45223	1881,0701.2984	Ledger.
45224	1881,0701.2985	Account.
45225	1881,0701.2986	Account.
45226	1881,0701.2987	Account of barley.
45227	1881,0701.2988	Medical.
45228	1881,0701.2989	Ledger.
45229	1881,0701.2990	Receipt. 13/2/18.
45230	1881,0701.2991	Account.
45231	1881,0701.2992	Contract.
45232	1881,0701.2993	Ledger.
45233	1881,0701.2994	Economic.
45234	1881,0701.2995	Account of silver.
45235	1881,0701.2996	Account. -/3/-.
45236	1881,0701.2997	Account.
45237	1881,0701.2998	Economic.
45238	1881,0701.2999	Account.
45239	1881,0701.3000	Literary.
45240	1881,0701.3001	Joined to 43839.
45241	1881,0701.3002	Historical(?).
45242	1881,0701.3003	Account.
45243	1881,0701.3004	Account.
45244	1881,0701.3005	Contract; lease of a house. Cam 8/12/[]. Babylon.
45245	1881,0701.3006	Field plan.
45246	1881,0701.3007	Chronicle; refers to year 3 of Tiglath-pileser.
45247	1881,0701.3008	Astronomical.
45248	1881,0701.3009	Unidentified.
45249	1881,0701.3010	Incantations; Maqlu I. (+) 43826 + 43835. Abusch, AMD 10, 23-49.
45250	1881,0701.3011	Receipt.
45251	1881,0701.3012	Account of dates or grain.
45252	1881,0701.3013	Account of dates or grain.
45253	1881,0701.3014	Receipt. 26/-/-.
45254	1881,0701.3015	Economic.
45255	1881,0701.3016	Unidentified.

45256	1881,0701.3017	Receipt.
45257	1881,0701.3018	Account.
45258	1881,0701.3019	Economic.
45259	1881,0701.3020	Receipt. -/11/16.
45260	1881,0701.3021	Account of dates. -/12/-.
45261	1881,0701.3022	Account of wheat. Npl 22/9/3. (Sippar).
45262	1881,0701.3023	Promissory note for dates. Babylon.
45263	1881,0701.3024	Economic.
45264	1881,0701.3025	Economic.
45265	1881,0701.3026	Ledger.
45266	1881,0701.3027	Account.
45267	1881,0701.3028	Ledger.
45268	1881,0701.3029	Account.
45269	1881,0701.3030	Medical.
45270	1881,0701.3031	Economic; gold and jewellery, probably for garments of the gods. (Sippar).
45271	1881,0701.3032	Account.
45272	1881,0701.3033	Account of oxen. -/8/-.
45273	1881,0701.3034	Memorandum.
45274	1881,0701.3035	Promissory note for dates.
45275	1881,0701.3036	Economic.
45276	1881,0701.3037	Medical.
45277	1881,0701.3038	List of men.
45278	1881,0701.3039	Receipt. 25/4/-.
45279	1881,0701.3040	Account.
45280	1881,0701.3041	Account. 27/-/-.
45281	1881,0701.3042	Promissory note for barley.
45282	1881,0701.3043	Economic.
45283	1881,0701.3044	Economic.
45284	1881,0701.3045	Letter.
45285	1881,0701.3046	Economic.
45286	1881,0701.3047	Economic.
45287	1881,0701.3048	Account of jewellery for garments of the gods. Nbk. (Sippar).
45288	1881,0701.3049	Account of birds.
45289	1881,0701.3050	Receipt.
45290	1881,0701.3051	Ledger.
45291	1881,0701.3052	Ledger.
45292	1881,0701.3053	Account.
45293	1881,0701.3054	Account.
45294	1881,0701.3055	Receipt. 7/-/-.
45295	1881,0701.3056	Account.
45296	1881,0701.3057	Receipt for sheep. Nbk.
45297	1881,0701.3058	Account of dates or grain.
45298	1881,0701.3059	Receipt. Npl 17/1/11. (Sippar).

45299	1881,0701.3060	Receipt.
45300	1881,0701.3061	List of men.
45301	1881,0701.3062	Account.
45302	1881,0701.3063	Receipt.
45303	1881,0701.3064	Receipt.
45304	1881,0701.3065	Account.
45305	1881,0701.3066	Ledger.
45306	1881,0701.3067	Account of dates or grain.
45307	1881,0701.3068	Receipt for tools. Nbk 2/[]/2.
45308	1881,0701.3069	Economic.
45309	1881,0701.3070	Account.
45310	1881,0701.3071	Economic.
45311	1881,0701.3072	Account.
45312	1881,0701.3073	Medical.
45313	1881,0701.3074	Economic.
45314	1881,0701.3075	Economic.
45315	1881,0701.3076	Economic.
45316	1881,0701.3077	Economic.
45317	1881,0701.3078	Unidentified.
45318	1881,0701.3079	Account.
45319	1881,0701.3080	Account of dates or grain. 20/9/-.
45320	1881,0701.3081	Economic.
45321	1881,0701.3082	Contract. Cyr 12/2/8.
45322	1881,0701.3083	Account of cows. -/-/8.
45323	1881,0701.3084	Account.
45324	1881,0701.3085	Memorandum.
45325	1881,0701.3086	Economic.
45326	1881,0701.3087	Economic.
45327	1881,0701.3088	Account of sheep.
45328	1881,0701.3089	Economic. -/1/-.
45329	1881,0701.3090	Account of birds.
45330	1881,0701.3091	Economic.
45331	1881,0701.3092	Account of silver.
45332	1881,0701.3093	Receipt.
45333	1881,0701.3094	Ledger.
45334	1881,0701.3095	Letter.
45335	1881,0701.3096	Account.
45336	1881,0701.3097	Economic.
45337	1881,0701.3098	Contract.
45338	1881,0701.3099	Economic.
45339	1881,0701.3100	Receipt.
45340	1881,0701.3101	Account.
45341	1881,0701.3102	Account.
45342	1881,0701.3103	Account.
45343	1881,0701.3104	Account.

45344	1881,0701.3105	Account.
45345	1881,0701.3106	Account.
45346	1881,0701.3107	Economic.
45347	1881,0701.3108	Account.
45348	1881,0701.3109	Account.
45349	1881,0701.3110	Economic.
45350	1881,0701.3111	Account.
45351	1881,0701.3112	Account of animals. Npl -/-/8. (Sippar).
45352	1881,0701.3113	Medical.
45353	1881,0701.3114	Economic.
45354	1881,0701.3115	Unidentified.
45355	1881,0701.3116	Receipt. Nbk -/1/6. (Sippar).
45356	1881,0701.3117	Medical.
45357	1881,0701.3118	Astronomical.
45358	1881,0701.3119	Account.
45359	1881,0701.3120	Account of birds.
45360	1881,0701.3121	Account of dates or grain.
45361	1881,0701.3122	Receipt.
45362	1881,0701.3123	Account.
45363	1881,0701.3124	Economic.
45364	1881,0701.3125	Economic.
45365	1881,0701.3126	Letter.
45366	1881,0701.3127	Account of jewellery.
45367	1881,0701.3128	Economic.
45368	1881,0701.3129	Economic.
45369	1881,0701.3130	Contract.
45370	1881,0701.3131	Astronomical.
45371	1881,0701.3132	Astronomical.
45372	1881,0701.3133	Bilingual incantation, Marduk's Address (Udug-ḫul 11). + 46401. Geller, BAM 8, 340-392, pls. 80-81; Lambert, MC 24, no. 177.
45373	1881,0701.3134	Incantation; Marduk's Address (Udug-ḫul 11). + 46318 + 46323 + 46368 + 46484. Geller, BAM 8, 340-392, pls. 77, 79, 80, 87-90; Lambert, MC 24, no. 196.
45374	1881,0701.3135	Unidentified.
45375	1881,0701.3136	Bilingual incantation.
45376	1881,0701.3137	Lexical; syllabary.
45377	1881,0701.3138	Incantation; Marduk's Address (Udug-ḫul 11), colophon. + 45402 + 46369 + 46375 + 46383 + 46434 + 46435 + 46437 + 46454 + unnum. Geller, BAM 8, 340-392, pls. 75, 76, 79, 81, 82, 85; Lambert, MC 24, no. 173.
45378	1881,0701.3139	Lexical; syllabary.
45379	1881,0701.3140	Literary.

45380	1881,0701.3141	Lexical.
45381	1881,0701.3142	Literary; Love Lyrics. + 45384 + 45390 + 45406 (+) 46500. Cf. Finkel, AuOr 9 (1991), 92.
45382	1881,0701.3143	Incantation; Marduk's Address (Udug-ḫul 11). + 46332 + 46393 + 46423 + 46440 + 46461 + 46497. Geller, BAM 8, 340-392, pls. 74, 80-82, 86, 87, 90; Lambert, MC 24, no. 191.
45383	1881,0701.3144	Missing.
45384	1881,0701.3145	Joined to 45381.
45385	1881,0701.3146	Bilingual incantation; Muššu'u tablet III; prayer on upper edge; colophon; edition of Bēl-zēru-līšir. Alex III 17/6/10. Babylon. + 46291 + 46358 + 46388 + 46439. CT 17, 12-13 (46291 + 46358 only); cf. Finkel, AuOr 9 (1991), 95-96; Böck, Muššu'u, 133-146 and pls. VIII-IX.
45386	1881,0701.3147	Lexical; syllabary.
45387	1881,0701.3148	Missing.
45388	1881,0701.3149	Literary.
45389	1881,0701.3150	Incantation, Sag-ba sag-ba, complete, with catch-line and colophon; cf. Römer, Fs Sjöberg, pp. 465-479.
45390	1881,0701.3151	Joined to 45381.
45391	1881,0701.3152	Bilingual incantation; four columns; colophon.
45392	1881,0701.3153	Bilingual incantation, Udug-ḫul 2, colophon. + 45398 + 45399 + 45404 + 45407 + 45408. Geller, BAM 8, 59-88, pls. 9-10.
45393	1881,0701.3154	Incantation, ritual and colophon; Qutaru; edition of Tanittu-Bēl; Udug-ḫul 1 and 11, colophon. Alex III []/12?/13. Babylon. + 46277 + 46331. Cf. Finkel, AuOr 9 (1991), 103; Farber, Lamaštu, 47, pls. 78-80; Geller, BAM 8, 44-58, 340-392.
45394	1881,0701.3155	School practice text; turns sideways. + 46283.
45395	1881,0701.3156	Bilingual incantation; Muššu'u tablet III. (+) 46413 + 46472 + 46527. Cf. Finkel, AuOr 9 (1991), 95; Böck, Muššu'u, 133-146 and pls. VI-VII.
45396	1881,0701.3157	Lexical; syllabary. + 46286 + 46294 + 46327 + 46339 + 46356 + 46385. CT 11, 10.
45397	1881,0701.3158	Lexical; syllabary. CT 11, 13.
45398	1881,0701.3159	Joined to 45392.
45399	1881,0701.3160	Joined to 45392.
45400	1881,0701.3161	Lexical; syllabary; personal names.
45401	1881,0701.3162	Bilingual incantation, Udug-ḫul 2. (+) 46329 (+) 46333 + 46360 + 46477 + 46512 + 46517 (+) 46353. Geller, BAM 8, 59-88, pls. 18-19. Geller has 46560 for 46360.
45402	1881,0701.3163	Joined to 45377.

45403	1881,0701.3164	Incantation; Marduk's Address (Udug-ḫul 11). + unnum. Geller, BAM 8, 340-392, pls. 74, 87; Lambert, MC 24, no. 176.
45404	1881,0701.3165	Joined to 45392.
45405	1881,0701.3166	Bilingual incantations; Muššu'u tablet IV; edition of Tanittu-Bēl; colophon. + 46289 + 46387 + 46416 + 46419 + 46446 + 46509 + 1881,0728 unnum. (+) 46361 (+) 46458. Cf. Finkel, AuOr 9 (1991), 95 and 96-97; Böck, Muššu'u, 147-180 and pls. XVI-XVII (not 46361 or 46446).
45406	1881,0701.3167	Joined to 45381.
45407	1881,0701.3168	Joined to 45392.
45408	1881,0701.3169	Joined to 45392.
45409	1881,0701.3170	Incantation.
45410	1881,0701.3171	Lexical; syllabary. + 46344 + 46350 + 46495. CT 11, 11.
45411	1881,0701.3172	Land sale; mentions the Great Gate of Uraš; sealed; finger-nail marks. Dar 15/4?/17. Tamerat Purattu. Nisaba 28, no. 119.
45412	1881,0701.3173	Field sale; finger-nail marks. Dar 12 /5/18.
45413	1881,0701.3174	Astronomical.
45414	1881,0701.3175	Joined to 38624.
45415	1881,0701.3176	Field sale.
45416	1881,0701.3177	Land sale; sealed; finger-nail marks. Nbk 6?/7/33. Babylon. Nisaba 28, no. 54.
45417	1881,0701.3178	Land sale. (Babylon?).
45418	1881,0701.3179	Astrological omens.
45419	1881,0701.3180	Ritual; ušburruda. Abusch and Schwemer, AMD 8/1, text 7.9 b, pl. 48.
45420	1881,0701.3181	Lexical; Ea; sign list and literary extracts.
45421	1881,0701.3182	Literary(?) or school text(?).
45422	1881,0701.3183	Medical.
45423	1881,0701.3184	School text(?); two columns.
45424	1881,0701.3185	Omens; terrestrial.
45425	1881,0701.3186	Contract; sale of a slave. -/12b/-. Babylon.
45426	1881,0701.3187	Astronomical; compilation of Saturn observations; two columns. Steele, JHA 2019.
45427	1881,0701.3188	Literary(?) or school text(?).
45428	1881,0701.3189	Omens.
45429	1881,0701.3190	Field sale.
45430	1881,0701.3191	Astrological omens.
45431	1881,0701.3192	Field plan. Dar 10/[]/30.
45432	1881,0701.3193	Field plan.
45433	1881,0701.3194	Field plan.
45434	1881,0701.3195	Field sale.

45435	1881,0701.3196	Account.
45436	1881,0701.3197	Contract.
45437	1881,0701.3198	Field sale.
45438	1881,0701.3199	Joined to 43899.
45439	1881,0701.3200	Astronomical.
45440	1881,0701.3201	Economic. 3/[]/15.
45441	1881,0701.3202	Economic.
45442	1881,0701.3203	Economic.
45443	1881,0701.3204	Ritual.
45444	1881,0701.3205	Unidentified.
45445	1881,0701.3206	Account.
45446	1881,0701.3207	Commentary.
45447	1881,0701.3208	Lexical?; two columns.
45448	1881,0701.3209	Contract; lease of a house. Nbk 4/[]/42. Babylon.
45449	1881,0701.3210	Economic.
45450	1881,0701.3211	Lexical; Ḫḫ I; literary extracts.
45451	1881,0701.3212	Field plan.
45452	1881,0701.3213	Lexical.
45453	1881,0701.3214	Promissory note for silver. Dar 21/3/-.
45454	1881,0701.3215	Contract; land sale.
45455	1881,0701.3216	Astrological omens.
45456	1881,0701.3217	Joined to 43975.
45457	1881,0701.3218	Omens.
45458	1881,0701.3219	Ritual.
45459	1881,0701.3220	Unidentified.
45460	1881,0701.3221	Economic. 26/4/-.
45461	1881,0701.3222	Field sale.
45462	1881,0701.3223	Promissory note for barley.
45463	1881,0701.3224	Lexical?; two columns.
45464	1881,0701.3225	Medical.
45465	1881,0701.3226	Lexical.
45466	1881,0701.3227	Economic.
45467	1881,0701.3228	Account.
45468	1881,0701.3229	Unidentified.
45469	1881,0701.3230	Contract.
45470	1881,0701.3231	Omens; terrestrial.
45471	1881,0701.3232	Literary.
45472	1881,0701.3233	Ledger.
45473	1881,0701.3234	Account.
45474	1881,0701.3235	Lexical.
45475	1881,0701.3236	Economic.
45476	1881,0701.3237	Economic. 23/[]/1.
45477	1881,0701.3238	Literary.
45478	1881,0701.3239	Prayer to Marduk.
45479	1881,0701.3240	Economic.

45480	1881,0701.3241	Promissory note for dates.
45481	1881,0701.3242	Contract.
45482	1881,0701.3243	Incantation against witchcraft; colophon. Abusch and Schwemer, AMD 8/2 text 7.22 b, pl. 20.
45483	1881,0701.3244	Bilingual incantations; Muššu'u VIII; colophon. + 46299 + 46319 + 46367 + 46394 + 46397 + 46507 + 46525 + 1881,0728 unnum. Cf. Finkel, AuOr 9 (1991), 99-100; Böck, Muššu'u, 261-313 and pls. XXXVIII-XXXIX.
45484	1881,0701.3245	Bilingual incantation. + 47139.
45485	1881,0701.3246	Incantation.
45486	1881,0701.3247	Medical.
45487	1881,0701.3248	Field sale. Dar.
45488	1881,0701.3249	Economic.
45489	1881,0701.3250	Unidentified.
45490	1881,0701.3251	Field plan.
45491	1881,0701.3252	Medical.
45492	1881,0701.3253	Lexical; syllabary.
45493	1881,0701.3254	Lexical; Ea; sign list.
45494	1881,0701.3255	Contract for a purchase.
45495	1881,0701.3256	Economic. -/8/-.
45496	1881,0701.3257	Letter.
45497	1881,0701.3258	Economic.
45498	1881,0701.3259	Contract.
45499	1881,0701.3260	Sale of fields; finger-nail marks. Nbn 5/3/11. Bīt-Sa-a-lu. + 46840 + 46901.
45500	1881,0701.3261	Field plan?
45501	1881,0701.3262	Astronomical.
45502	1881,0701.3263	Letter?
45503	1881,0701.3264	Economic.
45504	1881,0701.3265	Incantation.
45505	1881,0701.3266	Medical.
45506	1881,0701.3267	Economic.
45507	1881,0701.3268	Economic.
45508	1881,0701.3269	Economic.
45509	1881,0701.3270	Astronomical.
45510	1881,0701.3271	Lexical; gán.
45511	1881,0701.3272	Astronomical.
45512	1881,0701.3273	Promissory note for silver. Nbn -/12/-. Babylon.
45513	1881,0701.3274	Economic. -/-/5.
45514	1881,0701.3275	Economic.
45515	1881,0701.3276	Astronomical.
45516	1881,0701.3277	Sumerian literary.
45517	1881,0701.3278	Contract; lease of a house.
45518	1881,0701.3279	Field plan.

45519	1881,0701.3280	Economic.
45520	1881,0701.3281	Economic.
45521	1881,0701.3282	Astrological omens.
45522	1881,0701.3283	Medical.
45523	1881,0701.3284	Economic.
45524	1881,0701.3285	Medical.
45525	1881,0701.3286	Literary; mentions various cities.
45526	1881,0701.3287	Division of a dowry field. Cyrus []/[]/6. Wunsch, AOAT 330, 372-373.
45527	1881,0701.3288	Dream omens; Zaqīqu. Oppenheim, Iraq 31, 159-165 and pl. XXXVI.
45528	1881,0701.3289	Literary; Enūma eliš I. + 46614 + 47173 + 47190 + 47197. King, STC pl. I-VI (only 45528 + 46614); Kämmerer and Metzler, AOAT 375, 84, Tafel I Y+, 85, Tafel II N+, pls. III-VI (only 47313 + 47190 + 47197); Lambert, BCM, p. 476, pl. 5.
45529	1881,0701.3290	Land sale. 27/10/2. Babylon.
45530	1881,0701.3291	Lexical.
45531	1881,0701.3292	Contract. Dar -/-/10.
45532	1881,0701.3293	Mathematical.
45533	1881,0701.3294	Mathematical.
45534	1881,0701.3295	Receipt for three dowry slaves. Nbn. Wunsch, AOAT 330, 372.
45535	1881,0701.3296	Receipt for three dowry slaves. [Nbn]. Wunsch, AOAT 330, 372.
45536	1881,0701.3297	Contract; lease; mentions Elam. 5/9/9.
45537	1881,0701.3298	Economic.
45538	1881,0701.3299	Letter.
45539	1881,0701.3300	Bilingual incantation, Udug-ḫul 5. + 46759. CT 16, 12-16 (45539 only); Geller, BAM 8, 174-216, pl. 44.
45540	1881,0701.3301	Economic.
45541	1881,0701.3302	Economic.
45542	1881,0701.3303	Economic.
45543	1881,0701.3304	Literary.
45544	1881,0701.3305	Lexical; Ḫḫ II.
45545	1881,0701.3306	Lexical.
45546	1881,0701.3307	Literary.
45547	1881,0701.3308	Contract; transfer of land as part of a dowry. [Npl 21/2/7]. + 46991 + 47272. Wunsch, Bab Arch 2, nos. 10c and 10d (46991 unpub.).
45548	1881,0701.3309	Lexical.
45549	1881,0701.3310	Sealing; uninscribed; impression of a stamp seal; double string knot behind.

45550	1881,0701.3311	Hemerology; calendar of lucky and unlucky days throughout the year; originally probably six + six columns; only Simanu to Šabaṭu preserved. + 46909.
45551	1881,0701.3312	Field sale; finger-nail marks. Dar I []/[]/12. Babylon.
45552	1881,0701.3313	Field sale; turns sideways. (Babylon).
45553	1881,0701.3314	Field sale.
45554	1881,0701.3315	Contract; provision of a dowry for his daughter by Marduk-rā'im-kitti; sealed; finger-nail marks. Dar I []/[]/31. Babylon. Nisaba 28, no. 176.
45555	1881,0701.3316	Sale of a slave girl and her daughter. Dar 24/8/35. URU Bīt-šá-x-x.
45556	1881,0701.3317	Ritual.
45557	1881,0701.3318	Sale of a prebend.
45558	1881,0701.3319	Contract.
45559	1881,0701.3320	Medical. + 45574.
45560	1881,0701.3321	Quitclaim about a dowry field. Dupl. 46788. Nbn 23/[]/16. Babylon. Wunsch, AOAT 330, 372-373.
45561	1881,0701.3322	Land sale. Nbk 14/11?/30. (Babylon).
45562	1881,0701.3323	Incantation.
45563	1881,0701.3324	Field sale.
45564	1881,0701.3325	Contract; lease.
45565	1881,0701.3326	Contract. -/5/4.
45566	1881,0701.3327	Bilingual incantation; Muššu'u tablet V. Cf. Finkel, AuOr 9 (1991), 98; Böck, NABU 2001, 80-81, no. 86; Böck, Muššu'u, 181-220 and pl. XXVI.
45567	1881,0701.3328	Field sale.
45568	1881,0701.3329	Literary; colophon.
45569	1881,0701.3330	Contract. Dar -/-/32.
45570	1881,0701.3331	Economic.
45571	1881,0701.3332	Unidentified.
45572	1881,0701.3333	Lexical; syllabary.
45573	1881,0701.3334	Incantation.
45574	1881,0701.3335	Joined to 45559.
45575	1881,0701.3336	Incantation.
45576	1881,0701.3337	Account.
45577	1881,0701.3338	Joined to 42561.
45578	1881,0701.3339	Joined to 42418.
45579	1881,0701.3340	Economic.
45580	1881,0701.3341	Astronomical.
45581	1881,0701.3342	Omens; extispicy.
45582	1881,0701.3343	Measurement of a house.
45583	1881,0701.3344	Economic. Dar. Sippar.
45584	1881,0701.3345	Literary.
45585	1881,0701.3346	Joined to 43309.
45586	1881,0701.3347	Economic.

45587	1881,0701.3348	Economic.
45588	1881,0701.3349	Joined to 43433.
45589	1881,0701.3350	Economic.
45590	1881,0701.3351	Joined to 42451.
45591	1881,0701.3352	Account of dates.
45592	1881,0701.3353	Joined to 42418.
45593	1881,0701.3354	Limestone cylinder fragment. Probably an archaic "Kudurru". Beginning of last (and only) line: šu-nigin 30+[]. Pre-Sargonic. Tell Ibrahim = Kūtû?
45594	1881,0701.3355	Sealing, uninscribed; impressions of three stamp seals.
45595	1881,0701.3356	Sealing, uninscribed; three impressions of a stamp seal.
45596	1881,0701.3357	Sealing; fragment.
45597	1881,0701.3358	Sealing, uninscribed; impression of a stamp seal.
45598	1881,0701.3359	Literary cylinder; hymn to Nabû. + 45601. Gesche, AOAT 275, 688.
45599	1881,0701.3360	Old Babylonian. Lexical; personal names; lenticular tablet.
45600	1881,0701.3361	Medical prescription. (+) F.231. Finkel, Fs Lambert, 167-168, text 14 A.
45601	1881,0701.3362	Joined to 45598.
45602	1881,0701.3363	Hollow cylinder; royal inscription.
45603	1881,0701.3364	Hollow cylinder; royal inscription.
45604	1881,0701.3365	Cylinder; royal inscription.
45605	1881,0701.3366	Hollow cylinder; royal inscription.
45606	1881,0701.3367	Uninscribed decorated fragment, probably part of a small incense altar.
	1881,0701.3368 ff.	Nos. 3368-3392 are uninscribed objects; for 3383, 3385 and 3392 see Walker and Collon, Tell-ed-Der 3, 108, nos. 119-121.
100691	1881,0701.3393	Brick of Gudea. (Tello). CBI, no. 6.
90792a	1881,0701.3394	Brick of Gudea. (Tello). CBI, no. 6.
	1881,0701.3395	Clay dog with a votive inscription of Ninurta-rē'ušu to Gula for the life of Nazi-maruttaš. Nazi-maruttaš. Sippar. Sollberger, Gs Speiser, 191-195; Walker and Collon, Tell-ed-Der 3, 98, no. 23.
45607	1881,0701.3396	Neo-Assyrian. Brick of Šamši-Adad V. (Ashur or Nineveh). CBI, no. 161.
	1881,0701.3397 ff.	Nos. 3397-3405 are uninscribed objects.
90599	1881,0701.3406	Neo-Assyrian. Brick of Sargon II. (Babylon). + 90629. CBI, no. 76.
90646	1881,0701.3407	Brick of Nebuchadnezzar II. CBI, no. 106.
90684	1881,0701.3408	Brick of Nebuchadnezzar II. CBI, no. 106.
	1881,0701.3409 ff.	Nos. 3409-3421 are uninscribed objects.

91001	1881,0701.3422	Clay cover for the "Sun-god tablet" of Nabû-apla-iddina; also numbered 12137a. For other items in this group see 91000-91004 (1881,0428.33-34b). Sippar King, BBSt, 120-129 and pl. C, no. XXXVI; Walker and Collon, Tell ed-Dēr 3, 102-103, no. 61.

1881,0706 collection

The 1881,0706 collection was purchased from Joseph M. Shemtob. See J. E. Reade in CBTBM VI, p. xv. The register gives the provenance as Babylon for nos. 1-687 and as Babylonia for nos. 688-741.

45608	1881,0706.1	Astronomical Diary for SE 102. + 45717. LBAT 299-300; Sachs and Hunger, ADART II, no. -209 D.
45609	1881,0706.2	Astronomical; Goal Year Text; not datable. LBAT 1362; Hunger and Sachs, ADART VI, no. 163.
45610	1881,0706.3	Astronomical Diary for SE 101. LBAT 297; Sachs and Hunger, ADART II, no. -210.
45611	1881,0706.4	Astrological. LBAT 1616.
45612	1881,0706.5	Joined to 35320.
45613	1881,0706.6	Astronomical Diary for SE 129. LBAT 340; Sachs and Hunger, ADART II, no. -182.
45614	1881,0706.7	Lexical; Ḫḫ IX. MSL 9, 181.
45615	1881,0706.8	Astronomical Diary for SE 148. LBAT 527; Sachs and Hunger, ADART III, no. -163 A.
45616	1881,0706.9	Joined to 34362.
45617	1881,0706.10	Astronomical Diary for SE 121. + 45682. LBAT 326 (45617 only); Sachs and Hunger, ADART II, no. -190 B.
45618	1881,0706.11	Prayer to Marduk no. 1. Oshima, BPM, 142-157; Lambert, MC 24, no. 86.
45619	1881,0706.12	Historical inscription of Nebuchadnezzar II; three or more columns. Berger, AOAT 4/1, Nebukadnezar Tontafel-Fragment VI,1; S. Smith, RA 21, 78.
45620	1881,0706.13	Astrological omens; commentary; Enūma Anu Enlil, eclipses. + 1881,0706.38 + 45764. Reiner, Fs Borger (CM 10), 298-299.
45621	1881,0706.14	Joined to 35759.
45622	1881,0706.15	Astronomical Diary for SE 208. LBAT 482; Sachs and Hunger, ADART III, no. -103 A.
45623	1881,0706.16	Prayer.
45624	1881,0706.17	Liver omens; kakku. + 45831.
45625	1881,0706.18	Astronomical Diary. SE -/-/239. Sachs and Hunger, ADART III, no. -72.
45626	1881,0706.19	Astronomical; Goal Year Text for SE 131. LBAT 1246; Hunger and Sachs, ADART VI, no. 28.

45627	1881,0706.20	Astronomical Diary for SE 156. LBAT 398; Sachs and Hunger, ADART III, no. -155 B.
45628	1881,0706.21	Astronomical; lunar eclipse report for eclipse of 19 January 67 BC; prayer on upper edge. SE Arsaces 244. LBAT 1448; Stephenson, HEER, 161-162, 183, 204-205, 210; Hunger and Sachs, ADART V, no. 27.
45629	1881,0706.22	Issue of silver. SE Arsaces 10/12b/186. CT 49, 33, no. 143; van der Spek, Raḫimesu, 210-211, no. 1.
45630	1881,0706.23	Promissory note for barley. Dar 1/4/24. Babylon.
45631	1881,0706.24	Letter order; archive of Murānu; sealed. SE n.d. CT 49, 44, no. 171; Jursa, Persika 9, 156, 199; Mitchell and Searight, no. 648; Nisaba 28, no. 679.
45632	1881,0706.25	Astronomical Diary for SE 169; prayer on upper edge. LBAT 415; Sachs and Hunger, ADART III, no. -142 B.
45633	1881,0706.26	Receipt for payment of silver; sealed. SE Demetrius I 4/10/151. Babylon. CT 49, 32, no. 138; Nisaba 28, no. 661.
45634	1881,0706.27	Commentary on extispicy; ḫašu; prayer on upper edge. RN lost 12+/2/[]. Babylon. CT 41, 42; Nougayrol, RA 65, 81; cf. Oelsner, Materialien, 212.
45635	1881,0706.28	Astronomical Diary for SE 109. LBAT 306; Sachs and Hunger, ADART II, no. -202 A.
45636	1881,0706.29	Astronomical Diary for SE 125. + 45876. LBAT 332 (45636 only); Sachs and Hunger, ADART II, no. -186 B.
45637	1881,0706.30	Incantation. + 45814.
45638	1881,0706.31	Astronomical observations; eclipses or other lunar data. LBAT 1457; Hunger and Sachs, ADART V, no. 47.
45639	1881,0706.32	Lexical; god-list.
45640	1881,0706.33	Joined to 35115.
45641	1881,0706.34	Ritual and colophon. SE Antiochus III 1/7/1[]7?
45642	1881,0706.35	Copy of a letter to Ashurbanipal from the scholars of Borsippa; colophon: tablet of Bēl-uballissu copied by his son Nabû-mušētiq-uddi. Frame and George, Iraq 67, 265-270.
45643	1881,0706.36	Incantation.
45644	1881,0706.37	Field sale.
	1881,0706.38	Joined to 45620.
45645	1881,0706.39	Astronomical Diary for SE 189. LBAT 454; Sachs and Hunger, ADART III, no. -122 C.
45646	1881,0706.40	Joined to 34892.
45647	1881,0706.41	Joined to 34926.
45648	1881,0706.42	Lexical; Ea II. MSL 14, 245.

45649	1881,0706.43	Astronomical Diary for SE 58. LBAT 526.
45650	1881,0706.44	Astronomical Diary for SE 168. LBAT 407; Sachs and Hunger, ADART III, no. -143 B.
45651	1881,0706.45	Astronomical; Goal Year Text for SE 155. LBAT 1260; Hunger and Sachs, ADART VI, no. 44.
45652	1881,0706.46	Astrological; Enūma Anu Enlil 56, planets; copy (ḫe-pí eš-šú); colophon. + 1881,0706.222 + 283 + 398. LBAT 1553; Reiner, Fs Borger (CM 10), 298.
45653	1881,0706.47	Astronomical; fixed stars, relationship unclear. LBAT 1512.
45654	1881,0706.48	Astronomical Diary for SE 141. + 45747. LBAT 365 (45654 only); Sachs and Hunger, ADART II, no. -170 A; Stephenson, HEER, 14.
45655	1881,0706.49	Astronomical procedure text for the moon; System A. LBAT 88; ACT 200f; Ossendrijver, BMAPT, no. 59.
45656	1881,0706.50	Astronomical Diary for SE 229. + 1881,0706.58 + 65 + 69. LBAT 511; Sachs and Hunger, ADART III, no. -82 B.
45657	1881,0706.51	Mythological-calendrical text; four columns; colophon; dupl. 35188+.
45658	1881,0706.52	Astronomical; Mercury observations, perhaps for Philip years 5-6. + 45658. LBAT 1385; Hunger and Sachs, ADART V, no. 101 (not 45802).
45659	1881,0706.53	Astronomical Diary for SE 234. + 45685. LBAT 515-516; Sachs and Hunger, ADART III, no. -77 B.
45660	1881,0706.54	Astronomical Diary. LBAT 677.
45661	1881,0706.55	Astronomical; Goal Year Text for SE 149-151. + 46170. LBAT 1259 (45661 only); Hunger and Sachs, ADART VI, no. 41.
45662	1881,0706.56	Joined to 40094.
45663	1881,0706.57	Astronomical Diary. LBAT 646.
	1881,0706.58	Joined to 45656.
45664	1881,0706.59	Astrological; fixed star names of planets. + 45683. LBAT 1571-1572; Reiner, Fs Borger (CM 10), 298.
45665	1881,0706.60	Astrological; commentary on Enūma Anu Enlil 23 (24) and 24 (25). LBAT 1551; van Soldt, Solar Omens, 3 and 15 (Ca), 16 and 48 (Ce); Weidner, AfO 22, 65-66; Reiner, Fs Borger (CM 10), 298.
45666	1881,0706.61	Late astrology; intermediate astronomy; cf. 34059. LBAT 1617.
45667	1881,0706.62	Astronomical; lunar eclipse table. + 45856. LBAT 1451 (45667 only); Hunger and Sachs, ADART V, no. 33.
45668	1881,0706.63	Mathematical; table of squares of regular numbers. LBAT 1636; Aaboe, JCS 19, 83 and 85.

45669	1881,0706.64	Astronomical Diary.
	1881,0706.65	Joined to 45656.
45670	1881,0706.66	Promissory note for barley.
45671	1881,0706.67	Mantic dream ritual and incantation; two columns.
45672	1881,0706.68	Registered as "13 lines, illegible"; only traces of 5 lines now visible.
	1881,0706.69	Joined to 45656.
45673	1881,0706.70	Astronomical Diary. LBAT 173; Sachs and Hunger, ADART I, no. -375 A.
45674	1881,0706.71	Astronomical; Venus and lunar data from 463 to 392 BC. + 1881,0706.79 + 81 + 86 + 87 + 88 + 89 + 90 + 251 + 254 + 620 (+) 32299 (+) 42083. LBAT 1387; Hunger and Sachs, ADART V, no. 56.
45675	1881,0706.72	Lexical; syllabary.
45676	1881,0706.73	Astronomical Diary for SE 141. + 1881,0706.74 + 227 + 517 + 540. LBAT 369; Sachs and Hunger, ADART II, no. -170 H.
	1881,0706.74	Joined to 45676.
45677	1881,0706.75	Lexical; Ea; sign list.
45678	1881,0706.76	Astronomical Diary.
45679	1881,0706.77	Lexical.
45680	1881,0706.78	Omens; terrestrial. + 45835.
	1881,0706.79	Joined to 45674.
45681	1881,0706.80	Astronomical Diary. LBAT 607.
	1881,0706.81	Joined to 45674.
45682	1881,0706.82	Joined to 45617.
45683	1881,0706.83	Joined to 45664.
45684	1881,0706.84	Historical-literary text. Grayson, BHLT, 93-97.
45685	1881,0706.85	Joined to 45659.
	1881,0706.86	Joined to 45674.
	1881,0706.87	Joined to 45674.
	1881,0706.88	Joined to 45674.
	1881,0706.89	Joined to 45674.
	1881,0706.90	Joined to 45674.
45686	1881,0706.91	Ritual and incantations against field pests; dupl. Gurney, STT 243 and Weisberg, OIP 122, 168. + 55561. George and Taniguchi, Iraq 72, 126-132; cf. Lambert and Millard, Atra-ḫasīs, p. 27.
45687	1881,0706.92	Astronomical; Jupiter observations for SE 112-137. LBAT 1408; Hunger and Sachs, ADART V, no. 78.
45688	1881,0706.93	Astronomical; System A ephemeris; lunar eclipses from SE 137 to 160. LBAT 50; ACT 60, colophon Zj; Aaboe, KDVSMM 40/6 (1979) 11-15; Kugler, Mondrechnung, 55-60 and 117.
45689	1881,0706.94	Joined to 43025.

45690	1881,0706.95	Literary; "Nebuchadnezzar King of Justice". CT 46, 41-45, no. 45; Lambert, Iraq 27, 1-11; Schaudig, AOAT 256, 579-588.
45691	1881,0706.96	Astronomical Diary for SE 206. LBAT 478; Sachs and Hunger, ADART III, no. -105 B.
45692	1881,0706.97	Joined to 34223.
45693	1881,0706.98	Astronomical Diary for SE 187. + 45853. LBAT 450-451; Sachs and Hunger, ADART III, no. -124 B; van der Spek, RAL XLVIII, 404-405.
45694	1881,0706.99	Astronomical; new moons and full moons for SE 235. LBAT 68; ACT 123, colophon Zk; Kugler, Mondrechnung, 41-50 and pl. IV.
45695	1881,0706.100	Literary.
45696	1881,0706.101	Astronomical; Normal Star Almanac for SE 111. LBAT 1020; Hunger and Sachs, ADART VII, no. 47.
45697	1881,0706.102	Astrological omens; commentary; colophon. LBAT 1564; Pinches, PSBA 31 (1909) 25 and pl. IV; Weidner, HBA 118-121; Reiner, Fs Borger (CM 10), 299.
45698	1881,0706.103	Astronomical; Almanac for SE 236; prayer on upper edge. SE -/-/236. LBAT 1174; Rochberg-Halton, Or NS 58, 120-121; Hunger in Swerdlow, Astronomy, 94-96; Hunger and Sachs, ADART VII, no. 191.
45699	1881,0706.104	Joined to 35070.
45700	1881,0706.105	Joined to 34926.
45701	1881,0706.106	Joined to 34938.
45702	1881,0706.107	Astronomical procedure text for Jupiter and Venus. ACT 812; LBAT 140-145; Ossendrijver, BMAPT, no. 46.
45703	1881,0706.108	Astronomical Diary for SE 171 (Arsaces). + 45741 + 45748. LBAT 416-418; Sachs and Hunger, ADART III, no. -140 A.
45704	1881,0706.109	Late astrological; obv. fixed star names of planets; rev. omens? (+) 45711. LBAT 1618-1619.
45705	1881,0706.110	Medical. + 45779.
45706	1881,0706.111	Joined to 35531.
45707	1881,0706.112	Joined to 34629.
	1881,0706.113	Registered as "broken"; probably written off in the 1890s.
45708	1881,0706.114	Astronomical Diary for SE 186. + 1881,0706.158. LBAT 447; Sachs, PTRSL A.276, 49, fig. 9; Sachs and Hunger, ADART III, no. -125 A.
45709	1881,0706.115	Astronomical Diary for SE 174. + 1881,0706.192. LBAT 422; Sachs and Hunger, ADART III, no. -137 A.
	1881,0706.116	Joined to 40091.

45710	1881,0706.117	Joined to 34892.
45711	1881,0706.118	Late astrological; obv. fixed star names of planets; rev. omens? (+) 45704. LBAT 1618-1619.
45712	1881,0706.119	Astronomical Diary for SE 216. LBAT 491; Sachs and Hunger, ADART III, no. -95 C.
45713	1881,0706.120	Astronomical Diary for SE 155. LBAT 395; Sachs and Hunger, ADART III, no. -156 C.
45714	1881,0706.121	Lexical; Nabnītu excerpt; tablet W. MSL 16, 309, 339, 346.
45715	1881,0706.122	Astrological; Enūma Anu Enlil; planets and stars; colophon; AE 115; dated by Arsaces LUGAL KUR.KUR.MEŠ. SE Arsaces 5?/9/179. Reiner, Fs Borger (CM 10), 299.
45716	1881,0706.123	Astronomical; Almanac for SE 197. LBAT 1147; Hunger and Sachs, ADART VII, no. 181.
45717	1881,0706.124	Joined to 45608.
45718	1881,0706.125	Joined to 34655.
45719	1881,0706.126	Literary cylinder; hymn to Nabû. Gesche, AOAT 275, 688.
45720	1881,0706.127	Late astrology and number speculation. Steele, JCS 67, 209-210.
45721	1881,0706.128	Astronomical; schematic astronomical procedure relating daylight and shadows. Steele, SCIAMVS 14 (2013), 3-39
45722	1881,0706.129	Astronomical Diary for SE 129. + 55549 + 78826. LBAT 342 (as "78825" only); Sachs, PTRSL A.276, 49, fig. 12; Sachs and Hunger, ADART II, no. -182 C (with "+ 78825").
45723	1881,0706.130	Astronomical Diary for SE 63. LBAT 267; Sachs and Hunger, ADART II, no. -248; Stephenson, HEER, 134.
45724	1881,0706.131	Joined to 35089.
45725	1881,0706.132	Joined to 35110.
45726	1881,0706.133	Astronomical; planetary observations; one section 122 SE?; reverse lost; two or three columns; large fragment in very poor condition.
45727	1881,0706.134	Bilingual incantation.
45728	1881,0706.135	Astronomical procedure text; planets; colophon of Lâbâši. Artaxerxes. Kugler, SSB I, p. 45 and pl. II; Brown, CM 18, 305; Britton, AOAT 297, 21, 26.
	1881,0706.136	Joined to 45706.
45729	1881,0706.137	Astronomical; Almanac for SE 246. + 1881,0706.148 + 618. LBAT 1181; Hunger and Sachs, ADART VII, no. 200.
45730	1881,0706.138	Joined to 43023.

45731	1881,0706.139	Astronomical Diary for SE 155. + 45862. LBAT 393-394; Sachs and Hunger, ADART III, no. -156 B.
45732	1881,0706.140	Astronomical.
	1881,0706.141	Joined to 35726.
	1881,0706.142	Joined to 34799.
45733	1881,0706.143	Omens; commentary; cf. 35401.
45734	1881,0706.144	Joined to 35629.
45735	1881,0706.145	Unidentified; two broken fragments accidentally joined in antiquity; cf. 45776 and 46043.
45736	1881,0706.146	Medical. + 1881,0706.379 + 408.
45737	1881,0706.147	Magic ritual; é.gal.ku4.ra. + 46086.
	1881,0706.148	Joined to 45729.
45738	1881,0706.149	Astronomical Diary.
45739	1881,0706.150	Astrological. + 46123.
45740	1881,0706.151	Astronomical; Jupiter observations from Artaxerxes II year 43 to Alexander year 13. (+) 35531 + 45706 + 46031. LBAT 1398; Hunger and Sachs, ADART V, no. 66.
45741	1881,0706.152	Joined to 45703.
45742	1881,0706.153	Lexical; Erimḫuš V. + 45781 + 45837 + 45916 + 1881, 0706.600. MSL 17, 66.
45743	1881,0706.154	Astrological; Enūma Anu Enlil, eclipses. Reiner, Fs Borger (CM 10), 299.
	1881,0706.155	Joined to 34629.
45744	1881,0706.156	Bilingual incantation, Udug-ḫul 4, colophon. CT 16, 50; Geller, BAM 8, 133-173.
45745	1881,0706.157	Astronomical Diary for SE 175. LBAT 429; Aaboe, Centaurus 24 (1980), 23; Sachs and Hunger, ADART III, no. -136 B; Stephenson and Clark, AEAR, 31; Stephenson, HEER, 64-65 (fig. 3.9), 129-130, 136-137; Stephenson and Steele, JHA 37 (2006) 55-69.
	1881,0706.158	Joined to 45708.
45746	1881,0706.159	Prayer to Marduk no. 1; dupl. Lambert, AfO 19, 55-60; colophon noted in Strassmaier, ZA 7, 204 and Kugler, SSB 2, 447. (+) 34366. SE Arsaces []/7/277 (= AE 213); note Arsaces written 1.ḪAL-šá-kam, where ḪAL = buru8 = arû, to vomit. Babylon. Oshima, BPM, 142-157; Lambert, MC 24, no. 85.
45747	1881,0706.160	Joined to 45654.
45748	1881,0706.161	Joined to 45703.
45749	-	Ritual tablet for mīs pî; colophon. S. Smith, JRAS 1925, 37-60; Walker and Dick, SAALT I, 68-82. The original registration number of this tablet is unknown. It certainly does not correspond to 1881,0706.162 +.

-	1881,0706.162	+ 1881,0706.234 + 270. This tablet cannot be found at present. The register describes 1881,0706.162 as "calculations", a term generally used for astronomical texts.
45750	1881,0706.163	Astronomical Diary for SE 204; prayer on upper edge. + 45983 + 45984. LBAT 472-474; Sachs and Hunger, ADART III, no. -107 C.
45751	1881,0706.164	Commentary on astrological omens; cf. 42286. Reiner, Fs Borger (CM 10), 299.
	1881,0706.165	Joined to 34926.
45752	1881,0706.166	Astronomical Diary for SE 215. LBAT 488; Sachs and Hunger, ADART III, no. -96 C.
45753	1881,0706.167	Liver omens; kakku.
45754	1881,0706.168	Lexical; explanatory god-list; Diri commentary.
45755	1881,0706.169	Medical ritual; directions and rituals, apparently for treatment of diseases of women, barrenness, etc.; É-gal-ku4-ra.
45756	1881,0706.170	Astronomical; planetary observations; two columns; large, but in poor condition.
45757	1881,0706.171	Joined to 33024.
45758	1881,0706.172	Astronomical Diary for SE 45. LBAT 247; Sachs and Hunger, ADART I, no. -266 B.
45759	1881,0706.173	Lexical; synonym list.
45760	1881,0706.174	Astronomical Diary for SE 194. Sachs and Hunger, ADART III, no. -117 A.
45761	1881,0706.175	Astronomical Diary for SE 174. LBAT 423; Sachs and Hunger, ADART III, no. -137 B.
45762	1881,0706.176	Astronomical Diary for SE 193. Sachs and Hunger, ADART III, no. -118 B.
45763	1881,0706.177	Astronomical Diary for SE 55. + 45960 (+) 45959. LBAT 253 (45763) and 182 (45960); Sachs and Hunger, ADART II, no. -256.
45764	1881,0706.178	Joined to 45620.
45765	1881,0706.179	Astrological; Enūma Anu Enlil. Reiner, Fs Borger (CM 10), 299.
45766	1881,0706.180	Astronomical Diary. LBAT 208; Sachs and Hunger, ADART I, no. -322 A.
45767	1881,0706.181	Astronomical Diary for SE 128. Sachs and Hunger, ADART II, no. -183 D.
45768	1881,0706.182	Astronomical Diary for SE 156. LBAT 397; Sachs and Hunger, ADART III, no. -155 A.
45769	1881,0706.183	Joined to 34362.
45770	1881,0706.184	Astronomical Diary for SE 238. LBAT 518; Sachs and Hunger, ADART III, no. -73.

45771	1881,0706.185	Astronomical Diary for SE 204. (+) 34707 (+) 45961. LBAT 475; Sachs and Hunger, ADART III, no. -107 D.
45772	1881,0706.186	Astronomical Diary for SE 35. LBAT 240; Sachs and Hunger, ADART I, no. -276.
45773	1881,0706.187	Astronomical; Goal Year Text for SE 207. LBAT 1292; Hunger and Sachs, ADART VI, no. 78.
45774	1881,0706.188	Astronomical Diary for SE 153. LBAT 390; Sachs and Hunger, ADART III, no. -158 D.
45775	1881,0706.189	Astronomical observations; large, but in poor condition.
45776	1881,0706.190	Astronomical Diary?; with fragments of a second tablet accidentally joined in antiquity; cf. 45735 and 46043.
	1881,0706.191	Joined to 34104.
	1881,0706.192	Joined to 45709.
45777	1881,0706.193	Joined to 42799.
45778	1881,0706.194	Astronomical Diary for SE 204.
45779	1881,0706.195	Joined to 45705.
45780	1881,0706.196	Astronomical observations.
45781	1881,0706.197	Joined to 45742.
45782	1881,0706.198	Astronomical Diary for SE 145. Sachs and Hunger, ADART II, no. -166 A.
45783	1881,0706.199	Astronomical?
45784	1881,0706.200	Literary cylinder; hymn to Nabû. Gesche, AOAT 275, 688.
45785	1881,0706.201	Astronomical Diary for SE 150. Sachs and Hunger, ADART III, no. -161 C.
45786	1881,0706.202	Astronomical; Goal Year Text for SE 129. (+) 45909 (+) 46113 + 46146. LBAT *1244-*1245 and 1304; Hunger and Sachs, ADART VI, no. 27.
45787	1881,0706.203	Astronomical; Goal Year Text for SE 105. + 46057. LBAT 1229-1230; Hunger and Sachs, ADART VI, no. 14.
45788	1881,0706.204	Astronomical Diary.
	1881,0706.205	Joined to 35570.
45789	1881,0706.206	Mathematical; table of reciprocals.
45790	1881,0706.207	Astronomical; lunar ephemeris; System A. ACT 16b.
45791	1881,0706.208	Prayer.
45792	1881,0706.209	Astronomical.
45793	1881,0706.210	Cylinder; inscription of Esarhaddon on the restoration of the Eanna temple at Uruk; previously numbered 12173 and 91031. Esar. Borger, AfO Bieh. 9, 73-75 “Uruk A”; Frame, RIMB 2.6.31.15.1; Leichty, RINAP 4.133.1.

	1881,0706.211	Joined to 34171.
45794	1881,0706.212	Astronomical; Goal Year Text for SE 168. + 45834. LBAT 1265a; Hunger and Sachs, ADART VI, no. 51.
45795	1881,0706.213	Astronomical Diary. + 1881,0706.260 + 46222.
45796	1881,0706.214	Unidentified; mostly illegible.
45797	1881,0706.215	Astronomical Diary.
45798	1881,0706.216	Astronomical Diary.
45799	1881,0706.217	Liver omens; manzāzu tablet V. U. S. Koch-Westenholz, Babylonian Liver Omens, 103, no. 5a, and pl. VIII.
45800	1881,0706.218	Astronomical Diary.
45801	1881,0706.219	Astronomical Diary.
45802	1881,0706.220	Joined to 45658.
45803	1881,0706.221	Historical(?), Seleucid; mentions šatammu; possibly lengthy historical section of an Astronomical Diary.
	1881,0706.222	Joined to 45652.
45804	1881,0706.223	Astronomical Diary for SE 147. + 45973 + 46038. Sachs and Hunger, ADART II, no. -164 A.
45805	1881,0706.224	Astronomical.
45806	1881,0706.225	School text; lexical; god-list. 1/7/-.
45807	1881,0706.226	Astronomical; Greek letter phenomena of Saturn; two columns. (+) 42878. Steele, JHA 41 (2010) 261-268.
	1881,0706.227	Joined to 45676.
45808	1881,0706.228	Astronomical Diary for SE 49. + 55518. LBAT 248; Sachs and Hunger, ADART I, no. -262.
45809	1881,0706.229	Joined to 34691.
45810	1881,0706.230	Astronomical; procedure text involving ziqpu stars.
45811	1881,0706.231	Lexical.
45812	1881,0706.232	Astrological; Enūma Anu Enlil; eclipses; adir. Reiner, Fs Borger (CM 10), 299.
45813	1881,0706.233	Astronomical Diary for SE 188. Sachs and Hunger, ADART III, no. -123 C.
	1881,0706.234	Joined to 45749.
45814	1881,0706.235	Joined to 45637.
45815	1881,0706.236	Astronomical; Goal Year Text; not datable. Hunger and Sachs, ADART VI, no. 164.
45816	1881,0706.237	Astronomical Diary. LBAT 170; Sachs and Hunger, ADART I, no. -380 B.
45817	1881,0706.238	Astronomical Diary.
45818	1881,0706.239	Astronomical procedure text for the moon; System B. SE 243. + 45838. + 46192. ACT 194a and 221, colophon Zkc; Jones, AHES 29 (1983) 1-11; Ossendrijver, BMAPT, no. 94.
45819	1881,0706.240	Astronomical Diary for SE 146. Sachs and Hunger, ADART II, no. -165 B.

45820	1881,0706.241	Joined to 34809.
45821	1881,0706.242	Joined to 42961.
45822	1881,0706.243	Astronomical Diary.
45823	1881,0706.244	Unidentified; mostly illegible.
45824	1881,0706.245	Astronomical; Goal Year Text; not datable. Hunger and Sachs, ADART VI, no. 165.
45825	1881,0706.246	Astronomical?
45826	1881,0706.247	Astronomical Diary.
45827	1881,0706.248	Astronomical; Almanac for SE 189. + 46094. LBAT 1141-1142; Hunger and Sachs, ADART VII, no. 176.
45828	1881,0706.249	Astronomical Diary.
45829	1881,0706.250	Astronomical Diary for SE 150. (+) 34140 (+) 34180. Sachs and Hunger, ADART III, no. -161 A.
	1881,0706.251	Joined to 45674.
45830	1881,0706.252	Astronomical Diary for SE 179. Sachs and Hunger, ADART III, no. -132 A.
45831	1881,0706.253	Joined to 45624.
	1881,0706.254	Joined to 45674.
45832	1881,0706.255	Astronomical Diary.
45833	1881,0706.256	Astronomical Diary.
45834	1881,0706.257	Joined to 45794.
45835	1881,0706.258	Joined to 45680.
45836	1881,0706.259	Astronomical Diary; historical section mentions Demetrius.
	1881,0706.260	Joined to 45795.
45837	1881,0706.261	Joined to 45742.
45838	1881,0706.262	Joined to 45818.
45839	1881,0706.263	Astronomical; Almanac for SE 190. LBAT 1144; Hunger and Sachs, ADART VII, no. 177.
45840	1881,0706.264	Astronomical Diary for SE 58. + 45945 (+) 33445. LBAT 261; Sachs and Hunger, ADART II, no. -253 A.
45840 a	1881,0706.264 a	Astronomical.
45841	1881,0706.265	Astronomical Diary.
45842	1881,0706.266	Incantation and ritual; cf. 45671.
45843	1881,0706.267	Liver omens; weapon of Enlil.
45844	1881,0706.268	Astronomical.
45845	1881,0706.269	Astronomical; lunar eclipse report for eclipse of 1 June 120 BC; prayer on upper edge. SE Arsaces 14/2/192. LBAT 1442; Stephenson, HEER, 172, 183, 189; Hunger and Sachs, ADART V, no. 22.
	1881,0706.270	Joined to 45749.
45846	1881,0706.271	Astronomical Diary for SE 132. + 46062. LBAT 350 (45846 only); Sachs and Hunger, ADART II, no. -179 E.

	1881,0706.272	Joined to 34580.
45847	1881,0706.273	Astronomical Diary for SE 216. LBAT 492; Sachs and Hunger, ADART III, no. -95 E. Stephenson, HEER, 159-160.
45848	1881,0706.274	Astronomical Diary for SE 147. + 45907. Sachs and Hunger, ADART II, no. -164 C.
	1881,0706.275	Nothing registered.
45849	1881,0706.276	Astronomical; new moons and full moons for two years. (+) 46237. ACT 123a, colophon Zka.
	1881,0706.277	Joined to 34580.
45850	1881,0706.278	Astronomical Diary for SE 187. + 1881,0706.363. LBAT 449; Sachs and Hunger, ADART III, no. -124 A.
45851	1881,0706.279	Joined to 34081.
45852	1881,0706.280	Astronomical Diary for SE 120. + 46079. Sachs and Hunger, ADART II, no. -191 A.
45853	1881,0706.281	Joined to 45693.
45854	1881,0706.282	Astronomical Diary for SE 122. LBAT 328 (obv. only); Sachs and Hunger, ADART II, no. -189 A.
	1881,0706.283	Joined to 45652.
45855	1881,0706.284	Joined to 36308.
45856	1881,0706.285	Joined to 45667.
45857	1881,0706.286	Astronomical Diary for SE 199; prayer on upper edge. LBAT 461; Sachs and Hunger, ADART III, no. -112.
45858	1881,0706.287	Astronomical Diary. Sachs and Hunger, ADART I, no. -329 B.
45859	1881,0706.288	Lexical; Hg VII A-B. MSL 9, 185.
45860	1881,0706.289	Lexical; Nabnītu Excerpt III. MSL 16, 316.
45861	1881,0706.290	Astronomical; lunar procedure text for the length of the Saros. Brack-Bernsen and Steele, Centaurus 47 (2005) 181-206; Steele, AOAT 297, 405-420.
45862	1881,0706.291	Joined to 45731.
45863	1881,0706.292	Astronomical Diary for SE 232. LBAT 513; Sachs and Hunger, ADART III, no. -79.
	1881,0706.293	Joined to 34789.
45864	1881,0706.294	Astrological omens; Sin.
45865	1881,0706.295	Astronomical; Jupiter, first visibility; System B. ACT 625. Probably (+) 42002.
45866	1881,0706.296	Joined to 34887.
	1881,0706.297	Joined to 34789.
45867	1881,0706.298	Astrological omens; apodoses mention eclipses.
45868	1881,0706.299	Omen apodoses (public). (+) 45939.
45869	1881,0706.300	Unidentified; possibly a copy.

45870	1881,0706.301	Astronomical Diary for SE 128. + 45904 (+) 46017. Sachs and Hunger, ADART II, no. -183 C.
45871	1881,0706.302	Astrological omens; commentary.
45872	1881,0706.303	Liver omens, pān tākalti tablet VI. U. S. Koch-Westenholz, Babylonian Liver Omens, 343, no. 64.
45873	1881,0706.304	Astronomical?
45874	1881,0706.305	Astronomical Diary for SE 200. (+) 46196. LBAT 464; Sachs and Hunger, ADART III, no. -111 D.
45875	1881,0706.306	Astronomical Diary.
45876	1881,0706.307	Joined to 45636.
45877	1881,0706.308	Astronomical; Goal Year Text; not datable. Hunger and Sachs, ADART VI, no. 166.
45878	1881,0706.309	Astronomical Diary. Sachs and Hunger, ADART I, no. -322 C.
45879	1881,0706.310	Astronomical Diary for SE 151. Sachs and Hunger, ADART III, no. -160 C.
45880	1881,0706.311	Astronomical; Goal Year Text; not datable. Hunger and Sachs, ADART VI, no. 167.
45881	1881,0706.312	Astronomical; Goal Year Text for SE 175. LBAT 1271; Hunger and Sachs, ADART VI, no. 55.
45882	1881,0706.313	Astronomical Diary.
45883	1881,0706.314	Literary; Gilgameš IV. CT 46, 30, no. 22; Landsberger, RA 62, 96-97; Garelli, Gilgameš, 124 (copy by Wiseman), 127-128; George, Gilgamesh II, pl. 71.
45884	1881,0706.315	Mathematical table. ACT 1001; Ossendrijver, JCS 66, 149-165 and pls.
45885	1881,0706.316	Astronomical Diary.
45886	1881,0706.317	Astronomical?
45887	1881,0706.318	Lexical.
45888	1881,0706.319	Astronomical.
45889	1881,0706.320	Astronomical Diary.
45890	1881,0706.321	Astronomical Diary. + 1881,0706.343.
45891	1881,0706.322	Omens; Šumma izbu 9. Leichty, TCS 4, 238; De Zorzi, Šumma izbu, 938.
45892	1881,0706.323	Letter from Bēl-bullissu. SE 23/12/183. CT 49, 32, no. 142.
45893	1881,0706.324	Joined to 42944.
45894	1881,0706.325	Astrological; Enūma Anu Enlil 6. Reiner, Fs Borger (CM 10), 299; Verderame, Nisaba 2, 202 and Fol. IX 5.
45895	1881,0706.326	Astronomical Diary.
45896	1881,0706.327	Astronomical Diary.
45897	1881,0706.328	Astronomical?
45898	1881,0706.329	Astronomical Diary for SE 153. LBAT 389; Sachs and Hunger, ADART III, no. -158 B.

45899	1881,0706.330	Joined to 35500.
	1881,0706.331	Joined to 34580.
45900	1881,0706.332	Astrological; commentary on Enūma Anu Enlil 14; colophon of Bēl-aba-uṣur / Bēl-balāssu-iqbi. Steele and Brack-Bernsen, in Fs Slotsky, 257-262.
	1881,0706.333	Joined to 34580.
45901	1881,0706.334	Joined to 34616.
45902	1881,0706.335	Astronomical; procedure text? and ephemeris? ACT 1007.
45903	1881,0706.336	Astrological.
45904	1881,0706.337	Joined to 45870.
45905	1881,0706.338	Astronomical.
45906	1881,0706.339	Astronomical Diary. LBAT 214.
45907	1881,0706.340	Joined to 45848.
45908	1881,0706.341	Unidentified; mostly illegible.
45909	1881,0706.342	Astronomical; Goal Year Text for SE 129. (+) 45786 (+) 46113 + 46146. LBAT *1244-*1245 and 1304; Hunger and Sachs, ADART VI, no. 27.
	1881,0706.343	Joined to 45890.
	1881,0706.344	Joined to 35531.
45910	1881,0706.345	Astronomical Diary.
45911	1881,0706.346	Astronomical Diary for SE 171 (Arsaces). + 1881, 0706.453 + 454 + 578 + 581. LBAT 421; Sachs and Hunger, ADART III, no. -140 D.
45912	1881,0706.347	Astronomical?
45913	1881,0706.348	Lexical; Ḫḫ I. MSL 9, 157.
45914	1881,0706.349	Astronomical Diary.
45915	1881,0706.350	Astronomical; star list.
45916	1881,0706.351	Joined to 45742.
45917	1881,0706.352	Omens; extispicy?
45918	1881,0706.353	Omens; Šumma ālu?;] ina É.BI is-si [.
45919	1881,0706.354	Astronomical; Almanac for SE 241. LBAT 1176; Hunger and Sachs, ADART VII, no. 194.
45920	1881,0706.355	Mathematical or astronomical; procedure or problems.
45921	1881,0706.356	Astronomical Diary.
45922	1881,0706.357	Astronomical; MUL.APIN. Hunger and Pingree, AfO Beih. 24, MUL-APIN text L; Reiner, Fs Borger (CM 10), 299; Hunger and Steele, MUL.APIN, 21.
45923	1881,0706.358	Astronomical Diary.
45924	1881,0706.359	Astronomical?
45925	1881,0706.360	Astronomical.
45926	1881,0706.361	Astronomical Diary for SE 131. Sachs and Hunger, ADART II, no. -180 B.

45927	1881,0706.362	Astronomical Diary for SE 27. + 1881,0706.384 + 46260. LBAT 229; Sachs and Hunger, ADART I, no. -284.
	1881,0706.363	Joined to 45850.
45928	1881,0706.364	Astronomical.
45929	1881,0706.365	Astronomical; Almanac for SE 234. Hunger and Sachs, ADART VII, no. 190.
45930	1881,0706.366	Astronomical; lunar table. Aaboe, KDVSMM 38/6 (1971) 13-20, pl. I; Aaboe, KDVSMM 40/6 (1979) 9.
45931	1881,0706.367	Astronomical Diary. + 45966.
45932	1881,0706.368	Omens.
45933	1881,0706.369	Joined to 34755.
45934	1881,0706.370	Astronomical.
45935	1881,0706.371	Astronomical procedure; random? numbers on reverse; rounded tablet, late Seleucid script.
45936	1881,0706.372	Astronomical Diary.
45937	1881,0706.373	Astronomical Diary.
45938	1881,0706.374	Unidentified.
45939	1881,0706.375	Astrological omens. (+) 45868.
45940	1881,0706.376	Astronomical Diary for SE 170. LBAT 414; Sachs and Hunger, ADART III, no. -141 G.
45941	1881,0706.377	Akkadian incantation.
45942	1881,0706.378	Astronomical Diary.
	1881,0706.379	Joined to 45736.
45943	1881,0706.380	Astronomical.
45944	1881,0706.381	Astronomical.
45945	1881,0706.382	Joined to 45840.
45946	1881,0706.383	Unidentified; mostly illegible.
	1881,0706.384	Joined to 45927.
45947	1881,0706.385	Astronomical Diary.
45947a	1881,0706.385a	Astronomical Diary for SE 189. Sachs and Hunger, ADART III, no. -122 B.
	1881,0706.386	Joined to 34580.
45948	1881,0706.387	Ritual for ridding land of an evil influence; colophon. Maul, Bagh Forsch 18, 324ff.
45949	1881,0706.388	Astronomical Diary for SE 64. LBAT 268; Sachs and Hunger, ADART II, no. -247; A. Stephenson, HEER, 199.
45950	1881,0706.389	Literary cylinder; cf. 45969.
45951	1881,0706.390	Astronomical?
45952	1881,0706.391	Astronomical Diary. + 46195.
45953	1881,0706.392	Astronomical; Almanac for SE 234. + 46021. LBAT 1167-1168; Hunger and Sachs, ADART VII, no. 190.
45954	1881,0706.393	Astronomical Diary.
45955	1881,0706.394	Joined to 35024.

45956	1881,0706.395	Astronomical Diary.
45957	1881,0706.396	Omens; birds?; upper edge; colophon. SE Antiochus III & Antiochus []/[]/100+.
45958	1881,0706.397	Astronomical Diary.
	1881,0706.398	Joined to 45652.
	1881,0706.399	Joined to 42961.
45959	1881,0706.400	Astronomical Diary for SE 55. (+) 45763 + 45690. LBAT 254; Sachs and Hunger, ADART II, no. -256.
45960	1881,0706.401	Joined to 45763.
45961	1881,0706.402	Astronomical Diary for SE 204. (+) 34707 (+) 45771. LBAT 476; Sachs and Hunger, ADART III, no. -107 D.
45962	1881,0706.403	Astronomical Diary, mentions death of Alexander. LBAT 209; Sachs and Hunger, ADART I, no. -322 B.
45963	1881,0706.404	Lexical.
45964	1881,0706.405	Astronomical Diary.
45965	1881,0706.406	Astronomical Diary.
45966	1881,0706.407	Joined to 45931.
	1881,0706.408	Joined to 45736.
45967	1881,0706.409	Astronomical Diary.
45968	1881,0706.410	Astronomical Diary.
45969	1881,0706.411	Literary cylinder; cf. 45950.
45970	1881,0706.412	Lexical; syllabary.
45971	1881,0706.413	Astronomical Diary.
45972	1881,0706.414	Astronomical; Almanac for SE 195. + 46013. LBAT 1146; Hunger and Sachs, ADART VII, no. 180.
45973	1881,0706.415	Joined to 45804.
45974	1881,0706.416	Astronomical; ACT ephemeris with colophon; cf. 46042.
45975	1881,0706.417	Astronomical Diary.
	1881,0706.418	Missing; not found by L W King in the 1890s.
45976	1881,0706.419	Astronomical; System A ephemeris; excerpts for at least SE 181 to 185. ACT 75.
45977	1881,0706.420	Joined to 42744.
45978	1881,0706.421	Astronomical Diary.
45979	1881,0706.422	Astronomical Diary.
45980	1881,0706.423	Astronomical procedure text; Mercury, evening and morning star for SE 133 to 153. + 1881,0706.434. ACT 301 and 820a; Ossendrijver, BMAPT, no. 1.
45981	1881,0706.424	List of workmen.
45982	1881,0706.425	Astronomical; Almanac for SE 355; this is the latest known tablet expressly dating by the Seleucid Era. SE -/-/355. LBAT 1198; Sachs, AOAT 25, 386-389, pl. XVI; Hunger and Sachs, ADART VII, no. 215.
45983	1881,0706.426	Joined to 45750.

45984	1881,0706.427	Joined to 45750.
45985	1881,0706.428	Joined to 34892.
45986	1881,0706.429	Literary; Praise of Babylon; cf. 36646. + 46063 + 46121 + 46166.
45987	1881,0706.430	Astronomical Diary.
45988	1881,0706.431	Astronomical Diary for SE 139.
45989	1881,0706.432	Astronomical Diary; historical section mentions Arsaces. SE.
45990	1881,0706.433	Astronomical procedure text for the moon; kunnu, turru, ḫepi, etc.; cf. TCL 6, no. 11.
	1881,0706.434	Joined to 45980.
45991	1881,0706.435	Omens.
45992	1881,0706.436	Joined to 34629.
45993	1881,0706.437	Astronomical; Goal Year Text for SE 205. Hunger and Sachs, ADART VI, no. 75.
45994	1881,0706.438	Astrological omens.
45995	1881,0706.439	Joined to 35110.
45996	1881,0706.440	Astronomical Diary.
45997	1881,0706.441	Bilingual literary; hymn to Nanâ. Reiner, JNES 33, 221-236.
45998	1881,0706.442	Astronomical Diary for SE 189. + 46049. Sachs and Hunger, ADART III, no. -122 A.
45998a	1881,0706.442a	Astronomical Diary; fragment.
45998b	1881,0706.442b	Astronomical Diary; fragment.
45999	1881,0706.443	Astronomical; Jupiter observations for SE 130-132. Hunger and Sachs, ADART V, no. 80.
46000	1881,0706.444	Astrological; Enūma Anu Enlil; Sin. Reiner, Fs Borger (CM 10), 299.
46001	1881,0706.445	Hemerology.
46002	1881,0706.446	Literary; Gilgameš VII. CT 46, 31, no. 23; Landsberger, RA 62, 123 and 128; George, Gilgamesh II, pl. 77.
46003	1881,0706.447	Astronomical Diary for SE 151. LBAT 385; Sachs and Hunger, ADART III, no. -160 A; Stephenson, HEER, 157.
46004	1881,0706.448	Astronomical Diary.
46005	1881,0706.449	Historical cylinder; duplicate not yet identified.
46006	1881,0706.450	Astronomical Diary for SE 64. LBAT 269; Sachs and Hunger, ADART II, no. -247 B.
46007	1881,0706.451	Astronomical Diary.
46008	1881,0706.452	Joined to 42744.
	1881,0706.453	Joined to 45911.
	1881,0706.454	Joined to 45911.
46009	1881,0706.455	Astronomical Diary. LBAT 172; Sachs and Hunger, ADART I, no. -379.

46010	1881,0706.456	Astronomical; System A; lunar ephemeris. ACT 13a.
46011	1881,0706.457	Medical; colophon.
46012	1881,0706.458	Astronomical; Mercury observations; Goal Year Text?
46013	1881,0706.459	Joined to 45972.
46014	1881,0706.460	Astronomical.
46015	1881,0706.461	Astronomical; lunar ephemeris; System A; eclipses or excerpts for several years. ACT 55; Aaboe, KDVSMM 38/6 (1971) 20-26 and KDVSMM 40/6 (1979) 15-16.
46016	1881,0706.462	Joined to 35629.
46017	1881,0706.463	Astronomical Diary for SE 128. (+) 45870 + 45904. Sachs and Hunger, ADART II, no. -183 C.
46018	1881,0706.464	Joined to 35189.
46019	1881,0706.465	Astronomical; Mercury, morning star for (at least) five years; System A1. ACT 305.
46020	1881,0706.466	Omens; apodoses.
46021	1881,0706.467	Joined to 45953.
46022	1881,0706.468	Astronomical; procedure?
46023	1881,0706.469	Astronomical Diary for SE 162; historical section mentions Demetrius. + 46027.
46024	1881,0706.470	Astronomical Diary.
46025	1881,0706.471	Astrological omens. Reiner, Fs Borger (CM 10), 299
46026	1881,0706.472	Omens; Šumma izbu 14. De Zorzi, Šumma izbu, 698.
46027	1881,0706.473	Joined to 46023.
46028	1881,0706.474	Sumerian literary.
46029	1881,0706.475	Astronomical Diary for SE 200. + 46035 + 46084. LBAT 463 (part of 46035); Sachs and Hunger, ADART III, no. -111 B.
46030	1881,0706.476	Astronomical Diary for SE 62. + 1881,0706.495. LBAT 266; Sachs and Hunger, ADART II, no. -249 B.
46031	1881,0706.477	Joined to 35531.
46032	1881,0706.478	Omens; Iqqur īpuš, Ayyaru. Cf. Reiner, Fs Borger (CM 10), 299.
46033	1881,0706.479	Joined to 34926.
46034	1881,0706.480	Astronomical Diary.
46035	1881,0706.481	Joined to 46029.
46036	1881,0706.482	Omens.
46036a	1881,0706.482a	Astronomical Diary.
46037	1881,0706.483	Astronomical?
46038	1881,0706.484	Joined to 45804.
46039	1881,0706.485	Astronomical; planetary and lunar procedure text?
46040	1881,0706.486	Astronomical Diary for SE 216. LBAT 490; Sachs and Hunger, ADART III, no. -95 A.

46041	1881,0706.487	Astronomical; Normal Star Almanac for SE 211. Hunger and Sachs, ADART VII, no. 97.
46042	1881,0706.488	Astronomical; lunar ephemeris; System A. + 48088. ACT 7a. 48088 is unpublished.
46043	1881,0706.489	Astronomical; Almanac for SE 244; two broken fragments accidentally joined in antiquity; cf. 45776 and 45735 and see the photograph in Reade, Iraq 55, 54 fig. 17. + 46105. LBAT 1178 (copy of 46043 rev. only) and 1186 (46103); Hunger and Sachs, ADART VII, no. 197; Reade, Iraq 55, 54 fig. 17 (photograph of 46043).
46044	1881,0706.490	Astronomical.
46045	1881,0706.491	Astronomical Diary.
46046	1881,0706.492	Joined to 33746.
46047	1881,0706.493	Joined to 43025.
46048	1881,0706.494	Economic? Now disintegrating.
	1881,0706.495	Joined to 46030.
46049	1881,0706.496	Joined to 45998.
46050	1881,0706.497	Astronomical; Almanac for SE 254. LBAT 1184; Hunger and Sachs, ADART VII, no. 204.
46051	1881,0706.498	Astronomical Diary for SE 126. Sachs and Hunger, ADART II, no. -185 B.
46052	1881,0706.499	Astronomical Diary.
46053	1881,0706.500	Astronomical Diary.
46054	1881,0706.501	Omens.
46055	1881,0706.502	Astronomical Diary; historical section mentions Arsaces. SE.
46056	1881,0706.503	Astronomical procedure text for Jupiter. ACT 819a; Ossendrijver, BMAPT, no. 39.
46057	1881,0706.504	Joined to 45787.
46058	1881,0706.505	Astronomical Diary.
46059	1881,0706.506	Literary.
46060	1881,0706.507	Ritual. George, BTT, pl. 51; Linssen, CM 25, 324.
46061	1881,0706.508	Astronomical Diary.
46062	1881,0706.509	Joined to 45846.
46063	1881,0706.510	Joined to 45986.
46064	1881,0706.511	Astronomical Diary.
46065	1881,0706.512	Astronomical Diary; historical section mentions Antiochus.
46066	1881,0706.513	Astronomical Diary.
46067	1881,0706.514	Medical.
46068	1881,0706.515	Astronomical Diary.
46069	1881,0706.516	Astronomical?
	1881,0706.517	Joined to 45676.

46070	1881,0706.518	Tintir V. George, BTT, pl. 17; Gurney, Iraq 36, 40 and pl. VII.
46071	1881,0706.519	Unidentified.
46072	1881,0706.520	Incantation and ritual.
46073	1881,0706.521	Literary.
46074	1881,0706.522	Unidentified; mostly illegible.
46075	1881,0706.523	Unidentified; mostly illegible.
46076	1881,0706.524	Astronomical; lunar ephemeris; System A. ACT 6.
46077	1881,0706.525	Astronomical Diary.
46078	1881,0706.526	Sealing, two personal names, with stamp seal impressions. Mitchell and Searight, no. 345; Nisaba 28, no. 663.
46079	1881,0706.527	Joined to 45852.
46080	1881,0706.528	Astronomical Diary? Sachs, PTRSL A.276, 49, fig. 14.
46081	1881,0706.529	Astronomical Diary.
46082	1881,0706.530	Joined to 42768.
46083	1881,0706.531	Astronomical; star catalogue. Sachs, JCS 6, 146-150; Brown, CM 18, 305; Roughton et al., AHES 58 (2004) 537-572.
46084	1881,0706.532	Joined to 46029.
46085	1881,0706.533	Incantation.
46086	1881,0706.534	Joined to 45737.
46087	1881,0706.535	Astronomical Diary.
46088	1881,0706.536	Astronomical; flake from two column tablet.
46089	1881,0706.537	Astronomical Diary.
46090	1881,0706.538	Chronicle.
46091	1881,0706.539	Omens; terrestrial.
	1881,0706.540	Joined to 45676.
46092	1881,0706.541	Astrological; Enūma Anu Enlil; eclipses. Reiner, Fs Borger (CM 10), 299.
46093	1881,0706.542	Astronomical; Goal Year Text for SE 131. + 1881, 0706.611.
46094	1881,0706.543	Joined to 45827.
46095	1881,0706.544	Tintir V 100-104.
46096	1881,0706.545	Astronomical Diary.
46097	1881,0706.546	Joined to 34859.
46098	1881,0706.547	Astronomical; Goal Year Text; not datable. Hunger and Sachs, ADART VI, no. 168
46099	1881,0706.548	Astronomical; Mercury observations for at least SE 6-7. + 46172. Hunger and Sachs, ADART V, no. 67.
46100	1881,0706.549	Astronomical; Goal Year Text; not datable. Hunger and Sachs, ADART VI, no. 169.
46101	1881,0706.550	Astronomical?
46102	1881,0706.551	Omens; extispicy?; apodoses.

46103	1881,0706.552	Astronomical; Goal Year Text; not datable. + 1881, 0706.613. Hunger and Sachs, ADART VI, no. 170.
46104	1881,0706.553	Astronomical Diary.
46105	1881,0706.554	Joined to 46043.
46106	1881,0706.555	Astronomical; Almanac for SE 179. LBAT 1136; Hunger and Sachs, ADART VII, no. 172.
	1881,0706.556	Joined to 34859.
46107	1881,0706.557	Astronomical Diary.
46108	1881,0706.558	Omen apodoses.
46109	1881,0706.559	Astrological?; Enūma Anu Enlil? Reiner, Fs Borger (CM 10), 299.
46110	1881,0706.560	Astronomical Diary. Sachs, PTRSL A.276, 49, fig. 14.
46111	1881,0706.561	Literary cylinder. (+) 42768.
46112	1881,0706.562	Astronomical; new moons? for SE 176? ACT 119.
46113	1881,0706.563	Astronomical; Goal Year Text for SE 129. + 1881, 0706.606 + 46146 (+) 45786 (+) 45909. LBAT *1244-*1245 and 1304; Hunger and Sachs, ADART VI, no. 27.
46114	1881,0706.564	Colophon only. SE Antiochus IV and Antiochus []/[]/139.
	1881,0706.565	Joined to 42961.
46115	1881,0706.566	Astronomical Diary. + 46147.
46116	1881,0706.567	Astronomical procedure text for the moon; System A; prayer on upper edge. ACT 207a, colophon Zra; Ossendrijver, BMAPT, no. 69.
46117	1881,0706.568	Astronomical Diary.
46118	1881,0706.569	Colophon.
46119	1881,0706.570	Literary; instructions for wisdom; secrets; scribeship.
	1881,0706.571	Joined to 35843.
46120	1881,0706.572	Chronicle of the years SE 140-141, mentioning pulitai (Greek citizens). SE. BCHP 13.
46121	1881,0706.573	Joined to 45986.
46122	1881,0706.574	Astronomical?
46123	1881,0706.575	Joined to 45739.
46124	1881,0706.576	Astronomical?
46125	1881,0706.577	Astronomical Diary.
	1881,0706.578	Joined to 45911.
46126	1881,0706.579	Astronomical; Goal Year Text for SE 129. + 46163. LBAT 1274; Hunger and Sachs, ADART VI, nos. 59 and 171.
46127	1881,0706.580	Astronomical Diary for SE 200. Sachs and Hunger, ADART III, no. -111 C.
	1881,0706.581	Joined to 45911.
46128	1881,0706.582	Missing.

46129	1881,0706.583	Astronomical Diary.
46130	1881,0706.584	Astronomical Diary.
46131	1881,0706.585	Astronomical Diary.
46132	1881,0706.586	Astronomical?
46133	1881,0706.587	Joined to 35110.
46134	1881,0706.588	Astrological omens.
	1881,0706.589	Joined to 34580.
46135	1881,0706.590	Joined to 34081.
46136	1881,0706.591	Liver omens; padānu. + 46155.
46137	1881,0706.592	Astronomical.
46138	1881,0706.593	List of market prices. Slotsky and Wallenfels, Tallies and Trends, text 17.
46139	1881,0706.594	Medical omens; Sa-gig III. Heeßel, AOAT 43, 140.
46140	1881,0706.595	Astronomical; Goal Year Text.
46141	1881,0706.596	Astronomical Diary; mentions Demetrius and Arsaces. SE. + 46182 + 46186 + 46213 + 46273.
46142	1881,0706.597	Joined to 43023.
46143	1881,0706.598	Astronomical Diary.
46144	1881,0706.599	Lexical; giš.
	1881,0706.600	Joined to 45742.
46145	1881,0706.601	Joined to 35110.
46146	1881,0706.602	Joined to 46113.
46147	1881,0706.603	Joined to 46115.
46148	1881,0706.604	Astronomical Diary.
46149	1881,0706.605	Joined to 35086.
	1881,0706.606	Joined to 46113.
46150	1881,0706.607	Astronomical?
46151	1881,0706.608	Astronomical?; mentions ŠU.SI.MEŠ and LÚ.NUN.MEŠ.
46152	1881,0706.609	Astronomical Diary.
46153	1881,0706.610	Astronomical Diary for SE 335? LBAT 523.
	1881,0706.611	Joined to 46093.
46154	1881,0706.612	Astronomical Diary. Sachs, PTRSL A.276, 49, fig. 14.
	1881,0706.613	Joined to 46103.
46155	1881,0706.614	Joined to 46136.
46156	1881,0706.615	Astronomical Diary; mentions LÚ.GAL GAL ú-qa (Antigonus).
46157	1881,0706.616	Literary cylinder; hymn to Nabû; two columns; minute writing; ru-ru-ru between columns. + 1881,0706 unnum.
46158	1881,0706.617	Astronomical Diary.
	1881,0706.618	Joined to 45729.
46159	1881,0706.619	Astronomical; flake.
	1881,0706.620	Joined to 45674.

46160	1881,0706.621	Lexical; Ḫḫ I; month names spelled out.
46161	1881,0706.622	List of market prices. Slotsky and Wallenfels, Tallies and Trends, text 12.
46162	1881,0706.623	Astronomical?; mentions 24 streets.
46163	1881,0706.624	Joined to 46126.
46164	1881,0706.625	Joined to 42761.
46165	1881,0706.626	Astronomical Diary.
46166	1881,0706.627	Joined to 45986.
46167	1881,0706.628	Astronomical; microzodiac rising time scheme for Aquarius and Pisces. Steele, Rising time schemes, 73-74.
46168	1881,0706.629	Ritual; ŠIM.ḪÁ; IM.1 (south).
46169	1881,0706.630	Joined to 35110.
46170	1881,0706.631	Joined to 45661.
46171	1881,0706.632	Astrological; certain stars connected with 'rising' (ZI-ut (tibût) (māt) Subartu, etc); cf. 46187.
46172	1881,0706.633	Joined to 46099.
46173	1881,0706.634	Astronomical.
46174	1881,0706.635	Astronomical Diary.
46175	1881,0706.636	Historical(?); or perhaps part of an Astronomical Diary; mentions 1.ar-šú.
46176	1881,0706.637	Joined to 35495.
46177	1881,0706.638	Incantation.
46178	1881,0706.639	Astronomical; procedure text?
46179	1881,0706.640	Astronomical?
46180	1881,0706.641	Astronomical; Goal Year Text; not datable. + 46217. Hunger and Sachs, ADART VI, no. 172.
46181	1881,0706.642	Astronomical Diary.
46182	1881,0706.643	Joined to 46141.
46183	1881,0706.644	Astrological omens; mentions Mars.
46184	1881,0706.645	Astronomical Diary.
46185	1881,0706.646	Joined to 35673.
46186	1881,0706.647	Joined to 46141.
46187	1881,0706.648	Astrological?; cf. 46171.
46188	1881,0706.649	Omens; physiognomic.
46189	1881,0706.650	Joined to 35110.
46190	1881,0706.651	Astronomical?
46191	1881,0706.652	Astronomical Diary.
46192	1881,0706.653	Joined to 45818.
46193	1881,0706.654	Astronomical Diary.
46194	1881,0706.655	Ritual.
46195	1881,0706.656	Joined to 45952.
46196	1881,0706.657	Astronomical Diary for SE 200. (+) 45874. LBAT 465; Sachs and Hunger, ADART III, no. -111 D.
46197	1881,0706.658	Incantation.

46198	1881,0706.659	Unidentified.
46199	1881,0706.660	Commentary.
46200	1881,0706.661	Astronomical Diary.
46201	1881,0706.662	Astronomical.
46202	1881,0706.663	Bilingual incantation.
46203	1881,0706.664	Astronomical Diary.
46204	1881,0706.665	Ritual; mentions NENNI A NENNI.
46205	1881,0706.666	Astronomical Diary.
46206	1881,0706.667	Astronomical; Normal Star Almanac. SE. Hunger and Sachs, ADART VII, no. 146.
46207	1881,0706.668	Tintir V. George, BTT, pl. 17.
46208	1881,0706.669	Literary.
46209	1881,0706.670	Astronomical.
46210	1881,0706.671	Astronomical; Normal Star Almanac for SE 157. LBAT 1033; Hunger and Sachs, ADART VII, no. 70.
46211	1881,0706.672	Astronomical(?) or historical(?).
46212	1881,0706.673	Astronomical; Goal Year Text; not datable. Hunger and Sachs, ADART VI, no. 173.
46213	1881,0706.674	Joined to 46141.
46214	1881,0706.675	Incantation?
	1881,0706.676	Joined to 42961.
46215	1881,0706.677	Joined to 42961.
46216	1881,0706.678	Joined to 35189.
46217	1881,0706.679	Joined to 46180.
46218	1881,0706.680	Astronomical; Goal Year Text; not datable. Hunger and Sachs, ADART VI, no. 174.
46219	1881,0706.681	Lexical; explanatory god-list.
46220	1881,0706.682	Astronomical Diary.
46221	1881,0706.683	Astronomical Diary.
46222	1881,0706.684	Joined to 45795.
46223	1881,0706.685	Astrological; Enūma Anu Enlil, Sin. Reiner, Fs Borger (CM 10), 299.
46224	1881,0706.686	Astronomical Diary.
46225	1881,0706.687	Astronomical Diary.
46226	1881,0706.688	List of plants, utensils and personnel in the garden of Marduk-apla-iddina (Merodach-baladan). CT 14, 50; Meissner, ZA 6, 289ff.; Brinkman, Fs Oppenheim, 48.
46227	1881,0706.689	Astronomical Diary for SE 231. Sachs and Hunger, ADART III, no. -80.
46228	1881,0706.690	Medical omens; Sa-gig XL. Labat, TDP 216-230 and pl. LXIII; Heeßel, AOAT 43, 146.
46229	1881,0706.691	Astronomical Diary. + 1882,0704.83 + 98 + 113. LBAT 189*; Sachs, PTRSL A.276, 48, fig. 8; Sachs and Hunger, ADART I, no. -346.

46230	1881,0706.692	Astrological; Rikis gerri Enūma Anu Enlil. Reiner, Fs Borger (CM 10), 299; Gehlken, CM 43, p. 277.
46231	1881,0706.693	Astronomical; observations; Mercury for SE 54-56, Mars for SE 54-55, so that the Goal Years are SE 101-102. LBAT 1373; Hunger and Sachs, ADART V, no. 73.
46232	1881,0706.694	Ritual, incantation, and physiognomic omens. Fincke, Fs Geller, 203-231.
46233	1881,0706.695	Mathematical; extended table of reciprocals.
	1881,0706.696	Joined to 34709.
46234	1881,0706.697	Astrological; Enūma Anu Enlil, Sin. Reiner, Fs Borger (CM 10), 299.
46235	1881,0706.698	Joined to 35339.
46236	1881,0706.699	Joined to 35045.
46237	1881,0706.700	Astronomical; new moons and full moons for two years. + 1882,0704.92 + 140 (+) 45849. ACT 123a, colophon Zka.
46238	1881,0706.701	Astrological; Enūma Anu Enlil 47. Reiner, Fs Borger (CM 10), 299; Gehlken, CM 43, p. 123, pl. 26.
46239	1881,0706.702	Astrological; Enūma Anu Enlil 20. Rochberg-Halton, AfO Beih. 22, EAE 20; Reiner, Fs Borger (CM 10), 299; Fincke, Kaskal 14, 55-74.
	1881,0706.703	Joined to 34713.
46240	1881,0706.704	Astronomical.
	1881,0706.705	Joined to 34572.
46241	1881,0706.706	Joined to 38359.
46242	1881,0706.707	Joined to 35339.
46243	1881,0706.708	Astronomical; procedure text; eclipses and shadows.
46244	1881,0706.709	Omen apodoses; public or Enūma Anu Enlil, Dilbat (Venus); mentions SA.GAZ. Reiner, Fs Borger (CM 10), 299.
46245	1881,0706.710	Sumerian literary.
46246	1881,0706.711	Medical; prescription or list of plants.
46247	1881,0706.712	Medical; list of 7 stones; NA4 ša IGI ...
46248	1881,0706.713	Lexical; Ḫḫ V.
46249	1881,0706.714	Receipt for birds.
46250	1881,0706.715	Receipt?
46251	1881,0706.716	Contract; note two non-Babylonian names, f.ta-na-ḫa-at and 1.ú-ḫa-ri-pi-'.
46252	1881,0706.717	Astrological. Reiner, Fs Borger (CM 10), 299.
46253	1881,0706.718	Astronomical Diary.
46254	1881,0706.719	Astronomical Diary.
46255	1881,0706.720	Astronomical; Almanac for SE 186. LBAT 1140; Hunger and Sachs, ADART VII, no. 175.
46256	1881,0706.721	Astronomical; procedure.

46257	1881,0706.722	Astronomical Diary; mentions Arsaces LUGAL and ma-dak-tú. SE.
46258	1881,0706.723	Lexical.
46259	1881,0706.724	Astronomical?
46260	1881,0706.725	Joined to 45927.
46261	1881,0706.726	Incantation; NENNI A NENNI.
46262	1881,0706.727	Astronomical; mentions stars.
46263	1881,0706.728	Astronomical Diary.
46264	1881,0706.729	Astronomical; System A, lunar ephemeris. Steele, Fs Walker, 293-318, text G.
46265	1881,0706.730	Omens.
46266	1881,0706.731	Lexical; Ea II. MSL 14, 245.
46267	1881,0706.732	Astronomical?
46268	1881,0706.733	Omen apodoses (public).
46269	1881,0706.734	Literary.
46270	1881,0706.735	Astronomical; Goal Year Text or planetary observations.
46271	1881,0706.736	Commentary.
46272	1881,0706.737	Astronomical; Vorläufer?; early procedure text?; mentions ziq-pi.
46273	1881,0706.738	Joined to 46141.
	1881,0706.739	Joined to 35500.
46274	1881,0706.740	Lexical; syllabary.
46275	1881,0706.741	Astrological; mentions Akkad, Elam, ša tamlê. Reiner, Fs Borger (CM 10), 299.

1881,0727 collection

The 1881,0727 collection comes from the excavations of Hormuzd Rassam. See J. E. Reade in CBTBM VI, p. xxxi. The tablets are already catalogued in Bezold, Cat. 4 pp. 1808-1809. The register gives the provenance of these tablets as Babylon.

1881,0727.200	Lexical; syllabary.
1881,0727.201	Contract between f.Kaš-šá-a and her husband Marduk-šuma-iddina. Nbk 26/8/39. Babylon.
1881,0727.202	Hymn.
1881,0727.203	Bilingual hymn.
1881,0727.204	Contract. Šamaš-šum-ukin 9/1/11. Babylon. Brinkman and Kennedy, JCS 35, 28, K.44.
1881,0727.205	Incantation, prayer and ritual; colophon. Hunger, AOAT 2, no. 467.
1881,0727.209	Memorandum.
1881,0727.210	Lexical; dupl. DT 111
1881,0727.212	Astrological; eclipses.
1881,0727.213	Joined to 36479.

1881,0728 collection

The 1881,0728 collection comes from the excavations of Hormuzd Rassam. See J. E. Reade in CBTBM VI, p. xxxi. The register gives the provenance of the whole collection as Babylon.

46276	1881,0728.1	Bilingual incantation; Muššu'u tablet V; edition of Tanittu-Bēl; colophon. Alex III 25/2?/13. Babylon. + 46278 + 46341. Cf. Finkel, AuOr 9 (1991), 97-98; Böck, NABU 2001, 80-81, no. 86; Böck, Muššu'u, 181-220 and pls. XX-XXI.
46277	1881,0728.2	Joined to 45393.
46278	1881,0728.3	Joined to 46276.
46279	1881,0728.4	Tintir IV. George, BTT, pl. 11.
46280	1881,0728.5	Literary; Love Lyrics. + 46342 + 46359 + 46486.
46281	1881,0728.6	Incantation; Lamaštu. + 46335 + 46420 + 46460 + 46469. Farber, Lamaštu, 46, pls. 36-43.
46282	1881,0728.7	School text; lexical; Ea I, II, III, Diri VII. MSL 14, 173; 245; 301; MSL 15, 197; Landsberger, Gs Speiser, 133; Gesche, AOAT 275, 688.
46283	1881,0728.8	Joined to 45394.
46284	1881,0728.9	Lexical; syllabary. CT 11, 19.
46285	1881,0728.10	Lexical; list of personal names. Pinches, Assyrian Grammar, 64.
46286	1881,0728.11	Joined to 45396.
46287	1881,0728.12	Lexical; syllabary. + 46292 + 46322 + 46450 + 46470. CT 11, 13 (not 46450).
46288	1881,0728.13	Bilingual incantation; prayer on upper edge. + 46505 + unnum. Schramm, GBAO 2, p. 90, text B8 (46355 only). + 46355 + 46362 + 46363 + 46390 + 46392 + 46405 + 46414 + 46447 + 46505 + 46526 + unnum. CT 17, 3 (46288 + 46363 + 46390 + 46392 + 46405 only); cf. Finkel, AuOr 9 (1991), 96 n. 7; Schramm, GBAO 2, p. 90, texts B3 and B8 (but 46414 not copied); Schramm, GBAO 2, p. 90, text B8 (46355 only).
46289	1881,0728.14	Joined to 45405.
46290	1881,0728.15	Lexical; syllabary. + 46337. CT 11, 12.
46291	1881,0728.16	Joined to 45385.
46292	1881,0728.17	Joined to 46287.
46293	1881,0728.18	Ritual.
46294	1881,0728.19	Joined to 45396.
46295	1881,0728.20	Bilingual incantation; Muššu'u tablet VII. Böck, Muššu'u, 241-260 and pl. XXXII; Lambert, BCM, p. 157.

46296	1881,0728.21	Bilingual incantation; Udug-ḫul 5; edition of Tanittu-Bēl; colophon. + 1881,0728.96 + 46374 + 46408. CT 16, 12-16; cf. Finkel, AuOr 9 (1991), 96 n. 1; Geller, BAM 8, 174-216, pl. 42.
46297	1881,0728.22	Bilingual incantation; Muššu'u tablet VII; also Udug-ḫul 7; edition of Tanittu-Bēl; colophon. + 46328 + unnum. Cf. Finkel, AuOr 9 (1991), 95 and 98; Böck, Muššu'u, 241-260 and pls. XXX-XXXI; Lambert, BCM, p. 157; Geller, BAM 8, 249-287, pls. 57-58.
46298	1881,0728.23	List of days worked by named persons.
46299	1881,0728.24	Joined to 45483.
46300	1881,0728.25	Promissory note for silver.
46301	1881,0728.26	Bilingual incantation; Muššu'u tablet I; edition of Tanittu-Bēl; colophon. Alex III []/[]/13. CT 17, 25-26; MSL 9, 23; cf. Finkel, AuOr 9 (1991), 94; Böck, Muššu'u, 93-111, pls. II-III.
46302	1881,0728.27	Lexical; syllabary. CT 11, 12.
46303	1881,0728.28	List of commodities for building, by weight, mostly woods.
46304	1881,0728.29	Measurements of a field.
46305	1881,0728.30	Lexical; syllabary. CT 11, 11.
46306	1881,0728.31	Bilingual incantation; Muššu'u VIII; edition of Tanittu-Bēl; colophon. Cf. Finkel, AuOr 9 (1991), 99-100; Böck, Muššu'u, 261-313 and pl. XL.
46307	1881,0728.32	Astronomical?
46308	1881,0728.33	Account of silver.
46309	1881,0728.34	Inventory of household furniture.
46310	1881,0728.35	Lexical.
46311	1881,0728.36	Lexical; syllabary; personal names. CT 11, 13 (obverse only).
46312	1881,0728.37	Sumerian literary.
46313	1881,0728.38	Literary. + 46514.
46314	1881,0728.39	Astronomical; weather predictions.
46315	1881,0728.40	Memorandum about pots.
46316	1881,0728.41	Division of property. Dar 5/5/21. Babylon.
46317	1881,0728.42	Omens; Šumma ālu, tablet 14; sūqu and ḫarrānu; colophon.
46318	1881,0728.43	Joined to 45373.
46319	1881,0728.44	Joined to 45483.
46320	1881,0728.45	Bilingual incantation.
46321	1881,0728.46	Lexical; god-list.
46322	1881,0728.47	Joined to 46287.
46323	1881,0728.48	Joined to 45373.
46324	1881,0728.49	Contract(?); mostly illegible; captions for a seal and a finger-nail mark.

46325	1881,0728.50	Unidentified.
46326	1881,0728.51	Prayer.
46327	1881,0728.52	Joined to 45396.
46328	1881,0728.53	Joined to 46297.
46329	1881,0728.54	Bilingual incantation, Udug-ḫul 2. (+) 45401 (+) 46333 + 46360 + 46477 + 46512 + 46517 (+) 46353. Geller, BAM 8, 59-88, pls. 18-19.
46330	1881,0728.55	Bilingual incantation; Muššu'u tablet II; colophon; prayer on upper edge. + 46391 + 46476 + 1881,0728 unnum. Cf. Finkel, AuOr 9 (1991), 95-96; Böck, Muššu'u, 113-131 and pl. IV.
46331	1881,0728.56	Joined to 45393.
46332	1881,0728.57	Joined to 45382.
46333	1881,0728.58	Bilingual incantation, Udug-ḫul 2. + 46360 + 46477 + 46512 + 46517 (+) 45401 (+) 46353. Geller, BAM 8, 59-88, pls. 18-19.
46334	1881,0728.59	Incantation; Marduk's Address (Udug-ḫul 11).
46335	1881,0728.60	Joined to 46281.
46336	1881,0728.61	Ritual for the 4th day, for the temple é-túr-kalam-ma at Babylon; prayer on upper edge. + 46371. Lambert, Unity and Diversity, 98-135.
46337	1881,0728.62	Joined to 46290.
46338	1881,0728.63	Literary account of a dream; prayer on upper edge. + 46340 + 46372 + 46425 + 46455.
46339	1881,0728.64	Joined to 45396.
46340	1881,0728.65	Joined to 46338.
46341	1881,0728.66	Joined to 46276.
46342	1881,0728.67	Joined to 46280.
46343	1881,0728.68	Lexical and literary extracts. + 46366.
46344	1881,0728.69	Joined to 45410.
46345	1881,0728.70	"Aluzinnu text"; dupl. 2R 60, no. 1.
46346	1881,0728.71	Literary.
46347	1881,0728.72	Unidentified.
46348	1881,0728.73	Lexical; syllabary.
46349	1881,0728.74	School text; lexical.
46350	1881,0728.75	Joined to 45410.
46351	1881,0728.76	Lexical; syllabary.
46352	1881,0728.77	"Aluzinnu text"; dupl. 2R 60, no. 1.
46353	1881,0728.78	Bilingual incantation, Udug-ḫul 2. (+) 45401 (+) 46329 (+) 46333 + 46360 + 46477 + 46512 + 46517. Geller, BAM 8, 59-88, pls. 18-19.
46354	1881,0728.79	Lexical; syllabary. CT 11, 10.
46355	1881,0728.80	Joined to 46288.
46356	1881,0728.81	Joined to 45396.
46357	1881,0728.82	Lexical; personal names.

46358	1881,0728.83	Joined to 45385.
46359	1881,0728.84	Joined to 46280.
46360	1881,0728.85	Joined to 46333.
46361	1881,0728.86	Bilingual incantations; Muššu'u tablet IV. (+) 45405 + 46289 + 46387 + 46416 + 46419 + 46446 + 46509 + 1881,0728 unnum. (+) 46458.
46362	1881,0728.87	Joined to 46288.
46363	1881,0728.88	Joined to 46288.
46364	1881,0728.89	Literary.
46365	1881,0728.90	Mantic dream ritual.
46366	1881,0728.91	Joined to 46343.
46367	1881,0728.92	Joined to 45483.
46368	1881,0728.93	Joined to 45373.
46369	1881,0728.94	Joined to 45377.
46370	1881,0728.95	Unidentified.
	1881,0728.96	Joined to 46296.
46371	1881,0728.97	Joined to 46336.
46372	1881,0728.98	Joined to 46338.
46373	1881,0728.99	Lexical; Ea; sign list.
46374	1881,0728.100	Joined to 46296.
46375	1881,0728.101	Joined to 45377.
46376	1881,0728.102	Bilingual incantation, Udug-ḫul 16.
46377	1881,0728.103	Bilingual incantation.
46378	1881,0728.104	Literary.
46379	1881,0728.105	Lexical; personal names beginning EN.
46380	1881,0728.106	Lexical; giš.
46381	1881,0728.107	Incantation.
46382	1881,0728.108	Lexical; syllabary. CT 11, 8.
46383	1881,0728.109	Joined to 45377.
46384	1881,0728.110	Contract; sale of a house. []-uṣur 7?/9/-.
46385	1881,0728.111	Joined to 45396.
46386	1881,0728.112	Lexical; Ea; sign list.
46387	1881,0728.113	Joined to 45405.
46388	1881,0728.114	Joined to 45385.
46389	1881,0728.115	Contract.
46390	1881,0728.116	Joined to 46288.
46391	1881,0728.117	Joined to 46330.
46392	1881,0728.118	Joined to 46288.
46393	1881,0728.119	Joined to 45382.
46394	1881,0728.120	Joined to 45483.
46395	1881,0728.121	Lexical.
46396	1881,0728.122	Ledger.
46397	1881,0728.123	Joined to 45483.
46398	1881,0728.124	Incantation.
46399	1881,0728.125	Incantation; colophon.

46400	1881,0728.126	Lexical; professions.
46401	1881,0728.127	Joined to 45372.
46402	1881,0728.128	Astronomical; procedure.
46403	1881,0728.129	Incantation.
46404	1881,0728.130	Unidentified.
46405	1881,0728.131	Joined to 46288.
46406	1881,0728.132	Contract for barley. Cam 14/3/1.
46407	1881,0728.133	Lexical; syllabary. CT 11, 5.
46408	1881,0728.134	Joined to 46296.
46409	1881,0728.135	Sumerian literary.
46410	1881,0728.136	Lexical, Aa V/3 = 28; colophon. + 46495. MSL 14, 421.
46411	1881,0728.137	Lexical; birds.
46412	1881,0728.138	Literary extracts.
46413	1881,0728.139	Bilingual incantation and colophon; Muššu'u tablet III. 14/[]/[]. + 46472 + 46527 (+) 45395.
46414	1881,0728.140	Joined to 46288.
46415	1881,0728.141	Commentary. + 46493 + 46523.
46416	1881,0728.142	Joined to 45405.
46417	1881,0728.143	Incantation?
46418	1881,0728.144	Lexical; syllabary.
46419	1881,0728.145	Joined to 45405.
46420	1881,0728.146	Joined to 46281.
46421	1881,0728.147	Incantation; Marduk's Address (Udug-ḫul 11); colophon of Tanittu-Bēl. Alexander. + 46485 + 46492 + 46510 (+) 46421a (+) 46429. Geller, BAM 8, 340-392, pls. 82, 85, 86; Geller, NABU 2016, 134-135, no. 80; Lambert, MC 24, no. 189.
46421a	1881,0728.147a	Incantation; Marduk's Address (Udug-ḫul 11); prayer on upper edge. (+) 46421 + 46485 + 46492 + 46510 (+) 46429. Geller, BAM 8, 340-392.
46422	1881,0728.148	Incantation.
46423	1881,0728.149	Joined to 45382.
46424	1881,0728.150	Bilingual incantation; Muššu'u tablet II. Cf. Finkel, AuOr 9 (1991), 95; Böck, Muššu'u, 113-131 and pl. V.
46425	1881,0728.151	Joined to 46338.
46426	1881,0728.152	Ledger.
46427	1881,0728.153	Medical.
46428	1881,0728.154	Sumerian literary.
46429	1881,0728.155	Incantation; Marduk's Address (Udug-ḫul 11). (+) 46421 + 46485 + 46492 + 46510 (+) 46421a. Geller, BAM 8, 340-392; Lambert, MC 24, no. 189.
46430	1881,0728.156	Economic.
46431	1881,0728.157	Lexical; syllabary.

46432	1881,0728.158	Account of dates over a number of years. 22/12/27.
46433	1881,0728.159	Account.
46434	1881,0728.160	Joined to 45377.
46435	1881,0728.161	Joined to 45377.
46436	1881,0728.162	Field plan.
46437	1881,0728.163	Joined to 45377.
46438	1881,0728.164	Obv. Tintir V; rev. theology? George, BTT, pl. 19.
46439	1881,0728.165	Joined to 45385.
46440	1881,0728.166	Joined to 45382.
46441	1881,0728.167	Letter from Nabû-dān to f.Ṭunāya. CT 22, 28, no. 147; Hackl et al., AOAT 414/1, no. 104.
46442	1881,0728.168	Incantation; Marduk's Address (Udug.ḫul 11). Geller, BAM 8, 340-392, pl. 76; Lambert, MC 24, no. 179.
46443	1881,0728.169	Astronomical?
46444	1881,0728.170	Ritual.
46445	1881,0728.171	Incantation or prayer.
46446	1881,0728.172	Joined to 45405.
46447	1881,0728.173	Joined to 46288.
46448	1881,0728.174	Unidentified; mostly illegible.
46449	1881,0728.175	Lexical; personal names.
46450	1881,0728.176	Joined to 46287.
46451	1881,0728.177	Economic.
46452	1881,0728.178	Lexical.
46453	1881,0728.179	Economic.
46454	1881,0728.180	Joined to 45377.
46455	1881,0728.181	Joined to 46338.
46456	1881,0728.182	Economic.
46457	1881,0728.183	Commentary.
46458	1881,0728.184	Bilingual incantation; Muššu'u tablet IV. (+) 45405 + 46289 + 46387 + 46416 + 46419 + 46446 + 46509 + 1881,0728 unnum. (+) 46361. Cf. Finkel, AuOr 9 (1991), 96-97; Böck, Muššu'u, 147-180 and pls. XVI-XVII.
46459	1881,0728.185	Lexical; Ḫḫ I. + 64390. MSL 5, 3.
46460	1881,0728.186	Joined to 46281.
46461	1881,0728.187	Joined to 45382.
46462	1881,0728.188	Unidentified.
46463	1881,0728.189	Economic.
46464	1881,0728.190	Lexical; Malku I; cf. 46514?
46465	1881,0728.191	Temple list.
46466	1881,0728.192	Astronomical.
46467	1881,0728.193	Incantation. + 46491.
46468	1881,0728.194	Lexical; syllabary.
46469	1881,0728.195	Joined to 46281.
46470	1881,0728.196	Joined to 46287.

46471	1881,0728.197	Incantation.
46472	1881,0728.198	Joined to 46413.
46473	1881,0728.199	Astronomical.
46474	1881,0728.200	Lexical and literary extracts.
46475	1881,0728.201	Lexical; personal names. + 1881,0728 unnum.
46476	1881,0728.202	Joined to 46330.
46477	1881,0728.203	Joined to 46333.
46478	1881,0728.204	Astronomical?
46479	1881,0728.205	Practice signs.
46480	1881,0728.206	Bilingual incantation.
46481	1881,0728.207	Lexical.
46482	1881,0728.208	Astronomical?
46483	1881,0728.209	Lexical; syllabary. + 46532. CT 11, 5 (46483 only).
46484	1881,0728.210	Joined to 45373.
46485	1881,0728.211	Joined to 46421.
46486	1881,0728.212	Joined to 46280.
46487	1881,0728.213	Bilingual incantation; Muššu'u tablet II. + 1881,0728 unnum. Cf. Finkel, AuOr 9 (1991), 95; Böck, Muššu'u, 113-131 and pl. V.
46488	1881,0728.214	Lexical; syllabary. CT 11, 5.
46489	1881,0728.215	Sumerian literary.
46490	1881,0728.216	Literary.
46491	1881,0728.217	Joined to 46467.
46492	1881,0728.218	Joined to 46421.
46493	1881,0728.219	Joined to 46415.
46494	1881,0728.220	Bilingual incantation. Schramm, GBAO 2, p. 90, text B10.
46495	1881,0728.221	Joined to 45410.
46496	1881,0728.222	Lexical; syllabary. CT 11, 11.
46497	1881,0728.223	Joined to 45382.
46498	1881,0728.224	Astronomical.
46499	1881,0728.225	Incantation; Marduk's Address (Udug-ḫul 11). Geller, BAM 8, 340-392, pl. 77; Lambert, MC 24, no. 178.
46500	1881,0728.226	Literary; Love Lyrics. (+) 45381.
46501	1881,0728.227	Incantation; Marduk's Address (Udug-ḫul 11). Geller, BAM 8, 340-392, pl. 88; Lambert, MC 24, no. 180.
46502	1881,0728.228	Commentary.
46503	1881,0728.229	Lexical.
46504	1881,0728.230	Incantation.
46505	1881,0728.231	Joined to 46288.
46506	1881,0728.232	Lexical; syllabary. CT 11, 12.
46507	1881,0728.233	Joined to 45483.
46508	1881,0728.234	Literary.
46509	1881,0728.235	Joined to 45405.
46510	1881,0728.236	Joined to 46421.

46511	1881,0728.237	Literary.
46512	1881,0728.238	Joined to 46333.
46513	1881,0728.239	Old Babylonian. Barley loan. Samsuiluna. + 46516.
46514	1881,0728.240	Joined to 46313.
46515	1881,0728.241	Incantation.
46516	1881,0728.242	Joined to 46513.
46517	1881,0728.243	Joined to 46333.
46518	1881,0728.244	Lexical; Ea I 32-39.
46519	1881,0728.245	Contract. Art 2/5/1.
46520	1881,0728.246	Incantation.
46521	1881,0728.247	Incantation.
46522	1881,0728.248	Prayer.
46523	1881,0728.249	Joined to 46415.
46524	1881,0728.250	Medical. + 46531.
46525	1881,0728.251	Joined to 45483.
46526	1881,0728.252	Joined to 46288.
46527	1881,0728.253	Joined to 46413.
46528	1881,0728.254	Bilingual incantation.
46529	1881,0728.255	Lexical; Ea; sign list.
46530	1881,0728.256	Sumerian literary.
46531	1881,0728.257	Joined to 46524.
46532	1881,0728.258	Joined to 46483.
46533	1881,0728.259	Personal name; ball shaped tablet.
46534	1881,0728.260	Personal name; ball shaped tablet.

1881,0830 collection

The 1881,0830 collection comes from the excavations of Hormuzd Rassam. See J. E. Reade in CBTBM VI pp. xxxi-xxxii. The register gives no provenance for much of the collection, but gives the provenance

Babylon to nos. 3-7, 9-29, 32-45, 47-49, 51-247, 250-287, 289-383, 385-409, 411-507, 562,
Babylon or Abu-habbah to no. 50,
Babylon or Dailem to nos. 46, 563-568,
Dailem to nos. 8, 31, 248, 249, 288, 384, 410, 518, 569, 591, 592, 607, 619, 624, 625, 651, 679, 686, 687, 688.

46535	1881,0830.1	Cylinder; inscription of Nebuchadnezzar II. Ball, PSBA 11 (1889) 248-253; Berger, AOAT 4/1, Nebukadnezar Zylinder II,1, no. 9; dupl. Langdon, VAB 4, 84-85, Neb. no. 6.
46536	1881,0830.2	Cylinder; inscription of Nebuchadnezzar II. Berger, AOAT 4/1, Nebukadnezar Zylinder II,1, no. 13.
46537	1881,0830.3	Sumerian grammatical text; dupl. K.5423 (CT 19, 28). Bertin, JRAS 1886, 81-88; Langdon, RA 13, 94-95; cf. Oelsner, Materialien, 230.

46538	1881,0830.4	Field plan. Nbk -/5/28.
46539	1881,0830.5	Field plan. Dar 10/12/34.
46540	1881,0830.6	Field plan. Dar 27/-/-.
46541	1881,0830.7	Medical omens.
46542	1881,0830.8	Field sale. Šamaš-šum-ukin 21 /12/15. Dilbat. Brinkman and Kennedy, JCS 35, 32, K.104.
46543	1881,0830.9	Late Babylonian copy of an inscription of Hammurabi; colophon of Rēmūt-Gula. King, LIH, no. 59; Frayne, RIME 4,.3.6.3.
46544	1881,0830.10	Land sale; sealed. Dar I []/[]/19. Nisaba 28, no. 122.
46545	1881,0830.11	Field sale; sealed. Dar I []/5/23. Nisaba 28, no. 128.
46546	1881,0830.12	Account of silver payments.
46547	1881,0830.13	School text; lexical, god-list, An = Anum; proverbs?; colophon. Gesche, AOAT 275, 326-328, 688.
46548	1881,0830.14	Lexical; god-list; colophon.
46549	1881,0830.15	Mathematical; table of measures of barley; complete but damaged.
46550	1881,0830.16	Mathematical; table demonstrating the computation of reciprocals. Fincke and Ossendrijver, ZA 106, 185-197; Friberg and Al-Rawi, NMCT, Sec. 2.1.
46551	1881,0830.17	Lexical; Ea; sign list and literary extracts.
46552	1881,0830.18	Prayer.
46553	1881,0830.19	Hemerology; colophon; copy of a tablet from Borsippa, by Nabû-šum-ukīn. Livingstone, CUSAS 25, p. 9.
46554	1881,0830.20	Mantic dream ritual.
46555	1881,0830.21	Contract; land sale. Nisaba 28, no. 130.
46556	1881,0830.22	Lexical; Ḫḫ XVII (plants).
46557	1881,0830.23	Lexical; obv. Ḫḫ I; rev. geographical list. MSL 9, 157 (as 46657).
46558	1881,0830.24	Incantation; Marduk's Address (Udug-ḫul 11). Geller, BAM 8, 340-392, pl. 90; Lambert, MC 24, no. 201.
46559	1881,0830.25	God-list. CT 29, 44-47.
46560	1881,0830.26	Astronomical?; mentions Babylon and Bēl; two columns.
46561	1881,0830.27	Mathematical; extended table of reciprocals.
46562	1881,0830.28	Hemerology. Livingstone, CUSAS 25, p. 10.
46563	1881,0830.29	Medical omens; Sa-gig XXIX. Cf. Finkel, Gs Sachs, 147 n. 29; Heeßel, AOAT 43, 318-327 and 464.
46564	1881,0830.30	Lexical; Ea; sign list; literary extract.
46565	1881,0830.31	Lexical; Ea; sign list.
46566	1881,0830.32	Astrological; Enūma Anu Enlil, Sin; star ... DAR/TE-ma DU; parallel to K.11721, etc. Reiner, Fs Borger (CM 10), 299.

46567	1881,0830.33	School text; literary, Enūma eliš V; lexical; Ḫḫ XIX-XXIII. Lambert, BCM, p. 97, pl. 20.
46568	1881,0830.34	Field sale.
46569	1881,0830.35	Field plan. Nemet-Nejat, LB Field Plans, no. 25.
46570	1881,0830.36	Mathematical; tablet of reciprocals, in unusual format.
46571	1881,0830.37	Field plan.
46572	1881,0830.38	Lexical; Ḫḫ III. MSL 9, 159.
46573	1881,0830.39	Field plan.
46574	1881,0830.40	Joined to 43839.
46575	1881,0830.41	Promissory note for dates; sealed. Dar II 26/6/2. URU Šul-lu-me-e. + 47013. Mitchell and Searight, no. 382; Nisaba 28, no. 243.
46576	1881,0830.42	Lexical; Ḫḫ IV. MSL 9, 168.
46577	1881,0830.43	Copy of an Old Babylonian Sumerian building inscription of Sin-kašid; copied from the head of a nail.
46578	1881,0830.44	Field plan. + 46763. Nemet-Nejat, LB Field Plans, no. 55.
46579	1881,0830.45	Lexical; Ea; sign list.
46580	1881,0830.46	Court record about a dowry; captions for seals, but not sealed. Wunsch, Bab Arch 2, no. 11.
46581	1881,0830.47	Contract; transfer of property. Wunsch, Bab Arch 2, no. 30.
46582	1881,0830.48	Field sale. -/7/-.
46583	1881,0830.49	Contract.
46584	1881,0830.50	Land sale; 18 GI.MEŠ; year 30 over erasure of 29; no king's name. (Dar I) 9/2/30. Kūtû.
46585	1881,0830.51	Field sale; sealed; finger-nail marks. d.l. Nisaba 28, no. 31.
46586	1881,0830.52	Sale of a palm-grove in the area of Esagil-mansi (Borsippa region); the first witness is šākin ṭēmi of Borsippa. Nbk 6/5/19. Borsippa.
46587	1881,0830.53	Contract for wet-nursing; sealed. SE []/[]/100+. + 47261. Mitchell and Searight, no. 346; Nisaba 28, no. 592.
46588	1881,0830.54	Field plan. Nemet-Nejat, LB Field Plans, no. 64.
46589	1881,0830.55	Prayer.
46590	1881,0830.56	Incantation for the moon god.
46591	1881,0830.57	Field plan. 8/6/30. Nemet-Nejat, LB Field Plans, no. 69.
46592	1881,0830.58	Lexical; Ea; sign list.
46593	1881,0830.59	Lexical; Ea; sign list and colophon practice.
46594	1881,0830.60	Omens; Šumma ālu?
46595	1881,0830.61	Field sale; caption for a finger-nail mark. Nbn 4/8/10? Alu-ša-Nabû-bān-zēri.

46596	1881,0830.62	Medical; ú-ru-a-na.
46597	1881,0830.63	Field plan. Nemet-Nejat, LB Field Plans, no. 62.
46598	1881,0830.64	Joined to 43899.
46599	1881,0830.65	Lexical; Ea; sign list and personal names.
46600	1881,0830.66	Cylinder; inscription of Nabonidus; Ebabbar cylinder; dupl. Schaudig, AOAT 256, text 2.13 ii 7-29. Sippar. Da Riva, GMTR 4, 126.
46601	1881,0830.67	Mathematical; table of coefficients, similar to 36776. (+) 46610.
46602	1881,0830.68	Field sale. 11/[]/11.
46603	1881,0830.69	Lexical; Syllabary A, list of archaic signs and Neo-Babylonian equivalents; picture signs as in Kraus, TDP pl. 35; cf. 46609. (+) 46609. Pearce, Iraq 45, 136-137; Finkel and Seymour, Babylon, 86, fig. 64.
46604	1881,0830.70	Field plan. Dar 3/6b/30.
46605	1881,0830.71	Sale of a woman.
46606	1881,0830.72	Bilingual incantation, Udug-ḫul 4. Geller, BAM 8, 133-173, pl. 38.
46607	1881,0830.73	Joined to 41237.
46608	1881,0830.74	Account of oil.
46609	1881,0830.75	Lexical; Syllabary A; list of archaic signs and Neo-Babylonian equivalents with numerical values for each sign; picture signs as in Kraus, TDP pl. 35; cf. 46603. (+) 46603. Pearce, Iraq 45, 136-137; Finkel and Seymour, Babylon, 86, fig. 64.
46610	1881,0830.76	Mathematical; possibly table of coefficients? (+) 46601.
46611	1881,0830.77	Astronomical; very late Seleucid type script; also inscribed on left edge.
46612	1881,0830.78	Mathematical; multiplication table.
46613	1881,0830.79	Lexical; Ea; sign list.
46614	1881,0830.80	Joined to 45528.
46615	1881,0830.81	Mathematical; problem; in poor condition but complete.
46616	1881,0830.82	Account of dates. 20/[]/10.
46617	1881,0830.83	Promissory note for silver.
46618	1881,0830.84	Marriage contract. Nbn 11/7/14. Wunsch, Bab Arch 2, no. 2.
46619	1881,0830.85	Lexical; Ea; sign list.
46620	1881,0830.86	Account.
46621	1881,0830.87	Lexical; Ḫḫ IV. MSL 9, 168.
46622	1881,0830.88	Omens; Iqqur īpuš, Nisannu.
46623	1881,0830.89	Promissory note for seed. Nbn 23/5/-.
46624	1881,0830.90	Field plan. Dar 8/5/28. + 46748 + 46979. Nemet-Nejat, LB Field Plans, no. 43.

46625	1881,0830.91	Lexical; god list.
46626	1881,0830.92	Contract.
46627	1881,0830.93	Lexical, commentary on Nabnītu XXV (= L). MSL 16, 225.
46628	1881,0830.94	Astrological. Reiner, Fs Borger (CM 10), 299.
46629	1881,0830.95	Contract. AM 26/1/[].
46630	1881,0830.96	Omens; Šumma ālu?
46631	1881,0830.97	Lexical; syllabary; literary extract.
46632	1881,0830.98	Lexical; Ea; sign list.
46633	1881,0830.99	Promissory note for silver. Nbk 20/9/5.
46634	1881,0830.100	Contract; hire of oxen. Nbk 23?/10/38. Babylon.
46635	1881,0830.101	Contract; transfer of land as part of a dowry. Npl 21/2/7. Wunsch, Bab Arch 2, no. 10b.
46636	1881,0830.102	Contract; lease of a field. Nbk 14/7/23. Babylon.
46637	1881,0830.103	Contract; sale of a house. Nbk 12/4/15. Babylon.
46638	1881,0830.104	Promissory note for silver. Nbk 4/3/21.
46639	1881,0830.105	Quittance. Nbk 9/12/20. Babylon.
46640	1881,0830.106	Contract; sale of dates. Nbk 14/6/1. Alu-ša-Šamaš-iddin.
46641	1881,0830.107	Contract for purchase of barley. Nbk 21/12/4. Babylon.
46642	1881,0830.108	Promissory note for 3 1/2 shekels of silver. Nbk 21/9/28
46643	1881,0830.109	Receipt of bricks; mentions 16th year of Nebuchadnezzar.
46644	1881,0830.110	Purchase of a slave. Nbk 2/1/13. Upija.
46645	1881,0830.111	Promissory note for dates. Nbk 7/[]/30. Babylon.
46646	1881,0830.112	Promissory note for silver. Ner 5/8/2. Babylon. Wunsch, Bab Arch 2, no. 27.
46647	1881,0830.113	Promissory note for barley. Nbn 14/7/11. Babylon.
46648	1881,0830.114	Record of additional witnesses to two land sale contracts. Nbn 7/6/9. Babylon. Wunsch, AOAT 330, 372.
46649	1881,0830.115	Promissory note for silver. Nbn -/-/5.
46650	1881,0830.116	Promissory note for dates. Nbn 12/[]/13.
46651	1881,0830.117	Promissory note for dates. Nbn 9/5/7. Babylon.
46652	1881,0830.118	Promissory note for 7 1/2 shekels of silver. Cyr 12/9/4.
46653	1881,0830.119	Barley as rent. Cyr 2/3/5. Alu-ša-Bēl-ušallim.
46654	1881,0830.120	Dowry conversion. Cyr 23/[]/8. Babylon. Wunsch, AOAT 330, 373, 375.
46655	1881,0830.121	Promissory note for silver. Cyr 9/8/8. Babylon.
46656	1881,0830.122	Contract for vats. Cam 8/7/6. Babylon.
46657	1881,0830.123	Promissory note for silver. Cam 28/11/acc. Babylon.
46658	1881,0830.124	Promissory note for dates. Cam 7/6b/3. Alu-ša-Iddin-Bēl.

46659	1881,0830.125	Promissory note for dates. Nbn 17/6/13. Borsippa. Zadok, Nisaba 21, 237.
46660	1881,0830.126	Deposition.
46661	1881,0830.127	Promissory note for 1 1/2 shekels of silver. Dar 11/4?/-.
46662	1881,0830.128	Promissory note for 5 shekels of silver.
46663	1881,0830.129	Letter order from Bulluṭ; sealed. Antig 1/10/3. (Borsippa). Mitchell and Searight, no. 657; Nisaba 28, no. 462.
46664	1881,0830.130	Promissory note for dates. Nbn -/6/11?
46665	1881,0830.131	Promissory note for dates. Nbn 1/6/16. Alu-ša-Aplāya.
46666	1881,0830.132	Promissory note for dates. Nbn 5/8/13. Babylon.
46667	1881,0830.133	Contract. Nbn 10+/10/3.
46668	1881,0830.134	Issue of garments. Nbn 8?/5/13. Babylon.
46669	1881,0830.135	Field sale. Nbn 29/12b/12. Babylon.
46670	1881,0830.136	Promissory note for silver. Nbn 25/1/12. Babylon.
46671	1881,0830.137	Contract. 18/6/4.
46672	1881,0830.138	Promissory note for silver. Dar 2/2?/4.
46673	1881,0830.139	Contract. Dar 25/2/5.
46674	1881,0830.140	Promissory note for dates. Dar 4/6/7.
46675	1881,0830.141	Promissory note for silver. Dar 10/11/7.
46676	1881,0830.142	Promissory note for silver. Cyr 22?/1/5.
46677	1881,0830.143	Promissory note for dates. Cam -/-/7.
46678	1881,0830.144	Promissory note for dates. Cam 13/12/7.
46679	1881,0830.145	Contract. Cam 5/12/5. Babylon.
46680	1881,0830.146	Promissory note for dates. Cam 8/6/4. Babylon.
46681	1881,0830.147	Contract about dates. Cam 25/6/5? Alu-ša-Iddin-Bēl.
46682	1881,0830.148	Promissory note for silver. Cam 25/10/4. Babylon.
46683	1881,0830.149	Contract; sale of a house. Cam 4/7/7. Babylon.
46684	1881,0830.150	Promissory note for silver. Dar 16/9/22. Babylon.
46685	1881,0830.151	Inventory of a dowry. Cam 14/4?/7. Alu-ša-Zababa-erība. Wunsch, AOAT 330, 373.
46686	1881,0830.152	Promissory note for dates. Dar []/6/2. Alu-ša-Zababa-erība. Wunsch, AOAT 330, 372.
46687	1881,0830.153	Contract about a legal dispute about dates; sealed; finger-nail marks. Dar II 11/5/3. Babylon. Nisaba 28, no. 244.
46688	1881,0830.154	Promissory note for silver. Dar 27/2/23.
46689	1881,0830.155	Promissory note for silver. Dar 4/2/22.
46690	1881,0830.156	Promissory note for dates. Dar 1/4?/8?
46691	1881,0830.157	Promissory note for 2/3 mina of silver; sealed. Dar II 27/4/10. Babylon. Mitchell and Searight, no. 404; Nisaba 28, no. 246.
46692	1881,0830.158	Promissory note for silver. Dar.

46693	1881,0830.159	Promissory note for dates. Dar -/-/27.
46694	1881,0830.160	Promissory note for dates. Dar 1/10/18.
46695	1881,0830.161	Promissory note for silver. Dar 1/9/20. Alu-ša-Bēl.
46696	1881,0830.162	Promissory note for silver. Dar 9/-/-.
46697	1881,0830.163	Contract. Dar 3/9/25. URU Gi-ru-ú.
46698	1881,0830.164	Promissory note for silver. Dar 6/[]/18. Wunsch, AOAT 330, 373.
46699	1881,0830.165	Promissory note for barley. Dar 7/9/18. URU Gi-ru-ú.
46700	1881,0830.166	Promissory note for silver. Dar 5/9/20. Babylon.
46701	1881,0830.167	Promissory note for dates. Dar 10/11/20.
46702	1881,0830.168	Promissory note for silver. Dar 14/8/21. URU Dūru-ša-[].
46703	1881,0830.169	Field plan. Nemet-Nejat, LB Field Plans, no. 3; Nemet-Nejat, JANES 7 (1975) 95-101.
46704	1881,0830.170	Promissory note for silver. Dar -/-/16. Borsippa.
46705	1881,0830.171	Letter from Nabû-aḫḫē-iddin to Rēmūt. CT 22, 26, no. 137; Hackl et al., AOAT 414/1, no. 105.
46706	1881,0830.172	Promissory note for dates. Dar 28/[]/31. Babylon.
46707	1881,0830.173	Promissory note for bales of straw. Dar 2/2/35. Babylon.
46708	1881,0830.174	Promissory note for dates. Dar 12/[]/35.
46709	1881,0830.175	Transfer of dowry property. Dar 24/12/23. Babylon. Wunsch, AOAT 330, 373.
46710	1881,0830.176	Promissory note for barley to be delivered in Bīt-Aḫtiya. Dar 22/12a/35. URU Bīt-Šaḫidu.
46711	1881,0830.177	Dowry record with receipt clause. Dar 18/11/14. Wunsch, AOAT 330, 374.
46712	1881,0830.178	Promissory note for silver. Dar -/-/19. Babylon.
46713	1881,0830.179	Contract; lease of a date-grove belonging to a dowry. Nabû-[] 1/6b/10. Wunsch, AOAT 330, 372.
46714	1881,0830.180	Promissory note for dates or grain.
46715	1881,0830.181	Mathematical problem?; left side left blank for calculations.
46716	1881,0830.182	Promissory note for silver. Art 14/4/31. Babylon.
46717	1881,0830.183	Promissory note for silver. Dar 12/[]/18. Dūru-ša-karrabbi.
46718	1881,0830.184	Lexical; Ḫḫ III-IV. MSL 9, 159, 168.
46719	1881,0830.185	Field plan. Nemet-Nejat, LB Field Plans, no. 2.
46720	1881,0830.186	Lexical; colophon.
46721	1881,0830.187	Promissory note for dates. Nbn 2+/5/16. Babylon. Wunsch, Bab Arch 2, no. 31.
46722	1881,0830.188	Deposition about grain.
46723	1881,0830.189	Memorandum about ox-hides issued on 27th day of month vii to named persons.

46724	1881,0830.190	List of workmen.
46725	1881,0830.191	List of workmen on the 15th day of month iii.
46726	1881,0830.192	Division of property.
46727	1881,0830.193	Promissory note for silver. Dar -/-/30.
46728	1881,0830.194	Contract; lease of a house. Dar 12/1/35?
46729	1881,0830.195	Letter; names of sender and addressee illegible. CT 22, 7, no. 29.
46730	1881,0830.196	Letter from Gula-[] to [] and Nabû-šumu-ēreš. CT 22, 31-32, no. 172; Hackl et al., AOAT 414/1, no. 106.
46731	1881,0830.197	Letter from Marduk-šumu-iddin to Minû-ana-Bēl-dānu.. CT 22, 24, no. 123.
46732	1881,0830.198	Letter order from Bulluṭ about disbursal of dates; sealed (Antigonus) 3/11/6. CT 49, 12, no. 59; Mitchell and Searight, no. 624; Nisaba 28, no. 463.
46733	1881,0830.199	Receipt of dates; sealed (Antigonus) -/-/4. CT 49, 17, no. 98; Mitchell and Searight, no. 611; Nisaba 28, no. 511.
46734	1881,0830.200	Memorandum? Dar 5?/2/15.
46735	1881,0830.201	School text; obv. literary excerpt: fable of the duqduqqu-bird (wren); rev. lexical, list of city names, including i-ši-in (sic) and šu-ru-up-pak; the obverse is inscribed in portrait format, the reverse in landscape format in two columns. Jiménez, BDP, 334, 338; Lambert, MC 24, no. 278.
46736	1881,0830.202	School text; incantations; bilingual incantation, Udug-ḫul 16; lexical (gi). Gesche, AOAT 275, 688; Geller, BAM 8, 499-541, pl. 129; Lambert, MC 24, no. 217.
46737	1881,0830.203	Contract about grain. Dar 30/6/17. Alu-ša-Marduk-šumu-līšir.
46738	1881,0830.204	Account of debts, etc.
46739	1881,0830.205	Inventory of household furniture.
46740	1881,0830.206	School text; house plan; lexical, Ḫḫ I. Wiseman, AnSt 22, 144-145; Gesche, AOAT 275, 688.
46741	1881,0830.207	Promissory note for silver. Dar I 15/12/20+. Borsippa. Zadok, Nisaba 21, 237.
46742	1881,0830.208	Account of wool.
46743	1881,0830.209	Contract; lease of a house.
46744	1881,0830.210	Transfer of land as part of a dowry. Dar 18/[]/17. Wunsch, AOAT 330, 373.
46745	1881,0830.211	Account of silver.
46746	1881,0830.212	Contract.
46747	1881,0830.213	Letter from Lâbâši; sealed; Philip 13/[]/[]. CT 22, 33, no. 181; Mitchell and Searight, no. 607; Nisaba 28, no. 443.

46748	1881,0830.214	Joined to 46624.
46749	1881,0830.215	Memorandum about silver and barley.
46750	1881,0830.216	Memorandum of 5 dan-nu-ut, month iv day 23, ud-du-ni.
46751	1881,0830.217	Memorandum?
46752	1881,0830.218	Account of silver.
46753	1881,0830.219	Contract.
46754	1881,0830.220	Promissory note for dates.
46755	1881,0830.221	Memorandum with list of names.
46756	1881,0830.222	List of workmen.
46757	1881,0830.223	Promissory note for silver 26/[]/5. Babylon.
46758	1881,0830.224	Field plan. Nemet-Nejat, LB Field Plans, no. 13.
46759	1881,0830.225	Joined to 45539.
46760	1881,0830.226	Field plan. Nemet-Nejat, LB Field Plans, no. 10.
46761	1881,0830.227	Memorandum about silver issued.
46762	1881,0830.228	Letter; names of sender and addressee lost. Hackl et al., AOAT 414/1, no. 107.
46763	1881,0830.229	Joined to 46578.
46764	1881,0830.230	Field plan. Dar 10/5/-.
46765	1881,0830.231	Promissory note for silver. Dar 26/4/-. Babylon.
46766	1881,0830.232	Joined to 43975.
46767	1881,0830.233	Contract. 7/-/-. Babylon.
46768	1881,0830.234	Medical omens; Šumma UZU.BE.
46769	1881,0830.235	Contract.
46770	1881,0830.236	Contract. 16/-/-.
46771	1881,0830.237	Promissory note for barley. Dar 5/11/-.
46772	1881,0830.238	Contract. Nbk -/2/-. Babylon.
46773	1881,0830.239	Contract.
46774	1881,0830.240	Contract.
46775	1881,0830.241	Contract. -/-/11.
46776	1881,0830.242	Sumerian literary.
46777	1881,0830.243	Memorandum of entries by day.
46778	1881,0830.244	Account of dates or grain.
46779	1881,0830.245	Contract for bricks. Nbk 1/12/-.
46780	1881,0830.246	Field plan. Dar 3/8/[]. Nemet-Nejat, LB Field Plans, no. 45.
46781	1881,0830.247	Omens from the flight of birds. + 46810 + 46917. Reiner, Fs Borger (CM 10), 300.
46782	1881,0830.248	Lexical; Ea; sign list.
46783	1881,0830.249	Lexical; Ea; sign list.
46784	1881,0830.250	Lexical; Ea; sign list.
46785	1881,0830.251	Mathematical; table of measures of length.
46786	1881,0830.252	Sumerian literary; šu'illa to Marduk; dupl. Weissbach, Miscellen, pls. 13-14.

46787	1881,0830.253	Marriage contract. Dar 26/8/[]. Wunsch, Bab Arch 2, no. 4.
46788	1881,0830.254	Quitclaim about a dowry field. Dupl. 45560. Nbn [23]/[]/16. Babylon. Wunsch, AOAT 330, 372-373.
46789	1881,0830.255	Account of oxen, etc.
46790	1881,0830.256	Contract.
46791	1881,0830.257	Land sale. Babylon.
46792	1881,0830.258	Lexical; Ea; sign list; literary extract.
46793	1881,0830.259	Promissory note for barley; sealed. Dar II 4/[]/17? Nisaba 28, no. 254.
46794	1881,0830.260	Field plan. Dar. Nemet-Nejat, LB Field Plans, no. 31.
46795	1881,0830.261	Lexical, Aa IV/2 = 23. MSL 14, 373.
46796	1881,0830.262	Astronomical. -/-/6.
46797	1881,0830.263	Promissory note for dowry silver. Dar 15/11/14. Babylon. Wunsch, AOAT 330, 374.
46798	1881,0830.264	Contract. Cam -/-/6. Babylon.
46799	1881,0830.265	Sale of ḫanšû land; archive of Bēl-ēṭir; finger-nail marks. Šamaš-šum-ukin 3/10/12. Kiš. + 46928 + 47309. Brinkman and Kennedy, JCS 35, 29, K.59; Nielsen, NABU 2006, 44-45, no. 44; Nielsen, JCS 62, 98-102.
46800	1881,0830.266	Contract. Dar 25/[]/28. Babylon.
46801	1881,0830.267	Contract; lease of a field.
46802	1881,0830.268	Astronomical.
46803	1881,0830.269	Literary; Enūma eliš I. King, STC pl. IX-XI; Lambert, BCM, p. 47.
46804	1881,0830.270	Bilingual epic; Lugal-e II 77-87. van Dijk, Lugal, text m2.
46805	1881,0830.271	Field sale.
46806	1881,0830.272	Field plan. Dar 17/12/22. Nemet-Nejat, LB Field Plans, no. 28.
46807	1881,0830.273	Account.
46808	1881,0830.274	Inventory of household furniture. Nbk -/3/-.
46809	1881,0830.275	Field sale.
46810	1881,0830.276	Joined to 46781.
46811	1881,0830.277	Mantic dream ritual.
46812	1881,0830.278	Field plan. Nemet-Nejat, LB Field Plans, no. 27.
46813	1881,0830.279	Account of dates. + 46895.
46814	1881,0830.280	Medical. + 46815.
46815	1881,0830.281	Joined to 46814.
46816	1881,0830.282	Promissory note for seed. Dar -/7/-.
46817	1881,0830.283	Promissory note for wheat. Dar 18/1/10.
46818	1881,0830.284	Field plan. RN lost []/5/[]. Nemet-Nejat, LB Field Plans, no. 8.
46819	1881,0830.285	Medical; list of plants; prescription ingredients.
46820	1881,0830.286	Medical; prescription ingredients.

46821	1881,0830.287	Literary.
46822	1881,0830.288	Lexical; Diri V. MSL 15 166.
46823	1881,0830.289	Lexical; Ḫḫ VIII. MSL 9, 173.
46824	1881,0830.290	Field plan. [Xerxes] 25+/5/[]. Nemet-Nejat, LB Field Plans, no. 46.
46825	1881,0830.291	Field sale. + 47167.
46826	1881,0830.292	Literary.
46827	1881,0830.293	Contract; transfer of land as part of a dowry. [Npl 21/2/7]. Babylon. Wunsch, Bab Arch 2, no. 10a.
46828	1881,0830.294	Medical; èš-abzu níg-nam-mú-a and bušānu incantations; dupl. Köcher, BAM VI, 533.
46829	1881,0830.295	Contract; sale of land; sealed. RN lost 12/9/9.
46830	1881,0830.296	Promissory note for dates. Dar 14/7/8. Wunsch, Bab Arch 2, no. 32.
46831	1881,0830.297	Medical.
46832	1881,0830.298	Field sale. Nbn -/-/11. Babylon.
46833	1881,0830.299	Contract. Dar 28/4/9.
46834	1881,0830.300	Mathematical; multiplication tables for 3 and 40, using gam for a-rá.
46835	1881,0830.301	School text; lexical; reverse: Ḫḫ XVI, XVII, XIX, XX, XXI. + 47022. MSL 10, 4, 81, 127 and 11, 3, 10.
46836	1881,0830.302	Account.
46837	1881,0830.303	School text; lexical; Ḫḫ XXI. MSL 11, 10.
46838	1881,0830.304	Contract; gift of slaves by a mother to her daughter. Cyr []/[]/8. Wunsch, Bab Arch 2, no. 28.
46839	1881,0830.305	Economic.
46840	1881,0830.306	Joined to 45499.
46841	1881,0830.307	Lexical; Ea; sign list.
46842	1881,0830.308	Mathematical.
46843	1881,0830.309	Field plan. Dar []/[]/23. Nemet-Nejat, LB Field Plans, no. 32.
46844	1881,0830.310	Promissory note for dates. Cam? 14/6/-.
46845	1881,0830.311	Letter.
46846	1881,0830.312	Contract. 26/[]/3.
46847	1881,0830.313	Deposition? Nbn.
46848	1881,0830.314	Promissory note for silver. Dar 13/3/20+. Babylon.
46849	1881,0830.315	Sale of a prebend. Dar.
46850	1881,0830.316	School text; lexical; Ḫḫ IX. MSL 9, 18.
46851	1881,0830.317	Account; names and weights.
46852	1881,0830.318	Medical; prescription ingredients.
46853	1881,0830.319	Account of barley.
46854	1881,0830.320	Account of purchases.
46855	1881,0830.321	Contract.
46856	1881,0830.322	Promissory note for silver; sealed. RN lost []/[]/35. Mitchell and Searight, no. 591; Nisaba 28, no. 237.

46857	1881,0830.323	Medical ritual; É-gal-ku4-ra.
46858	1881,0830.324	Field plan 6/12/5. + 47065. Nemet-Nejat, LB Field Plans, no. 26.
46859	1881,0830.325	Account of seed.
46860	1881,0830.326	Contract; list of witnesses.
46861	1881,0830.327	Literary.
46862	1881,0830.328	Contract; lease of a house. Nabû-[] -/-/16? Babylon.
46863	1881,0830.329	Contract.
46864	1881,0830.330	Lexical, commentary on Ḫḫ XX. MSL 11, 11.
46865	1881,0830.331	Incantation; Muššu'u tablet V. Böck, NABU 2001, 80-81, no. 86; Böck, Muššu'u, 181-220 and pl. XXVII.
46866	1881,0830.332	Field sale.
46867	1881,0830.333	Promissory note for silver.
46868	1881,0830.334	Contract. Dar 5/6/-. Babylon.
46869	1881,0830.335	Sale of field.
46870	1881,0830.336	Omens; extispicy?; copy (ḫe-pí).
46871	1881,0830.337	Astronomical; MUL.APIN. Reiner, Fs Borger (CM 10), 300; Hunger and Steele, MUL.APIN, 20.
46872	1881,0830.338	Literary.
46873	1881,0830.339	Contract; deed about a woman. Nbn 12/5/8. Borsippa. Zadok, Nisaba 21, 237.
46874	1881,0830.340	Receipt for 5 1/2 shekels of silver; drawing of a bird on the reverse.
46875	1881,0830.341	Promissory note for silver. RN lost 12/5/2.
46876	1881,0830.342	Sale of a slave. Dar 25/-/-.
46877	1881,0830.343	Promissory note for dates; drawing of two circles above date formula. Nbk 11/6?/39.
46878	1881,0830.344	Promissory note for silver. Dar 17/1/11.
46879	1881,0830.345	Account.
46880	1881,0830.346	Contract; lease of a house. Artaxerxes 28/8/29. Babylon.
46881	1881,0830.347	Literary.
46882	1881,0830.348	Incantation.
46883	1881,0830.349	Contract; pledge of a house. Dar I 19/8/28. Borsippa. Zadok, Nisaba 21, 237.
46884	1881,0830.350	Inventory of household furniture.
46885	1881,0830.351	Medical; prescription ingredients.
46886	1881,0830.352	Contract. -/-/23. Babylon.
46887	1881,0830.353	Promissory note for dates. Dar 24/5/18.
46888	1881,0830.354	Contract; lease of a house. Dar 7/8/14.
46889	1881,0830.355	Joined to 41223.
46890	1881,0830.356	Contract; sale of a house. Dar []/[]/[2]5+. + 47125. Nisaba 28, no. 133.
46891	1881,0830.357	Contract.
46892	1881,0830.358	Literary; mār Enlil and deities.

46893	1881,0830.359	Lexical; syllabary.
46894	1881,0830.360	Promissory note for silver; sealed; finger-nail marks. Art II/III 9/8/7. Mitchell and Searight, no. 643; Nisaba 28, no. 265.
46895	1881,0830.361	Joined to 46813.
46896	1881,0830.362	Medical; mentions seven stones.
46897	1881,0830.363	Joined to 43824.
46898	1881,0830.364	Promissory note for silver; u'iltim. Art 3/[]/11. Babylon.
46899	1881,0830.365	Contract; sale of a house.
46900	1881,0830.366	Lexical; place names.
46901	1881,0830.367	Joined to 45499.
46902	1881,0830.368	Field sale; land measured in GI. Dar 10/12/22.
46903	1881,0830.369	Astronomical.
46904	1881,0830.370	Lexical; Ea; sign list.
46905	1881,0830.371	Promissory note for silver.
46906	1881,0830.372	Copy (ḫe-pí) of a list of temple personnel? of Esangila; colophon.
46907	1881,0830.373	Iqqur īpuš, Ulūlu. Reiner, Fs Borger (CM 10), 300.
46908	1881,0830.374	Contract. -/-/9. Babylon.
46909	1881,0830.375	Joined to 45550.
46910	1881,0830.376	Contract. Babylon.
46911	1881,0830.377	Incantation; Šà-zi-ga. Biggs, TCS 2, p. 24-26, no. 8 and pl. 3.
46912	1881,0830.378	Field plan.
46913	1881,0830.379	Lexical; Ea; sign list.
46914	1881,0830.380	Medical.
46915	1881,0830.381	List of workmen.
46916	1881,0830.382	Promissory note for silver; dated arki Aššur-nādin-šūmi. Aššur-nādin-šūmi 24/5?/12. Borsippa. Brinkman and Kennedy, JCS 35, 16, Fn.2; Brinkman, NABU 1992, 68-69, no. 88.
46917	1881,0830.383	Joined to 46781.
46918	1881,0830.384	Old Babylonian. Loan contract; sealed. Samsuiluna 10/12/28.
46919	1881,0830.385	Contract for a garment. Dar I 15/6/15. Borsippa. Zadok, Nisaba 21, 237-238.
46920	1881,0830.386	Lexical; Ea; sign list and personal names.
46921	1881,0830.387	Promissory note for silver. Nbn 2/11/6. Babylon.
46922	1881,0830.388	Receipt for silver.
46923	1881,0830.389	Contract.
46924	1881,0830.390	Letter from Aplāya to Šadūnu. CT 22, 7, no. 32.
46925	1881,0830.391	Contract. Dar 30/5/36.
46926	1881,0830.392	Promissory note for silver. Dar -/7/-. Babylon.
46927	1881,0830.393	Receipt for barley. Dar 6/7/-.

46928	1881,0830.394	Joined to 46799.
46929	1881,0830.395	Field sale. Cam 14?/5/6.
46930	1881,0830.396	Field plan. Nemet-Nejat, LB Field Plans, no. 61.
46931	1881,0830.397	Letter; names of sender and addressee lost. Hackl et al., AOAT 414/1, no. 158.
46932	1881,0830.398	Letter order from Bullut; sealed. (Antigonus). CT 49, 17, no. 97; Nisaba 28, no. 465.
46933	1881,0830.399	Account of baskets.
46934	1881,0830.400	Memorandum; distribution of dates or grain.
46935	1881,0830.401	Promissory note for silver. Dar 2/1/4.
46936	1881,0830.402	Receipt for silver. Dar I 24/[]/21. Borsippa. Zadok, Nisaba 21, 238.
46937	1881,0830.403	Contract; lease of a house. [Dar?] 7/[]/34. Babylon.
46938	1881,0830.404	Promissory note for silver. Nbn. Babylon.
46939	1881,0830.405	Account.
46940	1881,0830.406	Promissory note for silver. Dar 12/2/16.
46941	1881,0830.407	Promissory note for dates. Dar I 13/2/16. Borsippa. Zadok, Nisaba 21, 238.
46942	1881,0830.408	Promissory note for dates. Dar 29/6/3.
46943	1881,0830.409	Receipt for house rent; finger-nail mark. Dar I 5/7/32. Borsippa. Zadok, Nisaba 21, 238.
46944	1881,0830.410	Letter from [] to the qīpu. Hackl et al., AOAT 414/1, no. 157.
46945	1881,0830.411	Promissory note for barley. Nbk 7/12/-.
46946	1881,0830.412	Receipt for silver. Dar I 23/3/27. Borsippa. Zadok, Nisaba 21, 238.
46947	1881,0830.413	Receipt for silver.
46948	1881,0830.414	Promissory note for onions. Dar I 22/9/33. Borsippa. Zadok, Nisaba 21, 238.
46949	1881,0830.415	Promissory note for silver. Dar 15/12/11. Babylon.
46950	1881,0830.416	Contract. Dar 26/1/30. Babylon.
46951	1881,0830.417	Field sale. RN lost -/-/14.
46952	1881,0830.418	Contract. Nbn -/-/8.
46953	1881,0830.419	Contract; lease of a house. Cyr -/1/-. Babylon.
46954	1881,0830.420	Omens.
46955	1881,0830.421	Receipt of silver for house rent. Dar I 12/1/25. Borsippa. Zadok, Nisaba 21, 238.
46956	1881,0830.422	Bilingual epic; Lugal-e VII 281-289 and 328-332. van Dijk, Lugal, text z.
46957	1881,0830.423	Contract. Dar 21/2/-.
46958	1881,0830.424	Contract. Nbk 23/1/36. Babylon.
46959	1881,0830.425	Promissory note for onions.
46960	1881,0830.426	Mathematical.
46961	1881,0830.427	Lexical, Aa IV/2 = 23. MSL 14, 373.

46962	1881,0830.428	Receipt for part of a dowry. Dar. Wunsch, AOAT 330, 373.
46963	1881,0830.429	Promissory note for dates. Nbn 16/7/15. Babylon. + 47091.
46964	1881,0830.430	Contract; lease of a house. AM? []/[]/1?. Babylon.
46965	1881,0830.431	Contract.
46966	1881,0830.432	Field plan. RN lost 8+/12/10+. Nemet-Nejat, LB Field Plans, no. 47.
46967	1881,0830.433	Contract. Dar -/-/17.
46968	1881,0830.434	Account.
46969	1881,0830.435	Field sale.
46970	1881,0830.436	Contract.
46971	1881,0830.437	Joined to 43974.
46972	1881,0830.438	Maqlu tablet IX (ritual tablet). Abusch, AMD 10, 205-225.
46973	1881,0830.439	Omens; Šumma izbu. De Zorzi, Šumma izbu, 927-928.
46974	1881,0830.440	Field sale. Dar 14/7/16. Babylon.
46975	1881,0830.441	Quittance. AM 22/9/1. Babylon.
46976	1881,0830.442	Promissory note for dates.
46977	1881,0830.443	Promissory note for barley. Ner 4/9/acc.
46978	1881,0830.444	Joined to 43897.
46979	1881,0830.445	Joined to 46624.
46980	1881,0830.446	Promissory note for silver. Dar 5/8/3. Babylon.
46981	1881,0830.447	Memorandum of elongated oval shape. 10 me / 1,30 / 1 lim. The 10 is written with 10 vertical wedges.
46982	1881,0830.448	Promissory note for 1/2 mina 2 shekels of silver. Nbn 10/12/8.
46983	1881,0830.449	Deposition. Dar -/1/10. Babylon.
46984	1881,0830.450	Joined to 43975.
46985	1881,0830.451	Contract.
46986	1881,0830.452	Contract.
46987	1881,0830.453	Contract.
46988	1881,0830.454	Inventory of a dowry.
46989	1881,0830.455	Sale of a woman. + 47124.
46990	1881,0830.456	Joined to 43975.
46991	1881,0830.457	Joined to 45547.
46992	1881,0830.458	Field plan. Nemet-Nejat, LB Field Plans, no. 12.
46993	1881,0830.459	School text; lexical; Ḫḫ XXIII. MSL 11, 68.
46994	1881,0830.460	Contract.
46995	1881,0830.461	Field plan. Nemet-Nejat, LB Field Plans, no. 54.
46996	1881,0830.462	Contract.
46997	1881,0830.463	Field plan. Nemet-Nejat, LB Field Plans, no. 17.
46998	1881,0830.464	Field sale.

46999	1881,0830.465	Medical ritual and incantation. + 47169. Abusch and Schwemer, AMD 8/2 text 8.27 h, pl. 50.
47000	1881,0830.466	Contract; lease from month viii? of year 7? to month vii of year 8; lower left corner of tablet; sealed. Art II/III []/[]/7? Mitchell and Searight, no. 488; Nisaba 28, no. 266.
47001	1881,0830.467	Dowry record. Dar []/9/[]. Babylon. Wunsch, AOAT 330, 373.
47002	1881,0830.468	Promissory note for dates. []/8/[]. Babylon.
47003	1881,0830.469	Lexical; Ea; sign list.
47004	1881,0830.470	Deposition.
47005	1881,0830.471	Lexical; Ea; sign list.
47006	1881,0830.472	Contract. Dar? 15/[]/26.
47007	1881,0830.473	Account of dates or grain.
47008	1881,0830.474	Lexical; Ḫḫ XXIII. MSL 11, 67.
47009	1881,0830.475	Lexical; god-list.
47010	1881,0830.476	Sale of a canal inspector's prebend. 17/10/-.
47011	1881,0830.477	Bilingual incantation; Bīt rimki III 62-69; dupl. Borger, JCS 21, 1-15.
47012	1881,0830.478	Letter from Bēl-ēṭer to Nabû-bullissu. Hackl et al., AOAT 414/1, no. 108.
47013	1881,0830.479	Joined to 46575.
47014	1881,0830.480	Field plan. Dar []/[]/12. Nemet-Nejat, LB Field Plans, no. 35.
47015	1881,0830.481	Field sale.
47016	1881,0830.482	Promissory note for dates or grain.
47017	1881,0830.483	Sale of a woman. 10/-/-.
47018	1881,0830.484	Contract.
47019	1881,0830.485	Field plan. Dar 30/5?/[]. Nemet-Nejat, LB Field Plans, no. 33.
47020	1881,0830.486	Promissory note for barley. Cam -/10/1. Babylon.
47021	1881,0830.487	Promissory note for silver.
47022	1881,0830.488	Joined to 46835.
47023	1881,0830.489	Contract.
47024	1881,0830.490	Lexical; Ea III; colophon. MSL 14, 301; Landsberger, Gs Speiser, 133.
47025	1881,0830.491	Contract. Nbk -/2/21.
47026	1881,0830.492	Contract. Nbn 7/3/-.
47027	1881,0830.493	Bilingual; mentions Esangila.
47028	1881,0830.494	Field sale.
47029	1881,0830.495	Field plan. Nemet-Nejat, LB Field Plans, no. 68.
47030	1881,0830.496	Omens?
47031	1881,0830.497	Incantation.
47032	1881,0830.498	Love Lyrics. Fincke, NABU 2013, 125-127, no. 76.
47033	1881,0830.499	Literary; mentions KÁ pa-pa-ḫi, Ningal, etc.

47034	1881,0830.500	Incantation.
47035	1881,0830.501	Account.
47036	1881,0830.502	Field plan. Nemet-Nejat, LB Field Plans, no. 30.
47037	1881,0830.503	Contract; land sale; sealed; finger-nail marks. [Darius I]. Nisaba 28, no. 131.
47038	1881,0830.504	Contract.
47039	1881,0830.505	Sealing; uninscribed; impression of a cylinder seal.
47040	1881,0830.506	Mathematical; memorandum of numbers; 6 24 24 6.
47041	1881,0830.507	Memorandum.
	1881,0830.508ff.	Nos. 508-517 are uninscribed objects.
	1881,0830.518	Fragment of a stone mortar with one line of inscription; d.nin-ḫur-sag. Old Babylonian?
	1881,0830.519ff.	Nos. 519-561 are uninscribed objects.
47042	1881,0830.562	Mathematical; unusual table in format: 1 n1 ŠEŠ.MEŠ IGI n1 n2 1 n2 LÚ n3; large tablet; turns sideways; inscribed on the edges. + 47064.
47043	1881,0830.563	Lexical; Ea; sign list.
47044	1881,0830.564	Economic.
47045	1881,0830.565	Economic.
47046	1881,0830.566	Ritual.
47047	1881,0830.567	Field plan. Nemet-Nejat, LB Field Plans, no. 48.
47048	1881,0830.568	Lexical; Ea; sign list and personal names.
47049	1881,0830.569	School practice.
47050	1881,0830.570	Contract; date mentioned. 1/6/-.
47051	1881,0830.571	School practice tablet; numbers.
47052	1881,0830.572	Lexical; god list.
47053	1881,0830.573	Lexical; Ea; sign list.
47054	1881,0830.574	Bilingual incantation.
47055	1881,0830.575	Field sale; sealed. [Dar I]. Nisaba 28, no. 129.
47056	1881,0830.576	Lexical; Ḫḫ I.
47057	1881,0830.577	Lexical; personal names.
47058	1881,0830.578	Field plan. Dar 8/[]/30. + 47131. Nemet-Nejat, LB Field Plans, no. 4.
47059	1881,0830.579	Lexical; Ea; sign list.
47060	1881,0830.580	Lexical; syllabary.
47061	1881,0830.581	Lexical.
47062	1881,0830.582	Lexical; Ea; sign list.
47063	1881,0830.583	Contract. 10/[]/5.
47064	1881,0830.584	Joined to 47042.
47065	1881,0830.585	Joined to 46858.
47066	1881,0830.586	Field plan. + 1881,0830.596.
47067	1881,0830.587	Field plan.
47068	1881,0830.588	Lexical; syllabary. + 1881,0830.626.

47069	1881,0830.589	School text; bilingual incantations, extracts including Udug-ḫul 10; diagram. + 47113. Geller, BAM 8, 323-339, pl. 160.
47070	1881,0830.590	Lexical; Ea; sign list.
47071	1881,0830.591	Lexical; Ea; sign list.
47072	1881,0830.592	Lexical; god-list.
47073	1881,0830.593	Lexical; Ea; sign list.
47074	1881,0830.594	Contract.
47075	1881,0830.595	Literary; colophon.
	1881,0830.596	Joined to 47066.
47076	1881,0830.597	Field sale.
47077	1881,0830.598	Lexical; god-list.
47078	1881,0830.599	Unidentified; mentions Zarpanītu.
47079	1881,0830.600	Literary.
47080	1881,0830.601	Literary catalogue.
47081	1881,0830.602	Field plan.
47082	1881,0830.603	Field sale.
47083	1881,0830.604	Field sale.
47084	1881,0830.605	Marriage contract. Wunsch, Bab Arch 2, no. 6.
47085	1881,0830.606	Literary.
47086	1881,0830.607	Lexical; Ea; sign list.
47087	1881,0830.608	Field plan. Nemet-Nejat, LB Field Plans, no. 52.
47088	1881,0830.609	Contract.
47089	1881,0830.610	Field plan. Nemet-Nejat, LB Field Plans, no. 18.
47090	1881,0830.611	Literary.
47091	1881,0830.612	Joined to 46963.
47092	1881,0830.613	Medical.
47093	1881,0830.614	Economic.
47094	1881,0830.615	Field plan. Nemet-Nejat, LB Field Plans, no. 19.
47095	1881,0830.616	Field plan.
47096	1881,0830.617	Lexical; Ea; sign list.
47097	1881,0830.618	Lexical; syllabary.
47098	1881,0830.619	Letter.
47099	1881,0830.620	Economic.
47100	1881,0830.621	Contract.
47101	1881,0830.622	Lexical, Lú = ša.
47102	1881,0830.623	Account; one face inscribed in landscape format, the other in portrait format.
47103	1881,0830.624	Lexical; Ea; sign list.
47104	1881,0830.625	Medical.
	1881,0830.626	Joined to 47068.
47105	1881,0830.627	Incantation.
47106	1881,0830.628	Lexical.
47107	1881,0830.629	Field plan.
47108	1881,0830.630	Account. Dar 17/[]/4.

47109	1881,0830.631	Mathematical; multiplication tables.
47110	1881,0830.632	Field plan. Nemet-Nejat, LB Field Plans, no. 37.
47111	1881,0830.633	Lexical; Ea; sign list.
47112	1881,0830.634	Medical.
47113	1881,0830.635	Joined to 47069.
47114	1881,0830.636	Contract.
47115	1881,0830.637	Land sale(?).
47116	1881,0830.638	Economic.
47117	1881,0830.639	Bilingual incantation.
47118	1881,0830.640	Astronomical?
47119	1881,0830.641	Astronomical.
47120	1881,0830.642	Lexical; syllabary.
47121	1881,0830.643	Lexical and literary extracts.
47122	1881,0830.644	Lexical; Ea; sign list.
47123	1881,0830.645	Field sale.
47124	1881,0830.646	Joined to 46989.
47125	1881,0830.647	Joined to 46890.
47126	1881,0830.648	Lexical.
47127	1881,0830.649	Lexical; Ea; sign list.
47128	1881,0830.650	Literary.
47129	1881,0830.651	Lexical; Ea; sign list.
47130	1881,0830.652	Lexical.
47131	1881,0830.653	Joined to 47058.
47132	1881,0830.654	Contract; sealed. Nisaba 28, no. 308.
47133	1881,0830.655	Field plan. Nemet-Nejat, LB Field Plans, no. 16.
47134	1881,0830.656	Historical; fragment of a copy of the Cyrus Cylinder (90920). Finkel, Cyrus cylinder, 129-133.
47135	1881,0830.657	Account.
47136	1881,0830.658	Medical.
47137	1881,0830.659	Joined to 43975.
47138	1881,0830.660	Lexical; personal names.
47139	1881,0830.661	Joined to 45484.
47140	1881,0830.662	Economic.
47141	1881,0830.663	Incantation?
47142	1881,0830.664	Medical?
47143	1881,0830.665	Late Babylonian copy of an early royal inscription; 3 signs only.
47144	1881,0830.666	Lexical; list of plant parts. + 47308.
47145	1881,0830.667	Contract; lease of a house.
47146	1881,0830.668	Contract.
47147	1881,0830.669	Contract -/12/-. Babylon.
47148	1881,0830.670	Literary.
47149	1881,0830.671	Astronomical.
47150	1881,0830.672	Temple ritual.
47151	1881,0830.673	Contract.

47152	1881,0830.674	Astronomical.
47153	1881,0830.675	Medical.
47154	1881,0830.676	Tintir V 39-42.
47155	1881,0830.677	Field sale.
47156	1881,0830.678	Astrological omens.
47157	1881,0830.679	Lexical; Ea; sign list.
47158	1881,0830.680	Incantation; Ḫulbazizi.
47159	1881,0830.681	Field plan. Nemet-Nejat, LB Field Plans, no. 41.
47160	1881,0830.682	Promissory note for silver. 1/[]/10+.
47161	1881,0830.683	Contract; sealed. Nisaba 28, no. 309.
47162	1881,0830.684	Economic.
47163	1881,0830.685	Joined to 41237.
47164	1881,0830.686	Lexical; personal names.
47165	1881,0830.687	Old Babylonian. Receipt.
47166	1881,0830.688	Incantation.
47167	1881,0830.689	Joined to 46825.
47168	1881,0830.690	Lexical; Ḫḫ XVII (plants). MSL 10, 80.
47169	1881,0830.691	Joined to 46999.
47170	1881,0830.692	Mathematical; multiplication table.
47171	1881,0830.693	Field plan. Nemet-Nejat, LB Field Plans, no. 36.
47172	1881,0830.694	Contract.
47173	1881,0830.695	Joined to 45528.
47174	1881,0830.696	Incantation.
47175	1881,0830.697	Lexical; syllabary.
47176	1881,0830.698	Historical; fragment of a copy of the Cyrus Cylinder (09020). Finkel, Cyrus cylinder, 129-133.
47177	1881,0830.699	Hemerology; Babylonian Almanac; part of a multi-column tablet listing the days of each month of the year; fragment from the reverse.
47178	1881,0830.700	Contract.
47179	1881,0830.701	Contract; sealed. Nisaba 28, no. 310.
47180	1881,0830.702	Economic.
47181	1881,0830.703	Account of dates or grain.
47182	1881,0830.704	Field sale.
47183	1881,0830.705	Economic.
47184	1881,0830.706	Mathematical.
47185	1881,0830.707	Incantation, Šurpu III?
47186	1881,0830.708	Literary.
47187	1881,0830.709	Incantation.
47188	1881,0830.710	Account of grain.
47189	1881,0830.711	Account.
47190	1881,0830.712	Joined to 45528.
47191	1881,0830.713	Unidentified.
47192	1881,0830.714	Incantation.
47193	1881,0830.715	Field sale.

47194	1881,0830.716	Contract.
47195	1881,0830.717	Unidentified; rulings after every line.
47196	1881,0830.718	Incantation.
47197	1881,0830.719	Joined to 45528.
47198	1881,0830.720	Promissory note for dates. Dar 18/6/24.
47199	1881,0830.721	Contract. Dar 5/[]/20.
47200	1881,0830.722	Lexical; Ea; sign list; stones.
47201	1881,0830.723	Sumerian literary.
47202	1881,0830.724	Contract.
47203	1881,0830.725	Incantation; Lamaštu?
47204	1881,0830.726	Omens; Šumma ālu.
47205	1881,0830.727	Division of property.
47206	1881,0830.728	Contract.
47207	1881,0830.729	Lexical; Ea; sign list and literary extracts.
47208	1881,0830.730	Lexical; Ea; sign list.
47209	1881,0830.731	Contract.
47210	1881,0830.732	Economic.
47211	1881,0830.733	Practice words and phrases.
47212	1881,0830.734	Lexical; sign list.
47213	1881,0830.735	Administrative? Mostly illegible.
47214	1881,0830.736	Lexical; Ea; sign list.
47215	1881,0830.737	Lexical; Ea; sign list.
47216	1881,0830.738	Unidentified.
47217	1881,0830.739	Lexical; Ḫḫ I.
47218	1881,0830.740	Unidentified. Lines end in UD 9, UD 10, UD 11, etc. (+) 47219.
47219	1881,0830.741	Unidentified. Lines end in UD 4, UD 8, UD 9, etc. (+) 47218.
47220	1881,0830.742	Missing.
47221	1881,0830.743	Literary extracts.
47222	1881,0830.744	Lexical; Ea; sign list.
47223	1881,0830.745	Lexical; Ea; sign list.
47224	1881,0830.746	Lexical; personal names.
47225	1881,0830.747	Lexical; syllabary.
47226	1881,0830.748	Field plan. Nemet-Nejat, LB Field Plans, no. 60.
47227	1881,0830.749	Lexical; Ea; sign list.
47228	1881,0830.750	Contract.
47229	1881,0830.751	Lexical; Ea; sign list; personal names; donkeys.
47230	1881,0830.752	Lexical?; two columns.
47231	1881,0830.753	Mathematical; factorisation table.
47232	1881,0830.754	Lexical; personal names.
47233	1881,0830.755	Lexical; explanatory god-list.
47234	1881,0830.756	Mathematical; problem text; division between brothers.
47235	1881,0830.757	Lexical; Ea; sign list.

47236	1881,0830.758	Economic. 10/[]/20.
47237	1881,0830.759	Lexical; Ea; sign list.
47238	1881,0830.760	Medical.
47239	1881,0830.761	Unidentified.
47240	1881,0830.762	Lexical; Ea; sign list.
47241	1881,0830.763	Lexical; personal names.
47242	1881,0830.764	Literary; bilingual.
47243	1881,0830.765	Bilingual incantation.
47244	1881,0830.766	Old Babylonian. Contract; sale of a house.
47245	1881,0830.767	Medical.
47246	1881,0830.768	Lexical; Ḫḫ; animals.
47247	1881,0830.769	Account.
47248	1881,0830.770	Field plan.
47249	1881,0830.771	Sealing for one side of a jar; inscribed with numerals only; two? cylinder seal impressions.
47250	1881,0830.772	Account.
47251	1881,0830.773	Lexical; Ea; sign list.
47252	1881,0830.774	Lexical; personal names.
47253	1881,0830.775	Promissory note.
47254	1881,0830.776	Contract.
47255	1881,0830.777.	Fragment of envelope of a letter.
47256	1881,0830.778	Contract.
47257	1881,0830.779	Lexical.
47258	1881,0830.780	Lexical.
47259	1881,0830.781	Lexical; Ea; sign list and literary extracts.
47260	1881,0830.782	Lexical; Ea; sign list.
47261	1881,0830.783	Joined to 46587.
47262	1881,0830.784	Lexical; Ea; sign list.
47263	1881,0830.785	Receipt for payment of silver.
47264	1881,0830.786	Economic.
47265	1881,0830.787	Incantation? + 47267.
47266	1881,0830.788	Lexical; Ea; sign list and personal names.
47267	1881,0830.789	Joined to 47265.
47268	1881,0830.790	Medical.
47269	1881,0830.791	Lexical; personal names.
47270	1881,0830.792	Lexical.
47271	1881,0830.793	Receipt of barley(?); sealed. (Borsippa). Mitchell and Searight, no. 592; Nisaba 28, no. 529.
47272	1881,0830.794	Joined to 45547.
47273	1881,0830.795	Lexical.
47274	1881,0830.796	List of workmen. -/-/acc.
47275	1881,0830.797	Lexical; Ea; sign list.
47276	1881,0830.798	Obv. lexical, GI; rev. days by number.
47277	1881,0830.799	Mathematical; combined multiplication table.
47278	1881,0830.800	Contract.

47279	1881,0830.801	Medical.
47280	1881,0830.802	Lexical; Ea; sign list.
47281	1881,0830.803	Contract.
47282	1881,0830.804	Lexical; god-list; Zababa repeated.
47283	1881,0830.805	Contract.
47284	1881,0830.806	Economic.
47285	1881,0830.807	Incantation.
47286	1881,0830.808	Lexical; god-list.
47287	1881,0830.809	Lexical; two columns.
47288	1881,0830.810	Economic.
47289	1881,0830.811	Lexical; Ea; sign list.
47290	1881,0830.812	Contract.
47291	1881,0830.813	Incantation.
47292	1881,0830.814	Literary; Enūma eliš I. Cf. Pinches, JRAS 1902, p. 205 n. 1; Kämmerer and Metzler, AOAT 375, 87, Tafel I UU, pl. XII; Lambert, BCM, p. 47, pl. 4.
47293	1881,0830.815	Lexical; two columns.
47294	1881,0830.816	Astronomical Diary.
47295	1881,0830.817	Account of lambs.
47296	1881,0830.818	Astronomical?
47297	1881,0830.819	Contract.
47298	1881,0830.820	Field sale; fragment of upper edge; obv. inscribed in landscape format, rev. in portrait format.
47299	1881,0830.821	Contract. Dar 6/[]/10.
47300	1881,0830.822	Account.
47301	1881,0830.823	Contract. Dar I []/[]/33. Borsippa. Zadok, Nisaba 21, 238.
47302	1881,0830.824	Account.
47303	1881,0830.825	Economic.
47304	1881,0830.826	Promissory note for dates. Dar I []/3/28. Borsippa. Zadok, Nisaba 21, 238.
47305	1881,0830.827	Memorandum.
47306	1881,0830.828	Receipt.
47307	1881,0830.829	Contract. 4/[]/24+.
47308	1881,0830.830	Joined to 47144.
47309	1881,0830.831	Joined to 46799.
47310	1881,0830.832	Economic.
	1881,0830.833ff.	Nos. 833-841 are uninscribed objects.
47311	1881,0830.842	Promissory note for dates owed as tithe to Nabû; mentions Bulluṭ / Nabû-ēṭir; sealed. Philip 10/11/3. Borsippa. CT 49, 2, no. 9; Mitchell and Searight, no. 606; Nisaba 28, no. 441.
	1881,0830.843ff.	Nos. 843-845 are uninscribed objects.
	1881,0830.846ff.	Nos. 846-922 are bricks of Nebuchadnezzar II. See CBI, no. 106.

	1881,0830.923ff.	Nos. 923-928 are uninscribed objects.
47312	1881,0830.563a	Old Babylonian. Field sale; sealed. Ammiṣaduqa 4/9/?
47313	1881,0830.564a	Old Babylonian. Contract; sealed with captions.
47314	1881,0830.565a	Old Babylonian. Contract; sealed with captions.
47315	1881,0830.566a	Old Babylonian. Contract; sealed. Samsuditana 13/9/11?
47316	1881,0830.567a	Envelope of a letter; sealed. The inner tablet is 47329. SE Ant II 11/9/54. + 47323. CT 49, 25, no. 122; Jursa, Persika 9, 156, 191-192; Mitchell and Searight, no. 687; Nisaba 28, no. 669.
47317	1881,0830.568a	Old Babylonian. Contract; sealed. Samsuditana 15/10/17.
47318	1881,0830.569a	Old Babylonian. Contract; sale of a house. Abiešuḫ 10/11/?
47319	1881,0830.570a	Old Babylonian. Contract; sealed. Ammiṣaduqa 10/2/11.
47320	1881,0830.571a	Old Babylonian. Contract; sealed.
47321	1881,0830.572a	Old Babylonian. Contract; sealed. Samsuditana 7/[]/19.
47322	1881,0830.573a	Old Babylonian. Contract; sealed. Samsuditana 5/5/?.
47323	1881,0830.574a	Joined to 47316.
47324	1881,0830.575a	Old Babylonian. Contract; sealed. Ammiditana 8/7/?.
47325	1881,0830.576a	Old Babylonian. Contract; sealed. + 1881,0830.592a.
47326	1881,0830.577a	Old Babylonian. Contract; sealed. Ammiditana 8/2/?.
47327	1881,0830.578a	Old Babylonian. Contract; sealed. Ammiditana 1/2/?.
47328	1881,0830.579a	Old Babylonian. Contract; sealed. Ammiditana 18/12/23.
47329	1881,0830.580a	Letter to Murānu; the envelope is 47316. SE Ant II 11/9/54. CT 49, 26, no. 123; Jursa, Persika 9, 156, 191-192.
47330	1881,0830.581a	Old Babylonian. Contract; sealed.
47331	1881,0830.582a	Old Babylonian. Contract; sealed. Samsuditana 16/12/10.
47332	1881,0830.583a	School text; literary; lexical.
47333	1881,0830.584a	Old Babylonian. Contract about sheep; sealed. Ammiṣaduqa 1/12/14.
47334	1881,0830.585a	Old Babylonian. Contract; sealed.
47335	1881,0830.586a	Old Babylonian. Contract; sealed with captions; year illegible. 10+/12/?.
47336	1881,0830.587a	Old Babylonian. Contract for barley; sealed with captions. Samsuditana ?/7/?.
47337	1881,0830.588a	Old Babylonian. Contract; sealed with caption.
47338	1881,0830.589a	Old Babylonian. Contract; sealed.

47339	1881,0830.590a	Old Babylonian. Fragment of the envelope of a contract; 6 witnesses.
47339a	1881,0830.591a	Old Babylonian. Fragment of the envelope of a contract; sealed with caption.
47339b	1881,0830.591b	Contract; witnesses.
	1881,0830.592a	Joined to 47325.

1881,1008 collection

The 1881,1008 collection was presented by C. D. Cobham, HM Commissioner at Larnaca, Cyprus, via C. T. Newton. The fact that four (or maybe all five) of these items were copied by Bellino indicates the early origins of the collection. At present we have no information on how Cobham acquired the collection. The register gives no provenances.

91141	1881,1008.1	Cylinder; inscription of Nebuchadnezzar II. Grotefend, AGWG 6 (1853) 65 (Bellino's copy); Berger, AOAT 4/1, Nebukadnezar Zylinder II, 2, no. 2; Barnett and Walker, Iraq 36, 27, no. 23.
47340	1881,1008.2	Record of a debt of barley, repayable in Kūtû; sealed; finger-nail marks; Aramaic note; vitrified. Art II 7/10/3. Šinna'ē. Strassmaier, 8th Orientalist Congress, no. 25; Bertin 2873; Grotefend, ZKM 1, 212-222 and pl., A (Bellino's copy D); Barnett and Walker, Iraq 36, 27, no. 16; Stolper, Fs Reiner, 390-391; Stolper, Fs Larsen, 520, 522-523, 541 (Bellino's copy D); Nisaba 28, no. 229.
47341	1881,1008.3	Contract; sale of a house; caption for lost finger-nail mark. Dar I 10?/[]/[]. [Babylon?]. Stolper, Fs Larsen, 520, 527-529, 544 (Bellino's copy H).
47342	1881,1008.4	Brick of Nebuchadnezzar II. CBI, no. 95.
47343	1881,1008.5	Promissory note for silver secured by pledge of real estate; sealed. Art I 17/9/40. Manaḫu. Strassmaier, 8th Orientalist Congress, no. 31; Bertin 2858; Grotefend, ZKM 3, 179-183 and pl., D (Bellino's copy G); Oppert and Ménant, DJ, 280-284; Barnett and Walker, Iraq 36, 2, no. 19; Stolper, Fs Reiner, 394-395; Stolper, Fs Larsen, 520, 526-527, 542 (Bellino's copy G); Mitchell and Searight, no. 503; Nisaba 28, no. 223.

1881,1103 collection

The 1881,1103 collection comes from the excavations of Hormuzd Rassam. See J. E. Reade in CBTBM VI, p. xxxi. Of the tablets listed here the register gives the following provenances:

Babylon nos. 1-48, 66-72, 74-76, 79, 82, 83, 85, 91, 93, 100-102, 104, 107, 108, 111, 113, 121, 126, 129-131, 133-136, 138, 141-143, 146, 150, 160, 166(?), 168, 174, 257, 270, 397, 830-957, 959, 961-967, 969, 971-975, 978-982, 984-989, 991-999, 1000-1-26, 1028-1030, 1033, 1035, 1037, 1038, 1042-1045, 1047-1050, 1052-1055, 1057, 1060, 1061, 1063-1067, 1069, 1071-1085, 1087, 1089-1094, 1096-1109, 1111-1118, 1120-1134, 1136, 1137, 1139-1143, 1148, 1150, 1151, 1153-1155, 1157-1162, 1164-1167, 1170, 1171, 1173-1176, 1178-1189, 1191, 1193, 1195, 1196, 1199-1201, 1204-1219, 1221-1290, 1292-1355, 1357-1368, 1370-1401, 1403-1411, 1414, 1415, 1417, 1419-1424, 1428-1431, 1433, 1435-1444, 1446-1457, 1459-1464, 1468, 1470-1475, 1477-1486, 1488-1497, 1500-1616, 1618-1642, 1645, 1649, 1650, 1655, 1657, 1658, 1660-1662, 1664, 1665, 1667, 1669, 1670, 1673-1677, 1679, 1681, 1683, 1686, 1688-1691, 1695, 1697-1699, 1702-1711, 1713, 1714, 1718, 1720-1726, 1728, 1729, 1731-1733, 1735-1744, 1746-1753, 1755, 1757, 1760-1763, 1769, 1774, 1776-1784, 1786-1796, 1798-1820, 1822-1850, 1852-1874

Birs Nimrud nos. 103, 235, 259, 260, 269, 271, 29, 297, 305, 313, 315, 323, 329, 330, 399, 405, 422, 478-480, 496, 604, 958, 960, 970, 976, 977, 983, 990, 1027, 1039, 1040, 1046, 1056, 1086, 1088, 1095, 1138, 1144-1147, 1149, 1156, 1168, 1169, 1172, 1190, 1192, 1194, 1197, 1198, 1202, 1203, 1220, 1291, 1356, 1369, 1402, 1413, 1425, 1434, 1465, 1617, 1696, 1701, 1712, 1715, 1719, 1734, 1754, 1756, 1759, 1821

Dailem nos. 49-64, 73, 77, 78, 80, 81, 84, 86-90, 92, 94-96, 98, 99, 105, 106, 109, 110, 112, 114-120, 122, 124, 125, 127, 128, 137, 139, 140, 144, 145, 148, 154, 155, 157-159, 165, 169-171, 173, 176-179, 181, 182, 184-195, 209, 213, 215, 216, 218, 220, 223, 236, 237, 240, 246, 261, 262, 278, 286, 287, 298$_2$99, 301, 304, 310-312, 314, 320-322, 325, 328, 409, 412, 415, 416, 419, 469-472, 474, 476, 485, 488, 490, 492-494, 525, 607, 644, 968, 1031, 1032, 1034, 1036, 1041, 1051, 1058, 1059, 1062, 1068-1070, 1110, 1119, 1135, 1152, 1163, 1177, 1412, 1416, 1418, 1426, 1427, 1432, 1445, 1458, 1466, 1467, 1469, 1476, 1487, 1498, 1499, 1643, 1644, 1646-1648, 1651-1654, 1656, 1659, 1663, 1666(?), 1668, 1671, 1672, 1678, 1680, 1682, 1684, 1685, 1687, 1692-1694, 1716, 1717, 1727, 1730, 1745, 1764-1768, 1770-1773, 1775, 1784, 1797, 1851

Borsippa no. 65.

	1881,1103.1ff.	Nos. 1-48 are uninscribed objects.
47344	1881,1103.49	Promissory note for dates. Dar I 5/7/30. Dilbat. Bertin 2680.
47345	1881,1103.50	Promissory note for barley. Art I/II 14/9/39. Dilbat. Stolper, Iraq 54 (1992) 130-131; Bertin 2868.
47346	1881,1103.51	Promissory note for silver. Nbk 7/12/12. Dilbat. Bertin 1070.

47347	1881,1103.52	Receipt for barley fodder. Ner 16/9/acc. Evetts, Ner. 6; Bertin 1185; Sack, AOAT 236, no. 6.
47348	1881,1103.53	Promissory note for silver. Kandalanu 21/11/17+. Dilbat. Brinkman and Kennedy, JCS 35, 51, L.180; Bertin 1030.
47349	1881,1103.54	Promissory note for barley and dates. Nbk 29/12/39. Dilbat. Bertin 1148.
47350	1881,1103.55	Promissory note for barley. Dar I 5?/9/27. Dilbat. Bertin 2628.
47351	1881,1103.56	Promissory note for dates. Cyr 8/4/5?. Alu-ša-Ea-zēra-ibni. Bertin 1665.
47352	1881,1103.57	Sale of a woman. Nbk 17/6/30. Dilbat. Bertin 1078.
47353	1881,1103.58	Promissory note for silver. Šamaš-šum-ukin 21/7/7. Dilbat. Brinkman and Kennedy, JCS 35, 27, K.21; Bertin 1004.
47354	1881,1103.59	Sale of a jenny and her foal by Iddin-Nabû / Nabû-ina-kāri-lūmur to Nergal-ab-uṣur / Ubārīja; scribe is Nabû-zēr-ibni / Nabû-šum-iddin / Šangû-Adad. Dar I 26/2/31. Dilbat. Weszeli, WZKM 86, 477-478; Weszeli and Baker, WZKM 87, 237-238 and 245, no. 5; Bertin 2696.
47355	1881,1103.60	Promissory note for dates. Dar I 12/6/34. Dilbat. Bertin 2733.
47356	1881,1103.61	Account of barley rations. Nbk []/[]/36. Nbk 315; Bertin 1136.
47357	1881,1103.62	Promissory note for dates. Nbk 26/5/37. Dilbat. Bertin 1141.
47358	1881,1103.63	Promissory note for silver. Dar I 27?/1/29. Dilbat; marked "D". Bertin 2667.
47359	1881,1103.64	Receipt for rent? 16/12/31. Dilbat; marked "D". Bertin 2988.
47360	1881,1103.65	Bilingual incantation; marked "B".
47361	1881,1103.66	Sale of a woman; Indian(?) script on reverse; fingernail marks. Art I/II 11/12/23. Babylon. Pinches, PSBA 5 (1883) 103ff; Bobrinskoy and Torrey, JAOS 56, 86-88, 490-491; Bertin 2864.
47362	1881,1103.67	Contract; partnership agreement; sealed. Art I/II 8/2/28. Babylon. Mitchell and Searight, no. 500; Nisaba 28, no. 287.
47363	1881,1103.68	Letter from Iṣṣūr to Iddin-Uraš. CT 22, 7, no. 33; Hackl et al., AOAT 414/1, no. 159.
47364	1881,1103.69	"Aluzinnu text", list of gods and their seats; dupl. 2R 60, no. 1.
47365	1881,1103.70	Lexical; list of gods and epithets; especially Ea; partly duplicates 2R 58, 5 (K.4366) and CT 25, 48.

47366	1881,1103.71	Contract; siege text. Šamaš-šum-ukin 9/10/19. Babylon. Pinches, JTVI 26 (1893) 163-165; Oppenheim, Iraq 17, 77; Brinkman and Kennedy, JCS 35, 35, K.133; Frame, JCS 51, 105.
47367	1881,1103.72	Promissory note for silver. Kandalanu 8/12/17. Babylon. Brinkman and Kennedy, JCS 35, 46, L.114.
47368	1881,1103.73	Sale of prebend. Dar I 4/8/31.
47369	1881,1103.74	Promissory note for barley. Nbk 23/9/14. Babylon.
47370	1881,1103.75	Promissory note for dates. Dar 18/[]/3. Babylon.
47371	1881,1103.76	Contract for wool. Nbk 2/2/4. Babylon.
47372	1881,1103.77	Memorandum.
47373	1881,1103.78	School text; lexical; Ḫḫ XV, XVI, XVII. MSL 9, 5 and 10, 4, 81.
47374	1881,1103.79	Account of silver; tēlītu tax.
47375	1881,1103.80	Promissory note for silver. Dar I 18/1?/11. Dilbat.
47376	1881,1103.81	Promissory note for silver. Nbk 8/3/12. Dilbat.
47377	1881,1103.82	Deposition. Nbk 9/1/20.
47378	1881,1103.83	Promissory note for dates or grain. Babylon.
47379	1881,1103.84	Promissory note for barley. Cyr 20/8/6. Dilbat.
47380	1881,1103.85	Consolidated account.
47381	1881,1103.86	Contract. Šamaš-šum-ukin -/-/10.
47382	1881,1103.87	Promissory note for barley. Art I/II 20/1/26. Dilbat.
47383	1881,1103.88	Contract. Art I/II 27/3/32. Babylon.
47384	1881,1103.89	Field sale. Nbk 25/12/7. Dilbat.
47385	1881,1103.90	Contract; lease of a field. Dar I 11/2/[]. Dilbat.
47386	1881,1103.91	Receipt for wool. Dar 11/5/35.
47387	1881,1103.92	Promissory note for dates. Dar I 9/6/27.
47388	1881,1103.93	Promissory note for silver. Nbk 11/-/-.
47389	1881,1103.94	Promissory note for silver. Dar I 8/8?/35. Dilbat.
47390	1881,1103.95	Contract.
47391	1881,1103.96	Promissory note for silver. Dar I 2/12/4. Dilbat.
47392	1881,1103.97	Promissory note for dates or grain. Dar 8/[]/17.
47393	1881,1103.98	Promissory note for dates. Nbk -/-/13. Dilbat.
47394	1881,1103.99	Promissory note for barley. Nbk -/6/-. Dilbat.
47395	1881,1103.100	Economic. Dar 21/7/20. Alu-ša-Bēl.
47396	1881,1103.101	Letter from Bulṭāya to Iddin-Bēl. Hackl et al., AOAT 414/1, no. 100.
47397	1881,1103.102	Letter from Bēl-iddin to Nabû-ittanna. CT 22, 12, no. 57.
47398	1881,1103.103	Contract; hire of tools; sealed. Art II/III 21/1/1. Borsippa? Nisaba 28, no. 257a.
47399	1881,1103.104	Promissory note for silver. Cam 18/2/1. Babylon.
47400	1881,1103.105	Sale of a field on the Ḫarru-ša-Uraš (near Dilbat?). Xerxes 7/5/9. URU Nār-Bēlet-ekalli. + 47596.
47401	1881,1103.106	Account of income. Art I/II/III 26/3/5. Dilbat.

47402	1881,1103.107	Contract. Xerxes 14/3/1. Babylon. Waerzeggers, AfO 50, 156.
47403	1881,1103.108	Promissory note for barley.
47404	1881,1103.109	Field sale. Nbk 10/6/35. Dilbat.
47405	1881,1103.110	Field sale. Nbk 2/12/33. URU Kār-Nusku-ekallim.
47406	1881,1103.111	Literary; Marduk theology. CT 24, 50; Maul, Fs Borger (CM 10), 369; Lambert, BCM, p. 264.
47407	1881,1103.112	Letter.
47408	1881,1103.113	School practice tablet. Dupl. 47577.
47409	1881,1103.114	Letter from Libluṭ to Šaḫû. Hackl et al., AOAT 414/1, no. 160.
47410	1881,1103.115	Letter from Marduk-zēru-ibni to Rēmūt, Bēlšunu and Marduk-ēṭer. CT 22, 22, no. 112; Hackl et al., AOAT 414/1, no. 161.
47411	1881,1103.116	Contract; lease of a field.
47412	1881,1103.117	Account.
47413	1881,1103.118	Letter from Sūqāya to Aplaya. CT 22, 35, no. 191; Hackl et al., AOAT 414/1, no. 195.
47414	1881,1103.119	Medical; prescription ingredients. 24/6/no year
47415	1881,1103.120	Account; distribution of silver.
47416	1881,1103.121	Ritual.
47417	1881,1103.122	Promissory note for dates.
47418	1881,1103.123	Promissory note for barley. Art 22/6/6. Alu-ša-Iddin-apli.
47419	1881,1103.124	Mathematical; problem text.
47420	1881,1103.125	School text; lexical; Ḫḫ IX-XII. MSL 9, 181, 189, 195, 203.
47421	1881,1103.126	Mathematical; diagram of rectangle and triangles; rough calculations on reverse.
47422	1881,1103.127	List of workmen.
47423	1881,1103.128	Transcript of legal proceedings. Dar 7/1/6. Dilbat. Sandowicz, WZKM 108, 229-239; Sandowicz, dubsar 11, no. 45.
47424	1881,1103.129	Contract; lease of a house. Nbk 20/[]/22. Babylon.
47425	1881,1103.130	Field plan. Nemet-Nejat, LB Field Plans, no. 56.
47426	1881,1103.131	Account of silver.
47427	1881,1103.132	Promissory note for silver. Cyr 11/9/2. Kār-Nabû.
47428	1881,1103.133	Promissory note for silver. Nbk 27/10/30. Babylon.
47429	1881,1103.134	Prayer.
47430	1881,1103.135	Medical.
47431	1881,1103.136	Mathematical; obv. geometrical diagram with a square and four inset circles; rev. calculation of areas in ŠE.NUMUN; colophon. + 48969. Robson, Fs Slotsky, 211-226.
47432	1881,1103.137	Promissory note for dates. Xerxes 7?/6/4. Dilbat.

47433	1881,1103.138	Account of dates. Dar 3/8/30.
47434	1881,1103.139	Contract; lease of a field. Nbk 27/4/17. Dilbat.
47435	1881,1103.140	Promissory note for dates. Xerxes 5/[]/[].
47436	1881,1103.141	Ritual for the repair of the statue of a god. Walker and Dick, SAALT I, 228-245.
47437	1881,1103.142	Field plan. Dar 26/6/23. Nemet-Nejat, LB Field Plans, no. 24#.
47438	1881,1103.143	Lexical, Aa?
47439	1881,1103.144	Lexical; Ea; sign list and personal names.
47440	1881,1103.145	Division of property. 13/12/-.
47441	1881,1103.146	Contract.
47442	1881,1103.147	Copy of a broken (ḫe-pí) contract for the sale of land in Babylon; finger-nail marks; the original contract was dated 1/11/8 Nabopolassar.
47443	1881,1103.148	Lexical; Ḫḫ II, 14-31; note that the text is given twice, once in each column. MSL 9, 157.
47444	1881,1103.149	Commentary.
47445	1881,1103.150	Ritual for the repair of the statue of a god. Walker and Dick, SAALT I, 228-245.
47446	1881,1103.151	Consolidated account of distribution of barley. Npl 26/1/4. Uruk. Kennedy, JCS 38, 181, T.4.1; Da Riva, AfO 50, 245-254.
47447	1881,1103.152	Astrological; commentary to Enūma Anu Enlil 16-20?; colophon of the scribe Šema'a. Art 23/11/19. Rochberg-Halton, AfO Beih. 22, 284-290; cf. Finkel, Gs Sachs, 155; Reiner, Fs Borger (CM 10), 300.
47448	1881,1103.153	Omens; Šumma ālu; šumma NA SISKUR.SISKUR ana DINGIR-šú.
47449	1881,1103.154	School text; obv: lexical, syllabary; rev: lexical, syllabary; literary, partial duplicate to the Sargon birth legend. CT 13, 43; cf. Grayson, BHLT, 8 n. 11; Pinches, PSBA 18 (1896) 257.
47450	1881,1103.155	Lexical; Ea; sign list.
47451	1881,1103.156	Bilingual incantation against witchcraft; ušburruda; colophon of the scribe Šema'a. Schwemer, Or NS 78, 44-58; cf. Finkel, Gs Sachs, 154; Abusch and Schwemer, AMD 8/2 text 7.12 a, pls. 12-13.
47452	1881,1103.157	Lexical; Ea; sign list.
47453	1881,1103.158	Lexical; Ea; sign list.
47454	1881,1103.159	Lexical; Ea; sign list.
47455	1881,1103.160	Field sale; sealed; finger-nail marks. Dar []/7?/20. Babylon. Nisaba 28, no. 125
47456	1881,1103.161	Iqqur īpuš; colophon of the scribe Marduk-pir'u-uṣru. Art 14/2/9. Cf. Finkel, Gs Sachs, 154.

47457	1881,1103.162	Incantations and rituals of the É-gal-ku4-ra and igi-bi-ḫúl-a-ke4 types; inim-inim-ma ḫu-ud pa-ni DÙ.DÙ.BI; colophon of Marduk-šum-iddin / Bēl-upaqqa.
47458	1881,1103.163	Commentary.
47459	1881,1103.164	Ritual; colophon. Cf. Finkel, Gs Sachs, 154.
47460	1881,1103.165	Lexical; Ea; sign list.
47461	1881,1103.166	Astrological; Enūma Anu Enlil 68; colophon; copy made for Esangila. Reiner, Fs Borger (CM 10), 300.
47462	1881,1103.167	Aḫutu ālu omens; colophon of the scribe Marduk-pir'u-uṣru. Cf. Finkel, Gs Sachs, 154
47463	1881,1103.168	Astrological; explanatory text; dupl. 41361; colophon of the scribe Šema'a. + 49124. Livingstone, MMEWABS, 6, etc; cf. Finkel, Gs Sachs, 154.
47464	1881,1103.169	Lexical; Ḫḫ II. MSL 9, 157.
47465	1881,1103.170	Field sale; finger-nail marks. Nbn 22/12/4. Dilbat.
47466	1881,1103.171	Field sale; finger-nail marks.
47467	1881,1103.172	Lexical; Ea III. MSL 14, 301; Landsberger, Gs Speiser, 133.
47468	1881,1103.173	Field sale; mentions 19th year.
47469	1881,1103.174	Contract; lease of a house in Babylon; sealed. Philip 20/8/5? Babylon. Mitchell and Searight, no. 487; Nisaba 28, no. 335.
47470	1881,1103.175	Field sale; finger-nail marks. 8/[]/10. Babylon.
47471	1881,1103.176	Contract for sale of a prebend; finger-nail marks. Dar I 24/10/[]. Dilbat.
47472	1881,1103.177	Account of silver distributed in month ix; sealed. Npl -/9/5. (Dilbat?). Nisaba 28, no. 183.
47473	1881,1103.178	Field sale. Bēl-ibni 7/12/acc. Dilbat. Brinkman and Kennedy, JCS 35, 14, E.2.
47474	1881,1103.179	Ritual blessing the furnishings of the temple; copy (ḫe-pí-eš-šú); space left on the obverse, possibly for a drawing; colophon.
47475	1881,1103.180	Transcript of legal proceedings about land and a house; sealed. Ner []/[]/2. Dilbat. Mitchell and Searight, no. 293; Nisaba 28, no. 3; Sandowicz, dubsar 11, no. 16.
47476	1881,1103.181	Practice syllabic writing.
47477	1881,1103.182	Field sale; finger-nail marks.
47478	1881,1103.183	Account of seed. Dar 29/2/21.
47479	1881,1103.184	Court record. Cam 27/6/5.
47480	1881,1103.185	Transcript of legal proceedings about a promisory note for silver. Šamaš-šum-ukin 24+/4/2. Dilbat. + 47783. Brinkman and Kennedy, JCS 35, 26, K.9; Sandowicz, dubsar 11, no. 36.

47481	1881,1103.186	Promissory note for dates. Dar I 1/6/34. Dilbat.
47482	1881,1103.187	Field sale; mentions šākin ṭēmi of Dilbat. Kandalanu 19?/6b/13+. Brinkman and Kennedy, JCS 35, 50, L.170.
47483	1881,1103.188	Promissory note for barley. Dar I 6/2?/25. Dilbat.
47484	1881,1103.189	Promissory note for dates. Dar I 5/10/23. Dilbat.
47485	1881,1103.190	Field sale. Dar I 19/1/9. Dilbat.
47486	1881,1103.191	Field sale. Nbn 10/12/14. Dilbat.
47487	1881,1103.192	Field sale; finger-nail marks.
47488	1881,1103.193	Field sale; finger-nail marks. (+) 48769 + 49027. Dar I 7/[]/19. Babylon. (+) 48769 + 49027.
47489	1881,1103.194	Lexical; Ea; sign list and stones.
47490	1881,1103.195	Lexical; še; and literary extracts.
47491	1881,1103.196	Medical; women's illnesses; colophon of the scribe Šema'a. 27/10/-. Cf. Finkel, Gs Sachs, 154.
47492	1881,1103.197	Marriage contract. Wunsch, Bab Arch 2, no. 7.
47493	1881,1103.198	Medical.
47494	1881,1103.199	Astrological explanatory text listing stars and cities, and the use of constellations for prediction. Reiner, Fs Borger (CM 10), 300; Hunger, Fs Pingree, 16-32.
47495	1881,1103.200	Prayer.
47496	1881,1103.201	Astrological omens; Sin.
47497	1881,1103.202	Astrological omens; apodoses; šar Akkad.KI BAD.
47498	1881,1103.203	Hemerology. Jiménez, JCS 68, 197-227.
47499	1881,1103.204	Mathematical; problem text; perhaps cf. 47547.
47500	1881,1103.205	Dialogue contract about a woman. Dar II 26/12b/7. Borsippa. Zadok, Nisaba 21, 239.
47501	1881,1103.206	Sumerian literary.
47502	1881,1103.207	Medical.
47503	1881,1103.208	Account.
47504	1881,1103.209	Prayer.
47505	1881,1103.210	Account. -/4/-. Babylon.
47506	1881,1103.211	Medical; colophon. + 48972. Cf. Finkel, Gs Sachs, 154#.
47507	1881,1103.212	Middle Babylonian?, ballad of Ištar; colophon of Taqīšum / Meme-Enlil. Black, JAOS 103, 25-34.
47508	1881,1103.213	Field sale. Nbn -/6b/[10]. Babylon.
47509	1881,1103.214	Ritual against epilepsy, list of stones and šu'illa incantation. + 48370. Schuster-Brandis, AOAT 46, pp. 265-270, Text 7, pl. 8.
47510	1881,1103.215	Contract; exchange of property. Nbn 20/6/1. Dilbat.
47511	1881,1103.216	Field sale.
47512	1881,1103.217	Mathematical; non-standard multiplication table with heading: maš.šá gam x ina še-im.
47513	1881,1103.218	Field sale; finger-nail marks.

47514	1881,1103.219	Medical; prescription ingredients; prayer on upper edge.
47515	1881,1103.220	Contract.
47516	1881,1103.221	Field plan. Dar []/[]/35. Nemet-Nejat, LB Field Plans, no. 6.
47517	1881,1103.222	Marriage contract. Ner 1/1/1. Babylon. Evetts, Ner. 13; Sack, ZA 68, 136; Sack, AOAT 236, no. 13.
47518	1881,1103.223	Promissory note for barley. Xerxes 23/1/16. Dilbat.
47519	1881,1103.224	Omens about dogs; Šumma izbu 23; Šumma ālu 47. + 47763. De Zorzi, Šumma izbu, 899; Freedman, If a city, vol. 3, 59, 255-256.
47520	1881,1103.225	Contract. Dar []/6/30.
47521	1881,1103.226	Field sale.
47522	1881,1103.227	Lexical; practcal vocabulary. MSL 10, 102.
47523	1881,1103.228	Mathematical; school practice; numbers.
47524	1881,1103.229	Memorandum on issues of beer? in month iii to two persons. 15/3/-.
47525	1881,1103.230	Promissory note for silver. Dar 1/3/18.
47526	1881,1103.231	Field plan. Nemet-Nejat, LB Field Plans, no. 65.
47527	1881,1103.232	Economic.
47528	1881,1103.233	Late Babylonian copy of an Old Babylonian land-sale contract dated to 10+/9/30 Samsuiluna; the original contract had a captioned seal-impression; colophon.
47529	1881,1103.234	Commentary on Marduk's Address (Udug-ḫul 11); colophon of the scribe Marduk-pir'u-uṣru. + 47685. Cf. Finkel, Gs Sachs, 154; Geller, Melosthesia, 60-64; Geller, BAM 8, 341, 396-397, pls. 42-44, 69-71, 77; Lambert, MC 24, no. 214.
47530	1881,1103.235	Literary; The Defeat of Enutila, Enmešarra and Qingu. Lambert, BCM, pp. 326-329, pl. 56.
47531	1881,1103.236	Receipt for barley. Dar I 11/2/4. Dilbat.
47532	1881,1103.237	Promissory note for dates; <Xerxes> 27/5/3 (king of Persia, Media and Babylon). Alu-ša-rab-šarri.
47533	1881,1103.238	Memorandum; list of names.
47534	1881,1103.239	Promissory note for dates. Dar 15/9/4. Babylon.
47535	1881,1103.240	Marriage contract. Šamaš-šum-ukin 14/8/13. Brinkman and Kennedy, JCS 35, 30, K.74.
47536	1881,1103.241	Promissory note for deposit of barley; sealed; fingernail marks. Alex III 21/6?/9. Borsippa. CT 49, 2, no. 7; Nisaba 28, no. 438.
47537	1881,1103.242	Contract; sale of a field. Šamaš-šum-ukin 7+/2?/[]. Borsippa. Brinkman and Kennedy, JCS 35, 36, K.150; Zadok, Nisaba 21, 239.
47538	1881,1103.243	Account.
47539	1881,1103.244	Promissory note for oil. Dar 7/12/27. Babylon.

47540	1881,1103.245	Account. 5/12/28. Babylon.
47541	1881,1103.246	Field plan. Nemet-Nejat, LB Field Plans, no. 57.
47542	1881,1103.247	Contract. Nbk 2/3/24. Babylon.
47543	1881,1103.248	Circular memorandum; obverse, 1.d.AG-ḫi-in-ni-' LÚ paq-du; reverse, two lines illegible.
47544	1881,1103.249	Memorandum; personal names.
47545	1881,1103.250	Memorandum; circular.
47546	1881,1103.251	Letter; sealed. Art III 21+/6/5. CT 49, 1, no. 4; Nisaba 28, no. 434.
47547	1881,1103.252	Mathematical; problem text; perhaps cf. 47499.
47548	1881,1103.253	Account.
47549	1881,1103.254	Mathematical; school practice; numbers.
47550	1881,1103.255	Account of silver.
47551	1881,1103.256	Incantation.
47552	1881,1103.257	Contract; transfer of land to secure a dowry; sealed. Dar 22/8/28. Babylon. Wunsch, Bab Arch 2, no. 18; Nisaba 28, no. 136.
47553	1881,1103.258	School text; lexical; Ḫḫ XI-XII. MSL 9, 195, 203.
47554	1881,1103.259	Commentary; explanatory.
47555	1881,1103.260	Receipt for cows.
47556	1881,1103.261	Contract. Dar? 23/[]/3. Dilbat.
47557	1881,1103.262	Contract. + 47764.
47558	1881,1103.263	Promissory note for barley.
47559	1881,1103.264	Promissory note for dates or grain. Dar 2/[]/5.
47560	1881,1103.265	Promissory note for silver. Art I/II 13?/8/31. Borsippa.
47561	1881,1103.266	Astronomical.
47562	1881,1103.267	Memorandum about foodstuffs.
47563	1881,1103.268	Account audit. Kandalanu 19/1/18. Babylon. Brinkman and Kennedy, JCS 35, 47, L.118.
47564	1881,1103.269	Literary.
47565	1881,1103.270	Promissory note for silver. Npl 13/12/17. Babylon.
47566	1881,1103.271	Account of silver.
47567	1881,1103.272	Receipt for silver. Nbk 5/2/32.
47568	1881,1103.273	Letter.
47569	1881,1103.274	Letter from Balāṭu to Ubartu; sealed. Nisaba 28, no. 212.
47570	1881,1103.275	Letter from Marduk-zēru-ibni to Šulāya. CT 22, 22, no. 113; Hackl et al., AOAT 414/1, no. 162.
47571	1881,1103.276	Contract.
47572	1881,1103.277	Account of silver.
47573	1881,1103.278	Promissory note for barley. Dar I 10/2/27. Dilbat.
47574	1881,1103.279	Promissory note for silver. Dar 2/12/29. Babylon.

47575	1881,1103.280	Memorandum of apotropaic stones: ud-da-a-tu4 šá GÚ šá 1.ap-la-a NA4.ZÁLAG NA4.AN.NE NA4. MU.ZA.
47576	1881,1103.281	Ball-shaped tablet with literary text inscribed in a spiral.
47577	1881,1103.282	School practice text; ball-shaped; duplicates 47408.
47578	1881,1103.283	Medical; gynaecological.
47579	1881,1103.284	Medical; list of stones; prescription ingredients. Schuster-Brandis, AOAT 46, p. 139, Kette 222.
47580	1881,1103.285	Medical; prescription ingredients.
47581	1881,1103.286	Account.
47582	1881,1103.287	Account of dates or grain.
47583	1881,1103.288	Medical; prescription ingredients.
47584	1881,1103.289	Letter from Kurbanni-Marduk to Nabû-gāmil. CT 22, 20, no. 101.
47585	1881,1103.290	Promissory note for silver. Cyr 10/8/5. Babylon.
47586	1881,1103.291	Contract. Dar I 20+/10/9+. Borsippa. Zadok, Nisaba 21, 239.
47587	1881,1103.292	Account. 5/7/-.
47588	1881,1103.293	Mathematical; factorisation table (powers of 3); two columns; reverse blank.
47589	1881,1103.294	Letter; sealed. Art III 25/6/4. CT 49, 1, no. 3; Nisaba 28, no. 433.
47590	1881,1103.295	Letter; sealed. Art III 21/6/4. CT 49, 1, no. 1; Nisaba 28, no. 431.
47591	1881,1103.296	Letter; sealed. Art III 25/10/4. CT 49, 1, no. 2; Mitchell and Searight, no. 519; Nisaba 28, no. 432.
47592	1881,1103.297	Astrological; Enūma Anu Enlil. Reiner, Fs Borger (CM 10), 300 (wrongly as 45793).
47593	1881,1103.298	Ration list?); two lines on the upper edge written upside down; marked "D"; probably Seleucid period (script). No RN 25/4/26.
47594	1881,1103.299	Field sale; finger-nail marks.
47595	1881,1103.300	Promissory note for silver. Dar 8/[]/25. + 47861.
47596	1881,1103.301	Joined to 47400.
47597	1881,1103.302	Sale of a woman. Dar 29/12b/-.
47598	1881,1103.303	Contract.
47599	1881,1103.304	Medical; prescription ingredients.
47600	1881,1103.305	Memorandum about bread. 12/4/-.
47601	1881,1103.306	Medical omens. + 47797.
47602	1881,1103.307	Incantation to Šamaš and ritual. Abusch and Schwemer, AMD 8/2 text 8.32 a, pl. 63.
47603	1881,1103.308	Account.
47604	1881,1103.309	Contract.
47605	1881,1103.310	Receipt. 15/[]/23. Dilbat.

47606	1881,1103.311	Promissory note for silver. Dar 12/1/13. Dilbat.
47607	1881,1103.312	Promissory note for dates.
47608	1881,1103.313	Memorandum about barley.
47609	1881,1103.314	Contract; lease of a house. -/12/-.
47610	1881,1103.315	Account of dates or grain.
47611	1881,1103.316	Contract; lease of a field. Art 11/4/11.
47612	1881,1103.317	Mathematical; geometrical diagrams (circles and chords) with numbers. (+) 47613.
47613	1881,1103.318	Mathematical problem; geometrical diagrams (circles and chords) with numbers. (+) 47612.
47614	1881,1103.319	Contract. Cam. Babylon.
47615	1881,1103.320	Sale of a slave.
47616	1881,1103.321	Promissory note for barley. -/-/31.
47617	1881,1103.322	Promissory note for silver. Šamaš-šum-ukin 21+/6/14 (year written MU-tú 14-KÁM). Dilbat. Brinkman and Kennedy, JCS 35, 31, K.82.
47618	1881,1103.323	Medical.
47619	1881,1103.324	Label with two line inscription; šá d.Bēl repeated; pierced top to bottom at the left side.
47620	1881,1103.325	Memorandum about grain distribution.
47621	1881,1103.326	Letter.
47622	1881,1103.327	Ritual, mentioning stars.
47623	1881,1103.328	Memorandum about birds.
47624	1881,1103.329	Lexical, commentary.
47625	1881,1103.330	Lexical; Reciprocal Ea A. MSL 14, 524.
47626	1881,1103.331	Sale of a donkey. Cam 10/6b/acc. Babylon.
47627	1881,1103.332	Letter from Itti-Bēl-[] to Bēl-ēter. CT 22, 14-15, no. 70; Hackl et al., AOAT 414/1, no. 163.
47628	1881,1103.333	Mathematical problem text; begins AN.ZA.QAR la ni-bi a-na AN.[]; mostly figures; colophon: ana KA Bēlšunu / Lâbâši / Egibi, etc.
47629	1881,1103.334	Contract.
47630	1881,1103.335	Contract.
47631	1881,1103.336	Astronomical Diary.
47632	1881,1103.337	Mathematical; reused tablet fragment with a number and a geometrical diagram drawn at one end (pentagon inscribed in a circle).
47633	1881,1103.338	Omens.
47634	1881,1103.339	Contract. 9+/[]/9.
47635	1881,1103.340	Contract.
47636	1881,1103.341	Astronomical Diary.
47637	1881,1103.342	Contract. Nbn -/7/14.
47638	1881,1103.343	Contract about a boat and boatmen; sealed. Cam 5/10/[]. + 47641. Nisaba 28, no. 151.
47639	1881,1103.344	Promissory note for barley. Cyr 21/4/-.

47640	1881,1103.345	Letter order from Marduk-bēlšunu and Bēl-bullissu, exorcists. SE []/[]/56?. Nisaba 28, no. 672.
47641	1881,1103.346	Joined to 47638.
47642	1881,1103.347	Horoscope. SE 4/5/88. Rochberg, Babylonian Horoscopes, no. 13.
47643	1881,1103.348	Contract about silver. Art I/II 8/12/31+.
47644	1881,1103.349	Contract.
47645	1881,1103.350	Incantation; colophon.
47646	1881,1103.351	Astronomical.
47647	1881,1103.352	Contract; witnesses only; sealed. RN lost 20+/8/[]. Babylon. Nisaba 28, no. 181.
47648	1881,1103.353	Bilingual incantation.
47649	1881,1103.354	Astronomical.
47650	1881,1103.355	Astronomical Diary for SE 141. Sachs and Hunger, ADART II, no. -170 G.
47651	1881,1103.356	Lexical, Lú = ša; and literary extracts.
47652	1881,1103.357	Incantation.
47653	1881,1103.358	Contract -/-/6.
47654	1881,1103.359	Account.
47655	1881,1103.360	Cylinder; inscription of Ashurbanipal on the restoration of the city wall of Babylon. (Babylon). (+) 47656. Frame, RIMB 2.6.32.1.12.
47656	1881,1103.361	Cylinder; inscription of Ashurbanipal on the restoration of the city wall of Babylon. (Babylon). (+) 47655. Frame, RIMB 2.6.32.1.13.
47657	1881,1103.362	Incantation.
47658	1881,1103.363	Astronomical.
47659	1881,1103.364	Astronomical Diary.
47660	1881,1103.365	Bilingual epic; Lugal-e I 3-16 and 37-45; probably written by Kabti-ilāni-Marduk. (+) 48598. van Dijk, Lugal, text u1.
47661	1881,1103.366	Commentary.
47662	1881,1103.367	Literary.
47663	1881,1103.368	Bilingual incantation. + 48670.
47664	1881,1103.369	Ritual.
47665	1881,1103.370	Astronomical Diary; prices.
47666	1881,1103.371	Literary.
47667	1881,1103.372	Lexical; personal names.
47668	1881,1103.373	Commentary; grammatical? + 48447.
47669	1881,1103.374	Contract?; witnesses only.
47670	1881,1103.375	Incantation; Šà-zi-ga; cf. Biggs, TCS 2, p. 66.
47671	1881,1103.376	Field plan 2/7/30. Nemet-Nejat, LB Field Plans, no. 50.
47672	1881,1103.377	Medical. + 47742 + 48443 + 48666 + 49148.
47673	1881,1103.378	School text; lexical; Ḫḫ XI. MSL 9, 195.

47674	1881,1103.379	Sumerian literary. + 48471.
47675	1881,1103.380	Literary; Love Lyrics.
47676	1881,1103.381	Lexical; Ea; sign list.
47677	1881,1103.382	Omens; extispicy.
47678	1881,1103.383	Astronomical or terrestrial omens.
47679	1881,1103.384	Chronicle; dupl. of the Weidner Chronicle (Grayson, TCS 5, Chronicle 19).
47680	1881,1103.385	Lexical; Ḫḫ II. MSL 9, 157.
47681	1881,1103.386	Lexical; Ea; sign list and literary extracts.
47682	1881,1103.387	Lexical; Ea; sign list and literary extracts. Pinches, Assyrian Grammar, p. 64.
47683	1881,1103.388	Astronomical or astrological omens.
47684	1881,1103.389	Omens; physiognomic; two columns. + 48455 + 48474.
47685	1881,1103.390	Joined to 47529.
47686	1881,1103.391	Lexical; Ea; sign list.
47687	1881,1103.392	Medical; colophon of the scribe Šema'a. + 48517. Finkel, Gs Sachs, 153-155 and 158-159.
47688	1881,1103.393	Astrological; Enūma Anu Enlil 64. Reiner, Fs Borger (CM 10), 300; Reiner and Pingree, BPO 4, 9-12, 19, 22, 74-77.
47689	1881,1103.394	Account.
47690	1881,1103.395	Medical.
47691	1881,1103.396	Medical ritual.
47692	1881,1103.397	Contract about an orchard; sealed. Art 16/[]/10+. Babylon. Nisaba 28, no. 232a.
47693	1881,1103.398	Lexical, commentary on Aa II/3 = 11. + 48828 + 49041. MSL 14, 278 and pl. 3 (48828 only).
47694	1881,1103.399	Contract.
47695	1881,1103.400	Prescriptions against witchcraft. + 47781. Abusch and Schwemer, AMD 8/2 text A.1, pls. 89-90.
47696	1881,1103.401	Ritual; Bīt salā' mê; two columns; colophon. Art []+1/8/[]. + 48027 (+) 47798 + 48337 + 1881,1103. 506. Ambos, Der König, 157-173 and 264-265.
47697	1881,1103.402	Astrology; market predictions.
47698	1881,1103.403	Bilingual historical-literary text of Nebuchadnezzar I; dupl. 47805+ (Frame, RIMB.2.4.8.4).
47699	1881,1103.404	Copy of two royal inscriptions in Akkadian; colophon: ki-ma KA 2 NA4 NA.RÚ.A LIBIR.RA.MEŠ ša NA4.GIŠ.ŠIR.GAL.
47700	1881,1103.405	Ledger.
47701	1881,1103.406	Incantation. + 48966.
47702	1881,1103.407	Account. 2/12/15. + 47813.
47703	1881,1103.408	Literary; catalogue of incipits of hymns to Ištar(?) Ruled after every line.

47704	1881,1103.409	Lexical; Ea; sign list; measurements.
47705	1881,1103.410	Mathematical; problem text.
47706	1881,1103.411	Economic; [GI]Š.SAR ḫal-la-tu.
47707	1881,1103.412	Lexical; Ḫḫ III-IV. MSL 9, 159, 168.
47708	1881,1103.413	Account; amounts and names.
47709	1881,1103.414	Mathematical.
47710	1881,1103.415	Account. 26/6/-.
47711	1881,1103.416	Account.
47712	1881,1103.417	Mathematical; table of reciprocals?
47713	1881,1103.418	Lexical; Ea; sign list and literary extracts.
47714	1881,1103.419	Contract.
47715	1881,1103.420	Receipt for seed.
47716	1881,1103.421	Field plan. + 48497. Nemet-Nejat, LB Field Plans, no. 44.
47717	1881,1103.422	Astronomical or astrological omens.
47718	1881,1103.423	Promissory note for silver. Dar 5/6/-. Babylon.
47719	1881,1103.424	Medical.
47720	1881,1103.425	Astronomical Diary.
47721	1881,1103.426	Horoscopes for SE 53 and 61. SE Antiochus II 8/2/61. Rochberg, Babylonian Horoscopes, no. 6.
47722	1881,1103.427	Joined to 33850.
47723	1881,1103.428	Astronomical procedure text mentioning various planets; begins: [x x x x] ḫal-qa ana DÙ-ka BE-ma MÚL-BABBAR ina u4-mu GAR-an.
47724	1881,1103.429	Astronomical; Normal Star Almanac for SE 31. LBAT 995; Hunger and Sachs, ADART VII, no. 4.
47725	1881,1103.430	Astronomical Diary. LBAT 168; Sachs and Hunger, ADART I, no. -381 B.
47726	1881,1103.431	Joined to 33508.
47727	1881,1103.432	Joined to 33448.
47728	1881,1103.433	Astronomical omens. + 47932.
47729	1881,1103.434	Contract.
47730	1881,1103.435	Astrological; commentary on Enūma Anu Enlil 26 (27). + 47891 + 47906 + 47918 + 48108 + 48927. van Soldt, Solar omens, 68 and 83 (Cb); Reiner, Fs Borger (CM 10), 300.
47731	1881,1103.436	Contract; quit-claim for field rent; sealed. SE [Ant III] & Sel 4/1/123. [Borsippa]. CT 49, 30, no. 136; van der Spek, Grondbezit, 232-236, no. 9; Nisaba 28, no. 601.
47732	1881,1103.437	Lexical; list of cuneiform signs of Syllabary A and associated numbers; probably eight columns of 50 lines. + 48191. Pearce, Iraq 45, 136-137.

47733	1881,1103.438	School text; lexical, Ḫḫ II; Weidner Chronicle (Grayson, TCS 5, Chronicle 19); unidentified. Finkel, JCS 32, 74-75, 79-80; Gesche, AOAT 275, 688.
47734	1881,1103.439	Astronomical procedure text for the moon. Ossendrijver, BMAPT, no. 61B.
47735	1881,1103.440	Astronomical Diary. Sachs and Hunger, ADART I, no. -391; J. Koch, AfO 38/39, 107-109.
47736	1881,1103.441	Bilingual incantation, Udug-ḫul 13-15, colophon. CT 16, 18; Geller, BAM 8, 434-498.
47737	1881,1103.442	Chronicle, mentioning temple robberies in the years SE 34 and 90. Joannès, Fs Oelsner, 193-211; BCHP 17.
47738	1881,1103.443	Astronomical; Normal Star Almanac for SE 128. LBAT 1024; Hunger and Sachs, ADART VII, no. 55.
47739	1881,1103.444	Astronomical Diary.
47740	1881,1103.445	List of workmen.
47741	1881,1103.446	Lexical; syllabary.
47742	1881,1103.447	Joined to 47672.
47743	1881,1103.448	Astrological; Enūma Anu Enlil 17; colophon. Rochberg-Halton, AfO Beih. 22, EAE 17; Reiner, Fs Borger (CM 10), 300.
47744	1881,1103.449	Joined to 33451.
47745	1881,1103.450	Theodicy. Lambert, MC 24, no. 253.
47746	1881,1103.451	Medical.
47747	1881,1103.452	Astronomical Diary.
47748	1881,1103.453	Astronomical Diary for SE 179; prayer on upper edge. + 47885. Sachs and Hunger, ADART III, no. -132 C.
47749	1881,1103.454	Late Babylonian historical epic about Kurigalzu and Qatantum. Finkel, Anatolian Studies 33 (1983) 75-80.
47750	1881,1103.455	Unidentified.
47751	1881,1103.456	Astronomical Diary for SE 168. Sachs and Hunger, ADART III, no. -143 C.
47752	1881,1103.457	Lexical; Ḫḫ VIII. MSL 9, 173.
47753	1881,1103.458	Medical omens, Sa-gig XXVI. Heeßel, AOAT 43, 278-291; Finkel, JCS 46, 87.
47754	1881,1103.459	Ritual.
47755	1881,1103.460	Literary and medical extracts: bilingual incantation, Muššu'u tablet IV; Šurpu IX incipits; medical prescriptions; astrological medicine. (+) 35072 (+) 47913. Cf. Finkel, AuOr 9 (1991), 97 n. 9; Böck, Muššu'u, 147-180 (47913 only); Geller, Melosthesia, 85-87 (47755 only).
47756	1881,1103.461	Prayer; prayer on upper edge.
47757	1881,1103.462	Incantation; namburbû; copy (ḫe-pí).

47758	1881,1103.463	Incantation.
47759	1881,1103.464	Medical.
47760	1881,1103.465	Lexical; Aa III/5 = 20; colophon; copy of Barsip, written by Lūṣî-ana-Marduk. CT 12, 14-15; MSL 14, 343; Landsberger, Gs Speiser, 134; Ungnad, AfO 14, 262.
47761	1881,1103.466	Astrological; commentary.
47762	1881,1103.467	Astrological; numbers and star names; circular tablet. Steele and Horowitz, Fs Brack-Bernsen, 225-232.
47763	1881,1103.468	Joined to 47519.
47764	1881,1103.469	Joined to 47557.
47765	1881,1103.470	Contract.
47766	1881,1103.471	Contract.
47767	1881,1103.472	Contract.
47768	1881,1103.473	Unidentified.
47769	1881,1103.474	Lexical and personal names.
47770	1881,1103.475	Medical; list of protective amulet stones. + 47904. Schuster-Brandis, AOAT 46, p. 148, Kette 154-162, p. 192, series kunuk ḫalti tablet I (both as 47904).
47771	1881,1103.476	Lexical; Ea; sign list and personal names.
47772	1881,1103.477	Practice vertical wedge.
47773	1881,1103.478	Lexical, Ana ittišu I 4-21.
47774	1881,1103.479	Sale of fields; sealed. Alex III []/[]/10 Mitchell and Searight, no. 599; Nisaba 28, no. 331.
47775	1881,1103.480	Lexical; Ḫḫ III. + 47815. MSL 9, 159.
47776	1881,1103.481	Literary.
47777	1881,1103.482	Ritual.
47778	1881,1103.483	School text; lexical, Syllabary A, Ḫḫ XIII; place-names; acrographic list; letter. Gesche, AOAT 275, 328-329, 689; Pinches, PSBA 18 (1896), 251-253 and pl. I (wrongly as 81-11-3, 478).
47779	1881,1103.484	Lexical, Aa IV/4 = 25. CT 12, 21; MSL 14, 384.
47780	1881,1103.485	Lexical; Ea; sign list and personal names.
47781	1881,1103.486	Joined to 47695.
47782	1881,1103.487	Namburbû?; colophon.
47783	1881,1103.488	Joined to 47480.
47784	1881,1103.489	Lexical; personal names.
47785	1881,1103.490	Lexical.
47786	1881,1103.491	Sumerian literary.
47787	1881,1103.492	Lexical; Ea; sign list; Ana ittišu?
47788	1881,1103.493	Lexical; Ea; sign list and literary extracts.
47789	1881,1103.494	Lexical; Ea; sign list.
47790	1881,1103.495	Lexical, Lú = ša?. + 1881,1103.499.

47791	1881,1103.496	Contract; loan from tithe income; sealed. SE (Sel II) 23/[]/70. (Borsippa). Mitchell and Searight, no. 700; Nisaba 28, no. 582.
47792	1881,1103.497	Lexical; animals.
47793	1881,1103.498	Astrological; Enūma Anu Enlil, Sin; lunar halo. Reiner, Fs Borger (CM 10), 300.
	1881,1103.499	Joined to 47790.
47794	1881,1103.500	Lexical; god-list.
47795	1881,1103.501	Contract; sale of a house; sealed. d.l. [Babylon]. (+) 48712. Wunsch, Bab Arch 2, no. 29; Nisaba 28, no. 114a.
47796	1881,1103.502	Late Babylonian copy of an earlier inscription. + 48794.
47797	1881,1103.503	Joined to 47601.
47798	1881,1103.504	Ritual; Bīt salā' mê; two columns; colophon. Art []+1/8/[]. + 1881,1103.506 + 48337 (+) 47696 + 48027. Ambos, Der König, 157-173 and 262-263.
47799	1881,1103.505	Astrological; Enūma Anu Enlil 57? Reiner, Fs Borger (CM 10), 300.
	1881,1103.506	Joined to 47798.
47800	1881,1103.507	Incantation; colophon. Dar 10/4/25.
47801	1881,1103.508	Incantation.
47802	1881,1103.509	Medical; prescription.
47803	1881,1103.510	Literary.
47804	1881,1103.511	Medical.
47805	1881,1103.512	Bilingual historical-literary text of Nebuchadnezzar I; dupl. 32291+(+) 32507+ and 47698 and 54135+. + 48032 + 48035 + 48037 + 48046. Lambert, JCS 21, 128-131 and 138; Lambert, RAI XIX, 427-440; Frame, RIMB 2.4.8.4.
47806	1881,1103.513	Ušburruda incantation. + 48445 + 48977 + 49040. Schwemer, Iraq 72, 72-74.
47807	1881,1103.514	Field plan. + 49000. Nemet-Nejat, LB Field Plans, no. 58.
47808	1881,1103.515	Astrological medicine; list of diseases.
47809	1881,1103.516	Omens; Šumma ālu? Scorpions.
47810	1881,1103.517	Omens; Šumma ālu; about a man's house.
47811	1881,1103.518	Omens; Šumma ālu; IGI and apodoses.
47812	1881,1103.519	Directions for rituals in connexion with the New Year Festival; obv. 1st and 7th days of Nisannu are mentioned and Nabû ša ḫa-re-e; rev. contains details of a number of sacrifices and the gods to which they are offered. + 48477 + 48588 + 48663.
47813	1881,1103.520	Joined to 47702.

47814	1881,1103.521	Cylinder; inscription of Nabonidus; duplicate not yet identified. Da Riva, GMTR 4, 126.
47815	1881,1103.522	Joined to 47775.
47816	1881,1103.523	Astronomical; Normal Star Almanac for SE 58; contains references to lunar and solar eclipse possibilities. SE -/-/58. LBAT 999; Hunger and Sachs, ADART VII, no. 15.
47817	1881,1103.524	Ritual for delivering man possessed of devil; rev. outline drawing of man followed by devil; catch line and colophon.
47818	1881,1103.525	Account; unusual finger-nail marks.
47819	1881,1103.526	Account.
47820	1881,1103.527	Copy of a broken tablet of dates and grain accounts dated or mentioning month i of 35th year of Artaxerxes; amounts and personal names. Art I/II -/1/35.
47821	1881,1103.528	Joined to 34671.
47822	1881,1103.529	Lexical; god-list; personal names; professions. + 47988 + 48251 (+) 47986. Pinches, PSBA 18 (1896) 256; Pinches, Assyrian Grammar, 64, 38a-b; both 47822 only.
47823	1881,1103.530	Unidentified.
47824	1881,1103.531	Omens.
47825	1881,1103.532	Lexical; Ea; sign list; personal names.
47826	1881,1103.533	Contract.
47827	1881,1103.534	Bilingual incantation, Udug-ḫul 2, colophon. + 47838 (+) 47845. Geller, BAM 8, 59-88, pls. 16-17.
47828	1881,1103.535	Account.
47829	1881,1103.536	Lexical; Ḫḫ I; colophon.
47830	1881,1103.537	Lexical.
47831	1881,1103.538	Account.
47832	1881,1103.539	Promissory note for barley.
47833	1881,1103.540	Ledger.
47834	1881,1103.541	Account; months and days; ina qatê Bēl-kāṣir.
47835	1881,1103.542	Account; mentions month ii day 24.
47836	1881,1103.543	Lexical.
47837	1881,1103.544	Promissory note for dates.
47838	1881,1103.545	Joined to 47827.
47839	1881,1103.546	Account; months and days and personal names.
47840	1881,1103.547	List of workmen.
47841	1881,1103.548	Account of dates or grain.
47842	1881,1103.549	Economic.
47843	1881,1103.550	Astronomical?
47844	1881,1103.551	Astronomical Diary?
47845	1881,1103.552	Bilingual incantation; Udug-ḫul 2; colophon. (+) 47827. Geller, BAM 8, 59-88, pls. 16-17.

47846	1881,1103.553	Contract.
47847	1881,1103.554	Account; mentions 11th and 12th years.
47848	1881,1103.555	Lexical; Ea; sign list; professions.
47849	1881,1103.556	Field sale.
47850	1881,1103.557	Contract. Art 22/7/[].
47851	1881,1103.558	Astronomical; calendrical table involving intervals of 13 and 277 days. Hunger, WZKM 86, 191-196.
47852	1881,1103.559	Bilingual incantation, Udug-ḫul 3. + 47855 + 48673. CT 17, 47-48 (47852 + 47855 only); Geller, BAM 8, 89-132, pls, 23-24.
47853	1881,1103.560	Account of dates or grain. Nabû-[] 22/[]/5.
47854	1881,1103.561	Lexical; god-list.
47855	1881,1103.562	Joined to 47852.
47856	1881,1103.563	School text; incantation; lexical. 18/7/-.
47857	1881,1103.564	Astrological omens; Enūma Anu Enlil 21.
47858	1881,1103.565	Liver omens.
47859	1881,1103.566	Late Babylonian copy of a tablet copied from a stele; Sumerian incantation against gall. Alster, Or NS 41, 349ff and 357.
47860	1881,1103.567	Astrological; i.NAM.giš.ḫur.an.ki.a; coefficient list; colophon. Dar 12/11/33. Livingstone, MMEWABS, 17-52; Robson, OECT XIV, 204-205, List J.
47861	1881,1103.568	Joined to 47595.
47862	1881,1103.569	Lexical; Ea; sign list.
47863	1881,1103.570	Astronomical Diary.
47864	1881,1103.571	Astronomical.
47865	1881,1103.572	Astronomical Diary or summary of observations; edge: EN-NUN šá gi-ne-e.
47866	1881,1103.573	Lexical.
47867	1881,1103.574	Lexical; god-list.
47868	1881,1103.575	Field sale. Wunsch, CM 20A-B, no. 180.
47869	1881,1103.576	Astronomical; Normal Star Almanac for SE 96. Hunger and Sachs, ADART VII, no. 31.
47870	1881,1103.577	Astrological omens.
47871	1881,1103.578	Astronomical Diary.
47872	1881,1103.579	Astronomical Diary.
47873	1881,1103.580	Astronomical Diary.
47874	1881,1103.581	Joined to 35475.
47875	1881,1103.582	Medical. + 49022.
47876	1881,1103.583	Medical.
47877	1881,1103.584	Medical.
47878	1881,1103.585	Astronomical Diary.
47879	1881,1103.586	Contract.

47880	1881,1103.587	Medical; one section begins šumma amēlu ina KA-šú; copy (ḫe-pí ḫe-pí ḫe-pí for nine lines); two columns.
47881	1881,1103.588	Astronomical.
47882	1881,1103.589	School text; unidentified; colophon. Gesche, AOAT 275, 330-331, 689.
47883	1881,1103.590	Omens; terrestrial.
47884	1881,1103.591	Astronomical.
47885	1881,1103.592	Joined to 47748.
47886	1881,1103.593	Astronomical procedure text for Saturn; System B; colophon. + 47914.
47887	1881,1103.594	"Aluzinnu text", omens; dupl. 2R 60, no. 1.
47888	1881,1103.595	Astronomical Diary for SE 177. Sachs and Hunger, ADART III, no. -134 A.
47889	1881,1103.596	School text; literary; Enūma eliš V. Lambert, BCM, p. 123, pl. 34.
47890	1881,1103.597	Mathematical(?) problem text with diagram; for the diagram cf. 33333B, 37171, 39198 and 40680.
47891	1881,1103.598	Joined to 47730.
47892	1881,1103.599	Bilingual epic; Lugal-e IV 137-148 and 174-181; colophon. van Dijk, Lugal, text u.
47893	1881,1103.600	Astrological omens.
47894	1881,1103.601	Medical; mentions giš-kàd-úr-šú.
47895	1881,1103.602	Lexical; god-list.
47896	1881,1103.603	Sumerian literary.
47897	1881,1103.604	Lexical; Ḫḫ III. MSL 9, 159.
47898	1881,1103.605	Bilingual incantation.
47899	1881,1103.606	Lexical; Ea; sign list and literary extracts; colophon; la ta-qab-bi, scribe, Nabû-šar-[].
47900	1881,1103.607	Lexical; god list; personal names.
47901	1881,1103.608	Lexical; Ea; sign list.
47902	1881,1103.609	Ritual for the New Year Festival in Babylon. + 48320. Pongratz-Leisten, Bagh Forsch 16, 233-235; Lambert, RA 91, 52-56; Linssen, CM 25, 9, 85, 324.
47903	1881,1103.610	Bilingual incantation, Udug-ḫul 12. Geller, BAM 8, 399-433, pl. 94.
47904	1881,1103.611	Joined to 47770.
47905	1881,1103.612	Omens; Šumma ālu 50-53.
47906	1881,1103.613	Joined to 47730.
47907	1881,1103.614	Mantic dream ritual. (+) 48093 (+) 48097.
47908	1881,1103.615	Astrological medicine.
47909	1881,1103.616	Astronomical; Normal Star Almanac for SE 113. Hunger and Sachs, ADART VII, no. 48.
47910	1881,1103.617	Literary cylinder; hymn to Nabû. Lambert, Fs Matouš II, 75-111; Gesche, AOAT 275, 689.

47911	1881,1103.618	Literary cylinder.
47912	1881,1103.619	Astronomical; lunar functions related to solar eclipses; Xerxes 11 to Artaxerxes I 8. (+) 36737. Aaboe and Sachs, Centaurus 14 (1969) 11-20 and pls. IV-V, text D; cf. ACT, p. 10 n. 44; Britton, Centaurus 32 (1989) 1-52 (as Text S).
47913	1881,1103.620	Bilingual incantations; Muššu'u tablet IV; astrological medicine. (+) 35072 (+) 47755. Cf. Finkel, AuOr 9 (1991), 97 n. 9; Böck, Muššu'u, 147-180 and pl. XIX.
47914	1881,1103.621	Joined to 47886.
47915	1881,1103.622	Astrological omens; colophon.
47916	1881,1103.623	Joined to 33457.
47917	1881,1103.624	Astronomical Diary.
47918	1881,1103.625	Joined to 47730.
47919	1881,1103.626	Astronomical; list with risings and settings of stars, similar to 36382.
47920	1881,1103.627	Astronomical.
47921	1881,1103.628	Lexical; Ea; sign list.
47922	1881,1103.629	Division of property.
47923	1881,1103.630	Astronomical; lunar System B(?), columns Psi', T, B. Steele, AHES 60 (2006) 123-153, text I.
47924	1881,1103.631	Joined to 33451.
47925	1881,1103.632	Field sale. Wunsch, CM 20A-B, no. 69.
47926	1881,1103.633	Legal declaration by the šatammu of Esangila about a land grant made by Seleucus II; two columns. SE Ant IV [& Ant] []/[]/139. Babylon. + 1881,1103.641. van der Spek, JESHO 57, 213; CTMMA IV 213-227.
47927	1881,1103.634	Joined to 33507.
47928	1881,1103.635	Astronomical; Goal Year Text for SE 177. Hunger and Sachs, ADART VI, no. 56.
47929	1881,1103.636	Astronomical Diary for SE 17. Sachs and Hunger, ADART I, no. -294.
47930	1881,1103.637	Astrological omens; colophon. Reiner, Fs Borger (CM 10), 300.
47931	1881,1103.638	Joined to 33833.
47932	1881,1103.639	Joined to 47728.
47933	1881,1103.640	Medical; prayer on upper edge.
	1881,1103.641	Joined to 47926.
47934	1881,1103.642	Field sale. [Xerxes] 30/7/[].
47935	1881,1103.643	Lexical; sign-list, Idu. CT 12, 27.
47936	1881,1103.644	Field sale.
47937	1881,1103.645	Lexical.
47938	1881,1103.646	Excerpts, omens and ritual; Šumma ālu, tablet 72 (=80); namburbû; unidentified; colophon. CT 39, 26-

		27; Freedman, If a city, vol. 1, 340 and vol. 3, 4; Caplice, Or NS 36, 9; Hunger, AOAT 2, no. 427.
47939	1881,1103.647	Namburbû.
47940	1881,1103.648	Liver omens; pān tākalti tablet X; colophon. U. S. Koch-Westenholz, Babylonian Liver Omens, 377, no. 70 and pl. XXV.
47941	1881,1103.649	Lexical; Ea; sign list.
47942	1881,1103.650	Lexical.
47943	1881,1103.651	Deposition. Nbk 19/5/15.
47944	1881,1103.652	Lexical.
47945	1881,1103.653	Account of barley.
47946	1881,1103.654	Lexical; Ea; sign list.
47947	1881,1103.655	Incantation; colophon.
47948	1881,1103.656	Commentary.
47949	1881,1103.657	Lexical; Ea; sign list.
47950	1881,1103.658	Omens; extispicy; Šumma isru.
47951	1881,1103.659	Astronomical?
47952	1881,1103.660	Incantation.
47953	1881,1103.661	Unidentified.
47954	1881,1103.662	Lexical, commentary on Nabnītu I. + 48894 + 1881, 1103 unnum. MSL 16, 341, 347-348.
47955	1881,1103.663	Contract.
47956	1881,1103.664	Unidentified.
	1881,1103.665	Missing. Marked "not found" in register (i.e. in the 1890s).
47957	1881,1103.666	Lexical; Ea; sign list.
47958	1881,1103.667	Lexical; Ea; sign list and literary extracts.
47959	1881,1103.668	Lexical; Ea; sign list; measurements.
47960	1881,1103.669	Account.
47961	1881,1103.670	Lexical; god-list. + 49150.
47962	1881,1103.671	Contract.
47963	1881,1103.672	List of workmen.
47964	1881,1103.673	Lexical; Ḫḫ IX. MSL 9, 181.
47965	1881,1103.674	Unidentified.
47966	1881,1103.675	Astrological omens.
47967	1881,1103.676	Lexical; Ea; sign list.
47968	1881,1103.677	Astronomical?
47969	1881,1103.678	Contract. Dar -/7/-. Sippar.
47970	1881,1103.679	Lexical.
47971	1881,1103.680	Lexical; Ea; sign list and literary extracts.
47972	1881,1103.681	Unidentified.
47973	1881,1103.682	Lexical; Ea; sign list.
47974	1881,1103.683	Lexical; Ea; sign list.
47975	1881,1103.684	Account of meat. 15/11/18.
47976	1881,1103.685	Astronomical; circular astrolabe fragment?

47977	1881,1103.686	Incantation.
47978	1881,1103.687	Unidentified; ruled between each line.
47979	1881,1103.688	Medical.
47980	1881,1103.689	Economic.
47981	1881,1103.690	Lexical; Ḫḫ; giš. + 47994.
47982	1881,1103.691	Unidentified; mentions kip-pa-tu4.
47983	1881,1103.692	Literary.
47984	1881,1103.693	Unidentified.
47985	1881,1103.694	Omens; physiognomic.
47986	1881,1103.695	Lexical; god-list. (+) 47822 + 47988 + 48251.
47987	1881,1103.696	Lexical.
47988	1881,1103.697	Joined to 47822.
47989	1881,1103.698	Lexical; Ea; sign list. + 47995.
47990	1881,1103.699	Unidentified.
47991	1881,1103.700	Literary.
47992	1881,1103.701	Mathematical; tabulated numbers increasing in each line by 1: colophon mentions Nabû-balāssu-iqbi. + 48055.
47993	1881,1103.702	Contract; ina ḫud libbišu; quppu.
47994	1881,1103.703	Joined to 47981.
47995	1881,1103.704	Joined to 47989.
47996	1881,1103.705	Unidentified.
47997	1881,1103.706	Bilingual incantation. + 48038.
47998	1881,1103.707	Lexical.
47999	1881,1103.708	Lexical; personal names.
48000	1881,1103.709	Unidentified.
48001	1881,1103.710	Unidentified.
48002	1881,1103.711	Unidentified.
48003	1881,1103.712	Literary; tree fable?
48004	1881,1103.713	Contract. Dar I 10/[]/16. Borsippa. Zadok, Nisaba 21, 239.
48005	1881,1103.714	Literary.
48006	1881,1103.715	Economic.
48007	1881,1103.716	Literary.
48008	1881,1103.717	Obv. list of witchcraft diagnoses; rev. list of incantation incipits; colophon(?). + 48028. Abusch and Schwemer, AMD 8/2 text 8.44 a, pl. 69.
48009	1881,1103.718	Contract. Wunsch, CM 20A-B, no. 67.
48010	1881,1103.719	Lexical.
48011	1881,1103.720	Bilingual epic; Lugal-e I 32-35. Geller, BSAOS 48 (1985) 215-223.
48012	1881,1103.721	Lexical.
48013	1881,1103.722	Unidentified.
48014	1881,1103.723	Astronomical?
48015	1881,1103.724	Lexical; giš.

48016	1881,1103.725	Economic.
48017	1881,1103.726	Incantation, Udug-ḫul 1. Geller, BAM 8, 44-58, pl. 7.
48018	1881,1103.727	Economic.
48019	1881,1103.728	Unidentified.
48020	1881,1103.729	Unidentified.
48021	1881,1103.730	Lexical; gi.
48022	1881,1103.731	Unidentified.
48023	1881,1103.732	Astrological omens.
48024	1881,1103.733	Lexical; Ea; sign list and literary extracts.
48025	1881,1103.734	Literary.
48026	1881,1103.735	Lexical; Ea; sign list.
48027	1881,1103.736	Joined to 47696.
48028	1881,1103.737	Joined to 48008.
48029	1881,1103.738	Promissory note for silver. Cyr 28/1/5.
48030	1881,1103.739	Prayer and ritual.
48031	1881,1103.740	Promissory note for silver. -/-/3.
48032	1881,1103.741	Joined to 47805.
48033	1881,1103.742	Circular tag, with only two damaged lines of text on the obverse.
48034	1881,1103.743	Promissory note for barley.
48035	1881,1103.744	Joined to 47805.
48036	1881,1103.745	Omens; Šumma ālu 34. Freedman, If a city, vol. 2, 223.
48037	1881,1103.746	Joined to 47805.
48038	1881,1103.747	Joined to 47997.
48039	1881,1103.748	Medical.
48040	1881,1103.749	Astronomical. + 48045 + 48048.
48041	1881,1103.750	Letter.
48042	1881,1103.751	Commentary.
48043	1881,1103.752	Omens.
48044	1881,1103.753	Sealing with two impressions of a stamp seal.
48045	1881,1103.754	Joined to 48040.
48046	1881,1103.755	Joined to 47805.
48047	1881,1103.756	Incantation; mentions zi-ku5-ru-da.
48048	1881,1103.757	Joined to 48040.
48049	1881,1103.758	Omens.
48050	1881,1103.759	Unidentified.
48051	1881,1103.760	Omens; extispicy.
48052	1881,1103.761	Liver omens; ubānu.
48053	1881,1103.762	Bilingual epic; Lugal-e IV; colophon. Mirelman, Iraq 79, 155-162.
48054	1881,1103.763	Contract.
48055	1881,1103.764	Joined to 47992.
48056	1881,1103.765	Lexical; syllabary.
48057	1881,1103.766	Sumerian literary.

48058	1881,1103.767	Lexical.
48059	1881,1103.768	Literary.
48060	1881,1103.769	Lexical.
48061	1881,1103.770	Field sale; sealed. d.l. Babylon. + 49103. Nisaba 28, no. 311.
48062	1881,1103.771	Economic.
48063	1881,1103.772	Astronomical Diary. + 48069. LBAT 192 (48063 only); Sachs and Hunger, ADART I, no. -338.
48064	1881,1103.773	Unidentified.
48065	1881,1103.774	Economic.
48066	1881,1103.775	Literary.
48067	1881,1103.776	Astronomical Diary.
48068	1881,1103.777	Joined to 33841.
48069	1881,1103.778	Joined to 48063.
48070	1881,1103.779	Economic.
48071	1881,1103.780	Incantation.
48072	1881,1103.781	Astronomical; Normal Star Almanac for SE 190. Hunger and Sachs, ADART VII, no. 88.
48073	1881,1103.782	Unidentified.
48074	1881,1103.783	Medical.
48075	1881,1103.784	Astronomical Diary.
48076	1881,1103.785	Unidentified.
48077	1881,1103.786	Medical.
48078	1881,1103.787	Astronomical.
48079	1881,1103.788	Astronomical; lunar table.
48080	1881,1103.789	Economic. -/4/-. Babylon.
48081	1881,1103.790	Astrological omens. Reiner, Fs Borger (CM 10), 300.
48082	1881,1103.791	Astrological omens.
48083	1881,1103.792	Economic.
48084	1881,1103.793	Literary.
48085	1881,1103.794	Literary.
48086	1881,1103.795	Bilingual incantation?
48087	1881,1103.796	Astronomical Diary.
48088	1881,1103.797	Joined to 46042.
48089	1881,1103.798	Astrological; Enūma Anu Enlil 65; colophon. Reiner, Fs Borger (CM 10), 300; Reiner and Pingree, BPO 4, 6-7, 67.
48090	1881,1103.799	Astronomical; lunar eclipse table for at least 280-278 BC. LBAT 1432; Hunger and Sachs, ADART V, no. 15.
48091	1881,1103.800	Astronomical; lunar six.
48092	1881,1103.801	Lexical; Ea; sign list.
48093	1881,1103.802	Mantic dream ritual. (+) 47907 (+) 48097.
48094	1881,1103.803	Literary.
48095	1881,1103.804	Astronomical.

48096	1881,1103.805	Account of dates or grain.
48097	1881,1103.806	Mantic dream ritual. (+) 47907 (+) 48093.
48098	1881,1103.807	Unidentified; mostly illegible.
48099	1881,1103.808	Astronomical.
48100	1881,1103.809	Unidentified; turns sideways.
48101	1881,1103.810	Astrological. Reiner, Fs Borger (CM 10), 300.
48102	1881,1103.811	Astrological omens.
48103	1881,1103.812	Astronomical?
48104	1881,1103.813	Astronomical; Normal Star Almanac for SE 19. Hunger and Sachs, ADART VII, no. 2.
48105	1881,1103.814	Astronomical?
48106	1881,1103.815	Astronomical.
48107	1881,1103.816	Astronomical?
48108	1881,1103.817	Joined to 47730.
48109	1881,1103.818	Astrological omens.
48110	1881,1103.819	Lexical; Ea; sign list.
48111	1881,1103.820	Astronomical.
48112	1881,1103.821	Account.
48113	1881,1103.822	Astrological; Enūma Anu Enlil; Sin ina IGI.IGI.LÁ-šú GIM UD.1.KAM. Reiner, Fs Borger (CM 10), 300.
48114	1881,1103.823	Economic.
48115	1881,1103.824	Astrological; MUL šamê SUR-ma ša U18 ana MIR; inūšu; catalogue? Reiner, Fs Borger (CM 10), 300.
48116	1881,1103.825	Medical.
48117	1881,1103.826	Account.
48118	1881,1103.827	Unidentified.
48119	1881,1103.828	Economic.
48120	1881,1103.829	Astronomical.
48121	1881,1103.830	Astronomical Diary.
48122	1881,1103.831	Lexical; Ea; sign list.
48123	1881,1103.832	Lexical; syllabary.
48124	1881,1103.833	Astronomical Diary; prices.
48125	1881,1103.834	Old Akkadian administrative text; issues? of barley? CT 50, 49, no. 183.
48126	1881,1103.835	Omens; Šumma ālu; referring to a man's house.
48127	1881,1103.836	Astrological; ITI x KUR-ma EN ITI y DU (... u-še-er ...). Reiner, Fs Borger (CM 10), 300.
48128	1881,1103.837	Lexical; Forerunner to Ḫḫ XIII. CT 14, 12; MSL 8/1 103.
48129	1881,1103.838	Lexical; Ea; sign list.
48130	1881,1103.839	Lexical; Ea; sign list.
48131	1881,1103.840	Unidentified.
48132	1881,1103.841	Unidentified.
48133	1881,1103.842	Economic.
48134	1881,1103.843	Lexical; god-list.

48135	1881,1103.844	Lexical; kuš. + 1881,1103.856.
48136	1881,1103.845	Unidentified.
48137	1881,1103.846	Astrological; Enūma Anu Enlil, Šamaš?, Sin? Reiner, Fs Borger (CM 10), 300.
48138	1881,1103.847	Lexical; Ea; sign list.
48139	1881,1103.848	Economic.
48140	1881,1103.849	Promissory note for barley. -/7/8.
48141	1881,1103.850	Economic.
48142	1881,1103.851	Mathematical astronomy; procedure text, Moon system A: G from Phi.
48143	1881,1103.852	Astronomical?
48144	1881,1103.853	Lexical.
48145	1881,1103.854	Medical. + 48203.
48146	1881,1103.855	Astrological; Enūma Anu Enlil, Sin; eclipse. Reiner, Fs Borger (CM 10), 300.
	1881,1103.856	Joined to 48135.
48147	1881,1103.857	Astronomical; Mercury table. Aaboe, Fs Hartner, 1-8.
48148	1881,1103.858	Astronomical Diary. Reiner, Fs Borger (CM 10), 300.
48149	1881,1103.859	Commentary.
48150	1881,1103.860	Contract. 11/[]/16.
48151	1881,1103.861	Astronomical Diary.
48152	1881,1103.862	Astronomical.
48153	1881,1103.863	Astronomical?
48154	1881,1103.864	Astronomical? 23/6/-.
48155	1881,1103.865	Lexical; Ea; sign list.
48156	1881,1103.866	Economic.
48157	1881,1103.867	Lexical.
48158	1881,1103.868	Mathematical; table of reciprocals. + 48893 + 49130.
48159	1881,1103.869	Astronomical Diary or related text; Lunar Six data.
48160	1881,1103.870	Incantation.
48161	1881,1103.871	Astronomical Diary.
48162	1881,1103.872	Literary.
48163	1881,1103.873	Unidentified; mostly illegible.
48164	1881,1103.874	Astronomical Diary.
48165	1881,1103.875	Astronomical.
48166	1881,1103.876	Astronomical; microzodiac rising time scheme. Steele, NABU 2018, 132, no. 84.
48167	1881,1103.877	Lexical; giš.
48168	1881,1103.878	Incantation. Lambert, MC 24, no. 225.
48169	1881,1103.879	Receipt.
48170	1881,1103.880	Astronomical Diary.
48171	1881,1103.881	Astronomical?
48172	1881,1103.882	Unidentified.
48173	1881,1103.883	Mathematical.
48174	1881,1103.884	Unidentified.

48175	1881,1103.885	Astronomical.
48176	1881,1103.886	Temple ritual, É-tur-kalamma.
48177	1881,1103.887	Economic.
48178	1881,1103.888	Astronomical.
48179	1881,1103.889	Contract; sealed. d.l. Nisaba 28, no. 312
48180	1881,1103.890	Astronomical.
48181	1881,1103.891	Astronomical?
48182	1881,1103.892	Astronomical.
48183	1881,1103.893	Unidentified.
48184	1881,1103.894	Unidentified.
48185	1881,1103.895	Unidentified; lists LÚ.GIG NENNI three times.
48186	1881,1103.896	Lexical; gi, and literary extracts.
48187	1881,1103.897	Literary.
48188	1881,1103.898	Hemerology?
48189	1881,1103.899	Astronomical.
48190	1881,1103.900	Astronomical?
48191	1881,1103.901	Joined to 47732.
48192	1881,1103.902	Mathematical.
48193	1881,1103.903	Lexical; Ea; sign list.
48194	1881,1103.904	Literary.
48195	1881,1103.905	Bilingual incantation.
48196	1881,1103.906	Measurements of fields.
48197	1881,1103.907	Lexical; syllabary.
48198	1881,1103.908	Mathematical.
48199	1881,1103.909	Letter.
48200	1881,1103.910	Receipt.
48201	1881,1103.911	Astronomical?
48202	1881,1103.912	Literary.
48203	1881,1103.913	Joined to 48145.
48204	1881,1103.914	School text; literary and lexical extracts. 28/12/-.
48205	1881,1103.915	Astronomical, Normal Star Almanac?
48206	1881,1103.916	Sumerian literary.
48207	1881,1103.917	Lexical; Ea; sign list.
48208	1881,1103.918	Field sale.
48209	1881,1103.919	Lexical; Ea; sign list.
48210	1881,1103.920	Contract.
48211	1881,1103.921	Lexical.
48212	1881,1103.922	Sumerian literary.
48213	1881,1103.923	Incantation.
48214	1881,1103.924	School text; hymn to Šamaš, 175-184; unidentified. + 48226.
48215	1881,1103.925	Promissory note for silver. Dar -/11/8. Babylon.
48216	1881,1103.926	Astronomical?
48217	1881,1103.927	Lexical; place names.
48218	1881,1103.928	Astronomical.

48219	1881,1103.929	Contract.
48220	1881,1103.930	Literary.
48221	1881,1103.931	Promissory note for barley. Nbn []/6/10. Babylon.
48222	1881,1103.932	Lexical.
48223	1881,1103.933	Lexical; giš, and personal names.
48224	1881,1103.934	Unidentified.
48225	1881,1103.935	Astronomical; Goal Year Text (Jupiter section).
48226	1881,1103.936	Joined to 48214.
48227	1881,1103.937	Unidentified.
48228	1881,1103.938	Bilingual incantation; Udug-ḫul 10. Geller, BAM 8, 323-339, pl. 82.
48229	1881,1103.939	Astronomical.
48230	1881,1103.940	Astronomical?
48231	1881,1103.941	Economic.
48232	1881,1103.942	Cylinder; inscription of Nebuchadnezzar II; dupl. Langdon, VAB 4, 144-147, Neb. no. 17 i 3-14, ii 1-23.
48233	1881,1103.943	Hollow cylinder; royal inscription, possibly of Nebuchadnezzar II, two columns; mostly illegible.
48234	1881,1103.944	Cylinder; inscription of Nabonidus; hollow; two columns; dupl. Schaudig, AOAT 256, 2.9, p. 387 (Ebabbar-Zylinder).
48235	1881,1103.945	Astronomical?
48236	1881,1103.946	Commentary.
48237	1881,1103.947	Lexical; Ea; sign list.
48238	1881,1103.948	Practice vertical wedge.
48239	1881,1103.949	Commentary on omens from the behaviour of the sacrificial lamb (cf. 49561); prayer on upper edge; drawing(?) on lower reverse. (+) 48561.
48240	1881,1103.950	Lexical; Ea; sign list.
48241	1881,1103.951	Lexical; Ea; sign list.
48242	1881,1103.952	Lexical; Ea; sign list.
48243	1881,1103.953	Astronomical?
48244	1881,1103.954	Lexical; Ea; sign list and literary extracts.
48245	1881,1103.955	Lexical; Ea; sign list.
48246	1881,1103.956	Lexical; Ea; sign list.
48247	1881,1103.957	Lexical; Ea; sign list.
48248	1881,1103.958	Lexical; practice wedges.
48249	1881,1103.959	Medical.
48250	1881,1103.960	Lexical; Ea; sign list.
48251	1881,1103.961	Joined to 47822.
48252	1881,1103.962	Astronomical.
48253	1881,1103.963	Astronomical; Normal Star Almanac. + 48333.
48254	1881,1103.964	Lexical; god-list; personal names.
48255	1881,1103.965	Hemerology. (+) 49020.

48256	1881,1103.966	Lexical; Ea; sign list.
48257	1881,1103.967	Obverse mostly lost except for a diagram (circle divided by six diameters); reverse colophon: copied from an Assyrian original. 8/[]/33 Darius I.
48258	1881,1103.968	Prayer.
48259	1881,1103.969	Lexical; Ea; sign list.
48260	1881,1103.970	Lexical; Ea; sign list.
48261	1881,1103.971	Lexical, commentary on Aa II/5. (+) 48380.
48262	1881,1103.972	Mathematical.
48263	1881,1103.973	Memorandum.
48264	1881,1103.974	Lexical; Ea; sign list.
48265	1881,1103.975	Lexical; Ea; sign list and literary extracts.
48266	1881,1103.976	Omens?
48267	1881,1103.977	Lexical; Ea; sign list.
48268	1881,1103.978	Literary.
48269	1881,1103.979	Economic.
48270	1881,1103.980	Literary.
48271	1881,1103.981	Medical.
48272	1881,1103.982	Lexical; Ea; sign list.
48273	1881,1103.983	Lexical; Ea; sign list.
48274	1881,1103.984	Lexical; Ea; sign list.
48275	1881,1103.985	Lexical; Ḫḫ I; literary extracts. + 48319.
48276	1881,1103.986	Astrological omens; Enūma Anu Enlil 19.
48277	1881,1103.987	Lexical.
48278	1881,1103.988	Incantation.
48279	1881,1103.989	Lexical; Ea; sign list and literary extracts.
48280	1881,1103.990	Lexical; god-list and professions.
48281	1881,1103.991	Astronomical?
48282	1881,1103.992	Unidentified.
48283	1881,1103.993	Literary.
48284	1881,1103.994	Astronomical?
48285	1881,1103.995	Astronomical.
48286	1881,1103.996	Letter.
48287	1881,1103.997	Incantation. + 48288.
48288	1881,1103.998	Joined to 48287.
48289	1881,1103.999	Bilingual incantation.
48290	1881,1103.1000	Astronomical Diary.
48291	1881,1103.1001	Astronomical Diary or related text.
48292	1881,1103.1002	Mathematical astronomy; synodic table, Moon system A, unusual format.
48293	1881,1103.1003	Astronomical?
48294	1881,1103.1004	Astronomical Diary.
48295	1881,1103.1005	Economic.
48296	1881,1103.1006	Account.
48297	1881,1103.1007	Memorandum.

48298	1881,1103.1008	Lexical?
48299	1881,1103.1009	Lexical; Nabnītu I. MSL 16, 339, 345.
48300	1881,1103.1010	Astronomical table (probably lunar).
48301	1881,1103.1011	Astronomical Diary or related text.
48302	1881,1103.1012	Unidentified.
48303	1881,1103.1013	Astronomical.
48304	1881,1103.1014	Promissory note for dates. Nbn -/-/11.
48305	1881,1103.1015	Astronomical?
48306	1881,1103.1016	Unidentified.
48307	1881,1103.1017	Unidentified.
48308	1881,1103.1018	Medical.
48309	1881,1103.1019	Promissory note for silver. Dar 18/6/11
48310	1881,1103.1020	Letter.
48311	1881,1103.1021	Omens; terrestrial; referring to a man's house.
48312	1881,1103.1022	Medical.
48313	1881,1103.1023	Astronomical Diary for SE 200+ (Arsaces); prayer on upper edge.
48314	1881,1103.1024	Economic.
48315	1881,1103.1025	Unidentified.
48316	1881,1103.1026	Lexical.
48317	1881,1103.1027	Unidentified.
48318	1881,1103.1028	Mathematical.
48319	1881,1103.1029	Joined to 48275.
48320	1881,1103.1030	Joined to 47902.
48321	1881,1103.1031	Unidentified.
48322	1881,1103.1032	Field plan. Dar I []/12/24. Nemet-Nejat, LB Field Plans, no. 66.
48323	1881,1103.1033	Economic.
48324	1881,1103.1034	Lexical; Ḫḫ I.
48325	1881,1103.1035	Field plan. Nemet-Nejat, LB Field Plans, no. 20.
48326	1881,1103.1036	Lexical; Ea; sign list.
48327	1881,1103.1037	Lexical.
48328	1881,1103.1038	Mathematical.
48329	1881,1103.1039	Lexical; Ea; sign list.
48330	1881,1103.1040	Medical.
48331	1881,1103.1041	Lexical; Ea; sign list.
48332	1881,1103.1042	Lexical; Ḫḫ III.
48333	1881,1103.1043	Joined to 48253.
48334	1881,1103.1044	Lexical; Ea; sign list.
48335	1881,1103.1045	Lexical.
48336	1881,1103.1046	Literary.
48337	1881,1103.1047	Joined to 47798.
48338	1881,1103.1048	Lexical; Ea; sign list and professions.
48339	1881,1103.1049	Literary.
48340	1881,1103.1050	Astronomical?

48341	1881,1103.1051	Lexical; personal names.
48342	1881,1103.1052	Unidentified.
48343	1881,1103.1053	Field plan.
48344	1881,1103.1054	Commentary on Šumma ālu. + 48536.
48345	1881,1103.1055	Economic.
48346	1881,1103.1056	School text in cursive script.
48347	1881,1103.1057	Contract.
48348	1881,1103.1058	Lexical; Ea; sign list.
48349	1881,1103.1059	Contract. 29/[]/3.
48350	1881,1103.1060	Lexical and literary extracts.
48351	1881,1103.1061	Field sale; finger-nail marks. Neb II. Wunsch, CM 20A-B, no. 5 B.
48352	1881,1103.1062	Lexical; syllabary.
48353	1881,1103.1063	Literary extracts.
48354	1881,1103.1064	Lexical; Ea; sign list and personal names.
48355	1881,1103.1065	Lexical; Ea; sign list and personal names.
48356	1881,1103.1066	Literary.
48357	1881,1103.1067	Promissory note for dates or grain. Dar -/-/9. Dilbat.
48358	1881,1103.1068	Practice wedges.
48359	1881,1103.1069	Lexical; personal names.
48360	1881,1103.1070	Contract. Xerxes 10/5/[].
48361	1881,1103.1071	Literary.
48362	1881,1103.1072	Lexical; Ea; sign list.
48363	1881,1103.1073	Economic.
48364	1881,1103.1074	Account of silver. -/2/-.
48365	1881,1103.1075	Lexical; Ea; sign list.
48366	1881,1103.1076	Account.
48367	1881,1103.1077	Lexical; list of diseases?
48368	1881,1103.1078	Lexical; personal names.
48369	1881,1103.1079	Lexical; Ea; sign list.
48370	1881,1103.1080	Joined to 47509.
48371	1881,1103.1081	Lexical; Ea; sign list.
48372	1881,1103.1082	Lexical; Ea; sign list.
48373	1881,1103.1083	Medical.
48374	1881,1103.1084	Incantation.
48375	1881,1103.1085	Commentary on bird omens?
48376	1881,1103.1086	Incantation.
48377	1881,1103.1087	Medical.
48378	1881,1103.1088	Lexical; Ea; sign list.
48379	1881,1103.1089	Historical?; mentions Babylon. + 48383.
48380	1881,1103.1090	Lexical, commentary on Aa II/5. (+) 48261.
48381	1881,1103.1091	Lexical; god-list.
48382	1881,1103.1092	Economic.
48383	1881,1103.1093	Joined to 48379.
48384	1881,1103.1094	Lexical; Ea; sign list.

48385	1881,1103.1095	Lexical; Ea; sign list and literary extracts.
48386	1881,1103.1096	Prayer.
48387	1881,1103.1097	Unidentified.
48388	1881,1103.1098	Lexical.
48389	1881,1103.1099	Lexical; Ea; sign list.
48390	1881,1103.1100	Unidentified.
48391	1881,1103.1101	Lexical; Ea; sign list.
48392	1881,1103.1102	Economic.
48393	1881,1103.1103	Ritual; mentions UZU šá ŠAḪ.
48394	1881,1103.1104	Practice wedges.
48395	1881,1103.1105	Unidentified; mentions é-sag-íl-la.
48396	1881,1103.1106	Incantation.
48397	1881,1103.1107	Bilingual incantation; Muššu'u VIII. Cf. Finkel, AuOr 9 (1991), 99-100; Böck, Muššu'u, 261-313 and pl. XL.
48398	1881,1103.1108	Literary.
48399	1881,1103.1109	Economic.
48400	1881,1103.1110	Incantation.
48401	1881,1103.1111	Unidentified.
48402	1881,1103.1112	Lexical; Ea; sign list and literary extracts.
48403	1881,1103.1113	Unidentified.
48404	1881,1103.1114	Lexical.
48405	1881,1103.1115	Astronomical.
48406	1881,1103.1116	Economic.
48407	1881,1103.1117	Literary.
48408	1881,1103.1118	Astronomical.
48409	1881,1103.1119	Contract; lease of a house.
48410	1881,1103.1120	Deposition. Nbn.
48411	1881,1103.1121	Lexical; god-list.
48412	1881,1103.1122	Field sale.
48413	1881,1103.1123	Lexical; Ea; sign list.
48414	1881,1103.1124	Incantation.
48415	1881,1103.1125	Economic.
48416	1881,1103.1126	Unidentified.
48417	1881,1103.1127	Astronomical Diary or related text.
48418	1881,1103.1128	Literary.
48419	1881,1103.1129	Medical. + 48568 + 48811.
48420	1881,1103.1130	Unidentified.
48421	1881,1103.1131	Literary.
48422	1881,1103.1132	Astrological commentary?
48423	1881,1103.1133	Omens.
48424	1881,1103.1134	Economic.
48425	1881,1103.1135	Incantation.
48426	1881,1103.1136	Literary.
48427	1881,1103.1137	Lexical.

48428	1881,1103.1138	Bilingual incantation.
48429	1881,1103.1139	Promissory note for silver. -/-/15. Dilbat.
48430	1881,1103.1140	Literary.
48431	1881,1103.1141	Unidentified.
48432	1881,1103.1142	Promissory note for dates. Dar 25/12b/5. Dilbat.
48433	1881,1103.1143	Audit. Nbn 11/12a/15. Babylon.
48434	1881,1103.1144	Letter order from Mušēzib-Marduk to Bēl-kāṣir; sealed. Nisaba 28, no. 213.
48435	1881,1103.1145	Namburbû ritual and incantation about a meteor. Maul, Bagh Forsch 18, 461ff.
48436	1881,1103.1146	Small round tablet with list of workmen.
48437	1881,1103.1147	Economic; crushed into an unusual shape.
48438	1881,1103.1148	Small round tablet with list of workmen; half lost; erasures on reverse.
48439	1881,1103.1149	Medical; stones as prescription ingredients.
48440	1881,1103.1150	Memorandum.
48441	1881,1103.1151	Memorandum; small cone-shaped tablet.
48442	1881,1103.1152	Field sale.
48443	1881,1103.1153	Joined to 47672.
48444	1881,1103.1154	Medical.
48445	1881,1103.1155	Joined to 47806.
48446	1881,1103.1156	Lexical(?); two columns.
48447	1881,1103.1157	Joined to 47668.
48448	1881,1103.1158	Lexical; gi.
48449	1881,1103.1159	Omens; Šumma ālu.
48450	1881,1103.1160	Astrological; commentary; Enūma Anu Enlil. (+) 48986.
48451	1881,1103.1161	Part of envelope of a letter.
48452	1881,1103.1162	Unidentified.
48453	1881,1103.1163	Astronomical.
48454	1881,1103.1164	Mathematical; measures.
48455	1881,1103.1165	Joined to 47684.
48456	1881,1103.1166	Field sale. + 48703.
48457	1881,1103.1167	Astronomical?
48458	1881,1103.1168	Lexical; Ea; sign list.
48459	1881,1103.1169	Economic.
48460	1881,1103.1170	Literary.
48461	1881,1103.1171	School text; personal names. + 48463.
48462	1881,1103.1172	Astrological omens.
48463	1881,1103.1173	Joined to 48461.
48464	1881,1103.1174	Practice wedges.
48465	1881,1103.1175	Lexical; Ea; sign-list.
48466	1881,1103.1176	Lexical; Ea; sign list and personal names.
48467	1881,1103.1177	Literary.
48468	1881,1103.1178	Lexical; Ea; sign list.

48469	1881,1103.1179	Astronomical?
48470	1881,1103.1180	Lexical; Ea; signs, and literary extracts.
48471	1881,1103.1181	Joined to 47674.
48472	1881,1103.1182	Literary.
48473	1881,1103.1183	Lexical; Ea; sign list.
48474	1881,1103.1184	Joined to 47684.
48475	1881,1103.1185	Account.
48476	1881,1103.1186	Lexical; Ea; sign list.
48477	1881,1103.1187	Joined to 47812.
48478	1881,1103.1188	Literary.
48479	1881,1103.1189	Physiognomic omens.
48480	1881,1103.1190	Lexical; Ea; sign list.
48481	1881,1103.1191	Incantation; É-gal-ku4-ra.
48482	1881,1103.1192	Lexical; Ea; sign list.
48483	1881,1103.1193	Lexical; Ḫḫ III. MSL 9, 159.
48484	1881,1103.1194	Lexical; Ea; sign list. + 1881,1103.1203.
48485	1881,1103.1195	Bilingual prayer. Gabbay and Mirelman, ZA 107, 22-34.
48486	1881,1103.1196	Contract.
48487	1881,1103.1197	Lexical; Ea; sign list and literary extracts.
48488	1881,1103.1198	Lexical; god-list and literary extracts. (+) 48489.
48489	1881,1103.1199	Lexical; Ea; sign list; god-list; practice wedges. (+) 48488.
48490	1881,1103.1200	Lexical; personal names; literary extracts; numbers; practice signs; practice wedges.
48491	1881,1103.1201	Omens; extispicy.
48492	1881,1103.1202	Lexical; Ea; sign list.
	1881,1103.1203	Joined to 48484.
48493	1881,1103.1204	Physiognomic omens.
48494	1881,1103.1205	Medical.
48495	1881,1103.1206	Lexical; Ḫḫ II. MSL 9, 157.
48496	1881,1103.1207	Medical incantation and ritual.
48497	1881,1103.1208	Joined to 47716.
48498	1881,1103.1209	Chronicle of market prices. Grayson, TCS 5, Chronicle 23.
48499	1881,1103.1210	Contract for birds. Dar 1/11/30. Alu-ša-Bēl.
48500	1881,1103.1211	Ledger.
48501	1881,1103.1212	Account of silver.
48502	1881,1103.1213	Unidentified.
48503	1881,1103.1214	Astronomical.
48504	1881,1103.1215	Astronomical.
48505	1881,1103.1216	Astronomical.
48506	1881,1103.1217	Contract.
48507	1881,1103.1218	Contract.
48508	1881,1103.1219	Account.

48509	1881,1103.1220	Lexical; Ea; sign list.
48510	1881,1103.1221	Lexical; Ea; sign list.
48511	1881,1103.1222	Medical omens.
48512	1881,1103.1223	Lexical; god-list.
48513	1881,1103.1224	Lexical and literary extracts.
48514	1881,1103.1225	Sale of a sheep. 6/9/-.
48515	1881,1103.1226	Lexical; Ea; sign list.
48516	1881,1103.1227	Lexical; professions (LÚ.KAB.SAR).
48517	1881,1103.1228	Joined to 47687.
48518	1881,1103.1229	Medical.
48519	1881,1103.1230	Incantation.
48520	1881,1103.1231	Lexical; geographical list.
48521	1881,1103.1232	Unidentified.
48522	1881,1103.1233	Lexical; syllabary.
48523	1881,1103.1234	Lexical; Ea; sign list and personal names.
48524	1881,1103.1235	Late Babylonian copy of the Laws of Hammurabi.
48525	1881,1103.1236	Medical.
48526	1881,1103.1237	Lexical; Ea; sign list.
48527	1881,1103.1238	Sumerian literary.
48528	1881,1103.1239	Literary.
48529	1881,1103.1240	Lexical; Ea; sign list.
48530	1881,1103.1241	Unidentified.
48531	1881,1103.1242	Account of dates or grain.
48532	1881,1103.1243	Commentary. + 48963.
48533	1881,1103.1244	Mathematical; problem text.
48534	1881,1103.1245	Field sale.
48535	1881,1103.1246	Medical.
48536	1881,1103.1247	Joined to 48344.
48537	1881,1103.1248	Lexical; Ea; sign list and literary extracts.
48538	1881,1103.1249	Account of dates or grain.
48539	1881,1103.1250	Lexical; Ea; sign list.
48540	1881,1103.1251	Economic.
48541	1881,1103.1252	Lexical; Ea; sign list.
48542	1881,1103.1253	Bilingual incantation.
48543	1881,1103.1254	Literary; bilingual proverbs; copied from a damaged original (ḫe-pí); probably same composition as K.4160+ (Lambert, BWL 233-234).
48544	1881,1103.1255	Astronomical; star list.
48545	1881,1103.1256	Promissory note for silver with pledge of a house. Cyr 19/12/5? Babylon.
48546	1881,1103.1257	Lexical; personal names.
48547	1881,1103.1258	Medical.
48548	1881,1103.1259	Lexical; Ea; sign list.
48549	1881,1103.1260	Bilingual incantation.
48550	1881,1103.1261	Incantation.

48551	1881,1103.1262	Lexical; Ea; sign list.
48552	1881,1103.1263	Astrological omens.
48553	1881,1103.1264	Lexical; personal names.
48554	1881,1103.1265	Field plan. Nemet-Nejat, LB Field Plans, no. 34.
48555	1881,1103.1266	Lexical; Ea; sign list.
48556	1881,1103.1267	Field sale.
48557	1881,1103.1268	Medical.
48558	1881,1103.1269	Incantation.
48559	1881,1103.1270	Literary.
48560	1881,1103.1271	Lexical; Ea; sign list.
48561	1881,1103.1272	Commentary on omens from the behaviour of the sacrificial lamb; cf. 48239. (+) 48239.
48562	1881,1103.1273	Contract for a dowry. d.l. Wunsch, AfO 44/45, 95, no. 28.
48563	1881,1103.1274	Lexical; Ea; sign list and literary extracts.
48564	1881,1103.1275	Astronomical Diary?
48565	1881,1103.1276	Contract.
48566	1881,1103.1277	Lexical; Ea; sign list.
48567	1881,1103.1278	Economic.
48568	1881,1103.1279	Joined to 48419.
48569	1881,1103.1280	Lexical; Ḫḫ XI 324-331.
48570	1881,1103.1281	Lexical; Ḫḫ VIII. + 48578. MSL 9, 173 (48578 only).
48571	1881,1103.1282	Economic.
48572	1881,1103.1283	Field sale.
48573	1881,1103.1284	Economic.
48574	1881,1103.1285	Economic.
48575	1881,1103.1286	Commentary on Šumma ālu.
48576	1881,1103.1287	Lexical; Ea; sign list and numbers.
48577	1881,1103.1288	Account of dates or grain.
48578	1881,1103.1289	Joined to 48570.
48579	1881,1103.1290	Omens; extispicy. + 49154.
48580	1881,1103.1291	Lexical; Ea; sign list.
48581	1881,1103.1292	Medical.
48582	1881,1103.1293	Incantation.
48583	1881,1103.1294	Lexical; Ea; sign list.
48584	1881,1103.1295	Economic.
48585	1881,1103.1296	Sumerian literary.
48586	1881,1103.1297	Lexical; Ea; sign list.
48587	1881,1103.1298	Lexical; Ea; sign list.
48588	1881,1103.1299	Joined to 47812.
48589	1881,1103.1300	Incantation.
48590	1881,1103.1301	Incantation.
48591	1881,1103.1302	Literary.
48592	1881,1103.1303	Medical.
48593	1881,1103.1304	Lexical; god-list.

48594	1881,1103.1305	Contract.
48595	1881,1103.1306	Medical.
48596	1881,1103.1307	Literary.
48597	1881,1103.1308	Incantation.
48598	1881,1103.1309	Bilingual epic; Lugal-e I 17-25 and 27-33; probably written by Kabti-ilāni-Marduk. (+) 47660. van Dijk, Lugal, text k2.
48599	1881,1103.1310	Astronomical Diary.
48600	1881,1103.1311	Mathematical.
48601	1881,1103.1312	Contract.
48602	1881,1103.1313	Astronomical; lunar table; System B.
48603	1881,1103.1314	Ledger.
48604	1881,1103.1315	Literary.
48605	1881,1103.1316	Economic.
48606	1881,1103.1317	Lexical; Ḫḫ IV. MSL 9, 168.
48607	1881,1103.1318	Unidentified.
48608	1881,1103.1319	Promissory note for silver. Dar -/-/1.
48609	1881,1103.1320	Field sale. 11/[]/21.
48610	1881,1103.1321	Incantation.
48611	1881,1103.1322	Astronomical Diary; Artaxerxes.
48612	1881,1103.1323	Incantation.
48613	1881,1103.1324	Economic.
48614	1881,1103.1325	Astronomical Diary or related text.
48615	1881,1103.1326	Practice wedges.
48616	1881,1103.1327	Lexical; Ea; sign list.
48617	1881,1103.1328	Economic.
48618	1881,1103.1329	Literary.
48619	1881,1103.1330	Astronomical Diary.
48620	1881,1103.1331	Unidentified.
48621	1881,1103.1332	Lexical; Ea; sign list.
48622	1881,1103.1333	Astronomical Diary or related text.
48623	1881,1103.1334	Astronomical Diary or related text.
48624	1881,1103.1335	Astronomical?
48625	1881,1103.1336	Field sale. Nbn? 20+/2/10.
48626	1881,1103.1337	Contract.
48627	1881,1103.1338	Astrological omens; moon.
48628	1881,1103.1339	Mathematical; problem text?
48629	1881,1103.1340	Economic.
48630	1881,1103.1341	Astronomical.
48631	1881,1103.1342	Astronomical?
48632	1881,1103.1343	Account.
48633	1881,1103.1344	Astrological omens; stars; TE-tablet.
48634	1881,1103.1345	Account.
48635	1881,1103.1346	Account.
48636	1881,1103.1347	Economic.

48637	1881,1103.1348	Lexical, commentary on Aa I.
48638	1881,1103.1349	Economic.
48639	1881,1103.1350	Field sale. + 48646.
48640	1881,1103.1351	Lexical; Ea; sign list and literary extracts.
48641	1881,1103.1352	Field sale.
48642	1881,1103.1353	Account.
48643	1881,1103.1354	Letter.
48644	1881,1103.1355	Astronomical; lunar six observations; Nebuchadnezzar II. Steele, NABU 2018, 129-130, no. 82.
48645	1881,1103.1356	Commentary.
48646	1881,1103.1357	Joined to 48639.
48647	1881,1103.1358	Astronomical?
48648	1881,1103.1359	Lexical; Ḫḫ I.
48649	1881,1103.1360	Lexical.
48650	1881,1103.1361	Medical.
48651	1881,1103.1362	Economic.
48652	1881,1103.1363	Literary.
48653	1881,1103.1364	Economic.
48654	1881,1103.1365	Account.
48655	1881,1103.1366	Lexical; Ea; sign list.
48656	1881,1103.1367	Astronomical?
48657	1881,1103.1368	Incantation.
48658	1881,1103.1369	Medical.
48659	1881,1103.1370	Lexical, commentary on Aa II/6 (pirsu 14).
48660	1881,1103.1371	Bilingual incantation.
48661	1881,1103.1372	Sumerian literary.
48662	1881,1103.1373	Mathematical.
48663	1881,1103.1374	Joined to 47812.
48664	1881,1103.1375	Incantation.
48665	1881,1103.1376	Practice wedges.
48666	1881,1103.1377	Joined to 47672.
48667	1881,1103.1378	Lexical; Ea; sign list.
48668	1881,1103.1379	Mathematical; factorisation table.
48669	1881,1103.1380	Literary.
48670	1881,1103.1381	Joined to 47663.
48671	1881,1103.1382	Bilingual incantation, Udug-ḫul 9. Geller, BAM 8, 302-322, pl. 75.
48672	1881,1103.1383	Commentary.
48673	1881,1103.1384	Joined to 47852.
48674	1881,1103.1385	Receipt of silver as rent. Art II 14/7/32.
48675	1881,1103.1386	Lexical; Ḫḫ I.
48676	1881,1103.1387	Account of dates.
48677	1881,1103.1388	Medical.
48678	1881,1103.1389	Astronomical.
48679	1881,1103.1390	Unidentified.

48680	1881,1103.1391	Medical.
48681	1881,1103.1392	Omens.
48682	1881,1103.1393	Lexical; Ea; sign list.
48683	1881,1103.1394	Lexical; Ea; sign list.
48684	1881,1103.1395	Unidentified.
48685	1881,1103.1396	Economic.
48686	1881,1103.1397	Lexical; Ea; sign list.
48687	1881,1103.1398	Incantation.
48688	1881,1103.1399	Omens; Šumma ālu; 30-31. + 48859. Freedman, If a city, vol. 2, 132, 148.
48689	1881,1103.1400	Lexical; Ea; sign list and literary extracts.
48690	1881,1103.1401	Lexical; Ḫḫ XVI (stones). MSL 10, 3.
48691	1881,1103.1402	Lexical; Ea; sign list.
48692	1881,1103.1403	Field plan. Nemet-Nejat, LB Field Plans, no. 42.
48693	1881,1103.1404	Medical.
48694	1881,1103.1405	Practice signs.
48695	1881,1103.1406	Literary.
48696	1881,1103.1407	Ritual. + 49098a.
48697	1881,1103.1408	Contract. Dar. Babylon.
48698	1881,1103.1409	Literary extracts.
48699	1881,1103.1410	Astronomical; colophon.
48700	1881,1103.1411	Astronomical.
48701	1881,1103.1412	Incantation.
48702	1881,1103.1413	Medical; prescription ingredients.
48703	1881,1103.1414	Joined to 48456.
48704	1881,1103.1415	Lexical. + 48841.
48705	1881,1103.1416	Field sale; finger-nail marks. RN lost []/[]/2?
48706	1881,1103.1417	Medical.
48707	1881,1103.1418	Contract. -/-/19.
48708	1881,1103.1419	Letter.
48709	1881,1103.1420	Economic.
48710	1881,1103.1421	Medical; materia medica and gynaecology.
48711	1881,1103.1422	Astronomical Almanac. SE 198 (Arsaces). + 48912 + 48947.
48712	1881,1103.1423	Contract; sale of a house; sealed; finger-nail marks. d.l. [Babylon]. (+) 47795. Wunsch, Bab Arch 2, no. 29; Nisaba 28, no. 114b.
48713	1881,1103.1424	Lexical; Ea; sign list.
48714	1881,1103.1425	Unidentified.
48715	1881,1103.1426	Uninscribed tablet; complete; of the size and shape of a private letter.
48716	1881,1103.1427	Lexical.
48717	1881,1103.1428	Incantation.
48718	1881,1103.1429	Literary; colophon.
48719	1881,1103.1430	Medical.

48720	1881,1103.1431	Lexical; Ea; sign list.
48721	1881,1103.1432	Economic.
48722	1881,1103.1433	Field sale.
48723	1881,1103.1434	Lexical.
48724	1881,1103.1435	Lexical.
48725	1881,1103.1436	Literary; colophon.
48726	1881,1103.1437	Literary.
48727	1881,1103.1438	Commentary; medical omens; Sa-gig VII. + 48741.
48728	1881,1103.1439	Commentary?
48729	1881,1103.1440	Commentary; medical omens; Sa-gig VII.
48730	1881,1103.1441	Hemerology.
48731	1881,1103.1442	Incantation.
48732	1881,1103.1443	Lexical; Ea; sign list and literary extracts.
48733	1881,1103.1444	Lexical; Ea; sign list and literary extracts.
48734	1881,1103.1445	Deposition.
48735	1881,1103.1446	Lexical; Ea; sign list.
48736	1881,1103.1447	Commentary on Šumma ālu.
48737	1881,1103.1448	Literary.
48738	1881,1103.1449	Omens.
48739	1881,1103.1450	Medical.
48740	1881,1103.1451	Incantation.
48741	1881,1103.1452	Joined to 48727.
48742	1881,1103.1453	Incantation.
48743	1881,1103.1454	Lexical; Ḫḫ I. MSL 5, 6.
48744	1881,1103.1455	Lexical; Ea; sign list.
48745	1881,1103.1456	Astronomical?
48746	1881,1103.1457	Medical; names of diseases.
48747	1881,1103.1458	Lexical; Ea; sign list.
48748	1881,1103.1459	Astronomical?
48749	1881,1103.1460	Lexical; Ea; sign list and literary extracts.
48750	1881,1103.1461	Lexical; Ea; sign list.
48751	1881,1103.1462	Lexical; Ea; sign list.
48752	1881,1103.1463	Commentary on an astrological text.
48753	1881,1103.1464	Incantation; colophon.
48754	1881,1103.1465	Astrological omens.
48755	1881,1103.1466	Unidentified.
48756	1881,1103.1467	Contract.
48757	1881,1103.1468	Ritual.
48758	1881,1103.1469	Deposition. Nbk 3/1/3. Babylon.
48759	1881,1103.1470	Lexical; Ea; sign list.
48760	1881,1103.1471	Astrological omens.
48761	1881,1103.1472	Bilingual incantation.
48762	1881,1103.1473	Lexical; Ea; sign list.
48763	1881,1103.1474	Lexical; Ea; sign list.
48764	1881,1103.1475	Lexical; Ea; sign list.

48765	1881,1103.1476	Economic.
48766	1881,1103.1477	Medical.
48767	1881,1103.1478	Deposition.
48768	1881,1103.1479	Lexical; Ea; sign list.
48769	1881,1103.1480	Field sale; finger-nail marks. + 49027 (+) 47488.
48770	1881,1103.1481	Medical. + 48783.
48771	1881,1103.1482	Omens.
48772	1881,1103.1483	Prayer.
48773	1881,1103.1484	Literary.
48774	1881,1103.1485	Ritual.
48775	1881,1103.1486	Medical.
48776	1881,1103.1487	Lexical; Ea; sign list.
48777	1881,1103.1488	Medical.
48778	1881,1103.1489	Prayer.
48779	1881,1103.1490	Medical.
48780	1881,1103.1491	Contract.
48781	1881,1103.1492	Astronomical; colophon.
48782	1881,1103.1493	Medical.
48783	1881,1103.1494	Joined to 48770.
48784	1881,1103.1495	Field plan. Nemet-Nejat, LB Field Plans, no. 38.
48785	1881,1103.1496	Field plan.
48786	1881,1103.1497	Medical.
48787	1881,1103.1498	Lexical; Ea; sign list.
48788	1881,1103.1499	Prayer.
48789	1881,1103.1500	Contract; hire of a slave.
48790	1881,1103.1501	Late astrology.
48791	1881,1103.1502	Lexical; Ea; sign list.
48792	1881,1103.1503	Namburbû.
48793	1881,1103.1504	Medical.
48794	1881,1103.1505	Joined to 47796.
48795	1881,1103.1506	Lexical; personal names.
48796	1881,1103.1507	Medical.
48797	1881,1103.1508	Medical.
48798	1881,1103.1509	Medical.
48799	1881,1103.1510	Medical.
48800	1881,1103.1511	Economic.
48801	1881,1103.1512	Lexical; Ea; sign list.
48802	1881,1103.1513	Lexical.
48803	1881,1103.1514	Unidentified.
48804	1881,1103.1515	Lexical; Ea; sign list.
48805	1881,1103.1516	Medical.
48806	1881,1103.1517	Mathematical.
48807	1881,1103.1518	Omens.
48808	1881,1103.1519	Ledger.
48809	1881,1103.1520	Medical.

48810	1881,1103.1521	Economic.
48811	1881,1103.1522	Joined to 48419.
48812	1881,1103.1523	Lexical; Ea; sign list.
48813	1881,1103.1524	Lexical; Ea; sign list and literary extracts.
48814	1881,1103.1525	Lexical, commentary on Aa.
48815	1881,1103.1526	Economic.
48816	1881,1103.1527	Medical.
48817	1881,1103.1528	Lexical; Ea; sign list.
48818	1881,1103.1529	Lexical; Ea; sign list.
48819	1881,1103.1530	Lexical; Ea; sign list.
48820	1881,1103.1531	Medical.
48821	1881,1103.1532	Astronomical.
48822	1881,1103.1533	Medical.
48823	1881,1103.1534	Medical.
48824	1881,1103.1535	Account.
48825	1881,1103.1536	Unidentified.
48826	1881,1103.1537	Lexical; Ea; sign list.
48827	1881,1103.1538	Contract; sealed. [Borsippa?]. Nisaba 28, no. 644.
48828	1881,1103.1539	Joined to 47693.
48829	1881,1103.1540	Practice wedges.
48830	1881,1103.1541	Economic.
48831	1881,1103.1542	Lexical; Ea; sign list.
48832	1881,1103.1543	Medical.
48833	1881,1103.1544	Bilingual incantation.
48834	1881,1103.1545	Contract. Cam 15/10/-.
48835	1881,1103.1546	Lexical; god-list.
48836	1881,1103.1547	Lexical; Ea; sign list.
48837	1881,1103.1548	Astronomical.
48838	1881,1103.1549	Unidentified.
48839	1881,1103.1550	Economic.
48840	1881,1103.1551	Lexical; Ḫḫ I.
48841	1881,1103.1552	Joined to 48704.
48842	1881,1103.1553	Contract.
48843	1881,1103.1554	Economic.
48844	1881,1103.1555	Lexical; personal names.
48845	1881,1103.1556	Unidentified.
48846	1881,1103.1557	Economic.
48847	1881,1103.1558	Contract.
48848	1881,1103.1559	Lexical; Ea; sign list.
48849	1881,1103.1560	Bilingual incantation.
48850	1881,1103.1561	Unidentified.
48851	1881,1103.1562	Lexical; Ea; sign list.
48852	1881,1103.1563	Literary.
48853	1881,1103.1564	Lexical; Ea; sign list.
48854	1881,1103.1565	Promissory note for silver. Nbn 18/[]/13+. Babylon.

48855	1881,1103.1566	Lexical; Ea; sign list.
48856	1881,1103.1567	Contract.
48857	1881,1103.1568	Contract.
48858	1881,1103.1569	Receipt.
48859	1881,1103.1570	Joined to 48688.
48860	1881,1103.1571	Unidentified; mostly illegible.
48861	1881,1103.1572	Astronomical?
48862	1881,1103.1573	Literary.
48863	1881,1103.1574	Graeco-Babyloniaca; lexical, Syllabary A. Geller, ZA 87, 73-74 and 90, no. 6 (copy); Westenholz, ZA 97, 267.
48864	1881,1103.1575	Joined to 33462.
48865	1881,1103.1576	Joined to 33493.
48866	1881,1103.1577	Joined to 33493.
48867	1881,1103.1578	Lexical; stones.
48868	1881,1103.1579	Omens.
48869	1881,1103.1580	Astronomical; compilation of planetary observations.
48870	1881,1103.1581	Astronomical Diary or related text.
48871	1881,1103.1582	Incantation.
48872	1881,1103.1583	Lexical; Ḫḫ IV. MSL 9, 168.
48873	1881,1103.1584	Unidentified.
48874	1881,1103.1585	Economic.
48875	1881,1103.1586	Unidentified.
48876	1881,1103.1587	Lexical, similar to Ana ittišu II.
48877	1881,1103.1588	Astronomical; Mercury observations.
48878	1881,1103.1589	Unidentified.
48879	1881,1103.1590	Bilingual incantation.
48880	1881,1103.1591	Economic.
48881	1881,1103.1592	Literary; colophon. + 49070.
48882	1881,1103.1593	Astrological omens.
48883	1881,1103.1594	Incantation; Seleucid colophon. Lambert, MC 24, no. 215.
48884	1881,1103.1595	Ritual.
48885	1881,1103.1596	Joined to 33493.
48886	1881,1103.1597	Astronomical; Goal Year Text or Almanac; lunar six values.
48887	1881,1103.1598	Incantation.
48888	1881,1103.1599	Astronomical Diary; mentions Arsaces, Bagayasha and Timotheos. SE. BCHP 18c.
48889	1881,1103.1600	Literary; colophon.
48890	1881,1103.1601	Joined to 32205.
48891	1881,1103.1602	Astronomical?
48892	1881,1103.1603	Field sale.
48893	1881,1103.1604	Joined to 48158.
48894	1881,1103.1605	Joined to 47954.

48895	1881,1103.1606	Lexical; giš.
48896	1881,1103.1607	Astronomical; Normal Star Almanac.
48897	1881,1103.1608	Unidentified; mostly illegible.
48898	1881,1103.1609	Joined to 33450.
48899	1881,1103.1610	Unidentified.
48900	1881,1103.1611	Lexical; Ea; sign list.
48901	1881,1103.1612	Account.
48902	1881,1103.1613	Medical.
48903	1881,1103.1614	Literary.
48904	1881,1103.1615	Astronomical Diary.
48905	1881,1103.1616	Account of silver.
48906	1881,1103.1617	Lexical; Ea; sign list.
48907	1881,1103.1618	Incantation.
48908	1881,1103.1619	Literary.
48909	1881,1103.1620	Lexical; Ḫḫ XV. MSL 9, 4.
48910	1881,1103.1621	Promissory note for wheat. Nbn 18/4/2. Babylon.
48911	1881,1103.1622	Practice numbers.
48912	1881,1103.1623	Joined to 48711.
48913	1881,1103.1624	Incantation.
48914	1881,1103.1625	Lexical; giš, and literary extracts.
48915	1881,1103.1626	Medical.
48916	1881,1103.1627	Astronomical?
48917	1881,1103.1628	Astronomical procedure text.
48918	1881,1103.1629	Joined to 33514.
48919	1881,1103.1630	Omens; terrestrial.
48920	1881,1103.1631	Lexical and literary extracts.
48921	1881,1103.1632	Astronomical; Almanac.
48922	1881,1103.1633	Astronomical Diary or related text; Lunar Six data.
48923	1881,1103.1634	Joined to 33450.
48924	1881,1103.1635	Lexical; personal names.
48925	1881,1103.1636	Lexical; gi.
48926	1881,1103.1637	Incantations, Maqlu V. Abusch, AMD 10, 1311-150.
48927	1881,1103.1638	Joined to 47730.
48928	1881,1103.1639	Astronomical; star list.
48929	1881,1103.1640	Practice wedges and signs.
48930	1881,1103.1641	Missing.
48931	1881,1103.1642	Lexical; Ea; sign list.
48932	1881,1103.1643	Field sale.
48933	1881,1103.1644	Field sale. Art I/II []/[]/30. Babylon.
48934	1881,1103.1645	Unidentified.
48935	1881,1103.1646	Economic.
48936	1881,1103.1647	Economic.
48937	1881,1103.1648	Unidentified.
48938	1881,1103.1649	Astronomical?

48939	1881,1103.1650	Contract; land sale; finger-nail marks. Dar 17/5/[]. Babylon.
48940	1881,1103.1651	Field sale.
48941	1881,1103.1652	Field sale.
48942	1881,1103.1653	Unidentified.
48943	1881,1103.1654	Field sale.
48944	1881,1103.1655	Lexical; Ea; sign list.
48945	1881,1103.1656	Lexical; Ea; sign list and numbers.
48946	1881,1103.1657	Lexical; Ea; sign list and personal names.
48947	1881,1103.1658	Joined to 48711.
48948	1881,1103.1659	Contract.
48949	1881,1103.1660	Lexical; Ea; sign list.
48950	1881,1103.1661	Ritual.
48951	1881,1103.1662	Medical.
48952	1881,1103.1663	Contract. Dilbat.
48953	1881,1103.1664	Lexical; Ea; sign list.
48954	1881,1103.1665	Lexical; Ea; sign list.
48955	1881,1103.1666	Field sale.
48956	1881,1103.1667	Field plan. Nemet-Nejat, LB Field Plans, no. 40.
48957	1881,1103.1668	Lexical; Ea; sign list.
48958	1881,1103.1669	Lexical; personal names.
48959	1881,1103.1670	Lexical; Ea; sign list.
48960	1881,1103.1671	Promissory note for silver. Kandalanu 29/12/8+. Brinkman and Kennedy, JCS 35, 51, L.188.
48961	1881,1103.1672	Mathematical; problem text.
48962	1881,1103.1673	Astronomical?
48963	1881,1103.1674	Joined to 48532.
48964	1881,1103.1675	Promissory note for dates or grain.
48965	1881,1103.1676	Account.
48966	1881,1103.1677	Joined to 47701.
48967	1881,1103.1678	Lexical; Ea; sign list.
48968	1881,1103.1679	Promissory note for silver; sealed. Dar II/III 14/[]/[]. Nisaba 28, no. 257.
48969	1881,1103.1680	Joined to 47431.
48970	1881,1103.1681	Astronomical.
48971	1881,1103.1682	Lexical; Ḫḫ I.
48972	1881,1103.1683	Joined to 47506.
48973	1881,1103.1684	Incantation.
48974	1881,1103.1685	Marriage contract.
48975	1881,1103.1686	Economic.
48976	1881,1103.1687	Field sale. -/-/6.
48977	1881,1103.1688	Joined to 47806.
48978	1881,1103.1689	Economic.
48979	1881,1103.1690	Account.
48980	1881,1103.1691	Medical.

48981	1881,1103.1692	Field plan. RN lost []/[]/34. Nemet-Nejat, LB Field Plans, no. 9.
48982	1881,1103.1693	Astronomical?
48983	1881,1103.1694	Promissory note for dates.
48984	1881,1103.1695	Unidentified.
48985	1881,1103.1696	Medical.
48986	1881,1103.1697	Astrological; commentary; Enūma Anu Enlil. (+) 48450.
48987	1881,1103.1698	Economic.
48988	1881,1103.1699	Commentary.
48989	1881,1103.1700	Field sale. RN lost 1/[]/13. Dilbat. + 49016 + 49055 + 49140.
48990	1881,1103.1701	Astronomical.
48991	1881,1103.1702	Literary.
48992	1881,1103.1703	Promissory note for silver.
48993	1881,1103.1704	Field plan.
48994	1881,1103.1705	Economic.
48995	1881,1103.1706	Field plan. Nemet-Nejat, LB Field Plans, no. 14
48996	1881,1103.1707	Account of barley.
48997	1881,1103.1708	Medical.
48998	1881,1103.1709	Lexical; Ea; sign list.
48999	1881,1103.1710	Incantation.
49000	1881,1103.1711	Joined to 47807.
49001	1881,1103.1712	Economic.
49002	1881,1103.1713	Account.
49003	1881,1103.1714	Lexical.
49004	1881,1103.1715	Lexical; Ea; sign list.
49005	1881,1103.1716	Mathematical.
49006	1881,1103.1717	Astronomical.
49007	1881,1103.1718	Economic.
49008	1881,1103.1719	Memorandum.
49009	1881,1103.1720	Astrological omens; Enūma Anu Enlil.
49010	1881,1103.1721	Contract.
49011	1881,1103.1722	Contract.
49012	1881,1103.1723	Economic.
49013	1881,1103.1724	Medical prescriptions.
49014	1881,1103.1725	Contract; lease of a house.
49015	1881,1103.1726	Astronomical.
49016	1881,1103.1727	Joined to 48989.
49017	1881,1103.1728	Lexical; Ḫḫ III?
49018	1881,1103.1729	Commentary.
49019	1881,1103.1730	Economic.
49020	1881,1103.1731	Hemerology. (+) 48255.
49021	1881,1103.1732	Lexical.
49022	1881,1103.1733	Joined to 47875.

49023	1881,1103.1734	Receipt(?); sealed. (Borsippa). Nisaba 28, no. 530.
49024	1881,1103.1735	Economic.
49025	1881,1103.1736	Medical.
49026	1881,1103.1737	Medical.
49027	1881,1103.1738	Joined to 48769.
49028	1881,1103.1739	Economic.
49029	1881,1103.1740	Commentary on extispicy; isru.
49030	1881,1103.1741	Bilingual incantation.
49031	1881,1103.1742	Contract. 13/[]/29.
49032	1881,1103.1743	Lexical; Ḫḫ II.
49033	1881,1103.1744	Economic.
49034	1881,1103.1745	Lexical; Ea; sign list.
49035	1881,1103.1746	Lexical; Ea; sign list.
49036	1881,1103.1747	Field plan 3/5/-. Nemet-Nejat, LB Field Plans, no. 15.
49037	1881,1103.1748	Omens.
49038	1881,1103.1749	Missing.
49039	1881,1103.1750	Literary.
49040	1881,1103.1751	Joined to 47806.
49041	1881,1103.1752	Joined to 47693.
49042	1881,1103.1753	Commentary on Šumma ālu I.
49043	1881,1103.1754	Omens; terrestrial.
49044	1881,1103.1755	Commentary; medical omens; Sa-gig VII?
49045	1881,1103.1756	Astronomical?
49046	1881,1103.1757	Medical.
49047	1881,1103.1758	Literary.
49048	1881,1103.1759	Literary; two columns; colophon. Art.
49049	1881,1103.1760	Lexical; Ea; sign list.
49050	1881,1103.1761	Practice wedges.
49051	1881,1103.1762	Literary; charm to ward off evil.
49052	1881,1103.1763	Namburbû or expiatory ritual.
49053	1881,1103.1764	Letter.
49054	1881,1103.1765	Field sale.
49055	1881,1103.1766	Joined to 48989.
49056	1881,1103.1767	Contract; sale of a house.
49057	1881,1103.1768	Field sale; finger-nail marks. RN lost 8/9/[].
49058	1881,1103.1769	Medical.
49059	1881,1103.1770	Economic.
49060	1881,1103.1771	Economic.
49061	1881,1103.1772	Economic.
49062	1881,1103.1773	Contract; land sale; finger-nail marks.
49063	1881,1103.1774	Lexical; Ea; sign list.
49064	1881,1103.1775	List of workmen.
49065	1881,1103.1776	Account.
49066	1881,1103.1777	Omens; monthly.
49067	1881,1103.1778	Lexical; Ea; sign list and literary extracts.

49068	1881,1103.1779	Field plan.
49069	1881,1103.1780	Incantation.
49070	1881,1103.1781	Joined to 48881.
49071	1881,1103.1782	Incantation.
49072	1881,1103.1783	Lexical.
49073	1881,1103.1784	Lexical; Ea; sign list.
49074	1881,1103.1785	Medical.
49075	1881,1103.1786	Unidentified.
49076	1881,1103.1787	Lexical; personal names.
49077	1881,1103.1788	Unidentified.
49078	1881,1103.1789	Prayer.
49079	1881,1103.1790	Receipt for wheat.
49080	1881,1103.1791	Astronomical.
49081	1881,1103.1792	Lexical; syllabary; literary extracts.
49082	1881,1103.1793	Lexical; Ea; sign list.
49083	1881,1103.1794	Clay fragment with curious marks, not cuneiform script but perhaps worm tracks; compare 33022 and 39264.
49084	1881,1103.1795	Joined to 33451.
49085	1881,1103.1796	Lexical; Ea; sign list.
49086	1881,1103.1797	Astronomical.
49087	1881,1103.1798	Omens; Sa-gig or Šumma izbu or terrestrial?
49088	1881,1103.1799	Lexical?
49089	1881,1103.1800	Unidentified.
49090	1881,1103.1801	Astronomical Diary or related text.
49091	1881,1103.1802	Medical.
49092	1881,1103.1803	Incantation.
49093	1881,1103.1804	Astronomical.
49094	1881,1103.1805	Economic.
49095	1881,1103.1806	Lexical; syllabary.
49096	1881,1103.1807	Promissory note for silver. Dar 7/[]/8. Babylon.
49097	1881,1103.1808	Lexical; Ea; sign list.
49098	1881,1103.1809	Astronomical Diary.
49098a	1881,1103.1809a	Joined to 48696.
49099	1881,1103.1810	Unidentified.
49100	1881,1103.1811	Lexical; gi.
49101	1881,1103.1812	Unidentified.
49102	1881,1103.1813	Lexical; giš.
49103	1881,1103.1814	Joined to 48061.
49104	1881,1103.1815	Uninscribed envelope fragment, probably of a private letter.
49105	1881,1103.1816	Omens.
49106	1881,1103.1817	Field plan.
49107	1881,1103.1818	Astronomical.
49108	1881,1103.1819	Economic.

49109	1881,1103.1820	Unidentified.
49110	1881,1103.1821	Unidentified.
49111	1881,1103.1822	Letter from Šadûnu to Kūnāya. CT 22, 19, no. 91; Levavi, dubsar 3, no. 199.
49112	1881,1103.1823	Lexical; Ea; sign list.
49113	1881,1103.1824	Astronomical; lunar System A; column E for solar eclipses for at least SE 265-267.
49114	1881,1103.1825	Medical.
49115	1881,1103.1826	Economic.
49116	1881,1103.1827	Economic.
49117	1881,1103.1828	Lexical, Ana ittišu II 4-8.
49118	1881,1103.1829	Lexical; god-list.
49119	1881,1103.1830	Field sale.
49120	1881,1103.1831	Lexical; Ea; sign list.
49121	1881,1103.1832	Literary.
49122	1881,1103.1833	Promissory note for silver.
49123	1881,1103.1834	Mathematical.
49124	1881,1103.1835	Joined to 47463.
49125	1881,1103.1836	Promissory note.
49126	1881,1103.1837	Unidentified.
49127	1881,1103.1838	Unidentified.
49128	1881,1103.1839	Astronomical.
49129	1881,1103.1840	Incantation.
49130	1881,1103.1841	Joined to 48158.
49131	1881,1103.1842	Lexical; personal names.
49132	1881,1103.1843	Medical.
49133	1881,1103.1844	Medical.
49134	1881,1103.1845	Literary; colophon.
49135	1881,1103.1846	Lexical; Ea; sign list.
49136	1881,1103.1847	Account.
49137	1881,1103.1848	Ritual.
49138	1881,1103.1849	Lexical; personal names.
49139	1881,1103.1850	Lexical; god-list.
49140	1881,1103.1851	Joined to 48989.
49141	1881,1103.1852	Ritual to make clay cylinder seals inscribed with spells against fever. Duplicates 43359. + 65953 + 68455.
49142	1881,1103.1853	Account.
49143	1881,1103.1854	Medical.
49144	1881,1103.1855	Lexical; god list.
49145	1881,1103.1856	Sumerian literary.
49146	1881,1103.1857	Medical.
49147	1881,1103.1858	Literary?
49148	1881,1103.1859	Joined to 47672.
49149	1881,1103.1860	Lexical.

49150	1881,1103.1861	Joined to 47961.
49151	1881,1103.1862	Contract.
49152	1881,1103.1863	Contract.
49153	1881,1103.1864	Lexical; Ea; sign list.
49154	1881,1103.1865	Joined to 48579.
49155	1881,1103.1866	Bilingual incantation.
49156	1881,1103.1867	Lexical; Ea; sign list.
49157	1881,1103.1868	Literary.
49158	1881,1103.1869	Lexical.
49159	1881,1103.1870	Fragment of agate eye-stone; inscribed: [na]m-t[i-la-ni-šè] / a mu-un-n[a-ru]. Date uncertain.
49160	1881,1103.1871	Sealing, uninscribed, with three stamp seal impressions; traces of string on one side.
49161	1881,1103.1872	Sealing, uninscribed, with six stamp seal impressions; traces of string behind.
49162	1881,1103.1873	Sealing, uninscribed, with two stamp seal impressions; traces of string behind.
49163	1881,1103.1874	Sealing, uninscribed, with two stamp seal impressions; traces of string behind.
49163a	1881,1103.1875	Sealing, uninscribed, with two stamp seal impressions.
	1881,1103.1876ff.	1876-1966 are uninscribed objects from Babylon and Dailem.

Later collections

Many of the fragments catalogued in CBTBM VI-VIII have been joined to tablets catalogued here. The joins are mostly of fragments acquired through Rassam, Shemtob and Spartali. The following is a list of joins made since the publication of CBTBM VI-VIII.

51261	1882,0323.2295	Joined to 36699.
55433	1882,0704.3	Joined to 33334.
55484	1882,0704.57	Joined to 35188.
55485	1882,0704.58	Joined to 35401.
55503	1882,0704.77	Joined to 34809.
55505	1882,0704.80	Joined to 34809.
55507	1882,0704.84	Joined to 35407.
55531	1882,0704.114	Joined to 35015.
55542	1882,0704.125	Joined to 34854.
55551	1882,0704.136	Joined to 35188.
55561	1882,0704.151	Joined to 45686.
93030	1882,0704.196	Joined to 35586 (not joined to 34616 as said in CBTBM VI).
55633	1882,0704.234	Joined to 35188.
64190	1882,0918.4165	Joined to 38592.

65831	1882,0918.5822	Joined to 34575 (+) 132282 (+) 32762.
65953	1882,0918.5845	Joined to 45656.
77251	1883,0928.2	Aluzinnu text; (+) 35557 (not actually joining as said in CBTBM VIII).
78826	1888,0512.12	Joined to 45722 (not 78825 as said in CBTBM VIII).
82870	1883,0121.33	Joined to 34212.
99669	1883,0121.2031	Joined to 35401.
99677	1883,0121.2039	Joined to Rm.717 + 34188.
99679	1883,0121.2041	Joined to 34888.
99685	1883,0121.2047	Joined to 35401.

1958,0412 collection

The 1958,0412 collection was purchased from Mrs E. C. B. Chappelow, being part of the estate of her late husband A. C. Chappelow, who had inherited the tablets from Professor T. G. Pinches. See J. E. Reade in CBTBM VI, pp. xv-xvi, on the joins to the 1881,0625 collection and the probability of Pinches having purchased some of the collcction from Spartali in 1879-80.

132267	1958,0412.1	OB Sumerian literary; balag composition of Enlil. (+) 81014 + 132268. CT 58, 46-47, no. 39 B.
132268	1958,0412.2	OB Sumerian literary; balag composition of Enlil. Joined to 81014. CT 58, 46-47, no. 39 B.
132269	1958,0412.3	Astrological omens.
132270	1958,0412.4	Hymn to a goddess?
132271	1958,0412.5	List of rations for 53 women from month ix year 5 to month ii year 6 of Philip Arrhidaeus.
132272	1958,0412.6	Syllabary with glosses.
132273	1958,0412.7	Astronomical Diary for SE 225. Sachs and Hunger, ADART III, no. -86 B.
132274	1958,0412.8	Astronomical Diary.
132275	1958,0412.9	Astronomical; Goal Year Text for SE 201 and 202. Joined to 41958. Hunger and Sachs, ADART VI, no. 73.
132276	1958,0412.10	Astronomical Diary for SE 66. Sachs and Hunger, ADART II, no. -245 A. (+)MNB 1884 (see Durand, TBER, p. 83).
132277	1958,0412.11	Astronomical Diary for SE 74. Joined to 41464. Sachs and Hunger, ADART II, no. -237.
132278	1958,0412.12	Astronomical Diary for SE 221. Joined to 41529. Sachs and Hunger, ADART III, no. -90.
132279	1958,0412.13	Astronomical Diary for SE 34. Sachs, PTRSL A.276, 48, fig 4; Sachs and Hunger, ADART I, no. -277 C. (+) Wellcome WHMM R 68/3 (unpublished).

132280	1958,0412.14	Astronomical; lunar ephemeris; System A, several columns, for SE 142. Joined to 41865. Steele, AHES 60 (2006) 123-135 Text C.
132281	1958,0412.15	Astronomical; Normal Star Almanac for SE 100. Hunger and Sachs, ADART VII, no. 36.
132282	1958,0412.16	Astronomical. Lunar System A, several columns, for SE 144-149; (+) 32762 (+) 34575+. Steele, Fs Walker, 293-318, text C; Steele, AHES 60 (2006) 123-153, text D.
132283	1958,0412.17	Astronomical; Normal Star Almanac for SE 105. (+) 41545. Hunger and Sachs, ADART VII, no. 40.
132284	1958,0412.18	Astronomical; Normal Star Almanac. Joined to 41588. Hunger and Sachs, ADART VII, no. 30.
132285	1958,0412.19	Astronomical; Normal Star Almanac. Joined to 41900. Hunger and Sachs, ADART VII, no. 196.
132286	1958,0412.20	Astronomical; Goal Year Text for SE 158. (+) 34932 (+) 40866. Hunger and Sachs, ADART VI, no. 45.
132287	1958,0412.21	Astronomical; Normal Star Almanac for SE 151. Hunger and Sachs, ADART VI, no. 66.
132288	1958,0412.22	Astrological omens.
132289	1958,0412.23	Old Babylonian. Square tablet, reused, with 3 lines of numbers: the 18th power of 2 and its reciprocal and the 15th power of 2.
132290	1958,0412.24	Administrative note about payment of a tithe in staters of Alexander; sealed.
132291	1958,0412.25	Old Babylonian. Literary or lexical?
132292	1958,0412.26	Incantation to Marduk.
132293	1958,0412.27	Bilingual; additional notes on the left edge.
132294	1958,0412.28	Prism; inscription of Esarhaddon about the restoration of Babylon. Joined to 78224. Kouyunjik Catalogue 3rd Supplement; Millard; AfO 24, 117.
132295	1958,0412.29	Letter to Širku (Ši-iš-ku); sealed.

Bibliography and abbreviations

1R, 2R, 4R, 4R(2), 5R	The Cuneiform Inscriptions of Western Asia, volumes 1, etc., edited by Rawlinson, Norris, Smith and Pinches (London 1861-1891)
Aaboe, Episodes	A. Aaboe, Episodes from the Early History of Astronomy. New York 2001
AB	Assyriologische Bibliothek
AchHist	Achaemenid History (Leiden)
Abel and Winckler, KGV	L. Abel and H. Winckler, Keilschrifttexte zum Gebrauch bei Vorlesungen. Berlin 1890
Abraham, BPPE	K. Abraham, Business and Politics under the Persian Empire
ACT	O. Neugebauer, Astronomical Cuneiform Texts
ADART	A. J. Sachs and H. Hunger, Astronomical Diaries and Related Texts from Babylonia Volume I: Diaries from 652 B.C. to 262 B.C. (Wien, 1988). Volume II: Diaries from 261 B.C. to 165 B.C. (Wien, 1989). Volume III: Diaries from 164 B.C. to 61 B.C. (Wien, 1996). Volume V: Lunar and Planetary Texts (with an appendix by J. M. Steele) (Wien, 2001) Volume VI: Goal Year Texts (Wien, 2006) Volume VII: Almanacs and Normal Star Almanacs (Wien, 2014)
AE	Arsacid Era
AfO	Archiv für Orientforschung
AfO Beih.	Archiv für Orientforschung Beiheft
AfO Beih. 3	F. R. Kraus, Texte zur babylonischen Physiognomatik, Berlin 1939
AfO Beih. 9	R. Borger, Die Inschriften Asarhaddons, Königs von Assyrien. Graz 1956
AfO Beih. 22	F. Rochberg-Halton, Aspects of Babylonian celestial divination: the lunar eclipse tablets of Enūma Anu Enlil. Horn 1988
AfO Beih. 24	H. Hunger and D. Pingree, MUL.APIN, an astronomical compendium in cuneiform. Horn 1989
AfO Beih. 25	M. Jursa, Die Landwirtschaft in Sippar in neubabylonischer Zeit. Horn and Wien 1995
AfO Beih. 27	B. Böck, Die babylonisch-assyrische Morphoskopie. Horn and Wien 2000

AGWG	Abhandlungen der Königlichen Gesellschaft der Wissenschaften zu Göttingen, historisch-philologische C/Klasse
AHES	Archive for History of Exact Sciences
AIHS	Archives Internationales d'Histoire des Sciences
AJSL	Americal Journal for Semitic Languages and Literatures
Ambos, Baurituale	C. Ambos, Mesopotamische Baurituale aus dem 1. Jahrtausend v. Chr. Dresden 2004
Ambos, Der König	C. Ambos, Der König im Gefängnis und das Neujahrsfest im Herbst. Dresden 2013
AMD	Ancient Magic and Divination (Leiden)
AMI NF	Archäologische Mitteilungen aus Iran, Neue Folge (Berlin)
AnOr	Analecta Orientalia
AnSt	Anatolian Studies
AOAT	Alter Orient und Altes Testament
AOAT 1	M. Dietrich and W. Röllig (eds.), Lišān mitḫurti: Festschrift Wolfram Freiherr von Soden. Kevelaer and Neukirchen-Vluyn 1969
AOAT 2	H. Hunger, Babylonische und assyrische Kolophone. Kevelaer and Neukirchen-Vluyn 1968
AOAT 25	B. L. Eichler et al. (eds.), Kramer Anniversary Volume: Cuneiform Studies in Honor of Samuel Noah Kramer. Kevelaer and Neukirchen-Vluyn 1976
AOAT 43	N. Heeßel, Babylonisch-assyrische Diagnostik. Münster 2000
AOAT 46	A. Schuster-Brandis, Steine als Schutz- und Heilmittel. Münster 2008
AOAT 51	S. Paulus, Die babylonischen Kudurru-Inschriften von der kassitischen bis zur frühbabylonischen Zeit. Münster 2014
AOAT 222	M. T. Roth, Babylonian Marriage Agreements 7th–3rd Centuries B.C. Kevelaer and Neukirchen-Vluyn 1989
AOAT 236	R. H. Sack, Neriglissar – King of Babylon. Kevelaer and Neukirchen-Vluyn 1994
AOAT 252	J. Marzahn et al. (eds.), Assyriologica et semitica; Festschrift für Joachim Oelsner. Münster 2000
AOAT 256	H. Schaudig, Die Inschriften Nabonids von Babylon und Kyros' des Großen. Münster 2001
AOAT 275	P. Gesche, Schulunterricht in Babylonien im ersten Jahrtausend v. Chr. Münster 2000
AOAT 291	R. Da Riva, Der Ebabbar-Tempel von Sippar in frühneubabylonischer Zeit (640-580 v. Chr.). Münster 2000

AOAT 297	J. M. Steele and A. Imhausen (eds.), Under One Sky: Astronomy and Mathematics in the Ancient Near East. Münster 2002
AOAT 326	U. S. Koch, Secrets of Extispicy: The Chapter Multābiltu of the Babylonian Extispicy Series and Niṣirti bārûti Texts mainly from Aššurbanipal's Library. Münster 2005
AOAT 330	H. D. Baker and M. Jursa (eds.), Approaching the Babylonian Economy. Münster 2005
AOAT 375	T. R. Kämmerer and K. A. Metzler, Das babylonische Weltschöpfungsepos Enūma elîš. Münster 2012
AOAT 398	M. Sandowicz, Oaths and Curses: A Study in Neo- and Late Babylonian Legal Formulary. Münster 2012
AOAT 414/1	J. Hackl, M. Jursa and Martina Schmidl, Spätbabylonische Briefe, Band 1. Spätbabylonische Privatbriefe. Munster 2014
AOAT 451	R. Tarasewicz and S. Zawadzki, Animal Offerings and Cultic Calendar in the Neo-Babylonian Sippar. Münster 2018
AOATS	Alter Orient und Altes Testament Sonderreihe
AOATS 4	R. H. Sack, Amēl-Marduk 562-560 B.C. Kevelaer and Neukirchen-Vluyn 1972
AoF	Altorientalische Forschungen
ARRIM	Annual Review of the Royal Inscriptions of Mesopotamia Project
Art	Artaxerxes
AS	Assyriological Studies (Chicago)
AuOr	Aula Orientalis (Barcelona)
Bab Arch	Babylonische Archive (Dresden)
Bagh Forsch	Baghdader Forschungen (Berlin)
Bagh Mitt	Baghdader Mitteilungen (Berlin)
Barnett, Ashurbanipal	R. D. Barnett, Sculptures from the North Palace of Ashurbanipal at Nineveh (668-627 B.C.). London 1976
BCHP	I. L. Finkel and B. van der Spek, Babylonian Chronicles of the Hellenistic Period (on-line prepublication)
Bertin	Unpublished copies by G. Bertin held at the British Museum
Bezold, Cat. 4	C. Bezold, Catalogue of the Cuneiform Tablets in the Kouyunjik Collection of the British Museum, volume 4
BiOr	Bibliotheca Orientalis (Leiden)
Böck, Muššu'u	B. Böck, Das Handbuch Muššu'u "Einreibung". Biblioteca del Próximo Oriente Antiguo 3. Madrid 2007

BOR	The Babylonian and Oriental Record (London, 1886-1893)
Borger, WAO	R. Borger, Die Welt des Alten Orients. Göttingen 1975
Brinkman, MSKH I	J. A. Brinkman, Materials and Studies for Kassite History vol. I. Chicago 1976
Brinkman, PHPKB	J. A. Brinkman, A Political History of Post-Kassite Babylonia. AnOr 43. Rome 1968
BRM	Babylonian Records in the Library of J. Pierpont Morgan
BSOAS	Bulletin of the School of Oriental and African Studies (London)
Budge, Rise and progress	E. A. W. Budge, The rise and progress of Assyriology. London 1925
Cam	Cambyses; J. N. Strassmaier, Inschriften von Cambyses
CBI	C. B. F. Walker, Cuneiform Brick Inscriptions
CBTBM	Catalogue of the Babylonian Tablets in the British Museum
CCT	Cuneiform Texts from Cappadocian Tablets in the British Museum
Centaurus	Centaurus: International Magazine of the History of Mathematics, Science and Technology (Copenhagen)
Charpin, Archives	D. Charpin, Archives familiales et propriété privée en Babylonie ancienne: Étude des documents de “Tell Sifr”. Paris 1980
Civil, Farmer’s Instructions	M. Civil, The farmer’s instructions: A Sumerian agricultural manual. Aula Orientalis Supplementa 5. Barcelona 1994
CM	Cuneiform Monographs
Wiggermann, CM 1	F. A. M. Wiggermann, Mesopotamian protective spirits: the ritual texts. Cuneiform Monographs 1. Groningen 1992
Wunsch, CM 3	C. Wunsch, Die Urkunden des babylonischen Geschāftsmannes Iddin-Marduk. Cuneiform Monographs 3. Groningen 1993
Fs Borger, CM 10	S. M. Maul (ed.), Festschrift für R. Borger. Cuneiform Monographs 10. Groningen 1998
Brown, CM 18	D. Brown, Mesopotamian planetary astronomy-astrology. Cuneiform Monographs 18. Groningen 2000
Wunsch, CM 20	C. Wunsch, Das Egibi-Archiv. Cuneiform Monographs 20. Groningen 2000
Linssen, CM 25	M. J. H. Linssen, The cults of Uruk and Babylon. Cuneiform Monographs 25. Leiden 2004

Attia, CM 37	A. Attia et al. (eds.), Advances in Mesopotamian Medicine from Hammurabi to Hippocrates. Cuneiform Monographs 37. Leiden 2009
Gehlken, CM 43	E. Gehlken, Weather Omens of Enūma Anu Enlil; Thunderstorms, wind and rain (tablets 44-49). Cuneiform Monographs 43. Leiden 2012
Cohen, Canonical Lamentations	M. E. Cohen, The canonical lamentations of ancient Mesopotamia. Potomac 1988
Collon, CS III/V	D. Collon, Catalogue of the Western Asiatic Seals in the British Museum, Cylinder Seals III/V. London 1986 and 2001
Corò, PTES	P. Corò, Prebende templari in età Seleucide. History of the Ancient Near East / Monographs VIII. Padova 2005
Corò, STUBM	P. Corò, Seleucid tablets from Uruk in the British Museum. Venice 2018
CRAIB	Comptes rendus … Académie des Inscriptions et Belles-Lettres. Paris
Craig, ABRT I	J. A. Craig, Assyrian and Babylonian religious texts, I. Leipzig 1895
CT	Cuneiform Texts from Babylonian Tablets in the British Museum
CTMMA	Cuneiform Texts in the Metropolitan Museum of Art.
Cyr	Cyrus; J. N. Strassmaier, Inschriften von Cyrus
Dar	Darius; J. N. Strassmaier, Inschriften von Darius
Da Riva, GMTR 4	R. Da Riva, The Neo-Babylonian royal inscriptions: An introduction. Guides to the Mesopotamian Textual Record 4. Münster 2008
Da Riva, SANER 3	R. Da Riva, The inscriptions of Nabopolassar, Amel-Marduk and Neriglissar. Studies in Ancient Near Eastern Records 3. Berlin 2013
van Dijk, Lugale	J. van Dijk, LUGAL UD ME-LÁM-bi NIR-GÁL. Leiden 1983
De Zorzi, Šumma izbu	N. De Zorzi, La serie teratomantica Šumma izbu. History of the Ancient Near East / Monographs XV. Padova 2014
Doty, CAHU	L. T. Doty, Cuneiform archives from Hellenistic Uruk. Yale University dissertation 1977; University Microfilms International 1982
dupl.	duplicates
Ebeling, Glossar	E. Ebeling, Glossar zu den neubabylonischen Briefen. München 1953
Ebeling, Handerhebung	E. Ebeling, Die akkadische Gebetsserie "Handerhebung". Berlin 1953

Ebeling, KAR	E. Ebeling, Keilschrifttexte aus Assur religiösen Inhalts I und II. Leipzig 1915-23
Ebeling, LKA	E. Ebeling and F. Köcher, Literarische Texte aus Assur. Berlin 1953
Ebeling, Neubab. Briefe	E. Ebeling, Neubabylonische Briefe. München 1949
Epping, AaB	J. Epping, Astronomisches aus Babylon. Freiburg 1889
Evetts	B. T. A. Evetts, Inscriptions of the Reigns of Evil-Merodach, Neriglissar and Laborosoarchod. Babylonische Texte Heft VI B. Leipzig 1892
FAOS	Freiburger altorientalische Studien
Farber, Lamaštu	W. Farber, Lamaštu. An edition of the canonical series of Lamaštu incantations and rituals. Mesopotamian Civilizations 17. Winona Lake 2014
Farber, SKS	W. Farber, Schlaf, Kindchen, Schlaf! Mesopotamische Baby-Beschwörungen und -Rituale. Mesopotamian Civilizations 2. Winona Lake 1989
Finkel, Board Games	I. L. Finkel (ed.), Ancient Board Games in perspective. London 2007
Finkel and Seymour, Babylon	I. L. Finkel and M. J. Seymour (eds.), Babylon, myth and reality. London 2008
Frahm, GMTR 5	E. Frahm, Babylonian and Assyrian Text Commentaries: Origin and Interpretation. Guides to the Mesopotamian Textual Record 5. Münster 2011
Freedman, If a city	S. M. Freedman, If a city is set on a height: the Akkadian omen series Šumma alu ina mēlê šakin. Vols. 1, 2 and 3, Philadelphia 1998, 2006 and 2017
Friberg and Al-Rawi, NMCT	J. Friberg and F. N. H. Al-Rawi, New mathematical cuneiform texts. Cham 2016
Fs	Festschrift (memorial volumes are abbreviated as Gs, Gedenkschrift)
Fs Biggs	M. Roth et al. (eds.), Studies presented to Robert D. Biggs. From the workshop of the Assyrian Dictionary, vol. 2. Assyriological Studies 27. Chicago 2007
Fs Böhl	M. A. Beek et al. (eds.), Symbolae Biblicae et Mesopotamicae Francisco Mario Theodoro De Liagre Böhl dedicatae. Leiden 1973
Fs Borger	S. M. Maul (ed.), Festschrift für Rykle Borger. Cuneiform Monographs 10. Groningen 1998
Fs Brack-Bernsen	J. Steele and M. Ossendrijver (eds.), Studies on the Ancient Exact Sciences in Honor of Lis Brack-Bernsen. Berlin Studies of the Ancient World 44. Berlin 2018

Fs Diakonoff	M. A. Dandamayev et al. (eds.), Societies and languages of the Ancient Near East: Studies in honour of I. M. Diakonoff. Warminster 1982
Fs Fales	G. B. Lanfranchi et al. (eds.), Leggo! Studies presented to Frederick Mario Fales. Leipziger Altorientalische Studien 2. Wiesbaden 2012
Fs Finkelstein	M. de J. Ellis, Essays on the Ancient Near East in memory of Jacob Joel Finkelstein. Memoirs of the Connecticut Academy of Arts and Sciences 19. Hamden 1977
Fs Geller	S. V. Panayotov et al. (eds.), Mesopotamian Medicine and Magic. Studies in Honor of Markham J. Geller. Leiden 2018
Fs Hartner	Y. Maeyama and W. G. Saltzer (eds.), Prismata, Festschrift für Willy Hartner. Wiesbaden 1977
Fs Haupt	C. Adler and E. Ember (eds.), Oriental studies published in commemoration of … Paul Haupt. Baltimore and Leipzig 1926
Fs Hunger	M. Köhbach et al. (eds.), Festschrift für Hermann Hunger. WZKM 97. Wien 2007
Fs E. S. Kennedy	D. A. King and G. Saliba (eds.), From deferent to equant: A volume of studies in the history of science in the Ancient and Medieval Near East in honor of E. S. Kennedy. Annals of the New York Academy of Sciences 500. New York 1987.
Fs Kraus	G. van Driel et al. (eds.), Zikir šumim: Assyriological studies presented to F. R. Kraus. Leiden 1982
Fs Lambert	A. R. George and I. L. Finkel (eds.), Wisdom, gods and literature: Studies in Assyriology in honour of W. G. Lambert. Winona Lake 2000
Fs Matouš	B. Hruška and G. Komoróczy (eds.), Festschrift Lubor Matouš. Budapest 1978
Fs Neumann	K. Kleber et al. (eds.), Grenzüberschreitungen: Studien zur Kulturgeschichte des Alten Orients: Festschrift für Hans Neumann. dubsar 5. Münster 2018
Fs Oelsner	J. Marzahn et al. (eds.), Assyriologica et semitica: Festschrift für Joachim Oelsner. AOAT 252. Münster 2000
Fs Oppenheim	R. D. Biggs and J. A. Brinkman (eds.), From the workshop of the Chicago Assyrian Dictionary: Studies presented to A. Leo Oppenheim. Chicago 1964
Fs Pingree	C. Burnett et al. (eds.), Studies in the History of the Exact Sciences in Honour of David Pingree. Leiden 2004

Fs Postgate	Y. Heffron et al. (eds.), At the dawn of history: Ancient Near Eastern studies in honour of J. N. Postgate. Winona Lake 2017
Fs Reiner	F. Rochberg-Halton (ed.), Language, literature and history: Philological and historical studies presented to Erica Reiner. American Oriental Series 67. New Haven 1987
Fs Sigrist	P. Michalowski (ed), On the Third Dynasty of Ur: Studies in honor of Marcel Sigrist. JCS Supplemental Series 1, 2008.
Fs Sjöberg	H. Behrens et al. (eds.), DUMU-E2-DUB-DA-A: Studies in honor of Åke W. Sjöberg. Philadelphia 1989
Fs Slotsky	M. Ross (ed.), From the banks of the Euphrates: Studies in honor of Alice Lousie Slotsky. Winona Lake 2008
Fs Stol	R. J. van der Spek et al. (eds.), Studies in ancient Near Eastern world view and society, presented to Marten Stol. Potomac 2008
Fs Strommenger	B. Hrouda et al. (eds.), Von Uruk nach Tuttul: eine Festschrift für Eva Strommenger. Münchener Vorderasiatische Studien 12. München 1992
Fs van der Spek	K. Kleber and R. Pirngruber (eds.), Silver, money and credit: a tribute to Robartus J. van der Spek. PIHANS CXXVIII. Leiden 2016.
Fs Walker	C. Wunsch (ed.), Mining the archives: Festschrift for Christopher Walker. Bab Arch 1. Dresden 2002
Gabbay, HES 2	U. Gabbay, The Eršema prayers of the first millennium BC. Heidelberger Emesal-Studien 2. Wiesbaden 2015
Garelli, Assyriens	P. Garelli, Les Assyriens en Cappadoce. Paris 1963
Garelli, Gilgameš	P. Garelli, Gilgameš et sa légende (RAI VII). Paris 1960
Geller, ABM	M. J. Geller, Ancient Babylonian Medicine, theory and practice. Oxford 2010
Geller, BAM 7	M. J. Geller, Renal and rectal disease texts. Die babylonisch-assyrische Medizin in Texten und Untersuchungen, Band 7. Berlin 2005
Geller, BAM 8	M. J. Geller, Healing magic and evil demons. Die babylonisch-assyrische Medizin in Texten und Untersuchungen, Band 8, Berlin 2016
Geller, Melosthesia	M. J. Geller, Melosthesia in Babylonia: Medicine, magic and astrology in the Ancient Near East. Berlin 2014

George, BTT	A. George, Babylonian topographical texts. Orientalia Lovaniensia Analecta 40. Leuven 1992
George, Gilgamesh	A. George, The Babylonian Gilgamesh epic. Oxford 2003
GMTR	Guides to the Mesopotamian Textual Record (Münster)
Grayson, BHLT	A. K. Grayson, Babylonian Historical-Literary Texts
Gs	Gedenkschrift
Gs Black	H. D. Baker et al. (eds.), Your praise is sweet; a memorial volume for Jeremy Black. Oxford 2010
Gs Cagni	S. Graziani et al. (eds.), Studi sul Vicino Oriente antico dedicati alla memoria di Luigi Cagni, vols. I-IV (Napoli, 2000)
Gs Sachs	E. Leichty et al. (eds.), A scientific humanist: Studies in memory of Abraham Sachs. Philadelphia 1988
Gs Speiser	W. W. Hallo (ed.), Studies in memory of E. A. Speiser. AOS 53. New Haven 1968
Hunger and Steele, MUL.APIN	H. Hunger and J. Steele, The Babylonian astronomical compendium MUL.APIN. Abingdon and New York 2019
Iran	Iran: Journal of the British Institute of Persian Studies
Iraq	Iraq: Journal of the British School of Archaeology in Iraq (now the British Institute for the Study of Iraq)
JANES	Journal of the Ancient Near Eastern Society of Columbia University
JAOS	Journal of the American Oriental Society
JCS	Journal of Cuneiform Studies
Jean, Tell Sifr	C.-F. Jean, Tell Sifr, textes cunéiformes conservés au British Museum, réédités. Paris 1931
JEOL	Jaarbericht van het Vooraziatisch-Egyptisch Genotschap "Ex Oriente Lux" (Leiden)
JESHO	Journal of the Economic and Social History of the Orient (Leiden)
JHA	Journal for the History of Astronomy
Jiménez, BDP	E. Jiménez, The Babylonian Disputation Poems. Leiden 2017
JNES	Journal of Near Eastern Studies
JRAS	Journal of the Royal Asiatic Society (London), cited by year only
JTVI	Journal of the Transactions of the Victoria Institute (London)
Jursa, Bēl-rēmanni	M. Jursa, Das Archiv des Bēl-rēmanni. Leiden 1999
Kan	Kandalanu

Karvonen-Kannas, Figurines	K. Karvonen-Kannas, The Seleucid and Parthian terracotta figurines from Babylon. Monografie di Mesopotamia 4. Firenze 1995
Kaskal	Kaskal, Rivista di storia, ambiente e culture del Vicino Orienta Antico (Venezia/Firenze)
KDVSMM	Det Kongelige Danske Videnskabernes Selskab Matematisk-fysiske Meddelelser (Copenhagen)
Ker Porter, Travels	R. Ker Porter, Travels in Georgia, Persia, Armenia, Ancient Babylonia, etc. London 1821-1822
King, BBSt	L. W. King, Babylonian Boundary Stones. London 1912
King, BMS	L. W. King, Babylonian Magic and Sorcery. London 1896
King, LIH	L. W. King, The Letters and Inscriptions of Hammurabi, I-III. London 1898-1900
King, STC	L. W. King, The Seven Tablets of Creation, I-II. London 1902
Koch-Westenholz, Babylonian Liver Omens	U. S. Koch-Westenholz, Babylonian liver omens. The chapters Manzāzu, Padānu and Pān tākalti of the Babylonian extispicy series mainly from Aššurbanipal's Library. Carsten Niebuhr Institute Publications 27. Copenhagen 2000
Köcher, BAM II	F. Köcher, Keilschrifttexte aus Assur 2. Die babylonisch-assyrische Medizin in Texten und Untersuchungen, Band II. Berlin 1963
Köcher, BAM VI	F. Köcher, Keilschrifttexte aus Ninive 2. Die babylonisch-assyrische Medizin in Texten und Untersuchungen, Band VI. Berlin 1980
Köcher, Pflanzenkunde	F. Köcher, Keilschrifttexte zur assyrisch-babylonischen Drogen- und Pflanzenkunde. Berlin 1955
Kugler, Mondrechnung	F. X. Kugler, Die babylonische Mondrechnung. Freiburg 1900
Kugler, SSB	F. X. Kugler, Sternkunde und Sterndienst in Babel. Münster 1907-1935
Labat, Commentaires	R. Labat, Commentaires assyro-babyloniens sur les présages. Bordeaux 1933
Lambert, BCM	W. G. Lambert, Babylonian Creation Myths. Mesopotamian Civilizations 16. Winona Lake 2013
Lambert, BOQ	W. G. Lambert, Babylonian Oracle Queries. Mesopotamian Civilizations 13. Winona Lake 2007
Lambert, BWL	W. G. Lambert, Babylonian Wisdom Literature. Oxford 1960
Lambert, MC 24	W. G. Lambert, Cuneiform Texts from the Folios of W. G. Lambert, Part 1. Edited by A. R. George and

	J. Taniguchi. Mesopotamian Civilizations 24. Philadelphia 2019
Lambert, Unity and Diversity	W. G. Lambert in H. Goedicke and J. J. M. Roberts, Unity and diversity. Baltimore, 1975
Lambert and Millard, Atra-ḫasīs	W. G. Lambert and A. R. Millard, Atra-ḫasīs: the Babylonian story of the flood. Oxford 1969
Layard, ICC	A. H. Layard, Inscriptions in the cuneiform character. London 1851
Layard, MN II	A. H. Layard, The monuments of Nineveh, II. London 1853
Layard, Niniveh	A. H. Layard, Nineveh and its remains. London 1849
Layard, Niniveh and Babylon	A. H. Layard, Discoveries in the ruins of Nineveh and Babylon. London 1853
LBAT	Late Babylonian Astronomical and Related Texts, copied by T. G. Pinches and J. N. Strassmaier, prepared for publication by A. J. Sachs with the co-operation of J. Schaumberger
Lehmann-Haupt, AB 8	C. F. Lehmann-Haupt, Šamaššumukîn, König von Babylon 668-648 v.Chr. AB 8. Leipzig 1892
Levavi, dubsar 3	Y. Levavi, Administrative epistolography in the formative phase of the Neo-Babylonian empire. Spätbabylonische Briefe, Band 2. dubsar 3. Münster 2018
Livingstone, CUSAS 25	A. Livingstone, Hemerologies of Assyrian and Babylonian scholars. Cornell University Studies in Assyriology and Sumerology 25. Bethesda 2013
Livingstone, MMEWABS	A. Livingstone, Mystical and mythological explanatory works of Assyrian and Babylonian scholars. Oxford 1986
LM	Labaši-Marduk
Loftus, Travels	W. K. Loftus, Travels and researches in Chaldaea and Susiana. London 1857
Lorenz, Nebukadnezar III/IV	J. Lorenz, Nebukadnezar III/IV: Die politischen Wirren nach dem Tod des Kambyses im Spiegel der Keilschrifttexte. Dresden 2008
MARI	MARI: Annales de Recherches Interdisciplinaires (Paris)
Maul, Bagh Forsch 18	S. M. Maul, Zukunftsbewältigung: eine Untersuchung altorientalischen Denkens anhand der babylonisch-assyrischen Löserituale (Namburbi). Baghdader Forschungen 18. Mainz 1994
Mayer, Untersuchungen	W. Mayer, Untersuchungen zur Formensprache der babylonischen "Gebetsbeschwörungen". Studia Pohl: Series Major 3. Rome 1976
Meissner, BAP	B. Meissner, Beiträge zum altbabylonische Privatrecht. Leipzig 1893

Meissner, Supp.	B. Meissner, Supplement zu den assyrischen Wörterbüchern. Leiden 1898
Ménant, Notice	J. Ménant, Notice sur quelques empreintes de cylindres du premier empire de Chaldée. CRAIB 22, 210-233. Paris, 1878
Mesopotamia	Mesopotamia: Rivista di archeologia, epigrafia e storia orientale antica (Firenze)
Mitchell and Searight	T. C. Mitchell and A. Searight, Catalogue of the Western Asiatic Seals in the British Museum, Stamp Seals III, Impressions of stamp seals on cuneiform tablets, clay bullae and jar handles. Leiden 2008
MSL	Materialien zum sumerischen Lexikon: Materials for the Sumerian Lexicon
MVAG	Mitteilungen der Vorderasiatisch-Aegyptischen Gesellschaft
NABU	Nouvelles Assyriologiques Bréves et Utilitaires (Paris, 1987-)
Nbk	Nebuchadnezzar; J. N. Strassmaier, Inschriften von Nabuchodonosor
Nbn	Nabonidus; J. N. Strassmaier, Inschriften von Nabonidus
Nemet-Nejat, LB Field Plans	K. R. Nemet-Nejat, Late Babylonian field plans in the British Museum. Rome 1982
Ner	Neriglissar
Neugebauer, Exact Sciences	O. Neugebauer, The exact sciences in antiquity. New York 1952
Neugebauer, MKT	O. Neugebauer, Mathematische Keilschrifttexte. Berlin 1935-1937
Nisaba 20	S. Altavilla and C. B. F. Walker, Late Babylonian seal impressions on tablets in the British Museum, Part 1: Sippar. Nisaba 20. Messina 2009
Nisaba 28	S. Altavilla and C. B. F. Walker, Late Babylonian seal impressions on tablets in the British Museum, Part 2: Babylon and its vicinity. Nisaba 28. Messina 2016
Npl	Nabopolassar
OB	Old Babylonian
OECT	Oxford Editions of Cuneiform Texts
Oelsner, Materialien	J. Oelsner, Materialien zur babylonischen Gesellschaft und Kultur in hellenistischer Zeit. Budapest 1986
OLA	Orientalia Lovaniensia Analecta
OLP	Orientalia Lovaniensia Periodica
OLZ	Orientalistische Literaturzeitung
Or NS	Orientalia Nova Series (Rome)

Oppert and Ménant, DJ	J. Oppert and J. Ménant, Documents juridiques de l'Assyrie et de la Chaldée. Paris 1877
Orient	Orient: Journal of the Society for Near Eastern Studies in Japan
Oshima, BPM	T. Oshima, Babylonian Prayers to Marduk. Tübingen 2011
Oshima, BPPS	T. Oshima, Babylonian Poems of Pious Sufferers. Tübingen 2014
Ossendrijver, BMAPT	M. Ossendrijver, Babylonian Mathematical Astronomy: Procedure Texts. New York 2012
Persika 9	P. Briant and F. Joannès (eds.), La transition entre l'empire achéménide et les royaumes hellénistiques. Persika 9. Paris 2006
PIHANS	Publications de l'Institut historique-archéologique néerlandais de Stamboul
Pinches, Assyrian Grammar	T. G. Pinches, An Outline of Assyrian Grammar. London 1910
PSBA	Proceedings of the Society of Biblical Archaeology (London); cited by volume and year
PTRSL	Philosophical Transactions of the Royal Society of London
RA	Revue d'assyriologie et d'archéologie orientale (Paris)
RAI XV	J.-R. Kupper (ed.), La civilisation de Mari (XVe Rencontre Assyriologique Internationale, 1966)
RAI XIX	P. Garelli (ed.), Le palais et la royauté, archéologie et civilisation (XIXe Rencontre Assyriologique Internationale, 1971)
RAI XLV/2	W. W. Hallo and I. J. Winter (eds.), Seals and seal impressions (XLVe Rencontre Assyriologique Internationale, 1998)
RAI XLVIII	W. van Soldt, R. Kalvelagen and D. Katz (eds.), Ethnicity in Ancient Mesopotamia (XLVIIIe Rencontre Assyriologique Internationale, 2002)
Reiner and Pingree, BPO	E. Reiner and D. Pingree, Babylonian Planetary Omens BPO 1 = Bibliotheca Mesopotamica 2/1. Malibu 1975 BPO 2 = Bibliotheca Mesopotamica 2/2. Malibi 1981 BPO 3 = Cuneiform Monographs 1. Groningen 1998 BPO 4 = Cuneiform Monographs 30. Leiden 2005
Renger, Babylon	J. Renger (ed.), Babylon. Colloquien der Deutschen Orient-Gesellschaft 2. Saarbrucken 1999
Rich, Narrative Babylon	C. J. Rich, Narrative of a journey to the site of Babylon in 1811 … Second memoir on the ruins. London 1839

RIMB	The Royal Inscriptions of Mesopotamia, Babylonian Periods (Toronto)
RIME	The Royal Inscriptions of Mesopotamia, Early Periods (Toronto)
RINAP	The Royal Inscriptions of the Neo-Assyrian Period (Winona Lake)
RlA	Reallexikon der Assyriologie und Vorderasiatischen Archäologie
Rochberg, Babylonian Horoscopes	F. Rochberg, Babylonian Horoscopes. TAPS 88/1, 1998
SAA	State Archives of Assyria
SAALT	State Archives of Assyria Literary Texts
San Nicolò, BR 8/7	M. San Nicolò, Babylonische Rechtsurkunden des ausgehenden 8. und 7. Jahrhunderts v. Chr. München 1951
Sandowicz, dubsar 11	M. Sandowicz, Neo-Babylonian dispute documents in the British Museum. dubsar 11. Münster 2019
Schramm, GBAO 2	W. Schramm, Ein Compendium sumerisch-akkadischer Beschwörungen. Göttinger Beiträge zum Alten Orient 2. Göttingen 2008
Schwemer, StBot 58	D. Schwemer in A. Müller-Karpe et al. (eds.), Saeculum: Gedenkschrift für Heinrich Otten. Studien zu den Bogazköy-Texten 58. Wiesbaden 2015
SCIAMVS	SCIAMVS: Sources and Commentaries in the Exact Sciences (Kyoto)
Science	Science, Journal of the American Association for the Advancement of Science
SE	Seleucid Era
Segal, Incantation Bowls	J. B. Segal, Catalogue of the Aramaic and Mandaic incantation bowls in the British Museum. London 2000
SEL	Studi Epigrafici e Linguistici sul Vicino Oriente Antico. Verona
Slotsky and Wallenfels, Tallies and Trends	A. L. Slotsky and R. Wallenfels, Tallies and Trends: The Late Babylonian commodity price lists. Bethesda 2009
G. Smith, Assyrian Discoveries	George Smith, Assyrian Discoveries. London 1875
S. Smith, BHT	Sidney Smith, Babylonian Historical Texts. London 1924
S. A. Smith, MAT	Samuel Alden Smith, Miscellaneous Assyrian Texts of the British Museum. Leipzig 1887
Steele, Calendars and years	J. M. Steele (ed.), Calendars and years: Astronomy and time in the Ancient Near East. Oxford 2007
Steele, Rising time schemes	J. M. Steele, Rising time schemes in Babylonian astronomy. Cham 2017

Steinert, ABSTC — U. Steinert, Assyrian and Babylonian scholarly text catalogues: Medicine, Magic and divination. Die babylonisch-assyrische Medizin in Texten und Untersuchungen 9. Berlin 2018

Stephenson, HEER — F. R. Stephenson, Historical eclipses and earth's rotation. Cambridge 1997

Stephenson and Clark, AEAR — F. R. Stephenson and D. H. Clark, Applications of early astronomical records. Bristol 1978

Stephenson and Walker, Halley's Comet — F. R. Stephenson and C. B. F. Walker, Halley's Comet in History. London 1985

Stevenson, Ass.-Bab. Contracts — J. H. Stevenson, Assyrian and Babylonian contracts with Aramaic reference notes. New York 1902

Stolper, Annali Supp. 77 — M. W. Stolper, Late Achaemenid, Early Macedonian and Early Seleucid Records of Deposit and Related Texts. Supplemento n. 77 agli Annali dell'Istituto Universitario Orientale di Napoli, (1993), fasc. 4

Strassmaier, 8th Orientalist Congress — J. N. Strassmaier, Einige kleinere babylonische Keilschrifttexte aus dem Britischen Museum, in Actes du huitième congrès international des Orientalistes (1889), II/I Section sémitique (b) (Leiden 1893), 279-283, pls. 1-35

Strassmaier, Liverpool — J. N. Strassmaier, Die babylonischen Inschriften im Museum zu Liverpool nebst andern aus der Zeit von Nebukadnezzar bis Darius, in Actes du sixième congrès international des Orientalistes (1883), II/I Section sémitique (Leiden 1885), 569-624, pls. 1-176

Strassmaier, Warka — J. N. Strassmaier, Die altbabylonischen Verträge von Warka, in Abhandlungen und Vorträge des Fünften Internationalen Orientalisten-Congresses (1881), II/1 Semitische Section (Berlin 1882), 315-365, pls. 1-144

Swerdlow, Astronomy — N. M. Swerdlow (ed.), Ancient Astronomy and Celestial Divination. Cambridge, Mass. 1999

Syria — Syria, revue d'art oriental et d'archéologie (Paris)

TAPS — Transactions of the American Philosophical Society (Philadelphia)

TCS — Texts from Cuneiform Sources

TDP — R. Labat, Traité akkadien de diagnostics et prognostics médicaux. Leiden 1951

Thompson, Devils — R. Campbell Thompson, The devils and evil spirits of Babylonia, I-II. London 1903-4

Thureau-Dangin, RAcc — F. Thureau-Dangin, Rituels accadiens. Paris 1921

Thureau-Dangin, TMB — F. Thureau-Dangin, Textes mathématiques babyloniens. Leiden 1938

TSBA	Transactions of the Society of Biblical Archaeology (London)
TUAT NF 3	B. Janowski and G. Wilhelm (eds.), Texte aus der Umwelt des Alten Testaments, Neue Folge Band 3: Briefe. Gütersloh 2006
Unger, Babylon	E. Unger, Babylon, die heilige Stadt. Berlin and Leipzig 1931
unnum.	unnumbered
VAB	Vorderasiatische Bibliothek
van der Spek, Grondbezit	R. J. van der Spek, Grondbezit in het seleucidische rijk. Amsterdam 1986
van der Spek, Raḫimesu	R. J. van der Spek, Cuneiform documents on Parthian history: The Raḫimesu archive. Materials for the study of the standard of living. In J. Wiesehöfer (ed.), Das Partherreich und seine Zeugnisse, pp. 205-258. Stuttgart 1998
van Soldt, Solar omens	W. van Soldt, Solar omens of Enuma Anu Enlil: tablets 23 (24) - 29 (30). Leiden 1995
Verderame, Nisaba 2	L. Verderame, Le tavole I-VI della serie astrologica Enuma Anu Enlil. Nisaba 2. Messina 2002
von Soden, LTBA II	W. von Soden, Die lexikalischen Tafelserien der Babylonier und Assyrer in den Berliner Museum II. Berlin 1933
Waerzeggers, AH XV	C. Waerzeggers, The Ezida temple of Borsippa: priesthood, cult, archives. Achaemenid History XV. Leiden 2010
Waerzeggers, OLA 233	C. Waerzeggers, Marduk-rēmanni, local networks and imperial politics in Achaemenid Babylonia. OLA 233. Louvain 2014
Walker and Collon, Tell-ed-Dēr 3	C. B. F. Walker and D. Collon in L. de Meyer, Tell ed-Dēr III: Soundings at Abū Ḥabbah (Sippar)
Weidner, Gestirn-Darstellungen	E. F. Weidner, Gestirn-Darstellungen auf babylonischen Tontafeln. Wien 1967
Weidner, HBA	E. F. Weidner, Handbuch der babylonischen Astronomie I. AB 23. Leipzig 1915
Winckler, ABK	H. Winckler and E. Böhden, Altbabylonische Keilschrifttexte zum Gebrauch bei Vorlesungen. Leipzig 1892
Winckler, MAOV I	H. Winckler, Mitteilungen des Akademisch-Orientalistischen Vereins zu Berlin 1 (1887)
Wiseman, Chronicles	D. J. Wiseman, Chronicles of Chaldean Kings (626-556 B.C.). London 1961
Wiseman, Nebuchadrezzar and Babylon	D. J. Wiseman, Nebuchadrezzar and Babylon. Oxford 1985
WO	Die Welt des Orients (Göttingen)

WOO 6	G. J. Selz (ed.), The empirical dimension of Ancient Near Eastern Studies. Wiener Offene Orientalistik 6 (2011)
WVDOG	Wissenschaftliche Veröffentlichungen der Deutschen Orient-Gesellschaft
Wunsch, Bab Arch 2	C. Wunsch, Urkunden zum Ehe-, Vermögens- und Erbrecht. Bab Arch 2. Dresden 2003
WZKM	Wiener Zeitschrift für die Kunde des Morgenlandes
ZA	Zeitschrift für Assyriologie und vorderasiatische Archäologie
ZABR	Zeitschrift für Altorientalische und Biblische Rechtsgeschichte
Zadok, Nisaba 21	R. Zadok, Catalogue of Documents from Borsippa or related to Borsippa in the British Museum I. Nisaba 21. Messina 2009
Zadok, RGTC 8	R. Zadok, Geographical Names According to New- and Late-Babylonian Texts. Répertoire Géographique des Textes Cunéiformes 8. Wiesbaden 1985
ZKM	Zeitschrift für die Kunde des Morgenlandes